P S Y C H O L O G Y

F O U R T H   E D I T I O N

PSYCHOLOGY

FOURTH EDITION

HENRY GLEITMAN

W·W·NORTON & COMPANY·NEW YORK·LONDON

The text of this book is composed in Bembo, with the display set in Machine.
Composition by TSI Graphics.
Manufacturing by R. R. Donnelley.
Book design by Antonina Krass.
Layout by Roberta Flechner.

Cover design: Antonina Krass
Cover illustration: *David* by Michelangelo (photograph courtesy of the Bridgeman
Art Library, London)
Acknowledgments and copyrights appear on pages A94–A100, which constitute a continuation of the
copyright page.

Library of Congress Cataloging-in-Publication Data

Gleitman, Henry.
Psychology/Henry Gleitman.—4th ed.
p.   cm.
Includes bibliographical references and index.
1. Psychology.   I. Title.
BF121.G58   1994
150—dc20   94-36073

ISBN 0-393-96608-9

W. W. Norton & Company, Inc., 500 Fifth Avenue, New York, N.Y. 10110
W. W. Norton & Company Ltd., 10 Coptic Street, London WC1A 1PU

4 5 6 7 8 9 0

THE CONTENTS IN BRIEF

1 │ INTRODUCTION

PART ONE │ **ACTION**

2 │ BIOLOGICAL BASES OF BEHAVIOR
3 │ MOTIVATION
4 │ LEARNING

PART TWO │ **COGNITION**

5 │ SENSORY PROCESSES
6 │ PERCEPTION
7 │ MEMORY
8 │ THOUGHT AND KNOWLEDGE
9 │ LANGUAGE

PART THREE │ **SOCIAL BEHAVIOR**

10 │ THE BIOLOGICAL BASIS OF SOCIAL BEHAVIOR
11 │ SOCIAL COGNITION AND EMOTION
12 │ SOCIAL INTERACTION

PART FOUR | DEVELOPMENT

13 | PHYSICAL AND COGNITIVE DEVELOPMENT

14 | SOCIAL DEVELOPMENT

PART FIVE | INDIVIDUAL DIFFERENCES

15 | INTELLIGENCE: ITS NATURE AND MEASUREMENT

16 | PERSONALITY I: ASSESSMENT, TRAIT THEORY, AND THE BEHAVIORAL-COGNITIVE APPROACH

17 | PERSONALITY II: PSYCHODYNAMIC, HUMANISTIC, AND SOCIOCULTURAL APPROACHES

18 | PSYCHOPATHOLOGY

19 | TREATMENT OF PSYCHOPATHOLOGY

APPENDIX | STATISTICS: THE COLLECTION, ORGANIZATION AND INTERPRETATION OF DATA

CONTENTS

PREFACE   xxiii

CHAPTER **1** | INTRODUCTION   1

THE SCOPE OF PSYCHOLOGY   1   ELECTRICALLY TRIGGERED IMAGES   AMBIGUOUS SIGHTS AND SOUNDS   THE PERCEPTUAL WORLD OF INFANTS   DISPLAYS   COMPLEX SOCIAL BEHAVIOR IN HUMANS

A SCIENCE OF MANY FACES   5   DREAMS AS MENTAL EXPERIENCES   DREAMS AS BEHAVIOR   DREAMS AS COGNITION   DREAMS AND SOCIAL BEHAVIOR   DREAMS AND HUMAN DEVELOPMENT   DREAMS AND INDIVIDUAL DIFFERENCES   PERSPECTIVES ON PSYCHOLOGY

THE TASK OF PSYCHOLOGY   11

PART ONE | ACTION 13

CHAPTER **2** | BIOLOGICAL BASES OF BEHAVIOR   15

THE ORGANISM AS MACHINE   16   DESCARTES AND THE REFLEX CONCEPT   THE BASIC NERVOUS FUNCTIONS: RECEPTION, INTEGRATION, REACTION

NERVE CELL AND NERVE IMPULSE   18   THE NEURON   THE ELECTRICAL ACTIVITY OF THE NEURON

INTERACTION AMONG NERVE CELLS   24   THE REFLEX   INFERRING SYNAPTIC FUNCTION   THE SYNAPTIC MECHANISM

INTERACTION THROUGH THE BLOODSTREAM: THE ENDOCRINE SYSTEM   32

THE MAIN STRUCTURES OF THE NERVOUS SYSTEM
33   THE EVOLUTION OF CENTRAL CONTROL   THE PERIPHERAL AND
CENTRAL NERVOUS SYSTEMS

THE CEREBRAL CORTEX   38   PROJECTION AREAS   ASSOCIA-
TION AREAS   HOW NEAT IS THE HIERARCHY?

ONE BRAIN OR TWO?   48   EVIDENCE FROM SPLIT BRAINS
LATERALIZATION IN NORMAL SUBJECTS   TWO MODES OF MENTAL FUNC-
TIONING   WHAT THE BRAIN CAN TELL US ABOUT THE MIND

RECOVERY FROM BRAIN INJURY   53   REPAIR FROM
WITHIN   REPAIR FROM WITHOUT   REHABILITATION

SOME FINAL COMMENTS   56

SUMMARY   57

CHAPTER 3 | MOTIVATION   61

MOTIVATION AS DIRECTION   61   CONTROL SYSTEMS
SELF-REGULATION   HOMEOSTASIS

TEMPERATURE REGULATION   64   TEMPERATURE CONTROL
FROM WITHIN   TEMPERATURE CONTROL BY BEHAVIOR   THE AUTO-
NOMIC NERVOUS SYSTEM AND TEMPERATURE CONTROL   SENSING THE IN-
TERNAL ENVIRONMENT: THE HYPOTHALAMUS

THIRST   67   VOLUME RECEPTORS   OSMORECEPTORS

HUNGER   69   THE SIGNALS FOR FEEDING   HYPOTHALAMIC CON-
TROL CENTERS   FOOD SELECTION   OBESITY   ANOREXIA AND BULIMIA

FEAR AND RAGE   81   THREAT AND THE AUTONOMIC NERVOUS
SYSTEM   CENTRAL CONTROLS   DISRUPTIVE EFFECTS OF AUTONOMIC
AROUSAL   PAIN AND THE ENDORPHIN SYSTEM

SLEEP AND WAKING   88   WAKING   SLEEP AND BRAIN ACTIV-
ITY   THE STAGES OF SLEEP   THE FUNCTIONS OF SLEEP   DREAMS

WHAT DIFFERENT MOTIVES HAVE IN COMMON   95
THE PSYCHOLOGY OF REWARD AND THE AROUSAL LEVEL   THE BIOLOGY
OF REWARD

THE NATURE OF MOTIVES   101

SUMMARY   102

CHAPTER **4** | LEARNING 105

HABITUATION 106

CLASSICAL CONDITIONING 107 PAVLOV AND THE CONDI-
TIONED REFLEX THE MAJOR PHENOMENA OF CLASSICAL CONDITIONING
EXTENSIONS OF CLASSICAL CONDITIONING

INSTRUMENTAL CONDITIONING 115 THORNDIKE AND
THE LAW OF EFFECT SKINNER AND OPERANT BEHAVIOR THE MAJOR
PHENOMENA OF INSTRUMENTAL CONDITIONING

COGNITIVE LEARNING 126 A COGNITIVE VIEW OF CLASSI-
CAL CONDITIONING A COGNITIVE VIEW OF INSTRUMENTAL CONDITION-
ING

VARIETIES OF LEARNING 136 BIOLOGICAL CONSTRAINTS
ON ASSOCIATIVE LEARNING: BELONGINGNESS ADAPTIVE SPECIALIZATIONS
OF LEARNING SIMILARITIES IN WHAT DIFFERENT SPECIES LEARN

COMPLEX COGNITION IN ANIMALS 142 COGNITIVE
MAPS INSIGHTFUL BEHAVIOR

TAKING STOCK 147

SUMMARY 148

PART TWO | COGNITION 151

CHAPTER **5** | SENSORY PROCESSES 153

THE ORIGINS OF KNOWLEDGE 153 THE EMPIRICIST
VIEW THE NATIVIST REJOINDER DETECTION AND DECISION SENSORY
CODING

A SURVEY OF THE SENSES 165 KINESTHESIS AND THE
VESTIBULAR SENSES THE SKIN SENSES THE SENSE OF TASTE THE SENSE
OF SMELL HEARING THE SENSES IN OVERVIEW

VISION 176 THE STIMULUS: LIGHT GATHERING THE STIMULUS:
THE EYE THE VISUAL RECEPTORS INTERACTION IN TIME: ADAPTATION
INTERACTION IN SPACE: CONTRAST COLOR THE PHYSIOLOGICAL BASIS
OF COLOR VISION FEATURE DETECTORS

TAKING STOCK 197

SUMMARY 197

CHAPTER **6** | PERCEPTION 201

THE PROBLEM OF PERCEPTION 201

THE PERCEPTION OF DEPTH: WHERE IS IT? 202
BINOCULAR CUES MONOCULAR CUES THE PERCEPTION OF DEPTH
THROUGH MOTION INNATE FACTORS IN DEPTH PERCEPTION

THE PERCEPTION OF MOVEMENT: WHAT IS IT
DOING? 206 ILLUSIONS OF MOVEMENT PERCEIVED STABILITY

FORM PERCEPTION: WHAT IS IT? 208 THE INFORMA-
TION-PROCESSING APPROACH THE ELEMENTS OF FORM PERCEPTUAL
SEGREGATION PATTERN RECOGNITION THE PROCESSING SEQUENCE IN
FORM PERCEPTION

PERCEPTUAL PROBLEM SOLVING 222 THE LOGIC OF PER-
CEPTION WHEN LOGIC FAILS: IMPOSSIBLE FIGURES

PERCEPTUAL SELECTION: ATTENTION 225 SELECTION
BY PHYSICAL ORIENTATION CENTRAL SELECTION

THE PERCEPTION OF REALITY 228 EMPIRICISM AND
NATIVISM REVISITED SIZE AND SHAPE CONSTANCY LIGHTNESS CON-
STANCY

THE REPRESENTATION OF REALITY IN ART 234
SEEING AND KNOWING THE RENAISSANCE: SCENES THROUGH A WINDOW
FRAME THE IMPRESSIONISTS: HOW A SCENE IS PERCEIVED THE MOD-
ERNS: HOW A SCENE IS CONCEIVED

SUMMARY 239

CHAPTER **7** | MEMORY 243

STUDYING MEMORY 243 SOME PRELIMINARY DISTINCTIONS
ENCODING, STORAGE, RETRIEVAL

ENCODING 245 THE STAGE THEORY OF MEMORY A CHANGED
EMPHASIS: ACTIVE MEMORY AND ORGANIZATION

RETRIEVAL 255 THE RELATION BETWEEN ORIGINAL ENCODING
AND RETRIEVAL ELABORATIVE REHEARSAL MEMORY SEARCH IMPLICIT
RETRIEVAL

WHEN MEMORY FAILS 261   FORGETTING   CONCEPTUAL
FRAMEWORKS AND REMEMBERING   DISORDERED MEMORIES   EXPLICIT
AND IMPLICIT RETRIEVAL REVISITED

TAKING STOCK 278

SUMMARY 278

CHAPTER **8** THOUGHT AND
KNOWLEDGE 281

ANALOGICAL REPRESENTATIONS 281   MENTAL IMAGES
SPATIAL THINKING

SYMBOLIC REPRESENTATIONS 287   SYMBOLIC ELEMENTS
KNOWLEDGE AND MEMORY

THE PROCESS OF THINKING: SOLVING PROBLEMS
292   ORGANIZATION IN PROBLEM SOLVING   OBSTACLES TO PROBLEM
SOLVING   OVERCOMING OBSTACLES TO SOLUTION   RESTRUCTURING
ARTIFICIAL INTELLIGENCE: PROBLEM SOLVING BY COMPUTER

THE PROCESS OF THINKING: REASONING AND DECI-
SION MAKING 308   DEDUCTIVE REASONING   INDUCTIVE REA-
SONING   DECISION MAKING

COGNITION AND CONSCIOUSNESS 315   MENTAL
PROCESSES THAT GO ON BELOW THE SURFACE   WHAT'S CONSCIOUSNESS
GOOD FOR?

TAKING STOCK 319

SUMMARY 320

CHAPTER **9** LANGUAGE BY LILA R. GLEITMAN 323

MAJOR PROPERTIES OF HUMAN LANGUAGE 324
LANGUAGE IS CREATIVE   LANGUAGE IS STRUCTURED   LANGUAGE IS MEAN-
INGFUL   LANGUAGE IS REFERENTIAL   LANGUAGE IS INTERPERSONAL

THE STRUCTURE OF LANGUAGE 328   PHONEMES   MOR-
PHEMES AND WORDS   PHRASES AND SENTENCES

THE LINGUISTIC HIERARCHY AND MEANING 331
THE MEANING OF WORDS   ORGANIZING WORDS INTO MEANINGFUL
SENTENCES

COMPREHENSION 342   THE SENTENCE ANALYZING MACHINERY
THE INTERACTION OF SYNTAX AND SEMANTICS

THE GROWTH OF LANGUAGE IN THE CHILD   346
THE PROBLEM OF LANGUAGE LEARNING   IS LANGUAGE LEARNING THE AC-
QUISITION OF A SKILL?

LANGUAGE DEVELOPMENT   349   THE SOCIAL ORIGINS OF
SPEECH PRODUCTION   DISCOVERING THE FORMS OF LANGUAGE   THE
ONE-WORD SPEAKER   THE TWO-WORD (TELEGRAPHIC) SPEAKER   LATER
STAGES OF LANGUAGE LEARNING: SYNTAX   FURTHER STAGES OF LAN-
GUAGE LEARNING: WORD MEANING

LANGUAGE LEARNING IN CHANGED ENVIRONMENTS
360   WILD CHILDREN   ISOLATED CHILDREN   LANGUAGE WITHOUT
SOUND   LANGUAGE WITHOUT A MODEL   CHILDREN DEPRIVED OF ACCESS
TO SOME OF THE MEANINGS   THE CASE OF HELEN KELLER

LANGUAGE LEARNING WITH CHANGED ENDOW-
MENTS   367   THE CRITICAL PERIOD HYPOTHESIS   LANGUAGE IN
NONHUMANS

LANGUAGE AND ITS LEARNING   373

SUMMARY   374

PART THREE | SOCIAL BEHAVIOR 377

CHAPTER 10 | THE BIOLOGICAL BASIS
OF SOCIAL BEHAVIOR
379

THE SOCIAL NATURE OF HUMANS AND ANIMALS
379   NATURAL SELECTION AND SURVIVAL   BUILT-IN SOCIAL BEHAVIORS

BIOLOGICAL SOURCES OF AGGRESSION   383   CON-
FLICT BETWEEN SPECIES: PREDATION AND DEFENSE   CONFLICT BE-
TWEEN LIKE AND LIKE

THE BIOLOGICAL BASIS OF LOVE: THE MALE-
FEMALE BOND   390   SEXUAL BEHAVIOR   SEXUAL CHOICE
REPRODUCTION AND TIMING   EVOLUTION AND MATING SYSTEMS

THE BIOLOGICAL BASIS OF LOVE: THE PARENT-
CHILD BOND   399   THE INFANT'S ATTACHMENT TO THE
MOTHER   THE MOTHER'S ATTACHMENT TO THE INFANT

COMMUNICATING MOTIVES 401   EXPRESSIVE MOVEMENTS: ANIMAL DISPLAY   THE EXPRESSION OF EMOTIONS IN HUMANS   THE DIFFERENCE BETWEEN DISPLAY AND LANGUAGE

SOCIAL COGNITION IN PRIMATES 405

SELF-SACRIFICE AND ALTRUISM 407   ALTRUISM IN ANIMALS   ALTRUISM IN HUMANS

ETHOLOGY AND HUMAN NATURE 412

SUMMARY 412

CHAPTER 11 | SOCIAL COGNITION AND EMOTION 415

SOCIAL COGNITION AND SOCIAL REALITY 416   THE INTERPERSONAL NATURE OF BELIEF   SOCIAL COMPARISON   COGNITIVE PROCESSES AND BELIEF

ATTITUDES 420   ATTITUDES AND BEHAVIOR   ATTITUDE CHANGE   ATTITUDE STABILITY

PERCEIVING OTHERS 426   FORMING IMPRESSIONS   IMPRESSIONS OF OTHERS AS PATTERNS   IMPRESSIONS OF OTHERS AS COGNITIVE CONSTRUCTIONS   IMPRESSION MANAGEMENT

ATTRIBUTION 432   ATTRIBUTION AS A RATIONAL PROCESS   ERRORS IN THE ATTRIBUTION PROCESS

PERCEIVING ONESELF 437   THE SELF-CONCEPT   SELF-PERCEPTION AND ATTRIBUTION

EMOTION: PERCEIVING ONE'S OWN INNER STATES 439   THE JAMES-LANGE THEORY   THE ATTRIBUTION-OF-AROUSAL THEORY   BEYOND ATTRIBUTION-OF-AROUSAL THEORY   COMPLEX EMOTIONS   EMOTION AND THE THEATER

TAKING STOCK 449

SUMMARY 450

CHAPTER 12 | SOCIAL INTERACTION 453

RELATING TO OTHERS: ONE-ON-ONE INTERACTIONS 453   SOCIAL EXCHANGE AND RECIPROCITY   ALTRUISM   ATTRACTION   LOVE

SOCIAL INFLUENCE: MANY-ON-ONE INTERACTIONS
467   SOCIAL FACILITATION: SOCIAL INFLUENCE BY THE PRESENCE OF
OTHERS   CONFORMITY   BLIND OBEDIENCE   SOCIAL IMPACT THEORY

LEADERSHIP: ONE-ON-MANY INTERACTIONS   479
GREAT PERSON OR SOCIAL FORCES   LEADERSHIP IN THE LABORATORY

CROWD BEHAVIOR: MANY-ON-MANY INTERACTIONS
482   THE EMPHASIS ON THE IRRATIONAL: DEINDIVIDUATION   COGNI-
TIVE FACTORS AND THE PANICKY CROWD

SOME FINAL COMMENTS   486   COMMON THEMES   THE
GENERALITY OF SOCIAL PSYCHOLOGY

SUMMARY   489

PART FOUR | DEVELOPMENT 491

CHAPTER **13** | PHYSICAL AND COGNI-
TIVE DEVELOPMENT   493

WHAT IS DEVELOPMENT?   493   DEVELOPMENT AS DIFFEREN-
TIATION   DEVELOPMENT AS GROWTH   DEVELOPMENT AS ORDERLY PRO-
GRESSION

THE PHYSICAL BASIS OF DEVELOPMENT   499   THE
MECHANISM OF GENETIC TRANSMISSION   ENVIRONMENTS AT DIFFERENT
POINTS IN DEVELOPMENT   ENVIRONMENT AND MATURATION

PIAGET'S THEORY OF COGNITIVE DEVELOPMENT
505   SENSORY-MOTOR INTELLIGENCE   THE PREOPERATIONAL PERIOD
CONCRETE AND FORMAL OPERATIONS

WHAT IS THE COGNITIVE STARTING POINT?   511
SPACE AND OBJECTS IN INFANCY   NUMBER IN INFANCY   SOCIAL COGNI-
TION IN INFANCY: THE EXISTENCE OF OTHER MINDS

COGNITIVE DEVELOPMENT IN PRESCHOOLERS   516
THE MEANING OF MENTAL STAGE   NUMERICAL SKILLS IN PRESCHOOLERS
SOCIAL COGNITION IN PRESCHOOLERS: DEVELOPING A THEORY OF MIND
SEQUENCES OR STAGES?

THE CAUSES OF COGNITIVE GROWTH   522   THE NA-
TIVIST APPROACH: MATURATION   THE EMPIRICIST APPROACH: SPECIFIC

LEARNING   PIAGET'S APPROACH: ASSIMILATION AND ACCOMMODATION
THE INFORMATION-PROCESSING APPROACH: CHUNKING AND STRATEGIES

COGNITIVE DEVELOPMENT FROM A CROSS-
CULTURAL PERSPECTIVE   528

TAKING STOCK   530

SUMMARY   530

CHAPTER **14** | SOCIAL DEVELOPMENT
                   533

ATTACHMENT   534   THE ROOTS OF ATTACHMENT   PATTERNS OF
ATTACHMENT   THE EFFECT OF EARLY MATERNAL SEPARATION   WHEN
THERE IS NO ATTACHMENT AT ALL   ARE THE EFFECTS OF EARLY SOCIAL
DEPRIVATION REVERSIBLE?

CHILDHOOD SOCIALIZATION   544   CULTURAL VALUES
AND CHILD REARING   MECHANISMS OF SOCIALIZATION   THE FIRST
AGENTS OF SOCIALIZATION: THE PARENTS   THE CHILD'S EFFECT ON THE
PARENTS

THE DEVELOPMENT OF MORALITY   550   NOT DOING
WRONG   DOING GOOD   MORAL REASONING

THE DEVELOPMENT OF SEX AND GENDER   556   GEN-
DER ROLES   CONSTITUTIONAL FACTORS AND SEX DIFFERENCES   SOCIAL
FACTORS AND SEX DIFFERENCES   THEORIES OF GENDER TYPING   SEXUAL
ORIENTATION

DEVELOPMENT AFTER CHILDHOOD   569   ADOLESCENCE
ADULTHOOD

SUMMARY   576

PART FIVE | INDIVIDUAL DIFFERENCES 579

CHAPTER **15** | INTELLIGENCE: ITS NA-
                   TURE AND MEASURE-
                   MENT   581

MENTAL TESTS   582   THE STUDY OF VARIATION   EVALUATING
MENTAL TESTS   USING TESTS FOR SELECTION

INTELLIGENCE TESTING 589 MEASURING INTELLIGENCE
AN AREA OF APPLICATION: MENTAL RETARDATION INTELLIGENCE AND
AGE

WHAT IS INTELLIGENCE? THE PSYCHOMETRIC AP-
PROACH 599 THE STRUCTURE OF MENTAL ABILITIES

WHAT IS INTELLIGENCE? THE INFORMATION-
PROCESSING APPROACH 602 SIMPLE COGNITIVE CORRE-
LATES COMPLEX COGNITIVE COMPONENTS STRATEGIES AND INTELLEC-
TUAL FUNCTIONING

WHAT IS INTELLIGENCE? BEYOND IQ 607 PRACTICAL
INTELLIGENCE THE NOTION OF MULTIPLE INTELLIGENCES THE CUL-
TURAL CONTEXT OF INTELLIGENCE

NATURE, NURTURE, AND IQ 611 SOME POLITICAL ISSUES
GENETIC FACTORS ENVIRONMENTAL FACTORS HERITABILITY GROUP
DIFFERENCES IN IQ

TAKING STOCK 623

SUMMARY 624

CHAPTER **16** | PERSONALITY I: ASSESS-
MENT, TRAIT THEORY,
AND THE BEHAVIORAL-
COGNITIVE APPROACH 627

METHODS OF ASSESSMENT 629 STRUCTURED PERSONAL-
ITY TESTS UNSTRUCTURED PERSONALITY TESTS

THE TRAIT APPROACH 639 THE SEARCH FOR THE RIGHT
TAXONOMY THE TRAIT-SITUATION CONTROVERSY TRAITS AND
BIOLOGY

THE BEHAVIORAL-COGNITIVE APPROACH 658
RADICAL BEHAVIORISM SOCIAL LEARNING THEORY

SUMMARY 666

CHAPTER **17** | PERSONALITY II:
PSYCHODYNAMIC,
HUMANISTIC, AND
SOCIOCULTURAL
APPROACHES 669

THE PSYCHODYNAMIC APPROACH: FREUD AND PSY-
CHOANALYSIS 669 THE ORIGINS OF PSYCHOANALYTIC

THOUGHT   UNCONSCIOUS CONFLICT   THE ORIGINS OF UNCONSCIOUS
CONFLICT   WINDOWS INTO THE UNCONSCIOUS   A CRITICAL LOOK AT
FREUDIAN THEORY

THE PSYCHODYNAMIC APPROACH: PERSONALITY
DIFFERENCES 691 PATTERNS OF NEUROTIC CONFLICT   COPING
PATTERNS AND MENTAL HEALTH

THE HUMANISTIC APPROACH 695 THE MAJOR FEATURES
OF THE HUMANISTIC MOVEMENT   EVALUATING THE HUMANISTIC AP-
PROACH

THE SOCIOCULTURAL PERSPECTIVE 702 HUMAN DI-
VERSITY   HUMAN SAMENESS   COLLECTIVISM AND INDIVIDUALISM   CUL-
TURAL DIFFERENCES IN THE CONCEPT OF THE SELF

TAKING STOCK 710

SUMMARY 711

CHAPTER 18 PSYCHOPATHOLOGY 715

DIFFERENT CONCEPTIONS OF MADNESS 715 PSY-
CHOPATHOLOGY AS DEMONIC POSSESSION   PSYCHOPATHOLOGY AS A DIS-
EASE

THE UNDERLYING PATHOLOGY MODEL 722 SUBCAT-
EGORIES OF THE PATHOLOGY MODEL   CLASSIFYING MENTAL DISORDERS
EXPLAINING DISORDER: DIATHESIS, STRESS, AND PATHOLOGY

SCHIZOPHRENIA 726 SIGNS AND SYMPTOMS   THE SEARCH
FOR THE UNDERLYING PATHOLOGY   ULTIMATE CAUSES OF SCHIZOPHRE-
NIA   THE PATHOLOGY MODEL AND SCHIZOPHRENIA

MOOD DISORDERS 736 BIPOLAR AND UNIPOLAR SYN-
DROMES   ORGANIC FACTORS   PSYCHOGENIC FACTORS   MOOD DISOR-
DERS AND THE DIATHESIS-STRESS CONCEPTION

ANXIETY DISORDERS 744 PHOBIAS   OBSESSIVE-
COMPULSIVE DISORDER   GENERALIZED ANXIETY DISORDER   PANIC DIS-
ORDER   POST-TRAUMATIC STRESS DISORDER

DISSOCIATIVE DISORDERS 750 FACTORS UNDERLYING
DISSOCIATIVE DISORDERS   DISSOCIATIVE DISORDERS AND THE DIATHESIS-
STRESS CONCEPTION

SOMATOFORM AND PSYCHOPHYSIOLOGICAL DISOR-
DERS 752 SOMATOFORM DISORDERS   PSYCHOPHYSIOLOGICAL
DISORDERS

A CATEGORIZING REVIEW 756

SOCIAL DEVIANCE 757 THE SOCIOPATH SOCIOPATHY AND THE DISORDER CONCEPT

THE SCOPE OF PSYCHOPATHOLOGY 759

SUMMARY 760

CHAPTER **19** | TREATMENT OF PSYCHO-PATHOLOGY 763

BIOLOGICAL THERAPIES 763 PHARMACOTHERAPIES EVALUATING A MEDICATION PSYCHOSURGERY CONVULSIVE TREATMENTS

PSYCHOTHERAPY 772 CLASSICAL PSYCHOANALYSIS PSYCHODYNAMIC THERAPY BEHAVIOR THERAPY COGNITIVE-BEHAVIORAL THERAPIES HUMANISTIC THERAPIES SOME COMMON THEMES EXTENSIONS OF PSYCHOTHERAPY

EVALUATING THERAPEUTIC OUTCOME 789 DOES PSYCHOTHERAPY WORK? COMPARING DIFFERENT THERAPIES

A CENTURY OF THERAPY 795

SUMMARY 796

EPILOGUE 798

APPENDIX | STATISTICS: THE COLLECTION, ORGANIZATION, AND INTERPRETATION OF DATA BY NEIL A. MACMILLAN A1

DESCRIBING THE DATA A2 CATEGORICAL AND ORDINAL SCALES INTERVAL SCALES RATIO SCALES

COLLECTING THE DATA A4 THE EXPERIMENT THE OBSERVATIONAL STUDY THE CASE STUDY

SELECTING THE SUBJECTS A5 SAMPLE AND POPULATION RANDOM AND STRATIFIED SAMPLES SAMPLING RESPONSES

ORGANIZING THE DATA: DESCRIPTIVE STATISTICS A7 THE FREQUENCY DISTRIBUTION MEASURES OF CENTRAL TEN-

DENCY   MEASURES OF VARIABILITY   CONVERTING SCORES TO COM-
PARE THEM   THE NORMAL DISTRIBUTION

DESCRIBING THE RELATION BETWEEN TWO VARI-
ABLES: CORRELATION   A14   POSITIVE AND NEGATIVE COR-
RELATION   THE CORRELATION COEFFICIENT   INTERPRETING AND MISIN-
TERPRETING CORRELATIONS

INTERPRETING DATA: INFERENTIAL STATISTICS
A18   ACCOUNTING FOR VARIABILITY   HYPOTHESIS TESTING   SOME IM-
PLICATIONS OF STATISTICAL INFERENCE

SUMMARY   A27

GLOSSARY   A29

REFERENCES   A52

ACKNOWLEDGMENTS AND COPYRIGHTS   A94

INDEX   A101

PREFACE

This is the fourth edition of my book *Psychology.* One reason for this revision is the obvious fact that, like any other discipline, psychology advances and develops. When I began my graduate work fifty years ago, psychologists tended to be rather defensive about the status of the field and were perhaps a bit too loud in proclaiming that "Psychology is a science!" But by now there is no need for such defensive proclamations, for that assertion has become a simple statement of fact. In the last half a century psychology has assuredly become a "real" and vigorously progressive science.

As a field advances, so must all attempts to describe it. These advances, together with the suggestions by the many students and colleagues who have used this text, prompted a number of changes that I describe below.

THE OVERALL AIM: COHESION IN A DIVERSE FIELD

Before describing these changes, let me briefly review what has not changed: my original aims. In writing *Psychology,* I sought to present the field in all its diversity while yet conveying the sense in which it is a coherent intellectual enterprise. In pursuit of this goal, I did the following:

1. To present the different sub-areas of psychology, I organized the book around five main questions: How do humans (and where relevant, animals) act, how do they know, how do they interact, how do they develop, and how do they differ from each other?

2. To provide some intellectual cohesion, I considered each topic against the backdrop of one or two major ideas that could serve as an organizing and unifying framework. Thus the chapter on the biological bases of behavior opens with Descartes' conception of the organism as a machine and the next chapter treats various aspects of motivated behavior as manifestations of negative feedback. To relate the material across chapters, I used several overarching themes. For example, the various chapters that deal with cognition ("Sensory Processes," "Perception," "Memory," "Thought and Knowledge," and "Language") all consider variations on the two controversies of nature versus nurture and psychological atomism versus organization.

3. In many cases, the attempt at integration required taking a step backward to look at psychology's intellectual history, for a number of the field's endeavors are hard to explain unless one points to the paths that led up to them. Why did Thorndike study cats in puzzle boxes? Why did his conclusions have such an important effect on American psychology? Why were they challenged by Köhler and Tolman? It still pays to take a serious look at the work of such pioneers before turning to the present. Much as a river's water is clearer when it is taken from its source, so issues that have become more and more complex as detail has been piled upon detail become plainer and more evident when traced back to their origin.

GENERAL ORGANIZATION

Several organizational changes distinguish this edition from the previous ones. One concerns the discussions of Freud, psychoanalysis, and current dynamic approaches to personality, which are now brought together. Toward this end I eliminated the separate chapter on psychoanalysis, and dealt with that material within the general two-chapter discussion of personality (specifically, in Chapter 17). Another is a revision of the old chapter on thinking. This is now entitled "Thought and Knowledge" and deals with both the knowledge base of thought (that is, generic and semantic memory, which were formerly discussed in the chapter on memory) as well as the processes of thinking (that is, problem solving, reasoning, and decision making). As a result, the chapter on memory is primarily devoted to episodic memory. Further changes represent updatings (in some cases, major updatings) of the subject matter, which are best described within an outline of the overall structure of the book.

After an introductory chapter, the book is divided into five parts that reflect the perspectives from which most psychological phenomena can be regarded: Action, Cognition, Social Behavior, Development, and Individual Differences. In brief outline, they cover the following topics:

PART I: ACTION

This part focuses on overt behavior and its physiological basis. It begins by considering the biological underpinnings of human and animal action, leading to a discussion of the nervous system and its operation (Chapter 2) and some phenomena of motivation (Chapter 3). It then asks how organisms can modify their behavior to adapt to new circumstances, a topic which leads to a discussion of classical and instrumental conditioning, modern behavior theory, and more recent approaches that take a more cognitive slant (Chapter 4).

In Chapter 2 ("Biological Bases of Behavior") the discussion of cerebral structures is revised, with demonstrations of hierarchical organization integrated into the description of cerebral anatomy. Other changes concern a greater emphasis on evolutionary issues, and a greater stress on the emerging importance of cognitive neuropsychology. Chapter 3 ("Motivation") uses the concept of potentiation as an overall organizational principle. It also includes a section on pain and endorphins, topics that were formerly dealt with mostly in Chapter 2. Chapter 4 ("Learning") stresses recent developments in animal learning, including work on contingency and modern cognitive approaches to classical and instrumental conditioning. It also explores the adaptive evolutionary perspective, as in a discussion of similarities and differences in the ways various animals learn and remember.

PART II: COGNITION

This part deals with knowledge and how it is gained and used. It begins by asking how the senses provide us with information about the world outside (Chapter 5) and how this information is organized and interpreted to lead to the perception of objects and events (Chapter 6). Further questions concern the way this knowledge is stored in memory and retrieved when needed (Chapter 7), the way it is organized through thinking (Chapter 8), and the way knowledge is communicated to others through the medium of language (Chapter 9).

Many of the changes in this part reflect a greater concern with recent information-processing approaches and a greater stress on evolutionary adaptiveness. Chapter 5 ("Sensory Processes") contains a discussion of evolution and sensory equipment, as well as a new section on feature detectors (a topic formerly dealt with in Chapter 6). In Chapter 6 ("Perception"), the organization has been changed to give more prominence to modern approaches to pattern recognition, including a section on free-floating primitive features. Chapter 7 ("Memory") focuses primarily on episodic memory, including the modern emphasis on encoding and retrieval, the role of schemas in memory, the issue of false memories, and the difference between explicit and implicit memory. Chapter 8 ("Thought and Knowledge") begins with the database on which thinking rests, including topics that were formerly dealt with in the previous chapter: analogical representations (imagery and spatial thinking) and symbolic or digital representations (models of semantic memory, including a new section on parallel distributed processing).

PART III: SOCIAL BEHAVIOR

This part concerns our interactions with others. It begins with a discussion of built-in social tendencies in humans and animals, a topic to which ethology and evolutionary theory have made major contributions (Chapter 10). It then turns to modern social psychology, considering how people try to understand the social situation in which they find themselves, how they interpret their own internal states and emotions, and how they interact with others (Chapters 11 and 12).

There have been several changes in this section. In Chapter 10 ("The Biological Bases of Social Behavior") the treatment of social cognition in primates has been expanded and now includes a discussion of whether monkeys and apes have a "theory of mind." The section on human mating patterns has also been revised. Chapter 11 ("Social Cognition and Emotion") continues to focus on the way individuals interpret social events, including discussions of attitudes and attitude change, attribution, impressions of others, and the interpretation of one's own internal states, but it now also has an expanded discussion of emotions and facial expression. Chapter 12 ("Social Interaction") continues to treat the way individuals deal with others. In addition to discussions of social exchange, attraction and love, conformity, obedience, and crowd behavior, it has a new section on leadership and on social dilemmas.

PART IV: DEVELOPMENT

This section contains two chapters on development. Chapter 13 ("Physical and Cognitive Development") continues to focus on recent, post-Piagetian approaches to mental growth and includes material on counting and numerical skills in infants and pre-schoolers, work on social cognition in infants and pre-schoolers, including studies of false beliefs and their bearing on the child's development of a "theory of mind." Chapter 14 ("Social Development") has been updated with expanded discussions of such topics as moral development, empathy, sex, and gender. Among new developments treated in this chapter is the role of cultural factors in moral reasoning and recent discoveries about the physiological and genetic bases of homosexuality.

PART V: INDIVIDUAL DIFFERENCES

This part begins with a chapter on mental testing in general and intelligence testing in particular (Chapter 15), and then continues with two chapters on personality assessment and theory (Chapters 16 and 17). It continues by looking at several varieties of psychopathology and asking how they arise (Chapter 18), and concludes by examining various methods of treatment and therapy (Chapter 19).

Chapter 15 ("Intelligence") is updated in various ways, including a section on more recent attempts to understand intelligence in information-processing terms. New material includes discussions of the use of intelligence tests as neuropsychological instruments, reaction time as a measure of mental ability, and intelligence considered in a social and cultural context. As already noted, the two chapters on personality have been reorganized to include both early and more recent psychoanalytic conceptions, thus incorporating material that was formerly presented in a separate chapter on Freud and psychoanalysis. Chapter 16 ("Personality I") considers methods of personality assessment and discusses trait theory and behavioral-cognitive theory as two of five theoretical approaches to personality, with particular attention to the trait-situation controversy and to recent attempts to look for biological and genetic bases of personality differences. Chapter 17 ("Personality II") takes up three other theoretical approaches to personality—the psychodynamic, humanistic, and the sociocultural. It includes a full treatment of psychoanalytic formulations, beginning with Freud's original theories, continuing with more recent psychodynamic approaches, and concluding with a discussion of early and later critiques. A completely new section describes some recent attempts to put the study of personality in a social and cultural context.

Both Chapter 18 ("Psychopathology") and Chapter 19 ("Treatment of Psychopathology") have been drastically updated to include modern developments, such as new psychobiological theories, new pharmacological approaches to treatment, and new approaches to the evaluation of treatment outcome.

THE READER AND THE BOOK

It is sometimes said that students in the introductory course want to learn about things that are relevant to themselves and to their own lives. But why should this be a problem? When you come right down to it, there is something odd about the idea that psychology is not relevant to anyone's particular life history—specialist and nonspecialist alike. Psychology deals with the nature of human experience and behavior, about the hows and whys of what we do, think, and feel. Everyone has perceived, learned, remembered, and forgotten, has been angry and afraid and in love, has given in to group pressure and stood up to it. In short, everyone has experienced most of the phenomena that psychology tries to explain. This being so, psychology cannot fail to be relevant.

I've tried to point out this relevance by a liberal use of examples from ordinary experience and a frequent resort to metaphors of one kind or another, in the hope that in so doing I would show the direct relation of many psychological phenomena to the reader's own life. In these attempts, the most important guide has been my own experience as a classroom teacher. There is little doubt that one of the best ways of learning something is to teach it, for in trying to explain something to others, you first have to clarify it for yourself. This holds for the subject matter of every course I have ever taught, but most especially for the introductory course. Students in an advanced course will come at you with tough and searching questions; they want to know about the evidence that bears on a theory of, say, color vision or language acquisition, and about how that evidence was obtained. But students in an introductory course ask the toughest questions of all. They ask why anyone would ever want to know about color vision (or language acquisition or whatever) in the first place. And they also ask what any one topic has to do with any other. They ask such questions because they—unlike advanced students—have not as yet accepted the premises of the field. They wonder whether the emperor is really wearing any clothes. As a result, they make me ask myself afresh what the field of psychology is all about—what the emperor's clothes are really like when you look at them closely.

This book, as well as its predecessors, grew out of my attempts to answer such questions over the years in which I have taught the introductory course, to answer them not only to satisfy the students but also to satisfy myself.

SUPPLEMENTARY MATERIALS

To help serve the needs of students, instructors, and teaching assistants, several supplementary materials are available with this text.

1. For the student:

There is a complete study guide for students, prepared by two of my colleagues and collaborators, John Jonides of the University of Michigan and Paul Rozin of the University of Pennsylvania. This study guide, a revised version of the guide the same authors wrote for the three previous editions of *Psychology,* should prove very useful to students who want some help and guidance in mastering the material in the text. Moreover, for every chapter, it provides experiments and observational studies that students can carry out on their own to get some first-hand experience with psychology's subject matter.

2. For the instructor:

There is an instructor's manual, prepared by Kimberly Cassidy of Bryn Mawr College, Christine Massey of Swarthmore College, Hilary Schmidt of New Jersey Medical School, and myself, which offers specific suggestions for every textbook chapter, including discussion topics, a bibliography, an annotated film and media guide prepared by James B. Maas of Cornell University, and classroom demonstrations. Included in the demonstrations are materials necessary to perform some thirty in-class experiments covering a range of phenomena, from the speed of the nervous impulse to several perceptual demonstrations, the Stroop effect, a number of reasoning problems, demonstrations of first impressions in the perception of personality, and a demonstration of gender stereotypes. Transparencies, student worksheets, data summaries, and detailed instructions for the teacher are also included. These demonstrations are adapted from those that I and my collaborators, Paul Rozin and Lila Gleitman (both of the University of Pennsylvania), have used in our own teaching.

Paul Cornwell of Pennsylvania State University, Richard Day of McMaster University, and John Jonides of the University of Michigan, with the help of Tibor Palfai of Syracuse University, have prepared a test-item file, which includes questions for all chapters plus the statistical appendix. A proportion of these questions have been statistically analyzed at Syracuse and Pennsylvania State Universities; the resulting data are included in the printed test-item file. Of course, this test-item file is also available on diskette in MS-DOS and Macintosh formats.

ACKNOWLEDGMENTS

There remains the pleasant task of thanking the many friends and colleagues who helped so greatly in the various phases of writing this book and its predecessors. Some read parts of the manuscript and gave valuable advice and criticism. Others talked to me at length about various issues in the field, which I then saw more clearly. I am very grateful to them all. These many helpers, and the main areas in which they advised me, are as follows:

BIOLOGICAL FOUNDATIONS

Elizabeth Adkins-Regan, Cornell University; Norman T. Adler, University of Pennsylvania; Robert C. Bolles, University of Washington; Brooks Carder; Dorothy Cheney, University of Pennsylvania; John D. Corbit, Brown University; Alan N. Epstein, late of the University of Pennsylvania; Steven Fluharty, University of Pennsylvania; Charles R. Gallistel, University of California, Los Angeles; Harvey J. Grill, University of Pennsylvania; Jerre Levy, University of Chicago; Martha McClintock, University of Chicago; Peter M. Milner, McGill University; Douglas G. Mook, University of Virginia; Allen Parducci, University of California, Los Angeles; Judith Rodin, University of Pennsylvania; Paul Rozin, University of Pennsylvania; Jonathan I. Schull, University of Rochester and Swarthmore College; Robert Seyfarth, University of Pennsylvania; W. John Smith, University of Pennsylvania; Paul G. Shinkman, University of North Carolina; Peter Shizgall, Concordia University; Edward M. Stricker, University of Pittsburgh.

LEARNING

Ruth Colwill, Brown University; Frank Costin, University of Illinois; Richard B. Day, McMaster University; Paula Durlach, McMaster University;

Richard C. Gonzales, Bryn Mawr College; Robert Henderson, University of Illinois; Werner Honig, Dalhousie University; Francis W. Irwin, late of University of Pennsylvania; Nicholas Mackintosh, Cambridge University; Paul Rozin, University of Pennsylvania; Robert Rescorla, University of Pennsylvania; Jonathan I. Schull, University of Rochester and Swarthmore College; Barry Schwartz, Swarthmore College; Richard L. Solomon, University of Pennsylvania; John Staddon, Duke University.

SENSATION AND PERCEPTION

Linda Bartoshuk, Yale University; Michael Gamble, Malaspina College; Julian E. Hochberg, Columbia University; Leo M. Hurvich, University of Pennsylvania; Dorothea Jameson, University of Pennsylvania; R. Duncan Luce, University of California, Irvine; Neil A. MacMillan, Brooklyn College; James L. McClelland, Carnegie-Mellon; Jacob Nachmias, University of Pennsylvania; Edward Pugh, University of Pennsylvania; Irwin Rock, University of California, Berkeley; Burton S. Rosner, Oxford University; Robert Steinman, University of Maryland; Denise Varner, University of Washington; Brian Wandell, Stanford University; Jeremy M. Wolfe, Massachussetts Institute of Technology; James L. Zacks, Michigan State University.

COGNITION

Lynn A. Cooper, Columbia University; Robert G. Crowder, Yale University; Lila R. Gleitman, University of Pennsylvania; Douglas Hintzman, University of Oregon; Francis C. Keil, Cornell University; Deborah Kemler, Swarthmore College; Stephen M. Kosslyn, Harvard University; John Jonides, University of Michigan; Michael McCloskey, Johns Hopkins University; Douglas Medin, University of Illinois; Morris Moscovitch, University of Toronto; Ulric Neisser, Emory University; Daniel N. Osherson, Massachusetts Institute of Technology; David Premack, University of Pennsylvania; Daniel Reisberg, Reed College; Miriam W. Schustack, University of California, San Diego; Myrna Schwartz, University of Pennsylvania; Michael Turvey, University of Connecticut; Rose T. Zacks, Michigan State University.

LANGUAGE

Sharon L. Armstrong, Drake University; Anne Fowler, Bryn Mawr College; John Gilbert, University of British Columbia; Roberta Golinkoff, University of Delaware; Barbara Landau, Columbia University; Anne Lederer, University of Pennsylvania; Elissa Newport, University of Rochester; Ruth Ostrin, Medical Research Council, Cambridge, England; Ted Suppala, University of Rochester; Kenneth Wexler, Massachusetts Institute of Technology.

SOCIAL PSYCHOLOGY

Solomon E. Asch, University of Pennsylvania; Joel Cooper, Princeton University; Phoebe C. Ellsworth, University of Michigan; Frederick J.

Evans, Carrier Foundation, Bellemead, N.J.; Alan Fridlund, University of California, Santa Barbara; Larry Gross, University of Pennsylvania; Michael Lessac; Clark R. McCauley, Jr., Bryn Mawr College; Stanley Milgram, late of City College of New York; Martin T. Orne, University of Pennsylvania; Albert Pepitone, University of Pennsylvania; Dennis Regan, Cornell University; Lee Ross, Stanford University; John Sabini, University of Pennsylvania; Philip R. Shaver, University of Denver; R. Lance Shotland, Pennsylvania State University.

DEVELOPMENT

Thomas Ayres, Clarkson College of Technology; Renée Baillargeon, University of Illinois; Anne L. Brown, University of Illinois; Justin Aronfreed, University of Pennsylvania; Edwin Boswell, Ardmore, Pennsylvania; Adele Diamond, University of Pennsylvania; Carol S. Dweck, Columbia University; Margery B. Franklin, Sarah Lawrence College; Rochel Gelman, University of California, Los Angeles; Frederick Gibbons, Iowa State University; Ellen Gleitman, Devon, Pennsylvania; Susan Scanlon Jones, Indiana University; Ed Kako, University of Pennsylvania; Philip J. Kellman, Swarthmore College; Ellen Markman, Stanford University; Elizabeth Spelke, Cornell University; Douglas Wallen, Mankato State University; Sheldon White, Harvard University.

INTELLIGENCE

Jonathan Baron, University of Pennsylvania; James F. Crow, University of Wisconsin; Daniel B. Keating, University of Minnesota; Robert Sternberg, Yale University.

PERSONALITY

Hal Bertilson, Saint Joseph's University; Jack Block, Massachusetts Institute of Technology; Nathan Brody, Wesleyan University; Peter Gay, Yale University; Lewis R. Goldberg, University of Oregon, Eugene; Ruben Gur, University of Pennsylvania; Judith Harackiewicz, Columbia University; John Kihlstrom, University of Arizona; Lester B. Luborsky, University of Pennsylvania; Carl Malmquist, University of Minnesota; Jerry S. Wiggins, University of British Columbia.

PSYCHOPATHOLOGY

Lyn Y. Abramson, University of Wisconsin; Lauren Alloy, Temple University; Kayla F. Bernheim, Livingston County Counseling Services; John B. Brady, University of Pennsylvania; Gerald C. Davison, University of Southern California; Leonard M. Horowitz, Stanford University; Steven Mathysse, McLean Hospital; Sue Mineka, Northwestern University; Ann James Premack, University of Pennsylvania; Rena Repetta, New York University; Martin E. P. Seligman, University of Pennsylvania; Larry Stein, University of California, Irvine; Hans

H. Strupp, Vanderbilt University; Paul L. Wachtel, College of the City University of New York; Ingrid I. Waldron, University of Pennsylvania; Richard Warner, University of Southern California; David R. Williams, University of Pennsylvania; Julius Wishner, late of the University of Pennsylvania; Lisa Zorilla, University of Pennsylvania.

INTELLECTUAL HISTORY

Mark B. Adams, University of Pennsylvania; David DeVries, New York University; Claire E. Gleitman, Ithaca College; Alan C. Kors, University of Pennsylvania; Elisabeth Rozin, Upper Darby, Pennsylvania; Harris B. Savin, Philadelphia, Pennsylvania.

To state in detail how each of these people helped me is impossible. But I do want to express special thanks to a few whose comments helped me to see whole topics in a new light for this edition. I owe special thanks to Charles R. Gallistel of the University of California at Los Angeles, for enormously helpful comments on the entire book, especially the sensory and physiological chapters; to Doug Mook of the University of Virginia, who continued to give wise counsel on problems in the field of motivation; to Jeremy Wolfe of the Massachusetts Institute of Technology, who helped me to understand some important modern developments in the fields of sensation and perception; to Douglas L. Hintzman of the University of Oregon, whose sharp and incisive critique of my old chapter on memory forced me to see that entire area in a new light; to Ed Kako, who gave me some important insights into the nature of sexual orientation; and to Lisa Zorilla, who made me aware of some recent changes in the understanding of the biological basis of schizophrenia.

Yet another kind of thanks goes to Neil Macmillan, who wrote "Statistics: The Collection, Organization, and Interpretation of Data," an appendix for *Psychology*, with a fine sense of balance between the demands of the subject matter and the demands of expositional clarity.

Four persons contributed in a special way: Alan Fridlund, Daniel Reisberg, Jonathan Schull, and Paul Rozin. All four are distinguished scientists as well as dedicated teachers with considerable experience in the introductory course. They served as an editorial advisory group, counseling me on all aspects of this edition and sharing their knowledge of the subject matter as well as their experience in communicating it to beginning students. Alan Fridlund was particularly helpful in the areas of social processes, the emotions, and psychopathology. Daniel Reisberg provided sharp criticisms and new perspectives, especially in the area of cognition. Jonathan Schull did the same for the biological areas. And as always, my old friend Paul Rozin helped me see many facets of the field in a new way, especially those that involve issues of evolutionary and cultural development.

In thanking all these people I take particular pleasure from the fact that many of them were once undergraduate or graduate students of mine. I find something reassuring in the reflection that those I once taught are now teaching me, though it's almost certain that I have learned much more from them than they ever learned from me.

To one person I owe a special debt: my wife, friend, and collaborator, Lila R. Gleitman. She not only wrote Chapter 9, "Language"; she also read virtually all chapters of this manuscript and did what she always does to the things I do and think and write about—she makes them better. Much better. I can't thank her enough.

Several people helped on this edition in still other ways. One is my secretary, Janet White, who helped to track down innumerable papers, references, illustrations, and God knows what else and made sure that I hardly lost any of them. Further thanks go to many people at W. W. Norton: To Roy Tedoff, who managed the production of the book with his usual aplomb; to Antonina Krass, whose brilliance as a book designer continues to astound me; to Maura Conron and John McAusland, who executed some fine new drawings and illustrations; to Ruth Mandel, who provided her sharp artistic eye in the supervision of the photo and art research and gave so generously of her time in so many useful and pleasant discussions; to Roberta Flechner, for her remarkable efforts in arranging the layouts; and to Catherine Von Novak, Claire Acher, and Kari Gerster, who helped in many phases of the editorial and graphic aspects of the book, as they all worked together to fit the many pieces of the puzzle into a seamless whole.

I am especially indebted to two highly competent and indefatigable Norton editors. One is Cathy Wick, who provided invaluable advice, continual encouragement, and occasional psychotherapy and whose personal contact with many psychology instructors throughout the country was of enormous benefit. The other is Jane Carter, who served as manuscript editor, a person of excellent taste and judgment, who combines the skills of a first-rate organizer with those of a fine literary critic. Authors need reinforcement no less (and probably more) than do rats and pigeons. Both Cathy and Jane provided it, making me feel they appreciated both me and what I tried to do. I hope they know how very much I appreciated them in my turn. It was a genuine pleasure to work with them both.

My final thanks go to Norton's chairman of the board, Donald Lamm. I met him over thirty years ago when he first gave me the idea to write this book. We have both aged (somewhat) in the interim, but he is still the same sharp-eyed critic that he was three decades earlier. Age has not withered nor custom staled his infinite variety. His ideas are as brilliant and outrageous as ever; his puns are as bad as ever. And my esteem and affection for him are as great as ever.

Merion, Pennsylvania

September, 1994

PSYCHOLOGY

FOURTH EDITION

CHAPTER

INTRODUCTION

THE SCOPE OF PSYCHOLOGY 1

ELECTRICALLY TRIGGERED IMAGES ■ AMBIGUOUS SIGHTS AND
SOUNDS ■ THE PERCEPTUAL WORLD OF INFANTS ■ DISPLAYS ■
COMPLEX SOCIAL BEHAVIOR IN HUMANS

A SCIENCE OF MANY FACES 5

DREAMS AS MENTAL EXPERIENCES ■ DREAMS AS BEHAVIOR ■ DREAMS
AS COGNITION ■ DREAMS AND SOCIAL BEHAVIOR ■ DREAMS AND
HUMAN DEVELOPMENT ■ DREAMS AND INDIVIDUAL DIFFERENCES ■
PERSPECTIVES ON PSYCHOLOGY

THE TASK OF PSYCHOLOGY 11

hat is psychology? It is a field of inquiry that is sometimes defined as the science of mind, sometimes as the science of behavior. It concerns itself with how and why organisms do what they do; why wolves howl at the moon and children rebel against their parents; why birds sing and moths fly into the flame; why we remember how to ride a bicycle twenty years after the last try; why humans speak and make love and war. All of these are behaviors, and psychology is the science that studies them all.

THE SCOPE OF PSYCHOLOGY

The phenomena that psychology takes as its province cover an enormous range. Some border on biology; others touch on social sciences such as anthropology and sociology. Some concern behavior in animals; many others pertain to behavior in humans. Some are about conscious experience; others focus on what people do regardless of what they may think or feel inside. Some involve humans or animals in isolation; others concern what they do when they are in groups. A few examples will give an initial sense of the scope of the subject matter.

ELECTRICALLY TRIGGERED IMAGES

Consider the relation between biological mechanisms and psychological phenomena. Some investigators have developed a technique of electrically stimulating the brains of human patients who were about to undergo brain surgery. Such operations are generally conducted under local rather than general anesthesia. As a result, the patients are conscious, and their reports may guide the neurosurgeon in the course of the operation.

These and other procedures have shown that different parts of the brain have different psychological functions. For example, when stimulated in certain portions of the brain, patients have visual experiences—they see streaks of color or flickering lights. When stimulated in other regions, they hear clicks or buzzes. Stimulation in still other areas produces an involuntary movement of some part of the body (Penfield and Roberts, 1959; Penfield, 1975).

Related findings come from studies that look at the rate at which blood flows through different parts of the brain. When any part of the body is especially active, more blood will flow to it—to deliver oxygen and nutrients, and carry away waste products—and the brain is no exception. The question is whether the blood flow pattern depends on what the patient does. The answer is yes. When the patient reads silently, certain regions of the brain receive more blood (and are thus presumably more active) than others. A different blood flow pattern is found when the person reads aloud, yet another when he watches a moving light, and so on (Lassen, Ingvar, and Skinhoj, 1978).

AMBIGUOUS SIGHTS AND SOUNDS

Many psychological phenomena are much further removed from issues that might be settled by biological or medical investigations. To study these, one proceeds at the psychological level alone. An example is the perception of ambiguous visual patterns. Consider Figure 1.1, which is a photograph of a vase created for Queen Elizabeth on the occasion of her Silver Jubilee. It is usually seen as a vase, but it can also be seen as the profiles of the queen and her consort, Prince Philip.

The way ambiguous figures are perceived often depends on what we have seen just before. Take Figure 1.2, which can be seen as either a rat or an amiable gentleman with glasses. If we are first shown an unambiguous figure of a rat, the ambiguous picture will be seen as a rat. If we are first exposed to an unambiguous face, the ambiguous figure will be perceived as a face.

What holds for visual patterns also holds for language. Many utterances are ambiguous. If presented out of context, they can be understood in several different ways. Take the following sentence for example:

The mayor ordered the police to stop drinking.

This sentence may be a command to enforce sobriety among the population at large. It may also be a call to end drunkenness among members of the police force. Just how it is understood depends on the context. A prior discussion of panhandlers and skid row probably would lead to the first interpretation; a comment about alcoholism among city employees is likely to lead to the second.

THE PERCEPTUAL WORLD OF INFANTS

Phenomena of the sort we've just discussed document the enormous effect of prior experience on what we see and do. But this does not mean that all psychological accomplishments are acquired by past experience. Some seem to be part of the innate equipment that all of us bring into the world when we are born. Take the infant's reaction to heights for example.

Crawling infants seem to be remarkably successful in noticing the precipices of everyday life. A demonstration is provided by the **visual cliff**. This consists of a large glass table, which is divided in half by a wooden center board. On one

1.1 Reversible figure *Photograph of a vase celebrating the twenty-fifth year of the reign of Queen Elizabeth in 1977. Depending on how the picture is perceptually organized, we see either the vase or the profile of Queen Elizabeth and Prince Philip. (Courtesy of Kaiser Porcelain Ltd.)*

1.2 Perceptual bias *(A) An ambiguous form that can be seen either as (B) a rat or (C) a man with glasses. (After Bugelski and Alampay, 1961)*

A

B

C

A

B

1.3 The visual cliff *(A) An infant is placed on the center board that is laid over a heavy sheet of glass, and his mother calls to him. If he is on the "deep" side, he will not crawl across the apparent cliff. (Courtesy of Richard D. Walk) (B) A similar reaction in a kitten. (Courtesy of William Vandivert)*

side of the board, a checkerboard pattern is attached directly to the underside of the glass; on the other side, the same pattern is placed on the floor three feet below. To adults, this arrangement looks like a sudden drop-off in the center of the table. Six-month-old infants seem to see it in much the same way. When the infant is placed on the center board and called by his mother, his response depends on where she is when she beckons. When she is on the shallow side, he quickly crawls to her. But when she calls from the apparent precipice, discretion wins out over valor and the infant stays where he is (see Figure 1.3).

This result suggests that, to some extent at least, the perception of depth is not learned through experience but is built into our system at the very start.

DISPLAYS

Thus far, all our examples have dealt with individuals in isolation. But much of the subject matter of psychology is inherently social. This holds for animals no less than humans. For virtually all animals interact with others of their species, whether as mates, parents, offspring, or competitors.

In animals, many social interactions depend on largely innate forms of communication. An example is courtship in birds. Many species of birds have evolved elaborate rituals whereby one sex—usually the male—woos the other. Just what this wooing consists of depends on the species. Some males court by making themselves conspicuous. The peacock spreads his magnificent tail feathers, the blue bird of paradise displays his plumage while hanging upside down from a branch, and the red frigate bird inflates his red throat pouch. Other males take a more romantic approach: The bower bird builds a special cabin that he decorates with colored fruit and flowers. The males of other species offer gifts. In all cases, the fundamental message is the same: "I am a male, healthy, and willing peacock (or bird of paradise, or frigate bird, or whatever), and hope that your intentions are similar to mine" (see Figure 1.4).

1.4 Courting birds *Birds have evolved many diverse patterns of courtship behavior that are essentially built-in and characteristic of a particular species. (A) The peacock displays his tail feathers. (Photograph by Ed Reschke/Peter Arnold, Inc.) (B) The blue bird of paradise shows off his plumage while hanging upside down from a branch. (Photograph by David Gillison/Peter Arnold, Inc.) (C) The frigate bird puffs up his red throat pouch. (Photograph by Fred Bavendam/Peter Arnold, Inc.)*

A

B

C

A

B

1.5 Displays *(A) Threat display of the male mandrill, a large West African baboon. (Photograph by George H. Harrison/Grant Heilman) (B) The human smile. (Photograph by Peter Hendrie/The Image Bank)*

Such social communications are based on built-in signals called ***displays,*** which are specific to a particular species. They are ways by which one individual informs another of his current intentions. Some are mating displays, as in the case of courtship displays. Others are threats ("Back off or else!"; see Figure 1.5A). Still others are attempts at appeasement ("Don't hurt me. I am harmless!"). Some built-in displays form the foundation of emotional expression in humans. An example is the smile, a response found in all babies, even those born blind who couldn't have learned it by imitation. It is often considered a signal by which humans tell each other: "Be good to me. I wish you well" (see Figure 1.5B).

COMPLEX SOCIAL BEHAVIOR IN HUMANS

Human social interactions are generally much more subtle and flexible than those of animals. Male peacocks have just one way of going courting: They spread their tail feathers and hope for the best. Human males and females are much more complex, in courtship and many other social interactions. They try one approach, and if it fails, they try another and yet another. If these fail, too, the partners do their best to save the other's face. For much of human social life is based on one person's rational appraisal of how another person will respond to her actions: "If I do this . . . he will think this . . . then I will have to do this . . . ," and so on. Such subtleties are beyond the peacock. If his usual courtship ritual fails, he has no alternate strategy. He won't try to build bowers or offer flowers; all he can do is to display his tail feathers again and again.

While human social behavior has a strong element of rationality, there are some apparent exceptions in which we seem to act with little thought or reason. This is especially likely when we are in large groups. Under some circumstances, people in crowds behave differently than they do when alone. An example is panic (see Figure 1.6). When someone shouts "Fire" in a tightly packed auditorium, the resulting stampede may claim many more victims than the fire itself would have. At the turn of the century, a Chicago theater fire claimed over six hundred victims, many of whom were smothered or trampled to death by the frantic mass behind them. In the words of a survivor, "The heel prints on the dead faces mutely testified to the cruel fact that human animals stricken by terror are as mad and ruthless as stampeding cattle" (Brown, 1965). The task for psychology is to try to understand why the crowd acted differently from the way each of its members would have acted alone.

1.6 Panic *Richard Bosman, 1982. (Collection of Robert H. Helmick; courtesy Brooke Alexander, New York)*

A SCIENCE OF MANY FACES

These illustrations document the enormous range of psychology, whose territory borders on the biological sciences at one end and touches on the social sciences at the other. This broad range makes psychology a field of multiple perspectives, a science of many faces.

To make this point concrete, we will focus upon one psychological phenomenon and show how it can be approached from several different vantage points. This phenomenon is *dreams*. Dreaming is a topic interesting in its own right, but it is also an especially good illustration of how psychology approaches any single phenomenon—not just from one point of view but from several.

Let us start out by describing dreaming as we all experience it. A dream is a kind of nocturnal drama to which the only price of admission is falling asleep. It is usually a series of scenes, sometimes fairly commonplace, sometimes bizarre and disjointed, in which the dreamer often figures as a participant. While this dream play unfolds, it is generally experienced as real. It seems so real in fact, that on waking one sometimes wonders whether the dream events might have happened after all. As a Chinese sage wrote over two thousand years ago, "Once upon a time, I, Chuang-tzu, dreamed I was a butterfly, fluttering hither and thither. . . . Suddenly I was awakened. . . . Now I do not know whether I was a man dreaming I was a butterfly, or whether I am a butterfly now dreaming I am a man"(MacKenzie, 1965).

How can such delicate, transient events ever become a suitable topic for scientific inquiry?

DREAMS AS MENTAL EXPERIENCES

One way of looking at dreams is as conscious, mental experiences. According to an old account that goes back to the Greek philosopher Aristotle, the dream happenings are mental re-evocations of sights and sounds that occurred during the dreamer's waking life. Aristotle believed that the succession of these dream images from the past is experienced as real while it occurs because there is no competition from the clamor of waking reality and because the intellect is "dulled" during sleep (Aristotle, ca. 330 B.C.).

Later investigators tried to relate what people dream about to what happens to them both before and during sleep. One question concerns the effect of recent waking experiences. Aristotle was apparently correct in his belief that such recent events often reemerge in dreams. This is especially so when the recent waking experience was highly emotional. For example, soldiers who have just gone through intense battle stress may relive their combat terrors in nightmare dreams (Pai, 1946).

Some writers have suggested that the dream images from the past are supplemented by external events that impinge upon the sleeper in the present. A widely cited example is the alarm clock, which is often said to turn into a peal of church bells or a fire engine in the dream. To test this hypothesis, several investigators have studied the effects of applying various forms of external stimulation during sleep. Numerous sleepers have been shaken, tickled, splashed with water, and shouted at—all to discover whether they would later report a dream that referred to these experiences. Sometimes they did, as in the dream reported on awakening after an experimenter shouted "Help" into the sleeper's ears: "I was driving along the highway at home. Heard yelling and we stopped. A car was turned sideways in the road. I went down and saw the car was turned over on the side of the road. . . . There was a woman badly cut. We took her to the hospital" (Hall, 1966, p. 6). It is hard to resist the conclusion that, at some level, the dreamer heard and understood the shout "Help" even while asleep and then incorporated it within his dream narrative.

DREAMS AS BEHAVIOR

Dreams as conscious, mental experiences are essentially private; they go on "inside" the individual. As such, dreams can be regarded as a form of behavior that is looked at from within, as if the actor were observing his own actions. Yet psychologists study most aspects of behavior from "outside," for much of what we do is directly apparent and overt and can therefore easily be seen by others. Humans and animals act. They run and fly and scurry about; they eat and fight and mate; they often perform new acts to attain their ends.

OVERT BEHAVIOR

Can we study dreaming from the outside by taking this action-oriented view? On the face of it, the prospects don't seem too bright, for during sleep the body is by and large immobile. Even so, there is a way. For there is one thing the sleeper does while dreaming that is overt and can be observed from the outside: She moves her eyes.

This fact emerged after it became clear that there are two kinds of sleep: quiet sleep and active sleep. During quiet sleep, both breathing and heart rate are slow and regular, and the eyes are motionless. But during active sleep the pattern is different. Breathing and heart rate accelerate, and—most characteristic of all—the eyes move back and forth behind closed eyelids in quick irregular darts. Periods of quiet and of active sleep (often called REM sleep because of the rapid eye movements) alternate throughout the night, with a total of perhaps ninety minutes devoted to REM (see Figure 1.7).

The crucial fact about REM sleep is that this is the period during which dreams occur. When subjects—the persons whose behavior is being studied—are aroused during REM sleep, about 85 percent of the awakenings lead to reports of a vivid dream. In contrast, subjects awakened from non-REM sleep recall dreams much less often (Dement, 1974).

There is little doubt that the rapid eye movements go along with dreaming. But some investigators take a further step. They suggest that these movements provide a clue to what the sleeper is dreaming of. In their view, the eye movements indicate that the sleeper is "looking at" whatever he sees in his dream world. Some evidence for this intriguing (though quite controversial) hypothesis comes from studies which show that the direction of the eye movements observed during a given REM period is appropriate to what the subject recalls having seen while dreaming. For example, when the predominant direction of eye movements was up and down, one subject dreamed that he was throwing basketballs, looking up at the net and shooting, then looking down to pick another ball off the floor. In contrast, another REM period, in which the eye movements were mostly from side to side, produced a dream in which the subject was watching two people throwing tomatoes at each other (Dement and Kleitman, 1957).

1.7 Quiet and active sleep Record of eye movements picked up by electrodes at the side of each eye. The record shows the eye-movement pattern during active sleep, the period when sleepers dream. Both eyes move rapidly and in synchrony. (After Dement, 1974)

AWAKE

QUIET SLEEP

REM SLEEP (dreaming)

1.8 Sleep and the EEG *The figure shows EEG records during waking, during increasingly deep stages of quiet sleep, and during active sleep. (Courtesy of William C. Dement)*

BIOLOGICAL UNDERPINNINGS OF BEHAVIOR

Evidence based on eye movements is one clue to the nature of dreaming. Another clue concerns its biological basis. Most psychologists take it for granted that whatever we do or think has some physical basis in the activity of our brains. Some promising first steps in this direction pertain to dreams. These came after the development of a number of methods for monitoring what people do when they are fast asleep. An important tool is the electroencephalogram, or EEG, which measures the overall activity of the sleeper's brain. The EEG traces the quick fluctuations of electrical activity over time, and its graphic record is sometimes called brain waves. Happily for sleep investigators, it soon proved possible to attach the multitude of required electrodes to the subjects without disturbing their sleep (see Figure 1.8).

The results showed that the EEG patterns of sleep and waking differ markedly. As the subject falls into deeper and deeper stages of sleep, the brain waves become slow, large, and rather regular, indicating a lower level of brain activity. But this holds only for periods of quiet sleep. As this is interrupted by active (that is REM) sleep, the EEG becomes quite similar to that found when the subject is awake. This makes good sense, for it suggests that during REM sleep the brain is reasonably aroused and active—as well it should be since this is the time when we are busily engaged in dreaming.

DREAMS AS COGNITION

Like many other psychological phenomena, dreams reflect what we know, what we have experienced, remembered, or thought about—activities that psychologists call *cognition.* To be sure, the dream happenings didn't really take place. We didn't really fly through the air or have tea with Queen Elizabeth. But the components of the dream were surely drawn from the dreamer's own knowledge, which contains information about flying and the queen of England. How was this knowledge retrieved and woven into the dream story? How was the dream recalled on later awakening? And why is it that most of us remember so few of our dreams?

Some psychologists have tried to attack these and related questions by asking about the factors that make for better dream recall. They have come up with some evidence that people who remember more of their dreams are more likely to have better and sharper visual mental images in their waking life; perhaps their dreams are more memorable because they are experienced in a more vivid pictorial form (Cory et al., 1975). Another factor is the extent to which the dream experience is interfered with by what happens immediately after the sleeper awakes. In one study, subjects were asked to call the weather bureau immediately after waking up; after this, they had to write down a detailed description of any dreams they had that night. The results showed that weather reports and dreams don't mix. The subjects who made the call generally remembered that they had had a dream, but most of them could not remember what it was that they had dreamed about (Cohen and Wolfe, 1973).

DREAMS AND SOCIAL BEHAVIOR

Human life is rarely solitary but is spent among a world of others—strangers and friends, partners and rivals, potential and actual mates. What holds for waking existence, holds for dreams as well. Most of them involve interaction with others. Some feature themes of aggression, such as competition, attack, and submission. Others concern friendship and sometimes sex. But whatever the plot, the cast usually includes some others. More than 95 percent of our dreams are peopled with others, and most revolve around our relations with them (Hall and Van de Castle, 1966).

DREAMS AND THE CULTURE

Dreams concern major themes in the person's own life, but they take place within a larger framework, the dreamer's own culture. In our own society, a common dream is of appearing naked among strangers and being embarrassed. But in a culture where it is normal to wear no clothes, such a dream would be unlikely. Nor are many urban Americans likely to have nightmares in which they are chased by cows, which happens to be a common dream in western Ghana (Barnouw, 1963).

Culture affects not only what the dream is about but also how the dreamer thinks about it when she recalls it later on. In some societies, including our own, dreams are generally dismissed as nonsensical fancies, irrelevant to real life. Many preliterate cultures have a different view (see Figure 1.9). Some regard dreams as supernatural visions and behave accordingly. Others take dreams very seriously even though they think of them as naturally occurring events. The Senoi, a tribe in Malaya, act as if they had all taken several courses in psychoanalysis. They believe that dreams indicate something about their inner lives and can provide clues for heading off problems before they become serious. Every morning Senoi children tell their father what they dreamed about the night before. The father then helps the children interpret their dreams. These may reveal some incipient conflict with others, as in a dream of being attacked by a friend. If so, the father may advise the child on how to correct matters, for example, by giving the friend a present (Stewart, 1951).

DREAMS AND INTERNAL CONFLICT

The social aspect of dreaming lies at the heart of a famous (and controversial) theory of dreams proposed by Sigmund Freud. According to Freud, dreams are the product of an elaborate clash between two contending forces—the unconscious primitive urges of our biological heritage and the civilizing constraints imposed by society. In dreams we sometimes see one, sometimes the other side of the battle. Various forbidden impulses—mostly sex and aggression—emerge, but they are soon opposed by the thou-shalt-nots of our early upbringing. The result is a compromise. The forbidden material breaks through but only in a stealthy, censored masquerade (see Figure 1.10). This disguise explains why dreams are so often odd and senseless. Their senselessness is only on the surface, a cunning mask that lets us indulge in the unacceptable wish without realizing that it is unacceptable (Freud, 1900).

DREAMS AND HUMAN DEVELOPMENT

Thus far we have discussed dreams as they are experienced by adults. But of course dreams occur in childhood as well as in adulthood. Psychologists who are concerned with the course of human mental development have considered the different ways in which children and adults think about their dreams.

Developmental psychologists want to know how children acquire the basic intellectual operations that are part of adult human thought—how they learn to

1.9 Iroquois cornhusk mask for dream ceremony *The Iroquois Indians regarded dreams as an important means for revealing hidden desires and held formal dream-remembering ceremonies during which special masks were worn. (Courtesy of Staatlicher, Museum für Völkerkunde, Munich)*

1.10 Symbolism in dreams *A film about Freud's early career includes a dream sequence in which he enters a deep tunnel that eventually leads him to a cavern where his mother sits, smiling, on a Cleopatra-like throne. The dream is a compact symbolic expression of how Freud saw himself: an explorer of subterranean unconscious motives who uncovered the hidden childhood lusts of all men and women. (From John Huston's 1963 film,* Freud, *with Montgomery Clift. Courtesy The Museum of Modern Art/Film Stills Archive)*

That very night in Max's room a forest grew

and grew—

The distinction between dreams and waking reality is not always clear in childhood *(From Sendak, 1963)*

count, to understand that events have causes, and so on. For example, they ask how children learn that there is a difference between two realms of phenomena, those that we call subjective (thoughts, beliefs, and of course, dreams) and those that we call objective (the world of tangible things "out there"). To ask how this distinction is made is another way of asking how we attain our adult notion of objective reality, how we come to know that the tree in the garden—unlike a dream—will still be there after we blink our eyes.

This distinction is by no means clear in early childhood. Thus young children initially have great trouble in distinguishing dreams from waking life. A three-year-old awakes and tells her parents how much she loved the elephants at the circus yesterday. The parents correct her; she was not at the circus yesterday. But the child indignantly sticks to her story and appeals to her brother for corroboration, for "he was there too." When her brother shakes his head in denial, she begins to cry, angrily insisting that she told the truth. Eventually she learns that there is a whole group of experiences that older people call "just dreams," no matter how real they seem to her (Levy, 1979).

The fact that the child finally recognizes the circus elephants—and the nightmare robbers and witches—as dreams does not mean that she has acquired an adult conception of what dreams are. Young children tend to think of them as physical objects. When asked whether dreams can be tall, a four-year-old replied, *"Yeah.* How tall? *Big, big, big,* (spread arms). Where are dreams? *In your bedroom.* In the daytime? *No they're outside. . . .* What are they like? *They're made of rock.* Could they be heavy? *Yeah; and they can't break either"* (Keil, 1979, pp. 109–10).

It's quite a while before children think of dreams the way adults do. By six or seven, they believe that dreams are sent through the air, perhaps by the wind or by pigeons. Eventually they recognize that, as one eleven-year-old put it, "You dream *with the head* and the dream is *in the head"* (Piaget, 1972).

This realization that dreams are subjective events is no small achievement. As we will see later, the recognition that some experiences are subjective, inner happenings is not limited to dreams but extends to many other conceptual attainments about the basic nature of the physical and psychological universe.

The Dream   *by Pablo Picasso, 1932*
(Courtesy of the Ganz Collection/Scala/
Art Resources)

DREAMS AND INDIVIDUAL DIFFERENCES

There is a further aspect of dreams: They are a reflection of the fact that people are different. People vary in what they characteristically do and think and feel. And some of these differences between people are reflected in their dreams. Some simply pertain to the differing circumstances in the dreamers' lives. This point was made some two thousand years ago by the Roman poet Lucretius who noted that at night lawyers plead their cases, generals fight their battles, and sailors wage their war with the winds (Woods, 1947).

More interesting are differences that reveal something about the personalities of the dreamers. An example is a comparison of the dreams of normal people and of patients with a diagnosis of schizophrenia, a condition generally regarded as the most serious psychiatric disorder in our time. The difference between the two groups was enormous. The schizophrenics reported dreams that were highly bizarre and often morbid: The dreamer is eaten alive by an alligator; there are nuclear wars and world cataclysms. Themes of bodily mutilation were fairly common, as in a dream in which a woman killed her husband and then stuffed parts of his body into a camel's head. In contrast, the normals' dreams were comparatively mild and ordinary. This result fits in with what we know about schizophrenia. Schizophrenics often jump from one idea to the other without maintaining a firm line of thought. As a result, their behavior often appears bizarre. And they often report great personal turmoil and distress. It seems that their extremely bizarre and morbid dreams are simply an exaggeration of a condition already present in their waking lives (Carrington, 1972).

PERSPECTIVES ON PSYCHOLOGY

We have seen that dreams can be looked at as conscious, mental experiences, as overt behaviors, as aspects of cognition, as indications of social patterns, as reflections of human development, and as expressions of the dreamer's individuality. What holds for dreams holds for most other psychological phenomena: They can all be viewed from several perspectives. Each perspective is valid, but none is complete without the others, for psychology is a field of many faces, and to see it fully, we must look at them all.

Given the many-faceted character of psychology, it is not surprising that those who have contributed to it came from many quarters. Some had the proper title of psychologist with appropriate university appointments in that discipline, including two of its founding fathers, Wilhelm Wundt of Germany and William James of the United States. But psychology was not built by psychologists alone—far from it. Among its architects are philosophers, beginning with Plato and Aristotle and continuing to our own time. Physicists and physiologists played important roles and still do. Physicians contributed greatly, as did specialists in many other disciplines, including anthropology and, more recently, linguistics and computer science. Psychology, the field of many faces, is by its very nature a field of many origins.

In presenting the subject matter of psychology as it is today, we must try to do justice to this many-sidedness. In an attempt to achieve that, this book has been organized around five topics that emphasize somewhat different perspectives on the field as a whole and that mirror the different ways in which we have just looked at dreams: *action, cognition, social behavior, development,* and *individual differences.*

Wilhelm Wundt (1832–1920) *(Courtesy of Stock Montage)*

William James (1842–1910) *(Courtesy of The Warder Collection)*

THE TASK OF PSYCHOLOGY

Psychology is sometimes popularly regarded as a field that concentrates on the secret inner lives of individual persons—why Mary hates her mother and why George is so shy with girls. But questions of this sort are really not psychology's main concern. To be sure, there is an applied branch of psychology that deals with various adjustment problems, but it is only a special part of the field. The primary questions psychology asks are of a more general sort. Its purpose is not to describe the distinctive characteristics of a particular individual. Its main goal is to get at the facts that are general for all of humankind.

The reason is simple. Psychology is a science and, like all other sciences, it looks for *general principles*—underlying uniformities that different events have in common. A single event as such means little; what counts is what any one event—or object or person—shares with others. Ultimately of course, psychology—again, like all other sciences—hopes to find a route back to understanding the individual event. It tries to discover, say, some general principles of adolescent conflict or parent-child relations to explain why George is so shy and why Mary is so bitter about her mother. Once such explanations are found, they may lead to practical applications: to help counsel and guide, and perhaps to effect desirable changes. But, at least initially, the science's main concern is with the discovery of the general principles.

Is there any field of endeavor whose primary interest is in individual persons, with the unique George and Mary who are like no other persons who ever lived or ever will live? One such field is literature. The great novelists and playwrights have given us portraits of living, breathing individuals who exist in a particular time and place. There is nothing abstract and general about the agonies of a Hamlet or the murderous ambition of a Macbeth. These are concrete, particular individuals, with special loves and fears that are peculiarly theirs. But from these particulars, Shakespeare gives us a glimpse of what is common to all humanity, what Hamlet and Macbeth share with all of us. Both science and art have something to say about human nature, but they come to it from different directions. Science tries to discover general principles and then to apply them to the individual case. Art focuses on the particular instance and then uses this to illuminate what is universal in us all.

Science and art are complementary. To gain insight into our own nature we need both. Consider Hamlet's description:

> What a piece of work is a man, how noble in reason, how infinite in faculties; in form and moving how express and admirable, in action like an angel, in apprehension like a god: the beauty of the world, the paragon of animals! (*Hamlet,* Act II, scene ii).

To understand and appreciate this "piece of work" is a task too huge for any one field of human endeavor, whether art, philosophy, or science. What we will try to do here is to sketch psychology's own attempts toward this end, to show what we have come to know and how we have come to know it—and perhaps even more important, how much we have not learned as yet.

PART ONE

ACTION

CHAPTER

BIOLOGICAL BASES OF BEHAVIOR

THE ORGANISM AS MACHINE 16

DESCARTES AND THE REFLEX CONCEPT ■ THE BASIC NERVOUS
FUNCTIONS: RECEPTION, INTEGRATION, REACTION

NERVE CELL AND NERVE IMPULSE 18

THE NEURON ■ THE ELECTRICAL ACTIVITY OF THE NEURON

INTERACTION AMONG NERVE CELLS 24

THE REFLEX ■ INFERRING SYNAPTIC FUNCTION ■ THE SYNAPTIC
MECHANISM

INTERACTION THROUGH THE BLOOD-STREAM: THE ENDOCRINE SYSTEM 32

THE MAIN STRUCTURES OF THE NERVOUS SYSTEM 33

THE EVOLUTION OF CENTRAL CONTROL ■ THE PERIPHERAL AND
CENTRAL NERVOUS SYSTEMS

THE CEREBRAL CORTEX 38

PROJECTION AREAS ■ ASSOCIATION AREAS ■ HOW NEAT IS THE
HIERARCHY?

ONE BRAIN OR TWO? 48

EVIDENCE FROM SPLIT BRAINS ■ LATERALIZATION IN NORMAL
SUBJECTS ■ TWO MODES OF MENTAL FUNCTIONING ■ WHAT THE BRAIN
CAN TELL US ABOUT THE MIND

RECOVERY FROM BRAIN INJURY 53

REPAIR FROM WITHIN ■ REPAIR FROM WITHOUT ■
REHABILITATION

SOME FINAL COMMENTS 56

SUMMARY 57

The study of mind has many aspects. We may ask what human beings know, we may ask what they want, and we may ask what they do. Much of psychology is an attempt to answer the last question: What is it that humans do and why do they do it? In this section we will deal with the approach to mind that grows out of an interest in what all animals do, an approach that emphasizes behavior as the basic subject matter of psychology. We will focus on the particular version of this approach that is based on the notion that mind can be understood as a reflex machine. We shall see how the reflex notion has led to impressive achievements in our understanding of the structure and function of the nervous system, and how this notion has been modified to encompass the phenomena of motivation and of learning in animals and humans.

 hat are the biological foundations of mental life? The first steps toward an answer came from the study of human and animal action. The ancients, no less than we, wondered why humans and animals behave as they do. What is it that leads to animal movement, impels the crab to crawl, the tiger to spring? Prescientific folk could only answer *animistically*: There is some inner spirit in the creature that impels it to move, each creature in its own fashion. Today we know that any question about bodily movement must inevitably call for some reference to the nervous system, for to us it is quite clear that the nervous system is the apparatus that most directly determines and organizes an organism's reactions to the world in which it lives.

Modern advances in the study of this system have given us insights into its functioning that would have amazed the scientists who lived even a century ago, let alone the ancients. Some of the new techniques allow us to observe the operations of small components of individual nerve cells (see Figure 2.1). Others

2.1 Observing the nervous system through a microscope *A nerve cell in the spinal cord. (Photograph by Cabisco/Visuals Unlimited)*

2.2 Observing the living brain with PET scans *(A) Horizontal plane of brain used in taking the PET (Positron Emission Tomography) scan. (B) Four PET scans taken while the subject rests, listens to someone talk, listens to music, or both. These scans indicate the degree of metabolic activity in different parts of the brain, viewed in horizontal cross-section as shown in the diagram with the front of the head on top. Red indicates the most intense activity and blue the least. Listening to speech activates the left side of the brain, listening to music activates the right side, and listening to both activates both sides. (PET scans taken by Dr. John Mazziotta, UCLA School of Medicine, et al./Science Photo Library/Photo Researchers)*

Horizontal
plane

A

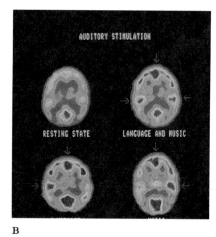

B

permit us to eavesdrop on the workings of living human brains without seriously disturbing their owners (see Figure 2.2A and B). Our advances have been considerable. But to put them in perspective, we must first look at some of the historical origins of our current conceptions.

We will soon ask many detailed questions about the structure and function of the nervous system—the apparatus that underlies human and animal action. But before we do so, we must address a more general question: Broadly speaking, what must this system accomplish?

THE ORGANISM AS MACHINE

René Descartes *(Courtesy National Library of Medicine)*

In modern times this question was first raised seriously by the French philosopher René Descartes (1596–1650), and his answer provides the broad outline within which we think about such matters even now. Descartes lived in a period that saw the beginning of the science of mechanics. Kepler and Galileo were beginning to develop the ideas about the movements of heavenly bodies that some thirty years later led to Newton's *Principia*. Radically new views of humanity and its universe were being put forth. There were laws of nature that determined the fall of stones and the motions of planets: rigid, precise, and immutable. The universe was run by a system of pushes and pulls originally set in motion by God, the Great Watchmaker. At a more lowly level, these natural laws were mirrored in the workings of ingenious mechanical contrivances that were all the rage in the wealthy homes of Europe: cuckoo clocks that would call the hour, water-driven gargoyles with nodding heads, statues in the king's garden that would bow to the visitor who stepped on a hidden spring. The action of a lever, the release of a spring—these mechanisms could explain the operation of such primitive devices. Could human thought and action be explained in similar mechanical terms?

DESCARTES AND THE REFLEX CONCEPT

To Descartes all action, whether human or animal, was essentially a response to some event in the outside world. His human machine would work as follows: Something from the outside excites one of the senses; this in turn excites a nerve that transmits the excitation upward to the brain, which then relays the excitation downward to a muscle; the excitation from the senses thus eventually leads to a contraction of a muscle and thereby to a reaction to the external event that started the whole sequence. In effect, the energy from the outside is *reflected* back by the nervous system to the animal's muscles—the term **reflex** finds its origin in this conception (see Figure 2.3).

Conceived thus, human doings could be regarded as the doings of a machine. But there was a problem. The same external event produces one reaction today and another tomorrow. The sight of food leads to reaching movements, but only when we are hungry. In short, the excitation from one of the senses will excite a nerve leading to one muscle on one occasion, but on another occasion it will excite a different nerve that may move an entirely different muscle. This suggests that Descartes' mechanism must have a central switching system, supervised by some operator who sits in the middle to decide what incoming pipe to connect with which pipe leading to the outside.

To explain these behavioral options mechanically was both difficult and dangerous. Descartes was deeply religious, and he was very much troubled by the theological implications of his argument should he bring it to its ultimate conclusion. In addition he was prudent—Galileo had difficulties with the Inquisition because his scientific beliefs threatened the doctrines of the Church. Descartes therefore shrank from taking the last step in his own argument, the reduction of human beings to the status of machines. Instead, he proposed that human mental processes were only semiautomatic. To handle the switching function he proposed that the soul, operating through a particular structure in the brain, determines the choice of possible nervous pathways.

Descartes asserted that, while animals were machines, humans were more than mere robots. But later thinkers went further. They felt that the laws of the physical universe could ultimately explain all action, whether human or animal, so that a scientific account required no further "ghost in the machine"—that is, no reference to the soul. They ruthlessly extended Descartes' logic to human beings, arguing that humans differ from animals only in being more finely constructed mechanisms.

Descartes' machine is an example of an influential scientific metaphor that affected the thought of many subsequent generations. Much of the history of science is the history of such metaphors. An illustration from physics is the description of the atom as a miniature solar system in which electrons circle the atomic nucleus just as the planets orbit the sun. Descartes' machine was similarly modeled on the water-driven machines of his day in which some motion was transformed into some other motion through a system of gears or levers until it finally led to the movement of the mechanism. Later theorists complicated the machine metaphor by borrowing from the technology of their time in likening the brain to a giant telephone switchboard. The details of the metaphor changed, but in some important regards the metaphor itself stayed the same: For the machinery that was thought to underlie psychological processes was always one in which some kind of energy (now electrical or chemical) was ultimately transformed into some bodily movement. The details changed, but the proposed machine was always one whose inputs come from the environment and whose ultimate product is action.★

2.3 Reflex action as envisaged by Descartes *In this sketch by Descartes, the heat from the fire, A, starts a chain of processes that begins at the affected spot of the skin, B, and continues up the nerve tube until a pore of a cavity, F, is opened. Descartes believed that this opening allowed the animal spirits in the cavity to enter the nerve tube and eventually travel to the muscles that pull the foot from the fire. While the figure shows that Descartes anticipated the basic idea of reflex action, it also indicates that he did not realize the anatomical distinction between sensory and motor nerves. (From Descartes, 1662)*

★ In some later chapters we will turn to a rather different metaphor that likens mind and brain to a computer. (See Chapters 4 through 8.)

THE BASIC NERVOUS FUNCTIONS: RECEPTION, INTEGRATION, REACTION

Psychologists today still agree with Descartes that much of behavior can be understood as reactions to outside events: The environment poses a question and the organism answers it. This approach, like Descartes', leads to a tripartite classification of nervous functions: *reception* through the senses, *reaction* from the muscles and glands, and *conduction* and *integration* to mediate between these two functions.

As here conceived, the chain of events that leads to action typically begins outside of the organism. A particular physical energy impinges upon some part of the organism sensitive to it. This event we call a *stimulus* (a term that derives from the name of a wooden implement with a nail at one end used by Roman farmers some two thousand years ago to goad their sluggish oxen). The stimulus excites *receptors,* specialized structures capable of translating some physical energy into a nervous impulse. Once a receptor is stimulated, the excitation is conducted farther into the nervous system. Bundles of nerve fibers that conduct excitation toward the brain or spinal cord are called *afferent nerves* (from the Latin, *affere,* "to bring to"). These fibers transmit their message still farther; in the simplest case, to other fibers that go directly to the *effectors,* the muscles and glands that are the organs of action. Nerve fibers that lead to the effectors are called *efferent nerves* (from the Latin, *effere,* "to bring forth").

The transmission path from receptors to effectors is usually more circuitous than this, however. The afferent fibers often bring their messages to intermediate nerve cells, or *interneurons,* in the brain or spinal cord. These interneurons then either transmit the message to the efferent nerve cells or send it on to yet other interneurons. Typically, many thousands of such interneurons are "consulted" before the command to action is finally issued and sent down the path of the efferent nerve fibers. All this, in simple outline, is really a modern restatement of Descartes' reflex conception.

We now turn to a more detailed discussion of the nervous system. We will deal with progressively larger units of analysis, first discussing the smallest functional and structural units of nervous activity (the nerve impulse and the nerve cell), then the interaction among different nerve cells (at the synapse), and finally, the functional plan of the major structures of the nervous system.

NERVE CELL AND NERVE IMPULSE

Neuroscientists know that the basic unit of nervous function is the *nerve impulse,* the firing of an individual nerve cell, or *neuron.* Our discussion begins with a brief look at the anatomy of the neuron.

THE NEURON

The neuron is the simplest element of nervous action. It is a single cell with three subdivisions: the *dendrites,* the *cell body,* and the *axon* (see Figure 2.4). The dendrites are usually branched, sometimes enormously so. The axon may extend for a very long distance, and its end may fork out into several branches. Impulses from other cells are received by the dendrites; the axon transmits the impulse to yet other neurons or to effector organs such as muscles and glands. Thus, the dendrites are the receptive units of the neuron, while the axon endings may be regarded as its effector apparatus.

Many axons are surrounded by a *myelin sheath,* a tube mainly composed of fatty tissue, that insulates it from other axons. The tube is not continuous but consists of a number of elongated segments, with small uncoated gaps in the sheath, the *nodes of Ranvier,* which allow for a considerable increase in the speed of transmission (see Figure 2.4).

A few details about neurons will give a feeling for their size and number. The diameter of an individual neuron is very small; cell bodies vary from 5 to about 100 microns in diameter (1 micron = 1/1,000 millimeter). Dendrites are typically short, say a few hundred microns. The axons of neurons can be very long: Some motor neuron axons extend from the head to the base of the spinal cord, others from the spinal cord to the fingers and toes. To get a sense of the cell body relative to the axon in a motor neuron, imagine a basketball attached to a garden hose that stretches the whole fourteen-mile length of Manhattan.

Different kinds of neurons are specialized for different tasks. We will mention only a few of the varieties. Some neurons are attached to specialized *receptor cells* that can respond to various external energies, such as pressure, chemical changes, light, and so on. These receptor cells translate (more technically, *transduce*) such physical stimuli into electrical changes, which then trigger a nervous impulse in other neurons. Receptor cells are like money changers, exchanging the various energies impinging from the outer world into the only currency acceptable within the nervous system—the nervous impulse.

Neurons that convey impulses from receptors toward the rest of the nervous system are called *sensory neurons.* Sometimes the receptor is a specialized part of the sensory neuron, as in the neurons that are responsible for sensing pressure on the skin. But in many cases, transduction and transmission are separate functions that are entrusted to different cells. In vision and hearing, receptor cells transduce optic stimulation and air pressures into electrical changes in the cell. These changes in the receptors trigger impulses in sensory neurons that then transmit their information to other neurons in the nervous system.

Other neurons have axons that terminate in effector cells. An important example is the *motor neurons* that activate the *skeletal musculature,* the muscles that control the skeleton, such as those of the arms and legs. The cell bodies of the motor neurons are in the spinal cord or brain, and their long axons have terminal branches whose final tips contact individual muscle cells. When a motor neuron fires, a chemical event produced at its axon tips causes the muscle fibers to contract.

A

Nucleus

Dendrites

Cell body

Nodes of Ranvier

Axon

Myelin sheath

Terminal endings

2.4   The neuron   *(A) A schematic diagram of the main parts of a "typical" neuron. Part of the cell is myelinated; that is, its axon is covered with a segmented, insulating sheath. (After Katz, 1952) (B) Highly magnified nerve cell in the human brain showing cell body and several dendrites. The long vertical bands are branches from other nerve cells. (Photograph by Manfred Kage/Peter Arnold, Inc.)*

B

A

B

C

2.5 Different kinds of neurons (A) A motor neuron of the human spinal cord. (B) A neuron in the human cerebral cortex, the part of the brain concerned with such higher mental functions as perception and planning. (After Kolb and Whishaw, 1980). (C) A specialized neuron in the cerebellum, a part of the brain that controls motor coordination. This kind of cell has been said to gather impulses from as many as 80,000 other neurons. The photomicrograph is from the cerebellum of a twelve-month-old infant. It has been stained by a special chemical that shows the extent of the branching of the cell's dendrites. (© Guigoz/Dr. A. Privat/Petit Format/Science Source/Photo Researchers)

In complex organisms, the vast majority of nerve cells are **interneurons,** which have a functional position that is between sensory neurons and motor neurons. Interneurons come in many shapes and forms. They usually show considerable branching, which produces an enormous number of synaptic contacts (see Figure 2.5).

The total number of neurons in the human nervous system has been estimated to be as high as 1,000 billion (Nauta and Feirtag, 1986).★ Given that each neuron may be connected to as many as 10,000 other neurons, it is no wonder that the human brain is often said to be the most complex object in the known universe.

THE ELECTRICAL ACTIVITY OF THE NEURON

The biological function of neurons is to receive and transmit impulses. But how do they perform these functions? How do they transmit signals, influence each other, and cause muscles to contract? We now know that they do so electrically. But the unraveling of this mystery required the development of new scientific instruments to measure and depict not just anatomy, but electrical activity—the movements of charged particles. Direct measurement of these electrical currents in neurons only became possible with several key advances in the twentieth century. One such advance was the development of ever finer microelectrodes, some of which have tips tapered to a diameter of 1 micron. Such electrodes can puncture a neuron without squashing it and detect weak electrical currents without disrupting them. Equally important was the development of the oscilloscope, a device that amplifies and expands weak electrical signals, and displays them as glowing lines on a fluorescent screen. The resulting pattern then charts electrical changes which occur during a very short interval of cellular activity. Another contribution came considerably earlier than the twentieth century; it was made by evolution, which provided the squid, an animal endowed with several giant axons with diameters up to 1 millimeter—a great convenience for electrophysiological work on the nervous impulse.

★ While this number may seem prodigious, it is somewhat sobering to realize that there is no way of getting more; a neuron, once lost, can't be replaced. But some recent findings sound a more optimistic note, at least for male songbirds. Their brains shrink in the winter (when they don't sing) and expand in the spring (when they do). This annual increase in brain size is partially caused by the formation of new neurons during the spring to replace old neurons that die off in the fall (Nottebohn, 1987).

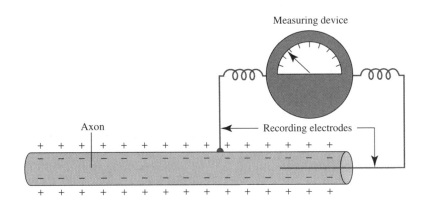

2.6   Recording the impulse   *A schematic drawing of how the impulse is recorded. One electrode is inserted into the axon; the other records from the axon's outside. (After Carlson, 1986)*

THE RESTING POTENTIAL

Figure 2.6 shows one microelectrode inserted into an axon while another records from the surface of the fiber. In this manner one can record the electrical potential (the voltage) across the cell membrane. One fact emerges immediately. There is a difference in potential between the inside and the outside of the fiber when the cell is at "rest" (that is, not firing). The inside is electrically negative with respect to the outside. This ***resting potential*** is about −70 millivolts relative to the outside of the cell. This means that in its normal state the cell membrane is ***polarized.*** Its outside and inside are like the electrical poles of a miniature battery, with the outside positive and the inside negative.

THE ACTION POTENTIAL

What happens when the neuron is aroused from rest? To find out, neuroscientists stimulate the surface of the fiber by means of a third microelectrode, which applies a brief electrical pulse. This pulse reduces the potential across the membrane for an instant. If the pulse is weak, nothing further will happen. As the strength of the pulse slowly increases, the resting potential drops still more, but again with no further effect, until the pulse is strong enough to decrease the potential to a critical point, the ***threshold*** (about 55 millivolts in mammals).

Now a new phenomenon occurs. The potential suddenly collapses; in fact, it overshoots the zero mark and for a brief moment the axon interior becomes positive relative to the outside. This flare lasts only about 1 millisecond and quickly subsides. The neuron then returns to the resting state. This entire sequence of electrical events is called the ***action potential*** (Figure 2.7).

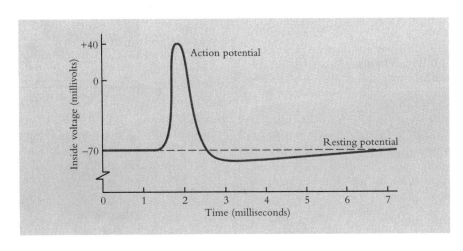

2.7   The action potential   *Action potential recorded from the squid's giant axon. (After Hodgkin and Huxley, 1939)*

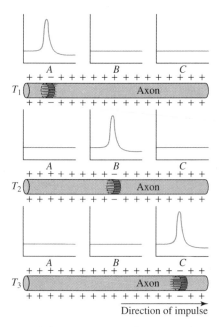

2.8 The action potential as it travels along the axon *The axon is shown at three different moments in time—T₁, T₂, and T₃—after the application of a stimulus. The electrical potential is shown at three different points along the axon—A, B, and C. (After Carlson, 1986)*

The action potential is recorded from only one small region of the axon. What happens elsewhere in the fiber? Consider Figure 2.8 An ***adequate stimulus***—that is, one that is above threshold—is applied to point *A,* and the potential is measured at *A,* as well as at other points along the axon, say at *B* and *C.* At first, an action potential is observed at *A,* while *B* and *C* are still at rest. A bit later, *A* returns to normal, while *B* shows the action potential. Still later, *B* returns to normal but an action potential is found at *C.* (Of course, these time intervals are exceedingly brief.) The change in potential is evidently infectious, with each region quickly setting off its neighbor.

By now there is no doubt that the action potential is the physical event that corresponds to the nervous impulse. Consider the speed of the nervous impulse, which was measured in the middle of the nineteenth century, many years before anyone knew anything about the underlying electrophysiology of neural action. In humans, this was found to be about 50 meters per second. If action potentials and nerve impulses are one and the same, then the two should travel at the same speed. And in fact they do.

Explaining the action potential How do we explain the action potential? Modern electrophysiology proposes a model based on physical and chemical interactions at the cell membrane. The neuron is enclosed in a very thin membrane, which serves as a gatekeeper governing the movement of various particles into the cell and out of it. The particles are ***ions,*** atoms or molecules that have gained or lost electrons, thus acquiring a positive or negative charge. Different ions exist at various concentrations on either side of the membrane. In particular, there is a higher concentration of positively charged sodium ions (Na^+) on the outside of the neuron than on the inside. This difference is produced by a mechanism embedded in the cell membrane that pumps sodium ions out of the cell's interior. This excess of positively charged sodium ions on the outside of the cell (and imbalances of other ions as well) creates the electrical imbalance that is the resting potential—negative on the inside and positive on the outside (see Figure 2.9).

To explain the action potential, we have to note a further fact. In addition to the slow-acting ion pumps, the neuronal membrane also contains special ion gates. These are usually closed to sodium ions, which would otherwise rush into

2.9 Ion gates and the action potential *(A) When a stimulus is above threshold, special ion gates of the membrane open, and positively charged sodium ions (Na^+) surge inside. (B) Immediately thereafter, the gates that admitted Na^+ close, and the electrical balance is restored, because some other positively charged ions—specifically potassium ions (K^+)—are now forced out. The whole process is repeated at an adjacent point in the axon. (After Starr and Taggart, 1989)*

the cell, but when the neuron is stimulated, this changes: Some of the sodium gates are electrically controlled, and they only stay closed if the resting potential is negative. When the resting potential is reduced to the threshold, the sodium gates spring open temporarily. Sodium ions rush in, creating a temporary excess of positively charged particles on the inside of the membrane—the positive swing of the action potential. But immediately afterwards the ionic gates close again, like electrical doors at supermarkets and airports. The newly entered sodium ions are forced out of the cell's interior, and the resting potential soon returns to normal.

Why does this excitation spread to neighboring regions? The reason is that the temporarily positive electrical potential at any point on the axon opens ionic gates at neighboring regions. The resulting entrance of sodium ions at the neighboring region shifts its electrical potential, which then opens the gates of the region adjacent to it, and so on. The upshot is that the impulse—the chain-reaction of action potentials—moves down the entire length of the axon. The whole thing is like a spark traveling along a fuse, except that whereas the fuse is consumed by the spark, the ionic gates rapidly reclose and the membrane potential is restored within milliseconds. The neuron is soon ready to fire again, and if a super-threshold stimulus is still present, fire it will.

All-or-none law One point should be stressed. The electrical response of the axon—that is, the action potential—is unaffected by the intensity of the stimulus, once the stimulus is at threshold level or above. Increasing the stimulus value above this level will neither increase the intensity of the action potential nor affect its speed of conduction to other points in the fiber. This phenomenon is sometimes referred to as the **all-or-none law** of axon reaction. The all-or-none law clearly implies that the stimulus does not provide the energy for the nervous impulse. It serves as a trigger and no more: Given that the trigger is pulled hard enough, pulling yet harder has no effect. Like a gun, a neuron either fires or does not fire. It knows no in-between.★

Stimulus intensity We have seen that the axon obeys the all-or-none law, that stimulus intensity has no effect once threshold is passed. Does this law make sense? Much of our everyday experience seems to deny it: We can obviously tell the difference between the buzz of a mosquito and the roar of a jet plane. How can we square such facts with the all-or-none law?

In many cases what happens is that the more intense stimulus excites a *greater number of neurons.* This is precisely what we should expect, for we know that different neurons vary enormously in their thresholds. Thus, a strong stimulus will stimulate more neurons than a weak stimulus. A weak stimulus will stimulate all neurons whose thresholds are below a given level; a strong stimulus will stimulate all of those, plus others whose threshold is higher.

While remaining strictly obedient to the all-or-none law, however, the individual neuron is nevertheless affected by stimulus intensity. This becomes apparent when we apply a continuous stimulus for somewhat longer intervals. Now we obtain not one impulse but a whole volley. We notice that the size of the action potentials remains the same whatever the stimulus intensity. What changes instead is the **impulse frequency.** The stronger the stimulus, the more *often* the axon will fire. This effect holds until we reach a maximum rate of firing, after which further increases in intensity have no effect (see Figure 2.10). Different neurons have different maximum rates; the highest in humans is of the order of 1,000 impulses per second.

At 160% of
threshold intensity

At 270% of
threshold intensity

500 msec

2.10 Stimulus intensity and firing frequency *Responses of a crab axon to a continuous electric current at three levels of current intensity. The time scale is relatively slow. As a result, the action potentials show up as single vertical lines or "spikes." Note that while increasing the current intensity has no effect on the height of the spikes (the all-or-none law) it leads to a marked increase in the frequency of spikes per second. (After Eccles, 1973)*

★ The all-or-none law holds for the action potential—that is, for conduction along the axon. As we will see shortly, however, the situation is different at the dendrites and cell body, where potentials are graded, being built up or lowered in a continuous rather than an all-or-none fashion.

Interaction among nerve cells *An isolated nerve cell. The cell body is in contact with other cells through numerous extensions. The figure illustrates how nerve fibers cross each other to form an elaborate network. (Photograph by David M. Phillips / Visuals Unlimited)*

Sir Charles Sherrington *(Courtesy National Library of Medicine)*

INTERACTION AMONG NERVE CELLS

In a way, the neurons of our nervous system are like 1,000 billion speakers, endlessly prattling and chattering to one another. But each of them has only one word with which to tell its story, the one and only word it can utter. It can choose only whether to speak its word or keep silent, to speak it often or more rarely. Looked at in isolation, the individual speakers seem like imbeciles with a one-word vocabulary, babbling and being babbled at. But when taken as a whole, this gibbering becomes somehow harmonious. The trick is in the integration of the individual messages, the interplay of the separate components. The really interesting question for psychology, then, is not how a neuron manages to produce its word, but rather how it can talk to others and how it can listen.

THE REFLEX

To study the interactions among different neurons, we begin with the simplest illustration of such interactions—the *reflex.* Descartes pointed out that some of our actions are automatic, controlled by mechanical principles, not by the "will." Later progress in neuropsychology was made by studying animal motion that persists after the brain is gone. (What farmer had not seen a chicken running around the barnyard without its head?) Around 1750, the Scottish physician Robert Whytt showed that such movements are controlled by the spinal cord. He found that a decapitated frog will jerk its leg away from a pinprick, but when deprived of *both* brain and spinal cord, it no longer responded. Presumably, the frog's leg movement depended on the spinal cord.

The study of reflexes received some additional impetus during the French Revolution. Pierre Cabanis, friend and physician to some of its leaders, wondered whether consciousness survives beheading. He concluded that it does not and that the body's twitches after execution are mere reflex actions, automatisms without consciousness. This grim business was taken up again some forty years later by the German scientist Theodor Bischoff, who performed a series of rather macabre experiments on the freshly separated head of an executed criminal. Even fairly intense stimuli produced no effects during the first minute after decapitation. Among the stimuli Bischoff employed, with perhaps greater devotion to science than human sensitivity, was the word "Pardon!" shouted into the ears of the severed head (Fearing, 1930).

Today we can list a host of reflexes, built-in response patterns executed automatically, without thought and without will and even without a functioning brain. Vomiting, the rhythmic contraction of the intestines (peristalsis), erection of the penis, blushing, limb flexion in withdrawal from pain, sucking in newborns—the catalog is very large. Some reflexes are produced by circuits (reflex arcs) composed of only two neurons, one sensory and one motor. More typically the chain is longer, with one or more interneurons interposed between the afferent and efferent ends.

INFERRING SYNAPTIC FUNCTION

Initially, many neurologists believed that the reflex pathway was across a long and essentially continuous strand of nervous tissue—in essence, along one neuron—but by the end of the nineteenth century most became convinced that there is a gap between neurons, the *synapse,* across which they must communicate. The critical studies establishing the role of the synapse and its place in nerve interaction were performed at the turn of the century by the English physiologist Sir Charles Sherrington (1857–1952). Sherrington's work was conducted at the level of behavior rather than that of electrophysiology. What he observed directly was reflex action in dogs, cats, and monkeys. How the synapse worked, he inferred. In this sense Sherrington acted more like a psychologist than a physiologist: He focused on behavior in order to gain insight into its underlying mechanisms.

Sherrington set out to study the *simple reflex,* that is, the reflex considered in splendid neurological isolation, unaffected by activities elsewhere in the nervous system. Of course he was well aware that such simplicity does not really exist, for even the lowliest spinal reflex is modified by higher centers in the spinal cord or the brain. An itch in your side will initiate a scratch reflex, but if you are the catchman in a trapeze act you will probably inhibit it. To remove the effect of higher centers, Sherrington used the *spinal animal,* usually a dog, whose spinal cord had been completely severed in the neck region. This cut all connections between the body (from the neck down) and the brain, so that spinal reflexes could be studied pure.

EXCITATION

Sherrington's method was simple. He applied mild electric shocks to some point on the spinal animal's skin and observed whether this stimulus evoked a particular reflex response (Figure 2.11). Sherrington asked whether conduction across neurons had the same characteristics as conduction within neurons. He discovered that it did not.

One line of evidence to support this conclusion came from *temporal summation* (see Figure 2.12). Sherrington showed that while one stimulus below threshold will not elicit the reflex, two or more of them (all equally subthreshold) may do so if presented in succession. The important point was that such temporal summation effects occurred even when the individual stimuli were spaced at intervals of up to half a second or thereabouts. How could this be? Sherrington argued that the most plausible interpretation is that some form of summation occurs at a crossover point between neurons. This crossover point soon came to be called the synapse.

Sherrington supposed that there is some kind of excitatory process (presumably caused by the liberation of a then still undiscovered chemical substance from the ends of the axon) that accumulates at the synapse and builds up until it reaches a level high enough (the threshold level) to trigger the next neuron into

2.11   Saddle-shaped area of spinal dog
When a stimulus whose strength is above threshold is applied at any point in the "saddle," the animal will perform a scratching movement. (After Sherrington, 1906)

2.12   Arguments for synaptic transmission *(A) Temporal summation. A subthreshold stimulus will not elicit the reflex, but two or more stimuli will if presented successively at intervals of up to half a second. This indicates that the effects of the first stimulus were somehow stored and added to the effects of the second. (B) Spatial summation. Subthreshold stimuli applied to different points in the saddle area will not evoke a reflex if presented separately, but they will if presented simultaneously. This indicates that the excitatory effects from different regions are all funneled into the same common path.*

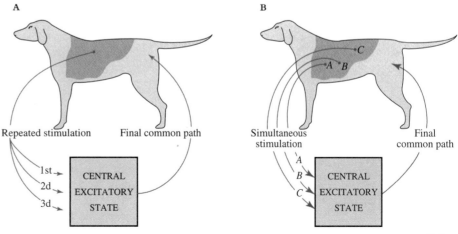

action. This hypothesis clearly accounts for temporal summation. Every time cell *A* fires, a tiny amount of the excitatory substance is liberated into the total synaptic gap between cell *A* and cell *B*. With enough repetitions of the stimulus, the total quantity of what Sherrington called the ***central excitatory state*** exceeds the threshold of cell *B*, which then fires (Figure 2.12A).

Further evidence for Sherrington's general approach derives from the phenomenon of ***spatial summation,*** which highlights the fact that several neurons may funnel in upon one output. Consider two fairly adjacent points on a dog's flank, *A* and *B,* such that stimulating either of them alone will elicit a particular reflex if the stimulus is intense enough. Sherrington showed that subthreshold stimulation at *both* points will yield the reflex, even though this same weak stimulation would not suffice for either of these points in isolation. This indicates that two groups of nerve fibers converge upon one neural output—the ***final common path***. At this juncture, the excitatory chemicals released by the converging neurons "pile up" and their effects summate (Figure 2.12B).

INHIBITION

So far it would appear that neurons either vote "aye," thus adding to the central excitatory state at the synapse, or else abstain altogether. However, some neurons may signal "nay" and set up an inhibitory effect, actively opposing and preventing excitation. One of the clearest demonstrations of such an effect is the phenomenon of ***reciprocal inhibition***. Skeletal muscles typically come in antagonistic pairs—flexor and extensor (Figure 2.13). What happens to the flexor muscle when the extensor is excited and conversely? Patently, the antagonists must not both contract at the same time, like wrestlers straining against each other. For maximum mechanical efficiency, the force of the excited muscle should encounter little or no opposition from its antagonist.

Using a spinal animal, Sherrington provided an experimental demonstration. He found that stimulation of a sensory site that caused the flexor to contract had a further effect. It also caused the extensor to relax so that it actually became limp—limper in fact than it was in the normal resting state. Sherrington concluded that this unusually low level of muscular contraction could only be explained by assuming that a counteracting process nullifies the excitatory messages to the muscle fibers that maintain normal muscle tone—*inhibition*.

This finding suggested that a neuron can receive both excitatory and inhibitory messages. The two processes summate algebraically; they pull in

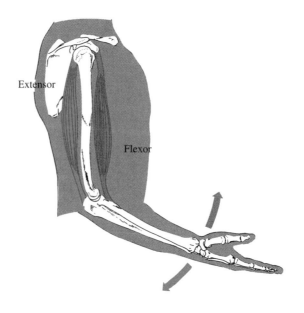

2.13 An example of muscle antagonists
The figure shows how the members of an antagonistic muscle pair (biceps and triceps) oppose each other in flexing and extending the forearm.

Extensor

Flexor

opposite directions and thus have opposite signs (with excitation positive, inhibition negative). Such inhibitory signaling is found throughout the nervous system, but let's stay with Sherrington's illustration of motor neurons. Whether a motor neuron fires (and thus activates a muscle fiber) depends upon the other neurons that send messages to it. Each of these cells gives a positive or negative signal or remains neutral and thereby determines whether the excitatory threshold of the motor neuron is reached, and therefore, whether it fires or does not.

THE SYNAPTIC MECHANISM

Sherrington could only guess at the specific physical mechanism that governs transmission at the synapse, but he did sketch some general guidelines. There had to be excitatory and inhibitory processes, accumulating over time, pooling effects from various neural inputs and adding algebraically. But what was their nature?

SYNAPTIC TRANSMISSION

Sherrington and some of his contemporaries guessed that neurons communicate with their neighbors by means of some chemical substance that is released when the impulse reaches the end of the axon. The proof came in 1920 when Otto Loewi performed a crucial experiment. He dissected two frogs, removed their hearts, and placed each of the two hearts in separate, fluid-filled jars in which they kept on beating. One of the hearts still had the vagus nerve attached to it; this nerve inhibits the heart muscle and slows down the heartbeat. Loewi electrically stimulated the vagus nerve for half an hour or so. All this time the other heart stayed in its own jar, and beat at its own, more rapid pace. After a while, Loewi took the fluid from the jar that held the first heart (whose beat had been slowed down by the vagus nerve) and poured it into the jar in which the second heart was kept. Almost immediately that second heart slowed down as well. The implication was clear. The stimulation of the vagus nerve liberated some substance whose effect on the heart muscle (a region that we now know acts just like a synapse) is to inhibit its function (see Figure 2.14). Loewi called that substance "vagus stuff." We now call it ***acetylcholine*** (usually abbreviated ACh), the first of a hundred or more chemical substances now identified as ***neurotransmitters*** (Loewi, 1960; Eccles, 1982).

Loewi's experiment had only shown that the transmission of the neural message involves a chemical substance. We now know quite a bit more about the way in which this transmission occurs in actual neurons. Let's begin by distinguishing between the ***presynaptic neuron*** and the ***postsynaptic neuron.*** The presynaptic neuron sends the neural message; the postsynaptic neuron receives

2.14 Schematic illustration of Loewi's discovery of the action of neurotransmitters *The hearts in two jars, I and II, are beating. (A) The vagus nerve that is still attached to the heart in jar I is stimulated, thus inhibiting the muscle and slowing down the heartbeat. (B) After an interval, the fluid in jar II is replaced by the fluid from jar I. The heart in jar II will now slow down almost immediately. (After Groves and Rebec, 1988)*

2.15 The synapse Electron micrograph of synaptic knobs, the tiny swellings of the axon terminals that contain the vesicles. (Lewis et al., 1969)

it. The process begins in the tiny knobs of the axon terminals of the presynaptic neuron (see Figure 2.15). Within these swellings are numerous tiny sacs, or **vesicles** ("little vessels"), which contain neurotransmitters. When the presynaptic neuron fires, some of the vesicles in its axon knobs burst and release their transmitter load into the **synaptic gap** that separates the two cells. The transmitter molecules diffuse across this gap and come to rest upon the dendrite or cell body of the postsynaptic cell (see Figure 2.16A and B).

Once across the synaptic gap, how do transmitters perform their transmitting function? They do so by activating specialized **receptor molecules** in the **postsynaptic membrane.** When one of these receptors is activated, it opens or closes certain ion gates in the membrane. For example, some neurotransmitters open the gates to sodium ions. As these sodium ions enter the postsynaptic cell, that cell's resting potential is *decreased* (see Figure 2.16C and D). (We'll consider inhibitory effects shortly.) As more and more transmitter molecules cross the synaptic bridge, they activate more and more receptors, which drop the resting potential of the postsynaptic cell further and further. These drops accumulate and spread along the membrane of the postsynaptic neuron. When the drop gets large enough, the threshold is reached, the action potential is triggered, and the impulse speeds down the postsynaptic cell's axon.

A similar mechanism accounts for inhibition. At some synapses, the presynaptic cell liberates transmitter substances that produce an *increase* in the resting potential of the postsynaptic neuron. This is in contrast to excitatory transmitter substances, which *decrease* the cell's resting potential.★ As a result, a larger drop in resting potential will now be necessary to set off the action potential in the postsynaptic cell. Since most neurons have synaptic connections with neurons that excite them as well as with others that inhibit them, the response of a given postsynaptic cell depends on a final tally of the excitatory and inhibitory "yeas" and "nays" that act upon it. If the net value is excitatory, and if this value exceeds the threshold, the cell will fire.

We can now see how these synaptic mechanisms account for Sherrington's discovery that conduction *within* neurons is governed by different principles than conduction *between* neurons. The ultimate reason is that the changes in potential

★ Whether a transmitter is excitatory or inhibitory depends on its relation to the postsynaptic membrane. The same transmitter can be excitatory at some synapses and inhibitory at others. Thus acetylcholine excites the muscle fibers of the skeleton while inhibiting those of the heart.

INTERACTION AMONG NERVE CELLS

2.16 Schematic view of synaptic transmission *(A) Neuron A transmits a message through synaptic contact with Neuron B. (B) The events in the axon knob (the mitochondria shown in the figure are structures that help to produce the energy the neuron requires for its functioning). (C) The vesicle is released, and neurotransmitter molecules stream toward the postsynaptic membrane. (D) Transmitter molecules settle on the receptor site, an ion channel opens, and Na⁺ streams in. (After Bloom, Lazerson, and Hofstadter, 1988)*

in the dendrites and cell body produced by the neurotransmitters are quite different from the action potential in the axon. For unlike the action potential (which is all or none), these changes are **graded.** They add up over time: Small changes accumulate to create larger changes as more and more transmitter molecules affect the postsynaptic cell (thus accounting for temporal summation). They also add up in space. Most neurons receive inputs from a great many presynaptic cells—in the brain, often from a thousand or more. As a result, transmitter molecules arrive at several different regions of the postsynaptic membrane, and their effects summate (thus accounting for spatial summation).

What happens to the transmitter molecules after they have affected the post synaptic neuron? It wouldn't do just to leave them where they are, for they might continue to exert their effects long after the presynaptic neuron had stopped firing. There are two mechanisms that prevent such false messages from being sent. Some transmitters are inactivated shortly after they've been discharged by a special "cleanup" enzyme that breaks them up into their chemical components. Others are removed from the synapse and recycled back into the presynaptic neuron.

NEUROTRANSMITTERS

On the face of it, one might think that the nervous system only needs two transmitters: one excitatory and the other inhibitory. But nature, as so often, turns out to be exceedingly generous, for in actual fact there are a great number of different transmitter substances. About a hundred or so have been isolated thus far, and many more are sure to be discovered within the next decade.

We will mention just a few of these neurotransmitters here. *Acetylcholine (ACh)* is released at many synapses and at the junction between motor neurons and muscle fibers (a junction that is a kind of synapse) and makes the fibers contract. Others include *serotonin (5HT)*, a transmitter that is involved in many of the mechanisms of sleep and emotional arousal, and *GABA* (or to give its full name, gamma-amino butyric acid), the most widely distributed inhibitory transmitter of the central nervous system. Yet others are *norepinephrine (NE)* and *dopamine (DA)* to which we will refer in later discussions of drug effects and certain mental disorders. For now, we only want to note that neurons differ in the transmitters they release as well as the transmitters that affect them. Thus neurons sensitive to dopamine will not respond to serotonin or to GABA, and vice versa. It is as if different neurons speak different languages. Some speak "Dopaminese," others speak "Serotonese," and so on.

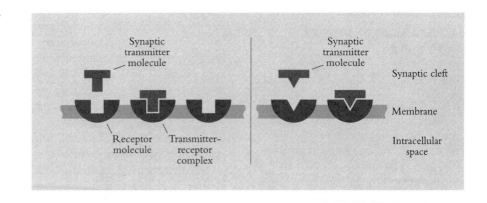

2.17 Lock-and-key model of synaptic transmission *Transmitter molecules will only affect the postsynaptic membrane if their shape fits the shape of certain receptor molecules in that membrane, much as a key has to fit into a lock. The diagram shows two kinds of transmitters and their appropriate receptors. (From Rosenzweig and Leiman, 1982)*

One attempt to understand the differences in chemical responsiveness is the **lock-and-key model** of transmitter action. This theory proposes that transmitter molecules will only affect the postsynaptic membrane if their shape fits into certain synaptic receptor molecules much as a key must fit into a lock (see Figure 2.17). But the mere fact that a given molecule fits into the receptor is not enough to qualify it as a transmitter. The key must not just fit into the lock; it must also turn it. In the language of neurophysiology, the transmitter molecule must produce the changes in membrane potential that correspond to excitatory and inhibitory processes.

POISONS, DRUGS, AND NEUROTRANSMITTER ACTIVITY

The fact that communication between neurons depends on different neurotransmitter substances has wide implications for both psychology and pharmacology. Drugs that enhance a transmitter's activity are technically called **agonists,** a term borrowed from Greek drama in which the agonist is the name for the hero. Drugs that impede such action are **antagonists,** a term that refers to whoever opposes the hero (so to speak, the villain).

Many such drugs operate by increasing or decreasing the amount of available transmitter substance. Some agonists enhance a transmitter's effect by blocking its **reuptake,** a process by which the transmitter molecules are more or less sucked back into the presynaptic neuron, thus terminating their effect on the postsynaptic membrane. Other agonists act by counteracting the cleanup enzyme, or by increasing the availability of some **precursor** (a substance required for the transmitter's chemical manufacture). Antagonists impede transmitter action through the same mechanisms operating in reverse: They speed reuptake, augment cleanup enzymes, and decrease available precursors. Still other drugs affect the synaptic receptors. Some are agonists that activate the receptors by mimicking the transmitter's action, much as a passkey opens a lock. Others are antagonists that prevent the transmitter effect by binding themselves to the synaptic receptor and blocking off the transmitter, thus serving as a kind of putty in the synaptic lock.

Acetylcholine, curare, and the black widow's venom An example of an antagonist that works by blocking receptors is **curare,** a substance discovered by certain South American Indians who dipped their arrows in a plant extract that contained it, with deadly effect on animal prey and human enemies. Curare blocks the action of acetylcholine at the synaptic junctions between motor neurons and muscle fibers. The result is total paralysis and eventual death by suffocation, since the victim is unable to breathe.

INTERACTION AMONG
NERVE CELLS

Curare, the black widow's venom, and paralysis (A) This Cofan man from Colombia is using a curare-tipped dart to hunt. The curare acts as an acetylcholine antagonist: It inhibits this neurotransmitter's action, which leads to paralysis and death. (Photograph by B. Malkin/Anthro-Photo File) (B) The venom of the black widow spider also affects its victim's acetylcholine supply, but instead of inhibiting acetylcholine action, it acts as an acetylcholine agonist, quickly exhausting the victim's supply of this neurotransmitter. The end, however, is the same: paralysis and death. (Photograph © 1992, Comstock)

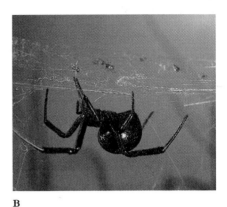

A   B

The venom of the black widow spider, while actually an agonist, achieves a similar result. This substance initially enhances the production of acetylcholine at the neuromuscular junction, but it does so at such an accelerated pace that the neuron's currently available supply of the transmitter is quickly exhausted. The ultimate result is the same muscular paralysis produced by a direct antagonist such as curare.

Norepinephrine and amphetamine   **Amphetamines** act as agonists. These drugs enhance the release of norepinephrine from the presynaptic neurons and also inhibit its reuptake. Norepinephrine is the transmitter for neurons that have to do with general bodily and psychological arousal. The greater the activity of such neurons, the more active and excited the individual is likely to be. It is therefore understandable that amphetamine ("speed") acts as a powerful stimulant. In moderate doses, it leads to restlessness, insomnia, and loss of appetite; larger doses and continued use may lead to frenetic hyperactivity and delusions. Certain other stimulants, cocaine in particular, have similar effects.

Dopamine, schizophrenia, and Parkinson's disease   Some transmitter blockades, like that produced by curare, lead to catastrophic results. But other blockades may be beneficial. An example is the effect of various **antipsychotic drugs,** such as **Thorazine** on the symptoms of schizophrenia, a serious mental disorder that afflicts about 1 percent of the population. In its more extreme forms, schizophrenia is characterized by delusions (believing what isn't so, such as conspiracies and persecution), hallucinations (perceiving what isn't there, such as hearing voices), or bizarre mannerisms and unusual postures that may be maintained for many hours. According to one hypothesis, schizophrenia is produced by an oversensitivity to the transmitter dopamine. Neurons that liberate dopamine have an arousing function in many parts of the brain. Adherents of the dopamine hypothesis believe that people who are overly responsive to this transmitter will be continually overaroused, which may ultimately lead to the symptoms of schizophrenia. One of the arguments for this theory comes from the fact that Thorazine, which blocks the effects of dopamine, has a pronounced effect in alleviating schizophrenic symptoms. While the dopamine hypothesis of schizophrenia is still a matter of dispute, many investigators do agree that disturbances in transmitter function play a role in the production of this and other mental disorders (see Chapter 18 for further discussion).

If the dopamine theory of schizophrenia is correct, the problem is an excess of (or an oversensitivity to) a certain transmitter, specifically dopamine. In other disorders, the problem is the very opposite. An important example is **Parkinson's** *disease,* which mostly afflicts people in their later years. It is characterized by tremors, rigidity, and serious difficulties in initiating voluntary movements. Here, too, the cause is related to dopamine, but now as a case of too little rather than of too much, for in Parkinson's disease there is a gradual degeneration of dopamine-releasing neurons in a pathway of the brain that is crucial for movement. Some of the symptoms of Parkinson's disease are counteracted by the administration of L-DOPA, a dopamine precursor that increases the supply of dopamine in the brain and allows the patient's surviving dopamine-releasing neurons to function more effectively. While this therapy alleviates many patients' symptoms, it does not constitute a real cure, for the progressive destruction of the dopamine-releasing neurons continues (Marsden, 1985).

INTERACTION THROUGH THE BLOODSTREAM: THE ENDOCRINE SYSTEM

Thus far, we have considered the primary instrument of communication within the body: the nervous system. But there is another organ system that serves a similar function: the *endocrine system* (see Figure 2.18 and Table 2.1). Various endocrine glands (such as the pancreas, adrenal glands, and pituitary) release their *hormone* secretions directly into the bloodstream and thus exert effects upon structures often far removed from their biochemical birthplace. As an example, take the *pituitary gland.* One of its components secretes a hormone that tells the kidney to decrease the amount of water excreted in the urine, a useful mechanism when the body is short of water (see Chapter 3).★

On the face of it, the integration that the endocrine glands give us seems to be very different from that provided by the nervous system. In the nervous system, neurotransmitters are sent to particular addresses through highly specific channels. In contrast, the chemical messengers employed by the endocrine system travel indiscriminately to all parts of the body until they finally reach the one organ that is their destination. There is also an enormous difference in the distance these messengers have to travel. While neurotransmitters must only cross the synaptic cleft, which is less than 1/10,000 mm wide, the endocrine messengers may have to traverse half the length of the entire body. But at bottom, the two communication systems have a good deal in common, for both systems deliver their messages by the release of chemical substances. In the nervous system, neurotransmitters excite or inhibit the postsynaptic cell; in the endocrine system, hormones affect specially sensitive cells in the target organ.

Several substances turn out to serve both as hormones and as neurotransmitters. For example, norepinephrine (also known as *noradrenaline*) is the transmitter released by certain neurons that make blood vessels constrict; it is also one of the hormones secreted by the adrenal gland and has similar results. The adrenal gland's release of norepinephrine, and its close relative adrenaline, is controlled by pituitary hormones, and adrenaline (as we all know) increases psychological as well as physiological arousal through its effects on the brain and body.

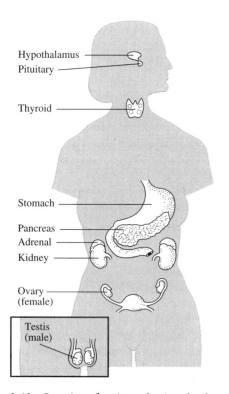

2.18   Location of major endocrine glands and hypothalamus

Hypothalamus
Pituitary
Thyroid
Stomach
Pancreas
Adrenal
Kidney
Ovary (female)
Testis (male)

★ In addition to the endocrine glands, there are also *duct glands* (such as salivary and tear glands) that channel their secretions through their ducts directly to the proper region of application.

TABLE 2.1   THE MAIN ENDOCRINE GLANDS AND THEIR FUNCTIONS

Gland	Functions of the released hormones
Anterior pituitary	Often called the body's master gland because it triggers hormone secretion in many of the other endocrine glands.
Posterior pituitary	Prevents loss of water through kidney.
Thyroid	Affects metabolic rate.
Islet cells in pancreas	Affects utilization of glucose.
Adrenal cortex	Various effects on metabolism; some effects on sexual behavior.
Adrenal medulla	Increases sugar output of liver; stimulates various internal organs in the same direction as the sympathetic branch of the ANS (e.g., accelerates heart rate).
Ovaries	One set of hormones (estrogen) produces female sex characteristics and is relevant to sexual behavior. Another hormone (progesterone) prepares uterus for implantation of embryo.
Testes	Produces male sex characteristics; relevant to sexual arousal.

THE MAIN STRUCTURES OF THE NERVOUS SYSTEM

Our general approach has been to move from the simple to the increasingly complex. We first looked at the operation of the smallest functional unit of the nervous system, the neuron, and then considered the way in which two or more neurons may interact. We now turn to a still more complex level of analysis as we discuss the function of large aggregates of neurons. What can we say about the function of those clumps of nervous tissue, each made up of many millions of neurons, which comprise the gross structures of the brain and spinal cord?

THE EVOLUTION OF CENTRAL CONTROL

The nervous system is analogous to a government, and its evolution can be understood as the gradual imposition of central control over local autonomy. A first step was the establishment of regional rule. Early in evolutionary history the cell bodies of many interneurons began to clump together to form *ganglia* (singular, *ganglion*). At first, these ganglia served primarily as relay stations that passed on sensory messages from the receptors to the muscles. But eventually the close proximity of the cells within these clumps of neural tissue led to the development of an ever-increasing number and complexity of synaptic interconnections. As a result, the ganglia became local control centers that integrated messages from different receptor cells and coordinated the activity of different muscle fibers. These regional centers were usually located close to the sites where important sensory information is gathered or where vital activity takes place.

THE EMERGENCE OF HIERARCHICAL CONTROL

As evolution progressed, the initial loose federation of ganglia gradually became increasingly centralized; some ganglia began to control others, and the ganglia located in the head became dominant. This is true even for the lowly flatworm. The flatworm has a head that contains its mouth and a tail that more or less corresponds to the end of its digestive tube. Under the circumstances, the flatworm is better off with taste and vision receptors in the head than elsewhere. Taste receptors are obviously more useful near the beginning of the digestive tube: They signal edibility and determine whether food should be accepted or rejected; distance receptors such as those of vision are also more effective if situated at the animal's front end: The flatworm already knows something about its rear, for it was there just a moment ago, but what is ahead is still unknown.

To integrate the messages from the various receptors in the head, more and more neural machinery was required and the ganglionic centers that processed the incoming information became increasingly complex. They eventually started to coordinate the activity of ganglia elsewhere in the body until they finally emerged as the head ganglia in status as well as location—in short, they became the brain.

This tendency toward increasing centralization continued within the brain itself. The various structures of the brain tend to function hierarchically; as we will see, there are higher centers that command lower centers, that in turn command still lower centers, and so on.

HIERARCHIES IN SMALL NEURAL CIRCUITS

The hierarchical principle is generally the rule throughout the entire nervous system, even in groupings of relatively few neurons. In some cases, the control function is handled by just one cell, which coordinates the activity of several others. Thus in the sea snail *aplysia* seven neurons determine the animal's circulation by exciting or inhibiting the heart muscles and the blood vessels: One of them acts as a command cell, while the other six act as subordinates doing the commander's bidding (Kandel, 1979).

More usually the command role at lower levels is assumed by small circuits called **central pattern generators** (or **CPGs**), which instigate certain crucial basic actions such as chewing, breathing, locomotion, and the like. Such actions use simple reflexes as their building blocks, with CPGs organizing them in special ways. Consider walking in a four-footed vertebrate: The four legs have to act in concert; when two of the legs are lifted off the ground, the other two have to exert special force to hold the body up. This intricate interplay of individual limb movements is orchestrated by CPGs, as are the various movements required for chewing and swallowing, for breathing, for some lower level aspects of copulation, and so on. The CPGs orchestrate lower level reflexes (and other neural activities) into whole, organized *acts* (Gallistel, 1980; Grillner and Wallèn, 1985).

DISINHIBITION

Another demonstration of the hierarchical principle comes from some cases of **disinhibition.** Higher centers often exert an inhibitory effect upon lower ones.

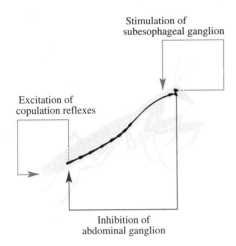

Stimulation of
subesophageal ganglion

Excitation of
copulation reflexes

Inhibition of
abdominal ganglion

**2.19   The disinhibitory mechanism in
the praying mantis**   *Excitation of the abdominal ganglion leads to copulatory movements
in the male. But the sight of the moving female
stimulates the subesophageal ganglion in the
male's head. This in turn inhibits the abdominal ganglion so that copulation stops. Decapitation severs the subesophageal ganglion. The
result is disinhibition and copulation resumes.
Here, dark green indicates excitation and dark
red inhibition. (Roeder, 1967)*

The inhibitory effect of such brain centers is often discovered indirectly, by noting an *increase* in the strength of a reflex after the influence of this higher center
is removed, an effect called disinhibition. A classic example is spinal reflexes in
frogs, which are more vigorous when all brain structures have been removed.

A rather ghoulish instance of disinhibition is provided by the love life of the
praying mantis (see Figure 2.19). The female mantis is a rapacious killer. She
seizes and devours any small creature unfortunate enough to move across her
field of vision. Since the male mantis is considerably smaller than the female, he
too may qualify as food. This cannibalism is quite puzzling. How can the mantis
survive as a species given a behavioral tendency that counteracts successful fertilization?

According to one hypothesis, the female's predatory pattern is triggered
almost exclusively by moving visual stimuli. The courting male's behavior is delicately attuned to this fact. As soon as he sees her he becomes absolutely immobile. Whenever she looks away for a moment he stalks her ever so slowly, but
freezes immediately when her eyes wheel back toward him—an inhibitory
effect upon overall reflex activity. When close enough to her, he suddenly leaps
upon her back and begins to copulate. Once squarely upon the female's back he
is reasonably safe (her normal killer reflexes are elicited only by moving visual
stimuli, and he is mostly out of sight). But the dangers he must surmount to
reach this place of safety are enormous. He must not miss her when he jumps;
he must not slip while upon her. Should he fall, he will surely be grasped and
eaten. Fairly often he does lose his balance, but even then all love's labor is not
lost—for his genes, if not for him. The female commences to eat her fallen mate
from the head on down. In almost all instances, the abdomen of the male now
starts vigorous copulatory movements that are often successfully completed.
Clearly, the male performs his evolutionary duty whatever his own private fate.
But what is the mechanism?

It appears that the intact male's copulatory reflexes are inhibited by the subesophageal ganglion, located in his head. When this nerve cluster is removed,
the animal will engage in endless copulatory movements even when no female
is present. The same thing happens if the female chances to seize her mate and
eat him. She first chews off his head and with it the subesophageal ganglion,
thus disinhibiting the male's copulatory pattern which now resumes in full force
(Roeder, 1935).★ Poets may appreciate this finding as further proof that true
love can survive the grave. But for our present purposes it is a demonstration of
the principle of hierarchical organization. As we will see, this principle is even
more important in vertebrate nervous systems than in the less developed neural
structures of invertebrates such as the mantis.

THE PERIPHERAL AND CENTRAL NER-
VOUS SYSTEMS

Taken as a whole, the human nervous system consists of a fine network of
fibers that gradually merge into larger and larger branches which converge
upon a central trunk line, like the tributaries of a stream. This system is composed of the central and peripheral nervous systems. The ***central nervous system***

★ A more recent study suggests that this cannibalistic pattern may only occur under artificial
conditions of captivity and when the female is virtually starved. Under more natural circumstances,
males seem to manage to mate quite successfully without losing their heads in the process. But
even if induced artificially, the phenomenon is an interesting if macabre illustration of the effect of
disinhibition (Liske and Davis, 1984).

2.20   Central and peripheral nervous system   *The central nervous system (in dark red) and the peripheral nervous system (in orange). (After Bloom, Lazerson, and Hofstadter, 1988)*

(usually abbreviated **CNS**) is made up of the brain and spinal cord. The **peripheral system**, as its name implies, comprises all nervous structures that are outside of the CNS (see Figure 2.20).

Anatomists distinguish between two divisions of the peripheral nervous system—the **somatic** and the **autonomic.** The somatic division is primarily concerned with the control of the skeletal musculature and the transmission of information from the sense organs. It consists of various nerves that branch off from the CNS—efferent fibers to the muscles and afferent fibers from the skin, the joints, and the special senses. The autonomic nervous system (ANS) serves the many visceral structures that are concerned with the basic life processes, such as the heart, the blood vessels, the digestive systems, the genital organs, and so on.

The cental nervous system can be described as a long tube whose front end is much thickened and has a number of structures attached to it. The portion of the tube below the skull is the **spinal cord,** while the portion located in the skull is the **brain.** Two structures are attached to the **brain stem.** One is the pair of **cerebral hemispheres,** which are very large and envelop the central tube completely; the other is the **cerebellum** (literally, "little brain"), which is located lower down and is much smaller (see Figure 2.21).

Neuroanatomists find it convenient to consider the brain in terms of three major subdivisions: the **hindbrain,** the **midbrain,** and the **forebrain** (see Figure 2.22).

THE HINDBRAIN

The hindbrain includes the **medulla** and the **cerebellum.** The medulla is the part of the brain stem closest to the spinal cord; it controls vital bodily functions such as heartbeat, circulation, and respiration. The cerebellum is a deeply convoluted structure that controls bodily balance and muscular coordination. It functions as a specialized computer whose 30 billion or more neurons integrate the information from the muscles, joints, and tendons of the body that are required both for ordinary walking and for the skilled, automatic movements of athletes and piano players.

The hindbrain is on a fairly low rung of the nervous system's hierarchical ladder. This is shown by the behavior of cats whose brain has been cut (technically, **transected**) at a point just above the hindbrain, severing the parts of the nervous

2.21   The central nervous system   *This diagram is a highly schematic representation of the main parts of the brain. (After Lickley, 1919)*

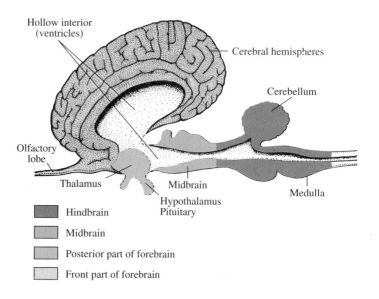

Hollow interior (ventricles)

Cerebral hemispheres

Cerebellum

Olfactory lobe

Thalamus

Midbrain

Hypothalamus
Pituitary

Medulla

■ Hindbrain
■ Midbrain
■ Posterior part of forebrain
■ Front part of forebrain

A

B
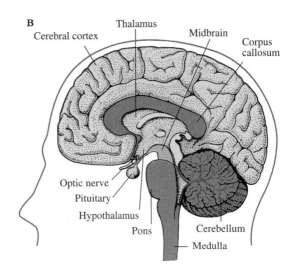

2.22   The human brain   *(A) A photograph of the brain cut lengthwise. (Photograph by Biophoto Associates, Photo Researchers) (B) A diagram of the brain, cut lengthwise. The colors are analogous to those used in Figure 2.21 to indicate hindbrain (dark blue), midbrain (aqua), and forebrain (light green). (After Keeton, 1980)*

system below the cut (that is, the hindbrain and the spinal cord) from all control by the portion above. The question is what the part below the cut can do now that it is on its own.

The answer is that the resulting hindbrain animal can still make the various limb and trunk movements that are required for standing, crouching, or walking. But it can't put them together. As a result, it is unable to stand or make walking movements unless supported by straps. Without support, a hindbrain cat will collapse, unable to come up with more than disorganized reflex twitches if stimulated. Reduced to a hindbrain, the animal has become a mere biological marionette without a puppet master: "It can move, but it cannot act" (Gallistel, 1980).

THE MIDBRAIN

The midbrain contains several neural centers that control some motor reactions and that also have some limited auditory and visual functions (such as controlling eye movements). True to its name, the midbrain can be regarded as a form of neural middle management that knits together the simple movements organized by the hindbrain to form larger wholes: They now are acts rather than movements. When a transection is made just above the midbrain, the resulting midbrain animal can now stand without support, walk, shiver, chew, swallow, and hiss. But these acts don't cohere into a broader behavioral scheme. The acts of a normal cat are organized into sequences that serve a larger goal: A hungry cat will walk to search for prey, will stalk the prey once found, and will then pounce, kill, and eat it. In contrast, a midbrain cat can't put its acts together. If starved, it won't look for food; if attacked, it won't flee. It acts, but it acts without point or purpose. Such observations suggest that the midbrain contains circuitry that coordinates lower-level building blocks, such as reflexes, and forms them into the most basic acts of the organism. But the orchestration of these basic acts into patterns of purposeful behavior is conducted at a higher level still.

FOREBRAIN: THALAMUS, HYPOTHALAMUS, AND LIMBIC SYSTEM

The forebrain is made up of the two **cerebral hemispheres,** the **thalamus,** the **hypothalamus,** and the **limbic system.** Anatomists usually distinguish several large sections within each hemisphere, called **lobes.** There are four such lobes,

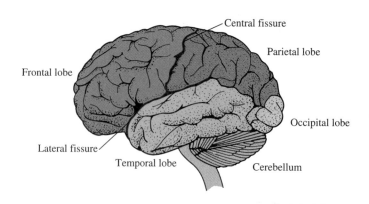

2.23   The cerebral hemispheres, side view

each named for the cranial bone nearest to it: the *frontal, parietal, occipital,* and *temporal* (see Figure 2.23). The thin outer layer of the cerebral hemispheres is called the *cerebral cortex* (see below).

Nestled under the cortex are several forebrain structures that represent the topmost regions of the brain stem. One is the *thalamus,* a large system of various centers that serves as a kind of reception area for the cerebral hemispheres. Fibers from the eyes, the ears, the skin, and some motor centers pass their information to the thalamus, which then forwards it upward to the cerebral cortex. Another major structure in this region is the *hypothalamus,* which is intimately involved in the control of behavior patterns that stem from the basic biological urges (e.g., feeding, drinking, maintaining an appropriate temperature, engaging in sexual activity, and so forth; see Chapter 3). Finally, the third set of structures in the subcortical forebrain is located near the center of the cerebral hemispheres in a region that borders on the brain stem (see Figures 2.22 and 2.24). These are often grouped together under the term *limbic system* (from the French *limbique,* "bordering"). Many limbic subsystems are part of what (in evolutionary terms) is an older unit, sometimes called the "old cortex." The limbic system has close anatomical ties with the hypothalamus and is involved in the control of emotional and motivational activities, and some aspects of learning and memory (see the discussion of the hypothalamus in Chapter 3).

When a transection is made leaving an animal with the hindbrain, the midbrain, and all structures of the forebrain but the cortex, it can organize its separate acts toward some purpose. A limbic cat searches for food when hungry, looks for a warmer place when cold, tries to escape when harmed, and so on. In many ways it behaves much as a normal cat. But there is a difference—its performance is inept. When attacked by another cat, it strikes back, but quite ineffectively. Its blows are poorly directed and easily avoided by its enemy. The limbic animal can coordinate its acts into a sequence that has an aim. But that sequence and the environment in which it is enacted must be very simple. If it is at all complex, the animal will fail. The limbic animal can act, and its acts have some purpose. But lacking a cortex, it is stupid (Bard and Rioch, 1937; Wetzel and Stuart, 1976; Gallistel, 1980).

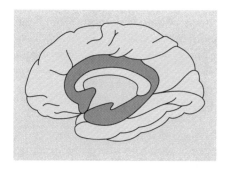

2.24   The limbic system   *A schematic diagram of the limbic system (in blue) shown in the side view. (After Russell, 1961)*

THE CEREBRAL CORTEX

We finally turn to the structure that has traditionally been regarded as the functional summit of the behaving organism (or at least, of the thinking organism): the *cerebral cortex.* The cells in the cortex are so densely packed that they are

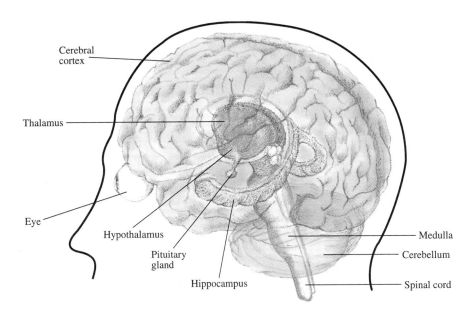

2.25 Important structures of the brain
Thalamus, hypothalamus, and other structures as if seen through a transparent hemisphere. (After Bloom, Lazerson, and Hofstadter, 1988)

capable of the most complex synaptic interconnections. While the cortex is only about 3 mm thick, it comprises a substantial proportion of the entire human brain because the cerebral hemispheres are deeply folded and convoluted. Thus crumpled up, the cerebral surface that can be packed into the cranial cavity is very much increased (see Figure 2.25).

The cortex is the most recent structure of the brain to emerge in the course of evolution. Fish have none at all, reptiles and birds have but a poor beginning, while in mammals there is considerable enlargement, especially in the primates. The cerebral cortex is that part of the nervous system that allows us to be intelligent. In cats, its presence may not be utterly necessary, although as we saw they are certainly in a bad way without it. But in our own species, its absence is catastrophic. For without a cortex there can be no planning, no complex sequence of motor movements, no perception of organized form, and no speech—in short, no semblance of anything that we call human.

PROJECTION AREAS

Among the first discoveries in the study of cortical function was the existence of the ***projection areas.*** These serve as receiving stations for sensory information or as dispatching centers for motor commands. ***Sensory projection areas*** are those regions of the cortex where the messages that come from the various senses (usually through some other relay stations) are first received. ***Motor projection areas*** are those from which directives that ultimately go to the muscles are issued. The term *projection* is here used in a geometrical sense: Motor and sensory areas of the body are projected (mapped) onto particular regions of the cortex, resulting in a rough topographical correspondence between the location in the body and the location of the receiving or dispatching center in the cortex.

MOTOR AREAS

The discovery of the cortical motor areas began over a hundred years ago, when several physiologists opened the skull of a lightly anesthetized dog and then applied mild electric currents to various portions of its cerebral cortex. They discovered a region in the frontal lobe in which stimulating a given point led to motion of the forelimb, stimulating another point led to motion of the trunk, and so forth. Stimulating the left hemisphere led to movements on the right side of the body; stimulating the right hemisphere caused movements on the left. This made good anatomical sense because most of the major efferent pathways from the brain cross over to the opposite side just as they leave the hindbrain.

Some sixty years later, similar studies were conducted on human subjects by the Canadian neurosurgeon, Wilder Penfield. The stimulation was administered in the course of a brain operation. Penfield's studies showed that the cortical motor area in humans is in a region of the frontal lobe that is quite similar to that found in dogs. Stimulation there led to movement of some parts of the body, much to the surprise of patients who had no sense of "willing" the action or of "performing it themselves." Systematic exploration showed that for each portion of the motor cortex, there was a corresponding part of the body that moved when its cortical counterpart was stimulated, with each hemisphere controlling the side of the body opposite to it. The results are sometimes expressed graphically by drawing a "motor homunculus," a schematic picture of the body with each part depicted on the motor projection area that controls its movement (Figure 2.26).

Inspection of the motor homunculus shows that equal areas of the body do not receive equal cortical space. Instead, parts of the body that are very mobile and capable of precisely tuned movement (for instance, the fingers, the tongue) are assigned greater cortical space than those employed for movements that are more gross and undifferentiated (for instance, the shoulder). Evidently, what matters is function, the extent and complexity of use (Penfield and Rasmussen, 1950).

Some related findings with various animals fit tidily into this picture. For example, consider the cortical representations of the forepaw in dogs and rac-

2.26   The motor projection area of the human cortex   *(A) The location of the motor projection area in a side view of the brain. (B) The head shows the plane of the cross section of the figure. (C) The motor projection area of one hemisphere shown in a cross section of the brain. The location and relative amount of cortical space allotted to each body region is graphically expressed as a motor homunculus. (After Penfield and Rasmussen, 1950)*

A

B

C

MOTOR HOMUNCULUS

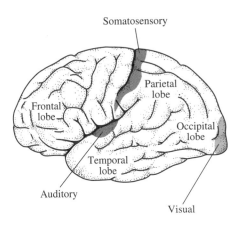

2.27 Sensory projection areas of the human cortex *The location of the so-matosensory, auditory, and visual projection areas in the brain. (After Cobb, 1941)*

The sensory homunculus *An artist's rendition of what a man would look like if his appearance were proportional to the area allotted by the somatosensory cortex to his various body parts. (Courtesy of The Natural History Museum, London)*

coons. Unlike the dog, the raccoon is a "manual" creature that explores the world with its forepaws; neatly enough, the forepaw cortical area in raccoons dwarfs its counterpart in dogs (Welker, Johnson, and Pubols, 1964).

SENSORY AREAS

Analogous methods have demonstrated the existence of cortical sensory areas. The **somatosensory area** is located in the parietal lobes (see Figure 2.27). Patients stimulated at a particular point of this area report a tingling sensation somewhere on the opposite side of their bodies. (Less frequently, they will report experiences of cold, warmth, or of movement.) Again, we find a neat topographic projection. Each part of the body's surface sends its sensory information to a particular part of the cortical somatosensory area, but again with an unequal assignment of cortical space. The parts of the body that are most sensitive to touch, such as the index finger and the tongue, enjoy a disproportionately large cortical space allocation. And again we find a crossover effect. Each part of the body is mapped onto the hemisphere on the side opposite to it: the right thumb onto the left hemisphere, the left shoulder onto the right hemisphere, and so on.

Similar projection areas exist for vision and for hearing and are located in the occipital and temporal lobes respectively (see Figure 2.27). Patients who are stimulated in the visual projection area report optical experiences, vivid enough, but with little form or meaning—flickering lights, streaks of color. Stimulated in the auditory area, patients hear things, but again the sensation is rather meaningless and chaotic—clicks, buzzes, booms, hums.

ASSOCIATION AREAS

Less than one-quarter of the human cortex is devoted to the projection zones. The remaining regions are the so-called **association areas,**★ which are implicated in such higher mental functions as planning, perceiving, remembering, thinking, and speaking. Most of the evidence comes from studies of patients who have incurred damage (technically, **lesions**) through tumors, hemorrhage, accident, or blockage of cerebral blood vessels (popularly known as a stroke).

METHODS FOR STUDYING LOCALIZATION

The traditional interpretation of the effect of lesions in association areas is that they impair the organization of messages that come from the sensory projection areas or that go to the motor projection areas. But just how do we know exactly where the lesions are? To be sure, their exact location will eventually be known through an autopsy, but both the physician (and no doubt the patient) would surely prefer to get an answer while the patient is still alive. Standard X-rays are of some help, but they only reveal very gross pathologies. Fortunately, several modern techniques have been developed that provide us with a much more precise picture of the anatomical structure of a living patient's brain.

One such technique is the **CAT scan** (an abbreviation for **Computerized Axial Tomography**). It employs a narrow beam of X-rays that is aimed through the patient's head and hits a detector on the opposite side. This beam moves

★ The term grew out of an earlier belief that neural messages from the different senses meet and become associated in these regions.

2.28 CAT scan *The CAT scan shows a subarachnoid hemorrhage, resulting from a ruptured blood vessel. The hemorrhage is the light area over the right side of the brain (left on image). It looks white because there was considerable bleeding; blood absorbs more radiation than ordinary brain tissue (Courtesy Radiography Dept., Royal Victoria Infirmary, Newcastle-upon-Tyre. Photo by Simon Fraser, Science Photo Library/Photo Researchers, Inc.)*

slowly in a circular arc, and the detector moves along with it. Since different brain tissues vary in density, they block the X-rays to different degrees. A computer eventually constructs a composite picture based on the X-ray views from all the different angles (see Figure 2.28).

Another development allows neurologists and psychologists to look into a living brain and observe some aspects of its functioning. This is the **PET scan** (or, to give its full name, **Positron Emission Tomography**), which utilizes the fact that brain tissue, like all other living tissue, uses more fuel the more active it is. The subject is injected with a radioactive sugar that resembles glucose (the only metabolic fuel the brain can use). Active cells of the brain will take up this substance, which will then signal its presence by emitting subatomic particles. (Needless to say, the dose is low enough so that there are no harmful effects). The more emission that occurs, the more metabolic activity is indicated. The resulting PET scan can thus tell the physician that a certain region of the brain is abnormally active or inactive and may suggest a tumor, a lesion, or a psychological disorder (see Figure 2.29). PET scans are also useful tools in studying localization of function in normal persons. For example, they will show varying degrees of activity in the general region of the visual projection area depending on the complexity of the scene that is being viewed (see Figure 2.30).

By now the most widely used neurodiagnostic technique is **Magnetic Resonance Imaging (MRI)**, which relies on a physical principle called nuclear magnetic resonance. This refers to the fact that the nuclei at the center of atoms have their own resonant frequencies: If you perturb them, they sing like tuning forks as they bounce back to normal. The nuclei of the atoms that make up the neurons in the brain sing differently from those of other tissues. An MRI scan disturbs these atoms by passing a very high frequency alternating magnetic field through the brain by means of electromagnets surrounding the patient's head. As the magnetic field fluctuates, the chorus of atomic voices is detected by magnetic sensors within the scanner. A computer will then put the data together to

2.29 PET scans and disorders *The scans show the difference in metabolic levels in normal, schizophrenic, and depressed individuals. Red indicates highest metabolic activity, with yellow next, followed by green, and then blue. During depression, for example, brain activity is considerably reduced, especially in the frontal areas. (NIH/SPL/Photo Researchers)*

2.30   PET scan and visual stimulation These scans show the difference in metabolic brain activity depending on whether the patient's eyes were closed, or whether she was viewing a simple or complex scene. (Photograph by Dr. John Mazziotta et al./Photo Researchers)

2.31   Magnetic Resonance Imaging (MRI) A patient goes through the MRI procedure, while a medical specialist watches the image on a screen (Photograph © Paul Shambroom)

form a picture of the brain that will show brain tumors and the blood clots and leaks that may signal strokes (see Figure 2.31).

As these and other medical procedures are refined in the next decade, they will offer a new window into the functioning of the normal human brain; at present, their greatest use is in locating cerebral lesions in clinical patients. By studying the disorders caused by such lesions, neuropsychologists have been able to make cautious inferences about the functions of the cortical association areas that have been damaged.

DISORDERS OF ACTION

Apraxia   Some lesions in the cortical association areas produce **apraxias** (from the Greek for "inability to act"), which are serious disturbances in the initiation or organization of voluntary action. In some apraxias, the patient is unable to perform certain well-known actions such as saluting or waving good-bye when asked to do so. In other cases, actions that normal persons regard as quite simple and unitary become fragmented and disorganized. When asked to light a cigarette, the patient may strike a match against a matchbox, and then strike it again and again after it is already burning; or he may light the match and then put it into his mouth. These deficits are in no sense the result of a motor paralysis, for the patient can readily perform each constituent of the action in isolation. His problem is in initiating the sequence or in selecting the right components and fitting them together (Luria, 1966; Kolb and Whishaw, 1990).

Apraxia is evidently an impairment of a neurological system that initiates and organizes individual movements into coherent, larger actions. When we looked at the behavior of transected cats, we saw how different levels of the brain organize limb movements into acts and acts into simple goal-directed sequences. The same hierarchical principle applies to cortical action. The association region whose lesion leads to apraxia is perhaps analogous to the command post of a regiment that draws up the battle plan and orders an attack. If the command post falls and no other takes its place, there can be no organized attack, even though the individual soldiers are still able to fire their guns and throw their hand grenades (Geschwind, 1975; Kolb and Milner, 1981).

The intention to move   Further evidence for the role of cortical association areas in setting up a plan for action comes from electrical recording studies. In one experiment, electrodes were placed on the scalps of human subjects, who were asked to press a button in response to various stimuli. Neurons in association areas of the frontal lobe adjacent to the motor cortex fired almost a second before subjects actually moved their fingers, suggesting that these association areas have a role in preparing that action (Deecke, Scheid, and Kornhuber, 1969).

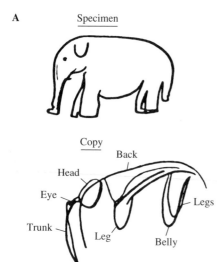

A Specimen

Copy

Back
Head
Eye
Legs
Trunk
Leg
Belly

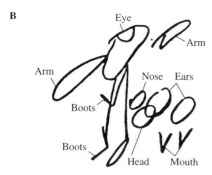

B

Eye
Arm
Arm
Nose Ears
Boots
Boots
Head Mouth

2.32 Drawings by a patient with visual agnosia *(A) Trying to copy an elephant. (B) Production when asked to draw a man. (From Luria, 1966)*

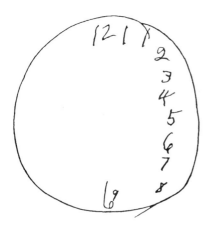

2.33 Unilateral neglect syndrome *A patient with damage to the right parietal cortex was asked to draw a typical clock face. In his drawing, the left side was ignored, and all the hours were squeezed into the right. (From Rosenzweig and Leiman, 1989)*

Other investigators measured cerebral blood flow as an index of cerebral activity (The rate of blood flow in a given region is known to correlate with the activity of that region.) When the movement became complex and involved all the fingers, the blood flow increased in both the motor projection and motor association areas. But when the subjects were asked to rehearse the movements mentally without actually performing them, the blood flow only increased in the frontal association areas (Roland et al., 1980).

DISORDERS OF PERCEPTION AND ATTENTION

In several other disorders caused by lesions in certain cortical association areas, the patient suffers a disruption in the way she perceives the world or attends to it.

Agnosia   One such disorder is **agnosia** (from the Greek for "without knowledge"). Whereas apraxia represents a disrupted organization of action, agnosia is characterized by a disorganization of various aspects of the sensory world. In visual agnosia, patients can see, but they are often unable to recognize what they see. They may have 20/20 vision, but they nevertheless suffer a kind of "psychic blindness." Some of these patients can perceive each separate detail of a picture, but they are unable to identify the picture as a whole. When shown a drawing of a telephone, one such patient painstakingly identified several parts and then ventured an appropriate guess: "A dial . . . numbers . . . of course, it's a watch or some sort of machine!" (Luria, 1966, p. 139). Sometimes the guess leads to a correct inference, as in the case of a patient shown a drawing of two giraffes: "The way this comes down, this could be an animal, four legs and a tail . . . a long neck comes up, an awfully long neck . . . here's a head because here's an eye . . . not a mouse God knows . . . what would have such an extraordinarily long neck? . . . a giraffe" (Wapner, Judd, and Gardner, 1978, p. 347). Agnosic patients have similar difficulties when asked to copy drawings. The individual parts are rendered reasonably well, but they cannot be integrated into a coherent whole (see Figure 2.32).

In some agnosias (technically known as **prosopagnosias,** from the Greek *proso,* "face"), the primary difficulty is in recognizing faces. Some of these patients are unable to distinguish familiar faces; others are even unable to recognize that a face *is* a face. When walking in the street, one such patient would pat the tops of fire hydrants, which he thought were the heads of little children. On one occasion he mistook his wife's head for a hat (Sacks, 1985; for further discussion, see Chapter 6).

Sensory neglect   In agnosia, the patient can see (or feel or hear), but he is unable to make sense of what his senses tell him. In some other disorders, the patient's problem is one of attention. He may perceive certain aspects of the world, but he systematically ignores them.

A striking example is the **unilateral neglect syndrome,** which typically results from certain lesions on the right side of the parietal lobe. Its main characteristic is the patient's systematic neglect of the left side. He acts as if the left side does not exist. This holds for features of the external world. When asked to read compound words such as *toothpick* or *baseball,* such a patient will read "pick" and "ball," ignoring the left half of the word; when asked to draw the face of a clock, he will squeeze all of the numbers onto the clock's right side (see Figure 2.33). And when he is eating, he will select and eat food only from the right side of the plate. A similar neglect applies to the left side of the patient's own body. When dressing, he will ignore the left shirt sleeve and pants leg; when shaving, he will leave the left side of his face unshaven (Heilman and Watson, 1977; Kolb and Whishaw, 1990).

2.34 Tan's brain *The embalmed brain of Broca's famous aphasic patient "Tan," so-called because this was the only syllable he was able to utter. Note the area of damage on the lower side of the left frontal lobe, now known as Broca's area. (Photograph by M. Sakka, courtesy Musée de l' Homme et Musée Dupuytren, Paris)*

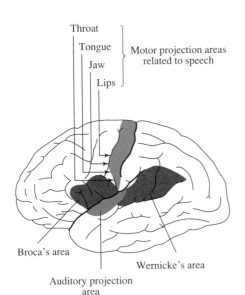

2.35 Broca's and Wernicke's areas *The diagram shows the two association areas most relevant to language. Destruction of Broca's area generally leads to expressive aphasia; destruction of Wernicke's area leads to receptive aphasia. Note the proximity to the relevant projection areas: Broca's area is closest to the regions that control the speech muscles, while Wernicke's area borders on the auditory projection zone.*

What accounts for the unilateral neglect syndrome? According to some theorists, the reason is essentially a failure of attention (Heilman and Watson, 1977). They believe that the syndrome is produced by the disruption of a cortical arousal system. If there is a lesion in the arousal system in just one hemisphere, the person will be less attentive to sensory stimulation coming from the side of the body (or the sensory system) that is controlled by that hemisphere.

DISORDERS OF LANGUAGE

Certain lesions in the cortical association areas lead to serious disruptions of the most distinctively human of all human activities—the production and comprehension of speech. Disorders of this kind are called **aphasias** (from the Greek for "lack of speech"). In right-handers, they are almost always produced by lesions in certain cortical areas of the left hemisphere.

Expressive aphasia In one form of aphasia, the patient's primary difficulty is with the production of speech. This is **expressive aphasia,** which is essentially a language apraxia. In extreme cases, a patient with this disorder becomes virtually unable to utter or to write a word. Less extremely, a few words or phrases survive. These may be routine expressions such as "hello" or emotional outbursts such as "damn it!" In still less severe cases, only a part of the normal spoken vocabulary is lost, but the patient's speech becomes fragmented, as finding and articulating each word requires a special effort. The result is a staccato, spoken telegram: "Here . . . head . . . operation . . . here . . . speech . . . none . . . talking . . . what . . . illness" (Luria, 1966, p. 406).

The similarity to the apraxias we have discussed before is very striking. There is no paralysis of speech muscles, for the patient is perfectly able to move lips and tongue. What is impaired is the ability to organize and plan these movements into a unified sequence, the ability to synthesize individual movements so as to form a word or to put one word after another so as to create a coherent sentence.

Expressive aphasias of the kind described here are generally produced by lesions in a region of the left frontal lobe called **Broca's area** (after a French physician, Paul Broca, who first noted its relation to speech in 1861; see Figures 2.34 and 2.35). This is an association area that borders on the part of the motor projection zone that controls the various speech muscles (jaw, tongue, lips, larynx, and so on) and presumably plays an important role in orchestrating their separate functions.

Receptive aphasia In expressive aphasia, patients generally understand what they hear but cannot answer. In another form of aphasia, the patients' problem is that they don't understand when they are spoken to, though they usually answer anyway. This condition is called **receptive aphasia,** which amounts to a kind of language agnosia. Unlike patients with expressive aphasia, those with receptive aphasia talk very freely and very fast, but while they utter many words, they say very little. The sentences they produce are reasonably grammatical, but they are largely composed of the little filler words that provide little information. A typical example is, "I was over the other one, and then after they had been in the department, I was in this one" (Geschwind, 1970, p. 904).

Receptive aphasia is usually associated with left-hemisphere lesions (in right-handers) in various association areas of the temporal and parietal lobes. Many authorities believe that the crucial locus is **Wernicke's area,** a region that borders on the auditory projection zone and is named after a nineteenth-century neurologist who first described various receptive aphasias (see Figure 2.35).

4 5

Aphasia and sign language   In all cases of aphasia we've discussed thus far, there is a disruption of a *spoken* language, such as English, or Hindi, or Swahili. But some people are deaf and communicate through *sign* language. A number of investigators have shown that such sign languages, for example American Sign Language (ASL), are as complex as any of their vocal counterparts (see Chapter 9, pp. 362–63; Klima and Bellugi, 1979). What happens to deaf people, whose only language is ASL, who suffer a stroke in the left hemisphere? The general finding is that they suffer from a condition that is essentially equivalent to aphasia. They can move their hands and fingers, but they have serious difficulties in using them effectively to produce signs. Some lesions seem to impair the ability to produce particular signed words. Others impair the ability to put these signs together to form grammatical signed sentences. It appears that the left-hemisphere lesions that produce aphasia affect some mental function that is not specific to the ear-mouth channel. That function is human language, which evidently depends on some cerebral machinery that is pretty much the same whether the language is produced by tongue and mouth or by hands and fingers (Bellugi, Poizner, and Klima, 1983; Mayeux and Kandel, 1991).

HOW NEAT IS THE HIERARCHY?

We have repeatedly noted that the nervous system is organized along the lines of a hierarchy, with higher centers controlling lower centers, which control yet lower ones. Where does the cortex fit in? Some nineteenth-century neurologists supposed that the cortex is at the very top of the hierarchy and hands down orders to all the rest. This view fits in with the view that those functions most severely disturbed by cortical lesions—language, thinking, memory, and perception—are the "higher" mental processes and that these presumably govern the "lower" ones (see pp. 44–46). To that extent, our notion of the cortex as the neurological apex may be a good first approximation to the actual state of affairs. But it's worth noting that the final picture will probably turn out to be considerably more complicated than this.

THE MOTOR SYSTEMS

Consider the motor system. Thus far we have acted as if there were only one. But in fact, there are two. One is the ***extrapyramidal*** system, which is the oldest in evolutionary terms. This system works in a fairly precise, hierarchical fashion. At the bottom are the motor neurons: the blue-collar workers of the nervous system that perform the actual work—exciting the muscles. They take their orders from lower-level central pattern generators in the spinal cord, who in their turn are controlled by a middle management system in the midbrain. On top of the system are the ***basal ganglia,*** a set of subcortical structures in the cerebrum that send their messages to the spinal cord through the midbrain, modulate various motor functions, and probably have an important share in motor planning and motor learning. All in all, this is a neat table of organization that would delight many corporate management consultants.

The second motor system is the ***pyramidal*** system. This has its origin in the motor cortex, which sends its tracts directly to the motor neurons that activate the muscles. The first question is, Why are there two systems instead of one?

One answer is that the two systems have different functions. The extrapyramidal system handles relatively gross movements of the head, limbs, and trunk, such as walking, while the pyramidal system supervises more precise actions, such as the delicate movements of a pianist's fingers. But is that answer really

Motor control of reptiles *The motor control system provided by the midbrain and basal ganglia are normally quite sufficient for the limb movements of alligators. Only those alligators that come out of Walt Disney Studios have motor control precise enough to allow dancing. Did their creators endow them with a pyramidal motor system? (From* Fantasia, *1940; courtesy of Photofest)*

adequate? If the cortex represents top management, why does it sidestep its own chain of command? It's as if the president of General Motors decided to tighten nuts and bolts on the factory floor whenever a particularly complex part of the engine is being assembled. On the face of it, it doesn't seem like the most efficient way to proceed.

Perhaps it isn't, but then the nervous system is not a human product. It was built by evolution, which doesn't care about efficiency or neat organizational charts but can only work on what exists at any given point in time. In the evolutionary history of the vertebrates, the extrapyramidal system (based on the midbrain and the basal ganglia) came first and governed the trunk and limb movements of our reptilian ancestors. There was little initially in the way of a second motor system to control the movements of the digits (or nose, or face). But such precise movements are probably less important to reptiles who move their limbs more or less as a whole.★ (There are few alligators who play the piano).

Under the circumstances, what evolved was a second motor system, grafted on top of the first, based on the more complex and adaptable neural tissues in the cortex. Starting from scratch, one might have come up with a more efficient system. But unlike automobile designers who can in principle start all over again (putting the engine in front or using an electrically powered engine), the evolutionary process has to work with what is there at the time. The trouble is that there is no way of going back to square one. As a result, evolution creates systems that are in essence jury-rigged. They may not be the most elegant one might devise, but many of them work reasonably well nevertheless.

THE CORTEX AND LOWER FUNCTIONS

Another demonstration that the neurological hierarchy is far from being neat and clear-cut comes from the fact that the cortex does not control many of the lower functions. For example, rats—and for that matter, humans—continue to eat and seek food even though they may have suffered extensive cortical damage. Foods that they found highly palatable or distasteful before the lesion will still be palatable or distasteful afterwards (Grill and Berridge, 1985). This is not to say that the cortex does not play any role in food seeking (or drinking, or engaging in sexual behavior, or any of the other "lower" functions). But there is no evidence that it *governs* them.

Given what we've learned thus far, it's safe to assume that the nervous system is not organized according to a single hierarchy. It is not an absolute monarchy, with a cortical king who governs all else below (e.g., Arbib, 1972). Instead, it is composed of a number of hierarchies whose controls and functions overlap, with some in the cortex and some in subcortical structures. These hierarchies interact continuously, with one in charge on one occasion but not on another. So it probably makes no sense to say that any one of them is the ruler. For the operation of the nervous system may well be analogous not to an absolute monarchy but to that of a complex twentieth-century society such as ours. The United States in the 1990s is not governed by *one* hierarchy, but by a number of interlocking ones. There are the three branches of the federal government, as well as the armed forces, the bureaucracies of the government agencies, the hierarchies of the large corporations, the labor unions, the lobbyists, the media, and so on and so on. We are governed by a complex interaction of them all, and

---

★ This may not be true of certain modern reptiles, such as crocodiles, who have excellent control of their jaw muscles: They transport their eggs in their mouths to deposit them in safe locations where their chances of survival are maximized.

who will make the decisions depends on many factors, including what is to be decided.

So who's *really* in charge? That may be the wrong question. For just as rulers ultimately depend on those they rule, so the "higher" structures of the nervous system depend critically on the subordinate ones. The ultimate problem is to discover how all the various parts interact and work together.

ONE BRAIN OR TWO?

Anatomically, the brain's two hemispheres appear to be quite similar, but there is abundant evidence that their functions are by no means identical. This asymmetry of function is called **lateralization,** and its manifestations include such diverse phenomena as language, spatial organization, and handedness—the superior dexterity of one hand over the other (Springer and Deutsch, 1981).

We have already seen that in right-handers aphasia is usually associated with lesions in the left hemisphere. Until fairly recently, neuroscientists interpreted this fact to mean that one hemisphere is *dominant* over the other. As a result, they called the (right-hander's) right hemisphere the "minor hemisphere," for they believed that it is essentially a lesser version of the left hemisphere.

More recent evidence has rescued the right hemisphere from this poor relation status, for it now appears that it has many important functions of its own. Right-handers with lesions in the right hemisphere often suffer from various difficulties in the comprehension of various aspects of space and form; they concentrate on details but cannot grasp the overall pattern. Some have trouble recognizing faces (Bogen, 1969). And as we've seen, some suffer from the unilateral neglect syndrome, systematically neglecting the left side of the world (see p. 45 above).

The results are more ambiguous for the 12 percent or so of the population that is left-handed (and also generally left-footed, and to a lesser extent, left-eyed and left-eared as well; Porac and Coren, 1981). Somewhat more than half of the left-handers have speech predominantly lateralized in the left hemisphere; in the rest, language is usually represented in both hemispheres. But overall, there seems to be less lateralization in left-handers than in right-handers, so that the functional capabilities of the left-handers' two hemispheres are more on a par. Thus, in left-handers, aphasia may often be produced by lesions to either hemisphere. But by the same token, left-handed aphasics have a greater chance for ultimate recovery, for the intact hemisphere is better able to take over the responsibilities formerly assigned to the hemisphere that suffered damage (Brain, 1965; Springer and Deutsch, 1981).

EVIDENCE FROM SPLIT BRAINS

Some of the most persuasive evidence about the different functions of the two cerebral hemispheres comes from studies originated by Nobel laureate Roger Sperry on people with **split brains** (Sperry, 1974, 1982): those whose corpus callosum has been surgically severed (see Figure 2.36). The corpus callosum is a massive bundle of nerve fibers that connects the two hemispheres so that they can pool their information and function as a harmonious whole. This neurological bridge (and some other subsidiary ones) is sometimes cut in cases

2.36 The split brain To control epilepsy, neurosurgeons sometimes sever the two hemispheres. This is accomplished by cutting the corpus callosum (in blue) and a few other connective tracts. The corpus callosum is shown here in a lateral cross section.

2.37 *A setup sometimes used in split-brain studies* *The subject fixates a center dot and then sees a picture or a word on the right or left side of the dot. He may be asked to respond verbally, by reading the word or naming the picture. He may also be asked to respond without words, for example, by picking out a named object from among a group spread out on a table and hidden from view, so that it can only be identified by touch. (After Gazzaniga, 1967)*

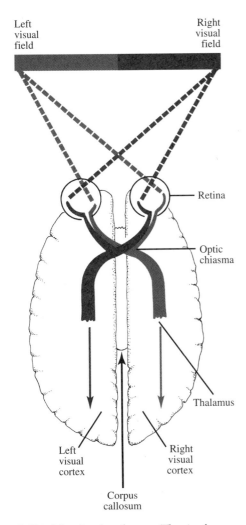

Left visual field

Right visual field

Retina

Optic chiasma

Thalamus

Left visual cortex

Right visual cortex

Corpus callosum

2.38 *The visual pathway* *The visual pathway is so arranged that all points in the right visual field send their information to the left hemisphere; all those in the left field send theirs to the right hemisphere. Information from one hemisphere is transmitted to the other by way of the corpus callosum.*

of severe epilepsy so that the seizure will not spread from one hemisphere to the other (Bogen, Fisher, and Vogel, 1965; Wilson et al.,1977). Once confined to a smaller cortical area, the seizures are less severe and less frequent. The surgery clearly relieves suffering, but it has a side effect—the two hemispheres of the split brain become functionally isolated from each other and in some ways act as two separate brains (Gazzaniga, 1967).

The effect of the split-brain operation is best demonstrated by setting a task that poses a question to one hemisphere and requires the answer from the other (see Figure 2.37). One method is to show a picture so that the neural message only reaches one hemisphere. This is done by flashing the picture for a fraction of a second to either the right or the left side of the patient's field of vision. The anatomical pathways of the visual system are such that if the picture is flashed to the right, it is projected to the left hemisphere; if presented to the left, it is projected to the right hemisphere (see Figure 2.38). The patient's job is merely to say what he sees. When the picture is on the right, he easily does so, for the information is transmitted to the same hemisphere that can formulate a spoken answer—the left hemisphere (which as we've seen is the primary site of language knowledge and of speech). The situation is different when the picture is flashed on the left. Now the visual image is sent to the right hemisphere, but this hemisphere can neither provide a spoken reply nor relay the information to the left hemisphere, which has the language capacity, because the bridge between the two has been cut (Gazzaniga, 1967).

This is not to say that the right hemisphere has no understanding of what it's been shown. One patient was unexpectedly shown a picture of a nude girl. When this picture was flashed to the left hemisphere, the patient laughed and correctly described what she had seen. When the same picture was presented to the right hemisphere, she said that she saw nothing, but immediately afterward she smiled slyly and began to chuckle. When asked what was so funny, she said, "I don't know . . . nothing . . . oh—that funny machine" (Gazzaniga, 1970, p. 106). The right hemisphere knew what it was laughing at. The left hemisphere heard the laughter but could only guess at the cause, for *it* didn't see what the right hemisphere had looked at.

The split-brain studies give further proof that language is largely the province of the left hemisphere. But this doesn't mean that the right hemisphere has no language capacity at all. When a patient is asked to name a picture that is flashed to the left side (that is, to the right hemisphere), he sometimes makes a haphazard guess. But immediately afterwards, he often frowns or shakes his head. The right hemisphere evidently has some—limited—ability to understand what it hears. It sees the pictured object, and while it cannot produce the correct name—say, "ashtray"—it knows enough to understand that the name it just came up with—say, "coffeepot"—couldn't possibly be right (Gazzaniga, 1967).

Further documentation of right-hemisphere language abilities comes from studies showing that split-brain patients can understand short written words flashed to the right hemisphere and can tell whether a small string of letters, such as *house* and *pouse*, is or is not an English word (Zaidel, 1976, 1983; for some alternative interpretations, see Gazzaniga, 1983; Levy, 1983).

LATERALIZATION IN NORMAL SUBJECTS

All the evidence for lateralization we've discussed thus far has come from patients with neurological deficits: some with lesions in one or another hemisphere, others with a severed corpus callosum. Can lateralization be demonstrated in normal populations? A considerable amount of recent research has shown that it can.

SELECTIVE STIMULATION OF THE TWO HEMISPHERES

One approach uses the same experimental procedure that was so successfully employed with the split-brain patients. Various stimuli are briefly presented to either the right or the left visual field of normal subjects. Some of the stimuli are items that are presumably better dealt with by the left hemisphere: words or letters. Others are items that call on the special capacities of the right hemisphere: faces or other complex forms. The subject's task is to recognize the items and indicate his response as quickly and as accurately as he can.

In studies of this sort, the experimenters' primary interest is in the subject's **reaction time,** that is, how long it takes him to respond. The logic of the experiment is simple. Suppose the stimulus is presented to the hemisphere that is most appropriate to it: words to the left, faces to the right. If so, this hemisphere can get to work immediately, decipher the stimulus, and come up with an answer. But suppose the stimulus is sent to the wrong cerebral address: words to the right and faces to the left. This calls for an extra step, for now the visual message must be forwarded to the other hemisphere by way of the corpus callosum. But this additional transmission step takes a certain amount of time. As a result, we would expect subjects to be faster in recognizing words presented to the left hemisphere than to the right hemisphere. By the same token, we would expect them to respond more quickly to faces shown to the right hemisphere rather than to the left. By now, a fair number of experiments have shown that this is essentially what happens (e.g., Geffen, Bradshaw, and Wallace, 1971; Moscovitch, 1972, 1979).

TWO MODES OF MENTAL FUNCTIONING

The preceding discussion indicates that language and spatial organization are usually handled in two different areas of the brain. Some psychologists believe that this difference in localization goes along with a distinction between two fundamentally different modes of thought: one that involves words, the other spatial processes. This distinction is certainly in line with everyday observation. We often think in words—about scientific problems, about politics, about who likes whom; the list is endless. But we also mentally manipulate the world with little benefit of language—as when we visualize our living room with rearranged furniture or when we work a jigsaw puzzle. Many problems can be solved by either mode. We may find our way to a friend's home by referring to a mental map or by memorizing a verbal sequence, such as "first right turn after the third traffic light." But the two modes are not always intersubstitutable. How a corkscrew works is hard to describe in words; the pros and cons of a political two-party system are impossible to get across without them.

The difference between verbal and spatial modes of thought is explicitly recognized in the construction of many tests of intelligence. Different test items are provided to assess each mode separately. Verbal aptitude may be gauged by questions that involve vocabulary ("What does *formulate* mean?") or the abstraction of underlying similarities ("In what ways are dinosaurs and horse-drawn carriages alike?"). Spatial ability may be tested by items that require the subject to construct a design by arranging a set of colored blocks or to visualize how a two-dimensional shape will appear when folded into a box (see Figure 2.39). In line with our previous discussion, performance on the various verbal tests is more impaired by lesions to the left hemisphere, while performance on spatial tests is more impaired by lesions to the right hemisphere (Levy, 1974).

Some theorists feel that there is a more fundamental difference in the functions of the two hemispheres that underlies the verbal-spatial distinction. In their view, the right hemisphere is specialized for the organization of space, whereas the left hemisphere concentrates upon organization in time. It is clear that spatial organization is critical for the perception of form or the ability to visualize three-dimensional shapes given a two-dimensional pattern. But upon reflection, temporal organization is no less critical for language. The person who is insensitive to what comes first and what comes second cannot possibly speak or understand the speech of others. *Tap* is not the same word as *pat,* and the sentence "Wellington beat Bonaparte" is crucially different from "Bonaparte beat Wellington." To summarize this view, the right hemisphere is more concerned with what goes where, the left more with what comes when (Bogen, 1969; Tzeng and Wang, 1984).

While the space versus time hypothesis is rather speculative, it is still more or less in line with the facts of hemispheric lateralization. The same is not always true of the many accounts written for the general lay audience. In the process of popularization, the facts have been progressively displaced by a rash of speculations that assert that the two hemispheres differ not just in their relative contributions to language function and spatial organization, but in many other underlying attributes as well. Thus it is sometimes claimed that the left hemisphere controls logical and sequential thought, that it analyzes, works with numbers, and deals in rationality. In contrast, the right hemisphere is said to be concerned with intuition, artistic creativity, and the comprehension of patterns that are grasped as a whole rather than being analyzed into their component parts. Some authors go as far as to relate the right-left hemispheric differences to the (alleged) difference between Western science and logic on the one hand and Eastern culture and mysticism on the other. By now, the popular myth has it that our own society overly encourages "left-brained" at the expense of "right-brained" functions and that we need special efforts to train the neglected right hemisphere (e.g., Ornstein, 1977). One author recommends "Ten Ways to Develop Your Right Brain," which include occasionally drowning out the presentation of information with music and giving a thirty-second explanation of something and asking people to guess what you're getting at (Prince, 1978, cited in Springer and Deutsch, 1981). Whether such procedures actually help to strengthen intuitive

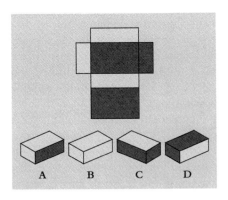

2.39   An item from a test of spatial relations   *The subject has to decide which of the figures,* A, B, C, *or* D, *can be made by folding the pattern above. (The correct answer is* D. *After Cronbach, 1970a)*

thinking or complex pattern perception is exceedingly doubtful. But in any case, there is no reason to believe that the two hemispheres correspond to the distinctions (assuming such distinctions can really be made) between rational vs. intuitive thought, or analytic vs. artistic processes, or the difference between Western and Eastern philosophies of life (Levy, 1985; Efron, 1990). As Jerre Levy, a prominent investigator of hemispheric lateralization, puts it: ". . . The popular myths are misinterpretations and wishes, not the observations of scientists. . . . Normal people have not half a brain nor two brains but one gloriously differentiated brain with each hemisphere contributing its specialized abilities. We have a single brain that generates a single mental self" (Levy, 1985, p.44).

WHAT THE BRAIN CAN TELL US ABOUT THE MIND

The study of hemispheric lateralization illustrates an important trend in recent work on brain localization. Until recently, the main focus of twentieth-century investigators who studied the effects of brain lesions was on the light such effects might throw upon the functions that various parts of the brain perform. In effect they asked what the mind—or rather, damage to the mind—can tell us about the brain. But some modern workers, including many of those concerned with hemispheric lateralization, take the reverse approach. They ask what the brain can tell us about the mind.

To adherents of this approach—often called *cognitive neuropsychologists*—a crucial source of evidence comes from the *dissociation* of symptoms, a term that is used when a patient is impaired in one function but relatively unaffected in another. The neuropsychologists' reasoning is simple: If a patient with a lesion in one region of the brain suffers damage to one mental function but is unaffected in another function, while a person with a lesion in a different region shows the reverse pattern of impairments—which is just what happens with right- versus left-hemisphere lesions and spatial versus verbal ability—then we conclude that the two underlying psychological functions are essentially different.

Another example of such a dissociation of symptoms comes from certain patients with visual agnosias. Some of these patients are unable to identify or recognize inanimate objects. When confronted with pictures of vases and glasses and asked which go with each other, they fail completely. But when shown pictures of animate objects, such as dogs and cows, they do perfectly well. Other patients suffer from the reverse deficit: They have great difficulties in recogniz-

Cerebral localization then and now
(A) According to a now completely discredited theory developed during the nineteenth century, the degree to which people possessed such characteristics as foresight, courage, and the desire to have children could be assessed by looking at the shape of their skulls. The figure shows a model of a human head, indicating the supposed functions of the brain regions below. (Courtesy of The Science Museum/ Science & Society Picture Library) (B) Modern neuropsychologists are more modest; they try to determine the function of different parts of the brain by correlating lesions in those regions with psychological losses. The figure shows a Magnetic Resonance Imaging (MRI) scan of a patient's head. (Photograph by Leonard Lessin/Peter Arnold, Inc.)

A   B

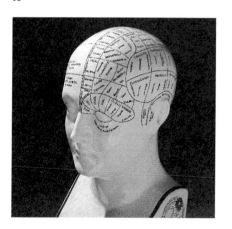

ing and identifying animate objects but little or none in dealing with inanimate ones. Findings of this sort suggest that our perception of animate and inanimate objects depends on different underlying psychological processes (McCarthy and Warrington, 1990; Shallice, 1988; but see Farah, 1990).

It's too early to say whether cognitive neuropsychology will succeed in determining which psychological processes belong together and which are independent of each other. Its adherents believe that it will, that the dissociation technique is a procedure that will carve cognition at its seams. To the extent that it will, psychology will be the richer.

RECOVERY FROM BRAIN INJURY

As we've seen, much of our knowledge of the brain comes from an analysis of the effects of various cerebral lesions. We now ask how people recover from cerebral injury and by what mechanisms they do so. It is self-evident that this topic is of great medical and general interest. But in addition, the facts about recovery have considerable scientific importance, for they throw yet further light on how the human brain works.

REPAIR FROM WITHIN

Recovery from cerebral lesions varies enormously. Consider aphasia. In some cases, there is considerable recovery; for example, a stroke patient with aphasia may regain normal fluency and comprehension after a couple of months, though a certain difficulty in finding words (sometimes called *anomia*) usually remains. When shown a picture of a key, the patient may be unable to think of its name and say, "I know what it does . . . you use it to open a door" (Kolb and Whishaw, 1990). But in other cases, the recovery is considerably less, and the prospects for improvements are not too bright; if the individual has not recovered a year or so after the brain injury, the hopes for further gains are relatively small.

How can we explain these great variations in the degree to which patients recover from brain damage?

RECOVERY OF DAMAGED BUT LIVING NEURONS

A critical factor is whether some—or even all—of the neurons in the affected area were damaged rather than being destroyed outright. If there is damage but little or no destruction, many of the symptoms may be reversible. An example of such a reversible condition is the damage produced by the pressure brought on by the swelling following a head injury, an infection, or a tumor. If these conditions are removed, for example by draining some cerebral fluid to relieve cranial pressure, the damaged neurons may recover, and the patient's symptoms will become less severe or even disappear entirely (Moscovitch and Rozin, 1989).

SPROUTING OF COLLATERALS

The outlook is much less favorable when neurons have been destroyed. For as we've seen, there is no replacement warranty for dead neurons; a neuron lost is lost forever. But even so, some possibilities of improvement remain. One possibility is the formation of new connections. The axons of some healthy neurons adjacent to the damaged cells may grow new branches, called **collateral sprouts,** that may eventually attach themselves to the synapses left vacant by the cells lost through injury (Veraa and Grafstein, 1981). Consider the effects of a certain lesion in the hypothalamus of a rat. In the first few days after the lesion, the animal just lies on its belly, unable to stand, let alone walk around, but after a few weeks there is recovery (Golani, Wolgin, and Teitelbaum, 1979). Some authors believe that some of the axons cut by this lesion gradually sprout new collateral branches that fill in for cells that were permanently destroyed. As a result, a smaller number of neurons can now do the work formerly done by many (Stricker and Zigmond, 1976).

Whether such sproutings will always be beneficial is by no means clear. Recovery will occur only if the newly grown branches attach themselves to the appropriate terminals. If the connections are made willy-nilly, the animal may end up worse off than it was before. This is analogous to what happens if a cable of telephone wires is cut. The trick is to reconnect the wires appropriately, otherwise there will be telephonic chaos. As yet, we don't know exactly when sprouting will be helpful and when it won't, though there is evidence that both kinds of results can occur (Scheff and Cotman, 1977; Wall, 1980).

SUBSTITUTION OF FUNCTION

Another factor that can produce recovery is the taking over of the function of the damaged regions by other parts of the brain. This seems to occur in certain cases of recovery from aphasia; here the right hemisphere comes to perform some of the tasks originally handled by the left. Evidence comes from patients who show nearly complete recovery of language function subsequent to left-hemisphere lesions; in most of these cases, there is an increase in the blood flow to the right hemisphere (Knopman et al., 1984, cited in Rosenzweig and Leiman, 1989).

It appears then that the brain has a certain plasticity of function. Jobs performed by one region of the brain can be taken on by other parts when injury requires it. This plasticity is generally greater in the young. At least up to age eight, children who become aphasic regain speech function, even if their impairment immediately after the brain injury was quite severe (Woods and Teuber, 1978).

Substantia nigra dopamine tissue

Fetal brain

Adult brain

2.40   Steps in the grafting procedure
Fetal brain tissue is dissected from a fetal brain, transferred to a dish with a saline solution, and then treated to separate the fetal brain cells from connective tissue, blood vessels, and other tissue. It is then transferred to a syringe and injected into the appropriate region of an adult brain (After Björklund et al., 1983)

REPAIR FROM WITHOUT

Thus far, we've talked about cases in which the nervous system manages to repair itself, at least to some extent. Is there a way in which we can help that repair along?

We've seen that the brain cannot replace dead neurons. But there are some recent animal studies which suggest that someday neurologists may be able to provide some such replacement by transplanting neural tissue from outside. Thus far, this work is still in the early experimental stages, but initial results give some grounds for hope (Fine, 1986).

Several groups of investigators have created various kinds of lesions in the brains of rats and then transplanted tissues from the brains of rat fetuses into the affected areas (see Figure 2.40). The donors were fetuses rather than adults

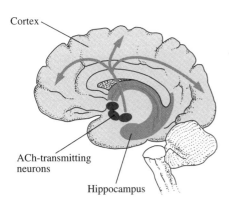

Cortex

ACh-transmitting
neurons

Hippocampus

**2.41   Acetylcholine pathways apparently
involved in Alzheimer's disease**   *Acetyl-
choline-transmitting neurons located in regions
at the base of the forebrain activate many regions of the cortex as well as the hippocampus.
The degeneration of these neurons may be a
major cause of Alzheimer's disease. (After
Coyle, Price, and Delong, 1983)*

because fetal tissue is still relatively unformed and plastic. In one group of studies, the investigators partially destroyed a pathway of dopamine-releasing fibers
in the midbrain. This pathway projects upwards to a region at the base of the
cerebral hemispheres that is intimately involved in the control of voluntary
movement. This is the same pathway whose gradual degeneration produces
Parkinson's disease in humans. The effect of the lesion on rats is essentially similar to that found in humans: a serious drop in the level of dopamine in the brains
of the affected rats concurrent with massive motor disturbances (see p. 31–32).
The implantation of tissues from the appropriate regions of the donors' brains
led to an increase in the host brains' level of dopamine and considerable
improvement in motor performance—a result that offers hope for a better therapy for Parkinson's disease than exists at present (Björklund, et al., 1983).

Another group of studies is of potential relevance to *Alzheimer's disease,*
which afflicts 5 to 10 percent of all persons over age sixty-five (Kolb and
Whishaw, 1990). This devastating disease is characterized by a progressive decline
in intellectual functioning that begins with serious memory problems, continues
with increasing disorientation, and culminates in total physical and mental helplessness. While Alzheimer's disease leads to degenerative changes throughout the
brain, the worst destruction seems to befall a pathway of acetylcholine-releasing
neurons that have their origin in a region at the base of the forebrain and extend
to many cortical association areas as well as to the hippocampus (a structure that
is important for memory). When enough of these cells are dead or dying, the
cortical and hippocampal regions to which they project are no longer activated.
As a result, there is loss of memory and cognitive functioning (see Figure 2.41;
Coyle, Price, and DeLong, 1983).★

Can degenerative changes of this sort be reversed by brain transplants? They
can in rats, at least to some extent. Some investigators worked on rats that had
been subjected to lesions in acetylcholine-releasing pathways analogous to those
destroyed in Alzeheimer patients. Others used animals of a fairly advanced age
(in rats, this is about two years of age). Both the lesioned and the aged rats
showed substantial impairments on various tests of memory and spatial learning.
Initially they couldn't learn certain simple mazes or retain what they had learned
from one occasion to the next. But after appropriate brain transplants, there was
significant improvement (Björklund and Stenevi, 1984; Gage and Björklund,
1986).

Just how do these brain grafts lead to recovery? There are probably several
answers. In part, the transplanted tissue may provide new cells for the host brain;
in part, the graft may stimulate some of the host's intact neurons to release more
transmitter substances; finally, the grafted tissue may encourage axon sprouting
(Freed, de Medicacelli, and Wyatt, 1985).

What are the chances that these or similar techniques can be applied to
human patients? As of yet, we can't say. There are obvious technological hurdles.
But it's worth noting that if and when the transplantation techniques are ready
for clinical application, there will be some serious ethical problems as well,
because the most probable donors would be aborted human fetuses. The many
ethical (as well as political) issues that surround this subject are highlighted by a
1988 federal decision that denied all federal money for research using fetal tissue
obtained from abortions (Lewin, 1988). One of the very first acts of the Clinton
administration in 1993 was the lifting of this ban.

★ Students interested in neuroanatomical details may want to know that the dopamine pathway
involved in Parkinson's disease extends from the substantia nigra to the caudate nucleus, while the
acetylcholine pathway involved in Alzheimer's disease originates in the nucleus basalis of Meynert.

REHABILITATION

Recovery through processes of self-repair can only go so far, especially in adults, and transplantation therapy is as yet only a hope for the future. Can anything be done for the patient to help the recovery process along? The patient can sometimes be taught—very slowly and very patiently—to use impaired functions and to develop compensatory skills to make up for those lost or damaged. An example is making a patient sit on her good arm, thus forcing her to use the one that is semi-paralyzed. Days and weeks of practice will bring slow gains, but these gains often add up and help the patient develop self-sufficiency. How much this rehabilitation can accomplish depends on the injury and on the patient's capacity and will to continue the training process (see Figure 2.42). Sometimes sheer persistence (and no doubt some good fortune in the site and extent of the lesion) leads to remarkable results.

To sum up, while we know much more about the brain than we did only a decade or two ago, medical technology is as yet unable to do much to aid the recovery of the injured brain. But it looks as if we're on the threshold of a new era of progress in this crucial area. Considering that the population of the industrial world is aging at an unprecedented rate, with a concomitant increase in the proportion of persons with degenerative brain disorders, that era can come none too soon.

2.42 Rehabilitation *Sometimes sheer persistence (and no doubt some good fortune in the site and extent of the lesion) leads to remarkable results. An example is the case of Patricia Neal, an Academy Award–winning actress who had a stroke at the age of 39. The stroke paralyzed one leg and left her unable to speak, read, or write. But an intensive rehabilitation program enabled her to recover sufficiently so that four years later she could star in other films. (Neal, 1974; courtesy of Rex USA)*

SOME FINAL COMMENTS

Most of this chapter was about the neurological underpinnings of behavior. We have obviously come a long, long way since Descartes. Today we know a great deal about the biological foundation on which all human striving rests: the hundred billion neurons whose collective firings make up our human mind. Without these aggregates of neurons, there would be no *Hamlet,* no Sistine Chapel, no 9th Symphony, and of course no Auschwitz and no Cambodian massacres either.

The nervous system and its operation underlie whatever we do and think and feel. But does this mean that all psychological questions are at bottom neurological ones? Does it mean that all our ultimate answers will be in terms of action potential and neurotransmitters?

The proper reply is no. The answer to any question always depends on the level at which the question is phrased. Some questions are indeed most properly answered at the level of physiology (e.g., "What causes color blindness?"). But many others are properly stated at quite a different level. Suppose a historian asks why Napoleon didn't invade England. To answer with a paragraph—or book—about Napoleon's neurons and synaptic connections would be absurd. An appropriate answer might be that the weather was untoward, or that he didn't think he had enough ships, or that he didn't trust his admirals, or whatever. Any of these answers might be false, but they are at the right level. A statement about neuronal firing in Napoleon's frontal cortex would be completely off the mark and not only because we simply don't as yet know enough about the nervous system: Even if we could chart each firing, this answer is not going to satisfy the historian.

What holds for historians asking questions about a particular event holds for psychologists asking about the human (and even animal) mind. When they ask about how humans and animals act, perceive, think, remember, and feel, they typically want answers at the psychological level. Of course they're aware that all our actions take place within a framework set by our nervous system. But even so, they believe that psychological explanations are usually cast at a different (so to speak, higher) level than neurological explanations. Just how such psychological explanations are formulated will be the topic of many subsequent chapters.

One of the oldest of old and tired riddles is "Why does the chicken cross the road?" The answer—"Because it wants to get to the other side"—is exceedingly silly, but it is surely much less silly than the answer "Because its cerebral neurons fired that way."

SUMMARY

1. Since Descartes, many scientists have tried to explain human and animal movement within the framework of the *reflex* concept: A stimulus excites a sense organ, which transmits excitation upward to the spinal cord or brain, which in turn relays the excitation downward to a muscle or gland and thus produces action. Descartes' general classification of nervous function is still with us as we distinguish between *reception, integration,* and *reaction.*

2. Later investigators showed that the smallest unit of the nervous system is the *neuron,* whose primary anatomical subdivisions are the *dendrites, cell body,* and *axon.*

3. The main function of a neuron is to produce a *nerve impulse,* an electrochemical disturbance that is propagated along the membrane of the axon when the cell's normal *resting potential* is disrupted by a stimulus whose intensity exceeds the *threshold.* This stimulus produces a brief depolarization of the cell, which leads to an *action potential.* The action potential obeys the *all-or-none law:* Once threshold is reached, further increases of stimulus intensity have no effect on its magnitude. But the nervous system can nevertheless distinguish between different intensities of stimuli all of which are above threshold. One means for doing this is *frequency:* The more intense the stimulus, the more often the neuron fires.

4. To understand how neurons communicate, investigators have studied *reflex action,* which is necessarily based on the activity of several neurons. Results of studies with *spinal animals* led Sherrington to infer the processes that underlie conduction across the *synapse,* the gap between the axon of one neuron and the dendrites and cell body of the next. Conduction within neurons was shown to obey different laws than conduction between neurons (that is, across the synapse). Evidence included the phenomena of *spatial* and *temporal summation.* Sherrington concluded that the excitation from several neurons funnels into a common reservoir to produce a *central excitatory state.*

5. Further studies argued for a process of inhibition. Evidence came from *reciprocal inhibition* found in antagonistic muscles. Further work showed that a reflex can be activated either by increasing excitation or by decreasing inhibition.

6. Sherrington's inferences of synaptic functions have been confirmed by modern electrical and chemical studies. Today we know that transmission across the synapse is accomplished by *neurotransmitters,* chemical substances that are liberated at the axon terminals of one neuron and exert excitatory or inhibitory effects on the dendrites and cell body of another. These transmitters cross the *synaptic gap* and affect *receptor molecules* located on the *postsynaptic membrane.* This creates *graded potentials* that summate and spread. When they reach threshold value, they produce an action potential in the axon of the second neuron.

7. Important examples of neurotransmitters include *acetylcholine, norepinephrine,* and *dopamine.* The effect of transmitters is enhanced by *agonists* and reduced or blocked by *antagonists.*

8. In addition to the nervous system, there is another group of organs whose function is to serve as an instrument of communication within the body. This is the *endocrine system,* whose glands secrete their *hormones* directly into the bloodstream, which will eventually carry them to various target organs.

9. A crude anatomical outline of the vertebrate nervous system starts out with the distinction between the *peripheral (somatic* and *autonomic)* and *central nervous systems.* The central nervous system consists of the *spinal cord* and the *brain.* Important parts of the brain are the *hindbrain* (including *medulla* and *cerebellum), midbrain,* and *forebrain* (including the *thalamus, hypothalamus, cerebral hemispheres,* and *cerebral cortex).* Of special interest is a group of subcortical structures of the forebrain called the *limbic system.*

10. In general, the brain tends to function hierarchically, with higher centers commanding lower centers. Hierarchical control at the bottom levels is seen in *central pattern generators* or *CPGs.* Another demonstration of the hierarchical principal is the phenomenon of *disinhibition* produced by the destruction of higher centers that inhibit a reflex.

11. Hierarchical control in the central nervous system of mammals is shown by studies of animals with transections at various points in the brain. Animals whose brain is cut so that only the hindbrain remains, can still move but don't integrate their movements. Animals that have hindbrain and midbrain but that lack the forebrain show integrated movements but without any goal. Animals that only lack the cortex integrate movements and goals but pursue their goals ineptly.

12. The *cerebral cortex* is generally believed to underlie the most complex aspects of behavior. The *projection areas* of the cortex act as receiving stations for sensory information or as dispatching centers for motor commands. The sensory projection areas for vision, hearing, and the bodily senses are respectively located in the *occipital, temporal,* and *parietal* lobes; the motor projection area is in the *frontal* lobe. The remaining regions of the cortex are called *association areas.* Their function concerns such higher mental processes as planning, remembering, thinking, and speaking.

13. A number of modern neurological tools, including the *CAT scan,* the *PET scan,* and the *MRI* make it possible to diagnose and study lesions in the brains of living patients. Certain lesions of association areas lead to *apraxia,* a serious disturbance in the organization of voluntary action. Other lesions produce *agnosia,* a disorganization of perception and recognition. Still other cause *asphasia,* a profound disruption of language function, which may involve speech production, speech comprehension, or both. A lesion in *Broca's area* leads to *expressive aphasia;* one in *Wernicke's area* leads to *receptive aphasia.*

14. The hierarchical organization of the nervous system does not have the neatness of a corporate organizational chart. This is because evolution generally builds on what is there to begin with rather than starting from scratch. An example is the fact that we have two *motor systems,* the older *extrapyramidal system* headed by the *basal ganglia* and the more recent *pyramidal system* headed by the motor cortex.

15. In many ways, the two hemispheres are mirror images of each other. But to some extent, their function is not symmetrical. In most right-handers, the left hemisphere handles the bulk of the language functions, while the right hemisphere is more relevant to spatial comprehension. One source of evidence for this difference in hemispheric function, or *lateralization,* comes from the study of *split-brain* patients in whom the main connection between the two hemispheres, the *corpus callosum,* has been surgically cut. Further evidence is provided by the reaction times of normal persons when stimuli calling on verbal or spatial abilities are presented to either hemisphere.

16. Until recently, most neuroscientists asked what damage to the mental functions can tell us about the brain. More recently, investigators concerned with *cognitive neuropsychology* have taken the opposite approach and asked what damage to the brain can tell us about the mental functions. A major tool in this endeavor is the study of the *dissociation* of symptoms.

SUMMARY

17. Recovery from cerebral lesions varies considerably from one patient to another. Some recovery is produced by *collateral sprouting,* whereby healthy neurons adjacent to the region of injury will grow new branches. In addition, some functions of the damaged regions are sometimes taken over by other, undamaged, parts of the brain. Recent work on the transplanting of neural tissue offers some hope that neurobiologists may ultimately be able to provide some replacement for damaged tissue.

CHAPTER **3**

MOTIVATION

MOTIVATION AS DIRECTION 61

CONTROL SYSTEMS ▪ SELF-REGULATION ▪ HOMEOSTASIS

TEMPERATURE REGULATION 64

TEMPERATURE CONTROL FROM WITHIN ▪ TEMPERATURE CONTROL BY BEHAVIOR ▪ THE AUTONOMIC NERVOUS SYSTEM AND TEMPERATURE CONTROL ▪ SENSING THE INTERNAL ENVIRONMENT: THE HYPOTHALAMUS

THIRST 67

VOLUME RECEPTORS ▪ OSMORECEPTORS

HUNGER 69

THE SIGNALS FOR FEEDING ▪ HYPOTHALAMIC CONTROL CENTERS ▪ FOOD SELECTION ▪ OBESITY ▪ ANOREXIA AND BULIMIA

FEAR AND RAGE 81

THREAT AND THE AUTONOMIC NERVOUS SYSTEM ▪ CENTRAL CONTROLS ▪ DISRUPTIVE EFFECTS OF AUTONOMIC AROUSAL ▪ PAIN AND THE ENDORPHIN SYSTEM

SLEEP AND WAKING 88

WAKING ▪ SLEEP AND BRAIN ACTIVITY ▪ THE STAGES OF SLEEP ▪ THE FUNCTIONS OF SLEEP ▪ DREAMS

WHAT DIFFERENT MOTIVES HAVE IN COMMON 95

THE PSYCHOLOGY OF REWARD AND THE AROUSAL LEVEL ▪ THE BIOLOGY OF REWARD

THE NATURE OF MOTIVES 101

SUMMARY 102

I n this chapter, we will examine some of the simple motives that human beings share with other animals. These motives steer our behavior in certain directions rather than others, toward food, say, rather than toward shelter.

Our main concern will be with motives that are essentially unlearned and that pertain primarily to the individual alone rather than to his interaction with others. Some of these motives can be understood as attempts at *self-regulation.* They include temperature maintenance, thirst, and hunger, which grow out of the organism's efforts to safeguard certain bodily necessities: a temperature that stays within certain limits, its water supply, its nutrient levels. Others are motives that are attempts at *self-preservation* in response to threat, such as the energetic exertions that accompany the emotions of fear and rage. Yet another motive is the need for sleep, which is sometimes thought to grow out of efforts at *self-restoration.*

These various motives are obviously very different, but they nevertheless have an underlying similarity, for they all direct behavior by making some acts more probable than others: When hungry, we generally seek food and eat it rather than engaging in other activities. The same holds for perception: When hungry, food and food-related stimuli in the environment are more likely to be looked for and noticed than are others. Similarly for feeling: When hungry, food is much more pleasant than when we are sated. This tendency to make some behaviors, perceptions, and feelings more probable than others is sometimes called *potentiation* (that is, increasing a potential). This chapter is an attempt to show how modern physiological psychologists try to account for these phenomena.

MOTIVATION AS DIRECTION

Most human and animal actions are directed. We don't simply walk, reach, shrink, or flee; we walk and reach *toward* some objects, shrink and flee *away* from others. The objects that are approached or withdrawn from may be in the organism's here and now, as when a kitten jumps toward a rolling ball. But often enough, the object exists in an as yet unrealized future. The hawk circles in the sky in search of prey, but there is none in sight as yet. In such a case, an inner motive (a purpose, a desire) apparently leads to actions that bring the hawk closer to its food.

Directed action seems difficult to reconcile with Descartes' notion of humans and animals as reflex machines, however complex their internal wiring. This problem is most pronounced for actions that are directed toward some future goal, for it is hard to see how an automaton can be imbued with purpose or desire. But difficulties arise even in the simplest case in which the direction is toward (or away from) an immediately present object. Consider the kitten reaching for the ball. What matters is not whether this flexor muscle is contracted or that extensor muscle relaxed, but rather whether the overall pattern of muscular activity gets the creature closer to the final end state—near the ball. The kitten may swipe at the ball with its right paw or its left, may crouch more on one side than on the other—all that matters is that, whatever the specific motor response, it will be directed toward the ball. Descartes' statues walked out and bowed when a visitor stepped on a hidden spring, but did they bow *to* the visitor? Suppose the visitor were to push the spring and then jump quickly to the left. The statue would surely lumber through its prescribed routine exactly as before, in stony disregard of the altered circumstance.

It is evident that a simple automaton is incapable of directed action. Can the machine be modified to overcome this lack? The answer is yes.

CONTROL SYSTEMS

Modern engineers have developed an immense technology based on machines that control their own activities and are in that sense directed. The basic principle upon which these devices are built is the notion of a **feedback system.** When such a machine is in operation, it performs some kind of action that may be mechanical, electrical, thermal, or whatever but that in all cases engenders some changes in the external environment. If these changes in turn influence the further operation of the machine—if they feed back upon the machine—we have a control system based on **feedback.**

In **positive feedback systems,** the feedback strengthens the very response that produced it. The result is an ever-increasing level of activity. An example is what happens when a microphone is held too close to its amplifier. The microphone picks up whatever static is generated by the amplifier. It then feeds this static back to the amplifier, which makes the noise yet louder (that is, amplifies it). This louder noise is then picked up by the microphone and fed back to the

Motivation as directed action *This painting was commissioned by a man dramatically rescued from a shark attack in Havana harbor. As here depicted, every member of the small boat's crew directs his efforts towards the swimmer's rescue. (*Watson and the Shark *by John Singleton Copley, 1778; gift of Mrs. George von Lengerke Meyer; courtesy of the Museum of Fine Arts, Boston)*

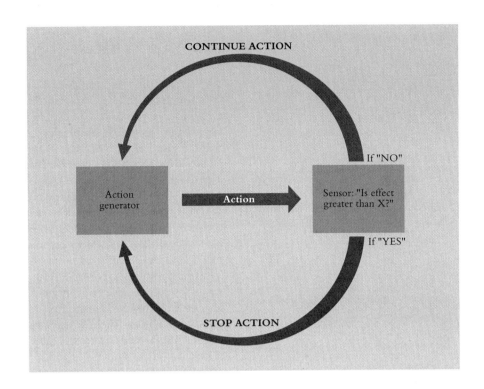

3.1 Negative feedback *In negative feedback systems, the feedback stops or reverses the action that produces it. A sensing device indicates the level of a certain stimulus. If that level exceeds a certain setpoint, the action stops. The effect is self-regulation.*

amplifier, which makes it even louder, and so on, until it produces an unbearably loud wail that is the bane of poorly designed public-address systems.

Of greater relevance to our present concern is **negative feedback** in which the feedback stops, or even reverses, the original response of the machine that produced the environmental change. Negative feedback underlies a large number of industrial devices called **servomechanisms** that can maintain themselves in a particular state (Figure 3.1). A simple example is the system that controls most home furnaces. A thermostat turns on a switch that controls the furnace for all temperatures below a given setting and turns it off for all that are above it. In the winter, the result is a steady house temperature, for the furnace will burn fuel only if the temperature is below the critical level; once this is reached, the furnace shuts off, deactivated by its own negative feedback. In a sense, the thermostatically controlled furnace has a goal: It "aims" at a particular temperature.

Negative feedback systems exist at all levels of the nervous system and are responsible, at least in part, for directed action. In this chapter we will see how such systems underlie motivated actions of many kinds. Some concern the organism's regulation of various vital functions—temperature maintenance, food and water intake, and the like. Others involve the organism's reaction to threats from outside, whether fearful escape or raging attack.

SELF-REGULATION

Can we apply the principles of negative feedback to the understanding of motivated action in which the direction is imposed from within? We will begin by considering those motives that grow directly out of the organism's regulation of its own internal state, such as its temperature, its water level, and its supply of nutrients.

HOMEOSTASIS

Descartes had emphasized the external environment—the stimuli that impinge on the organism from without and trigger its reactions. Some two hundred years after Descartes, another Frenchman, the physiologist Claude Bernard (1813–1878), emphasized the fact that the organism exists in an internal environment as well as an external one—the organism's own bodily fluids, its blood and its lymph. Bernard pointed out that this internal environment is kept remarkably constant despite considerable fluctuations of the environment outside. This striking constancy is shown by the salt and water balance of the body, its oxygen concentration, its pH (a measure of acidity), its concentration of various nutrient substances such as glucose, and its temperature (in warm-blooded animals). In healthy organisms, all of these fluctuate within very narrow limits, and these limits define the organism's conditions for health and survival. Thus 60 to 90 milligrams per 100 cubic centimeters of blood is the acceptable range for the glucose concentration in the bloodstream of a healthy person. A drop below this level means coma and eventual death; a prolonged rise above it indicates disorders such as diabetes. The modern term for this stable internal equilibrium is *homeostasis* (literally, "equal state") and the mechanisms whereby it is achieved are sometimes said to reflect the "wisdom of the body" (Cannon, 1932).

TEMPERATURE REGULATION

A relatively simple example of homeostatic balance is temperature regulation in birds and mammals. These animals are called warm-blooded because they have a large repertoire of homeostatic adjustments that keep their internal body temperatures at a fairly constant level, despite wide temperature variations in the surrounding environment.

TEMPERATURE CONTROL FROM WITHIN

If the internal temperature of a warm-blooded animal is too high, various reflexive reactions produce heat loss. One is peripheral *vasodilatation,* a widening of the skin's capillaries. This sends warm blood to the body's surface and results in heat loss by radiation. Other reactions that lead to cooling are sweating (in humans) and panting (in dogs), both of which produce heat loss by evaporation.

An opposed pattern is called into play when the internal temperature is too low. Now there is no sweating or panting, and instead of peripheral vasodilatation there is *vasoconstriction.* The capillary diameters narrow, so that the blood is squeezed away from the cold periphery and heat is conserved. Other reflexive reactions include a ruffling of the fur to create a thick envelope of protective air. (The goose-flesh feeling is our feeble remnant of this reflex response, of little use to us now in our naked condition.)

All of these reflexive reactions—as indeed all homeostatic adjustments—are essentially *compensatory.* They compensate for the swings of body temperature by

Vasodilatation
Sweating
Panting, etc.

Parasympathetic

Upper
set-point

Lower
set-point

Sympathetic

Vasoconstriction
Shivering
Fur-ruffling, etc.

3.2 Reflexive temperature regulation in mammals *When the temperature deviates from an internal setpoint, various reflexive reactions will occur to restore the temperature to this setpoint.*

External temperature control and mother love in rats *After rat pups are born, they huddle under the mother's belly for warmth. Why does the mother allow this? It's not just maternal affection. The hormones circulating through the mother after she gives birth overheat her, so she is quite content to have the cool bodies of her offspring against her own. (Photograph by Jane Burton; © 1987, Bruce Coleman, Inc.)*

pushing the system in the opposite direction. In this regard, they are completely analogous to the thermostatic controls of a furnace or an air conditioner. If a warm-blooded animal is too hot, vasodilatation, panting, and the like lead to heat loss; if it is too cold, vasoconstriction, ruffling of the fur, and so on compensate by producing heat conservation. Similarly for the negative feedback systems that control the temperature of a building: When the house gets too cold, the furnace is switched on; when it gets too hot, the air conditioner goes on.

These self-regulatory, reflexive, compensatory reactions are called into play when the temperature deviates too far from some internal temperature setpoint (again analogous to mechanical heating and cooling devices; see Figure 3.2). But in some animals this setpoint can be changed. For example, a certain ground squirrel spends the winter in hibernation. When the outside temperature falls, and his internal setpoint drops, he finds a secluded burrow and settles into his winter torpor—a useful mechanism in times when food is very scarce. But while his new setpoint is low, it still functions. When the weather gets cold enough, he wakes up to keep from freezing to death (Heller, Cranshaw, and Hammel, 1978).

TEMPERATURE CONTROL BY BEHAVIOR

The homeostatic mechanisms we have just described are essentially involuntary. They may be actions, but we don't feel that they are *our* actions; in fact, some of them concern only a fraction of the body's subsystems. For example, vasodilatation and vasoconstriction do not involve the skeletal musculature at all. But there is no question that when the need arises, these reflexive compensatory mechanisms are supplemented by voluntary actions that involve the organism as a whole. If a rat is placed in a cold cage, it will search for suitable materials and build a nest. That humans perform similar voluntary acts in the service of temperature regulation goes without saying: They wear coats when they are cold and wear as little as custom permits (or turn on an air conditioner) when they are hot. The important point is that these voluntary actions are still in the service of that same internal environment whose constancy is so crucial to survival. But there is one important difference: Now the organism actively changes its external environment so that its internal environment can stay the same.

THE AUTONOMIC NERVOUS SYSTEM AND TEMPERATURE CONTROL

To understand how the nervous system marshals its forces to protect us against extreme heat and cold we'll begin by looking at the involuntary side of temperature regulation. What controls the various reactions of the internal organs that accomplish this? The most direct control is exerted by the autonomic nervous system (ANS), which sends commands to the **glands** and to the **smooth muscles**★ of the viscera (internal organs) and blood vessels.

The ANS has two divisions: the **sympathetic** and the **parasympathetic.** These two divisions often act as antagonists. Thus, the excitation of the sympathetic division leads to an acceleration of heart rate and inhibition of peristalsis (rhythmic contractions) of the intestines. Parasympathetic activation has effects that are the very opposite; cardiac deceleration and stimulation of peristalsis. This same antagonism is seen in temperature regulation. The sympathetic division acts to counteract cold; it triggers vasoconstriction, shivering, and fur-ruffling. In contrast, the parasympathetic helps to cool the body when it is overheated; it stimulates panting, sweating, and vasodilatation (see Figure 3.14, p. 82). We'll have more to say about the tug-of-war between the two autonomic divisions when we discuss fear and rage. For now, we merely note that the autonomic nervous system is an important agent in directing the control of the internal environment.

SENSING THE INTERNAL ENVIRONMENT: THE HYPOTHALAMUS

The sympathetic and parasympathetic divisions control the various compensatory levers that help to maintain the internal environment. But what governs *them?* A crucial center is the hypothalamus (see Figure 3.3), which represents a veritable triumph of anatomical miniaturization. In a full-grown person, it is only about the size of a pea, but it contains the controls for many of the biological motives.

Several regions within the hypothalamus control the two divisions of the autonomic nervous system whose excitation leads to cooling and heating effects. But how does the hypothalamus decide which of the two divisions should act and by how much? Under normal conditions, temperature regulation is nearly perfect. This means that the hypothalamus can somehow sense the body's temperature, can sense deviations from the normal level, and can then determine in which direction it should throw the autonomic two-way switch (for example, choosing vasoconstriction over vasodilatation) to restore the thermal balance. But how does it do this?

The answer is that the hypothalamus contains its own thermometer: receptor cells that respond to the temperature of the bodily fluids in which the brain is bathed. When a cat's anterior hypothalamus is heated by a warm wire, there is panting and vasodilatation despite the fact that the cat's body temperature may be well below normal (Magoun et al., 1938). This suggests that the thermoreceptors are hooked up to the reflex controls so as to yield negative feedback—a hypothalamic thermostat. The heating wire fools the hypothalamus by changing

Hypothalamus

3.3 ***The hypothalamus*** *Cross-section of the human brain with the hypothalamus indicated in blue (After Keeton, 1980)*

★The individual fibers of these muscles look smooth when observed under a microscope, in contrast to the fibers of the skeletal muscles, which look striped.

its temperature independently of the temperature of the skin and body; the overheated hypothalamus then causes sweating, regardless of the actual body temperature. The effect is analogous to what would happen if a blow dryer were directed at a home thermostat. The furnace would shut itself off, even though the house were actually freezing.

Vasoconstriction and vasodilatation are involuntary compensatory reactions, more in the domain of physiology than that of behavior. Does the hypothalamic feedback device have similar effects upon actions that reach out into the external world (for instance, wearing a fur coat)? Indeed it does. As one example, consider a study that utilized the fact that rats in a cold chamber will press a bar for a brief burst of heat (Weiss and Laties, 1961; see Figure 3.4). The question was whether rats that had learned this skill in a cold environment would bar-press for heat if one cooled their brains rather than their bodies. The test was to run cold liquid through a very thin U-shaped tube implanted in the neighborhood of the anterior hypothalamus (Satinoff, 1964). The rats turned on the heat lamp when their brains were cooled even though the outside temperature was reasonably neutral.

Tricking the hypothalamus (and certain regions just adjacent to it) can evidently affect integrated behavior patterns just as it does autonomic reactions like vasodilatation. The hypothalamus defines an internal need for the rest of the nervous system, and this need then becomes an important criterion that determines whether a given act is appropriate and, if so, potentiates it.

It is worth noting that the region that controls involuntary temperature regulation is not identical to the one that controls voluntary warming and cooling behaviors. When that region was destroyed (an area just in front of the hypothalamus) the animals stopped pressing levers to turn heat lamps on or off, but there was no effect on involuntary reactions such as shivering and vasoconstriction. The result was reversed when another region was destroyed (this time an area at the side of the hypothalamus); now the autonomic reactions were abolished but the voluntary behaviors remained (Satinoff and Rutstein, 1970; Satinoff and Shan, 1971; Van Zoeren and Stricker, 1977). It thus appears that there are separate circuits to handle two different ways of solving the same homeostatic problem; here, as in many other areas, evolution has provided multiple safeguards to protect the organism's vital functions (Satinoff, 1978).

3.4 Performing a learned response to keep warm *A rat kept in a cold environment will learn to press a lever that turns on a heat lamp for a few seconds after each lever press. (Weiss and Laties, 1961)*

THIRST

What holds for temperature holds for most other homeostatic regulations as well. Consider the body's water supply. We continually lose water—primarily through the kidneys, but also through the respiratory system, the sweat glands, the digestive tract, and, occasionally, by hemorrhage.

How does the system act to offset these losses? One set of reactions is entirely internal. Thus, a loss of water volume leads to a secretion of the **antidiuretic hormone (ADH)** by the pituitary gland. ADH instructs the kidneys to reabsorb more of the water that passes through them. As a result, less water is passed out of the body in the urine. (Conversely, alcohol inhibits ADH, a fact that may explain why rest rooms are so heavily used at bars.)

But as with temperature regulation, internal compensatory readjustments can only restore the bodily balance up to a point. ADH can help protect the body against further water loss, but it cannot bring back what was lost already. Eventually, the corrective measures must involve some behavior by which the organism reaches out into the external world so as to readjust its internal environment. This behavior is drinking—in humans, an average of two to three quarts of water per day.

VOLUME RECEPTORS

How does the body know about its own condition? How does it know that what it needs is water? There are a number of receptors that provide this information. Some are located in the brain and monitor the total volume of blood and other bodily fluids outside of the cells. According to some investigators, the receptors perform this task by responding to a substance called **angiotensin,** which is produced by the kidneys when there is a decrease in the total amount of liquid that passes through them (Epstein, Fitzsimons, and Rolls, 1970). Other volume receptors are located inside the heart and its surrounding veins, and they are excited by drops in blood pressure that occur when there is a decrease in the total amount of body fluid. Their effect was shown by studies on dogs in which a small balloon was inserted into the large vein that leads to the heart. When this balloon was inflated, the dogs drank copiously. The balloon impeded the blood flow into the heart and caused a decrease in fluid pressure. This set off the pressure receptors that sent the brain the signals that led to drinking (Fitzsimons and Moore-Gillow, 1980; Rolls and Rolls, 1982).

OSMORECEPTORS

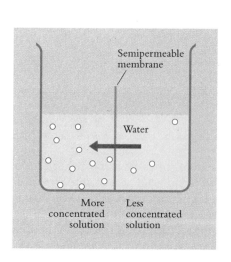

3.5 Dehydration by osmosis *If two solutions are separated by a membrane that allows the free flow of water but impedes the flow of substances that are dissolved in the water, water flows from the less concentrated region into the more concentrated one.*

Still another group of receptors keep track of the water *within* the body's cells. This depends on the concentration of certain minerals (especially sodium) that are dissolved in the fluid outside the cell. Suppose the sodium content of the outside fluid is markedly increased (for example, by drinking salt water). While water can pass freely through the cell membrane, many dissolved minerals cannot. The water will flow in the direction that keeps the total concentration of dissolved materials equal on both sides of the membrane. As a result, any increase in the sodium content of the outside fluid dehydrates the cells as water is drawn out of them—a process called *osmosis* (see Figure 3.5). This is why drinking salt water makes us *more* rather than less thirsty.

A number of studies have shown that the hypothalamus contains receptor cells (called **osmoreceptors**) that are sensitive to these osmotic processes and

Osmotic dehydration *Although surrounded by water, sailors in a lifeboat are nevertheless dying of thirst, for drinking the sea-
water would only lead to further dehydration.
(Scene from* Mutiny on the Bounty, *1935;
courtesy Photofest)*

respond to the concentration of their surrounding fluid solutions. Proof comes
from studies in which tiny drops of salt water are injected into certain regions in
or around the hypothalamus of a rat. The injection immediately leads to drinking. This is because the injection changes the concentration of the fluid that surrounds the receptor cell. It will now contain more dissolved materials (here,
sodium) than the cell itself. As a result, water leaks out by osmosis, the receptor
fires, and the animal begins to drink (Blass and Epstein, 1971; Rolls and Rolls,
1982).

It appears that there are at least three separate receptor systems that monitor
the body's water levels; future research may find even more. Why so many?
Here, as in the case of temperature regulation, we find that evolution has provided us with multiple defenses. There is a redundancy of mechanisms, so that if
one fails another can take its place. We will find even greater redundancy when
we turn to a more complex system of self-regulation: maintaining the body's
nutrient levels by feeding.

HUNGER

All animals have to eat, and much of their lives revolve around food—searching
for it, hunting it, ingesting it, and doing their best not to *be* it for others. There
is no doubt that feeding is ultimately in the service of homeostasis, for no matter what food an animal eats or how he gets it, the ultimate biological consequence is always the same—to maintain appropriate nutrient supplies in the
internal environment. But what are the actual mechanisms that determine
whether humans and animals eat or stop eating? To put it another way, what
makes us hungry and what satiated?

THE SIGNALS FOR FEEDING

There are numerous signals that control food intake. Among the most
important of these are stimuli that arise from within the animal's own
body and somehow inform the brain of the current state of the nutrient sup-

plies. That some such messages are sent is certain. Without them, neither humans nor animals would be able to control their food intake, and they generally do. If food is freely available, they usually eat just about the right amount to keep a roughly constant weight as adults. What is regulated is caloric intake rather than the total volume of food that is eaten. This was demonstrated in a study in which the experimenter varied the caloric level of the diet fed to rats by adulterating their food with nonnutritive cellulose. The more diluted the food, the more of it was eaten, in a quantity roughly adequate to keep the total caloric content constant (Adolph, 1947).

RECEPTORS IN THE BRAIN

How does the animal manage to adjust its food intake to its caloric needs? From the start, investigators focused on *glucose* (or blood sugar), which is the major source of energy for bodily tissues. The first hypothesis that comes to mind is that the critical signal is the glucose concentration in the bloodstream. But this is clearly wrong, for while persons with diabetes have abnormally high levels of blood glucose, they tend to be hungry much of the time. A plausible alternative is that what matters is not the amount of glucose as such, but the amount of glucose that is available for metabolic use (Mayer, 1955). Many authors believe that the receptors that detect changes in the way this metabolic fuel is utilized are in the brain itself, most likely in the hypothalamus. Evidence for such *glucose receptors* and their location comes from studies in which the hypothalamus was injected with a chemical that made its cells unable to respond to glucose. The result was ravenous eating. This treatment presumably silenced the glucoreceptors whose failure to fire was then interpreted as a fuel deficiency, which led to feeding (Miselis and Epstein, 1970).

RECEPTORS IN THE STOMACH AND INTESTINES

Why does an animal stop eating? The receptors in the brain can't be the only reason. For they respond to fuel deficiency in the bloodstream, and this deficiency will not be corrected until after the meal has been at least partially digested. Yet humans and animals will terminate a meal much before that. What tells them that it's time to stop?

Common sense suggests that feeding stops when the stomach is full. This is true enough, but it is only part of the story, for animals will stop eating even when their stomach is only partially full. This will only happen, however, if they have ingested a nutritious substance. If the stomach is filled with an equal volume of nonnutritive bulk, the animal will continue to eat. This suggests that the stomach walls contain receptors that are sensitive to the nutrients dissolved in the digestive juices. They signal the brain that nutrient supplies to the internal environment are on their way as food is about to enter the intestines. The result is satiety (Deutsch, Puerto, and Wang, 1978).

SIGNALS FROM THE SMALL INTESTINE

Further satiety signals come from the *duodenum,* the first part of the small intestine. When food passes out of the stomach into the intestines, the duodenum begins to release a hormone from its mucous lining. There is good evidence that this hormone—*cholecystokinin,* or *CCK*—sends "stop eating" messages to the brain (Gibbs and Smith, 1984). When CCK is injected into the abdominal cavity of hungry rats and dogs, they stop feeding; when it is administered to people, it produces a sense that they've had enough (Stacher, Bauer, and Steinringer, 1979).

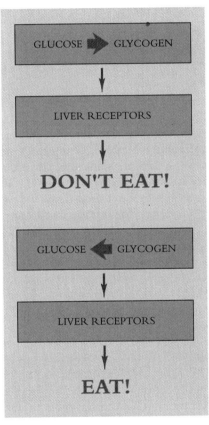

3.6 *The relation between the glucose-glycogen balance in the liver and eating*

SIGNALS FROM THE LIVER

Yet another source of information about the body's nutrient levels comes from the organ that acts as the manager of the body's food metabolism—the liver.

Immediately after a meal, glucose is plentiful. Since the body can't use it all, much of it is converted into other forms and put in storage. One such conversion goes on in the liver, where glucose is turned into **glycogen** (often called animal starch) and various fatty acids. Glycogen and fat cannot be used up as a metabolic fuel. This is fine right after a meal when glucose is still abundant, but the glucose will soon be used up so the stored energy has to be tapped eventually. When that happens, the chemical reaction goes the other way. Now the stored energy has to be turned into usable glucose.

Several studies suggest that the liver contains receptors that can sense in which direction the metabolic transaction goes, from glucose cash to stored energy deposits, or vice versa. If the balance tips toward storage, the receptors signal satiety and the animal stops eating. If the balance tips toward glucose production, the receptors signal hunger and the animal eats (Figure 3.6). The evidence that this happens in the liver comes from hungry dogs that were injected with glucose. When the injection was into the vein that goes directly to the liver, the dogs stopped eating. When the injection was anywhere else, there was no comparable effect (Russek, 1971; Friedman and Stricker, 1976).

Such evidence suggests that the internal stimuli for hunger and satiety arise at a rather earlier stage in the process of food extraction and storage than had been traditionally believed. If so, food-related homeostasis is not a last-ditch affair in which the system waits until the internal environment is already in precarious imbalance. Instead, the built-in hunger mechanism seems to be more prudent. It has an anticipatory character that corrects metabolic insufficiencies before they can possibly affect the internal environment.

A further example of the anticipatory quality of the hunger signal comes from some recent studies showing that an important stimulus for starting a meal is a particular pattern in the level of blood glucose—specifically, a fifteen minute drop in the glucose level followed by a quick rise. Such a change indicates a fall in the available fuel supply, followed by the body's own attempt to rectify that situation—presumably by converting some glycogen to glucose. This signal does not say that the fuel tank is currently empty, but rather that it soon will be if it's not filled up again. Given this signal, both animals and humans act appropriately. When such a change in the blood glucose level occurs in rats, the animals start to eat (Campfield and Smith, 1990 a, b). When it occurs in human subjects, they say that they are hungry and want something to eat (Campfield and Rosenbaum, 1992).

SIGNALS FROM THE OUTSIDE

The self-regulation of food intake is remarkable, but it is not perfect. Humans and animals eat to maintain nutritive homeostasis; put another way, they eat because their bodies need food. But they sometimes eat because they like the taste of a particular food. We eat dessert even though we may be full; our need for nutrients is gone, but not our appetite.

Such facts show that eating is not solely determined by stimuli that come from within the body. For these are supplemented by various external signals. We clearly do not eat for calories alone. Taste—and also smell and texture—is a powerful determinant of food intake for humans as well as animals. But palatability is not the only external signal for eating. Other signals are determined through learning. The expected mealtime is one example; the company of fel-

Peasant Wedding Feast *(Peter Brueghel the Elder, 1527; courtesy the Kunsthistorisches Museum)*

low eaters is another. A hen who has had her fill of grain will eagerly resume her meal if joined by other hens who are still hungry (Bayer, 1929).

External stimuli—say, the smell of a sizzling steak—can be a powerful inducement to start eating, but their effectiveness depends in part on the internal state of the organism. Sights, smells, and tastes can restore one's appetite, but if the meal was large enough, even the tastiest dessert will no longer be tempting. In line with this fact of everyday experience is a finding about food-sighting neurons in the hypothalamus of monkeys. In one group of studies, investigators implanted microelectrodes in the hypothalamus of waking monkeys and found some neurons in that area that fired when the animal was shown a peanut or a banana. But these cells only fired when the monkey was hungry. When the animal was first fed to satiety and *then* shown the same foods, the hypothalamic neurons did not respond. It would seem that at least in the hypothalamus, the eye is *not* bigger than the stomach (Mora, Rolls, and Burton, 1976; Rolls, 1978).

The fact that the attractiveness of food depends on the degree of hunger reminds us of what hunger—and indeed all the biological motives—are all about. They potentiate and orchestrate all kinds of food-related behaviors whose ultimate biological function is to get us through life as healthy and as well-fed as possible. Animals don't know that their body needs various nutrients to convert into glucose and other vital metabolic necessities; after all, neither they nor most of us have ever read a text on digestive physiology. Nature has built that information into their and our nervous systems so that hunger is unpleasant and eating when hungry is pleasant. The fact that the most enjoyable dessert becomes unbearably cloying after two or three portions is another demonstration of the potentiating role of motives that determine what we feel no less than what we do.

HYPOTHALAMIC CONTROL CENTERS

We have seen that there are many different signals for food intake. It was natural to suppose that these various messages are all integrated at one point in the nervous system where a final decision is made to eat or not to eat. The natural candidate for such a feeding center was the hypothalamus, which was already known to house controls for temperature regulation and water balance and which gave evidence of containing glucoreceptors. Physiological psychologists soon devised a dual-center theory of hypothalamic control of feeding that was analogous to the temperature system. It postulates two antagonistic centers, one corresponding to hunger, the other to satiety.

DUAL-CENTERS FOR FEEDING

According to dual-center theory, the hypothalamus contains an "on" and an "off" command post for eating. Two anatomical regions are implicated. One is located in the *lateral region* of the hypothalamus; it was said to function as a hunger center whose activation leads to food search and eating. The other is the *ventromedial region,* which was thought to be a satiety center whose stimulation stops eating.

The evidence for these claims came from the effects of lesions. Rats whose lateral hypothalamus has been destroyed suffer from *aphagia* (from the Greek for "no eating"). They refuse to eat and drink and will starve to death unless forcibly tube-fed for weeks (Teitelbaum and Stellar, 1954). Interestingly enough, eventually there is some recovery of function. After a few weeks the animals begin to eat again, especially if tempted by such delectables as liquid eggnog (Teitelbaum and Epstein, 1962).

Lesions to the ventromedial region produce effects that are in many ways the very opposite. Animals with such lesions suffer from *hyperphagia* (from the Greek for "excess eating"). They eat voraciously and keep on eating. If the lesion is large enough, they may become veritable mountains of rat obesity, finally reaching weights that are some three times as great as their preoperative levels. Tumors in this hypothalamic region (although very rare) have the same effect on humans (Miller, Bailey, and Stevenson, 1950; Teitelbaum, 1955, 1961).

While ventromedial lesions lead to rapid weight gain, this levels off in a month or two after which the animal's weight remains stable at a new (and of course much greater) level. Once this new weight is reached, the animal eats enough to maintain it but no more (Hoebel and Teitelbaum, 1976). This suggests that the lesion produced an upward shift in a *set-point* for weight regulation—a point that defines a kind of target value that determines food intake. As we will see, this interpretation may be relevant to explain some of the phenomena of human obesity (Nisbett, 1972; see Figure 3.7).

Details aside, dual-center theorists regard the two hypothalamic regions as mutually inhibitory centers of which one serves as an on-switch for eating, the other as an off-switch. There is a great deal of recent evidence that these switches are in turn activated by a number of internal and external signals. All of these signals act upon the feeding centers—some to trigger eating, others to inhibit it. Whether the organism eats will then depend on the summed value of them all: the level of various available nutrients in the blood stream, satiety signals from the stomach, food palatability, learned factors, and so on (Stellar, 1954).

DUAL CENTERS RECONSIDERED

The dual-center theory of feeding has held center stage for several decades. But it has come in for some reconsideration in recent years. The main grounds concern the effects of hypothalamic lesions. Some critics believe that some of the effects of these lesions are not directly on behavior, but rather on food metabolism (Stricker and Zigmond, 1976). Take the effects of ventromedial lesions. According to the original dual-center view, the only reason why rats with such lesions overeat is damage to some off-switch for feeding. But another interpretation lays at least some of the blame on a disruption of fat metabolism.

3.7 Hyperphagia (A) Curve showing the weight gain of hyperphagic rats after an operation creating a hypothalamic lesion. The weight eventually stabilizes at a new level. (After Teitelbaum, 1955) (B) Photograph of a rat several months after the operation. This rat weighed over 1,000 grams. (Courtesy Neal E. Miller, Rockefeller University)

Under normal conditions, animals store some of their unused nutrients in the form of fats. This tendency to save for later use can sometimes go too far, however. One effect of ventromedial lesions is that they produce an overreaction of certain branches of the parasympathetic system. This triggers an oversecretion of the hormone *insulin,* which in its turn increases the proportion of usable nutrients, especially glucose, that are turned into fat and cached away as adipose tissue. The trouble is that so much is stored that not enough is left over to serve as metabolic fuel. As a result, the animal stays hungry; it has to eat more to get the fuel that it needs. But since most of what it eats is turned into fat and stored away, the process continues and the animal has to keep on eating. It is in the position of a rich miser who has buried all of his possessions and has therefore no money to live on. Evidence comes from studies showing that animals with ventromedial lesions get fatter than normals even when both groups are fed the identical amount (Stricker and Zigmond, 1976).

Some authors argue that analogous indirect effects underlie the aphagia produced by lesions of the lateral hypothalamus (Stricker and Zigmond, 1976). But there is some evidence that the two hypothalamic centers also affect feeding directly. Thus cells in the ventromedial hypothalamus (the presumed "off" center) fire more slowly long after a meal and more quickly when the animal's stomach has been distended by a balloon—which is just what one would expect if these cells signal satiety (Anand and Pillai, 1967). Correspondingly, cells in the lateral hypothalamus (the presumed "on" center for feeding) fire more quickly when a hungry animal sees food, and the infusion of a certain neurotransmitter into this region leads to increased eating (Rolls, Burton, and Mora, 1976; Stanley, Magdalin, and Leibowitz, 1989).

Putting all of this together, the best guess is that the two hypothalamic centers serve two functions: They control feeding behavior, and they also give the commands to the autonomic nervous system that affect food metabolism, such as the increase or decrease of insulin secretion.

FOOD SELECTION

We've seen that the mechanisms that determine feeding are at least partially under the control of homeostasis. To that extent they resemble those that govern drinking and temperature regulation. But in many ways they are considerably more complex. One reason is that the control of food intake depends on two decisions. The animal (or its nervous system) must not only decide *whether* to eat, but also *what* to eat. How do animals and humans make this selection?

To some extent the selection is built into the nervous system. Take, for example, the response to sweet and bitter tastes. When a human newborn's mouth is moistened with a sweet solution (say, sugar water), the infant's facial expression suggests pleasure; when the solution is bitter (say, quinine water), the newborn screws his face into a grimace and turns away (Steiner, 1974; see Figures 3.8A and B). This selectional bias makes good biological sense, for it leads to the best nutritional bet: In the natural environment, sweet substances generally have more nutritional value than others. In contrast, bitter tastes are found in many poisonous plants. Occasionally though, the nutritional bet is lost: Saccharin is sweet and is generally preferred to less sweet substances, but it contains no calories.

Can built-in preferences account for all of an animal's food choices? They might, if the animal lives on one (or only a very few) food items, such as the

A

B

3.8 The response of newborn human babies to different tastes *Drops of different solutions were placed on the infants' mouths to record their reaction to (A) a sweet taste (sugar solution) and (B) a bitter taste (quinine solution). (From Steiner, 1977; photographs courtesy of Jacob Steiner)*

A   B   C

3.9 Food selection *(A) Some animals such as zebras eat only plants. (Photograph by Laura Riley/Bruce Coleman) (B) Others such as lions eat only other animals. (Photograph by Stan Osolinski/Oxford Scientific Films) (C) A few others subsist on a diet of just one food substance. In the case of the koala of Australia, this consists of eucalyptus leaves, which provide the animal with water as well as nutrients. (Photograph by Helen Williams/Photo Researchers)*

koala, whose diet consists almost entirely of eucalyptus leaves (Figure 3.9). But the majority of animals are less specialized than the koala; their diet is made up of all sorts of foods. How do these animals know which substances in the world provide calories and which do not? Furthermore, how do they identify the various nutrients they require over and above calories: various vitamins, minerals, amino acids, and so on? This is the problem of food selection. For carnivores, the food selection problem is relatively easy. Since the animals they feed on have nutritional needs like their own, carnivores are assured of getting a balanced diet. Lions run no risk of vitamin deficiency unless they insist on eating vitamin-deficient zebras (Rozin, 1976c, 1982).

The food selection problem is more difficult for omnivores like ourselves who are culinary generalists and eat a wide variety of plant foods. The problem is that many plants lack some essential nutrients that animals need for survival. Worse yet, other plants contain poisons—an adaptive device that protects them from plant-eaters, mostly insects. To get the necessary nutrients, omnivores must somehow identify a large range of edible plants that, taken together, will satisfy all of their dietary needs, but they must also identify those that are toxic. How can this be done? Some animals have hit upon a rather simple solution. When it comes to food, they are **neophobic**—that is, afraid of anything new. When rats (who like humans are food generalists) are confronted with some substance they've never tasted before, they will initially shy away from it altogether. But eventually, they'll taste a very small amount, as it were, to test it. If it is a poison, they will get sick. But since they only ate a little, they will most probably recover. They will later associate the taste of that food with their sickness and will avoid this taste from then on.★ On the other hand, if the food turns out to be safe, the animals will return in a day or two, take larger bites, and add this particular taste to their repertoire of acceptable food flavors (Rozin, 1976c).

Many children exhibit a somewhat similar neophobia about foods once they are about two years old. From then on, they tend to be culinary conservatives who stick to foods they know and make sour faces if confronted with something new. But in humans this neophobia is less pronounced than it is in rats and is not too hard to override. One factor is built-in taste preferences, particularly for sweets. Babies may dislike new foods, but they are certainly willing to make exceptions for chocolate pudding. But even more important is the fact that people live in a culture that allows them to benefit from the pooled experience of

★Such acquired taste aversions have some important implications for our understanding of the learning process, which will be discussed in a later section (see Chapter 4, pp. 136–39).

Inborn aversions? (*The FAR SIDE cartoon by Gary Larson is reprinted by permission of Chronicle Features, San Francisco, California, all rights reserved*)

previous generations. Most animals have to learn anew whether a given food is safe, but a child can rely on her parents.★ She may fuss and scream about the spinach and cauliflower on her plate, but at least she doesn't have to worry that they might be poisonous. After a while, she will learn to eat the foods her culture prefers (Mother's apple pie) and to avoid those to which the culture has aversions or taboos (pork to Muslims and Jews).

Here, as so often, human culture plays a crucial role in channeling the satisfaction of biological needs. For leopards, food satisfies a caloric need; for humans, it serves many other functions as well. It can be a source of aesthetic satisfaction, is often used to make various symbolic statements, may underline social distinctions, and can help to cement social and family groups. After all, is there any American who believes that there are some special metabolic needs that arise in late November which require the specific nutrients a turkey provides?

OBESITY

Both homeostatic and nonhomeostatic determinants of food intake are relevant to a problem partially created by the affluence of modern industrialized society—*obesity.* Obesity is sometimes defined as a body weight that exceeds the average for a given height by 20 percent. Judged by this criterion, about one-third of all Americans are obese. Most of them would rather be slim, and their wistful desires offer a ready market for a vast number of diet foods and fads. In part, the reason is health (at least it is sometimes said to be). But more important are social standards of physical attractiveness. There are no corpulent matinee idols, no fat sex goddesses (Stunkard, 1975).

Most authorities agree that there are several reasons why people become fat. In some cases, the cause is a bodily condition. In others, it is simply a matter of eating too much.

BODILY FACTORS IN OBESITY

Most of us take it for granted that body weight is a simple function of caloric intake and energy expenditure. To some extent this is undoubtedly true, but it is not the whole story. There is also good evidence that a number of other constitutional factors may predispose one person to get fat, even if he eats no more (and exercises no less) than his slender next-door neighbor. One reason may be a more proficient digestive apparatus; the person who manages to digest a larger proportion of the food he ingests will necessarily put on more weight than his digestively less efficient fellows. Another reason may be a lower metabolic level; the less nutrient fuel that is burned up, the more that is left for fatty storage. These constitutional differences may help to explain why some people gain weight much more readily than others (Sims, 1986).

In some individuals there may be a biochemical pattern in which too much of the nutrient intake is converted into fat, leaving too little to burn as metabolic fuel. As we already saw, this pattern necessarily leads to increased hunger and

★To some extent this is true even of rats. Young rats rely on the smell of their mothers' breath to decide whether to eat a novel food. When a new food item is encountered, rat pups will only eat it if they can smell it when sniffing at their mothers' mouth (Galef, 1988).

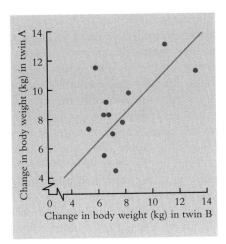

3.10 Similarity of weight gains in identical twins *Weight gains for twelve pairs of identical twins after 100 days of the same degree of overfeeding. Each point represents one twin pair, with the weight gain of twin A plotted on the vertical axis and the weight gain of twin B plotted on the horizontal axis. Weight gains are plotted in kilograms (1 kg = 2.2 lbs). The closer the points are to the diagonal line, the more similar the weight gains of the twins are to each other. (After Bouchard et al., 1990)*

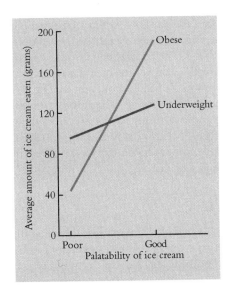

3.11 Eating, palatability, and obesity *In the experiment, obese and underweight subjects were given the opportunity to eat ice cream. If the ice cream tasted good, the obese subjects ate more than the underweight ones. The reverse was true if the ice cream did not taste good. (After Nisbett, 1968)*

overeating, which in turn leads to further fat deposits and yet further overeating (Friedman, 1990 a, b).

Some recent studies suggest that such constitutional differences in metabolic efficiency depend partially on genetic makeup. One was a study on the effects of overeating on twelve pairs of identical male twins. Each of these men was overfed by about 1,000 excess calories per day above the amount required to maintain his initial weight. The activities of each subject were kept as constant as possible, and there was very little exercise. This regimen continued for a period of 100 days. Needless to say, all twenty-four men gained weight, but the amount they gained varied substantially: from about ten to thirty pounds. A further difference concerned the parts of the body where the newly gained weight was deposited. For some subjects, it was the abdomen; for others, it was the thighs and buttocks. The important finding was that the amount each person gained was very similar to the weight gain of his twin (see Figure 3.10). Similarly for the location on the body where the weight was deposited. If one twin gained in the abdomen, so did his twin; if another deposited the fat in his thighs and buttocks, his twin did too. These findings are a strong indication that people differ in how their bodily machinery handles excess calories and that this metabolic pattern is probably inherited (Bouchard et al., 1990).

BEHAVIORAL FACTORS

In some persons, obesity is evidently produced by a bodily condition. But for many others, the cause lies in behavior: They simply eat too much. The question is why. It is virtually certain that there is no one answer, for chronic overeating has not one cause but many.

The externality hypothesis Some years ago, a number of investigators subscribed to the **externality hypothesis,** which held that obese people are comparatively unresponsive to their own internal hunger state and are much more susceptible to signals from without (Schachter and Rodin, 1974). One line of evidence came from studies that seemed to show that obese subjects are rather finicky when it comes to food. If offered a fine grade of vanilla ice cream, they eat *more* than normal subjects. But if offered vanilla ice cream that has been adulterated with bitter-tasting quinine, they eat *less* than do normals (Nisbett, 1968; see Figure 3.11).

Advocates of the externality hypothesis argued that this discrepancy in the sensitivity to external and internal cues for eating might be a contributing cause of obesity. Since he is presumably rather insensitive to the internal state of his body, the obese person will eat even though his body needs no further calories, so long as there are enough external cues (such as the taste of a fine grade of ice cream) that prompt him on. And in food-rich twentieth-century America, such cues are certainly plentiful (Schachter, 1971).

More recent studies have thrown doubt on the externality hypothesis. To begin with, the evidence for the greater sensitivity of obese persons to external cues turns out to be rather inconsistent. But to the extent that this oversensitivity does exist, its explanation may be quite different from what was originally supposed; it may be an *effect* of the obesity rather than its cause (Nisbett, 1972; Rodin, 1980, 1981).

In our society many people who are overweight consciously try to restrain their eating. Since obesity is a social liability, they make resolutions, go on diets, buy low-calorie foods, and do what they can to clamp a lid on their intense desire to eat. But the clamp is hard to maintain, for any external stimulus for eating will threaten the dieter's resolve. In effect, there is a "disinhibition" of eating (Herman and Polivy, 1980).

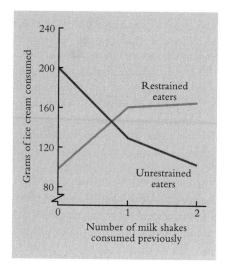

3.12 The diet-busting effect in restrained eaters *In the experiment, restrained and unrestrained eaters were asked to consume 0, 1, or 2 milk shakes in what they thought was an experiment on taste perception. They were later asked to judge the taste of ice cream and allowed to sample as much of it as they wished. The figure shows that restrained eaters ate considerably more ice cream if they had previously consumed one or more milk shakes. (After Herman and Mack, 1975)*

An interesting demonstration of this disinhibition is provided by a study of "restrained" and "unrestrained" eaters. Persons judged as restrained said they were on a diet or expressed concerns about their weight. Restrained and unrestrained subjects participated in what was described as an experiment on the perception of tastes. Initially, some subjects had to taste (and consume) one or two 8 oz. milk shakes, while control subjects tasted none. After this, the subjects were asked to judge the taste of ice cream. While performing this task, they were left alone with an unlimited supply of ice cream. How much would they eat? Unrestrained eaters ate a sensible, homeostatically appropriate amount: The more milk shakes they previously consumed, the less ice cream they ate in the subsequent test. But the exact opposite was true of the restrained eaters. The more milk shakes they previously consumed, the more ice cream they ate now. The prior exposure disinhibited their restraint and led to a motivational collapse—a phenomenon all too familiar to would-be dieters that some investigators have dubbed the "what-the-hell" diet-busting effect (Herman and Mack, 1975; see Figure 3.12).

The setpoint hypothesis   The hypothesis regarding disinhibition of restrained eating tries to explain some of the effects of obesity. But it has little to say about its cause. One possibility is that people differ in their setpoints for weight. These may reflect differences in constitution, which in turn may be partially determined by heredity (Foch and McClearn, 1980). These setpoints determine the weight an individual's system aims at as it regulates its internal economy. But if so, then many a person who is fat by the standards of official what-your-weight-should-be tables may weigh exactly what their own setpoints say they should weigh. If they starve themselves, they'll drop to a weight below that level. But in the long run they probably won't stay there, for there'll always be a tendency to go back to the setpoint weight (Nisbett, 1972).

Some authors point out that the tendency to maintain a given body weight affects energy expenditure as well as caloric intake. Thus when obese people starve themselves, they don't lose anywhere near as much weight as they should on the assumption (known to all dieters) that 3,500 calories equals one pound. The reason is that the body compensates for the caloric loss by a drastic reduction in metabolism (Keesey and Powley, 1986). Repeated bouts of weight loss followed by weight gain lead to even greater efficiency in using food reserves. After several alternations between dieting and overeating, it takes considerably more days on the diet to get back to the original weight (Brownell, et al., 1986). This probably accounts for the "yo-yo" phenomenon sometimes observed in people who go on diets, break them, and then start dieting again (Carlson, 1991).

THE TREATMENT OF OBESITY

What can be done to help people who are overweight? Everyone knows that it's relatively easy to lose weight over the short run; the problem is to keep it off for good. Can it be done? Some authors are optimists and believe that obesity is a behavioral problem that can be remedied by training people to develop self-control and acquire appropriate habits of diet and exercise. Other authorities are more pessimistic, for they believe that weight depends largely on a person's setpoint, which he can't escape in the long run. Attempts at treatment include psychoanalysis, various forms of behavior therapy (techniques for modifying the individual's behavior by the systematic use of certain principles of learning; see Chapters 4 and 19), and self-help groups (such as, Weight Watchers International). There is considerable dispute over the extent to which any of these methods leads to long-term change, although there is some suggestion that the self-help groups do a fairly good job, especially for those who are only

3.13 Relation of obesity to mortality
The figure presents the mortality rate in a sample of 5,209 people in Massachusetts for men and women from 45 to 74 years old between 1948 and 1964. The percent overweight is calculated by reference to mean weights for a given height. The figure shows that overweight does not increase the overall mortality risk, at least not for overweight percentages that are less than 50. (From Andres, 1980)

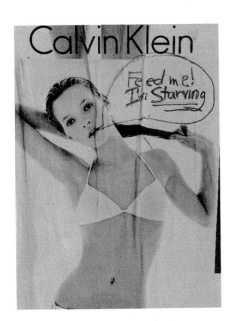

Thin is beautiful—or is it? *The Boston organization Boycott Anorexic Marketing is a group of women who believe that the glamorization of ultrathin models in advertising tends to encourage the development of eating disorders in young women. To call attention to this relationship, such groups sometimes annotate the ads of those they see as culprits. (Kate Moss in an advertisement for Calvin Klein; photograph courtesy of Jane Carter, 1994)*

mildly overweight (Booth, 1980; Stuart and Mitchell, 1980; Stunkard, 1980; Wilson, 1980).

At this point it is difficult to decide whether the optimists have a better case than the pessimists (Logue, 1986). But suppose the pessimists turn out to be correct—suppose that there is a setpoint which decrees that weight is fate. If so, can we offer any hope to those who are overweight?

To begin with, one may question the widely held belief that being overweight is necessarily a disorder. It is often asserted that being overweight is a health hazard and that over one-third of the U.S. population are too heavy (U.S. Public Health Service, 1966). But apart from cases of gross obesity, the relation between overweight and life expectancy is still a matter of debate (Fitzgerald, 1981; see Figure 3.13). Some authors argue that for the great majority of individuals, obesity is a social and aesthetic problem, rather than a problem of physical health. (This is especially so for women, who are much more likely to regard themselves as overweight than are men; Gray, 1977; Fallon and Rozin, 1985). Seen in this light, being slender is a social ideal, but we should not forget that it is an ideal of *our* society. Other cultures set different standards. The women painted by Rubens, Matisse, and Renoir were considered beautiful by their contemporaries; today they would be considered overweight. But does it really make sense to aspire to the body form of a fashion model if it is not one's own and perhaps can't be? Many people who regard themselves as overweight try to become lithe and slender but often fail anyway. Perhaps the best advice for them is to accept themselves as they are.

ANOREXIA AND BULIMIA

In some cases, the desire to be thin may be so extreme that it leads to eating disorders whose health hazards are much more serious than those produced by being somewhat overweight. One such condition is **anorexia nervosa,** which afflicts about 1 in 200 young women of the middle and upper classes in our society. Where the obese person is too fat and almost always eats too much, the anorexic is too thin (often dangerously so) and eats much too little. There are some cases of anorexia (literally "lack of appetite") that are caused by various organic conditions; for example in cancer patients, undergoing chemotherapy can produce nausea and various food aversions. In contrast, anorexia nervosa is not produced by any known organic pathology but is at least in part brought on by psychological factors. Its defining feature is "the relentless pursuit of thinness through self-starvation, even unto death" (Bruch, 1973, p. 4).

Anorexics are intensely and continually preoccupied by the fear of becoming fat. They eat only low-calorie food, if they eat at all. In addition, they often engage in strenuous exercise, often for many hours each day. Of course, this regimen leads to extreme weight loss, sometimes reaching levels that are less than 50 percent of the statistical ideal. Further symptoms include the cessation of menstruation, hyperactivity, sleep disorders, and avoidance of sex. In perhaps 10 percent of the cases, the end result of this self-starvation is death.

What leads to anorexia nervosa? Many authors believe that the primary causes are psychological and center on food and not eating because of our modern obsession with slimness (Logue, 1986). In some patients, the main cause is a fear of being sexually unattractive or of sex. In others, the primary focus involves a rebellion against the parents and a fierce desire to exercise some degree of autonomy and control. As one patient put it: "When you are so unhappy and you don't know how to accomplish anything, then to have control over your body becomes a supreme accomplishment. You make out of your body your

A

B

C

Changing conceptions of the relation between body weight and attractiveness *An under-lying cause of many eating disorders in Western women is their belief that being slender is beautiful. But is it? It depends. (A) The Venus of Willendorf, a prehistoric statuette unearthed near Willendorf, Austria, that was sculpted some 30,000 years ago. Some archeologists believe that it depicts a fertility goddess; others, that it represents the female erotic ideal of the ice age. (Courtesy Naturhistorisches Museum, Wien) (B) The Three Graces, painted by the Flemish master Peter Paul Rubens in 1639. (Courtesy Museo del Prado) (C) Paulina Porizkova, a model in the 1980s. (Photograph © M. Carraro/Gamma Liason)*

very own kingdom where you are the tyrant, the absolute dictator" (Bruch, 1978, p. 61).

Other authorities believe that the primary problem is organic. One possibility is some kind of hypothalamic malfunctioning, together with a hormonal disturbance, as shown by the fact that anorexics have unusually low levels of reproductive and growth hormones. As yet, we don't know whether the hormonal imbalances are the effect or the cause of the psychological problems and the self-starvation diet (Garfinkel and Garner, 1982).

Another eating disorder is **bulimia,** which is characterized by repeated eating binges that are often followed by attempts to purge the calories just consumed by self-induced vomiting or by taking laxatives. Unlike anorexics, bulimics are of roughly normal weight, but their repeated binge-and-purge bouts can lead to a variety of problems. To begin with, many bulimics suffer considerable depression after a binge. In addition, the repeated binges may produce disruptions of the electrolyte balance that may ultimately lead to cardiac, kidney, and urinary infections. Bulimia is fairly common currently among college students (in one survey, it was found in 19 percent of the women and 5 percent of the men). The binge-and-purge cycle is a perfect expression of our contradictory attitudes toward food and eating. On the one hand, there are the easily available high-calorie foods that we are constantly urged to buy ("Treat yourself to a bar of _____. You deserve it!"); on the other hand, we are constantly reminded that to be sexually attractive we must be thin (Logue, 1986).

We've seen that the regulation of food intake in all animals is a complexly regulated process characterized by multiple, overlapping mechanisms acting at a variety of levels of organization. But the eating disorders show us that in our own species in which a highly developed cerebrum modulates the hypothalamic control centers, social and psychological factors can in some cases cause these mechanisms to bite the hand that tried to feed them, resulting in grave bodily harm and even death.

FEAR AND RAGE

Thus far, our emphasis has been on motives that are largely based on internal, homeostatic controls: A disruption of the internal environment impels the organism to perform some action that ultimately restores its internal balance. But there are a number of motives that have little to do with homeostatic equilibrium. Sex is one example. While internal hormone levels play an important role, the desire is essentially aroused (as it were, "turned on") by external stimuli of various kinds; homeostatic imbalances have nothing to do with it. We will discuss this in a later chapter that deals with motives that are primarily social (see Chapter 10). Here we will consider another motive that is almost entirely instigated from without rather than within: the reaction to intense threat, which results in attempts to escape or to fight back in self-defense and which is often accompanied by the violent emotions of rage and fear.

To the extent that this motive (much like sex) is nonhomeostatic and is primarily instigated by external stimuli, it is of course quite different from the motives of self-regulation, such as hunger, thirst, and temperature maintenance. But in one regard this motive is just the same as the homeostatic motives, for like them it has a potentiating function—it activates particular tendencies to react and decreases others. A man confronted by a hungry tiger has little on his mind except how to remove himself from the scene, or if he has a weapon and the skill to use it, how to remove the tiger. For the time being, food, drink, and sex will be very low on his list of priorities.

THREAT AND THE AUTONOMIC NERVOUS SYSTEM

What are some of the biological mechanisms that underlie our reactions to threat? We'll begin our discussion by looking at the functions of the autonomic nervous system. We previously saw how the interaction of sympathetic and parasympathetic excitations permits adjustments of the visceral machinery in the control of temperature. But the opposition between the two autonomic branches is more fundamental yet. According to the American physiologist Walter B. Cannon (1871–1945), they serve two broad and rather different functions. The parasympathetic system handles the *vegetative* functions of ordinary life: the conservation of bodily resources, reproduction, and the disposal of wastes. In effect, these reflect an organism's operations during times of peace—a lowered heart rate, peristaltic movements of stomach and intestines, secretion of digestive glands. In contrast, the sympathetic system has an *activating* function. It summons the body's resources and gets the organism ready for vigorous action (Cannon, 1929).

As an example of this opposition, consider the role of the two autonomic divisions in governing the delivery of nutrient fuels and oxygen as well as the removal of waste products to and from the musculature. Parasympathetic excitation slows down the heart rate and reduces blood pressure. Sympathetic excitation has the opposite effect and also inhibits digestion and sexual activity. In addition, it stimulates the inner core of the adrenal gland, the **adrenal medulla,** to pour epinephrine (adrenaline) and norepinephrine into the bloodstream.

Walter B. Cannon *(Courtesy National Library of Medicine)*

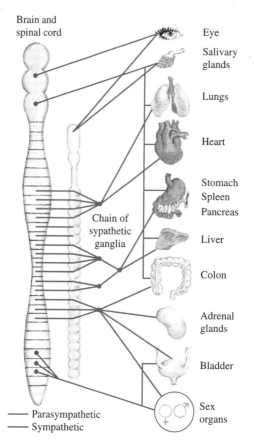

Brain and
spinal cord

Eye

Salivary
glands

Lungs

Heart

Stomach
Spleen
Pancreas

Liver

Colon

Adrenal
glands

Bladder

Sex
organs

Chain of
sypathetic
ganglia

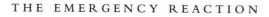
Parasympathetic
Sympathetic

3.14   The sympathetic and parasympathetic branches of the autonomic nervous system   *The parasympathetic system (shown in red) facilitates the vegetative functions of the organism: It slows the heart and lungs, stimulates digestive functions, permits sexual activity, and so on. In contrast, the sympathetic system (shown in blue) helps to place the organism on an emergency basis: It accelerates heart and lung actions, liberates nutrient fuels for muscular effort, and inhibits digestive and sexual functions.*

Note that the fibers of the sympathetic system are interconnected through a chain of ganglionic fibers outside of the spinal cord. As a result, sympathetic activation has a somewhat diffuse character; any sympathetic excitation tends to affect all of the viscera rather than just some. This is in contrast to the parasympathetic system whose action is more specific. (After Cannon, 1929)

PARASYMPATHETIC SYSTEM

Constriction of pupil

Secretion of tear glands

Salivation

Inhibition of heart action

Constriction of respiratory passages

Stomach contraction: secretion of digestive fluids

Intestinal peristalsis

Contraction of bladder

Erection

SYMPATHETIC SYSTEM

Dilation of pupil

Inhibition of tear glands

Inhibition of salivation

Acceleration of heart action

Opens respiratory passages

Inhibits stomach contractions and digestive secretion

Inhibits intestinal peristalsis

Relaxes bladder

Inhibits erection

3.15   Sympathetic emergency reaction
A cat's terrified response to a frightening encounter. (Photograph by Walter Chandoha)

These have essentially the same effects as sympathetic stimulation—they accelerate the heart rate, speed up metabolism, and so on. As a result, the sympathetic effects are amplified yet further (see Figure 3.14).

THE EMERGENCY REACTION

Cannon pointed out that intense sympathetic arousal has a special function. It serves as an ***emergency reaction*** that mobilizes the organism for a crisis—for flight or fight. Consider a grazing zebra, placidly maintaining homeostasis by nibbling at the grass and vasodilatating in the hot African sun. Suddenly it sees a lion approaching rapidly. The vegetative functions must now take second place, for if the zebra does not escape it will have no internal environment left to regulate. The necessary violent exertions of the skeletal musculature will now require the total support of the entire bodily machinery, and this support is provided by intense sympathetic activation. There is more nutrient fuel for the muscles, and it is now delivered more rapidly. At the same time, waste products are jettisoned more quickly, and all unessential organic activities are brought to a halt. If the zebra does not escape, it is not because its sympathetic system did not try.

Cannon produced considerable evidence suggesting that a similar autonomic reaction occurs when the pattern is one of attack rather than of flight. A cat about to do battle with a dog shows accelerated heartbeat, piloerection (its hair standing on end, normally a heat-conserving device), and pupillary dilation—all signs of sympathetic arousal, signs that the body is girding itself for violent muscular effort (Figure 3.15).

Cannon emphasized the biological utility of the autonomic reaction, but his principle cannot tell us which choice the animal will make, whether it will choose fight or flight. This depends in part upon built-in predispositions, in part upon the specific situation. For example, a rat first tries to escape but fights when finally cornered. Emergency situations may produce still different reactions from those we have already seen. Some animals become paralyzed by fright and stand immobile—an adaptive reaction since predators are more likely to detect and strike prey that is in motion. Other animals have even more exotic means of self-protection. Some species of fish pale when frightened, which makes them harder to spot against the sandy ocean bottom. This effect is produced by the direct action of adrenal epinephrine upon various pigmented substances in the animal's skin (Odiorne, 1957).

These reactions are of course also found in humans, as bodily concomitants of intense emotion. In fear, our hearts pound, our palms sweat, and we sometimes shiver—all sympathetic activities. It is hardly surprising that such autonomic responses (as pulse rate and respiration) are often used as indicators of emotional states. The *galvanic skin response (GSR)* is a particularly favored measure. It is a drop in the electrical resistance of the skin, particularly of the palm (related to, but not identical with, the activity of the sweat glands), that is a sensitive index of general arousal.

The GSR and other indices of autonomic activity are part of the technology of the polygraph test, sometimes called the "lie detector test." Such tests obviously cannot detect lies as such. What they do instead is uncover autonomic arousal to certain key questions or phrases. The responses to these critical items (e.g., "Did you stab anyone with a knife on . . . ?") are then compared with the responses to control items—questions that are likely to produce an emotional reaction but are irrelevant to the issue at hand (e.g., "Before age nineteen did you ever lie to anyone?").

The fundamental assumption on which the lie-detection enterprise rests is that innocent persons will be more concerned by the control items than by the critical questions and will therefore show more intense autonomic arousal to the former than to the latter (Figure 3.16). But this assumption is in serious dispute (Lykken, 1979, 1981). By and large, while polygraph operators do rather well in identifying guilty individuals, certain persons—especially those called sociopathic personalities—seem to have a special knack at beating lie detector tests (Waid and Orne, 1982; see Chapter 18, pp. 758–59). In addition, the polygraph does rather poorly in exonerating individuals who are innocent (Saxe, Dougherty, and Cross, 1985). Evidence of this kind, as well as ethical considerations, led Congress to pass legislation in 1988 that severely restricted the use of lie-detector tests in the courts, in government, and in industry.

3.16 Lie detection by use of autonomic measures (A) *Various devices measure autonomic arousal—a tube around the chest measures respiration rate, electrodes attached to the hand measure GSR, and an arm band measures blood pressure and pulse. (Photograph by Mary Shuford) (B) A recording of respiration, GSR, and a measure of blood pressure and pulse. The record was obtained from a store employee caught stealing merchandise. At issue was the amount of the theft. To determine this, all parties agreed to be guided by the results of a lie detector test. The subject was asked questions about the amount, such as "Did you steal more than $1,000?" and "Did you steal more than $2,000?" The record shows a high peak just after $3,000 and before $4,000. Later the subject confessed that the actual amount was $4,000. (After Inbau and Reid, 1953)*

A

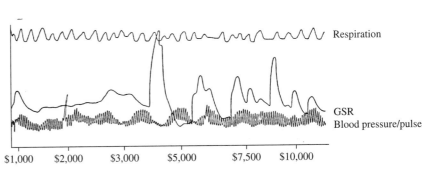

B

Respiration

GSR
Blood pressure/pulse

$1,000 $2,000 $3,000 $5,000 $7,500 $10,000

"Did you steal more than _____?"

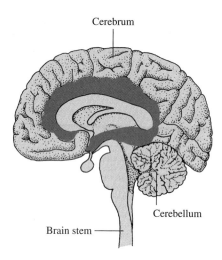

3.17   Limbic system of the human brain
Schematic view of the limbic system (in blue) in cross section. (After Keeton and Gould, 1986)

Cerebrum

Cerebellum

Brain stem

CENTRAL CONTROLS

The autonomic nervous system, in both its sympathetic and parasympathetic branches, is by no means as autonomous as its name implies; rather, it is largely guided by other neural centers. Some of these centers are among the oldest and most primitive portions of the cerebral cortex. These primitive cortical structures comprise the *limbic system,* a group of structures in the brain intimately involved in the control of the emotional reactions to situations that call for flight, defense, or attack (Figures 3.17 and 3.18). Electrical stimulation of certain portions of the limbic system transforms a purring cat into a spitting, hissing Halloween figure. Stimulation of the same region in humans often produces feelings of great anxiety or of rage, as in a patient who said that she suddenly wanted to tear things to pieces and to slap the experimenter's face (Magnus and Lammers, 1956; King, 1961; Flynn et al., 1970).

Psychologically there seem to be different kinds of attack, and they are evidently initiated by different control centers. In cats, the stimulation of one hypothalamic region produces predatory attack: quiet stalking followed by a quick, deadly pounce. The stimulation of another region leads to the Halloween pattern: a counterattack in self-defense (probably related to what in humans is called rage). When this rage pattern is triggered, the cat ignores a nearby mouse and will spring viciously at the experimenter by whom it presumably feels threatened (Egger and Flynn, 1963; Clemente and Chase, 1973). Predatory attack is another matter entirely: The lion who pounces on the zebra is probably not at all enraged but is merely engaged in the prosaic business of food gathering. (Whether the zebra is comforted by the fact that the lion is not angry at it is another question.)

3.18   The limbic system and some related structures   *The brain is pictured here as if the hemispheres were essentially transparent. One of the structures particularly relevant to emotional reactions is the amygdala, a walnut-sized structure that has been implicated in the production of aggressive behavior and fear reactions. (After Bloom, Lazerson, and Hofstadter, 1988)*

Frontal lobe

Olfactory lobe

Hypothalamus

Amygdala

Limbic cortex

Thalamus

Hippocampus

Reticular formation

Spinal cord

DISRUPTIVE EFFECTS OF AUTONOMIC AROUSAL

Our preceding discussion emphasized the biological value of the emergency system. But strong autonomic arousal can also be disruptive and even harmful to the organism. This negative side of the matter is especially clear in humans. In our day-to-day lives we rarely encounter emergencies that call for violent physical effort. But our biological nature has not changed just because our modern world contains no sabertooth tigers. We still have the same emergency system that served our primitive ancestors, and its bodily consequences can take serious tolls.

The disruptive effect of fear and anger upon digestion or upon sexual behavior is a matter of common knowledge. During periods of marked anxiety there are often complaints of constipation or other digestive ills. The same holds for impotence or frigidity. This is hardly surprising, since digestive functions and many aspects of sexual activity (for example, erection) are largely controlled by the parasympathetic system and are thus inhibited by intense sympathetic arousal. Moreover, the aftereffects of emotional arousal can sometimes be more permanent, causing profound and long-lasting bodily harm. Various disorders such as peptic ulcer, colitis, asthma, and hypertension can often be traced back to emotional patterns in the patient's life and are then considered psychophysiological disorders in which a psychological cause produces a bodily effect (see Chapter 18). Such psychophysiological effects are sometimes even more grievous and irrevocable, as in cases of hypertension and coronary disease, which can lead to heart attacks and death (see Chapter 18).

PAIN AND THE ENDORPHIN SYSTEM

We've considered the biological basis of self-defense, but have thus far said little about the stimuli that set it off. Some of the stimuli that lead to fear or counterattack have surely acquired their significance through learning (to which we will turn in the next chapter). But some of them seem to produce the sympathetic emergency reaction without any prior experience. An important example of such a built-in trigger for fear and rage is pain.

PAIN AS AN AID TO SURVIVAL

It seems paradoxical, but pain—especially pain that is acute rather than chronic—has survival value, representing a biological boon rather than a bitter burden. This fact is highlighted by the rare cases of individuals born with a virtual insensitivity to pain. As a child, one such individual bit off the tip of her tongue while chewing, incurred serious burns when kneeling on a hot radiator, and suffered severe pathological dislocations in her hips and spine because she failed to shift her weight appropriately or turn over in her sleep. Such traumas eventually led to massive infections that caused her death at the age of twenty-nine (Melzack, 1973).

PAIN RELIEF THROUGH ENDORPHINS

Pain's adaptive value is as a signal to react—to withdraw from the burning flame, to run away, to fight in self-defense, to nurse one's wounds (Bolles and Fanselow, 1982). But once the pain stimulus has set off the appropriate reaction, continued

3.19 Acupuncture *Acupuncture is a complex system of treatment that grew up in ancient China and was based on the idea that disease is a disturbance of vital energies that circulate in particular channels. Their balance was to be restored by manipulating metal needles at special points along these channels. (A) From a seventeenth-century Chinese treatise illustrating the liver tract with twenty-eight special points. (From Blakemore, 1977) (B) A contemporary patient receiving treatment. (Photograph © Pierre Boulat/Woodfin Camp & Associates)*

pain may get in the way of whatever it is that has to be done. Under the circumstances, it would be adaptive if the organism could now alleviate its own pain.

The existence of such a biological process of self-administered pain alleviation has long been suspected. There is good evidence that pain can be alleviated or even abolished by psychological means that serve as an **analgesic** (a pain reliever). There are many stories of athletes or soldiers who suffer injuries but don't feel the pain until the game or the battle is over. Related effects have been produced in the laboratory. Thus rats subjected to various forms of stress, such as being forced to swim in cold water, become less sensitive to pain (Bodnar et al., 1980). Similar results have been shown in humans: Paradoxically enough, mild electric shock to the back or limbs can serve as an analgesic. So can acupuncture, an ancient Chinese treatment in which needles are inserted in various parts of the body (see Figure 3.19; Mann et al., 1973). This procedure seems to suppress pain in animals as well as humans (Nathan, 1978). In all these cases, the question is why.

The answer seems to be a matter of brain chemistry. It's long been known that the experience of pain can be dulled or entirely eliminated by various drugs, such as morphine and other opiates. These drugs are typically applied from the outside. But on occasion, the brain is its own best pharmacist. For when assailed by various kinds of stress (one of which is extremely painful stimulation), the brain can sometimes produce its own brand of opiates, which it then administers to itself. These are the **endorphins,** (a contraction of the word *endogenous*—that is, internally produced—and the word *morphines*), a group of neurotransmitters that are secreted by certain neurons within the brain. These transmitters stimulate yet other neurons, which in their turn modulate messages from the pain receptors sent up to the brain by a spinal cord tract (see

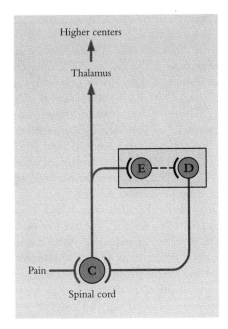

Higher centers

Thalamus

Pain

Spinal cord

3.20 Pain and pain relief *Highly schematic diagram of a proposed neural circuit to explain certain pain relief phenomena, with dark green indicating excitation and dark red indicating inhibition. Pain stimuli excite neurons in the spinal cord (C) that carry pain information upwards to the thalamus. But they also excite endorphin-releasing neurons (E) in the midbrain, which, through several intermediate steps, excite descending neurons (D) that inhibit the pain pathway in the spinal cord. This pain-relief system can also be activated by the administration of morphine or by the electrical stimulation of the region of the midbrain that contains the E-neurons. (After Groves and Rebec, 1988)*

Figure 3.20). Regular opiates such as morphine are chemically very similar to the endorphins and will therefore activate the same pain-inhibiting neurons (though, in fact, some of the brain's own endorphins are considerably more powerful than the artificially produced morphines dispensed by physicians; Snyder and Childers, 1979; Bloom, 1983).

Placebos Many investigators believe that the endorphins together with social factors play a role in the pain reduction produced by a ***placebo,*** a chemically inert substance that the patient believes will help him, such as the old family doctor's little sugar pill. There is good evidence that such placebos do sometimes alleviate pain and may have other beneficial effects (see Chapter 19 for a discussion of placebos in the context of psychotherapy). They may even contribute to the pain relief produced by "real" pharmacological agents such as morphine. In one experiment (Evans, 1974) some patients were given a sugar pill described as "aspirin" and in another case, they were given a sugar pill described as "morphine." In both cases, the pills produced substantial relief—about 50 percent of the relief produced when the actual drugs are given! This suggests that when the actual drugs are given in normal therapeutic situations, as much as 50 percent of the pain relief may be a nonpharmacological placebo effect.

To prove that the endorphins are involved in these and similar instances in which pain is reduced by "psychological" means, investigators turned to ***naloxone.*** This is a drug known to inhibit the effect of morphine and other opiates; it is generally given to addicts who have overdosed on the potent (and of course, illicit) opiate, heroin. A number of studies have shown that naloxone also blocks the pain alleviation produced by acupuncture (Mayer et al., 1976). The same holds for placebos dispensed to patients who believe they are taking a pain killer. In one such study, patients were given a placebo after having a wisdom tooth extracted. This helped some of the patients, but had no effect when the patients were given naloxone in addition to the placebo (Levine, Gordon, and Fields, 1979). Some more recent studies have shown that, while naloxone attenuates such placebo effects, it does not abolish them completely. This indicates that there are some avenues to pain relief that do not involve the morphine system (Watkins and Mayer, 1982; Grevert and Goldstein, 1985). An example is hypnosis, which is sometimes used as a surgical anesthetic. The mechanisms that produce this pain relief are still under investigation, but they evidently do not involve endorphins since the analgesic effect of hypnosis is not abolished by naloxone (Moret et al., 1991; De Beneedittis et al., 1989).

ENDORPHINS AND EXERCISE

Some authors believe that the exhilarating effect of repeated stressful exercise, such as jogging and marathon running, is also related to the endorphins. The runner continues to exert herself until she is exhausted and in pain. This builds up endorphins, which counteract the pain and produce a mood swing in the opposite direction. Eventually there may be something like an addiction—the jogger has to have her jogging fix to enjoy the endorphin-produced euphoria. Whether this interpretation is correct is still unknown, though there is evidence that stressful exercise does increase the secretion of endorphins (Hawkins, 1992; Thoren et al., 1990; Carr et al., 1981).

To sum up, both pain and pain relief are biologically adaptive. Pain is a crucial warning signal that tells an animal that it had better do something quickly to avert bodily harm. But once the warning is given, further pain may be incapacitating. A wounded deer must be able to ignore its wounds if it wants to escape the hunters.

SLEEP AND WAKING

Thus far, our main concern has been with the *directive* function of motives. This direction can be primarily imposed from within, as in the case of the homeostatic motives such as thirst and hunger. It can also be initiated by stimuli from the outside, as in fear and rage. Either way, the effects on behavior are readily described in terms of a negative feedback system. In the case of homeostatic motives, the organism acts so as to change the state of the internal environment; it eats or drinks until its water balance or nutrient level is restored. In the case of rage and fear, it acts to change the conditions of the external environment that prompted the disturbance: The cat runs away to remove itself from a barking dog, or it hisses and scratches in a frantic attempt to remove the dog.

Motives also have another function. They *arouse* the organism, which then becomes increasingly alert and vigorous. A given motive will thus act like both the tuner and the volume control of a radio. A thirsty animal seeks water rather than food or a sexual partner. And the thirstier it is, the more intensely it will pursue its goal. Psychologists have used various terms to describe this facet of motivation. Some call it **activation;** others prefer the term **drive.** They all agree that increased drive generally leads to increased behavioral vigor. Thus, rats will run faster to water the longer they have been water-deprived.

We will now look at some of the biological mechanisms of activation as we consider waking arousal and sleep.

WAKING

In a sense, the sympathetic branch of the autonomic nervous system can be considered an arousal system for various physiological processes of the body. Similar arousal systems operate to alert the brain, to activate the cortex so that it is fully responsive to incoming messages. In effect, they awaken the brain.

Just where these arousal systems are in the brain is still a matter of some debate. Until fairly recently, they were believed to have their origin in the midbrain but more recent work has focused on several structures in the mid- and hindbrain, which have branches that ascend to the rest of the brain.* Activity in these regions not only leads to awakening, but also produces increasing levels of arousal once awake (Aston-Jones, 1985).

Stimulation from the subcortical arousal systems is not the only source of cortical activation. Stimulation can also come from the cortex itself. Descending fibers from the cortex may excite the subcortical structures, which then activate the cortex more fully. This circuit—cortex to lower arousing systems to cortex—probably plays an important role in many phenomena of sleep and waking. We sometimes have trouble in falling asleep because we "can't shut off our thoughts." Here cortical activity triggers the subcortical arousal system, which activates the cortex, which again excites the lower level subcortical system, and so on. The role of the cortex in rousing itself is also shown by the fact that some stimuli—a baby's cry, the smell of fire, the sound of one's own name—are more likely to wake us than others, regardless of their intensity. The same circuit can also produce the lowering of arousal. When our cortex is unstimulated by

Observing sleep *All-night recordings of EEGs of patients in sleep labs have revealed the several stages of sleep. (Photograph by Grant Leduc/Monkmeyer)*

*Some forty years ago it was generally beleived that a major component of this arousal system was the reticular formation of the midbrain (e.g., French, 1957), but this position has now been discarded.

3.21 Schematic diagram of EEG recording *A number of scalp electrodes are placed on a subject's head. At any one time, there are small differences in the electrical potential (that is, the voltage) between any two of these electrodes. These differences are magnified by an amplifier and are then used to activate a recording pen. The greater the voltage difference, the larger the pen's deflection. Since the voltage fluctuates, the pen goes up and down, thus tracing a brain wave on the moving paper. The number of such waves per second is the EEG frequency.*

events, the arousal level may drop so low that we find ourselves dropping off into the state that is the very opposite of high arousal—sleep.

SLEEP AND BRAIN ACTIVITY

The primary focus of this chapter is on motivation and thus on the direction and activation of behavior that motives bring about. In this context, sleep is of considerable interest because it seems to represent the very opposite of arousal. But it has a more direct relevance as well. The desire for sleep is one of the most powerful of motives; if kept awake long enough, the urge to sleep will eventually take precedence over most motives (which is one of the reasons why jailers sometimes use enforced sleeplessness to force confessions out of prisoners). What can we say about this state in which most of us spend a third of our lives? Sleep cannot be observed from within, since it is almost by definition a condition of which the sleeper is unaware. (The rare dreams in which we know that we are dreaming are an interesting exception.) Since we cannot study sleep from within, we must perforce study it from without. One way of doing this is by observing what the brain does while its owner is asleep.

Eavesdropping on the brain of waking or sleeping subjects is possible because the language of the nervous system is electrical. When electrodes are placed at various points on the skull, they pick up the electrical changes that are produced by the summed activity of the millions of nerve cells in the cerebral cortex that is just underneath. In absolute terms these changes are very small; they are therefore fed to a highly sensitive amplifier whose output in turn activates a series of pens. These pens trace their position on a long roll of paper that moves at a constant speed (Figure 3.21). The resulting record is an *electroencephalogram,* or EEG, a picture of voltage changes over time occurring in the brain.

Figure 3.22 shows an EEG record that begins with the subject in a relaxed state, with eyes closed, and "not thinking about anything in particular." The record shows *alpha waves,* a rather regular waxing and waning of electrical potential, at some eight to twelve cycles per second. This alpha rhythm is very characteristic of this state (awake but resting) and is found in most mammals. When the subject attends to some stimulus with open eyes or when he is involved in active thought (for instance, mental arithmetic) with his eyes closed, the picture changes. Now the alpha rhythm is *blocked;* the voltage is lower, the frequency is much higher, and the pattern of ups and downs is nearly random.

THE STAGES OF SLEEP

Several decades of work involving continuous, all-night recordings of EEGs and other measures have shown that there are several stages of sleep and that these vary in depth. Just prior to sleep, there tends to be an accentuated alpha rhythm. As the subject becomes drowsy, the alpha comes and goes; there are increasingly long stretches during which the pattern is random. The subject is now in a light, dozing sleep from which she is easily awakened (Stage 1 in

3.22 Alpha waves and alpha blocking
(After Guyton, 1981)

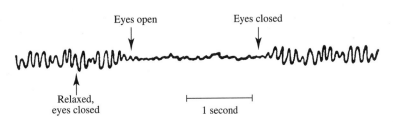

Eyes open   Eyes closed

Relaxed,
eyes closed

1 second

3.23   The stages of sleep   *The figure shows EEG records taken from the frontal lobe of the brain, during waking, quiet sleep, and active sleep. (Courtesy of William C. Dement)*

Figure 3.23). Over the course of the next hour she drifts into deeper and deeper stages, in which the EEGs are characterized by the complete absence of alpha and by waves of increasingly higher voltage and much lower frequency (Stages 2 through 4 in Figure 3.23). In the last stages, the waves are very slow. They occur about once every second and are some five times greater in amplitude than those of the alpha rhythm. At this point the sleeper is virtually immobile and will take a few seconds to awaken, mumbling incoherently, even if shaken or shouted at. During the course of the night, the sleeper's descent repeats itself several times. She drops from dozing to deep, slow-wave sleep, reascends to Stage 1, drops back to slow-wave sleep, and so on for some four or five cycles.

The oscillations between different sleep stages are not merely changes in depth. When the sleeper reascends into Stage 1, he seems to enter a qualitatively different state entirely. This state is sometimes called **active sleep** to distinguish it from the **quiet sleep** found during the other stages. Active sleep is a paradoxical condition with contradictory aspects. In some ways it is as deep as sleep ever gets. The sleeper's general body musculature is at its most flaccid, and he is at his least sensitive to external stimulation (Williams, Tepas, and Morlock, 1962). But judged by some other criteria, the level of arousal during active sleep is almost as high as during alert wakefulness. One sign is the EEG, which in humans is rather similar to that found in waking (Jouvet, 1967). Another is the appearance of dreams (of which more later), which are found in active rather than quiet sleep and during which we often feel as if we were active and thoroughly awake.

Of particular interest are the sleeper's eye movements during Stage 1 sleep; these can be recorded by means of electrodes attached next to each eye. During quiet sleep, the eyes drift slowly and no longer move in tandem. But during active sleep a different pattern suddenly appears. The eyes move rapidly and in unison behind closed lids, as if the sleeper were looking at some object outside. These jerky, rapid eye movements (REMs) are one of the most striking features of active sleep, which is often called **REM sleep.** Young human adults enter this stage about four times each night (Figure 3.24).

A   Non-REM   REM

Eye movements

3.24   REM and non–REM sleep   *(A) Eye movements during non-REM and REM sleep. The REM periods are associated with dreaming. (B) The alternation of non-REM and REM periods throughout the course of the night (REM periods are in color). Rapid eye movements and dreams begin as the person repeatedly emerges from deeper sleep to the level of Stage 1. (After Kleitman, 1960)*

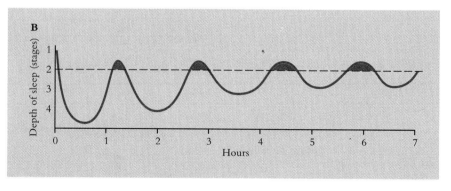

THE FUNCTIONS OF SLEEP

What functions are served by sleep, whether in its active or quiet form? Surprisingly enough, the answer is still unknown.

SLEEP DEPRIVATION

One way of trying to assess the benefits that sleep may bring is to observe what ills befall if it is prevented. This is the logic of sleep-deprivation experiments in which humans and animals are kept awake for days on end. The results suggest that there is indeed a need for sleep. If deprived of sleep, the organism seeks sleep just as it seeks food when it is starved. When sleep is finally allowed, the subjects sink down upon the nearest cot and try to make up for the sleep they have lost.

The need of the sleep-deprived person is not just for sleep in general but also for the two major sleep states that comprise it. This is shown by studies on selective sleep deprivation in which the experimenter prevents one kind of sleep (for example, REM) but not the other. If he wants to deprive the subjects of REM sleep only, he simply wakes them up whenever the EEG and eye movements signal the beginning of a REM period. After the subjects wake up, they go back to sleep, are reawakened when they next enter the REM state, go back to sleep, are reawakened, and so on through the night. After a few nights of this, the subjects are allowed to sleep freely. They will now spend more time in REM than they normally do, as if to make up for the state of which they were deprived (Figure 3.25). The same holds for selective deprivation of the deep, slow-wave sleep of Stages 3 and 4. If lost one night, it is made up on another (Webb, 1972).

SLEEP AS A RESTORATIVE PROCESS

The sleep-deprivation experiments suggest that there is a need for sleep, but they do not tell us why. One possibility is that sleep is restorative, that it is a period during which some vital substance is resynthesized in the nervous system. In one form or another, this view was held at least as early as the Renaissance, as witness Shakespeare who regarded sleep as "a balm of hurt minds" that "knits up the ravel'd sleave of care." That sleep has some such function seems probable even though we have only a sketchy notion of what might be restored and how.

Some authors focus on the restorative functions of deep, slow-wave sleep (Stages 3 and 4). A number of studies suggest that slow-wave sleep is enhanced under conditions such as physical fatigue, where there is a greater need for bodily revival. There is some evidence that marathon runners sleep longer during the two nights after the race; their largest increase is in the time they spend during slow-wave sleep (Shapiro et al., 1981). This result fits in with the finding that a growth-promoting hormone that boosts protein synthesis (and thus helps to replace body tissue) is secreted primarily during slow-wave sleep (Takahashi, 1979). The matter is still under debate, for there is some evidence that the increase in slow-wave sleep may not be due to bodily fatigue at all. It appears that intense exercise leads to an increase in brain metabolism. If so, it is the brain rather than the body that requires rest and restoration (Horne, 1988).

We are just as far from a definite answer when we ask what REM sleep is good for. There have been many suggestions. One possibility is that as the sleeper enters each night's REM sleep she consolidates whatever she learned on the day before. On this view, what happens during REM sleep is analogous to what goes on in a library after the reading rooms are closed: The books are catalogued

3.25 The effect of lost REM sleep *The figure shows an increase in the time cats spend in REM sleep after various periods of REM-sleep deprivation. The animals were deprived of REM sleep (but not non-REM sleep) for from 5 to 72 days by being awakened as soon as their EEG indicated the beginning of a REM period. On the first day when the animals were finally allowed to sleep undisturbed, there was an increase in the proportion of time spent in REM sleep rather than non-REM sleep. (Data from Cohen, 1972)*

Biological rhythms in the vegetable world
The figure shows a morning glory opening over a four-hour period. This timing is driven by the plant's circadian biological clock. (Photographs by Takahisa Hirano/Nature Production)

and put back on the proper shelves, so that they can be looked up and found the next day. Evidence for some such process comes from rats who were first taught some task and then systematically deprived of REM sleep. When tested the next day, these animals performed worse than did control rats who suffered no REM deprivation (McGrath and Cohen, 1978; Smith, 1985).

SLEEP AS A CLOCK-DRIVEN PROCESS

Whether sleep really has a restorative function is by no means clear. But even if it does, that cannot be the whole story. For there is little doubt that the need for sleep partially depends on the time of day, regardless of the amount of prior sleep deprivation. People who go without sleep for several nights find that they feel more tired in the late evenings but more awake in the mornings, even though they didn't sleep the night (or nights) before. This shows that sleep is a **clock-driven** process (see Figure 3.26). In this regard, it resembles a number of other biological rhythms that seem to depend on built-in internal clocks. Some of these rhythms extend over a whole year, such as the seasonal patterns that determine migration, mating, and hibernation in many animals. Others are much shorter, such as the short rhythms of respiration and heart beat. In sleep, the rhythm spans about a twenty-four-hour day and is therefore called **circadian** (from the Latin, *circa,* "nearly," and *dies,* "day"). It originates from a clock circuit in the hypothalamus, which seems to be set by inputs from the optic nerve that inform the system of whether it is day or night. Disruptions of these clocks (e.g., through jet lag) can produce seriously debilitating motivational effects.★

3.26   The ticking of the brain's biological clock   *Activity of single cells in the superchiasmatic nucleus of a rat's hypothalamus. The regular day-night fluctuations in the firing rate of these cells demonstrate that the brain has a built-in biological clock. (From Carlson, 1991)*

SLEEP AS AN EVOLUTIONARY RELIC

The fact that sleep is related to the day-night cycle has led some investigators to suggest that it is a behavioral relic from earlier eons. They argue that while the desire for sleep is clearly an insistent motive, there is no reason to believe that it

★Some promising new treatments for certain emotional illnesses are based on the new realization that disturbances of biological clocks and sleep patterns can have radical effects upon moods (see Chapter 18, pp. 739–40).

serves a vital bodily need. They agree that the sleepless person seeks sleep just as the starved one craves food. But they point out that while starvation eventually leads to death, there is no evidence that even prolonged sleep deprivation will have such dire effects; it will make people drowsy, a bit confused, and desperately anxious for sleep, but little more. They suggest that sleep may be an evolutionary relic of former times, a built-in response system that once had an important adaptive function although it no longer does. A daily period of enforced near-immobility spent in some hiding place may have been quite useful to our animal ancestors; it would have helped them to conserve their energies and have kept them out of the way of possible predators. It is of little use to us now that we have·electric light bulbs and need fear no predators except those of our own kind, but it is no less powerful even so (Webb, 1974).

To sum up, while we know a great deal about the phenomena of sleep and some of the mechanisms that bring it about, we are as yet unsure about its functions. The desire for sleep is a powerful motive, and some twenty-five years of an average lifetime are devoted to it. But we're still not clear what it is really good for. (For discussion, see Webb, 1979, 1982; Horne, 1988).

Jacob's Dream *Dreams have often been regarded as a gateway between everyday reality and a more spiritual existence. An example is the biblical patriarch Jacob, who dreamed of angels descending and ascending a ladder between heaven and earth. (From the Lambeth Bible, England, twelfth century; courtesy of the Lambeth Palace Library)*

DREAMS

REM sleep was discovered fairly recently, but its discoverers almost immediately related it to a phenomenon surely known to humans since prehistoric times: dreaming.

DREAMING AND REM SLEEP

When sleeping subjects are awakened during REM sleep, they generally report a dream: a series of episodes that seemed real at the time. Not so for quiet (that is, non-REM) sleep. When awakened from quiet sleep, subjects may say that they were thinking about something, but they rarely relate the kind of inner drama we call a dream (Cartwright, 1977). Further evidence links the duration of the dream events to the length of the REM period. Subjects who are awakened five minutes after the onset of REM tend to describe shorter dreams than subjects awakened fifteen minutes after the REM period begins. This result argues against the popular notion that dreams are virtually instantaneous, no matter how long they take to relate when later recalled. In actual fact, the dream seems to take just about as long as the dream episode might have been in real life (Dement and Kleitman, 1957; Dement and Wolpert, 1958).

These findings suggest that the average adult dreams for about one and a half hours every night, the time spent in REM sleep. How can we square this statement with the fact that in everyday life many people seem to experience dreams only occasionally and that some deny they ever dream? The answer is that dreams are generally forgotten within minutes after they have occurred. In one study, subjects were awakened either during REM sleep or five minutes after a REM period had ended. In the first condition, detailed dream narratives were obtained on 85 percent of the narratives; in the second, there were none (Wolpert and Trosman, 1958).

Why dreams leave such fragile memories is something of a puzzle. One possibility is that the memory of the dream is ordinarily inaccessible because of a failure to relate the dream episode (when it occurs) to the many other memories of waking life (Koulack and Goodenough, 1976). This interpretation may explain some odd experiences in which we seem to remember something that we know did not occur. These may be recollections of a dream without the realization that it was a dream and not a real event. If so, it suggests that the insubstantial

Dreams *Salvador Dali depicts a dreamlike world in which various bizarre and disjointed images are interpreted by the dreamer to have symbolic meaning. (The Great Paranoic, by Salvador Dali, 1936; courtesy Museum Boymans-van Beuningen, Rotterdam)*

nature of our dream memories is a boon rather than a misfortune; it protects us from confusing the memories of our real, waking past with those of our dreams (Goodenough, 1978; Johnson and Raye, 1981).

DO DREAMS HAVE A FUNCTION?

The ancients believed that dreams have a prophetic function. In our own time, several theorists have argued that their function is related to the sleeper's personal problems. The most influential account was that of Sigmund Freud, who maintained that during dreams a whole host of primitive and forbidden impulses—mostly concerning sex and aggression—start to break through the barriers we erect against them while awake. The result is a compromise. The prohibited materials emerge, but only in a heavily masked and censored form. Freud believed that this explains why our dreams are so often strange and apparently senseless. According to Freud, they are only odd on the outside. If we look beneath the surface, we can recognize the disguised meaning, the hidden, unacceptable wishes that are cleverly masked and lie underneath (Freud, 1900).

During the last thirty years, more and more evidence has come up that has thrown considerable doubt on Freud's dream theory (for details, see Chapter 17). Today, many authors believe that dreams don't have the complex functions that Freud (let alone the ancients) maintained. An influential modern account is the ***activation-synthesis hypothesis,*** which holds that the dream is simply a reflection of the brain's aroused state during active sleep. During this period, the cerebral cortex is active, and its activity is manifested in conscious experience— the dream. But this dream experience necessarily has a special form. The cortex may be active, but it is largely shut off from sensory input. Under the circumstances, its activity is not constrained by the demands of external reality. Memory images become more prominent than they are in waking life, for they do not have to compete with the insistent here and now provided by the senses. The recent experiences of the day are evoked most readily, and they will then arouse a host of previous memories and intermingle with them. The cortex is sufficiently active to connect and interpret these raw materials so that we experience a running, inner narrative. But this is often accomplished in a primitive, disjointed way; perhaps the cortex is not active enough to provide more than a crude organization (Hobson and McCarley, 1977; Hobson, 1988).

A recent modification of the activation-synthesis hypothesis tries to explain why dreams feature certain sensations rather than others. One that is rarely present is the sensation of pain. We may dream of being chased and even caught by lions, but we rarely if ever experience any pain. Now if dreams are the brain's attempts to make sense of random images evoked during sleep, as the activation-synthesis hypothesis proposes, shouldn't the dream narrative incorporate pain when it is so obviously called for? According to the modified activation-synthesis hypothesis, the reason why pain (and a number of other sensations) is rarely incorporated into the dream narrative is that pain sensations are a crucial sentinel on duty against the reality outside. If there is genuine pain, the sleeper awakes so that he can deal with whatever genuine danger exists. A sleeper who is bitten by a wolf better wake up immediately. If instead he weaves the pain of the bite into the fabric of his dream, he risks never waking at all (Symons, 1993).

A final point pertains to the dreamer's own needs, conflicts, and preoccupations. These surely matter. For if the cerebral activity of active sleep is unconstrained by sensory reality, the content of dreams is likely to reflect the individuality of the dreamer. The raw materials of the dream are peculiarly *hers*: her thoughts, *her* memories, *her* emotions. Since objective sensory input is absent, these subjective sources are more prominent than they are in waking life. This is probably one of the reasons why dreams have so often been thought to have a deeper, more personal meaning (see Chapter 17).

WHAT DIFFERENT MOTIVES HAVE IN COMMON

The preceding sections have dealt with a number of motives that impel to action—hunger, thirst, fear, and so on. Some, such as hunger, are in the service of homeostasis and serve to maintain the internal environment. Others, such as fear and rage, are triggered by stimuli in the environment and are relevant to self-preservation. For a few others—the main example is sleep—the function is still unknown. These various motives are clearly very different, as are the goals toward which they steer the organism—food, water, escape from threat, a good night's sleep. Since all of them are motives, they all potentiate behavior (almost by definition), and so they affect what we do, what we see, and what we feel. But over and above this, is there something that all these motives and goals have in common?

THE PSYCHOLOGY OF REWARD AND THE AROUSAL LEVEL

A number of theorists have suggested that all—or at least most—motives can be described as a search for some *optimum level of arousal* or of general stimulation. One of the early controversies in this area was over the question of what the optimum level is.

DRIVE-REDUCTION THEORY

According to the *drive-reduction theory* proposed by Clark L. Hull some fifty years ago, the optimum level of arousal that organisms seek is essentially zero. Hull and his students were impressed by the fact that many motives seem directed at the reduction of some internal state of bodily tension that, if continued, would lead to injury or even death. Examples are food deprivation, water deprivation, pain, and so on. Hull believed that this is true for all motives. In his view, all built-in rewards produce some reduction of bodily tension (or, as he called it, of drive). This position amounts to the assertion that what we normally call pleasure is at bottom nothing else but the reduction of pain or discomfort. According to this view, what organisms strive for is the absolute minimum of all arousal and stimulation, a biopsychological version of the Eastern search for *Nirvana.*

In some ways, Hull's theory can be regarded as a homeostatic conception carried to its extreme. As Hull saw it, anything an organism does is ultimately directed at getting rid of some noxious state—pain, nutrient deficit, or whatever. One immediate difficulty is posed by sex, a motive that is clearly not homeostatic in the sense in which hunger and thirst are. To explain sexual satisfaction in drive-reduction terms, Hull and his students argued that what is rewarding about sexual activity is the drop in tension that occurs during orgasm (Hull, 1943).

AN OPTIMUM AROUSAL ABOVE ZERO

Hull's drive-reduction theory suggests that, in general, organisms seek minimum levels of stimulation, preferring peace and quiet to states of tension and arousal. But, in fact, this does not seem to be true. For there is little doubt that some experiences are actively sought after, like the taste of sweets and erotic stimulation. These are both felt to be positive pleasures rather than the mere removal of some irritant. Consider saccharin, a sweet substance that has no nutritive value and thus no effect on the bodily tension and deficit that underlie hunger. But rats and other animals will nevertheless drink a saccharine solution avidly (Sheffield and Roby, 1950).

Other findings concern sexual activity. In one study, male rats were run in a maze that had two end boxes. One was empty, while the other contained a sexually receptive female. When the male encountered the female, he usually mounted her. But an unsympathetic experimenter invariably separated the pair before ejaculation could occur. This meant that sexual tension was increased rather than decreased. But the males nevertheless chose the side of the maze that held the female and did so again and again. This shows that sexual stimulation is rewarding in its own right. Whether this point really requires experimental substantiation is debatable, considering that so many humans engage in sexual foreplay and try to lengthen the time before orgasm (Sheffield, Wulff, and Backer, 1951).

Such evidence demonstrates that drive reduction is not the only goal of motivated behavior. Similar conclusions emerge from work on curiosity and manipulation. Monkeys will go to considerable lengths to puzzle out how to open latches that are attached to a wooden board (see Figure 3.27). But when the latches are unlocked, nothing opens because the latches never closed anything in the first place. Since unlatching gets the animal nothing, the response was presumably its own reward. In this regard, monkeys act much like human beings, who in countless ways indicate that they often do things as ends in themselves, rather than as means to other ends.

Hull's theory is clearly untenable. To be sure, we do try to reduce arousal if our arousal level is unduly high, as in intense hunger or fear or pain. But in

3.27 Curiosity and manipulation
Young rhesus monkeys trying to open a latch. The monkeys received no special reward for their labors but learned to open the devices just "for the fun of it." (After Harlow, 1950; photograph courtesy of University of Wisconsin Primate Laboratory)

many other cases we apparently try to increase it. Hull's theory notwithstanding, this suggests that there is an above-zero optimum level of arousal. If we are above this optimum (for example, in pain), we try to reduce arousal. But if we are below it, we seek stimulation to ascend beyond it. This optimum undoubtedly varies from time to time and from one motive to another as befits their different biological functions, as in hunger arousal versus sexual arousal. Optimum arousal levels may also differ from person to person. According to some authors, some people are sensation seekers who generally look for stimulation, while others prefer a quieter existence (Zuckerman, 1979; see Chapter 16).

DRUGS AND ADDICTION

The normal ways of coping with an arousal level that is too high or too low are by actively engaging with the world outside. If we are overaroused, we move toward quiescence: We still our hunger, escape from pain, or go to sleep. If we are under aroused, we seek stimulation. In some cases, this may reach rather high-pitched levels—by prolonged sex play, by watching an effective horror movie, by riding on a roller coaster. But there is another way to create a drastic change of arousal. We can use drugs that artificially give us a "high" or a "low."

Drugs that change arousal level   Our present focus is on two major classes of drugs that have powerful effects: those that act as behavioral ***depressants*** and those that act as ***stimulants.***

Let's begin with the depressants. They include various sedatives (for example, barbiturates), alcohol, and the opiates (opium, heroin, and morphine).★ Their general effect is to depress the activity of all the neurons in the central nervous system. On the face of it that may seem surprising, since all of us have seen loud and aggressive drunks who seem anything but lethargic or depressed. The paradox is resolved if we recognize that their hyperexcitability is a case of disinhibition. At the first stage of inebriation (or at low doses of alcohol ingestion), the depression hits inhibitory synapses in the brain before it affects the excitatory ones. The usual constraints are relaxed, and the individual may engage in activities that he normally would not. Sexual inhibitions will be loosened, as will inhibitions against aggression. There may also be some initial euphoria. But with further alcohol ingestion, the depressive effects will hit all of the cerebral

---

★Strictly speaking, the opiates belong to a separate class. For unlike alcohol and other sedatives, they serve as narcotics (that is, pain relievers) and act on separate opiate receptors. In addition, one of their number—heroin—seems to be able to produce an unusually intense euphoric "rush," sometimes likened to intense sexual excitement, when taken intravenously.

A

B

C

***Seeking stimulation**   People have invented many activities to experience the paradoxical joy of fear and danger. (A) Some of these activities induce excitement but are known to be safe in reality, such as riding on roller coasters. (Photograph by Georg Gerster, Comstock) (B) Others are more dangerous but provide greater thrills, such as skydiving. (Photograph by Guy Sauvage, Agence Vandystadt/Photo Researchers) (C) In yet other activities the fear and danger are experienced vicariously, as in watching horror movies. Here, the heroine (played by Jodie Foster) is about to be attacked in the 1993 movie* Silence of the Lambs. *(Photograph courtesy of Photofest)*

centers. Now the excitement produced by disinhibition will give way to a general slowdown of activity. Attention and memory will blur, and bodily movement and speech will become increasingly uncoordinated, until finally the person will become completely incapacitated and lose consciousness.

The behavioral stimulants, which include amphetamine and cocaine, boost behavioral activity and can lead to an intense elevation of mood—a euphoric "rush" or "high" accompanied by feelings of enormous energy and increased self-esteem. This is especially so for cocaine, which some turn-of-the-century physicians (including Sigmund Freud) regarded as a miracle drug that produced boundless energy, exhilaration, and euphoria with no untoward side effects. This is unfortunately far from true, for the initial euphoria is bought at a considerable cost. Contrary to initial claims, amphetamines and cocaine often produce addictions that eventually become the user's primary focus in life. In addition, repeated use of cocaine (and amphetamines) can lead to extremely irrational states that resemble certain kinds of schizophrenia, in which there are delusions of persecution, irrational fears, and hallucinations (Siegel, 1984).

Tolerance and withdrawal   In many individuals, repeated drug use leads to **addiction.** One result is an increased **tolerance** for the drug, especially for the opiates, so that the addict requires ever-larger doses to obtain the same effect. A second consequence of addiction goes hand in hand with increased tolerance. When the drug is withheld, there are **withdrawal symptoms.** In general, these are the precise opposite of the effects produced by the drug itself. Thus heroin users deprived of their drug feel hyperexcitable; they are extremely irritable, are restless and anxious, and suffer insomnia. Similarly for the behavioral stimulants: The cocaine or amphetamine user's manic energy and elation give rise to severe emotional depression coupled with profound fatigue when the drug is withdrawn. The same antithesis holds for many physical symptoms. One characteristic of the opiates is that they lead to marked constipation. (They've been used for centuries to relieve diarrhea and dysentery.) But when the drug is withdrawn, the addict suffers violent diarrhea and related gastrointestinal symptoms (Julien, 1985; Volpicelli, 1989).

By its nature, addiction tends to be self-perpetuating. To begin with, the addict wants to regain the intense pleasure of his drug-induced euphoria (even though this euphoria will become harder and harder to obtain because of his increased tolerance). Even more important, perhaps, is the fact that the addict (especially the opiate addict) wants to escape the pangs of drug withdrawal. To dull those pains, he has to take another dose of the drug. But this may only strengthen the addiction and lead to even more intense withdrawal next time, and so on.

Further factors that underlie addiction are various local and psychological problems—in the family, at the workplace, or whatever (Alexander and Hadaway, 1982). Such problems often existed before the drug use began, and another dose or another drink is a way of escaping them for a while. But they can only be worsened by the addiction.

THE OPPONENT-PROCESS THEORY OF MOTIVATION

What accounts for the phenomena of drug use and drug addiction? Some suggestions come from the **opponent-process theory,** which offers a broad outline of how many motives are acquired.★ The opponent-process theory emphasizes the fundamental opposition of the various emotional feelings associated with pain and pleasure (such as fear and terror on the one hand, and joy and euphoria on the other). Its basic premise is that the nervous system has a general tendency to counteract any deviation from normal that is reminiscent of homeostasis. If there is too much of a swing to one pole of the pain-pleasure dimension, say toward joy and ecstasy, an opponent process is called into play that tilts the balance toward the negative side. Conversely, if the initial swing is toward terror or revulsion, there will be an opponent process toward the positive side. The net effect is that there will be an attenuation of the emotional state one happens to be in, so that ecstasy becomes mild pleasure and terror loses some of its force.

A further assumption of this theory is that repetitions of the initial emotional state will produce an increase in the power of the opponent process that is its antagonist (Solomon and Corbit, 1974; Solomon, 1980). This may explain the development of tolerance, the concomitant growth of the withdrawal state, and the resulting vulnerability to the vicious cycle of addiction. According to the theory, the emotional reaction produced by a behavioral stimulant such as amphetamine triggers an opponent process that pulls in the opposite direction. The more often the drug is taken, the stronger this opponent process becomes. The result is increased tolerance so that ever larger doses of the drug are required to produce an emotional high. The effect of the opponent process is revealed more starkly when the drug is withheld and there is no further pull toward the positive side of the emotional spectrum. Now all that remains is the opponent process whose strength has increased with every dose. This pulls the reaction in the opposite direction, resulting in the anguish of withdrawal (Solomon, 1980).

THE BIOLOGY OF REWARD

Thus far, we have discussed what the various motives that humans and animals strive to satisfy have in common psychologically. But one may also ask whether there are some underlying *physiological* commonalities. A number of investigators have asked whether there is a special region of the brain whose activation gives rise to what humans call "pleasure," a **pleasure center** that is triggered whenever a motive is satisfied, regardless of which motive it is. They have tried to answer this question by studying the rewarding effects of electrically stimulating various regions in the brain.

This general area of investigation was opened up in 1954 when James Olds and Peter Milner discovered that rats would learn to press a lever to give them-

★The term *opponent process* was originally used in the field of color vision where it designates neural processes that pull in opposite directions (See Chapter 5, pp. 192–94).

3.28 Self-stimulation in rats *The rat feels the stimulation of a pulse lasting less than a second. (Courtesy of Dr. M. E. Olds)*

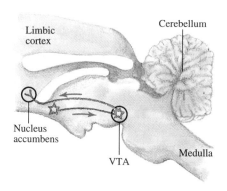

3.29 Pathways implicated in the rewarding effect of brain stimulation *The figure is a schematic cross-section of the lower part of a rat's brain, showing a descending pathway that stimulates dopamine-releasing neurons in the ventral tegmental area (VTA) that ascend to the nucleus accumbens. (After Rosenzweig and Leiman, 1989)*

selves a brief burst of electrical stimulation in certain regions of the limbic system (Olds and Milner, 1954; see Figure 3.28). Similar rewarding effects of self-stimulation have been demonstrated in a wide variety of animals, including cats, dogs, dolphins, monkeys, and human beings. To obtain it, rats will press a lever at rates up to 7,000 presses per hour for hours on end. When forced to opt between food and self-stimulation, hungry rats will typically opt for self-stimulation, even though it literally brings starvation (Spies, 1965).

SPECIFIC AND GENERAL PLEASURE CENTERS

What explains the rewarding effect of self-stimulation? Two possibilities suggest themselves. One is that brain stimulation mimics certain *specific* natural rewards. Stimulation in one region might fool the brain into assuming there had been eating, stimulation in another that there had been copulation, and so on. Another possibility is that self-stimulation provides a more *general,* nonspecific kind of pleasure, something that all rewards share. Drinking, eating, and copulating are obviously different, but perhaps the different motivational messages they send to the brain ("have just drunk, eaten, copulated") ultimately feed into a common neurological system that responds to all of them in much the same way ("that sure felt good").

There is evidence that the stimulation of certain areas provides rather specific rewards. For example, animals will work to obtain electrical stimulation of the lateral zone of the hypothalamus (the "hunger center") but how much they will work to get this reward depends on their hunger level. If they haven't eaten for a while, they will work much harder than they would otherwise. This suggests that the brain regards stimulation in this region as equivalent to food. Analogous effects are found for regions that are concerned with drinking or sexual behavior (Olds and Fobes, 1981).

THE DOPAMINE HYPOTHESIS OF REWARD AND DRUG EFFECTS

What is the physiological underpinning of the self-stimulation effect? A number of investigators believe that the key is in some dopamine releasing pathways in the brain. It is known that self-stimulation is most effective when it is applied to a bundle of nerve fibers called the **medial forebrain bundle (MFB).** According to some theorists, action potentials in some of these fibers will trigger activity of a second (and as yet unknown) group of cells that extend from a certain region in the midbrain (the **ventral tegmental area,** or **VTA**) to one in the base of the forebrain (the **nucleus accumbens**) and release dopamine at their axon terminals (see Figure 3.29). That dopamine is involved is shown by the fact that when drugs that serve as dopamine antagonists are injected into the nucleus accumbens (that is, into the region of the second group's axon terminals), brain stimulation is much less effective. Conversely, if drugs that serve as dopamine agonists are injected into that same area, the opposite effect occurs: Brain stimulation is very much more effective (Gallistel, Shizgal, and Yeomans, 1981; Stellar and Stellar, 1985; Wise and Rompre, 1989).

To explain these findings, some authors assume that the dopamine-triggered activation of fibers originating in the nucleus accumbens is interpreted by the brain as the neurological equivalent of "Good . . . let's have it again"—which may well be just another version of the general pleasure-center theory. One virtue of this hypothesis is that it helps to explain some of the phenomena of drug addiction. Both cocaine and amphetamine are dopamine agonists that enhance the levels of dopamine at the synapse. Cocaine does so by blocking dopamine reuptake (so that the transmitter stays around for a longer period); amphetamine has the same effect and also enhances the release of dopamine at the axon terminal. So once in the bloodstream, both drugs will eventually enter the nucleus accumbens and trigger the "Good . . . let's have it again" fibers. The opiates (and possibly alcohol) exert their effect by entering the VTA. Whether the drug is a depressant, such as heroin, or a stimulant, such as cocaine, the key to the addiction is that the drug provides something akin to pleasure (Wise, 1987; Wise and Bozarth, 1987; for discussion, see Gallistel, 1986).

As yet, we don't know how to put the various pieces of the brain-stimulation puzzle together to create a coherent picture of its physiological underpinnings. But there's reason to believe that when we do, we may understand much more than why rats (and dogs and dolphins) press levers that give certain portions of their brains small jolts of electric current. We may understand the neurological basis of natural rewards and motives, what it is in the brain that makes humans and animals record certain events as events they want to reexperience (such as eating when one is hungry, copulating when one is sexually aroused, and so on). And we may also understand something about the underlying biology of certain "unnatural" rewards like drugs to which some individuals may become addicted.

THE NATURE OF MOTIVES

To sum up, during the past fifty years, there has been enormous progress in our understanding of the psychology and physiology of the biological motives. But as yet, there is no agreement on what it is that the different biological motives have in common, in what ways a comfortable temperature, sufficient water and food, safety, a night's sleep, or sexual satisfaction are alike. Negative feedback can't be the answer, for while it underlies some motives, such as temperature regulation, thirst, and hunger, it can't easily account for others, such as sleep or sex. Nor can we find a common characteristic in arousal level. For some motives, such as sex, the optimum arousal level is high; for others, such as sleep, it is low. Perhaps all we can say is that these different satisfactions are things we seek and want, and for good biological reasons (though in the case of sleep that reason is still unknown).

It may be that there is no one characteristic that the various satisfactions of the biological motives have in common (although advocates of a general pleasure center would probably disagree). Like all scientists, psychologists are much happier when they get neat explanations, and one underlying explanation would be much neater than several different ones. But Nature did not design organisms to make psychologists happy; she designed organisms to do what they need to do to survive and to propagate their genes.

A final point: This chapter was concerned with a number of built-in motives—the biological goals we must attain in order to survive. But whenever we looked at a motive in detail (as in the case of human food selection), we saw that the specific nature of these goals depends not only on our biology but also on what we have learned and been taught. Just what we drink is not only a matter of our water balance: Except for Count Dracula, few members of our Western culture drink blood. By the same token, while we have to maintain certain nutrient levels, most of us would not be satisfied with a diet of grasshoppers. Similar concerns apply to what we fear and hate, or how we behave in sexual matters and when, where, and with whom. In all these cases, experience builds upon biology and gives form to the built-in basics with which we start. We learn—from the experience of our own lifetime and through culture, from the lifetime of hundreds of prior generations.

Evolution gave us a set of built-in, biological goals and a few built-in mechanisms for attaining them. Learning provides the way to modify these goals and to find ever more complex means to achieve them. We turn next to the mechanisms by which such learning occurs in humans and animals.

SUMMARY

1. Most human and animal actions are motivated. *Motives* have a two-fold function: They *direct* behavior toward or away from some goal by *potentiating* certain perceptions, behaviors, and feelings rather than others. They also serve to *activate* the organism, which becomes more aroused the greater the strength of the motive.

2. The biological basis of directed action is *negative feedback* in which the system "feeds back" upon itself to stop its own action. Built-in negative feedback is responsible for many reactions that maintain the stability of the organism's internal environment, or *homeostasis.* Special cells in the hypothalamus sense various aspects of the body's internal state, such as temperature. If this is above or below certain *setpoints,* a number of self-regulatory reflexes controlled by the *sympathetic* and *parasympathetic* divisions of the *autonomic nervous system* are triggered (for example, shivering). In addition, directed, voluntary acts (such as putting on a sweater) are also brought into play.

3. Similar homeostatic mechanisms underlie a number of other biological motives, such as *thirst.* The organism is informed about its water balance by *volume receptors* that monitor the total volume of its bodily fluids and by *osmoreceptors* that respond to the concentration of certain minerals dissolved in these fluids. Water losses are partially offset by reflex mechanisms, including the secretion of the *antidiuretic hormone (ADH),* which instructs the kidneys to reabsorb more of the water that passes through them. In addition, the organism readjusts its own internal environment by directed action— drinking.

4. The biological motive that has been studied most extensively is *hunger.* Many of the signals for feeding and satiety come from the internal environment. Feeding signals include nutrient levels in the bloodstream (which probably affect *glucoreceptors* in the brain) and metabolic processes in the liver (especially the *glucose-glycogen* balance). Satiety signals include messages from receptors in the stomach and the small intestine (particularly a satiety hormone, *cholecystokinin,* or *CCK*). Other feeding and satiety signals are external, including the *palatability* of the food.

5. Many authors believe that the control of feeding is lodged in two antagonistic centers in the hypothalamus whose excitation gives rise to hunger and satiety respectively. As evidence, they point to the effect of lesions. Destruction of the supposed hunger center leads to *aphagia,* a complete refusal to eat. Destruction of the supposed satiety center produces *hyperphagia,* a vast increase in food intake. The original *dual-center* theory has been modified by findings that suggest that the two centers affect not only the behavior of feeding but also food metabolism.

6. Homeostatic factors determine *that* an animal eats, but they have less of an effect on *what* it eats. Food selection is determined by a variety of factors, including built-in preferences and learning. Many animals are *neophobic*—afraid of anything that is new. They will only sample new foods in small amounts, developing a learned *taste aversion* if they turn out to be poisonous and adding them to their diet if they prove to be safe.

7. One feeding-related disorder is *obesity.* Some cases are produced by various constitutional factors, including genetically based metabolic efficiency and an overabundance of fat cells. Others are the result of various behavioral factors. According to the *externality hypothesis,* overweight people are comparatively insensitive to internal hunger signals and oversensitive to external ones such as palatability. An alternative is the *setpoint hypothesis,* which asserts that overweight people have a higher internal setpoint for weight.

SUMMARY

8.   Other eating disorders are *anorexia nervosa* in which there is a pattern of relentless self-starvation, sometimes to the point of death, and *bulimia,* which is characterized by repeated binge-and-purge bouts.

9.   In contrast to thirst and hunger, which are largely based on homeostatic factors from within, a number of motives are instigated from without. An example is the intense reaction to external threat. Its biological mechanisms include the operations of the *autonomic nervous system.* This consists of two antagonistic branches. One is the *parasympathetic nervous system,* which serves the vegetative functions of everyday life, such as digestion and reproduction. It slows down the heart rate and reduces blood pressure. The other is the *sympathetic nervous system,* which activates the body and mobilizes its resources. It increases the available metabolic fuels and accelerates their utilization by increasing the heart rate and respiration. Intense sympathetic activity can be regarded as an *emergency reaction,* which underlies the overt reactions of *fight* or *flight* and their usual emotional concomitants, rage or fear.

10.   The sympathetic emergency reaction is not always adaptive. It can produce temporary disruptions of digestive and sexual functions, and can also lead to more permanent psychophysiological disorders.

11.   Among the stimuli that set off the sympathetic emergency reaction is *pain.* This has survival value for it is a signal to react to danger. But since continued pain may interfere with appropriate action, a counteracting process alleviates pain. The mechanism involves the *endorphins,* a group of neurotransmitters secreted within the brain that stimulate nerve tracts that inhibit the transmission of pain messages. The endorphins may explain the pain-relieving effect of *placebos,* substances that the patient believes will help him even though they are chemically inert.

12.   While the sympathetic system arouses the more primitive physiological processes of the body, several subcortical structures arouse and wake the brain. These waking systems are opposed by antagonistic processes that lead to sleep. During sleep, brain activity changes as shown by the *electroencephalogram* or *EEG.* Each night, we oscillate between two kinds of sleep. One is *quiet sleep,* during which the cortex is relatively inactive. The other is *active sleep,* characterized by considerable cortical activity and *rapid eye movements* or *REMs,* a pattern of internal activity during which dreams are experienced. *Sleep-deprivation* studies show that when one or the other kind of sleep is prevented, it is to some extent made up later on. This suggests that there is a need for each of the two sleep states, but the biological functions served by either are as yet unknown. One hypothesis is that one or both forms of sleep serve a *restorative function,* but this can't be the only reason, since sleep is a *clock-driven* process that partially depends on the time of day, regardless of the individual's state of exhaustion. Another hypothesis is that sleep represents an *evolutionary relic* of ancestral adaptive patterns.

13.   According to *drive-reduction theory,* all built-in motives act to reduce stimulation and arousal. Today most authors believe instead that organisms strive for an *optimum level of arousal.* If below this optimum, they try to increase arousal by various means.

14.   One way of coping with an arousal level that is too high or too low is by the use of drugs. Some drugs act as *depressants,* including alcohol and the opiates. Others, such as the *amphetamines* and *cocaine,* act as *stimulants.* In many individuals, repeated drug use leads to *addiction,* accompanied by increased *tolerance* and *withdrawal effects* if the drug is withheld.

15.   The *opponent-process theory of motivation* tries to explain these and many other phenomena by arguing that all shifts of arousal level produce a counteracting process that acts to moderate the ups and downs. When the original instigator of the shift is removed, the opponent process is revealed more clearly, as in withdrawal effects.

16.   Work on the rewarding effects of certain regions of the brain has led to speculations about possible *pleasure centers* in the brain. There is evidence that stimulation of certain areas leads to specific reward effects. According to the *dopamine hypothesis of reward,* the neural underpinnings of such reward effects lie in the activation of fibers that originate in a brain structure called the *nucleus accumbens* and are triggered by dopamine. According to the hypothesis, their activation is the neurological equivalent of "Good ... let's have it again!"

CHAPTER

4

LEARNING

HABITUATION 106

CLASSICAL CONDITIONING 107

PAVLOV AND THE CONDITIONED REFLEX ■ THE MAJOR PHENOMENA OF
CLASSICAL CONDITIONING ■ EXTENSIONS OF CLASSICAL CONDITIONING

INSTRUMENTAL CONDITIONING 115

THORNDIKE AND THE LAW OF EFFECT ■ SKINNER AND OPERANT
BEHAVIOR ■ THE MAJOR PHENOMENA OF INSTRUMENTAL CONDITIONING

COGNITIVE LEARNING 126

A COGNITIVE VIEW OF CLASSICAL CONDITIONING ■ A COGNITIVE VIEW
OF INSTRUMENTAL CONDITIONING

VARIETIES OF LEARNING 136

BIOLOGICAL CONSTRAINTS ON ASSOCIATIVE LEARNING: BELONGINGNESS
■ ADAPTIVE SPECIALIZATIONS OF LEARNING ■ SIMILARITIES IN WHAT
DIFFERENT SPECIES LEARN

COMPLEX COGNITION IN
ANIMALS 142

COGNITIVE MAPS ■ INSIGHTFUL BEHAVIOR

TAKING STOCK 147

SUMMARY 148

Thus far, our discussion has centered on the built-in facets of human and animal behavior, the general neural equipment that provides the underpinning for everything we do, and the specific, innate feedback systems that underlie directed action. But much of what we do and are goes beyond what nature gave us and is acquired through experience in our lifetime. People learn—to grasp a baby bottle, to eat with a knife and fork, to read and write, to love or hate their neighbors, and eventually, to face death. In animals, the role of learning may be less dramatic, but it is enormously important for them too.

What can psychology tell us about the processes whereby organisms learn? Consider Descartes' reflex-machine conception, which we discussed in the preceding chapters. Reflexes are built-in links between afferent neural messages coming from outside and efferent commands to the muscles or glands. In effect they represent connections that are *hardwired,* a term that derives from the computer industry and refers to a circuit that is built into the machine itself. Such hardwired connections underlie many of the behavior patterns of both animals and humans and are presumably established because they proved to be adaptive in the species' evolutionary past. However, much of what we and animals do is not based on the evolutionary past but rather on what we and they experience in our own lifetimes. A squirrel has a built-in tendency to bury nuts in the fall and to look for them in the winter. But this alone will not get the squirrel through the winter; the animal must also remember where it buried the nuts in the first place. Hardwired connections are clearly not enough, for no squirrel is born knowing that it buried a walnut under Farmer MacDonald's tree.

A number of investigators have tried to reconcile the phenomena of learning with the reflex-machine conception. The adherents of this approach, whose modern exponents are sometimes called *behavior theorists,* argue that the organism's hardwired repertory of behaviors is supplemented by continual *rewirings* that are produced by experience. Some of these rewirings consist of new connections between stimuli. Thus, the sight of the mother's face may come to signify the taste of milk. Other rewirings involve new connections between acts and their consequences, as when a toddler learns that touching a hot radiator is followed by a painful burn. The behavior theorists set themselves the task of discovering how such rewirings come about.

The behavior theorists' interest in the learning process was admirably suited to the intellectual climate during the first part of this century, especially in the United States. For here was a society that was deeply committed to the individual's efforts to improve himself by pushing himself on to greater efforts and acquiring new skills—in numerous public schools and colleges, in night classes for recent immigrants, dance classes for the shy, courses for those who wanted to "win friends and influence people," and martial-arts classes for those less interested in winning friends than in defeating enemies. There was—and in many ways still is—an enormous faith in the near-limitless malleability of human beings, who were thought to be almost infinitely perfectible by proper changes in their environment, especially through education. Under the circumstances, it was hardly surprising that learning became (and remains) one of the paramount concerns of American psychology.

Habituation in Siamese fighting fish
Male Siamese fighting fish adopt a fighting posture when they see another male, but after a while they habituate to his presence. (Photograph by Bette Splendens/Oxford Scientific Films)

Alarm

No alarm

4.1 Innate fear of hawks or habituation?
Young turkeys run for cover when a silhouette model is pulled in the direction of the model's short end, which makes it look like a bird of prey, but not when it is pulled in the opposite direction, which makes it look like a goose. (After Tinbergen, 1951)

How should the learning process be studied? At least initially, most behavior theorists felt that there were some basic laws that come into play, regardless of what is learned or who does the learning—be it a dog learning to sit on command or a college student learning integral calculus. This early conception was very influential. It led to the view that even the most involved learned activities are made up of simpler ones, much as complex chemical compounds are made up of simpler atoms. Given this belief, it was only natural that the early investigators concentrated their efforts on trying to understand learning in simple situations and in (relatively) simple creatures like dogs, rats, and pigeons. By so doing, they hoped to strip the learning process down to its bare essence so that its basic laws might be revealed.

As we will see, some of the beliefs of the early behavior theorists had to be modified in the light of later discoveries. They never succeeded in finding *one* set of laws that underlie *all* phenomena of learning in *all* organisms, including humans. But even so, their search led to the major discoveries that form the basis of much of what we know today. It is to these that we now turn.

HABITUATION

Perhaps the simplest of all forms of learning is **habituation.** This is a decline in the tendency to respond to stimuli that have become familiar due to repeated exposure. A sudden noise usually startles us—an adaptive reaction, for sudden and unfamiliar stimuli often spell danger. But suppose the same noise is repeated over and over again. The second time, the startle will be diminished, the third time it will hardly be evoked, and after that, it will be ignored altogether. We have become habituated to the noise. Much the same holds for many other everyday events. We have become so accustomed to the ticking of a clock in the living room that we are utterly unaware of it until it finally stops. By the same token, city dwellers become completely habituated to the noise of traffic but are kept awake by the crickets when they take a vacation in the country.★

What is the adaptive significance of habituation? One of its major benefits is that it narrows down the range of stimuli that elicit escape reactions. After all, organisms have to eat and drink and mate to survive, and they can't do so if they spend all their time running away from imaginary enemies. Habituation allows them to ignore the familiar and focus their emergency reactions on things that are new and may signal danger (Wyers, Peeke, and Herz, 1973; Shalter, 1984).

An example of the role of habituation in focusing escape reactions is the response of ground-living birds to the sight of birds flying above. Some early experiments studied the reaction of young turkeys to a cardboard silhouette of a bird pulled overhead on a string. The silhouette had a short end and a long end (see Figure 4.1). When pulled so that the long end pointed forward (which made it look like a goose with an outstretched neck), the young turkeys were nonchalant. But when it was pulled in the opposite direction, the birds became terrified and ran for cover. Now the short end pointed forward, and the silhou-

★There is some debate about whether habituation is really a different kind of learning from certain others we'll describe later, such as classical and instrumental conditioning. According to some authors, it only refers to a certain experimental procedure used to establish the effect (Rescorla and Holland, 1976).

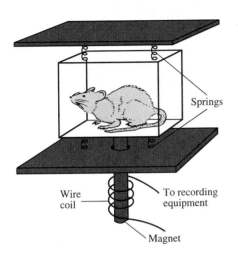

4.2 An apparatus that measures the startle response in rats *A small chamber is balanced on springs. The bottom of the chamber is attached to a magnet that is surrounded by a coil of wire. Sudden movements of the rat will lead to movements of the chamber that produce an electrical current in the wire. (After Hoffman and Fleshler, 1964)*

Springs

Wire coil

To recording equipment

Magnet

ette resembled a hawk. Some authors took this result as evidence that ground-living birds have a built-in fear reaction to birds of prey (Tinbergen, 1951). But further studies suggested that the effect was a result of novelty and habituation. In the turkey's environment, long-necked geese and ducks flying overhead were fairly common, while hawks were hardly ever seen. As a result, the turkeys had become habituated to the one and not the other. The young birds began with a fear reaction to just about everything. Given time and habituation, familiarity bred neglect. As a result, their fear reaction could be narrowed down to the rather infrequent stimuli—the short-necked hawks overhead—that the animal indeed has good reason to fear (Schleidt, 1961).

Laboratory studies have shown that habituation comes in two varieties. One is a short-term effect that dissipates in a matter of minutes. A second is more long term; it may persist for days or weeks. That these two are different makes intuitive sense. We gradually habituate to a certain noise; but if a year elapses without the noise, that same sound might well frighten us again. These two facets of habituation were demonstrated in a study of rats that were exposed to a high-pitched, loud tone presented for two seconds (Leaton, 1976). Initially, the stimulus produced a marked startle response. The rat literally jumped up in the air when it heard the tone (see Figure 4.2). To measure **short-term habituation,** the experimenters presented three hundred of these tones within the space of five minutes. Presented in this manner, the startle quickly wore off. After one hundred or so presentations, the animal ignored the now familiar tones. The experimenters next asked whether this nonchalance wore off after longer intervals. It evidently did, for when tested after a twenty-four-hour interval the rats jumped just as much as they did at the start of their last short-term training—a phenomenon called **spontaneous recovery.** To demonstrate **long-term habituation,** the investigators presented the same tone just once a day over an eleven-day period. They found that the startle response gradually declined over days. This shows that there is a long-term memory effect as well as a short-term effect. In some fashion, the animal compares what it now hears and sees with what else it has previously heard and seen, either in its immediate or its more remote past. To the extent that the current stimulus matches what is in its memory, it is judged to be familiar and thus not "startling" (Wagner, 1979; Whitlow and Wagner, 1984). We will have occasion to revisit the distinction between short- and long-term memory storage in a later chapter (see Chapter 7).

CLASSICAL CONDITIONING

In habituation, an organism learns to recognize an event as familiar, but it doesn't learn anything about the relation between that event and any other circumstances. Such learned relationships among events linked in space or time are often called **associations.**

There's little doubt that much of what we learn consists of various associations between events: between thunder and lightning, between the nipple and food, between the sound of a thumping motor and a large automobile repair bill. The importance of associations in human learning and thinking has been emphasized since the days of the Greek philosophers, but the experimental study of associations did not begin until the end of the nineteenth century. A major step in this direction was the work on conditioning performed by the great Russian scientist, Ivan Petrovich Pavlov (1849–1936).

Ivan Petrovich Pavlov in his laboratory, with some colleagues and best friend
(Courtesy of The Bettman Archive)

PAVLOV AND THE CONDITIONED REFLEX

Ivan Petrovich Pavlov had already earned the Nobel Prize for his work on digestion before he embarked upon the study of conditioning that was to gain him even greater fame. His initial interest was in the built-in nervous control of the various digestive reflexes in dogs; most important to us, the secretion of saliva. He surgically diverted one of the ducts of the salivary gland, thus channeling part of the salivary flow through a special tube to the outside of the animal's body where it could be easily measured and analyzed. Pavlov demonstrated that salivation was produced by several innate reflexes and serves to prepare the food for digestion. This is triggered by food (especially dry food) placed in the mouth.

In the course of Pavlov's work a new fact emerged. The salivary reflex could be set off by stimuli that at first were totally neutral. Dogs that had been in the laboratory for a while would soon salivate to a whole host of stimuli that had no such effect on their uninitiated fellows. Not only the taste and touch of the meat in the mouth, but its mere sight, the sight of the dish in which it was placed, the sight of the person who usually brought it, even that person's footsteps—eventually all of these might produce salivation. Pavlov soon decided to study such effects in their own right, for he recognized that they provided a means of extending the reflex concept to embrace learned as well as innate reactions. The approach was simple enough. Instead of waiting for accidental events in each animal's history, the experimenter would provide those events himself. Thus he would repeatedly sound a bell and always follow it with food. Later he observed what happened when the bell was sounded and no food was given (Pavlov, 1927; Figure 4.3).

The fundamental finding was simple: Repeated bell-food pairings led to salivation when the bell was presented alone (that is, unaccompanied by food) on occasional test trials. To explain this, Pavlov proposed a distinction between unconditioned and conditioned reflexes. **Unconditioned reflexes** he held to be

4.3 Apparatus for salivary conditioning
The figure shows an early version of Pavlov's apparatus for classical conditioning of the salivary response. The dog was held in a harness; sounds or lights functioned as conditioned stimuli, while meat powder in a dish served as the unconditioned stimulus. The conditioned response was assessed with the aid of a tube connected to an opening in one of the animal's salivary glands. (After Yerkes and Morgulis, 1909)

essentially inborn and innate; these are unconditionally elicited by the appropriate stimulus regardless of the animal's history. An example is food in the mouth, which unconditionally elicits salivation. In contrast, **conditioned reflexes** were acquired; thus they were conditional upon the animal's past experience and, according to Pavlov, based upon newly formed connections in the brain.

According to Pavlov, every unconditioned reflex is based upon a (presumably built-in) connection between an **unconditioned stimulus (US)** and an **unconditioned response (UR).** In Pavlov's laboratory, these were food in the mouth (the US) and salivation (UR). The corresponding terms for the conditioned reflex are **conditioned stimulus (CS)** and **conditioned response (CR).** The CS would be an initially neutral stimulus, that is, some stimulus (here, the bell) that does not elicit the CR without prior conditioning. The CR (here again, salivation) is the response elicited by the CS after some such pairings of CS and US. These various relationships are summarized in Figure 4.4 and constitute the basis of what is now known as **classical conditioning.★**

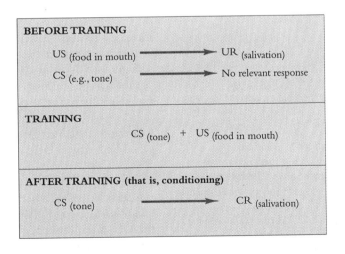

4.4 Relationships between CS, US, CR, and UR in classical conditioning

---

★The adjective "classical" is used, in part, as dutiful tribute to Pavlov's eminence and historical priority and, in part, to distinguish this form of conditioning from *instrumental conditioning* to which we will turn later.

THE MAJOR PHENOMENA OF CLASSICAL CONDITIONING

Pavlov saw conditioning as a way of extending the reflex concept into the realm of learning. Later workers (especially in the United States) were not as convinced that the so-called conditioned reflex is in fact some kind of reflex, even one that is modified. As a result, they substituted the more neutral term "response" for "reflex," as in "unconditioned response." But until quite recently, most of them shared Pavlov's conviction that conditioning was essentially a change in what the animal does, and so they also focused on the acquisition of the conditioned response. As we will see, later workers came to see conditioning in rather different ways. But we will begin by describing Pavlov's empirical discoveries with a minimum of editorial comment, for these findings laid the foundations for all subsequent theories of classical conditioning and indeed of much of learning generally.

ACQUISITION OF CONDITIONED RESPONSES

Pavlov noted that the tendency of the conditioned stimulus (CS) to elicit the conditioned response (CR) goes up the more often the CS and the unconditioned stimulus (US) have been paired together. Clearly then, presenting the US together with (or more typically, subsequent to) the CS is a critical operation in classical conditioning. Such a pairing is said to *reinforce* the connection; trials on which the US occurs and trials on which it is omitted are called **reinforced** and **unreinforced trials** respectively.

Measuring the strength of the CR   There are a number of ways in which the strength of a CR can be measured. One is **response amplitude:** In Pavlov's experiments, this was the amount of saliva secreted when the CS was presented without the US. Another measure is **probability of response:** the proportion of trials on which the CR is made when the CS is presented alone. Yet another measure is **response latency:** the time from the onset of CS to the CR. In contrast to amplitude and probability of response, which increase as CR strength increases, response latency varies inversely with CR strength: The shorter the latency, the stronger the CR.

Figure 4.5 is an idealized learning curve in which the strength of the CR is plotted against successive reinforced trials. In this and other conditioning trials, the general trend is very clear and unsurprising. The strength of the response increases with the number of reinforced trials: The more often a bell's ringing is followed by food for the dog, the greater the amount of saliva the dog produces when he hears the bell.

Second-order conditioning   Once the CS-US relation is solidly established, the CS can serve to condition yet further stimuli. To give one example, Pavlov first conditioned a dog to salivate to the beat of a metronome, using meat powder as the US. After a number of such pairings, he presented the animal with a black square followed by the metronome beat, but without ever introducing the food. Eventually the sight of the black square alone was enough to produce salivation. This phenomenon is called **second-order conditioning.** The metronome, which served as the CS in first-order conditioning, now functioned as the US for a second-order conditioned response. In effect, the black square had become a signal for the metronome, which in turn had previously signaled the appearance of food.

4.5   An idealized learning curve
Strength of the CR is plotted against the number of reinforced trials. The curve presents the results of many such studies, which by and large show that the curve is negatively accelerated: Strength of the CR rises with increasing number of trials, but each trial adds less strength than the trial just before it.

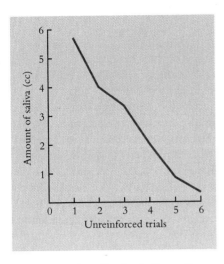

4.6 Extinction of a classically conditioned response *The figure shows the decrease in the amount of saliva secreted (the CR) with increasing number of extinction trials—that is, trials on which the CS is presented without the US. (After Pavlov, 1928)*

4.7 Generalization gradient of a classically conditioned response *The figure shows the generalization of a conditioned blinking response in rabbits. The CS was a tone of 1,200 hertz, and the US was electric shock. After the conditioned response to the original CS was well established, generalization was measured by presenting various test stimuli, ranging from 400 hertz to 2,000 hertz and noting the percent of the trials on which the animals gave the CR. The figure shows the results, averaged over several testing sessions. (After Moore, 1972)*

EXTINCTION

The adaptive value of conditioning is self-evident. A zebra's chance of future survival is enhanced by conditioning. There's much to be gained by a conditioned fear reaction to a place from which a lion has pounced some time before (assuming, of course, that the zebra managed to survive the CS-US pairing in the first place). On the other hand, it would be rather inefficient if a connection once established could never be undone. The lion might change its lair, and its former prowling place might now be perfectly safe for grazing.

Pavlov showed that a conditioned reaction can be undone. He demonstrated that the conditioned response will gradually disappear if the CS is repeatedly presented without being reinforced by the US; in his terms, the CS-US link undergoes *experimental extinction.* Figure 4.6 presents an extinction curve from a salivary extinction experiment. As usual, response strength is measured along the *y*-axis, while the *x*-axis indicates the number of extinction trials (that is, trials without reinforcement). As extinction trials proceed, the salivary flow dries up. In effect, the dog has learned that the CS is no longer a signal for food.

A conditioned response that has been extinguished can be resurrected. One means is through *reconditioning,* that is, by presenting further reinforced trials. Typically, reconditioning requires fewer reinforced trials to bring the CR to its former strength than were necessary during the initial conditioning session, even if extinction trials had been continued until the animal stopped responding altogether. The conditioned response was evidently not really abolished by extinction but instead was somehow masked.

The fact that the conditioned response is only masked rather than abolished by extinction is also shown by the phenomenon of *spontaneous recovery.* An extinguished CR will usually reappear after a rest interval during which the animal is left to its own devices. This effect is reminiscent of a similar phenomenon in habituation. In both cases, the sheer passage of time leads to the spontaneous recovery of a response: In the one case, the resurrected response had previously been habituated; in the other, it had been extinguished. The interpretation of these effects is still a matter of some debate. According to a recent analysis, the animal gradually loses interest in the CS as extinction proceeds and no longer looks or listens to it. After an interval away from the situation, it attends to the CS once again and therefore resumes responding. In principle, a similar analysis might account for the spontaneous recovery of habituation (Robbins, 1990).

GENERALIZATION

So far our discussion has been confined to situations in which the animal is tested with the *identical* stimulus that had served as the CS during training. But of course in the real world the stimuli are never really identical. The master's voice may signal food, but the exact intonation will surely vary from one occasion to another. Can the dog still use whatever it has learned before? If it can't, its conditioned response will be of little benefit. In fact, animals do respond to stimuli other than the original CS, so long as these are sufficiently similar.

This phenomenon is called *stimulus generalization.* A dog may be conditioned to respond to a tone of 1,000 hertz (cycles per second); nevertheless, the CR will be obtained not just with that tone, but also with tones of different frequencies, like 900 or 1,100 hertz. But the CR evoked by such new stimuli will show a *generalization decrement;* it will be weaker than the CR elicited by the original CS. The greater the difference between the new stimulus and the original CS, the larger this decrement will be. The resulting curve is called a *generalization gradient* (see Figure 4.7).

DISCRIMINATION

Stimulus generalization is not always beneficial. A tiger may be similar to a kitten; but someone who generalizes from one to the other is likely to be sorry. What he must do instead is discriminate—and not try to pet the tiger.

The phenomenon of *discrimination* is readily demonstrated in the laboratory. A dog is first conditioned to salivate to a CS, for example, a black square (CS^+). After the CR is well established, reinforced trials with the black square are randomly interspersed with nonreinforced trials with another stimulus, say, a gray square (CS^-). This continues until the animal discriminates perfectly, always salivating to CS^+, the reinforced stimulus, and never to CS^-, the nonreinforced stimulus. Of course the dog does not reach this final point immediately. During the early trials it will be confused, or more precisely, it will generalize rather than discriminate. It will tend to salivate to CS^- (which, after all, is quite similar to CS^+); by the same token, it will often fail to salivate when presented with CS^+. Such errors gradually become fewer and fewer until perfect discrimination is finally achieved. Not surprisingly, the discrimination gets harder and harder the more similar the two stimuli are. As similarity increases, the tendency to respond to CS^+ will increasingly generalize to CS^-, while the tendency not to respond to CS^- will increasingly generalize to CS^+. As a result, the dog will require many trials before it finally responds without error.

One might think that the difficulty in forming a discrimination is that the animal has trouble telling the two stimuli apart. But that is usually not the reason. The dog's problem is not that it can't form a sensory discrimination between CS^+ and CS^-. What is at fault is not its eyesight, for it can distinguish between the dark-gray and light-gray squares visually. Its difficulty is in discovering and remembering which stimulus is *right*—which goes with the US and which does not. Eventually the animal learns, but this doesn't mean that it has learned to see the stimuli differently. What it has learned is their significance; it now knows which stimulus is which.

EXTENSIONS OF CLASSICAL CONDITIONING

Thus far, we have mainly looked at laboratory phenomena such as dogs salivating to bells, lights, and metronomes. Needless to say, conditioning would be of little interest if it only applied to those phenomena. But in actual fact, its scope is very much larger than this.

To begin with, classical conditioning has been found in a large variety of animal species other than dogs, including ants and anteaters, cats and cockroaches, pigeons and people. Thus, crabs have been conditioned to twitch their tail spines, fish to thrash about, and octopuses to change color. Responses conditioned in laboratory studies with humans include the galvanic skin response (where the US is typically a loud noise or electric shock) and the blink-reaction of the eyelid (where the US consists of a puff of air on the open eye; Kimble, 1961).

Nor is classical conditioning restricted to the laboratory, for it plays a considerable role in our everyday life. Many of our feelings and urges are probably the result of classical conditioning. We tend to feel hungry at mealtimes and less so during the times between; this is so even if we fast a whole day. Another example is sexual arousal. This is often produced by a partner's special word or gesture whose erotic meaning is very private and is surely learned.

4.8   Response suppression   *A rat is trained to press a lever at a steady rate to gain food. The figure plots the extent to which this response is suppressed after successive presentations of a three-minute light CS that is immediately followed by electric shock. After twelve such trials, suppression is at 100 percent, and the animal doesn't respond at all during the three minutes when the CS is presented. (Data from Kamin, 1969)*

CONDITIONED FEAR

Of special importance is the role of classical conditioning in the formation of various emotional reactions, especially those concerned with fear. A common consequence of a conditioned fear reaction is *response suppression.* The CS will evoke fear, which in turn will suppress whatever other activities the animal is currently engaged in. This is the basis of a widely used technique to study fear conditioning, the **conditioned emotional response (CER)** procedure. A hungry rat is first taught to press a lever for an occasional food reward. After a few training sessions, the rat will press at a steady rate. Now classical conditioning can start. While the animal is pressing, a CS is presented—a light or a tone that will stay on for, say, three minutes. At the end of that period, the CS terminates and the rat receives a mild, brief electric shock (the US). Some twenty minutes later, the same CS-US sequence is repeated. After this, there is another twenty-minute interval during which neither the CS nor the US are presented, followed by yet another CS-US sequence, and so on (Estes and Skinner, 1941; Kamin, 1965). After twelve such trials, the response is completely suppressed—the rat will no longer press the lever (see Figure 4.8).

It is a plausible guess that many adult fears are based upon classical conditioning, acquired in much the same way that fear is acquired in the laboratory. These fears may be relatively mild or very intense (if intense enough, they are called **phobias**). They may be acquired in early childhood or during particular traumatic episodes in later life. An extreme example is an Air Force pilot who bailed out of his plane but whose parachute failed to open until five seconds before he hit the ground. In such traumatic episodes, conditioning apparently occurs in a single trial. This seems reasonable enough, for it would certainly be unadaptive if the pilot had to bail out on ten separate occasions, each time barely escaping death, before he finally developed a conditioned fear reaction (Sarnoff, 1957).★

THE RELATION BETWEEN CR AND UR

The phenomenon of fear conditioning brings us to an important question that we have neglected up to now: What is the relation between the CR and the UR? In salivary conditioning, the CR and the UR seem to be rather similar, a fact that fits in very nicely with Pavlov's attempt to extend the reflex conception to encompass learned modifications of behavior. But on closer examination, the CR and the UR are rarely if ever identical. This is quite apparent in fear conditioning. When exposed to electric shock, the US, the animal makes little jumps and its heart beats faster; when it hears or sees the CS that signals the shock, it stops moving, tenses itself, and its heart beats more slowly. The difference between the CR and the UR is found even in salivary conditioning. To be sure, Pavlov's dogs salivated both when they heard the CS and when they experienced the US. But when the dog responds to the US, its saliva is more copious and much richer in digestive enzyme than when it reacts to the CS.

All of this makes good biological sense. The CS often serves as a preparatory signal for the US, but does not become a substitute for it. The response to the CS (the CR) is essentially a preparation for the US; while the response to the US (that is, the UR) performs the task for which the organism is now prepared (for discussion, see Zener, 1937; Holland, 1984; Hollis, 1984).

★A number of theorists suggest that there is a built-in predisposition or preparedness to acquire certain phobias, such as a fear of snakes, more readily than others. (See Chapter 18, p. 746.)

CONDITIONING AND DRUG EFFECTS

In some situations, the CR is not just different from the UR, but is actually its very opposite. This effect is often encountered in studies on the conditioning of drug effects. Suppose a person gets many doses of insulin, which depletes blood sugar. After a number of such insulin injections, the bodily reaction to various stimuli that accompany the drug (such as the sight of the needle) is the exact opposite of the response to the drug itself: Given those stimuli, the blood-sugar level goes *up*. Put in conditioning terms, the US is the insulin, the UR is a decrease in blood sugar, the CS is the sight of the needle (or some other stimulus that generally accompanies the injection), and the CR is an increase in blood sugar level. Note that in this situation the CR is the exact opposite of the UR. It is as if the body prepares itself for the chemical agent it is about to receive and does so by adopting a compensatory reaction that tilts the other way (Siegel, 1977).

This compensatory-reaction hypothesis has some important consequences for our understanding of drug addiction. Consider opiates such as morphine or heroin, which we discussed in the previous chapter. These have various effects, such as relief from pain, euphoria, and relaxation. But after repeated administrations, stimuli that usually precede the injection of these drugs (for example, the sight of the hypodermic needle) produce effects that go in the opposite direction: depression, restlessness, and an increased sensitivity to pain. Some authors believe that these effects represent a compensatory reaction in which the response to the CS counteracts the reaction triggered by the US. As a result, the user develops **drug tolerance.** To make up for the conditioned compensatory reaction, the addict must inject herself with increasingly larger doses of the drug to obtain the same effect that was produced when she took it for the first time.

Now suppose the user takes the drug in a *new* environment. She now risks a dangerous overdose. She has increased her drug dose to overcome the compensatory reaction of various conditioned stimuli. But in a new environment, there may be a generalization decrement. Since many of the old conditioned stimuli are altered or missing, there will be a weaker CR, thus a weaker compensatory response. The result may be death by overdose—a lethal side effect of classical conditioning.

That effects of this sort may play some such role in some cases of drug mortality is suggested by interviews with heroin overdose survivors. A number of these reported that on the occasion when they had injected themselves to near-fatal effect, their dose was no greater than usual. What differed were the circumstances under which they took the drug—the place, the company, and so on. Parallel results come from work with rats given heroin injections for a month and then subjected to a larger dose in the same place or in a different environment. When the environment was altered, the larger dose was much more harmful (Siegel et al., 1982; Siegel, 1983).

The compensatory-reaction hypothesis is still a subject of considerable debate, however, for it is as yet unclear under what conditions a CR will be similar to the UR and under what others it will be the very opposite. In all likelihood both phenomena occur, and they depend on a number of different mechanisms, many of which are still unknown.★ But whatever the ultimate upshot, it is clear that classical conditioning is much more than a laboratory curiosity lim-

The compensatory-reaction hypothesis and drug use *In an addict, the sight and feel of the hypodermic needle (or other drug-related stimuli) become a CS for the counterre-action to the drug, and larger doses of the drug become necessary to get the same high. But if the dose is taken in an unfamiliar environment, then the compensatory reaction may not set in and the addict may overdose. (Courtesy of the Museum of the City of New York)*

★The compensatory-reaction hypothesis is similar to the opponent-process theory discussed in the previous chapter in assuming that various drug reactions are accompanied by processes that pull in the opposite direction. According to one hypothesis, such compensatory reactions are equivalent to conditioned opponent processes, and many instances of what is often regarded as habituation may actually involve the covert conditioning of compensatory processes, which are responsible for reducing the intensity of the reaction to the repeatedly presented stimulus (Schull, 1979).

ited to dogs, metronomes, and saliva. It is a phenomenon of enormous scope, a basic form of learning that pervades much of our everyday life and is shared by flatworms and people alike (Eikelboom and Stewart, 1982; Hollis, 1982; Rescorla and Holland, 1982).

INSTRUMENTAL CONDITIONING

Habituation and classical conditioning are two of the main forms of simple learning. Another is *instrumental conditioning* (which is also called *operant conditioning*). An example of instrumental conditioning comes from the zoo. When a seal learns to turn a somersault to get a fish from the zoo attendant, it has learned an *instrumental response.* The response is instrumental in that it leads to a sought-after effect—in this case, the fish.

There are some important differences between instrumental and classical conditioning. The most important is the fact that in instrumental learning, reinforcement (that is, reward) depends upon the proper response. For the seal the rules of the game are simple: no somersault, no fish. This is not true for classical conditioning. There the US is presented regardless of what the animal does. Another difference concerns response selection. In instrumental learning, the response must be selected from a sometimes very large set of alternatives. The seal's job is to select the somersault from among the numerous other things a seal could possibly do. Not so in classical conditioning. There the response is forced, for the US unconditionally evokes it.

We could loosely summarize the difference between the two procedures by a description of what is learned in each. In classical conditioning the animal must learn about the relation between two stimuli, the CS and the US: Given CS, US will follow. In instrumental learning, the animal has to learn the relation between a response and a reward: Given this response, there will be reinforcement. But such statements are only crude descriptions. To get beyond them, we must discuss instrumental learning in more detail.

THORNDIKE AND THE LAW OF EFFECT

The experimental study of instrumental learning began a decade or two before Pavlov. It was an indirect consequence of the debate over the doctrine of evolution. Darwin's theory was buttressed by impressive demonstrations of continuity in the bodily structures of many species, both living and extinct: Despite their apparent differences, a bird's wing, a seal's flipper, and a human arm have the same bone structure. But his opponents could argue that such evidence was not enough. To them the essential distinction between humans and beasts was elsewhere: in the human ability to think and reason, an ability that animals did not share. To answer these critics, it was important to find proof of mental as well as bodily continuity across the animal kingdom.

For evidence, the Darwinians turned to animal behavior. At first, the method was largely anecdotal. Several British naturalists (including Darwin himself) collected stories about the intellectual achievements of various animals as related by presumably reliable informants. Taken at face value, the results painted a flattering picture of animal intellect, as in accounts of cunning cats scattering bread crumbs on the lawn to entice birds (Romanes, 1882). But even if such observations could be trusted (and they probably could not), they did not prove that the

Edward L. Thorndike *(Courtesy of The Granger Collection)*

4.9 Puzzle box *This box is much like those used by Thorndike. The animal steps on a treadle attached to a rope, thereby releasing a latch that locks the door. (After Thorndike, 1911)*

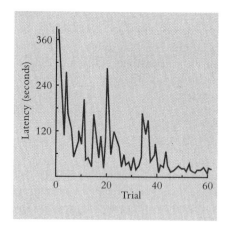

4.10 Learning curve of one of Thorndike's cats *To get out of the box, the cat had to move a wooden handle from a vertical to a horizontal position. The figure shows the gradual decline in the animal's response latency (the time it takes to get out of the box). Note that the learning curve is by no means smooth but has rather marked fluctuations. This is a common feature of the learning curves of individual subjects. Smooth learning curves are generally produced by averaging the results of many individual subjects. (After Thorndike, 1898)*

animals' performances were achieved in the way a human might achieve the same thing: by reason and understanding. To be sure of that, one would have to study the animals' learning processes from start to finish. To see a circus seal blow a melody on a set of toy trumpets is one thing; to conclude from this observation that it appreciates the tune is quite another.

There was clearly a need for controlled experimental procedures whereby the entire course of learning could be carefully scrutinized. That method was provided in 1898 by Edward L. Thorndike (1874–1949) in a brilliant doctoral dissertation that became one of the classic documents of American psychology (Thorndike, 1898).

CATS IN A PUZZLE BOX

Thorndike's method was to set up a problem for the animal. To gain reward the creature had to perform some particular action determined by the experimenter. Much of this work was done with hungry cats. The animal was placed in a *puzzle box,* an enclosure from which it could escape only by performing some simple action that would unlatch the door, such as pulling a loop or wire, or pressing a lever (Figure 4.9). Once outside, the animal was rewarded with a small portion of food and then placed back into the box for another trial. This procedure was repeated until the task was mastered.

On the first trial, the typical cat struggled valiantly; it clawed at the bars, it bit, it struck out in all directions, it meowed, and it howled. This continued for several minutes until the animal finally hit upon the correct response by pure accident. Subsequent trials brought gradual improvement. The mad scramble became shorter and the animal took less and less time to perform the correct response. By the time the training sessions were completed the cat's behavior was almost unrecognizable from what it had been at the start. Placed in the box, it immediately approached the wire loop, yanked it with businesslike dispatch, and hurried through the open door to enjoy its well-deserved reward. The cat had certainly learned.

How had it learned? If one merely observed its final performance one might credit the cat with reason or understanding, but Thorndike argued that the problem was solved in a very different way. For proof he examined the learning curves. Plotting the time required on each trial (that is, the *response latency*) over the whole course of training, he usually found a curve that declined quite gradually (Figure 4.10). Had the animals "understood" the solution at some point during training, one might expect learning curves that showed a sudden drop as the cat finally got the point. ("Aha!" muttered the insightful cat, "It's the lever that lets me out," and henceforth howled and bit no more.) But what really happened was that the cat achieved the correct response pattern in small increments, with no evidence of a sudden insight followed by perfect performance.

THE LAW OF EFFECT

Thorndike proposed that what the animal had learned was best described as an increase in the strength of the correct response. Initially, the cat had the tendency to perform a large set of responses, perhaps because of prior learning, perhaps because of built-in predispositions. As it happened, virtually all of these led to failure. As trials proceeded, the strength of these incorrect responses gradually weakened. In contrast, the correct response, which at first was weak, increasingly grew in strength. In Thorndike's terms, the correct response was gradually "stamped in," while futile ones were correspondingly stamped out. The improvements in the learning curves "represent the wearing smooth of a path in the brain, not the decisions of a rational consciousness" (Thorndike, 1911).

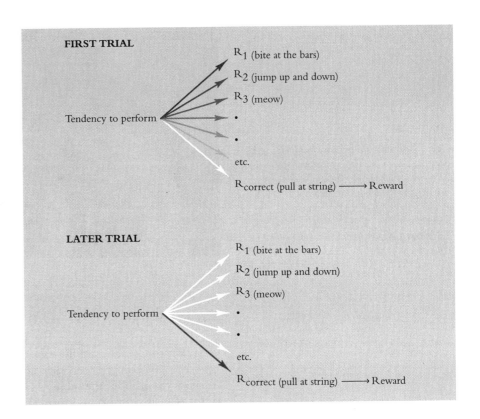

4.11 The law of effect *The figure is a schematic presentation of Thorndike's theory of instrumental learning. On the first trial, the tendency to perform various incorrect responses (biting the bars, jumping up and down) is very strong, while the tendency to perform the correct response (pulling the string) is weak or nonexistent. As trials proceed, the strength of these responses changes. The incorrect responses become weaker and weaker, for none of these responses is immediately followed by reward. In contrast, there is a progressive strengthening of the correct response because this is followed more or less immediately by reward.*

According to Thorndike, some responses get strengthened and others weakened as learning proceeds. But what produces these different effects? Thorndike's answer was a bold formulation called the *law of effect.*

The relevant features of his analysis are schematized in Figure 4.11, which indicates the tendency to perform the various responses, whether correct (R_c) or incorrect (R_1, R_2, R_3, etc.). The critical question is how the correct response gets strengthened until it finally overwhelms the incorrect ones that are at first so dominant. Thorndike's proposal, the law of effect, held that the consequences (that is, the effect) of a response determine whether the tendency to perform it is strengthened or weakened. If the response is followed by reward, it will be strengthened; if it is followed by the absence of reward (or worse yet, by punishment) it will be weakened. There was no need to postulate any further intellectual processes in the animal, no need to assume that the animal noticed a connection between act and consequence, no need to believe that it was trying to attain some goal. If the animal made a response and reward followed shortly, that response was more likely to be performed at a subsequent time.

This proposal fits neatly into the context of evolutionary thinking so dominant at the time. Thorndike emphasized the adaptive nature of the animal's activity, which is gradually shaped to serve its biological ends. But the relationship to evolutionary theory is even closer, for, as Thorndike pointed out, the law of effect is an analogue of the law of the survival of the fittest. In the life of the species, the individual whose genetic makeup fits it best for its environment will survive to transmit its characteristics to its offspring. In the life of the individual, learning provides another adaptive mechanism through the law of effect, which decrees that only the fittest *responses* shall survive. As Thorndike put it, "It is a process of selection among reactions . . . by eliminating the unsuitable reaction directly by discomfort, and also by positively selecting the suitable one by pleasure. . . . It is of tremendous usefulness. . . . He who learns and runs away, *will live to learn another day* . . ." (Thorndike, 1899, p. 91). In short, the reward is to new and adaptive responses as survival is to new and adaptive mutations.

A   B

4.12 Animals in operant chambers *(A) A rat trained to press a lever for water reinforcement. (Photograph by Mike Salisbury) (B) A pigeon pecking at a lighted key for food reinforcement. Reinforcement consists of a few seconds' access to a grain feeder that is located just below the key. (Photograph by Susan M. Hogue)*

B. F. Skinner *(Photograph by Nina Leen, Life Magazine, © Time Warner, Inc.)*

SKINNER AND OPERANT BEHAVIOR

Thorndike initiated the experimental study of instrumental behavior, but the psychologist who shaped the way in which many modern behavior theorists think about the subject is B. F. Skinner (1904–1990). Skinner was one of the first theorists to insist on a sharp distinction between classical and instrumental conditioning. In classical conditioning, the animal's behavior is *elicited* by the CS; to that extent, the salivation is set off from the outside. But Skinner insisted that in instrumental conditioning the organism is much less at the mercy of the external situation. Its reactions are *emitted* from within, as if they were what we ordinarily call *voluntary.* Skinner called these instrumental responses **operants:** They operate on the environment to bring about some change that leads to reward. Like Thorndike, Skinner believed in the law of effect, insisting that the tendency to emit these operants is strengthened or weakened by its consequences (Skinner, 1938).

Behavior theorists have always searched for ever-simpler situations in the hope that the true laws of learning will show up there. Skinner's way of simplifying the study of operant behavior was to create a situation in which the same instrumental response could be performed repeatedly. The most common example is the experimental chamber (popularly called the Skinner box) in which a rat presses a lever or a pigeon pecks at a lighted key (Figure 4.12). In these situations, the animal remains in the presence of the lever or key for, say, an hour at a time, pressing and pecking at whatever rate it chooses. All of the animal's responses are automatically recorded; stimuli and reinforcements are presented automatically by programming devices. The measure of response strength is the **response rate,** that is, the number of responses per unit of time.

THE MAJOR PHENOMENA OF INSTRUMENTAL CONDITIONING

Many of the phenomena of instrumental learning parallel those of classical conditioning. Consider reinforcement. In classical conditioning, the term refers to an operation (establishing a CS-US contingency) that strengthens the CR. In instrumental learning, reinforcement refers to an analogous operation: having the response followed by a condition that the animal prefers. This may be the presentation of something good, such as grain to a hungry pigeon. The

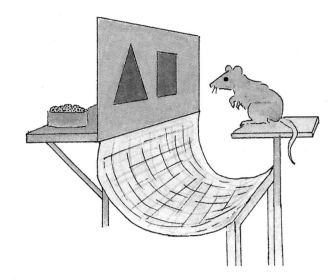

4.13 Studying discriminative stimuli with the jumping stand *The rat has to jump to one of two cards, say a triangle or a square, behind which is a ledge that contains food. If the choice is correct, the card gives way and the animal gets to the food. If the choice is incorrect, the card stays in place and the rat bumps its nose and falls into the net below. (After Lashley, 1930)*

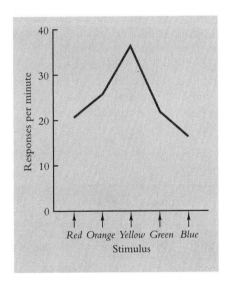

4.14 Stimulus generalization of an instrumental response *Pigeons were originally reinforced to peck at a yellow light. When later tested with lights of various colors, they showed a standard generalization gradient, pecking more vigorously at colors more similar to yellow (such as green and orange) than at colors farther removed (such as red and blue). Prior to being reinforced on the yellow key, their tendency to peck was minimal and roughly equal for all colors. (After Reynolds, 1968)*

grain is an example of an **appetitive stimulus** (a stimulus for which the animal so to speak "has an appetite"). In Thorndike's terms, it is something that the animal does everything to attain and nothing to prevent. Reinforcement may also be the termination or prevention of something bad, such as the cessation of an electric shock. Such a shock is an example of an **aversive stimulus,** one that the animal does everything to avoid and nothing to attain.

We can also distinguish between **positive reinforcement** and **negative reinforcement.** In positive reinforcement the response produces an appetitive stimulus—a rat pressing a lever to get food. In negative reinforcement the instrumental response eliminates or prevents an aversive stimulus—a rat jumping over a barrier to escape an electric shock.

Just as in classical conditioning, the probability of an instrumental response increases with an increasing number of reinforcements. And, again as in classical conditioning, the response suffers extinction when reinforcement is withdrawn.

GENERALIZATION AND DISCRIMINATION

The instrumental response is not elicited by external stimuli but is, in Skinner's terms, emitted from within. But this doesn't mean that external stimuli have no effect. They do exert considerable control over behavior, for they serve as **discriminative stimuli.** Suppose a pigeon is trained to hop on a treadle to get some grain. When a green light is on, hopping on the treadle will pay off. But when a red light is on, the treadle-hopping response will be of no avail, for the pigeon gets no access to the food container. Under these circumstances, the green light becomes a positive discriminative stimulus and the red light a negative one (here indicated by S^+ and S^- respectively). The pigeon will hop in the presence of the first and not in the presence of the second. But this discrimination is made in an instrumental and not a classical conditioning context. The green light doesn't signal food the way a CS^+ might in Pavlov's laboratory. Instead, it signals a particular relationship between the instrumental response and the reinforcer, telling the pigeon as it were "If you hop now, you'll get food." Conversely for the red light: The S^- tells the animal that there's no point in going through the treadle-hopping business right now.

A variety of techniques have been used to study the role of discriminative stimuli in affecting learned instrumental behaviors. Many of the results mirror those of generalization and discrimination in classical conditioning (see Figure 4.13). An example is the study of stimulus generalization using operant techniques. Figure 4.14 shows a typical stimulus generalization gradient for color in pigeons. The birds were trained to peck at a key illuminated with yellow light after which they were tested with lights of varying wavelengths. The resulting gradient is orderly. As the test light became less similar to the original S⁺, the pigeons were less inclined to peck at it (Guttmann and Kalish, 1956).

SHAPING

How does an animal learn the instrumental response that will lead to reinforcement? The law of effect tells us that once that response has been made, then reinforcement will act to strengthen it. But what happens if that response isn't ever made in the first place? As it happens, pecking and lever pressing are fairly easy as such responses go; many animals hit upon them of their own accord. But we can make the response much more difficult. For example, we could set the rat's lever so high on the wall that it must stretch up on its hindlegs to depress it. Now the animal might never make the response on its own. But it could learn this response and even ones more outlandish if its behavior were suitably *shaped*. This is accomplished by the method of *successive approximations.*

Take the problem of the elevated lever. First, we train the animal to approach the tray in which the food is delivered whenever the food-dispensing mechanism gives off its characteristic click. At random intervals, the click sounds and a food pellet drops into the tray; this continues until the rat shows that it is properly trained by running to pick up its pellet as soon as it hears the click. Shaping can now begin. We might first reinforce the animal for walking into the general area where the lever is located. As soon as it is there, it hears the click and devours the pellet. Very soon it will hover around the neighborhood of the lever. We next reinforce it for facing the lever, then for stretching its body upward, then for touching the lever with its paws, and so on until we finally complete its education by reinforcing it for pressing the lever down. The guiding principle throughout is immediacy of reinforcement. If we want to reinforce the rat for standing up on its hindlegs, we must do it the instant after the response; even a one-second wait may be too long, for by then the rat may have fallen back on all fours, and if we reinforce it then, we will reinforce the wrong response.

By means of this technique, animals have been trained to perform exceedingly complex response chains (see Figure 4.15). Pigeons have been trained to play

Shaping *The routines of circus animals are generally established through the method of successive approximation. (Photograph © Hank Morgan)*

4.15 Animals in show business (A) A pig trained by means of operant techniques to push a market cart. The animal was first reinforced for putting its front feet up on the handle, until it could raise up on the handle and push the cart while walking on its hind feet. (Photograph courtesy of Animal Behavior Enterprises) (B) Squirrels trained to stand on their hind legs and hold onto the bar and, hence, to waterski for a fixed interval so as to get reinforced. (Photograph by Gerald Davis / Contact Press Images)

A

B

Ping-Pong and dogs to plunk out four-note tunes on a toy piano. Such successes encouraged some enterprising psychologists to develop live advertising exhibits, featuring such stars as Priscilla, the Fastidious Pig to promote the sale of certain farm feeds (Breland and Breland, 1951). Priscilla turned on the radio, ate breakfast at a kitchen table, picked up dirty clothes and dropped them in a hamper, vacuumed the floor, and finally selected the sponsor's feed in preference to Brand X—a convincing tribute to the sponsor and to the power of reinforcement.

CONDITIONED REINFORCEMENT

So far, our examples of reinforcement have included food or water or termination of electric shock, whose capacity to reinforce responses is presumably based upon built-in mechanisms of various kinds. But instrumental learning is not always reinforced by events of such immediate biological consequence. For example, piano teachers rarely reinforce their students with food or the cessation of electric shock; a nod or the comment "good" is all that is usually required. How does the Thorndikian approach explain why the word "good" is reinforcing?

Thorndike and Skinner would answer that a stimulus will acquire reinforcing properties if it is repeatedly paired with a primary reinforcer. It will then provide *conditioned reinforcement* if administered after a response has been made.

Numerous experiments give evidence that neutral stimuli can acquire reinforcing properties. For example, chimpanzees were first trained to insert poker chips into a vending machine to acquire grapes. Having learned this, they then learned to operate another device that delivered poker chips (Cowles, 1937; see Figure 4.16). Examples of this kind indicate that the critical factor in establishing a stimulus as a conditioned reinforcer is its association with primary reinforcement. It is then not surprising that the effect increases the more frequently the two have been paired. As we might also expect, a conditioned reinforcer will gradually lose its powers if it is repeatedly unaccompanied by some primary reinforcement. All of this argues that conditioned reinforcement is established by a process that is akin to, if not identical with, classical conditioning. The conditioned reinforcer serves as a CS that signals some motivationally significant US.

If conditioned reinforcers are so readily extinguished in the laboratory, why do they seem so much more permanent in human life? Nods do not lose their reinforcing value just because they haven't been paired with any primary reinforcer for a month or more. In part, the answer may be that the nod or the smile has enormous generality. It is associated not with one but with many different desirable outcomes. Even if extinguished in one context, it would still be maintained in countless others.

4.16 Conditioned reinforcement in chimpanzees *Chimpanzee using a token to obtain food after working to obtain tokens. (Courtesy Yerkes Regional Primate Research Center of Emory University)*

DELAY OF REINFORCEMENT

According to the law of effect, a response will be strengthened if it is followed by a reward. But the mere fact that a reward will follow is not enough. In general, the reward must follow the response rather quickly, for a reinforcer becomes less and less effective the longer its presentation is delayed after the response is made.

The relation between the delay and the effectiveness of a reward has been studied experimentally in various ways. One experimenter trained several groups of rats to press a lever that was withdrawn from the box immediately after the correct response. Food was delivered after different delays of reinforcement ranging from 0 to 30 seconds for the various groups. Learning was clearly

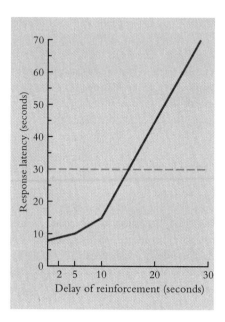

4.17 The effect of a delay in reinforcement The graph shows the response latency for rats pressing a lever after 50 trials on which they received a food reward following a delay of 0, 2, 5, 10, or 30 seconds. The dotted line indicates the animals' average latency at the very first trial. It is clear that animals trained with delays up to 10 seconds improved over trials, and the shorter the delay the greater was their improvement. But animals trained with a delay of 30 seconds did not improve; on the contrary, their performance was markedly worse after 50 trials than it was initially. (Data from Perin, 1943)

4.18 Performance on two fixed-ratio schedules The figure records the pigeon's cumulative responses—how many key pecks it made after 5 minutes in the operant chamber, after 10 minutes, and so on. The steeper the record, the faster the response rate. The left-hand panel shows performance on FR 65, the right on FR 185. The small diagonal slashes indicate times when the animal received reinforcement. Note the characteristic pause after the fixed ratio has been run off and that the duration of this pause increases with increasing ratios. (Adapted from Ferster and Skinner, 1957)

faster the shorter the interval. These results are summarized in Figure 4.17, which shows the declining effectiveness of reinforcement with increasing delay. Note that there was no learning at all when the interval was 30 seconds; in instrumental learning, late is sometimes no better than never (Perin, 1943).

To what extent does the delay-of-reward principle apply to humans? It depends upon which aspects of human behavior we consider. At one level there is an enormous gap between what we see in the rat and what we know of ourselves. Rats and humans live according to different time scales entirely. Reinforcement may come many days after an action and still have an effect, as in the case of a monthly paycheck, because people can relate their present to their past by all sorts of symbolic devices. Unlike the rat, humans can transcend the here and now.

The fact that people sometimes overcome long delays of reinforcement should not blind us to the fact that they often do not. Many of our actions are dictated by immediate reward, regardless of the long-term outcome. To give only one example, consider cigarette smoking. By now, most smokers are probably convinced of the ultimate dangers they are courting. In fact, they may experience some discomfort: They may cough and have trouble breathing when they wake up. Yet despite all this, many of them continue to smoke. The problem is that the positive reinforcement of the act is immediate, while discomfort or worse comes later. Transcending the gradient of reward is no easy task.

SCHEDULES OF REINFORCEMENT

So far, we've only dealt with cases in which reinforcement follows the response every time it is made. But outside of the laboratory, this arrangement is surely the exception and not the rule. The fisherman does not hook a fish with every cast, and even a star tennis player occasionally loses a match to one of her less accomplished rivals. All of these are cases of *partial reinforcement* in which a response is reinforced only some of the time.

One way of studying phenomena of this kind is in the operant situation. Here reinforcement can easily be scheduled in different ways—after every response, after some number of responses, after some interval, and so on. The *schedule of reinforcement* is simply the rule set up by the experimenter that determines the occasions on which a response is reinforced.

Ratio schedules One example of such a rule is the *fixed-ratio schedule* (abbreviated FR 2, FR 4, FR 50, as the case may be) in which the subject has to produce a specified number of responses for every reward, like a factory worker paid by piecework. Such schedules can generate very high rates of responding, but to get the organism to that level requires some finesse. The trick is to increase the ratio very gradually, beginning with continuous reinforcement and slowly stepping up the requirement. By such procedures, pigeons (and probably factory workers) have been led to perform at schedules as high as FR 500.

When the fixed ratio gets high enough, a new pattern develops. Following a reinforcement, the pigeon will pause for a while before it starts to peck again. The higher the ratio, the longer the pause (see Figure 4.18). In a way, the

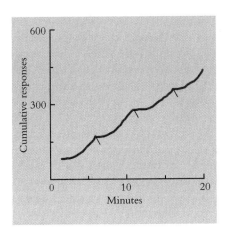

4.19 Performance on a fixed-interval schedule *The cumulative record of a pigeon's performance on a fixed-interval schedule, FI 5. The small diagonal slashes indicate reinforcements. Note the scalloped shape that is characteristic of performance on an FI schedule after the animal has been on that schedule for a few sessions. (After Ferster and Skinner, 1957)*

pigeon is like a student who has just finished one term paper and has to write another. It is very hard to start again, but once the first page is written, the next ones come more readily. The pause following reinforcement can be eliminated by changing the schedule to a *variable ratio (VR).* In VR schedules, reinforcement still comes after a certain number of responses but that number varies irregularly, averaging out to a particular ratio (for example VR 50, that is, a reward on average after every fifty responses). Now there is no way whereby the pigeon can know which of its pecks will bring reward. It might be the first, the tenth, or the hundredth peck following the last reinforcement. Since the number of prior pecks is no longer a clue, the pause disappears. A glance at a gambling casino gives proof that VR schedules affect humans much as they do pigeons. The slot machines are set to pay off occasionally, just enough to maintain the high rate of behavior that keeps the casino lucrative to its owners and not to its clients.

Interval schedules   Ratio schedules are based on numbers of responses. Another set of schedules is defined by intervals of time. In a *fixed-interval schedule (FI),* the animal is reinforced for the first response performed after a certain interval has passed following the last reinforcement, but it is not reinforced for any response performed before then. For example, if the interval is two minutes (FI 2), the pigeon may peck all it wants after a reinforcement, but all its work is of no avail until the two minutes are up. After this, the first peck will be rewarded, and the cycle will start all over again. An example of an FI schedule in ordinary life is looking in the mailbox. Since mail delivery occurs once a day, the schedule is FI 24 hours.

After an animal has been on an FI schedule for a while, it shows a characteristic response pattern. Immediately after reinforcement, its response is very low, but this rate will gradually pick up and get faster and faster as the end of the interval approaches (see Figure 4.19).

The animal's response rate will become very stable and uniform if the animal is put on a *variable-interval schedule (VI)* (see Figure 4.20). This differs from an FI schedule in that the interval varies irregularly around some average period, say four minutes (VI 4). Unpleasant examples of such schedules in ordinary life involve aversive stimuli such as surprise quizzes in the classroom and speed traps on the highway.

Partial reinforcement and extinction   Some of the most dramatic effects of partial reinforcement are seen during subsequent extinction. The basic fact can be stated very simply: A response will be much harder to extinguish if it was acquired during partial rather than continuous reinforcement. This phenomenon is often called the *partial-reinforcement effect* (Humphreys, 1939).

A good illustration is provided by an experiment in which several rats were trained on a runway for food (Weinstock, 1954). All animals received the same number of trials but not the same number of reinforcements. One group was reinforced on every trial, another only on 30 percent of the trials. Figure 4.21 (on page 124) shows what happened to these two groups during extinction. The rats reinforced 100 percent of the time gave up very much sooner than their partially reinforced fellows. Numerous other experiments have given substantially the same result on all manner of subjects, including humans.

4.20 Performance on a variable-ratio schedule *The cumulative record of a pigeon's performance on a variable ratio schedule—VR 173. Again, the small slashes indicate reinforcements. As the record shows, response rates are very high, and there are no pauses after reinforcement. (After Ferster and Skinner, 1957)*

4.21 The partial-reinforcement effect
The figure shows runway speeds during extinction trials on two groups of rats. One group had previously been reinforced on every trial; the other had only been reinforced on 30 percent of the trials. The figure shows that the group trained under full reinforcement (in dark red) stops running considerably before the group that was trained under partial reinforcement (in blue). (After Weinstock, 1954)

On the face of it, the partial-reinforcement effect is paradoxical. If the strength of an instrumental response increases with increasing reinforcements, we should expect that groups reinforced 100 percent of the time would continue to respond for longer than those reinforced only partially. In fact, the very opposite is true. Why? Speaking informally, we might suggest that the partially reinforced rat has come to expect that reward may occur even after several unrewarded trials; it has learned that "if you don't succeed, try, try again." In contrast, the rat reinforced 100 percent of the time has never encountered unreinforced trials before. If this interpretation of the partial-reinforcement effect is correct, we would expect an irregular sequence of reinforcements to be harder to extinguish than a regular one, even if the proportion of reinforcements is the same in both cases. This is precisely what happens. Thus ratio schedules engender greater resistance to extinction if they are variable rather than fixed.

To see the partial-reinforcement effect in action, consider a simple problem in child rearing. Many parents find that their six-month-old does not want to go to sleep. Put into his crib at night, he howls his vehement protests until he is lifted out again. Sooner or later his parents resolve that this has to stop. The baby is put back in the crib, and the wails begin. The parents stay firm for a while, but eventually they weaken (after all, the baby might be sick). Brought out of his crib, the baby gurgles happily, and the process of partial reinforcement has begun. Next time, the parents will have an even harder time. According to one study (and to common sense), the answer is consistent nonreinforcement. Two determined parents plotted an extinction curve for their twenty-one-month-old child's bedtime tantrums. One day they simply decided to put their little tyrant to bed and then leave the bedroom and not go back. On the first occasion, the child howled for forty-five minutes; the next few times the cries were much diminished, until finally after ten such "trials," the child went to sleep smiling and with no complaints at all (Williams, 1959).

AVERSIVE CONDITIONING

So far, our discussion of instrumental learning has largely centered on cases where the reinforcing stimulus is appetitive—the kind we normally call reward. But aversive stimuli are no less relevant to instrumental learning; they represent the opposite side of the coin—the stick rather than the carrot, punishment rather than reward. These aversive stimuli may be electric shock for laboratory rats or swats on the rear for infants. While the stimulus may differ, there is little doubt that organisms learn whatever they must to minimize such unpleasantries, to get as few shocks, swats, and insulting reproofs as they possibly can.

Punishment Psychologists distinguish between several kinds of instrumental learning that depend on the use of aversive stimuli. The most familiar from everyday life is ***punishment training.*** Here, a response is followed by an aversive stimulus, which will then tend to suppress the response on subsequent occasions. One factor that determines the resulting response suppression is the extent to which reinforcement is delayed, which we've already discussed in the context of reward. Consider a cat that has developed the unfortunate habit of using a large indoor plant as its private bathroom. The irate owner discovers the misdeed an hour or so later and smacks the cat when he sees it in the kitchen. It's hardly surprising that the punishment will not produce the hoped for hygienic result, for the animal has no way of connecting the crime with the punishment. For punishment to have its desired effect, it must be administered shortly after the unwanted response is performed.

Escape and avoidance Aversive stimuli can weaken response tendencies (as in punishment training), but they can also be used to strengthen them. This hap-

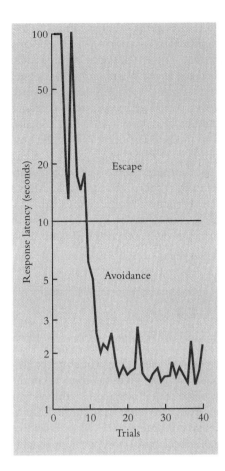

4.22 **The course of avoidance learning in a dog** *The figure shows response latencies of one animal in a shuttle box (where latency is the time from the onset of CS to the animal's response). A warning stimulus indicated that shock would begin 10 seconds after the onset of the signal. For the first nine trials the dog escaped. It jumped over the hurdle after the shock began. From the tenth trial on, the dog avoided: It jumped before its 10 seconds of grace were up. The jumping speed increased until the animal jumped with an average latency of about 1½ seconds. (Latency is plotted on a logarithmic scale. This compresses the time scale so as to put greater emphasis on differences between the shorter response latencies.) (After Solomon and Wynne, 1953)*

pens in *escape* and *avoidance learning.* In escape learning, the response stops some aversive event that has already begun. In avoidance learning, the subject can forestall the aversive event altogether. An example of escape learning is when a rat learns to press a lever to get rid of an electric shock. An example of avoidance learning is when a dog learns to jump over a hurdle in a shuttle box when it hears a tone that signals impending shock; if it jumps within some grace period, it will manage to avoid the shock entirely (see Figure 4.22).

Aversive reinforcement and the law of effect Both punishment training and escape learning readily fit into the Thorndike-Skinner conception of instrumental learning. Punishment training simply represents the opposite side of the law of effect: Where positive reinforcers strengthen the response that precedes them, aversive stimuli weaken it. The interpretation of escape learning is even easier: The response is followed by the termination of an aversive stimulus, which then serves as reward.

The interpretation of avoidance learning is more difficult. Consider a dog who jumps back and forth over a hurdle to avoid shock. What is the reinforcement? It is not the *cessation* of shock as it is in escape learning, for the animal doesn't get shocked to begin with. Could it be the *absence of shock?* This too won't work, for *not* receiving punishment can only be a source of satisfaction if punishment has been threatened. After all, most of us spend our entire lives without being drowned, beaten, or otherwise put to bodily harm, but we don't therefore regard ourselves as being in a state of perpetual bliss. It's not absence of shock as such that is the reward. It is rather the *absence of shock (or any other aversive event) when shock is expected.*

Avoidance learning in human life An enormous amount of ordinary human activity involves avoidance. We stop at red lights to avoid getting traffic tickets, pay bills to avoid interest charges, carry umbrellas to avoid getting wet, and devise excuses to avoid having lunch with a bore. We probably perform dozens of such learned avoidance responses each day, and most of them are perfectly useful and adaptive (Schwartz, 1989). But some avoidance learning is essentially maladaptive and is often based on more potent aversive stimuli than a boring lunch. An extreme example is phobias. As already mentioned, some people have intense fears—heights, open spaces, dogs, elevators, and so on. As a result, they will develop elaborate patterns to avoid these things. In some cases, the phobia may be caused by traumatic experiences in the past as in the case of a woman who was trapped for several hours in a swaying elevator stuck between the fortieth and forty-first floor of an office building and never used an elevator thereafter. Such an avoidance reaction is of little future use, for elevators ordinarily function perfectly well. But the trouble is that the avoidance response is self-perpetuating. It will not extinguish even if the aversive stimulus is no longer there. The reason is that the person (or animal) will not stay in the previously dangerous situation long enough to discover whether the danger is indeed still there. The woman who avoids elevators will never find out that they are now perfectly safe, for she won't ever use them again—a rather inconvenient behavior pattern if her own office happens to be above the forty-first floor.

Avoidance learning *No doubt the infant will learn to avoid the flame. (Photograph by Erika Stone)*

125

Is there any way to extinguish avoidance responses? (The question is of considerable practical interest because it has implications for therapy of phobias and related conditions.) In animals, the answer is yes. The technique is to force them to test reality so that they can discover that the aversive stimulus is no longer there. In a number of studies, animals were first trained to jump back and forth in a shuttle box to avoid a mild shock. After they had learned the avoidance response, they were exposed to the stimulus that previously had signaled impending shock. They immediately tried to jump to the other side of the box, but they couldn't; their avoidance response was blocked by a floor-to-ceiling barrier that forced them to remain in the compartment. They necessarily remained and were visibly frightened. But, in fact, there was no shock. After a few such trials without shock, the avoidance reaction was extinguished. The idea is much like getting back on the horse that threw you—a good prescription for aspiring jockeys, assuming the horse won't throw them again (Baum, 1970; Mineka, 1979).

COGNITIVE LEARNING

To the early theorists, the essential thing about classical and instrumental conditioning was that both procedures modify behavior. This held for classical conditioning, which Pavlov saw as an extension of reflex action whereby the elicitation of certain responses (the URs) is passed from one set of stimuli (the USs) to another (the CSs). It also held for instrumental conditioning, which Thorndike and Skinner regarded as the strengthening of certain responses by the mechanical effect of reinforcement.

From the earliest days of behavior theory, however, there was an alternative view which asserted that what really matters when animals (and humans) learn is not the *change* in behavior as such, but the acquisition of new *knowledge.* One of the most prominent exponents of this view was Edward C. Tolman (1886–1959), who argued that in both classical and instrumental conditioning an animal gains various bits of knowledge, or ***cognitions.***

These bits of knowledge are organized so that they can be used when needed. This is very different from asserting that the animal acquires a tendency to perform a certain response. As Tolman saw it, the response an animal acquires in the course of a learning experiment is only an index that a given cognition has been gained. It is an indispensable measuring stick, but it is not what is being measured. Rather the essence of what is learned is something within the animal, a private event that will only become public when the animal acts upon its newly acquired knowledge. Today such cognitions are often called ***representations,*** which correspond to (represent) certain events, or relations between events, in the animal's world (Dickinson, 1987).

Evidence that animals acquire cognitions came from a number of experiments designed to determine whether instrumental learning can occur without the performance of the relevant response. Many early behavior theorists claimed that performance is an indispensable ingredient for instrumental learning, insisting that the animal learns by doing and in no other way. Several studies, however, suggest that this is not the case. For example, rats have been ferried from one end of a large room to another in transparent trolley cars. Later tests showed that they had learned something about the general features of the room even though they had not performed any relevant responses during their trolley-car ride (Gleitman, 1963). They had acquired what Tolman called a "cognitive map" that represents what is where and what leads to what (Tolman, 1948).

Edward C. Tolman *(Courtesy Psychology Department, University of California, Berkeley)*

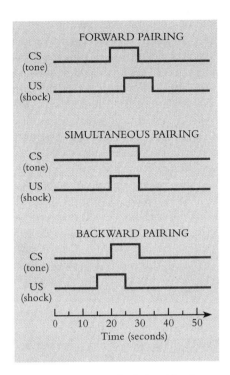

4.23 *Some temporal relationships in classical conditioning*

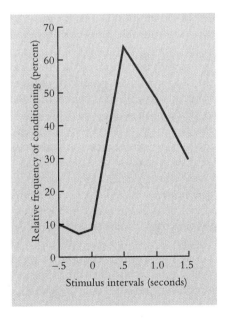

A COGNITIVE VIEW OF CLASSICAL CONDITIONING

The cognitive approach has had considerable impact on current conceptions of animal learning. One of its effects was a reinterpretation of classical conditioning. Pavlov believed that the essential feature of classical conditioning is the newly achieved ability of one stimulus to elicit a response that was originally evoked by another. If it does, a well-conditioned animal should respond to the CS just as it does to the US. But as we have seen before, this is not the case. Even in Pavlov's original experiment, the UR and the CR were not really identical (the composition of the two salivary secretions differed), and in others, they could even be exact opposites (as in conditioning in which the US is heroin). We conclude that the animal acquires a representation about the relation between the two stimulus events. Instead of substituting for the US, the CS becomes a sign that the US will follow (Tolman, 1932; Rescorla, 1988).

TEMPORAL RELATIONS BETWEEN THE CS AND THE US

It appears that what is learned in classical conditioning is an association between two events: the CS and the US. But how is this association acquired? In line with many philosophers who had thought about association, Pavlov believed that a necessary condition is temporal **contiguity,** that is, togetherness in time. As we will see, the answer is not quite as simple as that.

One way of finding out whether the CS-US association is based on contiguity in time is to vary the interval between the two stimuli as well as the order in which they are presented. A number of procedures do just that. In some, the CS precedes the US **(forward pairing),** in others it follows the US **(backward pairing),** and in yet others the two stimuli are presented at the same time **(simultaneous pairing).** (See Figure 4.23.)

The general results of these procedures are as follows: Conditioning is best when the CS *precedes* the US by some optimum interval that is generally rather short (see Figure 4.24).* Presenting the CS and the US simultaneously is generally much less effective, and the backward procedure is even worse. On the other hand, the effectiveness of forward pairing declines rapidly when the CS-US interval increases beyond the optimum interval (Rescorla, 1988).

How can we make sense of these facts? A reasonable suggestion is that the CS serves a signaling function: It prepares the organism for a US that is to come. Let

4.24 *The CS-US interval in classical conditioning* The figure shows the results of a study on the effectiveness of various CS-US intervals in humans. The CR was a finger withdrawal response, the CS a tone, and the US an electric shock. The time between CS and US is plotted on the horizontal axis. Negative intervals mean that the US was presented before the CS (backward pairing), a zero interval means that the two stimuli were presented simultaneously, and a positive interval means that the CS began before the US (forward pairing). The vertical axis indicates the degree of conditioning. (After Spooner and Kellogg, 1947)

*The precise value of that optimum interval depends on the particulars of the situation; it usually varies from about half a second to about ten seconds. In one form of classical conditioning, learned taste aversion, the optimum CS-US is very much longer and may be of the order of an hour or more. This phenomenon poses obvious difficulties for a contiguity theory of conditioning—and much else besides—and will be discussed in a later section (see pp. 136–39).

us consider forward, simultaneous, and backward pairing in this light by likening the subject's situation to that of a driver setting out upon an unfamiliar road. Suppose our driver wants to go from Denver to Salt Lake City and that some 150 miles out of Denver there is a dangerous hairpin turn over a ravine. How should the driver be warned of the impending curve? Presumably there will be a sign, "Hairpin Turn," which should obviously appear just a bit before the turn (analogous to forward pairing with a short CS-US interval). If the interval is too long it will be almost impossible to connect the sign with that which it signifies. The driver will understandably lose some of her faith in the Highway Department if it sets up the sign, "Hairpin Turn," just outside the Denver city limits while the turn itself is three hours away (forward pairing with a long CS-US interval). Her faith will be really shaken if she sees the sign prominently displayed just at the sharpest bend of the turn (simultaneous pairing). She will finally begin to suspect a degree of malevolence if she discovers the sign innocently placed on the road a hundred feet or so beyond the turn (backward pairing), though she should probably be grateful that she did not find it at the bottom of the ravine.

CONTINGENCY

It would seem that in classical conditioning an organism learns that one stimulus is a signal for another. The next task is to describe just what such a sign relationship between two events consists of.

Consider a dog in Pavlov's laboratory who is exposed to several presentations of a beating metronome followed by some food powder. The poor beast doesn't know that he is supposed to form a CS-US connection. All he knows is that every once in a while food appears. There are all sorts of stimuli in the laboratory situation. Of course he hears the metronome, but he also hears doors slamming and a babble of (Russian) voices in the background, and he feels the strap of the conditioning harness. How does he discover that it is the metronome that is the signal for food rather than the scores of other stimuli that he was also exposed to? After all, no one told him that metronome beats are Professor Pavlov's favorite conditioned stimuli.

A useful way of trying to understand what happens is to think of the animal as an amateur scientist. Like all scientists, the dog wants to predict important events. (When his human counterparts succeed, they publish; when the dog succeeds, he salivates.) How can he predict when food will appear? He might decide to rely on mere contiguity and salivate to any stimulus that occurs along with food presentation. But if so, he'd have to salivate whenever he was strapped in his harness or whenever he heard voices, for these stimuli were generally present when he was fed. But if the dog had any scientific talent at all, he would realize that the harness and the voices are very poor food predictors. To be sure, they occur when food is given, but they occur just as frequently when it is not. To continue in his scientific quest, the dog would look for an event that occurs when food appears and that does not occur when food is absent. The metronome beat is the one stimulus that fulfills *both* of these conditions, for it never beats in the intervals between trials when food is not presented. Science (or rather classical conditioning) has triumphed, and the dog is ready to announce his findings by salivating only when the CS is presented.

Contingency versus contiguity　The preceding account is a fanciful statement of an influential analysis of classical conditioning developed by Robert Rescorla (Rescorla, 1967). According to Rescorla, classical conditioning depends not only on CS-US pairings but also on pairings in which the *absence* of CS goes along with the *absence* of US. These two experiences—metronome/meat and

TABLE 4.1 CONTINGENCY IN CLASSICAL CONDITIONING

Three tables illustrating three different CS/US contingency arrangements in a hypothetical experiment in which the CS is a tone and the US is meat powder. Each table presents a different tone/meat contingency based on twenty trials. The column labeled *p* shows the probabilities that meat will occur under a particular stimulus condition.

Meat contingent upon tone			
	Meat	*No Meat*	p
Tone	8	2	.80
No Tone	2	8	.20

Meat contingent upon absence of tone			
	Meat	*No Meat*	p
Tone	3	7	.30
No Tone	7	3	.70

Meat and tone independent			
	Meat	*No Meat*	p
Tone	5	5	.50
No Tone	5	5	.50

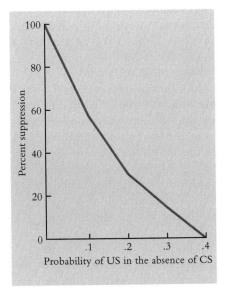

no metronome/no meat—allow the dog to discover that the occurrence of the US is **contingent** (that is, dependent) upon the occurrence of the CS. According to Rescorla, conditioning does not occur because the US is *contiguous* with the CS but rather because it is *contingent* upon the CS. By determining this contingency, the animal can forecast what is going to happen next.

Contingency need not be perfect. In nature it rarely is. A dark cloud generally precedes a storm, but it doesn't always. As a result, weather predictions are never perfect. But we can nevertheless make some predictions about the weather that are better than chance, for it's more likely to rain when the sky is dark than when the sun is shining. The same holds in the conditioning laboratory in which we can arrange whatever relationship between CS and US we choose. We could decide that the metronome will be followed by food on 80 percent of the trials, but that food will occur unheralded by the metronome on 20 percent of the trials. We have now created an imperfect contingency that will be harder to detect. But it is a contingency even so, for food is more likely after the CS than otherwise. To recognize such imperfect contingencies, the animal must keep track of four possible stimulus combinations that he will encounter. These combinations are: metronome/meat, metronome/no meat, no metronome/meat, no metronome/no meat. To determine if getting meat is contingent upon the metronome, the animal must somehow compute two probabilities: the probability of getting meat when the metronome is sounded and the probability of getting meat when it is not. If the first probability is greater than the second, then getting meat is contingent on the metronome (the metronome's ticking predicts that meat will arrive). If it is smaller than the second, getting meat is contingent upon the *absence* of the metronome (the metronome's ticking predicts that meat will *not* arrive). Such a negative contingency is analogous to the relation between a sunny sky and rain—rain is more likely when the sun is *not* shining. An important final possibility is that the two probabilities are identical. If so, there is no contingency, and the two events are independent (see Table 4.1).

If this line of thinking is correct, then temporal contiguity as such will not produce conditioning. For according to this view, conditioning will only occur if the probability of a US when the CS is present is greater than the probability of a US when the CS is absent. To demonstrate this, Rescorla exposed rats to various combinations of a tone CS and a shock US in a conditioned suppression experiment. In one set of conditions, the probability of receiving a shock when the tone was sounded was always the same (about .40). What varied was the probability that a shock would occur when no tone was sounded. The results were clear-cut. If the likelihood of a shock when the tone was on was the same as the likelihood of a shock when the tone was off, there was no conditioning. But if the likelihood of a shock was smaller when the tone was off than when it was on, conditioning did take place. The greater the difference in these probabilities, the stronger the level of conditioning the animal achieved (see Figure 4.25). The critical factor is evidently not contiguity, because the sheer number of CS-US pairings was identical for all groups. What matters is whether the tone was an informative signal that told the animal that shock was more likely now than at other times (Rescorla, 1967, 1988).

The absence of contingency What happens when there is no contingency whatsoever? On the face of it, there is nothing to learn. But in a situation in which

4.25 Contingency in classical conditioning *The figure shows the results of fear conditioning as a function of contingency. The probability of the US in the presence of the CS was always .40, but the probability of the US in the absence of the CS varied from 0 to .40. Conditioning was measured by the degree of response suppression. (After Rescorla, 1966)* there is fear and danger (for example, getting an electric shock) the animal does learn something after all: It learns it can never feel safe at any time.

Consider two situations: In the first, there is a CS that signals that shock is likely to follow. When the CS appears, the animal will become more fearful. But there is a compensation. When there is no CS, the animal can relax, for now shock is less likely. The absence of the CS has become a *safety signal.* In a second situation, the arrangement is different. This time, there is no stimulus that predicts when shock will occur. Now the animal is worse off than it was when there was a CS-US contingency, for it now has good reason to be afraid at all times because there is no safety signal. This unpleasant state of affairs leads to a number of harmful physiological consequences. For example, rats who are exposed to unsignaled electric shock are much more likely to develop stomach ulcers than rats who receive just as many shocks, but with a signal that predicts their occurrence (Seligman, 1968; Weiss, 1970, 1977).

The difference between signaled and unsignaled shock may be related to the distinction between *fear* and *anxiety* made by clinical psychologists concerned with human emotional disorders. As they use the terms, fear refers to an emotional state that is directed at a specific situation or object—flying in airplanes, snakes, or whatever. In contrast, anxiety is a chronic fear that has no particular object but is there at all times. A number of authors suggest that this unfocused anxiety state is in part produced by unpredictability. Patients whose dentists tell them "this may hurt" but at other times assure them "you won't feel anything now" will probably have fewer dental anxieties than those whose dentists never tell them anything (Seligman, 1975; Schwartz, 1989).

THE ROLE OF SURPRISE

It appears that in classical conditioning animals learn that certain stimuli are signals for impending events. They do so by noting the contingency between these stimuli and the events they forecast (that is, the USs). But how does the animal manage to keep track of all the information he gets in the conditioning procedure to decide which stimulus he should respond to? We have likened the animal to a scientist who tries to infer cause-and-effect relations. But of course this is just a metaphor. For it's very unlikely that the rats, dogs, and pigeons in classical conditioning laboratories keep a conscious mental record of their experiences, tallying trials on which the CS was followed by the US and trials on which the CS occurred and the US did not, and then computing probabilities and making appropriate deductions the way scientists do. Although in some ways they behave as if they do just that, the means whereby they achieve their results are almost certainly more automatic and mechanical than those employed by the human scientist.

The best guess is that classical conditioning in animals (and probably in humans too) is based on rather simple processes that operate on a trial-by-trial basis but that somehow combine to produce a more complex result. The question is just what those simple mechanisms might be. To answer this question, we must consider the factors that underlie the connection between a CS and a US. According to several theorists, the critical ingredient is the extent to which the US is *surprising* (that is, unexpected). If the US is unexpected, the animal will form a connection between it and the CS that preceded it: the greater the surprise, the stronger the connection. If there is no surprise at all, there will be no connection made at all (Kamin, 1968; Rescorla and Wagner, 1972).

Blocking Evidence for the role of surprise comes from a series of studies performed by Leon Kamin, who discovered a phenomenon called the **blocking effect.** Kamin showed that when a stimulus is *redundant,* providing information that an organism already has, it will not become connected to the CS. If the an-

TABLE 4.2 BLOCKING

Group	Stage 1	Stage 2	Test	Result
I	Noise → shock	(Noise + Light) → shock	Light alone	No conditioned fear
II	—	(Noise + Light) → shock	Light alone	Conditioned fear

imal already knows that the US is coming, it will not be surprised and conditioning will not take place.

Kamin's basic experiment was run in three stages. In Stage 1, the rats heard a hissing noise that was followed by shock. As one might expect, this noise became a CS for conditioned fear. In Stage 2, the shock was preceded by *two* stimuli that were presented simultaneously: One was the same old hissing noise used in Stage 1; the other was a light. Stage 3 was a test in which the light was presented alone to see whether it would also produce a conditioned fear reaction. The results showed that it did not. When the light came on, there was no response suppression even though that stimulus had been a perfect predictor of shock. Somehow the old established stimulus (the noise) had blocked out the new stimulus (the light).

To prove that this blocking effect was indeed caused by the animals' previous experience with the tone, Kamin ran a control group. These controls never went through Stage 1, but began at Stage 2 (that is, light plus noise followed by shock) from the very outset, with no previous exposure to noise alone. When these control animals were later tested with the light alone, they exhibited a substantial conditioned fear response (Kamin, 1969; see Table 4.2 and Figure 4.26).

The blocking effect follows directly from the notion that the formation of a CS-US association depends on the extent to which the animal is surprised by the US. In Kamin's procedure, a well-established CS (the noise) is presented together with a new stimulus (the light); then *both* are followed by shock. In this situation, the new stimulus—the light—adds no further information. The animal already knows that it will be shocked. When the shock comes, the rat may be sad, it may be resigned, but it will not be surprised. As a result, it will not connect the light stimulus with the shock.

Here again the animals are a bit like human scientists who try to infer cause-and-effect relations. Consider the early scientists who asked themselves where maggots come from. Whenever they saw maggots, they saw rotten meat, and they never saw maggots anywhere else. As a result, they assumed that the maggots' appearance was contingent upon rotting meat (which they took as evidence for the theory that life is generated spontaneously). Once having discovered this contingency, they were blinded to other contingencies that were also present, such as the fact that the meat had been lying around for a while (so flies could lay their eggs in it). Something similar holds for rats in classical conditioning. Once they've discovered a stimulus that signals the appearance of a US, they no longer connect other stimuli to the US, for they're no longer surprised when the US appears. The old stimuli block out the new, much as a scientist's old theory prejudices her to (blocks out) further facts.

4.26 The effect of blocking *Results for the test phase of Kamin's blocking experiment in which the animals were presented with the light alone. Group I (in dark red) showed virtually no response suppression (and hence no fear conditioning), indicating that the initial pairing of noise and shock in Stage 1 had blocked the recognition of the light-shock contingency during Stage 2. Group II (in blue) had no such prior pairings and showed no blocking effect. (After Kamin, 1969)*

A COGNITIVE VIEW OF INSTRUMENTAL CONDITIONING

We have seen that what is learned in classical conditioning is a representation about the relation between two stimulus events, the CS and the US. There is reason to believe that a similar cognitive account applies to instrumental conditioning. As with classical conditioning, this interpretation goes back to Tolman. Thorndike and Skinner had argued that instrumental learning involves the strengthening of a particular response, such as pressing a bar in a Skinner box. In contrast, Tolman believed that the animal acquires an internal representation of the relation between the response and the reinforcer that follows it: It doesn't just learn to press a bar; it learns that the bar leads to a food pellet. In effect, it acquires an association between an act and its outcome. This act-outcome representation may or may not be used on a later occasion, depending on the circumstances, such as the animal's needs and motives (Tolman, 1932).

EVIDENCE FOR ACT-OUTCOME ASSOCIATIONS

Early evidence that animals do acquire act-outcome cognitions of this sort comes from a study in which rats were run in an enclosed maze that had a black end box on one side and a white one on the other (see Figure 4.27). Both ends contained food, and the animals chose indifferently between them on several trials. Subsequently, the animals were placed into each box by hand without actually running the maze. In one end box they now found food as before; in the other they were shocked. After all this, the animals were again allowed to run down the original maze. Now virtually all of them chose the side away from the end box in which they had been shocked. Clearly, the rats had learned which turn led to which box, but this cognition led to selective action only after the two boxes had acquired their new significance. In effect, the animals had to combine two experiences. During the first phase of the experiment, they presumably learned to associate a particular turn with a particular end box. During the second phase, they further learned that a particular end box brought shock. The results of the final test indicate that they were able to put these two experiences together—an argument against the view that all instrumental learning depends on the strengthening or weakening of particular response tendencies (Tolman and Gleitman, 1949).

Similar *latent learning* effects have been obtained in a number of other studies. A classic example is an experiment in which rats were run through a maze without a reward for ten days. On the eleventh day food was finally placed in the goal box, and on the very next trial there was an abrupt decline in errors. Presumably the rats had learned something about the maze during the preceding days. But they did not show that they had learned until the reward was introduced. What they learned over the first ten days was only latent but not yet manifest (Tolman and Honzik, 1930).

A more recent experiment has provided some elegant further evidence for Tolman's general view (Colwill and Rescorla, 1985). Hungry rats were trained to make two different responses, each of which produced a different food reward. On some days, their experimental chamber contained a standard

4.27 *Proving that rats learn what leads to where* (I) Floor plan of a maze in the first phase of an experiment during which rats could learn that a left turn leads to end box A, a right turn to end box B. (II) The second phase of the experiment in which the two end boxes were detached from the rest of the maze and the animals were shocked in one of them, say, A. (III) The third phase of the experiment in which the animals were returned to the original situation. If they could put the two experiences together, then, having learned that a left turn led to A and that A led to shock, they should turn right—that is, away from shock. The results showed that they did. (After Tolman and Gleitman, 1949)

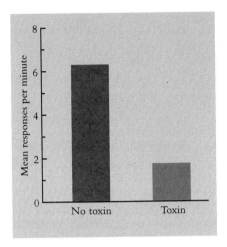

4.28 Act-outcome cognitions The figure shows the results on the final test of an experiment in which two different responses were reinforced by two different food rewards. Subsequently, one of the two rewards was paired with a toxin. There was a marked decline in the response leading to the reward that was devalued by the toxin (in blue) as compared with the response leading to the reward that was not devalued (dark red). (After Colwill and Rescorla, 1985)

Skinner-box lever that projected from one wall. When this lever was pressed, it led to a pellet made of rat chow. On other days, instead of a lever there was a chain that dangled from the ceiling. When this chain was pulled, the rat was rewarded with a few drops of a sugar solution. After a few days of training the rats were busily bar pressing and chain pulling, indicating that instrumental learning had been effective. But exactly what was it that had been learned? One possibility is that they acquired a tendency to perform the two responses. Another is that they acquired a cognition about the act-outcome relation: Bar pressing leads to rat-chow pellets, and chain pulling leads to sugar water.

To decide between these alternatives, the experimenters changed the desirability of one of the rewards after a week or so of instrumental training. They injected the rats with a mild toxin after they drank the sugar solution, creating a taste aversion for the sugar but not for the pellets (see Chapter 3, p. 76, and pp. 136–39). The question was what the animals would do when again given the chance to press a bar or pull a lever. The results showed that the rats learned which response led to which reward. They no longer pulled the chain that led to the sugar water (now a no-longer-desirable reward) but continued to press the lever that produced the chow pellet (Colwill and Rescorla, 1985; see Figure 4.28).★

CONTINGENCY IN INSTRUMENTAL CONDITIONING

We saw that classical conditioning depends on the contingency between the CS and the US rather than on their contiguity. A similar relation holds for instrumental conditioning. Here the relevant contingency is between an act and its outcome. If the act is lever pressing and the outcome is a food pellet, then the contingency is determined by comparing the probability of getting a pellet when the lever has been pressed with the probability of getting it when the lever has not been pressed. If the first probability is greater than the second, getting food is contingent upon lever pressing. If the two probabilities are equal, there is no contingency—lever pressing and getting pellets are independent.[†]

Response control in infants One line of evidence for the role of contingency in instrumental conditioning comes from studies of human infants. A group of two-month-old infants was provided with an opportunity to make something happen. The infants were placed in cribs above which a colorful mobile was suspended. Whenever the infants moved their heads, they closed a switch in their pillows. This activated the overhead mobile, which promptly turned for a second or so and did so every time the pillow switch was closed. The infants soon learned to shake their heads about, thus making their mobiles turn. They evidently enjoyed doing so; they smiled and cooed happily at their mobiles, clearly delighted at seeing them move. A second group of infants was exposed to a similar situation, but there was one difference—they had no control over the mobile's movement. Their mobile turned just about as often as the mobile for the first group, but it was moved for them, not by them. After a few days, these infants no longer smiled and cooed at the mobile, nor did they seem particularly

---

★For half the rats, a taste aversion was established for the chow pellets rather than the sugar water. When subsequently tested, these rats pulled the chain (which led to the sugar water) and did not press the lever (which led to the pellets).

[†]If the second probability is greater than the first, then getting the pellet is contingent upon *not* pressing the lever. This kind of contingency is common whenever one wants the learner to refrain from doing something, for example: "I'll give you a cookie if you stop whining."

4.29 Response control Infants who can make a mobile move, smile and coo at it, while those who have no control over its motion, stop smiling.

interested when it turned. This suggests that what the infants liked about the mobile was not that it moved but that they made it move. This shows that infants can distinguish between response-controlled and response independent outcomes, which is a strong argument for the contingency approach. It also shows that infants, no less than we, prefer to exercise some control over their environment. The reason for this is by no means clear, but it appears that even a two-month-old infant wants to be master of her own fate (Watson, 1967; see Figure 4.29).

Helplessness in dogs The mobile-turning infants illustrate the joy of mastery. Another, highly influential series of studies demonstrates the despair of no mastery at all. Their focus is on *learned helplessness,* an acquired sense that one can no longer control one's environment so that one gives up trying (Seligman, 1975).

The classic experiment on learned helplessness employed two groups of dogs, *A* and *B*, who received strong electric shocks while strapped in a hammock. The dogs in group *A* were able to exert some control over their situation. They could turn the shock off whenever it began by pushing a panel that was placed close to their noses. The dogs in group *B* had no such power. For them, the shocks were inescapable. But the number and duration of these shocks were exactly the same. For each dog in group *A* there was a corresponding animal in group *B* whose fate was "yoked" to that of the first dog. Whenever the group *A* dog was shocked, so was the group *B* dog. Whenever the group *A* dog turned off the shock, the shock was turned off for the group *B* dog. This arrangement guaranteed that the actual physical punishment meted out to both groups was precisely the same. What was different was what they could do about it. Group *A* was able to exercise some control; group *B* could only endure.

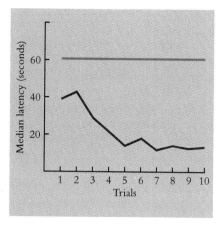

4.30 Learned helplessness The figure shows the shuttle box performance of two groups of dogs. On each trial, the animal could escape or avoid a shock. If it jumped within ten seconds after the CS, it avoided the shock altogether; if it did not jump within sixty seconds, the trial was terminated. The figure shows how quickly the animals jumped. The animals in Group A (dark red) had previously received electric shocks that they could escape by performing an instrumental response. The animals in Group B (blue) received the same shocks, but were unable to do anything about them. (After Maier, Seligman, and Solomon, 1969)

The question was how the group *B* dogs would fare when presented with a new situation that provided them with an opportunity to help themselves. To find out, both groups of dogs were presented with a standard avoidance learning task in a shuttle box (Figure 4.30). The dogs in group *A* learned just about as quickly as did naïve dogs who had no prior experimental experience of any kind. During the first trials, they waited until the shock began and then scrambled over the hurdle; later, they jumped before their grace period was up and thus avoided shock entirely. But the dogs in group *B*, who had previously suffered inescapable shock in the hammock, behaved very differently. Initially, they behaved much like other dogs; they ran about frantically, barking, and howling. But they soon became much more passive. They lay down, whined quietly, and simply took whatever shocks were delivered. They neither avoided nor escaped; they just gave up trying. In the hammock setup they had been objectively helpless; there really was nothing they could do. But in the shuttle box, their helplessness was only subjective, for there was now a way in which they could make their lot bearable. But they never discovered it. They had learned to be helpless (Seligman and Maier, 1967).

Helplessness and depression Martin Seligman, one of the discoverers of the learned helplessness effect in animals, asserts that a similar mechanism underlies the development of certain kinds of depression in human patients. (For further discussion of depression, see Chapter 18, pp. 742–43.) He believes that such patients share certain features with animals who had been rendered helpless. Both fail to initiate actions and instead "just sit there"; both are slow to learn that something they did was successful; both lose weight and have little interest in others. To Seligman and his associates these parallels suggest that the underlying cause is the same in both cases. Like the helpless dog, the depressed patient has come to feel that his acts are of no avail. And Seligman argues that, like the dog, the depressed patient was brought to this morbid state of affairs by an initial exposure to a situation in which he was objectively helpless. While the dog received inescapable shocks in its hammock, the patient found himself powerless in the face of bereavement, business failure, or serious illness (Seligman, Klein, and Miller, 1976). In both cases, the problem is a lack of contingency between acts and unfortunate outcomes.

Some biological consequences of helplessness The lack of contingency between acts and outcomes can have important medical consequences. Of particular interest are the biological effects of learned helplessness that are produced when humans and animals discover that they have no control over stressful events in their lives.

There's an old adage that patients who "give up hope" have a poorer chance of surviving than those who continue fighting. Several medical investigations suggest that there are some grounds for this belief. People who are hopeless and depressed are more likely to contract and succumb to major illness than those who try to cope. Thus, people who suffer the loss of a loved one are more likely to die in the year after their bereavement than control subjects of the same age. Finally, there is evidence that despair and helplessness in the face of important personal losses increase the risk of cancer in subsequent years (Horne and Picard, 1979; Shekelle et al., 1981; see Figure 4.31).

What might be responsible for these relationships? Some recent studies suggest that learned helplessness impairs the **immune system** of the body. The immune system produces a number of cells that fight various foreign invaders and tumors. Among these is a group called "killer cells," which deal with tumors. The killer cells recognize that the tumors are foreign and promptly dispatch them. Steven Maier and his associates have shown that the production of such killer cells is impaired when rats are put in a situation that induces learned helplessness. One group of animals was given a number of shocks from which they could escape by turning a tread wheel. A second group received the same shocks as the control rats but could do nothing about them. They suffered the same degree of physical stress, but unlike their counterparts in the control group, they learned that they had no control over their fate and so they became helpless. Later tests showed that animals who had been rendered helpless in this fashion produced fewer killer cells and were thus less able to stop tumor growth. This result fits in with other findings which show that learned helplessness in rats increases susceptibility to injected tumors (Visintainer, Volpicelli, and Seligman, 1982; Maier, Laudenslager, and Ryan, 1985).

Just why learned helplessness affects the immune system is still unknown. But whatever the mechanism, the fact that it does suggests that learning about the contingencies (and in the case of learned helplessness, the lack of contingencies) between one's own actions and subsequent events in the world has profound effects on bodily functioning.

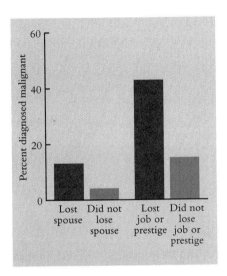

4.31 Psychological loss and lung cancer *Diagnoses were performed on over 100 patients whose X-rays showed a lesion in the lungs. Some of these patients had suffered serious psychological losses in the previous five years, for example, loss of a spouse, parent, or sibling; retirement; loss of a job; or loss of prestige. Others had not experienced any such losses. The figure presents the percent of the cases whose lung lesions turned out to be malignant. As the figure shows, malignancy was more likely for the patients who had suffered one of the serious losses listed above (in dark red) than for those who had not suffered any of these losses (in blue). (After Horne and Picard, 1979)*

VARIETIES OF LEARNING

Until fairly recently, most investigators were primarily interested in discovering some general laws of learning—whether associative or cognitive or possibly both—regardless of the particular animal that did the learning. To be sure, many of them believed that humans and other primates are capable of more complex cognition than lower animals, but outside of that they had little concern with the diversity of the animal kingdom, for in their view general laws should hold across the zoological board. By the same token, they also felt that these laws should apply to whatever is learned, whether it is learning to hunt or to escape hunters, to recognize members of one's own species or to speak the language of one's own group.

During the past two decades, this position has come under serious attack from investigators who adopt what has been called the *adaptive evolutionary perspective* (e.g., Roper, 1983; Bolles and Beecher, 1988; Rozin and Schull, 1988). A major impetus to their view came from the discovery of the role of "belongingness" in the formation of associations by animals.

BIOLOGICAL CONSTRAINTS ON ASSOCIATIVE LEARNING: BELONGINGNESS

In the early days of behavior theory, there was a widespread belief that animals are capable of connecting just about any CS to any US (in classical conditioning) or of associating virtually any response with any reinforcer (in instrumental conditioning). But during the last three decades, more and more evidence has accumulated that has undermined this position, which is sometimes called the **equipotentiality principle.** For as it turns out, not all associations are equally easy to learn. There are evidently certain built-in predispositions (often called **biological constraints**) that determine what a given animal can learn and what sorts of learning it will find difficult. These constraints are built into the system and help the animal adjust to the requirements of the environment in which it evolved (Rozin and Kalat, 1971, 1972; Seligman and Hager, 1972).

CS-US RELATIONS IN CLASSICAL CONDITIONING

According to the equipotentiality principle, the associations between the CS and the US are essentially arbitrary. But this turns out to be false. For there is now evidence that associations between two items are more readily formed if the items somehow belong together. An important example of the role of **belongingness** comes from classical conditioning, where a number of investigators have shown that certain CSs are more readily related to certain USs than to others. In their view, the animal has a built-in predisposition, sometimes called a **preparedness,** to form certain associations rather than others. The bulk of this evidence comes from learned taste aversions (García and Koelling, 1966; Domjan, 1983).

Belongingness and learned taste aversions It has long been known that rats are remarkably adept at avoiding foods they ate just before falling sick. This is the rea-

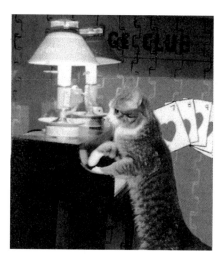

Arbitrary learning by operant techniques *Animals can be trained to prefer all manner of arbitrary responses by operant techniques as in the case of this cat that plays the piano. But there are important biological constraints that make some responses more difficult to learn than others. The cat has trouble learning to press the piano keys for food because its natural tendency is to importune people (or as a kitten, its mother) to feed it. (Photograph courtesy of Animal Behavior Enterprises)*

VARIETIES OF LEARNING

Learned food aversions in birds   In contrast to rats and humans, whose learned food aversions are usually based on taste and odor, most birds rely on visual cues. The figure shows the reaction of a bird who has just eaten a monarch butterfly, which contains distasteful and poisonous substances. The distinctive wing pattern of this butterfly provides the cue for an immediately acquired food aversion, for after one such mistake the bird will never again seize another monarch. (Courtesy of Lincoln P. Brower, University of Florida)

son why it is very difficult to exterminate wild rats with poison: The rat takes a small bite of the poisoned food, becomes ill, generally recovers, and thereafter avoids that particular flavor: The animal has become bait shy. Similar effects are easily produced in the laboratory. The subjects (usually rats) are presented with a given flavor, such as water containing saccharin. After drinking some of this water, they are exposed to X-ray radiation—not enough to kill them, but enough to make them ill and nauseous. After they recover, they are given a choice between, say, plain water and a saccharine solution. They will now refuse to drink the saccharin even though they they much preferred this sweet-tasting drink prior to their illness.

Such learned taste aversions are usually believed to be based on classical conditioning in which the CS is a certain flavor (here, saccharin) and the US is being sick. The question is whether other stimuli such as lights or tones serve equally well as CSs for such taste aversions. A number of studies by John Garcia and his coworkers have shown that they do not, thus refuting the equipotentiality principle.

One of the earliest studies to make this point is an experiment by Garcia and Koelling in which thirsty rats were allowed to drink saccharine-flavored water. The water came from a drinking tube; whenever the rat licked the nozzle, a bright light flashed and a clicking noise sounded. Subsequently, some rats received a shock to their feet. Others were exposed to a dose of illness-producing X-rays. All of the animals developed a strong aversion to the saccharine water. When again presented with water that was sweet and was accompanied by bright flashes and clicks, they hardly touched the drinking nozzle. All rats had presumably acquired a classically conditioned aversion. The US was either shock or illness. The CS was a stimulus compound comprised of the flavor, the light, and the noise. But did the rats learn to avoid all of these stimulus features or only some?

To find out, the experimenters tested the rats in a new situation. They gave some of the rats water that was saccharine-flavored but was unaccompanied by either light or noise. They gave others plain, unflavored water that was accompanied by the light and sound cues that were present during training. The results showed that what the rats had learned to avoid depended upon the US. If they had been shocked (and felt pain), they refused water that was accompanied by light and noise, but they had no objection to the sweet flavor. If they had been X-rayed (and became ill), the opposite was true—they avoided the saccharine

TABLE 4.3 BELONGINGNESS IN CLASSICAL CONDITIONING				
Training	In all groups: CS = saccharine taste + light + sound			
US:	Shock		X-ray illness	
Test Water with:	Saccharine taste	Light + sound	Saccharine taste	Light + sound
Results	No effect	Aversion	Aversion	No effect

flavor but were perfectly willing to drink when the water was preceded by light and noise (Table 4.3).

These results indicate that rats tend to link stimuli in certain fitting ways: In rats, taste goes with illness, sights and sounds with externally induced pain. This makes good biological sense. In the world of the rat, an omnivorous creature that selects its food mainly on the basis of its flavor, taste may well be the most reliable cue that warns of impending illness. If so, a built-in bias to associate sickness with preceding tastes is likely to have survival value. In effect, the rat cannot help but ask itself, "What did I eat?" whenever it has a stomachache (Garcia and Koelling, 1966).

If this is so, one might expect rather different results for animals who select their food on the basis of cues other than taste. An example comes from some species of birds that rely heavily on vision when choosing food. In one study, quail drank blue, sour water and were then poisoned. Some of the birds were later tested with blue, unflavored water; others were tested with water that was sour but colorless. The quail developed a drastic aversion to blue water. But they drank just about as much sour water as they had prior to being poisoned. Here, the learned food aversion was evidently based on color rather than on taste (Wilcoxin, Dragoin, and Kral, 1971). Thus, it appears that the built-in belongingness relation is species specific. Certain birds have a natively given bias to link sickness with visual cues, while rats and other mammals link it to taste. This bias prepares them to learn certain relations more readily than others (Seligman, 1970). In both cases, the preparedness fits in with the way the animal identifies food in its native habitat. (For an extension of the preparedness concept to phobias, see Chapter 18.)

Learned taste aversions and the CS-US interval That the equipotentiality principle is clearly false constitutes yet another argument against the role of contiguity in conditioning. In Garcia and Koelling's experiment, the noise and the flashing light were no less contiguous to the illness-producing X-rays than was the flavor of the water. But even so, only the flavor became an effective CS.

A further argument against the role of contiguity came from studies of the CS-US interval in learned taste aversions. In most studies of classical conditioning, the most effective CS interval tends to be relatively short, on the order of a few seconds or less. But Garcia and other investigators showed that in learned taste aversions the optimum interval is about an hour and that learning will occur with intervals as long as twenty-four hours (Garcia, Ervin, and Koelling, 1966; Rozin and Kalat, 1971; Logue, 1979). Just why it is possible to associate illness with tastes experienced an hour or more earlier is still a matter of debate (see Revusky, 1971, 1977, 1985; Rozin and Kalat, 1971; Domjan, 1980). But whatever the mechanism that underlies it, the biological utility of this phenomenon is clear enough: Both the beneficial and harmful effects of ingested food are delayed by the fairly slow processes of absorption and digestion. Under the circumstances, a mechanism that allows an animal to connect its internal malaise with tastes experienced some time ago makes excellent adaptive sense.

Taste aversions in humans   Taste aversions quite similar to those found in rats are also found in humans. When people get sick to their stomachs they often develop an aversion to the taste of food they ate before they became ill. They may know that their malaise was the result of an intestinal flu and that the raspberry ice cream or the clam chowder that they now find so repellent was in fact quite innocent. But this rational understanding does not alter their aversion, which may last for years (Logue, 1986).

The study of human taste aversions has implications for a number of real life concerns. One such area is the anorexia that is often found in cancer patients who undergo chemotherapy. The administration of the therapeutic drugs often produces nausea, which in turn may lead to an aversion to foods eaten prior to the treatment. This was demonstrated by a study in which cancer patients were given a novel-tasting ice cream before a chemotherapy session. Many of these patients developed a strong aversion to that novel flavor, even though they knew that their nausea was caused by the chemotherapy. This suggests some ways to alleviate the anorexia, such as minimizing meals—especially meals with novel foods—prior to treatments (Bernstein, 1978).

ACT-OUTCOME RELATIONS IN INSTRUMENTAL CONDITIONING

The preceding discussion showed that the CS-US relation in classical conditioning is not always arbitrary. A similar nonarbitrariness characterizes many instrumental learning situations (Shettleworth, 1972).

Consider a pigeon pecking away in a Skinner box. Here surely is the very prototype of arbitrary instrumental learning. But in fact, the relation between pecking and what is pecked at is far from arbitrary. One line of evidence comes from the fact that it is exceedingly hard to train pigeons to peck so as to escape or avoid electric shock (Hineline and Rachlin, 1969). This doesn't mean that shock escape or shock avoidance are inadequate reinforcers for pigeons—far from it. The birds readily learn to hop or flap their wings in order to get away from shock. What they have trouble learning is to peck to bring about the same outcome. According to Robert Bolles, this is because many animals have built-in defense reactions to danger. The pigeon is no exception. Its species-specific defense reaction is speedy locomotion, preferably airborne flight. The bird can learn new avoidance responses, but only to the extent that these fit in with its natively given danger reaction. Hopping, flying, and wing-flapping qualify, for they are merely modifications of the basic defense pattern. But pecking does not, and it is therefore very hard to learn as an escape or an avoidance response (Bolles, 1970).

If pigeons have so much trouble learning to peck to escape or avoid, why are they so readily trained to peck for food? The reason is that pecking is what pigeons do naturally when they consume food. In effect, pigeons pecking for a food reward are simply performing an anticipatory eating response. That something of this sort goes on is shown by how they peck when other reinforcers are used. In one study, thirsty pigeons had to peck at a key to obtain water. Their pecks were quite different from those seen with food reinforcement; they resembled the beak movements pigeons make while drinking (Figure 4.32). In another study, key-pecking brought access to a sexually receptive mate. Now

4.32   Key pecking for food and water   *(A) The pictures show a pigeon's beak movements as it pecks a key to obtain water. The movements resemble those the bird makes when it drinks. (B) These pictures show quite different beak movements made when the bird is hungry and pecks a key for food. Now the movements resemble those the animal makes when it eats. (Photographs by Bruce Moore, from Jenkins and Moore, 1973)* the pigeons cooed as they pressed the key. All of this means that key-pecking is not an arbitrary instrumental response. In effect, the pigeon "eats" the key when working for food, "drinks" it when working for water, and "courts" it when working for sex. There clearly is an intimate relation between the response and its reinforcer (Schwarts, 1989).

A number of psychologists believe that such findings indicate that key-pecking in a Skinner box is a classically rather than an instrumentally conditioned response. Evidence for this belief comes from a study in which naïve pigeons were left in a box whose key lit up periodically. The pigeons received food if they did *not* peck at the key during a six-second interval. But if they did peck, the key light went out and no food was presented. Here, food reward was contingent upon *not* pecking. But the pigeons pecked anyway. They simply couldn't help themselves (Williams and Williams, 1969). The CS-US contingency (here, lit key and food) evidently outweighed the response-outcome contingency (here, not pecking and food), which may be another way of saying that the response was in large part a classically conditioned CR (Schwartz and Gamzu, 1977).

THE "MISBEHAVIOR" OF ORGANISMS

Yet further evidence against the equipotentiality principle in instrumental conditioning comes from some observations by psychologists who trained animals to perform as live advertising exhibits (see pp. 120–21). By and large, their efforts were quite successful, but in some cases the animals "misbehaved." An example is a raccoon that was supposed to pick up several coins and then deposit them into a small piggy bank. The animal was first reinforced with food to pick up a coin. This was easy enough. After this, the raccoon was reinforced for dropping the coin into a container. This was more difficult, for the animal refused to let the coin go; it would rub it against the container, pull it back out, clutch it for a while, and release it only after considerable hesitation. The next step was even worse. Now the animal was required to pick *two* coins and then deposit them both. The raccoon refused. Instead of acting like a model savings bank customer, it rubbed the two coins together, dipped them into the container, pulled them out again, rubbed them together, and so on. It appeared that the raccoon reverted to a species-specific behavior pattern: Raccoons in the wild tend to rub food objects together and dunk or "wash" them. This same behavior emerged in the training, despite reinforcement contingencies to the contrary. Here, as in our previous examples, the relation between the instrumental response and its reinforcer is not arbitrary. The psychologists wanted the animal to learn an arbitrary response (deposit two coins) by reinforcing it with food. But the animal's own behavior drifted toward the response it was biologically predisposed to perform under these conditions (Breland and Breland, 1961).

ADAPTIVE SPECIALIZATIONS OF LEARNING

The preceding discussion demonstrates that the way in which animals associate events is not arbitrary. They come biologically prepared to acquire certain linkages rather than others. This clearly shows that the laws of associative learning must be modified to encompass the relationship between the CS and the US, and between the reinforcer and the response. But some theorists go further: They assert that in addition to the general forms of learning—conditioning and cognitive learning—there are some forms of learning that are specific to the species that does the learning and to what it is that gets learned.

A

B

Biological constraints on learning (A) *The chicken pulls the loop on the jukebox to start the music, then "dances" on the platform by scratching the floor. The scratching is not reinforced but is a built-in tendency of the chicken when it seeks food. (B) The "gold-mining pig" tends to toss the nuggets around and root them even though this delays its reinforcement. Rooting is a natural tendency of the pig in food-seeking situations; in this case, it leads to "misbehavior" since it interferes with the desired operant response. (Photographs courtesy of Animal Behavior Enterprises)*

DIFFERENCES IN WHAT DIFFERENT SPECIES LEARN

Proponents of this position argue that diversity is the rule in the biological world as different species adapt to different ecological niches. Different animals have vastly different anatomies and built-in behavior repertoires: lions stalk, antelopes run, and hyenas wait around and scavenge for left-overs. Proponents of the evolutionary perspective argue that a similar diversity may well apply to the processes of learning, that some animals can readily learn in ways that others cannot (Roper, 1983; Gallistel, 1990).

An oft-cited example is Clark's nutcracker, a food-storing bird that makes its home in the American Southwest and is a distant cousin of jays and crows. In the summer this bird buries thousands of pine nuts in various hiding places over an area of several square miles. All through the winter and early spring, the nutcracker flies back again and again to dig up its thousand of hidden caches. By now, several experiments have demonstrated that the bird does not mark the burial sites in any special way. It relies primarily on memory—a prodigious feat that few of us could rival. Some investigators have argued that this remarkable spatial memory might represent a special adaptation of the learning process. There is no doubt that the nutcracker is anatomically specialized as a food hoarder: It has a special pouch under its tongue that it fills with pine nuts when flying to find a hiding place. Why couldn't there be a similar evolutionary adaptation of the learning and memory process? Some further evidence suggests that there is: Related birds such as jays and pigeons that don't store food show poorer spatial memory than the nutcracker (Shettleworth, 1983, 1984; Olson, 1991).

Some interesting facts about the neurological basis of spatial memory in birds make a similar point. In birds the brain center essential for such functions is the hippocampus. Injury to this structure markedly impairs spatial memory: When lesioned in the hippocampus, food storing birds can't locate their caches. In line with the evolutionary perspective, it turns out that food-storing species possess a hippocampus that's twice the size of those found in species that don't store food.

A related fact concerns a sex difference in the size of this structure in the cowbird, a parasite that lays its eggs in the nest of another species. The female first finds a potential host nest, then returns to it a few days later to lay a single egg. During any one breeding season, she will repeat this process some forty times. This obviously requires some significant spatial ability; she first has to locate a potential host nest and must then find it again. No such ability is required in the male, who takes no part in the female's nest-finding activities. Appropriately enough, this behavioral difference between the sexes is mirrored in the size of their hippocampus. The female's is larger than the male's (Sherry, Jacobs, and Gaulin, 1992; Sherry et al., 1989).

A number of other phenomena of animal learning may well be understood as analogous biological adaptations. Seen in this light, the ability of many birds to learn the song of their own species and the remarkable navigation capacity of pigeons and geese are special forms of learning, their particular biological adaptations to their own environment (Marler, 1970; Gallistel, 1990).

SIMILARITIES IN WHAT DIFFERENT SPECIES LEARN

Some of the more extreme adherents of adaptive specialization are sufficiently impressed with the differences in what and how various species learn as to deny that there are any truly general learning processes. But in fact

Adaptive specialization of learning   A black-capped chickadee hiding a seed in one of many holes in a specially constructed laboratory tree. This bird has been shown to have a remarkable spatial memory: It hides over 100 seeds per day, each in a different location, and remembers where these seeds were deposited for up to 14 days. (From Dr. David Sherry; photograph courtesy of Susan Bradnam)

Convergent evolution *Animals that are exposed to similar environmental pressures may evolve similar adaptations. This holds for the convergent evolution of wings in animals of very different ancestry, such as insects, birds, and bats. It may also hold for some characteristics of learning, which may explain why many of the major phenomena of conditioning are found in such widely different animals as rats and honey bees. (A) A flying desert locust. (Photograph by Stephen Dalton/ NHPA) (B) A barn owl. (Photograph courtesy of Joe MacDonald/Bruce Coleman, Inc.) (C) A fishing bat. (Photograph by Stephen Dalton/Photo Researchers, Inc.)*

the similarities in how different creatures learn are no less striking than the differences. For example, there is evidence that the major phenomena of conditioning are found in honey bees just as they are in rats and pigeons (Couvillon and Bitterman, 1980). Such similarities suggest that while there are surely specialized adaptations, there are also some general mechanisms that govern learning throughout much of the animal kingdom. Such general learning processes would presumably underlie classical and instrumental conditioning, as well as the more complex cognitive processes found in higher mammals.

Given the fact that the nervous system of a bee is vastly different from that found in any animal with a backbone and has a totally different evolutionary history, it is quite unlikely that the same physiological mechanisms will underlie the way bees, rats, and pigeons learn. So how can we possibly explain the many similarities in the learning patterns of these and other animals? A possible answer is offered by the principle of **convergent evolution:** the idea that animals under similar environmental pressures often evolve similar adaptations.

Biologists appeal to this principle to explain why a very similar characteristic—such as the wing—evolves in organisms of very different ancestry—such as insects, birds, and bats. Although the wings of these creatures are anatomically very different (four specialized appendages of the outer skeleton in insects, two modified forelegs in birds, and two special skins between thumb and index finger in bats), they are wings all the same, for they all beat the air and serve as organs of flight. Their essential similarity is not produced by an underlying equivalence of anatomy or ancestry; it is instead created by equivalence of the world in which all three kinds of animals live. For all three must move through the air, and so they must obey the same laws of aerodynamics.

What holds for wings may also hold for some general laws of learning. Their physiological underpinnings may well be different in bees and rats. But whatever the underlying biology may turn out to be, one thing is the same and that is the world in which all these animals live. In that world, some significant events are contingent upon others and some important outcomes depend upon actions. Since this is so, one might well expect the evolution of mechanisms for extracting these relationships—that is, classical and instrumental conditioning. Many of the specific properties of conditioning that we have discussed already would be a natural consequence of the relationship between events in the real world. As one example, consider the superiority of forward to backward conditioning—a natural consequence of the fact that in our world time only flows in one direction, with the cause always preceding the effect.

Such considerations suggest that while there may be some species-specific differences in the what and how of learning, there are also some general processes such as classical and instrumental conditioning. Whether the physiological mechanisms that underlie such general processes are the same in different animals is still an open question.

COMPLEX COGNITION IN ANIMALS

The work on animal cognitions that we discussed earlier showed that animals may know something without manifesting this knowledge in their actions. But it did not focus directly on the intellectual capacities that this knowledge revealed. Evidence that bears on this point comes from a number of sources. One concerns spatial memory in animals; the other relates to insightful learning.

4.33   A radial-arm maze   *One pellet is placed at the end of each arm, so the rat is rewarded most for choosing each arm once. (From Olton and Samuelson, 1976)*

COGNITIVE MAPS

A number of contemporary investigators have extended Tolman's notion of a cognitive map that represents the spatial layout of the animal's world and indicates what is where and what leads to what (Tolman, 1948). By now we know that this spatial knowledge can be quite complex. One investigator studied rats in radial-arm mazes, consisting of a central platform from which 8 pathways extended like spokes in a wheel (Figure 4.33). Each arm of the maze contained a food pellet. A hungry rat was placed on the center platform and allowed to move about at will. It generally explored a bit, then chose one of the arms, ran to its end, found the food pellet, and ate it. The question was what would it do after it returned to the center? Its optimal strategy was *not* to revisit the arm on which it had just been, for this arm was now empty. Instead, it should visit each arm just once, thus getting the most food for the least effort. But to accomplish this, the rat must not only have learned the spatial layout; it must also have remembered where on that layout it had been and where it hadn't. The results show that the rats had these capacities. Given a radial maze of 8 arms, they chose an average of 7.9 different arms in 8 choices (Olton and Samuelson, 1976; Olton, 1978, 1979).

What rats can do, chimpanzees can do even better. Proof came from a chimpanzee version of an Easter-egg hunt. The experimenter took one animal at a time and carried it through a zig-zag course of a familiar, one-acre compound, while accompanied by an assistant who hid pieces of fruit in eighteen different locations. During this time, the chimpanzee merely watched through the bars of its carrying cage. A few minutes after the last piece of fruit had been hidden, the animal was released. It immediately dashed to one hiding place after another, unearthed the fruit hidden in each, and ate it. In general, the chimpanzee remembered most of the hiding places after only one trial of passive watching (Menzel, 1973, 1978).

Studies such as these suggest that the notion of a cognitive map may be more than a figure of speech. Perhaps something analogous to a map of the spatial environment is formed in the nervous system. Some authors have tried to find a physiological basis for such a mapping pattern in a certain region of the limbic system in the brain containing neurons that seem to be sensitive to spatial information (O'Keefe and Nadel, 1978).

INSIGHTFUL BEHAVIOR

Thorndike had argued that problem solving in animals comes about by blind trial and error. But his conclusion was soon challenged by an early study of chimpanzees undertaken by the German psychologist Wolfgang Köhler (1887–1968).

Köhler believed that animals can behave intelligently. To be sure, Thorndike's cats had shown little sign of understanding, but perhaps cats are not the best subjects if one wants to determine the upper reaches of animal intellect. A closer relative of human beings, such as chimpanzees, might prove a better choice. Even more important, Köhler believed that Thorndike had loaded the dice in favor of blind trial and error, for the problems he had posed his cats were often impossible to solve in any other way. Thus, even an intellectual supercat could never hit on the idea of yanking the wire that pulled the door latch except by pure chance; there was no other way, for all the strings and pulleys were hidden from the animal's view. To Köhler the real question was whether animals would

Wolfgang Köhler   *(Courtesy The Warder Collection)*

A   B   C   D

4.34 Tool using in chimpanzees *(A) Using a stick as a pole to climb up to a banana. (B) Using a stick as a club to beat down a banana. (C and D) Erecting three- and four-story structures to reach a banana. (From Köhler, 1925)*

4.35 Tool making in chimpanzees *Sultan making a double stick. (From Köhler, 1925)*

behave intelligently when the conditions were optimum—when all of the ingredients of the solution were visibly present.

Köhler's procedure was simple. A chimpanzee was placed in an enclosed play area. Somewhere out of its reach was a desirable lure (usually some fruit, such as a banana). To obtain it, the ape had to employ some nearby object as a tool. In this the animals were remarkably successful. They learned to use sticks as rakes to haul in bananas placed on the ground just outside the cage, but beyond the reach of their arms. Sticks were equally useful to club down fruit hung too high overhead. Some chimpanzees used the sticks as a pole as well; they stood it upright under the banana, frantically climbed up its fifteen-foot length, and grasped their reward just as the stick toppled over (a considerable intellectual as well as gymnastic feat, demonstrating the virtues of a healthy mind in a healthy body). The chimpanzees also learned to use boxes as "climb-upon-ables," dragging them under the banana and then stepping atop them to claim their prizes. Eventually they even became builders, piling boxes on top of boxes and finally erecting structures that went up to four (rather shaky) stories, as Köhler spurred them on to ever-greater architectural accomplishments by progressively raising the height of the lure (Figure 4.34).

Occasionally the apes became toolmakers as well as tool-users. For example, when in need of a stick, they might break off a branch of a nearby tree. Even more impressive was the manufacture of a double stick. A particularly gifted chimpanzee called Sultan was faced with a banana far out of his reach. There were two bamboo sticks in his cage, but neither of them was long enough to rake in the lure. After many attempts to reach the banana with one stick or another, Sultan finally hit upon the solution. He pushed the thinner of the two sticks into the hollow inside of the thicker one and then drew the banana toward himself, his reach now enlarged by the length of two sticks (Figure 4.35).

Köhler denied that such achievements were the result of a mechanical strengthening and weakening of response tendencies. On the contrary, the animals behaved as if they had attained what he called **insight** into the relevant relationships—as if they *saw* what led to what. Köhler offered several lines of evidence. To begin with, when the problem was once solved, the animals usually performed smoothly and continuously thereafter as if they "knew what they were doing," in marked contrast to Thorndike's cats who went on fumbling for many trials. In further opposition to Thorndike's findings, the insightful solution often came quite suddenly, sometimes after a pause during which the chimpanzee only moved its head and eyes as if studying the situation. Once the correct response was made, further errors were rare.

The most convincing evidence for the view that the chimpanzees learned by insight rather than by blind trial and error came from tests in which the situation was changed to determine what the animals would transfer from the original task. Such **transfer of training** tests provide a useful method that serves to define what has been learned in any given situation. Teachers use just this approach to find out what their students have understood. Consider a young child who quickly answers "7" when confronted by the symbols "3 + 4 = ?" Has he really grasped the notion of addition? A simple test might be to present him with another problem, "4 + 3 = ?" If he is now bewildered, he presumably has learned merely to give a specific answer to a specific question, but if his reply again is "7," he may be on the way to genuine arithmetic insight. Köhler used similar tests on his chimpanzees. For example, he took animals who had previously learned to use a box as a platform and presented the high lure again, but now with all boxes removed. The animals were quick to find other objects, such as a table or a small ladder, which they promptly dragged to the proper place. These were not the only substitutes. On one occasion, Sultan came over to Köhler, pulled him by the arm until he was under the banana, and then showed that in a pinch even the director of the Prussian anthropoid station would do as a climb-upon-able.

To Köhler, the main criterion for insight was wide and appropriate transfer. But is this kind of transfer really so hard to explain in behavior theory's terms? Can't one say that it is simply some form of stimulus generalization? A dog who has previously been conditioned to salivate to a tone of 1,000 hertz will also salivate when presented with 1,500 hertz. How is this different from the kind of transfer that we regard as a sign of understanding.

The answer is that in stimulus generalization transfer is only based on perceptual similarity. A variety of stimuli are seen (or heard or felt) as more or less alike and so they are responded to in a similar fashion. But in the case of the "3 + 4" example, the transfer is based on something else, on a common principle, on an abstract conceptual relationship. The important thing is not that "3 + 4" and "4 + 3" (not to speak of "2 + 5," "1 + 6," and so on) look alike. The important thing is that they are alike in meaning.

ABSTRACT CONCEPTS IN ANIMALS

A number of studies have shown that various primates can respond to certain abstract, conceptual aspects of a situation that transcend perceptual characteristics. Some demonstrations have been obtained by David Premack who has tried to map the upper limits of the cognitive capacities in several chimpanzees, including his prize pupil, Sarah (Premack, 1976; Premack and Premack, 1983). An example of such an abstract concept is the notion "same-different." Consider a situation in which an animal is shown three items. One serves as the sample, the other two as alternatives. The animal's task is to choose the alternative that matches the sample. Suppose the alternatives are a triangle and a square. If so, the triangle is the correct choice if the sample is also a triangle; conversely, if the sample is a square. This procedure is called **matching to sample** (see Figure 4.36).

There is little doubt that animals other than primates can be taught to match if they are given enough trials to learn. Thus, pigeons can be taught to peck at a green rather than a yellow key if the sample is green and to peck at the yellow key if the sample is yellow. But does that mean that they understand what sameness means? The question is whether they somehow understand that the relation between two yellow keys is the same as the relation between two equal tones or two identical triangles, that in all cases the two items are the same. To

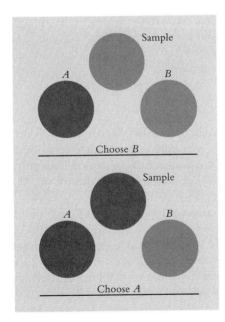

4.36 Matching to sample *The figure shows the procedure of a typical matching-to-sample experiment. The top circle in each panel represents the sample. The subject's task is to choose the one circle from the two at the bottom that matches the sample in color. In the top panel of the figure, the correct choice is B; in the bottom panel, it is A.*

test whether the animal has this abstract concept of sameness, we have to determine whether there is any transfer from one matching-to-sample situation to another one in which the particular stimulus items are quite different. Take the pigeon that has learned to match green-green. Does this training help the pigeon to match red-red or, better yet, triangle-triangle? By and large, the answer seems to be no (Premack, 1978; but see also Zentall and Hogan, 1974). It can recognize that two reds are the same. But it does not recognize that this sameness is the identical relation that exists between two other equal stimulus items.

The situation is quite different in chimpanzees. Having matched to sample on only three prior problems, Sarah and a few other animals readily handled new problems, performing perfectly on the very first trial. Even more impressive is the fact that Sarah learned to use two special tokens to indicate *same* and *different*. She was first shown two identical objects, such as two cups, and was then given a token whose intended meaning was *same*. Her task was to place this *same* token between the two cups. She was then presented with two different objects, such as a cup and a spoon, was given yet another token intended to mean *different*, and was required to place this *different* token between the cup and the spoon. After several such trials, she was tested with several pairs of items, some identical and some different, had to decide whether to place the *same* or the *different* token between them, and did so correctly (see Figure 4.37).

Such accomplishments show that chimpanzees can develop a way of thinking about the world that goes beyond the specific perceptual relations of the concrete moment. Like pigeons, they can of course respond to these concrete relationships, for example, the relationship between, say, red and red, circle and circle, A-flat and A-flat. But unlike pigeons, chimpanzees can also deal with some **higher-order relationships,** the relations that hold between the various concrete relationships. They can therefore recognize that the relation between red and red is identical to that between circle and circle, and for that matter between hippopotamus and hippopotamus—that in all of these the relation is *sameness*.

ACCESSING WHAT ONE KNOWS

The formation of abstract concepts is certainly one of the characteristics of what we normally call intelligence. But it is not the only one. Another criterion is whether the animal has some **access** to its own intellectual operations. This point is particularly relevant in the light of our previous discussion of adaptive specializations of learning.

Consider a pigeon who finds its way home over long distances. That bird is a brilliant navigator. It refers to the stars, to the sun, to a number of landmarks, and somehow calculates the correct path with remarkable accuracy. But we don't therefore regard the bird as especially intelligent. The reason is that we are convinced that it doesn't really know what it is doing. Its brain constitutes a marvelous navigational computer. But the bird can't use that computer for any purpose other than that for which it was installed by evolution. It has no access to its own intellectual machinery.

In this regard, a pigeon is quite different from a human being. At least to some extent, we do have access to our own mental functioning. We think and remember, and we also know that we think and remember. And we can use these and other intellectual capacities very broadly. This access to our own intellectual functions is by no means total; as we will see later on, it is especially limited in childhood (see Chapter 13). Our present point is only that this access is one of the defining features of intelligent behavior and is a characteristic of that intellectual generalist, the human being (Rozin, 1976a).

Some studies by Premack and his collaborators suggest that intellectual access is not confined to humans. They showed Sarah several videotaped scenes of a

Means *same*

Means *different*

4.37 The same-different problem
(After Premack and Premack, 1972)

4.38 Knowing about problem solving
(A) End of brief videotaped segment showing Sarah's trainer reaching for bananas that are too high for him. (B) Two pictured alternatives. One shows the trainer reaching along the ground with a stick. The other shows him stepping on a box. Sarah tended to choose the picture that showed the correct solution—in the present case, the trainer stepping on the top of the box. (From Premack and Woodruff, 1978)

trainer struggling with different problems. In one scene, he tried to reach a banana suspended high above him. In another, he vainly stretched his arm toward a banana on the floor outside of a cage. After Sarah saw the tapes, she was shown different photographs of the trainer engaged in one of several actions. In one picture he was climbing on a box, in another he was shoving a stick under the wire mesh of the cage, and so on. Sarah's job was to pick the photograph that depicted the appropriate solution to the problem. Thus, if she was first shown a scene in which the trainer struggled to reach an overhead banana, she had to choose the picture of a man stepping on a box. Sarah did quite well, succeeding in twenty-one out of twenty-four trials (Figure 4.38).

Sarah's success in this task suggests that the chimpanzee's problem-solving ability goes further even than Köhler had thought. To be sure, Sarah can solve a variety of spatial problems and can do so insightfully. But her ability may go beyond this. She not only solves problems, she also seems to know something *about* problem solving. She recognizes that the trainer has a problem, what this problem is, and how it should be dealt with successfully. To this extent, she has some access to her own intellectual processes (a point we'll return to later in discussing the extent to which monkeys, chimpanzees, and three-year-old humans have a "theory of mind"; see Chapters 10 and 13).

TAKING STOCK

What is the upshot of the scientific study of animal learning that began with the studies of Pavlov and Thorndike some ninety years ago? It is clear that they and their intellectual descendants have discovered many vital phenomena of learning. Whether the principles they uncovered in their study of habituation, classical conditioning, and instrumental conditioning underlie all forms of learning is still a matter of debate. For certain complex intellectual achievements in animals and humans such as insightful understanding, abstract concepts, and—especially—human language, may well be acquired in some different ways. But there is no question that the study of how CS-US and response-reinforcer relations are acquired and represented in animals will give important clues about the fundamental nature of some basic learning processes found in both humans and animals.

When we began our discussion, our initial focus was on *action*, on how classical and instrumental conditioning change what animals *do:* how Pavlov's dogs came to salivate to ticking metronomes they had never heard before; how Thorndike's cats came to perform all sorts of novel tricks. But as we saw, these changes of overt behavior are only one aspect of what happened to these animals—they are the consequence of having learned rather than its essence. For unlike Pavlov and Thorndike, who focused on overt behavior, modern investigators of animal learning have shown that at bottom classical and instrumental conditioning (and many other forms of learning too) depend on *cognition*. Rats—and dogs and pigeons—learn which events predict which other events and which actions produce which outcomes. These and other phenomena make it clear that psychological functions involve not just what animals and humans *do*, but also what they *know*.

Psychology must necessarily deal with both action and knowledge. In our discussion of animal learning we have straddled them both, for the field represents a kind of bridge between these two major concerns. We will now cross the bridge completely and move on to the study of cognition as a topic in its own right.

SUMMARY

1. The simplest of all forms of learning is *habituation,* a decline in the tendency to respond to stimuli that have become familiar through repeated exposure. In habituation the organism learns that it has encountered a stimulus before. In *classical conditioning,* first studied by I. P. Pavlov, it learns about the *association* between one stimulus and another. Prior to conditioning, an *unconditioned stimulus* or *US* (such as food) elicits an *unconditioned response* or *UR* (such as salivation). After repeated pairings of the US with a *conditioned stimulus* or *CS* (such as a buzzer), this CS alone will evoke a *conditioned response* or *CR* (here again, salivation) that is often similar to the UR.

2. The strength of conditioning is assessed by the readiness with which the CS elicits the CR. This strength increases with the number of *reinforced trials,* that is, pairings of the CS and the US. When a CS-US relation is well established, the CS can be paired with a second neutral stimulus to produce *second-order conditioning.*

3. Nonreinforced trials (when the CS is presented without the US) lead to *extinction,* a decreased tendency of the CS to evoke the CR. Some contend that *spontaneous recovery* shows that the CR is masked, not abolished, by extinction.

4. The CR is elicited not only by the CS but also by stimuli that are similar to it. This effect, *stimulus generalization,* increases the greater the similarity between the CS and the new stimulus. To train the animal to respond to the CS but not to other stimuli, one stimulus (CS^+) is presented with the US, while another (CS^-) is presented without the US. The more similar the CS^+ is to the CS^-, the more difficult this *discrimination* will be.

5. Classical conditioning can involve many responses other than salivation, such as, conditioning to feel fear as assessed by the *conditioned emotional response (CER)* procedure. The CR is never identical, and sometimes not even similar to the UR, which suggests that the CS serves as a signal, not a substitute, for the US. In some cases, the CR is not just different from the UR but is its very opposite. A possible example is the development of *drug tolerance.* According to some authors, this is partially caused by a conditioned compensatory reaction to stimuli that habitually accompany the drug administration.

6. In classical conditioning, the US is presented regardless of whether the animal performs the CR or not. In another form of simple learning, *instrumental conditioning* (or *operant conditioning*), something analogous to the US—a reward or *reinforcement*—is only delivered upon performance of the appropriate instrumental response.

7. An early study of instrumental conditioning was conducted by E. L. Thorndike using cats that learned to perform an arbitrary response to escape from a *puzzle box.* As Thorndike saw it, what the animals learned involved no understanding but was rather based on a gradual strengthening of the correct response and a weakening of the incorrect one. To account for this, he proposed his *law of effect,* which states that the tendency to perform a response is strengthened if it is followed by a reward (reinforcement) and weakened if it is not.

8. During the past sixty years or so, the major figure in the study of instrumental conditioning was B. F. Skinner, one of the first theorists to insist on a sharp distinction between classical conditioning in which the CR is *elicited* by the CS and instrumental (or *operant*) conditioning in which the instrumental response, or *operant,* is *emitted* from within. Operants are strengthened by *reinforcement,* but their acquisition may require some initial *shaping* by the method of *successive approximations.*

9. While some reinforcers are stimuli whose reinforcing power is unlearned, others are *conditioned reinforcers* that acquire their reinforcing power from prior pairings with stimuli that already have that capacity. One of the factors that determines the strength of instrumental conditioning is the *delay of reinforcement:* The shorter the interval between the response and the reinforcement, the stronger the response will be.

10. During *partial reinforcement,* the response is reinforced only some of the time. Responses that were originally learned under partial reinforcement are harder to extin-

guish than those learned when the response was always reinforced. The rule that determines the occasions under which reinforcement is given is a *schedule of reinforcement*. In *ratio schedules*, reinforcement comes after a number of responses that may be fixed or variable. In *interval schedules*, the animal is reinforced for the first response made after a given interval since the last reinforcement, which again can be fixed or variable.

11.　Reinforcement can be provided by the presentation of *appetitive stimuli* or by the termination or prevention of *aversive stimuli*. Aversive stimuli can weaken or strengthen instrumental responses, depending on the relation between the aversive stimulus and the response. In *punishment training*, the response is followed by an aversive stimulus; as a result, the animal learns *not* to perform it. In *escape learning*, the response stops an aversive stimulus that has already begun; in *avoidance training*, it averts it altogether. In both cases, the animal will then learn to make the desired response.

12.　Pavlov, Thorndike, and Skinner believed that the essential aspect of both classical and instrumental conditioning is that they modify *action*. *Cognitive theorists* such as Köhler and Tolman believe that when humans and animals learn they acquire new bits of knowledge or *cognitions*. According to many theorists, what is learned in classical conditioning is an association between two events, the CS and the US, such that the CS serves as a signal for the US. One line of evidence comes from studies of the effect of the CS-US interval. The general finding is that conditioning is more effective when the CS precedes the US by some optimum interval, which is typically rather short.

13.　A number of investigators have asked how the animal learns that the CS is a signal for the US. The evidence shows that CS-US pairings alone will not suffice; there must also be trials on which the absence of CS goes along with the absence of US. This allows the animal to discover that the US is *contingent* (depends) upon the CS. The discovery of this contingency seems to depend on the extent to which the US is unexpected or "surprising," as shown by the phenomenon of *blocking*.

14.　Unlike Thorndike and Skinner who argued that instrumental learning involves the strengthening of an instrumental response, cognitive theorists believe that it is based on an association between an act and its outcome. Evidence for this view comes from studies in which animals are trained to perform two responses that lead to two different outcomes after which one of the outcomes is made less desirable. Subsequent tests indicate that the animals learned which response led to which result.

15.　Contingency is crucial in instrumental conditioning just as it is in classical conditioning. In instrumental conditioning, the relevant contingency is between a response and an outcome. When there is no such contingency, the organism learns that it has no *response control*. Threatening conditions in which there is no response control may engender *learned helplessness*, which often generalizes to other situations.

16.　According to Pavlov, Skinner, and other early behaviorists, the connections established by classical and instrumental conditioning are essentially *arbitrary*. This led them to believe that just about any CS can become associated with any US and that just about any response can be strengthened by any reinforcer, a position often called the *equipotentiality principle*. This position is challenged by the fact that certain CSs are more readily associated with some USs than with others, as shown by studies of *learned taste aversions*. These studies suggest that animals are biologically prepared to learn certain relations more readily than others. Similar preparedness effects occur in instrumental conditioning: Some responses are more readily strengthened by some reinforcers than by others.

17.　According to some investigators there are some forms of learning that are species specific so that some animals can readily learn what others cannot. Adherents of this view point to specialized adaptations in various birds, including remarkable memory for hoarded food, song learning, and navigation abilities.

18.　Cognitive theorists point out that animals are capable of rather complex cognitions. Evidence comes from work on spatial memory in rats and chimpanzees which shows that these animals can acquire rather elaborate *cognitive maps*. Further work concerns the ability to abstract *conceptual* relationships. Early evidence came from Köhler's studies of *insightful learning* in chimpanzees, who showed wide and appropriate transfer when later tested in novel situations. Later work showed that chimpanzees can acquire certain *higher-order* concepts such as "same-different" and seem to have some access to their own cognitive operations.

PART TWO

COGNITION

CHAPTER **5**

SENSORY PROCESSES

THE ORIGINS OF KNOWLEDGE   153

THE EMPIRICIST VIEW ▪ THE NATIVIST REJOINDER ▪ DETECTION AND DECISION ▪ SENSORY CODING

A SURVEY OF THE SENSES   165

KINESTHESIS AND THE VESTIBULAR SENSES ▪ THE SKIN SENSES ▪ THE SENSE OF TASTE ▪ THE SENSE OF SMELL ▪ HEARING ▪ THE SENSES IN OVERVIEW

VISION   176

THE STIMULUS: LIGHT ▪ GATHERING THE STIMULUS: THE EYE ▪ THE VISUAL RECEPTORS ▪ INTERACTION IN TIME: ADAPTATION ▪ INTERACTION IN SPACE: CONTRAST ▪ COLOR ▪ THE PHYSIOLOGICAL BASIS OF COLOR VISION ▪ FEATURE DETECTORS

TAKING STOCK   197

SUMMARY   197

The approach to mental life we have considered thus far emphasizes action, whether natively given or modified by learning. It is an approach that asks what organisms do and how they do it. We now turn to another approach to mental functioning that asks what organisms know and how they come to know it.

Both humans and many animals are capable of knowledge, though in our own species, knowing (or cognition) is vastly more refined. We know about the world directly around us, perceiving objects and events that are in our here and now, like the rose that we can see and smell. We also know about events in our past at least some of which are stored in our memory and can be retrieved at some later time; the rose may fade, but we can recall what it looked like when it was still in bloom. Our knowledge can be transformed and manipulated by thinking; we can somehow sift and analyze our experiences to emerge with new and often abstract notions, so that we can think of the faded rose petals as but one stage in a reproductive cycle which in turn reflects the procession of the seasons. Finally, we can communicate our knowledge to others by the use of language, a uniquely human capacity that allows us to accumulate knowledge, each building upon the discoveries of the preceding generation.

T o survive, we must know the world around us. For most objects in the world are charged with meaning: Some are food, others are mates, still others are mortal enemies. The ability to distinguish between them—say, between a log and a crocodile—is literally a matter of life and death. To make these distinctions, we have to use our senses. We must do our best to see, hear, and smell the crocodile so that we can recognize it for what it is before it sees, hears, smells, and (most especially) touches and tastes us.

THE ORIGINS OF KNOWLEDGE

The study of sensory experience grows out of an ancient question: Where does human knowledge come from? Most philosophers in the past subscribed to one of two opposed positions. The **empiricists** maintained that all knowledge is acquired through experience. In contrast, the **nativists** argued that many aspects of our knowledge are based on innately given characteristics of the human mind (or, as we would now say, of the brain).

THE EMPIRICIST VIEW

A major proponent of the empiricist position was the English philosopher John Locke (1632–1704). Locke maintained that all knowledge comes through the senses. There are no innate ideas; at birth, the human mind is a blank tablet, a *tabula rasa,* upon which experience leaves its marks.

> Let us suppose the mind to be, as we say, a white paper void of all characters, without any ideas:—How comes it to be furnished? Whence comes it by that vast store which the busy and boundless fancy of man has painted on it with an almost endless variety? Whence has it all the materials of reason and knowledge? To this I answer, in one word, from experience. In that all our knowledge is founded; and from that it ultimately derives itself (Locke, 1690).

Locke's view fit in well with the emerging liberalism that was the dominant sentiment of the rising middle classes during the eighteenth century. The merchants and manufacturers of Western Europe had little use for the hereditary privileges of a landed aristocracy or for the divine right of kings to govern (and worse, to tax) as they chose. Under the circumstances, they readily grasped at any doctrine that proclaimed the essential equality of all men. If all men enter life with a *tabula rasa,* then all distinctions among them must be due entirely to differences in their environments.

DISTAL AND PROXIMAL STIMULI

Given the assumption that all knowledge comes through the senses, it was natural enough to ask about the kind of knowledge that the senses can give us. What is the information that the senses receive? Consider vision. We look at a tree some distance away. Light reflected from the tree's outer surface enters through the pupil of the eye, is gathered by the lens, and is cast as an image upon the photosensitive region at the rear of the eye called the *retina.* The stimuli that are involved in this visual sequence can be described in either of two ways. We can talk about the *distal stimulus,* an object or event in the world outside, such as the tree. (This is typically at some *distance* from the perceiver, hence the term *distal.*) We can also talk about the *proximal stimulus,* the pattern of stimulus energies that takes its origins at the distal stimulus and finally impinges on a sensory surface of the organism (hence, the term *proximal,* that is, "nearby.") In our example, this proximal stimulus would be the optical image the tree casts on the retina.

As perceivers, our interest obviously centers upon the distal stimulus, the real object in the world outside. We want to know about the tree, not its retinal image. Our interest is in the tree's real size, its distance away from us, the kind of leaves it has, and so on. But we can only learn about the distal stimulus through the proximal stimuli to which it gives rise. There is no way of really seeing the tree out there without a retinal image of the tree. The same holds for the other senses. We can only smell a rotten egg (the distal stimulus) because of hydrogen sulfide molecules suspended in the air that flows over the sensory cells in our nasal cavities (the proximal stimulus).

The senses are the only portals we have to the world outside; the proximal stimuli are the only messengers that are allowed to pass information through them. Such heirs of Locke as Bishop George Berkeley (1685–1753) were quick to show that this fact has enormous consequences. For one thing, the sensory information provided by the proximal stimulus seems to lack many of the qualities that presumably characterize the external object (that is, the distal stimulus) to which this information refers. For example, Berkeley pointed out that we

John Locke *(Courtesy of the National Portrait Gallery, London)*

Bishop George Berkeley *(Detail from* The Bermuda Group *by John Smibert; courtesy of Yale University Art Gallery, gift of Isaac Lothrop of Plymouth, Mass.)*

5.1 Distal and proximal stimuli *The young girl and her father are distal stimuli, real objects in the world outside. The proximal stimuli they give rise to are the images they cast on the retina. In the example, the little girl is about one-third the size of her father. But since the father is three times farther removed from the observer's eye than the child, the size of the retinal image he casts is the same as the one cast by the child.*

cannot tell the size of the physical object from the size of its retinal image. Our tree might be a miniature plant nearby or a giant one in the distance. By the same token, we cannot tell whether an object is in motion or at rest from its retinal image alone, for motion of the image may be caused by motion of the external object or by movements of the observer's eye. It appears that the knowledge that comes by way of the retinal image is very meager (see Figure 5.1).

SENSATIONS

Considerations of this sort led later empiricists to assume that the raw materials out of which knowledge is constructed are ***sensations,*** the primitive experiences that the senses give us and upon which we must then build. Green and brown are examples of visual sensations. An example of an auditory sensation would be a loud A-flat. An example of a gustatory (that is, taste) sensation would be a bitter taste. According to the empiricists, all our perceptual experience is ultimately composed of such sensations—a mosaic of colored patches, tones of different pitch and loudness, sweets and sours, and so on.

Can this description possibly do justice to the richness of our perceptual world? The fact is that we do see trees (and innumerable other objects) and not mere patches of green and brown. While Bishop Berkeley might argue that our vision cannot inform us about depth or true size, in actual life we seem to have little difficulty in telling how far an object is away from us. (Were it otherwise, every automobile would become a wreck within minutes of leaving the showroom.) And we can in fact perceive the true size of an object. After all, even Berkeley would have had little trouble in distinguishing between a tiger in the distance and a kitten close by.

How did the empiricists reconcile these facts with their assumptions about the nature of sensation? Their answer was learning.

THE ROLE OF ASSOCIATION

The empiricists assumed that the organized character and the meaningfulness of our perceptual world are achieved by prior experience. The key to this accomplishment was held to be ***association,*** the process whereby one sensation is linked to another. The basic idea was very simple: If two sensations occur

5.2 The use of linear perspective in Renaissance art The School of Athens by Raphael, 1509–1511. (Stanze della Segnatura, Vatican; courtesy Scala/Art Resource)

Immanuel Kant (Courtesy of Culver Pictures, Inc., New York)

together often enough, eventually one of them will evoke the idea of the other. According to the empiricists, this associative linkage is the cement that binds the separate components of the perceptual world to each other.★

An example is provided by the various **distance cues.** Some of these had been noted by the painters of the Renaissance who discovered several techniques for rendering a three-dimensional world on a two-dimensional canvas. Among them was linear perspective—objects appear to be farther away as they decrease in size (Figure 5.2). To an empiricist, the explanation is a matter of prior association. Visual cues of perspective generally precede reaching or walking; eventually, the visual cue alone will produce the memory of the appropriate movement and thus the experience of depth.

THE NATIVIST REJOINDER

The major theoretical alternative to the empiricist conception is **nativism,** which asserts that many aspects of perceptual experience are part of our natural endowment and do not depend on learning. This general position has a long ancestry with roots that go back as far as Plato. In more recent times, an influential rejoinder to empiricism came from the German philosopher Immanuel Kant (1724–1804). Kant argued that knowledge cannot come from sensory input alone; there must also be certain preexisting "categories" according to which this sensory material is ordered and organized. Examples are space, time, and causality—categories that, according to Kant, are built into the mind (or, as we would now say, into the nervous system). In Kant's view, there is no way in which we can see the world except in terms of these categories. It is as if

★ It is obvious that the notion of association was at the root of many of the theories of learning we discussed in the last chapter. For example, Pavlov's conceptions of classical conditioning are in many ways derived from the views of the early associationists.

we looked at the world through colored spectacles that we could never take off; if they were red, then redness would necessarily be part of everything we see. According to Kant, experience provides the sensory input that is then ordered according to these preexisting categories. But the categories themselves, and the way in which they order the sensory information, are natively given.

PSYCHOPHYSICS

The dispute between empiricists and nativists focused attention on the role of the senses and prodded later investigators into efforts to discover just how these senses function. The question they were concerned with can be stated very simply: What is the chain of events that begins with a stimulus and leads up to reports such as "a bitter taste," a "dull pressure," or a "brightish green"? The details of this sequence are obviously very different for the different senses. Vision differs from hearing, and both differ from taste—in the stimuli that normally excite them, in their receptors, in the qualities of their sensations. Even so, we can analyze the path from stimulus to sensory experience in quite similar ways, whatever the particular sense may be.

In all cases, one can crudely distinguish three steps in the sequence. First, there is the proximal stimulus. Second, there is the neural chain of events that this stimulus gives rise to. The stimulus is converted (technically, *transduced*) into an electrical signal, which is then translated into a nerve impulse.* Once converted in this manner, the message is transmitted further and often is modified by other parts of the nervous system. Third, there is some sort of psychological response to the message, often in the form of a conscious, sensory experience (or sensation).

The sequence can be looked at from several points of view. One concerns the *psychophysical* relations between some property of the (physical) stimulus and the (psychological) sensory experience it ultimately gives rise to, quite apart from the intervening neural steps. Another approach concerns *psychophysiology.* Here the questions concern the neural consequences of a given stimulus input—how it affects the receptors and the neural structures higher up in the brain. For now, we will confine our discussion to psychophysical matters, leaving psychophysiological issues for later on.

The object of *psychophysics* is to relate the characteristics of physical stimuli to attributes of the sensory experience they produce. For example, there are a variety of stimuli to which the human organism is sensitive. They include chemicals suspended in air or dissolved in water, temperature changes on the skin, pressure on the skin or within various parts of the body, pressure in the form of sound waves, and electromagnetic radiations within the visible range (the spectrum). In each case, the sensory system will not respond unless the stimulus energy is above some critical level of intensity called the *absolute threshold.*

The range of stimuli to which a given sensory system reacts is actually quite limited. Human sight is restricted to the visible spectrum and human hearing to sound waves between 20 and 20,000 hertz (that is, cycles per second). But there are many organisms that respond to different ranges of stimulation and thus see and hear a world different from ours. Many insects see ultraviolet light, while dogs and cats hear sound waves of much higher frequency than we can. The bat has carried high-frequency hearing to a point of exquisite perfection. As it glides through the night it emits high-pitched screams of up to 100,000 hertz that are used as a kind of sonar. They bounce off small objects in the air such as insects, echo back to the bat, and thus enable it to locate its prey.

---

* This is typically a two-stage affair. The transduction process produces a graded potential in specialized receptor cells, which in their turn trigger a nerve impulse in other neurons.

MEASURING SENSORY INTENSITY

Measuring the magnitude of a stimulus is in principle easy enough. We measure the physical stimulus energy—in pounds, in degrees centigrade, in lumens, in decibels, or whatever. But such matters become more difficult when we try to assess psychological intensity, the magnitude of a sensation rather than that of a stimulus.

Gustav Theodor Fechner (1801–1887), the founder of psychophysics, believed that sensations cannot be measured directly. In his view, sensations and the stimuli that produce them belong to two totally different realms—to use the terms many philosophers employ, that of the body and that of the mind. If this is so, how can one possibly describe them by reference to the same yardstick? Fechner argued that while sensations can't be compared to physical stimuli, they can at least be compared to each other. A subject can compare two of his own sensations and judge whether the two are the same or are different.

Consider the sensation of visual brightness produced by a patch of light projected on a certain part of the eye. We can ask, what is the minimal amount by which the light intensity of this patch must be increased so that the subject experiences a sensation of brightness just greater than the one he had before? This amount is called the *difference threshold.* It produces a *just noticeable difference,* or *j.n.d.* The j.n.d. is a psychological entity, for it describes a subject's ability to discriminate. But it is expressed in the units of the physical stimulus that produced it. (In our example, this would be lux, a unit of illumination.) Fechner had thus found an indirect means to relate sensory magnitude to the physical intensity of the stimulus.

Before proceeding we should note that the absolute threshold may be considered as a special case of a difference threshold. Here the question is how much stimulus energy must be added to a *zero* stimulus before the subject can tell the difference between the old stimulus ("I see nothing") and the new ("Now I see it").

Gustav Theodor Fechner *(Courtesy National Library of Medicine)*

THE WEBER FRACTION

To Fechner, measuring j.n.d.s was only the means to a larger goal—the formulation of a general law relating (physical) stimulus intensity to (psychological) sensory magnitude. He believed that such a law could be built upon an empirical generalization first proposed by the German physiologist E. H. Weber (1795–1878) in 1834. Weber proposed that the size of the difference threshold is a constant ratio of the standard stimulus. Suppose that we can just tell the difference between 100 and 102 candles burning in an otherwise unilluminated room. If Weber is right, we would also be able just to distinguish between 200 and 204 candles, 400 and 408, and so forth. Put in other words, the nervous system is sensitive to a percentage change rather than a change in absolute values— a 2 percent candle difference, rather than a difference of 2 or 4 or 8. Fechner was so impressed with this relationship that he referred to it as ***Weber's law,*** a label by which we still know it. Put algebraically, Weber's law is usually written as

$$\frac{\Delta I}{I} = c$$

where ΔI is the amount that has to be added to a stimulus of intensity I (that is, the standard stimulus) in order to produce a just noticeable increase, and where c is a constant. The fraction $\Delta I / I$ *is often referred to as the* ***Weber fraction.***

Fechner and his successors performed numerous studies to determine whether Weber's law holds for all of the sensory domains (or, more technically

E. H. Weber *(Courtesy National Library of Medicine)*

TABLE 5.1 REPRESENTATIVE (MIDDLE-RANGE) VALUES FOR THE WEBER FRACTION FOR THE DIFFERENT SENSES

Sensory modality	*Weber fraction* $(\Delta I/I)$
Vision (brightness, white light)	1/60
Kinesthesis (lifted weights)	1/50
Pain (thermally aroused on skin)	1/30
Audition (tone of middle pitch and moderate loudness)	1/10
Pressure (cutaneous pressure "spot")	1/7
Smell (odor of India rubber)	1/4
Taste (table salt)	1/3

SOURCE: Geldard, 1962.

sensory modalities). The answer seems to be yes, at least for much of the normal range of stimulus intensity within each sense.* The nervous system is evidently geared to notice relative differences rather than absolute ones.

Weber's law allows us to compare the sensitivity of different sensory modalities. Suppose we want to know whether the eye is more sensitive than the ear. How can we tell? We certainly cannot compare j.n.d.s for brightness and for loudness. To mention only one problem, the values will be in different units— millilamberts for the first, decibels for the second. The problem is circumvented by using the Weber fractions for the two modalities. Being fractions, they are dimensionless and can therefore be used to compare the sensitivity of different senses. If $\Delta I/I$ is small, the discriminating power of the sense modality is great; proportionally little must be added to the standard for a difference to be observed. The opposite holds when $\Delta I/I$ is large. It turns out that we are keener in discriminating brightness than loudness; the Weber fraction for the first is 1/60, for the second it is only 1/10. Weber fractions for other sense modalities are presented in Table 5.1.

FECHNER'S LAW

Weber's law indicated that the more intense the stimulus, the more stimulus intensity has to be increased before the subject notices a change. By making a number of further assumptions, Fechner generalized Weber's finding to express a broader relationship between sensory and physical intensity. The result was *Fechner's law,* which states that the strength of a sensation grows as the logarithm of stimulus intensity—

$$S = k \log I$$

—where S stands for psychological (that is, subjective) magnitude, I for stimulus intensity, and k for a constant that depends on the value of the Weber fraction.

This law has been challenged on several grounds which are beyond the scope of this book. For our purposes, it is sufficient to note that a logarithmic law such as Fechner's makes good biological sense. The range of stimulus intensities to which we are sensitive is enormous. We can hear sounds as weak as the ticking of a watch twenty feet away and as loud as a pneumatic drill operating right next

* Weber's law tends to break down at the two extremes of the intensity range, especially at the lower end (for example, for visual stimuli only slightly above absolute threshold). At these intensities, the Weber fraction is larger than it is in the middle range.

to us. Our nervous system has to have a mechanism to compress this huge range into some manageable scope, and this is precisely what a logarithmic transformation does for us.

DETECTION AND DECISION

The goal of psychophysics is to chart the relationships between a subject's perceptual responses and various characteristics of the physical stimulus. But are these physical characteristics the only factors that determine what the subject does or says in a psychophysical experiment? What about her expectations or wishes? The early psychophysicists believed that such factors could be largely disregarded. But a more recent approach to psychophysical measurement insists that they cannot. This is *signal-detection theory,* a very influential way of thinking about the way people make decisions.

RESPONSE BIAS

To understand how beliefs and attitudes come into play in a psychophysical experiment, consider a study of absolute thresholds. On every trial, harried subjects are forced into a decision. Is a stimulus there or isn't it? The decision is often difficult, for at times the stimulus is so weak that the subjects may be quite uncertain of their judgment. Under the circumstances, their *response bias* will exert an effect. Such a response bias is a preference for one response over another (here "yes" or "no"), quite apart from the nature of the stimuli. Thus, some subjects will approach the task with a free-and-easy attitude, cheerfully offering "yes" judgments whenever they are in doubt. Others will take a more conservative line and will never respond with a "yes" unless they are quite certain. This will produce a difference in obtained thresholds that will necessarily be lower for the subjects who are more liberal with their "yes" responses. But this only reflects a difference in response bias, not in sensory sensitivity. Both groups of subjects can presumably hear or see or feel the stimuli equally well. They only differ in their willingness to report a stimulus when they are unsure.

SIGNAL DETECTION

Such considerations make it clear that thresholds obtained with traditional techniques reflect two factors. One is sensitivity—how well the subject can hear or see the stimulus. The other is response bias—how readily the subject is willing to say "yes, I heard" when he is not certain. How can these two factors be separated?

The early psychophysicists tried to cope with this problem by using only subjects who were highly trained observers. In absolute threshold studies, such subjects were models of conservatism; they would never say "yes" unless they were completely certain. To maintain this attitude, the experimenters threw in an occasional "catch trial" on which there was no stimulus at all (Woodworth, 1938).

Signal-detection theory has developed a more systematic way of dealing with response bias. To begin with, it has provided a somewhat different testing procedure, the *detection experiment,* in which catch trials are part of the regular procedure rather than just an occasional check to keep the subjects on their toes (Green and Swets, 1966).

One version of this procedure is related to the measurement of the absolute threshold. Here the question is whether the subject can detect the presence of a

TABLE 5.2 THE FOUR POSSIBLE OUTCOMES OF THE DETECTION EXPERIMENT

	Stimulus present	Stimulus absent
Responds "yes"	Hit	False alarm
Responds "no"	Miss	Correct negative

TABLE 5.3 PAYOFF MATRIX THAT WILL PRODUCE A "YES" BIAS

	Stimulus present	Stimulus absent
Subject says "yes"	+ 10¢	− 1¢
Subject says "no"	− 10¢	+5¢

stimulus. We take a fairly weak stimulus and present it on half the trials. On the other half of the trials (interspersed in random order), we present no stimulus at all. We will now look at two kinds of errors. One is a *miss,* not reporting a stimulus when one is present. The other is a *false alarm,* reporting a stimulus when in fact none is present. By the same token, there are two different kinds of correct responses: reporting a stimulus when it is actually there (a *hit*) and not reporting one when none is present (a *correct negative*) (see Table 5.2).

THE PAYOFF MATRIX

The detection experiment can tell us what factors underlie response bias. One such factor is differential payoff. Suppose we (literally) pay a subject for every hit and correct negative but penalize him for every miss and false alarm according to a prescribed schedule of gains and losses called a *payoff matrix.* Thus the subject might gain 10 cents for every hit and 5 cents for every correct negative, while losing 10 cents for every miss and only 1 cent for every false alarm. Such a payoff matrix will lead to a bias toward "yes" judgments (Table 5.3). To make this clear, let's consider an extreme case. Suppose there are, say, fifty trials on which the subject has no sensory information on the basis of which he can decide whether the stimulus is present or not. If he consistently says "yes," he will on the average be correct on twenty-five trials (thus collecting $2.50) and wrong on the other twenty-five (thus losing $0.25) for a net gain of $2.25. In contrast, consistent "no" judgments will lead to a net loss (collecting $1.25 for the correct negatives and losing $2.50 for the false alarms).

Illustrations of the effect of payoff matrices abound in real life. There the differential payoff is usually reckoned in units larger than pennies. Consider a team of radiologists poring over an X-ray to look for a tiny spot that indicates the start of a malignant tumor. What are the penalties for error here? If the physicians decide there is no spot when there actually is one, their miss may cost the patient's life. If they decide that they see a spot when in fact there is none, their false alarm has other costs, such as the dangers of more elaborate clinical tests, let alone those of an operation. What the physicians ultimately decide will depend both on what their eyes tell them as they inspect the X-ray and also on the relative costs of the two possible errors they may commit.

SEPARATING SENSITIVITY AND RESPONSE BIAS

The preceding discussion showed that a subject's responses are jointly determined by her sensitivity to the stimulus and her response bias. If asked whether she hears a stimulus when presented with a thunderclap, she is almost certain to say "yes" even if her response bias is to say "no," for there is very little room for doubt given the intensity of the stimulus. But if the stimulus is relatively faint, the bias will show itself clearly and she is very likely to say "no."

Is there any way in which the effects of stimulus sensitivity and response bias can be disentangled? The detection experiment provides a means. The first step is to vary response bias while keeping sensitivity constant. This can be done by changing the payoff matrix. Another way is to vary the proportion of trials on which no stimulus is presented—the fewer such trials, the greater the yes bias.

When response bias is varied in this fashion, the results are quite systematic. If we induce the subject to be more conservative, we find a reduction in the proportion of trials on which he is guilty of a false alarm. But at the same time, we also find a reduction in the proportion of hits. Similarly, upward shifts in the yes bias lead to an increase in the proportion of both hits and false alarms. These effects can be expressed graphically by plotting the two proportions against each other. The resulting function is known by the rather arcane designation of

5.3 The ROC curve *The proportion of hits is plotted against the proportion of false alarms. The stimulus is kept constant but the response bias is systematically varied by asking subjects to adopt a more liberal attitude with their yeses. This bias becomes progressively larger as we move upward on the vertical axis (proportion of hits) and to the right on the horizontal axis (proportion of false alarms). Note that as the proportion of hits increases, so does the proportion of false alarms.*

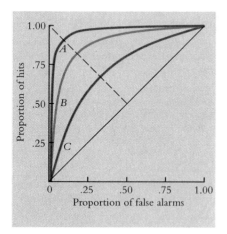

5.4 ROC curves for stimuli of different intensities *The figure shows ROC curves for three stimuli of increasing intensity (with A the strongest and C the weakest). Note that the stronger the stimulus, the more its ROC curve is displaced from the main diagonal. We can think of this diagonal as the ROC curve produced by a stimulus to which the subject is utterly insensitive. The displacement of the ROC curve from the main diagonal provides a pure index of sensitivity. It is measured along the second diagonal (broken line).*

receiver-operating-characteristic curve, which is almost always abbreviated **ROC curve** (Figure 5.3).

The next step is to get an index of sensitivity that is uncontaminated by response bias. To do so, we obtain separate ROC curves for different levels of stimulus intensity (with each curve based on a separate detection experiment). The results are very striking. The stronger the stimulus, the more its ROC curve is bowed away from the **main diagonal** (Figure 5.4).

Why should this be so? To answer this question, consider a hypothetical detection experiment using a visual stimulus but a blind subject. Here the subject's sensitivity is obviously zero, so that his judgments must be based entirely upon response bias. For this blind subject, the stimulus does not exist, so that he is just as likely to obtain a hit as to strike a false alarm. In consequence, his ROC curve is necessarily the main diagonal. His yes bias can go up or down, but his proportion of hits and of false alarms will always be equal. Evidently, the main diagonal represents total insensitivity, an absolute inability to distinguish the presence of a stimulus from its absence. As sensitivity goes up, the ROC curve moves away from the diagonal. Thus, the displacement of the ROC curve from the main diagonal provides a pure measure of sensitivity for the stimulus on which the ROC curve is based; it is measured along the second diagonal (Figure 5.4)

SIGNAL DETECTION AND THE DECISION PROCESS

There is one question that we have not really considered. Why does the subject have so much trouble distinguishing between the presence of a stimulus and its absence? Signal-detection theory proposes an intriguing answer. It asserts that there really is no such thing as a zero stimulus.

Signal-detection theorists assume that all psychophysical judgments are based on underlying neural activity in the sensory system, which is called the *sensory process.* Sensory processes can vary in magnitude and can occur either as the result of an actual, external stimulus or as the result of *background noise* from within the subject's own body. Take an experiment in hearing. The subject's auditory system may be stimulated from outside by the tone or from inside by the throbbing of the pulse, by spontaneous cell firing in the nervous system, or what have you.

The intensity of both the stimulus and the background noise varies. On average, the stimulus plus background noise produces a sensory process of greater magnitude than does the background noise alone, an average value that rises with increasing stimulus strength. But not always: On some trials the intensity of the background noise alone exceeds that of the stimulus plus background noise (see Figure 5.5).

The subject's task is to decide whether a given sensory process comes from the stimulus plus noise or the background noise alone, whether she hears a faint tone from outside or her own heartbeat (or spontaneous neural firing or whatever) from within. The subject must make her decision based on a response criterion—a particular intensity of sensory process—attributing more intense sensory processes to the stimulus, less intense ones to background noise. But since the intensity of the sensory processes from these two sources overlap, there is no way she can avoid errors. For any criterion she chooses, she will misattribute some of her sensory experiences.

She can't avoid errors, but she can control the direction in which she errs; that direction will depend on her response bias. If she wants to minimize misses (saying "no" when a stimulus is actually presented), she will have to lower the

5.5 *The decision process according to signal-detection theory* (A) *A frequency distribution of the sensory process when there is only background noise. The intensity of the sensory process is plotted on the horizontal axis and the frequency with which that intensity occurs on the vertical. The intensity varies, but generally hovers around a mean* M_n. *(B) A frequency distribution of the sensory process when the stimulus is presented; again, intensity fluctuates, with the mean,* M_s, *greater than the mean of the background noise alone. (C) The two frequency distributions overlap: On some trials the intensity of the background noise alone exceeds that of the stimulus plus background noise. So whatever noise level the respondent chooses as her criterion, some of her judgments will be in error. (D) Since errors are unavoidable, the nature of these errors will depend of the subject's response bias, her tendency to opt for misses over false alarms and vice versa, and the effect this will have on her choice of a criterion. If she wants to minimize misses, she has to shift her criterion to the left; if she wants to minimize false alarms, she has to shift it to the right.*

intensity of her criterion. This will decrease the number of misses, but it will also necessarily increase the number of false alarms. The opposite will happen if she wants to minimize the number of false alarms.

EXTENSIONS TO OTHER FIELDS

The general approach of signal-detection theory has applications to many areas of psychology outside of psychophysics. It is relevant whenever a person has to decide between two alternatives but can't be sure of the outcome. An example is the selection of college applicants. One error of admissions is a miss: An applicant is rejected who would have done well. Another error is a false alarm: An applicant is accepted who will be unable to graduate (for details, see Chapter 15). The important point is that in virtually all decision making some errors are inevitable and that these errors can be either misses or false alarms. There is always a trade-off between these two kinds of errors. If one wants to minimize the misses (rejected applicants who would have done perfectly well had they been accepted), one has to change the response bias toward "yes," which then inevitably increases the number of false alarms (accepted applicants who will flunk out). Conversely, if one wants to minimize the number of false alarms, one necessarily must increase the number of misses. Just which trade-off is chosen depends on the payoff matrix.

SENSORY CODING

Thus far, our focus has been on the psychophysical relationships between the physical properties of the stimulus and the sensory experience it gives rise to. But sensory psychologists are not content with this alone. They also want to learn something about the intervening neural steps. One crucial issue that comes up in all such enterprises is the nature of the *sensory code* through which the nervous system represents various sensory experiences. A code is a set of rules whereby information is transformed from one set of symbols to another. An example is the Morse code used by telegraphers, in which letters are transformed into patterns of dots, dashes, and spaces, so that dot-dash stands for A, dash-dot-dot-dot for B, dot-dot-(space)-dot for C, and so on. What Samuel Morse did for telegraphy, the nervous system does for all the senses. Instead of dots and dashes, the nervous system encodes (that is, translates) the various properties of the stimulus into various characteristics of the nervous impulse. Many of the efforts of sensory psychophysiologists are directed at cracking these codes.

We'll shortly consider some of the discoveries that pertain to the codes within the different senses. But before doing so, we should consider some general issues that apply to them all. One question concerns the code for *psychological intensity,* such as changes in loudness and brightness. By and large, it appears that the relevant code is firing frequency: the more intense the stimulus, the greater the rate of neural firing (and the more intense the subjective experience; Borg et al., 1967). Another signal for sensory intensity is the sheer number of neurons that are triggered by the stimulus. The more intense the stimulus, the more neurons it activates, which presumably leads to an increase in the psychological magnitude.

Another question concerns the code for *sensory quality.* The different senses obviously produce sensations of different quality. For example, the sensations of pressure, A-flat, red, or sour clearly belong to altogether different sensory modalities. To what factor shall we ascribe these differences in experienced quality? Is it the difference in the stimuli that produces these sensations? In 1826, the German physiologist Johannes Müller (1801–1858) argued that the answer is no. To be sure, visual sensations are usually produced by light waves, but occasionally other stimuli will serve as well. Strong pressure on the eyeballs leads us to see rings or stars (to the chagrin of boxers and the delight of cartoonists). Similarly, we can produce visual sensations by electric stimulation of various parts of the nervous system. Such facts led Müller to formulate his famous *doctrine of specific nerve energies.* According to this law, the differences in experienced quality are caused not by differences in the stimuli but by the different nervous structures that these stimuli excite. Thus, were we able to rewire the nervous system so as to connect the optic nerve to the auditory cortex and the auditory nerve to the visual cortex, we might be able to see thunder and hear lightning.

Some of Müller's successors extended his doctrine to cover qualitative differences within a given sense modality. For example, blue, green, and red are qualitatively different even though all three are colors. To the heirs of Müller, such a qualitative difference could only mean one thing: There had to be some decisive difference in the neural processes that underlie these different sensations, perhaps at the level of the receptors, perhaps higher up. This belief ultimately led to some fundamental discoveries about the physiological basis of various sensory experiences, such as color and pitch (Boring, 1942).

Müller's doctrine tells us that differences in sensory quality reflect a difference in some underlying neural process, but it leaves some room for debate about what the particular process is. In essence, there are two theoretical approaches. One is the *specificity theory,* which asserts that different sensory qualities are signaled by different neurons. These quality-specific neurons might be receptors, or they might be further up in the nervous system. In either case, they are somehow "labeled" with their quality, so that whenever they fire, the nervous system interprets their activation as "red" or "sour" or whatever their particular sensory quality might happen to be. The alternative position is the *across-fiber pattern theory.* This asserts that the code for quality comes from an overall pattern of activation across a whole set of fibers. In some sensory systems such as taste, the reactions of the sensory fibers are not terribly specific: Most of them respond to very many substances. What differs is the pattern of activation these substances produce, and this differential pattern may be the neural code that gives rise to the sensory quality. As we will see, the nervous system uses both specificity and pattern codes in different sensory systems (Goldstein, 1989; Rosenzweig and Leiman, 1989).

A SURVEY OF THE SENSES

The development of psychological methods, coupled with various physiological techniques, gave psychology a powerful set of tools with which to study the various senses. Our primary focus will be on just one sense, which we will consider in detail: vision. But we will first look briefly at several other sensory systems that provide us with information about various aspects of the world and about our own position within it.

KINESTHESIS AND THE VESTIBULAR SENSES

One group of senses informs the organism about its own movements and its orientation in space. Skeletal movement is sensed through *kinesthesis,* a collective term for information that comes from receptors in the muscles, tendons, and joints. Another group of receptors signals the rotation of the head. These are the receptors in the *semicircular canals,* which are located within the *vestibules* of the inner ear (Figure 5.6). The three canals contain a viscous liquid that moves when the head rotates. This motion bends hair cells that are located at one end of each canal. When bent, these hair cells give rise to nervous impulses. The sum total of the impulses from each of the canals provides information about the nature and extent of the head's rotation.

One vital function of the semicircular canal system is to provide a firm base for vision. As we walk through the world, our head moves continually. To compensate for this endless rocking, the eyes have to move accordingly. This adjustment is accomplished by a reflex system that automatically cancels each rotation of the head by an equal and opposite motion of the eyes. These eye movements are initiated by messages from the three semicircular canals, which are then relayed to the appropriate muscles of each eye. Thus, the visual system is effectively stable, operating as if it rested on a solid tripod.

THE SKIN SENSES

Stimulation of the skin informs the organism of what is directly adjacent to its own body. Not surprisingly, skin sensitivity is especially acute in those parts of the body that are most relevant to exploring the world that surrounds us directly: the hands and fingers, the lips and tongue. These sensitivities are reflected in the organization of the cortical projection area for bodily sensations. As we have seen, the allocation of cortical space is quite unequal, with a heavy emphasis on such sensitive regions as face, mouth, and fingers (see Chapter 2).

How many skin senses are there? Aristotle believed that all of the sensations from the skin could be subsumed under just one rubric, that of touch. But today most investigators believe that there are at least four different skin sensations: *pressure, warmth, cold,* and *pain.* How are these different sensory experiences coded by the nervous system? Here, as in the study of many other senses, the first line of inquiry was suggested by Müller's doctrine of specific nerve energies: If the sensory qualities are different, see whether there are different receptors that underlie them.

A

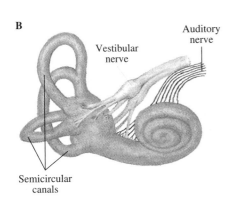

B

Vestibular nerve

Auditory nerve

Semicircular canals

5.6 The vestibular sense *(A) The location of the inner ears, which are embedded in bone on both sides of the skull. The vestibules are indicated in orange. The rest of the inner ear is devoted to the sense of hearing. (After Krech and Crutchfield, 1958) (B) Close-up of the vestibular apparatus. (After Kalat, 1984)*

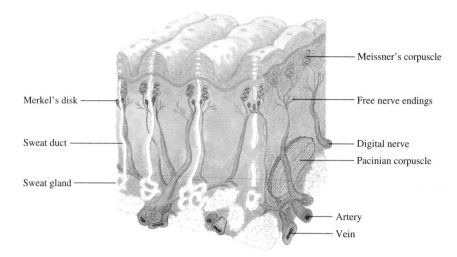

Meissner's corpuscle

Free nerve endings

Digital nerve

Pacinian corpuscle

Artery

Vein

Merkel's disk

Sweat duct

Sweat gland

5.7   A cross section through the skin   *The figure shows a number of structures that serve as receptors in hairless skin; for example, on the fingertips and palms. (After Carlson, 1986)*

Are there different receptors that correspond to these different sensations? The answer is a qualified yes. There is good reason to believe that various sensations of pressure are produced by a number of different specialized receptors in the skin (see Figure 5.7). Some of these receptors are wrapped around hair follicles in the skin and sense movements of the hair. Others are capsules that are easily bent by slight deformations of the skin. Some of these capsules respond to continued vibration, others to sudden movement across the skin, still others to steady indentation. It's clear that there is not one touch receptor but several.

Less is known about the underlying receptor systems for warmth, cold, and pain. Some of these experiences are probably signaled by free nerve endings in the skin that have no specialized end organs. These free nerve endings have been thought to provide information about warmth, cold, and pain, but some of them may also be additional pressure receptors (Sherrick and Cholewiak, 1986).

THE SENSE OF TASTE

The sense of taste has a simple function. It acts as a gatekeeper for the organism's digestive system by providing information about the substances that may or may not be ingested. Its task is to keep poisons out and usher foodstuffs in. In most land-dwelling mammals, this function is performed by specialized receptor organs, the **taste buds,** which are sensitive to chemicals dissolved in water. The average person possesses about 10,000 such taste buds, located mostly in the tongue but also in other regions of the mouth. Fibers from these receptors convey the message to the brain, first to the medulla and then further up to the thalamus and cortex.

TASTE SENSATIONS

Most investigators believe that there are four basic taste qualities: **sour, sweet, salty,** and **bitter.** In their view, all other taste sensations are produced by a mixture of these primary qualities. Thus, grapefruit tastes sour and bitter, while lemonade tastes sweet and sour. What are the stimuli that produce these four basic qualities? As yet, we don't have a full answer. We do know that the salty taste is usually produced by inorganic molecules dissolved in water and the sour taste by acids. The story is more complicated for sweet and bitter sensations. Both are generally produced by complex organic molecules, but as yet there are no clear-cut rules that predict the resulting taste sensation. For example, "sweet" is produced by various sugars, but also by saccharin, a chemical compound that

Taste buds

Section of a mammalian tongue   *The taste buds, which look like small hairy balls, are embedded in the walls of deep narrow pits in the tongue. (Courtesy of Ed Reschke)*

is structurally very different from sugar. Additional problems are posed by effects of concentration. Some substances, such as saccharin, that taste sweet in low concentrations taste bitter when their concentration is increased.

CODING FOR TASTE QUALITY

What neural processes underlie the different taste qualities? According to specificity theory, these qualities are signaled by different fibers that carry the messages from the taste receptors to the brain. Electrical recording studies using rats and hamsters have shown that some of these fibers respond best when stimulated by sugar, others when stimulated by salt, still others by (very diluted) hydrochloric acid, and yet others by quinine, corresponding to the four primary taste sensations. According to specificity theorists, the fiber that responds best to sugar (the "sugar-best fiber") signals sweet, the "quinine-best fiber" signals bitter, and so on. To the extent that any substance stimulates several taste fibers (and most substances do), the result will be a taste mixture. Evidence for this view comes from a comparison of two sugars: sucrose and fructose. Both rats and humans prefer sucrose to fructose, even though both sugars stimulate the sugar-best fibers (the ones that presumably signal "sweet"). The preference probably comes about because fructose also stimulates the salt-best fiber. As a result, its taste is a mixture of sweet and salty, which is less preferred. Whether these results are best explained by the specificity theory or by some version of the pattern theory is still a matter of debate (Bartoshuk, 1988; see Figure 5.8, adapted from Nowlis and Frank, 1981).

TASTE AND SENSORY INTERACTION

The sense of taste provides an illustration of a pervasive principle that holds for most (perhaps all) of the other senses and that we will here call **sensory interaction.** It describes the fact that a sensory system's response to any given stimulus rarely depends on that stimulus alone. It is also affected by other stimuli that impinge, or have recently impinged, upon that system.

One kind of sensory interaction occurs over time. Suppose one taste stimulus is presented continuously for fifteen seconds or more. The result will be **adaptation,** a phenomenon that is found in virtually all sensory systems. If the tongue is continually stimulated with the identical taste stimulus, sensitivity to that taste will quickly decline. For example, after continuous exposure to a quinine solution, the quinine will taste less and less bitter and may finally appear to be completely tasteless. This adaptation process is reversible, however. If the mouth is rinsed out and left unstimulated for, say, a minute, the original taste sensitivity will be restored in full.

In another form of interaction, the adaptation to one taste quality may lead to the enhancement of another, an effect that is sometimes regarded as a form of contrast. For example, adaptation to sugar makes an acid taste even sourer than before (Kuznicki and McCutcheon, 1979). A related effect is the change in the taste of ordinary tap water after prior adaptation to various substances. Adaptation to a salty solution will make water taste sour or bitter; adaptation to one that's sweet will make it taste bitter (McBurney and Shick, 1971).

THE SENSE OF SMELL

Thus far, our discussion has centered on the sensory systems that tell us about objects and events close to home: the movements and position of our own bodies, what we feel with our skin, and what we put in our mouths.

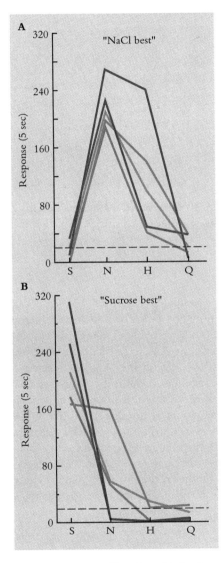

5.8 Response profiles of two kinds of taste fibers in the hamster *The figures show the number of responses to two kinds of fibers when stimulated by sucrose (S), sodium chloride (N), hydrochloric acid (H), and quinine (Q). In humans these substances give rise to the sensations of sweet, salty, sour, and bitter respectively. (A) Five fibers that respond best to sodium chloride. (B) Five fibers that respond best to sucrose. (From Frank, 1973)*

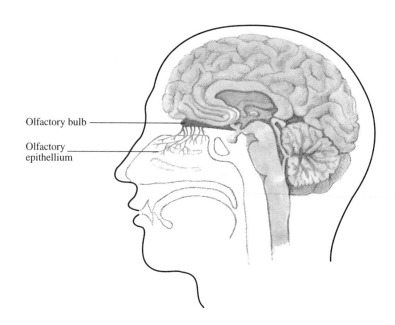

Olfactory bulb

Olfactory epithellium

5.9 The olfactory apparatus *Chemicals suspended in the air that flows through the nasal passages stimulate receptors in the olfactory epithelium that relay their information to a structure in the forebrain, the olfactory bulb. (After Amoore, Johnson, and Rubin, 1964; Carlson, 1986)*

But we clearly receive information from much farther off. We have three main receptive systems that enlarge our world by responding to stimuli at a distance: smell, hearing, and vision.

THE OLFACTORY STIMULUS

Smell, or to use the more technical term, *olfaction,* provides information about chemicals suspended in air that excite receptors located in a small area at the top of our nasal cavity, the *olfactory epithelium* (see Figure 5.9). There is still considerable debate about the nature of the chemicals that act as effective olfactory stimuli ("odorants") and the way in which they set off the olfactory receptors. Several classification schemes exist for describing all odors by reference to a number of primary smell sensations, for example, fragrant (rose), spicy (cinnamon), and putrid (rotten eggs). But as yet, there is no agreement about the underlying principle that makes certain chemicals arouse one of these olfactory experiences rather than another. At present, the best guess is that olfactory quality is not coded by particular receptors—with, say, one group of receptors responding to stimuli we call fragrant and another receptor group responding to stimuli we describe as putrid. Instead, the relevant sensory code for quality is probably a pattern of excitation across different receptor groups.

SMELL AS AN INTERNAL SENSE

Olfaction is a distance sense, but it is also a sense that can refer to things much closer by—in fact, to objects inside our own mouths (Rozin, 1982). We can smell the spaghetti on our plate, but we can also sense its flavor when we take a forkful in our mouths. That flavor—as indeed all flavors—depends largely on our sense of smell. For what we commonly call the "taste of food" is very rarely the sensation of taste alone; it is almost always a combination of taste, texture, temperature, and—most important of all—smell. When our nose is completely stuffed up by a cold, food appears to be without any flavor. While we can still experience the basic taste sensations, the aroma is lost, and so the food seems "tasteless." If smell is gone, we can no longer distinguish between vinegar and a fine red wine, or between an apple and an onion. For a gourmet (or a chef or a wine taster), a sensitive nose is even more essential than a sensitive tongue.

SMELL AS A DISTANCE SENSE

As a distance sense, smell plays a relatively minor part for humans. It is clearly less important to us than it is to many other species. In this regard we are similar to our primate cousins and to birds in that these animals all left the odor-impregnated ground to move up into trees, an environment in which other senses, especially vision, became more critical. In contrast, smell is of vital importance to many ground dwellers such as dogs. For them, it furnishes a guide to food and to receptive mates, and it may give warning against certain natural enemies. Modern psychophysical methods allow us to determine just how much more sensitive the dog's nose is compared to our own; it turns out that the dog-to-human ratio in sensitivity to smell is about a thousand to one (Marshall and Moulton, 1981; Cain, 1988).

Compared to dogs and most other land-dwelling animals, we are evidently olfactory incompetents. But that doesn't mean that smell is of no relevance to human life. It does warn us of impending danger, as when we sniff escaping gas; it greatly adds to our enjoyment of food; and it provides the basis of the perfume and deodorant industries. According to some reports, it even helps to sell luggage and used cars; plastic briefcases saturated with artificial leather scents and second-hand cars permeated with a "new car" odor are said to have greater market value (Winter, 1976). In addition, smell evidently plays a role in identifying other persons. In one study, a psychologist asked men and women to wear T-shirts for twenty-four hours without taking a shower or using perfumes or deodorants. After the twenty-four hours were up, each (unwashed) T-shirt was sealed in a separate bag. Every subject was then asked to sniff the contents of three of these bags without looking inside. One contained his or her T-shirt, a second the T-shirt worn by another man, a third the T-shirt worn by another woman. About three-quarters of the subjects were able to identify their own T-shirt based only on its odor, and could also correctly identify which of the other T-shirts had been worn by a man or by a woman (Russell, 1976; McBurney, Levine, and Cavanaugh, 1977). This sensitivity to human odors starts in the nursery. Thus babies apparently respond to the odor of their own mother's breast and underarm in preference to the odors of a strange mother (Russell, 1976; Cernoch and Porter, 1985). Generally speaking, females perform better than males on these and other olfactory-related tasks (a difference that seems to be present from earliest infancy), and younger people do better than older ones (Balogh and Porter, 1986; Cain, 1988).

PHEROMONES

In many species, olfaction has a function beyond those we have discussed thus far. It represents a primitive form of communication. Certain animals secrete special chemical substances called *pheromones* that trigger particular reactions in other members of their own kind. Some pheromones affect reproductive behavior. In many mammals, the female secretes a chemical (often in the urine) that signals that she is sexually receptive. In some species, the male sends chemical return messages to the female. For example, boars apparently secrete a pheromone that renders the sow immobile so that she stands rigid during mating (Michael and Keverne, 1968).

Other pheromones signal alarm. It appears that some animals can smell danger. To be more exact, they can smell a substance secreted by members of their own species who have been frightened. Thus rats who suffer an electric shock in an experimental chamber seem to exude a chemical that induces fear in other rats that are exposed to a whiff of the air from that same chamber (Valenta and Rigby, 1968).

Are there pheromones in humans? There may be some vestigial remains. One

(*Cartoon by Sidney Harris; © 1980, The New Yorker, Inc.*)

line of evidence concerns the development of ***menstrual synchrony.*** Women who live together, for example, in college dormitories, tend to develop menstrual cycles that roughly coincide with each other, even though their periods were very different at the start of the school year (McClintock, 1971). Some recent studies suggest that this synchrony is primed by olfactory cues. Female subjects exposed to the body odor of a "donor" woman gradually shifted their menstrual cycles toward that of the donor, even though the subjects and the donors never saw each other (Russell, Switz, and Thompson, 1980).

Of potentially greater interest is the possibility of discovering an olfactory sex attractant that operates like a kind of pheromone. Thus far, there has been little to whet the financial appetites of perfume manufacturers or the erotic hopes of male or female Lonely Hearts. At best, there may be some faint remnants. One line of evidence comes from olfactory thresholds to certain musk-like substances similar to that secreted by boars. Sexually mature women are vastly more sensitive to the smell of these compounds than are men or sexually immature girls. This sensitivity fluctuates with the woman's menstrual cycle and seems to reach a peak during ovulation. An intriguing speculation is that the receptive female's greater sensitivity to this odor points to the existence of a human male pheromone in our evolutionary past. Perhaps it is still present in a greatly attenuated form, but if so its effects are almost certainly too weak to be of any practical significance. Drenching himself in boar's musk and wearing Tom Cruise's unwashed T-shirt (or Mel Gibson's or Kevin Costner's) will not transform the universally rejected suitor into a matinee idol pursued by all women (even those—or especially those—near enough to smell him).

HEARING

The sense of hearing, or ***audition,*** is a close relative of other receptive senses that react to mechanical pressure, such as the vestibular senses or touch. Like these, hearing is a response to pressure, but with a difference—it informs us of pressure changes in the world that may take place many meters away. In effect, then, hearing is feeling at a distance.

SOUND

What is the stimulus for hearing? Outside in the world there is some physical movement that disturbs the air in which it occurs. This may be an animal scurrying through the underbrush or a rock dropping from a cliff or a set of vibrating vocal cords. The air particles directly adjacent to the movement are agitated, push other particles that are ahead of them, and then return to their original position. Each individual air particle moves back and forth for just a tiny bit, but this is enough to set up a series of successive pressure variations in the air. These travel in a wave form analogous to the ripples set up by a stone thrown into a pond. When these ***sound waves*** hit our ears, they initiate a set of further mechanical pressure changes that ultimately trigger the auditory receptors. These initiate various further neural responses in the brain which ultimately lead to an experience of something that is heard rather than felt. (This is yet another example of the operation of Müller's doctrine of specific nerve energies.)

Sound waves can vary in both ***amplitude*** and ***wavelength.*** Amplitude refers to the height of a wave crest: the greater the intensity of the vibration, the higher this crest will be. Wavelength is simply the distance between successive crests. Sound waves are generally described by their ***frequency,*** which is the number of cycles per second. Since the speed of sound is constant within any given medium, frequency is inversely proportional to wavelength (Figure 5.10).

Both amplitude and frequency are physical dimensions. Our brain translates

A

B

5.10 The stimulus for hearing (A) The figure depicts a momentarily frozen field of vibration in air. An insect vibrating its wings rapidly leads to waves of compression in the surrounding air. These waves travel in all directions like ripples in a pond into which a stone has been thrown. (B) The corresponding wave pattern is shown in simplified form. The amplitude of the wave is the height of each crest; the wavelength is the distance between successive crests. (From Gibson, 1966)

TABLE 5.4   INTENSITY LEVELS OF VARIOUS COMMON SOUNDS

Sound	Intensity level (decibels)
Manned spacecraft launching (from 150 feet)	180
Loudest rock band on record	160
Pain threshold (approximate)	140
Loud thunder; average rock band	120
Shouting	100
Noisy automobile	80
Normal conversation	60
Quiet office	40
Whisper	20
Rustling of leaves	10
Threshold of hearing	0

Rock and roll and hearing loss   *As rock guitarist Pete Townshend learned too late, prolonged exposure to loud noise, like that produced by his band, The Who, can cause serious hearing loss, as well as tinnitus, or, ringing in the ears. Many rock musicians, as well as fans, now wear ear plugs to prevent damage. (Photograph © RDR productions, 1981; Rex USA)*

these into the psychological dimensions of **loudness** and **pitch.** Roughly speaking, a sound will appear to be louder as its amplitude increases and will appear more high-pitched as its frequency goes up.

Amplitude and loudness   The range of amplitudes to which humans can respond is enormous. Investigators have found it convenient to use a scale that compresses this unwieldy range into a more convenient form. To this end, they developed a logarithmic scale that describes sound intensities in **decibels** (Table 5.4). Perceived loudness doubles every time the physical intensity (that is, the amplitude) goes up by 10 decibels. The physical stimulus intensity rises more steeply, increasing by a factor of 10 every 20 decibels (Stevens, 1955).

Frequency and pitch   The frequency of a sound wave is generally measured in **hertz** (Hz) (named after the nineteenth-century German physicist Heinrich Hertz), or waves per second. The frequencies associated with some musical tones are shown in Table 5.5. Young adults can hear tones as low as 20 hertz and as high as 20,000 hertz, with maximal sensitivity to a middle region in between. As people get older, their sensitivity to sound declines, especially at the higher frequencies.

TABLE 5.5   SOUND FREQUENCIES OF SOME MUSICAL TONES

Sound	Frequency (hertz)
Top note of grand piano	4214
Top note of piccolo	3951
Top range of soprano voice	1152
Top range of alto voice	640
Middle C	256
Bottom range of baritone voice	96
Bottom range of bass voice	80
Bottom note of contra bassoon	29
Bottom note of grand piano	27
Bottom note of organ★	16

★Can be felt but not heard
SOURCE: After Geldard, 1972.

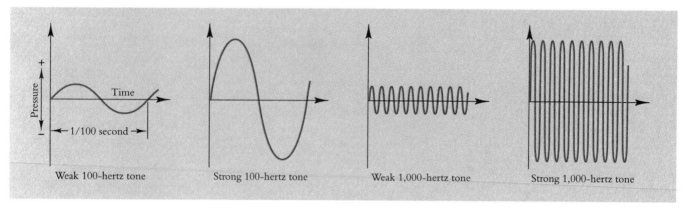

5.11 Simple wave forms vary in frequency and amplitude *Simple sound waves can be graphically expressed by plotting air-pressure change over time. The result is a sine curve. These curves show the sine waves for a weak and a strong 100-hertz tone (relatively low in pitch) and a strong and a weak 1,000-hertz tone (comparatively high pitch). (After Thompson, 1973)*

Simple and complex waves Thus far we have only dealt with simple wave forms, those that have only one frequency. Such waves are very rare in nature; they are produced by special electronic devices or by tuning forks. When such simple waves are expressed graphically, with pressure change plotted against time, they yield curves that correspond to the plot of the trigonometric sine function. Accordingly, such curves are called **sine waves** (Figure 5.11).

The sounds encountered in normal life are virtually never as simple as this. Instead, they are composed of many different waves, which differ in both frequency and amplitude. An example is the (relatively simple) **complex wave:**

This complex wave can be produced by the acoustic mixture of three simple tones that correspond to three sine waves, as shown below:

5.12 An irregular sound wave—an explosion *As in the previous figures, pressure change is plotted against time; but now there is no more regularity, so the wave form cannot readily be analyzed into its simpler components. (From Boring, Langfeld, and Weld, 1939)*

The point of this example is that the auditory system can analyze complex waves into their component parts. We can hear the separate notes that make up a chord; the tones are mixed, but we can unmix them. This ability has its limits. If the sound is made up of a great number of unrelated waves, it is perceived as noise, which we can no longer analyze (Figure 5.12).

GATHERING THE PROXIMAL STIMULUS

Most of the ear is made up of various anatomical structures whose function is to gather the proximal stimulus—they conduct and amplify sound waves so that

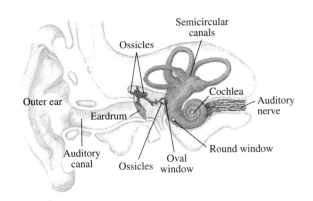

5.13   The human ear   *Air enters through the outer ear and stimulates the eardrum, which sets the ossicles in the middle ear in motion. These in turn transmit their vibration to the membrane of the oval window, which causes movement of the fluid in the cochlea of the inner ear. Note that the semicircular canals are anatomically parts of the inner ear. (After Lindsay and Norman, 1977)*

they can affect the auditory receptors (Figure 5.13). Sound waves collected by the outer ear are funneled toward a taut membrane that they cause to vibrate. This is the **eardrum,** which transmits its vibrations across an air-filled cavity, the **middle ear,** to another membrane, the **oval window,** that separates the middle from the **inner ear.** This transmission is accomplished by way of a mechanical bridge built of three small bones that are collectively known as the **ossicles.** The vibrations of the eardrum move the first ossicle, which then moves the second, which in turn moves the third, which completes the chain by imparting the vibratory pattern to the oval window to which it is attached. The movements of the oval window set up waves in a fluid that fills the **cochlea,** a coiled tube in the inner ear that contains the auditory receptors.

Why did nature choose such a roundabout method of sound transmission? The major reason is that the cochlear medium is a fluid, which, like all liquids, is harder to set into motion than air. To overcome this difficulty, the physical stimulus must be amplified. This amplification is provided by various features of the middle-ear organization. One involves the relative sizes of the eardrum and of that portion of the oval window moved by the ossicles; the first is about twenty times larger than the second. The result is the transformation of a fairly weak force that acts on the entire eardrum into a much stronger pressure that is concentrated upon the (much smaller) oval window.

TRANSDUCTION IN THE COCHLEA

Throughout most of its length the cochlea is divided into an upper and lower section by several structures including the **basilar membrane.** The auditory receptors are called **hair cells** and are lodged between the basilar membrane and other membranes above. Motion of the oval window produces pressure changes in the cochlear fluid that in turn lead to vibrations of the basilar membrane. As the basilar membrane vibrates, its deformations bend the hair cells and provide the immediate stimulus for their activity (Figure 5.14).

5.14   Detailed structure of the middle ear and the cochlea   *(A) Movement of the fluid within the cochlea deforms the basilar membrane and stimulates the hair cells that serve as the auditory receptors. (After Lindsay and Norman, 1977) (B) Cross-section of the cochlea showing the basilar membrane and the hair cell receptors. (After Coren and Ward, 1989)*

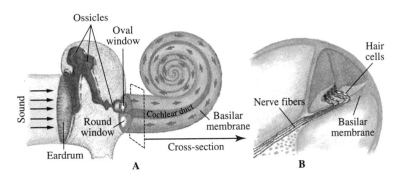

How does the activity of the auditory receptors lead to the sensory properties of auditory experience? Much of the work in this area has focused upon the perception of pitch, the sensory quality that depends upon the frequency of the stimulating sound wave.

Basilar place and pitch   According to the **place theory** of pitch, first proposed by Hermann von Helmholtz (1821–1894), different parts of the basilar membrane are responsive to different sound frequencies. In Helmholtz's view, the nervous system interprets the excitations from different basilar places as different pitches. The stimulation of receptors at one end of the membrane leads to the experience of a high tone, while the stimulation of receptors at the other end leads to the sensation of a low tone.

Today we know that Helmholtz was correct at least in part. The classic studies were performed by Georg von Békésy (1899–1972) whose work on auditory function won him the Nobel Prize in 1961. Some of Békésy's experiments used cochleas taken from fresh human cadavers. Békésy removed part of the cochlear wall so that he could observe the basilar membrane through a microscope while the oval window was being vibrated by an electrically powered piston. He found that such stimulation led to a wavelike motion of the basilar membrane (Figure 5.15). When he varied the frequency of the vibrating stimulus, the peak of the deformation produced by this wave pattern occurred in different regions of the membrane: High frequencies corresponded to regions close to the oval window, low ones to regions close to the cochlear tip (Békésy, 1957).

Sound frequency and frequency of neural firing   The place theory of pitch faces a major difficulty. As the frequency of the stimulus gets lower and lower, the deformation pattern it produces gets broader and broader. At very low frequencies (say, below 50 hertz), the wave set up by the tone deforms the entire membrane just about equally so that all receptors will be equally excited. But since we can discriminate low frequencies down to about 20 hertz, the nervous system must have some means for sensing pitch in addition to basilar location.

It is generally believed that this second means for sensing pitch is related to the firing frequency of the auditory nerve. For lower frequencies, the basilar membrane vibrates at the frequency of the stimulus tone and this vibration rate is then directly translated into the appropriate number of neural impulses per second, as evidenced by gross electrical recordings taken from the auditory nerve. The impulse frequency of the auditory output is further relayed to higher centers that somehow interpret it as pitch.

5.15   The deformation of the basilar membrane by sound   *(A) In this diagram, the membrane is schematically presented as a simple, rectangular sheet. In actuality, of course, it is much thinner and coiled in a spiral shape. (B) The relation between sound frequency and the location of the peak of the basilar membrane's deformation. The peak of the deformation is located at varying distances from the stapes (the third ossicle, which sets the membrane in motion by pushing at the oval window). As the figure shows, the higher the frequency of the sound, the closer to the stapes this peak will be. (After Lindsay and Norman, 1977; Coren and Ward, 1989)*

A

B

Hermann von Helmholtz (1821–1894)
(Courtesy National Library of Medicine)

Georg von Békésy (1899–1972)
(Courtesy Nobel Stiftelsen)

It appears then that pitch perception is based upon two separate mechanisms: Higher frequencies are coded by the place of excitation on the basilar membrane, lower frequencies by the frequency of the neural impulses. It is not clear where one mechanism leaves off and the other takes over. Place of excitation is probably relatively unimportant at frequencies below 500–1,000 hertz and has no role below 50 hertz, while impulse frequency has little or no effect for tones above 5,000 hertz. In all probability, sound frequencies in between are handled by both mechanisms (Green, 1976; Goldstein, 1989).

EVOLUTION AND SENSORY EQUIPMENT

As we've repeatedly noted, the particular stimuli to which different animals are sensitive vary markedly. For the sensory equipment of any species is an adaptation to the environment in which it lives. This holds both for what an animal can sense and what it cannot. It's hardly surprising that vision is only rudimentary in moles who live in lightless burrows but is exquisitely acute in eagles who have to detect their prey while circling in the sky several thousands of feet above. Many animals have senses that we lack altogether. Thus sharks are sensitive to electric currents leaking through the skin of fish hiding within crevices, rattlesnakes have specialized organs that can detect infrared radiation given off by small mammals nearby, and carrier pigeons use the earth's magnetic field to find their way home on cloudy nights when they can't navigate by the stars (Gould and Gould, 1988; Dyer and Gould, 1983; Wiltschko, Nohr, and Wiltschko, 1981).

An instructive example of the way in which evolution fashions a species' sensory system comes from some recent studies that have some of the flavor of a detective story perhaps entitled "The Case of the Missing Ear." Students of insect behavior long believed that the praying mantis is deaf, for it didn't seem to possess any ears. But electrophysiological evidence showed that some of the insect's nerve tracts fired in response to sounds. Their primary sensitivity was in the ultrasonic region, to tones between 25,000 and 50,000 hertz, which humans of course can't hear. So the mantis was evidently not deaf after all. The next question was, Where are its ears? To find out, the investigators coated the entire animal with a heavy layer of Vaseline after which the nerve no longer responded to sound. They next scraped off different portions of the Vaseline until they finally found a critical groove in the animal's thorax. When this was opened, the nerve resumed its response to auditory stimulation.

An ear had been found, but now this only deepened the puzzle. For there was only *one* ear, located in the animal's midline. In the animal kingdom, ears almost invariably come in pairs—a crucial prerequisite for sound localization. If the sound comes from the right, the right ear will be stimulated earlier and more intensely than the left; conversely, if the sound comes from the left. Information of this sort allows the the fortunate possessor of two ears to determine where a given sound is coming from. Given its one-eared status, the mantis can't do that. But if this is true, what is its one ear good for? And why is its primary sensitivity in the ultrasonic range?

The answer is bats. As we saw in a previous section (see p. 157), bats emit high-frequency sounds that operate like radar. These sounds echo back off the bodies of flying insects, thus enabling bats to locate their prey. The mantis's ear evidently serves as a bat detector. But if the mantis's single ear can't tell it where the bat is coming from, of what use is it? A clever study showed that sensing the likely direction of attack doesn't really matter. The investigators climbed on a ladder holding a mantis and then (gently) threw it into the air. When the mantis was aloft and flying, the investigators fired a batgun—a device that emits brief

175

Evasive flight pattern of a praying mantis
When the batgun fires (indicated by the arrow), the mantis takes evasive action, plummeting to the ground, away from what in nature would be a hungry bat. (From Yager and May, 1990)

pulses of ultrasonic sound, much like the screams of a hunting bat. High-speed photographs showed that whenever the batgun fired, most of the insects adopted an evasive flight pattern reminiscent of those used by fighter pilots—a steep, spiraling power dive likely to get them out of harm's way regardless of where the bat was coming from. The ultimate proof came from a study that pitted the insects against live bats. Over thirty mantises were thrown into the air in a wooded area in which several bats were hunting. When attacked by the bats, all insects that went into the spiral escaped unharmed; those that did not were generally captured (Yager and Hoy, 1986; Yager and May, 1990).

THE SENSES IN OVERVIEW

We've presented a brief sketch of all the senses except for vision, which we will take up in detail below. But before moving on, we should say a few words about the senses in general.

In our discussion of the various senses, we have come across many ways in which they differ—from each other and, to some extent, between different species. But we have also encountered a number of important phenomena that are not specific to any particular sensory system but are found more generally.

First, in most sense modalities (and among many animals) the processing of external stimulus energies begins with various **accessory structures** that gather these physical energies and fashion a "better" proximal stimulus for the receptors to work on. An example is provided by the semicircular canals which contain a liquid that is set in motion by head rotation and then stimulates the hair cell receptors of the vestibular system.

Second, in all sense modalities, the next step involves the receptors that achieve the **transduction** of the physical stimulus energy into an electrical signal. In some sensory systems, particularly hearing and vision, the nature of this transduction process is reasonably well understood. In other systems, such as smell, it is still unknown.

Third, the processing of stimulus input does not stop at the receptor level. There are typically further neural centers at which **coding** occurs. The stimulus information is coded (so to speak, translated) into the various dimensions of sensation that are actually experienced. Some of these dimensions involve intensity. In taste, we experience more or less bitter, in hearing—more or less loud. Other dimensions involve differences in quality. In taste, we can tell the difference between bitter, sweet, sour, and salty; in hearing, we can discriminate differences in pitch.

Fourth, any part of a sensory system is in continual **interaction** with the rest of that system. This process of interaction pertains both to the immediate past and to present activity in neighboring parts of the system. We considered some examples of sensory interaction in the taste system, including the phenomena of adaptation (with continued exposure, quinine tastes less bitter) and taste contrast (sugar on one side of the tongue makes salt on the other side taste saltier).

VISION

We now turn to a detailed discussion of vision, which in humans is the distance sense par excellence. The organization of this account will reflect characteristics that are common to most of the senses. Specifically, we will (1) describe the eye as a structure for gathering the visual stimulus, (2) examine the transduction of light energies by the visual receptors, (3) discuss some interaction processes found in vision, and (4) consider the coding processes that are involved in experiencing a particular sensory quality—in the case of vision, color.

THE STIMULUS: LIGHT

Most visual sensations have their point of origin in some external (distal) object. Occasionally, this object will be a light source that *emits* light in its own right; examples (in rather drastically descending order of emission energy) are the sun, an electric light bulb, and a glow worm. All other objects can only give off light if some light source illuminates them. They will then *reflect* some portion of the light cast upon them while absorbing the rest.

The stimulus energy we call light comes from the relatively small band of radiations to which our visual system is sensitive. These radiations travel in a wave form that is somewhat analogous to the pressure waves that are the stimulus for hearing. This radiation can vary in its *intensity,* the amount of radiant energy per unit of time, which is a major determinant of perceived brightness (as in two bulbs of different wattage). It can also vary in *wavelength,* the distance between the crests of two successive waves, which is a major determinant of perceived color. The light we ordinarily encounter is made up of a mixture of different wavelengths. The range of wavelengths to which our visual system can respond is the *visible spectrum,* extending from roughly 400 ("violet") to about 750 ("red") nanometers (1 nanometer = 1 millionth of a millimeter) between successive crests.

GATHERING THE STIMULUS: THE EYE

The next stop in the journey from stimulus to visual sensation is the eye. Except for the *retina,* none of its major structures has anything to do with the transduction of the physical stimulus energy into neurological terms. Theirs is a prior function: to fashion a proper proximal stimulus for vision, a sharp *retinal image,* out of the light that enters from outside.

Let us briefly consider how this task is accomplished. The eye has often been compared to a camera, and in its essentials this analogy holds up well enough (Figure 5.16). Both eye and camera have a *lens,* which suitably bends (or *refracts*) light rays passing through it and thus projects an image upon a light-sensitve surface

5.16   Eye and camera   As an accessory apparatus for fashioning a sharp image out of the light that enters from outside, the eye has many similarities to the camera. Both have a lens for bending light rays to project an inverted image upon a light-sensitive surface at the back. In the eye a transparent outer layer, the cornea, participates in this light-bending. The light-sensitive surface in the eye is the retina, whose most sensitive region is the fovea. Both eye and camera have a focusing device; in the eye, the lens can be thickened or flattened. Both have an adjustable iris diaphragm. And both finally are encased in black to minimize the effects of stray light; in the eye this is done by a layer of darkly pigmented tissue, the choroid coat. (Wald, 1950)

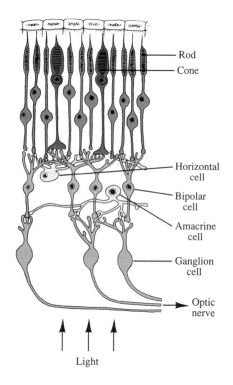

Rod
Cone

Horizontal cell

Bipolar cell

Amacrine cell

Ganglion cell

Optic nerve

Light

5.17 **The retina** *There are three main retinal layers: the rods and cones, which are the photoreceptors; the bipolar cells; and the ganglion cells, whose axons make up the optic nerve. There are also two other kinds of cells, horizontal cells and amacrine cells, that allow for sideways (lateral) interaction. As shown in the diagram, the retina contains an anatomical oddity. As it is constructed, the photoreceptors are at the very back, the bipolar cells are in between, and the ganglion cells are at the top. As a result, light has to pass through the other layers (they are not opaque so this is possible) to reach the rods and cones, whose stimulation starts the visual process. (After Coren and Ward, 1989)*

behind—the film in the camera, the retina in the eye. (In the eye, refraction is accomplished by both the lens and the **cornea,** the eye's transparent outer coating.) Both have a focusing mechanism: In the eye this is accomplished by a set of muscles that changes the shape of the lens; it is flattened for objects at a distance and thickened for objects closer by, a process technically known as **accommodation.** Finally, both camera and eye have a diaphragm that governs the amount of entering light: In the eye this function is performed by the **iris,** a smooth, circular muscle that surrounds the pupillary opening and that contracts or dilates under reflex control when the amount of illumination increases or decreases substantially.

The image of an object that falls upon the retina is determined by simple optical geometry. Its size will be inversely proportional to the distance of the object, while its shape will depend on its orientation. Thus, a rectangle viewed at a slant will project as a trapezoid.

THE VISUAL RECEPTORS

We have arrived at the point where the path from distal object to visual sensation crosses the frontier between optics and psychophysiology—the transformation of the physical stimulus energy into a nervous impulse. The structures that accomplish this feat have their visual receptor organs in the retina.

The retina is made up of several layers of nerve cells one of which is the receptor layer. Microscopic inspection shows two kinds of receptor cells whose names describe their different shapes—the **rods** and the **cones.** The cones are more plentiful in the **fovea,** a small roughly circular region at the center of the retina. While very densely packed in the fovea, they are less and less prevalent the farther out one goes toward the **periphery.** The opposite is true of the rods; they are completely absent from the fovea and are more frequent in the periphery. In all, there are some 120 million rods and about 6 million cones.

The receptors do not report to the brain directly, but relay their message upward by way of two intermediate neural links—the **bipolar cells** and the **ganglion cells** (Figure 5.17). The bipolar cells are stimulated by the receptors, and they, in their turn, excite the ganglion cells. The axons of these ganglion cells are collected from all over the retina, converging into a bundle of fibers that finally leaves the eyeball as the **optic nerve.** The region where these axons converge contains no receptors and thus cannot give rise to visual sensations; appropriately enough, it is called the **blind spot** (Figure 5.18).

VISUAL ACUITY

One of the most important functions of the visual sense is to enable us to tell one object from another. A minimum precondition for doing so is the ability to distinguish between separate points that are projected on the retina so that we do not see a blur. The ability to make such distinctions is called **acuity.** Under normal daylight conditions, this is greatest in the fovea, for it is there that the

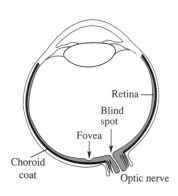

Retina
Blind spot
Fovea
Choroid coat
Optic nerve

5.18 **Fovea and blind spot** *The fovea is the region on the retina in which the receptors are most densely packed. The blind spot is a region where there are no receptors at all, this being the point where the optic nerve leaves the eyeball. (After Cornsweet, 1970)*

receptors are most closely bunched and thus provide the sharpest optical resolution. To "look at" an object means to move the eyes so that the image of that object falls upon both foveas. In peripheral vision we often see something without quite knowing what it is. To see it clearly, we swivel our eyes so that the image of the as yet unidentified something falls upon the foveal regions where our resolving power is greatest.

THE DUPLEX THEORY OF VISION

The fact that rods and cones differ in structure suggests that they also differ in function. Almost a hundred years ago, this notion led to the development of the **duplex theory of vision,** a theory that by now has the status of established fact. The idea is that rods and cones handle different aspects of the visual task. The rods are the receptors for night vision; they operate at low light intensities and lead to **achromatic** (colorless) sensations. The cones serve day vision; they respond at much higher levels of illumination and are responsible for sensations of color. The biological utility of such an arrangement becomes apparent when we consider the enormous range of light intensities encountered by organisms like ourselves who transact their business during both day and night. In humans, the ratio between the stimulus energy at absolute threshold and that transmitted by a momentary glance at the midday sun is 1 to 100,000,000,000. Evolution has evidently provided a biological division of labor, assigning two separate receptor systems to the upper and lower portions of this incredible range.

Fovea and periphery   Several facts provide important evidence in support of the duplex theory. Sensitivity to dim light is much greater in the periphery where rods are prevalent than in the center of the fovea where they are absent. This fact is familiar to sailors who know that the way to detect a faint star in the night sky is not to look at it directly, but to look off at an angle from where they think it might be. The quality of the visual sensation produced by such dim light is invariably achromatic, much like a black-and-white film.

Spectral sensitivity curves   Further evidence for the duplex theory comes from the study of spectral sensitivity. The human eye is insensitive to light waves shorter than about 360 and longer than about 700 nanometers. What is its sensitivity to the wavelengths in between? We know that photographic film (whether chromatic or achromatic) is more responsive to some regions of the visible spectrum than to others. Is the same true for the eye?

To answer this question, we ask subjects to detect a faint test light that is projected on a retinal region that contains mostly rods. The light can be independently varied in physical intensity and in wavelength. If the light is seen, it will necessarily appear gray, since only the rods are stimulated. The question is whether these rods are more sensitive to some wavelengths than to others.

To find out we determine the sensitivity for each separate wavelength. The result is the **spectral sensitivity curve** (see Figure 5.19) in which sensitivity is

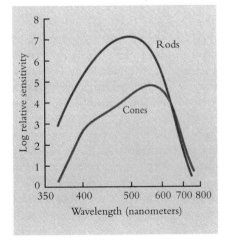

5.19   Sensitivity of rods and cones to light of different wavelengths   *Sensitivity was measured by determining the threshold for different frequencies of light projected on retinal areas rich in rods or cones. Sensitivity was then computed by dividing 1 by the threshold (the lower the threshold, the greater the sensitivity). Since sensitivity varied over an enormous range, the range was compressed by using logarithmic units. Note first that the cones, overall, are less sensitive than the rods. Note also that the point of maximal sensitivity is different for the two receptor systems. The cone maximum (560 nanometers) is closer to yellow, the rod maximum (510 nanometers) closer to green. (After Cornsweet, 1970)*

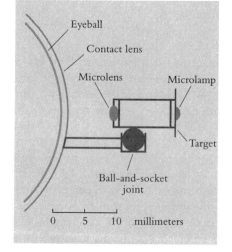

5.20 The dark adaptation curve as a composite of two separate processes *The figure shows separate dark adaptation curves for cones and rods. The dark green curve is for a light patch projected into the rod-free fovea and represents the cone-produced portion of the standard dark adaptation curve (as shown in Figure 5.19). The dark red curve is for a light patch projected well off the fovea into a cone-free region and represents the rod-produced component of the standard adaptation curve. The blue curve is the characteristic two-part adaptation curve, obtained when the test patch stimulates both rods and cones so that both rod-produced and cone-produced effects come into play. (After Cornsweet, 1970)*

plotted against wavelength. Maximal sensitivity for the rods is toward the short-wave region, with a peak at about 510 nanometers (which is seen as green).

What about the cones? We determine their spectral sensitivity by performing the same experiment, but with the test light projected on the all-cone fovea (Figure 5.20). The results show that the cones are much less sensitive than the rods. They also show that the cones' region of maximal sensitivity is toward the longer wavelengths, with a peak at about 560 nanometers (which is seen as yellowish green). Rods and cones evidently differ in their relative sensitivity to different wavelengths. For rods, the blues are easier to detect than the yellows and reds (although of course they all appear gray); the opposite holds for the cones.

VISUAL PIGMENTS

When light hits a visual receptor, its energy eventually triggers a nervous impulse. The first stage of this energy conversion involves a photochemical process. We are again reminded of the camera. In a photographic plate the sensitive elements are usually grains of silver salt such as silver bromide. When light strikes the film, some of it is absorbed by the silver bromide molecules with the result that the silver is separated from the compound (and eventually becomes visible after several darkroom manipulations). The visual receptors contain several ***visual pigments*** that perform an analogous function for the eye. One such substance is ***rhodopsin,*** which serves as the visual pigment for the rods.

Unlike a photographic emulsion, the visual pigments constantly renew themselves. Were it otherwise, a newborn infant would open his eyes, look at the bustling world around him, and never see again—his retina would be bleached forever. The bleached pigments are reconstituted to permit an unbroken succession of further retinal pictures.

5.21 Stabilized-image device *The subject wears a contact lens on which a tiny projector is mounted. At the rear of the projector is the stimulus target, which is projected onto the retina. This target will remain fixed at one point of the retina, for as the eyeball moves, so does the contact lens and its attached projector. As a result, the image on the retina remains stabilized. (After Pritchard, 1961)*

INTERACTION IN TIME: ADAPTATION

We now turn to some phenomena which prove that the visual system (as indeed all sensory systems) is much more than the passive observer that Locke had assumed it to be. On the contrary, the visual system actively shapes and transforms the optic input; its components never function in isolation, but constantly interact.

One kind of interaction concerns the relation between what happens now and what happened just before. The general finding is simple: There will be a gradual decline in the reaction to any stimulus that persists unchanged. For example, after continued inspection of a green patch, its greenness will eventually fade away. Similar adaptation phenomena are found in most other sensory systems. Thus, the cold ocean water feels warmer after we have been in it for a while.

5.22 Brightness contrast *Four (objectively) identical gray squares on different backgrounds. The lighter the background, the darker the gray squares appear.*

What does the organism gain by sensory adaptation? Stimuli that have been around for a while have already been inspected; if they posed a danger, this would have been detected already. Since these stimuli are of lesser relevance to the organism's survival, it pays to give them less sensory weight. What is important is change, especially sudden change, for this may well signify food to a predator and death to its potential prey. **Adaptation** is the sensory system's way of pushing old news off the neurophysiological front page.

An interesting adaptation effect in vision is provided by the **stabilized image.** In normal vision, the eyes constantly move. In consequence, no retinal region ever suffers prolonged exposure to the same stimulus; one moment, it will be stimulated by a dark object, the next moment, by a lighter one. Since every change of gaze leads to a change in the visual stimulus, there will be no visual adaptation. Even if one tries to hold one's eyes steady to fixate a stationary picture, adaptation effects will be rather minor. The fact is that we cannot truly hold our eyes motionless. Small tremors in the eye muscles lead to involuntary eye movements, and these necessarily alter the stimulus input for any given retinal region.

Several contemporary investigators, however, have developed a technique that achieves a truly stationary retinal image. The basic idea is as clever as it is simple. Since you can't stop the eye from moving, you move the stimulus along with the eye. One way to accomplish this is by means of a contact lens to which a tiny projector is attached. This projects a stimulus pattern upon the retina. The contact lens moves with every motion of the eyeball, but the projector moves with it. The result is a stabilized image. When the eye moves, so does the stimulus; thus each retinal region is continually exposed to the identical portion of the stimulus pattern (Figure 5.21). At first, the stabilized retinal image is seen very sharply, but after some seconds it fades away completely—a dramatic demonstration of the system's adaptation to unchanging stimulation. Interestingly enough, the image will reappear if the stimulus pattern is somehow altered, whether in intensity or in its retinal location (the latter by slippage of the contact lens). We can conclude that, in humans, continual involuntary eye movements serve the biologically useful purpose of keeping the visual world intact (Riggs et al., 1953).

INTERACTION IN SPACE: CONTRAST

Adaptation effects show that sensory systems respond to change over time. If no such change occurs, the sensory response diminishes. What holds for time holds for space as well. For here, too, the key word is *change*. In vision (as in some other senses), the response to a stimulus applied to any one region partially depends on how the neighboring regions are stimulated. The greater the difference in stimulation, the greater the sensory effect.

BRIGHTNESS CONTRAST

It has long been known that the appearance of a gray patch depends upon its background. The identical gray will look much brighter on a black background than it will on a white background. This is **brightness contrast,** an effect that increases the greater the intensity difference between two contrasting regions. Thus, gray appears brighter on black than on dark gray and darker against white than against light gray (Figure 5.22).

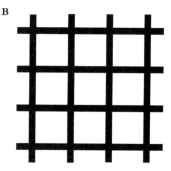

5.23 The effect of distance between contrasting regions *(A) The white lines in the grid are physically homogeneous, but they don't appear to be—each of the "intersections" seems to contain a gray spot. The uneven appearance of the white strips is caused by contrast. Each strip is surrounded by a black square, which contrasts with it and makes it look brighter. But this is not the case at the intersections, which only touch upon the black squares at their corners. As a result, there is little contrast in the middle of the intersections. This accounts for the gray spots seen there. (B) The same point is made by the second grid. Here there seem to be whitish spots at the intersections. The explanation is the same: The black lines are bounded by white and thus look darker by contrast. There is less contrast operating on the regions in the middle of the intersections. As a result, they don't appear as dark as the streets, looking like whitish spots. (After Hering, 1920)*

Contrast is also a function of the distance between the two contrasting regions—the smaller that difference, the greater the contrast (Figure 5.23). This phenomenon gives rise to a number of visual illusions and has been used by some contemporary artists to create striking effects (see Figure 5.24).

Such contrast effects serve to accentuate the edges between different objects in our visual world and thus allow us to see them more clearly. To explain why this is so we must consider some further facts about the optics of the eye and about brightness contrast.

ACCENTUATING EDGES

We've seen that brightness contrast exaggerates the brightness difference between two adjoining areas. A related effect is that it sometimes creates boundaries between regions where physically there are none.

A demonstration is provided by surfaces in which the physical light intensity varies from place to place according to some prearranged function. Consider Figure 5.25A, which contains strips of grays that range from very dark to very light. Within each strip, the physical light intensities are equal. But that is not how they appear. At the border between each strip and the neighboring one, there seems to be a band. A bright band is seen where the strip borders on a darker strip; a dark band is seen where the strip borders on a lighter strip. These results are summarized by Figure 5.25B in which the physical light intensities are plotted against stimulus position.

These phenomena are produced by the same contrast effects we discussed before. Contrast accentuates the difference between two adjacent regions. But this sharpening is maximal at the borders where the distance between the two contrasting regions is smallest. These bands (usually called **Mach bands,** after the nineteenth-century physicist Ernst Mach who discovered them) are the result.

It is generally agreed that the same process helps to overcome certain optical imperfections of the eye that produce fuzzy images even though the external

Ewald Hering *(Courtesy National Library of Medicine)*

5.24 Contrast *(A) Arcturus (1966) by Victor Vasarely. The luminous rays are not in the painting itself but are created by brightness contrast. Note that the painting consists of a series of frames, which surround other frames and become progressively darker as they go from center to periphery. (Courtesy of the Hirshhorn Museum and Sculpture Garden, Smithsonian Institution; gift of Joseph H. Hirshhorn, 1972. Photograph by Marianne Gurley) (B) The figure focuses on three of the frames in the painting. Consider squares 1, 3, and 4 in frame B. Squares 1 and 4 each have an entire side next to the brighter frame C above them. As a result, they look darker because of brightness contrast. But square 3 suffers little contrast, for it only touches on the brighter frame at its corner. It therefore looks brighter than the two squares 1 and 4 that are adjacent to it. For the same reason, squares 2 and 6 in frame A will seem to be darker than square 5. Since this happens for all the squares at the corners, the observer sees four radiating luminous diagonals. (Jameson, 1975)*

A

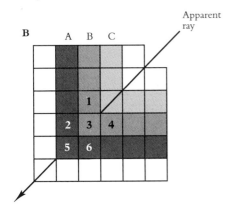

B A B C

Apparent ray

A

B

Stimulus intensity

Position on stimulus

stimulus is outlined sharply. The contours of the retinal image are sharpened, for the visual system recreates, and even exaggerates, boundaries by the same mechanisms that generate Mach bands.

A PHYSIOLOGICAL ACCOUNT OF CONTRAST

Brightness contrast and Mach bands provide some initial basis for the perception of shape: They enhance the differences between two adjacent regions and thus help to produce contours. But what is the mechanism that creates them?

Today we know that these effects are based on the mutual inhibition of cells in the retina and higher up. The conclusive demonstration that this is so had to await the techniques of modern electrophysiology. But many years before this, such sensory psychologists as Ernst Mach (1838–1916) and Ewald Hering (1834–1918) had postulated precisely such a process on the basis of what they observed in the sensory laboratory. In their view, the phenomena of contrast and Mach bands could be explained in no other way. In this regard, Mach and Hering resemble Sherrington, who inferred the synapse on the basis of behav-

5.25 Mach bands *(A) The series of gray strips is arranged in ascending brightness, from left to right. Physically, each strip is of uniform light intensity. This is graphically expressed in (B), which plots stimulus position against physical light intensity, showing a simple series of ascending steps. But this is not what is seen, for the strips do not appear to be uniform. For each strip, the left edge (adjacent to its darker neighbor) looks brighter than the rest, while the right edge (adjacent to its lighter neighbor) looks darker. The explanation is contrast. The edges are closer to their darker or lighter neighbors and will thus be more subject to contrast than the rest of the strip. The result is an accentuation of the contours that separate one strip from the next. (After Cornsweet, 1970; Coren, Porac, and Ward, 1978)*

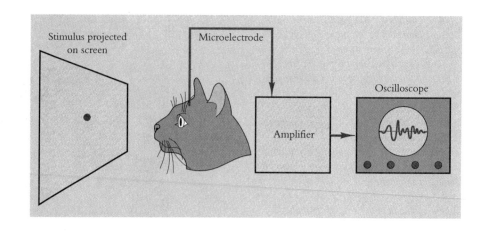

5.26   Recording from the visual system of a cat   *The experimental setup for recording neural responses from the visual system of a cat. An anesthetized cat has one eye propped open so that visual stimulation can be directed to particular regions of the retina. A microelectrode picks up neural impulses from a single cell in the optic system, amplifies them, and displays them on an oscilloscope. (After Schiffman, 1976)*

ioral data alone many decades before there was any means for providing physiological proof.

The modern physiological account of contrast effects is based on single-cell recording methods. The first step is to place a microelectrode in an anesthetized cat's optic nerve so that it picks up electrical activity from only one cell. The eye of the animal is then propped open and is stimulated by spots of light of varying intensities and at different locations (Figure 5.26). We find that there is a small region of the retina whose stimulation leads to an increase in the firing rate. The more intense the light, the greater the cell's response. But this central region is surrounded by a region in which illumination has the opposite effect. If we shine the light upon this region, the illumination depresses the cell's firing rate, and this depression increases with increasing light intensity (Figure 5.27). The entire area of the retina in which stimulation by light affects the cell's firing rate—whether up or down—is called the ***receptive field*** of that cell.

LATERAL INHIBITION AND BRIGHTNESS CONTRAST

These results make it clear that neighboring regions in the retina tend to inhibit each other. This tendency of a region of the visual system to oppose the responses from an adjacent region is called ***lateral inhibition***—in effect, it is inhibition exerted sideways. A simplified version of how this mechanism works is as follows: When any visual receptor is stimulated, it transmits its excitation upward to other cells that eventually relay it to the brain. But this excitation has a further effect. It also stimulates some neurons that extend sideways along the retina. These lateral cells make contact with neighboring cells whose activation they inhibit.

5.27   Receptive fields on the cat's visual system   *Using the setup shown in Figure 5.26, stimuli are presented to various regions of the retina. The panels show the firing frequency of a particular ganglion cell. Panel 1 shows the base-level firing rate when no stimulus is presented anywhere. Panel 2 shows the effect when a stimulus is presented anywhere within an inner, central region, A, on the retina. When stimulated in A, the cell's firing rate goes up. Panel 3 shows what happens in response to a stimulus presented anywhere within the ring-shaped region, B, surrounding region A. Stimulation in B causes the cell's firing rate to go down. Panel 4, finally, shows what happens when a stimulus is presented outside of either A or B, the regions that together comprise the cell's receptive field. Now there is no significant change from the cell's normal base level. (From Kuffler, 1953)*

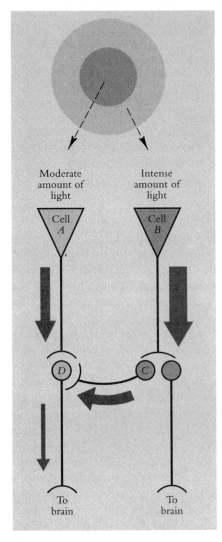

5.28 Lateral inhibition and contrast
Two receptor cells, A and B, are stimulated by neighboring regions of a stimulus. A receives moderate stimulation; B receives an intense amount of light. A's excitation serves to stimulate the next neuron in the visual chain, cell D, which transmits the message further toward the brain. But this transmission is impeded by cell B, whose own intense excitation exerts an inhibitory effect on its neighbors. B excites a lateral cell, C, which exerts an inhibitory effect on cell D. As a result, cell D fires at a reduced rate. (Excitatory effects are shown by dark green arrows, inhibitory ones by dark red arrows. In the human eye, the lateral inhibitors are the horizontal cells and the amacrine cells of the retina; see Figure 5.17.)

To see how lateral inhibition works, consider the retinal image produced by a gray patch surrounded by a lighter ring (Figure 5.28). For the sake of simplicity, we will only look at two neighboring receptor cells, *A* and *B. A* is stimulated by the gray patch and receives a moderate amount of light. *B* is stimulated by the lighter ring and receives much more light. Our primary interest is in the excitation that cell *A,* the one stimulated by the gray patch, relays upward to the brain. The more cell *A* is stimulated, the more excitation it will relay, and the brighter the patch will appear to be. The important point is that the excitation from cell *A* will not be passed on unimpeded. On the contrary, some of this excitation will be canceled by inhibition from neighboring cells. Consider the effect of cell *B,* whose stimulation comes from the lighter ring. That cell is intensely excited. One result of this excitation is that it excites a third cell, *C,* whose effect is inhibitory and exerted sideways (in short, a lateral inhibitor). The effect of this lateral cell *C* is to block the excitation that *A* sends upward.

Lateral inhibition is the basis of brightness contrast. Let's go back to the three cells in Figure 5.28. The more intensely cell *B* is stimulated, the more it will excite the lateral inhibitor, cell *C.* This explains why a gray patch on a black background looks brighter than the same gray patch surrounded by white. The black background does not stimulate cell *B;* as a result, the lateral inhibitor *C* is not active. But a white background does stimulate cell *B,* which excites cell *C,* which in its turn diminishes the excitation cell *A* sends upward to the brain to inform it of the apparent brightness of the gray patch. The upshot of all this is contrast: The brain gets a visual message that is an exaggeration; what is dark seems darker, what is light seem lighter.

COLOR

Despite their many differences, the sensory systems of hearing and of vision have some things in common. In both, the relevant stimulus energy is in wave form. And in both, wavelength is related to a qualitative psychological dimension—in one case pitch, in the other color. Much of the research in both domains has revolved around the question of how these two sensory qualities are coded. We will here consider only one of these domains, that of color.

CLASSIFYING THE COLOR SENSATIONS

A person with normal color vision can distinguish over seven million different color shades. What are the processes that allow him to make these distinctions? One step in answering this question is to find a classification system that will allow us to describe any one of these millions of colors by reference to a few simple dimensions. In this task we concentrate on what we see and experience, on psychology rather than physics. What we want to classify is our color sensations rather than the physical stimuli that produce them. In doing so, we cannot help but discover something about the way our mind—that is, our nervous system—functions. Whatever order we may find in the classification of our sensations is at least partially imposed by the way in which our nervous system organizes the physical stimuli that impinge upon it.

The dimensions of color   Imagine seven million or so colored paper patches, one for each of the colors we can discriminate. We can classify them according to three perceived dimensions: hue, brightness, and saturation.

Hue is a term whose meaning is close to that of the word "color" as used in everyday life. It is a property of what are called the **chromatic colors** (for exam-

400 nm   500 nm   600 nm   700 nm

5.29 The visible spectrum and the four unique hues *The visible spectrum consists of light waves from about 360 to 700 nanometers (1 nm = one millionth of a millimeter). White light contains all of these wavelengths. They are bent to different degrees when passed through a prism, yielding the spectrum with the hues shown in the figure. Three of the four unique hues correspond to part of the spectrum: unique blue at about 465 nm, unique green at about 500 nm, and unique yellow at about 570 nm. These values vary slightly from person to person. The fourth, unique red—that is, a red that has no apparent tinge of either yellow or blue—is called extraspectral because it is not represented by a single wavelength on the spectrum. It can only be produced by a mixture of wavelengths. (From Ohanian, 1993)*

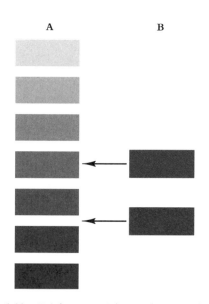

5.30 Brightness *Colors can be arranged according to their brightness. (A) This dimension is most readily recognized when we look at a series of grays, which are totally hueless and vary in brightness only. (B) But chromatic colors can also be classified according to their brightness. The arrows indicate the brightness of the blue and dark green shown here in relation to the series of grays.*

ple, red and blue) but not of the **achromatic colors** (that is, black, white, and all of the totally neutral grays in between). Hue varies with wavelength (Figure 5.29). Thus, ***unique blue*** (a blue that is judged to have no trace of red or green in it) occurs on the spectrum at about 465 nanometers, ***unique green*** (which has no blue or yellow) at about 500 nanometers, and ***unique yellow*** (which has no green or red) at about 570 nanometers.

Brightness varies among both the chromatic and achromatic colors. Thus, ultramarine is darker than light blue and charcoal gray is darker than light gray (Figure 5.30). But the brightness dimension stands out most clearly if we consider achromatic colors alone. These differ in brightness only, while the chromatic colors may differ in hue (as we have seen) and in saturation (which we will discuss next). Note that white and black represent the top and bottom of the brightness dimension. Thus, white is hueless and maximally bright; black is hueless and minimally bright.

Saturation is the "purity" of a color, the extent to which it is chromatic rather than achromatic. The more gray (or black or white) that is mixed with a color, the less saturation it has. Consider the various blue patches in Figure 5.31. All have the same hue (blue). All share the brightness of a particular, achromatic gray (which is also the same gray with which the blue was mixed to produce the less saturated blue patches, *A, B, C,* and *D*). The patches only differ in one respect: the proportion of blue as opposed to that of gray. The more gray there is, the less the saturation. When the color is entirely gray, saturation is zero. This holds for all colors. Thus red and pink differ largely in saturation, so that pink appears like a "washed out" red.

5.31 Saturation *The four patches A–D are identical in both hue and brightness. They only differ in saturation, which is greatest for A and decreases from A to D. The gray patch, E, on the far right matches all the other patches in brightness; it was mixed with the blue patch, A, in varying proportions to produce patches B, C, and D.*

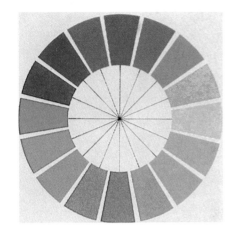

5.32   The color circle   *The relationship between maximally saturated hues can be expressed by arranging them in a circle according to their perceptual similarity. Note that in this version of the color circle, the spacing of the hues depends upon their perceptual properties rather than the wavelengths that give rise to them. In particular, the four unique hues are equally spaced, each 90 degrees from the next. (Hurvich, 1981)*

The color circle and the color solid   Some hues appear to be very similar to others. Suppose we only consider the color patches that look most chromatic—that is, those whose saturation is maximal. If we arrange these on the basis of perceptual similarity, the result is a circular series, the **color circle,** such that red is followed by orange, orange by yellow, yellow-green, green, blue-green, blue, and violet, until the circle finally returns to red (Figure 5.32).

The color circle embodies the perceptual similarities among the different hues. To complete our classificatory schema, we construct a **color solid,** which incorporates the color circle with the other two dimensions of perceived color, brightness and saturation (Figure 5.33). Each of our original seven million color patches can be fitted into a unique position in this solid (Figure 5.34). Our classificatory task is thus accomplished.

COLOR MIXTURE

With rare exceptions, the objects in the world around us do not reflect a single wavelength; rather, they reflect different ones, all of which strike the same region of the retina simultaneously. Let us consider the results of some of these mixtures.

Subtractive mixture   Before proceeding, we must recognize that the kind of mixture sensory psychologists are interested in is very different from the sort artists employ when they stir pigments together on a palette. Mixing pigments on a palette (or smearing crayons together on a piece of paper) is **subtractive mixture.** In subtractive mixture, one set of wavelengths is subtracted from another set.

5.33   The three dimensions of color
Brightness is represented by the central axis, going from darkest (black) to brightest (white). Hue is represented by angular position relative to the color circle. Saturation is the distance from the central vertical axis: The farther the color is from this axis, the more saturated it is. The maximal saturation that is possible varies from hue to hue; hence, the different extensions from the central axis. (Munsell Color, courtesy of Macbeth, a division of Kollmorgen Corporation)

5.34   The color solid   *Every color can be placed within a color solid that is based on the three dimensions of brightness, hue, and saturation. The inside of the solid is shown by taking slices that illustrate variations in hue, brightness, and saturation. (Munsell Color, courtesy of Macbeth, a division of Kollmorgen Corporation)*

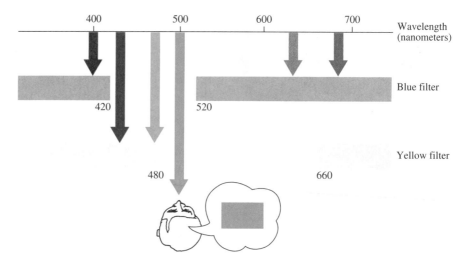

5.35 Subtractive mixture   *In subtractive mixture, the light passed by two filters (or reflected by two mixed pigments) is the band of wavelengths passed by the first minus that region subtracted by the second. In the present example, the first filter passes light between 420 and 520 nanometers (a broad-band blue filter), while the second passes light between 480 and 660 nanometers (a broad-band yellow filter). The only light that can pass through both is in the region between 480 and 520 nanometers, which appears green.*

The easiest demonstration is with colored filters, such as those used in stage lighting, which allow some wavelengths to pass through them while holding others back. Take two such filters, *A* and *B*. Suppose filter *A* allows passage to all light waves between 420 and 520 nanometers but no others. The broad range of light that comes through this filter will be seen as blue. In contrast, filter *B* passes light waves between 480 and 660 nanometers but excludes all others. The band of light waves that comes through this filter will be seen as yellow (Figure 5.35).

We now ask how we see light that has to pass through both filters. Filter *A* (the blue filter) blocks all light above 520 nanometers, while filter *B* (the yellow filter) blocks all light below 480 nanometers. As a result, the only light waves that can pass through this double barricade are those that can slip through the narrow gap between 480 and 520 nanometers, the only interval left unblocked by both filters. As it happens, light in this interval is seen as green. Thus, when the mixture is subtractive, mixing blue and yellow will yield green.

Thus far we have dealt with filters that let some wavelengths through while blocking others. The same account also applies to artists' pigments. Any pigment reflects only a certain band of wavelengths while absorbing the rest. Suppose we

A

B

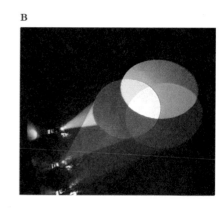

Color mixture   *The effect of (A) passing light through several filters (subtractive mixture) and (B) throwing different filtered lights upon the same spot (additive mixture). (Photographs by Fritz Goro / Life Magazine, © Time Warner, Inc.)*

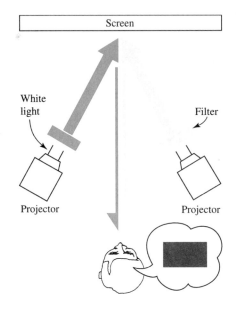

Screen

White
light

Filter

Projector

Projector

5.36 Additive mixture *In additive mixture, the light passed by two filters (or reflected by two pigments) impinges upon the same region of the retina at the same time. The figure shows two projectors throwing blue and yellow filtered light upon the same portion of the screen from which it is reflected upon the same region of the retina. In contrast to what happens in subtractive mixture, the result of adding these two colors is gray.*

mix pigment *A* (say, blue) with pigment *B* (say, yellow). The result is a form of subtraction. What we will see is the wavelengths reflected by the blue pigment (420 to 520 nanometers) minus the wavelengths absorbed by the yellow pigment (everything below 480 nanometers). The effect is exactly the same as if we had superimposed a blue filter over a yellow one. All that is reflected is light between 480 and 520 nanometers, which is seen as green.

Additive mixture In subtractive mixture, one set of wavelengths is removed from another set. This occurs before the light ever hits the eye. In another kind of mixture, the procedure is the very opposite. This is **additive mixture,** which occurs when different bands of wavelengths stimulate the same retinal region simultaneously. Here the mixture occurs in the eye itself. Such additive mixtures can be produced in the laboratory by using filtered light from two or more different projectors that are all focused on the same spot. In this procedure, the light from each source remains unmixed until it reaches the retina; the mixture occurs after this point and is produced by processes within the nervous system (Figure 5.36).

In real life, additive mixture has many uses. One is color television, in which the additive mixture is accomplished by three different sets of photosensitive substances. Another example is provided by the Pointillist painter Georges Seurat. His works are composed of dots of different colors that are too close together to be seen separately, especially when the picture is viewed from a distance (Figure 5.37). The result is that, while the colors remain separate on the canvas, they blend together in the viewer's eye.

5.37 Additive mixture in Pointillist art The Channel of Gravelines *(1890) by Georges Seurat. A detail of the painting (on the left) shows the separate color daubs which, when viewed from a distance, mix additively. The Pointillists employed this technique instead of mixing pigments to capture the bright appearance of colors outdoors. Pigment mixture is subtractive and darkens the resulting colors. (Courtesy Indianapolis Museum of Art, gift of Mrs. James W. Fesler in memory of Daniel W. and Elizabeth C. Marmon)*

A

B

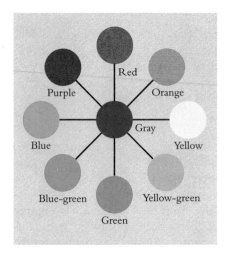

5.38 Complementary hues *Any hue will yield gray if additively mixed (in the correct proportion) with a hue on the opposite side of the color circle. Such hue pairs are complementaries. Some complementary hues are shown here linked by a line across the circle's center. Of particular importance are the two complementary pairs that contain the four unique hues: red-green and blue-yellow.*

COMPLEMENTARY HUES

An important fact about additive color mixture is that every hue has a **complementary,** another hue that, if mixed with the first in appropriate proportions, will produce the color gray. An easy way to find complementaries is by reference to the color circle. Any hue on the circumference will yield gray if mixed (additively) with the hue on the opposite side of the color circle (see Figure 5.38). Of particular interest are the complementary pairs that involve the four unique colors, red, yellow, green, and blue. Blue and yellow are complementaries that produce gray upon additive mixture; the same holds for red and green. Hues that are not complementary produce mixtures that preserve the hue of their components. Thus, the mixture of red and yellow leads to orange (which still looks like a yellowish red), while that of blue and red yields a violet (which looks like a reddish blue).

At the risk of repetition, note that all of this holds only for additive mixture. When blue and yellow are additively mixed in the right proportions, the observer sees gray. This is in contrast to what happens when the mixture is subtractive, as in drawing a blue crayon over a yellow patch. Now the result is green. The same holds for red and green. Additive mixture of the two yields gray; subtractive mixture produces a blackish brown.

COLOR ANTAGONISTS

The color-mixture effects we have just described suggest that color complementaries, such as blue and yellow on the one hand, and red and green on the other, are mutually opposed "antagonists" that cancel each other's hue. Some further phenomena lead to a similar conclusion.

One such phenomenon is the chromatic counterpart of brightness contrast. In general, any region in the visual field tends to induce its complementary color in adjoining areas. The result is **simultaneous color contrast.** For example, a gray patch will tend to look bluish if surrounded by yellow, yellowish if surrounded by blue, and so on (Figure 5.39).

In simultaneous contrast, the complementary relation involves two adjoining regions in space. In a related phenomenon, the contrast is with an immediately preceding stimulus; it is a contrast in time rather than in space. Suppose we stare at a green patch for a while and then look at a white wall. We will see a reddish spot. This is a **negative afterimage** (Figure 5.40). Negative afterimages have the complementary hue of the original stimulus (which is why they are called negative). Thus, fixation on a brightly lit red bulb will make us see a dark greenish shape when we subsequently look at a white screen.

5.39 Color contrast *The gray patches on the blue and yellow backgrounds are physically identical. But they don't look that way. To begin with, there is a difference in perceived brightness: The patch on the blue looks brighter than the one on the yellow, a result of brightness contrast. There is also a difference in perceived hue, for the patch on the blue looks somewhat yellowish, while that on the yellow looks bluish. This is color contrast, a demonstration that hues tend to induce their antagonists in neighboring areas.*

5.40 Negative afterimage *Stare at the center of the figure for a minute or two, and then look at a white piece of paper. Blink once or twice; the negative afterimage will appear within a few seconds, showing the rose in its correct colors.*

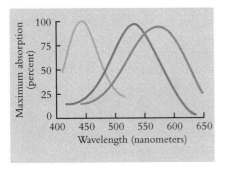

5.41 Sensitivity curves of three different cones in the primate retina *The retinas of humans and monkeys contain three different kinds of cones, each with its own photopigment that differs in its sensitivity to different regions of the spectrum. One absorbs more of the shorter wavelengths (and is thus more sensitive to light in this spectral region), a second more of the middle wavelengths, a third more of the longer ones. The resulting sensitivity curves are shown here. (After MacNichol, 1964)*

Afterimages are caused by events that occur in the retina and associated visual mechanisms. This is why, when the eye moves, the afterimage moves along with it. One reason for the effect is retinal adaptation. When we fixate a white disk on a black background, the pigments in the retinal region that correspond to the disk will be stimulated more intensely than those in surrounding areas. During subsequent exposure to a homogeneous white surface, the more deeply stimulated regions will respond less vigorously and will thus report a lesser sensory intensity. The result is a dark gray negative afterimage. But peripheral adaptation is probably not the whole story. In addition, there may be a rebound phenomenon. While the stimulus was still present, the excited regions may well have inhibited an antagonistic process. White held back black, blue inhibited yellow, and so on. When the stimulus was withdrawn, the inhibited processes rebounded, like a coiled spring that is suddenly released.

THE PHYSIOLOGICAL BASIS OF COLOR VISION

What is the physiological basis of color vision? We will consider this issue by subdividing it into two questions: (1) How are wavelengths transduced into receptor activity? (2) How is the receptor output coded so that it yields the psychological attributes of color, such as the sensory experience of unique blue?

COLOR RECEPTORS

The raw material with which the visual system must begin is light of various intensities. Since we can discriminate among different wavelengths, there must be different receptors (that is, different types of cones) that are somehow differentially attuned to this physical dimension.

It turns out that normal human color vision depends on three different kinds of cone elements (which is why our color vision is often called trichromatic). While each of these cone types responds to a broad range of wavelengths in the visible spectrum, their sensitivity curves differ in that one cone type is most sensitive to wavelengths in the short-wave region of the spectrum, the second to wavelengths in the middle range, and the third to the longer wavelengths (Bowmaker and Dartnall, 1980; MacNichol, 1986; see Figure 5.41).

The critical fact about all three cone elements is that their sensitivities overlap extensively so that most of the wavelengths of the visible spectrum stimulate each of the three receptor elements. This being so, how can we manage to discriminate different wavelengths? We can, because each receptor element will respond in differing degree depending upon the wavelength of the stimulus light. If the light is from the blue end of the spectrum, there will be maximum output from the cone element whose sensitivity is greatest in the short-wave region. If the light is from the orange end, it will elicit maximum activity from the cone element whose sensitivity is greatest in the long-wave region. As a result, each wavelength will produce a different ratio of outputs from the three types of receptors. Assuming that the nervous system can tell which receptor type is sending which message, wavelength discrimination follows.

COLOR CODING: THE OPPONENT-PROCESS THEORY

The preceding analysis can explain how lights of different wavelengths are discriminated from each other, but can it account for the reason why these lights look the way they do? One attempt to explain the psychological properties of color is the **Young-Helmholtz theory** (named for Thomas Young and Hermann von Helmholtz who proposed it in the nineteenth century). According to this theory, each of the three receptor types gives rise to the experience of one basic color. Stimulation of the short-wave receptor produces blue, stimulation of the medium-wave receptor produces green, and stimulation of the long-wave receptor produces red. According to the trichromatic theory, all other colors are essentially mixtures of the three colors that are said to be primary—red, green, and blue.

This interpretation of the way colors appear runs into a number of problems. The Young-Helmholtz theory asserts that all colors are produced by the mixture of the three primaries—red, green, and blue. But in fact, many colors don't look like mixtures of different proportions of red, green and blue. Some do, such as purple, which looks like a mixture of red and blue. But many others do not. The most troublesome example is yellow, which looks like a primary (that is, does not look like a mixture) but does not have primary status according to the trichromatic theory. An additional problem with this theory is that it cannot easily explain why the four unique hues form two complementary (and antagonistic) pairs: red-green and blue-yellow.

To account for phenomena of this kind we must assume some further neural mechanism that operates on outputs from the three cone types and ultimately codes them into the sensory qualities we know as color. Such a further mechanism is proposed by the **opponent-process theory** formulated by Leo Hurvich and Dorothea Jameson. This theory asserts that there are six psychologically primary color qualities—red, green, blue, yellow, black, and white—each of which has a different neural process that corresponds to it. These six processes are not independent, but instead are organized into three opponent-process pairs: red-green, blue-yellow, and black-white. The two members of each pair are antagonists. Excitation of one member automatically inhibits the other (Hurvich and Jameson, 1957).

The two hue systems According to the opponent-process theory, the experience of hue depends upon two of the opponent-process pairs—red-green and blue-yellow. Each of these opponent-process pairs can be likened to a balance. If one arm (say, the blue process) goes down, the other arm (its opponent, yellow) necessarily goes up. The hue we actually see depends upon the position of the two balances (Figure 5.42). If the red-green balance is tipped toward red and the blue-yellow balance toward blue (excitation of red and blue with concomitant inhibition of green and yellow), the perceived hue will be violet. This follows, because the resulting hue will be a combination of red and blue, which is seen as violet. If either of the two scales is evenly balanced, it will make no contribution to the hue experience. This will occur when neither of the two antagonists is stimulated and also when both are stimulated equally and cancel each other out. If both hue systems are in balance, there will be no hue at all and the resulting color will be seen as achromatic (that is, without hue).

Light of 450 nm

Hue: Blue + Red = Violet

5.42   The opponent-process hue systems   *The diagram shows how opponent-process theory interprets our response to light of a particular wavelength. In the example, the light is in the short-wave region of the visible spectrum, specifically, 450 nanometers. This will affect both the blue-yellow and red-green systems. It will tip the blue-yellow balance toward blue, and the red-green balance toward red. The resulting hue will be a mixture of red and blue (that is, violet).*

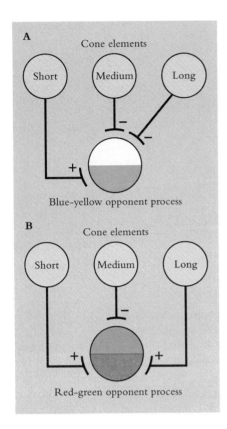

A Cone elements

Short　Medium　Long

Blue-yellow opponent process

B Cone elements

Short　Medium　Long

Red-green opponent process

*5.43　**From receptors to opponent-process pairs***　*A simplified presentation of a neural system in which all three receptor elements feed into two color opponent-process pairs. One pole of each opponent process is activated by excitation, while its opposite pole is activated by inhibition. (A) The blue-yellow system. This is excited by the short-wave receptors and inhibited by the medium- and the long-wave receptors. If excitation outweighs inhibition, the opponent-process signals blue; if inhibition outweighs excitation, it signals yellow; if excitation and inhibition are equal, there is no signal at all and we see gray. (B) The red-green system. This is excited by both the short-wave and the long-wave receptor elements, and is inhibited by the medium-wave elements. If excitation outweighs inhibition, the system signals red; if inhibition outweighs excitation, it signals green; if excitation and inhibition are equal, there is no signal and we see gray. The assumption that this system is excited by both short- and long-wave receptors is made because the experience "red" occurs at the two extremes of the spectrum: Short wavelengths produce the hues of violet or purple, which are perceived as having some red in them, while long wavelengths produce various oranges, which of course are also seen as having red in them. (For discussion, see Hurvich and Jameson, 1957)*

The black-white system　According to the opponent-process theory, the brightness or darkness of a visual experience is determined by the activity of a third pair of antagonists, black and white. Every wavelength contributes to the excitation of the white system, in proportion to its intensity and the sensitivity of daylight vision to this point of the spectrum. The black process is produced by inhibition of the antagonistic white process. This is best exemplified by some phenomena of brightness contrast. A piece of black paper placed against a dark gray background will look not black but a darker shade of gray. We can make it look pitch-black by presenting it against a brilliantly illuminated background. By doing so, we inhibit the white process within the enclosed region, which necessarily enhances the activity of its antagonist.

The relation between color receptors and opponent processes　Can we reconcile the fact that there are three elements at the receptor level with the claim that there are four chromatic color opponents? Hurvich and Jameson have suggested a neural system that tries to accomplish this. The basic idea is that the three receptor elements have both excitatory and inhibitory connections with neurons higher up that correspond to opponent processes and that one pole of each opponent process will be activated by excitation while its opposite pole will be activated by inhibition (for details, see Figure 5.43).

THE PHYSIOLOGICAL BASIS OF OPPONENT PROCESSES

When the theory was first developed, the opponent processes were only an inference, based upon the perceptual phenomena of color vision. Today there is evidence that this inference came close to the neurophysiological mark. The proof comes from single-cell recordings (in the retina or higher up), which show that some neurons behave very much as an opponent-process theory would lead one to expect.

As an example, take a study of single-cell activity in the visual pathway of the rhesus monkey, whose color vision is known to be very similar to ours. Some of its visual cells behave as though they were part of a blue-yellow system. If the retina is stimulated by blue light, these cells fire more rapidly. The opposite holds true if the same area is exposed to yellow light—the firing rate is inhibited

Blue   Yellow

5.44   Opponent-process cells in the visual system of a monkey   *The figure shows the average firing rate of blue-yellow cells to light of different wavelengths. These cells are excited by shorter wavelengths and inhibited by longer wavelengths, analogous to the cells in the human system that signal the sensation "blue." As the figure shows, shorter wavelengths lead to firing rates that are above the spontaneous rates obtained when there is no stimulus at all. Longer wavelengths have the opposite effect, depressing the cell's activity below the spontaneous firing rate. (Data from De Valois and De Valois, 1975)*

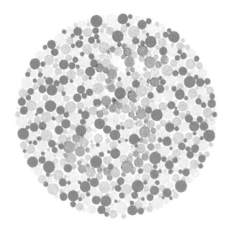

5.45   Testing for color blindness   *A plate used to test for color blindness. To pick out the number in the plate, an observer has to be able to discriminate certain hues. Persons with normal color vision can do it and will see the number 3. Persons with red-green color blindness cannot do it.*

(Figure 5.44). This is exactly what should happen if the underlying color mechanism mirrors the perceptual phenomena. Blue should have one effect and yellow the opposite. Other cells have been discovered that show a similar antagonistic pattern when stimulated by red or by green light (De Valois, 1965).

COLOR BLINDNESS

A small proportion of the total population consists of people who do not respond to color as most others do. Of these the vast majority are men, since many such conditions are inherited and sex-linked. Some form of color defect is found in 8 percent of all males as compared to only .03 percent of females.

Deficiencies in color vision come in various forms: Some involve a missing visual pigment, others a defective opponent process, and many involve malfunction at both levels (Hurvich, 1981). Most common is a confusion of reds with greens; least common is total color blindness in which no hues can be distinguished at all. Color defects are rarely noticed in everyday life, for color-blind people ordinarily use color names quite appropriately. They call blood red and dollar bills green, presumably on the basis of other cues such as form and brightness. To determine whether a person has a color defect, he or she must be tested under special conditions in which such extraneous cues are eliminated (Figure 5.45).

How do people with color defects see colors? We may know that a particular person cannot distinguish between red and green, but that does not tell us how these colors look to him. He cannot tell us, for he cannot know what sensory quality is lacking. The question would have remained unanswerable had it not been for a subject who was red-green color blind in one eye and had normal color vision in the other. This subject (who happened to be one of the rare females with a color defect) was able to describe what she saw with the defective eye by using the color language of the normal one. With the color-blind eye she saw only grays, blues, and yellows. Red and green hues were altogether absent, as if one of the opponent-process pairs were missing (Graham and Hsia, 1954).

FEATURE DETECTORS

Thus far, our primary concern has been with the visual attributes of brightness and color. But there are other characteristics that are no less important for our perception of the visual world—the various attributes of *con-*

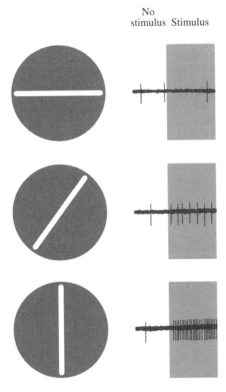

No
stimulus Stimulus

5.46   Feature detectors in the visual system of the cat   *The response of a single cortical cell when stimulated by a slit of light in three different orientations. This cell, a simple unit, was evidently responsive to the vertical. A horizontal slit led to no response, a tilted slit led to a slight response, while a vertical slit led to a marked increase in firing. (After Hubel, 1963)*

tours that are crucial for the recognition of a particular form. Some contours are curved while others are straight, some are angled upwards while others are oriented downwards, and so on. These characteristics are sensed by specialized detector cells that respond to certain characteristics of the stimulus and no others. The discovery of these cells has been one of the most exciting achievements of visual physiology during the past four decades. Electrophysiologists often record from single nerve cells (see Chapter 2). By such techniques they have discovered how particular cells in a sensory system respond to simple stimuli, such as light of a given wavelength (see p. 194). More recently, they have applied the same approach to the perception of contours, using stimuli that are much more complex and relational.

In some (relatively) lower animals, important aspects of form are detected at the level of the retina. In a classic study, recordings were taken from different ganglion cells of a frog's optic nerve while the animal was presented with various visual stimuli (Lettvin et al., 1959). The investigators found that certain ganglion cells respond only to particular and quite complex patterns of stimulation. For example, one kind of cell reacts most intensely to a small, dark object with convex edges that is moved into a particular retinal region and is then moved around within it. Moving stimuli that lack the appropriate shape have little or no effect, nor does a change in the general level of illumination. To a frog, the stimulus pattern that excites this particular cell (a "bug detector") represents its livelihood, for it is normally produced by a flying insect. This cell performs what amounts to a prewired sensory "abstraction," responding to buglike objects that move in a buglike manner, with a concomitant disregard for all other features of the stimulus. Could a frog ask for anything more?

The frog's bug detector is an example of a *feature detector,* which selectively responds to certain characteristics of a stimulus pattern. Other detectors have been found that respond to such features as direction of movement, the orientation of lines and edges, and so on. In higher animals such as cats and monkeys (and undoubtedly humans as well) most of this analysis takes place at a level beyond the retina, primarily in the cortex.

Two physiologists, Nobel Prize winners David Hubel and Torsten Wiesel, studied the activity of single cortical cells of cats in response to various visual stimuli. They found some cells that react to lines or edges of a particular orientation. Such cells would be excited by a thin sliver of light slanted at, say, 45 degrees, but not otherwise, regardless of the line's specific retinal location (Figure 5.46). Still other cells detect even more complex features. An example is a cell that reacts to right angles (Hubel and Wiesel, 1959). Yet other cells respond to directional motion; they will fire if a stimulus moves, from, say right to left, but won't fire if it moves from left to right.

ADAPTATION OF FEATURE DETECTORS

Most psychophysiologists believe that the excitation of feature detectors leads to such simple sensory experiences as the perception of movement, angular orientation, and the like. But they have no direct proof. The animals they test cannot describe what they see. And stimulating detector cells in (unanesthetized) human subjects and asking them to describe what they perceive while the cell is firing is obviously out of the question. Nevertheless, most investigators believe that what they pick up with their electrodes is somehow implicated in what we perceive.

Some evidence for the role of feature detectors in human perceptual experience comes from work on the phenomenon of adaptation. We previously encountered adaptation effects in the case of relatively simple sensory qualities such as hue. After prolonged fixation on a green patch, its apparent greenness will fade away and a neutral gray projected upon the same retinal region will look reddish (see pp.

A   Objective motion

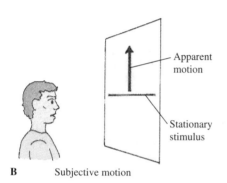

Apparent
motion

Stationary
stimulus

B   Subjective motion

5.47 **Aftereffect of movement** *(A) The subject first looks at a band of downward moving lines for a minute or two. (B) He then looks at a stationary horizontal line. This line will now appear to be moving upwards. This effect is probably produced by the adaptation of a movement detector that signals downward motion.*

190–91). Effects of this sort form the foundation of a theory of the opponent processes that underlie color. The same logic motivates the study of adaptation effects in more complex perceptual attributes (Anstis, 1975).

An example is the *aftereffect of visual movement.* If one looks at a waterfall for a while and then turns away to look at the riverbank, the bank and the trees upon it will seem to float upward, a dramatic effect that is readily produced in the perceptual laboratory (Figure 5.47). We might expect just this result on the assumption that the direction of perceived movement is signaled by the activity of two movement detectors that operate as opponent-process pairs. If these two detectors interact like the members of the color opponent-process pairs, then the stimulation of either one will automatically lead to the inhibition of the other. If one member of the pair has been stimulated for a long time (say, by exposure to a downward moving pattern), it will gradually adapt and will therefore fire less. As a result, the balance will swing toward the other member of the pair (that is, the upward movement detector). This changed balance will be revealed when the moving target is withdrawn and the subject looks at a stationary pattern. This (objectively stationary) pattern will now be perceived as moving upward. The effect is analogous to the red afterimage that follows prolonged fixation of a green patch. In both cases, there is adaptation of one member of an opponent-process pair.

Is there any way to determine whether a particular feature detector in humans is located in the retina or higher up in the brain? Needless to say, we can't resort to microelectrodes. But a number of investigators used another approach. They asked subjects to look at a stimulus that moved continuously in one direction, but to do so with one eye only; the other eye was covered. Would this lead to an aftereffect of movement when the subjects were then tested with the other eye? If so, the motion detectors that were adapted by the moving stimulus would have to be located at a point beyond the retina, in some region in the brain where the information from both eyes is somehow combined. The results proved that this was indeed the case. Looking at a moving stimulus with one eye led to an appropriate adaptation effect even when the test was conducted with the other eye (Mitchell, Reardon, and Muir, 1975).

FEATURE DETECTORS OF COMPLEX FORMS?

The organism is evidently endowed with appropriate neural devices that allow it to respond to such stimulus features as directional motion, edges, and orientation. But how does it organize these features into the countless objects in the world that we can recognize? It may be that there are some prewired systems that can detect complex shapes of various kinds, particularly those that have a special significance in the life of a given species. Something of this sort is clearly true for many lower animals whose analyzers are apparently tuned to the detection of the relatively few objects that matter to them; the frog's bug detector is a case in point.

It is of course inconceivable that such built-in mechanisms can account for all the forms higher animals—and especially humans—perceive and recognize. For unlike frogs, humans must discriminate among a multitude of patterns, and it is hardly possible that we carry specialized detectors for all of them—triangles, squares, apples, apple pies, champagne bottles, cabbages, kings—the list is endless. Nevertheless, it may well be that even the primates—and indeed, we ourselves—possess some special cells geared to detect stimulus relationships that are more complex than color, edges, and directional movement. Thus certain cells in a monkey's cortex have been shown to respond to pictures of a monkey's face, but not at all to nonface stimuli. Some other cells responded to pictures of a monkey's hand (Desimone et al., 1984). While there is no evidence that humans have analogous face or hand detectors, there is good reason to believe that the cortical systems that are responsible for recognizing faces are not the same as those that handle the perception of other visual forms. For as we saw in a previous chapter, certain cortical lesions may lead to a visual agnosia for faces (that is, to prosopagnosia, see p. 44) without affecting the perception of most other non-facelike objects (Farah, 1990). And as we'll see, there is evidence that infants prefer to look at shapes that resemble human faces rather than those that don't (see pp. 515–16).

Perhaps we do possess some cells that do for us what the bug detector does for the frog. But there is little doubt that the vast majority of the forms we recognize are assemblies of lower-level features glued together by experience. As we'll see in the next chapter, it's highly likely that these lower level feature detectors are the raw material out of which we construct the infinity of shapes we can perceive and recognize.

TAKING STOCK

We have looked at the way in which the different sensory systems respond to external stimuli, how they transduce the proximal stimulus and convert it into a neural impulse, how they code the incoming message into the various dimensions of our sensory experience, and how activity in any part of a sensory system interacts with the activity of other parts. All of this has led us to some understanding of how we come to see bright yellow-greens and hear high-pitched noises. But it has not yet addressed the question with which we started. How do we come to know about the objects and events outside—not just bright yellow-greens but grassy meadows, not just high-pitched noises but singing birds? That the sensory systems contribute the raw materials for such knowledge is clear enough. But how do we get from the sensory raw materials to a knowledge of the world outside? This question is traditionally dealt with under the heading of perception, the topic to which we turn next.

SUMMARY

1. The study of sensory processes grew out of questions about the origin of human knowledge. John Locke and other *empiricists* argued that all knowledge comes through stimuli that excite the senses. We can distinguish two kinds of stimuli. One is the *distal stimulus,* an object or event in the world outside. The other is the *proximal stimulus,* the pattern of physical stimulus energies that impinges on a given sensory surface. The only way to get information about distal stimuli outside is through the proximal stimuli these give rise to. This leads to theoretical problems, for we perceive many qualities—depth, constant size and shape—that are not given in the proximal stimulus. Empiricists try to overcome such difficulties by asserting that much of perception is built up through learning by *association.* This view has been challenged by *nativists,* such as Immanuel Kant, who believe that the sensory input is organized according to a number of built-in *categories.*

2. The path to sensory experience or *sensation* begins with a proximal stimulus. This is *transduced* into a nervous impulse by specialized receptors, is usually further modified by other parts of the nervous system, and finally leads to a sensation. One branch of sensory psychology is psychophysics, which tries to relate the characteristics of the physical stimulus to both the quality and intensity of the sensory experience.

3.   The founder of psychophysics, Gustav T. Fechner, studied sensory intensity by determining the ability of subjects to discriminate between stimulus intensities. Important measures of this ability are the *absolute threshold* and the *difference threshold*. The difference threshold is the change in the intensity of a given stimulus that is just large enough to be detected, producing a *just noticeable difference*, or *j.n.d.* According to *Weber's law,* the j.n.d. is a constant fraction of the intensity of the standard stimulus. Fechner generalized Weber's law to express a wider relationship between sensory intensity and physical intensity. This is *Fechner's law,* which states that the strength of a sensation grows as the logarithm of stimulus intensity.

4.   A way of disentangling sensory sensitivity and *response bias* is provided by *signal-detection theory.* In a typical *detection experiment,* the stimulus is presented on half of the trials and absent on the other half. In this procedure, there can be two kinds of errors: *misses* (saying a stimulus is absent when it is present) and *false alarms* (saying it is present when it is absent). Their relative proportion is partially determined by a *payoff matrix*. When this payoff matrix is varied, the effects can be graphically expressed by an *ROC* curve. According to signal-detection theory, distinguishing between the presence of a stimulus and its absence depends on a process in which the subject has to decide whether a *sensory process* is produced by the signal or some *background noise.*

5.   Investigations of the neural underpinning of sensation involve attempts to understand the *sensory codes* by which the nervous system represents sensory experiences. Of particular interest are qualitative differences that occur both between *sensory modalities* (e.g., A-flat versus red) and within them (e.g., red versus green). According to the *doctrine of specific nerve energies,* such qualitative differences are ultimately caused by differences in the nervous structures excited by the stimuli rather than by differences between the stimuli as such.

6.   Underlying neural processes are described by two alternative views: *specificity theory,* which holds that the different sensory qualities are signaled by different neurons, and *across-fiber pattern theory,* which asserts that these differences are coded by the overall pattern of activation across a whole set of neurons. The best evidence indicates that the nervous system uses both specificity and pattern codes in different sensory systems.

7.   Different sense modalities have different functions and mechanisms. One group of senses provides information about the body's own movements and location. Skeletal motion is sensed through *kinesthesis,* bodily orientation by the *vestibular organs* located in the *inner ears.*

8.   The various *skin senses* inform the organism of what is directly adjacent to its own body. There are at least four different skin sensations: *pressure, warmth, cold,* and *pain.*

9.   The sense of *taste* acts as a gatekeeper to the digestive system. Its receptors are *taste buds,* whose stimulation generates the four basic taste qualities of *sour, sweet, salty,* and *bitter.*

10.   Smell or *olfaction* is both an internal sense that provides information about substances in the mouth and (with the sense of taste) gives rise to the experience of flavor, and a distance sense that gives information about objects outside of the body. In humans, olfaction is a relatively minor distance sense, but in many animals it is a vital guide to food, mates, and danger. In many species, it permits a primitive form of communication based on *pheromones.*

11.   The sense of hearing or *audition* informs us of pressure changes that occur at a distance. Its stimulus is a disturbance of the air that is propagated in the form of *sound waves.* These can vary in *amplitude* and *frequency,* and may be *simple* or *complex.*

12.   A number of accessory structures help to conduct and amplify sound waves so that they can affect the auditory receptors. Sound waves set up vibrations in the *eardrum* that are then transmitted by the *ossicles* to the *oval window,* whose movements create waves in the *cochlea* of the inner ear. Within the cochlea is the *basilar membrane,* which contains the auditory receptors that are stimulated by the membrane's deformation. According to the *place theory,* the sensory experience of pitch is based on the place of the membrane that is stimulated, each place being responsive to a particular wave frequency and generating a particular pitch sensation. But since very low frequency waves deform

SUMMARY

the whole membrane just about equally, modern theorists believe that both the place of deformation and firing frequency of the auditory nerve are important. Higher frequencies depend upon the place stimulated on the basilar membrane, while lower frequencies depend upon neural firing frequency.

13. Vision is our primary distance sense. Its stimulus is light, which can vary in *intensity* and *wavelength*. Many of the structures of the eye, such as the *lens* and the *iris,* serve mainly as accessory devices to fashion a proper proximal stimulus, the *retinal image.* Once on the retina, the light stimulus is transduced into a neural impulse by the visual receptors, the *rods* and *cones. Acuity* is greatest in the *fovea* where the density of the receptors (here, cones) is greatest.

14. According to the *duplex theory of vision,* rods and cones differ in function. The rods operate at low light intensities and lead to colorless sensations. The cones function at much higher illumination levels and are responsible for sensations of color. Further evidence for the duplex theory comes from different *spectral sensitivity curves.*

15. The first stage in the transformation of light into a neural impulse is a photochemical process that involves the breakdown of various *visual pigments* that are later resynthesized. One such pigment is *rhodopsin,* the photochemically sensitive substance contained by the rods.

16. The various components of the visual system do not operate in isolation but interact constantly. One form of interaction occurs over time, as in various forms of *adaptation.* Visual adaptation is usually counteracted by eye movements, but their effects can be nullified by the *stabilized image* procedure.

17. Interaction also occurs in space, between neighboring regions on the retina. An example is *brightness contrast.* This tends to enhance the distinction between an object and its background. It also accentuates edges, as in the case of *Mach bands.* The physiological mechanism that underlies these effects is *lateral inhibition,* as shown by studies of *receptive fields.*

18. Visual sensations have a qualitative character—they vary in color. Color sensations can be ordered by reference to three dimensions: *hue, brightness,* and *saturation.* Colors can be mixed *subtractively* (as in mixing pigments) or *additively* (as in simultaneously stimulating the same region of the retina with two or more stimuli). The results of additive-mixture studies show that every hue has a *complementary hue* that, when mixed with the first, yields gray. Two important examples are red and green, and blue and yellow. These two color pairs are color antagonists, a fact shown by the phenomena of the *negative afterimage* and *simultaneous color contrast.*

19. The first question about the mechanisms that underlie color vision concerns the way in which the different light waves are transduced into a receptor discharge. There is general agreement that this is done by the joint action of three different cone types, each of which has a somewhat different sensitivity curve.

20. A second question concerns the way the receptor output is coded to produce color quality. A leading approach is the *opponent-process theory* of Hurvich and Jameson. This assumes that there are three neural systems, each of which corresponds to a pair of antagonistic sensory experiences: red-green, blue-yellow, and black-white. The first two determine perceived hue; the third determines perceived brightness. Further evidence for the opponent-process view comes from single-cell recordings of monkeys and some phenomena of *color blindness.*

21. Attributes of visual *contour* are vital to the recognition of form. Many of these attributes are sensed by *feature detectors,* both in the retina and in the brain. These are cells that respond to certain relational aspects of the stimulus, such as edges and corners, as shown by single-cell recordings. The *adaptation* of such feature detectors may explain certain changes of perceptual experience after prolonged exposure to a certain kind of stimulus, as in the *aftereffect of visual movement.*

CHAPTER 6

PERCEPTION

THE PROBLEM OF PERCEPTION   201

THE PERCEPTION OF DEPTH: WHERE IS IT?   202

BINOCULAR CUES ■ MONOCULAR CUES ■ THE PERCEPTION OF DEPTH THROUGH MOTION ■ INNATE FACTORS IN DEPTH PERCEPTION

THE PERCEPTION OF MOVEMENT: WHAT IS IT DOING?   206

ILLUSIONS OF MOVEMENT ■ PERCEIVED STABILITY

FORM PERCEPTION: WHAT IS IT?   208

THE INFORMATION-PROCESSING APPROACH ■ THE ELEMENTS OF FORM ■ PERCEPTUAL SEGREGATION ■ PATTERN RECOGNITION ■ THE PROCESSING SEQUENCE IN FORM PERCEPTION

PERCEPTUAL PROBLEM SOLVING   222

THE LOGIC OF PERCEPTION ■ WHEN LOGIC FAILS: IMPOSSIBLE FIGURES

PERCEPTUAL SELECTION: ATTENTION   225

SELECTION BY PHYSICAL ORIENTATION ■ CENTRAL SELECTION

THE PERCEPTION OF REALITY   228

EMPIRICISM AND NATIVISM REVISITED ■ SIZE AND SHAPE CONSTANCY ■ LIGHTNESS CONSTANCY

THE REPRESENTATION OF REALITY IN ART   234

SEEING AND KNOWING ■ THE RENAISSANCE: SCENES THROUGH A WINDOW FRAME ■ THE IMPRESSIONISTS: HOW A SCENE IS PERCEIVED ■ THE MODERNS: HOW A SCENE IS CONCEIVED

SUMMARY   239

In the previous chapter, we discussed some of the simpler attributes of sensory experience, such as red, A-flat, and cold. Locke and Berkeley thought that these experiences were produced by a passive registration of the proximal stimulus energies impinging upon the senses. But, as we have seen, the eye is more than a camera, the ear more than a microphone, for both sensory systems actively transform their stimulus inputs at the very start of their neurological journey, emphasizing differences and minimizing stimulation that remains unchanged. This active organization of the stimulus input is impressive enough when we consider the experience of simple sensory attributes, but it becomes even more dramatic when we turn to the fundamental problem traditionally associated with the term perception: how we come to apprehend the objects and events in the external reality around us, how we come to see, not just a bright red, but a bright red apple.

THE PROBLEM OF PERCEPTION

What must be explained in order to understand how we see the apple? Our initial reaction might be that the only problem is in grasping the perceptual meaning of the visual input, how we interpret it as an edible fruit—that grows on trees, that keeps the doctor away, that caused the expulsion from Eden, and so on. But how objects acquire perceptual meaning is by no means the only question, or even the most basic one, for the student of perception. The fundamental issue is not why a given stimulus is seen as a particular kind of object, but rather why it is seen as any object at all. Suppose we show the apple to someone who has never seen any fruit before. He will not know its function, but he will certainly see it as some round, red thing of whose tangible existence he has no doubt—in short, he will perceive it as an object.

How can he accomplish this feat? After all, the apple is a distal stimulus that (at least visually) is known to us only through the proximal stimulus it projects upon our retina, and this proximal stimulus is two-dimensional and constantly changing. It gets smaller or larger depending upon our distance from it; it stimulates different regions of the retina; it moves across the retina as we move our eyes. Before our observer can decide whether the object he's looking at is an apple (or a baseball or a human head, or whatever), he must somehow perceive the constant properties of this external object despite the continual variations in the proximal stimulus. To do this, he must organize the sensory world to which he is exposed into a coherent scene in which there are real objects (such as apples) and events (such as apples that fall from trees). To achieve this organization, he has to answer three important perceptual questions about what he sees (or hears and feels) in the world outside: Where is it? Where is it going? (And most important) What is it?

We will begin our discussion by turning to the first two questions, which concern the perception of depth and movement.

The problem of perception How do we come to perceive the world as it is—to see the flags as smaller than the boat, to see the wall extending continuously behind the people that block some portion of it from view, and so on? (Claude Monet, Terrace at Sainte-Adresse, 1867; courtesy The Metropolitan Museum of Art, purchased with special contributions and purchase funds given or bequeathed by friends of the Museum, 1967)

6.1 Retinal disparity *Two points, A and B, at different distances from the observer, present somewhat different retinal images. The distance between the images on one eye, a_1b_1, is different (disparate) from the distance between them on the other, a_2b_2. This disparity is a powerful cue for depth. (After Hochberg, 1978a)*

THE PERCEPTION OF DEPTH: WHERE IS IT?

Quite apart from the question of what an object is (which we'll take up later), we have to know where it is located. The object may be a potential mate or a saber-toothed tiger, but we can hardly take appropriate action unless we can also locate the object in the external world.

Much of the work on the problem of visual localization has concentrated on the perception of depth, a topic that has occupied philosophers and scientists for over three hundred years. They have asked: How can we possibly see the world in three dimensions when only two of these dimensions are given in the image that falls upon the eye? This question has led to a search for **depth cues,** features of the stimulus situation that indicate how far the object is from the observer or from other objects in the world.

BINOCULAR CUES

A very important cue for depth comes from the fact that we have two eyes. These look out on the world from two different positions. As a result, they obtain a somewhat different view of any solid object they converge on. This **binocular disparity** inevitably follows from the geometry of the physical situation. The disparity becomes less and less pronounced the farther the object is from the observer. Beyond thirty feet the two eyes receive virtually the same image (Figure 6.1).

Binocular disparity alone can induce perceived depth. If we draw or photograph the two different views received by each eye while looking at a nearby object and then separately present each of these views to the appropriate eye, we can obtain a striking impression of depth.

6.2   Linear perspective as a cue for depth
(Photograph by Roberta Intrater)

6.3   Interposition   *When one figure interrupts the contour of another figure, it provides a monocular cue for depth. This is interposition. Because of interposition, the red rectangle in the figure is perceived to be in front of the blue one.*

MONOCULAR CUES

Binocular disparity is a very powerful (and probably innate) determinant of perceived depth. Yet we can perceive depth even with one eye closed. Even more important, many people who have been blind in one eye from birth see the world in three dimensions. Clearly then, there are other cues for depth perception that come from the image obtained with one eye alone—these are the ***monocular depth cues.***

Many monocular depth cues have been exploited for centuries by artists and are therefore called ***pictorial cues.*** Examples include ***linear perspective, interposition,*** and ***relative size*** (Figures 6.2, 6.3, and 6.4). In each case, the eye exploits an optical consequence of the projection of a three-dimensional world upon a flat surface. Objects that are farther away are also inevitably blocked from view by any other opaque object that obstructs their optical path to the eye (interposition). Far-off objects necessarily produce a smaller retinal image than objects of the same size that are nearby (linear perspective and relative size).

6.4   Relative size   *(A) All other things being equal, the larger of two otherwise identical figures will seem to be closer than the smaller one. This is a consequence of the simple geometry of vision illustrated in (B). Two equally large objects, a and b, that are at different distances from the observer, will project retinal images of different size.*

6.5 Texture gradients as cues for depth
Uniformly textured surfaces produce texture gradients that provide information about depth: As the surface recedes, the texture density increases. Such gradients may be produced by sunflowers (A), or members of a gannet colony (B). (Photographs by Geoff Dore/ © Tony Stone Worldwide and G. R. Roberts)

An important set of pictorial cues is provided by ***texture gradients,*** whose role was emphasized by James J. Gibson (1904–1979), a very influential theorist in the psychology of perception. Such gradients are ultimately produced by perspective. Consider what meets the eye when we look at cobblestones on a road or clumps of grass in a meadow. Gibson pointed out that the retinal projection of such objects must necessarily show a continuous change, or texture gradient, that depends upon the spatial layout of the relevant surfaces (Figure 6.5). Such texture gradients are powerful determinants of perceived depth. Discontinuities in texture gradients provide information about further spatial relationships between the various textured surfaces. Thus, the change of texture density in Figure 6.6A produces the impression of an upward tilt, while that in Figure 6.6B yields perception of a sharp drop, a "visual cliff" (Gibson, 1950, 1966).

6.6 The effect of changes in texture gradients Such changes provide important information about spatial arrangements in the world. Examples are (A) an upward tilt at a corner; and (B) a sudden drop. (After Gibson, 1950)

THE PERCEPTION OF DEPTH THROUGH MOTION

Thus far we have encountered situations in which both the observer and the scene observed are stationary. But in real life we are constantly moving through the world we perceive. This motion provides a vital source of visual information about the spatial arrangement of the objects around us, a pattern of cues that once again follows from the optical geometry of the situation.

As we move our heads or bodies from right to left, the images projected by the objects outside will necessarily move across the retina. This motion of the retinal images is an enormously effective depth cue, called **motion parallax.** As we move through space, nearby objects appear to move very quickly in a direction opposite to our own; as an example, consider the trees racing backward as one looks out of a speeding train. Objects farther away also seem to move in the opposite direction, but at a lesser velocity (Helmholtz, 1909; see Figure 6.7).

According to James Gibson, such movement-produced changes in the optic image are a major avenue through which we obtain perceptual information about depth relations in the world around us. Motion parallax is just one example of the perceptual role played by these changes. Another is the **optic flow** that occurs when we move towards or away from objects in the world. As we approach them, they get larger and larger; as we move away from them, they get smaller. Figure 6.8A shows the flow pattern for a person looking out of the back of a train; Figure 6.8B shows the flow pattern for a pilot landing an airplane (Gibson, 1950, 1979).

INNATE FACTORS IN DEPTH PERCEPTION

In many organisms, important features of the perception of space are apparently built into the nervous machinery. An example is the localization of sounds in space. One investigator studied this phenomenon in a ten-minute-old baby. The newborn consistently turned his eyes in the direction of a clicking sound, thus demonstrating that some spatial coordination between eye and ear exists prior to learning (Wertheimer, 1961).

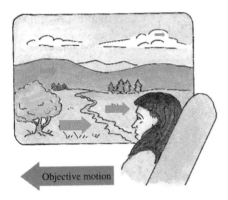

6.7   Motion parallax   *When an observer moves relative to a stationary environment, the objects in that environment will be displaced (and will therefore seem to move) relative to that observer. (The rate of relative displacement is indicated by the thickness of the mauve arrows. The thicker these arrows, the more quickly the objects seem to move. The observer's movement is indicated by a blue arrow.) (After Coren and Ward, 1989)*

6.8   Optic flow   *(A) The optic flow field as it appears to a person looking out of the rear window of a railroad car. (From Bruce and Green, 1985) (B) The optic flow field as it appears to a pilot landing an airplane. (From Gibson, 1950)*

There is evidence that some aspects of visual depth perception are also innately given (or come in at such an early age that if they are learned, they must be learned very quickly). The facets of depth that apparently come in first are those based on perceived movement, such as motion parallax. Another example is the response to **looming,** a rapid magnification of a form in the visual field that generally signals an impending impact. To study this looming effect experimentally, several investigators have simulated the visual consequence of rapid approach by various means, for example by a rapidly expanding shadow cast on a screen. When exposed to these expanding patterns, crabs flatten out, frogs jump away, and infant monkeys leap to the rear of their cages. Human infants as young as two or three weeks of age blink their eyes as if they sense a coming collision, stiffen, and cry (Schiff, 1965; Ball and Tronick, 1971; Yonas, 1981).

THE PERCEPTION OF MOVEMENT: WHAT IS IT DOING?

To see a large, unfriendly Doberman in front of you is one thing; to see him bare his teeth and rush directly at you is quite another. We want to know what an object is and where it is located, but we also want to know what it is doing. Put another way, we want to perceive events as well as objects. The basic ingredient of the perception of events is the perception of movement.

ILLUSIONS OF MOVEMENT

What leads to the perception of movement? One might guess that one sees things move because they produce an image that moves across the retina. But this answer is too simple. For in fact we sometimes perceive movement even when none occurs on the retina.

STROBOSCOPIC MOVEMENT

Suppose we briefly turn on a light in one location of the visual field, then turn it off, and after an appropriate interval (somewhere between 30 and 200 milliseconds) turn on a second light in a different location. The result is **apparent movement** (sometimes called **stroboscopic movement** or the **phi phenomenon**). The light is seen to travel from one point to another, even though there was no stimulation—let alone movement—in the intervening region (Figure 6.9). This phenomenon is perceptually overwhelming; given the right intervals, it is indistinguishable from real movement. It is an effect that has numerous technological applications, ranging from animated neon signs to motion pictures (Wertheimer, 1912). These results suggest that one stimulus for motion is relative displacement over time. Something is here at one moment and there at the next. If the time intervals are right, the nervous system interprets this as evidence that this something has moved.

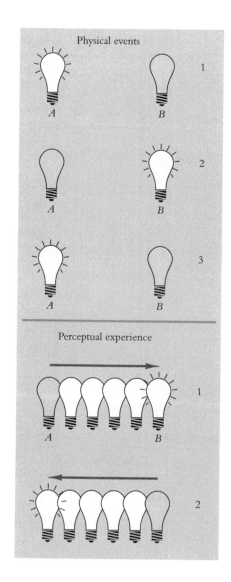

Physical events

Perceptual experience

6.9 Stroboscopic movement *The sequence of optical events that produces stroboscopic movement. Light A flashes at time 1, followed by light B at time 2, then back to light A at time 3. If the time intervals are appropriately chosen, the perceptual experience will be of a light moving from left to right and back.*

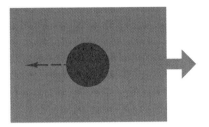

6.10 Induced movement *Subjects in an otherwise dark room see a luminous dot surrounded by a luminous frame. When the frame is moved to the right, subjects perceive the dot moving to the left, even though it is objectively stationary. (Duncker, 1929)*

Max Wertheimer *(1880–1943), one of the most influential figures in the psychology of perception. (Courtesy Omikron)*

INDUCED MOVEMENT

How does the perceptual system react when one of two objects is moving while the other is (physically) stationary? Consider a ball rolling on a billiard table. We see the ball as moving and the table at rest. But why not the other way around? To be sure, the ball is being displaced relative to the table edge, but so is the table edge displaced relative to the ball. One might guess that the reason is learning. Perhaps experience has taught us that balls generally move around while tables stay put. But the evidence indicates that what matters is a more general perceptual relationship between the two stimuli. The object that encloses the other tends to act as a frame, which is seen as stationary. Thus, the table serves as a frame against which the ball is seen to move.

In the billiard table example, perception and physical reality coincide, for the frame provided by the table is truly stationary. What happens when the objective situation is reversed? In one study subjects were shown a luminous rectangular frame in an otherwise dark room. Inside the frame was a luminous dot. In actual fact, the rectangle moved to the right while the dot stayed in place. But the subjects saw something else. They perceived the dot as moving to the left, in the opposite direction of the frame's motion. The physical movement of the frame induced the perceived movement of the enclosed figure (Figure 6.10).

The *induced movement* effect is familiar from everyday life as well. The moon apparently drifts though the clouds; the base of a bridge seems to float against the flow of the river current. In the second case, there may also be *induced motion of the self.* If the subject stands on the bridge that she perceives as moving, she perceives herself moving along with it. The same effect occurs when sitting in a train that's standing in a station. If a train on the adjacent track pulls out, we tend to feel ourselves moving though in fact we—and the train we're in—are stationary.

PERCEIVED STABILITY

Thus far, we have asked why things are seen to move. A related question is why they are generally seen as stable. The issue arises because our eyes are constantly moving, so that the retinal image shifts all the time. But if so, why do we perceive the world as stationary? One interpretation follows from the fact that eye movements don't produce relative displacements. When we move our eyes as we look at a chair, the retinal image of the chair is displaced, but so is the image of the room that serves as its framework; as a result, there is no relative displacement. But this cannot be the whole story. As Helmholtz showed a century ago, movement will be seen if the eyes are moved by muscles other than their own. Close one eye and jiggle the outside corner of the other eye (gently!) with a finger. Now the world will seem to move around, even though all relationships within the retinal image are kept intact. This shows that the perceptual system can respond to absolute displacement. But if it can do so when the eyes are pushed by a finger, why doesn't it do so when they are moved by the eye muscles that normally do the job?

Many students of visual perception believe that the nervous system achieves visual stability by compensating for retinal displacements that are produced by voluntary eye movements. Thus, when the brain signals the eye muscles to move, it computes the retinal displacement that such a movement would produce and then cancels out this amount in interpreting the visual input it receives. As a result, we see a stationary point at rest, even though our eyes are moving. The brain evidently keeps track of what it tells the eyes to do, say, to move 10 degrees to the right. It knows that the eye movement should produce a

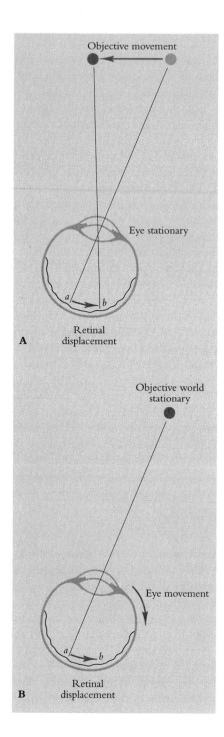

A

Objective movement

Eye stationary

Retinal displacement

B

Objective world stationary

Eye movement

Retinal displacement

6.11   Compensation for eye movements   *When the retinal image of some object is displaced, it may be because the object has moved, because the eye has moved, or both. In (A), there is objective movement that produces a retinal displacement, as the dot's projection shifts from point a to point b on the retina. But (B) shows that the same retinal displacement can be produced by moving the eye, in the opposite direction from that of the dot in (A), while the object itself remains stationary. From the retinal point of view, the displacements in (A) and (B) are identical. Fortunately, our brain allows us to see motion independent of eye movements by compensating for the displacements caused by changes in eye position. In (B), the brain would decide that there was no movement because the motion of the eye is precisely equal (and opposite) to the displacement on the retina.*

retinal displacement of 10 degrees in the opposite direction and subtracts this from the visual signal (Figure 6.11).

What happens when the brain signals the eyes to move but they can't obey because the eye muscles are paralyzed? A number of heroic experimenters have had themselves injected with paralytic drugs and reported that under these circumstances, the world did indeed jump around, just as the canceling out theory would predict. The brain ordered the eyes to move, say, 20 degrees to the right, but the eyes couldn't comply with the command; as a result, there was an inappropriate cancellation, and the world was seen to jump in the opposite direction (Matin et al., 1982).

FORM PERCEPTION: WHAT IS IT?

We've asked how we see where an object is and know where it is going. But we have not dealt with the most important question of all: How do we perceive and recognize what an object is?

In vision, our primary means for recognizing an object is through the perception of its form. To be sure, we sometimes rely on color (a violet) and occasionally on size (a toy model of an automobile), but in the vast majority of cases, form is the major avenue for identifying what it is we see. This reliance on form begins at a very early age. In a recent study using three-year-olds, an experimenter held up an oddly shaped wooden object that was painted blue and said: "Do you see this? This is a dax" (see Figure 6.12A). The children were perfectly happy to accept this new bit of information. After all, they'd never seen a dax before, so why shouldn't they believe what they were told?

The children were then shown a series of other objects. Some of these new objects had the same shape, but were made of a different substance and varied in size, color, and texture; others had a different shape, but were made of the identical substance and were of the same size, color, and texture as the original. The children were then asked: "Can you show me a dax?" Their answers showed that even at the age of three objects are defined by their shape. Shown an object of the same form, they unhesitatingly called it a dax, even if it was made of sponge rubber, was covered with chicken wire, or was ten times larger than the original (see Figure 6.12B and C). But an object of the same size, texture, and color as the original was rejected if its form was different (see Figure 6.12D). A dax is a dax is a dax—but only when it has the same shape (Landau, 1994).

The fact that the children recognized that a dax remains a dax, regardless of changes in color, texture, and size, illustrates one of the critical facts about form perception. Both humans and animals can often recognize a form even when

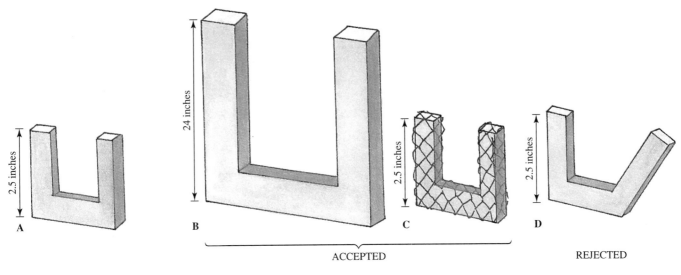

ACCEPTED   REJECTED

6.12 A dax is a dax is a dax
Three-year-olds who are told that (A) is a dax, conclude that figures (B) and (C) are daxes too but that figure (D) is not. To humans, form is evidently the main criterion for identifying an object. Color, size, and texture are less relevant. (Adapted from Landau, 1994)

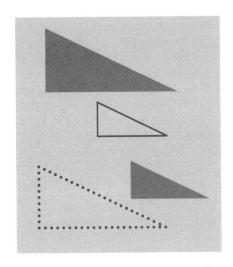

6.13 Form equivalence *The perceived forms remain the same regardless of the parts of which they are composed.*

many of its component parts are altered. Consider two similar triangles. It doesn't matter whether they are small, rendered as solids or as line drawings, made up of dots or dashes. The perceived form remains the same (Figure 6.13). A triangle is a triangle is a triangle, whatever the elements of which it is composed. This phenomenon is sometimes called the ***transposition of form*** or ***pattern.*** Similar effects occur in the temporal patterning of sounds: A melody remains the same even when all of its notes are changed by transposition to another key, and the same rhythm will be heard whether played on a kettledrum or a glockenspiel.

Phenomena such as these were among the chief arguments of **Gestalt psychology,** a school of psychology whose adherents believed that organization is basic to all mental activity and bolstered their view by many appeals to form perception. In particular, they insisted that a form is not perceived by somehow summing up all its individual components. On the contrary, they argued that a form is perceptually experienced as a *Gestalt,* a whole that is different from the sum of its parts.★ To recognize that a form is the same as one we have seen before, we must perceive certain relations among its component parts.

Most modern investigators of pattern recognition believe that the Gestalt psychologists had an important point. There is little doubt that a form is not just the sum of its parts: Three angles alone do not make a triangle, no more than a mouth, a nose, and two eyes suffice to make a face. The trouble is that it is hard to specify just what relations among the parts create the pattern. We can do it separately for each figure: For a triangle the three angles have to be properly aligned, for a face the nose has to be between the eyes, and so forth. But thus far no one has fully succeeded in formulating a general description of the relations between the parts that will do justice to all patterns. For these and similar reasons, most investigators of pattern recognition have focused less on the wholes than on the parts of which those wholes are composed. They hoped that by discovering the ways through which the proper parts are identified, the pattern can be identified as well.

We now turn to a discussion of the mechanisms by which particular patterns are recognized, whether it is in identifying a dax, the letter *W,* or a picture of an

---

★ The term *Gestalt* is derived from a German word that means "form" or "entire figure."

apple. We will consider some hypotheses about the processes by which the parts are transformed into patterns that we recognize as real objects and events in the world. While these hypotheses have not yet solved the transposition puzzle that Gestalt psychologists posed, they are important steps toward doing so.

THE INFORMATION-PROCESSING APPROACH

Form is evidently the major channel through which we identify objects. The question is how. Many modern psychologists who try to answer this question believe that form perception is based on several steps of *information processing* that transform (that is, process) the initial visual input into the cognitive end product: the perception of the objects in the world. This is generally thought to involve a series of successive stages of processing, in which each stage further transforms the outputs of the previous stage.

In part, the information-processing approach grew out of an analogy between the operations of the mind and the workings of a computer. Computers have some of the capabilities of human minds: They can acquire information, store it in memory, retrieve it, classify it, and transform it. By now the mind-as-computer has become a dominant scientific metaphor, largely replacing the metaphors of previous generations, starting with Descartes' water-powered statues as models of animal action through the more recent telephone switchboard analogies to explain the way the nervous system works. These earlier metaphors tried to explain transformations of energy: Certain energies (whether hydraulic, or chemical, or electrical) were converted into other energies until they were finally turned into a bodily movement. In contrast, the mind-as-computer metaphor tries to explain the transformation of symbols into other symbols.

Over the past four decades, the language of computers has also gradually crept into that of psychologists concerned with cognition; terms like *input, memory store, retrieval, subroutine,* and *coding* have become part of their everyday vocabulary. Attempts to understand such mental operations as recognizing a shape, recalling a name, or trying to solve a puzzle are often cast in the form of a flow chart. In the world of computer operators, such flow charts show the step-by-step operation of a computer program. Applied to the study of human cognitive processes, similar diagrams are meant to chart the flow of information as it is processed by the human mind (Neisser, 1967).

Much of our subsequent discussion of how forms are perceived will be organized along the lines of this information-processing approach.

THE ELEMENTS OF FORM

What's the first step in recognizing a form, whether it is a dax or an apple? Many investigators believe that the process begins with the response to certain primitive built-in features that serve as the elementary units of visual perception. In part, this belief is based on physiological findings we discussed in the previous chapter. Various cells in the brain act as feature detectors, which react to particular elements of visual form—lines or edges or a particular orientation. By now, there is good evidence that certain cortical cells signal other perceptual features. For example, some cells in the cortex are sensitive to binocular disparity (Hubel and Wiesel, 1970; Poggio and Fischer, 1978; Ferster, 1981). Other cells respond to directional movement; they fire if a line moves in one direction but won't fire if it moves in the direction that's opposite (e.g., Barlow and Hill, 1963; Vaultin and Berkeley, 1977).

Such evidence indicates that we're beginning to understand the built-in physiological mechanisms that underlie the primitive elements of visual perception. But how do we combine these building blocks so that we see not just colors, tilts, and edges, but the innumerable shapes and objects that we can perceive and recognize: circles and polygons, trees and houses, faces and hands? Many psychologists agree that this achievement comes in several stages, but their theoretical proposals vary in many specifics. What we will try to do here is to combine them in an (admittedly simplified) schematic overview.

FREE-FLOATING PRIMITIVES

How can we determine whether a given visual attribute is a primitive feature—a kind of sensory atom that serves as a building block for the perception of form? Single-cell recording studies may provide suggestions, but it would be much more convincing to have a psychological criterion, based on what human subjects actually perceive. Such a criterion has been provided in an influential series of studies by Anne Treisman (Treisman, 1986a, b, 1988).

Treisman argues that a given attribute is a primitive visual feature if a difference in that attribute leads to an immediate discovery, so that the item that is different just "pops out." One way of demonstrating this effect is by means of a *visual search task* in which subjects have to indicate whether a certain target is or is not present in a briefly presented display. When the target is an O amidst a number of *V*s, subjects find it very quickly (see Figure 6.14). What's more, the number of *V*s in which the O is embedded hardly affects the search time. This indicates that the visual system doesn't have to inspect each of the figures in turn to determine whether it has or does not have the relevant properties that define an O; the difference between the Os and *V*s jumps out immediately. The same holds for differences in color, orientation, or direction of movement (Treisman and Gelade, 1980; Treisman and Souther, 1985).

Color, curvature, orientation, and some other attributes thus seem to be primitive features that are processed quite automatically. But the objects we perceive are obviously made up of more than one visual feature. A leaf on a tree will give rise to a number of different visual features: of color, curvature, orientation, and—if it sways in the wind—movement. How are these different features put together? Treisman and her collaborators showed that this combination of features does not occur immediately but is accomplished in a later stage of processing. Subjects were presented with displays that contained items that combined several different features, for example a red F and a green X. The displays were flashed for about 200 milliseconds, and the subjects had to report what they saw. On a fair proportion of the trials, the subjects reported *illusory conjunctions,* such as having seen a green F or a red X. As Treisman sees it, these results indicate that at this early stage of processing, the various primitive features—color, shape, orientation, and so on—are free floating and exist in complete isolation from each other. It is as if each feature system had its own map with its own coordinate system, with no way of relating the different spatial maps to each other (Treisman and Schmidt, 1982).

According to Treisman, the integration of these separate feature systems is accomplished at a later stage of processing in which the several maps become coordinated and superimposed. Once this is done, there are no more illusory conjunctions, for now the system can determine what goes together with what—that there is a red F and a green X (rather than a green F and a red X), that the same leaf is at once green, curved with jagged edges, and fluttering in the breeze.

6.14 Pop-out in visual search *An O embedded in an array of Vs pops out immediately. Here, the visual system does not have to inspect each figure in turn to determine whether it is the target. Instead, it conducts a parallel search, inspecting all of the items simultaneously.*

6.15 Perceptual segregation *(A) A still life. (Photograph by Jeffrey Grosscup) (B) An overlay designating five different segments of the scene shown in (A). To determine what an object is, the perceptual system must first decide what goes with what: Does portion B go with A, with C, D, or E? Or with none of them?*

A   B

PERCEPTUAL SEGREGATION

The preceding discussion centered on the initial steps of form perception: deciding which primitive visual features go together. The next step is to decide what parts of the scene go together. Suppose the observer looks at the still life in Figure 6.15A. To make sense of the picture, her perceptual system must somehow group the many visual elements of the scene appropriately. For one thing, it has to determine what is focal (for example, the fruit and the bowl) and what can at least temporarily be relegated to the background (for example, the green shutters, the table, and perhaps the pitcher). But there is still more to be done. Some objects will necessarily be partially occluded by others that stand or lie in front of them. Consider the portions *A, B, C, D,* and *E* of Figure 6.15B. To determine what any given object can possibly be, we must first segregate the scene into its subcomponents, deciding whether portion *B* goes with *A* (half an apple combined with some grapes), with *C* (half an apple with a piece of orange), with *D* (half an apple with a banana), or finally with *E* (half an apple).

This **visual segregation** process is sometimes called **perceptual parsing,** since it performs the same function for vision that parsing performs for speech. When someone talks to us, our eardrums are exposed to a sound stream that is essentially unbroken. What hits the ears is a sequence of sounds such as:

Thestudentsaidtheteacherisafool.

The listener parses the sound pattern by grouping some sounds together with others, forming units called words:

The student said the teacher is a fool.

He may then parse further by grouping the words into larger units called phrases, as in:

The student, said the teacher, is a fool.

FORM PERCEPTION: WHAT IS IT?

6.16 Figure and ground *The first step in seeing a form is to segregate it from its background. The part seen as figure appears to be more cohesive and sharply delineated. The part seen as ground seems more formless and to extend behind the figure.*

6.17 Reversible figure-ground pattern *The classic example of a reversible figure-ground pattern. It can be seen as either a pair of silhouetted faces or a white vase.*

6.18 Figure-ground reversal in the visual arts *The Trojan War as depicted by Salvador Dali. The scene of wild carnage conceals the image of the Trojan Horse, whose outline follows the gateway to the city. (Courtesy Esquire)*

In some cases, he may even discover that there are alternate ways of parsing, as in:

The student said, the teacher is a fool.

The important point is that the parsing is not primarily in the stimulus. It is contributed by the listener, for the sound stream itself has no pauses between words and contains no commas. (When we don't understand a language, we don't "hear" the pauses, which is why foreigners speaking in their own language often sound as if they speak much faster than we do.) Until at least some basic parsing has been performed, the listener has no hope of comprehending what he has heard. To understand the meaning of the word *student,* he must first have segregated it from the surrounding sounds and heard it as a separate word.

What holds for words in speech, also holds for objects in the visual world: Visual segregation (or parsing) is the first step in organizing the world we see.

FIGURE AND GROUND

Visual segregation begins with the separation of the object from its setting, so that it is seen as a coherent whole that stands out against its background, as a tree stands out against the sky and the clouds. This segregation of *figure* and *ground* can be easily seen in two-dimensional pictures. In our still life, the apple is generally perceived as the figure, the tablecloth as the ground. But the same phenomenon also occurs with figures that have no particular meaning. Thus in Figure 6.16, the white splotch appears as the figure, which seems to be more cohesive and articulated than the blue region, which is normally perceived as the ground. This darker ground is seen as relatively formless and as extending behind the figure.

The differentiation between figure and ground is a perceptual achievement that is accomplished by the perceptual system. It is not in the stimulus as such. This point is made strikingly by *reversible figures* in which either of two figure-ground organizations is possible. A classic demonstration is shown in Figure 6.17, which can be seen either as a white vase on a blue background or as two blue faces in profile on a white background. This reversibility of figure-ground patterns has fascinated various artists, especially in recent times (see Figure 6.18).

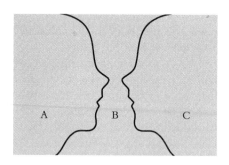

6.19 Fine detail is more readily seen in the figure than the ground *Subjects look at the vase-profiles figure as shown above and have to determine whether lines that are briefly flashed at points A, B, or C are tilted or vertical. If the vase is seen as the figure, they do much better when the stimuli are presented at B than at A or C. If the profiles are seen as the figure, they do much better when the lines are presented at A or C rather than at B. (After Weisstein and Wong, 1986)*

According to one proposal, the figure-ground distinction corresponds to two different kinds of neural processing. One (in regions seen as figure) involves the analysis of fine detail, while the other (in regions seen as ground) involves a cruder analysis appropriate to the perception of larger areas (Julesz, 1978). To test this hypothesis, subjects were presented with brief exposures to vertical and slightly tilted lines that were flashed on either of three locations of a line drawing of the vase-profile figure (see Figure 6.19). The subjects' task was to judge the orientation of the lines. In accordance with the detail-processing hypothesis, the subjects were much more accurate when the line was projected onto the area the subjects happened to see as the figure than when it was projected onto the area they saw as the ground (Weisstein and Wong, 1986).

PERCEPTUAL GROUPING

Reversible figure-ground formations demonstrate that a single proximal pattern may give rise to different perceptual organizations. The same conclusion follows from the related phenomenon of perceptual *grouping.* Suppose we look at a collection of dots. We can perceive the pattern in various ways depending upon how we group the dots: as a set of rows, or columns, or diagonals, and so on. In each case, the figural organization is quite different even though the proximal stimulus pattern is always the same.

What determines how a pattern will be organized? Some factors that determine visual grouping were first described by Max Wertheimer, the founder of Gestalt psychology. Wertheimer regarded these grouping factors as the laws of *perceptual organization* (Wertheimer, 1923). A few of these are discussed below.

Proximity The closer two figures are to each other (the greater their *proximity*) the more they will tend to be grouped together perceptually. So these six lines generally will be perceived as three pairs of lines:

Proximity may operate in time just as it does in space. The obvious example is auditory rhythm: Four drum beats with a pause between the second and third will be heard as two pairs.

Similarity Other things being equal, we also tend to group figures according to their *similarity.* Thus, in the figure below, we group blue dots together with blue dots, and red dots together with red dots. As a result, we see rows rather than columns in the left panel, and columns rather than rows in the right panel.

What aspects of stimulus similarity lead to grouping? Color is clearly one. Another is orientation. When similarity of form (for example, *T*s versus *L*s) is pitted against orientation (upright *T*s versus *T*s tilted by 45 degrees), subjects generally group by orientation (Beck, 1966; see Figure 6.20). Certain simple visual features such as color, brightness, and orientation are evidently more

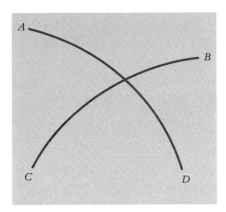

6.21 Good continuation *The line segments in the figure will generally be grouped so that the contours continue smoothly. As a result, segment A will be grouped with D and segment C with B, rather than A with B and C with D.*

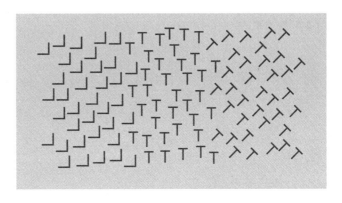

6.20 The effect of orientation and shape on perceptual grouping *The demarcation between the upright Ts and the tilted Ts is more easily seen than that between the upright Ts and the upright Ls. (From Beck, 1966)*

important for segmentation than more complex properties such as shape. This is because shape depends on more complex relations between the stimuli, such as the particular arrangement of the lines that defines the difference between a *T* and an *L* (Beck, 1982). This is just what we would expect if visual parsing is the first and thus most primitive step in visual organization.

Good continuation Our visual system seems to "prefer" contours that continue smoothly along their original course. This principle of grouping is called *good continuation* (Figure 6.21). Good continuation is a powerful organizational factor that will often prevail even when pitted against prior experience (Figure 6.22). This principle is used by the military for camouflage (Figure 6.23A). It also helps to camouflage animals against their natural enemies. (Figure 6.23B).

6.22 Good continuation pitted against prior experience *In (A), virtually all subjects see two complex patterns intersected by a horizontal line. Hardly anyone sees the hidden 4 contained in that figure—and shown in (B)—despite the fact that we have encountered 4s much more often than the two complex patterns that are probably completely new. (After Köhler, 1947)*

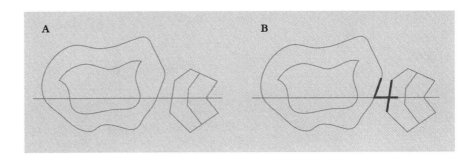

6.23 Good continuation as the basis of camouflage *In (A) camouflage is achieved by providing artificial contours that break up the outlines of the soldier's face and body. (Photograph by Larry Downing/Woodfin Camp & Associates) Good continuation helps to conceal the frog in (B) from predators who tend to see the frog as continuous with its background. (Photograph © Michael Fogden, Oxford Scientific Films)*

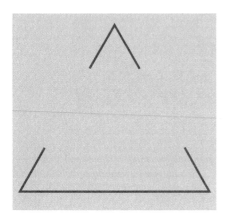

6.24 Closure *There is a tendency to complete—or close—figures that have a gap in them, as in the incomplete triangle shown here.*

Closure We tend to complete figures that have gaps in them. Figure 6.24 is seen as a triangle despite the fact that its sides are incomplete.

A closurelike phenomenon yields **subjective contours.** These are contours that are perceived, despite the fact that they don't physically exist (Figure 6.25). Some theorists interpret subjective contours as a special case of good continuation. In their view, the contour is seen to continue along its original path, and, if necessary, jumps a gap or two to achieve the continuation (Kellman and Shipley, 1991).

THE MAXIMUM-LIKELIHOOD PRINCIPLE

Proximity, similarity, good continuation, and closure are among the factors that determine whether we see portions of the visual world as belonging together or apart. Is there a general rule that underlies these different grouping factors? Different theorists have come up with a number of proposals. We'll consider only one of these, the **principle of maximum likelihood.** This principle goes back to the nineteenth-century physiologist Hermann von Helmholtz, but it has many modern adherents (Helmholtz, 1910; Gregory, 1974; Hochberg, 1981; Rock, 1983). It asserts that we tend to interpret the proximal stimulus pattern as that external (that is, distal) stimulus object that most probably produced it (Pomerantz and Kubovy, 1981; Hochberg, 1988).

How would the maximum-likelihood principle explain the grouping principles? Proximity is easy enough. Regions that are close together—and will therefore project images that are near each other on the retina—are generally portions of the same object. (Though there are exceptions, such as a worm on an apple.) The same holds for similarity. By and large, regions that are similar in color and texture also belong to the same object. (Though here too there are exceptions, such as a clown's costume or a patchwork quilt.)

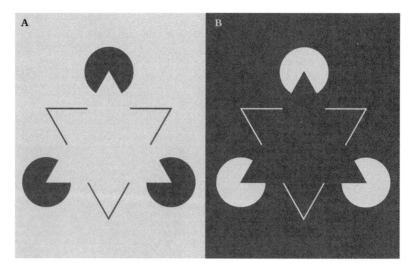

6.25 Subjective contours *Subjective contours are a special completion phenomenon in which contours are seen even where none exist. In (A) we see a tan triangle whose vertices lie on top of the three dark green circles. The three sides of this tan triangle (which looks brighter than the tan background) are clearly visible, even though they don't exist physically. In (B) we see the same effect with dark green and tan reversed. Here, there is a dark green triangle (which looks darker than the dark green background) with subjective green contours (Kanizsa, 1976)*

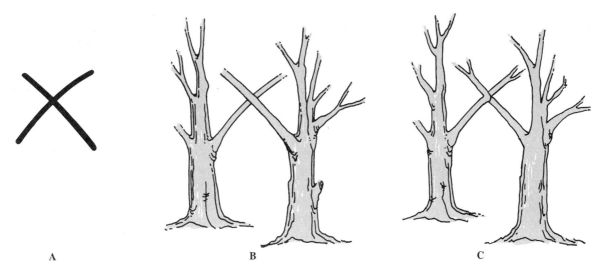

A   B   C

6.26   Good continuation and the maximum likelihood principle   (A) A figure that could be seen in two ways. (B) A likely alternative. (C) An unlikely alternative.

This principle can also explain grouping by good continuation. Consider Figure 6.26A. Most observers tend to perceive this as two smooth intersecting lines rather than as two triangular forms meeting at an angle (say, two fish kissing). Why should this be so? To answer this question, let's ask what Figure 6.26A might correspond to in the external world. One possibility is rather likely. It could easily be an image cast by two elongated objects, such as two branches of two trees that are at different distances from the observer (see Figure 6.26B). Alternatively, the figure might correspond to two angularly shaped objects, such as two elbow-shaped branches of trees that happen to be viewed from just the orientation at which their two branches are seen to meet (Figure 6.26C). Note that this is exceedingly unlikely, for any slight change of vantage point will shift the angles, so that this pattern will no longer hold. (Perceiving two passionate fish is even more unlikely.) Under the circumstances, the perceptual system makes the bet that is most likely to correspond to external reality: It groups by good continuation.

PATTERN RECOGNITION

We have considered the first steps in perceiving the form of an object: First, we respond to the primitive features of the scene and parse it so that we see the object as a figure, whose parts seem to belong together, standing out against its background. The next step is to determine *what* the object is, whether it is the letter *A,* or a dax, or an apple. To accomplish this, the visual system has to take the figure that emerges from the parsing process and compare its features to those of objects in our visual memory until it finally finds a match. The end result of these various steps is called ***pattern recognition.*** One of the major problems of the psychology of perception is to determine how this is accomplished.

We'll begin our discussion by considering some possible ways in which the visual system might accomplish this task.

PROCESSING STEPS FOR PATTERN RECOGNITION

Pandemonium   Some thirty years ago, an important approach to pattern recognition grew out of the efforts of computer scientists to develop machines that could "read" letters and numerals. Devices of this kind would have numerous practical applications, for example, sorting mail for the postal service or organizing bank records.

Many attempts to design such artificial recognition systems involved a chain of processing steps that began with the analysis of visual features. A very influential proposal of this sort was set forth by Oliver Selfridge (Selfridge, 1959). He envisioned a machine that could scan the optical image of a letter. How would it decide that this letter was, say, a *T?*

The machine could start out by looking for the presence or absence of certain visual features (for example, horizontal, vertical, or diagonal bars, curves to the right or left, and so on). It could then consult a list stored in its memory in which each capital letter is entered, together with the visual features that define it. By comparing the features in the stimulus with those of the letters on the list, it could begin to reach a decision: The more features that matched up, the stronger the activation. The final decision would then just be a matter of comparing the levels of activation, with the choice falling on the letter whose level of activation was greater than that of any of the others.

Selfridge called his model *Pandemonium,* because he regarded perceptual analysis as analogous to the work of various demons who pass on the results of their analysis to demons higher up, with feature-demons shouting at (in our terms, activating) letter-demons, and letter-demons in turn shouting at a decision-demon, who finally decides in favor of whichever letter-demon shouts the loudest (see Figure 6.27).

The simplest Pandemonium model only involves activation. But in later elaborations, inhibition of activation was also introduced. Suppose one of the features of a letter stimulus is a horizontal bar. In a Pandemonium model supplemented with inhibition, that feature would not only activate all of the letters

6.27 The Pandemonium model *The physical stimulus "R" gives rise to a visual image. This is then analyzed for the presence or absence of various component features, such as, vertical or horizontal lines, various corners, and so on. Each feature stimulates the stored letter patterns that contain it. In this example, one of the feature units stimulates the pattern "H," one stimulates, the pattern "A," two stimulate the pattern "P," and three the pattern "R." As a result, the "R" is more actively excited than the "H," "P," and "A," which leads to the decision that the letter is "R." The figure graphically renders Selfridge's metaphor of lower-level demons shouting out their messages to demons higher up. (Adapted from Lindsey and Norman, 1977)*

A

B

C

6.28 An ambiguous figure *(A) is ambiguous and is as likely to be seen as a young woman as an old woman. (B) and (C) are essentially unambiguous and depict the young woman and old woman respectively. If the subjects are first shown one of the unambiguous figures, they are almost sure to see the ambiguous picture in that fashion later on. (After Boring, 1930; Leeper, 1935)*

THE CAT

6.29 The effect of context on letter recognition *(After Selfridge, 1955)*

that contain this feature (such as F and E) but would also inhibit the activation of letters that do not contain that feature (such as W and Q). In the simplest version of Pandemonium, the demons merely try to shout as loudly as they can. In Pandemonium models in which there is inhibition, the demons do try to outshout each other, but in addition they also clap their hands over the mouths of other demons whose letters don't have the feature they have analyzed.

Top-down processing   Thus far we have discussed pattern recognition as a ***bottom-up process,*** which starts with primitive features and gradually builds up to larger units that are, so to speak, at the top. But there are reasons to believe that bottom-up processing is not enough. Pattern recognition often involves ***top-down processes*** in which the chain of events begins with the activation of higher units, which then affect units lower down. Evidence for this comes from the fact that recognition is often affected by higher-level knowledge and expectations.★

One demonstration of top-down processing in perception is provided by what are called ***context effects.*** In some cases, the context is provided by experiences in the past (often the immediately preceding past). A good example is provided by ambiguous figures. Consider Figure 6.28A, which can be seen as either an old woman in profile or a young woman whose head is turned slightly away. In one study, subjects were first shown one of two fairly unambiguous versions of the figure (Figures 6.28B and C). When later presented with the ambiguous figure (Figure 6.28A), they perceived it in line with the unambiguous version they had been shown before (Leeper, 1935).

In other cases, context effects depend on stimuli that are presented simultaneously with the stimulus in question. As an example, take the two words shown in Figure 6.29. The two middle "letters" of each word are physically identical, but they are usually seen as an *H* in *THE* and an *A* in *CAT.*

Similar context effects can make us hear speech sounds where in fact there are none. Something of this sort occurs in everyday life, for when people talk they sometimes cough or clear their throats so that the speech stream is interrupted. But even so, we usually hear and understand them and never notice that there were physical gaps in their actual utterance. In a laboratory demonstration of

★ Some investigators prefer the terms *data-driven* and *conceptually driven* for bottom-up and top-down respectively.

this phenomenon subjects listened to tape-recorded sentences in which the speech sounds were tampered with, as in the sentence:

The state governors met with their respective legislatures convening in the capital city.

In this sentence the experimenter replaced the middle *s* in the word *legislatures* with a cough-like noise. Yet virtually none of the subjects even noticed that any speech sound was missing. They somehow restored the deleted speech sound, and "heard" the *s* that was provided by the total context (Warren, 1970).

Bidirectional Activation Context effects demonstrate that there is some top-down processing. But this hardly means that bottom-up processing is unimportant—on the contrary. After all, if perceptual processing occurred only from the top down, we would always see what we expect and believe in—even if there were no stimulus whatever. To be sure, knowledge and expectations do help us interpret what we see and hear, but there has to be some sensory basis that informs these interpretations. Perceptual processing generally occurs in both directions: from top down, but also from the bottom up.

This bidirectional aspect of perceptual processing has been incorporated into some recent models of pattern recognition that operate from the top down and from the bottom up simultaneously. As an example, we'll take a problem in word recognition (see Figure 6.30). Suppose a perceiver is shown a three-letter word under very dim illumination. For the sake of simplicity, let's assume that in the first few milliseconds of the presentation, the system decides that the last two letters of the word are *AT,* but has as yet no information about the first letter. How does it choose between the many alternatives (e.g., *BAT, CAT, MAT, RAT, VAT,* and so on)? Let's suppose that the perceiver has just read a newspaper article on animals; this would presumably activate the words *BAT, CAT,* and *RAT.* These activations would in their turn lead to the inhibition of several other three-letter words that are inconsistent with the concept "animal," such as

6.30 Bidirectional activation *(A) Top-down processing. The first few milliseconds of perceptual analysis of the stimulus word* CAT*, given the last two letters but no information about the first letter. Activation of the concept "Animal" activates the words* CAT *and* RAT *(among others), which then activate their first-position letters* C *and* R*. It also inhibits incompatible words such as* MAT *(again, among others). Activation is indicated in dark green; inhibition in dark red. (B) Bottom-up processing. Some milliseconds later, further perceptual analysis of the first letter of the stimulus word has activated the feature curved-to-the-left, which activates the letter* C*, adds to the activation of the word* CAT*, and also inhibits the letter* R *and the word* RAT*. The end result is that the word* CAT *is more intensely activated than all other words and will reach recognition threshold. Activation is again in dark green and inhibition in dark red. To keep things simple, many mutually inhibitory effects (e.g., between the words* CAT *and* RAT*) are not shown in the figure.*

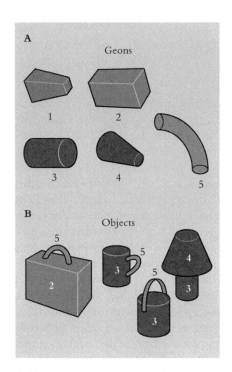

6.31 Some proposed geometric primitives (A) Some geons. (B) Some objects that can be created from these geons. (After Biederman, 1987)

6.32 Drawings by a patient with associative agnosia While the patient could see the models well enough to reproduce them fairly accurately, he was unable to recognize these objects. (From Farah, 1991)

MAT and *VAT.* They would also produce some top-down effects, such as activating the letters *B, C,* and *R.* After a few more milliseconds pass, some further perceptual analysis activates the curved-to-the-left feature. Now processing is bottom up and goes in the other direction. There will now be some further activation of the letter *C,* together with the inhibition of the letters *B* and *R.* This in turn will strengthen the word *CAT* and weaken *RAT* and *BAT,* until the activation of the word *CAT* gets above what is called the recognition threshold (McClelland, Rumelhart, and Hinton, 1986). In effect we have an augmented Pandemonium model in which demons at every level of the hierarchy—from above, below, and both sides—scream at each other until a single word-demon finally wins the shouting match.

AN INTERMEDIATE STEP: PERCEPTUAL COMPONENTS

In Pandemonium, the information-processing journey goes directly from the primitive features that are its starting point to the letters and numerals whose recognition is its goal. This may very well work for the relatively simple tasks for which it was devised (though it may encounter problems even there; e.g., Morton, 1969; Bruce and Green, 1985). But many theorists believe that recognizing the real objects of the world around us requires a processing sequence that involves some intervening steps. In their view, there are some intermediate perceptual components that are somewhat broader than lines, curves, and angles.

A model proposed by Irving Biederman lists some thirty such geometric components that he calls **geons** (a neologism for "geometric ions")—three-dimensional figures such as cylinders, cones, pyramids, and the like. According to Biederman, just about all objects can be analyzed—perceptually—into some number of such geons. When we encounter an object, we presumably perceive its component geons and their relationships, and then consult our visual memory to see whether there's an object that matches up. If there is, we recognize the object (Biederman, 1987; see Figure 6.31).

FROM GEONS TO MEANING

What the geons and their relationships give us is a complete *structural* description of an object—its complete geometry in three dimensions. Thus in Biederman's system, a certain geon on top of another is an appropriate visual description of the geometrical structure of, say, a desk lamp. But that's not enough to tell the system that the object *is* a desk lamp, that is, an article that casts light, can be switched on and off, and so on. The structural description does a fine job of representing the object's geometry; what it doesn't do is describe the object's meaning.

Evidence that object recognition goes though an all-but-final phase of structural description where the perceived object as yet has no meaning comes from patients who have suffered certain brain lesions (Farah, 1990). As we saw in a previous chapter, some cortical lesions produce visual agnosia; patients with this disorder can see but cannot recognize what they see (see Chapter 2, p. 44). In some cases of agnosia (technically termed **associative agnosia**), patients can perceive objects well enough to draw recognizable copies of them but are unable to identify them. One patient did a perfectly good job of copying drawings of a key, a bird, and a pig (see Figure 6.32). When asked to say what these were drawings of, he couldn't name the key and said that the bird was a tree stump and that the pig might be a dog or some other animal. He had evidently formed adequate structural descriptions of these objects. But his ability to process what he saw stopped there; what he perceived was stripped of its meaning.

THE PROCESSING SEQUENCE IN FORM PERCEPTION

To see an apple and recognize it for what it is is evidently an achievement that involves a number of steps. The first step is to detect the elementary features that make up the apple's form, such as certain curvatures. A subsequent—though often concurrent—step is visual segregation: The apple is seen as a figure against the ground of the table and whatever else is in the visual field. It is also seen as a unified whole, even if some of it is partially obscured by other objects in the field. After this come several steps in pattern recognition: The features of the figure are compared to certain other forms that are stored in memory until a match is found. This process first leads to intermediate visual components, the geons, which are then mentally assembled to form a structural description of the object. The final step is the perception of the actual object.

These processing steps are described here as if they always occur one after another and in this precise bottom-up order. In actuality, the situation is nowhere as neat as this, for many of these steps occur simultaneously rather than in sequence—to use the technical terms, demonstrating *parallel* rather than *serial processing* (see pp. 226–27). And even if they do occur in sequence, their order may well be the reverse from the one we described, for as we've seen there is top-down as well as bottom-up processing. But even so, our simplified account may provide a useful overview.

PERCEPTUAL PROBLEM SOLVING

Bidirectional models of the kind discussed above (pp. 220–21) fit in with the belief that much of perception is essentially a form of problem solving in which the observer tries to discover (consciously or, more commonly, without awareness) what it is that she sees. Seen in this light, the perceptual system starts out with both a stimulus and a hypothesis. The *perceptual hypothesis* is the perceiver's assumption about what the object out there really is. This hypothesis represents the top-down aspect of the process. It is tested as the system analyzes the stimulus (the bottom-up aspect) for some appropriate features. If these are found, the perceptual hypothesis gains plausibility and is either accepted or the stimulus is checked for further proof. If no such further confirming features are found, then a new hypothesis is considered, which is then tested by searching the stimulus for yet other features, and so on.

Occasionally, we become consciously aware that some such process operates. This sometimes happens when we are presented with a visual display that initially makes no sense. An example is Figure 6.33. At first glance most observers don't know what to make of it. But as they continue to look at the figure, they develop hypotheses about what it might be (e.g., maybe this part is the leg of some animal, maybe the animal has a spotted hide). If they are lucky, they eventually hit on the correct hypothesis (pintos on snow covered rocks). When they finally see the pintos, the top-down and bottom-up processes meet, and there is a perceptual insight, a visual "Aha!" Here the process of perceptual problem solving was quite conscious. But this is rare, for we usually see cars, trees, and people (and even pintos) without being aware that we are trying to solve any perceptual puzzles. But according to theorists who endorse the problem-solving approach to perception, much the same kind of thing occurs even then, though at much greater speed and outside of consciousness.

"By George, you're right! I thought there was something familiar about it." (Drawing by Chas. Addams; © 1957, 1985 The New Yorker Magazine, Inc.)

6.33   Perceptual problem solving   *This is a picture of something. What? (Painting, 1979, by Bev Doolittle; courtesy of the Greenwich Workshop, Inc.)*

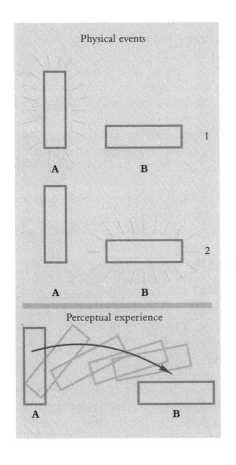

Physical events

Perceptual experience

6.34   The logic of stroboscopic movement: from upright to prone   *(A) Stimulus A flashes at time 1, followed by stimulus B at time 2, and back again. (B) With appropriate time intervals, this leads to the perception of a rectangle turning from an upright to a prone position and back. (After Kolers, 1972)*

THE LOGIC OF PERCEPTION

To the extent that perception involves a form of problem solving, it obeys a kind of logic. One of the laws of ordinary logic is that there can be no contradictions—a statement can't be both true and false at the same time. The perceptual system obeys a similar law. It operates to minimize perceptual contradictions and to make all parts mesh in a coherent whole. If the system detects a discrepancy, it does its best to rectify the situation (Rock, 1983).

An illustrative example comes from the study of stroboscopic motion. Subjects were briefly shown a rectangle standing upright in one location, followed by a brief exposure to a rectangle lying horizontally in another, and back and forth, with the two figures alternating continuously. If the intervals were appropriate, there was apparent (or stroboscopic) movement. But how can a figure be seen to move from one place to another, if its form is different in the two locations? The perceptual system comes up with a neat solution. The upright rectangle is seen to turn to the horizontal as it moves and then turn upward when it moves back again (see Figure 6.34).

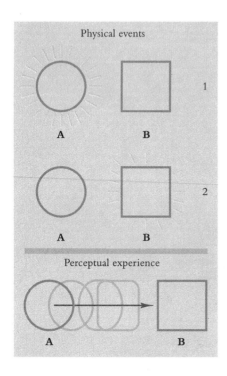

Physical events

1

A   B

2

A   B

Perceptual experience

A   B

6.35 **The logic of stroboscopic movement: from circle to square** *(A) Stimulus A flashes at time 1, followed by stimulus B at time 2, and back again. (B) With appropriate time intervals, this leads to the perception of a circle that changes in shape to become a square, and then changes again into a circle. (After Kolers and Pomerantz, 1971)*

In another study, the two alternating figures were a square and a circle. Again the subjects saw movement. But now the visual solution was different. The figures were seen to change smoothly from one shape to the other as they shuttled back and forth (see Figure 6.35; from Kolers and Pomerantz, 1971).

WHEN LOGIC FAILS: IMPOSSIBLE FIGURES

We've seen that the perceptual system is very clever. With a little top-down hint, it can reconstruct imperfect speech and discover hidden pintos. (In a pinch, it can even square a circle.) But even the cleverest system fails when it is confronted with a problem that is in principle insoluble. In perception such problems are posed by what are called *impossible figures* in which there is no way of resolving a perceptual contradiction (Penrose and Penrose, 1958).

Take Figure 6.36A. At the left, it is a perspective drawing of two rectangular beams joined in a U-shaped form; at the right, it is a picture of three round rods. If we look at either the left or the right separately, the figure makes sense. But as our glance travels from left to right, there is a gross inconsistency, for the two halves of the figure don't add up to a whole. Consider the third horizontal line from the top. At the left, it is the bottom edge of the upper horizontal beam; at the right it becomes the top edge of the middle rod. Now the perceptual system is stumped, for there is no perceptual hypothesis that can make the figure into a coherent whole.

In other examples, the impossibility takes a bit longer to appreciate. Take Figure 6.36B, which at first glance looks like a triangular, three-dimensional object. The trouble is that the perspectives are drawn differently at the different corners. If we mentally trace a path from one corner of the object to the second, then to the third, and finally try to return to the first, we find that there is no way to do so because the corners don't mate properly. The perceptual problem posed by Figure 6.36C is even more subtle. Here the inconsistency is based on yet another trick of perspective. As the figure is drawn, we can start at any place and go around the entire stair arrangement, always climbing upwards, until we get back to the starting point.

Impossible figures underline the fact that perceptual problem solving consists of making a sensible whole out of separate parts, an integration that is often achieved over time. When we attend to any one region of an impossible figure, we are unaware that there's a problem. The difficulty comes when our attention (and our eyes) travel from one region to another, and we try to fit the two regions together. Under normal circumstances, this process of building up a mental picture of what we see out there occurs without any conscious awareness. But we become aware of it when it is somehow blocked or frustrated, as in the case of impossible figures (Hochberg, 1970).

The preceding sections underlines a point we've made repeatedly: Perception involves both top-down and bottom-up processes. Without top-down processing, knowledge and expectation could never guide and influence our interpretations of what we see. And without bottom-up processing, the external stimulus would have no effect, and we would not perceive but only hallucinate.

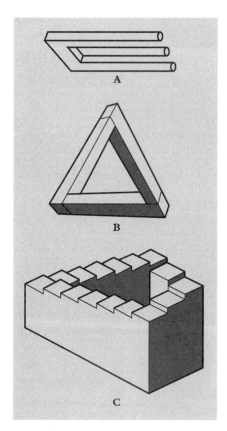

6.36 **Impossible figures** *(A) U-shape or three-pronged fork. (B) Impossible triangle. (C) Perpetual staircase. (Penrose and Penrose, 1958)*

PERCEPTUAL SELECTION: ATTENTION

Our perceptual system shapes and organizes the patchwork of different sensations into a coherent whole that has depth, motion, and form as well as meaning and results from both bottom-up and top-down processing. But in this processing not all parts of the perceptual world are given equal weight. We focus on the figure, not on the ground; we are more likely to notice shapes that are moving rather than those that are stationary. Thus, in addition to its other characteristics, perception is selective. We don't look at all the stimuli that are there to be looked at or focus upon them all. Our ability to take in and interpret the myriad stimulations around us is finite, and so our perceptual system is forced to choose among them. The various ways in which we exercise such choices and perceive selectively are often grouped together under the general label *attention*.

SELECTION BY PHYSICAL ORIENTATION

The most direct means of selecting input is to orient the various sensory systems physically toward one set of stimuli and away from another. The organism does not passively touch, see, or hear; it actively feels, looks, and listens. It turns its head and eyes, explores the world with its hands (or paws or lips or prehensile trunk), and if it has the necessary motor endowment, pricks up its ears. These orienting adjustments of the sensory machinery are the external manifestations of attention.

In humans, the major means of physically selecting the stimulus input are movements of the eyes. Peripheral vision informs us that something is going on, say, in the upper left of our field of vision. But our peripheral acuity is not good enough to tell us what it is precisely. To find out, our eyes move so that this region falls into the fovea. A number of investigators have developed techniques for recording eye movements made when looking at pictures. The records show that the subjects glance most frequently at the regions that are visually most informative (Figure 6.37). This gaze pattern may be different for different

A

B

6.37   Eye-movement records when looking at pictures   Both (A) and (B) are pictures that were looked at for 3 and 10 minutes respectively. With each picture is the record of the eye movements during this period. As the records show, most of the eye movements are directed toward the most visually informative regions. As a result, the eye-movement record is a crude mirror of the main contours of the picture. (From Yarbus, 1967)

6.38   Eye movements as a function of what the observer is looking for   *(A) A picture shown to subjects. Three-minute eye-movement records when the subjects were asked to estimate the wealth of the family (B) and when they were asked to estimate the ages of the people in the picture (C). (From Yarbus, 1967)*

observers, since what interests one person may not interest another. For example, a picture will be scanned quite differently if the observer is asked to estimate the ages of the people in it than when he's asked to estimate their economic status (see Figure 6.38A, B, and C).

These results show that the act of looking is purposeful. People don't scan the world in the wistful hope that their foveas will by chance hit on some interesting bit of visual news. They pick up some information from what they've vaguely seen in the periphery and from their general notions of what the scene is all about. They then move their eyes to check up on what they've seen and to refine their visual knowledge further (Yarbus, 1967; Rayner, 1978; Stark and Ellis, 1981).

CENTRAL SELECTION

Eye movements and other means for changing physical orientation determine the sensory input the perceptual system receives. But selective control of perception may also employ ***central selective processes,*** which determine whether a particular portion of the sensory input will be dealt with further, and if so, how it will be interpreted.

SELECTIVE LOOKING

A widely used method for studying visual attention is the ***visual search procedure*** that we saw used in studying primitive features. As with those studies, a subject is briefly shown an array of letters, digits, or other visual forms (usually called distractors) and has to indicate as quickly and accurately as she can whether a particular target is or is not present among them.

Parallel and serial processing   When the difference between the target and distractors involves just one feature, the search is very fast and seems almost effortless. An obvious example is searching for a green vertical among a number of green horizontals. Another is looking for an *S* in a group of other letters none of which contain any curves (e.g., *A, E, F, H,* and so on). Under these conditions, the search time is virtually independent of the number of distractors among which it appears. We saw earlier that some analysts take this as evidence that the single different feature is a primitive one. In information-processing terms the implication is that the search was conducted in ***parallel:*** All items in the display were processed simultaneously.

The situation is quite different when the target is defined by a ***conjunction of features,*** for example, a red *X* among distractors that include green *X*s, red *O*s, green *B*s, and so on. Now the system can't just look for the feature red or the feature diagonal; it has to find a red that goes with a diagonal, or a certain kind of diagonal (after all, the display might contain a red *R*). Under these conditions,

6.39 Serial processing in visual search When the task is to find a target that is defined by a conjunction of features (here a red O), the search is conducted serially. Each item is inspected in turn, and the search time increases as the number of false alternatives (red or green Vs, green Os) increases.

search time is longer and increases with the number of distractors in the display. The implication is that the search is **serial:** The processing system examines each item, one by one, to determine whether it does or does not have the required conjunction of features. Anne Treisman believes that this process involves some kind of attentional focus. This focus is necessarily limited, it can't encompass the entire visual field at once. Rather, it serves as a mental searchlight that passes over the items in the display, one after another (Treisman, 1988; see Figure 6.39).

Moving the mind's eye Not surprisingly, visual search becomes very much easier if the subject knows where to look, even if the search is for a conjunction of features. If she is told in advance that if a target is present it will be at, say, the three o'clock position from the center of the array, she will look there right away and come up with a quick and appropriate decision. But there are a number of studies that show that prior information about location will help the subject's search even if she does not move her eyes. In such experiments, the subject is first asked to look at a dot on a screen, and to keep her eyes on this *fixation point.* Shortly thereafter, an arrow appears for an instant and points to the critical location, after which the array is flashed on. What's crucial in this procedure is that the interval between the appearance of the arrow and the disappearance of the array is too short to permit a voluntary eye movement.★ But even so the arrow helps make the search much easier. It does not affect the physical orientation of the eyes; for, given the very brief intervals, the eyes never change position. But it evidently does affect an internal selection process, as if the mind's eye moves even though the eyes in the head are stationary (Egeth, Jonides, and Wall, 1972; Eriksen and Hoffman, 1972; Jonides, 1980, 1983).

SELECTIVE LISTENING

A different method for studying selective attention focuses on listening to speech and is modeled on a phenomenon often observed in real life, the *cocktail-party effect.* During conversations at a noisy party, one tunes in on the voice of the person one is talking to. The many other voices are somehow filtered out and are consigned to a background babble. This effect has been studied experimentally by asking subjects to attend to one of two simultaneously presented verbal messages. The usual procedure is **dichotic presentation.** The subject wears two earphones and receives different messages through each of them. To guarantee selective attention, the subject is generally asked to *shadow* the to-be-attended message. This means that he has to repeat it aloud, word for word, as it comes over the appropriate earphone. Under these conditions, the irrelevant message tends to be shut out almost entirely. The subject can hear speechlike sounds, but notices little else. He is generally unable to recall the message that came by way of the unattended ear. In fact, he often does not even notice if the speaker on the unattended ear shifts into a foreign language or if the selection is read backwards (Cherry, 1953).

THE FILTER THEORY OF ATTENTION

Results of this sort suggest that selective attention acts as a kind of filter. This filter is presumably interposed between the initial sensory registration and later stages of perceptual analysis. If the information is allowed through the attentional filter, it can then be further analyzed—recognized, interpreted, and stored in memory. But if it does not pass through, much of it is lost.

★ That interval is usually about 100 ms, while an eye movement takes about 150 to 200 ms to execute.

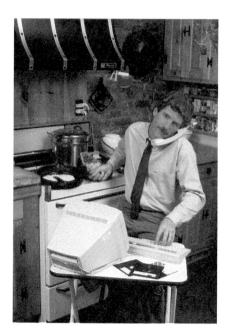

Attentional selection *Without some attentional selection, performance of any complex task would deteriorate. (Photograph © Jeff M. Dunn)*

Early versions of this theory suggested that the filtering effect is all-or-none. Subjects in a dichotic listening experiment were thought to understand no part of the message that entered by way of the unattended ear (Broadbent, 1958). This all-or-none theory turned out to be false, for there is good evidence that information that has some special significance is registered even if it is carried as part of the unattended message. The best example is the sight or sound of one's own name. No matter how intently we concentrate on the person next to us, we are quite likely to hear our own name in another conversation held on the other side of the room.

This everyday experience has been documented with the shadowing method. When subjects are forced to repeat a message that comes over one ear, word for word, they are almost completely oblivious to the irrelevant message that is fed into the other ear. But they do take notice when that irrelevant message contains the sound of their own name (Moray, 1959). This result suggests that the attentional filter does not block irrelevant messages completely. It only attenuates them, like a volume control that is turned down but not off. If the item is important enough (or perhaps familiar enough), then it may pass through the filter and be analyzed to some extent (Treisman, 1964).

Related evidence comes from a study in which subjects had to shadow sentences such as "They threw stones at the bank yesterday." Concurrently, the other ear was presented with either of two words: *river* or *money*. When questioned directly, the subjects couldn't recall which of these two words they had heard, if either. But some part of the meaning of these words must have come through nevertheless. The shadowed sentence contained the ambiguous word *bank,* which can be understood as either a financial institution or as the side of a river. Which interpretation was chosen depended upon whether the unattended ear was presented with the word *money* or *river.* This shows that the subjects extracted some meaning from the unattended message even though they never knew they did (McKay, 1973).

THE PERCEPTION OF REALITY

Of what use are all the mechanisms of perceptual organization we have considered throughout this chapter, whether innately given or based on learning? The answer is simple enough: They all help us to perceive reality. To be sure, the perceptual system may occasionally lead us astray, as in illusions of depth or movement, and sometimes it may actually leave us helpless, as in impossible figures. But these are fairly rare occasions. By and large, the processes that lead to the perception of depth, movement, and form serve the attainment of a larger goal—the perception of the real world outside.

To see the real world is to see the properties of distal objects: their color, form, size, and location, their movement through space, their permanence or transience. But as we have noted before, organisms cannot gain experience about the distal stimulus directly; all information about the external world comes to us from the proximal stimulus patterns that distal objects project upon the senses. The trouble is that the same distal stimulus object can produce many different proximal stimulus patterns. Its retinal image will get larger or smaller depending upon its distance; its retinal shape will change depending upon its slant; the amount of light it projects on the retina will increase or decrease depending on the illumination that falls upon it.

Under the circumstances, it may seem surprising that we ever manage to see the real properties of a distal object. But see them we do. The best proof is provided by **perceptual constancies:** An elephant looks large even at a distance, a postcard looks rectangular even though its retinal image is a trapezoid unless it is viewed directly head on, and a crow looks black even in sunlight. In all of these cases, we manage to transcend the vagaries of the proximal stimulus and react to certain constant attributes of the distal object such as its shape and its size.

EMPIRICISM AND NATIVISM REVISITED

How does the organism accomplish this feat? The attempts to answer this question are best understood as part of the continuing debate between the empiricist heirs of Locke on the one hand and the nativist descendants of Kant on the other.

THE EMPIRICISTS' ANSWER

Empiricists handle the problem of the constancies by asserting that the sensation produced by a particular stimulus is modified and reinterpreted in light of what we have learned through past experience. Consider perceived size. People five feet away look just about as tall as those at a fifty-foot distance. This is not merely because we know them to be average-sized rather than giants or midgets. The fact is that they really look equally tall provided there are cues that indicate their proper distance (Figure 6.40).

How can we explain this and similar phenomena? The most influential version of the empiricists' answer was formulated by Hermann von Helmholtz in the late nineteenth century. According to Helmholtz, the perceiver has two sources of information. To begin with, there is the sensation derived from the size of the object on the retina. In addition, there are a number of depth cues that indicate how far away the object is. Prior learning has taught the perceiver a general rule: The farther away things are, the smaller will be the sensation derived from the retinal image. The perceiver can now infer the true size of the object, given its retinal size, its distance, and the learned rule that relates the two. As a result she adjusts her perception of size, shifting it downward if the object is seen as close by and upward if it is seen as farther off. Helmholtz of course knew full well that we don't go through any conscious calculation of this sort when we look at objects and perceive their size. But he believed that some such process was going on anyway, and he therefore called it **unconscious inference** (Helmholtz, 1909).

It's worth noting that the unconscious inference theory is really an early version of the top-down processing hypothesis in perception. Both positions insist that perception is only partially determined by the sensory stimulation, that perception is in part a kind of mental construction, based on expectations and inferences of which the observer is often unaware. Thus contemporary theorists who argue that perception often involves a form of problem solving hold a view

A

B

6.40 Perceived size and distance (A) The actual image of the two men in the picture—which corresponds to the size of their retinal image—is in the ratio of 3 to 1. But this is not the way they are perceived. They look roughly equal in size, but at different distances, with one about three times farther off than the other. In (B) there are no cues that indicate that one man is farther away than the other—on the contrary. The figure was constructed by cutting the more distant man out of the picture and pasting him next to the other man, with the apparent distance from the viewer equal for the two. Now they look very different in size. (After Boring, 1964; Photograph by Jeffrey Grosscup)

6.41 An invariant relationship that provides information about size *(A) and (B) show a dog at different distances from the observer. The retinal size of the dog varies with distance, but the ratio between the retinal size of the dog and the retinal size of the textural elements made up of the bushes is constant. (Photographs by Jeffrey Grosscup)*

that is in many ways quite similar to that of Helmholtz (e.g., Hochberg, 1981, 1988; Rock, 1977, 1983, 1986).

THE NATIVISTS' ANSWER

The nativists' reply is that the perception of size is directly given. They argue that the stimulus for the perceived size of an object is not the size of the retinal image as such. It is rather some relationship between that size and certain other attributes that pertain to depth.

A very influential modern version of this approach is that of James J. Gibson (1950, 1966, 1979). Gibson believed that such vital characteristics of an object as its size, its shape, and its distance from the observer are signaled by various **higher order patterns of stimulation** to which the organism is innately sensitive.

As an example, let's return to size. To be sure, the size of the retinal image projected by an object must necessarily vary with its distance from the observer. But Gibson argued that this does not mean that there is no size information in the stimulus that hits the eye. One reason is that objects are usually seen against a background whose elements—leaves, pebbles, clumps of grass, or whatever—provide a texture. Since these elements are generally of about the same size, their size on the retina varies with distance and leads to texture gradients. As we've already seen, these texture gradients provide information about distance. But in addition, they also provide information about the relative size of objects in the world outside. For distance has the same effect on the retinal image of the object as it has on the retinal image of the adjacent textural elements of the object's background. In both cases, the retinal size decreases with increasing distance. As a result, there is a constant ratio between the retinal size cast by the object and the retinal size of its adjacent textural elements. According to Gibson, this ratio provides a **higher order stimulus relationship** that remains *invariant* over changes of distance, and we pick up the information provided by this ratio directly, without any intermediate cognitive steps (such as unconscious inference). Gibson called this process **direct perception.** (See Figure 6.41.)

The extent to which higher-order patterns of stimulation (such as the size ratio) provide information about various attributes of the world—of which size is only one—is still a matter of debate. Nor is it clear that perceivers are sensitive to all such higher-order patterns or that the response to such patterns is part of our native endowment. These issues are by no means settled, as we will see when we turn to the empirical study of the various perceptual constancies.★

James J. Gibson *(Courtesy of E. J. Gibson)*

★ Some psychologists point out that one's stand on the unconscious-inference versus direct-perception debate is not necessarily tied up with one's position on the nature-nurture issue, even though the two have often been conjoined in the past. At least in theory, there could be perceptu-

6.42 Shape constancy When we see a door frame at various slants from us, it appears rectangular despite the fact that its retinal image is often a trapezoid. (After Gibson, 1950)

SIZE AND SHAPE CONSTANCY

Size constancy is a term that describes the fact that the perceived size of an object is the same whether it is nearby or far away. A Cadillac Eldorado at a distance of 100 feet will look larger than a Volkswagen Beetle 20 feet away. An analogous phenomenon is *shape constancy,* which refers to the fact that we perceive the shape of an object more or less independently of the angle from which it is viewed. A rectangular door frame will appear rectangular even though most of the angles from which it is regarded will produce a trapezoidal retinal image (see Figure 6.42).

How can we explain size and shape constancy? An essentially nativist approach such as Gibson's would try to account for the phenomena by looking for some higher-order stimulus pattern that remains invariant despite changes in distance or angle of orientation. As we saw earlier in the chapter, in the case of distance such a proposed invariant is provided by the relation between the target stimulus and the texture of the background. Suppose we approach a door in a hallway. The door does not seem to change in size, even though its retinal image is expanding. In this case one thing remains unchanged: the ratio between the size of the images projected by the door and by the textural elements of the wallpaper in the hallway.

Such size ratios may well contribute to the constancy phenomenon, but they are probably not the only factor. For size constancy is found even when there are no apparent textural elements in either the target stimulus or the background that might provide the basis for a size ratio. As long as there are any cues to depth at all—such as perspective, interposition, binocular disparity, motion parallax, and so on—size constancy remains. As the number of these cues is progressively diminished, size constancy declines (Holway and Boring, 1947; Harvey and Leibowitz, 1967; Chevrier and Delorme, 1983).

An invariant size ratio is evidently unable to explain all cases of size constancy. But if so, what can? According to Helmholtz, we somehow take account of the object's distance and compensate for it (by unconscious inference). Helmholtz believed that the size-distance relationship is acquired through long experience. He argued that young children sometimes mistake objects at a considerable distance for miniatures. When they look from a tower, they see the people below as tiny dolls—a phenomenon that is also seen in adults

al inferences that appeal to principles that are genetically programmed. By the same token, a perceiver might learn to attend to a stimulus pattern that would provide direct information about some aspect of the real world, even if he had not done so initially (Pomerantz and Kubovy, 1986).

(Helmholtz, 1909; Day, Stuart, and Dickinson, 1980). Gibson would reply that at those distances the crucial textural elements are too far away to be visible. This might explain why size constancy breaks down when the distance between observer and target gets large enough, but it cannot explain why that breakdown occurs at an earlier point in children than in adults (Zeigler and Leibowitz, 1957).

Perhaps Helmholtz was right in asserting that size constancy is learned. But if so, it must be learned fairly quickly, for size constancy seems to be present rather early in life (at least for moderate distances—Bower, 1966; McKenzie, Tootell, and Day, 1980; Day and McKenzie, 1981). To test for size constancy in the first months of life, many investigators have resorted to the **habituation method** (for details, see Chapter 13). The infant is presented with a visual stimulus until she gets habituated (so to speak, bored) and looks away. She is subsequently presented with a new stimulus. If she spends relatively little time looking at it, the presumption is that she regards it as quite similar to the old boring stimulus. But if she inspects the new stimulus with some interest and for a longer time, she presumably sees it as essentially different from the old one to which she had become habituated.

A study that employed this method has shown size constancy in six-month-olds. The infants were first shown a model of a human life-sized head at a distance of 60 cm. After several trials with this figure, they habituated and looked elsewhere. The critical test involved two groups. Group I was shown the same head model at a distance of 30 cm—the distal size remained the same but the retinal size was changed. Group II was shown a head model identical in form but reduced by half and presented at a distance of 30 cm—here the distal size was changed while the retinal size remained the same (see Figure 6.43). The results showed that the infants in Group II spent much more time inspecting the stimulus than did those in Group I. It appears that a decrease in true size (with retinal image held constant) is regarded as more of a change than a change in retinal size (with distal size held constant)—a strong indication that some measure of size constancy is present by the age of six months (McKenzie, Tootell, and Day, 1980). Such findings are certainly compatible with the view that at least some instances of size constancy are part of our native endowment and are thus found at a very early age. But they are also compatible with the empiricist position, on the assumption that the relevant learning is acquired rather quickly.

What holds for size constancy, holds by and large for shape constancy as well. In both constancies, the observer requires some information in addition to the retinal image of the target stimulus: In size constancy, she has to know the distance to that target; in shape constancy, she must know the slant from which it is viewed. When deprived of information about the slant of, say, a square tilted backward, she will respond to the shape of its retinal image—perceiving a trapezoid rather than a square. In further analogy to size constancy, shape constancy is found at a rather early age. By three months of age, infants seem to regard a tilted square as essentially equivalent to a square viewed straight on (Caron, Caron, and Carlson, 1979; Cook and Birch, 1984). By five to six months, infants seem to see the similarity between a face photographed in front view to one in semi-profile (Fagan, 1976). As in size constancy, the shape constancy effect may be based on learning, but if so, the learning must occur rather quickly.

LIGHTNESS CONSTANCY

At this time, it's still an open issue whether size and shape constancy are based on a response to invariant higher-order stimulus patterns. But in another perceptual constancy, **lightness constancy,** the issue is mostly settled in

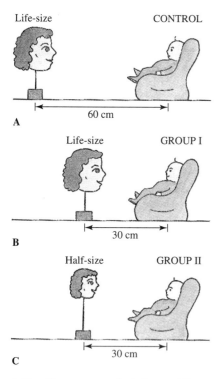

6.43 Size constancy in infants (A) Six-month-old infants were exposed to a model of a human head at a distance of 60 cm until they habituated. (B) One group was then tested with the same head model at a distance of 30 cm—same distal size but altered retinal size. (C) A second group was tested with the same head model reduced to half its size but at the original distance of 30 cm—same retinal size but altered distal size. The infants in (C) spent more time looking at the model than those in (B), an indication of size constancy.

6.44 Lightness constancy *Subjects are shown two identical gray papers, A and B. A is illuminated while B is in shadow. As a result, A reflects much more light than B. Even so, the two are perceived to be about equal in lightness, a manifestation of lightness constancy. (After Rock, 1975)*

favor of the nativist solution, for here an appropriate invariant relationship plays the major role.

Lightness constancy refers to the fact that humans and animals are able to perceive an object's lightness—whether it is white or gray or black—regardless of the illumination that falls upon it. On the face of it, this presents a problem. Virtually all objects reflect a certain proportion of the light that falls upon them. The exact proportion depends upon a physical property of the object itself, its *reflectance*. Some objects have a high reflectance (snow), others a low reflectance (coal). To say that an object is perceived as light or dark is really to say that we can tell something about its reflectance. Yet we cannot possibly see the reflectance directly; all we get from the object is the amount of light it actually reflects on any given occasion, the *luminance*. But this luminance depends not only upon the object's reflectance but also upon the *illumination* that falls upon it. A white shirt in shadow may well reflect less light than does a gray shirt in brilliant sunlight. Under these circumstances, we can still tell that the first is lighter than the second. A white shirt will not suddenly seem to turn gray when a cloud hides the sun; it appears just as white, but in shadow.

The apparent lightness of white shirts, and indeed all other objects, remains fairly constant despite rather drastic changes in the illumination that falls upon them. This phenomenon is readily demonstrated in the laboratory. Subjects are shown two gray papers of equal reflectance. One paper, *A*, receives twice the illumination of another paper, *B*, which is in shadow (Figure 6.44). But even so, the subjects judge the papers to be equally light, despite the fact that *A* reflects twice as much light as *B*.

How does lightness constancy come about? The explanation is that the perception of lightness depends in large measure on a higher-order stimulus relationship: the ratio of two luminances—the one reflected from the figure and the one reflected from the figure's background. The basic idea is that illumination changes normally affect both the object in the foreground and the background against which it is seen. As a result, the ratio between the two luminances will necessarily remain the same, whatever the illumination. Consider a black crow that stands in front of a brown garden wall (see Figure 6.45). The sun is democratic, shining equally on the crow and on the garden wall. If it suddenly emerges from behind a cloud, the illumination on the crow (and hence its luminance) will go up. But the same holds for the wall. Its luminance will also increase. This increase leads to an automatic decline in the apparent lightness of the crow. This is just another example of brightness contrast, which makes objects appear darker as the luminance of their background goes up (see Chapter 5).

6.45 Lightness constancy and brightness contrast *In (A) the illumination on both bird and wall is moderate; in (B) it is much greater. The fact that illumination goes up increases the amount of light reflected by the bird, but it also increases the amount of light reflected by the wall that serves as its background. The two increases tend to cancel each other. Any increase in the light intensity of the background tends to inhibit the apparent lightness of the figure. This compensation effect acts in the direction of lightness constancy: The crow continues to look black even in brilliant sunshine.*

6.46   Horemhab offering wine to Annubis, ca. 1339–1304 B.C.   *The conventions of Egyptian art required the main parts of the human body to be represented in their most characteristic view. Thus, heads are shown in profile, arms and legs from the side, but eyes are depicted in full-face view, as are the shoulders and the chest. (Courtesy of the Metropolitan Museum of Art, New York, Rogers Fund, 1923)*

THE REPRESENTATION OF REALITY IN ART

The mechanisms of perceptual organization evolved to serve in the struggle for survival that all organisms must wage. They allow us to see reality as it actually is. But it is part of our humanity that we have managed to turn these perceptual mechanisms to a use that goes beyond the necessities of sheer survival: the representation of reality in art.

As we've seen, there are many perceptual phenomena (for example, the recognition of form) that are enormously affected by memories of the past and expectations of the future. Clearly, there is a wide region where it is not quite clear where seeing ends and knowing begins. The psychology of visual art is yet another illustration of the overlap between seeing and knowing.

SEEING AND KNOWING

Consider Figure 6.46, a wall painting from Egypt some three thousand years ago. Why did the artist depict the figures as he did, with eyes and shoulders in front view and the rest of the body in profile? His fellow Egyptians were surely built as we are. But if so, why didn't he draw them "correctly"?

The answer seems to be that Egyptian artists drew, not what they could see at any one moment or from any one position, but rather what they believed was the most enduring and characteristic attribute of their model. They portrayed the various parts of the human body from the vantage point that shows each form in its most characteristic manner: the front view for the eyes and shoulders, the profile for the nose and feet. The fact that these orientations are incompatible was evidently of no concern; what mattered was that all of the components were represented as the artist knew them to be (Gombrich, 1961).

THE RENAISSANCE: SCENES THROUGH A WINDOW FRAME

The illustrations of Egyptian art show the enormous role of the known in the visual representation of the seen. One may argue that this simply reflects the fact that these artists never set themselves the task of mirroring nature as it appears to the eye. Does the artist copy more precisely if one of his main purposes is to do just that?

The most striking examples come from the Renaissance masters who conceived the notion that a picture should look just like a real scene that is viewed through a window from one particular orientation (see Figure 6.47). The paint-

6.47 Perspective in Renaissance art
The Annunciation by Crivelli *(ca. 1430–1495). Note the loving attention to perspective detail, such as roofs and arches extending far back. (Courtesy the National Gallery, London)*

6.48 The Cathedral of Rouen *by Claude Monet, 1893* *Monet, one of the leaders of the Impressionist movement, was engaged in a life-long attempt to catch fleeting sensations of light. If this painting of the cathedral at Rouen is viewed from a distance or out of foveal vision, the form becomes clearer and less impressionistic. What is lost is the brilliant shimmer of light and color. The oscillation between these two modes of appearance contributes to the total esthetic effect. (Courtesy of Musée d'Orsay)*

ing's frame is then the frame of this window into the artist's world. One major step toward achieving this end was the discovery of the geometrical laws of perspective that were discovered and codified by the Renaissance artist (Kubovy, 1986). This was supplemented by the systematic use of other pictorial cues for depth such as interposition.

In effect, the Renaissance masters seemed to believe that to catch visual reality one's picture should correspond to the image the model casts on the eye. This motivated their search for means to portray depth on a flat canvas. A similar issue motivated such empiricists as Locke and Berkeley whose concern was with the nature of perception. The empiricists asked how the painters' means of portraying depth—the pictorial cues—could lead to the experience of depth if the image on the eye is two-dimensional.

THE IMPRESSIONISTS: HOW A SCENE IS PERCEIVED

The Renaissance painters tried to represent a scene as it is projected on the eye. Other schools of painting set themselves a different task. Consider the French Impressionists of the late nineteenth century. They tried to recreate certain perceptual experiences that the scene evokes in the observer, the impression it makes rather than the scene itself. One of their concerns was to render color as we see it in broad daylight. Their method was to create a seeming patchwork of different daubs of bright colors (see Figure 6.48). These are clearly separate when looked at directly. But when viewed from the proper distance they change appearance, especially in the periphery where acuity is weak. The individual patches now blur together and their colors mix. But when the eyes move again and bring that area of the picture back into the fovea, the mixtures come apart and the individual patches reappear. Some authors believe that this continual alternation between mixed colors and separate dots gives these paintings their special vitality (Jameson and Hurvich, 1975).

This patchwork technique has a further effect. It enlists the beholder as an active participant in the artistic enterprise. Her active involvement starts as soon as she tries to see the picture as a whole rather than as a meaningless jumble of colored patches. This happens when the separate patches blur: when they are viewed from the periphery or from a few steps back. Now the picture suddenly snaps into focus and a whole emerges. This is both similar to and different from what happens in ordinary life. There we move our eyes to bring some part of the world to a region of greater acuity, the fovea. In the museum, we sometimes move our eyes (or our entire body) to bring a picture to a region of lesser acuity, away from the fovea. In either case, active movement leads to the perception of a figural whole (Hochberg, 1978b, 1980).

THE MODERNS: HOW A SCENE IS CONCEIVED

The impressionists tried to engender some of the perceptual experiences a scene evokes in the observer. Later generations went further and tried to capture not just how the scene is perceived but how it is conceived, how it is

6.49 **Violin and Grapes** *by Pablo Picasso, 1912* (*Courtesy Museum of Modern Art, New York, Mrs. David M. Levy bequest*)

6.50 **The Enigma of a Day** *by Georgio de Chirico, 1914 (Oil on canvas, 6′1¼″ × 55″, The Museum of Modern Art, New York. James Thrall Soby Bequest)*

known as well as seen. Modern art provides many examples, as in Pablo Picasso's still life showing superimposed fragments of a violin (Figure 6.49). Here perception and knowledge are cunningly merged in a sophisticated return to some of the ways of Egyptian artists (Gombrich, 1961).

Some Modern artists are not satisfied by adding conceptual elements to their visual representations. They want to create ambiguity by setting up visual puzzles that can't be solved. One way is to pit knowledge against visual perception, as in Picasso's faces that are seen in profile and front-face at the same time. Another is to build contradictions into the perceptual scene itself. An example is a painting by the turn-of-the-century Italian Giorgio de Chirico (Figure 6.50). One reason for the disturbing quality of his work is the fact that de Chirico often used incompatible perspectives. In his *The Enigma of a Day,* the structure on the left converges to one horizon, the structure on the right to a different horizon, while the crate in the middle does not converge at all. The result is an insoluble visual problem, an eerie world that cannot be put in order.

De Chirico's streets do not look like real streets, and Picasso's violins are a far cry from those one sees in a concert hall. In this regard, these Modern painters appear quite different from many of their predecessors whose representations were closer to the world as it appears to the perceiver. But we have to realize that with few exceptions, no artists, whether Renaissance masters, Impressionists, or Moderns, ever try to fool the observer into thinking that he is looking at a real scene. They neither can nor want to hide the fact that their painting is a painting. It may spring to life for a moment and look like a real person or a real sunset, or it may briefly conjure up a vivid memory of what a face or a violin looks like when viewed from several angles. But whether it emphasizes the seen or the known, it is also recognized as a flat piece of canvas daubed with paint.

According to some authors, this perceptual duality is an important part of the beholder's esthetic experience as he looks at a work of representational art. In a well-known poem by Robert Browning, a duke points to his "last duchess painted on the wall,/Looking as if she were alive." The key words are *as if*. One reason why visual art leads to an esthetic experience may be because it provides us with a halfway mark between seen reality and painted appearance, because it presents a visual *as if* (Hochberg, 1980).

In our discussion of visual art we have taken yet another step across the wide, shadowy region where perception and conception, seeing and knowing merge. In the next chapter we will cross the boundary altogether. There we will consider how we remember objects and events that no longer stimulate our senses.

SUMMARY

1. The fundamental problem of perception is how we come to apprehend the objects and events in the world around us. In the field of visual perception, the major issues concern the way in which we see *depth, movement,* and *form*.

2. The visual world is seen in three dimensions even though only two of these are given in the image that falls upon the eye. This fact has led to an interest in *depth cues*. Among these are *binocular disparity*, monocular cues such as *interposition* and *linear perspective, relative size,* and *texture gradients*. All of these cues are powerful determinants of perceived depth. More important still is the motion of our heads and bodies. This leads to *motion parallax* and various patterns in the *optic flow*, all of which provide vital information about how far objects are from each other and how far they are from ourselves.

3. Many aspects of depth perception are apparently built into the nervous machinery. Evidence comes from the behavior of very young humans or animals, as in reactions to *looming*.

4. Retinal displacement alone cannot explain the perception of movement, as shown by the phenomena of *apparent movement* and *induced movement,* and by the fact that the nervous system compensates for displacements produced by movements of the eye.

5. In vision, our primary means for recognizing an object is through its form, a fact already observed in young children. An important phenomenon in the psychology of form perception is *transposition of form:* A perceived form may remain the same even if all of its constituent parts are altered. This phenomenon is the keystone of *Gestalt psychology,* a theory that emphasizes the importance of wholes created by the relationship between their parts.

6. Many modern investigators believe that form perception is based on several steps of *information processing* that transform the initial visual input into its cognitive end product, the perception of objects in the world. This may begin with the automatic process-

ing of *primitive features*, which can be identified by the fact that they "pop out" in a *visual search task*. At the first stage of processing, these features exist in free-floating isolation as shown by *illusory conjunctions*.

7.   Before the perceiver can recognize a form, he must first engage in a process of *visual segregation* and *parse* the visual scene. This involves the segregation of *figure* and *ground*, which are not inherent in the proximal stimulus but are imposed by the perceptual system, as shown by *reversible figures*. Further segregation produces perceptual *grouping*, which depends upon factors such as *proximity, similarity, good continuation,* and *closure*. Some authors believe that all of these parsing phenomena are manifestations of a *maximum-likelihood principle*—the tendency to interpret a proximal stimulus pattern as that external stimulus object that most probably produced it.

8.   An important approach to *pattern recognition* grew out of efforts of computer scientists to develop machines that could identify visual forms such as letters. Most such attempts start with the view that pattern recognition typically involves two kinds of processes. One is *bottom-up processing,* which starts with the stimulus and "works up" by subjecting it to a feature analysis that begins with lower-level units (such as slanted lines) that then activate higher-level units (such as letters and words). The other is *top-down processing,* which is based on expectations and hypotheses, as shown by perceptual *context effects.* It begins with the activation of higher-level units that then activate lower-level ones.

9.   Most current theorists believe that after the initial steps of feature detection and segregation, the next step in pattern recognition is to match the features of the stimulus to forms stored in memory until a match is found. This generally involves *bidirectional activation* in which both top-down and bottom-up processes are utilized. This first leads to intermediate visual components, the *geons,* which are then mentally assembled to form a structural description of the object.

10.   Top-down processes provide *perceptual hypotheses* that are then tested by bottom-up processes. This kind of *perceptual logic* sometimes fails, as in the case of *impossible figures.*

11.   Perception is selective, for all aspects of a stimulus are not given equal weight. This selection is partially achieved by physical orientation, as in the case of eye movements. It is also achieved by a central process, *selective attention.* Methods for studying attention include *selective looking,* as demonstrated in *visual search procedures,* and *selective listening,* as in *dichotic presentation* in which one message is *shadowed.*

12.   Attempts to resolve the discrepancy between what the proximal stimulus gives us and what we actually see go back to two main approaches, the *empiricist* and the *nativist.* Empiricists explain this discrepancy by referring to *unconscious inference* based on a learned rule (in the case of size constancy, the rule that objects farther away cause smaller retinal sensations). Nativists emphasize *invariant higher-order stimulus relationships* that are directly given (in the case of size constancy, invariant size ratios in the retinal image).

13.   The ultimate function of perceptual organization is to help the organism perceive the outside world as it really is. This is illustrated by the *perceptual constancies* in which the perceiver responds to certain permanent characteristics of the distal object despite various contextual factors—illumination, distance, and orientation—that lead to enormous variations in the proximal stimulus. In *size* and *shape constancy,* the perceiver responds to the actual size and shape of the object more or less regardless of its distance and orientation. In *lightness constancy,* the perceiver responds to the object's reflectance and tends to ignore the level of illumination that falls upon it.

14.   The evidence indicates that lightness constancy is in large part based upon the same built-in processes that yield brightness contrast. The verdict is less clear-cut for size and shape constancy, but if those constancies are based on learning, that learning must occur quite early in life.

SUMMARY

15. The psychology of visual art is a further illustration of the overlap between perception and thinking. The artist represents both what she sees and what she knows. *Renaissance* painters represented scenes seen through a window frame; the *Impressionists* tried to recreate certain perceptual experiences the scene evokes in the beholder; while many Modern artists try to represent the scene as it is conceived and thought about.

CHAPTER 7

MEMORY

STUDYING MEMORY   243

SOME PRELIMINARY DISTINCTIONS ▪ ENCODING, STORAGE, RETRIEVAL

ENCODING   245

THE STAGE THEORY OF MEMORY ▪ A CHANGED EMPHASIS: ACTIVE
MEMORY AND ORGANIZATION

RETRIEVAL   255

THE RELATION BETWEEN ORIGINAL ENCODING AND RETRIEVAL ▪
ELABORATIVE REHEARSAL ▪ MEMORY SEARCH ▪ IMPLICIT RETRIEVAL

WHEN MEMORY FAILS   261

FORGETTING ▪ CONCEPTUAL FRAMEWORKS AND REMEMBERING ▪
DISORDERED MEMORIES ▪ EXPLICIT AND IMPLICIT RETRIEVAL REVISITED

TAKING STOCK   278

SUMMARY   278

Our discussion of visual perception has emphasized the way in which psychological events are organized in space. Locke and Berkeley to the contrary, our perceptual world is not a jumbled mosaic of isolated sensory fragments but an organized, coherent whole in which every piece relates to every other. We now turn to the subject of memory in which organization plays an equally prominent part. Where perception concerns the organization of space, memory—or at least many aspects of memory—concerns the organization of time.

Memory is the way in which we record the past for later use in the present. It is hard to think of humans (or any animal that is able to learn) without this capacity. Without memory, there would be no *then* but only a *now,* no ability to employ skills, no recall of names or recognition of faces, no reference to past days or hours or even seconds. We would be condemned to live in a narrowly circumscribed present, but this present would not even seem to be our own, for there can be no sense of self without memory. Each individual wakes up every morning and never doubts that he is he or she is she. This feeling of personal identity is necessarily based upon a continuity of memories that links our yesterdays to our todays.

STUDYING MEMORY

How do psychologists study memory? The first step is to realize that there is no such thing as one memory system or one set of memory processes. The term *memory* is simply a blanket label for a large number of processes that form bridges between our past and our present. But these processes differ in important ways.

SOME PRELIMINARY DISTINCTIONS

An important first distinction concerns the length of the time interval that is spanned in different tests of memory. Some of these intervals are measured in fractions of a second, others in seconds or minutes, and still others in months and years. Many psychologists believe that these different **retention intervals** are bridged by different memory systems. The major example concerns the distinction between **short-term** and **long-term memory.**

Another distinction concerns our conscious awareness of remembering. We are sometimes aware that we are tapping our memory, but often we are not. Suppose someone asks us what we had for dinner last night. When we answer, we are perfectly aware that we are at least trying to remember (whether we succeed or not is another question). In such cases, we are dealing with **explicit memory.** But we often call upon our memory without being at all aware that we do. For example, when we speak or listen, we understand the words we speak or hear because we have learned their meaning in the past. This means that while speaking or listening we must tap a mental dictionary in our memory system. But we are not conscious of consulting some kind of memory, even though we surely did. In such cases we are dealing with *implicit memory*.

Despite these significant distinctions, there are some general characteristics that pertain to all—or at least to most—kinds of memory. Before focusing on the different types of memory, let us start by examining what the various types of memory have in common.

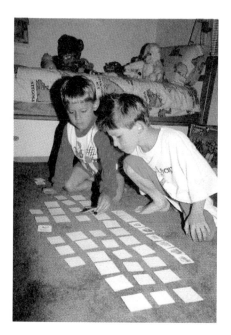

Card games and memory *Many card games make considerable demands on memory. Pictured here are children hard at work "playing" the game of "Memory." (Photograph by Kathy Hirsh-Pasek)*

ENCODING, STORAGE, RETRIEVAL

Any act of remembering implies success at three aspects of the memory process. Consider a person working on a crossword puzzle who is trying to think of an eight-letter word meaning "African anteater." If she comes up with the answer, *aardvark,* we can be sure that she succeeded in three aspects of remembering.

The first aspect of remembering has to do with acquiring the information in the first place. To remember, one must first have learned; the puzzle solver must first have encountered and noted this particular item of zoological exotica. During this acquisition phase, the item must be *encoded.* Taken from computer science, the term *encoding* refers to the form (that is, the code) in which an item of information is to be placed in memory. Our puzzle solver who once learned the word "aardvark" may have encoded it as a certain sound pattern or a particular letter sequence, in terms of its meaning or the context in which she first encountered the word, or all of these at once.

The next aspect of remembering is *storage:* To be remembered the encoded experience must leave some record in the nervous system (the *memory trace*); it must be squirreled away and held in some more or less enduring form for later use (probably in doing the next crossword puzzle).

The final phase is *retrieval,* the point at which one "tries to remember," to dredge up a particular memory trace from among all the others we have stored. There are two major methods to study retrieval. One is *recall* in which the subject is asked to produce an item or a set of items from memory, e.g., coming up with the answer to the question "What is the name of the boy who sat next to you in the third grade?" The experimental psychologist often tests for the recall of materials learned in the laboratory to assure that any failures aren't simply failures of original acquisition. The second method is *recognition:* A person is shown an item and has to indicate whether she has encountered it before, e.g., being able to answer the question "Is this one of the girls who played on your high-school field hockey team?" In the laboratory, the subject is usually asked to pick out the previously learned item from among several false alternatives. In multiple-choice or true-false tests a greater premium is obviously put on recognition, whereas essay or short-answer examinations emphasize recall.

Failures to remember can result from mishaps during any of the three phases of the memory process—encoding, storage, or retrieval. For example, if at the first encounter with *aardvark,* the learner encoded the term only as a sound pattern, there would be no memory trace of its meaning so that the puzzle item couldn't be solved. If both the sound and meaning were encoded and held for the length of the retention interval, the item might have been misfiled in memory—stored, say, with Asian carnivores rather than with African anteaters. If so, the item might be impossible to retrieve even though it is still stored in memory. That many of our failures to remember are failures of retrieval and not of storage often becomes clear at some later time. Our crossword expert might be unable to come up with the correct answer at the time, but when she later sees the solution, she realizes that she'd known it all along: "Of course. It's aardvark!"

Encoding, storage, and retrieval are the three aspects of the memory process. Encoding and retrieval represent the start and the end of this process, and are the two aspects that can be studied more or less directly and that we will focus upon in this chapter. (For some discussion of storage, see pp. 246, 265–67, 274–77).

ENCODING

In our discussion of how memories are encoded, we'll start out by considering an important theory of memory, which we will here call the *stage theory.* As we'll see, this theory has been in some ways superseded, but its formulations still provide the framework for much of our current thinking about the topic.

THE STAGE THEORY OF MEMORY

Memory has often been compared to a storehouse. This conception goes back to the Greek philosophers and to St. Augustine who described the "roomy chambers of memory, where are the treasures of countless images. . . ." This spatial metaphor, which likens memories to objects that are put into storage compartments, held for a while, and then searched for is a recurrent theme in both ancient and modern thought (Crowder, 1985a; Roediger, 1980).

The *stage theory of memory,* developed some twenty years ago, represents a modern variation on this same spatial metaphor but casts it within the framework of an information-processing approach. Unlike Augustine, who believed that there is one memory warehouse, this theory asserts that there are several such storage systems, each with different properties (Broadbent, 1958; Waugh and Norman, 1965; Atkinson and Shiffrin, 1968).

The belief that there are several memory stores comes from the fact that memory may reach back for years but may also concern events that occurred just moments ago. We usually think of memory in terms of a past that is reckoned in hours, days, or years. But a moment's reflection tells us that memory comes into play as soon as the stimulus has disappeared from the scene. An example is a telephone number we look up and retain just long enough to complete the dialing; here the interval between acquisition and retrieval is a matter of mere seconds, but it is a memory all the same.

These simple facts provide the starting points for the stage theory of memory. One of its assertions is that there are several memory systems. Of these, the most important are *short-term memory,* which holds information for fairly short intervals, and *long-term memory* in which materials are stored for much longer periods, sometimes as long as a lifetime.★

★ The original theory asserted that an additional stage—a *sensory register* in which sensory material is held for a second or two—precedes the others (Sperling, 1960; Atkinson and Shiffrin, 1968), but some later critics have challenged this assumption (e.g., Haber, 1983).

Overloading capacity   *The limited cognitive capacity of the working memory system has its physical analogue in the demands sometimes made upon us in modern technological society as caricatured in this scene from Charlie Chaplin's 1936 film,* Modern Times. *(Courtesy the Kobal Collection)*

THE STORAGE CAPACITY OF SHORT- AND LONG-TERM MEMORY

There is reason to believe that memories for relatively recent events differ in important ways from memories for events that are more remote in time. One difference concerns the *storage capacity* of the two postulated memory systems. The storage capacity of short-term memory is markedly different from that of long-term memory. The capacity of long-term memory is enormous: The size of an average college student's reading vocabulary (about 80,000 words) is documentation enough. In contrast, the capacity of short-term memory is exceedingly limited.

One way to determine the capacity of short-term memory is by measuring the *memory span,* the number of items an individual can recall after just one presentation. For normal adults, this span is remarkably consistent. If the items are randomly chosen letters or digits, the subject can recall about seven items, give or take about two. This quantity, seven plus or minus two, has been called the *magic number,* a widely quoted term originated by George Miller (Miller, 1956). According to Miller, this number represents the holding capacity of the short-term memory system, the number of items that will fit into its store at any one time. There is some debate about whether this number, seven plus or minus two, is really an accurate description of short-term capacity, but all investigators are agreed that the capacity of short-term memory is very small indeed.

SHORT-TERM MEMORY AS A LOADING PLATFORM

What is the relation between short-term and long-term memory? The stage theory of memory asserts that the road into long-term memory necessarily passes through the short-term store. Seen in this light, short-term memory can be regarded as a loading platform into the huge long-term warehouse. A parcel that stays on the platform long enough may be picked up and placed in the warehouse, but the vast majority of the parcels never make it.

Forgetting recent memories   Material in short-term memory is very short-lived. While reading the morning newspaper, we briefly note all kinds of extraneous matter: The coffee tastes bitter, a child is crying next door, there is a printer's error on the editorial page. But only a few moments thereafter these experiences are as if they had never been. One reason may be *decay:* The memory trace becomes eroded over time by some unknown physiological process, so its details become progressively less distinct (see p. 262). Another possibility is *displacement:* Items are somehow pushed out of memory by other items that enter later. The best evidence to date suggests that both factors play a role, that some packages on the platform rot away (decay), while others are shoved off by other packages (displacement). In either case, it is clear that they are generally not allowed to remain on the platform very long.

This rapid forgetting from short-term memory may be a blessing in disguise, for without it, our memory systems would be clogged with the clutter of useless information. Switchboard operators would be in poor shape if they were unable to forget a number immediately after they dialed it. Given its limited capacity, the loading platform has to be cleared very quickly to make room for new packages as they arrive (Bjork, 1970).

Transfer into long-term memory   According to stage theory, some items on the platform are moved into the long-term store by an essentially mechanical transfer process. As we've seen, most packages disappear before this transfer can

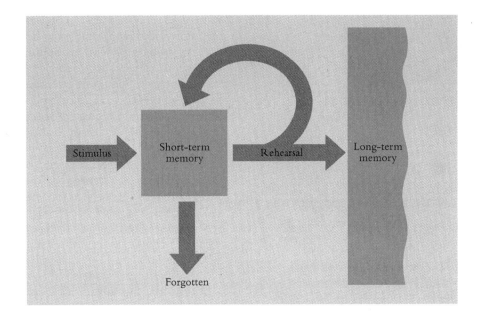

7.1 The relation between the short-term and long-term memory system as envisaged by stage theory *The figure is a schematic representation of the relation between the two memory systems as stage theorists conceive of them. Information is encoded and enters the short-term store. To enter the long-term store, it must remain in short-term memory for a while. The means for maintaining it there is rehearsal. (Adapted from Waugh and Norman, 1965)*

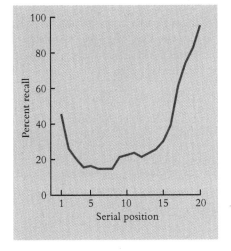

7.2 Primacy and recency effects in free recall *Subjects heard a list of twenty common words presented at a rate of one word per second. Immediately after hearing the list, the subjects were asked to write down as many of the words on the list as they could recall. The results show that the words at the beginning (primacy effect) and at the end (recency effect) were recalled more frequently than those in the middle. (After Murdock, 1962)*

happen, but a few do remain on the platform for a while and thus become candidates for memorial tenure. Stage theorists believe that one reason why they remain long enough to be transferred is *rehearsal.* By repeating an item over and over again, a subject will hold it in short-term memory, which increases the probability that this item will be transferred into the long-term store (see Figure 7.1).

These hypotheses about the relations between short- and long-term memory systems fit rather well with some facts obtained by the method of *free recall.* The subject hears a list of unrelated items, such as common English words, presented one at a time and is asked to recall them in any order that she wants to. If the items are presented only once, and if their number exceeds the memory span, the subject cannot possibly produce them all. Under these circumstances, the likelihood that any one item will be recalled depends upon where in the list it was originally presented. Items that were presented at the beginning or the end of the list are much more likely to be recalled than those that were in the middle. The *primacy effect* denotes the enhanced recall of items at the beginning; the *recency effect* designates the greater recall for those at the end (see Figure 7.2).

Stage theorists believed that the recency effect is produced because items that were presented at the end of the list are retrieved from short-term memory. These items are generally reported easily. They are still clear in memory because they were presented just a few seconds ago and no further items arrived to displace them. This allows the subject to recite these items quickly, before they disappear from the short-term store. According to stage theory, the recency effect simply reflects the fact that three or four items are still in the short-term store when the subject begins to recall and that these items are the first he reports.★

According to stage theory, the items at the beginning of the list are presumably retrieved from long-term memory. One reason for this interpretation of the primacy effect is that the early items have had more opportunity for rehearsal and thus for transfer into the long-term store. For example, if the first three items are *camera, boat,* and *zebra,* the subject could give his full attention to rehearsing *camera* after hearing it, silently repeating "camera, camera,

★ Some authors use the recency effect to estimate the capacity of the short-term store. If assessed in this manner, its capacity is about three items (Crowder, 1976).

7.3 The recency effect and short-term storage *Subjects heard several fifteen-word lists. In one condition (dark red), free recall was tested immediately after they heard the list. In the other condition (blue), the recall test was given after a thirty-second delay during which rehearsal was prevented. The long delay left the primacy effect unaffected but abolished the recency effect, indicating that this effect is based on retrieval from short-term storage. (After Glanzer and Cunitz, 1966)*

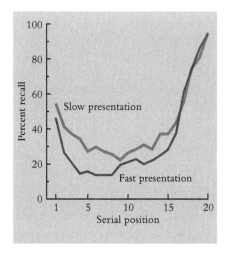

7.4 The primacy effect and long-term storage *The figure compares free-recall performance when item presentation is relatively slow (two seconds per item) and fast (one second per item). Slow presentation enhances the primacy effect but leaves the recency effect unaltered. The additional second per item presumably allows more time for rehearsal, which leads to long-term storage. (After Murdock, 1962)*

camera. . . ." When the second word arrives, he'll rehearse that too, but his attention will now be divided in half ("camera, boat, camera, boat, . . ."). He'll have to divide his attention still further after hearing the third word ("camera, boat, zebra, camera, boat, zebra . . ."), and so through the list. The result is that the earlier words get more attention than the later ones. The more attention a word gets, the more likely that word will make it to the long-term warehouse. Since the attention is greater for the words at the beginning than for those that come later on, those first words have an advantage.

Supporting evidence for these interpretations comes from various manipulations that affect the primacy and recency effects. One important factor is the interval between the last item on the list and the signal to recall. If this interval is increased to thirty seconds (during which the subjects perform some mental tasks such as counting backwards so they can't rehearse), the primacy effect remains unchanged but the recency effect is completely abolished. This is just what one would expect if the last items are stored in short-term memory from which forgetting is very rapid (see Figure 7.3). Other procedures diminish the primacy effect. An example is the rate at which items are presented. If this rate is relatively fast, the subject has less time for rehearsal. As a result, there is less transfer to long-term storage. We would therefore expect a reduced primacy effect but no particular change in the recency effect, and this is again what happens (see Figure 7.4).

OVERCOMING THE SHORT-TERM BOTTLENECK

Stage theory asserts that in order to enter long-term storage, items must first pass through short-term memory. But as we have seen, the short-term loading platform has a limited capacity. It can handle only a small number of packages at any one time. In view of this bottleneck, how do we manage to deposit so much material in the long-term store? Stage theory's answer is *organization*. The capacity limit of the loading platform is on the number of packages, which is exceedingly small (perhaps 7 ± 2). But what these packages contain is up to us. If we can pack the input more efficiently, we may squeeze more information into the same number of memory units.

Recoding into larger chunks As an example, consider a subject who tries to recall a series of digits that she heard only once:

$$149162536496481$$

If she treats this as a series of fifteen unrelated digits, she will almost surely fail. But if she recognizes that the digits form a pattern, specifically

$$1 \ 4 \ 9 \ 16 \ 25 \ 36 \ 49 \ 64 \ 81$$

her task becomes absurdly easy. She only has to remember the underlying relationship "the squares of the digits from 1 to 9," and the fifteen components of the series are easily recreated.

A similar example is the letter series

$$CIAFBIIBMTWA$$

This is again quite difficult if interpreted as a series of twelve unrelated letters. But if it is reorganized by three-letter groupings, specifically

$$CIA \ FBI \ IBM \ TWA$$

the recall task is again perfectly trivial.

The role of chunking in remembering a visual display   Could you possibly remember all the figures in this bewildering array? You might, if you knew Netherlandish proverbs of the sixteenth century, for that is what the painting depicts. To mention only some, there is (going from left to right): a man who "butts his head against the wall," another who is "armed to the teeth" and "ties a bell to the cat," and two women of whom "one spins while the other winds" (malicious gossips). Going further left, we see a woman who "puts a blue cloak over her husband" (deceives him), a man who "fills the hole after his calf was drowned," and another who "throws roses [we say pearls] before swine." Recognizing these scenes as illustrations of familiar proverbs will organize the visual array and thus help you to remember its many parts. (Detail of Netherlandish Proverbs by Pieter Brueghel, 1559; courtesy Gemäldegalerie, Staatliche Museen Preussischer Kulturbesitz, Berlin)

In both of these examples, the subject repackages the material to be remembered, **recoding** the input into larger units that are often called **chunks.** Each chunk imposes about the same load on memory as did each of the smaller units that are contained within it. But when eventually unpacked, each of these chunks yields much more information.

Much of the job of recoding items into larger chunks (or *chunking*) occurred in our early life. To an adult, a word is already a coherent whole, not merely a sequence of sounds. Still higher units of memorial organization are involved in the memory for sentences. The memory span for unrelated words is about six or seven items, but we may well recall a fairly long sentence after only a single exposure. This fact even holds for sentences that make little sense, such as *The enemy submarine dove into the coffee pot, took fright, and silently flew away.* This dubious bit of naval intelligence consists of fourteen words, but it clearly contains fewer than fourteen memorial packages: *The enemy submarine* is essentially one unit, *took fright* is another, and so on.

A CHANGED EMPHASIS: ACTIVE MEMORY AND ORGANIZATION

The stage theory of memory largely dominated the field for several decades. But as time went on, there was a reevaluation. An important challenge to stage theory came from some findings on the effect of rehearsal. Stage theory asserts that when an item is rehearsed, it is more likely to enter long-term memory. According to the stage theory, this transfer from the short-term loading platform to the long-term warehouse depends largely on how long that item has been on the platform. The longer it sits there, the greater will be its probability of being transferred. According to this view, rehearsal helps because it keeps the item in the short-term store for a longer period and keeps it from rotting away or being displaced before that transfer can happen. But there is evidence that entering long-term memory is by no means as automatic as this.

SHORT-TERM MEMORY AS AN ACTIVE PROCESS

It turns out that one form of rehearsal does relatively little in the long run. This is called **maintenance rehearsal** through which the subject mentally holds on to the material for a little while but does nothing more. We use this form of rehearsal when we try to retain a telephone number just long enough to complete the call. We repeat the number to ourselves until we begin dialing but then we promptly forget it. Experimental evidence on the effect of maintenance rehearsal comes from an ingenious study that varied the time in which items remained in short-term memory. The subjects listened to a number of lists of words, and they were asked to monitor each list for words beginning with a certain letter. The lists varied in length. At the end of each list, the subjects had to report the last word on the list that began with a particular letter. Suppose the letter was *G* and that the list was as follows:

> *Daughter,   Oil,   Garden,   Grain,   Table,*
> *Football,   Anchor,   Giraffe,   Pillow,   Thunder.*

In this situation, the subject has to hold one *G*-word in short-term memory until the next one appears. Thus *Garden* will be replaced by *Grain*, which will make way for *Giraffe* and so on until the end of the list is reached at which time the subject has to come up with the last *G*-word—in the present case, *Giraffe*. This arrangement guarantees that some of the *G*-words are held longer in short-term memory than others are; thus *Grain* will stay longer than *Garden*. The question was whether this increased stay in the short-term store increased the chance that *Garden* would be transferred to long-term memory. To find out, the experimenters gave a final—and quite unexpected—test after the end of the session during which many such lists had been presented. They simply asked the subjects to report as many of the *G*-words they had heard as they could. The results showed that the time an item had been in short-term memory had no effect—*Garden* was recalled just as often as was *Grain* (Craik and Watkins, 1973). It appears that maintenance rehearsal confers little or no benefit in aiding recall.

Active memory at work   *Cardplayers have to call on active memory to decide which cards were played most recently and which should be played next. (*The Cardplayers, *by Paul Cezanne; courtesy The Metropolitan Museum of Art, Bequest of Stephen C. Clark, 1960)*

WORKING MEMORY

The preceding discussion highlighted one of the problems of the stage theory of memory: Since maintenance rehearsal confers little or no benefit in aiding recall, the transfer from short- to long-term memory cannot be automatic. These and certain other phenomena we'll consider later led to a theoretical reorientation in the way psychologists think of memory processes. One change concerns the conception of short-term memory. Another is an emphasis on the role of processing and organization.

As we saw, stage theorists conceived of short- and long-term memory as depots in a traffic flow in which information was moved from a small short-term loading platform to the more spacious long-term store. Today, however, most theorists believe that long-term memories are formed by a more active process in which the subject's own ways of encoding and organizing the material play a major role. As a result, they regard short-term memory not so much as a temporary storage platform but rather as a mental workbench on which various items of experience are encoded—sorted, manipulated, and organized. According to this view, whether the materials will be retained in memory long enough to become retrievable later does not depend upon a simple transfer from one storage container to another. Instead, it depends on how this material is processed (that is, encoded and recoded). The more elaborate the processing, the greater the likelihood of later recall and recognition.

Considerations of this sort led many psychologists to abandon the concept of short-term memory as a mere storage depot (Crowder, 1982). It also led many of them to prefer the term *working memory* to the older designation short-term memory. The newer term focuses on the way in which memories are processed rather than on the hypothetical structures in which these memories are held. Seen in this light, the key difference is between those portions of our memory system that are currently activated (and acted upon)—that is, working memory—and those that are currently dormant—that is, long-term memory. This new conception can easily account for the findings that first led to the belief in a short-term memory store with a limited storage capacity. As modern investigators think about it, what's limited is not the storage area but rather the amount of processing that can be accomplished. There is only so much cognitive processing (or mental effort) the system can engage in at any time. This may concern something we want to remember, if only for a moment, like a telephone number before it is dialed. Or it may be some mental task such as multiplying two-digit numbers in our heads, where we have to keep track of the numbers, the partial products, and the point we're at in the problem.

If this is correct, the appropriate metaphor for a limited capacity of the working memory system is not really a loading platform that can hold only so many parcels. It is rather an overworked operative at the memory workbench who can only pack so many parcels—can only do so much chunking and organizing and linking materials to prior memories—at any one time. It's as if he (or she, or it) has only so many mental hands (Baddeley, 1976, 1986).

PROCESSING AND ORGANIZING: THE ROYAL ROAD INTO MEMORY

Our previous discussion has already pointed to the importance of how the subject encodes the incoming material for later recall. Certain ways of encoding (such as those produced by chunking) evidently promote better recall; others (such as those produced by maintenance rehearsal) are of much less help. What is it that the more helpful forms of encoding have in common?

Depth of processing An influential attempt to explain why some encodings help recall more than others argued that success in remembering depends on the depth at which the incoming information has been processed (Craik and Lockhart, 1972). The advocates of this ***depth-of-processing approach*** have performed many experiments that compare the effect of "shallow" and "deep" processing on later recall. For verbal materials, the term *shallow* is generally used for encoding of superficial characteristics such as the way a word sounds or the typeface in which it is printed, while *deep* refers to its meaning. In one such study, subjects were briefly shown forty-eight words as part of an experiment that they were told was concerned with perception and speed of reaction. As each word was presented, the subject was asked one of three possible questions. One had to do with the word's physical appearance ("Is it printed in capital letters?"), another concerned the word's sound ("Does it rhyme with train?"), while a third concerned the word's meaning ("Would it fit into the sentence: The girl placed the_____on the table?"). The first question would presumably lead to the shallowest encoding, the third to the deepest. After the subjects had gone through the entire list of forty-eight words, they were given an unexpected task: They were asked to write down as many of the words they had seen as they could remember. The results were in line with the depth-of-processing hypothesis. Words that called for the shallowest processing (typeface) were recalled worst of all; words that required an intermediary level (sound) were recalled a bit better; and words that demanded the deepest level (meaning) were recalled best of all (Craik and Tulving, 1975).

Some of the original formulations of the depth-of-processing hypothesis have come under attack. For example, some critics charged that there is really no satisfactory definition of depth (Baddeley, 1978). But even so, one of the major assertions of this approach remains a useful rule of thumb: The more attention we pay to the meaning of what we hear and see and read, the better we will remember it.

Organization The depth-of processing hypothesis emphasized the importance of meaning. A related view stresses *organization*. We already encountered the importance of organization when we took up chunking. Further evidence comes from a number of other findings that elaborate on the nature of chunking and of the organizational process.

Chunks—like the first nine squares, well-known acronyms such as FBI, and common English words—are taken from the subject's prior experience; all she has to do is to recognize them. But in many cases, the would-be memorizer will not be lucky enough to have all the material neatly prechunked; she has to perform some of the chunking herself if she wants to remember successfully.

Dramatic proof of the power of recoding came from a study in which a heroic subject devoted some 230 hours to the task of becoming a virtuoso at recalling strings of digits. In each session he heard random digits presented at a rate of one per second and then tried to recall the sequence. If his recall was correct, the sequence was increased by one digit; if it was incorrect, it was decreased by one digit. After more than twenty months of this, the subject's digit span had risen enormously: from an initial starting point of seven to a final level of almost eighty (Figure 7.5). What happened was that the subject had learned to recode the digit sequences into meaningful subparts, thus creating larger chunks. He was a long-distance runner who competed in major athletic events. This led him to express three- and four-digit groups as running times for various races (e.g., 3492 became "3 minutes 49 point 2 seconds, near world-record time"), a device supplemented with ages (893 became "89 point 3, very old man") and dates (1944 was "near end of World War II"). These recoded strings of digits became chunked groups in memory. This was neatly shown by the subject's

7.5 Chunking makes perfect *The figure shows an enormous increase in memory span after twenty months of practice during which the subject learned to code digit sequences into meaningful subparts. (After Ericsson, Chase, and Faloon, 1980)*

pause as he produced the digits in recall—virtually all of his pauses fell between the groups rather than within them (Ericsson, Chase, and Faloon, 1980).

Chunking is a way to relate incoming items to each other so that they can be more readily recalled. But these relationships will often go unrecognized unless we can relate the materials to what we already know. This organization may help us to understand what we hear or see, with powerful effects on later recall. An example is an experiment in which two groups of subjects were presented with a tape-recorded passage and were asked to try to understand and remember it. The passage was as follows:

> The procedure is actually quite simple. First you arrange things into different groups depending on their makeup. Of course, one pile may be sufficient depending on how much there is to do. If you have to go somewhere else due to lack of facilities that is the next step; otherwise you are pretty well set. It is important not to overdo any particular endeavor. That is, it is better to do too few things at once than too many. In the short run this may not seem important, but complications from doing too many can easily arise. A mistake can be expensive as well. The manipulation of the appropriate mechanisms should be self-explanatory, and we need not dwell on it here. At first, the whole procedure will seem complicated. Soon, however, it will become just another facet of life. It is difficult to foresee any end to the necessity for this task in the immediate future, but then one never can tell. (From Bransford and Johnson, 1972, p. 722)

Both groups of subjects heard the identical passage and were treated identically in all regards but one. One group heard the passage without any further information as to what it was about. The other group was told: "The paragraph you will hear will be about washing clothes." Not surprisingly, the two groups performed very differently on both tests of comprehension and of general recall (total number of ideas in the paragraph). Once they knew the sentences were about doing the laundry, the sentences in the paragraph could be related to what the subjects already knew. This meaningful encoding helped later recall (Bransford and Johnson, 1972).

MNEMONICS

The general principles of memorial organization we have just discussed also underlie a very practical endeavor whose roots go back to ancient times—the development of techniques for improving one's memory, often called *mnemonics.*

Mnemonics through verbal organization The ancients were well aware that it is much easier to remember verbal material if it is organized. They were particularly partial to the use of verse, or organization of word sequences that maintains a fixed rhythm and rhyme. Without such aids, preliterate societies might never have transmitted their oral traditions intact from one generation to the next. Homeric bards could recite the entire *Iliad,* but could they have done so had it been in prose? Verse is still used as a mnemonic when it seems necessary to impose some sort of order upon an otherwise arbitrary set of items ("Thirty days hath September, / April, June, and November").

Mnemonics through visual imagery Some of the most effective mnemonics ever devised involve the deliberate use of mental imagery. One such technique is the **method of loci,** which requires the learner to visualize each of the items she wants to remember in a different spatial location (locus). In recall, each location is mentally inspected and the item that was placed there in imagination is thus retrieved. This method provides a scheme that allows orderly retrieval. It requires a deliberate effort to relate the items that must be memorized to distinctive features of the retrieval scheme and to do so through visual imagery. The efficacy of this mnemonic system has been tested by several experimental studies. Subjects who recalled by the method of loci recalled up to seven times more than their counterparts who learned in a rote manner. In one such study, college students had to learn lists of forty unrelated concrete nouns. Each list was presented once for about ten minutes, during which the subjects tried to visualize each of the forty objects in one of forty different locations around the college campus. Tested immediately, they recalled an average of thirty-eight of the forty items; tested one day later, they still managed to recall thirty-four (Ross and Lawrence, 1968).

Why does imagery help?   Why are images such a powerful aid to memory? One of the reasons may be that they are yet another way of forming a new chunk in memory. By creating a mental image, the subject joins two unrelated items so that they form a new whole. When part of the chunk (the imagined locus) is presented, the entire chunk is retrieved, yielding the part required for recall.

Some evidence for this view comes from studies that show that mental images will only facilitate recall if they tend to unify the items to be associated into a coherent whole. Consider a subject who has to learn a list of noun-noun pairs such as eagle-locomotive and is instructed to use imagery as an aid to memory. She can construct mental pictures that bring the items into some kind of unitary relationship, for example, an eagle winging to his nest with a locomotive in his beak. But she may form an image whose constituents are merely adjacent and do not interact, such as an eagle at the side of a locomotive. Several recent experiments demonstrate that unifying mental images produce much better recall than nonunifying images (Wollen, Weber, and Lowry, 1972). A similar effect is found when the test items are real pictures. If shown a drawing of a doll standing on a chair waving a flag, subjects quickly reply "chair and flag" when asked to recall the objects that were pictured with the doll. Their recall score is substantially lower if they were shown a picture of the doll, chair, and flag, drawn as separate, unrelated objects (Figure 7.6).

The usefulness of mnemonics in everyday life   Mnemonic systems provide effective means for imposing organization upon otherwise disparate materials, such as a foreign vocabulary list or nonsense materials developed in the psychological laboratory. But we are not often confronted by such arbitrary pairings. A student

7.6   Interactive and noninteractive depictions   *Subjects shown related elements, such as a doll sitting on a chair and waving a flag (A), are more likely to associate the words* doll, flag, *and* chair *than subjects who are shown the three objects next to each other but not interacting (B). (After Bower, 1970a)*

reading a history text does not have to impose an organization. His job is to discover the organization that is already inherent in the material. When he does so, the various treaties and battles will fall into an appropriate mental scheme, linked to each other and to relevant historical matters that have been learned before. But imagery mnemonics will not help to provide this scheme. A visual image that links, say, General Custer and Chief Sitting Bull will be of little use in helping the student understand the conflict between the American Indians and the encroaching settlers.

In short, the best prescription for recall is to organize and understand the material at the time it is learned. If this material is devoid of inherent organization, some organization must be imposed upon it. In that case, mnemonic devices, especially imagery, are a useful tool. If the material is already organized, the best approach is to discover that organization and to chunk the various items in terms of it.

RETRIEVAL

That memory storage is not the same as memory retrieval is obvious to anyone who has ever blocked on a familiar name. We may know (that is, have stored) a name, a fact, an event, or whatever and still be unable to retrieve it on a particular occasion. In such cases, the memory trace is said to be inaccessible. Access to the trace may be restored by an appropriate *retrieval cue,* a stimulus that opens the path to the memory. This point has often been demonstrated experimentally. Subjects are presented with a long list of words that belong to various categories and are then tested for free recall. Suppose they don't recall a single word from a particular rubric. If now prompted by the category name, they readily produce several of the appropriate items (Tulving and Pearlstone, 1966).

The phenomenon of retrieving a memory that at first seemed altogether lost is well-known. The very words in which we describe our memorial functions testify to the distinction between storage and retrieval: We are reminded, we remember, we recollect—our very vocabulary suggests that what is now brought up was not available before. The recollection of temporarily inaccessible memories by appropriate retrieval cues is usually a rather humdrum event. We can't recall where we parked on a shopping trip, are reminded that our first stop was in a drugstore, and suddenly remember squeezing the car into a narrow space just across the street. But occasionally the effect is much more dramatic. Some persons reported having been unable to recall some of the simplest geographical features of the hometown they left years before. They finally returned for a visit, barely reached the outskirts, and suddenly all of the memories flooded back, often with a sharp pang of emotions that had been felt years before. Physical places are only one source of retrieval cues that may bring back the past. A word, a mood, a smell, a visit from a school friend not met for decades—any of these may trigger memories we thought were utterly lost.

Retrieval cues in the movies *A scene from Charlie Chaplin's 1931 film,* City Lights, *which shows the little tramp with a millionaire, played by Harry Myers, who befriends him one night while drunk, doesn't recognize him the next morning when he is sober, but greets him as an old friend when he gets drunk again the following night. While nowhere as extreme as this, such state-dependent memory effects have been observed in the laboratory. (Eich, 1980; courtesy Photofest)*

THE RELATION BETWEEN ORIGINAL ENCODING AND RETRIEVAL

What are the characteristics of an effective retrieval cue? It is obvious that not every reminder will in fact remind us, will in fact help us retrieve what is stored. The best guess is that success is most likely if the context at the

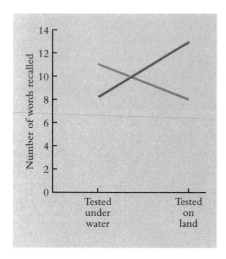

7.7 The effect of changing the retrieval situation *Scuba divers learned a list of 36 unrelated words above water (dark red) or 20 feet underwater (blue) and were then tested above or underwater. The figure shows that retention was better when the retrieval situation was the same as that in which encoding took place. (Godden and Baddeley, 1975)*

time of retrieval approximates that during original encoding. This is sometimes called the ***compatibility principle*** (or the ***encoding-specificity principle;*** Tulving and Osler, 1968; Tulving and Thomson, 1973; Hintzman, 1990).

A rather dramatic illustration of the compatibility principle is provided by a study of scuba divers who had to learn a list of unrelated words either on a boat or underwater and who were later tested for recall in either the same or the alternate environment in which they had learned. The results showed a clear-cut context effect: What was learned in the water was best recalled in the water, likewise for what was learned on deck (Godden and Baddeley, 1975; see Figure 7.7).

Similar effects can be obtained without going underwater. One experimenter presented subjects with a long list of words. A day later he brought them back for an unexpected recall test that took place in either the same room or in a different one, one that varied in size, furnishings, and so on. Recall was considerably better for subjects who were tested in the same physical environment. But the investigator found a simple way of overcoming this context effect. A different group of subjects was brought to the new room, but just prior to the recall test these subjects were asked to think about the room in which they had learned the lists—what is looked like, what it made them feel like. By doing so, they mentally recreated the old environment for themselves. On the subsequent recall test, these subjects performed no worse than those for whom there was no change of rooms. It appears that what matters is not so much that the retrieval cues physically match the conditions of acquisition; what counts is how the subject thinks about these conditions at the time he tries to recall (Smith, 1979).

ELABORATIVE REHEARSAL

The role of retrieval cues may help to explain why some ways of encoding are so much better than others for later recall. We've seen that organization helps, that chunking (which is a close relative of organization) helps, that deeper processing helps. But why? One might think that these superior ways of encoding allow us to store the material more efficiently. Perhaps they do. But they have an even more important effect—they make material easier to find when we later try to retrieve it. The key to good encoding is to provide means for later retrieval.

Evidence comes from a comparison of two forms of rehearsal. As we've previously seen, maintenance rehearsal, in which material is passively held in short-term memory, is of little help in recall. But there is another kind of rehearsal that has a powerful effect. That is ***elaborative rehearsal:*** the mental activities by means of which the subject organizes the items he wants to remember. He may organize them, recode them into fewer chunks, or relate them to each other and to other material in long-term memory—all of these are ways that help him store the material more efficiently. But this kind of rehearsal has another and even more important function: It increases the likelihood of later retrieval. If the subject is asked to recall, say, a list of words, then any one of these words that comes to mind will help him to retrieve more of the others. In addition, whatever else he saw and thought about at the time of rehearsal will also be connected to some of the items and may later serve as a retrieval cue. In the ancient world, all roads led to Rome and so the traveler could always find it. Much the same holds true for elaborative rehearsal. Every elaboration builds another path by which the material can later be reached; the more such paths that exist, the easier retrieval will be (Craik and Tulving, 1975).

A demonstration of the effect of elaborative rehearsal was provided by a study in which the degree of elaboration was varied. Subjects were presented with sentences in which one word was missing. Some of these were rather simple, such as: "He cooked the____." Others were more complex, such as: "The great bird swooped down and carried off the struggling____." The subjects' task was to decide whether a given target word (for example, *chicken*) could appropriately fit into the sentence frame. After sixty such trials, the subjects were (unexpectedly) asked to recall as many of the target words as they could. In line with the elaborative rehearsal hypothesis, the more complex sentence frames led to better recall. The richer encoding contexts presumably built more and better retrieval paths (Craik and Tulving, 1975).

We can now see just why understanding and comprehending material is so important for memorizing: Comprehension permits a kind of elaborative rehearsal that provides a much denser network of retrieval paths than any other mnemonic scheme.

MEMORY SEARCH

Many investigators believe that retrieval is generally preceded by an internal process call **memory search.** In most cases, this process occurs without our awareness and at great speed, as when answering the question: "Which president of the United States had the first name *Abraham?*" But there are times when we do become aware that some such process is going on, as we consciously sift and sort among our memories until we finally recall just who it was that did what to whom on which occasion many years ago.

SEARCH STRATEGIES

In a recent study of such conscious search processes, subjects were asked to try to recall the names of their high-school classmates after intervals of from four to nineteen years. Their recall accuracy was checked by consulting their high-school yearbooks. The subjects came up with a fair number of names in the first few minutes of this attempt. After this, they said that they couldn't remember any more. But the experimenters asked them to keep on trying anyway. And so they did, for ten sessions of one hour each. As they continued their efforts, they surprised themselves by dredging up more and more names, until they finally recalled about a third of the names of a class of three hundred (Williams and Hollan, 1982).

While going about this task, the subjects were asked to think aloud. Their comments fit the analogy of a physical search. They seemed to hunt for the sought-for names as one might search for a tangible object, inspecting one likely memory location after another. Their efforts were rarely haphazard, but seemed often based on well-formulated search strategies. For example, they mentally looked through their various classes, clubs, and teams, or scanned internal pictures to locate yet another person whom they would then try to name:

. . . It's like I want to think of, sort of prototypical situations and then sort of examine the people that were involved in those. And things like P.E. class, where there

External aids to memory   *People often rely on external memory aids. Some remind us of events in our past, such as family albums and high-school yearbooks. Others remind us of plans for future actions, such as calendars, memo pads, and shopping lists. (Brockton High-School yearbook, class of 1975, p. 108)* was . . . Ah . . . Gary Booth. Umm, and Karl Brist . . . Umm . . . I can think of things like dances. I guess then I usually think of . . . of girls . . . Like Cindy Shup, Judy Foss, and Sharon Ellis . . . I mean it's sort of like I have a picture of the high school dance. . . . (Williams and Hollan, 1982, p. 90)

THE TIP-OF-THE-TONGUE PHENOMENON

Needless to say, search isn't always successful. Some forgotten names are never retrieved, no matter how hard we try. But occasionally, we experience a kind of halfway point, when we seem about to recall something but don't quite. When this occurs, we feel as if the searched-for memory is on "the tip of the tongue," but we are unable to go beyond. There is no better description of this phenomenon than that by William James:

Suppose we try to recall a forgotten name. The state of our consciousness is peculiar. There is a gap therein; but no mere gap. It is a gap that is intensely active. A sort of wraith of the name is in it, beckoning us in a given direction, making us at moments tingle with the sense of our closeness, and then letting us sink back without the longed-for term. If wrong names are proposed to us, this singularly definite gap acts immediately so as to negate them. They do not fit into its mold. And the gap of one word does not feel like the gap of another, all empty of content as both might seem necessarily to be when described as gaps. (James, 1890, vol. 1, p. 251)

There is evidence that the tip-of-the-tongue experience described by James is a good reflection of how close to the mark we had actually come in our memory search, that we were really "getting warm," though unable to reach the exact spot. In one study college students were presented with the dictionary definitions of uncommon English words such as *apse, sampan,* and *cloaca.* The subjects were asked to supply the words that fit these definitions. The experimenters were concerned with those occasions on which subjects were unable to recall the target word but felt that they were on the verge of finding it (see Figure 7.8). Whenever this happened, they were asked to venture some guesses about what the target word sounded like. These guesses turned out to be closely related to

7.8   The tip-of-the-tongue phenomenon
This figure may provide an opportunity to demonstrate how something can be close to being retrieved from memory but not quite. (Adapted from Foard, 1975)

Instructions
Here are the dictionary definitions of twelve uncommon words. Please look at each definition in turn. Try to think of the word. There are several possibilities:

1. You may be pretty sure that you know the word. Or you may by quite sure that you don't know it. In either case, just move on to the next definition on the list.

2. You may feel that you know the word, but can't recall it just now. In fact, it may be "on the tip of your tongue." If so, quickly do the following:

    a. Guess the first letter of the word.

    b. Try to think of one or two words that sound similar to the one you're trying to find.

Follow this procedure as you go through the whole list of definitions. Then turn to the next left-hand page for the list of the words that fit these definitions.

Definitions
1. A blood feud in which members of the family of a murdered person try to kill the murderer or members of his family
2. A protecting charm to ward off spirits
3. An old coin of Spain and South America
4. A dark, hard, glassy volcanic rock
5. A secretion from the sperm whale used in the manufacture of perfume
6. A building used for public worship by Moslems
7. An Egyptian ornament in the shape of a beetle
8. The staff of Hermes, symbol of a physician or of the medical corps
9. A sword with a short curved blade, used by the Turks and Arabs
10. A Russian sled drawn by three horses
11. A navigational instrument used in measuring altitudes of celestial bodies
12. A narrow strip of land by which two larger bodies of land are connected

the target. Given that the target word was said to be at the tip-of-the-tongue, its initial letter was guessed correctly over 50 percent of the time. Similar results were found when the subjects were asked to guess at the number of syllables. When asked to supply some other words that they thought sounded like the target, the subjects were usually in the correct phonological neighborhood. Presented with the definition "a small Chinese boat" for which the proper answer is *sampan,* subjects who said they almost remembered but not quite supplied the following as sound-alikes: *saipan, Siam, Cheyenne,* and *sarong* (Brown and McNeill, 1966; Koriat and Lieblich, 1974).

IMPLICIT RETRIEVAL

Up to now, we've considered only methods of retrieval that are ***explicit,*** specifically recall and recognition. In both procedures, the subject is asked a question that refers to her prior experience. She may be tested for recall: "Tell me the name of one of your former high-school teachers." Or she may be asked for recognition: "Was Mr. Halberdam one of your former high-school teachers?" In either case, the question explicitly refers to the subject's remembered past. But retrieval can be ***implicit*** rather than explicit. An example comes from the performance of well-practiced skills. In general, the pianist need not be consciously aware of when and where he learned to finger the keys as he strikes a chord, nor does the golfer need consciously to remember where and how he perfected his golf swing while swinging the club. We know of course that the achievements of these skilled performers are honed by constant practice and thus depend on memory. To play the chord or hit the ball, both pianist and golfer necessarily retrieve something from memory, but these retrievals are implicit rather than explicit, for there is typically no awareness of "remembering" at the time.

IMPLICIT RETRIEVAL EFFECTS

Implicit retrieval has been the subject of many laboratory investigations (see Schacter, 1987, 1992; Roediger, 1990). In one such study the subjects were shown a number of words after which they were given two tests of memory. The first was a test of explicit memory in which a standard recognition procedure was employed. The second was a test of implicit memory in which the subjects' task was to identify words that were flashed on a screen for 35 milliseconds. Some of these words were the same as those that had been on the original list. The results of this second test showed ***repetition priming:*** Words that had been on the original list were identified more readily than words that had not. The crucial finding was that this priming effect held even for words that the subjects failed to recognize on the previous explicit retrieval. In short, subjects may show signs of implicit memory for items that they cannot consciously— that is, explicitly—remember, if their retrieval is tested implicitly (Jacoby and Witherspoon, 1982).

Similar implicit retrieval effects have been shown using a number of other priming procedures. An example is fragment completion in which subjects are presented with a word in which letters are missing (such as C_O_O_I_E for CROCODILE) and have to complete it with the first appropriate word that comes to mind. Here priming is indicated by an increased tendency to use words that were shown on a previous list (Jacoby and Dallas, 1981; Tulving, Schacter, and Stark, 1982; Graf and Mandler, 1984).

Implicit memory tasks seem to tap some different aspects of memory than do traditional tests of recall and recognition. One example concerns depth of processing, which affects explicit and implicit memory differently. We've previously seen that subjects who encode words for meaning (deep processing) tend to remember these words better than subjects who encode them by sound or visual appearance (shallow processing) and that they benefit more from elaborative rehearsal than from mere maintenance rehearsal. But recall and recognition are tests of explicit memory. When the test is for implicit memory, these effects do not hold. Thus repetition priming is unaffected by whether the items were encoded deeply or shallowly, or whether the subjects employed maintenance or elaborative rehearsal. All that matters is that the items have previously been seen (Jacoby and Dallas, 1981; Graf, Mandler, and Haden, 1982).

Another difference is in the effect of rather peripheral aspects of the stimulus. Suppose a subject is first exposed to a number of unrelated words and is then asked to indicate which of the words in a test set he had previously been shown. In such a probe of explicit memory it doesn't matter whether the visual appearance of the words is changed between original presentation and test in, say, size, or case, or font, as in

giraffe vs. **GIRAFFE**.

The subject's performance will be unaffected; he learned what the words are rather than what they looked like. The result is quite different when the memory is implicit. If the subject originally looked at the words without trying to learn them and is then asked to complete word fragments, he will do much better if the visual appearance of the letters is unchanged. If he originally saw *giraffe,* he'll be more likely to come up with the appropriate completion given

g_r_f_e rather than **G_R_F_E**.

Phenomena such as these suggest that explicit and implicit retrieval tasks tap different memory functions. According to one interpretation, explicit retrieval relies more on top-down processing (and is therefore said to be ***conceptually driven***): It depends greatly on the meaning of the items that have to be retrieved. In contrast, implicit retrieval is thought to be more dependent on bottom-up processing (and thus ***data driven***): It is largely based on relatively superficial aspects of the item (Jacoby, 1983). Some authors believe that these differences indicate the existence of two different memory systems, perhaps served by different areas of the brain. In large part, their view is based on the fact that brain-damaged patients with amnesia show massive deficits when engaged in explicit memory tasks but much less disruption when engaged in implicit ones (Squire and Cohen, 1984; see pp. 276–77).★

IMPLICIT RETRIEVAL AND FEELINGS OF FAMILIARITY

Thus far most of our discussion of the difference between implicit and explicit retrieval has centered on laboratory studies. But this distinction may help to explain a phenomenon we have all experienced in everyday life: the feeling that

Answers for tip-of-the-tongue demonstration

1. Vendetta
2. Amulet
3. Doubloon
4. Obsidian
5. Ambergris
6. Mosque
7. Scarab
8. Caduceus
9. Scimitar
10. Troika
11. Sextant
12. Isthmus

★ Some critics argue that the difference between the effects of implicit and explicit retrieval does not require the postulation of two different memory systems but merely reflects the compatibility between the conditions at the time of acquisition and recall (Roediger, 1990; Blaxton, 1989).

something is familiar, though we can't for the life of us recall where or when we encountered it. According to one hypothesis, the explanation is implicit retrieval. Something is retrieved, so there is the sense of familiarity. But the retrieval remains implicit, so there is no **source memory** and no knowledge of where the memory came from.

An elegant laboratory demonstration of this effect was produced in a study on "How to Become Famous Overnight." The subjects first took what they thought was a pronunciation test by reading a long list of unfamiliar names aloud. A day later, they were presented with a second list of names. This time their task was to decide whether the names were of famous people or not. Half of the names on the list were of moderately famous people (e.g., *Esther Williams*). The other half were the names of people who were not famous at all, but instead were picked from a telephone directory (e.g., *Sebastian Weisdorf*). The crucial point of the experiment was that some of these nonfamous names, such as *Sebastian Weisdorf*, had appeared on the original pronunciation list.

The results showed that familiarity sometimes breeds fame rather than contempt. At least it did for Sebastian Weisdorf, for he and others who had appeared on the first list were now erroneously judged to be famous. What happened was simple. The name *Sebastian Weisdorf* produced an implicit retrieval process with a consequent feeling of familiarity. But since the subject couldn't recall where or when she'd encountered that name before, she made the reasonable judgment: I probably read his name in a newspaper or heard it on TV—so he's famous.

In an important control experiment, the second list was presented immediately after the original pronunciation list. Now there was little confusion. To be sure, Sebastian's name triggered a sense of familiarity. But since the pronunciation list had been read just minutes before, the subject knew exactly why his name was familiar, and so she decided that Sebastian was not famous after all (Jacoby, et al., 1989).

Implicit retrieval may also help to explain the occasional experience of *déjà vu*—the feeling that we've met someone or visited some locale before, even though there is no question that we couldn't possibly have done so (e.g., we'd never been in the country where we encountered the familiar place). A possible interpretation is that the oddly familiar event aroused some memory trace—perhaps by association or through similarity or whatever—but that this arousal was entirely implicit. All that remained was an uncanny feeling of familiarity with no source memory whatsoever—the eerie sense of *déjà vu*.

WHEN MEMORY FAILS

In popular usage, the word *forgetting* is employed as a blanket term whenever memory fails. But as we've seen, memorial failures have many causes. Some arise from faulty encoding, while others arise at the moment of recall. In this section, we will discuss three broad topics that deal with memory failure. One concerns the lapse of time. Why is it easier to remember the recent past than it is to remember events from long ago? A second is the role of reconstruction in remembering, since much of remembering turns out to be a form of problem solving in which we draw on what we expect and believe to supplement what we actually remember. The third topic is somewhat different and concerns what happens to memory in certain cases of brain damage.

FORGETTING

At least on the face of it, forgetting increases with *retention interval,* the time that intervenes between original learning and the time of the test. Yesterday's lesson is better remembered than last week's. This fact was well known to Hermann Ebbinghaus (1850–1909), who began the experimental study of human learning by constructing lists of *nonsense syllables*—two consonants with a vowel in between that do not form a word, such as *zup* and *rif*—and then serving as his own subject as he memorized their serial order.★ He was the first to plot a *forgetting curve* by testing himself at various intervals after learning (using different lists for each interval) and then asking how much effort he had to expend to relearn the list to the level previously achieved. He found that there was a saving: Relearning the list took fewer trials than did the original learning. As one might expect, the saving declined as the retention interval increased. The decline was sharpest immediately after learning and became more gradual thereafter (Ebbinghaus, 1885; see Figure 7.9).

What accounts for the fact that the retention of the long-term memories seems to decline the longer the time since the memory was acquired? There are several theories designed to explain this and related phenomena.

DECAY

The most venerable theory of forgetting holds that memory traces gradually *decay* as time passes, like mountains that are eroded by wind and water. The erosion of memories is presumably caused by normal metabolic processes that wear down the memory trace until it fades and finally disintegrates.

Like most chemical reactions, many metabolic processes increase with increasing temperature. If these metabolic reactions are responsible for memorial decay, then forgetting should be a function of the body temperature during the retention interval. One study tried to provide an indirect test of this theory by varying body temperature. This prediction was tested with cold-blooded animals such as goldfish whose bodies take on the temperature of their surroundings. By and large, the results were in line with the hypothesis: The higher the temperature of the tank in which the fish were kept during the retention interval, the more forgetting took place (Gleitman and Rozin, as reported in Gleitman, 1971).

But other findings complicate this picture. There is good evidence that forgetting is determined not simply by normal metabolic processes during the retention interval, but by what actually happens to the subject during this time. Experiments on humans have shown that recall is substantially worse after an interval spent awake than after an equal period while asleep (Jenkins and Dallenbach, 1924). Later studies suggest that the favorable effect of sleep on retention only holds for quiet, slow-wave sleep (Ekstrand, 1972; Ekstrand et al., 1977).

Such results pose difficulties for a theory that assigns all of the blame for forgetting to decay, for they show that the normal metabolic processes that occur over time do not cause all of the loss. To explain such findings within a theory of decay, one would have to assert that the processes that erode the memory trace are slowed down (or counteracted) during one or all of the sleep states.

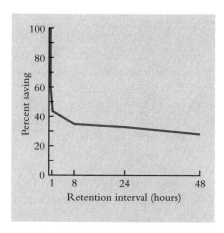

7.9 Forgetting curve *The figure shows retention after various intervals since learning. Retention is here measured in percentage saving, that is, the percent decrease in the number of trials required to relearn the list after an interval of no practice. If the saving is 100 percent, retention is perfect—no trials to relearn are necessary. If the saving is 0 percent, there is no retention at all, for it takes just as many trials to relearn the list as it took to learn it initially. (After Ebbinghaus, 1885)*

★ Ebbinghaus believed that his nonsense syllables were essentially meaningless, so that any associations among them were truly new and virginal and might thus reveal the laws of association in their pure form. By now we no longer accept this assumption: While *zup* is not an English word, it surely resembles some (e.g., *soup*), and to the extent that it does it is easier to remember. One may well doubt whether there is any verbal material that is completely meaningless; associative virginity is hard to find.

TABLE 7.1 RETROACTIVE INHIBITION EXPERIMENT

	Initial Period	Retention interval	Test period
Control Group	Learns list *A*	——————	Recalls list *A*
Experimental Group	Learns list *A*	Learns list *B*	Recalls list *A*

INTERFERENCE

A rather different theory of forgetting is ***interference.*** According to this view, a forgotten memory is neither lost nor damaged, but is only misplaced among a number of other memories that interfere with the recovery of the one that was sought. Seen in this light, our inability to remember the name of a high-school friend is analogous to what happens when a clerk cannot find a letter he received a year ago. The letter is still somewhere in his files, but it has been hopelessly buried in a mass of other letters that he filed both before and since. The greater the length of time since original acquisition, the greater the opportunity for new acquisitions to interfere (or in terms of the filing analogy, the greater the chance that the accumulation of other letters will get in the way).

Memorial interference is easily demonstrated in the laboratory. A major example is ***retroactive inhibition*** in which new learning hampers recall of the old. In a typical study, a control group learns some rote material, such as a list of nonsense syllables (List *A*), and is tested after a specified interval. The experimental group learns the same list as the control group and is tested after the same retention interval. But in addition it must also learn a second list (List *B*) that is interpolated during the retention interval (Table 7.1). The usual result is a marked inferiority in the performance of the experimental group; the interpolated list interferes with (inhibits) the recall of List *A*. (McGeoch and Irion, 1952; Crowder, 1976).

A similar effect is ***proactive inhibition*** in which interference works in a forward (proactive) direction. The usual procedure is to have an experimental group learn List *A* followed by List *B* and then to test for recall of List *B* after a suitable retention interval. The critical comparison is with a control group that learns only List B (Table 7.2). In general, the experimental group does worse on the recall test (e.g., Underwood, 1957). Such interference effects can have serious consequences. An example is the difficulty encountered by U.S. visitors in Britain when driving on the left side of the road. A more exotic example is recounted of a young woman who in moments of passion had the embarrassing tendency to cry out the name of a previous lover (Loftus, 1980, as cited in Baddeley, 1990).

TABLE 7.2 PROACTIVE INHIBITION EXPERIMENT

	Initial Period		Retention interval	Test period
Control Group	——————	Learns list *B*	· ——————	Recalls list *B*
Experimental Group	Learns list *A*	Learns list *B*	——————	Recalls list *B*

The child's world is in many ways utterly different from the adult's *According to some authors, childhood amnesia is partially produced by the enormous change in the retrieval cues available to the adult. (Photo courtesy of Suzanne Szasz)*

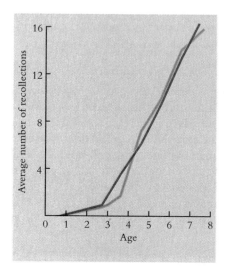

7.10   Number of childhood memories *College students were asked to recall childhood experiences. The figure plots the average number of events recalled as a function of the age at which they occurred for men (blue) and for women (dark red). Women recall a bit more at the earliest ages, which may reflect the fact that the maturation of girls is generally ahead of that of boys. (Data from Waldfogel, 1948)*

We should note that such interference effects (whether proactive or retroactive) depend on a number of other conditions. One is the similarity between the materials. If that similarity is low there will be little or no interference; thus learning to skate does not interfere with one's memory for irregular French verbs. But similarity alone will not necessarily produce interference. For if it did, then learning what's related to a given topic would hinder rather than help us remember; we'd never be able to learn French if we'd first learned Spanish, and so on. In fact, interference effects only occur if the things to be remembered are essentially inconsistent with each other. Such an inconsistency may occur in the very first stages of learning.

CHANGE OF RETRIEVAL CUES

Decay theory holds that the memory trace gradually fades away with time, while interference asserts that the trace gets lost among other traces acquired both before and after the forgotten material was learned. There is a further alternative which argues that memorial success or failure is primarily determined by the retrieval cues presented at the time of recall.

Changes in retrieval cues with increasing retention interval   We have already seen that a change in retrieval cues disrupts remembering. But can this effect explain why forgetting increases with an increasing retention interval? To maintain the hypothesis that the critical factor is cue alteration, one must assume that such an alteration becomes ever more likely with the passage of time. There are some cases for which this may well be true. Certain memories may have been acquired in a particular locale; over the years the neighborhood changes as some houses are torn down and new ones are built, thus altering the physical cues and thereby decreasing the chance of retrieval.

The retrieval cue hypothesis is a very plausible account of some aspects of forgetting. But it probably cannot explain them all. Forgetting increases as a function of the time since learning, even when the retrieval conditions appear essentially unchanged. Some evidence comes from studies with animal subjects where all facets of the situation are under the experimenter's control. In one study, rats were trained to run an alley for food reward. Some of them were tested one day after original learning, others after sixty-eight days. All of the physical conditions of the experiment—the location and illumination of the alley, the home cages, the animal's own weight—were kept identical throughout the entire period. Even so, the length of the retention interval had a massive effect. The animals tested some two months after training were much more hesitant in the alley than they were before, as if they had forgotten what they were supposed to do (Gleitman, 1971).

Childhood amnesia   Some authors appeal to the retrieval-cue hypothesis to explain the phenomenon of **childhood amnesia**—the fact that most of us can't recall events of our very early childhood. When college students are asked to report any events they can remember that occurred in early life, the average age of their earliest recollection is about three and a half years (Waldfogel, 1948; Sheingold and Tenney, 1982; see Figure 7.10). One possible cause is a massive change of retrieval cues. The world of the young child is utterly different from the world she will occupy some ten or fifteen years later. It is a world in which tables are hopelessly out of reach, chairs can be climbed upon only with great effort, and adults are giants in size and gods in ability. Whatever memories the child may store at this time are necessarily formed and encoded within this context; thus the appropriate retrieval context is necessarily absent from the adult's environment (Schachtel, 1947; Neisser, 1967).

Encoding differences may also have an effect. According to some authors, infants and very young children store memories—especially explicit memories—less efficiently than older children and adults. This may be because some relevant neural structures are not yet sufficiently mature (Nadel and Zola-Morgan, 1984). It may also be because these very young children have not yet developed the necessary schemas within which experiences can be explicitly organized, encoded, and rehearsed (White and Pillemer, 1979). Thus, while cue-change may account for some aspects of childhood amnesia, it almost surely does not account for it all (see also Howe and Courage, 1993).

WHEN FORGETTING SEEMS NOT TO OCCUR

The fact that there is forgetting doesn't mean that it always occurs. For memory doesn't always fail, even after very long intervals.

Long-lasting memories Some evidence was provided by Harry Bahrick who studied the long-term retention of materials in semantic memory. Bahrick was interested in what people remember from what they learned in school. To this end, he gave a Spanish reading-comprehension test to nearly 800 people who had studied Spanish for three or four years either in high school or in college. They were tested at intervals that ranged from one week to fifty years since their last Spanish course. The results showed that quite a bit is forgotten in the first two or three years after learning. But after this, the test performance levels off until much later in life, where aging effects probably account for the bulk of the later memory loss (see Figure 7.11). Educators will probably be gratified by the fact that even after fifty years the test performance reflects how well the language was learned originally. On average, students who had earned an A performed better than those who had received a C, even after half a century had passed (Bahrick, 1984). Similar findings come from a more recent study on the retention of knowledge acquired in an advanced psychology course, which

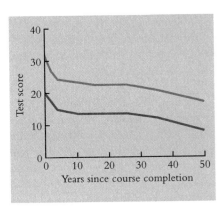

7.11 Forgetting a foreign language
The figure displays performance on a Spanish reading comprehension test administered from 0 to 50 years after taking Spanish in high school or college to persons who had previously earned a grade of A (blue) or C (dark red). (After Bahrick, 1984)

Childhood memories *While there is childhood amnesia for the events of the first two or three years, some early memories do remain, often in a jumbled and kaleidoscopic fashion. Thus the paintings of the Russian émigré artist Marc Chagall (1887–1985) show composite images of his early life in a Russian village, including a cow being milked, his mother, a child's naïve picture of a Russian village, and so on. (I and the Village, 1911, oil on canvas, 6'3⅝" × 59⅝". Collection, The Museum of Modern Art, New York, Mrs. Simon Guggenheim Fund)*

showed rather good retention of basic concepts—but not of *proper* names—after retention intervals up to twelve years (Conway, Cohen, and Stanhope, 1991).

The important finding is that some fraction of what had been learned originally remained intact without any further forgetting. In Bahrick's terms, these memories—vocabulary items, idioms, bits of grammar, psychological theories—moved into what he called a **permastore.** The semantic memory of an adult contains much information that is essentially permanent. We don't forget the meaning of ordinary words, or the rules of arithmetic, or many individual bits of information. In part, this may be because such materials are extremely well-learned in the first place. But in part, it may be because such items—and hopefully much of what we learn in school—have an inherent structure that protects them from being forgotten, a structure that Ebbinghaus's series of nonsense syllables certainly lacked (Neisser, 1989).

Flashbulb memories   Bahrick's findings concerned semantic memory. Are there episodic memories that are also essentially immune to being forgotten? According to Roger Brown and James Kulik, certain unexpected and emotionally important events produce *flashbulb memories,* which are extremely vivid and essentially permanent. They believe that such memories are like a photograph that preserves the scene when a flashbulb is fired. Some of the events that trigger the flash may be private and personal, such as an early morning telephone call that tells of a parent's death. Others may involve news of powerful national import such as the assassination of President Kennedy or the space shuttle disaster. Brown and Kulik found that most people recalled where they were at the time they learned of President Kennedy's assassination and also what they did, who told them, and so on. On the face of it, these detailed memories are surprising. That a president's assassination is an important and memorable event is obvious, but why should so many Americans recall the humdrum circumstances in which they personally found themselves at the time, such as "the weather was cloudy and gray," or "I was carrying a carton of Viceroy cigarettes, which I dropped"? According to Brown and Kulik, the reason is that such surprising and emotionally powerful events set off a mental flashbulb that preserves the entire scene along with perfectly mundane and unremarkable details (Brown and Kulik, 1977; see also Pillemer, 1984; McCloskey, Wible, and Cohen, 1988).

The flashbulb hypothesis has been the subject of considerable debate. The main issue is whether such memories are really created by a special mechanism

Events that have produced flashbulb memories   (A) *After the Kennedy assassination; (B) the space shuttle disaster. (Courtesy of the Bettmann Archive)*

that fixes the circumstances of the moment with a special "flashbulb" clarity. The best guess is that such a special mechanism does not exist. To begin with, there is some debate about the accuracy of these memories; they may be vivid, but that does not mean that they are fully correct (e.g., Neisser, 1982a, 1986; Thompson and Cowan, 1986; McCloskey, Wible, and Cohen, 1988). In addition, much of what was remembered may have been rehearsed in subsequent conversations with others, so that what was entered in memory did not in fact depend on a hypothetical flashbulb set off in the head. All in all, there is good reason to doubt the existence of a special flashbulb mechanism.

CONCEPTUAL FRAMEWORKS AND REMEMBERING

Thus far, our primary concern has been with memory failures that involve errors of omission in which we draw a blank, are unable to recall a name or recognize a face, and come up with nothing. We now turn to another kind of failure in which the memory error is one of *commission*. These are errors in which we give a distorted account by unwittingly reconstructing facts and events based on what we think and know rather than on what we really remember.

We've repeatedly stressed that remembering depends upon encoding and retrieval. These in turn are affected by still another factor: what the learner already knows. For all remembering takes place against a backdrop of prior knowledge that necessarily colors whatever enters memory. Without prior knowledge, we could not understand the words we hear, their connection with each other, or their relation to events in the world.

Similarly, organization helps us to remember, but this organization is almost always based on connecting what we hear and see with what we already know. It's easier to recall the first nine squares than the sequence 149162536496481 because we know about numbers and squares, and it's easier to recall some disconnected sentences that are preceded by the title "Doing the Laundry" than if they're not because we know about laundry routines. To give another example, consider a study in which subjects listened to a taped description of half an inning of a fictional baseball game. Some of the subjects were very knowledgeable about the game; others were not (though they had a rough idea of the rules of the game). When later asked to write down as much of the taped account as they could, the more expert subjects did far better than the subjects whose knowledge of the game was slight (Spilich et al., 1979).

Using prior knowledge in memory is analogous to top-down processing in perception. As in perception, such top-down effects can be enormously helpful. But again as in perception, our knowledge and expectations can lead us astray. For just as we can misperceive, so we can—and often do—misremember.

MEMORY DISTORTIONS

The most influential experiments on memory distortions were performed by the British psychologist Frederic Bartlett almost sixty years ago. Bartlett's subjects were asked to reproduce stories taken from the folklore of other cultures; thus, their content and structure were rather strange to Western ears. The reproductions showed many changes from the original. Some parts were subtracted, others were overelaborated, still others were additions that were completely new. In effect, the subjects had built a new story upon the memorial ruins of the original. This memorial reconstruction was generally more consonant with the cultural conceptions of the subjects than with the story they had actually heard.

For example, certain supernatural plot elements were reinterpreted along more familiar lines.

In another variant of the same experiment, Bartlett used the method of **serial reproduction.** A drawing was presented to one subject, who reproduced it from memory for the benefit of a second, whose reproduction was shown to a third, and so on for a chain of up to ten subjects (Bartlett, 1932). With this technique (an experimental analog of rumor transmission), each subject's memorial distortions became part of the stimulus for the next one down the line; the effect was to grossly amplify the reconstructive alteration (Figure 7.12).

The effect of schemas and scripts   Numerous experiments document Bartlett's claim that memories for events or narratives are strongly affected by the framework of prior knowledge in terms of which they are understood. In one study, subjects were asked to read a description of a home while taking either of two different viewpoints: that of a prospective home buyer or that of a burglar. Later recall showed that the different perspectives affected what was remembered: in the case of the "home buyers," a leaky roof; in the case of the "burglars," a valuable coin collection (Anderson and Pichert, 1978). In another study, there were errors of commission. Subjects were told about a person's visit to the dentist and then falsely recalled hearing some details that typically occur in a dentist's office (checking in with the receptionist, looking at a magazine in the waiting room, and so on), even though these were never explicitly mentioned (Bower, Black, and Turner, 1979).

In all these cases, the subjects' memory was affected by their knowledge of the world. They had some ideas of how home buyers, burglars, and dental patients are likely to behave, and they fit their particular recollections into the general outlines of this knowledge, filling in various gaps in memory without knowing that they did so. Following Bartlett, many contemporary psychologists describe such conceptual frameworks as **schemas.** As used in this context, the term refers to a general cognitive structure into which data or events can be entered, typically with more attention to broad brush strokes than to specific details. Many aspects of our experience are redundant: When prospective buyers look at a house they inspect the roof and basement; when patients visit the dentist, they generally check in with a receptionist, and so on. A schema is an effective summary of this redundancy and can therefore help us interpret and supplement the details of our remembered experience (Schwartz and Reisberg, 1991). A special subcase of a schema is a **script,** which describes a characteristic scenario of behavior in a particular setting, such as a restaurant script (whose sequence includes being seated, looking at the menu, ordering the meal, eating

7.12   Remembering studied by the method of serial reproduction   *Ten subjects were used in the experiment. Subject 1 saw the original figure and was asked to reproduce it after half an hour. His reproduction was shown to subject 2 whose reproduction was shown to subject 3, and so on through subject 10. The figure shows the original drawing and the 10 serial reproductions, illustrating a massive reconstruction process. (After Bartlett, 1932)*

The Persistence of Memory *by Salvador Dali. Memory persists, sometimes in distorted form. (Courtesy of the Museum of Modern Art)*

the food, paying the bill, and leaving), or the visit-to-the-dentist script we just described (Schank and Abelson, 1977).

Eyewitness testimony The schema-induced distortions we've discussed thus far were not particularly damaging. To be sure, the subject's memory for the particular details was faulty, but that hardly mattered since she recalled the gist. Under the circumstances, there was no harm done, since our ultimate object is to remember what a statement is all about, not its detailed phrasing. One might even argue that schematized remembering is beneficial since its efficiency lets us package, store, and retrieve more material than we could otherwise manage in an information-cluttered world.

The trouble is that this enhanced efficiency has a down-side, for sometimes the details are of considerable importance. They certainly are to lawyers and judges who are concerned with the accuracy of eyewitness testimony. Witnesses are sometimes quite confident of various circumstances they remember even though their recollections don't fit the actual facts. An accident occurred months ago, and its details have dimmed over time. As the witness tries to retrieve this past event, he may fill in the gaps by an inference of which he is quite unaware. In these cases (and many others), schematic distortion can have very damaging effects.

A series of studies by Elizabeth Loftus and her associates has highlighted this problem of schematized memory processes in eyewitness testimony. An important factor is the way in which recall is elicited. In one study, subjects viewed a brief film segment of a car accident. Immediately afterward they were asked a number of questions that were in either of two forms:

"Did you see the broken headlight?"
or
"Did you see a broken headlight?"

The results showed that subjects who were questioned about *the* headlight were more likely to report having seen one than subjects who were asked about *a* headlight. This was so whether the film actually showed a broken headlight or not. Here the schema is provided by the nature of our language. In effect, the

(Drawing by Chas. Addams; © 1979, The New Yorker Magazine, Inc.)

use of the definite article, *the,* makes the query a leading question, one which implies that there really was a broken headlight and that the only issue is whether the subject noticed it. No such presupposition is made when the indefinite article, *a,* is used (Loftus and Zanni, 1975).

Another study showed that leading questions during a first interrogation may change how the witnessed event is reported sometime later. Subjects were again shown film segments of a car accident. Shortly afterward some of them were asked leading questions such as, "Did you see the children getting on the school bus?" A week later, all subjects were asked the direct question, "Did you see a school bus in the film?" In actual fact, there was no school bus. But when compared to controls, subjects who were originally asked the leading question that presupposed the school bus were three to four times more likely to say that they had seen one. It would seem that a false memory of a bus had been implanted (Loftus, 1975).

These results are of considerable relevance both to the legal process and to the psychology of memory. To legal scholars they reemphasize the crucial importance of how questions are worded, not only in the courtroom but also in prior interrogations. To students of memory, they highlight the importance of prior knowledge and expectations in memory.

What produces schema-based distortions?   One possibility is that the distortions are reconstructions. According to this view, the subject reconstructs the past while trying to remember it by supplementing her partial knowledge with various inferences. Take the film clip of the auto accident. According to the reconstruction hypothesis, the subject has forgotten whether or not she saw a broken headlight. She fills the gap in her memory by making an inference: Since the experimenter asked her about the headlight, there must have been one. The subject tries to remember what she actually saw, but she ends up reporting what she decides she must have seen. Here, as in perception, top-down processing may produce a form of mental problem solving. In perception, the subject acts as if she asks herself: "What can it possibly be?" In memory, the equivalent question is: "What could it possibly have been?" In the first case, the inference concerns the present; in the second, it concerns the past. And in both cases, the inference may very well have been unconscious (see Chapter 6).

It is probably not surprising that reconstructive errors of this kind are more frequent the more time that elapses between the original encoding and the retrieval test. With increasing time, forgetting also increases, which in turn leads to greater reliance on inference to patch up the holes in memory (Anderson and Pichert, 1978; Spiro, 1980).

Can memories be altered after the event?   Some authors believe that schemas can do more than just fill gaps, as was shown in the case of the school bus study already described: They may actually alter memories. An example is a study in which subjects were shown slides of an automobile collision. Later on, the subjects were asked either of two questions: "How fast were the cars going when they hit each other?" or "How fast were the cars going when they smashed into each other?" A week later the subjects were asked whether they had seen any broken glass in any of the slides they had been shown. (In actual fact, there was none.) Subjects who had been asked about the cars that "smashed into each other" were much more likely to report having seen such glass than subjects who were asked about the cars that "hit each other" (Loftus and Palmer, 1974).

In this and similar studies, earlier memories seem to change to accord with later interpretation, as if the past were rewritten and updated to fit into our view of the present. Such retrospective alterations of memory are called ***accommodative distortions.*** Whether such phenomena really prove that old memories are easily erased and updated is still a matter of debate. But whatever the ultimate verdict on this point, one thing is clear: Such retrospective alterations change how a memory is *reported,* and for many purposes—including those of the courtroom—that is change enough (Belli, 1989; Loftus and Hoffman, 1989; Tversky and Tuchin, 1989; Zaragoza and McCloskey, 1989).

THE LIMITS OF MEMORY

There is ample evidence that memory is often fallible and subject to distortion. But the phenomena of retrieval tell us that more is retained in memory than we typically dig out and recall on any one occasion. This fact has led to a search for special techniques for recovering memories that have some particular importance, such as trying to help witnesses remember what a suspect said or did.

Memory, hypnosis, and the courtroom   A case in point is hypnosis. A number of law enforcement agencies have used this as a device to prompt witness recall in criminal investigations. A witness is hypnotized, told that he is back at a certain time and place, and asked to tell what he sees. On the surface, the results—in both the real world and in laboratory studies—are quite impressive. A hypnotized witness identifies an assailant as he mentally returns to the scene of the crime; a hypnotized college student is brought back to the age of six and relives his sixth birthday party with appropriately childlike glee. There is little doubt that these hypnotized people are convinced that they are actually reexperiencing these events, that what they recall really happened. But upon investigation, it often turns out that the hypnotically prodded memories are false. In one courtroom case, a suspect turned out to have been abroad at the time the hypnotized witness recalled having seen him during an assault (Orne, 1979). Similar points apply to the description of childhood events elicited under hypnosis. Convincing details such as the name of a first-grade teacher generally turn out to be quite false when later checked against available records. Some subjects were asked to draw a picture while mentally back at the age of six. At first glance, their drawings looked remarkably childlike. But when compared to the subjects'

7.13 Remembering studied through drawings done while under hypnosis *(A) Drawings done at age six. (B) Drawings done while subject was hypnotized and told that he was six years old. Note some interesting differences between the pictures, for example, the tepee, which is much more detailed in (B); the spelling of* balloon; *and a sense of overall design present in (B) and altogether lacking in (A). (From Orne, 1951)*

own childhood drawings made at that very age, it is clear that they are much more sophisticated. They represent an adult's conception of what a childish drawing is, rather than being the real thing (Figure 7.13; Orne, 1951).

How can we explain these results? First of all, it is clear that hypnosis does not have the near-magical powers often attributed to it (Barber, 1969; Orne and Hammer, 1974; Hilgard, 1977). Hypnosis does not enable us to relive our past at will (nor, for that matter, does it permit feats of agility or strength of which we are otherwise incapable). What it does do is to make people unusually anxious to believe in and cooperate with another person, the hypnotist, and to do what he asks of them (within the bounds of certain mutually understood limitations). If he asks them to remember, they will do their very best to oblige. They will doggedly stick to the task and rummage through their minds to find any possible retrieval cue. And so of course would we all, whether hypnotized or not, providing that we wanted to remember badly enough. But what if we don't succeed? If we are not hypnotized, we will eventually concede failure. But hypnotized people will not. They try to please the hypnotist who has told them to recall and has assured them that they can. And so they do what the hypnotist asks. They produce memories—by creatively adding and reconstructing on the basis of what they already know. As we have seen, such reconstructions are a common feature in much so-called remembering. The difference is that under hypnosis subjects become unusually confident that their memories are real (probably because of the hypnotist's suggestion).

Some evidence for this interpretation comes from a study on the susceptibility of those under hypnosis to leading questions. The experimenter employed the familiar technique of showing subjects videotapes of an accident and later asking them to recall certain details, in some cases while hypnotized and in others while not. Some of the probes were leading questions, while others were more objective in phrasing. As we just saw, such leading questions lead to errors even without hypnosis. But they lead to even more errors in hypnotized subjects than in controls. When asked whether they had seen "the license plate . . ." (which in fact was not visible), some of the hypnotized subjects not only said yes but actually volunteered partial descriptions of the license plate number. Findings of this sort cast serious doubts on the use of hypnosis in real-life judicial settings (Putnam, 1979; Smith, 1983).

The tape-recorder theory of memory Over and above what these findings tell us about hypnosis, they also have implications for what is sometimes called the tape-recorder (or, to update it, the videotape-recorder) theory of memory. According to this view, the brain contains a virtually imperishable record of all we have ever heard or seen or felt. The only trick is to find a way to turn the recorder back to some desired portion of the tape. But the evidence indicates that this suggestion is exceedingly implausible. All techniques that claim to provide such memory "playbacks"—the major example is hypnosis—have been found wanting. Under the circumstances, our best guess is that the tape-recorder theory is false. To be sure, we retain much more than we can retrieve at any given moment. But this doesn't mean we retain every bit of sensory information we encounter. Some is never entered, some is lost if not rehearsed and organized, and some is altered to fit in with incoming material (Loftus and Loftus, 1980; Neisser, 1982b).

Are there false memories? A special problem that has lately received much public attention concerns the reality of so-called ***repressed memories.*** In recent years, a considerable number of people have reported memories of traumatic childhood events, usually involving sexual abuse. As these people tell it, these memories had been pushed out of consciousness—that is, repressed—for many years, sometimes for as long as two or three decades. The memories surface much later, often while the person is being treated by a therapist who in many cases employs hypnosis. Are these memories accurate—that is, a true recounting of the actual history of what happened? This question has serious social and legal significance, all the more since many of the accusers have brought civil suits against the alleged perpetrators—parents or other relatives—or charged them in criminal court.

The authenticity of such long-repressed memories has been questioned in a recent paper by Elizabeth Loftus (Loftus, 1993). As she points out, there is some debate about whether memories can be repressed to such a massive extent and for so long a time; some even doubt whether the phenomenon of repression exists at all (e.g., Holmes, 1990). A further question concerns the role of psychotherapy. Many people who report the resurrection of repressed memories of child abuse are under the care of therapists who are convinced that their patients' psychological problems stem from childhood abuse and that these problems can only be dealt with if the patient faces them squarely by uncovering the buried memories of that abuse (e.g., Bass and Davis, 1988). Under these circumstances, there is a strong possibility of accommodative distortion and memory reconstruction. This possibility is further enhanced by the fact that many of these therapists use hypnosis as a means of uncovering the repressed childhood past.

None of this is said to minimize the social and moral problems produced by childhood sexual abuse and incest, the prevalence of which is clearly greater than previously supposed. Nor can we deny that some—perhaps very many—of the memories of childhood sexual abuse are valid. But we cannot take the veracity of these memories for granted: We know that it is possible to remember events from very long ago, but we also know that the possibility for error is greater in remembering the distant past than in remembering recent events. Likewise, we saw in our discussion of retrieval failures that some memories will come to light only if appropriately triggered with well-chosen cues, but we also saw that close questioning of a subject can *create* "memories" about things that never occurred, especially if the questions are asked of a hypnotized subject. We therefore have to be very cautious in accepting the accuracy of memories of long-past events, especially if those memories emerged through therapists' suggestions and hypnosis (Loftus, 1993; Kihlstrom, 1993; for a sharply divergent position, see Bass and Davis, 1988).

THE LIMITS OF DISTORTION

In the last chapter we saw that perception is an active process. It depends on incoming stimuli, but it does not provide a mere copy of that stimulus for the incoming sensory information is often reshaped and transformed. A similar point applies to memory. Memory depends on what is stored, but a given act of remembering provides us with more than a frozen slice of the past; it often reconstructs events to fill in gaps as we unwittingly try to fit our past into our present (Neisser, 1967).

But these acts of cognitive construction and reconstruction have some limits, in memory as well as in perception. For while there are numerous ways in which a memory can be distorted, such distortions don't always occur—far from it. After all, we do remember many details of experiences we've been exposed to, and many of those fit into no particular cognitive mold. And even in cases in which various schemas have led to distortions of recall, subsequent tests of recognition show that more is remembered than seems so at first (Alba and Hasher, 1983).

In sum, our memory is neither wholly distorted nor wholly accurate. The tape-recorder theory of memory is false. But so is the theory that everything we remember is changed and distorted by inference and reconstruction. In these regards, memory is again much like perception. Both are affected by processes that work from the top down as well as by those that start from the bottom up. Perception without any bottom-up processing (that is, without any reference to stimuli) would amount to continual hallucination. Memory without bottom-up processing (that is, without any reference to memory traces) would amount to perpetual delusion, a mere will-o'-the-wisp in which the remembered past is continually constructed and reconstructed to fit the schemas of the moment. Both top-down and bottom-up processes operate in both cognitive domains.

The use of schemas—that is, top-down processing—clearly has a cost, for it can lead to distortions of memory. But it also confers great benefits. Our cognitive machinery is limited: There's only so much that we can encode, store, and retrieve. As a result, we are forced to schematize and simplify so that we can impose order on the world we perceive and think about. But the very tools that help us to understand and remember occasionally backfire so that we misremember.

DISORDERED MEMORIES

Thus far, our discussion has largely centered on people with normal memories. But during the last thirty years, some of the most intriguing questions about human memory have been raised by studies of people with drastic defects in memory caused by various kinds of damage to the brain (Rozin, 1976b; Squire, 1987; Mayes, 1988).

ANTEROGRADE AMNESIA

Certain lesions in the temporal cortex (specifically, in the hippocampus and nearby regions of the limbic system) produce a memory disorder called *anterograde amnesia* (anterograde means "in a forward direction"). Patients with this disorder often have little trouble in remembering whatever they learned prior to the injury; their difficulty is in learning anything new thereafter. Such lesions can occur in various ways. They are found in certain chronic alcoholic patients who suffer from *Korsakoff's syndrome* (named after the Russian physician who first described it). They sometimes accompany senility. In the famous case of a patient generally known as H.M., they were a tragic side effect of neurosurgery undertaken to minimize severe epileptic seizures (see Figure 7.14).

7.14 Regions of the brain where damage can cause memory loss *A cutaway section of the human brain showing regions of the hippocampus and associated structures whose destruction caused H.M.'s massive memory deficits. Patients with Korsakoff's syndrome tend to have lesions in regions that lie higher up, including the thalamus, while patients with Alzheimer's disease show damage in the base of the forebrain. (Adapted from Mishkin and Appenzeller, 1987)*

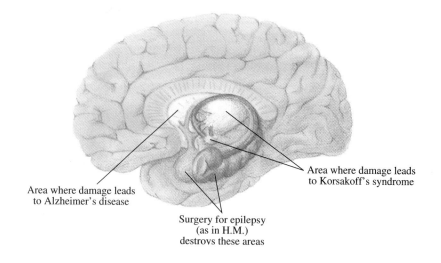

Area where damage leads to Alzheimer's disease

Surgery for epilepsy (as in H.M.) destroys these areas

Area where damage leads to Korsakoff's syndrome

H.M.'s hippocampal lesion occurred when he was twenty-nine. Following the surgery he had a normal memory span and thus, apparently, a normal working memory. But he seemed to be incapable of adding any new information to his long-term storage. He often could not recognize anyone he had not met before the surgery, no matter how often they met afterward. He was unable to find his way to the new house his family moved into after his operation. When told that his uncle had died he was deeply moved, but then forgot all about it and repeatedly asked when his uncle would come to visit. On each occasion he was told again of his uncle's death, and every time his grief was as intense as before; to him, each time he was told was the first (Milner, 1966; Milner, Corkin, and Teuber, 1968; Marslen-Wilson and Teuber, 1975; Corkin, 1984).

While H.M.'s long-term storage system was apparently almost completely closed to any new memories, his memories prior to the operation remained largely intact, especially for events that happened more than a year or so before the surgery. He could still read and write and engage in lively conversation. In many ways, his intellectual functioning was unimpaired. This is not uncommon in patients suffering damage to the hippocampus and related systems. Korsakoff's original patient could still play a competent game of chess though he could not remember how any given position on the chess board came about. But his memory loss was nevertheless profound and profoundly unsettling.

Some of H.M.'s comments give some idea of what such an amnesic state is like:

> Right now, I'm wondering, Have I done or said anything amiss? You see, at this moment everything looks clear to me, but what happened just before? That's what worries me. It's like waking from a dream; I just don't remember. (Milner, 1966)

And on another occasion:

> . . . Every day is alone in itself, whatever enjoyment I've had, and whatever sorrow I've had. (Milner, Corkin, and Teuber, 1968)

RETROGRADE AMNESIA

Various brain injuries may lead to *retrograde amnesia* (retrograde means "in a backward direction") in which the patient suffers a loss of memories for some period prior to the accident or the stroke. That period may be relatively brief, perhaps a matter of days or weeks. But in some cases, the retrograde amnesia covers a much longer span and may be reckoned in years. Some retrograde effects often go along with anterograde amnesia. Thus H.M. had difficulty remembering events that happened one to three years before his operation, but his memory was perfectly normal for those that occurred before then (Mayes, 1988).

What accounts for the loss of memories for events preceding the cerebral injury? According to some authors, one of the causes is a problem with *trace consolidation.* This is a hypothetical process by which newly acquired memory traces gradually become firmly established (consolidated). This might explain why retrograde amnesia primarily affects memories that were formed shortly before the injury. Such memories would not have time to consolidate and would thus be more liable to destruction. The consolidation effect may be on storage—young traces need time to become resistant to being forgotten, for until then they are as vulnerable as a cement mixture before it has hardened. The effect may also be on retrieval—like a newly acquired library book, it will be difficult to find until the librarian takes the time to fill out its card for the catalogue and to file it properly (Weingartner and Parker, 1984).

Whether retrograde amnesia can be explained in this manner is still a matter of debate. One trouble is the fact that retrograde amnesia often extends back for several years prior to the injury. If so, consolidation could not explain the deficit unless one assumes—and some authors do—that it is an exceedingly drawn-out process that may occur over very long time periods (Squire and Cohen, 1979, 1982; Squire, 1987).

EXPLICIT AND IMPLICIT RETRIEVAL REVISITED

For quite a while, it was thought that H.M. and other patients with the anterograde amnesic syndrome could not acquire any long-term memories at all. But further study demonstrated that this isn't true. They can be classically conditioned. They can also learn to trace the correct path through a maze and can acquire certain skills like mirror-tracing and reading mirror-imaged print. With practice, their performance gets better and better. But each time they are brought back into the experimental situation, they continue to insist that they have never seen the conditioning apparatus or the maze before and that they don't remember anything at all (Corkin, 1965; Weiskrantz and Warrington, 1979; Cohen and Squire, 1980).

How can we make sense of these findings? Anterograde amnesics are evidently quite competent at retaining skills such as mirror-tracing (they do just about as well as normals, despite their insistence that they don't remember anything about it; see Figure 7.15). On the other hand, they are utterly incompetent at many ordinary long-term memory tasks; for example, they don't recognize an experimenter they have met on twenty different occasions. The one kind of memory is spared; the other is not. What is the essential difference between such tasks?

Some authors believe that the essential distinction is between what computer scientists called *procedural* and *declarative knowledge.* Procedural knowledge is "knowing how": how to ride a bicycle or how to read mirror writing—areas in which the amnesic's memory is relatively unaffected. According to this view, such skills are essentially programs (that is, procedures) for executing certain motor or mental operations. In contrast, declarative knowledge is "knowing that": that there are three outs in an inning, that automobiles run on gasoline, that I had chicken for dinner last Thursday. To know something procedurally does not guarantee that one also knows it declaratively. Professional baseball players know how to swing a bat, but not all of them can explain just what it is that they know. Conversely, most physicists probably know (and can describe) the underlying mechanics of a baseball swing, but few will be able to perform competently when given a bat and asked to hit a ball. Neuroscientists who argue that this distinction explains what anterograde amnesics can remember and what they can't also believe that procedural and declarative memories depend on different neural systems (Cohen and Squire, 1980; Squire, 1986).

A somewhat different explanation centers on the distinction between explicit and implicit retrieval (see p. 259). The memories may be there, but they can only be retrieved implicitly so that the patient doesn't know that he has them. As a result, he cannot answer questions like "Do you remember?" or "Do you recognize?" when they pertain to events that occurred after he sustained the cerebral damage. Some evidence that the amnesic's deficit concerns explicit but

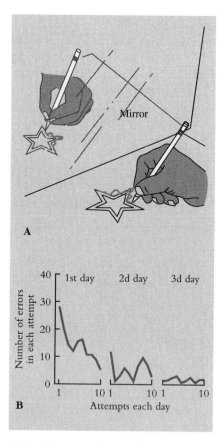

7.15 An example of what amnesics can learn (A) In mirror drawing, the subject has to trace a line between two outlines of a figure while looking at her hand in a mirror (Kolb and Whishaw, 1990). Initially, this is very difficult, but after some practice the subject gets very proficient at it. The same is true for amnesics. The graphs in (B) show H.M.'s improvement on this task over a period of three days. (Milner, Corkin, and Teuber, 1968)

Remote and recent memory in amnesics
(A) Sample items adapted from the "famous faces" test in which patients are asked to identify faces of individuals who reached fame in a particular decade (Albert, Butters, and Levin, 1979; Butters and Albert, 1982). The names of those pictured are listed on page 278. (B) Results on the famous faces test for H.M. (blue) and normal controls (dark red) for the years from 1920 to 1960. Note that, as one would expect, the performance of H.M. was essentially equivalent to that of normals in identifying persons reaching prominence between 1920 and 1930. Like the normals, he did poorly for faces that predate 1930 when he was still a preschool child. But he performed much more poorly than the two controls on faces from the period after his operation (which was performed during the early 1950s). (Adapted from Marslen-Wilson and Teuber, 1975)

1950s   1960s   1970s   1980s

B

not implicit memory comes from priming procedures. When amnesic patients are shown a number of words and are later asked to recall or recognize them, they fail completely. But the results are quite different when they are presented, with fragments of the words and asked to complete them by forming the first words that come to mind. Now there is evidence that something was remembered. The patient who was previously shown ELEPHANT and BOOKCASE will properly complete the fragments _L_P_A_T and B_O_C_S_, even though he will not recognize either word if explicitly asked whether he's just seen it before (Warrington and Weiskrantz, 1978; Diamond and Rozin, 1984). Interestingly enough, this effect will work only if the patient does not connect it with any intentional attempt to retrieve the word from memory. If he is explicitly asked to recall the previously presented words by using the fragments as cues, he will fail again (Graf, Mandler, and Squire, 1984).

Whether the explicit-implicit distinction is better or worse than the procedural-declarative one at capturing the essence of what the amnesic can and cannot learn is as yet unclear. It would seem that the two categories overlap, though they are probably not identical (Schacter, 1987). Perhaps there is no one distinction that does justice to the findings, since amnesia is almost surely not a unitary disorder; not every impaired memory is necessarily impaired in the same way (Squire and Cohen, 1984). In any case, there are many further questions. What is it about the development of declarative knowledge or of explicit, conscious access that makes them so vulnerable to brain damage? Why is procedural knowledge spared? As we begin to find some answers, it is likely that they will shed light not only on the amnesic disorders but on memory functions in general (Crowder, 1985).

Answers to "famous faces" test
1950s: *Mamie Eisenhower, Jonas Salk, Adlai Stevenson.* 1960s: *Nikita Khrushchev, Mohammed Ali, Golda Meir.* 1970s: *Anwar Sadat, Betty Ford, Patty Hearst.* 1980s: *Robert Bork, Walter Mondale, Bjorn Borg.*

Very Bad Memory

(Cartoon by Abner Dean)

TAKING STOCK

In looking back over this chapter, we are again struck by the intimate relationship between the fields of perception, memory, and thinking. It is often unclear where one topic ends and another begins. To give just one example, consider memory search. As we saw, trying to recall the names of one's high-school classmates apparently involves many of the same thought processes that are called upon when we try to figure out how to solve a geometry problem. To the extent that this is so, it is clear that much of memory involves thinking. And as we saw previously, the same is also true of perception. For there, too, the perceiver becomes a thinker as he tries to solve perceptual problems and make sense out of ambiguous or impossible figures. In the next chapter, we will consider the topic of thinking in its own right.

SUMMARY

1.   Any act of remembering implies success in each of three phases: *encoding, storage,* and *retrieval.*

2.   According to the *stage theory of memory,* there are several memory systems. Of these, the most important are *short-term memory* in which information is held for fairly short intervals and *long-term memory* in which information is stored for much longer periods. According to stage theory, to get to the long-term memory system, material must first pass through the short-term store.

3.   An important difference between short-term and long-term memory is in their capacity. That of long-term memory is enormous; that of short-term memory is very limited as shown by studies of memory span. The recall of an item heard just before may be from the short-term or long-term store. Studies of free recall with lists of unrelated items have provided a way of determining from where such items are retrieved. According to stage theory, the *primacy effect* obtained by use of this procedure is associated with retrieval from long-term storage, while the *recency effect* reflects retrieval from short-term memory.

4.   Since the stage theory assumes that the only gateway to long-term memory is through short-term memory, there will obviously be a bottleneck. This is overcome by *recoding* the incoming material into larger *chunks.*

5.   An important challenge to stage theory came from the fact that *maintenance rehearsal,* in which material is simply held passively in short-term memory, confers little or no long-term benefits in aiding recall, which indicates that the transfer from short-term to long-term memory cannot be automatic. This realization led to a theoretical reevaluation in the way memory is conceived today. One change concerns short-term memory, which is now often called *working memory* and is regarded as a mental workbench on which items are held while they are encoded. The other change is an increasing emphasis on the role of *depth of processing* and *organization* in remembering. This includes demonstrations that memory is better after deep processing than after shallow processing, that it is helped by chunking and other organizational devices, and that it is further aided by relating the material to be remembered with what is already known. These general principles of memorial organization underlie *mnemonics,* techniques for helping memory, which include various forms of verbal organization and the use of *visual imagery.*

6. Remembering depends in part upon the presence of appropriate *retrieval cues.* According to the principle of *compatibility* (also called *encoding specificity*), remembering is most likely if the context at the time of the retrieval is identical to that present at the time of original encoding. One reason why certain forms of encoding (for example, organization and understanding) are better than others is that they help in later retrieval. This also explains the effect of *elaborative rehearsal,* which, unlike maintenance rehearsal, helps in remembering because it provides appropriate retrieval paths.

7. Retrieval from long-term memory is often preceded by a process of *memory search.* In some cases, the search reaches a halfway point, where we seem to recall something but not quite, and we experience the *tip-of-the-tongue phenomenon.*

8. What we normally call remembering involves explicit retrieval, using such methods as recall or recognition in which the subject is explicitly asked a question that refers to memory. But retrieval can also be implicit, where the subjects are not asked or even made consciously aware that they are referring to some prior experience. Laboratory methods to test for implicit retrieval include repetition priming and fragment completion.

9. Other things being equal, forgetting increases the longer the time since learning. This point was first demonstrated by Ebbinghaus, who plotted the *forgetting curve* of associations between nonsense syllables. The causes of forgetting are still a matter of debate. One theory holds that traces gradually *decay* over time, though this view is complicated by the fact that forgetting is greater if the subject is awake rather than asleep during the retention interval. Another view argues that the fundamental cause of forgetting is *interference* produced by other, inappropriate memories. This approach leans heavily on two forms of interference produced in the laboratory, *retroactive* and *proactive inhibition.* Yet another theory asserts that forgetting is primarily caused by changes in *retrieval cues* at the time of recall. This position is sometimes used to explain the phenomenon of *childhood amnesia.*

10. Under some circumstances, forgetting doesn't seem to occur. There is evidence that some memories last for a very long time, as in the case of a language learned in school some remnants of which seem to remain in a *permastore.* Other evidence for long-lasting memories are *flashbulb memories* (as in remembering where one was at the time one heard that President Kennedy was assassinated or that the space shuttle had exploded) though these often prove inaccurate.

11. In many cases, remembering depends on prior knowledge, which affects encoding and later retrieval by relating the incoming material to various conceptual frameworks called *schemas* and *scripts.* The utilization of such frameworks can sometimes lead to *memory distortions* as originally shown by Frederic Bartlett. Modern studies of eyewitness testimony have elaborated this point by demonstrating that what is remembered can be seriously affected by building various presuppositions into the request for recall. Related work has shown that hypnotized subjects will reconstruct memories to please a hypnotist. Although genuinely convinced that what they recall really happened, the hypnotized subject often turns out to be incorrect and to be easily affected by leading questions.

12. There is some question about the mechanisms that underlie schema-based memory distortions. Some authors believe that they are mainly *reconstructions* in which gaps in memory are filled by conscious or unconscious inference. Others believe that schemas produce *accommodative distortions,* which don't just fill gaps but represent genuine alterations in one's memory.

13. Certain injuries to the brain, particularly to the hippocampus and surrounding regions, can produce disorders of memory. In *anterograde amnesia,* the patient's ability to fix material in long-term memory is damaged. In *retrograde amnesia,* the loss is for memories just prior to the injury and is sometimes attributed to a disruption of *trace consolidation.* An important current issue is why patients with severe anterograde amnesia can acquire certain long-term memories (learning a maze, benefiting from repetition priming) but not others (remembering that they have seen the maze or heard the word before). According to one hypothesis, the crucial distinction is between *procedural* and *declarative* knowledge; according to another, it is between *implicit* and *explicit retrieval.*

CHAPTER **8**

THOUGHT AND KNOWLEDGE

ANALOGICAL REPRESENTATIONS 281

MENTAL IMAGES ■ SPATIAL THINKING

SYMBOLIC REPRESENTATIONS 287

SYMBOLIC ELEMENTS ■ KNOWLEDGE AND MEMORY

THE PROCESS OF THINKING: SOLVING PROBLEMS 292

ORGANIZATION IN PROBLEM SOLVING ■ OBSTACLES TO PROBLEM SOLVING ■ OVERCOMING OBSTACLES TO SOLUTION ■ RESTRUCTURING ■ ARTIFICIAL INTELLIGENCE: PROBLEM SOLVING BY COMPUTER

THE PROCESS OF THINKING: REASONING AND DECISION MAKING 308

DEDUCTIVE REASONING ■ INDUCTIVE REASONING ■ DECISION MAKING

COGNITION AND CONSCIOUSNESS 315

MENTAL PROCESSES THAT GO ON BELOW THE SURFACE ■ WHAT'S CONSCIOUSNESS GOOD FOR?

TAKING STOCK 319

SUMMARY 320

I n ordinary language, the word *think* has a wide range of meanings. It may be a synonym for *remembering* (as in "I can't think of her name"), or for *attention* (as in the exhortation "Think"), or for *belief* (as in "I think sea serpents exist"). It may also refer to a state of vague and undirected reverie as in "I'm thinking of nothing in particular." These many uses suggest that the word has become a blanket term to cover virtually any psychological process that goes on within the individual and that is essentially unobservable from without.

But thinking also has a narrower meaning, which is graphically rendered in Rodin's famous statue of *The Thinker*. Here, the meaning of *think* is best conveyed by such words as *to reason* or *ponder* or *reflect*. Psychologists who study thinking are mainly interested in this sense of the term. To distinguish it from the others, they refer to **directed thinking,** a set of mental activities that are utilized whenever we plan a course of action, try to solve a problem, evaluate the truth of an assertion, or weigh the costs and benefits as we decide between alternatives. As we do so, we necessarily draw on the foundation upon which all thinking rests: what we already know.

ANALOGICAL REPRESENTATIONS

Whenever we think, we draw on what we already know, and shuffle and rearrange it to come up with a solution, an answer. To fix a mower, we call on our knowledge of gasoline-powered motors; to avert a social disaster, we refer to what we know about a thin-skinned acquaintance. But how should that knowledge be characterized? Many (perhaps all) of the components of this knowledge can be regarded as **mental representations** of the world and the individual's experiences with it.

These mental representations are the main elements of thought. They are the internal equivalent of the many **external representations** we encounter in ordinary life, those signs or symbols that "stand for" something else, such as maps, blue-prints, menus, price lists, stories—the list is very large. In all these cases, the representation is not equivalent to that which it stands for; it just signifies it: We don't literally drive on the map, nor do we eat the menu.

Psychologists, philosophers, and computer scientists have found it convenient to distinguish between two broad classes of representations, the **analogical** and the **symbolic.**★ Analog representations capture some of the actual characteristics of (and are thus analogous to) that which they represent. In contrast, symbolic representations bear no such relationship to the item for which they stand. As we will see, human thought uses both kinds of representations.

★ Many psychologists and computer scientists use the term *digital* for what we here call "symbolic." This is because computers usually encode such symbolic, nonpictorial representations in a discrete, all-or-none fashion by various combinations of the digits 0 and 1.

Thinking (Aristotle Contemplating the Bust of Homer, *1653, by Rembrandt; courtesy The Metropolitan Museum of Art, purchased with special funds and gifts of friends of the Museum, 1961)*

A

B

Consider a picture of a mouse and compare it to an actual mouse. The picture is in some ways quite different from the real animal. It represents a mouse rather than actually being one. But even so, the picture has many similarities to the creature that it represents, for it looks quite a bit like a real mouse. It is an analogical representation. In contrast, take the word *mouse.* This word stands for the same long-tailed, big-eared, and bewhiskered creature that the picture represents. But unlike the picture, the word has no physical similarity to the mouse whatever. It is an abstract representation, for the relation between the sound "mouse" (or the written, five-letter word *mouse)* and the little, long-tailed animal that it represents is entirely arbitrary and symbolic.

The same distinction applies to many other external representations. Consider the road sign "winding road ahead" shown below:

This sign is an analogical representation, for it (crudely) depicts the winding road it warns about. No such pictorial analogy applies to the abstract—symbolic—representation "$."

The same distinction that holds for external representations also holds for mental, internal ones. Some of our internal representations are images that are in some ways picturelike; others are thoughts that are more abstract and symbolic. We will begin our discussion by considering thought based on analogical representations: mental images and the related topic of visual and spatial thinking.

Some representations are pictorial, others are abstract *(A) A photograph of Ambroise Vollard, a French art dealer at the turn of the century. (B) A cubist portrait of Monsieur Vollard by Pablo Picasso. Note that while Picasso's rendering is by no means literal, there is enough of a pictorial similarity to the model that the portrait is still recognizable. While this painting is a pictorial representation, the model's name—Ambroise Vollard—is not. It stands for him, but it is not like him, for both names and words are abstract representations rather than pictorial ones. (Picasso's* Portrait of Ambroise Vollard, *1909. Pushkin Museum, Moscow; courtesy of Scala/Art Resource)*

MENTAL IMAGES

There is little doubt that much of our knowledge is based on analogical memories, often called *mental images,* that preserve some of the characteristic attributes of our senses. It's not just that we *know* that, say, people's waists are between their heads and their toes. Of course we do, but that isn't all. We are also able somehow to retrieve this "betweenness" from a mental image that has some of the characteristics of the original visual experience. As some authors (including Shakespeare) have put it, we see it in "our mind's eye." While similar claims have been made for other senses—hearing with the mind's ear (composers), feeling with the mind's fingers (blind persons)—our primary concern here will be with visual images.

RATING ONE'S OWN IMAGES

The first attempt to study visual imagery goes back a hundred years to Sir Francis Galton (1822–1911), the founder of the field of individual differences, who asked people to describe their own images and to rate them for vividness (Galton, 1883). The results showed that individuals differed widely. Some people said they could call up scenes at will and see them with the utmost clarity. Others (including some well-known painters) denied ever having images at all. One might expect that these differences in how people describe their own experiences would predict their performance on various tasks that seemed to call for visual memory. But in fact the results on this matter are ambiguous. Some studies do find the expected correlation, others find a reverse effect, while still others find no relationship at all (Marks, 1983; Reisberg and Leak, 1987; Di Vesta, Ingersoll, and Sunshine, 1971; Baddeley, 1976).

EIDETIC IMAGERY

Since self-judgments of imagery are of uncertain value, psychologists have turned to more objective procedures. In addition to asking what the image is like, they ask what it enables the subject to do. For example, is the image a mental picture from which he can read off information as if it were an actual visual scene outside? By and large, the answer is no. But there are some exceptions. The most striking is *eidetic imagery,* characterized by relatively long-lasting and detailed images of visual scenes that can sometimes be scanned and "looked at" as if they had real existence outside. In one study, a group of school children was shown a picture for thirty seconds. After it was taken away, the subjects were asked whether they could still see anything and, if so, to describe what they saw (Leask, Haber, and Haber, 1969). Evidence for eidetic imagery is contained in the following protocol of a ten-year-old boy, who was looking at a blank easel from which a picture from *Alice in Wonderland* had just been removed (Figure 8.1).

8.1   Test picture for study of eidetic imagery   *This picture from* Alice in Wonderland *was shown for half a minute to elementary schoolchildren, a few of whom seemed to have an eidetic image of it. (Illustration by Marjorie Torrey)*

Experimenter:	Do you see something there?
Subject:	I see the tree, gray tree with three limbs. I see the cat with stripes around its tail.
Experimenter:	Can you count those stripes?
Subject:	Yes (pause). There's about 16.
Experimenter:	You're counting what? Black, white or both?
Subject:	Both.
Experimenter:	Tell me what else you see.
Subject:	And I can see the flowers on the bottom. There's about three stems but you can see two pairs of flowers. One on the right has green leaves, red hair and a red hair band and there are some leaves in the upper left-hand corner where the tree is (Haber, 1969, p. 38).

Eidetic imagery is relatively rare. Only 5 percent of schoolchildren tested seem to have it, and the proportion is almost surely smaller in adults. According to one author, this difference between children and adults may only indicate that children tend to rely more on imagery in their thinking, perhaps because their verbal and conceptual memory systems are not as yet sufficiently developed (Kosslyn, 1980, 1984). In any case, there is no reason to believe that this form of imagery is an especially useful form of mental activity. Contrary to popular belief, memory experts don't generally have eidetic imagery (or photographic memory as it is sometimes popularly named); their skill is in organizing material in memory, rather than in storing it in pictorial form.

PICTURE-LIKE ASPECTS OF VISUAL MEMORY

With the possible exception of eidetic imagery, our memory of visually presented objects and events is not a simple reembodiment of stored visual sensation. Our perceptions are not like photographs, and so our visual memories (which are presumably based on these perceptions) can't be either. But they may nevertheless contain certain pictorial attributes that are also found in visual perception. A number of studies suggest that this is indeed the case.

Mental rotation One line of evidence comes from studies on **mental rotation.** Subjects were shown a letter or a number, either a normal version or a mirror-reversed form (that is *R* or *Я*). But in addition, the figures were tilted so that subjects might encounter an *R* rotated by, say, 180 degrees. Or they might be presented with *Я* rotated by, say, 60 degrees (see Figure 8.2). The subjects' task was to press one button if the stimulus was normal, another if it was mirror-reversed.

The reaction time proved to be a regular function of how far the characters were tilted away from the upright position. As the orientation of the letters changed from the upright (that is, 0 degree rotation) through 60 degrees to 180 degrees, reaction times increased. The same was true for the mirror-reversed letters. The authors interpret their results as evidence for a separate visual memory system. In their view, the subjects mentally rotated an image of the stimulus they were presented with until it was upright. Once they had brought it to this position, it could be compared to their visual memory of the normal and mirror-reversed characters. The fact that reaction time was a function of angle shows that this mental rotation takes time; in the present case, it took about 30 milliseconds for every 10 degrees of rotation (Cooper and Shepard, 1973; Shepard and Cooper, 1982).

Image scanning Another line of evidence comes from studies on **image scanning.** In one such study, the subjects were first shown the map of a fictitious island containing various objects: a hut, a well, a tree, a meadow, and so on (see Figure 8.3). After memorizing this map by copying it repeatedly, the subjects performed a reaction-time task. The experimenter named two objects on the map (say, the hut and the meadow). The subjects' task was to conjure up a mental image of the entire island and then to imagine a little black speck zipping from the first location to the second. The results showed that their reaction time was directly proportional to the distance between the two points. This result would be no surprise had the subjects scanned a physical map with their real eyes. That the same holds true when they scan an image with their mind's eye is rather remarkable (Kosslyn, Ball, and Reisser, 1978).

Images are not pictures The preceding discussion makes it clear that visual images are analogical representations that share some of the properties of pictures. In particular, some of the major spatial characteristics of the depicted scene are

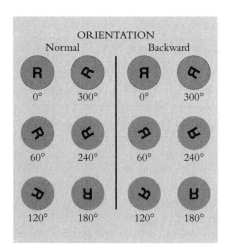

8.2 Mental rotation *Normal and backward versions of one of the characters used in the mental rotation study, showing the orientations in which it appeared as a test stimulus. (Adapted from Cooper and Shepard, 1973)*

8.3 Image scanning *Subjects were asked to look mentally at a map of a fictional island and then to imagine a speck zipping from one location to another. (After Kosslyn, Ball, and Reiser, 1978)*

8.4 Images are not pictures *The rabbit-duck figure, first used in 1900 by Joseph Jastrow. (After Attneave, 1971)*

maintained in the image. If two points in the scene are close to each other, they are functionally close in the image; if they are far apart, they are also functionally far apart in the image. What holds for perceived distance, also holds for such spatial relations as "betweenness." If point *B* in the scene is between points *A* and *C,* this relation is preserved in the image. It is functionally "between" in the image, so that one cannot mentally scan from point *A* to point *C* without passing through point *B.* In sum: Images preserve the general spatial layout of the scene that is depicted in the image.

But while images are picture-*like,* they are *not* pictures. Some evidence for this view comes from a study by Chambers and Reisberg who presented their subjects with a figure (that they had never seen before) that is normally reversible: If it is seen as oriented toward the left, it looks like the head of a duck; if oriented toward the right, it looks like the head of a rabbit (Figure 8.4). The subjects' first task was to form a mental image of this figure. At a later time, when the picture was no longer physically present, they were asked to call up this image and describe what it looked like. All subjects "saw" either a duck or a rabbit with their mind's eye, and some said they saw it very vividly. They were then asked whether their image might look like something else. Not one of the subjects came up with a reversal, even after many hints and considerable coaxing. The results were very different when the subjects subsequently drew the figure and looked at their own drawing. Now everyone came up with the perceptual alternative. To Chambers and Reisberg these results indicated that a visual image is not a picture. It is instead a mental product that is based on a picture, but that is already encoded to some extent—perhaps as a duck, perhaps as a rabbit. To the extent that it is so encoded, it has lost its pictorial innocence. It is no longer ambiguous because it has already been interpreted (see Chambers and Reisberg, 1985; for further discussion, see Finke, Pinker, and Farah, 1989; Reisberg and Chambers, 1990).

SPATIAL THINKING

Closely related to mental imagery is **spatial thinking,** the kind that we use when we want to determine a shortcut between two locations or when we mentally try to rearrange the furniture in the living room. How are such tasks accomplished? One means is by way of mental images. By consulting a mental picture, the traveler can read off shortcuts as she might from a mental map, and the decorator can save wear and tear on his back muscles by rearranging his images before moving the actual armchairs and sofas.

MENTAL MAPS THAT ARE PICTURE-LIKE

Most people have a general conception of the spatial layout of their environment. According to some investigators, part of this geographical knowledge is based on mental maps that have pictorial qualities. In one study, students were asked to estimate the distance between various locations on their university campus—for example, between their dormitory and the gymnasium, or between the student union and the library. It turned out that the subjects were quite accurate in their estimates. But even more interesting was the time it took to provide these estimates. The longer the distance, the longer the estimation time. It was as if the subjects measured distances with a mental ruler on a mental map, much as one might measure the length of a wall with a small ruler. The longer the wall, the more often the ruler would have to be moved from point to point and the more time the process would take (Jonides and Baum, 1978).

MENTAL MAPS THAT ARE BOTH SYMBOLIC AND CONCEPTUAL

Some kinds of spatial thinking are based on picture-like images, but others involve processes that are much more symbolic and conceptual. In one study, subjects were asked to indicate the relative locations of two cities. One of the pairs was San Diego, California, and Reno, Nevada. The subjects judged San Diego to be west of Reno, although it actually is farther east. Another pair was Montreal, Canada, and Seattle, Washington. Here the subjects judged Montreal to be farther north, although its actual location is south of Seattle. These results suggest that the subjects didn't base their answers on picture-like mental maps resembling the real maps shown in Figure 8.5. If they had, they would have said that Reno is west of San Diego. But in fact, they (falsely) asserted the very opposite.

How can we explain the subjects' errors? The most plausible explanation is that their judgments were affected by what they knew about the relative locations of the states or countries that contain the cities about which they were

8.5 Conceptual mental maps Subjects tend to judge San Diego to be west of Reno and Montreal to be north of Seattle. But these judgments are in error. (A) A map of California and Nevada with colored lines of longitude (angular distance from an arbitrary reference point in Greenwich, England) which shows that in fact San Diego is east of Reno. (B) A map of the United States and southern Canada with colored lines of latitude (angular distance from the equator) which shows that Seattle is slightly north of Montreal. (Stevens and Coupe, 1978)

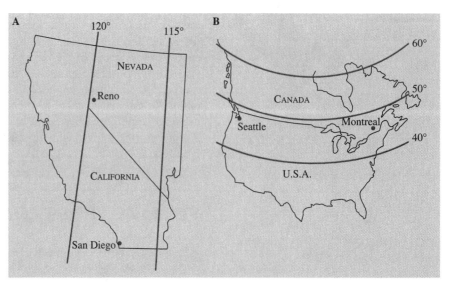

asked (e.g., Nevada is east of California, and Canada is north of the United States). And this knowledge was based on abstract, symbolic representations rather than representations that are analogical and pictorial. What the subjects knew about San Diego and Reno can be summarized by the three propositions shown below:

California is west of Nevada.
San Diego is in California.
Reno is in Nevada.

This way of representing spatial knowledge could easily lead to error, for it might suggest that the east-west relation that holds for the states also holds for all the cities within them. This would be true if the larger geographical units (California and Nevada) were conceptual categories such as *bird*. (If we know that owls and robins are birds, it automatically follows that they both have wings, beaks, and feathers.) Of course, states and countries are not at all equivalent to categories such as *bird*: Reno is not *a* Nevada but is *in* Nevada. Even so, most of us often store spatial information in such a rough-and-ready conceptual way. (One hopes that airplane navigators are an exception.) To the extent that we do store some geographical information under category rubrics, our spatial knowledge cannot be exclusively—or even largely—picture-like (Stevens and Coupe, 1978).

SYMBOLIC REPRESENTATIONS

Mental images are clearly not the only elements of thought, nor are they the most important ones. Around the turn of the century, several psychologists asked subjects to describe everything that "went through their minds" as they tried to solve various intellectual problems. The solution frequently came without a trace of imagery (and frequently also without words). The subjects reported that when their thought was both wordless and imageless, they often had a sense of certain underlying relationships, such as the experience of "this doesn't go with that" or a "feeling of *if* or *but*" (Humphrey, 1951).

SYMBOLIC ELEMENTS

The attempt to describe the components of this more abstract level of thinking is relatively recent, at least for psychologists. But some of the key items of such a description are already in the vocabulary of related disciplines, such as logic and linguistics. Examples are the terms *concept* and *proposition*.

CONCEPTS

The term *concept* is generally used to describe a class or category that subsumes a number (sometimes an infinite number) of individual instances or subtypes. An example is *dog,* which includes *poodle, beagle, dachshund,* and *Alsatian.* Other concepts designate qualities or dimensions. Examples are *length* and *age.* Still others are relational, such as *taller than.* Relational concepts don't apply to any one item in isolation. One can't be *taller than* except in relation to something else to which one's height is being compared. For our present purposes, these and many other concepts are regarded as symbolic rather than analogic mental representations.★

PROPOSITIONS

Concepts describe classes of events or objects or relations between them. They are what we generally think about. In so doing, we tend to combine them in various ways. The British empiricists emphasized one such mental combination: the simple associative train of thought in which one idea leads to another. A more important way of relating concepts is by asserting something about them, for example, "Dogs generally bite postmen." Such statements are called *propositions.* They make some assertion that relates a **subject** (the item about which an assertion is made, e.g., *dogs)* and a **predicate** (what is asserted about the subject, e.g., *bite postmen)* in a way that can be true or false.

KNOWLEDGE AND MEMORY

Concepts and propositions are the elements of symbolic thought. Many of them are stored in memory, where they constitute our accumulated knowledge, the "data base" that sustains and informs our thoughts. How is this knowledge organized in memory, how is it retrieved, explicitly or implicitly, and when is it used?

GENERIC MEMORY

Psychologists often distinguish between episodic and generic memory. **Episodic memory** is the memory for particular events (episodes) of one's own life, what happened when and where, as when recalling that one ate fried chicken the other night. This contrasts with **generic memory**, which is memory for items of knowledge as such, independent of the particular occasion on which one acquired them. For example, we remember the capital of France, the square root of 9, and the fact that Aaron Burr shot Alexander Hamilton in a duel, but rarely do we remember how or when we first acquired these bits of knowledge. In effect, a person's generic memory is the sum total of his acquired knowledge— the meanings of words and symbols, facts about the world, what objects look like, and various general principles, schemas, and scripts.

Most of the studies on memory we described in the last chapter are primarily about episodic memory. Consider an experiment in which subjects have to memorize a list of nouns such as *submarine, typewriter, elephant,* and so on. When the experimenter tests for later recall, her interest is in what the subjects learned at the time of the experiment—that the list they were presented with included *elephant* and *typewriter* but not *gazelle* and *thermometer.* This is not to say that the subjects brought no generic memories to bear on the tasks. After all, they knew and understood all the words on the list. But the experimenter was not interested in their generic memories. Had she been, she would have asked questions such as, "What is an elephant?" (Tulving, 1972).

One of the most important components of generic memory is **semantic memory,** which concerns the meanings of words and concepts. As some authors conceive it, our entire vocabulary is in this store: every word, together with its

---

★ As we will see in the next chapter, some authors believe that many concepts are better described by a *prototype* that serves as a kind of mental average of the various members of the conceptual category (see Chapter 9, pp. 333–34).

pronunciation, all of its meanings, its relations to objects in the real world, the way it is put together with other words to make phrases and sentences. How do we ever find any one bit of information in this bulky mental dictionary? One thing is certain: When we search for an item—say, a synonym for *quiet*—we don't go through *all* of the items in the semantic store, one after the other. If we did, the hunt might last for days or weeks. The fact that we can come up with *silent* in a second or less shows that we make use of a much more efficient retrieval system. To use a library analogy, the person who takes out a book doesn't have to rummage through all of the volumes on each shelf in order to find the one he wants. He can obtain his book much faster because there is an organized system according to which the books are arranged in the stacks.

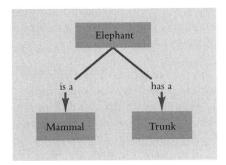

8.6 Network structure in semantic memory models *The figure shows a small section of a semantic memory model, with nodes ("elephant" "mammal" "trunk") connected through associative links. Some networks employ labeled associations that indicate the particular relations between the nodes (such as,* is a, has, *and so on).*

A HIERARCHICAL NETWORK

Semantic memory is surely organized, but just what does its organization consist of? To answer this question many investigators propose a **network model** in which the words and concepts stored in semantic memory are linked through a complex system of relationships (somewhat analogous to the networks we encountered previously when discussing pattern recognition). In such networks, the words or concepts are indicated by **nodes,** while the associations between them are indicated by lines or arrows (see Figure 8.6).

One of the first such network models was hierarchical. It assumed a semantic hierarchy in which a particular word (say, *canary*) is stored under the higher-order category that subsumes it (here, *bird*), which in turn is stored under a yet higher category (here, *animal),* and so on. Certain properties (or **features**) that describe each of these terms are then stored under the node that is most appropriate. Under canary, one presumably stores such features as: "is yellow," "can sing." Under bird, one might store features such as: "has wings," "has feathers." Similarly for yet higher categories such as animals or living things (see Figure 8.7; Collins and Quillian, 1969).

This hierarchical model was very neat but as so often, nature is much less neat than theorists would like her to be. To mention only one problem, membership in many semantic categories does not seem to be an all-or-none affair. Thus when subjects are asked to rate various birds according to the degree to which they are "typical birds," robins are rated to be most typical, chickens less so, and penguins birds by courtesy only (Rosch, 1973a, 1973b). These differences in typicality seem to affect the way in which semantic memory is accessed. For example, subjects are faster in agreeing that "X is a bird," if X is a typical bird like a canary rather than a marginal case like a penguin or an ostrich (Rips, Shoben, and Smith, 1973; Rips, Smith, and Shoben, 1978). Such effects suggest that the relation between items of information in the semantic memory is not as simple as the hierarchical position had supposed (e.g., Conrad, 1972; for further discussion, see Chapter 9, pp. 333–34).

8.7 A hierarchical theory of semantic memory *To decide whether the sentence "Ravens have feathers" is true, given the organization of the entries here pictured, one has to "look up" the information at the second level, under* bird.

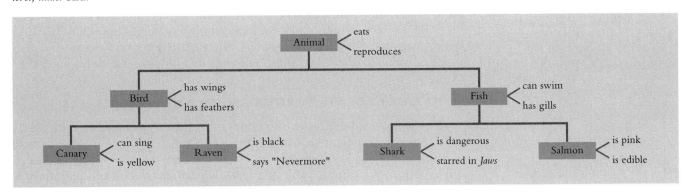

A NETWORK MODEL BASED ON SEMANTIC DISTANCE

The difficulties of the hierarchical model led to the formulation of several alternatives. One was a ***spreading activation model*** in which semantic relationships were built directly into the network. In this network, shorter arrows between two nodes indicate a closer semantic relationship—based on hierarchical position (as in *canary-sing*) or on similarity of meaning (*apple-orange*) or on well-learned associations (*Pepsi-Cola*). The model assumes that nodes can be activated and that this activation will spread to other nodes, much as electrical currents spread through a network of wires. This effect will be greater (and occur more quickly) for nodes that are nearby than for others that are farther off, for the activation tends to dissipate as it spreads (Collins and Loftus, 1975; see Figure 8.8).

How can this spreading activation hypothesis be tested? One line of evidence came from a study in which broad semantic categories were activated. Subjects were asked to think of a word that begins with a certain letter and belongs to some semantic category, such as *G-fruit*. The experimenter measures the reaction time from the presentation of the category term *fruit* and the response (say, *grapes*). Shortly thereafter subjects get tested once more. On some occasions, the same category is again called for, though with a different initial letter, as in *S-fruit*. Now the time it takes to retrieve a suitable word (say, *strawberries*) is quite a bit shorter than it was the first time. What seems to happen is that a semantic category is activated and remains that way for a while, like a section in a library that is lit up by a previous user who leaves the lights on when she departs. This part of the library will now become easier to find (Loftus, 1973).

Further evidence comes from several experiments on ***semantic priming***. In a classic study, the subjects were presented with two strings of letters, with one string printed above the other (Meyer and Schvaneveldt, 1971). Three examples are:

NURSE	NURSE	NARDE
BUTTER	DOCTOR	DOCTOR

The subjects' job was to press a "yes" button if both letter sequences were real words (that is, for NURSE-BUTTER and NURSE-DOCTOR), and a "no" button if one or both of the two were not (that is, for NARDE-DOCTOR). Our only interest is in the two pairs that required a "yes" response. (In such tasks, the "no" items are only there to make sure that the subject does what he is supposed to.) The results showed that the reaction time was shorter when the two words were related in meaning (as in NURSE-DOCTOR) than when they were unrelated (as in NURSE-BUTTER). It appears that the sight of the word NURSE primed the system to respond to related words such as DOCTOR but had no such facilitating effect on unrelated words such as BUTTER. This is in line with the Collins and Loftus model: The node corresponding to NURSE was activated, and this activation spread to nearby nodes (e.g., DOCTOR) on the network. Simply put, it means that words are stored and filed according to their semantic relatedness (Blank and Foss, 1978; McKoon and Ratcliff, 1979).

PARALLEL DISTRIBUTED PROCESSING

The network models we've discussed thus far share some important characteristics. Perhaps the most important of these is that each of the units of the network (that is, the nodes) corresponds to a particular representation. Take the concept *fire engine* in the small piece of a spreading activation network represented in

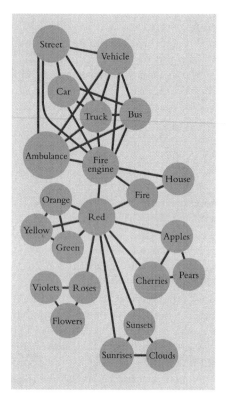

8.8 *The spreading activation model*
The figure shows a—very small—portion of the semantic network postulated by the spreading activation model. The shorter the path, the stronger the semantic relation. (After Collins and Loftus, 1975)

Figure 8.8. In that figure, *fire engine* corresponds to a particular node, as do the associated concepts *truck, ambulance, fire,* and *red*. But the past decade has seen the development of a new group of network models, often called **parallel distributed processing** models (or **PDP** models for short). In such models the relevant symbolic representations (here *fire engine*) do not correspond to any one unit of the network. They correspond instead to the state of the network as a whole. Within a PDP model, the concept *fire engine* is thus a property of the activation pattern of the entire network and is *distributed* over all of its units (hence, the model's name).★

How can we visualize the way in which concepts are distributed over the entire network? Consider a spy story in which Master Spy works out an ingenious plot to overthrow a government. The plan involves 100 different operatives, each of whom has his or her own instructions corresponding to a small part of the master plan. To protect himself and the others, Master Spy made sure that none of the operatives knew anything about the overall plan. All they know is their own little part. But once each operative has received the orders, he or she needs no further supervision. Now chance enters. Immediately after Master Spy has given the last operative instructions, he dies of a heart attack. So what happens to the overthrow plan? Since all operatives have their orders, the plot will presumably run by itself, without benefit of Master Spy. But where is the Master Plan? While Master Spy was alive we might have said that the Master Plan was in his mind, but now that he is dead where is it? It is not in the mind of any individual operative since each of them knows only a small part of the a whole. But in a way this Master Plan is still there, as a property of the entire spy network. And it is presumably still effective enough to topple the government. The plan emerges from the functioning of all 100 operatives, each doing their own small part simultaneously; it is distributed over them all, but is not (as a whole) in any one of their minds (Schwartz and Reisberg, 1991).

PDP models have been devised for many different cognitive operations, including pattern perception, memory processes, and aspects of thinking and language (McClelland and Rumelhart, 1986). In all of these cases, the relevant representation is a property of the network as a whole.

Such PDP networks have a number of theoretical advantages. One concerns the distinction between episodic and semantic memory. In traditional models, these two are regarded as essentially separate. But are they really? Let's go back to the concept *fire engine*. How is that general concept related to any one particular experience in which we see a fire engine racing at top speed with sirens blasting? In traditional networks, there is one node for *fire engine* in semantic memory and some other node (or nodes) in episodic memory that describes this most recent experience. But under such a conception it is difficult to explain how our semantic concepts ("fire engines in general") are affected by particular episodes ("this particular experience with a fire engine"). PDP memory models have no such problem, for they don't assume a separation of episodic and semantic memories. In such a model, the general concept simply corresponds to a particular set of connections between the units of the network and their activation strengths. Any new episode will simply change these patterns. If the episode is very similar to the ones preceding (e.g., "just another fire engine"), the change will be minor; if it's quite different (e.g., "What do you know—a *green* fire engine!"), the change will be more substantial.

The PDP approach is very ambitious. Its proponents believe that eventually all cognitive operations can be described in its terms. In their view, the complex

★ The term *parallel* refers to the fact that in such models the different parts of the network activate each other simultaneously (that is, in parallel) rather than one after another. Since the properties of the network depend on the connections among its component units, the PDP approach is sometimes called *connectionism*.

NAGMARA

BOLMPER

SLEVO

STIGNIH

TOLUSONI

8.9 *Anagrams* *Rearrange the letters on each line to form a word. (For the solution, see p. 294).*

8.10 *Matchstick problem* *Assemble all six matches to form four equilateral triangles, each side of which is equal to the length of one match. (For the solution, see p. 306).*

8.11 *Nine-dot problem* *Nine dots are arranged in a square. Connect them by drawing four continuous straight lines without lifting your pencil from the paper. (For the solution, see p. 307).*

phenomena of mental functioning are ultimately the result of much smaller mechanical events that go on at a lower, local level, much as an avalanche is produced by the movement of many small stones and rocks. They argue that this position fits what we know about the probable cerebral machinery that underlies cognition, asserting that neural networks are more similar to PDP networks than to networks modeled along traditional lines. These theoretical proposals have led to a great deal of vigorous debate, with strong advocates on both sides of the issue (e.g., Hetherington and Seidenberg, 1989; McCloskey, and Cohen, 1989; Pincker and Prince, 1988). As yet it is much too early to come to any final evaluation. This is an exciting area of current psychological theorizing in which new advances come at a very rapid rate, so that whatever we might say today will almost surely be out of date tomorrow.

THE PROCESS OF THINKING: SOLVING PROBLEMS

Thus far, our concern has been with the elements of which thought and knowledge are composed. We now turn from the question of *what* to the question of *how.* How does thinking operate as we try to solve the myriad of problems encountered in life, whether trying to fix a broken lawn mower, to smooth over an awkward social situation, or to solve an anagram?

ORGANIZATION IN PROBLEM SOLVING

Thinking is an activity, and like most activities of the organism it is organized. The would-be problem solver goes through a sequence of internal steps that are organized in a special way: They are directed toward a goal—the solution of the problem. Consider a taxi driver who is trying to decide on the best route from the city to the airport. The internal steps he goes through in making his decision are determined not merely by the step just before but by the original problem. This sets the overall direction that dominates all the later steps and determines how each of them is to be evaluated. The taxi driver considers the super highway and rejects it as he recalls some road construction along the way, thinks of a major avenue and dismisses it because of rush-hour traffic, and then decides on a cross-town highway. The original problem acts like a schematic frame, waiting to be filled in by a "fitting" solution.

Here, as in many other directed activities, the desired end determines the beginning. This same effect is seen in virtually all efforts at problem solving. Laboratory demonstrations include studies in which subjects have been asked to decipher anagrams (Figure 8.9), to manipulate various concrete objects so as to produce a desired result (Figure 8.10), or to find the solution to various geometrical problems (Figure 8.11). Considering this variety of problems, it is hardly surprising that there are differences in the way in which they are attacked and solved; a subject who tries to join nine dots with one continuous line will surely call upon a somewhat different set of mental skills than one who has to rearrange the letters *NAGMARA* into an English word. But in all cases, the problem solver's efforts are directed toward the goal.

The role of goal-determined organization in problem solving was highlighted in a classic study by the Gestalt psychologist Karl Duncker, who asked his sub-

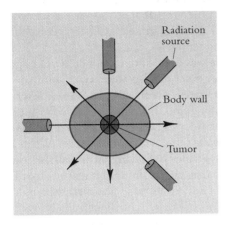

**8.12   The solution to the ray-tumor
problem**   *Several weak rays are sent from
various points outside so that they will meet at
the tumor site. There the radiation of the rays
will be intense, for all the effects will summate
at this point. But since they are individually
weak, the rays will not damage the healthy
tissue that surrounds the tumor. (After
Duncker, 1945)*

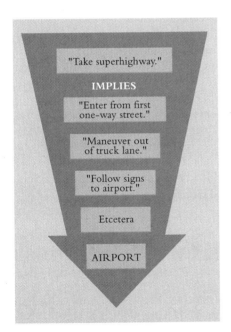

**8.13   Hierarchical organization of a
plan**   *Plans have subcomponents that have
subcomponents below them, as here illustrated
by the taxi driver's task.*

jects to "think out loud" while they tried to find the solution (Duncker, 1945).
One of Duncker's problems was cast in medical terms:

> Suppose a patient has an inoperable stomach tumor. There are certain rays which
> can destroy this tumor if their intensity is large enough. At this intensity, however,
> the rays will also destroy the healthy tissue which surrounds the tumor (e.g., the
> stomach walls, the abdominal muscles, and so on). How can one destroy the tumor
> without damaging the healthy tissue through which the rays must travel on their
> way?

Duncker's subjects typically arrived at the solution in several steps. They first
reformulated the problem so as to produce a general plan of attack. This in turn
led to more specific would-be solutions. For example, they might look for a
tissue-free path to the stomach and so propose to send the rays through the
esophagus. (A good idea which unfortunately will not work—rays travel in
straight lines and the esophagus is curved.) After exploring several other
general approaches and their specific consequences, some subjects finally hit
upon an appropriate general plan. They proposed to reduce the intensity of rays
on their way through healthy tissue and then turn up this intensity when the
rays reach the tumor. This broad restatement of what is needed eventually led
to the correct specific means, which was to send several bundles of *weak* rays
from various points outside so that they meet at the tumor where their effects
will summate (see Figure 8.12).

HIERARCHICAL ORGANIZATION

We've seen that problem solving is organized in a goal directed manner. This
organization is also *hierarchical*. Various mental operations are performed as
lower-level operations (what computer scientists call **subroutines**) that are run
under the control of higher-level ones. We have encountered the concept of
hierarchical organization before when discussing the neural organization of
behavior (see Chapter 2), as well as the role of chunking in memory (see
Chapter 7). A similar principle governs directed thinking. To the taxi driver, the
idea "take the cross-town highway" is a sort of master plan that implies various
subsidiary actions: entering from the appropriate one-way street, maneuvering
out of the truck lane, following the signs to the airport exit, and so on. To the
experienced driver, all of these substeps require no further thought, for they are
by now highly familiar and routinized. The result is a hierarchical organization
resembling that of a disciplined army. The colonel who orders his regiment to
attack does not have to specify the detailed commands his second lieutenants
issue to their platoons. Given the order from above, the subcommands follow
(Figure 8.13).

The ability to subsume many details under a larger chunk is one of the crucial
features of all directed activity, including the internal activity we call thought
and in particular the activity of problem solving. Take the fact that many problems that seem insuperable to the novice are absurdly easy to the expert. One
reason for this difference is that with long practice the necessary responses to
many of the lower-level subtasks in a problem (like those faced by the taxi
driver or by Duncker's subjects who tried to remove the tumor) become automatic. Initially they may well have been quite difficult and quite distinct, but
eventually they merged into lower-level chunks that are stored in memory as
subroutines, so that when later called upon they can be run off with a minimum
of attention. As we shall see, much of the difference between the expert problem solver in a given domain and the beginner is in the degree to which subcomponents of the activity have been turned into subroutines.

8.14 An apprentice telegrapher's learning curve *The curve plots the number of letters or digits the operator can receive per minute against weeks of practice. Note the plateau in the learning curve. The curve stays level from weeks 15 to 25 and then starts to rise again. According to Bryan and Harter, the new rise indicates the use of larger chunks. (After Bryan and Harter, 1899)*

ANAGRAM

PROBLEM

SOLVE

INSIGHT

SOLUTION

Solution to Anagrams (p. 292)

SKILLS AS THE DEVELOPMENT OF SUBROUTINES

How are subroutines formed? Their development in directed activity is particularly clear when we study how people become proficient at various skills. Some of these are mental skills such as reading or doing arithmetic. Others involve the perceptual and motor systems, as in playing tennis.

The first experimental study in this area was done about a hundred years ago by William Bryan and Noble Harter. These psychologists were trying to discover how telegraph operators master their trade. Their subjects were Western Union apprentices whose progress at sending and receiving Morse code messages was charted over a period of about forty weeks. Figure 8.14 plots one student's improvement at receiving, measured in letters per minute. What is interesting about this learning curve is its shape. Following an initial rise, the curve flattens into a plateau, after which it may rise again until it reaches another plateau, and so on. According to Bryan and Harter, such plateaus are an indication that the learner gradually transforms his task. At first he merely tracks individual letters, getting progressively faster in doing so as practice proceeds. But with time, the effective units he deals with become larger and larger: first syllables and words, then several words at a time, then simple phrases. The plateau represents the best the learner can do given that he is working with a unit of a lower level (say, letters); once this lower level is completely mastered, a higher level of organization—a larger chunk—is possible, and the learning curve shoots up once more (Bryan and Harter, 1897).

Similar effects are observed in the acquisition of many other skills, such as typing or driving a car. In such activities, becoming skillful involves a qualitative change in how the task is performed (Keele, 1982). To the novice, typing proceeds letter by letter; to the expert, the proper units are much larger, including familiar letter groupings, words, and occasionally phrases. Similarly, the beginning driver laboriously struggles to harmonize clutch, gas pedal, steering wheel, and brake to the considerable terror of innocent bystanders. After a while, those movements become quite routine and are subsumed under much higher (though perhaps equally dangerous) chunks of behavior, such as overtaking another car. An even simpler example is dressing. To the small child every article of clothing represents a major intellectual challenge; she beams with pride when she finally gets the knack of tying her shoelaces. To an adult the unit is "getting dressed," and its various components are almost completely submerged within the larger chunk. We decide to dress and before we know it we are almost fully clothed. Somehow our shoes get tied, but we never notice, unless a shoelace breaks.

It is hard to imagine any organized, skilled behavior in which this chunking process does not play a role. In Bryan and Harter's words:

> The ability to take league steps in receiving telegraphic messages, in reading, in addition, in mathematical reasoning and in many other fields, plainly depends upon the acquisition of league-stepping habits. . . . The learner must come to do with one stroke of attention what now requires a half a dozen, and presently, in one still more inclusive stroke, what now requires thirty-six. . . . Automatism is not genius, but it is the hands and feet of genius. (Bryan and Harter, 1899, p. 375)

What holds for behavioral skills is also true for problem solving. For when we try to solve a problem, we necessarily call upon all kinds of subroutines. The person who tries to rearrange the letters *KNINTGHI* to form an English word utilizes all sorts of chunks based on English spelling rules: placing vowels between consonants, eliminating clusters of more than three consonants, pursuing leads in the form of familiar letter combinations such as —*ING,* and so on.

MASTERS AND BEGINNERS

Some people solve certain problems better than others do. One reason is experience; the trained mechanic is more likely to hit on the cause of automotive failure than is his young apprentice. But what exactly does experience contribute? One obvious factor is knowledge. But no less important is chunking. Experts approach a problem in different ways than beginners. They think in larger units whose components are already contained within them. As a result the subcomponents require no further thought.

An interesting demonstration of how chunking makes the master comes from studies of chess players (de Groot, 1965; Chase and Simon, 1973a, 1973b). The chess world ranks its members according to a ruthlessly objective hierarchy of merit based on a simple record of who beats whom. Grandmasters are at the top, followed by masters, then experts, down to Class *D* players at the lowest rungs of the chess ladder. Adrian de Groot, a Dutch psychologist who was also a chess master, posed various chess problems to members of each merit category (including two former world champions) and asked them to select the best move. All of the masters chose continuations that would have won the game, while few of the other players did. But why? De Groot and many later theorists believed that the reason was in the way the players organized the problem. The chess master structures the chess position in terms of broad strategic concepts (e.g., a king-side attack with pawns) from which many of the appropriate moves follow naturally. In effect, the master has a "chess vocabulary" of more and larger chunks. If so, one would expect him to grasp a chess position in a shorter time. This is indeed the case. Players of different ranks were shown chess positions for five seconds each and were then asked to reproduce them a few minutes later. Grandmasters and masters did so with hardly an error; lesser players (including mere experts) performed much more poorly (see Figure 8.15). This is not because the chess masters had better visual memory. When presented with bizarre positions that would hardly ever arise in the course of a well-played game, they recalled them no better than novices did. Their superiority was in the conceptual organization of chess, not in the memory for visual patterns as such.

Some later studies show that the superiority of the chess masters is not entirely produced by better chunking. They are also better in evaluating chess posi-

8.15 Memory for chess positions in masters and average players (A) An actual chess position that was presented for five seconds after which the positions of the pieces had to be reconstructed. Typical performances by masters and average players are shown in (B) and (C) respectively, with errors indicated in red. (After Hearst, 1972)

A

Actual position

B

Typical master player's performance

C

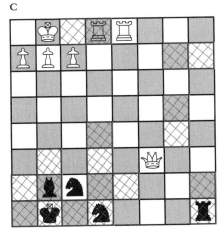

Typical average player's performance

tions and look further ahead in their mental calculations (Charness, 1981; Holding and Reynolds, 1982; Holding, 1985). But chunking clearly plays a major role in this mental skill, just as it does in telegraphy, typing, and various athletic pursuits (e.g., Allard, Graham, and Paarsalu, 1980).

Processes similar to chunking may also underlie much of the cognitive growth that occurs in childhood. As infants grow into toddlers, and toddlers into children, they gradually acquire many concepts that adults take for granted, so that they eventually comprehend space, time, and causality in much the way their parents do. It may be that the way in which they achieve this has much in common with the route that beginners take in becoming masters in a particular skill. We will return to this issue in a later discussion of cognitive development (see Chapter 13).

AUTOMATIZATION

The routinization of subcomponents in skilled activities, however, has a cost as well as a benefit. Its benefit is simple: It allows us to **automatize** the performance of many motor and mental operations (such as reading) so we can devote our attention to other tasks. The cost shows up when the automatized operations are inappropriate for the task at hand, for once they are set in motion, they are difficult to turn off.

An example is reading. When we see a billboard on a highway, we can't help but read what it says, whether we want to or not. The forms on the sign proclaim that they are letters and words; this is enough to trigger our automatized reading routines (La Berge, 1975). A striking demonstration of this phenomenon is the **Stroop effect** (Stroop, 1935). Subjects are asked to name the colors in which groups of letters are printed and to do so as quickly as they can (Figure 8.16). In one case, the letter groups are unrelated consonants or vowels. In this condition, the subjects have little trouble. After a little practice, they become very proficient at rattling off the colors, "red, blue, yellow. . . ."

The subjects' task becomes vastly more difficult in a specially designed condition in which the letters are grouped into words that are color names, such as *red, blue, yellow,* and so on. But diabolically enough, these are not the colors in which the color words are printed. Instead, *red* is printed, say, in green ink, *blue* in brown ink, *yellow* in red ink, and so on. Now the subjects respond much more slowly. Their task is to name the colors of the ink and say "green, brown, red," and so on, naming the *colors* in which the words are printed. But they can't help reading the *words* "red, blue, yellow, . . ." for reading is an automatized skill. As a result, there is violent response conflict. This conflict persists even after lengthy practice. One way subjects may finally manage to overcome it is by learning to unfocus their eyes. By this maneuver, they can still see the colors but can no longer recognize the words (Jensen,1965; see also Reisberg, Baron, and Kemler, 1980).

A	B
ZYP	RED
QLEKF	BLACK
SUWRG	YELLOW
XCIDB	BLUE
WOPR	RED
ZYP	GREEN
QLEKF	YELLOW
XCIDB	BLACK
SUWRG	BLUE
WOPR	BLACK
SUWRG	RED
ZYP	YELLOW
XCIDB	GREEN
QLEKF	BLUE
WOPR	GREEN
QLEKF	BLUE
WOPR	RED
ZYP	YELLOW
XCIDB	BLACK
SWRG	GREEN

8.16 The Stroop effect *The two lists, (A) and (B), are printed in four colors—red, green, blue, and yellow. To observe the Stroop effect, name the colors (aloud) in which each of the nonsense syllables in list (A) is printed as fast as you can, continuing downward. Then do the same for list (B), calling out the colors in which each of the words of the list is printed, again going from top to bottom. This will very probably be easier for list (A) than for list (B), a demonstration of the Stroop effect.*

OBSTACLES TO PROBLEM SOLVING

So far, we have primarily dealt with situations in which problem solvers succeed. How can we explain their all too many failures?

Problem solving is an organized, directed process, which utilizes hierarchical chunking. But there are a number of risks built into this process. As we've just seen, the benefits of chunking can be offset by the cost of its accompanying

8.17 *The standard method for solving the three-container problem* After Luchins, 1942)

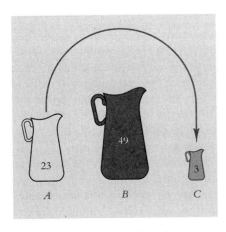

8.18 *A simpler method for solving certain three-container problems* (After Luchins, 1942)

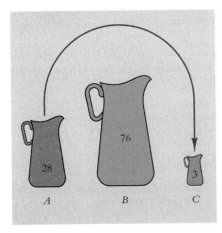

8.19 *A case where only the simple method works* (After Luchins, 1942)

automatization. But there are other risks as well. In order to use hierarchical chunks, one has to have a good sense of which chunks are appropriate and relevant; in order to work toward a goal, appropriate subgoals must be set. The trouble is that one's selections may be wrong. If so, the would-be problem solver may get stuck in a wrong approach and be unable to get unstuck. When finally told the answer, his reaction often shows that he was blind rather than ignorant: "How stupid of me. I should have seen it all along." He was victimized by a powerful ***mental set*** that was inappropriate for the problem at hand.

A well-known study shows how mental sets can make people rigid. They become ***fixated*** on one approach to a task, which makes it hard for them to think of it in any other way. The subjects were presented with a series of problems. They were told that they had three jars of known volume. Their job was to use these to obtain (mentally) an exact quantity of water from a well. In one problem, for example, the subjects had three containers—*A, B* and *C*—which held 21, 127, and 3 quarts respectively. Their task was to use these three jars to obtain 100 quarts. After a while, they hit upon the correct method. This was to fill jar *B* (127 quarts) completely, and then pour out enough water to fill jar *A* (21 quarts). After this, they would pour out more water from jar *B* to fill jar *C* (3 quarts), empty jar *C* and fill it again from jar *B*. The remaining water in jar *B* was the desired quantity, 100 quarts (Figure 8.17).

On the next few problems, the numerical values differed (see Table 8.1). But in all cases, the solution could be obtained by the same sequence of arithmetical steps, that is, $B - A - 2C$. Thus, $163 - 14 - 2 \times 25 = 99$; $43 - 18 - 2 \times 10 = 5$, and so on.

After five such problems, the subjects were given two critical tests. The first was a problem that required them to obtain 20 quarts, given jars whose volumes were 23, 49, and 3 quarts. Now most of the subjects showed a mechanization effect produced by mental set. They dutifully performed the laborious arithmetical labors they had used before, computing $49 - 23 - 2 \times 3 = 20$. They did so, even though there was a simpler method that takes only one step (Figure 8.18).

Subsequent to this was a second critical problem. The subjects were now asked to obtain 25 quarts, given jars of 28, 76, and 3 quarts. Note that here the only method that will work is the direct one, that is, $28 - 3 = 25$ (Figure 8.19). But the mental set was so powerful that many subjects failed to solve the problem altogether. They tried the old procedure, which is inappropriate ($76 - 28 - 2 \times 3$ does not equal 25), and could not hit on an adequate alternative! The set had made them so rigid that they became mentally blind (Luchins, 1942).

Similar effects have been demonstrated with other problems. In many of these there is no need to induce the misleading set by instructions or prior practice, for it is usually engendered by the perceptual arrangement of the problem itself.

TABLE 8.1 THE THREE-CONTAINER PROBLEM

Desired quantity of water (quarts)	Volume of empty jar (quarts)		
	A	B	C
99	14	163	25
5	18	43	10
21	9	42	6
31	20	59	4

8.20   Horse-and-rider problem   *The task is to place (B) on (A) in such a way that the riders are properly astride the horses. (After Scheerer, Goldstein, and Boring, 1941; for solution, see p. 307).*

Examples of such perceptually induced sets are the nine-dot problem (Figure 8.11) and the horse-and-rider problem (Figure 8.20).

SET AND MOTIVATION

In fairy tales the hero is sometimes required to solve a riddle or suffer death, but, being a fairy-tale hero, he invariably succeeds. In real life, he would have a harder time. For unfairly enough, problem solution becomes more difficult when the need for it is especially great. This is because of the relation between set and motivation. The greater the motivation toward solution, the stronger are the sets with which the problem is approached. If these sets happen to be appropriate, well and good. But if they are inappropriate, increased motivation will be a hindrance, for sets will then be that much harder to break. Since difficult problems—almost by definition—are problems that tend to engender the wrong set, their solution will be impeded as motivation becomes intense.

Evidence for these assertions comes from several experiments which show that flexibility goes down when motivation becomes intense enough. In one such study, the subjects were posed a practical problem. The problem was to mount two candles on a wall, given only the candles, a box of matches, and some thumbtacks (Figure 8.21). The solution is to empty one of the boxes, tack it to the wall, and then place the candles upon it. The difficulty of this particular problem is caused by **functional fixedness.** This is a set to think of objects in terms of their normal function: A box is to put things in and not on top of. The tendency to maintain this set (that is, functional fixedness) was increased by motivation. Subjects who expected no particular reward solved the problem more quickly than subjects who were told that they might win twenty dollars (Glucksberg, 1962).

OVERCOMING OBSTACLES TO SOLUTION

The preceding discussion highlighted some of the conceptual and motivational obstacles that lie in the face of problem solution. Apart from acquiring some further knowledge and some relevant cognitive chunks (and keeping

A

B

8.21   Functional fixedness   *(A) The problem is to mount two candles on the wall, given the objects shown. (B) To solve the problem, one has to think of a new function for the box. (After Glucksberg, 1962; photographs by Jeffrey Grosscup)*

calm about the $20 reward that accompanies success), is there anything one can do to surmount these obstacles? Thus far, no one has found a problem solver's panacea. But some psychologists have offered a few suggestions.

WORKING BACKWARDS

One useful method for solving problems is to work backwards. As an example, consider the following problem:

> Water lilies double in area every twenty-four hours. On the first day of summer, there is one water lily on a lake. It takes sixty days for the lake to become covered with water lilies. On what day is the lake half covered?

Here the problem solver will run into trouble if he tries to work it out by brute force: On Day 1, there is one lily; on Day 2, there are two; on Day 3, there are four, and so on. The trick is to shift gears and look at the problem backwards. If the lake is fully covered on Day 60, it must be half-covered on the day before, since lilies double in area every day, which means that the answer is Day 59 (after Sternberg and Davidson, 1983; see Figure 8.22).

FINDING AN APPROPRIATE ANALOGY

Another suggestion for solving difficult problems is to work by analogy, since many problems are similar to each other. The school counselor who advises teenagers is likely to find that the problem she hears about today reminds her of one she heard about a few months back, and her experience with the first generally helps her in understanding the second. What holds for the real world also holds for the laboratory. Sometimes new problems are solved by analogy with similar ones encountered earlier.

In one study subjects were first exposed to an analog of the ray-tumor problem described above (p. 293). They read a story about a general who had to attack a fortress but faced a dilemma: The fortress was protected against attack because all the roads that led to it were mined. While the mines were set to be detonated by a large body of men passing over them at one time, small groups of men would not set them off. Given this situation, the general divided his army into small groups and dispatched each of them to a different road. When he gave the signal, they each marched to the fortress, where they converged and attacked successfully. After reading this story, the subjects were given the ray-tumor problem (Gick and Holyoak, 1980, 1983).

The structural similarity between the ray-tumor problem and the general's dilemma is clear enough: In both cases, a force must be initially dispersed and later brought to convergence. But does exposure to the one problem help subjects to solve the other? It does, if they see the analogy. If they are given a hint that the military story may help them, about 80 percent of them solve the ray-tumor problem compared with only 10 percent of the control subjects. But if the subjects merely hear the general's story without being informed of its relevance, the beneficial effect is much weaker (about 20 percent). Mere exposure to an analogy is evidently not enough if the analogy is not recognized as such. But it may come to mind if it is somehow made more memorable. After hearing an additional story analog (the second featured an oil-well fire extinguished by the use of multiple converging hoses), the number of subjects who solved the ray-tumor problem rose to about 45 percent, even without getting explicit information about the analogy (Gick and Holyoak, 1983).

It's clear that analogies can help in finding a solution. The trick is to find the right analogy and to see its relevance.

8.22 The water-lily problem *Water lilies double in area every twenty-four hours. On the first day of summer, there is one water lily as in (A). On the sixtieth day, the lake is all covered, as in (B). On what day is the lake half-covered?*

8.23   The cheap-necklace problem   *You are given four separate pieces of chain that are each three links in length (A). It costs 2 cents to open a link and 3 cents to close a link. All links are closed at the beginning of the problem. Your goal is to connect all 12 links of chain into a single circle as shown in (B). The total cost must be no more than 15 cents. (From Wickelgren, 1974. The solution is described on p. 308).*

CHANGING THE REPRESENTATION

In many cases, a problem seems difficult because it is not correctly interpreted. To solve it, it has to be looked at in a new way. In effect, this is another case of changing set, but technically it is usually described as a change in the way the problem is ***represented.***

Below is an example:

> Suppose Joe and Frank have the same amount of money. How much must Joe give Frank so that Frank has $10 more than Joe?

Here the crucial recognition is that Frank's gain is necessarily Joe's loss. Every dollar Joe gives to Frank must be represented as a net change of two dollars: one gained by Frank and one lost to Joe. Since we need a net change of $10, the answer is $5. (For another problem in which the solution depends on a change of representation, see Figure 8.23).

RESTRUCTURING

We've already seen that the solution of a difficult problem often involves a shift in the way in which the problem is viewed. This shift may be very sudden and is then experienced as a flash of insight, a sense of "aha" that occurs when the misleading set is finally broken. ***Restructuring*** is especially clear in problems that impose a false set. To solve the nine-dot problem (Figure 8.11, p. 292) the subject has to move out of the square frame imposed by the dots. In a similar vein, the matchstick problem (Figure 8.10, p. 292) requires working in three dimensions rather than two. (See pp. 306, 307 for the solutions.)

Gestalt psychologists have proposed that this kind of perceptual restructuring lies at the heart of most problem solving in both animals and humans (see Chapter 6). So far, though little is known about the mechanisms that underlie the restructuring effect, there is reason to believe that it is a central phenomenon in the psychology of thinking. (For a contrary view, see Weisberg and Alba, 1981.) Such effects may also be related to the role of analogies we discussed previously: Restructuring can provide dramatically new bases for *finding* analogies.

CREATIVE THINKING

The creative thinker is one who generates a solution that is both new and appropriate. At the top of the pyramid are such giants as Archimedes, Descartes, and Newton, thinkers whose creations define whole chapters of intellectual history. On another level are the anonymous copywriters who develop new advertising slogans for spray deodorants. But whether great or humble, these real-life achievements are quite similar to those of the problem solver in the psychological laboratory. They represent a conceptual reorganization of what was there before.

According to the creators' own accounts, the critical insights typically occur at unexpected times and places. There is usually a period of intense preparation during which the thinker is totally immersed in the problem and approaches it from all possible angles. But illumination tends not to come then. Quite the contrary: After the initial onslaught fails, there is usually a period of retreat during which the problem is temporarily shelved. Rest or some other activity intervenes, and then suddenly the solution arrives, not at the writer's desk or the composer's piano, but elsewhere entirely—while riding in a carriage (Beethoven, Darwin), stepping onto a bus (the great mathematician Poincaré), or, in the

THE PROCESS OF THINK-ING: SOLVING PROBLEMS

8.24 Archimedes in his bathtub *A six-teenth-century engraving celebrating a great example of creative restructuring. The Greek scientist Archimedes (287–212 B.C.) tried to determine whether the king's crown was made of solid gold or had been adulterated with sil-ver. Archimedes knew the weight of gold and silver per unit volume but did not know how to measure the volume of a complicated object such as a crown. One day, in his bath, he no-ticed how the water level rose as he immersed his body. Here was the solution: The crown's volume is determined by the water it displaces. Carried away by his sudden insight, he jumped out of his bath and ran naked through the streets of Syracuse, shouting "Eureka! I have found it!" (Engraving by Walter H. Ryff, courtesy of The Granger Collection)*

8.25 A cognitive analysis of the appreci-ation of humor *The joke or cartoon sets up an expectation. The experience of humor arises (1) if this expectation is not fulfilled and (2) if the outcome nevertheless makes sense. (After Suls, 1972)*

most celebrated case of all, while sitting in a bathtub (Archimedes; see Figure 8.24).

Such effects have sometimes been attributed to a process of ***incubation*** (Wallas, 1926). According to this view, a thinker does not ignore the unsolved problem altogether when she turns away from it in baffled frustration; she con-tinues to work on it, but does so "unconsciously." This hypothesis adds little to our understanding, for it merely substitutes one mystery for another. Unless we know the why and wherefore of unconscious thought (whatever that may be), we know no more than we did before.

Many psychologists suspect that such incubation effects are produced in a less active way: Time away from a problem simply allows the problem solver to shake off false mental sets (Wickelgren, 1974; Anderson, 1990). Such false sets become increasingly restricting the longer she stays at the task, all the more so since her motivation is probably intense. Leaving the problem for a while may very well break these sets. As time elapses, the false set may be forgotten, and a drastic change of retrieval cues (the woods or the bathtub) will prevent its rein-statement. Once the false set is dropped, there is a chance that the true solution may emerge. Of course, that chance is much more likely to be realized if one is totally familiar with all the ins and outs of the problem and (especially) if one has the talents of a Beethoven or an Archimedes. Just taking a bath is unfortunately not enough.

RESTRUCTURING AND HUMOR

At least on the face of it, there is a certain similarity between insightful problem solution and humor. A joke does not strike us as funny unless we get the point. Conversely, insights sometimes have a comic aspect, especially when one recog-nizes how absurdly simple the solution really is.

Several writers suggest that the essential similarity lies in the fact that both insight and humor involve a dramatic shift from one cognitive organization to another (e.g., Suls, 1972, 1983; see Figure 8.25). The joke teller creates one expectation during the early stage of the narrative and then betrays it when he comes to the punch line. There is surprise followed by the realization that the unexpected ending makes some sense after all (H. Gleitman, 1990).

As an example, consider the story about a doctor, a lawyer, and an engineer—all of whom are to be executed on a guillotine. As they step up to the scaffold, each is given a choice of lying face up or face down. The doctor is the first and decides that one should confront one's fate directly, so he opts to lie face up. The blade drops, but then stops with a loud squeak just one foot above the doctor's throat. There is much amazement, and then the prisoner is released. Next is the lawyer. He is sure that legal precedent would lead to his own release if the blade were to stop for him as it had for the doctor, so he too lies face up. Again the blade stops short, and again the prisoner is released. It's now the engineer's turn. He decides his best bet is to go with whatever worked before. As he lies face up, he too can see the blade overhead. But then, just before the blade descends, he turns to the executioner and says, "Say, wait—I think I see what your problem is up there."

The story is set up to lead to the expectation of another ending, perhaps a third failure. The actual ending is unexpected and incongruous, but it makes sense even so—the engineer can't resist solving an engineering problem, even if it kills him. But incongruity as such is not enough, for without a viable cognitive alternative into which the ending fits, there will be no humor. If the engineer had asked the executioner to lend him a handkerchief, there would have been no joke at all, only puzzlement.

In other cases, the cognitive structure of the joke is more subtle. Consider the story about a mountain climber who slipped over a precipice and barely hung on to a long rope with a thousand-foot drop gaping underneath. There was no one with him, and he knew he couldn't hold on much longer. In his fear and despair, he looked up to the heavens and shouted: "Is there anyone up there who can help me?" There was a long pause and then a deep voice was heard from above: "You will be saved if you show your faith by letting go of the rope." The mountain climber looked down at the deep abyss beneath him, and then looked up again and cried: "Is there anyone *else* up there who can help me?

Here, the joke sets up a puzzle—what will the mountain climber do now? His response is unexpected. He both has faith and he doesn't. Not content with hearing from one deity, he wants to hear from yet another, trying to get a better bargain. A similar relation between humor and puzzles is apparent in many cartoons. For example, when a viewer first sees the famous skiing cartoon of Charles Addams, he tries to figure out what is going on. The solution is incongruous, but it fits and is therefore funny (see Figure 8.26).

8.26 Humor in a cartoon *(Drawing by Chas. Addams; © 1940, 1968 The New Yorker Magazine, Inc.)*

Surprise and reinterpretation are probably not the only cognitive factors required for humor to occur. Another ingredient is the comparison of the two cognitive structures that are juxtaposed. The critical element can be seen in *both* contexts. This simultaneous membership of an item in two radically different cognitive contexts seems to be a crucial aspect of humor. Thus, one of Oscar Wilde's dowagers, on interviewing a potential son-in-law, asks:

> Lady Bracknell: . . . Now to minor matters. Are your parents living?
> Jack: I have lost both my parents.
> Lady Bracknell: To lose one parent, Mr. Worthing, may be regarded as a misfortune; to lose both looks like carelessness.
> (Wilde, *The Importance of Being Earnest,* Act I)

The humor derives from the sudden jolt caused by the second meaning of *lost*, which is then contrasted with the first.

While cognitive restructuring is an important and perhaps a necessary condition for the production of humor, it is clearly not a sufficient one. A whole variety of emotional and motivational factors are also involved. Thus humor can serve as a relatively harmless outlet for aggressive or sexual wishes that can't be indulged directly, as in sarcastic wit and "dirty" jokes. A further condition is that the new and unexpected meaning (the point of the joke) has to be emotionally acceptable to the listener. Jokes about Hitler's extermination camps are not funny to anyone. This point holds even for the so-called "sick" joke. We can (barely) accept, "Yes, yes, Mrs. Lincoln, but how did you like the play?" because 1865 is over a hundred years in the past. An equivalent line about the former Mrs. John F. Kennedy is unpardonable.

ARTIFICIAL INTELLIGENCE: PROBLEM SOLVING BY COMPUTER

The preceding discussion emphasized the role played by hierarchical organization in thinking. But how does this organization come about? How does the problem solver hit upon the right plan of attack, and how does she recognize that it is right when she thinks of it? For that matter, how and when does

Computer-generated visual design By now, computers are used to assist in many human endeavors. The figure shows a computer design generated from a graphic program that incorporates various geometrical algorithms. (Courtesy of Lifesmith Classic Fractals)

"This one writes some fine lyrics, and the other one has done some beautiful music, but they just don't seem to hit it off as collaborators." (© 1978 by Sidney Harris—American Scientist Magazine)

restructuring occur? These questions are as yet unanswered, but there have been some promising leads.

One interesting avenue of research comes from attempts to program computers so as to simulate certain aspects of human thinking. The impetus for this work stems from the belief, held by many psychologists, that humans and computers are similar in one important regard—they are both information-processing systems. We have already seen several examples of the information-processing approach in our discussions of perception and memory. When we talk of items that are temporarily activated in working memory, are recoded into fewer and more compact chunks, and are later retrieved by various hierarchical search procedures, we are describing a system in which information is systematically converted from one form into another. There is a formal similarity between this sequence of inferred events in human memory and the actual steps of a computer program that handles the storage, recoding, and retrieval of various materials (such as library titles, tax returns, and so on). In an analogous way, what we call "thinking" may be the systematic manipulation of the hierarchically arranged conceptual chunks stored in our brain.

To be sure, the underlying physical machinery is very different. Computers use hardware made of magnetic cores and transistors, while biological systems are built of neurons. But this difference does not prohibit a similarity in their operations. Two different computers may differ in that one is built with electronic tubes and the other with transistors, but they may be fed the same programs even so—and they will both compute the same functions. Similarly—for at least some purposes—it may not matter that digital computers are built of steel and ceramic chips, while an organism's mental machinery is built of neurons. To students of **artificial intelligence,** the important point is that both computers and human beings are information-processing systems (Turing, 1950). They therefore regard it as likely that the study of one will help in the understanding of the other.

A further advantage of the computer simulation of thought comes from the fact that machines are painfully literal. The program must be spelled out in absolutely precise detail, for the computer will balk if presented with vague or overgeneralized instructions. This limitation is a blessing in disguise. It forces the scientist to formulate his notions in completely rigorous and explicit terms.

ALGORITHMS AND HEURISTICS

Several investigators have deliberately forced their "thinking" programs to be as humanlike as possible. The most prominent among these are Allen Newell and Nobel laureate Herbert Simon, who have programmed computers to play chess, to discover and prove theorems in symbolic logic, and to decipher cryptograms. They began by studying how human subjects deal with these problems, uncovering their typical strategies by using the think-aloud technique we discussed earlier. Newell and Simon then incorporated these problem-solving plans into the instructions fed to their computer. Interestingly enough, the computer does fairly well if it attacks these problems as human subjects say they do (Newell and Simon, 1972).

Newell and Simon found it useful to distinguish between two major kinds of solution strategies. One is an **algorithm,** a procedure in which all of the operations required to achieve the solution are specified step by step. Examples are the various manipulations of arithmetic. An algorithm guarantees that a solution will be found in time, but this time may be very long in coming. Consider a person working on a crossword puzzle who is trying to find a synonym for "sharp-tongued" that will fit into _c_ _bi_. An algorithm exists: Insert every possible alphabetic combination into the four empty spaces and check each result against an unabridged dictionary. While this procedure is certain to produce "acerbic," it should appeal to few puzzle solvers, for it will require the inspection of nearly 460,000 possibilities.

In actual practice, crossword puzzles are solved by procedures that, though not as sure, are much less slow. These are **heuristics,** strategies that buy efficiency at the cost of possible error, in contrast to algorithms that are guaranteed to work but are totally blind to efficiency. Such heuristics are tricks and rules of thumb that have often worked in the past and may do so again, such as guessing at a suffix given the word's grammatical class (*ic* is a good bet for an adjective), forming hypotheses on the basis of likely letter sequences in the language (if *c* is the second letter, the first must be an *s* or a vowel), and so on. The various procedures for overcoming obstacles to problem solving that we have discussed before, such as working backwards, finding analogies, and changing the way the problem is represented, are heuristics of a similar sort—they are by no means guaranteed to work, but they often do. The great majority of problems people face are solved by such heuristic procedures rather than by algorithms, for human life is short and human processing capacity is limited. Physicians reach their diagnoses by first considering a few hypotheses that seem most plausible and then testing those. If instead they looked at every possibility, the patient would be dead before being diagnosed.

If the problem is complex enough, even high-speed computers must resort to heuristics (Boden, 1977). Consider the analysis of a chess position some ten moves ahead. The total number of possibilities (based on moves, replies, replies to replies, and so on) has been estimated at an astronomical billion billion billion. Under the circumstances, an algorithm is out of the question. (Even if the inspection of each possibility took only one-millionth of a second, the inspection of all of them would not be completed for 1,000 billion years.) On the other hand, heuristics work remarkably well. Modern chess programs require the computer to search for moves that satisfy certain subgoals, such as material superiority (e.g., give a pawn for a queen but not vice versa), and various strategic objectives, such as occupation of the center squares (which limits the opponent's mobility). Notice that this approach resembles that of the human player. His ultimate goal is to checkmate his opponent, but he is not likely to achieve it unless he proceeds hierarchically; instead of evaluating each move in terms of the final goal, he considers it in the light of the subgoals that lead up to it. Chess programs that employ heuristics of this sort have become very powerful (Holding, 1985). They combine what is essentially brute force (the ability to search at extremely high speeds) with the ability to evaluate positions. Under the circumstances, it is not surprising that they are closing in on the game's human champions. One such program, Deep Thought, has already defeated several grandmasters (Byrne, 1989; see Figure 8.27).

8.27 Chess computers as expert systems
Grandmaster Arthur Bisguier inspecting a variety of chess microcomputers commercially available in 1982. By now, the best of these machines can hold their own against a player rated as a master but are unlikely to defeat players of Bisguier's stature. These chess computers can be regarded as expert systems because their knowledge is entirely limited to chess. (Photograph by Bruce Helm, U.S. Chess Federation)

EXPERT SYSTEMS

A promising new trend in the field of artificial intelligence is the development of **expert systems.** These are problem-solving programs with a very narrow scope. They deal only with problems in a highly limited domain, such as some subfield of organic chemistry, law, or medicine. Because they are so specialized, their memories can be stocked with a considerable amount of know-how in their own area.

An example is MYCIN, a computer program designed to assist physicians in the treatment of infectious diseases. MYCIN is not just a stored table that lists drugs to combat this or the other microorganism. It can diagnose, suggest therapies, and estimate their effectiveness. The physician "informs" the computer of the patient's symptoms and of the results of various blood tests and bacterial cultures. The computer then consults its memory for lists of potentially useful drugs and chooses among them by following various decision rules (which consider the patient's age, other medications, side effects, and so on) and makes a recommendation, indicating the statistical probability of success. If "asked," it will indicate how it arrived at its decision. If appropriately "instructed," it will add to or modify its rules; for example, it may add a note that a particular antibiotic ought not to be administered to a patient with a certain allergy (Shortliffe et al., 1973; Duda and Shortliffe, 1983; Buchanan and Shortliffe, 1985).

A number of studies have assessed the effectiveness of the MYCIN program by comparing its recommendations with those of over a dozen infectious disease specialists. The results indicate that the program performs at or near the level of expert physicians, at least in narrowly defined problem areas. Since MYCIN can be continually updated and improved, it is possible that it, or some similar program, may be used in medical practice before long. Whether the patients will take to MYCIN's bedside manner is another question. (And some physicians apparently have certain reservations; see Teach and Shortliffe, 1985.)

Is MYCIN intelligent? In a sense, it obviously isn't. Its very strengths are its weaknesses. It "knows" only about infectious diseases. If it is asked about a broken bone or a psychiatric condition, it will be utterly lost. It is a highly specialized expert that may eventually become a valuable, though rather limited, assistant. But it is not a model of the human intellect, for it simulates only a few human mental operations. Like other expert systems that are now being developed, MYCIN is meant to be an aid to human intelligence, not a substitute. All the same, its operations may be a microcosm of how the human mind solves some very limited problems, and so, in the end, it may provide a genuine contribution to our understanding of the psychology of human thought.

Solution of the matchstick problem *To arrange six matches (see Figure 8.10, p. 292) into four equilateral triangles, the matches have to be assembled into a three-dimensional pyramid. Most subjects implicitly assume the matches must lie flat. (After Scheerer, 1963)*

SOME LIMITATIONS OF ARTIFICIAL INTELLIGENCE

Computer simulation has added a new and exciting dimension to the study of cognitive processes. But so far at least, it still has some serious limitations as an approach to human thinking. We have just noted that expert systems such as MYCIN are both too rigid and too narrow-minded to be considered "truly intelligent." These and similar problems are even more apparent in computer programs that are more ambitious in scope than such expert systems.

Well-defined and ill-defined problems The problems that existing computer programs can handle are *well-defined.* There is a clear-cut way to decide whether a proposed solution is indeed the right one. Examples are algebraic proofs (Are the terms identical on both sides of the equation?), chess problems (Is the op-

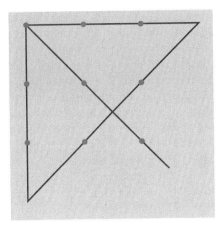

The solution of the nine–dot problem
The problem (see Figure 8.11, p. 292) is solved by going outside of the square frame into which the dots are perceptually grouped. The lines have to be extended beyond the dots as shown. Most subjects fail to hit on this solution because of a perceptual set imposed by the square arrangement.

Solution of the horse-and-rider problem
Solving the horse-and-rider puzzle (see Figure 8.20, p. 298) requires a change of perceptual set. (A) must be rotated 90 degrees so that the two old nags are in the vertical position. One can now see that the head of each (vertical) can join (horizontally) with the hindquarters of the other. The final step is to slide (B) over the middle of (A) and the problem is solved. (After Scheerer, Goldstein, and Boring, 1941)

posing king checkmated?), and anagrams (Is the rearranged letter sequence a word that appears in the dictionary?).

In contrast, many of the problems people face in real life are *ill-defined*. Consider an architect who is asked to design a modern college dormitory. Exactly what is a correct solution? Some proposals can obviously be rejected out of hand—for example, a design with no provisions for bathrooms—but there is no definite criterion for what is acceptable. The situation is similar for many other problems, such as completing a sonnet or organizing a lecture or planning a vacation. In all of these cases, the critical first step is to define the problem so that it can be solved and so that the solution can be evaluated. The architect begins by asking questions about the number of students who are to be housed, the facilities that must be included, the surrounding terrain, the available budget—all in an attempt to transform an ill-defined problem into a well-defined one. The progress of human knowledge is often a matter not of problem solution but of problem definition and redefinition: The alchemist looked in vain for a way to change lead into gold; now the modern physicist tries to discover the atomic structure of matter. As of yet, computer programs do not define their own problems. It's by no means clear that computers will ever be able to do so in the way people do.

The lack of common sense   Some computer scientists feel that the crucial difference between human and artificial intelligence concerns what is popularly called "common sense"—an understanding of what is relevant and what is not. People possess it, and computers do not. Consider a simple example: Let's assume that you build a computer program to perform some of the functions of a college registrar, such as keeping records of enrollments and grades. In principle it shouldn't be too hard to do so, and in many ways the program will do a much better job than a person might; it will never lose an entry or misfile it. Now let's suppose that you ask this computer a simple question: "How many psychology majors passed Computer Science 101 last semester?" The computer will search its memory and may come up with the answer "None." You become worried and restless and wonder whether psychology majors have some special disability. But if you understand the limitations of most computer programs, you will ask the computer a further question: "How many psychology majors enrolled in Computer Science 101 last semester?" When the computer comes up with the answer "None," you breathe a sigh of relief. But you will look at the computer wonderingly. A human registrar would never have answered the first question as the computer did. He would have understood the point of the question and would have responded relevantly and without extra prompting: "There were no psychology majors enrolled in the course." This is presumably because the human registrar—but not the computer—would immediately realize how misleading the original bare response "None" would be (Joshi, 1983; for a discussion of the problem of relevance, see Sperber and Wilson, 1986).

Computer scientists, well aware of the current limitations of artificial intelligence, sometimes tell a story about an interchange between an army general and the Pentagon's main computer in the war room:

Computer: The Russians (or the Chinese, or the Iraquis, or whoever) are coming!
General: By land or by sea?
Computer: Yes.
General: Yes what?
Computer: Yes, SIR!!!

The problem is that there is an enormous amount of knowledge about the world and its potential relevance to this or other questions that the computer is

Solution to the cheap-necklace problem
The obvious (but incorrect) approach to the problem (Figure 8.23, p. 300) is to try to link the four chains together: A to B to C to D and then back to A. The trouble is that this procedure costs too much. To solve the problem, one has to shift the representation and see that one of the chains (say, A) can provide the connecting links to connect the other three chains. The first step is to destroy a chain by opening all three links in A (at a total cost of 6 cents). The first link is used to connect B and C (creating a 7-link chain), the second to join this new chain with D (making an 11-link chain), and finally the third to join the ends of this 11-link chain together. It costs 9 cents to close these 3 links, for a total cost of 15 cents. One of the reasons why this problem is quite difficult is that its solution requires a detour: In order to make a larger chain (that is, the final necklace) one has to destroy one of the smaller ones. (From Wickelgren, 1974)

unlikely to have. This applies to expert systems such as MYCIN no less than to our computerized registrar. Suppose MYCIN's patient is a farmer. The program will probably not "realize" that some farmers are more likely to become infected with certain microorganisms because they get their water from wells. Of course that knowledge could be added to the program. But that's only the beginning. For MYCIN also recommends against the administration of a certain antibiotic to children under eight. This time, what MYCIN doesn't know is that this is because that particular antibiotic stains developing teeth. A human physician would obviously decide that if the disease is severe enough, cosmetic side effects should be ignored. Here once again, the relevant knowledge can be added to the program. But more and more such exceptions will be encountered, each of which will require the addition of yet another item of knowledge, together with the rules that tell the program when this knowledge is relevant and when it isn't. To give the computer the common sense of a human physician, one would have to give it the entire knowledge of that physician, including the basic sense of values that tells him that death is a worse outcome than dingy teeth.

The computer can answer questions, but it cannot understand why the questions were asked. In this regard human intelligence is different from artificial intelligence. For human thinking involves a heady mixture of exactness and inexactness, of algorithmic and heuristic procedures that computers have not as yet achieved and perhaps never will. There may be a permanent difference in kind—not just a present difference in power—between human and computer thinking. For while computers are getting ever more powerful—with enormous memorial stores, incredible processing speeds, and huge interlocking networks of commands—it's by no means clear that they are coming closer to reproducing the kaleidoscopic reach, the flexibility and the creativity of human thought, though in the current infancy of artificial intelligence it is of course too early to be secure about any such pessimistic assessment.

THE PROCESS OF THINKING: REASONING AND DECISION MAKING

In problem solving, a goal is set that has to be reached by some as yet unknown means. As we've seen, the goals that constitute the problem can vary widely. Some are mechanical (e.g., fixing an electrical short circuit), others are numerical (e.g., the water jug problem), still others are social (e.g., looking for a graceful way to refuse an invitation) or spatial (e.g., the taxi driver's search for the fastest route), and so on. One form of problem solving is of special interest. This is *reasoning,* in which the goal is to determine what conclusions can logically be drawn from certain premises.

How do people reason? For many years, the assumption was that the processes they use are intimately related to the formal laws of logic. Thus, George Boole, a famous nineteenth-century mathematician, entitled his treatise on the laws of logic "An Investigation into the Laws of Thought," with little doubt that the laws that governed the one also govern the other (Henle, 1962). Today, this belief is no longer held as widely. For by now there is ample evidence that people are very prone to errors of reasoning. As a result, some psychologists argue that the laws of logic have more to say about how people *should* think than about how they really *do* think, for in their view humans are not quite as rational as one would like to believe.

DEDUCTIVE REASONING

In **deductive reasoning,** the reasoner tries to determine whether certain conclusions can be drawn—that is, *deduced*—from a set of initial assertions. Logically, the decision of whether the deduction is valid depends entirely on the initial assertions coupled with some basic logical operations such as affirmation, negation, and so on. But do humans follow the appropriate laws of logic when they make their decisions?

A classical example of deductive reasoning is the analysis of **syllogisms,** an enterprise that goes back to Aristotle. Each syllogism contains two premises and a conclusion. The question is whether the conclusion logically follows from the premises (see Figure 8.28). Two examples of such syllogisms (one valid, one invalid) are:

> All *A* are *B*.
> All *B* are *C*.
> Therefore: All *A* are *C*. (valid)

> All *A* are *B*.
> Some *B* are *C*.
> Therefore: Some *A* are *C*. (invalid)

Or, stated in more concrete terms:

> All American Eagles are patriots.
> All patriots are red-blooded.
> Therefore: All American Eagles are red-blooded. (valid)

And:

> All heavenly angels are accomplished harp players.
> Some accomplished harp players are members of the American musicians' union.
> Therefore: Some heavenly angels are members of the American musicians' union. (invalid)★

Until the nineteenth century, most philosophers were convinced that the ability to evaluate syllogisms of this kind was an essential aspect of human rationality. Under the circumstances, it was a bit disheartening when experimental psychologists demonstrated that subjects make a considerable number of errors in evaluating syllogisms.

One cause of errors is produced by the subjects' tendency to perform inappropriate logical transformations. They hear the statement —"All *A* are *B*" and somehow interpret it as if it were symmetrical. As a result, they convert it to: "All *A* are *B,* and all *B* are *A*." Such invalid conversions will then of course lead to invalid judgments (Revlin and Leirer, 1980). An example is "All owls are birds," which of course does not permit the conclusion "All birds are owls."

8.28 Syllogistic argument *Insisting upon the execution of the Cheshire Cat, the King of Hearts argued that anything that has a head can be beheaded, including the Cheshire Cat, which at this stage of the story consists of nothing but a head. (Lewis Carroll, Alice in Wonderland, p. 55)*

★ Note that the validity of syllogisms only depends on whether the conclusion follows *logically* from the premises. The *empirical* plausibility of the conclusion (e.g., that the angels of heaven are unionized) has nothing to do with the matter.

INDUCTIVE REASONING

In deductive reasoning, we typically go from the general to the particular. We apply some general rule or rules ("All persons are mortal") and ask how it applies to a particular case ("Pat Smith is mortal"). But much of the reasoning we engage in is ***inductive reasoning*** in which this process is reversed. Here we go from the particular to the general. We consider a number of different instances and try to determine—that is, *induce*—what general rule covers them all.

Induction is at the very heart of the scientific enterprise, for the object of science is to determine what different events have in common. To do so, scientists formulate various *hypotheses*—tentative assumptions about what constitutes the general rule from which the individual observations can be derived. Hypotheses are developed by laymen as well as scientists. All of us try to see some general pattern in the world around us, as in trying to explain the behavior of a moody daughter or a troublesome automobile. The hypotheses we come up with may not be particularly profound ("She's a teenager" or "It's a lemon"), but profound or not they are attempts to comprehend an individual case by subsuming it under a more general statement.

What do people do to determine whether their hypotheses are correct? A number of investigators have concluded that there is a powerful ***confirmation bias.*** By and large, people seek evidence that will confirm their hypotheses, but they only rarely set out to see whether their hypotheses are false.

An illustration is provided by a study in which subjects were presented with three numbers—2-4-6—and were told that these numbers are an example of a series that conforms to a general rule that the subjects were asked to discover. To do this, they had to generate a three-number series of their own. Every time they produced such a series, the experimenter would tell them whether it did or didn't fit the rule. The subjects always indicated why they chose a particular series, and after a number of trials they announced their hypothesis. This continued until the subject succeeded or finally gave up.

The rule the experimenter had in mind was exceedingly simple: "any three numbers in increasing order of magnitude." It was so simple in fact that the sub-

The confirmation bias in science *Galileo vainly trying to persuade a group of university professors to look through his telescope. (From a National Theatre production of* Galileo *by Bertolt Brecht; photograph by Zoe Dominic)*

THE PROCESS OF THINK-ING: REASONING AND DECISION MAKING

"There it comes again."

(Illustration by Henry Gleitman)

jects took quite a while before they discovered what it was. But the real issue was how they went about their task. All of them soon developed one or another hypothesis. But whenever they did, they almost always generated a series that fit this hypothesis—to confirm it. They very rarely generated a series that was not consistent with their current hypothesis and would disconfirm it (Wason, 1960, 1968; Wason and Johnson-Laird, 1972).

The confirmation bias shown in the 2-4-6 experiment is a very pervasive phenomenon. It is not restricted to the psychologist's laboratory, for it is also found in the real-world behavior of scientists and engineers. They too tend to seek confirmations of their hypotheses and are disinclined to seek evidence that contradicts them. When Galileo provided visible proof that Jupiter has moons that rotate around it, some of his critics were so incensed at this challenge to their geocentric views of the universe that they refused even to *look* through his telescope (Mitroff, 1974; Mahoney, 1976; Mahoney and DeMonbreun, 1981).

There is little doubt that the confirmation bias can be a genuine obstacle to understanding, for in many ways, disconfirmations are more helpful in the search for truth than are confirmations. *One* disconfirmation shows that a hypothesis is false, but countless confirmations cannot really prove that it is true.

What accounts for the confirmation bias? A plausible guess is that humans have a powerful tendency to seek order in the universe. We try to understand what we see and hear, and to impose some organization upon it. The organization may not be valid, but it is often better than having none at all, for without some such organization we would be overwhelmed by an overload of information. But this benefit also has a corresponding cost, for our confirmation bias often condemns us to remain locked within our false beliefs and prejudices (Howard, 1983). We would be better off if we would be more ready to consider their falsity and would heed Oliver Cromwell's advice to a group of clergymen: "I beseech you, in the bowels of Christ, think it possible you may be mistaken."

DECISION MAKING

Deductive reasoning is about certainties: If certain premises are true, then certain conclusions will follow. There are no exceptions. If it is true that Pat Smith is a person and that all persons are mortal, then it inevitably follows that Pat Smith is mortal. The situation is very different in inductive reasoning in which we try to find a general rule when given a number of individual instances. Once we have arrived at this rule, we then try to apply it to new instances. But in contrast to deductions, inductions can never be certain but only probable. This even holds for Smith's mortality. For in actual fact, the proposition "All persons are mortal" is only an induction. To be sure, this induction is based on all of human history in which every single person who ever lived was ultimately observed to die. That Pat Smith will be an exception is therefore exceedingly unlikely—in fact, astronomically improbable. But death (or for that matter, taxes) is not an *absolute* certainty in the sense in which deductively derived truths always are.

In ordinary life, we are usually concerned with probabilities that are much less clear-cut, and evaluating these probabilities is often crucial. Baseball batters have to estimate the likelihood that a pitcher will throw a fast ball; brokers must judge the probability that a certain stock will rise; patients who contemplate elective surgery must do their best to weigh the relevant medical risks. How do people estimate the relevant probabilities? And how do they utilize these estimates to decide whether to swing at the pitch, buy the stock, or undergo the surgery? These questions are the province of an area of psychology (and other social sciences) called *decision making.*

COGNITIVE SHORTCUTS FOR ESTIMATING
PROBABILITIES

Technically, the probability that a particular event will happen is defined by a ratio: the frequency of that event (for example, the number of times a coin falls heads) divided by the total number of observations (the number of times the coin is tossed). But in actual practice we often don't know these frequencies. And even if we do, we often find it difficult to use them properly. According to Amos Tversky and Daniel Kahneman, we instead make use of various heuristics, which as we've seen are rules of thumb, cognitive shortcuts that often serve us well enough. But as Tversky and Kahneman point out, they sometimes lead to serious errors when they are used to estimate likelihoods (Tversky and Kahneman, 1973, 1974).★

The representativeness heuristic   One such rule of thumb is called the **representativeness heuristic.** When people have to make a judgment about the probability that a particular object or event belongs to a certain category, they often do this by comparing the similarity of the particular instance to a prototype of the category (that is, a representative case of that category). As a result, they may seriously misjudge the actual probabilities. A representativeness heuristic often comes into play when we have to make judgments about people. In one study, Kahneman and Tversky presented subjects with the following thumbnail sketch of an individual:

> Jack is a forty-five-year-old man. He is married and has four children. He is generally conservative, careful, and ambitious. He shows no interest in political and social issues and spends most of his time on his many hobbies, which include carpentry, sailing, and mathematical puzzles.

One group of subjects was told that this description was drawn at random from a group of seventy engineers and thirty lawyers, and were asked to indicate their judgment of the probability that the person described by the sketch was an engineer. A second group of subjects was given the identical task with only one difference: They were told that the description was drawn at random from a group of seventy lawyers and thirty engineers.

The results showed that both groups estimated that the odds that Jack was an engineer were more than 90 percent. They evidently concluded that the thumbnail sketch described a person with hobbies and interests that were more stereotypical of an engineer than of a lawyer. To that extent Jack seemed more representative of an engineer than of a lawyer. That the subjects took this information into account in making their judgment is not too surprising. What is surprising is that the group that was told that engineers accounted for only 30 percent of all the cases did not take this fact into account at all. It appears that the subjects completely ignored the **base rate,** the proportion of the category—here, engineers—that were in the original sample. The concrete description and its similarity to the stereotype overwhelmed all other factors in the estimate. Such failures to take base rates into account illustrate the general tendency to give more weight to the vivid, prototypical, and concrete case and less to the pale statistics (Kahneman and Tversky, 1972, 1973).

★ For a discussion of the relation between these probability estimates and the costs associated with different kinds of errors, see Chapters 5 and 15.

The availability heuristic Another rule of thumb used in inductive reasoning is the ***availability heuristic.*** This is a cognitive shortcut for estimating the frequency of certain events by considering how many such events come readily to mind (are currently available to memory). One study involved guesses of how often certain letters appear in different positions in English words. As an example, take the letter *R*. Considering all the words in the language, does *R* occur more frequently in the first position or in the third position of all the words in the language? Over two-thirds of the subjects said that it is more common in the first than the third position. In actuality the reverse is true. The reason for the errors is availability. The subjects made their judgments by trying to think of words in which *R* is the first letter (e.g., *r*ed, *r*ose, *r*ound) and of words in which it is the third (e.g., er*r*ing, bo*r*ing, ca*r*t, st*r*ong). They then compared the number they managed to generate in each category. But this method leads to a wrong estimate because our memorial dictionary (as well as Webster's) is organized according to the first rather than the third letter in each word. As a result, words that start with an *R* are much more easily retrieved (that is, more available) than those whose third letter is an *R*. As a result, their frequency is seriously overestimated (Tversky and Kahneman, 1973).

The availability heuristic can have serious practical consequences. What are the chances that the stock market will go up tomorrow or that a certain psychiatric patient will commit suicide? The stockbrokers and psychiatrists who have to decide on a particular course of action must base their choice on their estimate of these probabilities. But this estimate is likely to be affected by the availability heuristic. The stockbroker who remembers a few vivid days on which the market went up may overestimate the chances of an upswing; the psychiatrist who remembers one particular patient who unexpectedly slashed his wrists may underestimate the likelihood of eventual recovery of her other patients.

Vividness in memory is not the only factor that determines availability. Vividness in the way events are reported in the media have a similar effect. Consider estimates of various risks of death or bodily harm. In several studies, people were asked which of two causes of death is the more frequent. They generally overestimated the frequency of dramatic and sensational events, such as motor accidents, fires, tornadoes, and homicides and underestimated that of more unspectacular causes such as diseases. For example, they thought that the number of lives claimed by homicide was about the same as those caused by stroke, whereas the actual ratio is 1 to 11. Here the extent of the perceived risk is determined by how frequently and dramatically such events are reported by the media through which we learn about them, which in turn determines their availability. Fires and murders make front page stories, while strokes rarely do (Slovic, Fischoff, and Lichtenstein, 1982).

BIASES IN JUDGING OUTCOMES: FRAMING

The representativeness and availability heuristics can produce biases in estimates of the probability that some event will occur. Certain other psychological processes affect our judgement of the desirability of those events. An important example is the way the choice is ***framed.***

Consider the following example in which one group of subjects was presented with this problem:

> Imagine that the United States is preparing for the outbreak of an unusual Asian disease, which is expected to kill 600 people. Two alternative programs to combat the disease have been proposed. Assume that the exact scientific estimate of the consequences of the two programs are as follows:
>
> If Program A is adopted, 200 of these people will be saved.

If Program B is adopted, there is 1/3 probability that 600 people will be saved and 2/3 probability that no people will be saved.

Which of the two programs would you favor?

Given this problem 72 percent of the subjects opted for Program A. They preferred the guarantee of 200 lives saved to a one-third chance of saving them all.

The results were quite different for a second group of subjects who were given the same problem but with a different formulation of the two programs, again applied to 600 people. For this group of subjects, the alternatives were:

If Program A is adopted, 400 people will die.

If Program B is adopted, there is 1/3 probability that nobody will die and 2/3 probability that 600 people will die.

Given this formulation, 78 percent of the subjects chose Program B. To them the certain death of 400 people was less acceptable than a two-thirds probability that all 600 persons would die (Tversky and Kahneman, 1981).

The crucial point here is that the two problems are formally identical. The only difference between them is the way in which the alternative outcomes are framed. In the first case, they are characterized as gains, as "lives saved" (e.g., 200 out of 600). In the second case, they are characterized as losses, as "lives lost" (e.g., 400 out of 600). But these different descriptions obviously have a massive effect. In the first case (gains), they lead to the decision to take a certain gain and avoid any risk. In the second, they lead to the decision to take a risk in order to avoid a certain loss. People generally prefer a sure gain to a gamble to gain still more, but they will take risks to avoid a loss rather than settle for a certain smaller loss. The framing effect is a consequence of this bias (for details, see Kahneman and Tversky, 1984).

The framing process seems to occur in many situations outside of the laboratory. The most obvious examples concern the marketplace. In these days of paying in plastic, a number of retailers (for example, gas stations) have two prices for the same service or merchandise: one for cash, the other for credit. Retailers generally prefer to describe this price difference as a "cash discount" rather than as a "credit card surcharge." Needless to say, the dollar amount is identical; what differs is which of the two prices is treated as the "normal" reference point. By using the word *discount,* the reference standard is the credit card price; as a result, the discount is seen as a gain. Conversely, the term *surcharge* frames the cash price as the reference point; if so, the surcharge is seen as a loss. Since people are more willing to give up gains than to suffer losses, they don't mind paying by credit card and feel that they're getting a bargain if they pay in cash.

*"But we just don't have the technology to carry it out." (© 1976 by Sidney Harris—*American Scientist Magazine)

ARE PEOPLE REALLY IRRATIONAL?

The preceding discussion has considered a body of evidence that throws a rather poor light on human rationality. People make many errors in deductive reasoning; they often misunderstand or misconvert the premises and so come up with an incorrect conclusion. They make errors in inductive reasoning; they are primarily concerned with demonstrating that their hypotheses are correct and don't try to discover whether they are wrong. They are also very prone to error when they have to make decisions in the face of uncertainty; they use a number of heuristics that may lead to mistakes in estimating the probability of events. Intellectually, we evidently have much to feel modest about. But if so, how could humanity possibly have achieved what it has in mathematics, philosophy, and science?

One reason is that most of our great intellectual achievements are at bottom collective. They depend on countless prior generations, each of which bequeathed some bits of new knowledge and some new ways of gaining yet further knowledge to the generation that followed it. Because of them, we possess an immense arsenal of intellectual tools, including various techniques of formal thinking. Our mental machinery has some limited capacity for deductive and inductive reasoning, but this capacity is not finely honed until experience—the individual's own and that of his ancestors before him—makes it so.

Of course, this is not all. For even if we have the necessary intellectual tools, we may not use them. We may know statistics and still fall prey to the representativeness and availability heuristics; we may be trained in science and still be subject to the confirmation bias. But here, too, we are helped by the fact that much of human thought is a collective enterprise. An individual scientist may very well be biased toward confirmation and may not be inclined to look for evidence that disproves her hypothesis. But there are other scientists who will not have the same compunction. Many of them will not entertain the same hypothesis, and so they will be only too glad to do what's necessary to disprove *hers*. The collective upshot is likely to be a victory for rationality.

COGNITION AND CONSCIOUSNESS

The last few chapters have dealt with the ways in which we acquire, store, retrieve, and reorganize knowledge, as we perceive, remember, and think. But there is one topic that has come up in several contexts but has never been discussed in its own right—***consciousness.*** This subject crops up in all areas of cognition. We see the brilliant colors of a sunset, have a clear auditory image of a soprano's aria, and experience frustration when we try to think our way through a difficult algebra problem. To be sure, these experiences are produced by something from the outside, but at bottom they are *our* experiences. We can describe them to others, but ultimately no one else can ever share them. They are private, by definition.

On the face of it, one would expect psychology to be just the field to deal with such phenomena. After all, psychology is the science of mind, and consciousness is surely a part of mental life. In fact, when scientific psychology started out, it defined itself largely as the study of consciousness. But conscious experience turned out to be a murderously difficult topic. The early psychologists did their best to describe and analyze their conscious experiences. The trouble was that different psychologists came up with different descriptions, and there was no way to come to an agreement, precisely because conscious experience is essentially private. As a result, the study of consciousness was soon abandoned and by the early twentieth century was largely gone from psychological research. But as the previous chapters have suggested, modern psychologists are about to tackle the issue of consciousness again.

There is certainly much about consciousness that we don't understand: What exactly is consciousness? How is it possible for a biological mechanism, namely the human brain, to be conscious at all? Are other organisms conscious in the same sense we are? Could machines (perhaps complex computers) be conscious? These questions remain the subject of debate, and, generally speaking, philoso-

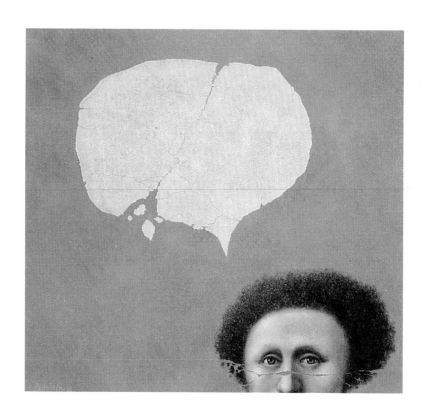

Nonconsciousness   *Some hints of what consciousness is about come from studies of mental processes that go on in the absence of consciousness. (Figure 14,1982, by Alfredo Castañeda; courtesy of Mary-Anne Martin/ Fine Art, New York).*

phers probably have more to say on such matters than psychologists do. (See, for example, Dennett, 1991; Rosenthal, 1993).

Even so, psychologists have of late made some progress in this area. Ironically, though, this progress has come, not from examining consciousness itself, but rather by studying what happens when consciousness is *absent*. In a way, this is similar to some other areas of psychology in which advances were also made by investigating functions that are impaired or lacking. For example, much of what we know about memory comes through the study of forgetting. By describing what can be done *without* consciousness, psychologists have tried to understand what consciousness does when it comes into play and just what it contributes to our mental functioning.

MENTAL PROCESSES THAT GO ON BELOW THE SURFACE

As we've seen before on several occasions, people can perform many mental functions without being conscious that they do so. They can perceive, remember, reason, and understand with no awareness of what they are doing and with no conscious supervision of these complex activities.

Before proceeding, a word about the word *unconscious*. The popular conception of the term goes back to the ideas of Sigmund Freud who applied it to ideas or memories that he believed are actively kept out of consciousness because they are threatening or because they provoke anxiety (see Chapter 17, p. 672). But the mechanisms we will discuss here are in no sense pushed down into a mental cellar; we are not aware of them in just the sense in which we are usually unaware of the intricate machinery of digestion that operates after we eat a meal. They are simply *non*conscious rather than *un*conscious in Freud's sense.

PERCEPTION WITHOUT AWARENESS

An obvious starting point is perception. When we look at the world we see many familiar objects—a chair, a dog, a friend, and so on. We respond appropriately to them all: We don't sit on the dog, throw a bone to the friend, or ask the chair about its golf game. This means that the relevant visual stimuli triggered the relevant visual memories. But we ourselves were not conscious that this happened. Very occasionally we may become aware of this process, for example, when the light is poor and the object is at some distance. If so, we may ask (and ask ourselves), "Is that you, Joe?" and are quite conscious of the answer. But ordinarily most perceptual identifications take place outside of our awareness.

A similar point is made by a surprising neurological finding. This is the phenomenon of **blindsight**, which has been observed in some patients who suffer from damage to the occipital cortex, the region of the cerebral cortex to which the pathway from the eye and thalamus project (see Chapter 2, pp. 38, 41). Lesions here will lead to a blindness in the area of the visual field that corresponds to the area of cortical destruction. If presented with visual stimuli in that region (which can be very large), the patient says he sees nothing and won't react even to flashes of very bright light. For all intents and purposes, this patient is blind in that area. But a series of studies by Larry Weiskrantz and his associates have shown that such patients are not truly without sight there. They presented various stimuli to the patients' affected field and asked them to point in the direction in which they were. The patients said the task was absurd: They were blind, so how could they guess? The investigators persisted, and the patients shrugged and guessed. It turned out that the guesses were surprisingly accurate. In further studies, the patients guessed whether stimuli placed in their blind field were, say, Xs or Os, or circles or squares. Here, too, their guesses were very much better than chance (Weiskrantz, 1986). Many investigators believe that the blindsight phenomenon depends on some connections between the visual system and other parts of the cortex (Weiskrantz, 1986; Rodman, Gross, and Albright, 1989; Cowey and Stoerig, 1992). But whatever its underlying neurological cause, the important psychological point concerns the fact that a mental process may take place without our being aware that it does. In a sense, Weiskrantz's patients could *see* but they were not *aware* of seeing.

MEMORY AND UNDERSTANDING WITHOUT AWARENESS

What holds for perception, holds for other cognitive processes as well. Take memory: We've already seen that we often rely on inferences to fill in gaps in our recollection (see Chapter 7). Very often such reconstructions occur quite unwittingly, without our ever being aware that we are referring to what we know or expect. This same lack of awareness crops up whenever we listen and understand. For in all cases we necessarily consult our memories without knowing that we do so.

Consider the sentence:

Susan put the vase down too firmly on the table and it broke.

What does the word *it* in this sentence refer to? The sentence is ambiguous, for it could be the vase or (less probably) the table. But most of us see only one of the two meanings: To us, *it* has to be the vase. But how do we know? To draw this conclusion, we surely rely on our knowledge that vases are often fragile and tables usually are not. This holds for every word in the sentence and indeed for all sentences we hear or speak: To understand them, we must construct their meaning from the pieces we retrieve from memory. Examples like this demonstrate that our understanding of ordinary language (and of pictures, and scenes, and events) is dependent on what's in our memories.

To understand, we have to consult our memories, but these consultations go on underground. They are memory retrievals, but they are implicit (see Chapter 7, pp. 259–61). They had better be, for if we consciously searched our memories every time we heard a sentence, we would probably never get to the end of any paragraph. For most of us the potential ambiguity of the vase-and-table sentence never comes to mind.

While much of our everyday memory retrieval is implicit and without awareness, it's of course clear that we can also retrieve memories consciously. This is especially so for episodic memories: When did we meet Jane last and what did we do, and so on. Here, conscious memory search and recollection occur quite regularly. But as we've seen, this is much less common in certain cases of brain damage. Patients suffering from Korsakoff's amnesia often have no conscious awareness of events they have witnessed or of things they have done. Yet these patients do remember these events in some sense—they are influenced, in their present beliefs and behaviors, by the specific content of prior episodes as shown by various demonstrations of implicit retrieval (see Chapter 7, pp. 276–77). Apparently amnesics can remember and are influenced by their memories, with no awareness that they are recalling the past.

ACTION WITHOUT AWARENESS

People can evidently perceive, retrieve memories, use memories, and make judgments—all without conscious awareness. As we've seen in our discussion of automatization, they can also act without awareness and they often do. With increasing practice, many tasks become automatic so that we become less and less aware of their details. To return to a previous example, we all know how to tie our shoes, but most of us have forgotten the steps needed to accomplish this feat. If asked to list the steps for shoelace tying (as if instructing a child), many of us will not be able to provide an adequate account. We tie our shoes without consciously knowing how and usually without being aware that we're doing so. This and many other operations are tasks that are by now on "autopilot."

How does practice create automaticity? One proposal is that, with practice, fewer *decisions* are required as one steps through a complex task. The well-practiced shoelacer doesn't have to choose what to do next after the first loop is formed. Instead, she can simply, and quite implicitly, draw on the memory of what she has done many times before. A complete subroutine has been stored in memory, encapsulating all of the steps of the procedure. Once the routine is launched, no decisions are needed—she simply repeats the familiar steps. (For a theoretical proposal on how such subroutines are formed, see Logan, 1988).

These various lines of evidence suggest that much of our mental life goes on behind the scenes, backstage and out of sight. By and large, we seem to be unaware of the *processes* by means of which we perceive, remember, think, and understand. What we are aware of instead are the *products* that emerge from these processes (Nisbett and Wilson, 1977).

When automatization breaks down *We are normally unaware of such highly practiced operations as tying our laces. But we quickly become conscious of them when something disrupts the routine, as in the case of the figure skater Tonya Harding who had some problems with her laces during the 1994 Winter Olympics and had to ask the judges for additional time. (John Gaps III /AP Wide World)*

WHAT'S CONSCIOUSNESS GOOD FOR?

It appears that many mental processes operate quite well without our awareness. But if so, what is consciousness good for? So far, psychologists (and philosophers and neuroscientists) can only offer some speculations.

One suggestion comes from the study of automatization. Nonconscious processing is very fast and efficient—whether going through the step-by-step routine of shoelace tying, or sending and receiving telegraphic messages, searching through memory, or drawing an obvious conclusion from the evidence. We achieve this efficiency in part simply by relying on familiar routines, rather than attending to each new decision. But as we saw earlier, by relying on routines we give up flexibility.

This leads to an obvious suggestion: Perhaps we need consciousness precisely for those tasks where we must preserve flexibility—that is, when we have to make choices. Nonconscious processing is fine when there are no choices and efficiency is the prime concern; much can be accomplished in a mind*less* fashion. Mind*ful*ness is required when we have to choose between one action and another. Mindfulness (that is, consciousness) becomes especially important when we must avoid becoming victims of habit, falling into the rut of continually relying on routine activities.

Seen in this light, consciousness is required for tasks that call for decisions, especially a succession of decisions—that is, tasks that don't allow a simple reliance on routine. It is also required to *choose* between actions, to fine tune our decisions, to make them exactly appropriate for the present situation. To take a lowly decision from everyday life: To avoid the embarrassment of telling and retelling the same joke to the same audience, we must *consciously* remember when we last told the joke and to whom (see Jacoby et al., 1989).

Another example is the principle of reciprocity, which guides behavior in many social systems (see Chapter 12, p. 454): In general, favors and gifts have to be repaid. But to apply this principle requires episodic memory (What have you done for me lately?) and that is largely supplied by conscious recollection. Here is yet another case in which the choice among actions (specifically, social actions) depends on consciousness.

At best, these are but small and very tentative steps on the road to an answer. After all, the puzzle of consciousness has perplexed some of the greatest minds in human history, and it would be surprising if it were unraveled in the foreseeable future. But even so, modern psychologists and neuroscientists are increasingly turning their attention to this issue, which is surely one of the most important in their field. Whether they will ultimately progress beyond the speculations of the great philosophers of centuries past is as yet unclear. But it's interesting that the suggestion that consciousness is required for choice hearkens back to Descartes whose mechanism for action required a soul (consciousness?) whenever a choice between two acts was required.

TAKING STOCK

In looking back over the three domains of cognition—perception, memory, and thinking—we can only repeat a theme we have struck before. There are no clear boundaries that demarcate these three domains. In describing perception, we often cross over the border into memory. For the way we perceive familiar objects—let alone such ambiguous figures as the young woman-old woman picture—is based in part on how we perceived them in the past. But perception also shades into thinking. We look at an ambiguous picture and eventually solve the perceptual puzzle as we recognize in it the image of spotted horses dappled by sunlight. Nor is it clear where memory leaves off and thinking begins. Much of remembering seems like problem solving. We try to recall to whom we lent a certain book, conclude that it has to be Jane, for we know no one else who is interested in the book's topic, and then suddenly have a vivid recollection of the particular occasion on which she borrowed it (and the way she swore that she'd return it right away). But if remembering is sometimes much like thinking, thinking can hardly proceed without reference to the storehouse of memory. Whatever we think about—which route to take on a vacation trip, how to fill out a tax form—requires retrieval of items from various memory systems.

All of this shows that there are no exact boundaries between perception, memory, and thinking. These areas are not sharply separated intellectual domains, but are simply designations for somewhat different aspects of the general process of cognition. We will now turn to the one aspect of cognition that we have thus far discussed only in passing—language. It, too, is intertwined with the other domains of cognition, but unlike perception, memory, and thinking, which are found in many animals, language is unique to human beings.

SUMMARY

1. All thought draws on our knowledge. The components of knowledge can be regarded as *mental representations,* which are either *analogical* or *symbolic.* Analogical representations capture some of the actual characteristics of that which they represent (e.g., a mouse and a picture of a mouse), while symbolic representations bear no such relationship to that which they represent (e.g., a mouse and the word "mouse").

2. An important example of analogical representation in thinking is provided by mental images. With the possible exception of *eidetic imagery,* visual memories are not a simple reembodiment of stored visual perceptions. But they have some picture-like attributes as shown by studies of *mental rotation* and *image scanning. Spatial thinking* is both symbolic and analogical as shown by studies on *mental maps.*

3. The elements of symbolic thought are *concepts* and *propositions.* Many of these are stored in *generic* memory, where they constitute the "database" for our thoughts. Unlike *episodic memory,* which concerns memory for particular events in one's life, *generic memory* concerns items of knowledge as such.

4. An important component of generic memory is *semantic memory,* whose organization has been described by various *network models.* Semantic memory has been studied by various techniques for assessing memory search, including memory activation. According to an early hypothesis, this network is hierarchical. Later proposals feature networks based on semantic distance and receive support from studies of *semantic priming.* The last decade has seen the development of a new group of network models based on *parallel distributed processing* (PDP) in which the relevant symbolic representations correspond to the state of the network as a whole.

5. Problem solving is a directed activity in which all steps are considered as they fit into the overall structure set up by the task. This structure is typically hierarchical, with goals, subordinate subgoals, and so on. This hierarchical structure is not unique to problem solving but may be a general characteristic of any directed activity.

6. Increasing competence at any directed activity goes together with an increase in the degree to which the subtasks of this activity have become chunked and *automatized.* In learning to send and receive Morse code, as in the attainment of many skills, learning curves exhibit *plateaus* followed by a later rise, suggesting the acquisition of progressively larger units. Similar chunking seems to occur in many forms of mental activity, including problem solving, and differentiates masters and beginners in many endeavors, such as playing chess.

7.   Problem solving is not always successful. One reason may be a strong, interfering *mental set,* which makes the subject *fixated* and is especially hard to overcome under conditions of intense motivation.

8.   Investigators of thinking have come up with a few suggestions to overcome obstacles to problem solving. One is working backwards from the goal; another is trying to find an analog; yet another is changing the mental representation of the problem. Sometimes the solution involves a radical *restructuring* by means of which a misleading set is overcome. Such restructurings may be an important feature of much of creative thinking. Accounts by prominent writers, composers, and scientists suggest that restructuring often occurs after a period of *incubation.* Restructuring may also play a role in humor, which often occurs when an unexpected cognitive organization turns out to make sense after all.

9.   An influential approach to problem solving comes from work on *artificial intelligence* in which computer scientists try to simulate certain aspects of human thinking. A number of solution strategies have been incorporated into several computer programs, including *algorithms* and *heuristics.* Some further extensions feature the use of *expert systems.* Among the limitations of current artificial intelligence programs as an approach to human thinking are their difficulty in dealing with ill-defined problems and their lack of common sense, a knowledge about many aspects of the world together with an understanding of what is relevant to the problem at hand.

10.   Studies of *deductive reasoning* show that people are prone to various errors in thinking. Errors of reasoning in dealing with *syllogisms* are caused by a number of factors, including the tendency to perform inappropriate logical transformations.

11.   In deductive reasoning, the thinker tries to deduce a particular consequence from a general rule or set of rules. In *inductive* reasoning, the direction is reversed, for here the thinker tries to induce a general rule from particular instances. An initial, tentatively held induction is a hypothesis. A number of studies have pointed to a powerful *confirmation bias* that makes subjects seek evidence that will confirm their hypotheses rather than look for evidence that would show their hypotheses to be false.

12.   *Decision making* involves the estimation of probabilities and the utilization of these estimates in deciding on a course of action. To make such estimates, people often make use of certain heuristics. These are cognitive rules of thumb that often serve us well enough but that may also lead to serious errors. One such rule of thumb is the *representativeness heuristic:* estimating the probability that an object belongs to a category by comparing the object to a prototype of the category, while ignoring other factors, such as *base rates.* Another rule of thumb is the *availability heuristic:* estimating the frequency of an event by how readily an example of such an event comes to mind.

13.   Some heuristics affect the judgment of the desirability of certain events. A major example is the way outcomes are *framed,* which affects whether they are interpreted as gains or losses. People generally prefer a sure gain to a gamble to gain still more, but they will take risks to avoid a loss rather than settle for a certain smaller loss.

14.   In recent years, psychologists have paid increasing attention to the problem of *consciousness.* Most of the progress in this area has come from studying some psychological processes that operate when consciousness is absent. One example is *blindsight,* which occurs in persons who have lost some portion of their visual cortex but can nevertheless perform many visual discriminations without being conscious that they do. Similar *nonconscious processing* occurs during innumerable occasions of everyday life when people retrieve memories implicitly. Yet another everyday occurrence of nonconscious processing is the performance of automatized tasks. These phenomena suggest that consciousness functions as a monitor that helps us to make choices between alternatives.

CHAPTER 9

L A N G U A G E

MAJOR PROPERTIES OF HUMAN LANGUAGE 324

LANGUAGE IS CREATIVE ■ LANGUAGE IS STRUCTURED ■ LANGUAGE IS MEANINGFUL ■ LANGUAGE IS REFERENTIAL ■ LANGUAGE IS INTERPERSONAL

THE STRUCTURE OF LANGUAGE 328

PHONEMES ■ MORPHEMES AND WORDS ■ PHRASES AND SENTENCES

THE LINGUISTIC HIERARCHY AND MEANING 331

THE MEANING OF WORDS ■ ORGANIZING WORDS INTO MEANINGFUL SENTENCES

COMPREHENSION 342

THE SENTENCE ANALYZING MACHINERY ■ THE INTERACTION OF SYNTAX AND SEMANTICS

THE GROWTH OF LANGUAGE IN THE CHILD 346

THE PROBLEM OF LANGUAGE LEARNING ■ IS LANGUAGE LEARNING THE ACQUISITION OF A SKILL?

LANGUAGE DEVELOPMENT 349

THE SOCIAL ORIGINS OF SPEECH PRODUCTION ■ DISCOVERING THE FORMS OF LANGUAGE ■ THE ONE-WORD SPEAKER ■ THE TWO-WORD (TELEGRAPHIC) SPEAKER ■ LATER STAGES OF LANGUAGE LEARNING: SYNTAX ■ FURTHER STAGES OF LANGUAGE LEARNING: WORD MEANING

LANGUAGE LEARNING IN CHANGED ENVIRONMENTS 360

WILD CHILDREN ■ ISOLATED CHILDREN ■ LANGUAGE WITHOUT SOUND ■ LANGUAGE WITHOUT A MODEL ■ CHILDREN DEPRIVED OF ACCESS TO SOME OF THE MEANINGS ■ THE CASE OF HELEN KELLER

LANGUAGE LEARNING WITH CHANGED ENDOWMENTS 367

THE CRITICAL PERIOD HYPOTHESIS ■ LANGUAGE IN NONHUMANS

LANGUAGE AND ITS LEARNING 373

SUMMARY 374

hen we consider the social forms and physical artifacts of human societies, we are struck by the diversity of cultures in different times and places. Some humans walk on foot, others travel on camels, and still others ride rockets to the moon. But in all communities and all times, humans are alike in having language. This essential connection, between *having language* and *being human,* is one reason why those interested in the nature of human minds have always been particularly intrigued with language.

To philosophers such as Descartes, language was that function which most clearly distinguished between beasts and humans, and was "the sole sign and only certain mark of thought hidden and wrapped up in the body." Descartes held that humans were utterly distinct from the other animals because all humans have language, while no other animals have anything of the sort. But this claim comes up against an immediate objection: There are about 4,000 languages now in use on earth (Comrie, 1987). Obviously, these are different from one another, for the users of one cannot understand the users of another. In what sense, then, can we speak of "language in general" rather than of French or English or Hindi? The answer is that human languages are at bottom much more alike than they seem at first glance to be. For example, all languages convey thought by the same *means:* They all use words and sentences to organize ideas. In contrast, animal communications often have something like words (for instance, a cat can purr happily and hiss angrily), but they never have complicated sentences (such as *I'm going to stop purring and start hissing unless you give me that catnip immediately*).

Another similarity is in the *ideas* human languages can express. When the United Nations ambassador from France makes a speech, numerous translators immediately whisper its equivalent in English, Russian, Arabic, and so on, to the listening ambassadors from other countries. The fact that the French speech can readily be translated suggests that, by and large, the same things that can be said in French can be said in English and Russian as well. This is true despite the fact that the Russian and English listeners may disagree with what the French diplomat is saying. But the translation will allow them to *know* that they disagree, so that they are in a position to stomp out of the room in a rage, or make a counterspeech—which will also be translatable. In our discussion of language, we will use English as our main example. But it is important to keep in mind that what we say about English generally goes for the other human languages as well.

The biblical account of the origin of different languages According to the Bible, all people once spoke a common language. But they built a tall structure, the Tower of Babel, and tried to reach the heavens. To punish them for their pride and folly, God made them unable to understand each other, each group speaking a different language. (Tower of Babel *by Jan Brueghel, the Elder, 1568–1625; courtesy of Kunsthistorisches Museum, Vienna)*

MAJOR PROPERTIES OF HUMAN LANGUAGE

There are five major properties of all human languages that psychology must describe: Language is **creative** (or **novel**), it is highly **structured** (or **patterned**), it is **meaningful,** it is **referential** (that is, it refers to and describes things and events in the real world), and it is **interpersonal** or **communicative** (involving the thoughts of more than one person at a time).

LANGUAGE IS CREATIVE

At first glance, language might seem to be merely a complicated habit, a set of acts by ear and mouth that have been learned by memorization and practice. According to this view, the explanation of talking is simple: Each of the memorized speech acts is simply performed whenever the appropriate circumstances arise. Our mothers said *That's a rabbit* when they saw a rabbit. Having observed this, we now say *That's a rabbit* when we see a rabbit. But this position of language as habit is hard to maintain, for speakers can and will utter and understand a great many sentences that they have never uttered or heard before. To see this point, it is only necessary to realize that, in addition to *That's a rabbit,* each of us can also say and understand:

> *That's a rabbit over there.*
> *A rabbit is what I see over there.*
> *Obviously, that's a rabbit.*
> *How clearly I recall that the word for that animal is* rabbit.
> *Well bless my soul, if that isn't a rabbit!*

And so on, with hundreds of other examples. A little child who has memorized all these sentences must be industrious indeed. But the situation is really incredibly more complicated than this, for we can talk about objects and creatures other than rabbits, including aardvarks and Afghans, apples and armies, and proceeding all the way to zebras and Zyzzogetons.

Furthermore, the sheer number of English sentences rules out habit as the explanation for language use. A good estimate of the number of reasonably short (20 words or fewer) English sentences is 10^{30}. Considering the fact that there are only 3×10^9 seconds in a century, a learner memorizing a new sentence every second would have learned only a minute fraction of them in the course of a lifetime. But the fact is that we can all say and understand most of them (Bloomfield, 1933; Chomsky, 1959).

In sum, we effortlessly create and interpret new sentences on the spot. Only a very few such as *How are you?*, *What's new?*, and *Have a nice day* are said and heard with any frequency. All the rest are at least partly new—new to the person who says them and new to his listeners as well. To express all the thoughts, we combine a limited—though large—number of words into sentences. Thus language is a system that allows us to reach a limitless end from limited means: Our stock of memorized, meaningful words is finite, but we nevertheless have the capacity to speak of an infinite number of new things and events. We can do so because our language system allows us to combine the old words in novel ways.

LANGUAGE IS STRUCTURED

While language use is creative in the sense that we can and do invent new sentences all the time, it is also restricted: There are unlimited numbers of strings of English words that—accidents aside—we would never utter. For example, we do not say *Is rabbit a that* or *A rabbit that's* even though these are fairly comprehensible ways to say *That's a rabbit*. Speakers construct their utterances in accord with certain abstract principles of language structure. These **structural principles** underlie the way in which we combine words to make up new sentences, and they are honored by every normal individual—without special thought and without any formal training in school. These principles are generally not known consciously, but are *implicit*. Even so, they govern our use of language and allow us to compose and understand boundless new sentences.

Language is not unique in being unlimited and structured, for a number of other behavior patterns have a similar potential for systematic and novel use. Consider arithmetic. Surely we don't know the sum of, say, 5,384 and 9,253 offhand. But we can readily calculate it, for we know a set of laws—the rules or principles of arithmetic. Similarly, we can drive cars to destinations where we have never traveled before, solve chess problems we have never previously encountered, and blush at embarrassments we have never experienced before. Thus many behavioral systems have the unbounded character that we have just shown for language.

We should point out that the structural principles of language (sometimes called **descriptive rules**) have to be distinguished from certain **prescriptive rules** handed down from various authorities about how they think we *ought* to speak or write. Prescriptive rules are the so-called rules of grammar that many of us learned painfully at school in the fourth grade (and thankfully forgot in the fifth), such as "Never say *ain't*" or "A sentence cannot end with a preposition." These recipes for speech and writing often do not conform to the actual facts about natural talking and understanding. For example, most of us have no qualms about ending sentences with a preposition (as in the sentence, *Who did you give the packages to?*) or even two prepositions (as in *What in the world are you*

The power of an "H" *A scene from the stage version of* My Fair Lady *in which the cockney flower girl, Eliza (Julie Andrews), is taught by Henry Higgins (Rex Harrison) to pronounce an "H" the way the British upper classes do. She thus becomes a lady. This shows that following prescriptive rules can sometimes confer important social advantages. (Labov, 1970b; photograph by Leonard Mc-Combe/LIFE Magazine, © Time Warner, Inc.)*

up to?). In some cases it sounds rather odd not to do so, as Winston Churchill pointed out when spoofing this "rule" by insisting that "This is the kind of language up with which I will not put!"

The **structural principles** we will be concerned with in this chapter are those that every normal speaker honors without effort or formal instruction—for example, the principle by which we invariably say *the rabbit* rather than *rabbit the*. It is these regularities that are fundamental to understanding language as a universal human skill. In fact, most human cultures outside of America and Western Europe do not have prescriptions for "proper" speech at all.

LANGUAGE IS MEANINGFUL

Each word in a language expresses a meaningful idea (or concept) about some thing (e.g., *camera* or *rabbit*), action (*run* or *rotate*), abstraction (*justice* or *fun*), quality (*red* or *altruistic*), and so on. The purpose of language is to express all these meanings to others, so we have no choice but to learn a conventional word for each.

But people talk in whole sentences rather than just one word at a time. This is because the grammatical patterns that we discussed in the previous section also contribute to meaningfulness. For example, the words *dogs, cats, bite* express very different meaningful thoughts depending on how they are put together: *Dogs bite cats,* or *Cats bite dogs.*

LANGUAGE IS REFERENTIAL

Language users know more than how to put words together into meaningful and grammatical sentences. They also know which words refer to which things, scenes, and events in the world. If a child said *"That's a shoe"* (a sentence whose grammar is impeccable and whose meaning is transparent) but did so while pointing to a rhinoceros, we would not think she had learned English very effectively. This is the problem of **reference:** how to use language to describe the world of real things and events—saying *shoe* to make reference to a shoe, but saying *rhinoceros* to refer to a rhinoceros.

The problem of reference is quite a complex one just because speech is not an automatic response of the nervous system. Even though the word *lemon* refers to lemons, one does not have to cry out *"Lemon!"* every time one sees a lemon. The source of language events has to do with the contents of the mind, what one is thinking about. Of course, if one sees a lemon, the probability that one is thinking about lemons is increased, but it is by no means a certainty. Seeing a lemon does not evoke the cry *Lemon!* in anything like the sense that seeing a lemon evokes salivation from a hungry viewer or in the sense that seeing a lemon in bright light evokes a bluish afterimage. Salivation and visual afterimages are direct psychophysiological reactions (responses) to identifiable events (stimuli). But sentences about lemons are not automatic reactions to seeing lemons. Sentences are expressions of our state of mind, and this can vary with relatively little regard to what is going on "out there in the real world."

LANGUAGE IS INTERPERSONAL

Many aspects of human language are within the individual and are thus the property of each single human mind. But language is a process that goes beyond the individual, for it is a social activity in which the thoughts of

Adam gives names to the animals *The belief that knowledge of word meanings sets humans above animals goes back to antiquity. An example is the biblical tale illustrated in this painting by William Blake, which shows Adam assigning names to the animals. According to some ancient legends, this act established Adam's intellectual superiority over all creation, including even the angels. In one such tale, the angels were unable to call the animals by name, but Adam could: "'Oh Lord of the world! The proper name for this animal is ox, for this one horse, for this one lion, for this one camel!' And so he called all in turn, suiting the name to the peculiarity of the animal" (Ginzberg, 1909, vol. 1, p. 62). Notice that Adam thinks that words sound like what they mean. (William Blake's* Adam Naming the Beasts; *Stirling Maxwell Collection, Pollok House, Glasgow Museums & Art Galleries)*

The stimulus-free property of language use   *How many sentences can you think of to describe this painting? (Henri Rousseau's* The Sleeping Gypsy, *1897, oil on canvas, 5' 1" × 6' 7." Collection, The Museum of Modern Art, New York. Gift of Mrs. Simon Guggenheim)*

one mind are conveyed to another. To accomplish these social ends, each speaker must know not only the sounds, words, and sentences of his language, but also certain **principles of conversation.** These principles govern the way in which language is used appropriately under varying circumstances.

Suppose, for example, that one sees a lion in the parlor and wants to tell a companion about this. It is not enough that both parties speak English. One has to estimate the listener's mental state, capacities, motivations, and relations to oneself in order to speak appropriately. If the companion is a sharpshooter with a revolver, one might say:

Quick, shoot! There is a lion in the parlor.

But if the companion is an artist, one might say:

Quick, draw! Lion of a gorgeous shade of ochre in the parlor.

To a biologist, one might say:

Quick, look! Member of the genus Panthera leo *in the parlor.*

And to an enemy,

Lovely morning, isn't it? See you later.

Clearly, what one says about a situation is not just a description of that situation, but depends upon one's knowledge, beliefs, and wishes about the listener. To communicate successfully, then, one must build a mental picture of "the other" to whom speech is addressed (Austin, 1962; Clark and Clark, 1977; Clark, 1978; Prince, 1981; Schiffrin, 1988).

The same problem arises for the listener, of course. To determine the sense of what one has heard, one must make an estimate of the speaker and the circumstances of her utterances. Suppose, for example, someone said "Can you pass me the salt?" To know how to respond appropriately, one must ask oneself (implicitly, of course) "Does this speaker think my arms are broken?" (in which case the answer should be "Yes, I can" or "No, I can't," depending on whether one's arms *are* in fact broken). But if one is hale and hearty, the ordinary supposition would be that this was just a polite way of requesting one to pass the salt. And now the answer should be, "Sure. Here you are," accompanied by the action of passing the salt (Searle, 1969; Clark, 1979; Sperber and Wilson, 1986).

In sum, the actual speech acts that pass between people are merely hints about

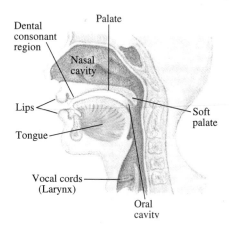

9.1 The human vocal tract *Speech is produced by the air flow from the lungs that passes through the larynx (popularly called the voice box) containing the vocal cords and from there through the oral and nasal cavities which together make up the vocal tract. Different vowels are created by movements of the lips and tongue, which change the size and shape of the vocal cavity. Consonants are produced by various articulatory movements that temporarily obstruct the air flow through the vocal tract. For some consonants the air flow is stopped completely. Examples are* p, *where the stoppage is produced by bringing both lips together, and* t *where it is produced by bringing the tip of the tongue to the back of the upper teeth. Some other consonants are created by blocking the air flow only partially, for example* th *(as in thick), which is produced by bringing the tip of the tongue close to the upper teeth but without actually touching them. (After Lieberman, 1975)*

the thoughts that are being conveyed. Talking would take just about forever if one literally had to say all, only, and exactly what one meant. Rather, the communicating pair takes the utterance and its context as the basis for making a series of complicated inferences about the meaning and intent of the conversation. A listener who fails to make these inferences is taken as an incompetent at best and a bore at worst. A person who blandly answers "Yes!" when you say "Could you tell me the time?" has failed to obey the principles of conversation that make communication possible (Grice, 1968; for overviews, see Leech, 1983; Horn, 1987).

THE STRUCTURE OF LANGUAGE

All human languages are organized as a hierarchy of structures. At the bottom of the hierarchy, each language consists of little snippets of sound, and at the other end, of sentences and conversations. We begin by describing the basic building blocks: the 40 or so phonemes, the 80,000 or so morphemes, and the hundreds of thousands of words.

PHONEMES

To speak, we move the various parts of the vocal apparatus from one position to another in a rapid sequence while expelling a column of air up from the lungs and out through the mouth (see Figure 9.1). Each of these movements shapes the column of air from the lungs differently and thus produces a distinctive speech sound (MacNeilage, 1972). Many of these differences among speech sounds are ignored by the listener. Consider the word *bus,* which can be pronounced with more or less of a hiss in the *s.* This difference is irrelevant to the listener, who interprets what was heard to mean 'a large vehicle' in either case. But some sound distinctions do matter, for they signal differences in meaning. Thus neither *butt* nor *fuss* will be taken to mean 'a large vehicle.' This suggests that the distinctions among *s, f,* and *t* sounds are relevant to speech perception, while the difference in hiss magnitude is not. The distinctions that are perceived to matter are called **phonemes.** They are the perceptual units of which speech is composed (Liberman, 1970; see Figure 9.2, which illustrates the hierarchy of linguistic structures).

9.2 The hierarchy of linguistic structures *Every sentence is composed of phrases, which are composed of morphemes (simple units of meaning such as strange and the plural -s), which in turn are composed of phonemes (the units of speech sound, such as p and ə). The phonemes are described by symbols from the phonetic alphabet because English spelling is not always true to the sounds of words.*

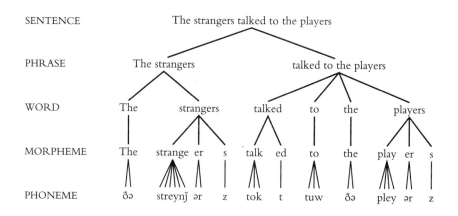

UNDERSTANDING UNFAMILIAR SPEECH

Because of the construction of the human speech apparatus, children can learn to pronounce a couple of hundred different speech sounds clearly and reliably. But each language restricts itself to using only some of them. English uses about forty.★ Other languages select differently from among the possible phonemes. For instance, German uses certain gutteral sounds that are never heard in English, and French uses some vowels that are different from the English ones. Once children have learned the sounds used in their native tongue, they usually become quite rigid in their phonemic ways: It becomes difficult for them to utter or perceive any others. This is one reason why foreign speech often sounds like a vague and undifferentiated muddle, rather than like a sequence of separable sounds.

Another difficulty in understanding unfamiliar speech—even in one's own language—has to do with the sheer rate at which the speech sounds are produced in sequence; adults can understand speech at the rate of 250 words per minute (Foulke and Sticht, 1969), which converts to about 16 phonemes per second. There are rarely gaps or silences that mark off one speech unit from the next in everyday speech. This holds not only for the successive phonemes, but for the words and phrases as well. All these units usually run into each other, so that it is difficult to tell where one ends and the other starts. Thus when one person speaks of a *gray tabby,* her listener may hear *a great abbey.*

COMBINING PHONEMES

As speakers of a language, we have learned the phonemes that constitute its sound elements. But we have learned something further as well—the way these phonemes can be combined into words. Some of these choices are a matter of historical accident. For instance, English happens to have a word *pledge,* composed phonemically of the sounds p–l–e–j. But it does not happen to have a word *medge,* composed of m–e–j. But some of the facts about how phonemes combine in words are systematic rather than accidental choices.

To see this point, consider the task of an advertising executive who tries to find a name for a new breakfast food. She will have to find some sequence of phonemes that has not already been used to mean something else. Will any new arrangement of phonemes do? The answer is no. To begin with, some, such as *gogrps* or *fpibs,* would be hard to pronounce. But even among phoneme sequences that can be pronounced, some seem somehow un-Englishlike. Consider the following possibilities: *Pritos, Glitos,* and *Tlitos.* They can all be pronounced, but one seems wrong: *Tlitos.* English speakers sense intuitively that English words never start with *tl,* even though this sequence is perfectly acceptable in the middle of a word (as in *motley* or *battling*). So the new breakfast food will be marketed as tasty, crunchy *Pritos* or *Glitos.* Either of these two names will do, but *Tlitos* is out of the question. The restriction against *tl*-beginnings is not a restriction on what human tongues and ears can do. For instance, one Northwest Indian language is named *Tlingit,* obviously by people who are perfectly willing to have words begin with *tl.* This shows that the restriction is a structural principle of English specifically. Few of us are conscious of this principle, but we have learned it and similar principles exceedingly well, for we honor them in our actual language use (Chomsky and Halle, 1968).

★ The English alphabet provides only twenty-six symbols (letters) to write these forty phonemes, so it often uses the same symbol for more than one. Thus, the letter *O* stands for two different sounds in *hot* and *cold,* an "ah" sound and an "oh" sound. This fact contributes to the difficulty of learning how to read English.

MORPHEMES AND WORDS

At the next level of the linguistic hierarchy (see Figure 9.2, p. 328), fixed sequences of phonemes are joined into morphemes. The **morphemes** are the smallest language units that carry bits of meaning. Like phonemes, the morphemes of a language can be combined only in certain ways. Some words consist of a single morpheme, such as *and, run,* or *strange.* But many morphemes cannot stand alone and must be joined with others to make up a complex word. Examples are *er* (meaning 'one who') and *s* (meaning 'more than one'). When these are joined with the morpheme *strange* (meaning 'alien' or 'odd') into the complex word *strangers* (*strange* + *er* + *s*), the meaning becomes correspondingly complex ('ones who are odd or alien'). Each of these morphemes has a fixed position within the word. Thus *er* has to follow *strange* and precede *s;* other orders (such as *erstranges* or *strangeser*) are not allowed (Aranoff, 1976).

The morphemes such as *strange* that carry the main burden of meaning are called **content morphemes.** The morphemes that add details to the meaning but also serve various grammatical purposes (such as the suffix *er* or the connecting word *and*) are called **function morphemes.**

The average speaker of English has acquired about 80,000 morphemes by adulthood (Miller and Gildea, 1987), knows the meaning of each, and how they are positioned within words. If we counted vocabulary by words rather than by morphemes, normal people would be credited with several hundred thousand of these, for then *strange, stranger, strangers,* etc., would each count as a separate item.

PHRASES AND SENTENCES

The system of words in a language is very rich and allows us to express an enormous variety of meanings with great precision. Nevertheless, we cannot memorize a new word for each of the hundreds of millions of thoughts that we want to express. Therefore, we combine our limited—though large—stock of words into whole sentences. We may remark either *The lion kicked the gnu* or *The gnu kicked the lion.* Both these sequences of words are meaningful, but there is a difference in the meaning that is of some importance—at least to the lion and the gnu. The term **syntax** (from the Greek, *arranging together*) is the name for the system that arranges (or groups) words together into meaningful phrases and sentences. This topic has been extensively investigated by the American linguist, Noam Chomsky (Chomsky, 1975, 1980, 1986; for overviews of syntactic theory, see Newmeyer, 1983; Sells, 1985; Radford, 1988).

Just as a morpheme is an organized grouping of phonemes and a word is an organized grouping of morphemes, so a **phrase** is an organized grouping of words. The phrases are the building blocks of which sentences are composed. Consider the sentence

Noam Chomsky

> *The French bottle smells.*

This sentence is **ambiguous:** It can be understood in two ways depending on how the words are grouped into phrases; either

> *(The French bottle) (smells).*

or   *(The French) (bottle) (smells).*

Thus by the choice of phrasing (that is, word grouping), the word *bottle* comes out a noun in the first interpretation, so that sentence is telling us something

9.3   How phrase structure can affect meaning   *On being asked what a Mock Turtle is, the Queen tells Alice "It's the thing Mock Turtle Soup is made from." Needless to say, this is a misanalysis of the phrase* mock turtle soup *as (mock turtle) (soup). It ought to be organized as* (mock) (turtle soup)—*a soup that is not really made out of turtles (and is in fact usually made out of veal). (Lewis Carroll,* Alice in Wonderland, *1969, p. 73)*

about French bottles. But *bottle* comes out a verb in the next interpretation, in which case the sentence is telling us about what the French put into bottles—namely, smells (that is, perfumes). For another example, see Figure 9.3.

The phrase is thus the unit that organizes words into meaningful groupings within the sentence. Just as for phoneme sequences and morpheme sequences, some phrase sequences (like those we just considered) are acceptable, while others are outlawed: for example, *(The French) (smells) (bottle).*

THE LINGUISTIC HIERARCHY AND MEANING

We have seen that language consists of a small number of sound units (the forty or so phonemes) organized into fixed sequences (the 80,000 or so morphemes and hundreds of thousands of words), which in turn are organized into the boundless number of phrases and sentences. In sum, as we ascend the linguistic ladder there are more and more units at every level. How can the human mind deal with this ever-expanding number of items? There is only one possible answer: We don't learn the billions of sentences in the first place. Instead, we acquire generalizations that allow us to construct any sentence. It is the fact that organization of units exists at each level of the hierarchy that makes language use possible in the first place. Without systematic knowledge of such patterns, we would not be able to learn, speak, or understand a language—there would just be too much to handle.

But why do humans go to the trouble of acquiring language? The answer, of course, is just that it allows us to convey boundless thoughts from one human mind to another human mind. Of primary interest, then, are the higher-level units and patterns of language: the meaningful words, phrases, and sentences. In the following sections, therefore, we will take up the questions of word and sentence meaning in detail.

THE MEANING OF WORDS

The question, "What do words mean?" is one of the knottiest in the whole realm of language (see Putnam, 1975; Fodor, 1983; 1988). The subfield that deals with this question, *semantics,* has thus far been able to give only a few, rather tentative answers. As so often, the first step is to eliminate some of the answers that appear to be false.

MEANING AS REFERENCE

One of the oldest approaches to the topic equates word and phrase meaning with *reference.* According to this position, the meaning of a word or phrase is whatever it refers to in the world. Thus this view asserts that words and certain phrases are essentially names. Proper names such as *Steffi Graf, Australia,* and the *Eiffel Tower* are labels for a particular person, place, and object. The reference theory of meaning claims that expressions such as *tennis player, continent,* and *building* function in a similar manner. According to this view, the only difference between such expressions and true proper names is that the former are more general; *tennis player* refers to various male and female players and to champions as well as duffers: *Steffi Graf* refers to one player and no one else.

The reference theory of meaning runs into several difficulties. One difficulty is that some words or phrases are perfectly meaningful even though it is hard to know exactly what they refer to. Some of these are abstract expressions such as *justice, infinity,* and *historical inevitability.* One cannot point to a real "infinity" somewhere out there in the world. Others are imaginary, such as *unicorn* and *the crown prince of South Dakota,* which presumably have no real-world referents at all. Yet these expressions do not seem to be "meaningless" or "semantically empty."

A famous example of the distinction between meaning and reference was pointed out by the German philosopher, Gottlob Frege (1892): The expression *the morning star* has one meaning (namely, 'the last star visible in the eastern sky as dawn breaks'), and the expression *the evening star* has quite a different meaning (namely, 'the first star visible in the western sky as the sun sets'). Yet both of these expressions refer to one and the same object in the sky (namely, the planet Venus). Thus two expressions can have different meanings and yet refer to the same thing. It follows that there is a distinction between the meaning of a word or phrase and the things that this word or phrase refers to in the world. The meaning of a word is the idea or concept that it expresses. The referents of the word are all those things in the real (or imaginary) world that fall under that concept.

THE DEFINITIONAL THEORY OF MEANING

We have just concluded that the meaning of a word is a concept (or **category**). Some words describe concepts that refer to only one thing or creature in the real or imaginary world, such as *Madonna* or *Pinocchio,* while other words such as *dog* or *unicorn* are more general, describing categories that have many referents. But is the meaning of a word always just a simple concept, irreduceable to simpler elements? Most theories of word meaning assert that only a relative handful of the words in a language describe elementary, "simple" concepts. The rest are labels for bundles of concepts. Thus the words *feathers, flies, animal, wings* might describe simple concepts, but all of these ideas are bundled together in the (relatively) complex word *bird.* One approach of this kind is the **definitional theory of meaning.** It holds that meanings are analyzable into a set of subcomponents, organized in our minds much as they are in standard dictionaries. This approach starts out with the fact that there are various meaning relationships among different words and phrases. Some words are similar in meaning *(wicked-evil);* others are opposites *(wicked-good);* still others seem virtually unrelated *(wicked-ultramarine).* According to the definitional proposal, these relationships can be explained by assuming that words are **bundles of semantic features** (Katz and Fodor, 1963; Katz, 1972). As an example, take the word *bachelor.* This word clearly has something in common with *uncle, brother, gander,* and *stallion.* As speakers of English, we know that all of these words carry the notion *male.* This point is forcefully made by considering various sentences that most English speakers will regard as odd (or, to use the technical term, *anomalous*). Thus, the sentence *My _____ is pregnant* sounds very peculiar if the missing word is any of the members of the bachelor-related group listed below:

	uncle	
	brother	
My	gander	is pregnant.
	stallion	
	bachelor	

Is this the entry for bird in your mental dictionary? *"bird . . . n. . . . [ME, fr. OE bridd] . . . 2: Any of a class (Aves) of warm-blooded vertebrates distinguished by having the body more or less completely covered with feathers and the forelimbs modified as wings. . . .*

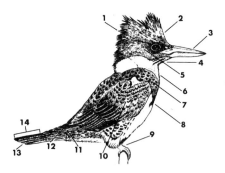

"bird 2 (kingfisher): 1 crest, 2 crown, 3 bill, 4 throat, 5 auricular region, 6 breast, 7 scapulars, 8 abdomen, 9 tarsus, 10 upper wing coverts, 11 primaries, 12 secondaries, 13 rectrix, 14 tail" (Merriam-Webster's Collegiate Dictionary, Tenth Edition)

Demonstrations of this sort suggest that words like *stallion* and *bachelor* are not simple in meaning, but rather are composed of a number of meaning atoms— the semantic features. Further demonstrations with anomalous sentences show that *bachelor* contains additional features such as 'unmarried' and 'adult.' This explains why the following sentences are also odd in meaning:

> *My sister is married to a bachelor.*
> *I met a two-year-old bachelor yesterday.*

The ultimate aim of this kind of analysis is to describe the meanings of words as packages that bundle together a limited set of primitive semantic attributes or **features.** For *bachelor*, these might be 'never married,' 'human,' 'adult,' and 'male'; for *stallion*, they would include 'adult,' 'male,' and 'horse.' Words like *stallion* and *bachelor* will be perceived to be related because when an individual looks up the features for each of these words in her mental dictionary (or **lexicon**), she will find that the meaning atom 'male' is listed for both of them. Taken together, the semantic features constitute a definition of a word. According to this theory, we carry such definitions in our heads as the meanings of words.

THE PROTOTYPE THEORY OF MEANING

The definitional theory faces a problem, for some members of a meaning category appear to exemplify that category better than others do. Thus a German shepherd seems to be a more doglike *dog* than a Pekinese, and an armchair seems to be a better example of the concept of *furniture* than a reading lamp. This seems to be at odds with the analysis we have described thus far, whose aim was to specify the necessary and sufficient attributes that *define* a concept. When a dictionary says that a bachelor is "an adult human male who has never been married," it claims to have said it all. Whatever fits under the umbrella of this definitional feature list is a bachelor. Whatever does not, is not. But if so, how can one bachelor be more bachelorlike (or one dog more doglike) than another?

The question is whether the semantic categories described by words are really as all-or-none as the definitional theory would have it. Several investigators have made a strong case for an alternative view, called the **theory of prototypes** (Rosch, 1973b; Rosch and Mervis, 1975; Smith and Medin, 1981).

The facts that the prototype theory tries to account for can easily be illustrated. Close your eyes and try to imagine a bird. It is pretty safe to guess that you just imagined something like a robin or a sparrow, not a buzzard, ostrich, or goose. There is something quintessentially *birdy* about a robin, while a goose does not seem such a good example of a bird. The definitional theory would have considerable trouble explaining why this is so. According to the definitional theory, some feature or features associated with the concept *bird* (such as 'has feathers,' 'lays eggs,' 'flies,' 'chirps') are both necessary and sufficient to pick out all birds and only birds. But if geese and robins are both said to be birds because they share these necessary and sufficient features, what makes the robin more birdy than the goose?

According to the prototype theory, the answer is that the meaning of many words is described as a whole set of features, no one of which is individually either necessary or sufficient. The concept is then held together by what some philosophers call a **family resemblance structure** (Wittgenstein, 1953). Consider the way in which members of a family resemble each other. Joe may look like his father to the extent that he has his eyes. His sister Sue may look like her father to the extent that she has his nose. But Joe and Sue may have no feature in common (he has his grandfather's nose and she has Aunt Fanny's eyes), and so the two of them do not look alike at all. But even so, the two are physically

Can a white rose be red? The Queen had ordered the gardeners to plant a red rose bush, but they planted a white one by mistake. They're now trying to repair their error by painting the white roses red. On the definitional theory of meaning, this seems reasonable enough. For the expressions red rose bush *and* white rose bush *differ by only a single feature—red* versus *white. But if so, why are they so terrified that the Queen will discover what they did? (From Lewis Carroll,* Alice in Wonderland, *1971, p. 62)*

9.4 The Smith brothers and their family resemblance *The Smith brothers are related through family resemblance, though no two brothers share all features. The one who has the greatest number of the family attributes is the most prototypical. In the example, it is Brother 9, who has all the family features: brown hair, large ears, large nose, moustache, and eyeglasses. (Courtesy of Sharon Armstrong)*

"Attention, everyone! I'd like to introduce the newest member of our family." (Drawing by Kaufman; © 1977 The New Yorker Magazine, Inc.)

related through a family resemblance, for each has some resemblance to their father (see Figure 9.4).

In sum, a family resemblance structure is like a collection of attributes. Probably no single member of the family will have them all. Nor will any two members of a family have the same ones (except for identical twins). But all will have at least some. Some individuals will have many of the family features. They are often called the "real Johnsons" or "prototypical Smiths." They are the best exemplars of the family resemblance structure because they have, say, the most Johnson-attributes and the least Jones-attributes. Other family members are marginal. They have only the nose or the little freckle behind the left ear.

Many investigators believe that what holds for the Smiths and the Johnsons may hold for many word concepts, such as *bird,* as well. For in fact, there is little doubt that, except for professional biologists, most people don't really know the features that all birds have in common (and which could thus serve as a definition for *bird*). Thus, contrary to our first guess, not all birds fly (ostriches don't fly). And not everything that lays eggs is a bird (giant tortoises lay eggs). Not all birds chirp (crows do not chirp, they caw), and some chirpers (crickets) are not birds. What are we left with from our list of defining features? Nothing but a pile of feathers! But feathers alone do not make something a bird. Hats have feathers, too. And, after all, if one plucked all the feathers out of a robin, it would be a mutilated robin, but it would still be a bird for all that. (You think this unfair? What would *you* call it? A hippopotamus?)

According to prototype theorists, birdiness is largely a matter of the total number of bird features a given creature exhibits. No one of these features is necessary and none is sufficient, but animals that have few (such as penguins and ostriches) will be judged to be poor members of the bird family, while those that have many (such as robins) will seem to be exemplary members. According to the theory, these judgments are based on a comparison with an internal **prototype** of the concept. Such prototypes represent mental averages of all the various examples of the concept the person has encountered. In the case of birds, people in our culture have presumably seen far more robins than penguins. As a result, something that resembles a robin will be stored in their memory system and will then be associated with the word *bird.* When the person later sees a new object, he will judge it to be a bird to the extent that it resembles the prototype in some way. A sparrow resembles it in many ways and so is judged to be "a good bird"; a penguin resembles it just a little and hence is "a marginal bird"; a rowboat resembles it not at all and hence is judged to be no bird.

Evidence for the prototype view comes from the fact that when people are asked to come up with typical examples of some category, they generally produce instances that are close to the presumed prototype (e.g., *robin* rather than *ostrich*). A related result concerns the time required to verify category membership. Subjects respond more quickly to the sentence *A robin is a bird* than to *An ostrich is a bird* (Rosch, et al., 1976; Rosch, 1978; for a related discussion, see Chapter 7).

COMBINING DEFINITIONAL AND PROTOTYPE DESCRIPTIONS

It appears that both the definitional and the prototype approaches to word meaning have something to offer. The prototype view helps us to understand why robins are better birds than ostriches. But the definitional theory explains why an ostrich is nevertheless recognized as a bird. Perhaps we can combine both views of meaning rather than choosing between them.

Consider the word *grandmother.* This word designates people who are 'mothers of a parent.' Thus *grandmother* clearly has a set of necessary and sufficient features that neatly define it. The definitional theory seems just right for words like

A

B

C

Prototypes *Members of the bird category. (A) A prototypical bird—the robin. (B) An atypical bird—the ostrich. (C) An exceedingly atypical bird—the penguin. (Photographs by Kenneth W. Fink, Laura Riley, Des and Jen Bartlett, all courtesy of Bruce Coleman)*

this. But now reconsider. Everyone knows that a grandmother is a person who bakes cookies, is old and gray, and has a kindly twinkle in her eye. When we say that someone is *grandmotherly,* we are referring to such prototypical attributes of grandmothers, not to geneology. But some grandmothers lack these typical properties. Zsa Zsa Gabor is a mother of a parent, but she is hardly gray or twinkly. And we all know some kindly lady who is gray and twinkly but never had a child; she may be grandmotherly, but she is not a grandmother (Lakoff and Johnson, 1980; Landau, 1982).

The most plausible assumption is that people have two partly independent mental representations for the meaning of a word. They know about prototypical attributes that are good symptoms of being a grandmother, such as being old and gray. They probably store a list (or perhaps a picture) of such attributes (or prototypical features) as a handy way of picking out likely grandmother candidates. But they also store defining grandmother features (e.g., 'mother of a parent'). These definitional features determine grandmother limits and tell one how to use the prototype appropriately (Miller and Johnson-Laird, 1976; Smith and Medin, 1981; Armstrong, Gleitman, and Gleitman, 1983).

ORGANIZING WORDS INTO MEANINGFUL SENTENCES

While individual words describe things, events, and so forth, the word groups that constitute phrases describe the endless varieties of complex categories for which the 80,000 words would be insufficient. Thus, once in a lifetime, we might want to speak of *three of the spotted ostriches on Joe Smith's farm.* We could not possibly memorize enough word items for all such complex categories that we could construct and might want to talk about, so we combine the words together in patterned ways to express our more complex concepts.

Sentence meanings are even more complex. They have to do with the various relations *among* the concepts that we want to express. Basic sentences introduce some concept that they are about (this is called the **subject** of the sentence) and then *propose* or *predicate* something of that concept (called the **predicate** of the sentence). Thus when we say *The boy hit the ball,* we introduce *the boy* as the subject or topic, and then we propose or predicate of the boy that he *hit the ball.* This is why sentence meanings are often called **propositions:** *The boy hit the ball* proposes (of the boy) that he hit the ball.

More generally, a simple proposition is usefully thought about as a sort of miniature drama in which the verb is the action and the nouns are the perform-

A grammar lesson at the Mad Hatter's Tea Party   *The meanings of words change in different linguistic constructions, so grammatical patterns are of great importance for communication.*

March Hare: "You should say what you mean."

Alice: "I do—at least I mean what I say—that's the same thing, you know."

Hatter: "Not the same thing a bit! Why, you might just as well say that 'I see what I eat' is the same thing as 'I eat what I see'!".

March Hare: "You might just as well say that 'I like what I get' is the same thing as 'I get what I like.'"

ers, each playing a different role. In our proposition about *boy-hitting-ball, the boy* is the "doer," *the ball* is the "done-to," and *hit* is the action itself. The job of a listener is much like that of a playgoer. The playgoer must determine which actors are portraying the various roles in the drama and what the plot (the action) is. Similarly, for each of the millions of heard sentences, the listener must discover exactly who did what to whom (Healy and Miller, 1970).

Propositions are of many different kinds, and therefore a language has many basic sentence types linked to the varying conceptions. For example, in sentences about *sneezing,* there need only be the phrase that expresses the subject of the sentence and the verb itself (e.g., *John sneezes*). But when we talk of *hitting,* we need to describe two entities in addition to the verb: the one who does the hitting and the one who gets hit. Correspondingly, sentences with *hit* will have two noun entities in addition to the verb (e.g., *The boy hit the ball*). And for acts of *giving,* which describe the transfer of objects from one person or place to another, we generally express three entities: the one who gives, the thing that is given, and the one who gets it (e.g., *The girl gives a bone to the dog*). Finally, some verbs such as *think* can express a relation between some entity and a whole proposition (rather than just a relation between two entities). We express this by putting a whole proposition—essentially, a little sentence—after the verb (e.g., *John thinks that Mary is a mongoose*). We see, then, that sentence structure is not just a collection of dry formulas. The varying forms of sentences are reflections of the variety of ways in which people conceptualize events, scenes, and relations (Fillmore, 1968; Bresnan, 1982; Jackendorf, 1987, 1990; Rappoport and Levin, 1988; Grimshaw, 1990; Fisher, Gleitman, and Gleitman, 1991).

PHRASE STRUCTURE

Consider again the simple sentence *The boy hit the ball.* It seems to be naturally organized into two main phrases. One is a **noun phrase** *(the boy)* and the other is a **verb phrase** *(hit the ball).* Even schoolchildren can demonstrate knowledge of these sentence parts by, say, enclosing the phrase units within parentheses *(the boy) (hit the ball)* (Read and Schreiber, 1982). Linguists use a different notation to convey this same partitioning of sentences into their natural parts. It is a **tree diagram,** so called because of its branching appearance, and similar to those we encountered in the discussion of hierarchical plans in directed thinking (see Chapter 8):

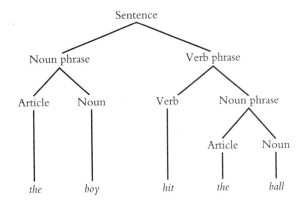

9.5 The structure of the sentence The
boy hit the ball   *This tree is called a
phrase-structure description, for it shows how
the sentence can be analyzed into phrase units.
Notice particularly that there are two noun
phrases in this sentence: One noun phrase
(the ball) is part of the verb phrase (hit the
ball); the other noun phrase (the boy) is not
part of the verb phrase. A description of this
kind also shows the word class types (e.g., article, noun, verb) of which each phrase consists. Finally, it shows the words of the sentence. Reading these (the bottom row in the
tree) from left to right, we get the actual sequence of words in the sentence being described. Thus (in its bottom row) the tree describes the actual words that speakers say and
listeners hear.*

The tree diagram notation is a useful way of showing that sentences can be
thought of as a hierarchy of structures (see Figure 9.2, p. 328). Each sentence
can be broken down into phrases, which can in turn be broken down into
words. The descending branches of the tree correspond to the smaller and
smaller units of sentence structure. The whole tree structure is called a **phrase
structure description** of the sentence.

It is important to get an idea of what phrase structure descriptions of simple
sentences look like. Figure 9.5 shows the phrase structure of the example sentence *The boy hit the ball.* At the very top of the tree this description asserts that
the example is a sentence; at the bottom it is a string of words, and in between it
is a sequence of phrases, subphrases and word-class names (e.g., *noun* and *verb*).
Similarly, Figure 9.6 shows the phrase structure of the passive sentence *The ball
was hit by the boy.* Clearly, these two figures look very different: The phrase
structures of the two sentences are not the same despite the fact that both mean
about the same thing. Because these descriptions do not, therefore, tell us everything about the sentence meanings, they are called **surface** phrase structure
descriptions. They describe the outward forms of sentences but not the full
meanings that lie beneath.

The fact that even schoolchildren with little formal training can analyze sentences into the phrase-sized pieces of Figures 9.5 and 9.6 suggests that this
analysis is not unnatural. Further evidence comes from various laboratory studies. One investigator asked whether recall is easier if the subject is helped to
think of the item in phrase-sized units. To find out, he asked subjects to memorize strings of nonsense words. One kind had no structure at all: *Yig wur vum rix
hum im jag miv.* The second kind was identical, except that various function
morphemes were added, resulting in sequences such as *The yigs wur vumly rixing
hum im jagest miv.*

On the face of it, the second sequence should be harder than the first to
memorize, for it is longer. But in fact the opposite was true. The function mor-

9.6 The structure of the sentence The
ball was hit by the boy   *Notice that the
phrase-structure descriptions in Figures 9.5
and 9.6 look quite different: The words in the
bottom row are arranged in different ways.
Thus the two trees succeed in describing the
fact that the active sentence and the passive
sentence sound quite different even though
they have quite a few words in common.*

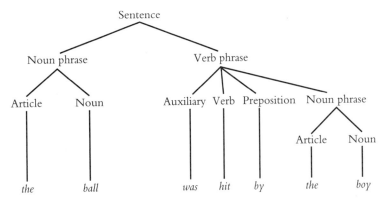

phemes in the second version allowed the subject to organize the sequence in terms of a phrase structure, and the phrase unit seems to be an efficient package for storing language-like information (Epstein, 1961; Levelt, 1970). Compare:

(The dogs) (were sadly serenading Naomi) (in mellowest tone).

and

(The yigs) (wur vumly rixing hum) (im jagest miv).

Of course, it was Lewis Carroll's use of this method in the poem "Jabberwocky" that made such nonsense as "'Twas brillig, and the slithy tove" appear to be meaningful. The mere existence of language structure gives the illusion of meaningfulness.

The effects we see here are examples of the "chunking" that aids human memory performance by organizing several individual pieces of information (here, the individual nonsense words) into a few higher units (the phrases) and in turn organizing the phrases into one yet higher-level unit (the sentence), which can now be treated as a single chunk to memorize (for further discussion, see Chapter 7).

UNDERSTANDING SIMPLE SENTENCES

What is the point of the formal diagrams of phrase structure as described by linguists and depicted in Figures 9.5 and 9.6? The answer is that if sentences are organized mentally just as they are in these diagrams, the listener can identify the characters in the sentence drama of who-did-what-to-whom by inspecting the subparts of the diagram. To see this point, consider a simplified diagram of the sentence *The boy hit the ball* (Figure 9.7A). How can the listener (or reader) find out who is the doer? Inspecting the diagram, the doer is whoever played this role:

Looking at this part of the tree in Figure 9.7A (dark red) we see that *the boy* was the doer. The done-to is whoever played this role:

Looking at this part of the tree in Figure 9.7A (dark green) we find that *the ball* was the done-to. But what was the action? Whatever occupies this place in the tree:

Looking at this part of the tree (blue), we see that *hit* was the action. Thus the phrase analysis of sentences is more than just a depiction of their parts. It begins to show how mental computations can inform the listener of what the speaker meant by the string of words she uttered. Figure 9.7B shows the structure as the listener would interpret it according to these semantic roles.

COMPLEX SENTENCES AND UNDERLYING STRUCTURE

So far we have looked only at very simple sentences and the way they are structured to express simple propositional ideas. But most of the sentences we say and understand are much more complicated than these first examples. One reason for this complexity is that we want to do more than express propositions that

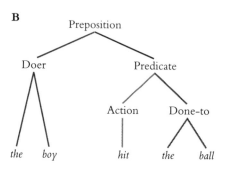

9.7 From structure to meaning *(A) The structure of the sentence* The boy hit the ball *(simplified); (B) The drama of who-did-what-to-whom as reconstructed by the listener from the structure in (A).*

describe some state of affairs in the world; we also want to express various attitudes and perspectives about these states of affairs. Another reason for complexity is that we often want to relate propositions to each other in subtle ways, and so we will utter two or more of them within the same sentence (as in *The boy who ate the hamburger hit the ball*).

As we will now see, this added complexity of meaning necessarily adds complexity to the sentence structures themselves. Yet the task of the listener—in addition to understanding the complexities—is still to recover the sentence drama of who-did-what-to-whom from the many ways in which this scenario is now hidden and disguised in the complex sentence.

To accomplish both these tasks, listeners mentally represent sentences in two different ways. The first is the **surface structure** of the sentence, which we have already discussed: This is the string of words actually uttered, organized into its various parts (as depicted in Figure 9.7A). The second is the **underlying structure** of the sentence.

Underlying structure, or the structure of sentence meaning, has two aspects. One we have discussed: the proposition, or basic thought, that the sentence is about (as depicted in Figure 9.7B). The proposition is the same in all the different sentences below, for they are all about the idea *boy-hitting-ball:*

1. *The boy hit the ball.*
2. *The boy did not hit the ball.*
3. *Did the boy hit the ball?*
4. *The ball was hit by the boy.*
5. *Wasn't the ball hit by the boy?*

Because all these sentences contain the same proposition, they are related in meaning. They are about the same doer, act, and done-to. But clearly they are not meaningfully identical. What differs is the stance or **attitude** the speaker is adopting toward the proposition. Namely, sentence (1) asserts the truth of the proposition about boy-hitting-ball, (2) denies it, (3) questions it, (4) asserts it but shifts the main focus of attention onto the ball rather than the boy, and (5) is a complex case of this focus-shift along with both the question and denial attitudes.

The whole logic of the sentence meaning, its underlying structure, is the proposition and attitudes taken together. Again, phrase structure trees will describe these underlying forms. This is because the meaning of the sentence (as well as its outward form) is naturally organized in terms of word groups (such as *the boy*) that act as coherent wholes in the meanings of sentences.

Figures 9.8 and 9.9 are tree diagrams of the underlying structure of two related sentences. One (Figure 9.8) is the active form: *The boy hit the ball;* its corresponding surface structure was shown in Figure 9.5 and again in a simplified form in Figure 9.7. The other (Figure 9.9) is the passive form: *The ball was hit by*

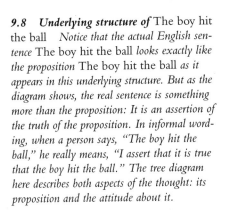

9.8 **Underlying structure of** The boy hit the ball *Notice that the actual English sentence* The boy hit the ball *looks exactly like the proposition* The boy hit the ball *as it appears in this underlying structure. But as the diagram shows, the real sentence is something more than the proposition: It is an assertion of the truth of the proposition. In informal wording, when a person says, "The boy hit the ball," he really means, "I assert that it is true that the boy hit the ball." The tree diagram here describes both aspects of the thought: its proposition and the attitude about it.*

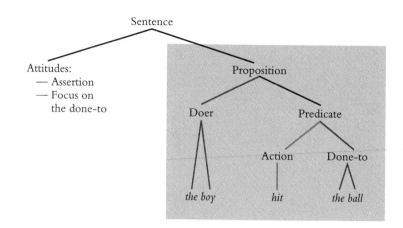

9.9 *Underlying structure of the passive sentence* **The ball was hit by the boy** *The similarity of meaning of this sentence to the one shown in Figure 9.8 is that both have the same proposition. The difference is that their list of attitudes is partly different.*

the boy; its corresponding surface structure was shown in Figure 9.6. Figures 9.8 and 9.9 are compact ways of describing the two aspects of sentence meaning—proposition and attitude. To begin with, they graphically show that the two sentences are related in meaning, for both contain the same proposition organized in the same way (the part of each diagram that is shaded pink). But these diagrams also show the subtle difference in their meaning: Their main focus is on different aspects of the proposition: The doer is emphasized in the first case, and the done-to is emphasized in the second.

There are many convincing demonstrations that what people remember primarily is the underlying structure, rather than the surface structure, of sentences. This is not surprising, for we usually care about what someone meant to say to us, not the exact way it was phrased. One investigator asked adult subjects to listen to stories. Afterward, she presented some isolated sentences and asked if these exact ones had appeared in the stories heard earlier (Sachs, 1967). For instance, a sentence in the original story might be

(1) *He sent a letter about it to Galileo.*

The later, test sentences were

(2) *Galileo sent a letter about it to him.*

and also

(3) *A letter about it was sent to Galileo by him.*

Neither (2) nor (3) had ever appeared in the original story. While the subjects generally knew that (2) was never presented, they often believed that (3) was. This is because the underlying structures of the two sentences (1) and (3) contain the same proposition *(He sent a letter about it to Galileo).* In contrast, sentence (2) contains a different proposition *(Galileo sent a letter about it to him).* In short, people remember the plot, but they often forget its exact presentation. They are more likely to recall propositions than the surface shapes of sentences.

THE MEANINGFUL RELATIONS AMONG SENTENCES

The idea that we mentally represent sentences in terms of underlying structure makes it possible to describe in quite a precise way how we understand the meaningful relations among many sentences that sound quite different; that is, that are different in their surface structures.

Paraphrases and opposites   As we have already seen, whenever two sentences have the same proposition in their underlying structure, they are related in meaning. But the precise nature of this relation depends on the sentence attitudes as well.

"Boy, he must think we're pretty stupid to fall for that again." (Courtesy of Leigh Rubin, Creators Syndicate, Inc. © 1990 Leigh Rubin)

If the only difference between two sentences is in the focus from which the action is regarded, as in the active versus the passive form, then the two sentences are **paraphrases**—their meanings are essentially equivalent. Thus

(1) *Wellington defeated Napoleon.*

and

(2) *Napoleon was defeated by Wellington.*

say the same thing in different words (though with a difference of emphasis).

Some differences in sentence attitude, on the other hand, alter the meaning radically, as in the case of assertion versus denial. The sentence

(3) *Wellington did not defeat Napoleon.*

obviously does not mean the same as sentence (1), but is its opposite. This is not to say, however, that (1) and (3) are unrelated in meaning, for they both take a stand (to be sure, an opposing stand) on the same proposition. They are related in a different way than sentence (1) is related to

(4) *Wellington ate hard-boiled eggs.*

A negative sentence attitude describes how (3) differs from (1), but a propositional difference describes how (4) differs from (1).

Ambiguity   Some of the preceding examples described sentences that differ in their surface structures but have the same proposition in their underlying structure. These turn out to be paraphrases, opposites, and so forth. What happens when the conditions are reversed, when the two sentences have the same surface structure but contain different propositions in their underlying structures? In this case, we will have two sentences that look for all the world as if they were a single sentence—on the surface they surely are, for they consist of the identical string of words. But this single word string has two meanings, depending on its two possible underlying structures. As a result, it is **ambiguous,** a single form that can be interpreted in two ways.

As examples, consider *Visiting relatives can be boring* and *Smoking volcanoes can be dangerous.* Each of these sentences has more than one meaning. The first can mean either that going to visit relatives can be boring or that relatives who come and visit can be boring. The more interesting case is the second example, because sheer sanity suggests it can mean only one thing—that a volcano with smoke billowing out of it is potentially dangerous since it might erupt (Figure 9.10A). But another interpretation comes to mind. One can envision a

9.10   Ambiguity of underlying structure

A

SURFACE: Smoking volcanoes can be dangerous

UNDERLYING PROPOSITIONS:
Volcanoes smoke. This can be dangerous.

B

SURFACE: Smoking volcanoes can be dangerous

UNDERLYING PROPOSITIONS:
Someone smokes volcanoes. This can be dangerous.

A   B

9.11 An analogy between linguistic and perceptual ambiguity Linguistic ambiguities are in some ways quite similar to perceptual ambiguities of the kind we encountered in Chapter 6. For in both cases, a stimulus can be interpreted in either of two different ways. (A) Ambiguity in visual perception. The same figure can be seen as either two profiles or a vase. (B) Ambiguity in sentence perception. The same sentence can refer to volcanoes that smoke or to volcanoes that are smoked.

deranged giant smoking away on a volcano, with effects the surgeon-general would regard as dangerous to his health (Figure 9.10B). This dual interpretation of a single string of words is analogous to the dual interpretation of single visual experiences that we discussed in Chapter 6 (see Figure 9.11).

Ambiguity is not restricted to underlying structure, however. It shows up from time to time at every level of the linguistic hierarchy. Surface-structure ambiguity can result from different phrase groupings of the same words (see Figure 9.3, p. 331). Another kind of ambiguity occurs in segmenting words from each other, as in *this guy* and *the sky* (see p. 340). Finally, there is word-meaning ambiguity. This occurs whenever words have more than one meaning. Thus *Someone stepped on his trunk* will give rise to different mental pictures depending on whether *his trunk* refers to a traveller with a suitcase, a tree surgeon, or a kneeling elephant.

COMPREHENSION

How do listeners understand the sentences they encounter? All they hear are sequences of words that occur one after another. But these sequences are only the surface forms of the sentences. To understand what the sentences mean, the listeners must somehow recover their underlying structure. How can they do this? After all, few listeners are lucky enough to encounter utterances such as *Focus on the done-to: John saw Mary.* Instead, they hear *Mary was seen by John.* How do they reconstruct the underlying logic from the surface forms?

In some ways, the problem of the listener is similar to that of the visual perceiver who has to determine the real shape of an object given its retinal image. This retinal shape changes with the object's orientation to the observer. But the observer can nevertheless perceive the object's actual shape, for he has a number of cues, such as perspective, that tell him about the orientation from which the object was viewed. Given these cues, the observer can now reconstruct the actual shape of the object perceptually (see Figure 9.12, and Chapter 6 for discussion).

Something analogous happens with language. Here, the underlying structures give rise to various surface forms. But these forms still bear telltale traces of the

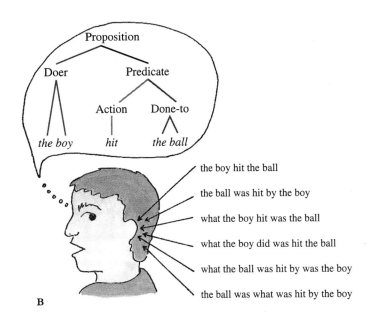

9.12 An analogy between linguistic paraphrase and perceptual constancy
Linguistic paraphrase is in some ways similar to perceptual constancies of the kind we discussed in Chapter 6. For in both cases, we interpret superficially different patterns of stimulation as roughly equivalent. (A) Shape constancy. When we look at a tabletop, the image that actually falls on our eye is a trapezoid whose exact shape depends on our orientation to the table. But shape constancy allows us to perceive the unchanging rectangular shape that gives rise to these images. (B) Paraphrase. The ear literally hears a variety of surface sentences, but the linguistic system interprets them all as containing the same proposition.

underlying structures to which they are related. These telltale traces are generally the appearance of certain function words, such as *by* or *who*. An example is the presence of a pattern such as *is verb-en by* (as in *is taken by, is given by,* and so on). This particular pattern is a good hint that we are dealing with a passive surface structure and that the focus therefore is on the done-to. Similarly, as we shall see, other function words, such as *who* and *or,* are a good clue that there is more than one proposition in the sentence being heard (Kimball, 1973).

THE SENTENCE ANALYZING MACHINERY

Just how are these clues utilized to reconstruct the underlying structure from the surface form? According to several psycholinguists, the **Sentence Analyzing Machinery** (let us call him—or her—SAM) operates in terms of several general strategies, two of which are discussed below. Depending on how easy or hard the sentence is to analyze by use of these strategies, the sentence will be correspondingly easy or hard for subjects to understand. (For general descriptions of sentence processing and comprehension, see Frazier and Fodor, 1978; Cairns, 1984; Tanenhaus, 1988; Joshi, 1991).

THE SIMPLEST FORM: DOER, ACT, DONE-TO

Several demonstrations have shown that SAM starts out with a strong bias about what kind of sentence he is about to hear: It is one in which the propositional roles appear in the order doer, act, done-to (or, using grammatical terminology, subject, verb, object).

The strategy of tentatively casting the first noun phrase in the role of the doer is quite useful, for in ordinary speech the active form of sentences (e.g., *John hits Fred*) is much more frequent than the passive *(Fred is hit by John)*. But infrequent or not, passive sentences do occur. Here, SAM's doer-first strategy necessarily fails, for in passive sentences the done-to comes before the doer. Now SAM has to correct himself. He recognizes his error when he gets far enough along to arrive at the words *is* and *by,* which occur in passive sentences. Having found these clues, he will revise his first guess and reassign the first noun phrase as

9.13 Deciding who is doer and who is done-to *Subjects were presented with sentences such as* The cat chases the dog *and* The dog is chased by the cat. *They were then shown either (A) or (B) and had to decide whether the sentence described the picture. Reaction times were faster for active than for passive sentences. (Slobin, 1966)*

done-to (and the second noun phrase as doer). But this revision takes some effort.

Evidence comes from studies of reaction time. The first-noun-did-it strategy necessarily implies that it will take a bit longer to understand a passive sentence than its corresponding active form. One investigator had subjects listen to sentences such as *The dog is chasing the cat* and *The cat is chased by the dog.* Immediately afterward, the subjects were shown one of two pictures—a dog chasing a cat or a cat chasing a dog. Their job was to decide whether the sentence did or did not describe the picture. The subjects reached the decision faster when the sentence was in the active rather than the passive form (Slobin, 1966; see Figure 9.13).

If SAM truly prefers to hear simple propositions in which the phrases occur in the order doer, act, done-to, he should also experience some difficulty with sentences in which one proposition occurs smack in the middle of another one, e.g., *The boy who ate a hamburger hit the ball.* Here, the proposition *The boy hit the ball* is interrupted by another proposition *(who ate a hamburger).* What is the effect of this interruption? Imagine SAM pursuing his doer, act, done-to strategy. For our new sentence, SAM does hear a noun phrase first *(the boy),* to which he happily assigns the role of doer. At this point, SAM is hoping to hear a verb, to which he can assign the role of action. But the next word in the complex sentence is *who,* surely not a verb. SAM must now do a kind of mental double take, analyzing the interrupting proposition *(who ate a hamburger)* before returning to finish the main sentence *(The boy . . . hit the ball).*

Of course we can all decipher such interrupted sentences, which are frequent in everyday speech, but careful measurement of reaction time shows that they require more effort than sentences like *The boy ate a hamburger and the boy hit the ball,* which presents the propositions one at a time, each in the order doer, act, done-to (Bever, 1970; Wanner and Maratsos, 1978; Wanner, 1988).

FUNCTION WORDS THAT SIGNAL PROPOSITION BOUNDARIES

In the example sentence just mentioned *(The boy who ate a hamburger hit the ball),* the boundary between the two propositions is signaled by the word *who.* Thus just as in the case mentioned earlier (the cueing of passive by the words *is* and *by),* it is the role of function words to reveal the structure of the sentence to the listener.

But in some cases, English allows us to omit such a function word in quick speech. For instance, we can say either *The princess kissed the frog whom the king knighted* or we can leave out the *whom,* saying *The princess kissed the frog the king knighted.* Evidently SAM gets a bit confused as to how to separate out the propositions when the clue from the function word is missing and so takes longer to understand such sentences (and occasionally misinterprets them altogether; Bever, 1970).

PUSHING SAM BEYOND HIS CAPABILITIES: A LINGUISTIC ILLUSION

We mention now a case where comprehension fails. Just as for the case of visual perception (see Chapter 6), some of the best evidence for understanding how the nervous system accomplishes its tasks in the usual case comes from looking at the rare cases where this machinery fails. Thus we saw that impossible figures defeat the observer, who sees a drawing of what appears to be an object but at the same time is perplexed because its parts don't seem to fit together in a natural way. Similar situations occur in sentence understanding, where the machinery

The horse (who was) raced past the barn (by the jockey)

—fell.

9.14 *Interpreting the sentence* The horse raced past the barn fell.

that works most of the time will go haywire for the occasional unusual sentence. Here is one such case:

The horse raced past the barn fell.

If you are like most English readers, your first impression will be that this is a totally ungrammatical sentence, one that has an "extra" verb *(fell)* that just doesn't fit. Yet there is good reason to believe that this sentence is both grammatical and meaningful (see Figure 9.14). Almost all listeners acknowledge it to be so once they have compared it to a related sentence. The trick is to notice that it is just a short form of

The horse who was raced past the barn fell.★

Why is *The horse raced past the barn fell* so hard to understand? The reason is that this sentence doesn't respond too readily to SAM's favorite analyzing strategies. For one thing, it doesn't consist of two separate cases of doer and action, one after the other, as in *The horse was raced past the barn, and the horse fell.* Instead, it inserts the second proposition *(who was raced past the barn)* in the middle of the first proposition *(The horse fell),* and this insertion comes after its doer (the *horse*) but before its action *(fell).* As if that weren't enough, the sentence makes things even more difficult by omitting the function words *who* and *was:* It says *raced past the barn* rather than *who was raced past the barn.* This is perfectly permissible—that is, grammatical—but as we have seen, such omissions make sentences much harder to understand. Finally, to add insult to injury, the proposition is in the passive *(the horse was raced past the barn)* rather than the active form in which doer is first and action is second (as in *Someone raced the horse past the barn).*

Every one of these features adds further complexity to the act of deciphering the sentence into the who-did-what-to-whom form. Rolled all together into one sentence, they overwhelm the processing capacity of the listener or reader. No wonder SAM doesn't comprehend.

Consider how SAM proceeds. Since he expects to hear a doer followed by an act, he goes down a garden path as he starts to listen, and then he interprets "The—horse—raced—past—the—barn" as one of his favorite cases in which *the horse* is doer, *raced* is the act, and *past the barn* is the place where the action takes place. But now, to his chagrin, SAM hears "fell." SAM cannot recover from his first guess and gives up. He is betrayed by the very machinery of normal comprehension that serves him so well in 99 percent of the cases, foiled by

★ If the sentence still seems hard to understand, try comparing it to the further sentences: *The horse taken past the barn fell* and *The horse who was taken past the barn fell.* These sentences are easier to understand because the form of the word *take (taken,* a so-called *passive participle)* could never be the main verb of the sentence. In contrast, *race* happens to have the same form for both past tense *(raced)* and passive participle (again, *raced),* much to the confusion of all!

9.15 Semantic cues to propositional thought *The passive sentence* The flowers are watered by the girl *takes no longer to understand than the active sentence* The girl waters the flowers, *since its meaning will surely be understood as pictured in (A) rather than in (B).*

the one unusual sentence that doesn't fit. Here, as so often, we learn something quite precise about the mental gymnastics of ordinary and successful understanding by looking at a case where SAM registers "TILT!" and does *not* understand.

THE INTERACTION OF SYNTAX AND SEMANTICS

Our discussion of comprehension has focused on how we use syntactic information as a clue to sentence meaning. But several authors have pointed out that this process may be heavily affected by semantic factors, ranging all the way from the meanings of the words uttered to the sense of the conversation as a whole (Marslen-Wilson, 1975; Crain and Fodor, 1985; Crain and Steedman, 1985; Stowe, 1987; Carlson and Tanenhaus, 1988; Trueswell, Tanenhaus, and Garnsey, in press). It is all these additional factors that keep conversation from being drowned in confusion by the pervasive ambiguity of word, phrase, and sentence structure.

To take a simple example, there is some evidence that the meaning of a passive sentence is recovered as quickly as the meaning of an active sentence if the words used give strong semantic cues to the overall propositional thought. Thus *The flowers were watered by the girl* can hardly be misunderstood to mean *The flowers watered the girl,* so the passive sentence in this case is rapidly understood through attention to its semantics (Slobin, 1966; see Figure 9.15).

In summary, the process of comprehension is marvelously complex, taking into consideration factors of multiple kinds. It is all the more amazing that understanding just about any sentence seems to be a snap. The difference in effort for the so-called easy ones and the so-called hard ones is usually just a few tenths of a second. Thus the facts of comprehension are one important instance of the intricacy of language knowledge that is somehow embodied in the brains of all normal adults.

THE GROWTH OF LANGUAGE IN THE CHILD

Now that we have surveyed the boundless forms and contents of language, and some of the computational complexities of comprehension, it seems impossible that any save the most brilliant person could possibly learn it. Yet we know that language is as natural and inevitable a part of human nature as chirping is to birds, roaring is to lions, and barking is to dogs. Whatever their talent, their motivation, or their station in life, normal children learn their native tongue to a high level of proficiency during the preschool years. This holds for children reared in poverty on the streets of New York and in the deserts of North Africa as much as it does for upper-class British children reared by nannies and sent to posh nursery schools.

THE PROBLEM OF LANGUAGE LEARNING

Language seems to pose awesome problems for the mere babes who must learn it. It is not even obvious which sounds are relevant and which can be ignored. The infant listening to adults is exposed to an enormous jumble of sounds. Some of these sounds constitute speech, but others are coughs, hums, whistles, and even animal imitations ("and the big cow said 'Moooooooooo'"): How does the learner ever sort through this jumble of noise to discover which of the sounds she hears are speech sounds and which are not?

Let's suppose the infant has somehow managed to solve this task, and knows which sounds are relevant to language. How does she relate these sounds to meanings? Here matters become even more complicated. One problem is that the same speech events seem to refer to different things at different times. Thus the caregiver may say "dog" when the child sees a Great Dane, but also when the child sees the very different looking Boston terrier or even a fluffy stuffed

Lewis Carroll's poignant tale of how an animal's mind would be different if it had language Alice came to a forest where nothing had a name. She met a fawn that walked trustingly by her side: "So they walked together through the wood, Alice with her arms clasped lovingly around the soft neck of the Fawn, till they came out into another open field [where things had names]. And here the Fawn gave a sudden bound into the air, and shook itself free of Alice's arm. 'I'm a Fawn!' it cried out in a voice of delight. 'And dear me! You're a human child!' A sudden look of alarm came into his beautiful brown eyes, and in another moment it had darted away at full speed." (Carroll, Through the Looking Glass, p. 227)

toy. How does the learner discover the category (namely, *dog*) that is to cover such widely different things? (Carey, 1985). Symmetrically, sometimes the child will hear different speech signals when she observes a single thing, for parents may refer to the pet in the house as "Spot," "the dog," "that animal," or even "that housewrecker." And oftentimes, when the child is attending closely to the dog, the adult may say something quite irrelevant, such as "Time for your nap, honey." Under the circumstances, how does the child ever discover that the word *dog* refers to dogs, while *nap* refers to sleeping? (Pinker, 1984; L. Gleitman, 1990; Waxman, 1994; P. Bloom, 1994).

It is clear that the young language learner is confronted with a confusing welter of sounds and information about the world. But she somehow makes sense out of all this jumble even so. If she is a learner of English, she extracts the general fact that the sound "see" means 'gaze with the eyes'; if she is a learner of Spanish, she extracts the different fact that the same sound "see" (as in "Si!") means 'yes.' The question is how.

IS LANGUAGE LEARNING THE ACQUISITION OF A SKILL?

Language learning is more than mere imitation. It is true that young children say "dog" and not "perro" or "chien" if they are exposed to English, so in this sense they are imitating the language community around them. But the real trick in word learning and use is creative: The word *dog* must apply to new dogs that the learners see. What served as a label for the pet bulldog must apply to the neighborhood poodle as well.

What goes for words goes for sentences too. Young children utter sentences they have never heard before. For instance, a mother may say to her child "I love you, Jane." But in response Jane may say "I hate you, Mommy" or "I'm going to crayon a face on this wall." These sentences are clear, though unwelcome, creative language acts of Jane's. They could not possibly have been learned by imitation.

Another popular hypothesis about language learning is that it is based on explicit **correction** or **reinforcement** by parents. According to this view, grammatical mistakes are immediately pointed out to the young learner, who subsequently avoids them. But in fact, this hypothesis is false (Morgan and Travis, 1989). In actual practice, mistakes in grammar and pronunciation generally go unremarked, as in the following exchange:

| two-year-old: | Mamma isn't boy, he a girl. |
| Mother: | That's right. |

The situation is quite different if the child makes an error of fact. In that case, the mother often does provide a correction:

| two-year-old: | And Walt Disney comes on Tuesday. |
| Mother: | No, he does not. |

(Brown and Hanlon, 1970)

These findings are perfectly reasonable. Parents are out to create socialized and rational beings, not little grammarians, and so they correct errors of conduct and fact, not errors of grammar.

LANGUAGE DEVELOPMENT

As we have just seen, imitation, correction, and reinforcement can't bear too much of the burden in explaining language learning. Children don't come to the task of acquiring their native tongue as little robots who can only notice and copy whatever they hear, whenever they hear it. How then are we to explain the growth of speech and comprehension? We will begin by tracing the child's progress during the first few years of life.

THE SOCIAL ORIGINS OF SPEECH PRODUCTION

Infants begin to vocalize from the first moments of life. They cry, coo, and babble. They make sounds such as "ga" and "bagoo" that sound very much like words—except that these babbles have no conventional meaning. This is shown by the fact that deaf infants, who cannot hear others' vocalizations, babble in the same way (Lenneberg, 1967). Moreover, deaf children in a home where sign language is used also babble manually; they produce gestures that look just like real signs, but as yet have no meaning (Petitto and Marentette, 1991). In the hearing infant, vocalization soon takes on a social quality, for three-month-olds will vocalize more when an adult vocalizes to them (Collis, 1975; K. Bloom, 1988).

Though true speech is absent in the first year of life, prelinguistic children have their own ways of making contact with the minds, emotions, and social behaviors of others. Quite early in life, babies begin to exchange looks, caresses, and sounds with caregivers. Several investigators have suggested that these are precursors and organizers of the language development to follow. The idea is that the gesture-and-babble interaction helps children to become linguistically socialized, to realize, for instance, that each participant in a conversation "takes a turn," and responds to the other (Bruner, 1974/1975; Tomasello and Ferrar, 1986; Baldwin, 1991).

Thus language knowledge is essentially social and interpersonal from the beginning (Fernald, 1992). Though the capacity to learn it is built into the brain of the individual child, useable knowledge of speaking and listening requires social interactions between more than one person at a time. To speak to another, one has to have an idea—no matter how primitive—that the other lives in the same, mutually perceived, world (Bates, 1976; Bates and MacWhinney, 1982).

DISCOVERING THE FORMS OF LANGUAGE

Infants' first attempts to speak are rather unimpressive. But careful analysis shows that they know more about language than they seem to at first glance. For at a very early age, they make some perceptual distinctions about the sounds they hear that are crucial to later language learning. Indeed, one remarkable study shows that infants are more attentive to hearing their caretaker's language than a foreign language by the fourth day of life (Mehler et al., 1988).

Social origins of speech *(Photograph by Erika Stone)*

THE RUDIMENTS OF PHONEME DISCRIMINATION

We have previously seen that all languages are built out of a few basic sound distinctions: the phonemes. But these linguistic sound atoms vary somewhat from language to language. Thus in English, there is a crucial difference between "l" and "r" (as in *lob* vs. *rob*). Though physically these sounds are quite similar, each of them falls within a different phoneme in English, whose speakers have no trouble producing and perceiving the distinction. In contrast, this distinction has no linguistic significance in Japanese, where "l" and "r" sounds fall within the same phoneme. In consequence, Japanese speakers can neither produce nor perceive a distinction between them. How does the infant learn which sound distinctions are the phonemes of his language?

The answer is that initially infants respond to just about all sound distinctions made in any language. They discover the phonemes of their native tongue by *learning to ignore* the distinctions that don't matter. Their first step in understanding, say, Japanese, is to learn not to become speakers of all the other 4,000 languages on earth (Jusczyk, 1985; Werker, 1991).

Evidence comes from studies which show that two-month-old babies can distinguish between such sounds as "ba" and "pa," "la" and "ra," and so forth. The experimenters used a version of the habituation method (see Chapter 13, pp. 512–13). The babies were given a pacifier, and whenever they sucked on it the syllable "ba" was broadcast over a loudspeaker. The infants quickly learned that their sucking led to the sound, and they began sucking faster and faster to hear it some more. After awhile, the babies habituated to the "ba" sound and their sucking rate diminished. At this point, the experimenters changed the broadcast sound from "ba" to "pa." The babies now started to suck again at a rapid rate. They had become dishabituated. This result indicates that they could discriminate between the two sounds (see Figure 9.16; Eimas et al., 1971).

Infants in the first year of life are sensitive to just about every contrast that occurs in *any* human language, but their sensitivity to foreign contrasts diminishes significantly by twelve months of age (Werker and Tees, 1984) and alteration in phonetic sensitivities is already observable at age six months (Kuhl et al., 1992). This is consistent with the idea that infants must be prepared by nature to learn any language on earth. After all, they arrive without a passport that tells them which language they are going to hear. But the diminished sensitivities of twelve-month-olds suggest that babies recalibrate their perceptions just as true speech and understanding begin, thus concentrating selectively on the distinctions that matter in their own linguistic community (Kemler-Nelson et al., 1989).

THE RUDIMENTS OF THE SENTENCE UNIT: "MOTHERESE"

We have seen that a crucial characteristic of language is that it includes syntax—general principles for combining the finite stock of words into infinitely many sentences. To discover the principles of syntax, infants first must recognize what a sentence is—where one ends and the next one begins.

One cue that may help infants is a special way of speaking that is almost universally employed by adults when they talk to babies. This special speech style has come to be called, somewhat whimsically, **Motherese** (Newport, Gleitman, and Gleitman, 1977). Of course, "Motherese" is something of a misnomer, for this style of speaking is adopted by fathers as well as mothers and by strangers as well as relatives when they are talking to an infant (Fernald et al., 1989). It is characterized by a special tone of voice, with high pitch, slow rate, and exaggerated intonations (Fernald and Kuhl, 1987). (Just hold a baby and talk to her; you will discover that you naturally use Motherese and will feel quite awkward if

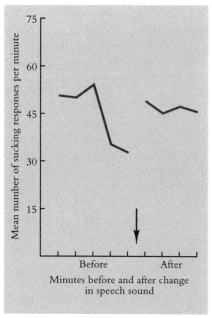

A

B

9.16 Sucking rate and speech perception in the infant (A) An infant sucks to hear "ba" or "ga." (Photograph courtesy of Philip Morse, Boston University) (B) The graph shows the sucking rate of four-month-olds to "ba" or "ga." The infants soon become habituated, and the sucking rate drops. When a new stimulus is substituted ("ga" for "ba" and "ba" for "ga"), the infant dishabituates and sucks quickly once again. Similar results have been obtained for one-month-olds. The point of the shift is indicated by the arrow. (From Eimas et al., 1971)

(Photograph by Erika Stone, 1989)

you try to sound the way you do when you talk to your Psych I professor.)

There is good evidence that infants prefer Motherese to adult-to-adult speech, even though they as yet understand neither. One investigator conditioned four-month-old babies to turn their heads to the left or right so they could listen to speech sounds that came out of two loudspeakers. When the baby turned his head toward the loudspeaker on the right, he heard Motherese (produced not by his own, but by another child's mother). When he turned to the left, he heard adult-to-adult talk. The infants soon began to turn their heads to the right, indicating a preference for Motherese despite the unfamiliarity of the speaker's voice (Fernald and Simon, 1984).

This remarkable coadjustment between adult and child—the caregiver finding it irresistible to speak in a special way to infants and the infants finding that style of speech bewitching to listen to—is a first hint of how our species is biologically adapted for the task of learning language. Indeed, such early observers as Charles Darwin (1877) had already noticed these protolinguistic interactions between mothers and their infants, and he called Motherese "the sweet music of the species."

The tones of Motherese and the responsive cooing of the infant are among the behavioral patterns related to the affective bonding between caregiver and child (Fernald, 1984). But Motherese may have more specific uses in language learning as well. Motherese has acoustic properties that make it useful for learning to recognize the phrases and sentence units in speech. Both in adult speech and in Motherese there are certain sound cues that can demarcate the boundaries between phrases and sentences. These include changes of pitch: The pitch tends to start high at the beginnings of sentences and to go down at their ends. Another characteristic is the presence of pauses (brief periods of silence) that often occur at the boundaries between phrases and between sentences. But these cues (and their co-occurrence) are much more reliable and clear in the exaggerated style of Motherese than in speech among adults. As a result, the Motherese style may help the infant to recognize sentence units and their phrase components (Morgan and Newport, 1981; Gleitman and Wanner, 1982; Morgan, 1986; Kemler-Nelson et al., 1989; Cutler, 1994).

Evidence comes from an experiment in which the investigators asked whether seven-month-olds prefer to hear speech in which these two cues (pitch fall and silent interval) occur together to speech in which they do not. To find out, they inserted extra-long pauses (one second in length) in recorded Motherese. The pause was inserted either at the end of sentences in that speech (where a fall in pitch naturally occurred) or some arbitrary distance earlier (three words from the end of the sentence, a place where the pitch usually did *not* fall). A loudspeaker on the child's left broadcast the speech in which the pauses co-occurred with the fall in pitch; a loudspeaker on the right broadcast the speech in which the pause was placed elsewhere. The infants showed a marked preference for the speech that came from the left in which the fall in pitch and the pause coincided (as shown by the fact that they turned their heads toward this rather than toward the other loudspeaker). This could hardly be because the infants preferred pauses at the end of sentences—for they presumably didn't know as yet what sentences are. What they preferred was speech in which a pause went along with a fall in pitch. A pause in the middle of sentences, where the pitch was still high, evidently sounded less natural (Hirsh-Pasek et al., 1987).

This preference for the coincidence of falling pitch and pause will be useful for the babies in later language learning. For they eventually must learn what is a sentence and what is not, and this coincidence will provide an important clue. It may well be that infants are specially attuned by nature to notice just those aspects of the sound stream that will be important to language learning—and that their caregivers are specially tuned by nature to make these properties available by exaggerating them in Motherese.

Learning language requires a receptive human mind. *Ginger gets plenty of linguistic stimulation but is prepared by nature only to be man's best friend. (The FAR SIDE cartoon by Gary Larson is reprinted by permission of Chronicle Features, San Francisco, California.)*

THE ONE-WORD SPEAKER

Children begin to understand a few words that their caregivers are saying as early as five to eight months of age. For example, some six-month-olds will regularly glance up at the ceiling light in response to hearing their mother say "light." Actual talking begins sometime between about ten and twenty months of age. Almost invariably, children's first utterances are one word long. Some first words refer to simple interactions with adults, such as *hi* and *peekaboo.* Others are names, such as *Mama* and *Fido.* Most of the rest are simple nouns, such as *duck* and *spoon,* adjectives such as *hot* and *big,* and action verbs such as *give* and *push.* And lest one think that child rearing is all pleasure, one of the first words is almost always a resounding *No.* The early vocabulary tends to concern things that can be moved around and manipulated or that move by themselves in the child's environment. For example, children are less likely to talk about ceilings than about rolling balls. And this early vocabulary refers more often to attributes and actions children can perceive in the outside world, such as shape or movement, than to internal states and feelings, such as pain or ideas (Nelson, 1973; Huttenlocher, Smiley, and Charney, 1983; Landau, 1994).

Missing altogether are the function words and suffixes, such as *the, and,* and *-ed.* These are among the most frequent items the child hears, but they are never uttered by beginners even so. There are several reasons for the lateness of these function items. One has to do with how hard they are to perceive. As we just saw, infants are especially interested in such properties of the sound wave as high pitch. But the function words are usually not stressed and occur with low pitch in the caregiver's speech (Kelly and Martin, 1994; Cutler, 1994). A second reason is that the function morphemes are grammatical items. Since young children say only one word at a time, they presumably have little need to utter morphemes whose central role is to organize groups of words into sentence form (Gerken, Landau, and Remez, 1990).

WORD MEANING AT THE ONE-WORD STAGE

It is hard to find out precisely what young children mean by the words they say. To be sure, we hear the tots say "rabbit" and "ball" but what exactly do these words mean to their young users? One reason for our relative ignorance about these earliest word meanings is that the same scene or event can often be described in many ways, depending on the particular words chosen. The very same creature can be described as *Peter, the rabbit, the animal, the creature with a tail,* and so forth. Therefore, even if a young child says "rabbit" on seeing a rabbit, he may mean 'tail' or 'animal' or 'white' or even 'runs by' for all we know.

The same problem that makes it hard for investigators to find out exactly what children mean ought to make it hard for children themselves to discover these meanings. Even if the helpful mother points out a rabbit to her child, saying "rabbit," the child still has a big job to do. He has to make up his mind whether the word *rabbit* means a particular animal (in which case *rabbit* is a name, such as 'Peter Rabbit'), anything that falls within the animal kingdom (in which case *rabbit* means 'animal'), anything within a particular species (so *rabbit* means 'rabbit'), or even some property, part, or action of a rabbit (in which case *rabbit* means 'white' or 'tail' or 'hops'; see Figure 9.17).

Because such problems for the learner are real, beginners often **undergeneralize** the meaning of a word: They may know that the word *house* refers to small toy buildings but not that it also refers to large real buildings. And they may **overgeneralize** the meanings of other words. They may think that the word *Daddy* refers to any man, not just their own father. These overgeneralizations

9.17 Symmetrical problems for child learners and investigators of child language *(A) The child's helpful mother points out a rabbit, saying "rabbit." The child sees a rabbit—but also sees an animal, an ear, and the ground beneath the rabbit. Which one does the mother mean by the word rabbit? (B) The mother's (and the investigator's) problem in understanding young children's speech is much the same. The child may say "rabbit" when she observes a rabbit, but for all the mother knows the child may have made an error in learning, and thus may mean something different by this word.*

and undergeneralizations are common for the first seventy-five or so words the child utters, but very rare thereafter (Rescorla, 1980). At later stages of learning, the child is almost always exactly on the mark in using words to refer to the right things in the world. We shall return later to how the child manages to be right overwhelmingly often despite the real problem of rabbits, rabbit parts, and the like. But for now it is important to realize that even the young overgeneralizer is surprisingly correct in what he has learned. Though he just about always observes the ground whenever he observes a rabbit (and hears the word *rabbit*)—because rabbits can't fly and thus are always found near the ground—still, he virtually never mistakenly learns that *rabbit* means 'ground' (or that *ground* means 'rabbit'). He just makes the category a bit too broad or narrow at first.

Developmental psychologists have different theories about the child's earliest word meanings. Some investigators take a *functional* approach. They believe that children use words to classify things together that act alike in their world— a ball is that which one throws and bounces in the playground (Nelson, 1973). Others argue for a *featural* approach. These investigators believe that children use words to designate things that look alike, that share certain perceptual features. Thus *ball* may be overgeneralized to anything that is round, including faces, balls, and the moon (Clark, 1973). Still others believe that early word meanings are based on *prototypes.* In their view, children call things "ball" to the extent that they resemble a particular ball which serves as the model (prototype) for the entire concept (Anglin, 1975; deVilliers, 1980; Keil and Batterman, 1984). Of course these primitive meanings will change and develop as the children acquire more and more information (Chi, Glazer, and Rees, 1982) and reorganize the categories of their physical and mental world (Carey, 1985; for overviews of word-meaning acquisition, see Clark, 1993; L. Gleitman and Landau, 1994).

PROPOSITIONAL MEANING AT THE ONE-WORD STAGE

There is another question about children's first words: Are these little foreshortened sentence attempts? That is, do children have a proposition and attitude in

Child on mother's lap

9.18 Set-up for the selective looking experiment *The child sits on the mother's lap and listens to a taped sentence while two video screens show two cartoon characters performing different actions. A hidden observer notes which screen the child is looking at. The mother wears a visor that covers her eyes, to make sure she does not see which screen shows which action and thereby give inadvertent clues to the child. (Courtesy of Roberta Golinkoff)*

mind when they say "Doggie!" as a dog runs by? To listening adults, it does seem as though children have in mind a comment, request, question, or command. Thus adults are inclined to interpret "Eat" as 'The duck is eating' when the child says it as he watches a duck eat, but as 'Eat this cookie!' if it is said as the child forces a cookie into a stuffed duck's beak. Many investigators of child language believe young children have propositional ideas in mind even when they are speaking only one word at a time (Shipley, Smith, and L. Gleitman, 1969; Bretherton, 1988).

One basis for this belief is that one-word speakers fill out their speech with accompanying gestures (Greenfield and Smith, 1976). A child may say "rabbit" and also reach toward a rabbit at the same time, so the meaning 'Give me that rabbit' or 'I want that rabbit' comes across to the watching, listening adult. Moreover, one-word speakers differentiate their requests, comments, and demands by intonation: Their pitch goes up when they seem to be requesting information and down when they seem to be making a demand (Gallagan, 1987).

The strongest evidence comes from recent experiments in which children as young as sixteen months of age (who themselves speak only one word at a time) look at brief movies that depict different happenings. The subjects sit on their mothers' laps and can see two video screens, one to their left and one to their right (Figure 9.18). Each screen shows cartoon characters known to the babies, engaged in various actions (Figure 9.19). On the screen to the left, Big Bird is tickling Cookie Monster, and on the screen to the right, Cookie Monster is tickling Big Bird. Half the children hear a voice saying "Oh look! Big Bird is tickling Cookie Monster." The other children hear the reverse sentence ("Oh look! Cookie Monster is tickling Big Bird"). Hidden observers now record which screen the children turn their attention to. The finding is that the toddlers look primarily at the screen that matches the sentence they have heard. To understand what matches and what does not match, their only clue is the syntax of the sentence they have heard. Thus the experiment proves that even babies who can speak only in single words understand the logic of simple sentences in terms of the drama of who-did-what-to-whom (Hirsh-Pasek et al., 1985; Naigles, 1990; L. Gleitman, 1990).

9.19 Stimuli for the selective looking experiment *One screen shows Big Bird tickling Cookie Monster, the other shows Cookie Monster tickling Big Bird.*

9.20   The ambiguities of two-word speech   *The two-word utterances of young children, while systematic and meaningful, are quite ambiguous. The three panels from the children's story* Higgledy Piggledy Pop, *by Maurice Sendak, show why one young child might want to learn more about adult syntax. (A) An adventurous dog takes a job as nurse to Baby. He must get Baby to eat, or he will be fed to the lion down in the basement. Here Baby refuses the food, saying "No eat!" (I will not eat). (B) Here, the dog eats up the food Baby has refused. Baby finds this objectionable and so cries out "No eat!" (Don't eat my porridge!). (C) Baby has angrily pushed the button so the dog-nurse will fall down to the waiting lion, but Baby has accidentally fallen also. To avoid being eaten by the lion, Baby cries out "No eat!" (Don't eat me up!). (From Maurice Sendak, 1979)*

THE TWO-WORD (TELEGRAPHIC) SPEAKER

Many drastic changes take place beginning at about the second birthday (Brown, 1973; Braine, 1976). The child's vocabulary begins to spurt, rising to many hundreds of words. Soon she begins to put words together into primitive sentences, and then we are aware most poignantly that another human mind is among us.

SYNTAX AND PROPOSITIONAL MEANING IN TWO-WORD SPEECH

Though we can clearly recognize propositional ideas in these first "sentences," these hardly sound like adult speech. Generally, each rudimentary sentence is only two words long, and each of its components is a content word. The function morphemes are still largely missing, and so these sentences sound like the short ones we often use in telegrams and newspaper headlines: "Throw ball!" "Daddy shoe," "No eat!" (Brown and Bellugi, 1964).

These sentences show some organization, however, despite their simplicity. From the earliest moments of "telegraphic speech," the words seem to be serially ordered according to the propositional roles. The child who says "Throw ball" usually does not say "Ball throw" to mean the same thing (Braine, 1963; L. Bloom, 1970; deVilliers and deVilliers, 1973). Thus young English speakers will put the doer of the action first and will say "Mommy throw!" if they want the mother to throw the ball; and they will put the done-to last and say "Throw ball!" in approximately the same circumstances. So mothers of two-year-old learners of English would probably be right in feeling a bit miffed if their child said "Throw Mommy!"

Two-year-olds' correct use of word order to express different sentence meanings is consistent with the comprehension that they showed even earlier (in understanding who did what to whom in the Cookie Monster and Big Bird videos). In fact, these short sentences are ordinarily so clear in meaning that one may wonder why children bother to learn anything more. But see Figure 9.20 for a demonstration of how ambiguous two-word speech sometimes is.

EXPLAINING TWO-WORD SPEECH

Why are children's early sentences so short? We have discussed one reason: The function words have low pitch and thus are less salient in the sound wave as

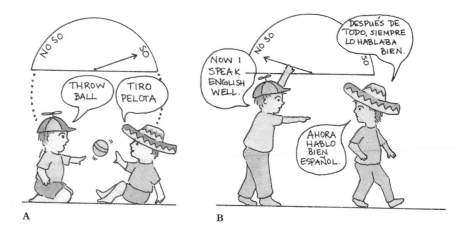

9.21 The parameter setting theory of language learning (A) Children hearing English and children hearing Spanish both come from nature's factory with the switch set to allow subject omission (SO). (B) The English speaker eventually resets his switch to disallow this (No SO); the Spanish speaker does not.

children perceive it. Accordingly, it is hard to learn them (Gleitman and Wanner, 1982). Another factor is the sheer problem of memory and information handling that makes construction of a complex sentence plan difficult, so the child reduces what she says to "the bare essentials" required to make communication go through (L. Bloom, 1970; P. Bloom, 1990).

But a third factor has been suggested recently. Several authors believe that learners are neurologically "programmed" to expect human language to have a certain specific syntactic organization. Variation away from this "universal linguistic structure" is only on a very few details (or **parameters**) in the real languages of the world (Wexler and Manzini, 1987; Crain and Nakayama, 1986). All the same, there is a little variation. One example has to do with expressing the subject noun phrase. In adult English, one must say "I am going to the store." One does not say "Am going to the store." But most of the languages of the world do not require the subject of the sentence to be uttered when its meaning is clear from the conversation. Thus in Spanish, one usually says "Hablo Español" (literally, "Speak Spanish") rather than the fuller "Yo hablo Español" ("I speak Spanish").★

Some investigators believe that children are preprogrammed to expect that the language they are learning will allow this dropping of the subject because this is the fact about *most* human languages. According to this view, the option of omitting the subject is a kind of "initial setting" in the mental machinery that is devoted to language learning. The learners come from nature's factory, so to speak, set to think that the language they are learning will be organized in such-and-such a way. For the case we are discussing, the first hypothesis of young English speakers, just like young Spanish speakers, is that one can omit the subject; so these learners say "Throw ball" instead of "I throw ball" (see Figure 9.21A). Learning that the subject is required in English is therefore a relatively late acquisition, for it violates the factory setting, which the child must "switch" after sufficient exposure to English. In contrast, Spanish-speaking children can just stick to their initial hypothesis and leave out obvious subjects for the rest of their lives (Figure 9.21B; Rizzi, 1982; White, 1985; Hyams, 1986).

★ The languages allowing the subject to be dropped are, not surprisingly, usually the ones that have an **agreement morpheme** attached to the verb itself (e.g., the -o in *hablo,* which signals first-person and thus identifies the missing doer as "I"). More generally, the approach to language acquisition (called **learnability theory**) that we are now discussing is a direct outgrowth of formal linguistic studies. Such approaches are based on an examination of the grammars of the languages of the world. Once these grammars are described, these investigators ask (again, generally by formal analysis): What must the child's mind be like, such that he or she could learn any of these language systems? (Chomsky, 1965; Wexler and Culicover, 1980; Baker and McCarthy, 1981; Borer and Wexler, 1987; Roeper and Williams, 1987; Pinker, 1984; Lust, 1987).

LATER STAGES OF LANGUAGE LEARNING: SYNTAX

By two-and-a-half years or so, children progress beyond the two-word stage. Their utterances now become longer (Figure 9.22). They can say little sentences that contain all three terms of a basic proposition, and function words have begun to appear. Their utterances are still short and simple, but—at least initially—they are quite correct as far as they go. Soon, however, a new phenomenon appears. Children start to make various kinds of errors in their word formation and in their syntax. An example concerns the *-ed* suffix which represents pastness. At the age of two and three, children use correct regular forms of the past tense (as in *walked* or *talked*), as well as correct irregular ones (such as *ran, came,* and *ate*). But at the age of four and five, these same children sometimes say "runned," "comed," and "eated" (Ervin, 1964; Prasada and Pinker, 1993). And they resist change even even when they hear their parents use the correct form, as in the following exchange:

Child:	My teacher holded the baby rabbits and we patted them.
Mother:	Did you say your teacher held the baby rabbits?
Child:	Yes.
Mother:	What did you say she did?
Child:	She holded the baby rabbits and we patted them.
Mother:	Did you say she held them tightly?
Child:	No, she holded them loosely.

(Bellugi, 1971)

What has happened to this child who in earlier years said "held" but now doggedly keeps saying "holded"? The answer seems to be that the child is now seeking general patterns that hold over the whole vocabulary or set of sentence structures. If some words choose to be exceptions to these patterns, so much the worse for these words. Thus the child now overgeneralizes the use of certain structures though, as we saw earlier, she no longer overgeneralizes the meanings of words. (For an alternative view, see Rumelhart and McClelland, 1986; for discussion, see Pinker and Prince, 1988).

Another example is the use of nouns as verbs. The child has heard "John bats the ball," where *bat* means 'hit with a bat,' so he invents "Don't Woodstock me!" to mean 'Don't hit me with a Woodstock toy' (Clark, 1982). A more complicated case is the invention of so-called **causative verbs** (Bowerman, 1982; Pinker, 1989). Children evidently notice that there are many ways to express causation in English. Given a sentence like "The door opened," one can express the causal agent in this affair by saying "John made the door open," "John got the door to open," or "John opened the door." So since children know sentences like "I giggle," they make an analogy from *open* and say, "Daddy giggled me" to mean "Daddy made me giggle."

9.22 The average length of the utterances produced by three children *The mean utterance length in three children between one-and-a-half and four years of age. The utterance length is measured in morphemes, where* dolls *counts as two morphemes (doll + s). Note the variations among the children, who were all within a normal range. (After Brown, Cazden, and Bellugi-Klima, 1969)*

FURTHER STAGES OF LANGUAGE LEARNING: WORD MEANING

We have already discussed some of the difficulties children *should* confront when they try to discover which word stands for which meaning. But in reality, they experience very little difficulty. Five-year-olds have a vocabulary of 10,000 to 15,000 words, whereas at fifteen months they had a vocabulary of

(Photograph by Roberta Intrater, 1980)

only about twenty-five words. This means they must be acquiring about ten words a day—every day, every week, every month. It is likely that none of us adults could do as well (Carey, 1978).

CAREGIVER AIDS TO WORD LEARNING

Part of the explanation for this remarkably rapid learning may come from the quite regular ways in which mothers talk to their children, for syntax often contains useful hints about what a word could mean. Let's return to the problem of learning which word means 'ear' and which means 'rabbit' (see Figure 9.17, p. 353). It turns out that when mothers refer to the whole rabbit, they use simple sentences ("This is a rabbit") and often point to the rabbit at the same time. But when they want to refer to the ear, they first refer to the whole rabbit, and then use such words as *his* in referring to the part: "This is a rabbit; these are his ears" (Shipley, Kuhn, and Madden, 1983).

PERCEPTUAL AND CONCEPTUAL BIASES IN CHILD LEARNERS

We see that caregivers' speech style helps language learners to decide which words are about the whole objects and which words are about their parts. It turns out that children have some biases, or "best guesses," of their own that also contribute to their solution of the word learning problem.

Much of the child's word learning is explained by how she is disposed to carve up *(categorize)* the world that she observes. Some ways of conceptualizing experience are natural to humans while others are less natural (Rosch, 1973a; Keil, 1979; Fodor, 1983). Thus the child can learn more easily if she assumes that each word represents some "natural" organization of experience.

One indication of this is the fact that young children acquire the "basic-level" words (e.g., *dog*) before the superordinates *(animal)* or subordinates *(Chihuahua)* (Rosch, 1978). One might think this is just because the basic-level words are used most frequently to children. But this does not seem to be the explanation. In some homes, the words *Spot* or *Rex* (specific names) are used much more often than *dog* (a basic-level term) for obvious reasons. And it is true that in this case the young learner will soon utter "Spot" and not "dog." But she has first learned it as a basic-level term all the same. This is shown by the fact that she will then utter "Spot" to refer to the neighbor's dog as well as her own. She overgeneralizes *Spot* just enough to convert it from a specific name to the basic level of categorization—evidently, the most natural level for carving up experience (Mervis and Crisafi, 1978; Shipley and Kuhn, 1983).

Further evidence comes from experimental attempts to teach new words to children. The method is to point to a new object and label it with a new (nonsense) word, and then to determine *what else* other than the first sample object the child will apply this new label to. Thus if an experimenter points toward an object and says "That's a biff," children will almost always guess that "biff" names the whole object rather than, say, some of its parts, or the material of which it is made, its color, and so forth (Markman and Hutchinson, 1984; Markman, 1989). This is despite the logical problem that when one points toward an object one simply can't help pointing toward its color (e.g., green) and substance (e.g., plastic or pewter) at the same time. Even more interesting, if one then shows this child other objects that are *shaped just like the original sample object* but differ from it in size or color, the child will take these as more biffs. But the same child will reject, as "not biffs," objects that have *even slightly different shapes*. Evidently, colors and textures are not as salient in the child's perceptual organization as shapes, so the slightest change in the latter will convince the learner that the new item is something wholly different from the one previously called "a biff" (Landau, Smith, and Jones, 1988).

THE INTERPLAY OF STRUCTURE AND MEANING IN WORD LEARNING

We have seen that children organize word meanings according to conceptual categories: the ways in which they understand the world. But children also seem to have pretty strong ideas about language itself: how a language can express these categories. One example concerns synonyms. Though many words are similar in meaning, it is hard to find exact and perfect synonyms in the simple vocabulary of any language. Young children apparently take this as a matter of principle: Any one concept can have only one word that refers to it (Clark, 1987; for an alternative view, see Gathercole, 1987).

Evidence again comes from experiments on new word learning. This time, the investigators showed some preschoolers a *familiar* kind of object, one that the children already had a word for (say, a cup made of pewter) and said "That's biff." Other children were shown an *unfamiliar* object (say, a pair of tongs made of pewter) and were also told "That's biff." Afterwards, the children were shown a collection of new objects and asked to select "more biffs." The children who had been introduced to tongs picked out all other tongs they saw, including those of different colors and substances (e.g., plastic ones as well as pewter ones). This again shows that children think that all objects with the same shape should have the same linguistic title. But the children who had been introduced to the cup behaved differently. They selected all pewter objects (that is, pewter tongs, cups, spoons, and so forth). These latter children apparently reasoned that they already knew a name for cups (namely, *cup*) and therefore *biff* could not mean 'cup.' So despite their initial bias that new words stand for whole objects, they had to find "something else" that the word meant. They did not believe that the new word was simply a synonym for the word they knew (Markman and Wachtel, 1988).

WORD CLASSES AND WORD MEANINGS

Children are disposed to organize the world into overarching categories—things, events, properties, and so forth. But what is more, they appear to believe that language will classify words according to related categories—nouns, verbs, and adjectives—in a way that is consistent with the conceptual categories (Braine, 1976; Pinker, 1984).

This phenomenon was demonstrated in an experiment with three- and four-year-olds in which the experimenter showed children a picture in which a pair of hands seemed to be performing a kneading sort of motion, with a mass of red confetti-like material that was overflowing a low, striped, container (Figure 9.23). The children were introduced to the picture in sentences that used non-sense words, but either as verbs ("In this picture can you see *sebbing?*"), common nouns *("Can you see a seb?"),* or mass nouns *("Can you see any seb?").*★ The children who had been asked to show *sebbing* made kneading motions with their hands, those asked to show a *seb* pointed to the container, and those asked about *any seb* pointed to the confetti (Brown, 1957; see also Katz, Baker, and MacNamara, 1974; Carey, 1982).

9.23 Word classes and word meanings
When asked "In this picture can you see any sebbing?" *(verb), children pointed to the hands; when asked "Can you see a seb?" (common noun), they pointed to the blue bowl; and when asked "Can you see any* seb?" *(mass noun), they pointed to the dark red confetti. (Adapted from Brown, 1957)*

★ A **common** or **count noun** is one that (1) requires a specifier such as *the* or *two* (compare *The dog walks down the street* with the ungrammatical *Dog walks down the street*), and (2) generally refers to the kinds of entities that can be counted (e.g., *One dog, two dogs*). A **mass noun** (1) occurs without a specifier (compare *Water flows through the pipes* with the ungrammatical *A water flows through the pipes*), and (2) generally refers to stuff that can't be counted, e.g., *water, confetti,* or *sand.*

Thus children use their growing knowledge of word classes and their semantic correlates to discover what a new word refers to, even though the scene itself can be interpreted in many ways (Pinker, 1984; L. Gleitman et al., 1988). Symmetrically, as we have seen with such examples as *Don't Woodstock me!* and *Daddy giggled me!,* they can use their knowledge of language structure to decide how to use these new words in novel sentence structures that their parents surely never taught them.

In sum, children proceed in their learning in two directions at once. They will use the forms of new words as clues to their meanings (e.g., "Since this new word was just used as a noun, it probably describes a thing"). But they will also use their knowledge of words to predict their forms ("Since this Woodstock toy is now an instrument for hitting me on the head, I can use it as a verb"). Using both kinds of evidence, the children efficiently "bootstrap" their way into knowledge of the tens of thousands of words and the ways these can be used in sentences (Grimshaw, 1981; Pinker, 1989; Fisher et al., 1994).

LANGUAGE LEARNING IN CHANGED ENVIRONMENTS

Thus far, our focus has been on language development as it proceeds normally. Under these conditions, language seems to emerge in much the same way in virtually all children. They progress from babbling to one-word speech, advance to the two-word telegraphic stage, and eventually graduate to complex sentence forms and meanings. The fact that this progression is so uniform and universal has led many psycholinguists to the view that children are biologically pre-programmed to acquire language. Further evidence for this view stems from studies of language development under certain unusual conditions, when children grow up in environments that are radically different from those in which language development usually proceeds. Which aspects of the early environment are essential for language learning? One line of evidence comes from reports of children who grew up in the wild or under conditions of virtual social isolation.

WILD CHILDREN

There are some remarkable examples of children who wandered (or were abandoned) in the forest and who survived, reared by bears or wolves. Some of these cases have been discussed by the psycholinguist Roger Brown (1958). In 1920, Indian villagers discovered a wolf mother in her den together with four cubs. Two were baby wolves, but the other two were human children, subsequently named Kamala and Amala. No one knows how they got there and why the wolf adopted them. Brown tells us what these children were like:

> Kamala was about eight years old and Amala was only one and one-half. They were thoroughly wolfish in appearance and behavior: Hard callus had developed on their knees and palms from going on all fours. Their teeth were sharp edged. They moved their nostrils sniffing food. Eating and drinking were accomplished by lowering their mouths to the plate. They ate raw meat. . . . At night they prowled and sometimes howled. They shunned other children but followed the dog and cat.

LANGUAGE LEARNING IN CHANGED ENVIRONMENTS

9.24 A modern wild boy Ramu, a young boy discovered in India in 1976, appears to have been reared by wolves. He was deformed, apparently from lying in cramped positions, as in a den. He could not walk, and drank by lapping with his tongue. His favorite food was raw meat, which he seemed to be able to smell at a distance. After he was found, he lived at the home for destitute children run by Mother Theresa in Lucknow, Uttar Pradesh. He learned to bathe and dress himself, but never learned to speak. He continued to prefer raw meat, and would often sneak out to prey upon fowl in the neighbor's chicken coop. Ramu died at the age of about 10 in February 1985. (New York Times, Feb. 24, 1985; photographs courtesy Wide World Photos)

They slept rolled up together on the floor. . . . Amala died within a year but Kamala lived to be eighteen. . . . In time, Kamala learned to walk erect, to wear clothing, and even to speak a few words. (Brown, 1958, p. 100)

The outcome was much the same for the thirty or so other wild children about whom we have reports. When found, they were all shockingly animal-like. None of them could be rehabilitated so as to use language at all normally, though some, including Kamala, learned to speak a few words (Figure 9.24).

ISOLATED CHILDREN

Kamala and Amala were removed from all human society. Some other children have been raised by humans, but under conditions that were almost unimaginably inhumane, for their parents were either vicious or deranged. Sometimes, such parents will deprive a baby of all human contact. "Isabelle" (a codename used to protect the child's privacy) was hidden away, apparently from early infancy, and given only the minimal attention necessary to sustain her life. Apparently no one spoke to her (in fact, her mother was deaf and did not speak). Isabelle was six years old when discovered. Of course she had no language, and her cognitive development was below that of a normal two-year-old. But within a year, this girl learned to speak. Her tested intelligence was normal, and she took her place in an ordinary school (Davis, 1947; Brown, 1958). Thus Isabelle at seven years, with one year of language practice, spoke about as well as her peers in the second grade, all of whom had had seven years of practice.

Rehabilitation from isolation is not always so successful. A child, "Genie," discovered in California about twenty years ago, was fourteen years old when found. Since about twenty months, apparently, she had lived tied to a chair, was frequently beaten, and never spoken to—but sometimes barked at, for her father said she was no more than a dog. Afterwards, she was taught by psychologists and linguists (Fromkin et al., 1974). But Genie did not become a normal language user. She says many words and puts them together into meaningful propositions as young children do, such as "No more take wax" and "Another house have dog." Thus she has learned certain basics of language. Indeed, her semantic sophistication—what she means by what she says—is far beyond young children. Yet even after years of instruction, Genie did not learn the function words that appear in mature English sentences, nor did she combine propositions together in elaborate sentences (Curtiss, 1977).

Why did Genie not progress to full language learning while Isabelle did? The best guess is that the crucial factor is the age at which language learning began. Genie was discovered after she had reached puberty, while Isabelle was only six. As we shall see later, there is some reason to believe there is a **critical period** for language learning. If the person has passed this period, language learning proceeds with greater difficulty.

LANGUAGE WITHOUT SOUND

The work on wild and isolated children argues that a necessary condition for learning language is some contact with other humans. If one's early life is spent entirely among animals, the effects are irreversible. If it is spent among people who do not talk to one, language may still be acquired later on if the crucial learning period has not been passed as yet. Our next question concerns the more specific factors of the learner's human environment. What aspects of this environment are essential for language to emerge?

It has sometimes been suggested that an important ingredient is exposure to language sounds. According to this view, language is intrinsically related to the way we organize what we hear. If so, language cannot develop in the absence of sound.

This hypothesis is false. For there is one group of humans that is cut off from auditory-vocal language—the deaf, who cannot hear it. Yet this doesn't mean that they have no language. Most deaf people eventually learn to read and write the language of the surrounding community of hearing persons. But they also have a manual-visual, or **gestural system.** One such system is **American Sign Language** (or **ASL**).

Are gestural systems genuine languages? One indication that they are is that these systems are not derived by translation from the spoken languages around them, but are independently created within and by communities of deaf individuals (Klima et al., 1979). Further evidence comes from comparing ASL to the structure and development of spoken languages. ASL has hand shapes and positions of which each word is composed, much like the tongue and lip shapes that allow us to fashion the phonemes of spoken language (Stokoe, 1960). It has morphemes and grammatical principles for combining words into sentences that are similar to those of spoken language (Supalla, 1986; see Figure 9.25).

Finally, babies born to deaf users of ASL (whether or not the babies themselves are deaf) pick up the system from these caregivers through informal inter-

A

B

C

9.25 Some common signs in ASL   (A) The sign for tree. *One difference between ASL and spoken language is that many of the signed words physically resemble their meanings. This is so for* tree, *in which the upright forearm stands for the trunk and the outstretched fingers for the branches. But in many cases, such a resemblance is not present. Consider (B), which is the modern sign for* help, *whose relation to its meaning seems as arbitrary as that between most spoken words and their meanings. Even so, such a relation was once present, as shown in (C), a nineteenth-century sign for* help. *At that time, the sign was not arbitrary; it consisted of a gesture by the right hand to support the left elbow, as if helping an elderly person cross a street. (B) grew out of (C) by a progressive series of simplifications in which signs tend to move to the body's midline and use shorter, fewer, and more stylized movements. All that remains of (C) is an upward motion of the right palm. (Frishberg, 1975; photographs of and by Ted Supalla)*

A

B

9.26 Self-made signs in a deaf boy never exposed to sign language A two-sign sequence. (A) The first sign means "eat" or "food." Immediately before, the boy had pointed to a grape. (B) The second sign means "give." The total sequence means "give me the food." (Goldin-Meadow, 1982; drawing courtesy Noel Yovovich)

action rather than by explicit instruction, just as we learn our spoken language (Newport and Ashbrook, 1977).★ And they go through the same steps on the way to adult knowledge as do hearing children learning English. It is hard to avoid the conclusion that ASL and other gestural systems are true languages (Klima et al., 1979; Supalla and Newport, 1978; Newport, 1984, 1990).

Thus language does not depend on the auditory-vocal channel. When the usual modes of communication are denied to humans of normal mentality, they come up with an alternative that reproduces the same contents and structures as other language systems. It appears that language is an irrepressible human trait: Deny it to the mouth and it will dart out through the fingers.

LANGUAGE WITHOUT A MODEL

The evidence we have reviewed shows that language emerges despite many environmental deprivations. Still, each case seemed to have one requirement—some adults who knew a language and could impart it to the young. But this must leave us puzzled about how language originated in the first place. Is it a cultural artifact (like the internal combustion machine or the game of chess) rather than a basic property of human minds, an invention that happened to take place in prehistoric times? Our bias has been the opposite, for we have argued that humans are biologically predisposed to communicate by language. But our case would have been much better if Kamala and Amala had invented a language of their own, down there in the wolf's den. Why didn't they? There are many ways to write off or ignore this case—maybe they were too busy learning to be good wolves, and maybe a human language is of no special use for learning to devour raw chickens. Is there a better test than those provided by the tragic cases of brutal mistreatment and neglect so far considered?

It certainly would be interesting if we could find a case of mentally normal children living in a socially loving environment but not exposed to language use by the adults around them. Feldman, Goldin-Meadow, and L. Gleitman (1978) found six children who were in such a situation. These children were deaf, and so they were unable to learn spoken language. Their parents were hearing; they did not know ASL and decided not to allow the children to learn a gestural language. This is because they shared the belief (held by some groups of educators) that deaf children can achieve adequate knowledge of spoken language by special training in lip reading and vocalization. The investigators looked at these children before they had acquired any knowledge of English, for a number of prior studies had shown that under these circumstances deaf children will spontaneously gesture in meaningful ways to others (Tervoort, 1961; Fant, 1972). The question was which aspects of communication these youngsters would come up with as they developed.

The results showed that the children invented a sizeable number of pantomimic gestures that the investigators could comprehend. For example, they would flutter their fingers in a downward motion to express *snow*, twist their fingers to express a twist-top *bottle*, and flap their arms to represent *bird* (see Figure 9.26).

The development of this "language" showed many parallels to ordinary language learning: The children gestured one sign at a time in the period (about

★ In fact, the expert sign-language translators seen on television are usually hearing children of deaf parents. They grow up in a bilingual environment, with ASL learned from their parents and English learned by contact with hearing children and adults, so they achieve perfect knowledge of both and thus are the best translators.

eighteen months of age) when hearing learners speak one word at a time. At two and three years of age they went on to two- and three-word sentences and so on. And in these basic sentences, the individual gestures were serially ordered by semantic role. This is strong evidence for a rudimentary syntactic organization, just like that of children who hear German or French—or see ASL—produced by adults.

On the other hand, we should not lose sight of the severe limitations of these homemade systems. First, they are limited to the elementary basics of language as we know it, with function words and elaborately organized sentences absent (Goldin-Meadow, 1982). And there is a yet more serious limitation that goes back to the social and interpersonal nature of ordinary language use: The parents of these children used gestures to them very rarely, and the adults' sporadic gesturing was in terms of isolated "words" and pointing to things in view, with no syntactic organization (Goldin-Meadow and Mylander, 1983). The result was that social interaction in this medium was quite restricted, for it takes more than one individual—inventive as he or she may be—to make a living language. We can be thankful, then, that these children once they reached the age of four or five began to receive instruction in reading English and were eventually introduced to a full sign language (ASL) by meeting other deaf individuals.★

In sum, these studies provide us with a fairly pure case of a group of children who were isolated from language stimulation, but not from love and affection. The findings show that the capacity to organize thought using the word and syntax principles of language is a deep-seated property of the human mind, at least in its basics if not in its elaborations. In this sense, we have no need to ask further about the origins of human language. Our best guess is that as human nature originated in evolutionary history, language inevitably made its appearance too. Yet the same studies show us the necessarily interpersonal and interactive nature of human communication, which must become stymied and dysfunctional in the end if there is no "other" with whom it can be used.

CHILDREN DEPRIVED OF ACCESS TO SOME OF THE MEANINGS

Children usually learn the meanings of words in situations in which they can determine the referents of those words. Thus it is certainly easier to learn the meaning of the word *horse* if that word is said in the presence of a horse. Only the rarer, and late-acquired, words like *zebu* usually have to be looked up in the dictionary (and even for these, we are helped if the dictionary provides a picture). To the extent that referents of the words and sentences help the learner, we should expect that blind learners have significant difficulties in learning a language. For often the mother may be talking of things that are too large, gossamer, or distant for the blind child to feel with her hands (e.g., mountains, clouds, or birds).

In this sense, blind children seem to suffer an environmental deprivation symmetrical with the one previously considered: The isolated deaf children heard no language *forms* from their parents, but they were free to observe all the things and events in the world that language describes. In contrast, blind children hear the language forms from their parents, but they are cut off from some opportu-

---

★ The degree of success with lip-reading and vocalization of English, as well as reading acquisition, by deaf children is variable, with the level attained closely related to the degree of deafness. Even the slightest hearing capability helps enormously. But there is growing evidence that the most natural alternative for profoundly deaf children is to learn and use ASL, for in this manual-visual medium they have no language handicap at all, as we showed in a previous section.

A

B

9.27 The meaning of "look" (A) A blindfolded, sighted three-year-old tilts her head upward in response to "Look up!" for to her the word look *means 'perceive by eye.' (B) A congenitally blind three-year-old raises her arms upward in response to "Look up!" for to her the word* look *means 'perceive by hand.' (Drawings by Robert Thacker)*

nities to observe their referents (and thus, presumably, to acquire word and sentence *meanings*).

All the same, recent evidence shows that blind children learn language as rapidly and as well as sighted children. One striking example is vision-related words like *look* and *see,* which blind children use as early (two-and-a-half to three years of age) and as systematically as sighted children. To be sure, there are some differences in how blind and sighted children understand these words. A young sighted listener, even if her vision is blocked by a blindfold, will tilt her covered eyes upward when asked to "Look up!" This suggests that to the sighted child, looking *must* refer to vision (Figure 9.27A). But a congenitally blind child, when also told to "Look up!," shows that she too has a sensible interpretation of *look,* though a somewhat different one. Keeping her head immobile, the blind youngster reaches upward and searches the space above her body with her hands (Figure 9.27B). Thus each of these children understands *look* differently. But the meanings resemble each other even so. Both children realize that *look* has something to do with perceiving the world by use of the sense organs. The children arrive at meaningful interpretations of words even though their information about the world is often quite different.

This fits with the general picture of language learning as we have discussed it, for all learners—not just blind ones—must (and do!) build their language knowledge from relatively sparse information about referents. Thus one child may see a Great Dane and a poodle when he hears "dog." Another child may be introduced to this same word when seeing a collie and a terrier. Based on these quite different experiences, both children will acquire the same category, as we know from the fact that both will apply it to Chihuahuas and Huskies the first time they see them. In light of this marvelous ability of children to categorize the world in terms that are important to their own perceptual and conceptual lives, perhaps it is not so surprising that the blind child understands *looking* to mean 'exploring with the hands' (Landau and L. Gleitman, 1985; see also Urwin, 1983; Mulford, 1986; Bigelow, 1987).

Before leaving this topic, we should again strike a cautionary note (as we did with the self-invented gestural language of deaf children). Even though blind learners' language forms and word meanings are strikingly like those of sighted children, up until age three they manifest many problems in understanding the particulars of conversations going on around them. This creates significant frustration (sometimes leading to severe behavioral problems) in blind toddlers. This is not surprising. Imagine what it would be like if all your companions were involved in face-to-face conversation, but you were connected to them only by telephone. Like blind children, you would experience confusion about what was being talked about, have trouble identifying the referents of pronouns, and so forth (Landau and L. Gleitman, 1985).

In sum, we see that those with sensory deprivation are relatively unscathed in the acquisition of syntax and meaning. Language principles are part of our nature and emerge in relative indifference to the type of environmental support. But we see also that these deprivations (at least early in life) have a significant impact on the interpersonal use of language for successful communication.

THE CASE OF HELEN KELLER

The most dramatic and compelling picture of children cut off from contact with a language community comes to us from the case of Helen Keller (1880–1968). At eighteen months, she was a bright toddler, learning her first few words. But she then suffered a devastating illness (never adequately diagnosed) that left her both deaf and blind. Thus Helen, unlike the congenitally deaf and blind children we have discussed (who never experienced hearing or seeing), was aware of suffering a catastrophic loss. She later wrote (speaking of herself in the third person):

> With appalling suddenness she [Helen] moved from light to darkness and became a phantom. . . . Helplessly the family witnessed the baffled intelligence as Phantom's hand stretched out to feel the shapes which she could reach but which meant nothing to her. . . . Nothing was part of anything, and there blazed up in her frequent fierce anger. . . . I remember tears rolling down her cheeks but not the grief. There were no words for that emotion or any other, and consequently they did not register. (Keller, 1955)

Helen thus suffered the double affliction of sudden darkness and silence, and lived the next five years of her life in many ways isolated from the world of other people. But in the end, she entered Radcliffe, studied algebra, Greek, and literature, wrote classic and elegantly crafted books on her life and experiences, became an illustrious educator, and was personally close to many of the important people of her time, including Mark Twain, Eleanor Roosevelt, and Alexander Graham Bell (Lash, 1980).

Helen Keller gave the credit for this triumphant return to life to her great teacher, Anne Sullivan. Sullivan, herself half-blind and raised in appalling conditions in a "poor house," had acquired a partial manual system. It was through this medium that she began to unlock the stifled mind of Helen: She finger-spelled onto her eager pupil's palm. Helen reported her awakening in this famous passage (in which Anne Sullivan is holding one of Helen's hands under a waterspout):

> . . . as the cool stream gushed over one hand, she [Anne Sullivan] spelled into the other the word water. . . . I stood still, my whole attention fixed upon the motions of her fingers. . . . Suddenly I felt a misty consciousness as of something forgotten—a thrill of returning thought; and somehow the mystery of language was revealed to me. . . . Everything had a name, and each name gave birth to a new thought. As we returned to the house every object which I touched seemed to quiver with life. (Quoted in Lash, 1980)

Helen Keller and her teacher Anne Sulli-van (*Photograph courtesy of the Perkins School for the Blind*)

As Anne Sullivan wrote, "She has learned that the manual alphabet is the key to everything she wants to know." Almost immediately, Helen was learning six new words a day. Eventually (though in the face of significant struggles because of the poor materials available for deaf children in these early days), Helen read raised letters and Braille, and went on to achieve a state of literacy and creativity with language that would put most of us to shame.

What can we learn from Helen Keller's case? It is not as though this child was completely unable to communicate or think before the arrival of Sullivan in her life. In Helen's biography, she underestimated her own status at that time, remembering herself as merely "a wild and destructive little animal." But Anne Sullivan saw something else. Like the deaf children we have described in the previous section, Helen had spontaneously invented many gestures to describe her wants and needs. For instance, "a desire for ice cream was shown by turning the freezer and a little shiver; . . . knotting hair on the back of her head symbolized her mother. . . . If she wanted bread and butter, she imitated the motions of cutting . . . and spreading." Sullivan recognized at least sixty such spontaneous "descriptive gestures" when she first met Helen (Lash, 1980).

So Helen's case is consistent with that of the deaf children we discussed earlier. Isolated from language forms, a human infant begins to invent her own. But Helen's case also reveals the crushing limitations of such a homemade language system for communicating with the surrounding community, which neither knows this idiosyncratic system nor understands its significance. Anne Sullivan,

Helen Keller conversing with Eleanor Roosevelt *Helen understood speech by noting the movements of the lips and the vibration of the vocal cords. (Photograph by Larry Morris/New York Times; courtesy of the Perkins School for the Blind)*

an incredibly sophisticated and talented teacher, differed from the loving but bewildered parents by capitalizing on the homemade signs in her first communicative contact with Helen. She wrote that "I use complete sentences . . . and fill out the meaning with gestures and her [Helen's] descriptive signs" (Lash, 1980). Anne Sullivan also knew that language learning has to be natural and communicative, and will not succeed by memorizing word lists out of context as had been common in the education of sensorily deprived children at that time. Thus she signed into Helen's palm "as we talk into the baby's ear." She wrote that the drill methods of her predecessors

> seem to be built up on the supposition that every child is a kind of idiot who must be taught to think. . . . Let him come and go freely, let him touch real things and combine his impressions for himself. . . . (Lash, 1980)

Thus we see that Sullivan's success depended not only on exploiting the child's natural disposition to organize language according to deep-seated principles of form and meaning, but on introducing language in the context of its—just as deep-seated—functions for communicating about things, events, and feelings with others (see Bates and MacWhinney, 1982).

We should also note one other resemblance between Helen's case and that of the other children we have discussed. Unlike Genie who was first exposed to English during adolescence and who failed to learn anything but rudimentary basics, Helen received language stimulation quite early in life. As in the case of Isabelle, her rehabilitation began at about age six and was richly successful. The medium of transmission Sullivan used to teach Helen Keller—signing onto the palm or cheek—is still employed today with great success for children who are both deaf and blind (C. Chomsky, 1984).

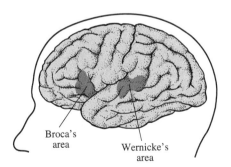

9.28   The language areas of the brain *Certain areas of the cerebral cortex (in most right-handers, in the left hemisphere) are devoted to language functions. These include Broca's area, whose damage produces deficits in speech production, especially of function words (expressive aphasia), and Wernicke's area, whose damage leads to deficits in comprehension of word meanings (receptive aphasia). For more details, see Chapter 2. (After Geschwind, 1972)*

LANGUAGE LEARNING WITH CHANGED ENDOWMENTS

We have now shown that language learning proceeds quite successfully despite severe environmental differences and deprivations. This suggests that there is an innate "mental machinery" for language that runs its course undeflected by any but the most radical environmental stresses (such as that suffered by Genie). But what happens if the nature of the learners themselves is changed? To the extent that language learning and use are determined by brain function, changing that brain should have strong effects (Lenneberg, 1967; Menyuk, 1977; L. Gleitman, 1986).

There are many indications that the nature and state of the brain have massive consequences for language functioning. An obvious instance is **aphasia,** as described in Chapter 2. We found there that if there is damage to a certain part of the left hemisphere of the brain **(Broca's area),** the victim loses use of the function words; and if the damage is to another part **(Wernicke's area),** the loss is to the content words (Figure 9.28).

Another attempt to look at the relationship between brain function and language is the study of mentally exceptional individuals, particularly children with Down's syndrome whose mental makeup appears to differ from that of ordinary learners. These children vary widely in their language attainments. Some of them achieve normal language growth. But those who fall at very low levels of the IQ range usually acquire only the basics of language and never attain the

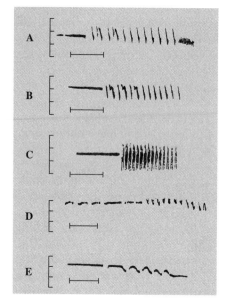

9.29 Critical period in the development of bird song *(A) A graphic presentation of the song of an adult, male white-crowned sparrow. The figure, a sound spectrograph, plots the frequency region of the bird's vocal output over time. Frequency is indicated by the vertical axis, in steps of 2,000 hertz. The horizontal time marker indicates half a second. The figure shows that the normal song begins with a whistle or two, continues with a series of trills, and ends with a vibrato. (B) The song of a bird raised in acoustic isolation but exposed to four minutes of normal song between the ages of 35 and 56 days. His adult song was almost normal. (C) The song of an isolated bird exposed to normal song between days 50 and 71. The adult song of this bird has some crude similarities to normal white-crowned sparrow song. There is a whistle followed by trills, but the details are very different. (D) and (E) show the songs of birds whose exposure to normal song occurred very early in life (days 3 to 7) or very late (after 300 days of age) respectively. Training at either of these times had no effect. (After Marler, 1970)*

elaborations (Lenneberg, 1967; Fowler, 1989). The general impression, then, is that children with Down's syndrome do not acquire language as fully as ordinary children, again an indication that the specifics of brain function are guiding and organizing the learning process. Yet it is difficult to speak with authority on this topic, for recent evidence shows that such children can evidently make considerable progress if provided with expanded social and educational supports.

We will turn our attention to quite a different distinction in the mental machinery that learners bring into the task of learning a language. This is their chronological age when they are exposed to linguistic stimulation. As the brains of humans are still growing and developing almost to the time of puberty, there is room to believe that young vs. old learners of a language approach the task equipped with rather different mental apparatus. Does this matter?

THE CRITICAL PERIOD HYPOTHESIS

According to the ***critical period hypothesis,*** there is an especially sensitive period in early life when language acquisition is easy. But according to this hypothesis, some characteristics of the brain change as the critical period draws to its close, so that later learning (both of a first language and of other ones) becomes more difficult (Lenneberg, 1967).

Critical periods seem to govern the acquisition of a number of important behavior patterns in many animals. One example is the attachment of the young of various animals to their mothers, which generally can be formed only in early childhood (see Chapter 14). Another example is bird song. Male birds of many species have a song that is characteristic of their own kind. They learn this song by listening to adult males of their own species. But this exposure will only be effective if it occurs at a certain period in the bird's life. This has been extensively documented for the white-crowned sparrow. To learn the white-crowned sparrow song in all its glory (complete with special trills and grace notes), the baby birds must hear an adult's song sometime between the seventh and sixtieth day of their life. The next forty days are a marginal period. If the fledgling is exposed to an adult male's song during that period but not before, he will acquire only some limited basics of the sparrow song, without the full elaborations heard in normal adults (see Figure 9.29). If the exposure comes still later, it has no effect at all. The bird will never sing normally (Marler, 1970).

Is there an analogy to this distinction in humans learning languages? Are adults less able to learn language than children because they have passed out of some critical period? Much of the evidence has traditionally come from studies of second-language acquisition, for the obvious reason that it is hard (though not impossible, as we will later see) to find adults who have not been exposed to a first language early in life.

SECOND LANGUAGE LEARNING

In the first stages of learning a second language, adults appear to be much more efficient than children (Snow and Hoefnagel-Hohle, 1978). The adult will venture halting but comprehensible sentences soon after arrival in the new language community. In contrast, many young children seem to be filled with confusion, astonishment, and even horror when they suddenly hear speech that they cannot understand at all; often they stop talking altogether for some weeks or even months. But in the long run the outcome is just the reverse. After one to two years, very small children speak the new language fluently and soon sound just like natives. This is much less common in adults.

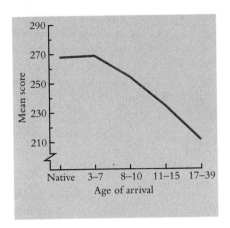

9.30 Critical period for second-language learning *Relation between age of arrival in the United States by 46 Korean and Chinese individuals, and their score (out of 276 test items) on a test of English grammar conducted five years later. (After Johnson and Newport, 1989)*

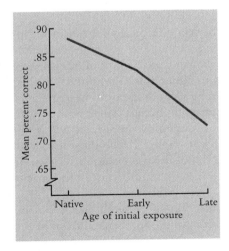

9.31 Critical period for first-language learning *Relation between time of first exposure to ASL by deaf individuals and their score on a test of ASL, conducted 30 or more years later. (After Newport, 1990)*

This point has been made by investigators who studied the long-run outcome of second-language learning, depending on the age of first exposure to the new language. The subjects were native Chinese and Korean speakers who came to the United States (and became immersed in the English-language community) at varying ages. These Far Eastern languages were chosen for study because they are quite dissimilar to English. The subjects were tested only after they had been in the United States for at least five years, so they had had ample exposure to English. Finally, all of them were students and faculty members at a large midwestern university, so they shared some social background (and presumably were all motivated to learn the new language so as to succeed in their university roles).

All of these subjects took a lengthy test. They listened to English sentences. Half of these were grossly ungrammatical (e.g. *The farmer bought two pig at the market; The little boy is speak to a policeman*). The other half were the grammatical counterparts of these same sentences. The task of the subjects was to indicate which sentences were grammatical in English and which were not. The results are shown in Figure 9.30. The learners who had been exposed to English before age seven performed just like native speakers of English. Thereafter there was an increasing decrement in performance as a function of age at first exposure. The older the subjects when they first came to the United States, the less well they seemed to have acquired English (Johnson and Newport, 1989).

LATE EXPOSURE TO A FIRST LANGUAGE

The results just described certainly lend credence to the critical period hypothesis. But there is an obvious problem. Perhaps the difficulties of learning had to do specifically with second language learning. For it is well known that knowledge of a first language in some ways interferes with learning the second language (Krashen, 1981; Flynn, 1987). Perhaps older learners don't get worse at learning language, but rather are more troubled by their sophisticated knowledge of their native tongue. To control for such interference explanations, we must therefore look at learning a *first* language late in life.

The best line of evidence comes from work on American Sign Language (ASL), which is often learned late in life. Children of deaf signers are exposed to ASL from birth. But many congenitally deaf children, such as those we discussed earlier, have hearing parents who choose not to allow their offspring access to ASL. Such children's first exposure to ASL may be quite late in life, when they eventually establish contact with the deaf community. These persons are thus essentially learning a first language at an unusually late point in maturational time.

Does this late start really matter? To find out, Elissa Newport studied the production and comprehension of various aspects of ASL in three groups of ASL signers. All her subjects had used ASL as their sole means of communication for at least thirty years, a virtual guarantee that they were as expert in the language as they would ever become. The only difference between them was in the age at which they began to learn this language. The subjects in the first group were exposed to ASL from birth because their parents were deaf signers. Those in the second group had learned ASL between the ages of four and six years of age. The third group was composed of subjects who had first come into contact with ASL after the age of twelve years. All subjects were about fifty years of age or older when tested, and clearly had had ample exposure to ASL at the time of the test.

The findings were dramatic (see Figure 9.31). All of these signers were quite fluent in ASL, but even so—thirty or more years after they began to use it— there was a strong effect of the age at first exposure. Those who had learned

ASL from birth used and understood all of its elaborations. Those whose first exposure had come after four years of age showed subtle deficits. Those whose exposure began in adolescence or adulthood had much greater deficits, and their use of function items was sporadic, irregular, and often incorrect (Newport, 1990).

It appears that young children show sensitivities to language that are a requirement for achieving native-level fluency. When exposure is late, there are significant deficits in learning that can be observed after many years of practice and use. These findings thus provide quite convincing evidence for a "sensitive" if not "critical" period for language learning.

IS THE CRITICAL PERIOD SPECIFIC TO LANGUAGE?

The notion of a critical period seems fairly plausible. What is less clear is that it is specific to language. One can take a broader view, which simply asserts that children are better at picking up any and all complex skills of which language is only one. As of now, we have insufficient evidence to choose between the narrow and the broad conceptions of the critical period. It may be specific to language alone. Or it may be nonspecific—so much so, perhaps, that to assert that such a period exists amounts to little more than the statement that you can't teach an old dog (or an old language learner) new tricks. Whatever the true answer, some kind of internal clock is doubtless ticking away and affecting the ability to acquire a new language. Hence if you have a passionate desire to acquire, say, Tlingit or Malay or Finnish, you would be well advised to buy your airline tickets immediately, for every moment seems to count.

(The FAR SIDE cartoon by Gary Larson is reprinted by permission of Chronicle Features, San Francisco, California)

LANGUAGE IN NONHUMANS

We have considered the role of the human biological endowment in language learning and use. The outcomes should leave us quite pessimistic about whether we can teach other animals to converse with us in our language (or, for that matter, whether we can learn to communicate with them in their own species-specific manner). As we will now see, not even our nearest animal relative, the chimpanzee, comes close to attaining human language even with the best of good will and the most strenuous educational procedures. Just as language deprivation did not forever destroy in Helen Keller the capacity to become a fully human user of language, so we cannot expect that language enrichment, no matter how extensive and systematic, can create this capacity full-blown in a chimpanzee.

At the same time, there is considerable overlap between our biological endowments and those of other primates. For this reason, we should not be too surprised if some rudiments of language-like skills can be made to grow in them. If so, this may offer some insight into the origins of our own communicative organization.

THE MEDIUM OF TRANSMISSION FOR CHIMPANZEE COMMUNICATION

Chimpanzee vocal tracts differ from our own, so they cannot literally speak as we do (Hayes, 1952). Several investigators overcame this obstacle by employing visual systems of various kinds. Some use artificial systems based on colored plastic chips or symbols on a computer screen (Premack, 1976; Rumbaugh,

1977). Others have adopted items from ASL (Gardner and Gardner, 1969, 1975, 1978; Terrace et al., 1979).

VOCABULARY

Chimpanzees using any of the visual systems just mentioned can acquire a substantial number of "words." Consider Washoe, a chimpanzee introduced to words at about age one year and treated just like a human child, with naps, diapers, and baths. She was taught ASL signs by having her hands physically molded into the desired position; other signs were learned by imitation (Fouts, 1972). After four years, she had learned about 130 signs for objects *(banana, hand),* actions *(bite, tickle),* and action modifiers *(enough, more).* This rate cannot compare with the human child who learns about 10,000 words in this period, but is impressive all the same (for discussion, see Savage-Rumbaugh et al., 1980).

Also of considerable interest is the finding that some of the chimpanzees use their new acquisitions in naturalistic interactions with their trainers, not just in laboratory tests. Moreover, Washoe appears to be teaching some of her human signs to an adopted chimpanzee baby (Fouts, Hirsch, and Fouts, 1982). If this result holds up, it is a very interesting case of "cultural transmission" by another species.

PROPOSITIONAL THOUGHT

Are chimpanzees capable of propositional thought? We know that they have mental representations of various objects and events in the world, for as we just saw, they can be taught words for them. But do they have anything like a notion of this-does-something-to-that?

One line of evidence comes from David Premack's (1976) studies on the concept of causation in chimpanzees. Premack showed his animals pairs of objects. In each pair the second object was the same as the first but had undergone some change. One pair consisted of a whole apple and an apple that was cut in pieces; another pair was a dry towel and a wet towel; a third was an unmarked piece of paper and a piece of paper covered with pencil marks. The chimpanzee's task was to place one of several alternatives between the objects—a knife, a bowl of water, or a pencil. The question was whether the animals would choose the item that caused the change (Figure 9.32). Premack's star pupil, Sarah, performed correctly on 77 percent of the trials, far more than would be expected by chance. Perhaps these animals have some primitive notions of the relation between certain objects, acts, and outcomes—knives cut up things, water wets them, and pencils mark them. To the extent that the apes have these concepts, they have the germs of propositional thought.

SYNTAX

Human speech is characterized by abstract syntactic principles. Can chimpanzees do anything of this sort? Can they organize their signs for *Mama, tickle,* and *Washoe* so as to say either *Mama tickles Washoe* or *Washoe tickles Mama?* The Gardners believe that Washoe has some such ability. As evidence, they refer to apparently novel sequences of signs produced by Washoe on her own. For instance, she once signed *listen eat* on hearing an alarm clock that signals mealtime, and she signed *water bird* upon seeing a duck.

A number of critics feel that such observations prove little or nothing. They are anecdotes that can be interpreted in several ways. Take the sequence *water bird.* On the face of it, its use seems like a remarkable achievement—a chimpanzoid equivalent of a compound noun that presumably means something like *bird*

A

B

9.32 A test for propositional thought in chimpanzees *(A) A chimpanzee is shown a whole apple and two halves of an apple. Its task is to place one of three alternatives between them: a pencil, a bowl of water, or a knife. (B) The animal chooses the knife, the instrument which produced the change from the uncut to the cut state. In other trials, when the animals were shown a blank piece of paper and a scribbled-upon piece of paper, in general, they would put the pencil in the middle. When shown a dry sponge and a wet sponge, they chose the bowl of water. (From Premack, 1976; photographs courtesy of David Premack)*

Chimpanzees signing *A young chimpanzee making the sign for (A) "hug" and (B) "apple." (Terrace, 1979; photographs courtesy of Herbert Terrace)*

that lives in water. But is this interpretation justified? Or did Washoe merely produce an accidental succession of two signs: *water* (perhaps water was seen just before) and *bird* (because of the duck)? It is hard to believe that she really understood the significance of the order (in English) in which the two words are uttered: a *water-bird* is a bird that lives in water, but *bird-water* is water for a bird. Since all we have is an anecdote, we cannot be sure.★

Recent claims for another species, the pygmy chimpanzee, are even stronger. It is claimed that these animals quite often come up with novel combinations of words and that their language knowledge in general is broader than that of common chimpanzees taught by similar methods (Savage-Rumbaugh et al., 1986; Savage-Rumbaugh, 1987). Our final assessment of primate linguistic intelligence will depend to some degree on further documentation of such effects.

Current evidence allows us to conclude only that chimpanzees can learn words and show some propositional thought. There is little satisfactory evidence that they can create (or understand) syntactic structures that are the human vehicles for expressing propositional thought. Thus—at least so far, though the debate continues—they cannot be said to be "linguistic animals." (For discussion of some of these issues, see Seidenberg and Pettito, 1979; Van Cantfort and Rimpau, 1982; Pinker, 1994).

IS IT LANGUAGE?

To sum up, recent years have seen a tremendous growth of scientific interest in the question of whether chimpanzees (and dolphins, gorillas, and other advanced animals) can acquire language. Of course, the idea of talking to animals is not a new one, appearing in the mythology of many cultures (not to speak of Dr. Doolittle). This idea for some reason has always held a fascination for many people who dream of interspecies communication (as witness the popularity of some recent movies in which chimpanzees not only talk and think, but also display impressive courage and an outstanding moral sense). The investigations we have discussed, however, go beyond such mythic motivations and are deeply grounded in the question of comparative (evolutionary) psychology. For it would be strange if we could see absolutely no link to the spectacular use of language by humans in the behavior of our closest neighbors on the evolutionary ladder (Cheney and Seyfarth, 1992).

What current evidence supports is that there are some precursors and prerequisites (such as primitive propositional thought) to our language capacities that are observable in trained chimpanzees. However, these very findings have led to great controversy. Some scientists have concluded from them that there is little qualitative difference in this regard between us and these primates—only a difference in degree. Others conclude that the chimpanzees' accomplishments are too sporadic and limited to be of much interest for understanding the minds of

---

★ Consider what is really being claimed by the investigators about the significance of *water-bird,* as uttered by the animal. It is that the combination itself has a set interpretation, above and beyond its individual words (i.e., that *water-bird* means 'a bird of the water' and not 'water for a bird'). This is not too plausible because this particular form/meaning interpretation is not inevitable, but rather is a fact about current-day English grammar, where we put the modifying word *(water)* before the main word *(bird)* to create such compounds. English was not always this way. Today we would say, for example, *penny-pincher* to mean 'one who pinches pennies' (that is, a miser). But in an earlier stage of English, the requirement was to put the main word first, and so people said *pinch-penny* for that same meaning. Are we to believe that the chimpanzee understands the current status of English morphology and syntax and so follows the new rule rather than the historically earlier one? Many critics would say it is easier—barring much, much stronger evidence—to say that the chimpanzee had just seen both water and a bird and so uttered these two signs one after the other without regard to (1) their particular serial order or (2) the semantic significance of that serial order.

either chimpanzees or humans. Many other scientists find no merit at all in calling these chimpanzee behaviors "language" in any useful sense. Their view is that these trained behaviors are no more convincing than the tricks of dancing circus poodles, whose accomplishments are never taken to prove that dogs, like humans, are two-legged animals.

Whether the chimpanzees' accomplishments should be called *language,* then, seems to depend on one's definition of that term. We can choose to say that trained chimpanzees use language. But in doing so, we have changed the technical meaning of the term so as to exclude from consideration the learning, speech, and comprehension machinery shown by every nonpathological human. Worse, we have even changed the common-sense meaning of the term *language.* For one thing is certain: If any of our children learned or used language the way Washoe or Sarah does, we would be terror-stricken and rush them to the nearest neurologist.

LANGUAGE AND ITS LEARNING

In our survey of the nature of language, we emphasized that human communication systems are at rock bottom the same all over the world. To be sure, the words themselves sound different, so the speakers of different languages cannot understand each other. Still, every language turned out to consist of a hierarchy of structures that represent a complex interweaving of meaning and form. The effect is that, if we share a language, we can communicate about all the endless social, emotional, and intellectual matters that concern us as humans.

Language is marvelously ornate and intricate—so much so that we must be boggled by the idea that human babies can learn any such thing. And yet they do, as we have seen. In all the nurturant (and even most of the horribly abusive) circumstances in which human babies find themselves, language makes its appearance and flourishes. Our nearest primate cousins even given the utmost in social and linguistic support do not approach the competence and sophistication of the most ordinary three-year-old human child. What makes this learning possible?

We have argued throughout that language is the product of the young human brain, such that virtually any exposure conditions will suffice to guide acquisition of any language in the world. In this sense, there appears to be a "bioprogram" for language learning (Chomsky, 1965; Lenneberg, 1967; L. Gleitman, 1981; Bickerton, 1984; Pinker, 1994). In retrospect, this is scarcely surprising. It would be just as foolish for evolution to have created human bodies without human "programs" to run these bodies as it would be to have created giraffe bodies without giraffe programs or white-crowned sparrow bodies without white-crowned sparrow programs.

But we must close by reemphasizing that specific languages must be learned by human babies, even though the capacity to accomplish this is given in large part by nature. This is because the manifestations of the human language capacity are certainly variable, particularly in the sounds of the individual words. To reiterate a point with which we began: Greek children learn Greek, not Urdu or Swahili. For this reason, we have had to view the language acquisition task as a complex interaction between the child's innate capacities and the social, cognitive, and specifically linguistic supports provided in the environment. Perhaps, in light of the efficiency and sure-handedness with which (as we saw) human babies accomplish this feat, you might feel disposed to buttonhole the next baby you meet in the street to compliment her for being born a human being.

SUMMARY

1. Language has five major properties. It is *creative* or novel: All normal humans can say and understand sentences they have never heard before. It is *structured:* Only certain arrangements of linguistic elements (phonemes, words, and so forth) are allowed. It is *meaningful:* Each word or combination of words expresses a meaningful idea (or concept). It is *referential:* It relates to things, scenes, and events in the extralinguistic world. It is *interpersonal:* It enables us to communicate with other people.

2. Languages are organized as a hierarchy of structures. The lowest-level units are *phonemes,* the sound elements of language. Each language uses somewhere between twelve and sixty phonemes and has specific arrangements of the phonemes it uses. Each language also has *morphemes,* which are the smallest language units that carry bits of meaning. There are *content morphemes,* which carry the bulk of meaning, and *function morphemes,* which carry the structure of the sentence. *Phrases* are groupings of morphemes that carry more complex meanings than single morphemes and words. Phrases are combined into *sentences* according to the principles of syntax. There are infinitely many phrases and sentences in a language.

3. Word and phrase meaning is not identical to word and phrase reference, for some expressions can refer to the same thing and yet have different meanings. The *definitional theory of meaning* holds that each word describes a bundle of more elementary semantic features. Each word is "defined" as some small set of features that are individually necessary and jointly sufficient to pick out that word from all other words in the language. The *prototype theory of meaning* responds to the fact that it is hard to find necessary and sufficient definitions for all words. The most widely held theory of word meaning today combines the definitional and prototype theories. The definitional part picks out properties that a concept must have. The prototype part concerns the most "typical" properties, the ones that most members of the concept share.

4. Human thought is in terms of whole *propositions,* consisting of a *subject* or topic, and a *predicate* (that which is said about the subject or topic). The linguistic expression of a proposition is a simple sentence, consisting of a *noun phrase* (representing the subject or topic) and a *verb phrase* (representing the predicate). Sentence structures are represented by hierarchical tree diagrams, which show the relations among the phrases and words that make up the full sentences.

5. Sentences have both a *surface structure,* which describes their structural parts (the phrases and words) and the order in which these are uttered in speech, and an *underlying structure,* which describes their meaning. The underlying structure consists of the sentence as interpreted into a proposition containing *doer, act,* and *done-to,* and various *attitudes* to this proposition, such as negative, doer focus, and question.

6. Sentence relations can be described according to various properties of surface and underlying structure. Two sentences that are the same in surface structure but different in underlying structure are *ambiguous.* Two sentences that are the same in underlying structure but different in surface structure are *paraphrases.*

7. Listeners hear only surface structure but, to comprehend, must recover the underlying structure. The psychological machinery in people's heads that accomplishes comprehension is called the *Sentence Analyzing Machinery,* or *SAM.*

8. Language learning is more than skill acquisition, for the learning cannot be fully described as a habit acquired through imitation and reinforcement. The proof is that children come to know more than they ever could have heard.

9. Infants are responsive to linguistic stimulation almost from birth. For instance, they have been shown to be responsive to differences among just about all the phonemes used in the various languages of the world. Learning a specific language's phoneme structure involves learning not to notice those distinctions not made in one's native lan-

SUMMARY

guage. Infants are especially responsive to a form of speech known as *Motherese*—talk used by parents—which is characterized by large pitch excursions and by pauses at phrase boundaries.

10. Most infants begin talking in *one-word sentences* at about one year of age and rapidly acquire a large vocabulary. They seem to have propositional ideas in mind, and some appreciation of syntactic structure, even at this early stage.

11. At about two years of age, children begin using rudimentary *two-word* or *telegraphic sentences* that contain content words but typically omit function morphemes and words. These first sentences are short because of the difficulty of planning complex speech events and perhaps because of learners' initial "preprogramming" concerning the design characteristics of human languages. Still, these short sentences have a good deal of structure.

12. Language learning takes place successfully in many radically different environments. It fails only if children are removed from all human company or violently isolated and abused. Even if one is deaf, one learns a language. In this case, the language will be a signed (visual-manual) language rather than a spoken (auditory-vocal) one.

13. Children isolated from opportunities to learn the language around them invent some of it for themselves. An example is deaf children not exposed to signed languages who invent pantomimic gestures for words and combine these into propositions.

14. In contrast to the cases of changed environmental conditions, which children of normal mentality generally overcome, are cases of changed conditions of mentality. When the brain is unusual or deficient, radical changes in language learning are seen.

15. An important case of a "changed brain" that learns a language is the second-language learner who is chronologically older than the usual first-language learner. The less mature brain and the mature brain appear to have different capacities. The finding is that the younger the second-language learner, the more likely he or she is to acquire the new language adequately.

16. Deaf children not exposed to signed languages present the opportunity to see whether age of exposure affects the learning of a *first* language. The age at which deaf children are first exposed to a signed language predicts their skill with this language, even if they are tested twenty or thirty years after they begin using one.

17. Because experimental evidence makes it clear that language learning is based on special properties of the young human brain, we should not expect to find that human language can be fully or even adequately learned by other higher animals such as chimpanzees and dolphins. Nevertheless, chimpanzees have been shown to have rather good word-learning capacities, though nowhere as good as those of a two-and-a-half-year-old human. They also seem to be able to think propositionally to some degree, that is, to think in terms of who-did-what-to-whom. There is little or no credible evidence, however, that chimpanzees can acquire even the rudiments of syntactic principles.

18. Summarizing all the evidence, language learning results from the interaction between a young human brain and various social, cognitive, and specifically linguistic supports provided in the environment. Language is perhaps the central cognitive property whose possession makes us "truly human." If aliens came from another planet but spoke like us, we would probably try to get to know them and understand them—rather than trying to herd them or milk them—even if they looked like cows.

PART THREE

SOCIAL BEHAVIOR

CHAPTER

THE BIOLOGICAL BASIS OF SOCIAL BEHAVIOR

THE SOCIAL NATURE OF HUMANS AND ANIMALS 379

NATURAL SELECTION AND SURVIVAL ■ BUILT-IN SOCIAL BEHAVIORS

BIOLOGICAL SOURCES OF AGGRESSION 383

CONFLICT BETWEEN SPECIES: PREDATION AND DEFENSE ■ CONFLICT BETWEEN LIKE AND LIKE

THE BIOLOGICAL BASIS OF LOVE: THE MALE-FEMALE BOND 390

SEXUAL BEHAVIOR ■ SEXUAL CHOICE ■ REPRODUCTION AND TIMING ■ EVOLUTION AND MATING SYSTEMS

THE BIOLOGICAL BASIS OF LOVE: THE PARENT-CHILD BOND 399

THE INFANT'S ATTACHMENT TO THE MOTHER ■ THE MOTHER'S ATTACHMENT TO THE INFANT

COMMUNICATING MOTIVES 401

EXPRESSIVE MOVEMENTS: ANIMAL DISPLAY ■ THE EXPRESSION OF EMOTIONS IN HUMANS ■ THE DIFFERENCE BETWEEN DISPLAY AND LANGUAGE

SOCIAL COGNITION IN PRIMATES 405

SELF-SACRIFICE AND ALTRUISM 407

ALTRUISM IN ANIMALS ■ ALTRUISM IN HUMANS

ETHOLOGY AND HUMAN NATURE 412

SUMMARY 412

In the preceding chapters, we asked what organisms do, what they want, and what they know. But thus far we have raised these questions in a limited context, for we have largely considered the organism as an isolated individual abstracted from the social world in which it lives. But many aspects of behavior are impossible to describe by considering a single organism. Courtship, sex, parental care, competition, and cooperation do not take place in isolation. They are not merely actions; they are interactions in which each participant's behavior is affected by the behavior of others.

In humans, the role of social factors is even more powerful than in animals. Most of our motives—the desire to be loved, to be esteemed, and in some cases, unhappily, to inflict pain—are social. Even motives that seem to involve only the isolated individual, such as hunger, thirst, and temperature maintenance, are social. For the ways we satisfy these motives are enormously affected by the social context, created by our forebears, in which we live. Thus, we eat food that is raised by a complex agricultural technology based on millenia of human discovery, and we eat it delicately, with knife and fork, according to the etiquette of a long-dead king.

The study of social behavior is the study of lives inextricably intertwined with those of others both living and dead. It is the study which proves that, to quote John Donne's famous sermon, "no man is an island complete unto himself."

 classic question posed by philosophers is, "What is the basic social nature of humankind?" Are greed, competition, and hate (or for that matter, charity, cooperation, and love) unalterable components of the human makeup, or can they be instilled or nullified by proper training? To answer these questions, we will have to consider not just humankind but some of its animal cousins as well.

THE SOCIAL NATURE OF HUMANS AND ANIMALS

Are human beings so built that social interaction is an intrinsic part of their makeup? Or are they essentially solitary creatures who turn to others only because they need them for their own selfish purposes? The English social philosopher Thomas Hobbes (1588–1679) argued for the second of these alternatives. In his view, man is a self-centered brute who, left to his own devices, will seek his own gain regardless of the cost to others. Except for the civilizing constraints imposed by society, men would inevitably be in an eternal "war of all against all." According to Hobbes, this frightening "state of nature" is approximated during times of anarchy and civil war. These were conditions Hobbes knew all too well, for he lived during a time of violent upheavals in England when Stuart royalists battled Cromwell's Puritans, when commoners beheaded

Thomas Hobbes *(Painting by John Michael Wright; courtesy of The Granger Collection)*

Charles Darwin *(Painting by J. Collier; courtesy of The National Portrait Gallery, London)*

their king in a public square, and when pillaging, burning, and looting were commonplace. Hobbes argued that in such a state of nature, human life is a sorry lot. There are "no Arts; no Letters; no Society; and which is worst of all, continuall fear, and danger of violent death; And the life of man solitary, poore, nasty, brutish, and short" (Hobbes, 1651, p. 186). Hobbes argued that under the circumstances, people had no choice but to protect themselves against their own ugly natures. They did so by entering into a "social contract" to form a collective commonwealth, the State.

Hobbes's psychological starting points are simple enough: People are by nature asocial and destructively rapacious. Society is a means to chain the brute within. Only when curbed by social fetters does humanity go beyond animal nature to become truly human. Given this position, the various social motives that bind us to others (such as love and loyalty) presumably are imposed through culture and convention. They are learned, for they could not possibly be part of our intrinsic makeup.

NATURAL SELECTION AND SURVIVAL

During the nineteenth century, Hobbes's doctrine of inherent human aggression and depravity was garbed in the mantle of science. The Industrial Revolution seemed to give ample proof that life is indeed a Hobbesian battle of each against all, whether in the marketplace, in the sweatshops, or in the far-off colonies. Ruthless competition among people was regarded as just one facet of the more general struggle for existence waged among all living things. This harsh view of nature had gained great impetus at the start of the nineteenth century when Thomas Malthus announced his famous law of population growth. According to Malthus, human and animal populations grow by geometrical progression (for example, 1, 2, 4, 8, 16, . . .) while the food supply grows arithmetically (for example, 1, 2, 3, 4, 5, . . .). As a result, there is inevitable scarcity and a continual battle for survival.

When Charles Darwin (1809–1882) read Malthus's essay, he finally found the explanatory principle he had been seeking to account for the evolution of living things. He, as others before him, believed that all present-day plants, animals, and even humans, were descended from prior forms. The evidence came from various sources, such as fossil records that showed the gradual transformation from long-extinct species to those now living. But what had produced these changes? Within each species there are individual variations; some horses are faster, others are slower. Many of these variations are part of the animal's hereditary makeup and thus are bequeathed to its descendants. But will an individual animal have descendants? That depends on how it fares in the struggle for existence. As a matter of fact, most organisms don't live long enough to reproduce. Only a few seedlings grow up to be trees; only a few tadpoles achieve froghood. But certain characteristics may make survival a bit more likely. The faster horse is more likely to escape predatory cats than its slower fellow, and it is thus more likely to leave offspring who inherit its swiftness. This process of ***natural selection*** does not guarantee survival and reproduction; it only increases their likelihood. In consequence, evolutionary change is very gradual and proceeds over eons (Darwin, 1872a).

PERSONAL AND GENETIC SURVIVAL

Natural selection leads to the "survival of the fittest." But just what does it mean to be fit? Thus far, our examples of better "fitness" involved attributes that make personal survival more likely: the faster horse, the more ferocious cat, and so on.

Genetic survival *The peacock's long tail feathers are a cumbersome burden that may decrease his chances of escaping predators and thus his own personal survival. But this is more than offset by his increased chances of attracting a sexual partner, thereby assuring survival of his genes. (Photograph © Ed Reschke, 1988; all rights reserved.)*

A woven nest *Many animals have genetically determined behavior patterns characteristic of their species. An example is nest weaving in the thick-billed African weaverbird. (Photo courtesy of Brian M. Rogers/Biofotos)*

But personal survival as such is not what the evolutionary game is about. The trick is to have reproductive success—to have offspring who will pass your genes along. A horse that manages to live two or three times longer than any of its fellows but that for some reason or another is infertile or stays celibate has not survived in an evolutionary sense. Personal survival (at least until sexual maturity) is a prerequisite for genetic survival, but it alone is not enough.

Seen in this light, it's clear that "fitness" is determined by all characteristics that enhance reproductive success, whether or not such characteristics contribute to the individual's own personal survival. Consider the magnificent tail feathers of the peacock. His long, cumbersome tail may somewhat decrease his chance to escape predators, but it hugely contributes to his evolutionary fitness. The peacock has to compete with his fellow males for access to the peahen; the larger and more magnificent his tail, the more likely she will respond to his sexual overtures. From an evolutionary point of view, the potential gain was evidently greater than the possible loss; as a result, long tail feathers were selected for. Much the same holds for many other characteristics that are of advantage in sexual competition. This is especially so among males (for reasons we'll discuss later on). Some of these characteristics are rather general, such as strength and aggressiveness. Others, such as the brightly colored plumage of many male birds and the large antlers of the stag, are more specialized. But whatever the particulars of a given attribute, its contribution to the animal's fitness is the extent to which it leads to reproductive success.

INHERITED PREDISPOSITIONS TO BEHAVIOR

The inherited characteristics that increase the chance for biological survival (that is, reproduction) may concern bodily structures such as the horse's hooves or the stag's antlers. But Darwin and his successors pointed out that natural selection may also involve behavior. Squirrels bury nuts and beavers construct dams; these behavior patterns are characteristic of the species and depend on the animals' *genes,* the basic units of heredity. Whether these genes are selected for or not depends upon the *adaptive value* (that is, the biological survival value) of the behavior they give rise to. A squirrel who has a genetic predisposition to bury nuts in autumn is presumably more likely to survive the winter than one who doesn't. As a result, it is more likely to have offspring who will inherit the nut-burying gene (or genes). The end product is an increase in the number of nut-burying squirrels.

Granted that behavior can be shaped by evolution, what kind of behavior is most likely to evolve? And, most important to us, what kind of built-in predispositions are most likely to characterize humankind? Many nineteenth-century thinkers answered in Hobbesian terms. They reasoned that people are animals and that in the bitter struggle for existence all animals are shameless egoists by sheer necessity. At bottom, they are all solitary and selfish, and human beings are no exception. To the extent that humans act sociably and on occasion even unselfishly—mating, rearing children, living and working with others—they learn to do so in order to satisfy some self-centered motive such as lust or hunger.

On the face of it, this Hobbesian view seems to fit evolutionary doctrine. But on closer examination, Darwinian theory does not imply anything of the sort. It holds that there is "survival of the fittest," but "fittest" only means most likely to survive and to have offspring; it says nothing about being solitary or selfish. Darwin himself supposed that certain predispositions toward cooperation might well be adaptive and would thus be selected for. We now know that something of this sort is true, for animals as well as human beings. As we shall see, there is considerable evidence that, Hobbes to the contrary, humans and animals are by nature social rather than asocial and that much of their social behavior grows out of natively given predispositions rather than running counter to them.

Konrad Lorenz *(Photograph by Nina Leen)*

BUILT-IN SOCIAL BEHAVIORS

Most systematic studies of built-in social behavior have been conducted within the domain of ***ethology,*** a branch of biology that studies animal behavior under natural conditions. Led by the Europeans Konrad Lorenz (1903–1989) and Niko Tinbergen (1907–1988), both Nobel Prize winners, ethologists have analyzed many behavior patterns that are built-in and ***species-specific,*** that is, characteristic of a particular species. Many of these built-in and species-specific behavior patterns are social; they dictate the way in which creatures interact with others of their own kind. Some involve a positive bond between certain members of the same species—courtship, copulation, care of the young. Others concern reactions of antagonism and strife—the struggle for social dominance, competition for a mate, and dispute over territory.

FIXED-ACTION PATTERNS

The early ethologists believed that many species-specific social reactions are based on genetically pre-programmed ***fixed-action patterns,*** which in turn are elicited by genetically pre-programmed ***releasing stimuli.*** An example of such a fixed-action pattern is the begging response of newly hatched herring gulls. They beg for food by pecking at the tips of their parents' beaks. The parent will then regurgitate some food from its crop and feed it to the young. But what is the critical stimulus that "releases" the chick's begging pecks? To find out, Tinbergen offered newly hatched gull chicks various cardboard models of gull heads and observed which ones they pecked at the most. The most successful model was one that was long and thin and had a red patch at its tip (see Figure 10.1). These are the very characteristics of an adult herring gull's beak, but the newly hatched chick has never encountered a parent's beak previously. Tinbergen concluded that evolution had done a good job in programming the chick to respond to certain stimulus features so as to recognize the parent's beak at first sight (Tinbergen, 1951).

10.1   Stimulus releasers for pecking
(A) The figure indicates the pecking rate of a herring gull chick when presented with various models. As the figure shows, a flat cardboard model is more effective than a real head, and a disembodied bill works almost as well. (Adapted from Keeton and Gould, 1933) (B) Best of all was a stick with spots on it moving back and forth horizontally, which the gull chick pecks at while ignoring a full representation of the parent's head. (Photograph courtesy of John Sparks, BBC [Natural History]).

A

B

Niko Tinbergen *(Photograph by Nina Leen)*

More recent studies suggest that the relation between releasing stimuli and species-specific fixed-action patterns is not quite as rigidly fixed and hardwired as Tinbergen's account suggests. For it appears that the baby gulls' begging response is partially shaped by experience. Right after hatching, the chicks peck at any red spot that moves horizontally across their field of vision, whether it is attached to a gull's head or not. But after two days in the nest with their parents, they peck only when confronted with a proper herring gull's beak. This suggests that the genes provide a crude first outline, as Tinbergen's work suggested. But then the chick's own experience must refine and build upon this outline (Hailman, 1967).

In many species, the releasing stimuli for any one animal's behavior are produced by another animal's behavior. What matters then is not just what some other animal looks like (e.g., the red spot on the gull parent's beak) but also what that other animal does. An important example of such behaviorally produced stimulus releasers are *displays.* Displays produce an appropriate reaction in another animal of the same species and are thus the basis of a primitive, innate communication system. The gull chick's begging peck is an elementary signal whose meaning is genetically given to both chick and parent: "Feed me! Feed me now!" (Tinbergen, 1951).

THE SOCIOBIOLOGICAL APPROACH

The analysis of chick pecking we have just discussed concentrated on the causes of behavior that are in the organism's own past (often the immediately preceding past): the particular stimuli that elicit the behavior, the physiological mechanisms that underlie it, and the developmental factors (such as learning) that help to shape it further. But there is another level of causation that precedes the particular organism's own past by countless generations: the animal's evolutionary history, which created the built-in bias toward that behavior through natural selection. In the last twenty years, a new branch of biology called *sociobiology* has arisen that focuses on these long-past causes with primary emphasis on the evolutionary basis of various social behaviors (Wilson, 1975). Most behavioral scientists agree that sociobiology has provided valuable insights about social behavior in animals. What is much more controversial is the sociobiologists' contention that similar analyses can be applied to human social patterns, a topic to which we turn in a later section (see pp. 396–99, 409–11).

BIOLOGICAL SOURCES OF AGGRESSION

We will begin our discussion of built-in social patterns by considering the biological basis of aggression. In humans, some of the causes of aggression are events in the immediate present, such as threats and frustrations that provoke anger and hostility. Our present concern is with sources that lie in our inherent makeup, the biological roots of aggression that derive from our evolutionary past. To uncover these, we have to study animals as well as humans, for the biological sources of human aggression are likely to be obscured by cultural factors and tradition.

10.2 Defending the nest *A royal tern attacks an egret that has come too close to its nest. (Photograph © M. P. Kahl)*

CONFLICT BETWEEN SPECIES: PREDATION AND DEFENSE

Most psychobiologists restrict the use of the term **aggression** to conflict between members of the same species. When an owl kills a mouse, it has slaughtered for food rather than murdered in hatred. As Lorenz points out, the predator about to pounce upon its prey does not look angry; the dog who is on the verge of catching a rabbit never growls, nor does it have its ears laid back (Lorenz, 1966). Neurological evidence leads to a similar conclusion. Rat-stalking (predatory attack) and arched-back hissing (aggression or self-defense) are elicited by the stimulation of two different areas of a cat's hypothalamus (Wasman and Flynn, 1962). Predatory attack is an outgrowth of the hunger motive and not of aggression; the hypothalamic site whose stimulation gives rise to rat-stalking also elicits eating (Hutchinson and Renfrew, 1966).

Somewhat closer to true aggression is the counterattack lodged by a prey animal against a predatory enemy (see Figure 10.2). Flocks of birds sometimes **mob** an intruding cat or hawk. A colony of lovebird parrots will fly in a body upon a would-be attacker, flapping their wings furiously and uttering loud, shrill squeaks. In the face of this commotion, the predator often withdraws to look for a less troublesome meal (Dilger, 1962). Defense reactions may also occur when a hunted animal is finally cut off from retreat. Even normally reticent creatures may then become desperate fighters, as in the case of the proverbial cornered rat.

Aside from these defense behaviors, aggression is the exception rather than the rule among members of different species. In an aquarium filled with tropical fish, like attacks like but leaves unlike alone. Vicious fights between unrelated species such as tigers and pythons have been photographed for wildlife films, but they are rare; the animals involved are either half-starved or they are goaded into the unnatural contest by having their escape route blocked (Lorenz, 1966).

A

B

10.3 Aggressive fighting *Male rats generally fight in fairly stereotypical ways, including (A) a "boxing position" that often escalates into (B) a leaping, biting attack. (From Barnett, 1963)*

CONFLICT BETWEEN LIKE AND LIKE

There is probably no group among the animal kingdom that has forsworn aggression altogether; fighting has been observed in virtually all species. Fish chase and nip each other; lizards lunge and push; birds attack with wing, beak, and claw; sheep and cows butt heads; deer lock antlers; rats adopt a boxing stance and eye each other warily until one finally pounces upon the other and begins a furious wrestling match with much kicking and leaping and occasionally serious bites (see Figure 10.3).

Among vertebrates, the male is generally the more aggressive sex. In some mammals, this difference in combativeness is apparent even in childhood play. Young male rhesus monkeys, for instance, engage in more vigorous rough-and-tumble tusslings than do their sisters (Harlow, 1962). A related result concerns the effect of *testosterone,* a male sex hormone. High testosterone levels in the bloodstream accompany increased aggressiveness in males; the reverse holds for decreased levels. This generalization seems to hold over a wide range of species including fish, lizards, turtles, birds, rats and mice, monkeys, and human males (Davis, 1964).

SECURING RESOURCES

What do animals fight about? Their struggles are generally about scarce resources—something valuable in their world that is in short supply. Such a resource may be a food source or a water hole; very often it is a mate. To secure a modicum of such resources many animals stake out a claim to a particular region, which they will then defend as their exclusive preserve, their private *territory.*

Take male songbirds, for example. In the spring, they endlessly patrol their little empires and furiously repel all male intruders who violate their borders. Contrary to the poet's fancy, the male bird who bursts into full-throated song is not giving vent to inexpressible joy, pouring out his "full heart in profuse strains of unpremeditated art." His message is more prosaic. It is a warning to male trespassers and an invitation to unattached females: "Have territory, will share."

A biological benefit of territoriality is that it secures an adequate supply of resources for the next generation. The songbird who chases his rivals away will probably leave more offspring than the one who doesn't, for his progeny will have a better start in life. Once his claim is staked out he can entice the female, offering his territory as a kind of dowry.

A side effect of territoriality is that it often serves to keep aggression within bounds. Good fences make good neighbors, at least in the sense that they keep the antagonists out of each others' hair (or fins or feathers). One mechanism that accomplishes this is rather simple. Once a territory is established, its owner has a kind of home-court advantage in further disputes (Krebs, 1982). On his home ground he is courageous; if he ventures beyond it, he becomes timid and is readily repulsed. As a result, there may be occasional border skirmishes but few actual conflicts. This behavior pattern is utilized by circus trainers who make sure that they are the first to enter the training ring and that the animals come in later. As a result, the ring becomes the trainer's territory and even the great cats are more readily cowed (Hediger, 1968).

Aggressive encounter between male bighorn rams (Courtesy of Stouffer Productions, Animals Animals)

Red deer stag roaring *(Photograph © Manfred Danegger)*

LIMITING AGGRESSION

A certain amount of aggression may be biologically adaptive. This is especially so for males who compete for access to females. For example, a more aggressive songbird will conquer a larger and more desirable territory, which will help him attract a mate. In addition, his territory confers further advantages such as more seeds or more worms, which further help his progeny who will get more and better food in their early days as nestlings. As a result, we would expect some selection for aggressiveness. But this holds only up to a point, for while aggression may confer some benefits, it also has its costs. Combat is dangerous and can lead to death or serious injury. In addition, it distracts the animal from other vital pursuits. The male who is continually fighting with his sexual rivals will have little time (let alone energy) left to mate with the female after his competitors have fled. Under the circumstances, natural selection strikes a compromise; there is aggression, but a number of factors keep it firmly in hand.

One way of avoiding catastrophic damage to life and limb is to assess the strength of the enemy. If he seems much stronger (or more agile, or better armed) than oneself, the best bet is to proclaim a cease-fire and concede defeat, or better yet, never to start the battle at all. Many male animals behave just that way. An example is provided by red deer stags who compete with each other for females. In the autumn, stags who hold a harem are challenged by other stags. In the first stage of this contest, the harem owner and the challenger roar at each other, sometimes for days on end. If the harem owner can keep on roaring longer and louder, the intruder will generally back off—a reasonable decision, since a stronger roar is most likely produced by a stronger stag (Krebs and Davies, 1987). Similar strategies for avoiding the costs of a bloody defeat are found in many species of sheep and deer whose males engage in a ritualized form of combat as if under an internal compulsion not to inflict serious wounds (see Figure 10.4).

The limitation on violence appears in other ways as well. Many conflicts are settled by blustering diplomacy before they erupt into actual war. For example, male chimpanzees try to intimidate each other by staring, raising an arm, or uttering fearsome shouts. This approach is found throughout the entire animal kingdom: Whenever possible, try to get your way by threat or bluff rather than by actual fighting. This holds even for creatures as large as elephants and as fierce

10.4 Ritualized fighting *Two South African wildebeest males in a harmless ritualized dual along an invisible but clearly defined mutual border between their territories. (Photograph by Hans Reinhard, © Bruce Coleman, Inc., 1988)*

A   B

10.5 Threat displays *(A) Some species threaten by making themselves appear larger and more impressive. (Photograph by Rod Williams, © Bruce Coleman, Inc., 1991) (B) Other species threaten by shouting at the top of their lungs, like howler monkeys, who scream at each other for hours on end. (Photograph © Ferrero)*

Appeasement displays in humans *A Yanamamö Indian youngster smiles appeasingly at another boy who threatens him. (Photograph © I. Eibl-Eibesfeldt, Forschungsstelle f. Humanethologie)*

as tigers. Both these and other creatures make use of **threat displays,** a much less costly method for achieving one's aim than actual combat (see Figure 10.5).

In some cases, serious fighting will occur even so, for animals no less than human generals may miscalculate their chances of victory. But some ways of limiting the cost of defeat still remain. In wolves, the loser may "admit defeat" by adopting a special submissive gesture, such as begging like a puppy or rolling on his back. This is an **appeasement display** that is functionally equivalent to our white flag of surrender. Unlike some human warriors, the victorious wolf is without rancor. He generally accepts the loser's submission, and all fighting stops (Lorenz, 1966). The adaptive value of such submissive signals is clear enough. They allow today's loser to withdraw from the field of battle so that he can come back in a year or two when he is older and wiser, and when he may very well win a rematch. The evolutionary rule is simple enough: Don't fight unless the probable gains (in reproductive success) outweigh the costs. If you lose and run away (or make an appeasement display), you may live to fight (and mate) another day.

DOMINANCE AND SUBMISSION

Animals that live in groups often develop a social order based on **dominance hierarchies.** Such hierarchies can be quite complex among troops of primates. For example, in baboons, the dominant male has usually achieved his status through victory in several aggressive encounters. After this, his status is settled for a while, and lower-ranking baboons generally step aside to let the "alpha male" pass, and nervously scatter if he merely stares at them.

In the early days of ethology, many investigators saw such hierarchies as a way of lessening aggression. In their view, once a hierarchy was formed, it was fairly stable. As a result, everyone "knew his place," thus minimizing combat and friction for the good of all (e.g., Lorenz, 1966). This view has been seriously challenged. To begin with, it is difficult to believe that baboons or rhesus monkeys have somehow entered into a Hobbesian social contract, as if they knew what was good for the group as a whole (or that they cared). Nor do such hierarchies abolish all internal friction. Much of an alpha male's life is spent in efforts to

A

B

10.6 Dominance hierarchies *(A) The two baboons at the right jointly threaten the larger baboon on the left who could defeat either of them alone but won't risk fighting them both. (Courtesy of L. T. Nash, Arizona State University) (B) A dominant male baboon with a harem of females and young. (Courtesy of Bruce Coleman)*

maintain his place at the top—harassing his subordinates, approaching them until they back away, staring at them until they look down, and if necessary, attacking them with teeth and nails. In these endeavors, the alpha male often depends on alliances with other males (often his own brothers) who will join him to fight off his rivals and who in turn are supported by him in their future aggressive encounters (Walters and Seyfarth, 1986; see Figure 10.6A).

Why should the animals spend so much time to achieve and maintain dominance? The answer is that rank has considerable privileges. The alpha male has first choice of sleeping site, enjoys easier access to food, and has priority in mating (see Figure 10.6B). Such perquisites undoubtedly make life more pleasant for the alpha male than for his less fortunate fellows. But even more important may be the long-run evolutionary value of rank, for in terms of genetic survival, the higher-ranking animal is more "fit." Since he has easier access to females, he will presumably leave more offspring (Smith, 1981; Silk, 1986).

Thus far, our primary focus has been on dominance relations among primate males. This followed the initial emphasis of investigators in this area who focused on male-male aggression. To be sure, the males' aggressive encounters are quite obvious, as they fight and strut and bellow. Many authors took this as evidence that the social order among most primates (and by implication, our own) was ultimately based on political struggles among males. But recent research shows that this conclusion is off the mark. For in many primate societies, females compete no less than males and develop hierarchies that are often more stable than those of males. Moreover, female rank has important long-term consequences, for mothers tend to bequeath their social rank to their offspring, especially to their daughters (Hrdy and Williams, 1983; Walters and Seyfarth, 1986).

TERRITORIALITY IN HUMANS AND HUMAN CULTURE

Is any of the preceding discussion of animals relevant to human behavior? At least on the surface there are parallels that have led some writers to suppose that concepts such as territoriality, dominance hierarchy, and the like apply to humans as well as to animals. There are certainly some aspects of human behavior that resemble territoriality. Even within the home, different members of a family have their private preserves—their own rooms or corners, their places at the dinner table, and so on. Other territorial claims are more temporary, such as a seat in a railroad car, whose possession we mark with a coat, a book, or a briefcase if we have to leave for a while.

A related phenomenon is **personal space,** the physical region all around us whose intrusion we guard against (Figure 10.7). On many New York subways, passengers sit on long benches. Except during rush hour, they will carefully choose their seats so as to leave the greatest possible distance between themselves and their nearest neighbor.

In one study, personal space was deliberately violated. Experimenters went to a library and casually sat next to a person studying there, even though a more distant chair was available. After some fidgeting, the victim tried to move away. If this was impossible, books and rulers were neatly arranged so as to create a physical boundary (Felipe and Sommer, 1966). A desire to maintain some minimum personal space is probably nearly universal, but the physical dimensions seem to depend upon various social factors. By and large, appropriate personal distance increases with age and socio-economic status (Collier, 1985). It is also affected by the standards of a particular culture. In North America, acquaintances stand about two or three feet apart during a conversation; if one moves closer, the other feels crowded or pushed into an unwanted intimacy. For Latin Americans, the acceptable distance is said to be much less. Under the circumstances, misunderstanding is almost inevitable. The North American regards the Latin American as overly intrusive; the Latin American in turn feels that the North American is unfriendly and cold (Hall, 1966).

One may ask whether these observations truly parallel the evidence from other species. There is no doubt that many people—though not all—care deeply about private ownership, whether of things, real estate, or more subtle private preserves. The question is whether this concern stems from the same evolutionary roots as does the territoriality of the songbird, whether humans really respond to a built-in "territorial imperative" that, according to some writers, is part of our genetic ancestry and cannot be disobeyed (Ardrey, 1966).

We conclude that while the overt behaviors may sometimes be similar, the underlying mechanisms are not. Territoriality in robins is universal and innately based, but in humans it is enormously affected by learning. For example, there are some societies in which private ownership is relatively unimportant; this certainly suggests that cultural factors play a vital role.

10.7 **Personal space** (A) Relatively even spacing in ring-billed gulls (Photograph by Allan D. Cruikshank © 1978/Photo Researchers) (B) Some ethologists believe that the maintenance of personal space in humans is a related phenomenon. Vacationers at a beach on the Baltic Sea in Germany keep a precise distance between each couple or family unit. (Photograph by J. Messerschmidt/Bruce Coleman)

A

B

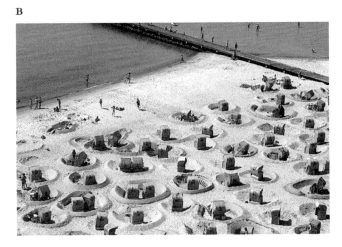

The preceding discussion has made it clear that there is some biological foundation for strife and conflict. The tendencies toward destruction are kept in bounds by a set of counteracting tendencies such as territoriality and ritualized fighting. As we shall see, they are also controlled and modified by learning, especially during childhood in humans, and their expression is greatly affected by situational factors (see Chapters 11 and 14).

But over and above these various checks on aggression, there is a positive force that is just as basic and deeply rooted in the biological makeup of animals and humans. The poets call it love. Scientists use the more prosaic term **bonding,** the tendency to affiliate with others of one's own kind.

The forces of social attraction are most obvious between mate and mate, and between child and parent. But positive bonds occur even outside of mating and child care. Examples are the social relationships cemented by *grooming* in monkeys and apes who sit in pairs while the groomer meticulously picks lice and other vermin out of the groomee's fur (Figure 10.8). The animals evidently like to groom and be groomed over and above considerations of personal hygiene; it is their way of forming a social bond, and it works. Grooming occurs most commonly among kin (brothers and sisters, cousins, and so on), although it may also occur among unrelated animals. But whether they be kin or unrelated, animals who groom most often are also the most closely bonded by other measures of primate togetherness: They sit together, forage for food together, and stick together in alliances against common antagonists (Walters and Seyfarth, 1986).

It has sometimes been suggested that a comparable human practice is small talk in which we exchange no real information but simply talk for the sake of "relating" to the other person. Other people are part of our universe, and we need them and want their company. Much the same is probably true for our primate cousins. They groom each other, whether or not they have vermin. We talk to each other, whether or not we really have something to say.

10.8 Grooming in baboons (Photograph by P. Craig-Cooper, Nature Photographers Ltd.)

SEXUAL BEHAVIOR

In some very primitive organisms, reproduction is asexual; thus amoebas multiply by a process of simple cell division. This form of procreation seems to work well enough, for amoebas are still among us. It appears that contrary to one's first impression, sex is not necessary (at least, not for reproduction). But if so, why do the vast majority of animal species reproduce sexually? Perhaps sexual reproduction is more enjoyable than the asexual varieties, but its biological advantage lies elsewhere. It comes from the fact that it assures a greater degree of genetic variability.

An amoeba that splits into two has created two replicas of its former self. Here natural selection has no differences to choose between, for the second amoeba can be neither better nor worse in its adaptation to the environment than the first, since the two are genetically identical.

Things are quite different in sexual reproduction. Here specialized cells, **sperm** and **ovum,** must join to form a fertilized egg, or **zygote,** which will then become a new individual. This procedure amounts to a kind of genetic roulette. To begin with, each parent donates only half of the genetic material: Within some limits, mere chance determines which genes are contained in any one

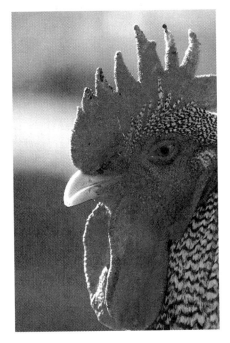

10.9   Advertising one's sex   *The comb and wattle of this barred rock rooster proclaim that he is a male. (Photograph by Garry D. McMichael, 1987/Photo Researchers)*

sperm or ovum. Chance enters again to determine which sperm will join with which ovum. As a result, there will be inevitable differences among the offspring. Now natural selection can come into play, perhaps favoring the offspring with the sharper teeth or the one with the more sexually attractive display, which will then enhance the survival of the gene that produced these attributes.

SEXUAL CHOICE

For sexual reproduction to occur, sperm and ovum have to meet in the appointed manner, at the proper time and place. Many structures and behavior patterns have evolved to accomplish these ends. Our first concern is with those that underlie sexual choice and determine who mates with whom.

ADVERTISING ONE'S SEX

The first job of a would-be sexual partner is to proclaim his or her sex. Many animals have anatomical structures whose function is precisely that, for example, the magnificent tail feathers of the male peacock or the comb and wattle of the rooster (see Figure 10.9). These structures are often crucial for appropriate mating behavior. In one species of woodpecker, the male has a mustache of black feathers while the female does not. An unkind ethologist trapped a female and attached a mustache. When she later flew back to her nest, her mate attacked her mercilessly, presumably under the impression that he was warding off an intruding male (Etkin, 1964).

In humans, structural displays of sex differences are less pronounced, but they are present nonetheless. A possible example is the female breast whose adipose tissue does not really increase the infant's milk supply. According to some ethologists, it evolved as we became erect and lost our reliance upon smell, a sense that provides the primary information about sex and sexual readiness in many mammals. Under the circumstances, there had to be other ways of displaying one's sex. The prominent breasts of the female may be one such announcement among hairless, "naked apes" (Morris, 1967).

COURTSHIP RITUALS

Advertising one's intentions   In many animals, sexual display involves various species-specific behavior patterns, called **courtship rituals.** These are essentially ways of advertising one's amorous intentions. Some of these rituals are mainly a means to exhibit the structural sex differences, as in the male peacock spreading his tail feathers. Others are much more elaborate. Thus penguins bow deeply to each other while rocking from side to side, and certain grebes complete an elaborate aquatic ballet by exchanging gifts of seaweed (Figure 10.10).

10.10   Courtship rituals   *(A) The male bower bird tries to entice the female into an elaborate bower decorated with berries, shells, or whatever else may be available, such as colored clothespins. (B) Grebes engage in a complex aquatic ballet. (C) The male tern courts by feeding the female. (Photographs from left to right by Philip Green; Bob and Clara Calhoun/Bruce Coleman; Jeff Foott/Bruce Coleman)*

A

B

C

In some species, courtship rituals may also involve alternating bouts of approach and withdrawal, of coy retreat and seductive flirtation. What accounts for these apparent oscillations between yes and no? There is an underlying conflict between attraction and fear; neither animal can really be sure that the other is not hostile. Each must therefore inform the other that its intentions are not aggressive. This is especially true of the male, who in many species performs various appeasement rituals that allay the female's fears.

Indicating one's species   Courtship rituals have a further function. They not only increase the likelihood that boy meets girl, but they virtually guarantee that the two will be of the same species. This is because these rituals are highly species-specific, as in the case of the gift-exchanging grebes. In effect they are a code whereby both members of the pair inform the other that they belong, say, to the duck species *anas platyrhynochos,* rather than to *bucephala clangula* or *tachyeres patachonicus,* or some other duck species that no self-respecting *anas platyrhynochos* would ever want to mate with. The effect of such species-specific courtship codes is that they make it more likely that the mating will produce fertile offspring. For contrary to popular view, different species can interbreed if they are related closely enough. But the offspring of such "unnatural" unions is often infertile; an example is the mule, a result of crossing a horse with a donkey. Species-specific courtship rituals probably evolved to avoid such reproductive failures.

The evolutionary origin of courtship rituals   We've discussed the general function of courtship rituals, but what can we say about the evolutionary history of a particular ritual or display? Displays leave no fossils, so there is no direct method for reconstructing their biological past. One possible approach is to compare displays in related species. By noting their similarities and differences, the ethologist tries to reconstruct the evolutionary steps in their history, much as a comparative anatomist charts the family tree of fins, wings, and forelegs.

An example of how this comparative method works is an analysis of an odd courtship ritual in a predatory insect, the dancing fly (Kessel, 1955). At mating time, the male dancing fly secretes a little ball of silk which he brings to the female. She plays with this silk ball while the male mounts her and copulates. How did this ritual arise? The courtship patterns in a number of related species give a clue. Most flies of related species manage with a minimum of precopulatory fuss; the trouble is that the female may decide to eat the male rather than mate with him. However, if she is already eating a small prey animal, the male is safe. Some species have evolved a behavior pattern that capitalizes on this fact. The male catches a small insect and brings it to the female for her to eat while he mates with her. In still other species, the male first wraps the prey in a large silk balloon. This increases his margin of safety, for the female is kept busy unwrapping her present. The dancing fly's ritual is probably the last step in this evolutionary sequence. The male dancing fly wastes no time or energy in catching a prey animal, but simply brings an empty ball of silk, all wrapping and no present. Copulation can now proceed unimpeded since the female is safely occupied—perhaps the first creature in evolutionary history to realize that it is the thought and not the gift that matters (Figure 10.11).

WHO MAKES THE CHOICE

The preceding discussions have centered on the various factors that bring male and female together. But, interestingly enough, the two don't have an equal voice in the ultimate decision. In most species, it is the female who makes the final choice in deciding whether or not to mate. The biological reason is simple—the female shoulders the major cost of reproduction. If she is a bird, she

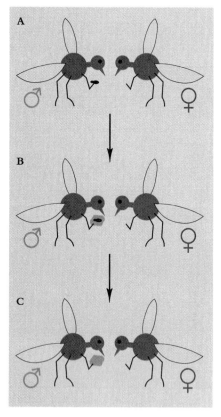

10.11   The evolution of courtship in dancing flies   *(A) In some species, the male catches a prey animal and gives it to the female to eat during copulation; this keeps her busy so she is less likely to eat him. (B) In other species, the male first wraps the prey in a balloon of secreted silk. This keeps the female even busier, since she has to unwrap the prey. (C) Finally, in the dancing fly, the male gives the female a ball of silk without anything in it. (After Klopfer, 1974)*

THE BIOLOGICAL BASIS OF LOVE: THE MALE-FEMALE BOND

10.12 *Male seahorse "giving birth"* (Photograph © Rudie H. Kuiter, Oxford Scientific Films)

supplies not only the ovum but also the food supply for the developing embryo. If she is a mammal, she carries the embryo within her body and later provides it with milk. In either case, her biological burden is vastly greater than the male's. If a doe's offspring fails to survive, she has lost a whole breeding season. In comparison, the stag's loss is minimal—a few minutes of his time and some easily replaced sperm cells. Under the circumstances, natural selection would favor the female who is particularly choosy about picking the best possible male, that is, the male whose genetic contribution will best ensure their offsprings' survival. From the male's point of view, the female seems coy or "plays hard to get." But in fact this is not just playacting, for, to the female, reproduction is a serious business with heavy biological costs (Trivers, 1972).

There are a few interesting exceptions. One example is the sea horse, whose young are carried in a brood pouch by the male (see Figure 10.12). In this animal, the male exhibits greater sexual caution and discrimination than the female. A similar effect is found in the phalarope, an arctic seabird whose eggs are hatched and whose chicks are fed by the male. Here a greater part of the biological burden falls on the male, and we should expect a corresponding increase in his sexual choosiness. This is just what happens. Among the phalaropes, the female does the wooing. She is brightly plumaged, and aggressively pursues the dull-colored, coyly careful male (Williams, 1966).

REPRODUCTION AND TIMING

Once male and female have met, the next step is to arrange for the union of their respective sperm and ovum. Terrestrial animals have evolved a variety of sexual mechanics to accomplish this end. In general, the male introduces his sperm cells into the genital tract of the female, where the ovum is fertilized. The problem is synchronization. The sperm has to encounter a ready ovum, and the fertilized egg can develop only if it is provided with the appropriate conditions. Under these circumstances, timing is of the essence. In birds and mammals, the timing mechanism depends on a complex feedback system between brain centers and hormones.

ANIMAL SEXUALITY AND HORMONES

Hormonal cycles Except for the primates, mammals mate only when the female is in heat, or *estrus.* For example, the female rat goes through a fifteen-hour estrus period every four days. At all other times, she will resolutely reject any male's advances. If he nuzzles her or tries to mount, she will kick and bite. But during estrus, the female responds quite differently to the male's approach. She first retreats in small hops, then stops to look back, and wiggles her ears provocatively (McClintock and Adler, 1978). Eventually, she stands still, her back arched, her tail held to the side, in all respects a willing sexual partner.

What accounts for the difference between the female's behavior during estrus and at other times? The crucial fact is a simple matter of reproductive biology. The time of estrus is precisely the time when the female's ova are ripe for fertilization. Evolution has obviously provided a behavioral arrangement that is exactly tuned to reproductive success.

The mechanism is an interlocking system of hormonal and neurological controls that involves the pituitary gland, the hypothalamus, and the ovaries. In effect, there are three phases: During the first, follicles in the ovary mature under the influence of pituitary secretions. The follicles produce the female sex hormone *estrogen.* As the concentration of estrogen in the bloodstream rises, the hypothalamus responds by directing the pituitary to change its secretions. In

3 9 3

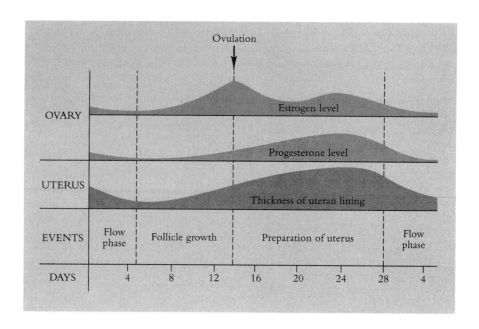

10.13   The main stages of the human menstrual cycle   The figure shows estrogen and progesterone levels and thickness of the uterus lining during the human menstrual cycle. The cycle begins with the growth of a follicle, continues through ovulation and a maximum estrogen level, is followed by a phase during which the uterus becomes prepared to receive the embryo, and ends with a flow phase during which the thickened uterus lining is sloughed off. (After Keeton, 1980)

consequence, follicle growth is accelerated until the follicle ruptures and releases the mature ovum. This triggers the second phase during which the animal is in estrus. Estrogen production climbs to a steep maximum and stimulates certain structures in the hypothalamus, which make the animal sexually receptive. The third phase is dominated by the action of another female sex hormone, ***progesterone,*** which is produced by the ruptured follicle. Its secretion leads to a thickening of the uterus lining, a first step in preparing the uterus to receive the embryo. If the ovum is fertilized, there are further steps in building an appropriate womb. If it is not, the thickened uterus walls are reabsorbed and another cycle begins. In humans and some primates, too much extra tissue is laid on to be easily reabsorbed; the thickened uterus lining is therefore sloughed off as ***menstrual flow*** (Figure 10.13).

Hormonal changes and behavior   Some hormonal changes affect behavior dramatically. When male rats are castrated, they soon lose all sexual interest and capacity, as do female rats without ovaries. But sexual behavior is quickly restored by appropriate injections of male or female hormones, specifically ***testosterone*** and estrogen.

Many investigators believe that behavioral effects of hormones are caused by neurons in the hypothalamus that contain receptors with which certain hormone molecules from the bloodstream combine. When this occurs, it leads to neural changes in the hypothalamus that trigger sexual appetite and behavior. This hypothesis has been tested by injecting minute quantities of various hormones into several regions of the hypothalamus. The total amounts were negligible and could hardly affect the overall hormone concentration in the blood. Will the hypothalamic sexual control system be fooled by the local administration of the hormone, as is its thermostatic counterpart when it is locally cooled or heated (see Chapter 3)? It evidently is. A spayed female cat will go into estrus when estrogen is implanted in her hypothalamus (Harris and Michael, 1964). Analogous effects have been obtained with ***androgens*** (that is, male hormones) administered to castrated male rats (Davidson, 1969; McEwen et al., 1982; Feder, 1984).

Hormones affect behavior, but the relation can also work the other way around. What an animal does and what it sees and feels will often have drastic effects on its hormonal secretions. An example is the effect of copulation on progesterone secretion in female rats. Some progesterone is secreted during the normal cycle, but not enough to permit the implantation of the fertilized egg in the uterus. Yet more progesterone is released as a reflex response to sexual stimulation. In rats, the male evidently has two reproductive functions. He supplies the sperm, but he also supplies the necessary stimulation that triggers the extra progesterone secretion without which there can be no pregnancy. This is shown by the fact that when the male rat ejaculates too quickly, no pregnancy results. There has been too little stimulation to set off the female's hormonal reflex (Adler, 1969).

HUMAN SEXUALITY AND HORMONES

The major difference between animal and human sexuality concerns the flexibility of sexual behavior. When does it occur, how, and with whom? Compared to animals, we are much less automatic in our sexual activities, much more varied, much more affected by prior experience. Human sexuality is remarkably plastic and can be variously shaped by experience and by cultural patterns (see Chapter 14).

The difference between animal and human sexual behavior is especially marked when we consider the effects of hormones. In rats and cats, sexual behavior is highly dependent upon hormone levels; castrated males and spayed females stop copulating a few months after the removal of their gonads (Figure 10.14). In humans, on the other hand, sexual activity may persist for years, even decades, after castration or ovariectomy, provided that the operation was performed after puberty (Bermant and Davidson, 1974).

The liberation from hormonal control is especially clear in human females. To be sure, women are subject to a physiological cycle, but this has relatively little impact on sexual behavior, at least when compared to the profound effects seen in animals. The female rat or cat is chained to an estrus cycle that commands her to be receptive during one period and prevents her from being so at all other times. There are no such fetters on the human female, who is capable of sexual behavior at any time during her cycle and also more capable of refusing.

Although we are evidently not the vassals of our hormones that most animals are, this is not to say that hormonal factors have no effect. Androgen injections into men with abnormally low hormone levels will generally increase their sex drive (Davidson, 1986). An important demonstration of this concerns the effects of androgen administration on gay men. The androgen-injected gay person becomes more sexually active; but, contrary to a common misconception, his renewed sexual vigor is toward other males just as before (Kinsey, Pomeroy, and Martin, 1948).

Another demonstration of hormonal effects comes from studies of the menstrual cycle. While women can respond sexually at virtually all points of their cycle, there are still some variations within that period. Sexual desire and activity tend to be highest during the middle of the cycle, when ovulation occurs (Hamburg, Moos, and Yalom, 1968; Bancroft, 1986). These effects are not very pronounced; they probably represent a small remnant of the old animal estrus cycle, buried under layers of evolutionary change.

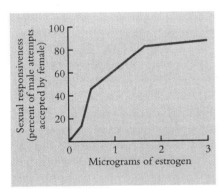

10.14   Estrogen and sexual behavior
The effect of estrogen injections on the sexual responsiveness of female rats was measured by the number of male attempts at mounting that were accepted by the female. The females' ovaries had been removed, so they could not produce estrogen themselves. The hormone was injected daily in the doses shown above. Sexual behavior was measured eight days after hormone treatment began. (After Bermant and Davidson, 1974)

EVOLUTION AND MATING SYSTEMS

In many species, the male and female part company after copulation and may very well never meet again. But in others, the partners remain together for a breeding season or even longer. In many cases, their arrangement involves *polygyny,* and the resulting family consists of one male, several females, and their various offspring. In a very few others, the mating system is *polyandry,* which works the other way around, with one female and several males. And in still others, the mating pattern is **monogamy,** with a reproductive partnership based on a special, more or less permanent tie between one male and one female.

MATING SYSTEMS IN ANIMALS

What accounts for the different mating systems found in different parts of the animal kingdom? A clue comes from the different patterns found in mammals and birds. Some 90 percent of all birds are monogamous: They mate and stay together throughout a breeding season. In contrast, more than 90 percent of all mammals are polygynous, with one male monopolizing a number of females. Why should this be so?

Evolutionary biologists seek the answer through some kind of evolutionary economics: The patterns that evolved are such as to maximize each individual's reproductive success. Consider the reproductive problem faced by birds. In many species, successful incubation requires both parents: one who sits upon the eggs, another who forages for food to nourish the bird that's sitting. After hatching, finding food for a nestful of hungry chicks may still require the full-time efforts of both birds. Under the circumstances, monogamy makes reproductive sense for both sexes: The father has to help the mother after she lays her eggs or else no chicks will survive into adulthood.

The situation is quite different for most mammals. Here there is no incubation problem; since the fetus grows within the mother's womb, she is still able to forage for her own food during the offspring's gestation. In addition, the mother has the exclusive job of feeding the offspring after birth, for only females can secrete the milk on which the infants live. Now the reproductive calculus leads to a different conclusion. The male does not have to invest time and effort in taking care of his offspring; instead, his best bet for maximizing his own reproductive success lies in mating with as many females as he possibly can. To accomplish this, he has to become attractive to females (by developing the most impressive antlers or whatever), and he has to win in the competition with many other males, all of whom have the identical goal. The end result is polygyny, with one successful male monopolizing a number of females.

There's an interesting anatomical correlate of mating arrangements in the animal kingdom. Almost invariably, polygyny is accompanied by **sexual dimorphism,** a pronounced anatomical difference in the size or bodily structures of the two sexes. The more polygynous the species, the more dimorphic it tends to be, with the males larger and often more ornamented than the females, as shown by the peacock's tail, the stag's antlers, and the male elephant seal's disproportionate size (Figure 10.15A). In contrast, monogamous species such as the gibbon show no such dimorphism (Figure 10.15B).

MATING PATTERNS IN HUMANS

A number of authors have tried to extend this general line of reasoning to account for the evolution of human sexual and mating behavior. One area of application concerns mate selection.

Mate selection   What determines who is a more desirable sexual or marital partner? Everyday observation suggests that in our society men and women choose on the basis of somewhat different criteria. One difference is the physical attractiveness of the partner which seems to be more important to men than to women. Another is age: By and large, men seem to prefer younger women, women to prefer men who are older than they. Yet another difference concerns the social and financial status of the partner, which seems to matter much more

Birds as monogamous   *Birds tend to mate and stay together during a mating season as both parents are needed for successful incubation of their young. Here a black-bowed albatross male courts a female on the nest that will serve as home for their offspring. (Photograph by Robert W. Hernández/The National Audubon Society Collection/Photo Researchers)*

A

B

10.15 Sexual dimorphism Polygynous species tend to be dimorphic. (A) A Hooker's sea lion bull with his harem. Note the bull's markedly larger size. (Photograph by Francisco J. Erize/Bruce Coleman Ltd.) (B) In Titi monkeys, which are monogamous, males and females are very similar in size and form. (Photograph © Jim Clare, Partridge Films/Oxford Scientific Films)

to women than it does to men. A number of studies by David Buss have shown that these male-female differences are not unique to our own society, but are found throughout the world, in countries as diverse as China, India, France, Nigeria, and Iran. In all cases, the results were the same: In evaluating the desirability of a potential mate, physical attractiveness and youth were more important to men, signs of good financial and social prospects were more important to women (Buss, 1989, 1992; Buss and Barnes, 1986).

Buss and his co-workers argue that these findings are consistent with an evolutionary point of view. As they see it, the mating preferences of both men and women were shaped by natural selection. The male's preference for a young female grows out of the fact that younger women tend to be more fertile than older ones (physical attractiveness is here seen as an outward sign of health and youth), while the female's preference for males of higher social and economic status is based on the potential benefits these resources may bring to her offspring. While Darwinian concerns may not be particularly relevant in determining the behavior of modern men and women, they did produce the mating preferences in our long dead prehistoric ancestors. They have therefore become a built-in preference pattern, even though their original biological point may no longer be relevant today.

Is this the only possible interpretation of Buss's findings? Some authors suggest that the greater value women seem to place on the status of their prospective mates may be a matter of economics rather than biology. Throughout much of the world men exercise greater economic influence and control than women do. (Just why is another issue.) To the extent that this is so, the male's economic position becomes critical to women because it determines both her and her children's economic future. This line of reasoning suggests that the gender difference in mate selection should be smaller in societies in which women have achieved a greater degree of economic parity. Whether this is actually so is still a matter of debate (Wallen, 1989).

Mating systems Another issue concerns human mating patterns. Sociobiologically oriented theorists start out with the observation that humans are somewhat dimorphic: On average, the human male is about 10 percent larger than the female. Since such dimorphism is correlated with polygyny in animals, one might expect some similar tendency in humans.

To bolster their case, sociobiologists refer to a number of findings that in their view point in this direction. One is the anthropological evidence. A review of

Polygynous tendencies in humans *The
archetype of the philandering male is Don
Juan, played here by John Barrymore. (From
the 1926 film* Don Juan, *with Mary Astor;
courtesy of the Motion Picture and Television
Photo Archive)*

185 cultures showed that the majority formally allowed polygyny. Only 16 percent of the cultures had monogamous marriage arrangements that permitted
only one spouse to each partner (Ford and Beach, 1951).★ Related findings
come from a number of studies of our own culture. These strongly suggest that,
on average, men have a greater desire for a variety of sexual partners than do
women (Symons, 1979).

Sociobiologists argue that these differences are ultimately rooted in our biological nature. In their view, men want greater sexual variety because for them it
is reproductively adaptive: The more women they mate with, the more children
they father. In contrast, women are much more cautious in evaluating potential
sexual partners and more interested in a stable, familial relationship—a good
reproductive strategy, since, as we've seen, the biological parental investment of a
human female is greater than a male's. Such built-in patterns are presumably no
longer relevant in a modern world in which birth control techniques have managed to uncouple sex from reproduction. But according to the sociobiologists,
these remnants of our biological past are still with us just the same. They were
once reproductively adaptive, and they continue to influence our behavior even
though their adaptive role is diminished or altogether gone.

This sociobiological account has been severely challenged. One line of attack
concerns the role of culture. Many critics argue that differences in sexual attitudes are a product of society rather than of biological predispositions and reflect
a cultural rather than a built-in double standard. In their opinion, polygyny is a
natural outgrowth of cultural conditions in which men are dominant and
women are perceived as property. As to the differences in men's and women's
desire for sexual variety, they regard it as a product of early social training: Boys
are taught that many sexual conquests are a proof of "manliness," while girls are
taught to value home and family and to seek a single partner.

By way of retort to this cultural critique, some writers point to the different
sexual practices of gay men and lesbians (Symons, 1979). It turns out that gay
men are much more interested in sexual variety than are lesbians. Until ten or
fifteen years ago, the sexual relations of gay men tended to be briefer, more
casual, and to involve many more partners than those of lesbians.† Thus one
study of 151 lesbians and 581 gay men in West Germany found that only 1 percent of the women reported having sexual relations with more than ten partners, while 61 percent of the men said they had (Schäfer, 1977). Such findings
have been interpreted as evidence for a biological rather than a cultural interpretation. This interpretation rests on the assumption that persons who have rejected the cultural norms for the sexual orientation of sex partners are unlikely to
have succumbed to a culturally induced standard for the *number* of partners.
Seen in this light, if gay men behave like heterosexual men and lesbians like heterosexual women, it is because of their biological nature—for in the last analysis,
they are men and women. But does this interpretation necessarily follow? It is
perfectly possible that the culture has taught gay men (no less than their heterosexual brothers) that being manly is to have a lot of sexual experiences and has
taught lesbians (no less than their heterosexual sisters) that a woman should be
faithful to just one partner (Gagnon and Simon, 1973).

Critics of the sociobiological approach have no quarrel with the sociobiologists' efforts to understand animal behavior in an evolutionary perspective.
Their critique is aimed at the attempt to extend these concepts to the human
level. After all, terms such as *monogamy* have quite a different meaning when

★ Note that this 16 percent figure applies to 185 different *cultures,* indicating that 30 of these cultures were monogamous. Of course, the percentage would be much higher if it were based on *individuals* rather than cultures, since the monogamous modern cultures (including our own) are much
more populous than most of the ones described in the anthropological literature.

† Some of these patterns have undoubtedly changed during the past decade in the wake of the
AIDS epidemic.

applied to, say, geese and humans. In geese, the term describes the fact that two parents stay together for one breeding season to hatch and raise their young; in humans, the term describes an arrangement that only makes sense in the context of a network of social and legal patterns. Evolution may have shaped many of our impulses and desires, but we simply don't know how these in turn have shaped the culture in which humans live and mate and bring up their children. Since this is so, it is rank speculation to assert that the reproductive economics that underlie an elephant seal's attempts to set up a harem are at bottom the same as those that account for the philandering found in some human males (Kitcher, 1985).

THE BIOLOGICAL BASIS OF LOVE: THE PARENT-CHILD BOND

There is another bond of love whose biological foundations are no less basic than those of the male-female tie—the relation between mother and child (and in many animals, the relation between father and child as well). In birds and mammals some kind of parental attachment is almost ubiquitous. In contrast to most fish and reptiles that lay eggs by the hundreds and then abandon them, birds and mammals invest in quality rather than quantity. They have fewer offspring, but they then see to it that most of their brood survives into maturity. They feed them, clean them, shelter them, and protect them during some initial period of dependency. While under this parental umbrella, the young animal can grow and become prepared for the world into which it must soon enter and can acquire some of the skills that will help it survive in that world. This period of initial dependency is longest in animals that live by their wits, such as monkeys and apes, and it is longest of all in humans.

THE INFANT'S ATTACHMENT TO THE MOTHER

In most birds and mammals, the young become strongly attached to their mother. Ducklings follow the mother duck, lambs the mother ewe, and infant monkeys cling tightly to the mother monkey's belly. In each case, separation leads to considerable stress: The young animals give piteous distress calls, and quack, bleat, and cry continuously until the mother returns. The biological function of this attachment is a simple matter of personal survival. This holds for humans as well as animals. For there is little doubt that in our early evolutionary history a motherless infant would probably have died an early death—of exposure, starvation, or predation. There are very few orphanages in nature.

The mechanisms that lead to this attachment will be discussed later (see Chapter 14). For now, we will only say that while some theorists believe that the main factor is the child's discovery that the mother's presence leads to the alleviation of hunger, thirst, and pain, there is strong evidence that the attachment is more basic than that. For the distress shown by the young—whether birds, monkeys, or humans—when they are separated from their mother occurs even when they are perfectly well-fed and housed. It appears that the infant's attachment to its mother is based on more than the satisfaction of the major bodily needs. The infant evidently comes predisposed to seek social stimulation, which is rewarding in and of itself.

Orangutan mother and child *(Photograph © Zefa Germany/The Stock Market, 1994)*

THE MOTHER'S ATTACHMENT TO THE INFANT

For the infant, the function of the mother-child bond is simple personal survival. For the mother, the biological function is again a matter of survival, but for her, the survival is genetic rather than personal, for unless her young survive into adulthood, her genes will perish. But what are the mechanisms that produce the mother's attachment? (And in many species, the father's attachment too). Robins and gibbons behave like proper parents: They care for their young and protect them. But they surely don't do this because they realize that their failure to act in this way would lead to genetic extinction. The real reason must lie elsewhere. One possibility is that there are some built-in predispositions toward parental behavior. If such predispositions do exist, they would then be favored by natural selection.

There is good evidence that the young of many animal species have a set of built-in responses that elicit caretaking from the parents. To give only one example, many baby birds open their mouths as wide as they can as soon as the parent arrives at the nest. This "gaping" response is their means of begging for food (see Figure 10.16). Some species of birds have special anatomical signs that help to elicit a proper parental reaction. An example is the Cedar Waxwing, whose bright red mouth lining evidently provides a further signal to the parent: I'm young, hungry, and a Cedar Waxwing!

Child care in humans is obviously more complex and flexible than it is in Cedar Waxwings, but it too has biological foundations. The mother-child relation grows out of a number of built-in reaction patterns, of child to mother and mother to child. The human infant begins life with a few relevant reflex patterns, including some that help him find the mother's nipple and suck at it once it is found. He also has an essentially innate signal system through which he tells the mother that he is in distress: He cries. Analogous *distress calls* are found in many animals, for when the young chirp, bleat, mew, or cry, the mother immediately runs to their aid and comforts them.

According to ethologists, evolution has further equipped the infant with a set of stimulus features that function as innate releasers of parental, and especially maternal, feelings. The cues that define "babyness" include a large, protruding forehead, large eyes, an upturned nose, chubby cheeks, and so on. Endowed with these distinctive properties, the baby looks "cute" and "cuddly," something to be picked up, fussed over, and taken care of. The case is similar for the young

10.16 Gaping in young birds (A) The gaping response of the young yellow warbler serves as a built-in signal that elicits the parents' feeding behavior. (Photograph by John Shaw/Bruce Coleman) (B) Cuckoos are parasites who lay their eggs in other birds' nests. The figure shows a young cuckoo being fed by its foster parent, a reed warbler. The young cuckoo, at about twenty-four hours old, instinctively ejects any eggs or young of its host from the nest, so that it alone is the sole occupant. Its large orange-red gaping mouth provides a powerful stimulus in eliciting feeding. The unwitting warbler will continue to feed the cuckoo even when it has grown to several times the "parent's" size. (Courtesy of Ian Wyllie, Monks Wood Experiment Station)

A

B

A

B

10.17   The stimulus features of "babyness"   *"Cute" characteristics of the "baby schema" are common to humans and a number of animals. (A) These include a rounded head shape, protruding forehead, and large eyes below the middle of the head (after Lorenz, 1943). (B) The Disney character Mickey Mouse became "cuter" over the years by subscribing more and more to the baby "schema," with his eyes and head becoming larger. (© Walt Disney Productions)*

of various animals who share aspects of the same "baby schema." Various commercial enterprises exploit these facts by devoting themselves to the deliberate manufacture of cuteness. Dolls and Walt Disney creatures are designed to be babied by children, while certain lap dogs are especially bred to be babied by adults (Figure 10.17).

Nature has provided the infant with yet another trick to disarm even the stoniest of parental hearts: the smile. In some fashion, smiling may begin within the first month; it is often considered a built-in signal by which humans tell each other "I wish you well. Be good to me." There is reason to believe that it is innate. Infants who are born blind smile under conditions that also produce smiling in sighted children, as when they hear their mother's voice. They obviously could not have learned this response by imitation.

COMMUNICATING MOTIVES

The preceding discussion has given ample testimony that many animal species exist within a social framework in much the same way that humans do. What one creature does often has a crucial effect on the behavior of another of its own kind. As we have seen, the major means of exerting such social influences is the signaling display.

EXPRESSIVE MOVEMENTS: ANIMAL DISPLAY

Displays represent a simple mode of communication whereby animals inform each other of what they are most likely to do in the immediate future. The crab waves its claws, and the wolf bares its fangs; these threat messages may save both sender and receiver from bodily harm if the message is heeded.

How do ethologists determine what message is conveyed by a given display? Since the sender is an animal, they cannot ask it directly. They can try, however, to infer the message by noting the correlation between a given display and the

A   B

The evolutionary origin of the human smile According to some authors, the human smile grew out of the "fear grin." This is an appeasement display found in monkeys and other primates, which usually signifies submission but may also indicate re-assurance when directed by a dominant animal to a subordinate (van Hooff, 1972). (A) The fear grin in a young chimpanzee. (Photograph © Tom McHugh/Photo Researchers, Inc., 1978) (B) A smile in an infant (Photograph © Luis Castaneda/The Image Bank)

animal's behavior just before and after its occurrence. For example, if a certain posture is generally followed by attack, then it is usually called a threat display; if it is usually followed by mating, it is probably a courtship signal, and so on.

Some ethologists interpret such correlations between displays and subsequent behavior by assuming that in effect displays communicate the animal's present motive state—its readiness to fight or to mate, its need for food or parental attention, and so forth. For this reason, displays are sometimes said to "express" the animal's inner state and are therefore described as ***expressive movements.***

THE EXPRESSION OF EMOTIONS IN HUMANS

In humans, built-in social displays are relegated to a lesser place. After all, we have the much richer communication system provided by human language. But even so, we do possess a set of displays that tells others something about our feelings and needs—our various emotional expressions.

THE UNIVERSALITY OF EMOTIONAL EXPRESSIONS

Humans have a sizable repertory of emotional expressions, most of them conveyed by the face. We smile, laugh, weep, frown, snarl, and grit our teeth. Are any of these expressive patterns our human equivalent of displays? If so, they should be universal to all humans and innately determined (Ekman, 1973; Ekman and Oster, 1979; Fridlund, Ekman, and Oster, 1983).

In one study, American actors posed in photographs to convey such emotions as fear, anger, and happiness. These pictures were then shown to members of different cultures, both literate (Swedes, Japanese, Kenyans) and preliterate (members of an isolated New Guinea tribe barely advanced beyond Stone Age culture). When asked to identify the portrayed emotion, all groups came up with quite similar judgments. The results were much the same when the procedure was reversed. The New Guinea tribesmen were asked to portray the emotions appropriate to various simple situations such as happiness at the return of a friend, grief at the death of a child, and anger at the start of a fight. Photographs of their performances were then shown to American college students who readily picked out the emotions the tribesmen had tried to convey (Figure 10.18).

10.18 Attempts to portray emotion by New Guinea tribesmen *Acting out emotions appropriate to various situations: (A) "Your friend has come and you are happy"; (B) "Your child has died"; (C) "You are angry and about to fight"; (D) "You see a dead pig that has been lying there for a long time." (© Paul Ekman, 1971)*

These results indicate that some emotional expressions may be common to all humans. This conclusion fits observations of children born blind. These children cry, smile, and laugh under essentially the same conditions that elicit these reactions in sighted children. In fact, much the same is true even of children born both blind and deaf. It would be hard to argue that these children had learned the emotional expressions considering that their sensory avenues of both sight and sound had been blocked off from birth (see Figure 10.19).

At least in part, such built-in expressions may serve a function similar to animal displays. They act as social signals by which we communicate our inner states to others, a way of saying what we are likely to do next.

THE ROLE OF CULTURE

These findings do not imply that smiling and other emotional expressions are unaffected by cultural conventions. According to some accounts, Melanese chieftains frown fiercely when greeting each other at a festive occasion, and Samurai mothers are said to have smiled upon hearing that their sons had fallen in battle (Klineberg, 1940). But such facts do not disprove the claim that facial expressions are built-in social signals; they only show that such signals can be artificially masked and modified. How and when such artifice comes into play, however, depends on the culture.

Some evidence for this view comes from studies in which American and Japanese subjects were presented with a harrowing documentary film of a primitive puberty rite. As they watched the film, their facial expressions were

10.19 The smile in blind children *(A) Smile in a child born blind. (Courtesy of The Lighthouse, N.Y.C.) (B) Smiling in a child born both blind and deaf. (Photograph © Tommy Thompson, 1992, Courtesy of Florida School for the Deaf and Blind, St. Augustine, Florida)*

403

A　　　　　　　　　　　**B**

10.20 Spontaneous facial expressions
(A) A Japanese and (B) an American student watched a film that depicted a rather gruesome scene. The figure shows their expressions when they were alone. Under these conditions, their facial expressions were virtually identical. But when they watched in the presence of another person, the Japanese masked his expression of unpleasant emotions more than the American did. (From Ekman and Friesen, 1975)

recorded with a hidden camera. The results showed that when alone, the facial reactions of the Japanese and American subjects were virtually identical (see Figure 10.20). But the results were quite different when the subject watched the film in the company of a white-coated experimenter. Now the Japanese looked more polite and smiled more than the Americans (Ekman, 1977; for further discussion, see Fridlund, 1990).

THE DIFFERENCE BETWEEN DISPLAY AND LANGUAGE

How are display repertories different from the communication achieved by human language? There is an obvious similarity. In both cases, the behavior of one organism affects that of its fellows. But the differences between these two communication systems far outweigh the similarities.

CREATING NEW MESSAGES

One obvious difference is in the complexity and flexibility of the two communicative systems. Consider the relative size of the two "vocabularies." Most mammals have some twenty to forty distinguishable display signals. This contrasts with an estimated vocabulary size of at least 50,000 words for the average human adult. The contrast is even sharper when we compare the way in which these vocabulary items are combined. Human language is based on a *productive* principle. Given the rules for putting words together (syntax), the speaker can construct any number of new messages that she has never heard before (see Chapter 9). Not so for animal displays. The display system is rigid. Each seal, robin, and rhesus monkey sends only messages that were sent by previous seals, robins, and rhesus monkeys. There is no room for originality in the language of display.

One reason is that in animal display systems there is no provision for rearrangements of parts so as to make a new whole. Consider the messages of the jackdaw. This bird has two distinct calls that beckon others to fly with it—a high-pitched call that sounds like *kia,* uttered when the jackdaw migrates southward in the autumn, and a lower-pitched call that sounds like *kiaw,* uttered when the bird returns home in the spring. Yet another jackdaw call is *zick-zick-zick,* which occurs during courtship. There is also an angry, rattlelike sound, emitted when the jackdaw is about to attack an enemy (Lorenz, 1952). These various calls are useful in helping the jackdaw communicate with its fellows, but they should not be considered as the analogues of words in a language. If they were, the jackdaw should be able to shuffle the individual calls to create new and ever more complex messages. They might produce a sentence in Jackdawese: *"Kia, rattle-rattle; Kiaw, zick-zick-zick."* Freely translated, this sentence might read, "Let's fly south to fight the enemy and then fly home to make love." No jackdaw—nor indeed, any animal but humans—has ever achieved such a linguistic feat.

THE CONTENT OF THE MESSAGES

Thus far, we've looked at the difference between the ways displays and true language systems express their messages. But there also tends to be a difference in what the messages convey. For the most part, displays are a way of telling a fellow creature what one is about to do. In effect, they are statements about the sender's interpersonal motives at a given time and place. If this is indeed what most displays are about, we can understand why the relative poverty of the system is no barrier to communication. There is no need for a large vocabulary or a productive combinatorial system because there is a limit on the number of things an animal wants to do to (or with) another of its own kind: flee, attack, feed or be fed by, groom or be groomed by, copulate, and a few others.★

In contrast, human language must precisely describe the world outside and is thus virtually unlimited in its topics. For this, a productive system is absolutely crucial. The variety of possible events and relationships in the world is infinite, and only a system that is capable of an infinite number of utterances can do justice to this variety.

Some evidence for a fundamental difference in the content of the messages of display and of human language comes from our own experience. We obviously don't use our display systems to tell others about the external world. We don't smile, blush, or embrace so as to inform each other about the Pythagorean theorem or the leak in the upstairs toilet. But conversely, we sometimes feel "at a loss for words" to express emotion and motive (the proper content of display messages). Such matters are often difficult to put into words, or at least words seem inadequate when we finally manage to do so. "I love you" is hard to say and, even if said, is somehow not enough. "I'm very sorry" is pallid as an expression of grief or consolation. In these situations, the more primitive display system is more appropriate because the signal to be sent concerns interpersonal feelings. The beloved is touched, the bereaved is cradled, and these "simple" gestures somehow seem right. Nothing more is gained by speech, because what matters has already been displayed.

(Photograph by Benny Ortiz)

SOCIAL COGNITION IN PRIMATES

Human social life obviously involves both motives and cognition (as we will discuss in the next chapter). Our lives revolve around what we desire from and of other people, be they friends or enemies, strangers or lovers, parents or children,

---

★ This statement has to be qualified, for some primates may have displays that signal different kinds of predators. Thus vervet monkeys have different alarm calls for eagles, leopards, and pythons (Seyfarth, Cheney, and Marler, 1980; Cheney and Wrangham, 1986). But while this adds some measure of complexity, it can't begin to compare to the incredible richness of human language.

Understanding kinship relationships in primates *This group of female vervet monkeys is looking at the mother of an infant who just gave an alarm call. Apparently, they know who in their group is related to whom. (Photograph courtesy of Dorothy Cheney)*

but also around what we know and think about them. Some recent studies of monkeys and apes indicate that there are many forerunners of such social cognitions in the animal world.

Consider the vervet, a small monkey that lives in groups of some fifteen animals or so and that makes its home primarily in the savanna woodlands of Africa. To a vervet, the most important thing in the world—right after not being eaten by an eagle or a leopard—is other vervets. Vervet monkeys can recognize other vervets in their troop by sight and sound. A demonstration comes from some elegant field studies performed by Dorothy Cheney and Robert Seyfarth. Cheney and Seyfarth set up camp near several vervet groups in Southern Kenya, tape recorded the screams of many of the vervets, and then played them back to their fellows at strategic times. On one occasion, they broadcast the distress cry of a juvenile to its mother and two other nearby females who also had offspring in the group. At the time all of the offspring were out of sight. The first result concerned the mother who looked in the direction of the (hidden) loud speaker and approached it, indicating that she recognized her screaming youngster's voice. More interesting yet was the behavior of the other two females. They did not look at the loudspeaker, nor did they look at each other, but instead looked *at the mother.* This suggests that they not only recognized the child's voice, but also recognized whose child it was, as if to say "It's *your* kid. So what are *you* going to do about it?" (Cheney and Seyfarth, 1982).

Evidence of this sort indicates that monkeys have a considerable degree of knowledge of the kinship and relationships in their group (e.g., Dasser, 1988). Further studies suggest that they also know a great deal about the dominance relationships in their group—who's up, who's down, and who's in-between. As a result, they can pretty well predict who's likely to chase or cuff them and who is not, and they can then behave according to these beliefs. But do monkeys think that other monkeys also have thoughts and beliefs? To ask this question is to ask whether these animals have what has often been called a "theory of mind," that is, whether they attribute states of mind such as beliefs and desires to others (Premack, 1978, 1988; Fodor, 1992; see also Chapter 4, p. 146–47).★ One way of determining whether they do is to see whether they can use deliberate deception to induce a false belief in another individual. There is a suggestion that some monkeys and apes are intelligent enough (and immoral enough) to do so.

Some suggestive evidence comes from several anecdotes about vervet monkeys. On one occasion, two vervet troops clashed at the boundary of their two territories. One of the two battling groups was about to lose when one of the combatants suddenly ran up a nearby tree and gave a leopard alarm call. In actual fact, there was no leopard around, but every one of the vervets acted as if there was and frantically raced for the nearest tree. The result was a return to the status quo with defeat averted and the old borders restored. The alarm caller's deception may have saved the day (Cheney and Seyfarth, 1990).

More compelling evidence comes from a laboratory study in which a chimpanzee saw a desirable piece of fruit being placed in one of two containers while the other was left empty. Unfortunately the containers were too far removed to be reached through the bars of the cage. As a result, the apes had to rely on the good offices of an attendant who stood outside the cage in easy reach of the containers. The trouble was that this attendant had not been there when the food was placed, so that he didn't know which of the two containers held the food. As a result, there was only one way in which the chimpanzees could get the food: They somehow had to tell the attendant—by looking at the correct

★ We will later encounter that same question raised about children below four or four-and-a-half years of age (see Chapter 13, pp. 515–16).

container or by pointing with hand or foot—which of the two containers was the correct one.

After a while, the animals learned to do this rather well, but then the experimenter introduced an unkind complication. He now used two attendants, one "good," the other "bad." The good one was all a chimpanzee could possibly ask for: Whenever he found food in a container, he gave it to the ape. The bad attendant was a self-seeking egotist: Whenever he found food in a container, he ate it himself. This eventually led the chimpanzees to develop a different strategy. They now gave proper signals to the good but not to the bad attendant. One of four chimpanzees went further and actively misled the bad attendant by pointing to the *incorrect* container with her foot (Woodruff and Premack, 1989; for some complicating evidence, see Premack, 1988). To the extent that these animals could deliberately deceive another individual, they demonstrated that they believed others have beliefs and that these beliefs may be (and in the case of the bad attendant, should be) different from their own. It is perhaps ironic that a certain level of immorality requires a fairly high degree of intellectual comprehension: Adam and Eve could not lie until *after* they had eaten from the tree of knowledge.

Such findings suggest that chimpanzees (and perhaps monkeys too) have something like a theory of mind. But there is little doubt that this chimpanzoid theory is rather primitive and doesn't begin to approach the complexities of our own adult conceptions of how other people think, feel, and believe. Our own human social interactions depend not just on what any of us think and believe about other people, but also on what we think or believe they think and believe about us. Such mutual cognitions are a commonplace of everyday life (e.g., "I think most of my acquaintances like me, and they probably think I like them too, but Joe and Jane seem to feel otherwise, and I don't really know why . . ." and so on). To us, the fact that others have thoughts and wishes and beliefs is an axiom. As we will see in the next chapter, it is an axiom from which most of our social behavior flows directly.

SELF-SACRIFICE AND ALTRUISM

The preceding pages have provided ample evidence that animals are certainly social: They fight and compete with each other, mate, reproduce, and communicate. Some even make judgments about what their fellows think and use that information to their own advantage. Still further work by ethologists suggests that under certain conditions they may even behave as if they were "unselfish altruists."

It's of course well known that many animals go to considerable lengths to defend their offspring. Various birds have evolved characteristic ways of feigning injury such as dropping one wing and paddling around in circles to draw a predator away from their nests (see Figure 10.21). On the face of it, such acts appear heroically unselfish, for the parents court the danger that the predator will seize them. But here again we come up with the difference between personal and genetic survival. For what seems unselfish from the vantage of the individual looks different from a biological point of view (Wilson, 1975). The mother bird who does not divert a potential attacker may very well live longer because she has played it safe. But from an evolutionary perspective what counts is not her own survival but the survival of her genes. And these are more likely to perish if she flies off to safety; while she hides in the bushes, the marauding cat will eat her chicks. As a result, she will have fewer offspring to whom she

10.21 A misleading display *In feigning injury, the killdeer, a small American bird, runs and flies erratically from predators that approach its nest, often flopping about as if it has a broken wing. (Photograph by Wayne Lankinen/Bruce Coleman)*

407

can pass on her genes, including the very gene or genes that underlie her maternal indifference. Those of her offspring that do survive will in turn have fewer offspring, and so on, until her genetic attributes disappear.

ALTRUISM IN ANIMALS

Seen in this light, parental self-sacrifice can be understood in evolutionary terms. Can a similar analysis be applied to unselfish acts that benefit individuals other than one's own children? Such apparently altruistic acts are found in various animal species.* A case in point is the warning signal given off by many species at the approach of a predator (see Figure 10.22). When a robin sees a hawk overhead, it gives an *alarm call,* a special cry that alerts all members of the flock and impels them to seek cover. This alarm call is based on a built-in, inherited tendency and is essentially unlearned. All robins emit this cry when in danger, and they do so even if raised in complete isolation from their fellows. There is no doubt that this alarm benefits all robins who hear it. They crouch low and hide, so their chances of escape are enhanced. But what does it gain the bird who sounds the alarm? Doesn't it place him in greater danger by increasing the likelihood that the hawk will detect *him?* Why does the robin play the hero instead of quietly stealing away and leaving his fellows to their fate? There are several possible factors, each of which may play a role.

ENLIGHTENED SELF-INTEREST

One possibility is that this act of avian heroism is not as unselfish as it seems, for it may well increase the warner's own chance of personal survival in the long run. If a particular robin spies a hawk and remains quiet, there is a greater chance that some bird in the flock will be captured, most likely another bird. But what about tomorrow? A hawk who has seized a prey in a particular location will probably return to the very same place in search of another meal. And this meal may be the very same robin who originally minded his own business and stayed uninvolved (Trivers, 1971).

KIN SELECTION

There is another alternative. Let us assume that our heroic robin is unlucky, is seized by the hawk, and dies a martyr's death. While this act may have caused the robin to perish as an individual, it may well have served to preserve some of that bird's genes. This may be true even if none of the birds in the flock are the hero's own offspring. They may be relatives who carry some of his genes, brothers and sisters who share half of the same genes, or nieces and nephews who share one-fourth. If so, the alarm call may have saved several relatives who carry the alarm-calling gene and who will pass it on to future generations of robins. From an evolutionary point of view, the alarm call had survival value—if not for the alarm caller or its offspring, then for the alarm-calling gene (Hamilton, 1964; Maynard-Smith, 1965).

According to this view, altruistic behavior will evolve if it promotes the survival of the individual's kin. This *kin-selection* hypothesis predicts that unselfish behavior should be more common among relatives than unrelated individuals. There is some evidence that this is indeed the case. Certain deer snort loudly

10.22 Alarm call *Ground squirrels give alarm calls when they sense a nearby predator. Such alarm calls are more likely to be given by females than males. The females usually have close relatives living nearby. As a result, their alarm call is more likely to benefit genetically related rather than unrelated individuals, which suggests that it is based on kin selection. (Photograph by Georg D. Lepp/Bio-Tec Images)*

---

*In modern biological usage, the term *altruism* is reserved for cases in which the good deed benefits neither the doers nor their own offspring.

when alarmed, which alerts other deer that are nearby. Groups of does tend to be related; bucks, who disperse when they get old enough, are less likely to be related. The kin-selection hypothesis would then predict that does should be more likely to give the alarm snort than bucks. This is indeed what happens. Similar results have been obtained for various other species (Hirth and McCullough, 1977; Sherman, 1977).

RECIPROCAL ALTRUISM

There is yet another possible mechanism that leads to biologically unselfish acts—*reciprocal altruism.* Some animals—and we may well be among them—may have a built-in Golden Rule: Do unto others, as you would have them do unto you (or unto your genes). If one individual helps another, and that other later reciprocates, the ultimate upshot is a benefit to both. For example, male baboons sometimes help each other in aggressive encounters, and the one who received help on one occasion is more likely to come to the other's assistance later on (Packer, 1977).

A built-in predisposition toward reciprocity may well be one of the biological foundations of altruism in some animals (and perhaps ourselves as well). If the original unselfish act doesn't exact too great a cost—in energy expended or in danger incurred—then its eventual reciprocation will yield a net benefit to both parties. A tendency toward reciprocal altruism of this kind, however, presupposes relatively stable groups in which individuals recognize one another. It also presupposes some safeguards against "cheating," accepting help without reciprocating. One such safeguard might be a link between a disposition toward altruism and a disposition to punish cheaters (Trivers, 1971).

ALTRUISM IN HUMANS

There is little doubt that humans are capable of considerable self-sacrifice. Soldiers volunteer for suicide missions, and religious martyrs burn at the stake. In addition to these awesome deeds of heroism are the more common acts of altruism—sharing food and money, offering help, and the like. Can such human acts of altruism be understood in the biological terms that apply to the alarm calls of birds and monkeys?

THE SOCIOBIOLOGISTS' VIEW

According to Edward Wilson, the founder of sociobiology, the answer is yes, at least to some extent. While Wilson emphasizes the enormous variations among human social systems, he notes that there are certain common themes, which he regards as grounded in our genetic heritage. Of these, the most important is based on kinship. Wilson and other sociobiologists suggest that, by and large, we will be most altruistic to our closest relatives. According to Wilson, the person who risks death in battle or through martyrdom probably helps to ensure the survival of the group of which he is a member—and thus of his own genes, since this group probably includes his own kin. As with the robin, the individual hero may die, but his genes will survive (Wilson, 1975, 1978).

Sociobiologists believe that this position is supported by the fact that kinship is of considerable importance in just about all human societies, as attested to by the elaborate terms used to describe the precise nature of kinship relations: brother, sister, uncle, aunt, cousin, second-cousin-once-removed, and so on. At least in our culture, the likelihood that one person will make a sacrifice for another increases the closer the two are genetically related to each other. In one

Braving death for an ideal *During the Civil War, a vastly outnumbered group of black Union soldiers attacked an impregnable fortress held by the Confederate forces, suffering enormous casualties. They were willing to die for the abolition of slavery and to show that blacks are just as capable of sacrificing themselves for an ideal as whites are. From the 1989 film* Glory, *directed by Edward Zwick. (Photograph courtesy of Photofest)* study, a fairly large sample of American women was asked who had helped them on occasions when they required assistance (of money, emotional support, and so on). The results showed that they were three times more likely to have been helped by their parents, siblings, or children (who share half their genes) than by half-siblings, aunts, uncles, nieces, nephews, and grandchildren or grandparents (who share only a quarter of their genes). This is not to say that genetically unrelated friends (let alone husbands) did not provide help, for indeed they did. But according to the authors, help among friends was probably based on reciprocal altruism. If a subject's friend gave her money (or time or emotional support), there was a mutual expectation that the assistance would be reciprocated at some later time. Among kin, such expectation of later repayment was less common (Essock-Vitale and McGuire, 1985).

Other sociobiologists have expanded this kinship-selection argument even further. As they see it, kinship selection underlies a human tendency toward *tribalism*—putting the welfare of one's own group ahead of others. This argument has further consequences. The individual's own resources are usually limited, but we have seen that even so he will often share them with his kin. But for the same reasons he is more likely to engage in conflict outside his immediate kin, and by extension, outside of his tribe.

> Me against my brother; me and my brother against our cousins; me, my brother, and my cousins against our friends; me, my brothers, cousins, and friends against our enemies in the village; all of these and the whole village against the next village. . . . (Old Arab proverb)

Seen in the light of this sociobiological perspective, human nature appears in a grim and unflattering light. Acts that seem altruistic turn out to be self-serving (at least genetically so). Kinship altruism may prompt us to help brothers, sisters, and cousins, but it turns us against all others of our kind. And reciprocal altruism may impel us to be generous, but only in so far as today's generosity is likely to be repaid tomorrow.

SOME PROBLEMS OF FACT AND THEORY: BIOLOGY OR CULTURE?

This sociobiological analysis of human altruism is highly controversial. To begin with, studies of different cultures show that the degree to which relatives help each other is not a simple function of their genetic closeness. It often depends much more on whether individuals *regard* themselves as close and related than on whether they actually are so genetically. Some evidence comes from the study of several cultures in which newly married couples live in the groom's father's household and eventually create an extended family with many brothers, sisters, uncles, aunts, and so on. A young boy in this family will get to know his paternal uncles—they will live in the same hut or one nearby. But he won't have much to do with his maternal uncles; they stayed behind in his maternal grandfather's household. Genetically, he is of course equally close to both, but when questioned about whom he is more likely to help or be helped by, he immediately says that it is the paternal uncle, whom he has known and lived with all his life (Sahlins, 1976).

Critics of sociobiology feel that these and similar findings show that human social behavior depends crucially on culture rather than genetics. To understand human altruism, we have to understand it in its own social terms. The Polynesian boy who feels close to his paternal but not his maternal uncle is responding to kinship as his culture describes it, rather than as something

SELF-SACRIFICE AND ALTRUISM

Human martyrdom *In their darkest hour, Joan of Arc, an unlettered peasant, arose to lead the French against the British during the Hundred Years' War. After several brilliant successes, she was finally captured and burned at the stake by the British. Can we really attribute the actions of a Joan of Arc to kin selection or reciprocal altruism? (From the 1957 film* Saint Joan, *directed by Otto Preminger and starring Jean Seberg; photo courtesy of Photofest)*

defined by his genes. The same holds for self-sacrifice. The ancient Romans fell on their swords when defeated, not to save their brothers' genes, but to save their honor. The early Christians defied death because of a religious belief rather than to maintain a particular gene pool. We cannot comprehend the ancient Romans without considering their concept of honor, nor can we explain the martyrdom of the early Christians without reference to their belief in the hereafter.

This is not to say that in unraveling the cultural contexts of these acts we have explained them fully. We surely have not. After all, not all defeated Romans fell on their swords, nor did all early Christians choose martyrdom. There is much about human altruism that is still a mystery. But any attempt to solve this mystery must include some reference to the cultural conditions in which such human acts occur. Our human genetic makeup is relevant, but this relevance is almost surely indirect. Our genes allow us to have a culture; they make us sociable; they give us the capacity for culture; they endow us with the enormous gift for learning on which culture rests. But they don't explain the products of culture directly. And according to Wilson's critics, one such human cultural product is altruism.

To sum up, Wilson and other sociobiologists have argued that human social behaviors such as altruism and self-sacrifice are at bottom biological adaptations that guarantee the survival of the reproductively fittest—in principle no different from the social patterns found in primates and in lower animals. The critics of this view do not deny the powerful influence of biology on human behavior. But they insist that human social behavior is so thoroughly infused by culture—by moral and religious beliefs, by customs, by art—that the analogy to animal behavior is more misleading than informative. This issue is still being hotly debated in the fields of psychology, biology, and anthropology, and we cannot solve it here. But we will return to it when we discuss altruistic behavior as it is studied by modern social psychologists (see Chapter 12, pp. 456–60).

SOME PROBLEMS OF ETHICS

There is a final issue that concerns some of the ethical implications of the sociobiological position. Suppose the sociobiologists' assertions about humans are true—that men are biologically predisposed toward philandering and women toward coyness, and that all of us are genetically biased toward hostile tribalism. All of these suppositions are vehemently disputed (see, for example, Lewontin, Rose, and Kamin, 1984; Kitcher, 1985, 1987). But for the sake of argument, let's assume that they are true. What then? Does this mean that these (supposed) biological facts justify sexism, or vindicate the double standard, or support a blind hostility toward everyone who is different from ourselves? The answer is an emphatic no. If the facts are as the sociobiologists claim they are (and we have repeatedly said that this is highly debatable), then philandering may be a biological predisposition in males and may be in that sense *natural.* But what is natural isn't necessarily good. A preference for sweets is biologically built in and has a perfectly understandable evolutionary function, for what's sweet is generally also nutritious. But in these days of caloric plenty, most of us learn to curb our natural appetite for sweets or suffer various unpleasant consequences. The same surely holds for whatever callous and self-seeking built-in tendencies we may have but that as civilized men and women we must morally deplore.

This point is recognized by a number of sociobiologists. Sarah Hrdy, an authority on primate behavior, stated it succinctly by quoting the character played by Katharine Hepburn in the film *The African Queen:* "Nature, Mr. Allnutt, is what we were put on this earth to rise above!" (Hrdy, 1988, p. 126).

ETHOLOGY AND HUMAN NATURE

Over three hundred years have passed since Hobbes described the "war of all against all," which he regarded as the natural state of all humankind. We are still far from having a definite description of our basic social nature. But at least we know that Hobbes's solutions are wrong or oversimplified. Humans are not built so as to be solitary. Other people are a necessary aspect of our lives, and a tendency to interact with others is built into us at the very outset. What holds for humans holds for most animals as well. The robin is pre-programmed to deal with other robins, the baboon with other baboons. Some of these interactions are peaceful, while others are quarrelsome. What matters is that there is always some intercourse between like and like. This social intercourse is an essential aspect of each creature's existence, as shown by an elaborate repertory of built-in social reactions that govern reproduction, care of offspring, and intraspecies competition at virtually all levels of the animal kingdom. No man is an island; neither is any other animal.

SUMMARY

1. Are humans inherently asocial and self-centered? Thomas Hobbes believed that they are. An alternative position, championed by Charles Darwin among others, is that both humans and animals have built-in social dispositions. The study of such innate bases of social reactions has largely focused on animal behavior and has been undertaken within the domain of *ethology.* An influential theoretical approach is *sociobiology,* which tries to explain the emergence of social behaviors in both animals and humans within the framework of evolutionary principles.

2. Most animals exhibit various *species-specific* behaviors, which were once thought to be based on *fixed-action patterns* that are triggered by *releasing stimuli.* An example is the begging response of newly hatched herring gulls. Many of these species-specific reactions are *displays,* which serve as communicative signals.

3. One realm of social behavior that has important biological roots is *aggression,* a term generally reserved for conflict between members of the same species. To secure a supply of resources for themselves and their descendants, many animals (usually the males) stake out a *territory* that they then defend. Various methods have evolved to keep aggression within bounds, including territoriality, which separates potential combatants in space, and *dominance hierarchies,* which separate them in social status. Further limitations on aggression include *threat* and *appeasement displays.*

4. While there are certain parallels between aggression among animals and among humans—for example, territoriality and *personal space*—there is reason to suppose that most of the underlying mechanisms are different in that human aggression depends in great part upon learning and culture.

5. Built-in predispositions figure heavily in various aspects of sexual reproduction. Various displays advertise the animal's sex, its readiness to mate, and its species. Examples are *courtship rituals,* which are highly species-specific and tend to prevent animals from interbreeding with members of other species.

6. Sexual behavior is partially controlled by several sex hormones. In mammals, a male hormone, *testosterone,* or a female hormone, *estrogen,* stimulates cells in the hypothalamus that trigger sexual activity. Female animals only mate when they are in *estrus,*

SUMMARY

the time during which the ovum is ready for fertilization. The female's estrus cycle depends on the interplay of estrogen, which stimulates the development of the ovum and makes the animal sexually receptive, and *progesterone,* another female hormone that prepares the uterus to receive the embryo.

7.   In humans, sexual behavior is more flexible and less dependent upon hormonal conditions than it is in animals. Thus, human females are capable of sexual behavior at any time in their cycle.

8.   Animals have evolved a number of different mating systems. In some, the pattern is *polygyny,* with one male and several females. In others, it is *monogamy,* with a more or less permanent tie between one male and one female. In a very few others, it is *polyandry,* with one female and several males. According to sociobiologists, the mating systems that evolved are such as to maximize each participant's reproductive success. Thus birds tend to be monogamous, while mammals are likely to be polygynous. Polygyny is generally accompanied by *sexual dimorphism,* a pronounced anatomical difference in the size or bodily structures of the two sexes.

9.   The majority of human cultures practice (or practiced) polygyny, and evidence from our own culture suggests that men have a greater desire for sexual variety than do women. Viewed from a sociobiological perspective, these differences are rooted in our biological nature. Seen from a cultural perspective, they are the product of early social training, which in turn is an outgrowth of cultural and economic conditions.

10.   In birds and mammals innate factors are an important determinant of another bond, that between parents—primarily mothers—and offspring. Parental reactions are elicited, at least in part, by various stimulus releasers produced by the young, such as *distress calls* and the human infant's smile.

11.   The key to most animal social behavior is communication by means of displays. Since displays communicate an animal's present motive state, they are often described as *expressive movements.* Displays are found in humans as well as animals. The major example is emotional expression. Many facial expressions seem to be partially based on built-in predispositions; one demonstration is smiling in children born blind. But such facial expressions are also affected by cultural conventions and can be voluntarily inhibited or "faked."

12.   While both display repertoires and human language are communications systems, they differ in some important regards. Display systems have a much smaller vocabulary, have no system for rearranging the individual signals to create new "sentences," and only convey something about the sender's present intentions. Human languages have a large vocabulary, have some syntactic system that can rearrange words to form an infinite number of sentences, and can convey messages about just about anything in the world.

13.   There has been some recent interest in *social cognition* in animals, especially monkeys and apes. These animals have a considerable knowledge of the kinship and dominance relations in their group and may have some primitive version of a "theory of mind" that allows them to attribute beliefs and desires to others.

14.   Some inherited behavior patterns, such as the *alarm calls* of certain birds, seem to be biologically unselfish since they don't directly contribute to the survival of the individuals or their offspring. The survival value of these behaviors often depends on *kin selection,* for such acts may save a number of relatives who carry the "altruist's" genes. Another mechanism that may lead to biologically unselfish acts is *reciprocal altruism.* Some authors have tried to explain human altruism in similar sociobiological terms, emphasizing the relation between kin selection and *tribalism.* This attempt, like other attempts by sociobiologists to interpret human social patterns based on analogies to animal behavior, is highly controversial.

CHAPTER **11**

SOCIAL COGNITION AND EMOTION

SOCIAL COGNITION AND SOCIAL REALITY 416

THE INTERPERSONAL NATURE OF BELIEF ■ SOCIAL COMPARISON ■ COGNITIVE PROCESSES AND BELIEF

ATTITUDES 420

ATTITUDES AND BEHAVIOR ■ ATTITUDE CHANGE ■ ATTITUDE STABILITY

PERCEIVING OTHERS 426

FORMING IMPRESSIONS ■ IMPRESSIONS OF OTHERS AS PATTERNS ■ IMPRESSIONS OF OTHERS AS COGNITIVE CONSTRUCTIONS ■ IMPRESSION MANAGEMENT

ATTRIBUTION 432

ATTRIBUTION AS A RATIONAL PROCESS ■ ERRORS IN THE ATTRIBUTION PROCESS

PERCEIVING ONESELF 437

THE SELF-CONCEPT ■ SELF-PERCEPTION AND ATTRIBUTION

EMOTION: PERCEIVING ONE'S OWN INNER STATES 439

THE JAMES-LANGE THEORY ■ THE ATTRIBUTION-OF-AROUSAL THEORY ■ BEYOND ATTRIBUTION-OF-AROUSAL THEORY ■ COMPLEX EMOTIONS ■ EMOTION AND THE THEATER

TAKING STOCK 449

SUMMARY 450

I n the preceding chapter, we considered the built-in bases of social behavior. Toward that end, we turned to the animal kingdom and looked at social interactions among robins and grebes, rats and baboons. None of these animals lives in isolation from its fellows, and their interactions tell us something about the biological foundations upon which all social life rests, whether in animals or ourselves. Both animals and humans compete in aggressive encounters, court and mate, provide for their young, and have a repertoire of built-in displays. But these similarities aside, there are of course enormous differences. While the social behavior of animals is relatively rigid and inflexible, that of humans is greatly affected by learning—based on personal experience as well as the experience of previous generations. And our social interactions are vastly more complex than those of any other animal.

In part, this is simply because human social behavior occurs within an elaborate web of cultural patterns. Unlike rats or baboons, we attend school, vote, buy stock, go to church, and join protest demonstrations. These and countless other actions only make sense because of a whole set of institutions around which most of our social life is organized.

But in addition there are cognitive factors. For most of our social interactions depend on how we understand the situation in which they occur. As we've seen, something of that sort also goes on at the animal level, especially among the primates, who show a considerable degree of social understanding and may even possess some forerunners of a theory of mind. But their level of social cognition—surprising as it may be—can't begin to compare to the richness and complexity of our own. A monkey's theory of mind is at best a mere rudiment of a human's. The world we live in is built upon an intricate network of interlocking social cognitions. We take for granted that others have desires and beliefs, and know that they in their turn know that we too have desires and beliefs. This cognitive mutuality can reach dizzying heights as in the calculations of a poker player musing about an opponent: "I think that he thinks that I think that he's bluffing."

The contrast between human and animal social behavior becomes even clearer when we turn away from primates to other animals, such as birds. Take the herring gull, which pecks at its neighbor when it comes too close. This is sometimes regarded as analogous to our desire to maintain our personal space, and in some ways it may be. But the differences between their actions and ours are no less striking than the similarities. Consider personal space in a railroad car. Suppose you are all alone in the car and a stranger approaches and sits next to you. Your reaction depends upon your interpretation of his action. Is it an attempt to start a conversation, an unwelcome intrusion, a sexual invitation? Or is it simply a response to the fact that all other seats in the car happen to be covered with soot? The point is that humans don't respond to other people's actions automatically; they respond to those actions as they interpret them. The herring gull has no such subtle problems; any other gull that invades its personal space has to be repelled and that is that.★

★ In actual fact, things aren't quite this simple even in birds, for their reactions also depend on various contextual factors (see Smith, 1977). But there is no doubt that these modifying factors are much less complex and flexible than they are in humans.

We react to any situation as we understand it to be The misunderstandings that may occur can form the plot of tragedy as well as comedy. In Shakespeare's Othello, *the hero strangles his wife because he wrongly believes she committed adultery. In the movie* Tootsie, *the hero disguises himself as a woman with resulting complications in his social relations. (From a production of* Othello *at the 1987 Stratford Festival in Ontario, Canada, with Howard Rollins and Wenna Shaw; photograph by Michael Cooper; and the 1982 film* Tootsie, *with Dustin Hoffman and Jessica Lange; courtesy of Photofest)*

The purpose of this chapter is to give some sense of the complexity of social cognition in humans. We will organize our account around one of the central questions of modern social psychology: How does an individual interpret social events and how does this interpretation affect his or her actions?

SOCIAL COGNITION AND SOCIAL REALITY

An individual's response to a social situation depends upon what he understands that situation to be. Romeo killed himself in front of Juliet's tomb because he thought that Juliet was dead; had he known that she was only drugged, the play would have had a happy ending. This simple point forms the basis for much of modern social psychology. But many modern social psychologists make an important further assertion: The way in which we interpret and try to comprehend such social events—that is, the nature of *social cognition*—is in principle no different from the way in which we interpret and try to comprehend any event whatsoever, whether social or not.

THE INTERPERSONAL NATURE OF BELIEF

Seen in this light, many facets of social psychology are simply an aspect of the psychology of thinking and cognition in general. But over and above this, social cognition has certain features that make it uniquely social. For there is no doubt that much of what we know, we know because of others. The primary medium of this cognitive interdependence is of course human language, which allows us to share our discoveries and pass them on to the next generation. As a result, we look at the world not just through our own eyes but also through the eyes of others, and we form our beliefs on the basis of what we've heard them say or what they have written. In fact, our very notion of physical reality is at least in part a matter of mutual agreement. This point was made very dramatically in a classic study performed by Solomon Asch (Asch, 1956).

In Asch's experiment, nine or ten subjects were brought together in a laboratory room and shown pairs of cards placed a few feet in front of them. On one card was a black line, say, 8 inches long. On the other card were three lines of varying lengths, say 6 1/4, 8, and 6 3/4 inches (Figure 11.1). The subjects were

11.1   The stimulus cards in Asch's social pressure experiment *The cards are drawn to scale. In the actual experiment, they were generally placed on the ledge of a blackboard, separated by forty inches. (Asch, 1956)*

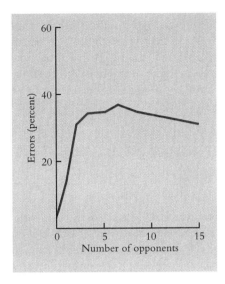

11.2 The effect of social pressure *The extent to which the subject yielded in relation to the size of the group pitted against him is demonstrated by this figure. In this situation, the effect of group size seems to reach a maximum at three, though other studies (such as Gerard, Wilhelmy, and Conolley, 1968) have found that conformity continues to rise beyond this point as the number of opponents increases. (After Asch, 1955)*

The subject in a social pressure experiment *(A) The true subject (center) listens to the instructions. (B) On hearing the unanimous verdict of the others, he leans forward to look at the cards more carefully. (C) After twelve such trials, he explains that "he has to call them as he sees them." (Photographs by William Vandivert)*

asked to make a simple perceptual judgment. They had to indicate which of the three lines on the one card was equal in length to the one line on the other card. Then the experimenter told the subjects that this procedure was only a minor prelude to another study and casually asked them, in the interest of saving time, to indicate their judgments aloud by calling them out in turn (the three comparison lines were designated by the numbers 1, 2, and 3 printed underneath them). This procedure continued for a dozen or so pairs of cards.

Considering the sizable differences among the stimuli, the task was absurdly simple except for one thing: There was only one "real" subject. All of the others were the experimenter's secret confederates. They had arranged their seating order so that most of them would call out their judgments before the real subject's turn came around. After the first few trials, they unanimously rendered false judgments on most of the trials thereafter. For example, the confederates might declare that a 6 1/4-inch line equaled an 8-inch line, and so on, for a dozen more trials. What did the real subject do?

Asch found that the chances were less than one in three that the real subject would be fully independent and would stick to his guns on all trials on which the group disagreed with him (Figure 11.2). Most subjects yielded to the group on at least some occasions, in fine disregard of the evidence of their senses—with rather uncomfortable implications for the democratic process. When interviewed after the experiment, most of the yielding subjects made it clear that the group didn't really affect how they *saw* the lines. No matter what everyone else said, the 8-inch line still looked longer than the 6 1/4-inch line. But the subjects wondered whether they were right, became worried about their vision and sanity, and were exceedingly embarrassed at expressing their deviance in public (Asch, 1952, 1956; Asch and Gleitman, 1953).

For our present purposes, our concern is not so much with what the subjects did, but rather with how they felt. In this regard, most of them were alike. Some yielded and some were independent (see Chapter 12), but assuming they did not suspect a trick (and a few of them did), they were generally very much disturbed. Why all the furor? The answer is that Asch's procedure had violated a basic premise of the subjects' existence: However people may differ, they all share the same physical reality. Under the circumstances, it is small wonder that Asch's subjects were deeply alarmed by a discrepancy they had never previously encountered. (Needless to say, the whole experiment was carefully explained to them immediately afterwards.)

What accounts for the assumption of a socially shared reality? We can only speculate. One possibility is that the notion that others perceive more or less the same world that we do is a built-in facet of the human animal. Another is that this notion is part and parcel of a more general consistency that provides the criterion for what we mean when we say that an object is "real." For example, when something is real, the senses provide consistent information about it. Macbeth sees a dagger but cannot touch it and therefore regards it as "a dagger of the mind, a false creation proceeding from the heat-oppressed brain." Another criterion is consistency across time. Real objects provide what one philosopher called a "permanent possibility of a sensation." You may look away

A **B** **C**

The interpersonal nature of reality *A scene from the 1939 film* Gaslight, *with Charles Boyer and Ingrid Bergman, in which a scheming husband terrifies his young wife into doubting her own sanity. (Courtesy of the Kobal Collection)*

from a tree, but it is still there when your gaze returns to it a moment later (Mill, 1865). At least in principle, the general notion of a fixed reality that is "out there" and independent of our momentary point of view is a rock-bottom concept that we all accept. If it is challenged, we become deeply disturbed. It may be that the definition of reality—perhaps from the very outset—includes not only agreement among different perceptions and memories within one person but also agreement with those of others. As a result, the belief that others see, feel, and hear pretty much as we do becomes a cognitive axiom of our everyday experience. When this axiom is violated, as it is in Asch's experiment, a vital prop is knocked out from under us, a prop so basic that we never even realized it was there.

SOCIAL COMPARISON

The Asch study shows what happens when the clear evidence of one's senses is contradicted by the verdict of a unanimous group. But suppose that our own perception does not provide a clear-cut answer. This will happen, for example, if the lines differ by only a small amount. If left to our own devices, we will try to obtain some further sensory evidence. We may look at the lines once more but from a different angle or try to measure them with a ruler. But if we can't do that, then it's only reasonable to listen to what others have to say. Their judgments can then be used in lieu of further information provided by our own eyes or hands. If the others now disagree with us, we may well change our own answer on their say-so. Several studies have shown that this is precisely what occurs in an Asch-type experiment in which the discrimination is fairly difficult. There is more yielding and very little emotional disturbance (Crutchfield, 1955; for further discussion of conformity effects, see Chapter 12, pp. 469–71).

This general line of reasoning may explain why people seek the opinion of others whenever they are confronted by a situation that they do not fully understand. To evaluate the situation, they need more information. If they cannot get it first hand, they will try to compare their own reactions to those of others (Festinger, 1954; Suls and Miller, 1977). The need for such *social comparison* is

Social comparison *The two museum visitors don't seem quite sure what to make of Marisol's sculpture* The Family *and compare reactions. (Photograph by Burt Glinn/© 1964 Magnum Photos)*

Solomon E. Asch   *(Courtesy of Swarthmore College)*

especially pronounced when the evaluations pertain to social issues, such as the qualifications of a political candidate or the pros and cons of sex education in public schools.

COGNITIVE PROCESSES AND BELIEF

The preceding discussion showed that people try to make sense of the world they encounter. But how? In effect, they do this by looking for some consistency among their own experiences and memories, and then by turning to other people for comparison and confirmation. If all checks out, then well and good. But what if there is some incongruity? The Asch study showed what happens when there is a serious incongruity between one's own experiences (and the beliefs based upon them) and those reported by others. But suppose the incongruity is among one's own experiences, beliefs, or actions? Many social psychologists believe that this will trigger some tendency to restore *cognitive consistency*—to reinterpret the situation so as to minimize whatever inconsistency may be there.

What kinds of mechanisms might explain this general tendency to reinterpret aspects of our experience so that they fit together sensibly? A very influential approach was developed by Leon Festinger, who proposed that any perceived inconsistency among various aspects of knowledge, feelings, and behavior sets up an unpleasant internal state that he called *cognitive dissonance,* which people try to reduce whenever possible (Festinger, 1957).

One of the earliest examples is provided by a study of a sect that was awaiting the end of the world. The founder of the sect announced that she had received a message from the "Guardians" from outer space. On a certain day, there would be an enormous flood. Only the true believers were to be saved and would be picked up at midnight of the appointed day in flying saucers. (Technology has advanced considerably since the days of Noah's Ark.) On doomsday, the members of the sect huddled together, awaiting the predicted cataclysm. The arrival time of the flying saucers came and went; tension mounted. Finally, the leader of the sect received another message: To reward the faithful, the world was saved. Joy broke out, and the believers became more faithful than ever (Festinger, Riecken, and Schachter, 1956).

Given the failure of a clear-cut prophecy, one might have expected the very opposite. A disconfirmation of a predicted event should presumably lead one to abandon the beliefs that produced the prediction. But cognitive dissonance theory says otherwise. By abandoning the belief that there are Guardians, the person who had once held this belief would have to accept a painful dissonance

(Drawing by Rea; © 1955, 1983, The New Yorker Magazine, Inc.)

between his present skepticism and his past beliefs and actions. His prior faith would now appear extremely foolish. Some members of the sect went to such lengths as giving up their jobs or spending their savings; such acts would lose all meaning in retrospect without the belief in the Guardians. Under the circumstances, the dissonance was intolerable. It was reduced by a belief in the new message, which bolstered the original belief. Since other members of the sect stood fast along with them, their conviction was strengthened all the more. They could now think of themselves not as fools, but as loyal, steadfast members of a courageous little band whose faith had saved the earth.

ATTITUDES

Many social beliefs are accompanied by strong feelings. Take the conviction that abortion is murder—a far cry from the many beliefs we hold that are completely unencumbered by emotion, such as our nonchalant assurance that the sum of the angles of a triangle is 180 degrees. Emotionally tinged social views of the former kind are generally called *attitudes.* Since various people often have different attitudes, they tend to interpret many social situations differently; the same crowd may look like a group of peaceful demonstrators to one observer and like a rioting mob to another.

As modern social psychologists use the term, an attitude is a rather stable mental position held toward some idea, or object, or person. Examples are attitudes toward nuclear power, the legalization of marijuana, school integration, or packaged breakfast foods. Every attitude is a combination of beliefs, feelings, and evaluations and some predisposition to act accordingly. Thus, people who differ in their attitudes toward nuclear power will probably have different beliefs on the subject (e.g., "nuclear power plants are—or are not—unsafe") and will evaluate the topic differently (from extreme pro to extreme con); these differences will also make them more likely to take some actions rather than others (e.g., to support or to protest the construction of a new nuclear plant).

ATTITUDES AND BEHAVIOR

Attitudes can be measured in a number of ways. The most widely used methods involve some form of self-report. For example, the subject might be given an *attitude questionnaire* with items that relate to the matter at hand. Thus, in a questionnaire on nuclear power and related issues, subjects might be given a statement such as: "Accidental explosions in nuclear plants pose some danger, but this risk is relatively small compared to the economic and social benefits of cheap and abundant energy." They would then be asked to select a number between, and say, +10 and −10 to indicate the extent of their agreement or disagreement. The sum of a person's responses to a number of statements that all tap the same concerns will then provide a quantitative expression of that person's attitude.

Do attitudes as measured by self-report predict what people actually do? This question has led to controversy, for some early reports suggested that the relationship is much weaker than one might think. During the thirties when there was considerable prejudice against Asians, Richard LaPiere traveled through the country with a Chinese couple and stopped at over fifty hotels and motels and at nearly two hundred restaurants. All but one hotel gave them accommodations,

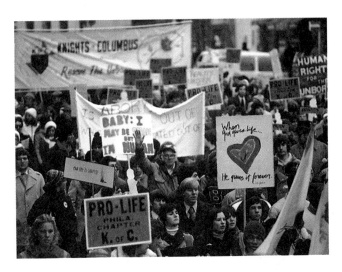

Attitudes *Attitudes are a combination of beliefs, feelings, and evaluations, coupled with some predisposition to act accordingly. (Left: photograph by Sylvia Johnson/Woodfin Camp, 1989. Right: photograph by Susan McElhinney, 1980/Woodfin Camp)*

and no restaurant refused them service. Later on the very same establishments received a letter that asked whether they would house or serve Chinese persons. Ninety-two percent of the replies were "No" (LaPiere, 1934). It appeared that there was a major inconsistency between people's attitudes as verbally expressed and their actual behavior.

The results of this and related studies led some social psychologists to doubt whether the attitude concept is particularly useful. If attitudes don't predict behavior, what is the point of studying them in the first place? (Wicker, 1969). But upon further analysis, this pessimism proved to be unwarranted. For later studies showed that under many circumstances attitudes do indeed predict what people do. Thus voter preferences during the four presidential campaigns of 1952 to 1964 as expressed in preelection interviews were a pretty good predictor of later behavior in the voting booth: 85 percent of the people interviewed voted in line with their previously expressed preference. For the most part, those who shifted had initial preferences that were rather weak (Kelley and Mirer, 1974).

It appears that attitudes often do predict behavior. But if so, how can we explain the fact that they don't always do so? One possible factor concerns situational pressures that may override other considerations. A similar qualification applies to the effect on behavior of personality characteristics (being sociable or withdrawn, bold or fearful, and so on). Just about everybody stops at a red light, regardless of whether they are bold or shy; and just about everybody is hushed at a funeral, regardless of whether they are sociable or withdrawn (see Chapter 16 for further discussion). What holds for personality characteristics also holds for attitudes. LaPiere's Chinese couple consisted of two young students who were attractive and well-groomed and who were accompanied by a white professor. Here, the situational pressures probably made refusal difficult and embarrassing.

An even more important factor is how specifically the attitude is defined. The less specific one's definition, the less likely it is to predict a particular bit of behavior. One study analyzed the relation between general attitudes to environmentalism and a particular act: volunteering for various activities of the Sierra Club. They found no relation. But when they tested the specific attitude toward the Sierra Club as such, they found a substantial correlation between attitude and action; those who had stated strongly positive views toward the club were much more likely to volunteer (Weigel, Vernon, and Tognacci, 1974). In a similar vein are the results of a study on women's attitudes to birth control. Positive attitudes toward birth control in general showed only a negligible correlation with the use of oral contraceptives during a two-year period. But attitudes toward using birth control pills in particular correlated quite well with their actual use during this period (Davidson and Jaccard, 1979).

A

B

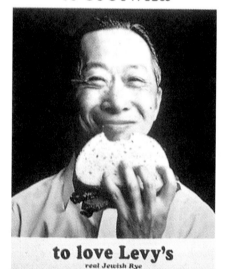

Attempts at persuasive communication
*Two advertising messages that try to change
consumer attitudes toward various products.
(A) links love with an expensive gift; (B)
asserts that a certain bread will appeal to any
ethnic group whatever. (Courtesy of De Beers,
Best Foods Baking Group)*

ATTITUDE CHANGE

While attitudes have a certain resilience, their stability is threatened at every turn, especially in modern mass society where our attitudes and beliefs are under continual assault. Hundreds of commercials urge us to buy one product rather than another, political candidates clamor for our vote, and any number of organizations exhort us to fight for (or against) arms control, or legalized abortion, or environmental protection, and so on. When we add these mass-produced appeals to the numerous private attempts at persuasion undertaken by our friends and relatives (let alone our would-be lovers), it is hardly surprising that attitudes sometimes do change. Social psychologists have spent a great deal of effort in trying to understand how such attitudinal changes come about.

PERSUASIVE COMMUNICATIONS

A number of investigators have studied the effectiveness of **persuasive communications.** These are messages that openly try to convince us to stop smoking, to outlaw abortion, to favor capital punishment, or—on a more humble level—to choose one brand of toothpaste rather than another. Among the factors that determine whether a given message has its desired effect are—not surprisingly—the person who sends the message and the message itself (Cialdini, Petty, and Cacioppo, 1981; McGuire, 1985).

The message source One factor that determines whether someone will change your mind on a given issue is who that someone is. To begin with, there is the element of *credibility*. Not surprisingly, communications have more of an effect if they are attributed to someone who is an acknowledged expert than to someone who is not. Thus a recommendation that antihistamines should be sold over the counter was more effective when ascribed to the *New England Journal of Medicine* than to a popular mass circulation magazine; a positive review of an obscure modern poem was more likely to lead to upward reevaluations of that poem if the review was attributed to T. S. Eliot rather than to another student (Hovland and Weiss, 1952; Aronson, Turner, and Carlsmith, 1963).

Expertise is important, but so is *trustworthiness.* For the would-be persuader will have a much harder time if we believe that she has something to gain from persuading us. A number of studies have shown that communicators are more effective when they argue for a position that seems to be against their own self-interest. In one study, students were shown statements that argued either for or against the strengthening of law enforcement agencies and that were attributed either to a prosecuting attorney or to a criminal. Statements in favor of stronger law enforcement had more effect when they were thought to be made by the criminal rather than by the prosecutor; the reverse was true for statements in favor of weaker law enforcement (Walster, Aronson, and Abrahams, 1966). When a used-car salesman tells you *not* to buy a car from his lot, you are likely to believe him. (Unless you believe that the other lot to which he refers you belongs to his brother-in-law.)

The message However important the messenger, the message she delivers is surely more important yet. What are the factors that determine whether that message will change attitudes? According to Petty and Caciopppo there are two routes to persuasion. One is what they call the **central route to persuasion** in which we follow the message with some care and mentally elaborate its arguments with yet further arguments and counterarguments of our own. We take this route if the issue is one that matters to us and if we're not diverted by other

Another attempt to persuade *An American advertisement from around 1900. (Frontispiece from* The Wonderful World of American Advertising, 1865–1900 *by Leonard de Vries and Ilonka van Amstel, Chicago: Follett, 1972)*

concerns. Here content and information are what matter, and strong arguments will indeed be more effective in changing our minds than will weak arguments. But the situation is quite different if the message comes by way of what Petty and Cacioppo call the **peripheral route to persuasion.** We'll be induced to take this route if we don't care much about the issue or if the message isn't clearly heard because of background noise or if we are otherwise distracted. In such circumstances, content and arguments matter little. What counts instead is how or by whom or in what surroundings the message is presented (Petty and Cacioppo, 1985).

The central route to persuasion involves reasoned thought. But just what is the peripheral route? According to some authors, it often represents a kind of mental shortcut. After all, there are only so many things we can pay attention to, and so we use some rules of thumb, or **heuristics,** to help us decide whether to accept or reject the message (Eagly and Chaiken, 1984; Chaiken, 1987). Such heuristics may include the speaker's apparent expertise, or likability ("nice people can be trusted"), or the sheer number or length of the arguments that are presented, regardless of how good they are. Such heuristics in reacting to persuasive communications are reminiscent of heuristics in decision making; both are mental shortcuts we resort to because our cognitive capacity is limited (see Chapter 8, p. 305, for a further discussion of heuristics).

COGNITIVE DISSONANCE AND ATTITUDE CHANGE

We've already seen that attitudes can affect behavior. But the relation can also go the other way. For in some situations, what an individual does will lead to a change in her attitudes. According to some social psychologists, this effect is produced by a tendency to reduce cognitive dissonance analogous to that which we've considered in the context of a change in beliefs. Suppose there is some inconsistency between a person's attitudes and her behavior. How can she reconcile the inconsistency? She can't change her behavior, for that's past and done with. All she can do is readjust her present attitude.

Justification of effort An illustration of this kind of readjustment comes from retrospective explanations of prior efforts. People often make considerable sacrifices to attain a goal—backbreaking exertion to scale a mountain, years and years of study to become a cardiologist. Was it worth it? According to dissonance theory, the goal will be esteemed more highly the harder it was to reach. If it were not, there would be cognitive dissonance. Support comes from common observation of the effects of harsh initiation rites, such as fraternity hazing. After the ordeal is passed, the initiates seem to value their newly found membership all the more. Similar effects have been obtained in the laboratory. Subjects admitted to a discussion group after going through a fairly harsh screening test put a higher value on their new membership than subjects who did not undergo such a screening (Aronson and Mills, 1959; Gerard and Mathewson, 1966).

Forced compliance A related result is the effect of **forced compliance.**★ The basic idea is simple. Suppose someone agrees to give a speech in support of a view that is contrary to his own position, as in the case of a bartender arguing for prohibition. Will his public act change his private views? The answer seems to de-

★ The term *forced compliance* was coined to describe the phenomenon when it was first demonstrated experimentally (Festinger and Carlsmith, 1959). It is a bit of a misnomer, however, since the subject is not really *forced* to lie about his attitudes but is instead persuaded or coaxed. Modern social psychologists prefer the more accurate—if more clumsy—designation *counter attitudinal advocacy.*

Justification of effort *Newly accepted members of a group tend to value their group membership all the more if their initiation was especially harsh, as in the case of soldiers who have gone through boot camp. (Courtesy of the U.S. Army)*

pend upon why he agreed to make the speech in the first place. If he was bribed by a large sum, there will be little effect. As he looks back upon his public denunciation of alcohol, he knows why he did what he did—$1,000 in cold cash is justification enough. But suppose he gave the speech with lesser urging and received only a trifling sum. If we later ask what he thinks about prohibition, we will find that he has begun to believe in his own speech. According to Festinger, the reason is the need to reduce cognitive dissonance. If the bartender asks himself why he took a public stand so contrary to his own attitudes, he can find no adequate justification; the few dollars he received are not enough. To reduce the dissonance, the compliant bartender does the only thing he can: He decides that what he said wasn't really all that different from what he believes.

A number of studies have demonstrated such forced compliance effects in the laboratory. In a classic experiment, subjects were asked to perform several extremely boring tasks, such as packing spools into a tray and then unpacking them, and turning one screw after another for a quarter turn. When they were finished, they were induced to tell another subject (who was about to engage in the same activities) that the tasks were really very interesting. They were paid either $1 or $20 for lying in this way. When later asked how enjoyable they had found the tasks, the well-paid subjects said that they were boring, while the poorly paid subjects said that they were fairly interesting. This result is rather remarkable. One might have guessed that the well-paid liar would have been more persuaded by his own arguments than the poorly paid one. But contrary to this initial intuition—and in line with dissonance theory—the exact opposite was the case (Festinger and Carlsmith, 1959). A number of other studies have performed variants on the original experiment with essentially the same results (e.g., Rosenfeld, Giacalone, and Tedeschi, 1984).

DISSONANCE RECONSIDERED

The reevaluation of prior decisions and the effect of forced compliance seem to be ways of reducing dissonance. But just what is the dissonance that is here reduced? One might regard dissonance as essentially equivalent to a logical inconsistency, like the inconsistency between the belief that the earth moves around the sun and the belief that the earth is at the center of the solar system. There is little doubt that cognitions are often adjusted to become consistent in just this sense. A person who hears the mumbled sentence "The woman shaved himself" is likely to hear it as "The man shaved himself" or "The woman shaved herself," so that noun and pronoun agree. The question is whether all cases of dissonance reduction boil down to an analogous tendency to keep cognitions logically consistent. The answer seems to be no, for recent evidence suggests that dissonance reduction is not always a cognitive matter. A number of studies indicate that we often try to reduce the dissonance between our acts and beliefs for more emotional reasons. One such factor is an effort to maintain a ***favorable self-picture*** (Aronson, 1969; Steele and Liu, 1983; Cooper and Fazio, 1984).

Consider the retrospective reevaluation of whether some achievement was worth its cost. People who have made a great sacrifice to attain some goal will value it more than those who achieved the goal with little effort. One hypothesis is that this dissonance reduction is produced by a tendency toward logical consistency—the worth of the goal has to match its cost, just as the noun must fit the pronoun. But there is a noncognitive reason that is just as plausible. An individual who goes through a difficult initiation rite to join a club and later discovers that the club is rather dull might well feel like a fool. To maintain a favorable self-picture, she adjusts her attitude to fit her own acts and overvalues her group membership.

Similar considerations apply to the effect of forced compliance. A subject who has argued for a position he doesn't hold will change his attitude to fit his

Attitude stability *Attitudes are generally resistant to change. One reason is that people generally stay in the same social environment, keeping company with others whose views of the world are essentially the same. (Photographs from left to right by Paul Fusco/ Magnum Photos, Inc.; Rex Features; James Foote/Photo Researchers Inc.)*

arguments (assuming he wasn't paid too much for presenting them). One interpretation of this effect is that it was an attempt to reduce a cognitive inconsistency. But the critical factor may have been emotional—a sense of guilt at having persuaded someone to spend an unpleasant hour at a boring task. If we can manage to change our own views just a bit (which is easier if we weren't paid too much for lying), we may salve our conscience. This guilt (and the consequent need to assuage it) will only arise, however, if we believe that our arguments convinced the poor fellow we lied to. And this guilt is likely to be much less if we don't much like that fellow; if so, we might well think that he had it coming. In one study, these predictions were upheld. There was no change of attitude (that is, no dissonance reduction) unless the subject believed that he had managed to convince the person he had lied to and did not dislike him (Cooper, Zanna, and Goethals, 1974).★

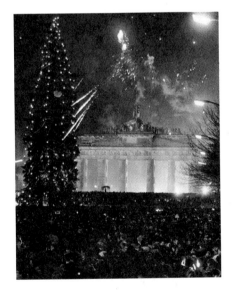

Radical attitude change produced by striking events *Occasionally a rare and momentous event changes attitudes. An example is the opening of the Berlin Wall in the winter of 1989, which signaled the end of the Cold War. (Photograph by Michael Probst, UPI/Bettman Newsphotos)*

ATTITUDE STABILITY

We've seen that attitudes can be changed by certain forms of persuasion (if the source is credible and trustworthy and if the message is appropriate) and by tendencies toward cognitive consistency (especially with regard to acts we've already performed). But on balance, the overall picture is one of attitude stability rather than of attitude change. Attitudes can be altered, but it takes some doing. By and large, there seems to be a tendency to hold on to the attitudes one already has.

Why should this be so? One reason for attitude stability is that people generally stay in the same social and economic environment. Their families, their friends and fellow workers, their social and economic situations tend to remain much the same over the years. Top-level executives know other top executives, and trade union members know other union members. On any one day, they may read or hear a speech that advocates a position contrary to their own, and they may even be affected. But on that evening and the day after, they will go back to the same old setting and will encounter the same old views that they held before. Under the circumstances, it is hardly surprising that attitude stability is more common than attitude change. To be sure, there are striking events that may transform our attitudes completely—not just our own, but also those of everyone around us. An example is the news of the attack on Pearl Harbor on December 7, 1941. Without a doubt, this led to an instant and radical change in Americans' attitudes toward Japan. But by their very nature, such events—and the extreme changes in attitudes they produce—are rare.

★ Seen in this light, dissonance reduction may be essentially equivalent to what Sigmund Freud called "rationalization" (see Chapter 17).

4 2 5

PERCEIVING OTHERS

Thus far our discussion of how people interpret the social world has focused upon the way in which they try to harmonize various events with their beliefs and attitudes. A similar approach has been applied to find out how we form impressions of other people and how we try to understand why they do what they do.

FORMING IMPRESSIONS

In the course of ordinary life we encounter many other people. The vast majority of them play the role of anonymous extras in each of our private dramas, especially in the big cities where we briefly cross the paths of countless strangers of whom we will never know anything. But a sizable number of other persons do impinge upon our lives, as bit players (a traffic cop of whom we ask directions), supporting cast (a casual acquaintance), and starring leads (friends, lovers, bosses, enemies). These we cannot help but evaluate and try to understand, as they, in their turn, evaluate and try to understand us. Much of the plot of our own dramas (and of theirs) depends upon the outcome of these mutual social attempts at understanding. How are they achieved?

Perceiving the characteristics of another person is in some ways analogous to perceiving certain stable attributes of a physical object, such as its shape or size. In our previous discussion of visual perception, we saw that to do this the observer must abstract the crucial relationships within the stimulus input so that he can see the form of the object, say, a catlike shape (see Chapter 6). He must also disregard various transient aspects of the situation, such as illumination, distance, and angle of regard, in order to perceive the stable characteristics of the object—its reflectance, size, and shape. By doing all this, the observer attains perceptual constancy and can answer such life-and-death questions as whether he is dealing with a kitten nearby or a tiger far away.

Something analogous occurs when we perceive—or rather, infer—such attributes of a person as his violent temper or warmth and so on. In effect, we are making a judgment as to what the person is "really" like, a judgment independent of the particular moment and occasion. His personal attributes (often called *traits*) are inferred invariant properties that seem to characterize his behavior in different situations. When we say that a person is irascible, we don't mean that he will utter an impolite expletive when someone deliberately steps on his toe. We mean that he will generally be short-tempered over a wide range of circumstances. To put it another way, the attempt to understand what another person is like boils down to an effort to note the *consistencies* in what he does over time and under different circumstances (see Chapter 16). The question is how this consistency is abstracted from the few bits of behavior of the other person we can actually observe.

IMPRESSIONS OF OTHERS AS PATTERNS

Several theorists assume that the processes whereby we try to understand another person are in many ways analogous to the way in which we perceive various attributes of physical objects. Consider visual form. This is a perceptual whole that depends upon the *relation* among the elements of which the form is composed; thus, a triangle can be composed of dots or crosses and still be perceived as the same triangle (see Chapter 6). According to Solomon Asch, a similar principle describes our conceptions of other people. In his view, these conceptions of others are not a simple aggregate of the attributes we perceive them to have. Instead, they form an organized whole whose elements are interpreted in relation to the overall pattern (Asch, 1952).

CENTRAL TRAITS

To test his hypothesis, Asch performed several studies of how people form impressions of others. His technique was to give subjects a list of attributes that they were told described a single person. Their task was to write a short sketch of the person so characterized and to rate this person on a checklist of antonyms (generous/ungenerous, good-natured/irritable). In one study, some subjects were given a list of seven traits: *intelligent, skillful, industrious, warm, determined, practical, cautious.* Other subjects received the same list except that *cold* was substituted for *warm*. The resulting sketches were quite different. The "warm person" was seen as "driven by the desire to accomplish something that would be of benefit," while the "cold person" was described as "snobbish, . . . calculating and unsympathetic." The checklist results were in the same direction. The person described as warm was seen as generous, happy, and good-natured. The "cold person" was characterized by the appropriate antonyms (Asch, 1946).

According to Asch, the warm/cold trait acted as a focus around which the total impression of the person was organized. To use his term, it was a **central trait** that determined the perception of the whole. Other traits seemed to be of lesser importance. For example, it made little difference whether the list of traits included *polite* or *blunt*.★

FIRST IMPRESSIONS

New items of information are often incorporated into patterns of organization that are already there. A familiar example is the effect of mental set. If subjects expect to be shown the name of an animal, then a very brief presentation of D–CK will be seen as DUCK rather than as DOCK (see Chapters 6 and 8). Our everyday experience suggests that a similar phenomenon occurs in person perception. Our first impression of someone often determines how we interpret what we find out about him later on.

This point has been illustrated by Asch in another version of his experiment with personal trait lists. One group of subjects was told to describe their impressions of a person who is intelligent, industrious, impulsive, critical, stubborn, and envious. Another group of subjects received the same list in the reverse order (that is, envious, stubborn . . . and so on). The results indicate that it pays to put one's best foot forward. If the list began on a positive note, it set up a favorable evaluative tone that seemed to overpower the later negative attributes; the opposite effect occurred when the unfavorable traits came first (Asch, 1946). According to Asch, the later attributes in the list take on different shades of meaning depending upon the context provided by the traits encountered earlier in the sequence. While similar **primacy effects** have been obtained by many other investigators (e.g., Luchins, 1957; Anderson, 1965), their interpretation is still a matter of debate (for discussion, see Ostrom, 1977; Schneider, Hastorf, and Ellsworth, 1979).

★ The question of why and when some traits are central and others not has received considerable attention. According to Julius Wishner, the effect is partially dependent on the observer's beliefs about which traits go with others (Wishner, 1960; Schneider, 1973).

First impressions *First impressions can be overcome, especially on screen and stage. A famous example is Shakespeare's* Much Ado About Nothing, *whose Beatrice and Benedick begin the play by bickering with each other and end it in each other's arms. (From the 1993 film directed by Kenneth Branagh, with Emma Thompson and Kenneth Branagh; photograph by Clive Coote)*

Primacy effects can be considerable, but they can be overcome. We sometimes do change our minds and come to respect or even love a person whom we detested on first meeting. The primacy effect only means that such alterations in judgment encounter a certain inertia. In old Hollywood movies, the fact that the hero and heroine took an instant dislike to each other was a tip-off to the audience that they would clinch by the final frame. But in real life, first impressions generally make more of a difference. If nothing else, they often preclude the chance of a later reevaluation.

IMPRESSIONS OF OTHERS AS COGNITIVE CONSTRUCTIONS

Asch tried to understand impression formation by an analogy to theories of perceptual patterning. A number of more recent authors have championed a view that is in many ways a modern version of Asch's approach, but they appeal to concepts derived from modern theories of memory and thinking rather than to principles of visual perception. In their view, our impressions of others are cognitive constructions based on various *schemas*—sets of organized expectations about the way in which different behaviors of people hang together. If we believe that someone is outgoing and gregarious, we will also expect her to be relatively talkative. She may or may not be, but the pattern we perceive is partially imposed by our schema of what an outgoing and gregarious person is like. Such schemas about persons are sometimes called *implicit theories of personality* (Bruner and Tagiuri, 1954; Schneider, 1973).

A demonstration of how such cognitive constructions operate used subjects who read several lists of attributes. One described a person said to be an extrovert, another a person who was an introvert. On a later recognition test, subjects falsely recognized adjectives that had not been on the original list if they fit in with the appropriate label. Thus terms such as *spirited* and *boisterous* that had not been presented previously were misremembered as being part of the original list that described the extrovert; terms such *shy* and *reserved* were falsely remembered as part of the list that described the introvert (Cantor and Mischel, 1979).

Phenomena of this kind suggest that the processes of social cognition, that is, the ways in which we gain knowledge of social events, are much like those of cognition in general. Suppose we briefly looked into a tool chest and were then shown a set of objects and asked which of them we had seen. We'd surely be more likely to misremember having seen a hammer than a baby bottle (assuming neither was actually in the chest). Our cognitive schema of a tool chest includes a hammer, just as our schema of an extrovert includes the attribute "boisterous."

THE PROS AND CONS OF TAKING MENTAL SHORTCUTS

Cognitive constructions such as schemas are mental shortcuts that confer obvious benefits. They allow us to circumvent our limited cognitive capacity so that we can cope with a complex world in which there is so much more to see, remember, and think about than we could possibly manage.

What holds for cognition in general also holds for social cognition. We are often forced to make judgments about people, but we rarely have the luxury of assembling all the necessary information that would allow us to make a sure and reasoned decision. As a result, we fill in the gaps by referring to broad schemas. Without such schemas, we would be unable to make any sense of our social world at all. Suppose we hear a man and a woman shout at one another but are too far away from them to make out what they're saying. If we know that the two are in the middle of a rocky love affair, we refer to our lover's quarrel schema and make one interpretation. If we know that the man is the woman's landlord and that she has refused to pay her rent because he hasn't fixed the faulty plumbing, we refer to our stingy landlord schema and make another interpretation.

Stereotypes and illusory correlations Given our limited cognitive capacity, schematic thinking provides us with a valuable mental tool that ordinarily works reasonably well. But the uncritical use of this tool can lead to errors that have serious social consequences. This is particularly clear in the case of social **stereotypes,** when schemas are simplified and applied to whole groups. Such stereotypes are categories by means of which we try to simplify the complex world in which we live, so that we talk about Greeks, and Jews, and African Americans (or student radicals, upwardly mobile yuppies, or little old ladies in tennis shoes) as if they were all alike. Such group stereotypes are often negative, especially if they are applied to minority groups.

The schema approach cannot explain how particular stereotypes come about, but it has some suggestions for how they are perpetuated. One possible factor is **illusory correlation.** Many characteristics of the world are correlated; they go together more often than would occur by chance alone—clouds and rainfall, accidents and sirens, and so on. But some of the correlations we perceive are illusory, a creation of our minds rather than a real relationship in the world outside. Such illusory correlations come about because certain co-occurrences are more readily noted and remembered than are others. One reason may be because they are the ones that are expected. Let's assume that we hold the stereotyped view that Englishmen are reserved. Suppose we now meet two Englishmen: Mr. Jones who is reserved and Mr. Brown who is outgoing and boisterous. Other things being equal, we are more likely to recall that Jones is an Englishman than that Brown is, for Jones fits our schema while Brown doesn't. As a result, we may continue to see a correlation where actually there is none (or overestimate a correlation that is in fact quite low).

Some evidence for this idea comes from a study in which subjects were presented with a number of statements that described members of different occupational groups, for example, "Doug, an accountant, is timid and thoughtful" or "Nancy, a waitress, is busy and talkative." Some of the characteristics were judged to fit the stereotype (e.g., accountant—perfectionist; stewardess—

Stereotypes *A British poster circa 1900, protesting competition from foreign goods on the home market in a cartoon featuring national stereotypes.*

attractive; salesman—enthusiastic), while others did not. But the sentences were so constructed that each occupation was systematically paired with each kind of adjective, so that in fact no correlation was encountered. The subjects were later asked to estimate how often each adjective described each occupational group in the sentences they had just read. Their estimates indicated that they believed that accountants were more often described as timid than were waitresses, stewardesses more often as attractive than librarians, and so on—a good example of an illusory correlation, suggesting how stereotypes can be maintained even in the face of contradictory evidence (Hamilton and Rose, 1980).

They're all alike A phenomenon related to stereotyping is the **outgroup homogeneity effect,** which describes how we perceive "us" (the **in-group**) versus "them" (the **out-group**). Take the assertions "All Jews are alike" or "All Gentiles are alike." The first is almost invariably made by a Gentile, the second by a Jew. The same holds for assertions such as "All women are alike," "All men are alike," "All blacks are alike," and "All whites are alike." Each member of a group tends to see members of the other group as more alike than members of his or her own.

The outgroup homogeneity effect is only too well known in the real social world. It can also be created in the laboratory. In one demonstration, subjects from two New Jersey universities (Rutgers and Princeton) viewed a videotape of a student who was waiting in an anteroom before participating in an experiment. The video showed him as he made a rather humdrum choice: to remain alone while waiting or to join a group of other students who were also waiting their turn. The subjects' task was to guess how many students would choose similarly (Quattrone and Jones, 1980).

Here was the trick: Some of the subjects from Rutgers were told that the student on the tape came from Princeton, while the rest were told that he, like them, was from Rutgers (similarly for Princetonians). The results were clear. If, say, the Rutgers students believed that the student was also from Rutgers, they didn't consider the videotaped choice at all representative—they thought that their fellow Rutgers students would make each choice about 50 percent of the time. On the other hand, if those same Rutgers subjects thought the student was from Princeton, then they concluded that whatever decision he made was more likely to characterize Princetonians as a whole. The equivalent result—students at Rutgers are alike, but those from Princeton differ—was found for Princetonians.

IMPRESSION MANAGEMENT

Thus far, we have talked about impression formation as it appears from the perspective of the person who tries to form that impression. We've seen that this process of impression formation is in some ways analogous to the perception of the physical environment. In both cases, we try to abstract some intrinsic attributes of an object from the welter of potentially distorting proximal stimulus features in which it appears: to perceive the real size of a distal object independent of its distance, to infer the characteristic feelings or motives of a person independent of the conditions of the moment.

But this analogy to visual perception can be pushed too far, for social perception is a more complex phenomenon. It is a two-way process in which all participants are potential stimuli as well as observers, are capable of being seen as well as of seeing. And most important, each participant knows this and knows that the others know it too. As a result, perceiving people is in an important sense very different from perceiving a physical object like a rock. The rock

"I have the impression that they're not very substantial people." (Drawing by Chas. Addams; © 1939, 1967, The New Yorker Magazine, Inc.)

doesn't know that we are looking at it, and it surely isn't trying to make a particular impression. But people often are.

In contrast to rocks, people are constantly working at **impression management,** a term coined by the sociologist Erving Goffman (Goffman, 1959; see also Schlenker, 1980). As Goffman saw it, much of social interaction is akin to a theatrical performance in which the actors are "putting on a front." Some "play hard to get," others wear elaborately contrived "casual looks," still others try to appear "above it all." Many of these impressions go along with social or professional roles. The medical student soon discovers that there is more to becoming a doctor than acquiring certain medical skills. He must also learn how to look like a doctor, how to instill confidence, how to develop a proper bedside manner. The audience for whom such productions are staged often includes the actors themselves. The would-be healer gradually comes to believe his own role, as one patient after another greets him as "Doctor" and treats his pronouncements with reverential awe.

Goffman pointed out that many of these social performances are jointly produced. To begin with, the actor is often supported by a team. The doctor's image is maintained not only by his own behavior but by that of various aides, nurses, and patients as well. Further support comes from the audience itself. We often go to considerable lengths to preserve another person's self-presentation, to allow her to "save face." If we want to break off an encounter at a cocktail party, we pretend that we are going to the bar for another drink. The other person may very well know that we have no intention of returning, and we may know that she knows, but this doesn't matter. Both participants tactfully play along. This kind of tact can reach consummate heights as in the case of the legendary English butler who accidentally surprised a lady in her bath and hurriedly mumbled, "I beg your pardon, Sir."

EMBARRASSMENT

An interesting variation on Goffman's impression-management theory concerns *embarrassment.* What are the conditions that produce this unpleasant experience? One factor may be a public failure, a loss of esteem in the eyes of others that produces a loss of esteem in our own eyes (Modigliani, 1971). But that can't be the whole story. For we are sometimes embarrassed even when our own self-picture is not involved. An example is **empathetic embarrassment,** becoming embarrassed for another person. This might happen when we see a friend in an amateur theatrical performance who suddenly can't remember his lines and stands frozen on the stage for what seems an eternity. Of course he is horribly embarrassed; of course he wants to sink through the floor—but the fact is that we are also embarrassed and that we too want to sink through the floor.

How can we explain this feeling? According to a recent account, the experience of embarrassment is partially caused by the disruption of a social interaction that no one knows how to repair (Parrot, Sabini, and Silver, 1988). As Goffman points out, all social intercourse is based on various prescribed scripts that provide a general frame within which each participant plays his part. When an actor forgets his lines and can't ad lib, the performance comes to a stop. This can happen in many other situations as well. Suppose Joe asks Mary for a date and she declines. If she answers with a flat "no," Joe will be embarrassed. He'll be much less embarrassed if she says, "I'd love to go out with you, but I'm afraid I'm involved with someone else." This excuse will serve to reduce Joe's embarrassment even if he knows that it's not true. What Mary has done by providing the false excuse is to allow the social interaction to proceed. If she simply says "no," Joe is left without anything to say. If she gives an excuse, he can withdraw with a modicum of grace. The show must go on, both on stage and in life, for it's too embarrassing if it does not.

Situation versus disposition? In ice
hockey, it's not always clear whether a player
who skates into another at full speed is deliberately trying to hurt him. The usual attribution is that he is, resulting in one of the many
fights that characterize hockey. (Courtesy
AP/Wide World Photos)

*"I've heard that outside working hours he's re-
ally a rather decent sort."* (Chas. Addams; ©
1975, The New Yorker Magazine, Inc.)

ATTRIBUTION

As previously pointed out, the attempt to understand what another person is
like is really an attempt to find the pattern, the consistency, in what he does. An
important step toward that end is to infer what caused his behavior on any particular occasion—for the meaning of any given act depends upon the cause. But
what cause do we see in what the other person does? Consider a football player
who violently bumps an opponent in the course of the game. If the bumping
occurred while the play was in progress, not much is revealed about the
bumper's personality; he was behaving according to the rules of the game. But if
the bump occurred some seconds after the official blew his whistle and the play
was over, the situation is different. Now the act is more revealing and may be
attributed to a grudge or a nasty disposition. The bumpee will conclude that the
bumper's action was internally caused and will then self-righteously become a
bumper when his own turn comes.

ATTRIBUTION AS A RATIONAL
PROCESS

The study of how such attributions are reached is one of modern social
psychology's important concerns (e.g., Heider, 1958; Kelley, 1967; Jones
and Nisbett, 1972; Kelley and Michela, 1980). According to Harold Kelley, one
of the first investigators in this area, the process through which such decisions
are reached is analogous to the way in which a scientist tracks down the cause of
a physical event (Kelley, 1967). An effect (such as an increase in gas pressure) is
attributed to a particular condition (such as a rise in temperature) if the effect
occurs when the condition is present but does not occur when that condition is
absent. Kelley believed that when people try to explain the behavior of others,
they implicitly refer to a similar principle of the covariation of cause and effect.
To answer the question "Why did he bump me?" the aggrieved player has to

consider the circumstances under which bumping is known to occur. Does it generally occur in circumstances just like now? Would most other football players do the same under much the same circumstances? If the answer to these and similar questions is yes, the act will probably be attributed to *situational factors:* essentially external causes, such as the social pressures of team play. But if the answer is no, the act will be attributed to some *dispositional quality,* something internal to the actor that is characteristic of him: He is a dirty player who took a cheap shot (Heider, 1958; Kelley, 1967).

As used in this context, the term *dispositional quality* refers to any underlying attribute that characterizes a given individual and makes him more disposed than others to engage in the particular bit of behavior we just observed. One kind of dispositional quality is the presence or absence of some ability (for example, falling because one is clumsy) or of some general personality trait (for example, leaving a very small tip for a waiter because one is stingy).

ERRORS IN THE ATTRIBUTION PROCESS

Kelley's analysis indicates that the rational way of trying to explain another person's behavior is to consider that behavior in the context of the total situation. But this is not always done. For there are a number of biases that lead to errors in the attribution process.

THE FUNDAMENTAL ATTRIBUTION ERROR

One error concerns the relative weights we give to situational and dispositional factors. While we do consider situational factors in judging the behavior of others, the evidence shows that we do so rather less than we should. There seems to be a strong bias to attribute behavior to dispositional qualities in the person while underrating the role of the external situation. This bias is so pervasive that it has been called the *fundamental attribution error* (Ross, 1977). The person on welfare is often judged to be lazy (a dispositional attribute) when he is really unable to find work (a situational attribute). Much the same holds for our interpretation of public affairs. We look for heroes and scapegoats and tend to praise or blame political leaders for acts over which in fact they had little control.

This general underemphasis of situational factors in interpreting why another person does what she does is illustrated in an experimental study in which college students were asked to participate in a simulated TV quiz show. Students were run in pairs and drew cards to decide who would be the "quiz master" and who the contestant. The quiz master had to make up questions, drawn from any area in which she had some expertise; the contestant had to try to answer them. Some of the questions were quite difficult (e.g., "What do the initials W. H. in W. H. Auden's name stand for?"). Under the circumstances, it's hardly surprising that the contestants' average score was only 4 correct answers out of 10.

The entire procedure was witnessed by other students who served as observers. When later asked to rate the two participants, the observers judged the quiz masters to be considerably more knowledgeable than the contestants. But why should this be so? To be sure, the contestants had been unable to answer many of the questions their partners asked. But the situation was obviously rigged, for the contestants were at the mercy of whatever questions their quiz masters posed. What happened clearly depended on the situation, on the role each participant was assigned. The observers knew that this role was determined by lot, for they witnessed the entire procedure. But even so, they couldn't help regarding the quiz masters as more knowledgeable than the con-

Attribution *People sometimes confuse the actor with his role, as in the case of Boris Karloff who often portrayed monsters such as Frankenstein's but who in real life was a gentle and cultured person. (Photographs courtesy of the Kobal Collection)*

433

testants—a tribute to the power of the fundamental attribution error (Ross, Amabile, and Steinmetz, 1977).★

THE ACTOR-OBSERVER BIAS

The tendency to underrate the importance of situational factors only occurs when we try to understand the behavior of others. The results are quite different when we ourselves are the actors rather than the observers. When we now try to explain our own acts, the causes seem less in us and more in the external situation. Someone trips, and we think he's careless or clumsy. But when we ourselves trip, we say the floor is slippery. This is the *actor-observer difference* in attribution—situational when we ourselves are the actors, dispositional when we are the observers (Jones and Nisbett, 1972).

A cognitive interpretation: Different information   One interpretation of the actor-observer difference is simply that we know ourselves better than we know anyone else. Let's say that on one evening we undertip a waiter in a restaurant. Should we make the dispositional attribution that we're stingy? Others who have never seen us in a similar situation might well conclude that we are. But we ourselves will disagree. We have observed ourselves in many restaurants and know that we normally tip properly. But if this is so, our recent act says nothing about our personal characteristics; rather, it must be caused by the situation— perhaps the waiter was rude, or we suddenly discovered that we didn't bring enough cash. Our attribution is different when we see someone else do the very same thing. We'll interpret *his* action dispositionally and conclude that he is stingy. After all, we haven't seen him in remotely as many restaurants as we've seen ourselves. So the one act of his that we did see weighs more heavily and can't be discounted. Some evidence in line with this hypothesis comes from a study which shows that the tendency to make dispositional attributions is somewhat less when the person we're describing is a close friend rather than a mere acquaintance (Nisbett et al., 1973).

A similar account may explain the outgroup homogeneity effect we discussed earlier: the tendency to see members of another group as more alike than members of one's own (see p. 430). Almost without exception, we know more about the members of our own group—including our differences from each other— than those of the outgroup. To the extent that we lack such detailed information about them, they seem "all the same."

A perceptual interpretation: Different perspective   There is another factor that contributes to the difference between actors and observers—the two have different physical perspectives (see Figure 11.3). To the observer, what stands out perceptually is the actor and his actions. The situation that calls out these actions is seen much less clearly, in part because the stimuli to which the actor responds are not as readily visible from the observer's vantage point. The reverse holds for the actor. He is not focused on his own behavior. One reason is that he cannot see his own actions very clearly (some, such as his own facial expressions, are literally invisible to him). What he attends to is the situation around him—the place, the people, and how he interprets them all. If we assume that whatever serves as the main center of attention (the figure rather than the ground) is more likely to be seen as the cause for whatever happens, then the differences in attribution follow: dispositional for the observer (who thus commits the fundamental attribution error), situational for the actor (Heider, 1958).

★ The actual details of the experimental procedure were somewhat more complex (among other things, because they involved the use of confederates), but they are irrelevant to the present discussion.

11.3 The actor-observer difference A schematic figure of a study on the effect of visual perspective on the actor-observer difference. Two actors (actually confederates) were engaged in a conversation and observed from three vantage points: from behind Actor A, from behind Actor B, and from midway between them. The results showed that the observer who watched from behind Actor A felt that B controlled the conversation, while the observer behind Actor B felt the reverse. The observer who watched from midway between the two felt that both were equally influential. (After Taylor and Fiske, 1975)

Actor A   Actor B

Some evidence for this position comes from a study in which two strangers met and engaged in a conversation that was videotaped. When later played back, only one of the two participants was shown (on the pretense that one of the cameras had malfunctioned while the sound was unaffected). As a result, one of the participants saw just what he had seen before: his fellow conversationalist. But the other saw something different: himself. When asked to describe his own behavior, the participant who saw the videotape of his partner gave the usual pattern of attribution—he said that his own actions were caused by the situation. The results were different for the participant who saw himself. The reversed perspective led to a reversal of the usual actor-observer difference. Having watched himself, the subject described his own behavior in dispositional terms (Storms, 1973).

THE SELF-SERVING BIAS

The two accounts of the actor-observer bias we've just discussed—different information and perspectives—are essentially cognitive; they argue that the bias results from limitations on what the individual can see, remember, and understand. But there is another interpretation that argues that in addition there are motivational factors. For our thoughts are all too often colored by our desires.

The best evidence comes from work on the *self-serving attributional bias,* which shows that people often deny responsibility for failures and take credit for successes, attributing the first to situational and the second to dispositional factors. The tennis player explains a loss by complaining that her serve was off and that the light was in her eyes, but she takes a win as proof of her ability and stamina. The student who fails says that the exam was unfair and happened to cover just those parts of the course that he hadn't studied for, but he believes that a good grade is a tribute to his talent and hard work.

This self-serving pattern has been documented very often (Bradley, 1978). In most studies, subjects were asked to perform various tasks and were then given fake information on whether they had achieved some criterion of success. In some, these tasks involved sensory or perceptual discriminations (e.g., Luginbhul, Crowe, and Kahan, 1975; Stevens and Jones, 1976); in others, they consisted of various tests that were said to measure social sensitivity (Miller, 1976; Sicoly and Ross, 1977); in yet others, they were competitive games played against fictitious opponents (Snyder, Stephan, and Rosenfield, 1976). The overall pattern of results was always the same: By and large, the subjects attributed

Self-serving bias John McEnroe protesting an umpire's call. (Courtesy of Reuters / Bettman Newsphotos)

their successes to internal factors (they were pretty good at such tasks, and they worked hard) and their failures to external factors (the task was too difficult, and they were unlucky).

What holds in the laboratory holds in the real world as well. This is especially true for the world of competitive sports. One study found evidence in the sports pages. The investigators analyzed the post-game comments of college and professional football and baseball players and coaches following important games. Eighty percent of the statements made by the winners were internal attributions: "Our team was great," "Our star player did it all," and so on. In contrast, the losers were less likely to give internal attributions (only 53 percent), but often explained the outcomes by referring to external, situational factors: "I think we hit the ball all right. But I think we're unlucky" (Lau and Russell, 1980, p. 32).

It is worth noting that these self-serving biases apply not just to the person's own failures or successes but extend to the perception of other persons and groups that he regards as in some ways his own: his friends, family members, social and political groups, and even hometown sports teams. Happily married couples are even more prone to a "spouse-serving attributional basis" than to a self-serving one: The spouse's successes reflect on his or her talents and character; the failures are caused by temporary external circumstances (Hall and Taylor, 1976; Holtzworth-Munroe and Jacobson, 1985). Similarly for people's favorite political candidate. Thus, if a candidate does poorly in a debate, her advocates will argue that she had an off day but that she will be sure to win a rematch, while her opponents will insist that it only proves their own favorite is the better of the two (Winkler and Taylor, 1979).

The above-average effect   An interesting example of the self-serving bias is the "above-average effect." When people are asked to compare themselves to all others on various favorable characteristics, the vast majority judge themselves to be "above average" in stark defiance of all statistical logic. Thus in 1976–1977 the College Board asked one million high-school students to rate themselves against their peers on leadership ability: Seventy percent said they were above average, while only two percent felt they were below. Similarly for athletic ability, which led to an equally illogical 60 percent above and 6 percent below. Similar findings have been obtained in people's judgments of talents ranging from managerial skills to driving ability.

What is going on here? The results should obviously be around fifty-fifty, but they are not. We may have a self-serving bias, but would so many of us defy all reason to that extent? What's happening is that people redefine the trait on which they are rating themselves so that they end up in the best possible light. Take driving ability. Suppose Henry is a slow, careful driver: He will tend to think that he's better than average precisely because he's slow and careful. But suppose Jane on the other hand is a fast driver who prides herself on her ability to whiz through traffic and hang tight on fast turns: She will also think that she's better than average because of the way she's defined driving skill. As a result, both Henry and Jane (and indeed most drivers) end up considering themselves above average. By appropriately redefining our talents to make each of us look good, we can all be self-serving. As one might expect, this effect only occurs when the traits on which people rate themselves are rather ambiguous (like driving ability). A strong above-average effect is also obtained for traits like "sophisticated," which allow a multitude of interpretations. It is much diminished given a less ambiguous trait such as "well read." (Dunning, Meyerowitz, and Holzberg, 1989).

Interpreting the self-serving bias   What accounts for the self-serving bias? The most obvious hypothesis is that it is just another case of impression management.

The experimenter asks a subject why she thinks she succeeded or why she failed. The subject doesn't want to lose face in public and therefore explains her performance to put herself in the best possible light, regardless of what she herself may actually think. In effect, she is trying to delude the experimenter rather than herself.

While such maneuvers probably play a role, however, they cannot account for the entire effect. For self-serving biases occur even when subjects experience failure but don't think the experimenter knows about it. Under these conditions, their public image is not threatened, so they have no reason to protect it. But they show a self-serving bias even so. Presumably they are trying to protect the picture they hold of themselves, now deluding themselves instead of—or in addition to—others (Greenberg, Pyszczynski, and Solomon, 1982; Schlenker, Hallam, and McCown, 1983).

PERCEIVING ONESELF

We have discussed some of the ways in which we see various qualities in others, as well as some of the ways in which we come to see such qualities in ourselves. We all have a conception of our own selves, what we are really like and why we do what we do—"I am a certain kind of person with such and such capacities, beliefs, and attitudes"—even if we sometimes glorify those capacities with a self-serving bias. But how do such self-concepts arise in the first place?

(Photograph by Suzanne Szasz)

THE SELF-CONCEPT

One crucial element is some reference to other people. For there is little doubt that there can be no full-fledged "I" without a "you" or a "they," for a crucial component of the self-concept is social. According to many authors, the child begins to see herself through the eyes of the important figures in her world and thus acquires the idea that she is a person—albeit at first a very little person—just as they are (Mead, 1934). As the social interactions become more complex, more and more details are added to the self-picture. In effect, the child sees herself through the mirror of the opinions and expectations of those others—mother, father, siblings, friends—who matter to her. Her later behavior cannot help but be shaped by this early "looking-glass self" (Cooley, 1902). Examples of such effects include the roles in which society casts children from the moment of birth: race, gender, ethnicity, and so on. (For different theoretical approaches to the development of the self-concept, see Chapters 10, 13, and 14.)

SELF-PERCEPTION AND ATTRIBUTION

According to the looking-glass theory, we learn who we are by finding out through others. But isn't there a more direct method? Can't we discover who we are and what we feel simply by observing ourselves?

According to some authors, the answer is no. In their view, our conceptions of self are attained through an attribution process no different from that which allows us to form conceptions of other people. The advocates of this *self-*

perception theory maintain that, contrary to common-sense belief, we do not know our own selves directly (Bem, 1972). In their view, self-knowledge can only be achieved indirectly, through the same attempts to find consistencies, discount irrelevancies, and interpret observations that help us to understand other people.

One line of evidence concerns the relation between attitude and behavior. Common sense argues that attitudes cause behavior, that our own actions stem from our feelings and our beliefs. To some extent, this is undoubtedly true. Those in favor of segregation are unlikely to join civil rights demonstrations. But under some circumstances, the cause-and-effect relation is reversed. For as already noted in our discussion of cognitive dissonance, sometimes our feelings or beliefs are the result of our actions.

A demonstration comes from the "foot-in-the-door" technique, originally perfected by traveling salesmen. In one study, suburban homeowners were asked to comply with an innocuous request, to put a three-inch square sign advocating auto safety in a window of their homes. Two weeks later, another experimenter came to visit those homeowners who had agreed to display the small sign. This time they were asked to grant a much greater request, to permit the installation of an enormous billboard on their front lawns, proclaiming "Drive Carefully" in huge letters while obstructing most of the house. The results showed that agreement depended upon prior agreement. Once having complied with the first, small request, the subjects were much more likely to give in to the greater one (Freedman and Fraser, 1966).

One interpretation of this and similar findings is a change in self-perception (Snyder and Cunningham, 1975). Having agreed to put up the small sign, the subjects now thought of themselves as active citizens involved in a public issue. Since no one forced them to put up the sign, they attributed their action to their own convictions. Given that they now thought of themselves as active, convinced, and involved, they were ready to play the part on a larger scale. Fortunately for their less-involved neighbors, the billboard was in fact never installed—after all, the request was only part of an experiment. But in real life we may not be let off so easily. The foot-in-the-door approach is a common device for persuading the initially uncommitted; it can be used to sell encyclopedias or political convictions. Extremist political movements generally do not demand violent actions from newcomers. They begin with small requests like signing a petition or giving a distinctive salute. But these may lead to a changed self-perception that ultimately may ready the person for more drastic acts.★

This line of argument may have some bearing on our understanding of how social systems function. The social world casts people in different roles that prescribe particular sets of behaviors; representatives of labor and management will obviously take different positions at the bargaining table. But the roles determine attitudes as well as behavior. If one has to act like a union representative, one starts to feel like one. The same holds for the corporate executive. This point has been verified in a study of factory workers both before and after they were elected a union steward or promoted to foreman. As one might have expected, the newly elected union stewards became more pro-union; the newly promoted foremen became more pro-management (Lieberman, 1956).

In short, our attitudes are affected by what we do and are expected to do. To some extent at least, the role makes the man or the woman. If one is appointed a judge, one begins to feel judicious.

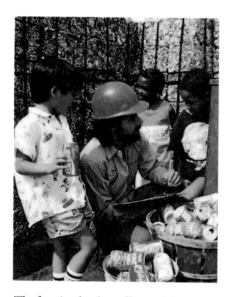

The foot-in-the-door effect and the environment   *The foot-in-the-door effect can start at an early age. The photo shows young children induced to do their bit for conservation. Whether the cans they collect now make much of a difference matters less than that these acts are likely to lead to greater efforts in the future as the children come to think of themselves as environmentalists. (Photograph by S. C. Delaney/EPA)*

★ These phenomena are very reminiscent of the effects of forced compliance and justification of past effort we discussed previously in the context of dissonance reduction. Under the circumstances, it may not be surprising that some authors have suggested that such effects are best explained by self-perception theory rather than by a tendency to reduce cognitive dissonance. The resulting controversy between adherents of the dissonance position and of the self-perception approach is beyond the scope of this book (Bem, 1967, 1972).

The misattribution of one's own inner state *According to one of the characters in Gilbert and Sullivan's operetta* Patience, *"There is a transcendentality of delirium—an acute accentuation of the supremest ecstasy—which the earthy might easily mistake for indigestion." (From a production by the New York Gilbert and Sullivan Players; photograph by Lee Snider, 1987)*

EMOTION: PERCEIVING ONE'S OWN INNER STATES

It appears that we come to know some of our own attitudes by a process of self-attribution. Some social psychologists have proposed that a similar process may affect the subjective experience of emotion. We say that we feel love, joy, grief, or anger. But are we always sure exactly what emotion we experience? In one of Gilbert and Sullivan's operettas, a character notes that the uninitiated may mistake love for indigestion. While this is probably an overstatement, something of the sort may be valid for all of us. We often have to interpret our internal states, have to decide whether the knot in our stomach is fear (say, of an impending examination), or is impatient anticipation (say, of a lovers' meeting). According to some psychologists, such interpretive processes are involved whenever we experience an emotion (Schachter and Singer, 1962; Mandler, 1975, 1984). To put their views in perspective, we will begin with a discussion of some earlier theories of emotion.

THE JAMES-LANGE THEORY

The topic of emotion has perplexed generations of investigators. Psychologists and biologists have had reasonable success in uncovering some of the objective, bodily manifestations of emotional states; examples are the emotional concomitants of fear and rage (see Chapter 3) and emotional expressions such as the smile (see Chapter 10). But what can we say about the way our emotions are experienced subjectively, how they feel "inside"?

Many nineteenth-century psychologists tried to catalogue various emotional experiences much as they had classified the different sensations provided by the senses (such as red, sour, A-flat). But their efforts were not very successful. People simply reported too many emotional experiences, and the classifications that were proposed did not seem to do justice to the richness of these subjective feelings. In addition, there were disagreements about the precise meaning of emotional terms. How does sadness differ from dolor or weariness or dejection? Different people reported different shades of meaning, and there seemed to be little hope of agreement as long as the description was confined to the subjective experience alone (which of course is private by definition).

A different approach to the problem was proposed by William James. To James, the crucial facet of emotion was that it is an aspect of what a person does. In fear, we run; in grief, we weep. The common-sense interpretation is that the behavior is caused by the emotion. James stood common sense on its head and maintained that the causal relation is reversed; we are afraid because we run:

> Common-sense says, we lose our fortune, are sorry and weep; we meet a bear, are frightened and run; we are insulted by a rival, are angry and strike. The hypothesis here . . . is that we feel sorry because we cry, angry because we strike, afraid because we tremble. . . . Without the bodily states following on the perception, the latter would be purely cognitive in form, pale, colorless, destitute of emotional warmth. We might then see the bear, and judge it best to run, receive the insult and deem it right to strike, but we should not actually feel afraid or angry. (James, 1890, v. 2, p. 449)

These phrases are the core of what is now known as the *James-Lange theory of emotions.* (Carl Lange was a contemporary of James who offered a similar account.) In effect, the theory asserts that the subjective experience of emotion

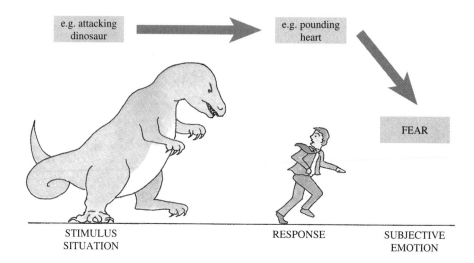

11.4 The sequence of events as conceived by the James-Lange theory of emotions *According to the James-Lange theory, the subjectively experienced emotion is simply our awareness of our own response to the anger- or fear-arousing situation. We see a dangerous object (an attacking dinosaur will do as well as any other); this triggers a bodily response (running, pounding heart), and the awareness of this response is the emotion (here, fear).*

is neither more nor less than the awareness of our own bodily changes in the presence of certain arousing stimuli. These bodily changes might be produced by skeletal movements (running) or visceral reactions (pounding heartbeat), though later adherents of James's theory emphasized the visceral responses and the activity of the autonomic nervous system that underlies them (Figure 11.4).

The James-Lange theory has been the focus of considerable controversy. One major criticism was raised by Walter Cannon, the pioneer in the study of autonomic functioning (see Chapter 3). Cannon pointed out that sympathetic reactions to arousing stimuli are pretty much the same, while our emotional experiences vary widely. Take the relation between rage and fear. Cannon pointed out that these two emotions are accompanied by just about the same autonomic discharge. So the James-Lange theory must have a flaw, since we are certainly able to distinguish between these two emotional experiences (Cannon, 1927).

A different objection concerns the effect of autonomic arousal. In several early studies, this was accomplished by injecting subjects with adrenaline. This triggered sympathetic activation with all its consequences—palpitations, tremor, and sweaty palms. According to the James-Lange theory, these are among the internally produced stimuli that give rise to the intense emotions of fear and rage. But in fact the subjects did not experience these emotions. Some simply reported the physical symptoms. Others said they felt "as if" they were angry or afraid, a kind of "cold emotion" that they knew was not the real thing (Landis and Hunt, 1932). These findings seemed to constitute a further argument against the James-Lange theory. The visceral reactions are evidently not a sufficient condition for the emotional experience.

THE ATTRIBUTION-OF-AROUSAL THEORY

In contrast to the James-Lange theory, which emphasizes the role of internal bodily feedback, an alternative account focuses on cognitive factors. After all, emotional experiences are usually initiated by certain external events—a letter with tragic news, a loved one's return. Events such as these bring grief or joy, but before they can possibly affect us emotionally they must be appraised and understood. Suppose we see a man who throws a spherical object toward us. Our emotional reaction will surely be different if we think the object is a ball than if we believe that it is a hand grenade. The emotion depends

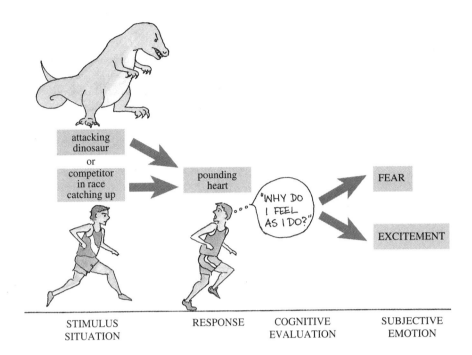

11.5 The sequence of events as conceived by Schachter and Singer's cognitive evaluation theory of emotions *According to Schachter and Singer, subjectively experienced emotion is the result of an evaluation process in which the subject interprets his own bodily reactions in the light of the total situation. Any number of external stimuli (ranging from attacking dinosaurs to competition in a race) may lead to the same general bodily reaction pattern—running and increased heart rate. The subjective emotion depends upon what the subject attributes these bodily responses to. If he attributes them to a danger signal (the dinosaur), he will feel fear. If he attributes them to the race, he will feel excitement.*

STIMULUS SITUATION   RESPONSE   COGNITIVE EVALUATION   SUBJECTIVE EMOTION

on some cognitive interpretation of the situation that in turn depends on what we see, what we know, and what we expect (Arnold, 1970).

Can a cognitive approach to emotion be combined with the James-Lange emphasis on bodily feedback? Proponents of a theory set forth by Stanley Schachter and Jerome Singer believe that it can. According to this ***attribution-of-arousal theory*** (sometimes called cognitive arousal theory) various stimuli may trigger a general state of autonomic arousal, but this arousal will provide only the raw materials for an emotional experience—a state of undifferentiated excitement and nothing more. This excitement is shaped into a specific emotional experience by cognitive appraisal and interpretation. In effect, this amounts to an attribution process. A person's heart beats rapidly and her hands tremble—is it fear, rage, joyful anticipation, or a touch of the flu? If the individual has just been insulted, she will interpret her internal reactions as anger and will feel and act accordingly. If she is confronted by William James's bear, she will attribute her visceral excitement to the bear and experience fear. If she is at home in bed, she will probably assume that she is sick. In short, according to Schachter and Singer's theory, emotional experience is produced, not by autonomic arousal as such, but rather by the interpretation of this arousal in the light of the total situation as the subject sees it (Schachter and Singer, 1962; Schachter, 1964; Mandler, 1984; see Figure 11.5).

THE MISATTRIBUTION OF AROUSAL

To test this general conception, Schachter and Singer performed a now classic experiment in which subjects were autonomically aroused but did not know what caused the arousal. The subjects were injected with a drug that they believed to be a vitamin supplement but that was really adrenaline (epinephrine). Some subjects were informed of the drug's real effects, such as increase in heart rate, flushing, tremor, and so on. Other subjects were misinformed. They were told only that the drug might have some side effects, such as numbness or itching. After the drug had been administered, the subjects sat in the waiting room while waiting for what they thought was a test of vision. In actual fact, the main experiment was conducted in this waiting room with a confederate posing

441

as another subject while the experimenter watched through a one-way screen. One condition was set up to produce anger: The confederate was sullen and irritable and eventually stalked out of the room. Another condition provided a context for euphoria: The confederate was ebullient and frivolous; he threw paper planes out of the window, played with a hula hoop, and tried to engage the subject in an improvised basketball game with paper balls. Following their stay in the waiting room, the subjects were asked to rate their emotional feelings (Schachter and Singer, 1962).

The critical question was whether the prior information about the drug's effects would influence the subjects' reactions. Schachter and Singer reasoned that those subjects who had been correctly informed about the physiological consequences of the injection would show less of an emotional response than those who had been misinformed. The informed subjects would attribute their tremors and palpitations to the drug rather than to the external situation. In contrast, the misinformed subjects had to assume that their internal reactions were caused by something outside—the elation of the euphoric confederate or the sullenness of the angry one. Given this external attribution, their emotional state would be in line with the environmental context—euphoric or angry as the case might be. The results were more or less as predicted. The misinformed subjects in the euphoria situation described themselves as more joyful than their correctly informed counterparts and were somewhat more likely than those counterparts to join in the confederate's mad antics. Analogous results were obtained in the anger situation.

CARRY-OVER OF AROUSAL

Some related effects result from a kind of spillover of arousal. Autonomic arousal usually takes awhile to subside; as a result, some bodily aftereffects of fear or anger or even physical exercise remain for quite a bit longer than we might expect. Such aftereffects may lead to *excitation transfer effects* (Zillman, 1983). In one study, some subjects first engaged in a bout of strenuous physical activity on an exercise bicycle. A few minutes after they finished pedaling, they were angered by a confederate in an adjacent room who administered a number of (mild) electric shocks as a way of signaling disagreement on various attitudes they discussed over an intercom. When subsequently given a chance to retaliate, they were more aggressive (that is, administered more severe shocks) than control subjects who were tested after their heart rate and blood pressure returned to base levels. (Needless to say, no retaliatory shocks were really delivered.) A similar effect was found for sexual excitement in response to erotic films; here too, arousal was enhanced by preceding physical exercise (Zillman, Katcher, and Milavsky, 1972; Cantor, Zillman, and Bryant, 1975). The explanation readily follows from Schachter's theoretical position. Some residual bodily aftereffects of the previous physical exercise are still present even though the subject doesn't know it. He is still aroused, but doesn't know why. As a result, he misattributes his arousal to the situation in which he currently finds himself and in so doing amplifies his own emotional feelings. If provoked, he becomes even angrier; if sexually aroused, he becomes more excited still (Valins, 1966).

BEYOND ATTRIBUTION-OF-AROUSAL THEORY

The attribution-of-arousal theory has come in for some criticism. A number of authors have pointed to various problems with the original study, such as that the effects they obtained were rather small or inconclusive and that

Excitation transfer *There is some evidence that the arousal immediately following intense exercise can lead to a misattribution of one's own reaction to emotion-producing stimuli. Whether competitive athletes to whom strenuous exercise is a matter of course are subject to this effect is an open question. (Photograph by Michael Nichols/Magnum)*

several later investigators did not succeed in replicating the full range of results predicted by attribution-of-arousal theory (Reisenzein, 1983). But the main point at issue goes beyond the details raised by that experiment. It concerns the theory's contention that visceral arousal can lead to any and all emotional experiences, depending upon the person's interpretation of the situation. Some later studies suggest that emotional experience is not quite as flexible as this. Thus injections of epinephrine may be more likely to lead to negative emotional experiences (such as fear and anger) than to positive ones (such as euphoria) regardless of the context in which they occur (Marshall and Zimbardo, 1979; Maslach, 1979; for a rebuttal, see Schachter and Singer, 1979).

The issue is by no means settled, but a plausible position is one that stands midway between the James-Lange and attribution-of-arousal theories. As we saw, the Schachter-Singer attribution-of-arousal approach starts out with the assumption that all human emotions have the same bodily underpinning. Some investigators, however, claim that there are differences in the autonomic patterns that accompany such emotions as anger, sadness, and fear (e.g., Ax, 1953; Funkenstein, 1956; Schwartz, Weinberger, and Singer, 1981). Other investigators make similar claims but base them mainly on differences in facial expressions. According to these authors, different bodily and facial patterns characterize a number of different **fundamental emotions** (Ekman, 1971, 1984; Izard, 1977). If so, the autonomic raw materials may not allow themselves to be shaped into virtually any emotional experience as Schachter and Singer had supposed.

FUNDAMENTAL EMOTIONS AND FACIAL EXPRESSION

The hypothesis that there are a few distinctive facial expressions that reveal a corresponding set of fundamental emotions goes back to Charles Darwin (Darwin, 1872b), who considered these expressions to be vestiges of basic adaptive patterns shown by our evolutionary forerunners. In effect, he argued that these expressions are a kind of read-out of an underlying emotional state that is a remnant of an ancestral reaction pattern. On this read-out view of facial expressions, our "anger" face, often expressed by lowered brows, widened eyes, and open mouth with exposed teeth, reflects the facial movements our ancestors would have made when biting an opponent. Similarly, our "disgust" face, often manifested as a wrinkled nose and protruded lower lip and tongue, reflects how our ancestors rejected odors or spit out foods (For elaborations, see Ekman, 1980, 1984; Izard, 1977; Tomkins, 1963.)

Just how many fundamental emotions are there? On the facial read-out approach this question can be answered by determining how many distinct facial expressions there are (see Figure 11.6). In Chapter 10, we saw that many

11.6 Six fundamental emotions *The photos depict the facial expressions that some investigators regard as characteristic of six fundamental human emotions: (A) happiness, (B) surprise, (C) sadness, (D) anger, (E) disgust, and (F) fear. (From Matsumoto and Ekman, 1989; photographs courtesy of David Matsumoto)*

A

B

C

D

E

F

of the same facial expressions are used and recognized in many cultures, that they emerge at a very early age, and that they are displayed in blind and deaf children who could not have learned them by observation (see Chapter 10, pp. 402–404). They must therefore be regarded as part of our built-in human heritage. From these expressions lists of fundamental emotions have been constructed. The numbers vary; one account lists seven: happiness, surprise, anger, sadness, disgust, fear, and contempt (Ekman, 1984). Others list from eight to ten and may include emotions like shame and guilt (e.g., Izard, 1971, 1991; Plutchik, 1980).

Further complications are added by the fact that human facial expressions are at least partially under voluntary control. As a result, they can be faked even if we're not emotional or if we experience a different emotion from that which we express. Hamlet was surely not the first to note that one may smile and smile and be a villain. In addition, read-out theorists hold that facial expressions can be at least partially suppressed, using various learned **display rules,** which typically represent a culture's view about what facial signals may or may not be shown overtly and in what contexts (see pp. 403–404; Ekman, Friesen, and O'Sullivan, 1988; Ekman, 1985; Ekman and Friesen, 1986).

FACIAL EXPRESSIONS AS COMMUNICATIONS

According to the read-out theory, the facial expressions indicate an underlying state (which to be sure can be hidden or faked). An alternative view proposes that facial expressions are primarily communicative displays. Adherents of this position argue that the pouty face signals that we want to be comforted or embraced, the angry face that we want others to take us seriously, obey us, or back off. Seen in this light, these various faces are not so much a revelation of an inner state as they are a message to others. The smile doesn't (necessarily) mean that we are *happy*, but rather that we are telling someone we want to be friends (e.g. Fridlund, 1991a; Mandler, 1984; Patterson, 1983).

Evidence for the communicative view comes from the fact that facial expressions occur mostly when we are in the presence of others and especially when we make eye contact with them. In one study, bowlers were observed when they made spares or strikes. The bowlers didn't smile at the moment of their success. Instead, they waited to smile until they turned around in the lane and met the gaze of their friends (Kraut and Johnston, 1979). What holds for adult bowlers also happens to ten-month-old infants playing with toys while their mothers watch on the sidelines. They smile most often when they turn to watch their mothers watching them (Jones, Collins, and Raag, 1991).

A possible objection to this position is that we sometimes make faces when we are alone. But we also talk in private, and the instances in which we do may be the very same ones that lead to private faces. Sometimes we talk to ourselves or make faces at ourselves; in such cases, we act as if we are both the sender and the recipient of the message (e.g., when scolding ourselves). And we sometimes talk to or smile at others who are currently only present in our imagination (Fridlund 1990, 1991b; Chovil, 1991).

Of course, the read-out and communicative theories are not mutually exclusive, for it may be that both processes operate. In part, facial expressions may simply be a read-out of what is going on inside; in part, they may be implicit messages we send to others.

FUNDAMENTAL EMOTIONS AND COGNITION

There are a number of further problems about the way in which emotional experiences arise. One concerns the fact that the number of fundamental emotions is rather small. The largest number that has been suggested is ten. But we

The face and emotion *A grieving Cypriot woman. (Photo by Constantine Manos/ Magnum)*

surely can distinguish between many more emotional experiences than this—for example, between sadness, resignation, regret, grief, and despair, and between happiness, jubilation, rapture, and serene delight. But how can we do this if we possess at most ten different fundamental emotions?

Advocates of the read-out approach argue that the fundamental emotions are often mixed and blended in various proportions, generating an additional number of complex emotions. Thus "jealousy" can be regarded as a mix of fear and anger, while anxiety is composed of the emotions of fear, guilt, sadness, and shame (Izard, 1991).

Further distinctions may be made by just the kind of interpretive process that Schachter and Singer described. A situation arouses the bodily states (and expressive reactions) corresponding to one of the fundamental emotions. This in turn produces an emotional experience—say of fear, or anger, or joy, or sadness. But its exact nature is then further shaped by the situation as the individual interprets it to be. And since the number of situations that the individual can face is countless, the number of emotional experiences that he can feel is countless as well—each with its own complexity and subtle shadings.

COMPLEX EMOTIONS

Thus far we have largely considered emotions that we might have shared with our primate predecessors and perhaps some even more primitive creatures earlier in our ancestral line. Many of these might well have had some version of what we call rage, fear, disgust, and joy; they fought competitors (rage), escaped from predators (fear), spat out noxious substances (disgust), and joined with mates (joy). But there are some emotions that seem peculiarly human, for they require a level of symbolic processing that is probably restricted to our own species. Examples are such emotional experiences as pity, anger, guilt, and regret, all of which depend on a complex attributional analysis of why we or someone else failed or succeeded in some endeavor, an analysis that even the cleverest chimpanzee is probably incapable of.

PITY, ANGER, AND GUILT

Consider the emotions of anger, pity, and guilt. Each of them is aroused by some misfortune: the loss of a job, failing an examination, and so on. According to Bernard Weiner, which particular emotion is felt depends on our perception of how this misfortune came about. If we believe that the outcome was essentially controllable, we feel anger; if we regard it as uncontrollable, we feel pity. If we hear that Joe failed an important exam because he went to a party the night before, we feel a bit angry (all the more so, if we really like him and wanted him to do well). But if he failed the exam because he had been ill all semester, we're more likely to feel sorry for him. In the first case, we feel that the failure was Joe's own fault, in the second, that he failed but couldn't help it (Weiner, 1982).

In these examples, the emotion is provoked by another person, for it is he who performed (or did not perform) the act that led to the unfortunate outcome. But a rather similar analysis applies when the emotional target is one's own self. Here too what matters is whether one could or could not control the outcome. If it was controllable, we feel guilt (which in a sense is anger directed at the self). If it was not controllable, we feel self-pity.

Still further complexities are introduced by the fact that certain emotions—such as anger and guilt—involve an appreciation of a moral order. Consider anger. Imagine that you are waiting in line, say, to buy a pair of World Series

Anger at moral transgression *Waiting in line to avoid righteous anger. (Drawing by Chas. Addams; © 1960, 1988, The New Yorker Magazine, Inc.)*

Anger as a social emotion *A four-year-old in self-righteous anger at a playmate who is using one of her toys and won't relinquish it. (Photograph by Suzanne Szasz)*

tickets. By the time you reach the ticket office you find out that there are no more tickets left; the man just in front of you bought the very last pair. Do you get angry at that man? You may get angry at your bad luck and curse the fates, but you won't get angry at him. You somehow recognize that his position in the line gave him the right to the tickets. The situation would be very different if he had pushed himself ahead of you. In that case you would become fiercely angry, because you would perceive his act as a moral transgression (Averill, 1978; Sabini and Silver, 1982).

To be sure, anger may well be based on a fundamental emotion that is related to within-species aggression. Dogs snarl and bare their fangs in rage. But in humans, anger is evidently more than this. We've seen that it involves the appreciation of another person's intentions and capacities. But beyond that, it also involves some sense of moral rights and transgressions. At this point, it is not rage, but outrage. Given all that, it clearly transcends its simple biological roots.

REGRET

Yet another emotion that transcends simple arousal or the few fundamental emotions is regret, a reaction produced by comparing the outcomes of whatever one did with what one might have done. It is the emotion of the might have been.

We've all had the experience of almost achieving some desired goal but just missing out. Somehow such near-misses are much more painful than attempts that don't come close at all. The person who gets a lottery ticket that differs from the winning number by just one digit feels much worse than the one whose number is way off the mark. The same holds for the football player who almost catches the winning touchdown pass or the actress who almost landed the star part. This general phenomenon has been documented in a number of studies in which subjects were presented with various scenarios and had to indicate their reactions. One example concerns a missed plane:

> Mr. Crane and Mr. Tees were scheduled to leave the airport on different flights, at the same time. They travelled from town in the same limousine, were caught in a traffic jam, and arrived at the airport thirty minutes after the scheduled departure time of their flights.

Mr. Crane is told that his plane left on time. Mr. Tees is told that his flight was delayed, and left five minutes ago.

Who is more upset? (Kahneman Tversky, 1982, p. 203)

It is no surprise that the virtually unanimous answer was Mr. Tees, who suffered the near-miss. But why should this be so, considering that the objective situation of the two men was identical, since they both missed their planes? Kahneman and Tversky believe the near-miss is more upsetting because it is much easier to imagine that one might have arrived five minutes earlier than half an hour earlier. If only the limousine had made just one more traffic light, if only the baggage had been unloaded a bit more quickly, if only. . . .

Kahneman and Tversky call this tendency to refer to such imaginary replays (or simulations) of what was and what might have been the *simulation heuristic;* it is yet another of the various mental shortcuts (e.g., the availability heuristic, see Chapter 8) that we use in making decisions and evaluating outcomes.

A number of further findings represent variations on the same general theme. In one study, subjects read about two people who died of exposure after surviving a plane crash in a remote area. Of one victim they learned that he made it to within one-quarter mile of safety; of the other, that he came within seventy-five miles. They were then asked to determine a fair amount of compensation for the victims' families. The subjects recommended a considerably higher sum for the family of the victim who came quite close than for the family of the victim who perished further away. They evidently felt that the fate of the first victim, the one who came so close, was worse (more "unfair" so to speak) than that of the second. In their imaginary reconstructions, they found it easier to construct a mental simulation for undoing the first victim's fate than for undoing the second's—if he'd only known how close he was, if he'd just been able to take a few more steps.

A similar account may explain why misfortunes that are caused by some exceptional departure from routine seem especially regrettable. That someone died on the Titanic is terrible enough, but it appears more terrible yet if she only got her ticket because of a last-minute cancellation by a passenger who suddenly fell sick. It's apparently easier to create a mental script for undoing an unusual circumstance than to imagine how more usual event patterns can be altered (Kahneman and Miller, 1986).

Regret *The sadness of "It might have been." (Drawing by Chas. Addams; © 1956, 1984, The New Yorker Magazine, Inc.)*

The experience of regret highlights the difficulty of referring all of our subjective emotional feelings to a few fundamental emotions. Regret is not just sadness, or a mixture of sadness with another fundamental emotion. Dogs may conceivably experience some inner state akin to what we call sadness; they seem to grieve for a lost master and look profoundly depressed after learned helplessness training. But it's hard to imagine that they could possibly feel regret. To credit them with that emotion is to suppose that they can mentally rummage through unrealized possibilities. But unlike dogs, humans are able to compare what is with what might have been. As a result, they can experience this special sadness.

EMOTION AND THE THEATER

There is a certain emotional experience that is in some ways quite unlike those we encounter in everyday life—the emotion we feel when watching a play or a movie. Is it a real emotion? Sometimes it seems to be. Some plays or movies can obviously move us to tears. As children, we weep at Lassie's illness; as adults, at Juliet's death. In retrospect, we may insist that while watching the play or the movie, we were really "into it" and had come to accept the characters' joys and sorrows as though they were real. But did we truly? Consider a great performance of *Oedipus Rex,* climaxed by that awesome scene in which Oedipus blinds himself. We may say that while watching the play we believed that what happened on stage was reality. In fact, we did no such thing. If we had, we would have experienced horror instead of tragic awe; we would have rushed for help, perhaps shouting, "Is there an ophthalmologist in the house?" In fact, we never believe that the stage Oedipus is real; at best, we are willing to suspend our disbelief, as the poet Coleridge put it so aptly. But in the fringes of our consciousness there is always the feeling that we are sitting in the theater's comfortable armchair. We may suspend disbelief, but this does not mean that we believe.

The emotions we experience in the theater cannot be identical to those we feel in the real world. But then, what are they? When we witness certain events in real life—a tearful reunion, a fistfight, a funeral—we experience real emotions. When analogous events occur on stage or on the screen, they trigger a similar arousal. But the cognitive context is quite different, for we still know that

Children at a Punch-and-Judy show
The younger child, upset over the fate of one of the puppets, is reassured by her older brother. (Photograph by Suzanne Szasz)

Emotion and the actor *A scene from Shakespeare's* King Lear *in which the old king, half-crazed with impotent fury, screams at the world during a raging storm. Lear was surely in a state of vehement frenzy. But was the actor who portrayed him? (Peter Ustinov and William Hutt in a 1979 production at Stratford, Ontario; photograph by Robert C. Ragsdale)*

we are sitting in a darkened theater. The experience is analogous to that "cold fear" produced by injecting adrenaline, that "as if" emotion that occurs in subjects who cannot attribute their arousal to any external cause.

The special esthetic flavor of the theatrical experience probably depends upon just this "as if." But this quality requires a delicate balance between disbelief and belief, between too little arousal and too much. On the one hand, there must be some sense of being "into it," or we will remain cold and dispassionate, like the bored usher who has seen the same show over and over again. On the other hand, too much arousal will also defeat the esthetic goal, for the "as if" feeling will then be lost altogether. A theatrically naïve audience may believe that what happens on stage is the real thing, as in children's theater where the four- and five-year-olds shout fearful warnings at Snow White when the evil old witch approaches. Their seven-year-old cousins are less naïve and thus more capable of enjoying a genuine dramatic experience. They feel aroused and excited, but they can reassure their young friends with an air of theaterwise sophistication, "Don't worry. It's not really real."

When a performance threatens to become too real, sophisticated adults may protect themselves by laughing nervously and thus breaking the spell altogether. This reaction to the loss of "psychical distance" (Bullough, 1912) is sometimes seen in theaters in the round, where the audience surrounds the playing area and those in the front row can almost touch the actors. If the play is a blood-and-guts melodrama, in-the-round staging may become too close for comfort. Suppose there is a well-acted scene in which a man almost murders his wife with an ax. The members of the audience directly adjacent to the two actors are very likely to avert their heads. The scene has become too real and the emotion too genuine. The audience responds by breaking contact.

The "as if" experience may also be an important ingredient in the emotion the actor feels as he plays his part. Many dramatic critics have asked the question, "What does the actor feel when he portrays the jealousy of an Othello or the rage of a Lear?" According to some schools of acting (such as the famous Actors' Studio of New York, which teaches "method" acting), the actor's job is to bring emotional reality to his role. In practice, the actor accomplishes this by vividly recalling some emotion-filled fragments of his own life that are appropriate to his present role and scene. The result is often a scene of genuine dramatic truth, felt by both actor and audience. But admirable as this may be, is it real in the sense in which everyday emotion is real? Again, the answer is almost surely no. No sane actor who ever played Othello really wanted to strangle the actress who portrayed Desdemona. Yet there is nevertheless this "as if" experience, a state of arousal perceived and interpreted against a cognitive context that includes both the situation of the character and that of the actor who plays that character (H. Gleitman, 1990).

The "as if" experience may be an important ingredient in the appreciation of several art forms. In theater, it is our simultaneous awareness of events that may move us deeply and yet that we know to be unreal. In the visual arts it is the simultaneous awareness of a scene or object that looks lifelike but that is nonetheless seen to be a flat, painted canvas (see Chapter 6).

TAKING STOCK

On looking back, we should note that many of the phenomena we've considered in this chapter may involve the operation of either (or both) cognition and motivation, or to use two old-fashioned terms, reason and passion. Consider the effect of forced compliance: Is it caused by a force toward cognitive consistency (that is, dissonance reduction) or by an attempt to minimize guilt? Or take the actor-observer bias in attribution: Is it produced by such cognitive factors as differential information and distinct perspectives or by the self-serving bias? Finally consider emotion: Here, if anywhere, motivational factors should be paramount, but we saw that even here—the very stronghold of passion—cognitive processes operate jointly with motivational ones to determine what we experience.

Both reason and passion determine what we think, and feel, and do. As we try to make sense of our social world, we try to be rational thinkers, but our cognitive limitations often force us to rely on various mental shortcuts and schemas that may lead to various errors and biases. But we are also people with motives, and passions, and a need to maintain self-esteem, so that we are sometimes wishful thinkers rather than rational ones.

SUMMARY

1. Social behavior depends in part on how people interpret situations they encounter. The processes that lead to such interpretations are in many ways similar to those that underlie cognitive processes in general.

2. Our conception of what is real is heavily affected by confirmation from others, as shown by Asch's study on the effects of group pressure and by the need for *social comparison,* especially in ambiguous situations.

3. To make sense of the world, people look for *cognitive consistency.* According to *cognitive dissonance theory,* they will do what they can to reduce any inconsistency (dissonance) they perceive by reinterpreting information to fit in with their beliefs, attitudes, and actions.

4. The interpretation of the situations people encounter is affected by their *attitudes,* which vary from one person to another. Attitudes are rather stable mental positions held toward some idea, object, or person, which combine beliefs, feelings, and predispositions with action.

5. Social psychologists have studied a number of approaches to changing attitudes. One concerns the effectiveness of *persuasive communications.* This depends in part on various characteristics of the message's source, including that source's trustworthiness and credibility. It also depends on characteristics of the message itself. Some contend that strong arguments will be more likely to change attitudes if the message comes in through the *central route* than if it enters through the *peripheral route,* where there is more reliance on rough-and-ready *heuristics.*

6. Another approach asserts that attitude change is often produced by an attempt to reduce cognitive dissonance. There is some evidence, however, that the dissonance reduction effects observed in *justification of effort* and *forced compliance* studies are a way of protecting the individual's *favorable self-picture* rather than a means to remove logical inconsistency.

7. While these various means for changing attitudes have some effect, attitudes tend to remain rather stable, in part because of cognitive consistency, which on the whole is a force for keeping things the way they are, and in part because people tend to stay in the same social and economic environment.

8. The way we perceive others is in some ways similar to the way we perceive and think of inanimate objects or events. Some theorists believe that impressions of others can be regarded as patterns whose elements are interpreted in terms of the whole, thus accounting for the role of *central traits* and of *primacy effects* in impression formation. More

SUMMARY

recent theorists emphasize the role of social cognition, which leads to the formation of *schemas* and *implicit theories of personality*.

9.   Our perception of people is further complicated by the fact that they know they are being perceived, which may lead to attempts at *impression management*. Failures at impression management may lead to embarrassment. This is partially caused by loss of self-esteem, but also by the disruption of a social interaction that no one knows how to repair, as in *empathetic embarrassment*.

10.   Attribution theory tries to explain how we infer the causes of another person's behavior, attributing them either to *situational factors* or to *dispositional qualities*. In part, this process is quite rational and depends on the conditions in which the behavior in question is seen to occur. But it can also lead to various errors. In judging others, we tend to make the *fundamental attribution error*, overestimating the role of dispositional qualities and underestimating that of situational factors. This attribution bias is reversed when we ourselves are the actors rather than the observers. Reasons for the *actor-observer difference* include the fact that we know ourselves better than anyone else and that actors and observers have different perspectives. An additional reason is the *self-serving bias*, which tends to make people deny responsibility for their failures while taking credit for their successes; it is probably also responsible for the *above-average effect*.

11.   According to self-perception theory, similar attribution processes determine how we perceive ourselves. In line with this theory is evidence that people realign their self-perceptions to fit their behavior, as shown in studies using the *foot-in-the-door technique*.

12.   An influential application of self-perception theory is Schachter and Singer's *attribution-of-arousal theory*, which is a revision of the *James-Lange theory of emotions*. According to the James-Lange theory, our subjective experience of emotion is simply an awareness of our own bodily changes (both autonomic and skeletal) in the presence of certain arousing stimuli. In contrast, proponents of the attribution-of-arousal theory argue that the emotion we feel is an interpretation of bodily responses and especially of our own autonomic arousal in light of the situation to which we attribute it. Misattribution effects of autonomic arousal include *excitation transfer*.

13.   Many investigators doubt that one arousal process underlies all emotions. They suggest that there are some six to ten *fundamental emotions* that correspond to different facial expressions. According to the *read-out theory*, these facial expressions are a direct read-out of an underlying emotional state. This theory is complicated by the fact that facial expressions can be at least partially suppressed in keeping with culturally acquired *display rules*. An alternative view proposes that facial expressions are primarily communicative, as shown by the fact that they occur primarily when we are in the presence of others or when we think about them.

14.   Certain complex emotions seem to be uniquely human because they require an unusual level of symbolic processing. Some depend on the judgments that a bad outcome was controllable (anger) or that it was not (pity). Others depend on the construction of cognitive scenarios that involve "what might have been" (regret). Still others depend on an "as if" experience, such as the emotion we feel while watching a performance in the theater.

CHAPTER **12**

S O C I A L
I N T E R A C T I O N

RELATING TO OTHERS: ONE-ON-ONE INTERACTIONS   453

SOCIAL EXCHANGE AND RECIPROCITY ■ ALTRUISM ■ ATTRACTION ■ LOVE

SOCIAL INFLUENCE: MANY-ON-ONE INTERACTIONS   467

SOCIAL FACILITATION: SOCIAL INFLUENCE BY THE PRESENCE OF OTHERS ■ CONFORMITY ■ BLIND OBEDIENCE ■ SOCIAL IMPACT THEORY

LEADERSHIP: ONE-ON-MANY INTERACTIONS   479

GREAT PERSON OR SOCIAL FORCES ■ LEADERSHIP IN THE LABORATORY

CROWD BEHAVIOR: MANY-ON-MANY INTERACTIONS   482

THE EMPHASIS ON THE IRRATIONAL: DEINDIVIDUATION ■ COGNITIVE FACTORS AND THE PANICKY CROWD

SOME FINAL COMMENTS   486

COMMON THEMES ■ THE GENERALITY OF SOCIAL PSYCHOLOGY

SUMMARY   489

I n the previous chapter, we discussed the ways in which we try to understand the social world around us. Our primary emphasis was on social cognition: our attitudes and how they are changed, our impressions of people, our interpretation of why they do what they do, and finally, the way that we ourselves interpret our own actions and experiences. In this chapter, our focus will be on action, or more precisely, *interaction*, as we ask how people deal with each other, influence each other, and act in groups.

We will consider four major kinds of interaction: Some are *one on one,* as when two friends have dinner or a customer tries to bargain with a used-car salesman; others are *many on one,* where many persons act upon one individual, as when a group of teenagers pressures one in their midst to wear the same clothes as all the others; still others are *one on many,* where one person acts on many others, as in various forms of leadership; we will finally consider interactions that can be described as *many on many,* as in riots or panics when many people affect many others and are affected by them in turn.

RELATING TO OTHERS: ONE-ON-ONE INTERACTIONS

How do people interact on a one-on-one basis? To a large extent, the answer depends on the relationship the actors have with each other. We deal one way with comparative strangers, another with people we know and like, and yet another with those we know but don't like. Still, according to many social scientists, there are some common threads that run through most of our relationships, no matter how tenuous or strong they may be. We'll begin by looking at the ways in which we interact with comparative strangers.

SOCIAL EXCHANGE AND RECIPROCITY

A number of theorists believe that one common principle that underlies the way people deal with others is ***social exchange.*** According to this view, each partner in a relationship gives something to the other and expects to receive something in return. Just what is exchanged depends on the relationship. If it is economic, as between buyers and sellers or employees and employers, the exchange will involve goods or labor for money. If it is between friends, lovers, or family members, the exchange will involve valued intangibles such as esteem, loyalty, and affection. According to social exchange theory, all (or at least, most) human relationships have this underlying give-and-take quality. If one partner

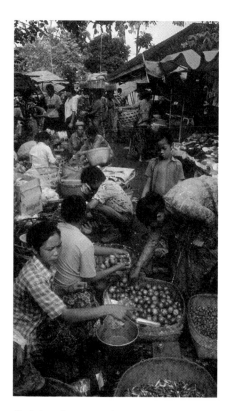

Social exchange *The process of social exchange is most obvious when it is economic.*

gives and receives nothing in return, the relationship will disintegrate sooner or later (Kelley and Thibaut, 1978).

The social exchange perspective is essentially economic and thus quite appropriate to the realm of material transactions. In the marketplace, money provides a common standard by which the value of commodities can be assessed. As a result, the value of what is given and received can be compared. This is much harder (and perhaps impossible) to accomplish when the exchange involves such "commodities" as praise or loyalty, let alone love. Whether the social exchange approach applies to all social interactions is therefore a matter of debate but that it applies to some is indubitable. One important example is the operation of the ***reciprocity principle.*** This is a basic rule that affects many aspects of social behavior. We feel that we somehow must repay whatever we have been given: a favor for a favor, a gift for a gift, a smile for a smile. As one author points out, this sense of social indebtedness is so deeply ingrained that it has been built into the vocabulary of several languages: thus, "much obliged" is a virtual synonym for "thank you" (Cialdini, 1984).

RECIPROCITY AND PERSUASION

According to Robert Cialdini, the reciprocity principle can become a powerful tool of persuasion (Cialdini, 1984). Cialdini points out that incurring a favor necessarily leads to a sense of indebtedness. We feel that we must repay a donor, even if we never wanted his gift in the first place. As a result, we are sometimes manipulated into compliance—saying "yes," or buying some merchandise or making donations—all despite the fact that we never really wanted to. As an example, Cialdini describes the techniques the Hare Krishna Society used to employ in soliciting donations. Members of this sect would approach airport travelers and press a flower into their hands. The traveler would typically want to return the unwanted gift, but the Krishna member would not take the flower back, insisting sweetly that "It is our gift to you." The member's next step would be to request a donation to the society. Many travelers felt that under the circumstances they had no choice. Since they took the gift (no matter how unwillingly), they felt that they had to reciprocate. Their only defense—and many travelers resorted to it—was to beware of Krishnas bearing gifts!

The reciprocal-concession effect Still another kind of behavior often affected by the reciprocity rule is bargaining. The seller states his price. The potential buyer says "No." Now the seller makes a concession by offering the item (the house, the car, or whatever) at a lower price. This very concession exerts a pressure on the buyer to increase her offer; since he offered a concession, she feels that she ought to give a little on her side too.

The reciprocal-concession effect has been the subject of several laboratory investigations. In one study, an experimenter approached people walking on a university campus and first made a very large request. He asked them to work as unpaid volunteer counselors in a juvenile detention center for two hours a week over a two-year period. Not a single subject agreed. The experimenter then made a much smaller request: that they accompany a group of boys or girls from the juvenile detention center on a single two-hour trip to the zoo. When this smaller request came on the heels of the large request that had been refused, 50 percent of the subjects consented. In contrast, only 17 percent of the subjects acceded to the smaller request when this was not preceded by the prior, larger demand. In the first case, there was an apparent concession; in the second, there was not. The sheer fact that the experimenter seemed to make a concession was enough to make the subjects feel that they should now make a concession of their own (Cialdini et al., 1975). This method for achieving compliance has been dubbed the ***door-in-the-face technique*** by way of contrast to the foot-in-the-door technique, in which compliance with a small request makes the subject more likely to comply with the larger one (see Chapter 11, p. 439). Both techniques take their names from the tricks of door-to-door salespeople (Cialdini, 1984).

Reciprocity and self-disclosure Clearly, the reciprocity principle can be used to persuade people to give of their time or money. But it can also be used to persuade people to give of themselves. Take **self-disclosure,** revealing something personal about oneself. In some ways, telling another person something about your own life is a bit like giving a present: A number of studies confirm that the other person generally feels obliged to disclose a bit about himself in return. A number of studies confirm what common sense surely predicts: As relationships deepen, self-disclosure becomes more frequent and intimate (Jourard, 1964; Altman, 1973; Rubin et al., 1980; Hansen and Schuldt, 1984).

There is a gender difference in patterns of self-disclosure. By and large, women are more willing to reveal themselves to other women than men are to men, at least in Western culture (Morton, 1978). According to some authors, friendships between women are in some ways more intimate and qualitatively different than those between men. What matters to women is sharing emotions; what matters to men is sharing some common activity (Sherrod, 1989). But these differences are clearly affected—and very probably produced—by cultural factors. Thus Chinese students in Hong Kong were more self-disclosing than a comparable group of Americans and showed none of the gender difference so familiar in our own culture (Wheeler, Reis, and Bond, 1989).

THE ROOTS OF RECIPROCITY

The reciprocity rule is extremely powerful and pervasive. When Cicero asserted that "There is no duty more indispensable than that of returning a kindness," he was not just talking about the Romans of his time, but also about us and about virtually all cultures and societies past and present. In the Trobriand Islands, inland islanders give vegetables to the fishermen on the shore, who will later repay the gift with fish, a further gift that in turn calls for a vegetable repayment, and so on—a reciprocity system in which "neither partner can refuse, neither

The gifts of the Magi *The social exchange position can be stretched too far, for sometimes we give without expectation of return. (The Star of Bethlehem, 1888–91, by Edward Burne-Jones; courtesy of The Birmingham Museums and Art Gallery)*

may stint, neither may delay" (Malinowski, 1926). Such exchanges often yield mutual gain, as in the case of the farmers and the fishermen who obtain nutritional benefits. But over and above such material advantages, the gift exchange has a further social function. It creates a web of mutual obligations that knits the members of a society together. In fact, there are a number of societies in which gift giving creates a ritualized cycle of obligations that are never completely canceled; any one gift represents a repayment for a previous gift with a little bit extra—an extra just enough to require still another gift in return, and so on (Gouldner, 1960).

How can we explain the fact that so much of human social life is governed by the reciprocity rule? One possibility is that it has biological roots. In a prior chapter, we discussed reciprocal altruism in various nonhuman animals (see Chapter 10, pp. 409). According to Leda Cosmides and John Tooby, human exchange rules are just a further elaboration of this pattern. As they see it, these rules and the reciprocity principle that follows from them grow out of a set of biological givens that are essentially built into our cognitive and motivational apparatus. The idea is that such a reciprocity principle is adaptive to both parties to the transaction and ultimately to their descendants. This being so, the biological make-up that allows the participants to act upon the principle will be selectively favored. Cosmides and Tooby believe that much of human intelligence evolved to help in understanding the uses and principles of social exchange. In their view, we did not become social because we are intelligent. Instead, we became intelligent because we are social (Cosmides and Tooby, 1992).

Reciprocity in human social life is obviously useful and adaptive, and on the face of it seems quite similar to reciprocal altruism in animals. But that does not necessarily mean that the two have the same roots. Reciprocity in both humans and animals may have evolved by some form of natural selection, but in humans the selection may have been by means of cultural rather than biological evolution. For it is likely that every viable culture requires principles of social exchange and reciprocity. Without these, a society can have no cooperation, no trade, no ties between one individual and another, and must necessarily end up in the war of all against all foretold by Thomas Hobbes. And if this happens, the society must therefore ultimately perish. As a result, all existing human societies should have some rules of social exchange, some principle of reciprocity, on the grounds of cultural rather than (or perhaps in addition to) biological evolution.

A final point: Thus far, we've only discussed the positive aspects of reciprocity—a gift for a gift, a smile for a smile. But there's a negative side as well, as promulgated in the Babylonian Hammurabi's Code—a tooth for a tooth, an eye for an eye. Some such tendency toward retaliation surely exists in every human culture. It might result from the same biological tendencies that lead to reciprocal altruism, which, as we saw in Chapter 10, requires some genetic safeguard against cheaters (see p. 409). Or it might result from cultural evolution. Either way, it's comforting to know that few modern societies insist upon the literal one-for-one reciprocity legislated by Hammurabi. If an accident victim loses two teeth, the guilty party may be forced to pay damages (or even to go to jail), but he won't be sent to a dentist to have two of his own teeth extracted.

ALTRUISM

Social exchange theory suggests (and the reciprocity principle derived from it insists) that no one ever gets anything for nothing. There is no such thing as a free lunch. But this harsh judgment on human nature seems to be contradicted by the fact that people sometimes act unselfishly. Or do they?

The Kitty Genovese tragedy *Many people watched Kitty Genovese being murdered on a street corner in Queens, but no one intervened. (The Streetlight by Roger Brown, 1983; private collection, New York; courtesy of Phyllis Kind Gallery, New York/Chicago)*

There is ample evidence that people often fail to help others who are in distress. The widespread indifference of pedestrians to the beggars and the homeless all around them is by now a daily fact of American city life. The classic example of public apathy to a stranger's plight is the case of Kitty Genovese who was attacked and murdered on an early morning in 1964 on a street corner in Queens, New York. The assault lasted over half an hour during which time she screamed and struggled while her assailant stabbed her repeatedly until she finally died. It later came out that thirty-eight of her neighbors had watched the episode from their windows, but none of them had come to her aid. No one even called the police (Rosenthal, 1964). Why was there this appalling inactivity?

THE BYSTANDER EFFECT

One factor may be a lack of altruistic motivation. Perhaps people in a big city simply don't care about the fate of strangers, no matter how terrible it may be. But according to Bibb Latané and John Darley, the failure to help is often produced by the way people understand the situation. It's not that they don't care, but that they don't understand what should be done. Here as in many other contexts, social action (and interaction) is heavily affected by social cognition.

Ambiguity   Consider the passerby who sees a man lying unconscious on a city street. How can he tell whether the man is ill or drunk? The situation is ambiguous. A similar confusion troubled some of the witnesses to the Genovese slaying. They later reported that they weren't quite sure what was going on. Perhaps it was a joke, a drunken bout, a lover's quarrel. If it were any of these, intervention might have proved very embarrassing.

Pluralistic ignorance   The situation is further complicated by the fact that the various witnesses to the Genovese tragedy realized that many others were seeing just what they did. For as they watched the drama on the street unfold, they saw the lights go on in many of the windows of adjacent buildings. As a result there was **pluralistic ignorance.** Each of the witnesses looked to the others to decide whether there really was an emergency. Each was ignorant of the fact that the others were just as unsure as they. The sheer fact that the various witnesses could see each other through the windows reassured them that nothing urgent was going on.

12.1   *The bystander effect*

Diffusion of responsibility   The fact that each observer knew that others observed the same event made it difficult to realize that the event was an emergency. But this fact had yet another consequence. It made intervention less probable even for those witnesses who did recognize (or at least suspect) that the situation was an emergency. For these persons were now faced with a ***diffusion of responsibility.*** No one thought that it was her responsibility to act. After all, while many of the observers might have felt some impulse to help, they also had self-centered motives that held them back: Some didn't want to get involved; others were afraid of the assailant; still others were apprehensive about dealing with the police. The conflict between the desire to help and to mind one's own business was finally resolved in favor of inaction through the knowledge that others witnessed the same event. Everyone assumed that since so many others saw just what they did, surely one of them would do something about it or had already done it (such as calling the police). As a result, no one did anything (see Figure 12.1).

This general line of reasoning has been tested in a number of experiments. In one, subjects were asked to participate in what they thought was a group discussion about college life with either one, three, or five other people. The subjects were placed in individual cubicles and took turns talking to each other over an intercom system. In actuality, there was only one subject; all the other discussants were tape recordings. The discussion began as one of the (tape-recorded) confederates described some of his own personal problems, which included a

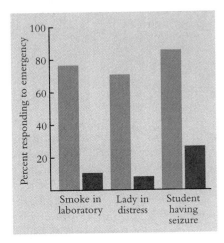

12.2 Group inhibition of bystander intervention in emergencies *When people are alone (in blue) they are more likely to respond in an emergency than when they are— or think they are—with others (in dark red), in part because of diffusion of felt responsibility. (Data from Darley, 1968; Latané and Rodin, 1969)*

tendency toward epileptic seizures in times of stress. When he began to speak again during the second round of talking, he feigned a seizure and gasped for help. The question was whether the subject would leave his own cubicle to assist the stricken victim (usually, by asking the experimenter's help). The results demonstrated the ***bystander effect:*** The larger the size of the group that the subject is in (or thinks he is in), the less likely he is to come to the victim's assistance (Darley and Latané, 1968; see Figure 12.2).

The bystander effect has been obtained in numerous other situations. In some, a fellow subject seems to have an asthma attack; in others, the experimenter appears to faint in an adjacent room; in still others, the laboratory fills with smoke. But whatever the emergency, the result is always the same: The larger the group the subject is in (or thinks he is in), the smaller the chance that he will take any action—in dramatic accord with the diffusion of responsibility hypothesis (Latané and Nida, 1981; Latané, Nida, and Wilson, 1981).

THE COSTS OF HELPING

The work on the bystander effect indicates that people often don't recognize that a need for help exists and that even when they do, they may not act because they think that others will. But suppose the situation is not ambiguous and that responsibility for helping is not diffused? Will they then help a stranger in distress?

One factor that determines whether they will or won't is the physical or psychological cost to the prospective helper. The greater that cost, the smaller the chance that he will in fact help. In some cases, the cost is physical danger. In others, it is simply time and effort. In one study, students had to go from one campus building to another to give a talk. They were told to hurry, since they were already late. As they rushed to their appointments, these students passed by a shabbily dressed man who lay in a doorway groaning. Only 10 percent stopped to help the victim. Ironically enough, the students were members of a theological seminary, and the topic of their talk was the parable of the Good

The Good Samaritan *(Painting by Jacopo Bassano, 1517/18–1592. Photograph © The National Gallery, London)*

Altruism *Helping victims of a highway collapse during the San Francisco earthquake of 1989. (Courtesy of the New York Public Library Picture Collection)*

Samaritan who came to the aid of a man lying injured on a roadside. It appears that if the cost—here in time—is high enough, even theological students may not behave altruistically (Darley and Batson, 1973).

What is costly to one potential helper may not be equally so to another. Take physical danger. It is probably not surprising that bystanders who intervene in cases of assault are generally much taller, stronger, and better trained than bystanders who do not intervene and are almost invariably men (Huston et al., 1981).

THE SELFISH BENEFITS OF UNSELFISHNESS

Providing help can yield benefits as well as costs. Some of the benefits are various signs of social approval, as in the case of a wealthy donor who is sure to make a lavish contribution as long as everyone watches. Other benefits have to do with avoiding embarrassment. Many city dwellers give two or three quarters to a beggar not because they want to help him but because it's easier to give than to say no. Occasionally the benefits of giving involve romance. In one study, the investigators posed as motorists in distress, trying to flag passing cars to provide help with a flat tire. The passing cars were much more likely to stop for a female than for a male, and the cars that stopped were generally driven by young men alone. The best guess is that the young men's altruism was not entirely unalloyed by sexual interest (West, Whitney, and Schnedler, 1975).

IS THERE ANY GENUINE ALTRUISM?

The preceding discussion paints a somewhat unflattering portrait of human nature. It seems that we often fail to help strangers in need of assistance and that when we do, our help is often rather grudging and calculated, and based on some expectation of later reciprocation. But that picture is too one-sided. For while people can be callous and indifferent, they are also capable of true generosity and altruism (see Figure 12.3). Sometimes people share food, give blood, contribute to charities, and administer artificial respiration to accident victims. Yet more impressive are the unselfish deeds of living, genetically unrelated donors who give one of their kidneys to a stranger who will otherwise die (Sadler et al., 1971). And still others are commemorated by Jerusalem's Avenue of the Righteous, dedicated to the European Christians who sheltered Jews during the Nazi Holocaust, risking (and often giving) their own lives to save those to whom they gave refuge (London, 1970).

Such acts of altruism suggest that human behavior is not always selfish. This probably undermines the claim that all social interactions can be understood as a form of exchange. To be sure, acts of altruism in which the giver gets *no* benefits at all—no gratitude, no public acclaim—are fairly rare.* The true miracle is that they exist at all. One aspect of our humanity is that we can go beyond the calls of social exchange and reciprocity.

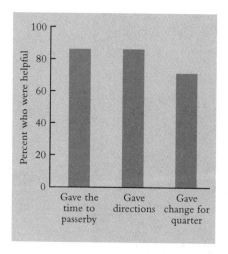

12.3 Small acts of helping in a large city *Various minor and prosaic acts of helping strangers are by no means uncommon even in a big city. (Data from Gerard, Wilhelmy, and Conolley, 1968)*

---

* It is sometimes argued that even the most self-sacrificing hero is at bottom no less selfish than anyone else. For even if no one else ever knows of his unselfish efforts, he himself does, thus gaining an increased sense of self-esteem and the satisfaction of knowing that the person he has helped is now better off. Thus at bottom the apparent altruist is selfish after all. This argument twists the ordinary meaning of the word "selfish." For at some level, every individual—including the noblest of martyrs—seeks certain rewards. If so, then whether someone should be considered selfish or unselfish depends not on whether he seeks some reward, but rather on *what* reward he seeks to obtain. A person who seeks the reward of seeing someone else feel better is by definition acting unselfishly (Sabini, 1992).

ATTRACTION

Thus far, we've primarily looked at social interactions with virtual strangers. What happens when the interactions are with people to whom we are closer and about whom we have stronger feelings? We'll begin by asking about the factors that attract us to others.

Could we ever hope to discover what it is that determines who will become friends or even lovers? On the face of it, it seems hard to believe that we will. For we've all been exposed to the romantic notions of our culture. We've all read countless novels and seen countless movies that show millionaires befriending tramps, princes marrying showgirls, and beauties enamored of beasts—each teaching the lesson that friendship and, most especially love, are not ruled by reason. But as we will see, while romantic love has some irrational and complex aspects, the factors that determine much of the attraction that humans have for each other are surprisingly simple.

PROXIMITY

One of the most important determinants of attraction and liking is sheer **proximity.** By now, dozens of studies have documented the fact that if you want to predict who makes friends with whom, the first thing to ask is who is nearby. Students who live next to each other in a dormitory or sit next to each other in classes develop stronger relations than those who live or sit only a bit farther away. Similarly, members of a bomber crew become much more friendly to fellow crewmen who work right next to them than to others only a few feet away (Berscheid and Walster, 1978; Berscheid, 1985).

What holds for friendship also holds for mate selection. The statistics are rather impressive. For example, there is evidence that more than half of the couples who took out marriage licenses in Columbus, Ohio, during the summer of 1949 were people who lived within sixteen blocks of each other when they went out on their first date (Clarke, 1952). Much the same holds for the probability that an engagement will ultimately lead to marriage; the farther apart the two live, the greater the chance that the engagement will be broken off (Berscheid and Walster, 1978).

Why should proximity be so important? One answer is that you can't like someone you've never met, and the chances of meeting that someone are much greater if he is nearby. But why should getting to know him make you like him?

One reason may be *familiarity.* There is a good deal of evidence that people tend to like what's more familiar. This seems to hold for just about any stimulus, whether it's a word in a foreign language, or a melody, or the name of a commercial product, or the photograph of a stranger's face—the more often it is seen or heard, the better it will be liked (Zajonc, 1968; Brickman and D'Amato, 1975; Moreland and Zajonc, 1982). Familiarity probably plays an important role in determining what we feel about other people as well. The hero of a well-known musical comedy explains his affection for the heroine by singing "I've grown accustomed to her face." In a more prosaic vein, the laboratory provides evidence that photographs of strangers' faces are judged to be more likable the more often they have been seen (Jorgensen and Cervone, 1978). Another study applied this general idea to the comparison of faces and their mirror images. Which will be better liked? If familiarity is the critical variable, then our friends should prefer a photograph of our face to one of its mirror image, since they've seen the first much more often than the second. But we ourselves should prefer the mirror image, which for us is by far the more familiar. The results were as

"Do you really love me, Anthony, or is it just because I live on the thirty-eighth floor?"
(Drawing by Claude; © 1959, 1987, The New Yorker Magazine, Inc.)

12.4   Familiarity and liking   *The figure shows two versions of a rather well-known lady. Which do you like better—the one on the right or the one on the left? (Courtesy Réunion des Musées Nationaux)* *(Please turn to p. 465.)*

predicted by the familiarity hypothesis (Mita, Dermer, and Knight, 1977; see Figure 12.4).

SIMILARITY

Do people like others who are similar to themselves, or do they prefer those who are very different? To put it differently, which bit of folk wisdom is more nearly correct: "Birds of a feather flock together" or—perhaps in analogy with magnets—"Opposites attract." It appears that birds have more to teach us in this matter than magnets do, for the evidence suggests that, in general, people tend to like others who are *similar* to themselves. For example, elementary school students prefer other children who perform about as well as they do in academics, sports, and music (Tesser, Campbell, and Smith, 1984), and "best friends" in high school resemble each other in age, race, year in school, and high-school grades (Kandel, 1978).

Whether similarity of personality characteristics such as sociability and extraversion play a similar role in determining attraction is still unclear. But there is no doubt that such relatively more objective attributes as race, ethnic origin, social and educational level, family background, income, and religion do affect marital choice and stability. This also holds for such behavioral patterns as the degree of gregariousness and drinking and smoking habits. One widely cited study showed that engaged couples in the United States are generally similar along all of these dimensions (Burgess and Wallin, 1943). The authors interpreted these findings as evidence for **homogamy**—a powerful tendency for like to marry like. Another study showed that homogamy plays a role in determining a couple's stability; couples who remained together after two-and-a-half years were more similar than those who had broken up (Hill, Rubin, and Peplau, 1976).

Is homogamy really produced by the effect of similarity on mutual liking? Or is it just a byproduct of proximity, of the fact that "few of us have an opportunity to meet, interact with, become attracted to, and marry a person markedly dissimilar from ourselves"? (Berscheid and Walster, 1978, p. 87). The answer is as yet unknown. But whether similarity is a cause of the attraction or is a side effect of some other factors that led to it initially, the end product is the same: Like pairs with like, and no heiress ever marries the butler except in the movies. We're not really surprised to discover that when a princess kisses a frog he turns into a prince. What would really be surprising is to see the frog turn into a peasant whom the princess then marries all the same.

Homogamy   *American Gothic by Grant Wood, 1930 (Photograph © 1992 The Art Institute of Chicago, all rights reserved)*

PHYSICAL ATTRACTIVENESS

There is little doubt that for a given time and culture there is considerable agreement as to how *physically attractive* a particular man or woman is. Nor is there any doubt that this factor is overwhelmingly important in determining a person's appeal—or at least his or her initial appeal—to members of the opposite sex. The vast sums of money spent on cosmetics, fashion, diets, and various forms of plastic surgery are one kind of testimony; our everyday experience is another. Under the circumstances, one may wonder whether there is any need to document the point experimentally, but in any case, such documentation does exist. In one study, freshmen were randomly paired at a dance and later asked how much they liked their partner and whether they wanted to go out with him or her at some future time. The main factor that determined each person's desirability as a future date was his or her physical attractiveness (Walster et al., 1966). Similar results were found in a study of the clients of a commercial video-dating service who selected partners after consulting files that included a photograph, background information, and detailed information about interests, hobbies, and personal ideals. When it came to the actual choice, the primary determinant was the photograph: Both male and female clients selected on the basis of physical attractiveness (Green, Buchanan, and Heuer, 1984).

Matching for attractiveness Physical attractiveness is clearly a very desirable quality. But if we all set our sights on only those who occupy the very top of this dimension, the world would soon be depopulated—there are simply not enough movie queens and matinee idols to go around. One would therefore assume that people behave in a more sensible fashion. They may well covet the most attractive of all possible mates, but they also have a fairly reasonable perception of their own social desirability (which is determined in part by their own physical attractiveness). In consequence, they will seek partners of roughly comparable social assets; while trying to get a partner who is most desirable, they also try to avoid rejection. This **matching hypothesis** predicts a strong correlation between the physical attractiveness of the two partners (Berscheid et al., 1971). This hypothesis is well supported by everyday observations ("They make such a fine couple!") and has been repeatedly documented in various empirical observations (Berscheid and Walster, 1974; White, 1980; Feingold, 1988).

What underlies physical attractiveness? Our discussion has assumed that physical attractiveness is a given and that people pretty much agree on who is and who is not attractive. But why should this be? Why should one set of particular features, one set of bodily proportions, represent the apex of attractiveness for so many people in our time and culture? As yet we don't know.

So far we are only beginning to discover just what it is that constitutes physical attractiveness in our own culture. According to one study, American college men judge photographs of women (whether white, black, or Asian) as more attractive if their face has certain features that are perceived as "cute" and tend to be found in children, such as relatively large and widely separated eyes, a small nose, and a small chin. If this result holds up in other cultures, a sociobiologist might suggest that this is because perceived youthfulness is a sign of fertility. The trouble is that there are a number of other features judged to be attractive that are associated with maturity rather than immaturity, for example, wide cheekbones and narrow cheeks (Cunningham, 1986).

In any case, there is little reason to suppose that the standards of attractiveness—of face or body—are the same across different times and places. To be sure, some similarities do exist. Signs of ill health and deformity (which might suggest a poor genetic bet) are considered unattractive in all cultures. The same

Attractiveness   People ornament themselves in virtually every culture but choose different ways of doing so. (A) Balinese dancer (Photograph by George K. Fuller), (B) Ahka girl from a village in Thailand (Photograph by George K. Fuller), (C) Masai girl in Kenya (John Moss/Photo Researchers)

Attractiveness in our own society   Cher accepting the Oscar for Best Actress in 1988. (Photograph © 1988, Smeal/Ron Galella Ltd.)

holds for signs of advancing age (which generally signal lower fertility, especially in females). In addition, all cultures want males to look male and females to look female, although the specific cues that weigh in this judgment (and that are considered attractive) vary widely. Beyond this, however, the differences probably outweigh the similarities.

LOVE

Attraction tends to bring people closer together. If they are close enough, their relation may be that of *love*. According to some authorities, psychologists might have been "wise to have abdicated responsibility for analysis of this term and left it to poets" (Reber, 1985, p. 409). But wise or not, in recent years psychologists have tried to say some things about this strange state of mind that has puzzled both sages and poets throughout the ages.

Psychologists have tried to distinguish between different kinds of love. Some of the resulting classification systems are rather complex. One such scheme tries to analyze love relationships according to the presence or absence of three main components: intimacy, passion, and commitment (Sternberg, 1986, 1988). Whether we're as yet at the stage at which we can really make the fine distinctions such systems propose is debatable. But most psychologists would agree that there are at least two crude categories. One is romantic—or passionate—love, the kind of love that one "falls into," that one is "in." The other is companionate love, a less violent state that emphasizes companionship and mutual trust and care.

ROMANTIC LOVE

Romantic love has been described as essentially passionate: "a wildly emotional state [in which] tender and sexual feelings, elation and pain, anxiety and relief, altruism and jealousy coexist in a confusion of feelings" (Berscheid and Walster, 1978). The extent to which the lovers feel that they are in the grip of an emotion they can't control is indicated by the very language in which they describe their love: They "fall in love," "are swept off their feet," and "can't stop themselves."

These tumultuous emotions are sharply focused on the beloved, who is almost always seen through a rosy glow. The lover constantly thinks about the beloved and continually wants to be in his or her company, sometimes to the point of near obsession. Given this giddy mixture of erotic, irrational, obsessed passions and idealized fantasy, it's understandable why Shakespeare felt that lovers have much in common with both madmen and poets. They are a bit mad because their emotions are so turbulent and their thoughts and actions so obsessive; they are a bit poetic because they don't see their beloved as he or she really is but as an idealized fabrication of their own desires and imaginings.

Romantic love and theories of emotions   A number of investigators have argued that if romantic love is an emotion, then theories such as Schachter and Singer's attribution-of-arousal theory (see Chapter 11, pp. 440–42) should apply to it just as they do to fear, anger, and euphoria. According to Schachter and Singer, an emotion has two components. One is a state of physiological arousal. The other is the appropriate cognitive context in the light of which that arousal is interpreted. According to some authors, much the same holds for romantic love (Walster and Berscheid, 1974; Walster and Walster, 1978).

Let's begin with the context. This includes our various ideas of what love and falling in love are all about. Our notions of romantic love—that there is the right person and no one else will do, that it can occur at "first sight," that one is often "helpless in the throes of love," that the beloved is a paragon of all possible virtues, and so on and so on—are at least in part cultural inventions. They were fashioned by a historical heritage that goes back to Greek and Roman times (with tales of lovers hit by Cupid's arrows), were revived during the Middle Ages (with knights in armor slaying dragons to win a lady's favor), and were finally mass-produced by the Hollywood entertainment machine (with a final fade-out in which boy and girl embrace to live happily ever after).★ This complex set of ideas about what love is, together with an appropriate potential love object—attractive, of the right age, more or less available, and so on—constitute the context that may lead us to interpret physiological arousal as love.

What leads to the relevant bodily arousal? One obvious source is erotic excitement, although other forms of stimulation may have the same effect. We previously saw that physiological arousal produced by sheer physical exertion can enhance sexual feelings (see Chapter 11, p. 442). In a similar vein, fear, pain, and anxiety may heighten general arousal and thus lend fuel to romantic passion. In a widely cited experiment, investigators compared the reactions of young men who crossed either of two bridges. One was a long, narrow, wobbly suspension bridge, precariously suspended over a shallow rapids 230 feet below. The other was a solid, well-built bridge, sitting only 10 feet above a small river. As each man crossed the bridge, he was approached by an attractive young woman who asked him to fill out a questionnaire for her to help her with a class project. Some of the men did indeed call the young woman later (ostensibly to discuss the experiment, but really to ask her for a date). But the likelihood of their doing so depended on the bridge on which they met. If it was the rickety suspension bridge—which presumably would elicit some fear and excitement—the chances were almost one in three that the men would call. If it was the safe, solid bridge, the chances were only one in twenty (Dutton and Aron, 1974; but see also Kenrick and Cialdini, 1977; Kenrick, Cialdini, and Linder, 1979).

Romantic love   *The blindness of romantic love is epitomized by Titania, Queen of the Fairies, in Shakespeare's* Midsummer Night's Dream. *Titania is made to fall in love with Bottom whose head has been turned into that of an ass. (*Titania Awakes, Surrounded by Attendant Fairies, Clinging Rapturously to Bottom, Still Wearing the Ass's Head, 1793/94, by Henry Fuseli; Kunsthaus, Zurich (Switzerland), Society of Zurich Friends of Art; © 1994 Kunsthaus Zurich. All rights reserved.)*

Revisiting Figure 12.4   *The familiarity-leads-to-liking hypothesis would predict a preference for the left panel—a retouched photograph of the Mona Lisa (see p. 462). The panel on the right is a mirror image of that photograph, which is presumably the less familiar of the two.*

★ While various Hindu myths and Chinese love songs make it clear that romantic love is found in other times and places than our own, it's unlikely that any other cultural epoch has taken it quite as seriously as ours does; thus love as a precondition for marriage is a relatively new and Western concept (e.g., De Rougemont, 1940; Hunt, 1959, Grant, 1976).

The rocky course of romantic love This general approach may help us understand why romantic love seems to thrive on obstacles. Shakespeare tells us that the "course of true love never did run smoothly" but if it had, the resulting love might have been lacking in ardor. The fervor of a wartime romance or of an extramarital affair is probably fed in part by danger and frustration, and many a lover's passion becomes all the more intense for being unrequited. In all these cases, there is increased arousal, whether through fear, frustration, or anxiety. This arousal continues to be interpreted as love, a cognitive appraisal that fits in perfectly with our ideas about romantic love, for these include suffering as well as rapture. An interesting demonstration of this phenomenon is the so-called Romeo-and-Juliet effect (named after Shakespeare's doomed couple whose parents violently opposed their love). This describes the fact that parental opposition tends to intensify the couple's romantic passion rather than to diminish it. In one study, couples were asked whether their parents interfered with their relationship. The greater this interference, the more deeply the couples fell in love (Driscoll, Davis, and Lipitz, 1972). The moral is that if parents want to break up a romance, their best bet is to ignore it. If the feuding Montagues and Capulets had simply looked the other way, Romeo and Juliet might well have become bored with each other by the end of the second act.

A related characteristic of romantic love is that it has some of the qualities of an adventure (Simmel, 1911; Sabini, 1992). Initially the word "romance" described a certain kind of tale written in medieval French (a language derived from Latin, or "Roman") about the wondrous feats of knights in armor who fought dragons and monsters and undertook quests to win some lady's love. In time, the word's meaning centered on the knight-meets-lady aspect of these stories and became more or less synonymous with "love affair." Some of its original sense still inheres in the way the term "romantic" is used today, for it often suggests some of the quality of fanciful adventure that the medieval romances described.

Rocky course of romantic love Parental opposition tends to intensify Romeo and Juliet's passion. Pictured here is the balcony scene from Prokofiev's ballet, Romeo and Juliet. (From a 1990 performance by American Ballet Theater; photograph by Martha Swope)

Romance and the knightly quest for adventure A painting based on a sixteenth-century Italian epic celebrating the heroic deed of Roger, a valorous knight doing battle with a sea monster to rescue the virtuous Angelica. (Roger and Angelique, by Jean-Auguste-Dominique Ingres, 1819; © Photo Réunion des Musées Nationaux)

Companionate love *When passion and obsession ebb, the companionship and affection of companionate love, as shown here, may follow. (Photograph © FPG International)*

COMPANIONATE LOVE

It's widely agreed that romantic love tends to be a short-lived bloom. That wild and tumultuous state, with its intense emotional ups and downs, with its obsessions, fantasies, and idealizations, rarely if ever lasts forever. Eventually there are no further surprises and no further obstacles except those posed by the inevitable problems of ordinary life. The adventure is over, and romantic love ebbs. Sometimes it turns into indifference (if not active dislike). But sometimes—and hopefully more often—it is transformed into a related but gentler emotion—*companionate love.* This is sometimes defined as the "affection we feel for those with whom our lives are deeply intertwined" (Berscheid and Hatfield, 1978, p. 176). In companionate love, the similarity of outlook, mutual caring, and trust that develop through day to day living become more important than the fantasies and idealization of romantic love, as the two partners try to live as happily ever after as it is possible to do in the actual world. This is not to say that the earlier passion doesn't occasionally flare up again. But it no longer has the obsessive quality that it once had, where the lover is unable to think of anything but the beloved (Neimeyer, 1984; Hatfield, 1988; Caspi and Herbener, 1990).

SOCIAL INFLUENCE: MANY-ON-ONE INTERACTIONS

Up to now, our discussion has focused upon one-on-one interactions: some between comparative strangers, others between friends and lovers. In such interactions, other people often affect what we do, as in the case of a salesman trying to sell a car to a potential customer or a would-be lover trying to persuade his beloved to reciprocate his affections. But there are instances in which the interaction is more complex and in which the social effects come from many people simultaneously.

Such situations are usually discussed under the general heading of ***social influence.*** In these cases, the interaction is of the form of many on one: The influence of many others converges upon one individual. In some cases, the influence of others may make us tailor our behavior to conform to theirs. In others, it will make us obey them and comply with their orders. And in still other instances, the others exert their influence upon us in an even simpler way—by their mere presence as an audience.

SOCIAL FACILITATION: SOCIAL INFLUENCE BY THE PRESENCE OF OTHERS

It has long been known that the presence of other people has an effect on us. An example is laughter: Every comedian knows that laughter is contagious; each guffaw triggers another and then yet another, a fact that led to the use of canned TV laughter on the theory that if the home audience hears the (dubbed) laughs of others, they will laugh along (Wilson, 1985). Similar effects have been demonstrated by many investigators who compared people on various tasks that they performed either alone or in the presence of others. The initial results suggested that the social effect is always beneficial. When with others who are engaged in the same task, people race bicycles faster, learn simple mazes more quickly, and perform more multiplication problems in the same period of time. Such effects have been grouped under the general title **social facilitation** (Allport, 1920).

Other studies, however, have indicated that the presence of others can sometimes be a hindrance instead of a help. While college students are faster at solving simple mazes when working with others, they are considerably slower when the mazes are more complex (Hunt and Hillery, 1973; Zajonc, 1965, 1980). An audience can evidently *inhibit* as well as facilitate. How can such divergent results be reconciled?

According to Robert Zajonc, the explanation is that the presence of others leads to a state of increased drive or arousal. Such an increase would resolve the apparent contradiction if we assume that it strengthens the tendency to perform highly dominant responses—the ones that seem to come "automatically." If so, then we should expect that the presence of others would improve performance when the dominant response is also the correct one—as in performing simple motor skills or learning simple mazes. But when the task gets harder—as in the case of complex mazes—then the dominant response is often incorrect. As a result, we should expect performance to get worse when others watch us, for in that case the dominant response (enhanced by increased arousal) will inhibit the less dominant but correct reaction. And this is just what happens.★

As an example from ordinary life consider an accomplished professional actor. Such a person generally thrives in front of an audience—the bigger the audience, the happier he is. For him, the dominant responses are precisely those demanded by his role; he knows his part and how to make the most of it, and so the audience brings his performance to even higher peaks. But the situation is very different for an unpracticed young amateur who is still stumbling over his lines and unsure of his part. His dominant responses are inappropriate to what he ought to be doing, and so he coughs, gives an embarrassed smile, and takes a few undecided half steps. He becomes aroused by the audience, but this arousal makes his performance even worse than it would be otherwise (Zajonc, 1965, 1980).

Some evidence comes from observations of pool players in a college union building. When good players were watched by an audience of four others, their accuracy rose from 71 to 80 percent. But when poor players were observed, their accuracy became even worse that it was before, dropping from 35 to 25 percent (Michaels et al., 1982).

Zajonc's general hypothesis may well be right, but there is still the question of why the presence of others should affect arousal. Some authors suggest that it triggers concern at being evaluated and perhaps embarrassed (e.g., Cottrell et al., 1968; Bond, 1982); others propose that it leads to distraction, which people then must try hard to overcome (Sanders, 1981). While such factors almost certainly play a role, they are probably not the only ones, for similar results have been obtained with lower animals. In one study, cockroaches learned to escape from a bright light by running down a simple alley or by learning a maze. Some performed alone; others were run in pairs. When on the runway, the animals performed better in pairs than alone—on this simple task, the dominant response was appropriate. The reverse was true for the maze—in this more complex task, the dominant response was incorrect and inappropriate (Zajonc, Heingertner, and Herman, 1969). The close parallel between these findings and

Social facilitation *Audiences generally enhance the performance of an accomplished professional. But the effect on novices is not always beneficial. (Photograph by Gale Zucker/Stock, Boston)*

★ This hypothesis goes back to some earlier findings on people who seem to be more anxious (and thus presumably more driven and aroused) than average. Such people do better than less anxious people when faced with relatively simple tasks and worse when faced with more complex ones (Spence and Spence, 1966).

Conformity *(Photograph by G. Frank Radway)*

those obtained with humans has led some authors to suggest that some of the factors that underlie social facilitation may be the same across species, although such cross-species factors are surely more primitive than, say, evaluation anxiety. (It is hard to believe that a cockroach is seriously concerned about what another cockroach thinks about him.) Zajonc suggests that this common factor is an increased alertness in the presence of another member of one's own species; such alertness increases arousal, which in turn augments the strength of dominant responses, with resulting enhancement or impairment of performance (Zajonc, 1980).

CONFORMITY

Social facilitation (and inhibition) may well be the simplest form of social influence. It shows that our behavior is affected by the mere presence of others just about regardless of what they do. But in other forms of social influence what others do matters very much indeed. An important example is *conformity* in which we go along with other people. We may regard ourselves as independent nonconformists, but in some situations we all conform whether in speech or dress or manner. In the last chapter, we saw that people may go along with a group even when the group is patently wrong, as in Asch's experiment when the subjects yielded to a majority that judged an 8-inch line to be equal to one whose length was 6 1/4 inches (Asch, 1952, 1955, 1956; see Chapter 11, pp. 416–17).

THE CAUSES OF CONFORMITY

Why do people conform? The evidence suggests that there are two main reasons: One is that they want to be right; another is that they want to be liked (or at least that they don't want to appear foolish).

One basis for following others is when we ourselves aren't sure what is right. In such cases, the group exerts influence because it provides information that we feel that we ourselves don't have. This holds for information about any difficult judgment, whether it is sensory, social, or moral. If we are nearsighted and aren't wearing glasses, we'll ask others to read distant street signs; if we are not sure of what to wear (or what to say, or who to vote for), we watch what others do to get some clues for how we ourselves should act. If people are made to believe that they are more competent and knowledgeable in some area than others are (for example, in seeing hidden figures), they are less likely to conform (e.g., Wiesenthal et al., 1976; Campbell, Tesser, and Fairey, 1986).

Another reason for going along with the crowd is not so much cognitive as motivational. For we sometimes conform even if we believe that we are right and the others are wrong. Consider the original Asch study in which a unanimous majority made a grossly incorrect judgment. The subject sees the world as it is, but she has every reason to believe that the others see it differently. If she now says what she believes, she can't help but be embarrassed; after all, the others will probably think that she's a fool and may then laugh at her.* Under the circumstances, many subjects prefer to disguise what they really believe and go along.

---

* This suspicion is by no means unjustified. In yet another variation of the Asch experiment, one confederate gave false responses when run with a group of sixteen real subjects who of course gave the correct answer. Under these circumstances, the group found the confederate's behavior ludicrous and laughed aloud at him (Asch, 1952).

(© 1974 Saturday Review, cartoon by Nurit Karlin)

NURIT KARLIN

"Twenty-two is out of step. Pass it on."

That something of this sort is going on was shown in another variant of the Asch experiment in which the subject came late while the experiment was already in progress. The experimenter told him that since he arrived late, it would be simpler for him to write his answers down in private rather than to announce them out loud. Under these circumstances, there was little yielding. The group stimuli were of the original unambiguous sort (e.g., 8 inches vs. 6 1/4 inches in height), so that there was no informational pressure toward conformity. And since the judgments were made in private, there was no (or little) motivational pressure either. As a result, there was a great deal of independence (Asch, 1952).

MAJORITIES AND MINORITIES

A unanimous majority evidently exerts a powerful effect on a solitary individual that makes him want to conform. What happens when the individual is no longer alone?

The ally effect   To answer this question, Asch varied his experiment by having one of the confederates act as the subject's ally; all of the other confederates gave wrong answers while the ally's judgments were correct. Under these conditions, the real subject yielded very rarely and was not particularly upset.

The moral seems simple enough: One person who believes as we do can sustain us against all others. But on closer examination, things are not quite as simple as that. For in another variation, the confederate again deviated from the majority, but she didn't do so by giving the correct answer. On the contrary, she gave an answer that was even further from the truth than was the group's. Thus, on a trial in which the correct answer was 6 1/4 inches and the group answer was 6 3/4 inches, the confederate's answer might be 8 inches. This response was obviously not arrayed on the side of the subject (or of truth), but it helped to liberate the subject even so. He now yielded very much less than when confronted by a unanimous majority. What evidently mattered was the group's unanimity; once this was broken, the subject felt that he could speak up without fear of embarrassment (Asch, 1952). Similar studies have been performed in other laboratories with essentially similar results (Allen and Levine, 1971; Allen, 1975; Nemeth and Chiles, 1988).

One person who shares our view can sustain us against all others. But if we can't find a supporter, the next best thing is to find another person who also opposes the majority, even if her opposition comes from the other side than our own. Thus, totalitarian systems have good reason to stifle dissent of any kind,

The ally effect *Not being alone sustains one against a majority but also in other struggles, such as against evil witches and all-powerful wizards. (From the 1939 movie,* The Wizard of Oz, *with Judy Garland, Ray Bolger, Jack Haley, and Bert Lahr; courtesy of Photofest)*

The effect of a consistent minority *A steadfast minority can gradually create genuine changes in what people think and feel as in the case of the American civil rights movement. A scene from the 1965 march from Selma to Montgomery. (Photograph by Dan Budnick/Woodfin Camp)*

whether of the right or the left. The moment one voice is raised in dissent, the unanimity is broken and then others may (and often do) find the courage to express their own dissent, whatever its form.

The role of a consistent minority Some authors believe that the impact of a minority may go beyond its role in breaking up unanimity. In their view, consistent minorities sometimes have yet another and distinctly different effect. History shows us that small minorities often create social innovations. They begin by challenging an established majority, as in advocating votes for women or civil rights. They often prevail in part because their members seem utterly unanimous in their determination and their confidence. As time goes on, these minorities tend to convert their erstwhile opponents to their own views. In this regard, their influence is rather different from that exerted by a majority. While a majority tends to produce overt conformity, its effect is essentially superficial; it changes what people do or say rather than what they think. In contrast, the effect of a unanimous and steadfast minority—while slower and less dramatic—may eventually affect more than overt behavior. It may lead to genuine changes in what people think and feel (Maass and Clark, 1984; Moscovici, 1985).

BLIND OBEDIENCE

There is another way of influencing the behavior of others that is much more direct than any we've considered thus far. It is by getting people to obey what we command them to do. Of particular interest is the case of *blind obedience* to orders that violate one's own conscience, actions in which the individual subordinates his own understanding of the situation to that of some authority. On the face of it, obedience might appear to differ from the forms of social influence we have considered thus far because commands are usually delivered on a one-to-one basis: The student obeys the teacher, the automobile driver obeys the policeman. But at bottom, the interaction is not truly one on one, because the teacher and the policeman speak with the authority of the

471

whole society behind them when they order us to hand in our homework or to pull over to the roadside. To the extent that this is so, obedience and conformity (and social facilitation and inhibition) are all instances of social influence.

A certain degree of obedience is a necessary ingredient of living in a society. In any society, no matter how primitive, some individuals have authority over others, at least within a limited sphere. Obedience is particularly relevant as societies get more complex, where the spheres within which authority can be exerted become much more differentiated. Teachers assign homework, doctors order intravenous feedings, and policemen stop automobiles. The pupils, nurses, and motorists generally obey. Their obedience is based on an implicit recognition that the persons who issued the orders were operating within their legitimate domain of authority. If this domain is overstepped, obedience is unlikely. Policemen can't order motorists to recite lists of irregular French verbs or to take two aspirins and go to bed.

Some tendency to obey authority is thus a vital cement that holds society together; without it, there would be chaos. But the atrocities of this century—the Nazi death camps, the Cambodian massacres, the so-called ethnic cleansing in Bosnia—give terrible proof that this disposition to obedience can also become a corrosive poison that destroys our sense of humanity. Some of these atrocities could not have been committed without the obedience of tens or hundreds of thousands and the acquiescence of many more. How could such obedience have come about?

Psychologists who try to answer this question have adopted two different approaches. One focuses on the personality structure of the blindly obedient individual and suggests that his acts are essentially irrational and stem from primitive, emotional sources. The other approach emphasizes the social situation in which the obedient person finds himself and proposes that some aspects of his behavior can be explained in cognitive terms, by asking how he interprets the situation in which he is placed.

OBEDIENCE AND PERSONALITY STRUCTURE

What makes people obey and thus participate in any of the unspeakable acts of which history tells us? One interpretation is that some personalities are more prone to obey than others, that the crucial determinant is within the person rather than in the situation.

An influential version of the person-centered hypothesis was proposed shortly after World War II by a group of investigators who believed they had discovered a personality type that is predisposed toward totalitarian dogma and is thus more ready to obey unquestioningly. Such *authoritarian personalities* are prejudiced against various minority groups and also hold certain sentiments about authority, including submission to those above, harshness to those below, and a general belief in the importance of power and dominance. These authoritarian attitudes are shown by a tendency to agree emphatically with statements such as: "Obedience and respect for authority are the most important virtues children should learn," "Most of our social problems would be solved if we could somehow get rid of the immoral, the crooked, and feeble-minded people," and "People can be divided into two distinct classes: the weak and the strong" (Adorno et al., 1950).

According to the investigators, this constellation of attitudes was an expression of underlying personality patterns formed in childhood. They found that people who scored high on minority prejudice and authoritarianism described their childhoods as dominated by a stern and harshly punitive father who insisted on absolute obedience. According to the investigators, the children reared in this manner developed what psychoanalysts call a "reaction formation"; they went to the opposite extreme and adopted obedience and submission to authority as exalted virtues (see Chapter 17, pp. 675–76). But their hostility was not submerged entirely; it found new outlets and was directed at safer targets, such as minority groups. As a result, they saw the outside world as populated by a horde of dangerous enemies who had to be crushed before they themselves were crushed by these "enemies"—African Americans, Latinos, Asians, Jews, foreigners, Bolsheviks, and so on.

The initial work on the authoritarian personality has been the subject of considerable criticism (for review, see Snyder and Ickes, 1985). Some critics focused on the fact that the sample on which the conclusions were based was limited to white middle-class Californians, others on the fact that the information about the subjects' childhoods was mainly based upon their own recollections, and so on. But while the original claims of the investigators may have been too extravagant, their studies did focus on an important set of relationships between social and political attitudes (Brown, 1965). Minority prejudice probably does tend to go together with authoritarian sentiments, and people with such sentiments do show a number of political characteristics that might be expected: They tend to be more obedient to authority, vote for conservative and law-and-order candidates, and accept the attitudes of those in power (Elms and Milgram, 1966; Izzett, 1971; Poley, 1974). In addition, there is some evidence that these authoritarian attitudes are often accompanied by certain ways of remembering and idealizing one's parents and a belief in stern childhood discipline. But whether this constellation of attitudes is caused by childhood experiences and emotions is still very much debatable. There is evidence that authoritarianism is more pronounced among people with less education and lower intelligence (Christie, 1954). As one writer put it in the sixties, "Authoritarianism may be the worldview of the uneducated in Western industrialized societies" (Brown, 1965, p. 523).

OBEDIENCE AND THE SITUATION

Can the person-centered hypothesis explain the atrocities of recent times? Are those who obey the order to massacre countless innocents sick individuals completely different from the rest of us? Some of them probably are (Dicks, 1972). But the frightening fact is that many seem to be cast in a much more ordinary mold; what is horrifying about them is what they do and not who they are. In a well-known account of the trial of Adolf Eichmann, the man who supervised the deportation of six million Jews to the Nazi gas chambers, the author comments on the grotesque "banality of evil": "The trouble with Eichmann was precisely that so many were like him, and that the many were neither perverted nor sadistic, that they were, and still are, terribly and terrifyingly normal" (Arendt, 1965, p. 276).

It appears that obedience to inhuman orders is in part a function of the total situation in which a person finds himself. Under some social systems—Hitler's Germany, Stalin's Russia, Pot's Cambodia—the conditions for compliance or tacit acceptance are so powerful that an outsider might well pause to wonder whether "there but for the grace of God go I."

The Milgram studies   The importance of situational factors in producing obedience is highlighted by the results of what may be the best known study in modern social psychology, conducted by Stanley Milgram (1963). Milgram's subjects were drawn from a broad spectrum of socioeconomic and educational levels; they were recruited by a local newspaper ad offering $4.50 per hour to persons willing to participate in a study of memory. Milgram's subjects arrived at the laboratory where a white-coated experimenter told them that the study in

Obedience   *The commandant of a concentration camp in Germany stands amid some of his prisoners who were burned or shot as the American army approached the camp during the last days of World War II. Most Nazis who held such positions insisted that they were "just following orders." (Courtesy of United Press International)*

which they were to take part concerned the effect of punishment on human learning.

The subjects were run in pairs and drew lots to determine who would be the "teacher" and who the "learner." The task of the learner was to master a list of associations. The task of the teacher was to present the stimuli, to record the learner's answers, and—most important—to administer punishment whenever the learner responded incorrectly. The learner was conducted to a cubicle where the experimenter strapped him in a chair, to "prevent excess movement," and attached the shock electrodes to his wrist—all in full view of the teacher. After the learner was securely strapped in place, the teacher was brought back to the main experimental room and seated in front of an imposing-looking shock generator. The generator had 30 lever switches with labeled shock intensities, ranging from 15 volts to 450 volts in 15-volt increments. Below each of the levers there were also verbal descriptions ranging from "Slight Shock" to "Danger: Severe Shock." The labels below the last two levers were even more ominous; they were devoid of any verbal designation and were simply marked "XXX" (Figure 12.5).

The teacher presented the items that had to be memorized. He was instructed to move on to the next item on the list whenever the learner responded correctly but to administer a shock whenever an error was made. He was told to increase the level of punishment with each succeeding error, beginning with 15 volts and going up by one step for each error thereafter until 450 volts was reached. To get an idea what the learner experienced, the teacher first submitted to a sample shock of 45 volts, the third of the 30-step punishment series, which gave an unpleasant jolt. During the experiment, all communications between teacher and learner were conducted over an intercom, since the learner was out of sight, strapped to a chair in the experimental cubicle.

Needless to say, the shock generator never delivered any shocks (except for the initial sample) and the lot drawing was rigged so that the learner was always a confederate, played by a mild-mannered, middle-aged actor. The point of the experiment was simply to determine how far the subjects would go in obeying the experimenter's instructions. Since the learner made a fair number of errors, the shock level of the prescribed punishment kept on rising. By the time 120 volts was reached, the victim shouted that the shocks were becoming too painful. At 150 volts he demanded that he be let out of the experiment. At 180 volts, he cried out that he could no longer stand the pain. At 300 volts, he screamed that he would give no further answers and insisted that he be freed. On the next few shocks there were agonized screams. After 330 volts, there was silence.

The learner's responses were of course predetermined. But the real subjects—the teachers—did not know that, so they had to decide what to do. When the victim cried out in pain or refused to go on, the subjects usually turned to the experimenter for instructions. In response, the experimenter told the subjects that the experiment had to go on, indicated that he took full responsibility, and pointed out that "the shocks may be painful but there is no permanent tissue damage."

How far do subjects go in obeying the experimenter? The results were astounding: About 65 percent of Milgram's subjects continued to obey the

A

B

C

D

12.5 The obedience experiment *(A) The "shock generator" used in the experiment. (B) The learner is strapped into his chair and electrodes are attached to his wrist. (C) The teacher receives a sample shock. (D) The teacher breaks off the experiment. (Copyright 1965 by Stanley Milgram. From the film* Obedience, *distributed by Penn State Audio-Visual Services.)*

experimenter to the bitter end. This proportion was unaffected even when the learner mentioned that he suffered from a mild heart condition. This isn't to say that the obedient subjects had no moral qualms—quite the contrary. Many of them were seriously upset. They bit their lips, twisted their hands, sweated profusely—but obeyed even so. Similar results were obtained when the study was repeated with subjects from other countries, Australia, Germany, and Jordan (Kilham and Mann, 1974; Mantell and Panzarella, 1976; Shanab and Yahya, 1977).

Is there a parallel between obedience in these artificial laboratory situations and obedience in the all-too-real nightmares of Nazi Germany or Cambodia? In some ways, there is no comparison, given the enormous disparities in scope and degree. But Milgram believed that some of the underlying psychological processes may be the same in both cases.

Being another person's agent In Milgram's view, one of the crucial factors is the fact that all of us are brought up in a world in which there is a continual stress on obedience to legitimate authority, first within the family, then in school, and still later within the institutional settings of the adult world. As a result, we all become well practiced in adopting the attitude of an agent who performs an action that is initiated by someone else. The responsibility belongs to that someone else and not to us. The good child does what she is told; the good employee may raise a question but will accept the boss's final decision; the good soldier is not even allowed to question why. All of them come to feel that they are just an agent who executes another's will: the hammer that struck a nail, not the carpenter who wielded it.

The feeling that one is a mere instrument with little or no sense of personal responsibility can be increased yet further. One means is by increasing the **psychological distance** between one's own actions and their end result. This phenomenon was studied in Milgram's laboratory. In one variation, two teachers were used. One was a confederate who was responsible for administering the shocks; the other was the real subject who was asked to perform such subsidiary tasks as reading the stimuli over a microphone and recording the learner's responses. In this new role, the subject was still essential to the smooth functioning of the experimental procedure. If he stopped, the victim would receive no further shocks. But even so, the subject might be expected to feel further removed from the ultimate consequence of the procedure, like a minor cog in a bureaucratic machine. After all, he didn't do the actual shocking! Under these conditions, over 90 percent of the subjects went all the way (Milgram, 1963, 1965; see also Kilham and Mann, 1974).

If obedience is increased by decreasing the subject's sense of personal responsibility, does the opposite hold as well? To answer this question, Milgram decreased the psychological distance between what the subject did and its effect upon the victim. Rather than being out of sight in an experimental cubicle, the victim was now seated directly adjacent to the subject who was told to administer the shock in a brutally direct manner. He had to press the victim's hand upon a shock electrode, holding it down by force if necessary. (His own hand was encased in an insulating glove to protect it from the shock; see Figure 12.6). Now compliance dropped considerably, in analogy to the fact that it is easier to drop bombs on an unseen enemy than to plunge a knife into his body when he looks you in the eye. But even so, 30 percent of the subjects still reacted with perfect obedience. (For further discussion of this and related issues, see Miller, 1986).

Cognitive reinterpretations In addition to emphasizing his role as a mere instrument, the obedient person develops an elaborate set of further cognitive devices to reinterpret the situation and his own part in it. One of the most common ap-

12.6 *Obedient subject pressing the learner's hand upon the shock electrode* (Copyright 1965 by Stanley Milgram. From the film *Obedience*, distributed by Penn State Audio-Visual Services)

proaches is to put on psychic blinders and try to shut out the awareness that the victim is a living, suffering fellow being. According to one of Milgram's subjects, "You really begin to forget that there's a guy out there, even though you can hear him. For a long time I just concentrated on pressing the switches and reading the words" (Milgram, 1974, p. 38). This dehumanization of the victim is a counterpart to the obedient person's self-picture as an agent of another's will, someone "who has a job to do" and who does it whether he likes it or not. The obedient person sees himself as an instrument; by the same token, he sees the victim as an object. In his eyes, both have become dehumanized (Bernard, Ottenberg, and Redl, 1965).

The dehumanization of the opponent is a common theme in war and mass atrocity. Victims are rarely described as people, but only as bodies, objects, numbers. The process of dehumanization is propped up by euphemisms and bureaucratic jargon. The Nazis used terms such as "final solution" (for the mass murder of six million people) and "special treatment" (for death by gassing); the nuclear age contributed "fallout problem" and "preemptive attack"; the Vietnam War gave us "free-fire zone" and "body count"; and the war in Bosnia-Herzegovina added "ethnic cleansing"—all dry, official phrases that are admirably suited to keep all thoughts of blood and human suffering at a reasonably safe distance.

By dehumanizing the victim, moral qualms are pushed into the background. For all but the most brutalized, though, these qualms can't be banished forever. To justify continued obedience, such queasy feelings may be suppressed by reference to some higher, overriding moral ideology. In Milgram's study, the subjects convinced themselves that science had to be served regardless of the victim's cries; in Nazi Germany, the goal was to cleanse humanity by ridding it of Gypsy and Jewish "vermin." In a related kind of self-justification, the fault is projected on the victims; they are considered to be subhuman, dirty, evil, and only have themselves to blame.

The slippery slope   The cognitive reorientation by which a person no longer feels responsible for her own acts is not achieved in an instant. Usually, inculcation is by gradual steps. The initial act of obedience is relatively mild and does not seriously clash with the person's own moral outlook. Escalation is gradual so that each step seems only slightly different from the one before. This of course was the pattern in Milgram's study, which created a *slippery slope* that subjects slid down unawares. A similar program of progressive escalation was evidently used in the indoctrination of death-camp guards. The same is true for the military training of soldiers everywhere. Draftees go through "basic training," in part to learn various military skills, but much more importantly, to acquire the habit of instant obedience. Raw recruits are rarely asked to point their guns at another person and shoot. It's not only that they don't know how; it's that most of them probably wouldn't do it.

Milgram's study, the person, and the situation   Modern social psychologists generally interpret Milgram's results as a pointed reminder that the situation in which people find themselves is a powerful determinant of what they do and may be more important than the sort of people that they are. Everyone knows that this is true for many ordinary situations of everyday life; virtually everybody stops at a red light, regardless of any quirks in their personalities. But that a situation such as Milgram's would lead two-thirds of his subjects to impose serious pain and harm on another person was a sobering surprise. Before Milgram published his results, he described his study to several groups of judges, including a group of forty psychiatrists. All of them predicted that he would encounter a great deal of defiance. In their view, only a pathological fringe of at most 2 percent of the subjects would go to the maximum shock intensity. As we now know, their predictions were far off the mark. In effect, they are yet another example of the fundamental attribution error—the belief that what people do is largely caused by who they are and to a much lesser extent by the situation in which they find themselves (see Chapter 11, pp. 433–35).

Clearly, Milgram's results highlight the role of the situation in determining what people do. They argue against an extreme version of the person-centered view, such as that expressed by the investigators who studied authoritarianism (see pp. 472–73). But this shouldn't blind us to the fact that personal factors also matter. The fact that two-thirds of Milgram's subjects obeyed to the bitter end is surprising as well as disturbing. But it's no less true that another third did not obey.

SOCIAL IMPACT THEORY

The preceding discussion dealt with several different forms of social influence, including social facilitation and inhibition, conformity, and obedience. According to Bibb Latané's *social impact theory,* all of these forms of social influence can be understood by thinking of the individual as exposed to a field of social forces that converge upon her much as a number of light bulbs cast light upon a target surface. How much light will be cast depends on their number, the strength of each bulb, and how close the bulbs are to the target. According to Latané, the impact of social forces converging on one individual works in a similar manner. The total impact will depend on the number of people who affect the target individual, how strong (in age, status, or power) each of these people is, and how close they are to her in space or time (see Figure 12.7).

Evidence for the role of strength comes from work on stage fright: Performers are more anxious when anticipating playing before audiences of higher than of lower status (Latané and Harkins, 1976). There is also evidence for the role of immediacy: Performing for a live audience produces more stage fright than performing for one that watches a video monitor in another room (Borden, 1980). Evidence for the effect of number is even more convincing, for

12.7 Convergence of social forces
(Freely adapted from Latané. 1981)

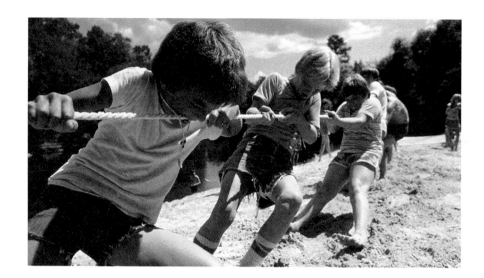

Social loafing *In a tug-of-war, everyone seems to pull as hard as he can, but the total force exerted by the group tends to be less than the solo rate times the number of its members. (Photograph by Jodi Cobb, 1985/Woodfin Camp)*

in virtually all many-on-one situations, the influence the "many" exert on the "one" goes up as their number increases. The larger the unanimous majority, the greater the conformity; the larger the audience, the greater the stage fright; the larger the crowd looking up at the sky, the more others look up too. Each additional individual increases the social impact, though with diminishing returns: Adding one person to a group of two will produce a much greater increase in social impact than adding one to a group of eight.

Thus far, we've only considered cases where the social influence exerted by several different sources converges upon one single target individual. In such cases, the impact goes up with their number (though, to be sure, with diminishing returns). What happens when that influence is spread out over more than one target? According to Latané, this will diffuse the impact, which will now be divided over all the targets: The more targets there are, the less social impact will hit any one of them (see Figure 12.8; adapted from Latané, 1981). Evidence

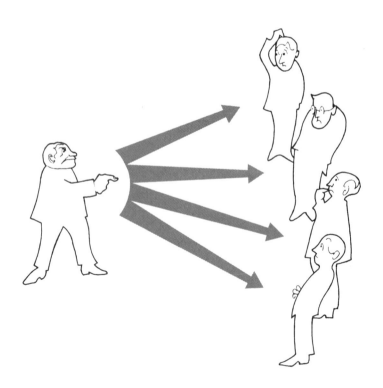

12.8 Diffusion of social impact *(Freely adapted from Latané, 1981)*

12.9 Diffusion of social impact and performance anxiety *Ratings of nervousness obtained prior to a college talent show from persons who performed alone or with two, four, seven, or ten others. (After Jackson and Latané, 1981)*

comes from a study of stage fright in participants at a college talent show. The acts at the show had from one to ten performers. The stage fright of these performers depended on the number of co-performers in the act: the greater their number, the less stage fright any one member of the act felt (Jackson and Latané, 1981; see Figure 12.9).

A similar dispersion of social impact is relevant to the bystander effect, which we discussed in another context (see pwp. 457–59). The likelihood that any one person will provide help in an emergency decreases as the number of bystanders increases. Here diffusion of social impact is partially produced by the diffusion of responsibility, for the obligation to help is spread out over all the onlookers, and each can ask, "Why me? Why not the others?"

A final example of diffusion of social impact comes from a phenomenon called **social loafing.** This describes the fact that when individuals work as a group on a common task, all doing the same thing, they often generate less effort than they would if they worked alone. An example is pulling at a rope. In one study, one man working alone pulled with an average force of 139 pounds, while groups of eight pulling together only averaged 546 pounds, which is less than four times the solo rate. In another study, students were asked to clap and cheer as loudly as they could; sometimes alone, sometimes in groups of two, four, or six. Here too the results showed social loafing: Each person cheered and clapped less vigorously the greater the number of others he was with (Latané, Williams, and Harkins, 1979). There is an old adage: "Many hands make light the work." The trouble is that they don't make it as light as they should.

LEADERSHIP: ONE-ON-MANY INTERACTIONS

The preceding section dealt with interactions that are many-on-one, such as those in which groups exert influence on an individual and produce conformity and compliance. We will now turn the tables and look at the reverse condition, the effect of one on many, where one individual exerts his or her influence on a number—sometimes a very large number—of others. The most important example of such one-on-many interactions is *leadership.*

Leadership occurs in a multitude of social contexts, including politics, the military, business and commerce, academia, sports teams, social clubs, and even the family. The ways this leadership may be exercised vary even more widely (Hollander, 1985; Bass, 1990). One difference concerns the size of the group being led, which may be as large as the People's Republic of China or as small as a boys' gang. Another concerns the leader's authority: Is that leader the ultimate authority (as was Stalin), or does that person report to another higher up in a chain of command (as a colonel reports to a general)? A further difference is whether the leader tries to influence his followers directly or whether he exerts his influence through a special group of loyal subordinates. Considering these many differences, is there anything one can say about leadership in general?

GREAT PERSON OR SOCIAL FORCES

From one perspective, history is essentially created by exceptional individuals, who, for better or worse, determine the course of human events. In the nineteenth century, the proponents of this great-person theory often cited

A

B

Leadership—person or situation? (A) *Some historians focus on the personality of the individual leader. To them, Napoleon was a military and political genius who shaped history. (B) Others see the leader in the context of the total situation in which he finds himself. To them, instead of history being made by Napoleon, Napoleon was massed by history.* (Napoleon on the Battlefield of Eylau, February 9, 1807, *1808, by Jean-Antoine Gros, Louvre, Paris*)

the case of Napoleon Bonaparte. According to some contemporary writers such as Thomas Carlyle, Napoleon was a political and military genius whose brilliant mind and unyielding will overcame all opposition for over two decades (Carlyle, 1841). But from another perspective, the success or failure of individuals is determined by the situations in which they find themselves. Thus, to the great Russian novelist Leo Tolstoy, Napoleon's initial successes were caused by circumstance: the ineptitude of the opposing generals, the zeal of the French soldiers, the huge armies under his command. And when he finally failed, it was not because his genius deserted him, but because of the ferocious Russian winter, the long supply lines, and so on (Tolstoy, 1868). The same controversy has emerged in the discussion of many other historical events. Would there have been a Bolshevik Revolution if Vladimir Lenin had remained in exile from Russia? Would the British have sued for peace with Hitler if Churchill had died before 1940? The two poles of the argument have surfaced again and again: On the one hand the genius of the leader seems to prevail, on the other the historical situation—sometimes described as "the spirit and needs of the times," sometimes as "economic necessity"—seems to control destiny (Hook, 1955; Jennings, 1972; Burns, 1978).

At a more mundane level, this debate among historians has its counterpart in an issue we considered in a previous discussion of attribution (see Chapter 11, pp. 432–37): Do we (and should we) attribute a person's actions to her dispositional qualities or to the situation? To be sure, the behaviors studied in the social psychologist's laboratory don't have the momentous quality of those performed by history's leaders; answering a quiz master's questions (see p. 433) is hardly on a par with fighting the Battle of Waterloo. But the underlying questions are quite similar. Do we attribute the subject's poorer performance to something in her (she is not as smart and knows less) or to something in the situation (she's not the one who picked the questions)? Similarly for issues in history: Do we attribute Napoleon's defeat to something in him (e.g., his genius finally flagged) or to something in the situation (e.g., the combined armies of England, Russia and his other enemies were too powerful)?

Put another way, the question is whether all—or most—successful leaders share any personal characteristics. The great-person theory would predict that they do, that a Napoleon would in all likelihood have achieved leadership even if he'd never entered the military. What evidence can social psychology offer?

LEADERSHIP IN THE LABORATORY

To determine whether there are, in fact, such leadership qualities, social psychologists have tried to relate various personal characteristics of group members to whether they are perceived as leaders and whether they are effective in this role. Leadership perception and performance have been assessed in many ways, including ratings by subordinates, peers, and supervisors. They have also been assessed by a number of laboratory studies in which small groups of four to six are given some joint task that has to be solved by discussion. Thus subjects may be told that they are explorers stranded 200 miles away from their base. To get back, they have to jettison some of their equipment (pup tent, tools, etc.). Each member first tells the others which item he would jettison first, which second, and so on. Then the group comes up with a consensus list. To assess leadership *perception,* each member is rated by all others on the degree to which he influenced the group. To assess leadership *performance,* each member's initial list is compared with the group's consensus list: To the extent that one member's list is closer to the final list than another's, his leadership is judged as more effective than his (Cammalleri et al., 1973; Bottger, 1984).

The next step is to see whether leadership perception and performance are related to any other personal characteristics. The verdict to date seems to be that there are indeed such relationships, although they are not as all-powerful as the great-person theory might lead one to suspect. Thus people who are seen as leaders tend to be more intelligent, more outgoing, and more dominant than those who are not regarded as leaders (e.g., Lord, deVader, and Alliger, 1986; Kenny and Zaccaro, 1983). But overall, the role of the situation seems to be at least as important as the leader's personal characteristics (Bass, 1981; Hollander, 1985).

What are the characteristics of the situation that make a leader effective? Relatively favorable situations are those in which the leader has considerable authority, the task to be performed is clear-cut, and the group members get along with each other and with the leader. To the extent that any of these conditions are reversed, the situation is unfavorable. It seems then that *both* the personal characteristics of the would-be leaders and the situations they confront determine how effective they will be.

"There are no great men, my boy—only great committees." (Drawing by Chas. Addams; © 1975 The New Yorker Magazine, Inc.)

But there is a complication: The person who becomes an effective leader of one group will not necessarily become the leader of another. This is especially true if the two groups have different missions. On reflection, this is pretty much what one might expect. The qualities that make for leadership in a corporate board meeting are surely different from those that make for leadership in a research laboratory. And both are different from those that make for leadership in a boys' gang. (For a more detailed proposal on the proper match-up between leaders and situations, see Fiedler, 1978).

How does any of this relate to the questions raised by speculative historians? Would the Nazi movement have risen to power in Germany without Adolf Hitler? Would Britain have continued to fight without Churchill's oratory? Social psychology obviously cannot answer momentous questions of this sort. Even to try would be exceedingly presumptuous. For surely issues of this sort require the combined efforts of all the social sciences—anthropology, economics, history, political science, social psychology, sociology—and even then, there may very well be no answers. For history—like life itself—has no control groups. It is a science that can only predict the past.

CROWD BEHAVIOR: MANY-ON-MANY INTERACTIONS

In this chapter we've considered three broad classes of social interaction. The first class involved one-on-one interactions between two persons who might be relative strangers or friends and lovers. In the second group, the interactions were of many on one, cases of social influence in which the impact of a number of others converged on an individual to produce social facilitation or inhibition, conformity or obedience. In the third, we looked at the effects of one on many in which one person influenced or led a group of others. We now turn to a fourth class of social interactions in which the relation is many on many. These are group interactions in which a number of people interact with a number of others simultaneously. An important example is *crowd behavior.*★ There is little doubt that under some circumstances people in crowds behave differently from the way they do when alone. In riots or lynch mobs, they express aggression at a level of bestial violence that would be inconceivable if they acted in isolation. In other situations, crowds may become frantically fearful, as in panics that may sweep a tightly packed auditorium when someone shouts "Fire." Yet another example is provided by occasional reports of crowds that gather to watch some disturbed person on a high ledge of a tall building and then taunt the would-be suicide and urge him to jump.

What does the crowd do to the individual to make him act so differently from his everyday self? In analogy to the attempt to explain blind obedience, we can distinguish between two contrasting views. One focuses on emotional factors and holds that the crowd transforms the individual completely so that he loses his individuality and becomes essentially irrational. Another position stresses cognitive aspects. It holds that crowd behavior is not quite as irrational as it appears at first, but that it can be explained—at least in part—as a function of the individual's cognitive appraisal of the total situation.

★ The many-on-one and many-on-many distinction is not hard and fast. At bottom, most many-on-many interactions are probably composed of a large number of many-on-one interactions, as each member in a panicky crowd or a rioting mob is influenced by the collective force of the mass of others.

A

B

Deindividuation *(A) Some deindividuation effects are harmless. (Photograph © 1983 by Michael Sheil/Black Star) (B) Others represent a menace to a humane, democratic society. (Photograph © Detroit Free Press, 1988, Pauline Lubens/Black Star)*

THE EMPHASIS ON THE IRRATIONAL: DEINDIVIDUATION

An early exponent of the role of irrational factors was Gustav Le Bon (1841–1931), a French writer of conservative leanings whose disdain for the masses was reflected in his theory of crowd behavior. According to Le Bon, people in a crowd become wild, stupid, and irrational, giving vent to primitive impulses that are normally suppressed. Their emotion spreads by a sort of contagion and rises to an ever-higher pitch as more and more crowd members become affected. Thus, fear becomes terror, hostility turns into murderous rage, and the crowd member becomes a savage barbarian—"a grain of sand among other grains of sand, which the wind stirs up at will" (Le Bon, 1895).

A number of social psychologists have tried to translate some of these ideas into modern terms. To them, the key to crowd behavior is ***deindividuation,*** a state in which an individual in a group loses awareness of himself as a separate individual. This state is more likely to occur when there is a high level of arousal and anonymity. Deindividuation tends to disinhibit impulsive actions that are normally under restraint. Just what the impulses are that are disinhibited by deindividuation depends on the group and the situation. In a carnival, the (masked) revelers may join in wild orgies; in a lynch mob, the group members will kill and torture (Festinger, Pepitone, and Newcomb, 1952; Zimbardo, 1969; Diener, 1979).

To study deindividuation experimentally, one investigation focused on the effect of anonymity in children who were trick-or-treating on Halloween. Some came alone; others came in groups. Some were asked for their names by the adults in the homes they visited; others were not. All children were then given an opportunity to steal pennies or candy when the adult left the room on some pretext. The children were much more likely to steal if they came in groups and were anonymous. Thus an increase in wrongdoing may have occurred because anonymity made the child less aware of himself as a separate individual—that is, made him deindividuated—with a resulting disinhibition of petty thievery. But there may have been a simpler and perfectly rational reason: Being anonymous, the child was less afraid of being caught (Diener et al., 1976).

COGNITIVE FACTORS AND THE PANICKY CROWD

Is crowd behavior really as irrational as the deindividuation approach suggests? Our primary focus will be on panics. Panics prove that people in groups sometimes act in ways that have disastrous consequences that none of them foresaw or desired. This shows that crowd behavior can be profoundly maladaptive, but does it prove that the individual members of the crowd acted irrationally? Several social psychologists have argued that it does not (Brown, 1965). They point out that in certain situations, such as fires in crowded auditoriums, the optimum solution for all participants (that is, escape for all) can only come about if they all trust one another to behave cooperatively (that is, not to run for the exits). If this trust is lacking, each individual will do the next best thing given her motives and her expectations of what others will do. She will run to the exit because she is sure that everyone else will do the same, hoping that if she runs quickly enough she will get there before them. The trouble is that all others make the same assumption that she does, and so they will arrive more or less together, jam the exit, and perish.

Panic   *In June of 1985, a riot broke out at a soccer match in Brussels resulting in the collapse of a stadium wall that killed 38 spectators and injured more than 200 others. The photo gives a glimpse of the resulting panic. (Photograph by Eamonn McCabe,* The Observer*)*

According to this cognitive interpretation, intense fear as such will not produce crowd panic, contrary to Le Bon's assertion. What matters are people's beliefs about escape routes. If they think that the routes for escape (the theater exits) are open and readily accessible, they will not stampede. Nor will panic develop if all escape routes are thought to be completely blocked, as in a mine collapse or a submarine explosion. Such disasters may lead to terror or apathetic collapse, but there will be none of the chaos that characterizes a panicky crowd. For panic to occur, the exits from danger must be seen to be limited or closing. In that case, each individual may well think that she can escape only if she rushes ahead of the others. If everyone thinks this way, panic may ensue (Smelser, 1963).

THE PRISONER'S DILEMMA

Roger Brown believes that some facets of escape panic can be understood in terms of a problem taken from the mathematical theory of games (Brown, 1965). It is generally known as the ***prisoner's dilemma*** (Luce and Raiffa, 1957). Consider the hypothetical problem of two men arrested on suspicion of bank robbery. The district attorney needs a confession to guarantee conviction. She hits on a diabolical plan. She talks to each prisoner separately and offers each a simple choice—confess or stay silent. But she tells each man that the consequences will depend, not just on what he does, but also on his partner's choice. If both confess, she will recommend an intermediate sentence of, say, eight years in prison for each. If neither confesses, she will be unable to prosecute them for robbery, but she will charge them with a lesser crime such as illegal possession of a gun and both will get one year in jail. But suppose one confesses and the other does not. In this case the two men will be dealt with very differently. The one who confesses will be treated with extra leniency for turning state's evidence; he will receive a suspended sentence and won't go to jail at all. But the one who remains silent will feel the full force of the law. The D.A. will recommend the maximum penalty of twenty years.

As the situation is set up, there are four possible combinations of what the prisoners may do. Both may remain silent; Prisoner A may confess while B does not; B may confess while A does not; or both may confess. Each of the four sets of decisions has a different consequence, or payoff, for each of the two prisoners. The four sets of decisions and the payoffs associated with each yield a payoff matrix as shown in Table 12.1.

Given this payoff matrix, what can the prisoners do? If both remain silent, the consequence is reasonably good for each of them. But how can either be sure that his partner won't double-cross him? If A remains silent while B tells all, B is even better off than he would be if both kept quiet; he stays out of jail entirely, while poor, silent A gets twenty years. Can A take the chance that B will not confess? Conversely, can B take this chance on A? The best bet is that each of

TABLE 12.1 PAYOFF MATRIX FOR THE PRISONER'S DILEMMA

		Prisoner B:	
		Stays silent	Confesses
Prisoner A:	Stays silent	1 year for *A* 1 year for *B*	20 years for *A* No jail for *B*
	Confesses	No jail for *A* 20 years for *B*	8 years for *A* 8 years for *B*

them will decide that it's too risky to trust the other, for they both know that the other will be mightily tempted to defect. As a result, neither takes the chance, and so they both defect from the common good and confess. The D.A. gets her conviction, and both men get eight years.

In a sense, the prisoners' behavior is maladaptive, for the outcome is far from optimal for each. But this doesn't mean that either of the two men behaved irrationally—on the contrary. Paradoxically enough, each picked the most rational course of action considering that he couldn't be sure how his partner would decide. Each individual acted as rationally as possible; the ironic upshot was an unsatisfactory outcome for both. In the best of all possible worlds they would have been able to trust each other, would have remained silent, and been in jail for a much shorter period. (But in the best of all possible worlds they wouldn't have robbed the bank in the first place.)

THE PRISONER'S DILEMMA AND PANIC

The underlying logic of the prisoner's dilemma applies to various social interactions whose payoff matrix is formally analogous. Brown has shown how it pertains to panic. In such cases there are more than two participants, but the essential ingredients are much the same. Each individual in the burning auditorium has two choices—she can wait her turn to get to the exit, or she can rush ahead. What are the probable outcomes? As in the case of the prisoners, they partially depend upon what others in the auditorium (especially those nearby) will do. If the individual rushes to the exit and everyone else does too, they will all probably suffer severe injuries and run some risk of death. If she takes her turn and others decorously do the same, the outcome is better; they will probably all escape, though they may suffer some minor injuries. The best outcome for the individual is produced if she ruthlessly pushes herself ahead of the others while the others continue to file out slowly. In this case she will surely escape without a blister, but the chances for the others to escape are lessened. Suppose the situation is reversed so that the individual waits her turn while everyone near her runs ahead? Now the others may very well get out without injury while she herself may die. These sets of decisions and their associated outcomes represent just another version of the prisoner's dilemma, and they are shown in the payoff matrix of Table 12.2.

Given the payoff matrix of Table 12.2, most people will probably opt to rush ahead rather than wait their turn. As in the case of the two prisoners, this solution is grossly maladaptive, but from the point of view of each separate individual it is, sadly enough, quite rational. We again face the peculiar irony of the prisoner's dilemma. As Brown notes, "This irony about escape behavior . . . is

TABLE 12.2 PAYOFF MATRIX FOR AN INDIVIDUAL AND OTHERS IN A BURNING AUDITORIUM

		Others (O):	
		Take turns	*Rush ahead*
Individual (I):	Takes turn	Minor injuries for *I* Minor injuries for *O*	Increased chance of death for *I* No injuries for *O*
	Rushes ahead	No injuries for *I* Increased chance of death for *O*	Severe injuries for *I* Severe injuries for *O*

always worked over by newspaper editorialists after panic occurs. 'If only everyone had stayed calm and taken his turn, then . . .' " (Brown, 1965, p. 741).

Brown's model of panic applies only if certain qualifications are met. As already noted, the danger must seem serious and the escape routes must appear inadequate. Another factor is the strength of social inhibitions. Most of us have been socialized to act with some respect for others; pushing ahead is socially disapproved and would therefore contribute a negative value to the relevant cells in the payoff matrix. The weight of this factor depends on the situation. If the fire seems minor, the embarrassment at behaving discourteously (or acting like a coward) might outweigh the fear of being the last to escape. If so, the payoff matrix will not be that of the prisoner's dilemma, and no panic will ensue.

SOCIAL DILEMMAS

In the classic prisoner's dilemma only two criminals are involved in the choice. But as the panic scenario illustrates, the dilemma can be expanded to include any number of individuals, each of whom has to decide whether to cooperate or to defect. Thus the prisoner's dilemma and its payoff structure can be applied to many serious social and economic issues (Dawes, 1980).

Consider the *social dilemma* posed by industrial pollution. Suppose ten companies make various plastic toys and in the process create sulfurous gases. Antipollution devices can be installed to remove the sulfur, but they are expensive. What will the companies do? If all ten toy manufacturers make the same environmentally sound choice, none will have a price advantage, and air and water quality will remain the same. If they all attempt to look out for themselves alone and omit antipollution devices, none still will have a price advantage but the environment will be terribly degraded. If the other nine toy manufacturers can be counted on to make the environmentally sound choice, one toy producer could omit the antipollution devices, undercut the competition on price, and only degrade air and water quality slightly. But if all but one of the other manufacturers choose to ignore environmental degradation, that one high-minded toy producer will probably be driven out of business.

In the modern world we face social dilemmas in many areas, including industrial pollution, deforestation, and the depletion of energy reserves. Is there anything we can do to encourage individuals to make the socially beneficial decision? As we saw in Chapter 5 (pp. 161, 163), we can skew the payoff matrix to create a bias. (This is largely what our district attorney did to encourage the prisoners to throw loyalty to the wind.) In the case of social dilemmas we can skew the payoff matrix by imposing penalties such as taxes or fines on individuals or companies that pollute, or we can enhance the appeal of altruistic behavior through education. Many of the social scientists who have studied social dilemmas suggest that teaching the ultimate benefits of cooperation and increasing our trust that others won't exploit us may be the most effective ways of changing the outcomes (e.g., Orbell, van de Kragt, and Dawes, 1988; Rapoport, 1988). Whether such methods will be sufficient to save "spaceship earth" from the follies of its inhabitants is another question (Dawes, 1980).

Social dilemmas *A roadside dump in Edgerton Kansas. (Photograph © Dave Gleiter/FPG International)*

SOME FINAL COMMENTS

In this and the preceding chapter we asked how the individual interprets the social world in which he lives and how he interacts with the other people in it. This led to a survey of many topics, including the way we perceive the motives and acts of others as well as those of our own selves, how we interact with others, how we conform and obey, and how we behave in crowds.

COMMON THEMES

Can we isolate some major threads that run through the many theories, phenomena, and experimental demonstrations we've examined thus far? One theme that has arisen several times is that of reason versus passion.★ We've repeatedly noted the fact that social behavior is affected by both cognitive and motivational factors. In our discussion of social cognition this point came up in relation to the self-serving bias, as well as the attribution-of-arousal theory of emotional experience. We encountered it again when dealing with social interaction. A case in point is conformity, which may be produced because the person thinks that others know more than he or because he is embarrassed to disagree with them. It arose once more in terms of crowd behavior, which may be produced by the disinhibition of various impulses or by the cognitive factors that underlie the prisoner's dilemma. Reason and passion are the twin engines of human behavior, all the more so if that behavior is social.

Another theme that comes up again and again is whether events are driven by individuals or by the situations in which individuals find themselves. We discussed this distinction in the context of social cognition: In studies on attribution the question is whether someone performs a certain action because of something in her (a dispositional attribute) or because of something in the situation. The same distinction comes up repeatedly when dealing with social interaction. The two contending hypotheses in studies of blind obedience were that it stems from a certain personality pattern (e.g., the authoritarian personality) or that it is produced by the situation (as the Milgram experiment demonstrated). Another example is leadership, where we encountered the same polarity under the heading of the great-person versus social-forces theories. In all these cases we saw a widespread tendency to overrate the role played by personal characteristics and to underrate those played by situational factors.

Both the person and the situation evidently enter into the equation. But we must not conclude that this equation is a simple sum of the two, for the real relation between person and situation is always an *interaction*. The particular traits of an individual may be relevant in one situation and not in another. The stubborn eloquence and force of will of Winston Churchill made him the undisputed leader of an embattled Britain during World War II. But in the years before that war when many Britons longed for peace at any price, these qualities made him an unpopular member of his own party.

THE GENERALITY OF SOCIAL PSYCHOLOGY

Social psychology has clearly contributed to our understanding of social behavior. But how broadly applicable is this understanding? Does it bring us closer to an understanding of basic human nature, or is it necessarily limited to our own time and place?

★ While items are often stated as polar opposites, in actuality there are no genuine either-or dualities in psychology. We are swayed in our judgments neither exclusively by reason nor exclusively by passion. The same holds for the nature-nurture distinction: Both nature and nurture exert a powerful influence.

Some authors argue that the discoveries of modern social psychology are limited to our social and cultural circumstances and cannot be generalized beyond them. Perhaps consistency, attribution of motives, self-perception, obedience, diffusion of responsibility, and so on are patterns of behavior that are specific to twentieth-century industrialized society, in particular, to that of modern North American society. If so, they may not describe how people act and think in other places and at other times (Gergen, 1973; Jahoda, 1979).

Some evidence in line with this view comes from a series of studies by Joan Miller on how Hindu individuals in India account for social behavior. Miller asked both American and Indian adults to describe "something a person you know well did recently that you regard as a wrong thing to have done" as well as others that "you considered good for someone else." After the subjects did so, they were asked to explain why the person performed these acts. She found a marked difference between the two groups. Many of the reasons cited by American subjects referred to general dispositions, such as "He is insecure," or "she is kind." In contrast, the Hindu subjects gave many more reasons that focused on the context and situation, such as "It was early in the morning," or "The man is unemployed. He is not in a position to give that money." It appears that the so-called fundamental attribution error—the tendency to attribute actions to dispositional rather than situational factors—is not as fundamental in India as it is in the United States (Miller, 1984; see also Aharon and Amir, 1988; Fletcher and Ward, 1988).

The culture-specific critique may be a valuable corrective to the notion that a genuine science of the psychology of social behavior can be developed in isolation from other social disciplines such as anthropology, sociology, economics, political science, and history. To understand the social situation the individual confronts, one has to refer to many cultural (or sociological or historical or political or economic) factors that transcend the individual (Pepitone, 1976; Price-Williams, 1985). We will return to this issue when we discuss the topic of personality, where we will consider different concepts of the self as they affect various aspects of cognition, emotion, and behavior (See Chapter 17, pp. 702–10).

Nevertheless, there are good reasons to believe that human social nature is much more stable than the culture-specific critique assumes it to be. Such diverse political theorists as Aristotle, Hobbes, and Machiavelli are still read despite the fact that they lived many centuries ago and under very different political systems than our own; they wrote about characteristics of human social behavior that we can recognize even today. History provides many other examples of enduring social reactions. There are records of panics in Roman amphitheaters when the stands collapsed, of riots during sporting events in Byzantium, and of murderous mobs in medieval Europe. The cast and costumes differ, but the basic plots remain much the same. Some of the ancients even used certain of our modern propaganda devices. When the city of Pompeii was destroyed by a volcano in 79 A.D., it was evidently in the midst of a municipal election. Modern archeologists have found some of the election slogans on the excavated walls: "Vote for Vatius, all the whoremasters vote for him" and "Vote for Vatius, all the wife-beaters vote for him." While the techniques of the anti-Vatius faction may be a bit crude for our modern taste, they certainly prove that the psychology of the smear campaign has a venerable history (Raven and Rubin, 1976).

Phenomena of this sort suggest that there are some invariant properties of human social behavior that have genuine generality.

Electioneering in Pompeii *Electoral inscriptions on the outer walls of houses in Pompeii. (From* The Buried Cities of Pompeii and Herculaneum; *photograph by Carlo Bevilacqua, © 1978 Instituto Geografico De Agostini; courtesy of the New York Public Library)*

SUMMARY

1. Social interactions can be classified as those that are *one on one* (our relations with both strangers and persons to whom we are closer), those that are *many on one* (including various manifestations of social influence), those that are *one on many* (including leadership), and those that are *many on many* (including crowd behavior).

2. According to some theorists, all one-on-one interactions depend on *social exchange*. Evidence comes from the operation of the *reciprocity rule*, which applies not only to material things such as food and gifts but also to intangibles such as *self-disclosure*.

3. In investigating *altruism*, social psychologists have found that people often fail to help others in an emergency. One reason is the *bystander effect:* The greater the number of people who are present, the less likely that any one of them will provide help, in part because of *pluralistic ignorance*, in part because of *diffusion of responsibility*.

4. Social psychologists have studied some of the factors that attract people to each other. They include *proximity, familiarity, similarity,* and *physical attractiveness.* There is evidence in favor of the *matching hypothesis,* which predicts a strong correlation between the physical attractiveness of the two partners. Love is an especially close relation between two partners. Some authors distinguish between *romantic love,* in which the emotions are intensely focused, and *companionate love,* which is less turbulent and more long-lasting.

5. A number of many-on-one situations involve *social influence.* In some cases, all that matters is the mere presence of others, which produces *social facilitation* and inhibition.

6. Another case of social influence is *conformity.* One reason for conformity is informational: We may believe that the group has knowledge we don't possess. Another reason is motivational: We go along because we want to be liked. A dissenting minority often leads to a massive reduction in the force toward conformity and may produce genuine changes in what people think and feel.

7. Still another form of social influence is obedience. Blind obedience has sometimes been ascribed to factors within the person, as in studies on the *authoritarian personality.* But situational factors may be even more important, as shown by Milgram's obedience studies. His findings suggest that obedience depends on the *psychological distance* between one's own actions and their end result. When this distance is increased—by decreasing one's sense of responsibility, by *dehumanization,* and by means of various *cognitive reinterpretations*—obedience increases too.

8. According to *social impact theory,* various phenomena of social influence can be understood by thinking of the individual as the target in a field of social forces. In certain situations—such as audience effects and conformity—social forces converge upon one individual. In others, the impact is diffused over several other targets, as in the bystander effect and *social loafing.*

9. An important example of *one-on-many* interactions is *leadership.* A major question in politics, warfare, and contemporary social psychology is what used to be called the *great-person* versus *social-forces* controversy: Does successful leadership depend on the special qualities of the leader or on the situation? The answer is that it is generally an interaction between the two.

10. In many-on-many interactions, a number of people interact with a number of others simultaneously. An example is crowd behavior, as in panics or riots. According to one account, the behavior of such crowds is essentially irrational and is based on *deindividuation.* According to another interpretation, it is not as irrational as it appears at first. The *prisoner's dilemma* shows that under certain conditions there can be collective irrationality even though all of the participants behave rationally as individuals. This has been applied to behavior in panics and to *social dilemmas.*

PART FOUR

DEVELOPMENT

CHAPTER **13**

PHYSICAL AND COGNITIVE DEVELOPMENT

WHAT IS DEVELOPMENT? 493

DEVELOPMENT AS DIFFERENTIATION ▪ DEVELOPMENT AS GROWTH ▪ DEVELOPMENT AS ORDERLY PROGRESSION

THE PHYSICAL BASIS OF DEVELOPMENT 499

THE MECHANISM OF GENETIC TRANSMISSION ▪ ENVIRONMENTS AT DIFFERENT POINTS IN DEVELOPMENT ▪ ENVIRONMENT AND MATURATION

PIAGET'S THEORY OF COGNITIVE DEVELOPMENT 505

SENSORY-MOTOR INTELLIGENCE ▪ THE PREOPERATIONAL PERIOD ▪ CONCRETE AND FORMAL OPERATIONS

WHAT IS THE COGNITIVE STARTING POINT? 511

SPACE AND OBJECTS IN INFANCY ▪ NUMBER IN INFANCY ▪ SOCIAL COGNITION IN INFANCY: THE EXISTENCE OF OTHER MINDS

COGNITIVE DEVELOPMENT IN PRESCHOOLERS 516

THE MEANING OF MENTAL STAGE ▪ NUMERICAL SKILLS IN PRESCHOOLERS ▪ SOCIAL COGNITION IN PRESCHOOLERS: DEVELOPING A THEORY OF MIND ▪ SEQUENCE OR STAGES?

THE CAUSES OF COGNITIVE GROWTH 522

THE NATIVIST APPROACH: MATURATION ▪ THE EMPIRICIST APPROACH: SPECIFIC LEARNING ▪ PIAGET'S APPROACH: ASSIMILATION AND ACCOMMODATION ▪ THE INFORMATION-PROCESSING APPROACH: CHUNKING AND STRATEGIES

COGNITIVE DEVELOPMENT FROM A CROSS-CULTURAL PERSPECTIVE 528

TAKING STOCK 530

SUMMARY 530

How do psychologists try to explain the phenomena they describe? Thus far, we've primarily dealt with two main approaches. The first is concerned with mechanism—it tries to understand how something works. The second approach focuses on function—it tries to explain what something is good for. But there is yet another approach to explanation in psychology that focuses on development. This approach deals with questions of history—it asks how a given state of affairs came into being.

In the next two chapters, our concern will be with this developmental perspective on psychological phenomena. We will ask how various psychological processes arise in the organism's history—how we come to see and remember, reason and think, feel and act as we now do; how it is that we are no longer children, but for better or worse have become adults in mind as well as in body.

t the beginning of the nineteenth century, many thinkers became increasingly interested in all forms of progressive change. They lived at a time of dramatic upheavals—the French Revolution, which ushered in a period of continued political unrest, and the Industrial Revolution, which transformed the social and economic structure of Europe and North America. These massive changes suggested an underlying pattern of social development—"progress" (Bury, 1932). Given this background, many scientists became interested in development wherever they saw it: in the history of the planet as it changed from molten rock to form continents and oceans; in the history of life as it evolved from early forms to myriad species of fossils and plants. One aspect of this intellectual movement was an increasing concern with the life history of individual organisms, starting from their embryonic beginnings and continuing as they developed toward maturity.

All animals develop, and so do we. The duckling becomes a duck, the kitten a cat, the human baby an adult. In this regard all humans are alike. It doesn't matter whether they are Gandhi or Hitler, Joan of Arc or Isaac Newton—they all started life as infants. Is there any common pattern in the developmental history of each human life? If so, what is it? The attempt to answer these questions is the province of developmental psychology.

WHAT IS DEVELOPMENT?

Many aspects of human development share certain characteristics, at least in a very general way, whether they involve *physical development,* the maturation of various bodily structures; *motor development,* the progressive attainment of various motor skills; *cognitive development*, the growth of the child's intellectual functioning; or *social development*, changes in the ways the child deals with others. We will consider three very general features that many aspects of development have in common: differentiation, growth, and orderly progression. We'll begin our discussion by looking at differentiation as this is revealed in the physical development of the embryo and in childhood behavior.

DEVELOPMENT AS DIFFERENTIATION

The concept of differentiation grows out of some early discoveries in embryology, the study of an organism as it develops from a single egg and assumes the complex shape and function of its adult form. The German biologist Karl Ernest von Baer (1792–1876) pointed out that embryological development involves a progressive change from the more general to the more particular, from the simpler to the more complex—in short, **differentiation.**

In embryonic development, anatomical differentiation is directly apparent. Initially there is one cell, then several cell layers, then the crude beginnings of the major organ systems, until the different organs and their component parts gradually take shape. Von Baer argued that this is the reason why embryos of very different species are so similar at early stages of development and utterly dissimilar at later stages (see Figure 13.1). Initially, the embryo only manifests the very general body plan characteristic of a broad class of animals. Thus a very young chick embryo looks much like the embryo of any other vertebrate animal at a similar stage of its development. The embryonic structures that will eventually become wings are quite similar to those structures that in a young human embryo will eventually become human arms. As embryonic development proceeds, special features begin to emerge and the chick embryo begins to look like a bird, then like some kind of fowl, and still later like a chicken (Gould, 1977).

Von Baer's differentiation principle was initially regarded as a description of anatomical development and nothing else. But a number of psychologists suggested that a similar principle also applies to the development of behavior. Consider the development of grasping movements in human infants. When reaching for a small block, they initially curl their entire hand around the block; still later, they oppose the thumb to all four fingers. By the time they are one year old, they can victoriously coordinate hand, thumb, and one or two fingers to pick up the block with an elegant pincer movement (although such ultimate triumphs of manual differentiation as picking up a tea cup while holding the little finger extended will probably have to wait until they are old enough to read a book on etiquette) (Halverson, 1931; see Figure 13.2).

DEVELOPMENT AS GROWTH

One of the most obvious characteristics of development is growth. Organisms grow as they change from a fertilized egg to a fetus, and after birth, they continue to grow in many different dimensions ranging from sheer physical size to mental complexity.

Tortoise   Chick   Rabbit   Human

13.1 Differentiation during embryonic development *The figure shows three stages in the embryonic development of four different vertebrates—tortoise, chick, rabbit, and human. At the first stage, all of the embryos are very similar to each other. As development proceeds, they diverge more and more. By the third stage, each embryo has taken on some of the distinctive characteristics of its own species. (From Keeton and Gould, 1993. Redrawn from Romanes, 1882)*

13.2 **The development of manual skills**
The diagram shows the progressive differentiation in the infant's use of the hand when holding an object. At sixteen weeks of age, he reaches for the object but can't hold on to it. At twenty weeks, he grasps it using the hand as a whole, with no differentiated use of the fingers. Between twenty-four and thirty-six weeks, the fingers and thumb become differentiated in use, but the four fingers operate more or less as a whole. By fifty-two weeks of age, hand, thumb, and fingers are successfully differentiated to produce precise and effective pincer movements. (Adapted from Liebert, Polous, and Strauss, 1974) Photos illustrate the same point at twenty-three, twenty-eight, and fifty-eight weeks. (Photographs by Kathy Hirsh-Pasek)

23 weeks   *28 weeks*   *58 weeks*

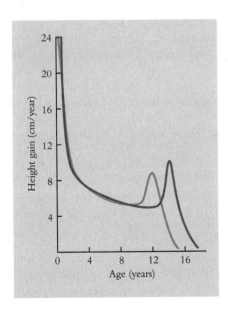

13.3 **Physical growth** Heights of British boys (dark red) and girls (blue) from birth until nineteen years of age. Physical growth continues for almost twenty years after birth with a special spurt at adolescence. (From Tanner, 1970)

GROWTH BEFORE BIRTH

Each human existence begins at conception when a sperm and egg cell unite to form the fertilized egg. This egg divides and redivides repeatedly, producing a cellular mass that attaches itself to the wall of the uterus. Two weeks after conception the mass of cells (now called an **embryo**) begins to differentiate into separate cell layers. From now until birth, growth and development proceed at a rapid pace. At one month after conception, the embryo is a fifth of an inch long and looks like a little worm. At two months after conception the mass of cells is about one inch in length and is now called a **fetus.** Just one month later, the fetus has grown to about three inches in length and has begun to look like a miniature baby with some functioning organ systems and a number of early reflexes, including sucking movements when the lips are touched. In another four months (that is, seven months after conception), the fetus has grown to sixteen inches, has a fully developed reflex pattern, can cry, breathe, swallow, and has a good chance of survival if it should be delivered at this time.

These stages of our prenatal life attest to the massive changes in sheer size and structural complexity that take place over this period. In addition to these gross gains, however, there are also many subtler ones that have far-reaching effects. Some of the most important of these concern the developing nervous system. In the later stages of prenatal growth, the neurons begin to mature, and their axons and dendrites form increasingly complex branches and interconnections with other nerve cells (Schacher, 1981).

GROWTH AFTER BIRTH

Physical growth continues for almost two decades after birth, with a special spurt at adolescence (see Figure 13.3). The growth of the child's body is accompanied by the no less striking growth of her mind—in the way she perceives, thinks, speaks, understands, and reacts to others. The details of these accomplishments will be discussed in later sections. For now we only note that many of these feats are based on the continuation of events that began before birth. Of particular importance is the growth of neural interconnections beginning in

495

13.4 Growth of neural interconnections
Sections of the human cortex in (A) a newborn, (B) a three-month-old, and (C) a fifteen-month-old. (Conel, 1939, 1947, 1955)

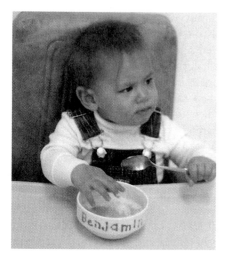

Capacity for learning *Learning from culture is not accomplished overnight. A ten-month-old baby is trying to master the intricacies of eating with a spoon. (Photograph courtesy of Kathy Hirsh-Pasek)*

fetal life and continuing long into infancy, as illustrated in Figure 13.4, which shows sections of the human cortex in a newborn, a three-month-old, and a fifteen-month-old child (Conel, 1939, 1947, 1955). According to a recent analysis, there is a tenfold increase in the average number of synapses per cortical neuron in the first year of life (Huttenlocher, 1979). This increasing neural complexity may well be one of the reasons for the increase in mental capacities as development proceeds.

THE SLOW RATE OF HUMAN GROWTH AND ITS EFFECTS

Nine months after conception the fetus enters the outer world. But is it really ready to do so? Left to its own devices, it obviously is not. It is singularly helpless and inept, more so by far than the young of most other mammals. To be sure, a newborn calf has to suckle and follow its mother, but it can walk at birth, and it can pretty well manage on its own after a fairly short period. But in humans (and to a lesser extent, in monkeys and apes), a considerable degree of development continues far beyond birth. For example, in most mammals the newborn's brain is just about fully formed—not so in primates and most especially not so in humans. Human newborns have achieved only 23 percent of their adult cranial capacity at birth and are still only at 75 percent of this final value when they are about two-and-a-half years old (Catel, 1953, cited in Gould, 1977). What holds for brain growth also holds for other aspects of physical development. At birth the bones of the skull are not yet joined together and certain wrist bones are still made of cartilage. In many ways, we are all born premature.

A number of authors believe that this retarded rate of development is what most distinctively makes us human, for the inevitable result is a protracted period of dependency. In some ways, this is quite inconvenient—for child and parent alike. But in many others, there are great benefits. For such a long period of dependency is tailor-made for a creature whose major specialization is its capacity for learning and whose basic invention is culture—the ways of coping with the world that each generation hands on to the next. As there is so much to learn, the young have much to gain by being forced to stay a while with those who teach them.

THE NEWBORN'S EQUIPMENT

What do newborns bring into the world to serve as a foundation for further psychological development? Here, we will only ask about motor and sensory capacities.

The infant's response capacities Initially infants have little control of their motor apparatus. Newborns can do very little—they thrash around in an uncoordinated manner and can't even hold up their heads. By four months of age they'll be able to sit up with support and reach for objects (which they often miss). But how do they manage in the meantime?

Part of the answer is that newborns have a neurological survival kit that will see them through their first period of helplessness: a set of early reflexes. Some reflexes of the very young infant have to do with clinging to the person who supports him. An example is the *grasp reflex*—when an object touches the infant's palm, he closes his fist tightly around it. If the object is lifted up, the infant hangs on and is lifted up along with it, supporting his whole weight for a

A vital reflex in the newborn The sucking reflex is initiated when an appropriate object is inserted three or four centimeters into the mouth. (Photograph by Kenneth Garrett 1984/Woodfin Camp)

minute or more. This and some related reflexes are sometimes regarded as a primitive heritage from our primate ancestors whose infants cling to their mothers' furry bodies.

Other infantile responses pertain to feeding. An example is the ***rooting reflex.*** When the cheek is lightly touched, the baby's head turns toward the source of stimulation, her mouth opens, and her head continues to turn until the stimulus (usually a finger or nipple) is in her mouth. When this point is reached, sucking begins.

Many infantile reflexes disappear after a few months. In some cases, the reflex is eventually replaced by a more directed response. Thus infants stop reflexive grasping when they are about three or four months old, but this doesn't mean that they will never again grasp objects in their hands. Of course they will. But when they do (at about five months of age), they do so because they want to— their grasp has become voluntary rather than reflexive. Such voluntary actions have to wait until various parts of the cerebral cortex have matured sufficiently to make them possible. But until this point, the infantile reflexes serve as a temporary substitute.

The infant's sensory capacities While newborns' motor capacities are initially very limited, their sensory channels function nicely from the very start. Evidence comes from changes in their rates of breathing, of sucking, and of similar indices in response to stimulation. Newborns can hear; they can discriminate between tones of different pitch and loudness. They also prefer their mother's voice to that of a strange female (DeCasper and Fifer, 1980; Aslin, 1987). Newborns can see: While quite short-sighted and unable to focus on objects farther off than about four feet, they can readily discriminate brightness and color, and they can follow a moving stimulus with their eyes (Bornstein, 1985; Aslin, 1987). In addition, they are sensitive to touch, smell, and taste (Crook, 1987).

All in all, infants seem to come rather well equipped to sense the world they enter. But do they come equipped to interpret what it is they see, hear, or touch? This is a disputed issue to which we will return in a later section. For now we merely note that young infants are quite competent to receive sensory inputs. Whether they have some built-in knowledge of what these inputs might signify (as nativists would argue) or have to acquire this knowledge by relating various sensory inputs to each other (as empiricists would have it) is another matter.

DEVELOPMENT AS ORDERLY PROGRESSION

In prenatal growth some events necessarily come before others. The embryo consists of primitive tissue layers before it develops organs; the skeleton is made of cartilage before it becomes bone. Developmental psychologists argue that similar patterns of orderly progression characterize psychological development after birth.

In ***motor development*** there is a regular sequence of achievements that begins with the ability to hold the head erect, followed by the ability to roll over, then to creep, crawl, sit up, stand up, take a step or two, and finally to walk, first shakily and then with increasing confidence. There is a good deal of variability in the age at which a given baby masters each skill. But a few months more or less make little difference for later development. What matters is that each step in the sequence comes before the next. No baby can walk before he can sit. (The

A

FETAL POSITION
0 month

CHIN UP
1 month

CHEST UP
2 months

REACH AND MISS
3 months

SIT WITH SUPPORT
4 months

SIT ON LAP
GRASP OBJECT
5 months

SIT ON HIGH CHAIR
GRASP DANGLING OBJECT
6 months

SIT ALONE
7 months

STAND WITH HELP
8 months

CREEP
10 months

WALK WHEN LED
11 months

PULL TO STAND
BY FURNITURE
12 months

CLIMB STAIR STEPS
13 months

STAND ALONE
14 months

WALK ALONE
15 months

13.5   *The development of locomotion* *(A) The average age at which babies master locomotor skills, from holding their chins up to walking alone. These ages vary considerably. (From Shirley, 1961) (B) A pictorial record of these milestones in the life of one child. (Photographs courtesy of Kathy Hirsh-Pasek)*

B

2 days

2 months

6 months

8 months

average age at which children reach each of these milestones of motor development is shown in Figure 13.5.)

Similar progressions are found in aspects of intellectual development. In the acquisition of language there is also an orderly sequence (see Chapter 9). Initially the baby coos, then he babbles, then he utters his first word or two, then he develops a small vocabulary but is limited to one-word utterances, after which both vocabulary and sentence complexity increase until they finally reach adult levels. As with motor development, there is a good deal of variability among different infants. Some may begin to talk by ten months, others as late as twenty, but age of initial language onset is no predictor of later linguistic competence. The important point is that linguistic development follows the same

10 months

10 months

14 months

TABLE 13.1 CHARACTERISTIC LINGUISTIC ACHIEVEMENTS IN THE FIRST 30 MONTHS	
Age	*Linguistic achievement*
3 months	cooing
4 months	babbling
10 months	first word
18 months	about 20 words; one-word utterances
24 months	about 250 words; two-word utterances
30 months	about 500 words; three-plus utterances

SOURCE: From Lenneberg, 1967, pp. 128–30.

general progression for all children. Here, as in so many other areas, development proceeds by an orderly sequence of steps, and this holds for the growth of our minds as well as our bodies. (See Table 13.1 to get a rough idea of the ages at which the first linguistic achievements of children occur.)

THE PHYSICAL BASIS OF DEVELOPMENT

What produces the many changes that constitute development? One important factor is the genetic blueprint that dictates much of the course of the organism's development from the moment of conception. Another factor is the organism's environment—both before and after it is born.

THE MECHANISM OF GENETIC TRANSMISSION

An organism's genetic makeup is encoded in the *genes,* the units of hereditary transmission. These genes are a set of instructions that determine growth and steer the organism's development from fertilized cell to mature animal or plant. They are stored within the *chromosomes* in the cell's nucleus, with each chromosome holding a thousand or more of such genetic commands. In organisms that reproduce sexually, the chromosomes come in pairs; one member of each pair is contributed by the mother, the other by the father (see Figure 13.6).

SEX DETERMINATION

The genetic commands that determine whether a given animal will be male or female are inscribed in a pair of sex chromosomes. In males, the two members are different: One is called an *X chromosome;* the other is somewhat smaller and is called a *Y chromosome.* In females, both members of the pair are X chromosomes. Which sex the child will be depends entirely on the father. For while every egg cell contains one X chromosome, sperm cells contain either an X chromosome or a Y chromosome. Depending upon which of the two kinds

13.6   The human chromosome pairs
The figure shows the twenty-three pairs of chromosomes in a human male. The twenty-third pair determines the individual's sex. In males, one member of each pair is an X chromosome, the other a Y chromosome. In females, both are X chromosomes. (Photograph courtesy of M. M. Grumbach)

Genetic effects on behavior *(Drawing by Shanahan; © 1989 The New Yorker Magazine, Inc.)*

Brown phenotype
Br–Br genotype

Blue phenotype
Bl–Bl genotype

Brown phenotype

13.7 Phenotype and genotype in the transmission of eye color *Eye color of the children of a brown-eyed and a blue-eyed parent if the brown-eyed parent's genotype is brown-brown. All of the children's eyes (phenotypes) will be brown, although their genotypes will be brown-blue. In the figure, genotypes are indicated by a pair of schematic eye-color genes under each face.*

joins up with the egg cell, the resulting fertilized egg (or *zygote*) may contain an XX pair (a female) or an XY pair (a male).

DOMINANT AND RECESSIVE GENES

Any given gene is located at a particular place on a given chromosome. Since chromosomes come in pairs, both members of each pair have corresponding loci at which there are genes that carry instructions about a particular characteristic (for example, eye color). These two related genes—one contributed by each parent—may or may not be identical. Consider eye color. If both of the genes for eye color are identical (blue-blue or brown-brown), the result is simple: The eye color will follow suit. But suppose they are different. Now the overt expression of the genetic blueprint depends upon other relationships between the two members of the gene pair. In humans, the gene for brown eyes is **dominant;** it will exert its effect regardless of whether the other member of the gene pair calls for brown or blue eyes. In contrast, the gene for blue eyes is **recessive.** This recessive gene will lead to blue eyes only if the gene on the corresponding locus of the paired chromosome also calls for blue eyes.

There are many other human traits that are based on a single gene pair, such as dark hair, dimples, and thick lips (dominant); and baldness, red hair, and straight nose (recessive). Some are more deleterious, and many of those are recessive. Examples range from mild conditions such as susceptibility to poison ivy and red-green color blindness, to hemophilia (in which the blood does not clot so that a person may bleed to death from a minor injury). Since these and most other damaging genetic characteristics are recessive, their expression is relatively rare. There will be no overt effect unless both parents transmit the recessive gene. This fact may partially account for the widespread cultural prohibition against incest. The more closely related the parents, the greater the chance that both will have the same recessive gene. As a result, their offspring run a much greater risk of serious genetic defects (let alone susceptibility to poison ivy).

The phenomenon of gene dominance illustrates a crucial distinction in the study of heredity. On the one hand, there is the overt appearance of an organism—its visible structure and behavior. This is the **phenotype,** the characteristic we actually observe in a given individual. But this phenotype is by no means equivalent to the organism's genetic blueprint, its **genotype.** As we have seen, two people who have brown eyes may well have different genotypes for eye color; one may be brown-brown, the other brown-blue (see Figure 13.7). Nonetheless, the phenotypes are the same, for if a gene for blue eyes is present, it will be masked by its counterpart that calls for brown eyes.

ENVIRONMENTS AT DIFFERENT POINTS IN DEVELOPMENT

Thus far, our focus has been on the genetic basis of the organism's development. What about the environment? It's obvious that a genetic blueprint without a proper environment will remain an unrealized potentiality—Isaac Newton could not possibly have rewritten the laws of the physical universe if he had been kept in a black, soundproof box from birth to adulthood. This underlines the fact (did anyone ever doubt it?) that development involves both heredity and environment. But the relation between the two is more subtle than may be apparent at first, for what is meant by "environment" continually changes as development proceeds.

THE ENVIRONMENT BEFORE BIRTH

Early embryonic development   The embryo has various tissues that will ultimately become its inner organs, muscles, skin, and nervous system. How does any given cell in the embryo know how to fulfill its proper destiny—to become part of a mouth, or of a spinal cord, or whatever? After all, every cell of the organism has the same genes, so that they all presumably get the same genetic instructions. But if so, how do they manage to develop differently?

Part of the answer is that the fate of any given cell is partially determined by the cells that are adjacent to it and form its physical environment. Evidence comes from studies of salamander embryos. At an early stage of their development, they have an outer layer of tissue whose cells can turn into skin or teeth. They will become teeth if they make contact with certain other cells in the mouth region that belong to an inner layer of the embryo. Proof comes from studies in which parts of the flank of a salamander embryo were cut out and then transplanted into the embryo's mouth region. Had those cells stayed where they were, they would have eventually developed into the skin of the flank region. Having been brought into a different cellular environment, however, they became teeth (Spemann, 1967).

Such findings show that the environment matters even in early embryonic development when the genetic forces are presumably at their strongest. But there is a further result that highlights the role of the cell's genetic constitution. In another study, the experimenters took a part of the flank of a frog embryo and transplanted it into the same mouth region of a salamander embryo they had used previously. The outcome has something to offer to both sides of the nature-nurture controversy. The transplanted cells became part of a mouth—in strict obedience to their new environment. But they became horny jaws rather than teeth—the mouth appendages of a frog rather than of a salamander—in appropriate homage to their genetic heritage. The cells could become the skin of a frog's sides or the horny jaw of its mouth, depending on the environment, but they could never escape their essential froghood (Spemann, 1967).

Studies such as these tell us that both heredity and environment are effective from the very start of life. The two interact to determine the further course of development.

The development of sexual structures   In an early stage of embryonic development, the environment consists of other cells. Somewhat later, development is affected by another kind of environment—the internal environment, which consists of the organism's own body fluids, especially its bloodstream (see Chapter 3). In mammalian embryos this is intimately linked up with the mother's blood supply. Various hormones that circulate within the embryo's blood or that of its mother will have a vital effect on the future course of development. An example is the development of sexual structures and behavior.

What determines whether an individual is biologically male or female? One might guess that the answer is just a matter of genetics—you are male if you are chromosomally XY and female if you are XX. But the actual story is more complicated than that. At about six weeks of age, the human embryo has primordial gonads and some external grooves and swellings that as yet give no indication of the baby's sex. A week or so later, the chromosomes initiate the differentiation of ovaries and testes, but the external genital apparatus still gives no clue as to whether its owner is male or female (see Figure 13.8). Now it is up to the hormones. In a genetic male, the XY chromosome pair leads to the formation of testes. Once formed, these produce **androgen,** the male sex hormone. The presence of this hormone in the bloodstream leads to the differentiation of the external genitals, and now the fetus is on the way to becoming a little boy.

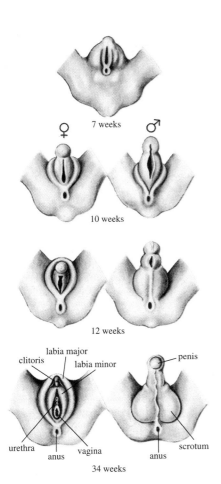

13.8   The development of external genitals in the human fetus   *At seven weeks, the genitalia of human male and female fetuses are virtually indistinguishable. Some differentiation is seen at ten weeks and becomes increasingly pronounced in the weeks thereafter. At thirty-four weeks, the distinctive characteristics of the different genitalia are fully apparent. (From Keeton and Gould, 1994)*

The creation of Eve *According to the Bible, Eve was created subsequent to Adam. But biologically, the order is reversed. (Panel from the Sistine Chapel ceiling, by Michelangelo, 1508–1512. Courtesy of Scala/Art Resource)*

The pattern is different for females. The formation of the female's external genitals does not depend on hormones except indirectly. As long as no androgen circulates in the bloodstream, the fetus will develop the appropriate female organs. In mammals, the basic development plan, shared by both sexes, evidently calls for the building of a female, and it will run its course in that direction if left undisturbed. To build a male, the developmental path has to be diverted by the appropriate hormones. It would seem that biologically—if not biblically—speaking, Adam was created after Eve (Money and Ehrhardt, 1972; Money, 1980).

The chromosome pairs define an individual's genetic sex. But the way in which that sex is actually shaped depends upon the organism's internal environment—the presence or absence of male hormones in its bloodstream.

THE ENVIRONMENT AFTER BIRTH

After birth, the crucial environmental events that affect development are those in the surrounding physical, social, and cognitive world. It is clear that the critical aspects of that environment are not the same at different ages. Imagine a three-month-old who hears an older sibling's loud (and no doubt well-intentioned) shout "Surprise!" as the parents put some new toy in the baby's crib.★ In all likelihood, the baby would cry in fear, for all he heard was a loud noise. At three years of age, the same shout would probably produce joyous squeals of anticipation, for now the sound has meaning and that meaning is vastly more important than its auditory intensity.

SENSITIVE PERIODS

It's clear that what is important at one stage in life may not be so at some later point. But various developmental theorists have expanded this idea to make a much stronger claim. They argue that there are certain ***critical periods*** in devel-

---

★ Some younger siblings argue that nothing an older sibling ever does could possibly be well intentioned. (Personal communication from the author's younger brother, G. Gleitman, in 1985).

opment during which certain important events will have an impact that they would not have (or would have to a much lesser extent) at earlier or later times.

The hypothesis of critical periods was derived from embryological development. Take the differentiation of organ tissue. We've previously seen that at a very early stage, parts of an embryo's outer tissue may become skin or teeth, depending upon the cells they are adjacent to. If transplanted at this time, they will take the shape appropriate to their new surroundings. But at a later point in time, this plasticity is gone. Skin and teeth have become unalterably differentiated; if the teeth are transplanted from mouth to flank and vice versa, then a skin flap will form in the mouth and the flank will sport teeth—proof positive that a critical period has been passed (Spemann, 1967).

Many developmental psychologists believe that similar critical periods exist after birth or hatching. An example is the attachment of the young of many species to their mother, an attachment that is generally much more readily formed at an early age (see Chapter 14). In humans, the main example is the acquisition of language, which as we've seen is also easier at younger ages (see Chapter 9). But the periods during which these developmental attainments are possible are not as rigidly fixed and all or none as the critical periods when the organism is an embryo. As a result, they are now called **sensitive periods** rather than critical periods.

ENVIRONMENT AND MATURATION

As noted earlier, development is orderly and progressive. Infants sit up before they can walk and babble before they can talk. What accounts for this well-nigh inevitable schedule of early developmental achievements?

A number of developmental psychologists believe that many of these achievements (especially of motor and sensory development) are produced by **maturation**—an inevitable unfolding of behavior patterns that is genetically programmed into the species and is independent of specific environmental conditions. They believe that this sequence of behavioral milestones is analogous to the ordered progression that characterizes physical growth. The particular rate of this behavioral schedule may vary somewhat from one baby to the next, but the steps in that schedule are essentially the same for all—crawling precedes walking, and uncoordinated reaching precedes precise grasping. Maturation theorists believe that these achievements result primarily from the growth and development of the infant's brain and musculature and that they have little to do with experience.

MATURATION AND PRACTICE

What is the evidence about the effect of practice on maturational processes? A number of investigators compared infant-rearing practices in different cultures. In some societies—for example, that of the Hopi and Navaho Indians—infants are swaddled and bound to a cradle or carrying board, with their activity severely inhibited for much of the first year of life (see Figure 13.9). Despite some initial reports to the contrary (Dennis, 1940), the bulk of the evidence suggests that such early restrictions do have a retarding effect on later motor milestones (e.g., among the Mayan Indians; Brazelton, 1972), while systematic practice in various motor activities leads to some acceleration (e.g., in certain Kenyan communities; Super, 1976).

Do these studies prove that the maturation concept should be discarded? Not really, for the effects of immobilization or special practice are relatively slight—

13.9   Learning, maturation, and walking   *A Shoshone infant strapped into a cradle. Swaddling has little effect on the child's ability to walk later on. (Shosone Indian Reservation, Wyoming; Photograph by Victor Englebert/Photo Researchers)*

the onset of walking may occur a bit earlier or later, but the child's ultimate performance is pretty much the same in either case. The important developmental achievement is to walk at all, and this is very probably based on maturation.

In line with this conclusion are studies using twins, one of whom was trained in such basic motor activities as walking or climbing stairs while the other was not. The results showed that while practice may help, it doesn't have long-run effects. If a twin practiced before she was "ready," she did indeed surpass her untrained twin. But the gains were short-lived. For once the other twin was given similar practice after reaching the appropriate maturational point, she quickly caught up with her specially educated twin and attained the same level of locomotor proficiency (Gesell and Thompson, 1929; McGraw, 1935).

All in all, it looks as if certain activities that are basic to the species occur largely as a function of maturation. They can be modified somewhat by experience, but they will emerge more or less on schedule regardless of specific practice. But a different verdict holds for skills that are specific to a particular culture or subgroup, such as swimming, climbing trees, playing tennis, or throwing a boomerang. Here early practice does seem to have lasting effects. This may be because such skills are more easily acquired at an early age (as is the case in learning a language, see Chapter 9, p. 368–70). It may also be that starting early provides the necessary motivation for the grueling efforts required for eventual mastery.

SPECIFIC VS. NON-SPECIFIC EXPERIENCE

Various achievements of early development seem to depend on maturation. But that does not mean that the organism's environment has no effect. For there is a good deal of evidence that certain kinds of very general experience exert important effects on a number of sensory and motor patterns. For example, animals reared in total darkness in early life will not develop certain structures of the visual system that allow them to see properly when they are later exposed to light (Gottlieb, 1976b).

Just as sensory deprivation can retard maturation (or deter it altogether) environmental enrichment can help it along. In one study, rat pups were placed in either an impoverished or an enriched environment right after they were weaned. The animals in the impoverished environment were individually housed in a standard laboratory cage with continual access to a water bottle and to food. In contrast, the animals in the enriched environment were housed in groups of about twelve in a large cage that was a veritable rats' playground: It contained a variety of objects that served as toys that the rats could climb upon, walk across, and run in and out of, and that were changed daily to provide additional opportunities for informal learning (Rosenzweig and Bennett, 1972; Renner and Rosenzweig, 1987; see Figure 13.10). After eighty days of exposure

13.10 Effects of environmental enrichment *After eighty days in the enriched environment of this rat playground, the animals had 23 percent more neural interconnections than control animals. (Photograph courtesy of Dr. Mark Rosenzweig)*

to these different environments, the brains of the animals were examined. The results showed that the brains of the environmentally enriched rats were heavier than those of the environmentally impoverished rats. It's not that the number of neurons in the brains of the two groups was any different. What differed instead was the number of neural branchings and interconnections. In one study, the enriched animals were estimated to have about 9,400 synapses per neuron, while the impoverished animals only had about 7,600 (Turner and Greenough, 1985). The increase in the number and complexity of synaptic junctions produced by exposure to a varied environment may well be the biological basis on which later behavioral development depends (Schapiro and Vukovich, 1976).

The organism's genetic instructions dictate the maturation of many of its early attainments. But these dictates cannot be obeyed without a proper environment in which maturation can take place.

PIAGET'S THEORY OF COGNITIVE DEVELOPMENT

Thus far, our discussion of development has focused on physical growth and changes in motor behavior. But the child grows in mind as well as body—in what she knows, how she comes to know it, how she thinks about it, and in the fact that she can tell it to others (sometimes interminably so). This intellectual growth from infancy to adulthood is generally called *cognitive development.*

We will organize our discussion of the child's mental growth around the work of the Swiss psychologist Jean Piaget (1896–1980). He was the first to develop methods for studying the ways in which infants and children see and understand the world, the first to suggest that these ways are profoundly different from those of adults, and the first to offer a systematic theoretical account of the process of mental growth from infancy to adulthood. As we will see, Piaget's formulations have aroused considerable controversy: Many of his empirical claims have been disputed, and most of his theoretical proposals have come under serious attack. But even so, we cannot begin the study of cognitive development without first considering Piaget's views, since these shaped the way in which all subsequent investigators thought about the subject.

Piaget believed that mental growth involves major qualitative changes. This hypothesis is relatively recent. According to the eighteenth-century empiricists, the child's mental machinery is fundamentally the same as the adult's, the only difference being that the child has fewer associations. Nativists also minimized the distinction between the child's mind and the adult's, for they viewed the basic categories of time, space, number, and causality as given *a priori*, being part of the native mental equipment that all humans have at birth. Thus both empiricists and nativists regarded the child as much like an adult; the first saw him as an adult-in-training, the second as an adult-in-miniature. In contrast, Piaget looked for qualitative differences and tried to chart the orderly progression of human intellect as the child grows into an adult.

Piaget's original training was as a biologist, which may be one of the reasons why his conception of intellectual development bears many resemblances to the way an embryologist thinks of the development of anatomical structures. The human fetus doesn't just get larger between, say, two and seven months—its whole structure changes drastically. Piaget argued that mental development is characterized by similar qualitative changes. He proposed that there are four main stages of intellectual growth, whose overall thrust is toward an increasing

Children as miniature adults *Children dressed as did the adults of their time and class as shown in this 1786 Dutch painting. (Helena van der Schalke, by G. ter Borch, Courtesy of the Rijksmuseum, Amsterdam)*

emancipation from the here and now of the immediate, concrete present to a conception of the world in increasingly symbolic and abstract terms. These stages are the period of **sensory-motor intelligence** (from birth to about two years), the **preoperational period** (two to seven years), the period of **concrete operations** (seven to eleven years), and the period of **formal operations** (eleven years and on). The age ranges are very approximate, however, and successive stages are often thought to overlap and blend into each other.★

SENSORY-MOTOR INTELLIGENCE

According to Piaget, at first there is nothing but a succession of transient, unconnected sensory impressions and motor reactions. As he saw it, mental life during the first few months contains neither past nor future, no distinction between stable objects and fleeting events, and no differentiation between the "me" and the "not me." The critical achievement of the first two years is the development of these distinctions.

OBJECT PERMANENCE

Consider an infant holding a rattle. To an adult, the rattle is an object, a thing, of whose existence he has no doubt, whether he looks at it or briefly looks away. The adult is sure of its existence, for he is certain that he will see it once more when he looks at it again. But does the rattle exist as a thing in the same sense to the infant? Does the infant have the notion of **object permanence**?

According to Piaget, there is little object permanence in the first few months of life. The infant may look at a new toy with evident delight, but if it disappears from view, he shows little concern (see Figure 13.11). It seems as if what's out of sight is also out of mind and does not really exist for the infant. Needless to say, infants eventually come to live in a world whose objects do not capriciously appear and disappear with each movement of their eyes. At about eight months of age, they start to search for toys that have been hidden or that have fallen out of their cribs. But for quite a while, their search pattern has some peculiar limitations.

Consider a nine-month-old who sees an experimenter hide a toy monkey in one place, say, under a cover to his right. He will happily push the cover off and snatch the monkey. The experimenter now repeats the process a few times, always hiding the monkey in the same place, under the same cover to the child's right; he'll keep on pulling the cover off and retrieving the monkey. Now the experimenter introduces a change in the procedure. Very slowly and conspicuously and in full view of the child, she now hides the toy in a different place, say, under a cover to the child's left. The child watches her every movement with grave attention—and then does exactly what he did before. He searches under the cover on the right where he previously found the monkey, even though he saw the experimenter hide the toy in another place just a moment before. This phenomenon is often called the **A-not-B effect,** where A designates the place where the object was first hidden, and B the place where it was hidden last. Piaget believed that the A-not-B effect showed that even the nine-month-old still lacks a full appreciation of the fact that objects exist in their own right. On

13.11 **Object permanence** *(A) A six-month-old looks intently at a toy. (B) But when the toy is hidden from view, the infant does not search for it. According to Piaget, this is because the infant does not as yet have the concept of object permanence. (Photographs by Doug Goodman 1986/Monkmeyer)*

★ These stages roughly correspond to the categories employed by modern developmental psychologists, regardless of their stand on Piaget's theory: infancy (from birth to about two-and-a-half years), early childhood (two-and-a-half to six years), middle childhood (six to eleven years), and adolescence and beyond (twelve years and up).

this view, the infant's notion of the object includes his own action in retrieving it, as if his reaching toward place *A* where he found it previously were as much a part of the monkey as the monkey's tail (Piaget, 1952; Flavell, 1985; Harris, 1987).

According to Piaget, the notion that objects exist on their own, and continue to exist even if they are not seen, heard, felt, or reached for, is a major accomplishment of the sensory-motor period. This notion emerges as the infant gradually interrelates his various sensory experiences and motor reactions. Eventually he coordinates the sensory spaces provided by the different modalities—of vision, hearing, touch, and bodily movement—into one real space in which all of the world's objects—himself included—exist.

SENSORY-MOTOR SCHEMAS

The newborn starts life with a rather limited repertoire of built-in reactions, such as gross bodily movements in response to distress, sucking and swallowing reflexes, and, after a few days, certain orienting responses such as head and eye movements. In Piaget's view, these recurrent action patterns are the first mental elements—or *schemas*—through which the infant organizes the world that impinges upon her. At first, these various schemas operate in isolation. A one-month-old infant can grasp a rattle and can also suck it or look at it. But she will perform these actions only if the stimulus object is directly applied to the relevant sensory surface. She will suck the rattle if it touches her mouth and will grasp it if it's pressed into her palm. But she is as yet unable to grasp whatever she's sucking or to look at whatever she's grasping. The coordination of all these patterns is not complete until she's about five months of age. How is this integration achieved?

According to Piaget, the answer lies in the two processes that in his view are responsible for all of cognitive development: *assimilation* and *accommodation.* At any given point, the child has to be able to interpret the environment in terms of the mental schemas she has at the time; the environment is assimilated to the schema. But the schemas necessarily change as the child continues to interact with the world around her; they accommodate to the environment. In the case of the sucking response, the initial schema only applies to the nipple. But with time, the infant starts to suck other objects, such as her rattle. Piaget would say that by doing this she has assimilated the rattle into her sucking schema. The rattle is now understood and dealt with as a "suckable." But the process does not stop there. After all, rattles are not the same as nipples; while both are suckable, they are not suckable in quite the same way. This necessarily leads to new discriminations. As a result, the sucking schema adjusts to (that is, accommodates) the new object to which it is applied. This process continues, with further assimilations followed by yet further accommodations, until finally looking, reaching, grasping, and sucking have all merged into one unified exploratory schema (Piaget, 1952).

BEGINNINGS OF REPRESENTATIONAL THOUGHT

According to Piaget, the last phase of the sensory-motor period (about eighteen to twenty-four months) marks a momentous change in intellectual development. Children begin to conceive of objects and events that are not immediately present by representing (that is "re-presenting") some prior experience with these to themselves. Such *mental representations* may be internalized actions, images, or words. But in all cases, they function as symbols that stand for whatever they may signify yet are not equivalent to it.

One demonstration of this change is the achievement of full object permanence. At eighteen months or so, children actively search for absent toys and are

Assimilation and accommodation *The three-month-old has assimilated the rattle into her sucking schema and has accommodated the schema so that it now includes the rattle as a suckable object. (Photograph by Steve Skloot/Photo Researchers)*

surprised (and sometimes outraged) if they don't find them under the sofa cover where they saw the experimenter hide them; it is reasonable to infer that they have some internal representation of the sought-for object. Even more persuasive are examples of **deferred imitation** in which children imitate actions that occurred some time past, such as a playmate's temper tantrum observed a day ago. A related phenomenon is make-believe play, which is often based on deferred imitation.

THE PREOPERATIONAL PERIOD

Given the tools of representational thought, the two-year-old has taken a gigantic step forward. A year ago, he could interact with the environment only through direct sensory or motor contact; now he can carry the whole world in his head. But while his mental world now contains stable objects and events that can be represented internally, it is still a far cry from the world of adults. The two-year-old has overcome the initial chaos of separate sensations and motor impressions. But according to Piaget, this was only to exchange it for a chaos of ideas (that is, representations) that he is as yet unable to relate in any coherent way. The achievement of the next five years is the emergence of a reasonably well-ordered world of ideas. In Piaget's view, this requires higher-order schemas that he calls **operations,** which allow the internal manipulation of ideas according to a stable set of rules. In his view, genuine operations do not appear until about seven or so, hence the term **preoperational** for the period from two to about seven years.

FAILURE OF CONSERVATION

Conservation of quantity and number   A revealing example of preoperational thought is the young child's failure to **conserve quantity.** One of Piaget's experimental procedures uses two identical glasses, *A* and *B*, which stand side by side and are filled with the same amount of some colored liquid. A child is asked whether there is more orangeade in one glass or the other, and the experimenter obligingly adds a drop here, a drop there until his subject is completely satisfied that there is "the same to drink in this glass as in that." Four-year-olds can easily make this judgment.

The next step involves a new glass, *C,* which is much taller but also narrower than *A* and *B* (see Figure 13.12). While the child is watching, the experimenter pours the entire contents of glass *A* into glass *C*. He now points to *B* and *C,* and asks, "Is there more orangeade in this glass or in that?" For an adult, the question is almost too simple to merit an answer. The amounts are obviously identi-

13.12   Conservation of liquid quantity
Patrick, aged four years, three months, is asked by the experimenter, "Do we both have the same amount of juice to drink?" Patrick says yes. (B) The experimenter pours the juice from one of the beakers into a new, wider beaker. When now asked, "Which glass has more juice?" he points to the thinner one. (Photographs by Chris Massey)

A

B

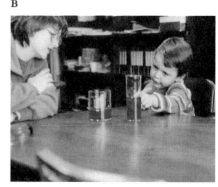

cal, since *A* was completely emptied into *C*, and *A* and *B* were set to equality at the outset. But four- or five-year-olds don't see this. They insist that there is more orangeade in *C*. When asked for their reason, they explain that the liquid comes to a much higher level in *C*. They seem to think that the orangeade has somehow increased in quantity as it was transferred from one glass to another. They are too impressed by the visible changes in appearance that accompany each transfer (the changing liquid levels) and do not yet realize that there is an underlying reality (the quantity of liquid) that remains constant throughout.

By the time children are about seven years old, they respond much like adults. They hardly look at the two glasses, for their judgment needs little empirical support. "It's the same. It seems as if there's less because it's wider, but it's the same." The experimenter may continue with further glasses of different sizes and shapes, but the judgment remains what it was: "It's still the same because it always comes from the same glass." To justify their answer, the children point to the fact that one can always pour the liquid back into the original glass (that is, *A*), and thus obtain the same levels. They have obviously understood that the various transformations in the liquid's appearance are reversible. For every transformation that changes the way the liquid looks, there is another that restores its original appearance. Given this insight, children at this age recognize that there is an underlying attribute of reality, the quantity of liquid that remains constant (is *conserved*), throughout the various perceptual changes. (For comparable results with malleable solids like clay, see Figure 13.13).

A related phenomenon is **conservation of number.** The child is first shown a row of six evenly spaced bottles, each of which has a glass standing next to it. The child agrees that there are as many bottles as there are glasses. The experimenter now rearranges the six glasses by setting them out into a much longer row while leaving the six bottles as they were. Here the turning point comes a bit earlier, at about five or six. Up to that age, children generally assert that there are more glasses because "they're more spread out" (see Figure 13.14). From about six on, there is conservation; the child has no doubt that there are just as many bottles in the tightly spaced row as there are glasses in the spread-out line. In all these conservation tasks, the older child's explanation emphasizes reversibility—liquid can be poured back in the taller glass, and the long line of glasses can be reassembled into a compact row.

Attending to several factors simultaneously   Why are preschool children unable to appreciate that the amount of a substance remains unaffected by changes of shape or that the number of objects in a given set does not vary with changes in the spatial arrangement? According to Piaget, part of the problem is the child's inability to attend to all of the relevant dimensions simultaneously. Consider conservation of liquid quantity. To conserve, the children must first comprehend that there are two relevant factors: the height of the liquid column and the

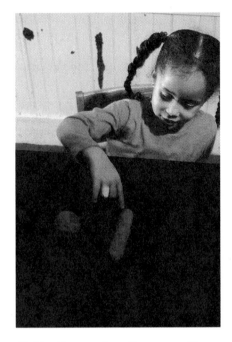

13.13   Conservation of mass quantity
In parallel to the failure to conserve liquid quantity is the preschooler's failure to conserve mass. Jennifer, aged four years and four months, is shown two clay balls which she adjusts until she is satisfied that there is the same amount of clay in both. The experimenter takes one of the balls and rolls it into a "hot dog." When now asked which is more, Jennifer points to the hot dog. (Photograph by Ed Boswell)

13.14   Conservation of number   (A) *The experimenter points to two rows of checkers, one hers, the other Tyler's. She asks, "Do I have as many checkers as you?" and Tyler (aged four years, five months) nods. (B) One row of checkers is spread out and the experimenter says, "Now, do we still have the same?" Tyler says no and points to the spread-out row, which she says has more. (Photographs by Chris Massey)*

A

B

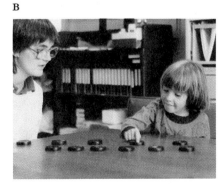

width. They must then appreciate that an increase in the column's height is accompanied by a decrease in its width. Initially, they center their attention only on the height and do not realize that the change in height is compensated for by a corresponding change in width. Later on, say at five, they may well attend to width on one occasion and to height on another (with corresponding changes in judgment). But to attend to both dimensions concurrently and to relate them properly requires a higher-order schema that reorganizes initially discrete perceptual experiences into one conceptual unit.

In Piaget's view, this reorganization occurs when the child focuses on the transformations from one experience into another, rather than on the individual experiences by themselves. The child sees that these transformations are effected by various reversible overt actions, such as pouring the contents of one glass into another. The overt action eventually becomes internalized as a reversible operation so that the child can mentally pour the liquid back and forth. The result is conservation of quantity (Piaget, 1952).

In summary, the preoperational child is the prisoner of his own immediate perceptual experience and tends to take appearance for reality. When a seven-year-old watches a magician, she can easily distinguish between her perception and her knowledge. She perceives that the rabbits come out of the hat, but she knows that they couldn't possibly do so. Her four-year-old brother has no such sophistication. He is delighted to see rabbits anytime and anywhere, and if they want to come out of a hat, why shouldn't they?

EGOCENTRISM

In Piaget's theory, the inability of preoperational children to consider two physical dimensions simultaneously has a counterpart in their approach to the social world. They cannot understand another person's point of view, for they are as yet unable to recognize that different points of view exist. This characteristic of preoperational thought is called *egocentrism.* As Piaget used the term, it does not imply selfishness. It is not that children seek to benefit at the expense of others; it is rather that they haven't fully grasped that there are other selves.

An interesting demonstration of egocentrism involves a literal interpretation of "point of view." If two adults stand at opposite corners of a building, each knows that the other sees a different wall. But according to Piaget, preoperational children don't understand this. In one study, children were shown a three-dimensional model of a mountain scene. While the children viewed the scene from one position, a small doll was placed at various other locations around the model. The child's job was to decide what the doll saw from its vantage point (see Figure 13.15). To answer, the child had to choose one of several drawings that depicted different views of the mountain scene. Up to four years of age, the children didn't even understand the question. From four to seven years old, their response was fairly consistent—they chose the drawing that showed what they saw, regardless of where the doll was placed (Piaget and Inhelder, 1956).

13.15 The three-mountain test of egocentrism *The child is asked to indicate what the teddy bear sees. The results suggest that the child thinks the teddy bear sees the scene just as she does, including the little house, which is of course obstructed from the teddy bear's vantage point. (After Piaget and Inhelder, 1967)*

CONCRETE AND FORMAL OPERATIONS

Seven-year-olds have acquired mental operations that allow them to abstract some of the essential attributes of reality such as number and substance. But according to Piaget, these operations are primarily applicable to the relations between concrete events (hence the term *concrete operations*). They do not really suffice when these relations must be considered entirely in the abstract. Eight- and nine-year-olds can perform various manipulations on specific numbers, but they generally fail to understand that certain results will hold for any

Jean Piaget *(Photograph by Yves De-Braine, Black Star)*

number whatsoever. They may realize that 4 is an even number and 4 + 1 is odd, and similarly for 6 and 6 + 1, 8 and 8 + 1, but they are by no means sure that the addition of 1 to *any* even number must always produce a number that is odd. According to Piaget, the comprehension of such highly abstract and formal relationships requires **formal operations,** operations of a higher order, which emerge at about eleven or twelve years of age. Given formal operations, the child's thought can embrace the possible as well as the real. He can now entertain hypothetical possibilities, can deal with what might be no less than what is.

An illustration of the role of formal operations comes from a study in which children had to discover what makes a pendulum go fast or go slow. They were shown how to construct a pendulum by hanging some object from a string. They were also shown how to vary the length of the string, the weight of the suspended object, and the initial force that set the pendulum in motion. Children between seven and eleven typically varied several factors at a time. They might compare a heavy weight suspended from a long string with a light weight suspended from a short string, and would then conclude that a pendulum swings faster the shorter its length and the lighter its weight. Needless to say, their reasoning was faulty, for the way to determine whether a given factor (e.g., weight) has an effect is to hold all others (e.g., length) constant. Children younger than about eleven cannot do this, for they can operate only on the concretely given. They are unable to consider potential cause-and-effect relationships, which must first be deliberately excluded and then tested for later on. In contrast, older children can plan and execute an appropriate series of tests. Their mental operations proceed on a more formal plane, so they can grasp the notion of "other things being equal" (Inhelder and Piaget, 1958).

The entry into the period of formal operations is the last important milestone in the child's intellectual progression that Piaget and his co-workers charted in some detail. Their account of the developmental steps that led up to this point has been enormously influential. But this doesn't mean that it has gone unchallenged. We will now consider some of the efforts to look at Piaget's description of human cognitive development with a more critical eye.

WHAT IS THE COGNITIVE STARTING POINT?

One critical challenge to Piaget's work concerns his views of what is given at the very start of life. A number of modern developmental psychologists contend that Piaget—who in this regard was much like the early British empiricists—had seriously underestimated the infant's native endowment. These critics deny that the infant's mind is the mere jumble of unrelated sensory impressions and motor reactions that Piaget declared it to be, for they believe that some of the major categories by which adults organize the world—such as the concepts of space, objects, number, and the existence of other minds—have primitive precursors in early life. They have buttressed their position by systematic studies of perception and action in very young infants.

SPACE AND OBJECTS IN INFANCY

Do humans come equipped with some built-in notion of space and objects? Some experiments with very young infants suggest that they do.

THE EFFECT OF OCCLUSION

One series of studies focused on the perceptual effect of **occlusion.** Consider Figure 13.16A, which shows an object that partially obscures (occludes) the view of an object behind it. When adults encounter this sight, they will surely perceive it as a child behind a gate. They are completely certain that when the gate is opened so that the partial occlusion is removed, they will see a whole child (Figure 13.16B) and would be utterly astounded if the opened gate revealed a child with gaps in her (Figure 13.16C). This ability to perceive partly hidden objects as they really are is continually called upon in our everyday life. Most of the things we see are partly concealed by others in front of them, but we perceive a world of complete objects rather than disjointed fragments (see Chapter 6).

What accounts for the adult's ability to perceive partly hidden objects? To some extent, it is surely a matter of learning. We know that people have no gaps in them and that even if they do, they can't stand unsupported in mid-air. But does this mean that Piaget is correct and that the infant starts life with no idea at all that there are external objects outside? Some authors believe it does not. In their view, the infant comes equipped with some primitive concept of a physical world that contains unitary objects whose parts are connected and stay connected regardless of whether the object is partially hidden. Their evidence comes from experiments which show that under some conditions four-month-old infants seem to perceive occluded objects in much the same manner that adults do. Most of these experiments employed the **habituation procedure** (Figure 13.17).

In one such study, the infants were shown a rod that moved back and forth behind a solid block that occluded the rod's central portion (Figure 13.18A). This display was kept in view until the infants became bored (that is, *habituated*), and stopped looking at it. The question was whether the infant perceived a complete, unitary rod, despite the fact that this rod was partially hidden. To find out, the experimenters presented the infants with two new and unoccluded displays. One was an unbroken rod that moved back and forth (Figure 13.18B). The other consisted of two aligned rod pieces that moved back and forth in unison (Figure 13.18C). If the infants saw the original display as a complete rod that moved behind the block, they would presumably regard the broken rod as a

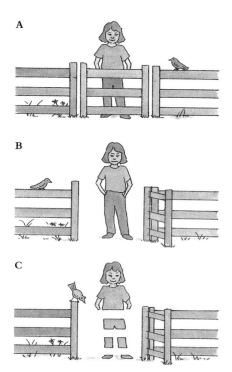

13.16 *The perceptual effect of occlusion* (A) A child occluded by a gate is perceived as a whole person behind a gate, so that she will look like (B) when the gate is opened, rather than being perceived as (C), a child with gaps in her body.

13.17 *The habituation procedure* (A) A four-month-old's face, looking at a small slowly rotating pyramid in front of her (the pyramid can be seen in the mirror that is behind the infant and above her head). (B) Habituation: The infant becomes increasingly bored and looks away. (C) Dishabituation: The infant sees a new object (the rotating cube shown in the mirror) and looks again. This dishabituation effect provides evidence that the infant perceives a difference between the first and the second stimulus (that is, the pyramid and the cube). (Photographs courtesy of Phillip Kellman)

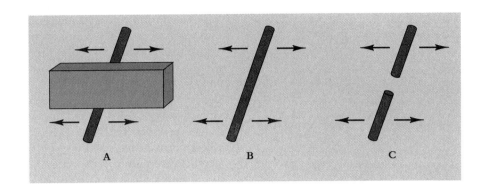

13.18 The perceptual effect of occlusion in early infancy *Four-month-olds were shown a rod that moved back and forth behind an occluding block as shown in (A). After they became habituated to this display and stopped looking at it, they were shown two new displays, neither of which was occluded. (B) was an unbroken rod that moved back and forth. (C) was made of two aligned rod pieces that moved back and forth together. The infants spent much more time looking at (C) than at (B). (After Kellman and Spelke, 1983)*

novel stimulus. If so, they would keep on looking at it for a longer time than at the (now unobstructed) complete rod. This is just what happened. The fact that the top and bottom of the rod in the original display were seen to move together behind the block apparently led to the perception that they were connected. This suggests that some notion of a real physical object exists even at four months of age (Kellman and Spelke, 1983; Kellman, Spelke, and Short, 1986).

KNOWING ABOUT OBJECTS

The preceding discussion suggests that very young infants see objects rather than disjointed fragments. Do they also understand certain rock-bottom principles of the physical world, such as the fact that two objects can't occupy the same space at the same time?

To answer that question, four-and-a-half-month-olds were shown a miniature stage in the middle of which was a medium-sized yellow box. In front of the box was a screen that was hinged on a rod attached to the stage floor. Initially, that screen was laid flat so that the box behind it was clearly visible, but the screen was then rotated upwards like a drawbridge, hiding the box from view (Figure 13.19A). There were two conditions. In one condition, the screen rotated backwards until it reached the no longer visible box, stopped, and then rotated forwards and returned to its initial position at which point the box became visible again (Figure 13.19B). In the other condition, the screen rotated backwards until it reached the occluded box and then kept on going as though the box were no longer there. Once it finished the full 180 degree arc, it reversed direction and swiveled all the way backwards, at which point the box was revealed again (the box being surreptitiously removed and replaced as required; see Figure 13.19C; Baillargeon, Spelke, and Wasserman, 1985; Baillargeon, 1987a).

To an adult, these two conditions present the observer with two radically different events. The first of these makes perfect physical sense: Since two objects can't occupy the same space at the same time, the screen necessarily stops when it encounters the solid box. But the second event is physically impossible: If one assumes the box is still where it was originally seen to be, the screen couldn't possibly pass through it.

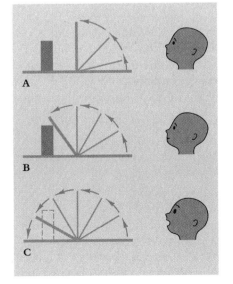

13.19 Knowing about objects *A four-and-a-half-month-old infant is looking at a stage on which he sees an upright, brightly colored box. In front of the box is a screen that initially lies flat and then starts to rotate upward (A). In the first condition (B), the screen stops rotating as soon as it hits the box. In the second condition (C), when the screen is at a point high enough to hide the box, the box is surreptitiously removed and the screen continues to rotate backwards. The infant seems to find this quite surprising as shown by the fact that he continues to look at the stage much longer than he did in the first condition. Infants seem able to distinguish possible from impossible events. (After Baillargeon, 1987a)*

A

B

C

13.20 A dissociation between what the infant knows and what the infant does
(A) A seven-month-old looks at a toy that has just been placed in B, one of the two wells. (B) He continues to look at well B after both wells are covered. (C) When finally allowed to reach for the toy, he uncovers well A in which he found the toy on a previous trial rather than well B in which he saw the toy being placed. In this particular sequence he actually still looks at B while uncovering A, suggesting a dissociation between what the infant knows and what he does. (Courtesy Adele Diamond)

This is all very well for adults, but do infants see the world the same way? The answer seems to be yes. They spent much less time looking at the stage in the first condition than they did in the second. In the first condition, the screen did what it was supposed to: It came to a halt when it came up against the—presumably still present—solid box. But in the second condition, the screen behaved rather oddly, for it apparently passed through a solid object. The four-month-olds evidently found the second condition more surprising—or puzzling—than the first. This suggests that these young infants had some notion of object permanence, for they evidently believed that the yellow box they had seen before continued to exist even though it was now occluded. It also suggests that young infants have some notions of the principles that govern objects in space; they evidently know that two objects (here, the screen and the yellow box) can't occupy the same place at the same time.

OBJECT PERMANENCE AND THE SEARCH PROCESS

All in all, there is reason to believe that, Piaget and the empiricists to the contrary, infants come remarkably well-equipped to see the world as it really is. But if so, how can we explain the findings that led Piaget to argue for the lack of object permanence in infancy, such as infants' persistent failure in retrieving objects that are out of sight? Most modern investigators feel that there is no real inconsistency. They hold that while infants may believe that objects exist, they are exceedingly inept in searching for them. Some evidence comes from work on the *A-not-B* effect (discussed earlier in this chapter), the infant's tendency to search at a place where he found a hidden toy previously rather than at a place where he has just seen a toy hidden (see Figure 13.20).

What accounts for the *A-not-B* effect? One factor may be the infants' inability to inhibit whatever response is currently dominant. Since they've repeatedly reached toward *A* before, that reaching pattern is presumably momentarily potent; if not held in check, it will override all competing response alternatives. In line with this hypothesis is the fact that in some cases infants look at *A* even though they reach for *B*, as if they knew where the object was but couldn't tell their arms what they had learned with their eyes (Baillargeon and Graber, 1987). Some investigators believe that the ability to override a dominant action tendency depends on the maturation of a certain region in the frontal lobe (specifically, the prefrontal cortex, a region just in front of the motor projection area). Evidence comes from work on monkeys with lesions in this area; they show the same deficits in analogous tasks (Diamond, 1988, 1989; Diamond and Goldman-Rakic, 1989).

Thus there is good reason to believe that Piaget was wrong about the infant's failure to have a notion of object permanence. All the evidence points to the conclusion that the very young infant has an idea that there are objects out in the world that have a separate existence apart from himself. What he does not have as yet is much of an idea of how to deal with those objects—for example, how to find them when they are hidden from view.

NUMBER IN INFANCY

Do infants have some notion of number? That is, do they recognize that a set of three cubes shares an important property with a set of three spheres—or three apples or three rattles or three teddy bears or three whatevers—namely, threeness? The ability to abstract this property underlies all numerical thinking. According to Piaget, this ability is not found before about six years

13.21 Some rudiments of number in six-month-olds *Six-month-olds were shown two panels that contained either two or three simple objects. Concurrently, a drum was sounded over a loudspeaker, producing rhythmic booms either in twos ("boom, boom") or in threes ("boom, boom, boom"). (A) When the drum was sounded "boom, boom," the baby looked at the panel that contained two items. (B) When the drum was sounded "boom, boom, boom," the baby looked at the panel that contained three items. This result suggests that the baby has some rudimentary concept of twoness and threeness, a concept that holds whether the items that are "counted" are visual objects or sounds. (Starkey, Spelke, and Gelman, 1983)*

of age, for in his view children are unable to conserve number until then. After all, a child who says that a row of four buttons that are spread out has more buttons in it than a row of four that are bunched more closely together has presumably failed to abstract the concept of numbers.

But more recent experiments have shown that indications of numerical ability are found not only in preschoolers but even in infants of six months or less. The demonstration comes from studies in which infants were presented with a series of slides that displayed different sets of three simple objects. One slide might show a comb, a fork, and a sponge, another might show a bottle, a brush, and a toy drum, and so on. Each slide also differed in the spatial arrangement of the items. They might be set up with two on top and one below, or with one above and two below, in a vertical column and so on. All the slides had in common was that each of them contained three items. Would the infants detect this common abstract property? To find out, the experimenters used the habituation technique: They presented these sets of threes until the infants became bored and stopped looking. Then they presented a series of new slides in which some of the slides showed two items, while others continued to show three. The results were dramatic: The infants spent more time looking at the slides that displayed two items rather than three (see Figure 13.21). Evidently they had abstracted the one property the original displays had in common: They were of threes. Since the two-item displays differed in this regard, they produced a dishabituation effect: They were evidently perceived as novel and so worth looking at (Starkey, Spelke and Gelman, 1983, 1990).

Results of this sort suggest that the ability to abstract number is part of our native endowment. Infants evidently can perceive numerical equivalence (at least with sets of up to four or five; e.g., Treiber and Wilcox, 1984). Do they also have some rudiments of the numerical reasoning that provides the basis for arithmetical operations? It appears that they do. In a recent study five-month-olds were shown a toy mouse on a small stage. After the infants had looked at this scene for a while, a screen came up from the floor and hid the mouse from view. Following this, the infants then saw the experimenter's hand appear from the wings, holding another mouse and placing it behind the screen. The final step was the test: The screen was lowered and revealed either one mouse or two. If the infants had some primitive understanding of the meaning of addition, they should have expected to see two mice and be surprised to see only one. In fact, this surprise is just what happened. The infants continued to look at the single mouse as if wondering why the other one wasn't there. Analogous results were found in a pint-sized subtraction task in which the experimenter presented two mice at first and then took one away. Here, the infants looked longer when they saw two mice as if none had been taken away (Wynn, 1992).

SOCIAL COGNITION IN INFANCY: THE EXISTENCE OF OTHER MINDS

To an adult, the existence of other minds is a basic axiom (e.g., Austin, 1970). We know that we have beliefs and desires, and take for granted that others also do. According to Piaget and the British Empiricists, this knowledge is entirely a product of learning. But while it's true that an enormous amount of what we know about others is acquired through learning, there is reason to believe that this learning builds upon a substantial substructure that is natively given.

To begin with, there is evidence that infants come into the world with some built-in predisposition to look at human faces. One group of investigators studied babies immediately (that is, nine *minutes*) after they were born. The experi-

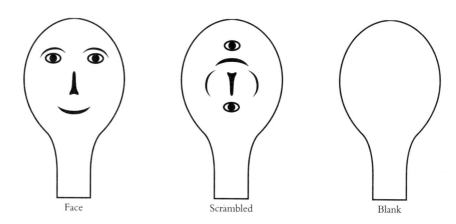

Face Scrambled Blank

13.22 Rudimentary face recognition in newborns *Newborn babies look longer at a pattern showing a schematic face than at a scrambled or a blank pattern. (From Johnson and Morton, 1991)*

menter held each baby in his lap and moved several patterns in front of their eyes. The infants turned their heads and looked longer at the pattern if it was of a schematic rather than of a scrambled face. Further studies suggest that this very early face recognition process is based on a subcortical mechanism that drops out within a month or two and is then replaced by more sophisticated recognition machinery that comes into its own as the visual cortex matures (Goren, Sarty, and Wu, 1975; Morton and Johnson, 1991; see Figure 13.22). The ability to recognize that certain sensory patterns characterize other human beings—that some visual patterns specify faces, that some auditory patterns define voices—is a necessary foundation on which all further social cognition rests. Before long the baby will know not just that such and such a sensory pattern characterizes another person but that it belongs to a particular person—its mother, father, or some other important caretaker.

The ability to recognize others is only the barest first step in understanding that there are other minds. An important next step is the infant's recognition that others live in the same physical world and can more or less see what she sees, hear what she hears, and so on. Evidence comes from work on shared attention. Thus nine-month-olds will tend to look in the direction of their mothers' gaze (Scaife and Bruner, 1975). When they are between twelve and eighteen months their ability to recognize where the mother is looking and what she is looking at becomes a conceptual achievement that goes beyond the perceptual here and now. In one study, each infant was held in his mother's lap while she looked at one of a number of toys arranged in front of her in a semicircle. But the child was held with his head toward the mother's body so that he could not see the target; all he could see was his mother's eyes. Evidently, that was enough—as soon as the mother's hold was released the infant squirmed around and looked at just the toy the mother had looked at a moment before (Butterworth and Cochran, 1980; Butterworth and Jarrett, 1991).

COGNITIVE DEVELOPMENT IN PRESCHOOLERS

The preceding discussion showed why many critics feel that Piaget underestimated the infant's native cognitive endowments. If these critics are right, the starting point of mental growth is higher than Piaget assumed it to be. But what about the process of development from then on? As Piaget described it, cognitive development goes through several distinct stages that are in some ways analogous to the stages found in embryological development. This stage notion of development has been the subject of considerable debate. No one doubts that there is mental growth, that the child changes in the way she thinks as she gets older. But is this growth best described as a progression through successive stages?

THE MEANING OF MENTAL STAGE

Piaget used the term *stage* in analogy to how it is understood in embryology. Embryological stages tend to be discrete rather than continuous. There is a qualitative difference between a tadpole and a frog; to be sure, the change from one to the other takes a while, but by the time the creature is a frog, its tadpole days are emphatically over. Piaget's basic claim was that the same discreteness characterizes cognitive development. A number of critics have questioned whether it really does.

As Piaget's account is usually understood, many cognitive capacities that mark one period of development are totally absent at prior periods. But this is questionable. Consider conservation of quantity or number. According to a simple discrete-stage hypothesis, these should be totally absent at an early age, say, five years old and younger. They should then emerge virtually full blown when the curtain finally opens on the next act of the developmental drama, the period of concrete operations. But a number of modern investigators deny that cognitive development is essentially all or none. As these critics see it, various cognitive achievements such as conservation have primitive precursors that appear several years earlier than the Piagetian calendar would predict (Gelman, 1978; Gelman and Baillargeon, 1983).

We will now consider two areas of cognitive growth during the preschool period—number and social cognition—from the perspective of these modern investigators.

NUMERICAL SKILLS IN PRESCHOOLERS

We've seen that infants can abstract the properties of twoness and threeness. This provides the initial basis for the further development of numerical abilities (Gelman, 1982; Gelman and Gallistel, 1978).

COUNTING

Consider counting. Some initial rudiments of this skill appear as early as two and a half. At this age, children may not yet know the conventional number terms. But nevertheless they may have grasped some aspect of what the counting process is all about. For example, some children employ an idiosyncratic number series. Thus one two-year-old consistently used "one, two, six," and another used "one, thirteen, nineteen." But what is important is that they used these series consistently. They realized that each of these number tags has to be applied to each object in the set on a one-to-one basis, that the tags must always be used in the same order, and that the last number applied is the number of items in the set. And this realization is the foundation on which counting rests (Gelman and Gallistel, 1978).

NUMERICAL REASONING

A child who can count (even if rather idiosyncratically) has taken a big step. But there is more to numerical understanding than counting. The child must also grasp some principles of numerical reasoning. She must understand that adding an item increases the total number of items in the set that is being counted, that subtracting one decreases it, and that adding one and then subtracting one leaves everything unchanged. The comprehension of these basic numerical truths will not suffice to make the child an arithmetician, but they are basic to all further advances in the numerical domain. The evidence suggests that preschoolers gradually acquire these conceptual basics. When comparing two sets of items, three- and four-year-olds can correctly point to the one that is smaller or larger if the number of items are small enough (Gelman, 1982; Gelman and Gallistel, 1978).

How can such results be reconciled with Piaget's claim that preschoolers fail in tasks that call for conservation of number? We have previously described the standard Piagetian finding: When preschoolers are asked to compare two rows that contain the same number of, say, toy soldiers, they often say that the longer row contains more soldiers, in an apparent confusion of length and number. But more recent studies show that children as young as three have surprising precursors of number conservation if the test conditions are suitably arranged (Gelman, 1972).

In one procedure, the children were shown two toy plates, each with a row of toy mice attached with velcro. One plate might have two mice, while the other had three. One plate was designated the "winner," the other the "loser." Each plate was then covered by a can and shuffled around while the children were instructed to keep track of the winner—a small-fry version of the venerable shell game. After each trial, the plates were uncovered, and the children received a prize if they could correctly identify the winner and the loser. After several such trials, the real test was conducted. The experimenter surreptitiously substituted a new plate for the original winner. In one case, the new plate contained the same number of mice as the original, but the row was made longer or shorter. In the other case, the row length stayed unchanged, but a mouse was added or subtracted. The results showed that spatial arrangement made little difference. But changes in number had dramatic consequences even at three and four years of age. The children were surprised, asked where the missing mouse was, and searched for it (Gelman, 1972; see Figure 13.23).

Other studies suggest that the children's apparent lack of conservation in Piaget's original studies may have been produced by the way in which the experimenter questioned them. In a typical number conservation experiment, a six-year-old is shown two rows, say, of buttons arranged in a neat one-to-one manner. When asked, "which row has more buttons or do they both have the same?" she quickly answers "The same!" Now the experimenter spreads out the buttons in one row, pushes the buttons in the other row more closely together, and asks again: "Which row has more buttons or do they both have the same?" But this is the same question he asked her before. The child may now interpret the fact that he repeated his question as an indication that her first answer, "they're the same" was wrong, and so she changes it. To be sure, this misinterpretation is only possible because the child is not really sure of her answer. If the number of buttons is small enough, the confusion will not arise (Siegal, 1991).

Here as in other cognitive realms, the achievements of later periods are built upon foundations established much earlier. If we look carefully enough, we see that the accomplishments of the concrete-operational period do not come out of the blue but have preludes in much earlier childhood years. It may well be true that there are milestones of intellectual growth which, as Piaget argued,

A

B

C

13.23 Gelman's mouse-plate test (A) *The experimenter points to the plate that has two mice and says it is the "winner," while three-year-old Carly watches. (B) After the experimenter covers the plates and rearranges the plates by a sleight-of-hand trick, (C) Carly points to the correct "winner" and then looks at the experimenter with surprise and says, "Hey—they're spreaded out!" (Photographs courtesy of Hilary Schmidt)* must be passed in an orderly sequence. But there are no neat demarcations between stages and no sharp transitions. The stages of cognitive development are not as all or none as the changes from tadpole to frog (let alone from frog to prince).

SOCIAL COGNITION IN PRESCHOOLERS: DEVELOPING A THEORY OF MIND

We've considered cognitive development during the preschool years as it pertains to the understanding of the world of things. But cognitive development also takes place in another realm—the understanding of the social world. During the same preschool period the child acquires the beginnings of what some theorists call a ***theory of mind,*** a term originally coined by Premack and Woodruff to interpret some phenomena observed in chimpanzees and then adopted more widely in the discussion of social cognition in human children and adults (Premack and Woodruff, 1978; Wellman, 1990; Leslie, 1992; Fodor, 1992).★

In human adults a theory of mind is a set of interrelated concepts we use as we try to make sense of our own mental processes and those of others, including the fact that both we and others have beliefs and desires, that beliefs can be true or false, that the beliefs and desires of others are not necessarily the same as our own, and that others know all this and also know that we know it too. These are rock-bottom axioms whose understanding is an absolute prerequisite for all social interactions. This holds for love, which is treasured precisely because both parties share both belief and desire: Joe loves Jane and Jane loves Joe, and both know that the other knows. It also holds for possible deception, whether practiced at the poker table, in foreign embassies, or in a used-car lot. The used-car salesman knows that his prospective customers know that his financial interests are not identical to theirs, and he also knows that they worry that he'll misrepresent his own beliefs about the road worthiness of his cars.

EGOCENTRISM REVISITED

Needless to say, three-year-olds are not yet capable of the advanced social machinations of international diplomacy and used-car sales. But have they got the first rudiments of a theory of mind?

Piaget would have answered with an emphatic "no." In his view, preschoolers couldn't possibly have anything resembling a theory of mind, since they are still dominated by egocentrism and haven't fully grasped that there are other selves. As a result, they are unable to appreciate the difference between another's point of view and their own. But recent studies show that a modicum of this ability is found in children between two and four.

One study used a picture-showing task. Children from one to three years of age were asked to show a photograph to their mother who was seated opposite them. At two-and-a-half and three years of age, all children turned the picture so that it faced the mother, which implies that they had some conception of the difference between one person's angle of regard and another's. If they had been

★ As they use the term, "an individual has a theory of mind if he imputes mental states to himself and others" (Premack and Woodruff, 1978). Premack and Woodruff make a good case that chimpanzees have such a theory of mind (though, to be sure, a rather primitive one) and there is some suggestion that monkeys also have some limited capacity to attribute beliefs and desires to other monkeys (Premack and Woodruff, 1978; Cheney and Seyfarth, 1990; see Chapters 4 and 10, pp. 148–49, 406). It is called a "theory" because it is an informal attempt at an explanation.

A   B   C

13.24   A simplified test of egocentrism
Poor performance on Piaget's test of egocentrism may have resulted from the fact that the spatial layout of his three-mountain task is unduly complicated. In a later study, three- and four-year-olds were shown various three-dimensional displays such as (A) and (B), as well as a three-mountain scene (C). Grover, a doll, was shown to drive a toy car around each layout. When he stopped the car, the child was asked to turn an identical display on another table until "you are looking at it the same way Grover is." The children did quite well with all displays except (C), the three-mountain scene. This one probably caused trouble because the children couldn't distinguish the mountains as readily as they could distinguish the toy objects in (A) and (B). (Borke, 1975; photograph courtesy of H. Borke)

totally egocentric, they should have shown their mothers the back of the picture, while continuing to look at it from the front (Lempers, Flavell, and Flavell, 1977; see also Figure 13.24).

PERCEPTIONS AND DESIRES

Evidence of this sort shows that the child has at least a rudimentary understanding that there are other minds. But how deep does this knowledge go? There is little doubt that even at three years of age the child has begun to be a little psychologist.

To begin with, she has some primitive understanding of how perception works. Two- and three-year-olds can hide things (to be sure, quite ineptly) so that another person can't find them, or they can help someone see a small picture by bringing it closer to his eyes (Flavell, Shipstead, and Croft, 1978; Lempers, Flavell, and Flavell, 1977). They evidently know that perception depends on the presence of an external stimulus.

They also know something about the mental state we call *motive* or *desire*. At about two-and-a-half years of age, a toddler can predict what another child will do if he knows what it is she wants. If Johnny is told that Annie wants a cookie, he will say that she'll look for one, will be happy if she finds one, and will continue to look if she doesn't.

TRUE AND FALSE BELIEFS

The child's task becomes much harder when we turn to *belief.* Adults take it for granted that another person's actions will depend not just on what he sees and desires, but also on what he believes. At first glance, the same seems to be true for the three-year-old. Suppose you tell Annie that Johnny wants to play with his puppy and thinks that it is under the piano. If you then ask her where Johnny will look, she'll say he'll look under the piano (Wellman and Bartsch, 1988). She seems to understand the concept of belief. But does she really?

A number of authors point out that there are two crucial components to the notion of belief. One is that beliefs can be true or false; the other is that different people can have different beliefs. According to several authors, the three-year-old doesn't understand this and won't until she is about four or four-and-a-half. To the extent that she doesn't, there is something seriously lacking in her theory of mind. Evidence for this comes from studies utilizing **false belief tests** (Dennett, 1978; Wimmer and Permer, 1983).

In a typical study of this kind, the child and a teddy bear sit in front of two boxes, one red and the other green. The experimenter opens the red box and puts some candy in it. She then opens the green box and shows the child—and the teddy—that this box is empty. The teddy bear is now taken out of the room

A

B

C

13.25 *The false belief test* *(A) The child watches as the experimenter makes the puppet "hide" the ball in the oatmeal container. (B) While the puppet is gone, the experimenter and the child move the ball to the box. (C) When the child is now asked, "Where does the puppet think the ball is?" she points to the box. (Photographs by Kimberly Canidy)*

(to play for a while) and the experimenter and the child move the candy from the red box into the green one. The teddy bear is brought back into the room, and the child is asked: "Where will the teddy look for the candy?" Virtually all three-year-olds and some four-year-olds will answer "In the green box." If you ask them why they say so, they'll say, "Because that's where it is." They evidently don't yet understand that beliefs can be false and that others may not share our own. At about four-and-a-half, they get the idea: "He'll look in the red box because that's where he thinks the candy is" (Wellman, 1990; Wimmer and Perner, 1983; Cassidy, 1993; see Figure 13.25).

Many authors have interpreted such results as an indication that the young child doesn't yet have a genuine theory of mind. But more recent evidence suggests that here, as in some other areas of cognitive development, the young preschooler knows more than it first appears. Some authors suggest that three- and four-year-olds do have a theory of mind, but they perform badly because they are confused by the experimental situation. One trouble is that they are pulled by their desire. To figure out what the teddy would do or think requires some mental cogitation; it's much easier to go in the direction of what it is that they want, the candy rather than the empty box (Fodor, 1992). To test this notion children were given a false belief test, but this time the object that was moved was something the children did not want—some broccoli. (They were also told that the teddy would have to eat whatever he found in the box). When now asked where the teddy would look, even the three-year-olds gave proof that they did understand something about beliefs. They correctly answered "In the red box." They were no longer seduced by desire and could therefore show that they did understand something about beliefs (Cassidy, 1993).

SEQUENCE OR STAGES?

What can we conclude about Piaget's stages of mental development? The evidence as a whole suggests that the child's mental growth does not proceed as neatly as a simple stage theory might lead one to expect (Flavell, 1985).

Does this mean that Piaget's cognitive milestones have no psychological reality? Not really: The sequence may not be as neat as one might wish, but there is little doubt that some such sequence exists. Consider the difference between seven-year-olds and preschoolers. Despite all the precursors of concrete operations at four or even earlier, there is no question that seven- and eight-year-olds have something preschoolers lack—the ability to apply their insights to a much wider range of problems (Fodor, 1972). Three-year-olds can tell the difference between two and three mice regardless of how they are spaced on the table. But they haven't fully grasped the underlying idea—that number and spatial arrangements are in principle independent and that this is so for *all* numbers and *all* spatial arrangements. As a result, they fail—and will continue to fail until they are six or seven years old—the standard Piagetian test for conservation of number in which they have to recognize that two rows of, say, nine buttons contain the same number of buttons, regardless of how the rows are expanded or compressed. This task baffles the preschool child, who finds the number in each row too large to count and gets confused. Seven-year-olds have no such problems. They can count higher, but that's not the issue. They know that there is no need to count, that the number of buttons in each row has to be identical, regardless of the way they are arranged. As a result, they can conserve number in general.

What holds for conservation of number holds for many other intellectual achievements. Most of them have precursors, often at much earlier ages than Piaget led us to suppose. But these preschool abilities usually represent isolated

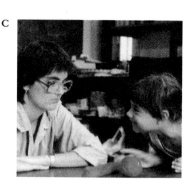

13.26 Development as maturation?
(A) Emerging from its crysalis for a butterfly and (B) walking for a child are largely matters of maturation. (C) Is the cognitive growth that underlies a seven-and-a-half-year-old's success in a Piagetian conservation task to be understood in similar terms? (Photographs by Pat Lynch/Photo Researchers; Ray Ellis/Photo Researchers; Chris Massey)

pockets of knowledge that can't be applied very widely. The seven- or eight-year-old's understanding of physical, numerical, and social reality is considerably more general, so much so that it seems qualitatively different from what went on before. By simplifying the task in various ways, experimenters can induce preschoolers to perform more creditably. But the fact remains that by the time the child is seven or eight years old, no such simplification is necessary. A seven- or eight-year-old conserves with barely a glance at the containers in which the liquid is sloshed around. He *knows* that the liquid quantity is unaffected no matter how the containers are shaped.

THE CAUSES OF COGNITIVE GROWTH

We described cognitive development as it proceeds from early infancy into the school years. But what explains these changes? As so often in the field of cognition, the attempts to come up with an adequate explanation have fluctuated between the two poles of the nature-nurture controversy.

THE NATIVIST APPROACH: MATURATION

As in the study of physical development, some investigators are inclined toward a nativist interpretation (see pp. 503–504). There is of course no doubt that native endowment plays some role in cognitive development as well. The human infant begins life with a potential that is quite different from that of his near and distant cousins in the rest of the animal kingdom, and no amount of training and nurturing can ever erase these differences in the equipment with which the varying species begin. Worms won't fly, platypuses won't form higher-order chunkings, and polar bears won't conserve liquid quantity, no matter what environments they are reared in. Our native equipment is thus a necessary precondition for all development. But can this endowment explain the orderly progression of cognitive development?

Some theorists believe that it can. They believe that development is largely driven by some form of physical maturation, a preprogrammed growth process based on changes in underlying neural structures that are relatively independent of environmental conditions. Could cognitive development be a matter of maturation (in part or whole) in the sense in which walking is (Figure 13.26)? As we saw earlier, there is a tenfold increase in the number of synaptic connections in the cortex between birth and twelve months of age, with further changes that last into the school years (see pp. 495–96). If the brain gets more complex, wouldn't cognition follow suit (Siegler, 1989)?

A number of authors have argued that maturational changes of this kind underlie many aspects of human cognitive development. This view is buttressed by the fact that, at least in broad outline, mental growth seems rather similar in children of different culture and nationalities. While children of different cultures master intellectual tasks such as conservation at somewhat different ages, they usually pass these landmarks in the same order. Thus Arab, Indian, Somali, and British children show the same progression from nonconservation of quantity to conservation (Hyde, 1959). This is reminiscent of physical maturation.

Different butterflies may emerge from their chrysalis at slightly different times, but none is a butterfly first and a chrysalis second. The timing of the transitions may well be affected by environmental conditions: in humans, by culture; in butterflies, by temperature. But according to the maturational hypothesis, the order of the stages is determined by the genetic code.

THE EMPIRICIST APPROACH: SPECIFIC LEARNING

The simplest alternative to a maturation-centered approach is one that emphasizes learning by exposure to the environment. The most extreme version of this view is that of the empiricists who followed in the footsteps of John Locke (see Chapter 5). To them, the human mind starts out as a blank tablet, a *tabula rasa,* upon which experience gradually leaves its mark. But can such a radical empiricist position explain the systematic sequence of cognitive development that Piaget and other investigators have chronicled?

Piaget argued that simple learning theories of the kind espoused by the early empiricists—and by their modern heirs such as Pavlov and Skinner—will not do. According to such theories, learning is the acquisition of relatively specific skills that in principle could be mastered at any age. But this is precisely what Piaget denied. According to Piaget, four-year-olds cannot possibly be taught how to use a measuring cup correctly, no matter how attractive the reinforcements or how many the number of trials. He argued that four-year-olds lack the prerequisite concepts of number and quantity (which they cannot attain before the concrete-operational level), so that any attempt to teach them is as fruitless as trying to build the third story of a house without a second story underneath it. This view has obvious relevance to educational policy. If Piaget is right, then there is little point in efforts to teach children this or that aspect of the curriculum before they are "ready" for it.

In an attempt to test this claim, several investigators have tried to determine whether children can be trained to reach certain cognitive landmarks such as conservation ahead of schedule. The results are a bit ambiguous. Formerly, most investigators concluded that specific training has little impact. In some cases, conservation was speeded up by special coaching, but later checks revealed that the children had not really understood the underlying principles and quickly reverted to their previous, nonconserving ways (e.g., Smedslund, 1961). But some later studies showed more substantial effects. In some cases, these were brought about by mere observation; for example, six-year-old nonconservers who watched conservers perform showed subsequent conservation of mass or number (Botvin and Murray, 1975; Murray, 1978). But the most likely interpretation is that the children already had most of the necessary conceptual ingredients at the time they were "trained." If so, then watching another child did not really teach conservation; it only helped to uncover what was already there (Gold, 1978; Gelman and Baillargeon, 1983).

Related findings come from a study conducted in a Mexican village whose inhabitants made pottery and whose children helped and participated in this activity from early on. When tested for conservation of mass, these children turned out to be more advanced than their North American counterparts (or those studied by Piaget in Switzerland). Having spent much of their lives working at a potter's wheel, they were more likely to know that the amount of clay is the same whether it is rolled into a ball or stretched into a long, thin sausage (Price-Williams, Gordon, and Ramirez, 1969). But these effects of pottery making were relatively specific. They led to an advance on tests of conservation of mass but to little else. (For further discussion, see Greenfield, 1976; Price-Williams, 1981; Rogoff, Gauvain, and Ellis, 1984.)

All in all, there is little doubt that environment plays some role in cognitive development. To acquire liquid conservation, one presumably has to live in a world in which liquids exist. If a frozen planet like Jupiter had inhabitants whose cognitive potential was like our own, their young would never know that when water is poured from a wide jar into a tall, thin beaker the amount of water stays unchanged. But this is not to say that the environment shapes human (or Jovian) children in the simple, passive way proposed by an extreme empiricist.

PIAGET'S APPROACH: ASSIMILATION AND ACCOMMODATION

Piaget's own view was that neither maturation nor specific learning could by themselves account for cognitive development. As he saw it, the child's mental progress is propelled by the twin engines of developmental change that we mentioned earlier, assimilation and accommodation. At any one stage, the environment the child faces is interpreted in terms of the mental schemas she has at that time—the environment is assimilated to the schemas. But these schemas cannot help but change as the child continues to interact with the world around her—the schemas accommodate to the environment. Without active involvement, there will be no such accommodation and hence no mental growth.

Piaget's conception of these two opposite processes, assimilation and accommodation, may be a useful way of emphasizing the fact that organism and environment interact in producing mental growth. But is it an explanation? Many psychologists argue that it is not, for Piaget offered no mechanism whereby schemas are changed through accommodation. Lacking such a mechanism, Piaget's proposal still leaves us with the unanswered question of why children go from one stage of thought to another.

THE INFORMATION-PROCESSING APPROACH: CHUNKING AND STRATEGIES

A recent suggestion for explaining cognitive development is in terms of information processing. According to this approach, all cognitive activities are ways of handling—that is, *processing*—information. Whenever a person perceives, remembers, or thinks, she has to acquire, retrieve, or transform information (see Chapters 6, 7, and 8). If adults think differently (and with greater success) than children, this is presumably because they process information differently.

In recent years, information-processing concepts have been applied to many aspects of cognitive development, including perception, language, thinking, and memory (Siegler, 1983). We will focus on just the development of memory and the awareness that other people have minds like our own.

THE CHILD AS A LIMITED MENTAL PROCESSOR

Memory in infancy Do infants possess memory? In one sense they do, for they can learn an instrumental response and retain it for several weeks. In one series of experiments, a string tied to the leg of a three-month-old set off the movement of an overhead mobile. After a few trials, the infant acquired the operant response of kicking, even when the string was removed. Two weeks later, the sight of the mobile was enough to make the infant kick his feet. If the experimenter jiggled the mobile (so to speak, as a reminder), the infant kicked even after a retention interval of two months (Rovee-Collior, 1990; Rovee-Collier and Hayne, 1987).

Such findings show that infants can retain experiences over time. While this means that they have some recognition memory, it is quite primitive and of the kind that we all share with many lower animals. What they lack is the explicit memory required to answer questions like "What did you have for dinner yesterday?" (see Chapter 7, p. 259). But however primitive, it serves as the foundation for the later memorial feats of the adult.

Memory in early childhood   By the time the child gets to be a toddler, it becomes reasonable to ask her explicit memory questions, such as: "Did you show your new doll to Grandma?" But on this and many other conventional tests of recall, younger children do worse than older ones. Take memory span—the number of items a subject can reproduce after just one presentation. This number is roughly equal to the child's age until she is about five: one item at eighteen months, three at three-and-a-half years, and four at four-and-a-half years, compared to a span of seven or eight in adulthood (see Figure 13.27).

What has happened during development that makes us so much better at remembering than young children are? Several theorists (sometimes called neo-Piagetians) believe that the reason is largely a matter of maturation. Initially, the child's mind is like a small computer with limited storage and processing capacity. But as her brain grows, so does her memory capacity. This in turn allows her to develop a whole set of cognitive skills that she could never have acquired previously (Pascale-Leone, 1978; Case, 1978, 1985). But there is reason to believe that maturational processes are only part of the story.

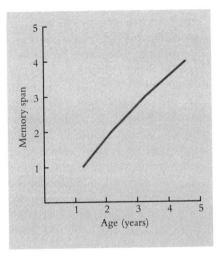

13.27   Memory span in young children *(After Case, 1978)*

THE CHILD AS NOVICE

There is evidence that the young child's poor performance at memory tasks is caused, at least in part, by the fact that she knows so little and has rather limited strategies for remembering the little that she does know (Flavell and Wellman, 1977; Brown et al., 1983; Chi, 1978, 1985).

In a previous section, we saw that in the course of acquiring skills, the performance of the learner changes qualitatively. For example, skilled typists have formed various higher-order chunks, so that they no longer respond to individual letters but to letter groupings and words (see Chapter 8). It may be that much of cognitive development can be understood as a similar process that all human beings go through as they go from infancy to adulthood.

This view assumes that the difference between child and adult is in large part a matter of expertise—the adult has had the time to develop many conceptual chunkings that the child still lacks. But suppose we found some task on which the child is the expert and the adult the novice? One investigator studied memory for chess positions in adults and ten-year-olds. Experts generally do much better in this task than novices because they can draw on more and larger chunks (see Chapter 8, pp. 295–96). But the study had a novel twist because here the children were the experts (they were recruited from local chess clubs), while the adults were the novices. Now that the tables were turned, what mattered was specific mastery rather than overall level of cognitive development. The children recalled many more chess positions than did the adults (Chi, 1978).

According to some authors, such findings suggest that intellectual growth is largely produced by the acquisition of more and more knowledge. But some of this knowledge is in the form of cognitive capital goods—tools for acquiring new knowledge. These are strategies for learning and thinking that become increasingly efficient and more widely applicable as the child gets older. As a result, he can become an expert in many areas.

THE CHILD AS A POOR STRATEGIST

Strategies for remembering When an adult is presented with a series of items and told to repeat them a moment later, she does her best to "keep them in mind." She rehearses, perhaps by repeating the items mentally, perhaps by organizing them in various ways. But the very young child doesn't do this, for he hasn't yet learned how. Some first precursors of rehearsal are found at age three. In one study, three-year-olds watched while an experimenter placed a toy dog under one of two containers. The experimenter told the children that he'd leave the room for a little while, but that they should tell him where the dog was hidden as soon as he came back. During the interval, some children kept looking at the hiding place and nodding "yes"; others kept their eyes on the wrong container while shaking their heads "no"; yet others kept their hands on the correct container. They all had found a way of building a bridge between past and present by performing an overt action—keeping the toy dog in their minds by marking its location with their bodies. Piaget, who believed that all mental activity is ultimately an outgrowth of overt action, might well have been pleased at this outcome (Wellman, Ritter, and Flavell, 1975).

Keeping one's hand on the to-be-remembered object may be a forerunner of rehearsal, but it's still a far cry from the real thing. Genuine rehearsal does not occur spontaneously until around age five or six. One experiment used subjects of five, seven, and ten years of age. The stimuli were pictures of seven common objects (e.g., a pipe, a flag, an owl, etc.), and the experimenter slowly pointed at three of them in turn. The children's job was to point at the three pictures in the same order after a fifteen-second interval. During this interval their eyes were covered (by a specially designed space helmet), so they couldn't bridge the interval by looking at the pictures or by surreptitiously pointing at them. Not surprisingly, the older children did better on the recall test than the younger ones (Figure 13.28). Was this because they had greater memory capacity? The main cause lay elsewhere. One of the experimenters was a trained lip reader who observed that almost all of the ten-year-olds were silently mouthing the words—that is, rehearsing—compared to only 10 percent of the five-year-olds. The older children remembered more than the younger ones, not because they had more "memory space," but because they used it better (Flavell, Beach, and Chinsky, 1966).

METACOGNITION

When young nonrehearsers are taught to rehearse, they will recall as well as their age-mates who rehearse on their own. But there is one problem. When later presented with another memory task, many of these subjects will abandon the rehearsal method they have just been taught. This is especially likely if the new task is somewhat different from the old. A child might be taught to remem-

13.28 Strategies for memorizing in children   (A) Nursery-school children, first-graders, and fifth-graders were shown a number of pictures and were asked to try to remember them. The figure shows recall as a function of age. (B) While the subjects watched the stimuli, the experimenters observed them for signs of rehearsal—naming the pictures, moving their lips while watching, and so on. The figure shows the proportion of all children who rehearsed. In the older children, there was quite a bit of rehearsal, but there was very little for the first-graders and virtually none for the nursery-school children. Absence of rehearsal has also been found for retarded subjects. (Data from Appel et al., 1972)

The child as expert *Ten-year-old chess champion Etienne Bacrot plays an adult opponent. To make the competition a bit more even, she wears a blindfold. (Photograph by Benainous, © Gamma)*

ber a set of names by reciting it aloud, but he won't apply the same principle to a shopping list. What is evidently lacking is a "master plan" for dealing with memory tasks in general, a strategy for using strategies (Flavell, 1970, 1977).

Normal adults adopt this higher-order strategy as a matter of course whenever they try to learn. They know that remembering telephone numbers, or traffic directions, or the names of the twelve cranial nerves are at bottom similar memory tasks. They also know that trying to commit them to memory requires certain mental activities—perhaps rehearsal or rhythmic and semantic grouping, all of which are lower-order strategies that are subsumed under the general memory master plan. But young children lack this general insight. They don't recognize what all memory tasks have in common. As a result, they don't realize that what helps in mastering one will also help in mastering the other. The adult's strategy of using strategies is an example of the higher-order cognitive processes that go under the general label of ***metacognition.***

Human adults can reflect on the cognitive operations whereby they gain knowledge. They know, they know that they know, and they also know a good deal about how they come to know it.★ But in children, metacognition is less well developed. Take memory. An adult has a fairly realistic idea of what he may or may not recall. When briefly shown pictures of four common objects, he will predict that he can recall them correctly after one presentation; when shown ten such pictures, he will predict that he cannot. First- and second-graders are much less realistic about what they can and cannot do (Yussen and Levy, 1975).

Metacognition is not limited to memory. Older children and adults manifest it in perception, so that they can do more than perceive—they can recognize the role of perspective, know the difference between reality and illusion, and become artists and art connoisseurs (Flavell, Flavell, and Green, 1983). They also manifest it in language, so that they can do more than talk and understand— they can play with language, as in puns or poems, recognize that some sentences are ill-formed, and become poets or linguists (Gleitman, Gleitman, and Shipley, 1972). They also manifest metacognition in thinking and problem solving. Of course, they think and solve problems, but they can do more—they can use general strategies for reaching solutions, know when they need more information, recognize a paradox, and become scientists or logicians. It may well be that

★ Metacognition is obviously related to the theory-of-mind phenomenon we discussed before (see pp. 519–21) because both require some understanding of one's own cognitive operations as well as those of others. In current writings, the term *metacognition* is generally used when referring to older children and adults, while *theory of mind* is used to refer to younger children, and sometimes to monkeys and apes.

From apprentice to master   *(A) At two, getting the right body part through the right hole of a shirt is still a major problem. (B) Only six months later, dressing is well on the way to becoming automatic, (C) though complete mastery is not quite there yet. (Photographs courtesy of Kathy Hirsh-Pasek)*

metacognitive processes of this kind are one of the distinguishing hallmarks of adult human intelligence (Gleitman, 1985).

COGNITIVE DEVELOPMENT FROM A CROSS-CULTURAL PERSPECTIVE

Thus far our primary emphasis has been on cognitive development among children in the Western world. Studies of cognitive development in non-Western cultures, especially those in which there is no formal schooling, have provided another perspective on theories of cognitive development.

We previously discussed evidence indicating that children from different cultures show a similar progression on the standard Piagetian tests (e.g., from non-conservation to conservation). But other studies suggest that there are also important cross-cultural differences in development. In some cultures (for example, that of Australian aborigines and of New Guinea tribesmen), a substantial number of adults fail tests of concrete operations, and evidence of formal operations is rare in cultures in which there is no formal schooling (Cole, 1975; Price-Williams, 1981). A related finding is the inability of most members of such cultures to deal with certain abstract problems such as syllogistic reasoning. Thus unschooled Kpelle farmers in Liberia were informed that "Spider and Black Deer always eat together. Spider is eating." When asked, "Is Black Deer eating?" they would typically fail to give the simple syllogistic "Yes." Instead, they would be noncommittal: "But I was not there. How can I answer such a question." If pushed, they would reply "Yes" but on irrelevant grounds: "The reason is that Black Deer always walks about all day eating green leaves in the bush. When it rests for a while, it gets up again and goes to eat" (Cole, et al., 1971, p. 187).

Such results are sometimes taken as signs that members of certain preliterate cultures are somehow deficient in abstract thinking because they lack some important experiences (especially formal schooling) that are a necessary prerequisite for the development of the relevant cognitive skills (Greenfield, 1966). But a number of investigators disagree. They point out that some of the peoples that do so poorly on standard cognitive tasks (such as Piaget's) are capable of some remarkable intellectual feats in the context of their own everyday lives. One example is provided by Polynesian sailors who reveal extraordinary skills of mental calculation in navigating their boats from one island to the next (Gladwin, 1970). Another comes from the !Kung San hunter-gatherers of the Kalahari desert, who perform remarkable feats of inference while hunting game: weighing the chances of tracking down a wounded giraffe against the cost of a drawn-out search, searching for clues in the pattern of crushed grasses, judging whether the blood on a twig fell before or after the twig was bent, and then evaluating the various interpretations to decide on a course of action (Blurton-Jones and Konner, 1976). It is clear that people who can perform tasks such as these are capable of abstract thought. But if so, how can we explain their poor performance on standard cognitive tests?

One possibility is that the test does not adequately assess non-Western peoples, in part, because the subjects often don't know just what kind of an answer the experimenter wants. Examples come from tests of classification. In one classic study the subjects were Central Asian Russian peasants some of whom had a few years of schooling while others had none. All of the subjects were shown sets of four pictures. In each set, three were of members of a well-defined category, such as tools (e.g., a saw, an ax, and a shovel) and a fourth (e.g., a piece of

A

B

Polynesian navigators *The seafarers of the Caroline Islands in the Pacific Ocean guide their sailing canoes over hundreds of miles of open ocean without benefit of compass or Western navigational mathematics. Instead, they rely on an elaborate navigational method that is based on a knowledge of star positions, ocean swells and currents, and the behavior of birds, and is carefully handed on from generation to generation. The figure shows a master navigator (A) guiding a boat, (B) teaching the star positions to students of all ages. (Reproduced from S. D. Thomas,* The Last Navigator, *New York: Holt, 1987. By permission of the publisher)*

wood) did not belong to that category but was functionally related to two of the other items. The subjects were asked to pick out the three pictures that belonged together. The schooled farmers behaved much as Western subjects do. They chose according to the abstract semantic category and grouped all the tools together. The unschooled farmers behaved quite differently. They chose on the basis of the concrete situation in which the objects would be used together, picking out the ax, the piece of wood, and the saw; those three go together (the tree must be felled, then sawed into pieces), but the shovel is irrelevant (Luria, 1971). Similar results have been found in studies of Kpelle subjects in Liberia (Glick, 1975).

On the face of it, this kind of classification seems overly concrete and yet another manifestation of the lack of abstract thought found in unschooled non-Westerners. But it may simply reflect the (non-Western) subject's understanding of what the task calls for. After all, we would all regard the ax-saw-wood grouping as perfectly reasonable if the subjects had been explicitly asked to put the items together by functional theme. It may be that the non-Western subjects understood the task in just that way. One investigator found that when unschooled Kpelle subjects were asked to sort objects (including tools and foods) into groups, they arranged them by function—a knife with an orange, a hoe with a potato, and so on. Asked why they sorted the objects as they did, they replied: "That is the way a wise man would do it." When the experimenter asked "How would a fool do it?" he received the response that he had originally looked for—food in one pile and tools in another (Glick, 1975).

Results of this kind suggest that cross-cultural differences in cognitive performance are partially artifacts of our procedures and the way we interpret them, produced by looking at non-Western behavior through Western eyes. But that is probably not all. For in part, they may also reflect a genuine difference in the way schooled and unschooled peoples think.

We've already cited evidence that shows that many cross-cultural differences in cognitive performance are at least in part attributable to differences in formal schooling. Other studies indicate that schooled West African children are more likely to conserve than unschooled ones (Greenfield, 1966), and schooled children in such diverse regions as Morocco, Yucatan, and Liberia do better on various tests of free recall than their unschooled counterparts (Cole, et al., 1971; Wagner, 1974, 1978).

Schooling evidently makes a difference, but why? First, schooled people are more likely to understand just what the experimenter has in mind. (For example, they are used to being asked a question by someone who already knows the answer but wants to find out whether they do). But another reason is more far-reaching. Western schools teach their students concepts and techniques that apply to many different contexts. The Polynesian navigator learns a complex system of mental calculation, but he doesn't think of applying that system or any of its cognitive components to anything except maritime navigation. The Western student acquires a set of very different skills. If he studies trigonometry, he doesn't expect to apply what he learns about sines and cosines to his everyday life outside of school. But he does assume—or at least his teachers hope that he assumes—that what he learns applies to all trigonometric relationships. The same applies to other parts of mathematics and to science, logic, and many other topics. They teach very general rules and operations that can be applied to a large number of problems. To the extent that he can do this, he operates at a more abstract level than an unschooled Kpelle or !Kung tribesman. As a result, he can use and create general strategies for reasoning and problem solving that apply across the board, thus acquiring the skills that are demanded by his complex technological society. But that kind of schooling will not serve him well if he wants to survive in the !Kung culture; courses in calculus and logic will be of little use in learning how to hunt giraffes (Scribner and Cole, 1973).

TAKING STOCK

As we review the various lines of evidence, we conclude that cognitive development is the joint outcome of both maturational and environmental factors. Certain earlier aspects of cognitive growth seem to be driven largely by maturation: Examples are the sensory-motor achievements of the first two years, the acquisition of language, and (perhaps) the development of certain simple concrete operations. These earlier achievements will unfold in a broad range of environments (though, if the environment is hostile enough, they may be impaired). The situation is different for various aspects of cognitive development that typically come in later and involve broadly generalizable, abstract skills, especially those that are often identified with Piaget's formal operations. For these, environmental and cultural conditions are of paramount importance. The conditions of our own culture and its formal schooling help the child to develop higher-order concepts that can serve as a foundation for yet higher ones and to acquire increasingly effective strategies for learning and thinking that become ever more widely applicable (and thus more abstract) as the child gets older.

SUMMARY

1. Embryological development involves progressive *anatomical differentiation*. According to many theorists, the differentiation principle also applies to the development of behavior. An example is the development of grasping during the infant's first year.

2. Development can be considered as a process of growth. After conception, the fertilized egg divides, redivides, and differentiates. In the process, it becomes an *embryo*, and then, two months later, a *fetus*. At birth, the infant comes equipped with a set of early reflexes and good sensory capacities. However, human newborns are further removed from adulthood than are the newborns of most other animal species. This leads to a long period of postnatal growth and dependency, which may be one of the factors that led to the development of human culture.

3. A general characteristic of development is that it is progressive. An example is *motor development* in which such steps as creeping, crawling, and walking occur in much the same sequence for all babies.

4. The changes that constitute development are produced by the interaction of genetic endowment and environmental factors. In humans, the genetic commands are contained in twenty-three pairs of *chromosomes*. One of these pairs determines the sex of the organism. If female, it is an XX pair; if male, an XY pair. Every chromosome contains thousands of *genes*, some *dominant* and some *recessive*. The genes determine an individual's *genotype*, but this is not equivalent to its *phenotype*, which corresponds to its visible structure and behavior.

5. What is meant by the term *environment* changes as development proceeds. In early embryonic development the environment of a given cell is the other cells with which it makes contact. Somewhat later, the embryonic environment includes hormonal conditions. An example is the formation of external genitals, which differentiate into those of a male in the presence of androgen, but become those of a female when androgen is absent. Similar effects occur after birth, since the same physical environment exerts different effects at different ages. Another example which shows that environment can exert radically different effects at different ages is provided by *sensitive periods*.

6. Some aspects of the orderly progression of development are determined by *maturation*, which is genetically programmed and is independent of specific environmental

SUMMARY

conditions. An example is walking. This and other early sensory and motor achievements seem to be relatively unaffected by specific practice. On the other hand, more general kinds of experience, such as sensory deprivation and sensory enrichment, seem to exert important effects.

7. All humans go through a process of *cognitive development.* According to Jean Piaget, they do so by passing through the same sequence of developmental stages.

8. In Piaget's account, the first stage is the period of *sensory-motor intelligence,* which lasts until about two years of age. During this period, the infant develops the concept of *object permanence,* builds up coordinated *sensory-motor schemas,* becomes capable of genuine *imitation,* and acquires increasingly complex *mental representations.*

9. The next period lasts till about six or seven. It is the *preoperational period* during which children are capable of representational thought but lack mental *operations* that order and organize these thoughts. Characteristic deficits include an inability to *conserve* number and quantity, and *egocentrism,* an inability to take another person's perspective.

10. At about seven, children begin to acquire a system of mental *operations* that allows them to manipulate mental representations with consequent success in conservation tasks and similar tests. But until they are about eleven, they are still in the period of *concrete operations,* which lacks an element of abstractness. After eleven, they enter the period of *formal operations.* As a result, they can consider hypothetical possibilities and become capable of scientific thought.

11. One critical challenge to Piaget's views concerns his beliefs of what is given at the very start of life. A number of critics deny that the infant's mind is the mere jumble of unrelated sensory impressions and motor reactions that Piaget declared it to be, for they believe that some of the major categories by which adults organize the world—such as the concepts of space, objects, number, and the existence of other minds—have primitive precursors in early life.

12. Studies of visual perception in infancy using the habituation procedure suggest that humans come equipped with some built-in notions of space and objects. Infants show appropriate reactions to perceptual *occlusion* and have some notions of the principles that govern objects in space. Piaget to the contrary, they have object permanence. But while they believe that objects exist, they are quite inept in searching for them.

13. Further studies show that infants can perceive *numerical equivalence* with sets of up to four or five, and also have some rudiments of *numerical reasoning.*

14. Other criticisms suggest that Piaget also underestimated the preschoolers' general cognitive abilities, as well as their *social cognition.* Three- and four-year-olds show less egocentrism than Piaget would have predicted. They also have the rudiments of a *theory of mind.* While they have difficulties on *false belief tests* until they're about four-and-a-half years of age, these may be side effects of the experimental situation.

15. Trying to explain cognitive growth has turned out to be even more difficult and controversial than trying to describe it. The nativist approach assumes that development is largely driven by *maturation.* Empiricists assume that the answer is *specific learning.* Piaget himself rejected both empiricist and nativist extremes, arguing that development involves a constant interchange between organism and environment, as the environment is *assimilated* to the child's current schema and the schema in turn *accommodates* to aspects of the environment. A current approach sees cognitive development as a change in *information processing* and argues that increased mental growth is based in part on the acquisition of better and larger chunks and of various strategies for thinking and remembering that depend on the development of *metacognition.*

16. Studies of cognitive development in non-Western cultures, especially those in which there is no formal schooling, have provided another perspective on theories of cognitive development. While some preliterate people do poorly on standard cognitive tasks, this may be because these subjects don't adequately assess these tasks, in part, because they don't know what kind of answer the experimenter is looking for. This is especially likely given the remarkable intellectual feats of these people in the context of their own everyday lives, as shown by the navigational skills of Polynesian sailors and the abilities of !Kung hunters to track game.

CHAPTER

CHAPTER 14

SOCIAL DEVELOPMENT

ATTACHMENT 534

THE ROOTS OF ATTACHMENT ■ PATTERNS OF ATTACHMENT ■ THE EFFECT OF EARLY MATERNAL SEPARATION ■ WHEN THERE IS NO ATTACHMENT AT ALL ■ ARE THE EFFECTS OF EARLY SOCIAL DEPRIVATION REVERSIBLE?

CHILDHOOD SOCIALIZATION 544

CULTURAL VALUES AND CHILD REARING ■ MECHANISMS OF SOCIALIZATION ■ THE FIRST AGENTS OF SOCIALIZATION: THE PARENTS ■ THE CHILD'S EFFECT ON THE PARENTS

THE DEVELOPMENT OF MORALITY 550

NOT DOING WRONG ■ DOING GOOD ■ MORAL REASONING

THE DEVELOPMENT OF SEX AND GENDER 556

GENDER ROLES ■ CONSTITUTIONAL FACTORS AND SEX DIFFERENCES ■ SOCIAL FACTORS AND SEX DIFFERENCES ■ THEORIES OF GENDER TYPING ■ SEXUAL ORIENTATION

DEVELOPMENT AFTER CHILDHOOD 569

ADOLESCENCE ■ ADULTHOOD

SUMMARY 576

I n the preceding chapter we discussed physical and cognitive development: the ways in which we progress from embryos to full-grown adults, from crawling infants to energetic tricyclists, from babbling babes to sophisticated eight-year-olds who understand all about liquid conservation. But children don't just grow in size and thought; they also develop in their relations to other people. To find out how they do this is the task of psychologists who study *social development.*

Physical, cognitive, and social development are different aspects of the human journey from birth to maturity. But even so, they are alike in one respect: In all three, we see an ever-increasing enlargement of the developing individual's universe. In biological development, the infant enlarges her physical horizons. As she grows in sheer size and strength, she develops the ability to move freely within her environment and becomes emancipated from her initial limitations in physical space. Cognitive development leads to an analogous expansion of horizons, but now of the mental rather than the physical world, as the growing child comes to transcend the immediate here and now to live in a world of ever more abstract ideas.

In social development, there is a similar pattern of continued expansion. In the first weeks of life, the baby's social world is limited to just one person, usually the mother. In time, her social horizons become enlarged to include both parents, then the rest of the family, then young peers in the nursery and in school. As adolescence sets in, friends of the opposite sex assume more and more importance, sexuality begins in earnest, and the individual soon becomes a parent in her own right and starts the reproductive cycle all over again. But the expansion of the child's social world goes yet further. As she grows older, she comes to understand the system of social rules through which she is linked, not just to her own family circle, but to a larger social universe. A major concern of this chapter is to chart the course of this social expansion through which babes in arms grow into citizens of the world.

Are there any general statements that describe this developmental progression? Much of the early work in the field was inspired by the theoretical scheme proposed by Sigmund Freud, the founder of psychoanalysis, whose work we'll consider in some detail in a later chapter (see Chapter 17). For now, we'll merely list two of his major claims that are particularly relevant to our present concerns. One is that the child's first social relationships are ultimately based on the gratification of basic creature needs, including certain infantile precursors to sexual satisfactions. Another is the belief that the relationship of young children to their parents determines all of their future social relationships. As we will see, both claims have turned out to be very questionable at best.

Attachment (Mother and Child, c. 1890, by Mary Cassatt; Courtesy of Wichita Art Museum, Wichita, Kansas; the Roland P. Murdock Collection)

14.1 The need for contact comfort *A frightened rhesus monkey baby clings to its terry-cloth mother for comfort. (Photograph by Martin Rogers/Stock, Boston)*

ATTACHMENT

Social development begins with the first human bond that is sometimes said to lay the foundations for all later relationships with others: the infant's *attachment* to the person who takes care of him.★ The infant wants to be near his mother, and if unhappy, he is comforted by her sight, her sound, and her touch. In this regard, human children have much in common with the young of many other species. Rhesus infants cling to their mother's body, chicks follow the hen, and lambs run after the ewe. As the young grow older, they venture farther away from the mother, gaining courage for ever more distant explorations. But for quite a while, the mother continues to provide a secure home base, a place to run back to should unmanageable threats be encountered.

THE ROOTS OF ATTACHMENT

What accounts for the infant's attachment to the mother? Until some thirty years ago, it was widely believed that the love for the mother is a secondary consequence of her association with basic creature satisfactions such as the alleviation of hunger, thirst, and pain. The most influential version of this approach was probably that of Sigmund Freud, who believed that the infant's upset at the mother's absence is based on the crass fear that his bodily needs would now go unsatisfied (see Chapter 17). The British psychiatrist John Bowlby called this the *cupboard theory* of mother love; it boils down to the view that the first love object is the breast or the bottle (Bowlby, 1969, 1973).

IS THE NEED FOR THE MOTHER PRIMARY?

The cupboard theory of the infant's tie to her mother has been criticized on several grounds. One problem is the fact that babies often show great interest in other people, even those who have never fed them or satisfied their other bodily needs. They seem to enjoy seeing others smiling or playing peek-a-boo. Does anyone seriously propose that infants want someone to play peek-a-boo with them because this game has previously been associated with food? It seems much more reasonable to assume that the infant comes predisposed to seek social satisfaction, which is rewarding in and of itself.

Another demonstration that love of mother goes beyond bodily needs comes from the work of Harry Harlow (1905–1981). Harlow raised newborn rhesus monkeys without their mothers. Each young monkey lived alone in a cage that contained two stationary figures. One of these models was built of wire; the other was made of soft terry cloth. The wire figure was equipped with a nipple that yielded milk, but no similar provision was made for the terry-cloth model. Even so, the monkey infants spent much more time on the terry-cloth "mother" than on the wire figure. The terry-cloth figure could be clung to and could provide what Harlow called "contact comfort" (Figure 14.1). This was especially clear when the infants were frightened. When placed in an unfamiliar room or faced with a mechanical toy that approached with clanking noises, they

★ Since the caregiver is typically the child's mother (she almost always was in earlier eras), we will from here on refer to the child's caregiver by that traditional term, *mother,* despite the fact that the actual caregiver may well be another person, such as the father or a babysitter.

14.2 Contact comfort in humans (Photograph by Suzanne Szasz)

Free-floating anxiety (Photograph by Suzanne Szasz)

invariably rushed to the terry-cloth mother and clung to her tightly. The infants never sought similar solace from the wire mothers, who were their source of food and nothing more (Harlow, 1958).

These results are in complete opposition to the cupboard theory. The monkey infant evidently loves its mother (whether real or terry cloth), not because she feeds it, but because she feels so "comforting." Some of the characteristics of the figure toward whom the monkey can direct its attachment are evidently preprogrammed. In monkeys, these presumably include the way the figure feels to the touch. Whether touch is equally important to human infants is as yet unclear, but very likely it plays some role. Frightened young humans run to their mothers and hug them closely just as rhesus infants do (Figure 14.2). Children also like stuffed, cuddly toys such as teddy bears, whom they hold tightly when they feel apprehensive. Perhaps Linus's security blanket is a kind of terry-cloth mother. It may or may not be; but contrary to the cupboard theory, it is not a substitute tablecloth.

BOWLBY'S THEORY OF ATTACHMENT

An important alternative to the cupboard theory was developed by John Bowlby, who proposed that attachment results because infants are born with a number of interrelated built-in tendencies that make them seek direct contact with an adult (usually the mother).

One facet of attachment seeking is positive. The infant evidently enjoys being with his mother and interacting with her. From birth on, he is well-equipped for social interaction. He quickly comes to recognize and prefer his mother's voice and even her smell (MacFarlane, 1975; DeCasper and Fifer, 1980). If he is contented, he is generally calm, he gurgles, and (starting at about six weeks) he will produce a full-blown social smile. The mother—and other important adults—will happily reciprocate; when the baby smiles, they smile back. As the infant gets older and acquires some locomotor control, he will do whatever he can to be in the adult's company—reaching toward the mother and father to be picked up, crawling toward them, and so on (Campos et al., 1983).

According to Bowlby, attachment seeking has a second, more negative cause. This is a built-in fear of the unknown and unfamiliar, which is yet another reason why the young of most mammals and birds become attached and stay close to some object that has become familiar to them. In the real world, the most likely object of attachment will be the mother. She has been around throughout the infant's short life and has therefore become familiar. And she has certain appropriate preprogrammed stimulus properties for the young of her species: If she is a duck, she quacks; if she is a rhesus monkey, she is furry.

Bowlby suggests that such a built-in fear of the unfamiliar has a simple survival value. Infants who lack it will stray away from their mothers and will be more likely to get lost and perish. In particular, they may well fall victim to predators, for beasts of prey tend to attack weak animals that are separated from their fellows.

Needless to say, infants don't know enough about the world to fear specific predators. But Bowlby argues that the built-in fear is initially quite unspecific. He conjectures that the fear aroused by the mother's absence is analogous to what psychiatrists call *free-floating anxiety.* This is a state in which the patient is desperately afraid but doesn't know what he is afraid of; he therefore becomes all the more afraid. Given this anxiety, even mild external threats become enormous to the child; the increased need for reassurance may lead to wild clinging and "childish" dependency, as in the dark or during a thunderstorm. This may occur even when the threat comes from the parents themselves. A child who is severely punished by his parents may become even more clinging and dependent than before. The parents caused the fear, but they are the ones who are approached for reassurance. This is analogous to the dog who licks the hand that whipped him. The whipping led to fear and pain, but whom can the dog approach for solace but his master?

IMPRINTING

According to Bowlby, the fear of the unfamiliar produces an attachment to a familiar object. In the real world of animals, this object is generally the mother. But it needn't be. Harlow's studies have already shown us that the focus of filial devotion is not rigidly determined by the genes, as witness the love borne for the terry-cloth mother.

A similar point is made by *imprinting* in birds, which has been studied extensively by the European ethologist Konrad Lorenz. Imprinting is a kind of learning that occurs very early in life and provides the basis for the chick's attachment to its mother. When a newly hatched duckling is first exposed to a moving stimulus, it will approach and follow this stimulus as soon as it is able to walk (at about twelve hours after hatching). If the duckling follows the object for about ten minutes, an attachment is formed; the bird is imprinted. In nature, the moving stimulus is the duckling's mother and all is well. But in the laboratory, it need not be. The duckling may be exposed to a moving duck on wheels, or to a rectangle sliding back and forth behind a glass window, or even to Konrad Lorenz's booted legs. In each case, the result is the same. The duckling becomes imprinted on the rectangle or on Lorenz; it follows one of these objects as if it were its mother, uttering piteous distress calls whenever it is not nearby. The real mother may quack enticingly so as to woo her lost offspring back, but to no avail; the imprinted duckling continues to follow the wooden duck or the moving rectangle or Lorenz (Hess, 1959, 1973).

Imprinting occurs most readily during a sensitive period that in ducklings lasts for about two days, with a maximum sensitivity at some fifteen hours after hatching (Hess, 1959). Subsequent to this period, imprinting is difficult to achieve (see Figure 14.3). According to Lorenz, this phenomenon reflects a decline in the plasticity of some part of the young bird's brain—a decline that is somehow tied to a physiological clock (Gottlieb, 1961). Another possible explanation is that ducklings are difficult to imprint after the sensitive period because by then they have become thoroughly afraid of all new objects. When exposed

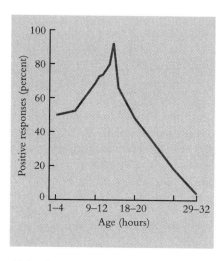

14.3 Imprinting and the critical period
The curve shows the relation between imprinting and the age at which a duckling was exposed to a male moving model. The imprinting score represents the percentage of trials on which the duckling followed the model on a later test. (After Hess, 1958)

Imprinting in ducklings *Imprinted ducklings following Konrad Lorenz. (Courtesy of Nina Leen)*

(Photograph by J. Blyenberg/Leo de Wys)

14.4 A diagrammatic sketch of the "Strange Situation" M *indicates the mother, and* S *the stranger. (Adapted from Ainsworth et al., 1978)*

to the wooden duck, the bird flees instead of following. Having lived for several days, it has learned something about what is familiar, and it can therefore appreciate—and fear—what is strange. Some evidence for this position comes from the fact that older ducklings can be imprinted on new objects if they are forced to remain in their presence for a while. One group of investigators exposed five-day-old ducklings to a moving rectangle. The ducklings tried to flee and huddled in a corner. After a while, their fear diminished. At this point, they began to follow the rectangle and gave distress calls when it was withdrawn. They had become imprinted even though they were long past the sensitive period (Hoffman, 1978; for still another interpretation, see Bateson, 1984).

PATTERNS OF ATTACHMENT

The attachment to the mother has a corollary: A separation from her evokes distress. During the first few months of life, the infant will accept a substitute, perhaps because there is as yet no clear-cut conception of the mother that differentiates her from all other people. But from somewhere between six and eight months of age, the infant comes to know who his mother is; he now cries and fusses when he sees her leave. The age at which children begin to register this protest against separation is pretty much the same across such diverse cultures as African Bushmen in Botswana, U.S. city dwellers, Indians in a Guatemalan village, and members of an Israeli kibbutz (Kagan, 1976).

ASSESSING ATTACHMENT

The reaction to separation provides a means for assessing the kind of attachment a particular infant has to her mother. A widely used procedure is the "Strange Situation" devised by Mary Ainsworth and her colleagues for children of about one year of age (Figure 14.4). The child is first brought into an unfamiliar room that contains many toys, and she is given an opportunity to explore and play while the mother is present. After a while, a stranger enters, talks to the mother, and then approaches the child. The next step is a brief separation—the mother goes out of the room and leaves the child alone with the stranger. A reunion follows—the mother comes back and the stranger leaves (Ainsworth and Bell, 1970; Ainsworth et al., 1978).

The behavior of one-year-olds in the Strange Situation falls into three major categories. One group (over two-thirds of the children in one of Ainsworth's studies) is described as "securely attached." As long as the mother is present, these children explore, play with the toys, and even make wary overtures to the stranger. They show some distress when the mother leaves, but greet her return with great enthusiasm. The remaining children show various behavior patterns that Ainsworth and her colleagues regard as signs of "insecure attachment." Some of these children are described as "resistant." They don't explore even in the mother's presence, become intensely upset and very panicky when she leaves, and act emotionally ambivalent during the reunion, running to her to be picked up and then angrily struggling to get down. A third group of children was described as "avoidant." They are distant and aloof from the very outset, show little distress when the mother leaves, and ignore her when she returns.

Ainsworth and other adherents of attachment theory believe that behavior in the Strange Situation reflects fairly stable characteristics, at least for the first few years of life. Thus children who were rated as securely attached in the Strange Situation at fifteen months of age were judged to be more outgoing, popular, and well-adjusted in nursery school at age three and a half (Waters, Wippman, and Sroufe, 1979). Attachment theorists regard these findings as evidence that the Strange Situation provides a good index of the mother-child relationship and that this relationship is a major determinant of later social and emotional adjustment. But do such findings really prove that the pattern of early attachment is the cause and what happens later is the effect? There are some alternative interpretations that are equally plausible.

One possibility is that the correlation is produced by the child's own (in part built-in) temperament. Some children are more irritable—or more gentle and sociable—than others, and this difference is likely to remain for a while at least. If so, the relationship between what the child did at fifteen months and later on is caused by something within the child rather than something in the attachment relation in early childhood (Kagan, 1984). Other authors suggest that the correlation is produced by the fact that the child's social environment stays pretty much the same. A mother who was gentle and loving when her child was fifteen months of age, probably remained gentle and loving during the next two years. Similarly for the mother who was short-tempered and rejecting. Under the circumstances, we can't be sure that the child's behavior in nursery school can be traced to the mother-child interaction two years earlier, for it could just as well be caused by the mother's current attitude (Lamb et al., 1985).

This discussion highlights a point we will come back to several times. Cause-and-effect relations in child development are almost impossible to disentangle, for virtually all the evidence we have is based on correlations: between what the child does at one age and what she does at another, or between different patterns of child rearing and this or another child behavior, and so on. To make definite cause-and-effect assertions requires experiments in which the relevant factors are controlled, and such experiments can't be performed for both practical and ethical reasons. To prove that a warm maternal relation between, say, six and twelve months, has important consequences at a later age, we'd have to raise two groups of randomly selected six-month-olds under two conditions: Give one group to a warm, accepting mother for six months, a second to a cold, rejecting mother for six months, and then have all the children raised by an in-between mother for the next six years, and then test them all. Such an experiment is obviously undoable (let alone unspeakable). Under the circumstances, we have to settle for correlational evidence.

ASSESSING THE ROLE OF THE FATHER

Ainsworth's general approach has provided a means for studying various other aspects of early social development. An example is the infant's relation to the father. Thus far, we've concentrated entirely on the child's attachment to the mother. Is the father left out in the cold? To find out, one investigator used the Strange Situation with fathers as well as mothers and found signs of distress when the father left and some clinging and touching when he returned (see Figure 14.5). It appears that the emotional life of the child is not exclusively wrapped up in the mother. But the mother seems to be more important, at least at an early age. There was more distress at the mother's departure than at the father's and more enthusiasm at her return (Kotelchuk, 1976).

It appears that young children become attached to fathers as well as to mothers, but further evidence indicates that the attachments to the two parents have some different characteristics. A number of studies have shown that fathers are more likely to play with their infants (and young children) than mothers are. In addition, their play is more physical and vigorous; they may lift or bounce their babies or toss them in the air. In contrast, mothers generally play more quietly with their infants and stress verbal rather than physical interactions. As a result, while the mother may be the parent the child is more likely to run to for care

(Photograph courtesy of Photo Researchers, Inc.)

A

B

C

14.5 Stranger anxiety *An eleven-month-old taken from his father's lap by a stranger (Photographs by Stephanie Arch, courtesy of Kathy Hirsh-Pasek)*

and comfort, the father is often the preferred playmate. This difference in the response to the two parents begins in early infancy, when there are more smiles for the mother and more giggles for the father. By the time the children are toddlers, two out of three pick the father as the one they want to play with. Mother is security and comfort; father is fun (Lamb, 1977; Clarke-Stewart, 1978; Parke, 1981).

What accounts for the differences in the way the two parents respond to their young child? One can make a case for both nature and nurture. In part, the distinction is surely based on social and economic circumstances. By and large, fathers are less involved in the actual caregiving process (though there is some evidence that this is changing; see Pleck, 1985; Ricks, 1985). As a result, their interactions with their children are quite different from those of the mother.

But cultural factors alone may not be the whole explanation. Some evidence comes from a comparison of fathers who were their infant's secondary caregivers (the usual role in our culture) and fathers who were the primary caregivers. The behavior of these two groups of fathers was quite similar. Both groups engaged in much more physical play with the infants than the mothers did (Field, 1978). This might suggest that some aspects of the father-mother difference are based on different biological predispositions. After all, rough-and-tumble play is much more common in male than in female primates, whether monkeys, apes, or humans (see Chapter 10). But one can well counter that the male-female behavioral difference is so deeply ingrained by learned societal patterns that it is very hard to dislodge. Nature and nurture are exceedingly hard to disentangle.

THE EFFECT OF EARLY MATERNAL SEPARATION

A number of authors believe that early separations from the mother may lead to lasting psychological damage. Thus John Bowlby (in common with many other attachment theorists) asserts that any disturbance of the initial attachment of the child to the mother will render the person more emotionally insecure in later life. In his view, separation is psychologically dangerous, for the continuity of the child's relationship to the first attachment figure is a necessary element of the child's ultimate mental health (Bowlby, 1973). This position has various social consequences. It has made many women uneasy about becoming

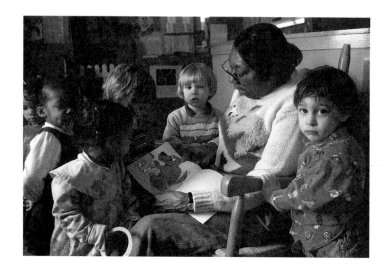

Attachment and day care   *While some contend that any early separation from the primary caregiver may adversely affect the child, others contend that its not the fact of day care that's important so much as it is the quality of day care (Photograph © Stephen Shames/ Matrix; The Caring Center, West Philadelphia)*

working mothers and leaving their children with another person or in a daycare center. It has also affected legal policies in cases of child placement, with a bias in favor of keeping children in homes (in which they had presumably formed attachments) despite evidence of neglect or abuse (Maccoby, 1980).

Given current social and economic conditions in the United States, it is hardly surprising that John Bowlby's views have led to considerable controversy. What with the majority of mothers now employed outside the home and a growing number of single-parent households, family life in the United States today is not that pictured in *Little House on the Prairie,* let alone in "Father Knows Best." According to one estimate, by the year 2000 one out of every five mothers of infants under one year of age will be in the labor force (Cole and Cole, 1993). Some form of out-of-home child care is clearly indispensable. But what are the consequences of this economic and sociological necessity for the psychological welfare of our children?

In line with Bowlby's views, some authors argue that children who have had extensive nonmaternal care (more than twenty hours per week) during their first year of life are more likely to show insecure patterns of attachment in the Strange Situation and were less compliant to adults (Barglow, Vaughn, and Molitor, 1987; Belsky, 1988; Belsky and Braungart, 1991). Does this mean that day care interfered with their optimum social and emotional development? Some authors don't think so. For one thing, they dispute the interpretation of these children's behavior in the test situation. Consider noncompliance to adult demands. Perhaps the day-care children were less compliant and obedient because they had become more independent and self-reliant. This interpretation is in line with other evidence that indicates that day-care children match or in some cases outstrip their non–day-care peers on measures of sociability, persistence, and achievement (Clarke-Stewart, 1989, 1993).

All of this makes good sense. The social world includes peers as well as primary caregivers, and some early experience with children of one's own age may well provide special benefits. But this conclusion probably has to be modified, for several studies suggest that what matters is the quality of the day care rather than the fact of day care as such. Children who, when four years old, attended centers that were well-equipped and spacious, with good adult-child ratios, well-trained teachers, and small classes showed better social and emotional development at eight years of age than children who had attended day-care centers that were poorer in these regards, even when such factors as social class and income were equated. But this result doesn't really prove that what happens at an earlier age still exerts an effect some years later. It may be that parents who select high-quality day care for their children also differ in some other regards from parents who don't make that selection. They may interact differently with their children or feel differently about them, and these differences may well persist over the four-year span (Vandell, Henderson, and Wilson, 1988).

WHEN THERE IS NO ATTACHMENT AT ALL

The preceding discussion suggests that attachment need not be to one single caregiver. But what happens when *no* attachment is formed at all? The results are apparently quite drastic. Some of the major evidence comes from studies of rhesus monkeys.

MOTHERLESS MONKEYS

We previously considered Harlow's studies on rhesus monkeys raised with substitute mothers made of terry cloth. Some later studies asked what happens when monkey infants are reared without any contact at all. The infants were isolated for periods that ranged from three months to one year. During this time, they lived in an empty steel chamber and saw no living creature, not even a human hand.

After their period of solitary confinement, the animals' reactions were observed in various test situations. A three-month isolation had comparatively little effect. But longer periods led to dramatic disturbances. The animals huddled in a corner of the cage, clasped themselves, and rocked back and forth. When they were brought together with normally reared age-mates, the results were pathetic. There was none of the active chasing and playful romping that is characteristic of monkeys at that age. Whenever the normals took an aggressive lunge at them, the monkeys reared in isolation were unable to fight back. They withdrew, huddled, rocked—and bit *themselves* (Figure 14.6).

This social inadequacy persisted into adolescence and adulthood. One manifestation was a remarkable incompetence in sexual and parental matters. Formerly isolated males were utterly inept in the business of reproduction: As Harlow put it, "Isolates may grasp other monkeys of either sex by the head and throat aimlessly, a semi-erotic exercise without amorous achievements," (Harlow, 1962). Formerly isolated females resisted the sexual overtures of normal males. Some were eventually impregnated, in many cases by artificial

14.6 Motherless monkeys *(A) A monkey reared in isolation, huddling in terror in a corner of its cage. (B) An isolated monkey biting itself at the approach of a stranger. (Courtesy of Harry Harlow, University of Wisconsin Primate Laboratory)*

A

B

means. When these motherless monkeys became monkey mothers themselves, they seemed to have no trace of love for their offspring. In a few cases, there was horrible abuse. The mothers crushed the infant's head to the floor, chewed off its toes or fingers, or bit it to death (Figure 14.7). Early social deprivation had evidently played havoc with the animals' subsequent social and emotional development (Suomi and Harlow, 1971; Harlow and Harlow, 1972; Harlow and Novak, 1973).

HUMANS REARED IN INADEQUATE INSTITUTIONS

Can we generalize from infant monkeys to human children? There is reason to suspect that there are some important similarities. After all, the monkey is related to *Homo sapiens,* however distantly; and like humans, monkeys go through a long period of development before they attain adulthood. In any case, it appears that human infants reared under conditions of comparative social isolation (although needless to say, not as drastic as that imposed on the monkeys) suffer somewhat analogous deficits.

The evidence comes from studies of infants who were reared in orphanages that supplied adequate nutrition and bodily care but provided rather little in the way of sensory and social stimulation. In one such institution the infants were kept in separate cubicles for the first eight months or so as a precaution against infectious disease. Their brief contacts with adults were restricted to the times when they were fed or diapered. Feeding took place in the crib with a propped-up bottle. There was little social give and take, little talk, little play, and little chance that the busy attendant would respond to any one baby's cry (Goldfarb, 1955; Provence and Lipton, 1962; Dennis, 1973).

When these infants were compared to others who were raised normally, there were no differences for the first three or four months. Thereafter, the two groups diverged markedly. The unstimulated infants showed serious impairments in their social development. Some were insatiable in their demands for individual love and attention. But the majority went in the opposite direction and became extremely apathetic in their reactions to people. They rarely tried to approach adults, either to hug and caress them or to get reassurance when in distress. A few others were reminiscent of Harlow's monkeys; they sat in a corner of their cribs, withdrawn and expressionless, and rocked their bodies.

It appears that many of these early deficits persist into later life. A number of studies have shown that in a fair number of cases—although by no means all—there are a number of intellectual deficits, for example in language and in abstract thinking, which persist into adolescence and beyond. There are also various long-term effects in the social and emotional sphere: heightened aggression, delinquency, and indifference to others (Yarrow, 1961).

More recent studies have focused on orphanages of much higher quality in which children were raised until they were two years or more. When later seen (after they were adopted or placed in foster homes) at age four or eight, these children had much better emotional and social adjustment (Tizard and Hodges, 1978).

14.7 Motherless monkeys as mothers
Female monkeys raised in isolation may become mothers by artificial impregnation. They usually ignore their infants. Sometimes, as shown here, they abuse them. (Courtesy of Harry Harlow, University of Wisconsin Primate Laboratory)

ARE THE EFFECTS OF EARLY SOCIAL DEPRIVATION REVERSIBLE?

It's clear that serious social deprivation in early life has unfortunate effects. But is that because the experience occurred early in life? And is the effect of that early experience irreversible? According to Freud—and many others—

A

B

14.8 Therapy to undo the effects of early isolation (A) A young, would-be therapist tenaciously clings to an unwilling isolate. (B) Some weeks later, there are strong signs of recovery as both patient and therapist engage in vigorous play. (Courtesy of Harry Harlow, University of Wisconsin Primate Laboratory)

the answer to both questions is yes. To Freud there was no question that "the events of [the child's] first years are of paramount importance for his whole subsequent life." In effect, this position is in some ways analogous to the Calvinist doctrine of predestination. According to John Calvin, each person is predestined to be blessed or damned before he is ever born. To Freud, the die is cast by the age of five or six.

UNDOING THE PAST IN ANIMALS

Some further evidence suggests that the dead hand of the past is not quite as rigid as Freud had supposed. For one thing, many of the effects of early isolation in monkeys turn out to be reversible. In one study, young rhesus monkeys were rehabilitated for social life after six months of isolation. They were placed together with carefully chosen monkey "therapists." These therapists were normally reared and were three months *younger* than their patients. They were thus too young to display aggression but old enough to seek and initiate social contact. At first, the previously isolated monkeys withdrew and huddled in a corner. But they hadn't counted on the persistence of their little therapists who followed them and clung to them. After a while, the isolates clung back, and within a few weeks patients and therapists were vigorously playing with each other (Figure 14.8). Six months later, the patients seemed completely recovered. Later studies showed that this kind of therapy worked even for monkeys isolated for an entire year. While the treated ex-isolates appeared to be more susceptible to stress than control animals, they usually played and fought and copulated in much the manner of normal monkeys (Suomi and Harlow, 1972; Novak and Harlow, 1975; Suomi, 1989).

A related finding concerns formerly isolated females who later became mothers. As we saw, these motherless females were total failures at the business of mothering. But while they ignored, rejected, or abused their first-borns, they were perfectly maternal to their second offspring—so much so, that they were virtually indistinguishable from normal rhesus monkeys. What could account for this discrepancy? One guess is that the first-borns served as "therapists" who helped their mothers become accustomed to another animal, especially an infant. This helped the mothers later, when dealing with a new offspring. The therapy was evidently not sufficient to protect the little therapists themselves, but that may only show that psychiatrists shouldn't treat their own mothers (Seay, Alexander, and Harlow, 1964).

UNDOING THE PAST IN HUMANS

With some luck and appropriate intervention, the past can evidently be overcome in animals, at least to some extent. Is the same true for humans? The evidence is by no means clear-cut, but the results of one study give grounds for optimism. The subjects were children at an overcrowded orphanage. There were few staff members and little individual attention. After about one-and-a-half years, some of the children were transferred out of the orphanage to an institution for mentally retarded women. Ironically, this institution provided the necessary means for emotional and intellectual rehabilitation. There was a richer and more stimulating environment, but most important, there were many more caregivers. Each of the transferred children was "adopted" by one adult—either an institutionalized woman or an attendant—who became especially attached to the child. This new emotional relationship led to improvements in many spheres of behavior. While the intelligence-test scores of the children who remained in the orphanage dropped during the succeeding years, those of the transferred children rose considerably. Similarly for their social adjustment: When they reached their thirties, the transferred subjects had reached an educational and occupational level that was about average for the country at the time. In contrast, half of the subjects who remained behind never finished the third grade (Skeels, 1966).

REASSESSING THE ROLE OF EARLY EXPERIENCE

In light of all this, we must evidently reassess our views on the all-importance of early social experience. That experience certainly provides a vital foundation upon which further social relationships are built. But experiences in infancy or childhood do not affect adult behavior directly. What happens instead is that each step in a sequence of social developments paves the way for the next. In monkeys, the mother's presence during the first six months allays the infants' fears of approaching other monkeys. As a result, they can play with their age-mates and enter the social apprenticeship of childhood and adolescence. In interacting with their peers, they gradually acquire the social skills of adult mon-keyhood. They can chase and be chased, can cope with aggression, and if necessary inhibit their own. These skills allow both sexes to mate when they reach maturity and also enable them to respond appropriately to their own offspring. Given this step-by-step progression, the motherless infants can be redeemed by introducing them to the subsequent peer stage by an unusual and special means—the unthreatening young therapists.

Something of a similar nature probably holds for human social development as well. The early years are crucial in the sense that certain social patterns are much more likely to be acquired then, such as the capacity to form attachments to other people. These early attachments are a likely prerequisite for the formation of later ones. The child who has never been loved by his parents will be frightened by his peers and probably hampered in his further social development. But while the earlier attachments (to mother and father) lay the foundation for later ones (to friends, lovers, and one's own children), the two are nevertheless quite different. As a result, there may be ways—as with Harlow's monkey therapists—of acquiring the social tools for dealing with one's later life that circumvent the handicaps of one's early childhood. For while the past affects the present, it does not predetermine it.

To sum up, the easiest way of getting to the second floor of a house is by way of the first floor. But in a pinch one can always bring a ladder and climb in through a second-floor window.

CHILDHOOD SOCIALIZATION

The infant's attachment to her caregiver marks her entrance into the social world. This is the starting point of *socialization,* the process by which the child acquires the patterns of thought and behavior that are characteristic of the society in which she is born. But socialization doesn't begin in earnest until somewhat later in childhood, when the individual starts to learn what she must and mustn't do as a member of her society. Our initial focus will be on the first agent of this socialization process, the child's family, which instills the first do's and don'ts of social life.

Socialization   *Most authors agree that parents exert some effect on the personality development of their children. What is at issue is what effects they have and how they achieve them. (Photographs courtesy of George Gleitman)*

CULTURAL VALUES AND CHILD REARING

Some of the goals of socialization are pretty much the same all over the world and probably were so throughout human history. The child may be an African bushman or a New York city dweller; in either case, he'll have to develop some control over his own bodily functions (for example, toilet training) and over his own impulses (for example, aggression). For wherever he lives, he'll have to learn that he has to live with others and that those others may have wants that take precedence over his own. As a result, there have to be some important similarities in the way all children are brought up.

But there are some important differences as well. Some of these simply reflect differences in the dominant values of the culture of which the parents are a part. This is hardly surprising. The child is socialized to become a member of a *particular* society, whether it be a band of nomadic herdsmen, a medieval village, or a tribe of Polynesian fishermen. Each of these societies will inevitably try to instill different characteristics in its young members-to-be. This point is especially clear when we consider the economy on which the society is based. Cultures that make their living through agriculture or animal husbandry tend to stress compliance, conformity, and responsibility as they raise their children. These attributes fit the adult role that the child must eventually assume—the patient, cooperative life of a farmer who must plough his soil or milk his cows at specified times so as to protect and augment an accumulated food supply. In contrast, hunting and fishing societies emphasize self-reliance and initiative—reasonable values for people who have to wrest their food from nature in day-to-day individual encounters (Barry, Child, and Bacon, 1959).

In our own culture, some differences in child rearing are associated with the parents' social class. Several comparisons of the ways in which middle-class and working-class parents rear their children point to one major difference: Working-class parents tend to stress the importance of controls from the outside, while middle-class parents try to instill control from within. When asked what parents should emphasize in raising their children, working-class parents mention "obedience," while middle-class parents are more likely to say "self-control." This makes sense if we consider the world the parents live and work in. By and large, members of the working class are in occupations in which their work is closely supervised—a boss or a foreman tells them what to do and they do it. In contrast, the work of middle-class persons is only loosely supervised, if at all, and it may be entirely self-directed. Thus parents try to make their children behave at home as they themselves do in the work place—the one is required to become obedient and to follow orders, the other to become his or her own boss and to learn self-control. A further result fits in neatly: The more closely supervised the father is at work, the more likely he is to use physical punishment—external control in one of its more extreme versions (Kohn, 1969; Hess, 1970).

Lessons in social behavior *Not all parent-child interactions are sweetness and light. (Photograph by Erika Stone)*

MECHANISMS OF SOCIALIZATION

We've asked about the goals of socialization. But what about the means whereby these goals are achieved? Different theorists emphasize different mechanisms that bring this about. Some stress the role of reward and the fear of punishment. Others point to the importance of imitation. Still others argue for the importance of the child's growing understanding of what she's supposed to

14.9   Learning by imitation   *Performing a traditional tea ceremony is learned by imitating an accomplished model. (Photograph by Michael Heron/Woodfin Camp)*

Modeling in real life   *(Photograph by Frostie/Woodfin Camp)*

do and why. The best guess is that all three of these kinds of mechanisms contribute to the child's socialization.

REINFORCEMENT THEORY

According to both operant behavior and psychoanalytic theory (see Chapters 4 and 17), the child is socialized by a calculus of pain and pleasure. She will continue to do (or wish or think or remember) whatever previously brought her gratification and will refrain from whatever led to punishment and anxiety.

SOCIAL LEARNING THEORY

But many psychologists believe that a theory exclusively based on such learning by reinforcement cannot possibly do justice to the socialization process. For we are animals with a culture, which makes us altogether unlike any of the animals studied in the learning laboratory. Thorndike's cats had to discover how to get out of the puzzle box by themselves (see Chapter 4): No other cat told them how to do it; no other cat could. But in the course of a lifetime, human beings learn a multitude of problem solutions that were discovered by those who came before them. They do not have to invent spoken language or the alphabet; they do not have to discover fire or the wheel or even how to eat baby food with a spoon. Other people show them.

A group of psychologists who are sometimes called *social learning theorists* regard *observational learning* as one of the most powerful mechanisms of socialization. The child observes another person who serves as a model and then proceeds to imitate what the model does, thus learning how to do something he didn't know before (Figure 14.9). The child sees an adult hammer a nail into a board and tries to duplicate the same feat (with any luck, not on the new dining room table). Many cultures explicitly use such imitative patterns as a way of inducting the child into adult ways. In one Central American society, young girls are presented with miniature replicas of a water jar, a broom, and a grinding stone. They observe how their mothers use the real objects and through constant imitation acquire the relevant skills themselves (Bandura and Walters, 1963).

How does a person learn a new response by imitation? There is little doubt that imitative learning is not a species of classical or instrumental conditioning. As social learning theorists point out, imitation may occur even though the observer does not copy the model's actions at the time that he sees them (learning without performance) and even though he neither receives a reward himself nor sees the model receive one (learning without reinforcement).

COGNITIVE DEVELOPMENTAL THEORY

Still another perspective on socialization is offered by the **cognitive approach,** which emphasizes the role of understanding in interpersonal conduct and thought. Cognitive theorists believe that there are many situations in which the child behaves neither as a creature impelled by irrational forces, as a puppet controlled by schedules of reward and punishment, nor as a sheep that follows an adult leader.

The child has some understanding of her own actions; she not only knows that some things are "bad" and others "good" but has some sense of why they are bad or good. Initially her understanding is quite dim, but as her mental development unfolds, so does her rational comprehension of how one does (or should) relate to others. As a result, much of social development is a consequence of cognitive development.

To illustrate the cognitive theory of socialization, consider imitation. Cognitive theorists argue that understanding plays a crucial role, both in learning by imitation and in performing a response one has learned by watching others. There's little doubt that imitative learning involves considerable cognitive complexity. One of the requirements seems to be a realization of the correspondence between one's own body and that of the model's. Suppose a boy imitates his father hitching up his trousers. In order to do so, he has to relate his own clothes and body to those of his father: My trouser belt is to my hands as his trouser belt is to his hands, and so on. In effect, the imitator takes the model's role. But he can do so only if the model's behavior fits into what Piaget would have called a well-developed cognitive "schema" (Piaget, 1951; Aronfreed, 1969). Under the circumstances, it is hardly surprising that children imitate more accurately as they get older, for their ability to utilize what they see the model do presumably increases with their cognitive development (Yando, Seitz, and Zigler, 1978).

The child's imitation of an adult model is not blind and irrational. The novice climber who follows a guide is not like a sheep that runs after a leader; he follows because he knows that the guide will bring him safely up and down the mountain slope. The child who imitates is no less rational, for she proceeds from the perfectly reasonable premise that, by and large, adults know more than she does (Kohlberg, 1969).

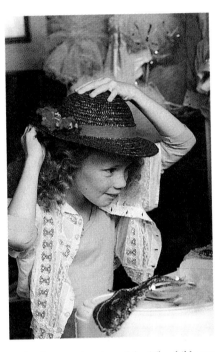

Imitating an absent model *The child may dress up to feel like an adult out of a desire for competence and mastery of the universe. (Photograph by Erika Stone)*

THE FIRST AGENTS OF SOCIALIZATION: THE PARENTS

Thus far, we have looked at socialization from the standpoint of the child who is being socialized, and we have considered how he learns the lessons that society tries to teach him—whether by reinforcement, by modeling, by understanding, or by all three. We now shift our focus to those that serve as society's first teachers: the child's parents. Do different ways in which they rear their children produce differences in the children's behavior? If so, how lasting are the effects?

FEEDING AND TOILET TRAINING

To answer questions of this sort, one must first decide which particular aspects of the parents' behavior one wants to focus on. Until forty or so years ago, developmental psychologists interested in these general issues concerned themselves with certain specific aspects of child rearing that Sigmund Freud and his followers had made much of, such as breast feeding and toilet training. They asked about the effects of different practices associated with feeding, weaning, and toilet training. Does breast feeding produce happier (or unhappier) infants? What about early weaning or early toilet training? As it turned out, the answer is that these child-rearing particulars have little or no effect (Orlansky, 1949; Zigler and Child, 1969; Zigler, Lamb, and Child, 1982).

DIFFERENT PARENTAL STYLES

In recent years, developmental psychologists have taken a different approach. Instead of concentrating on specific child-rearing practices, they have turned their attention to the general home atmosphere in which the child is raised (Baumrind, 1967, 1971; Maccoby and Martin, 1983).

In a number of studies, parents were asked to describe the way they dealt with their children and were also observed with them in various situations. Several patterns of child rearing emerged. One is the *autocratic pattern* in which the parents control the child strictly and often quite sternly. The rules they set down are essentially edicts whose infraction leads to severe (and frequently physical) punishment. Nor do they attempt to explain these rules to the child, who has to accept them as a simple manifestation of parental power: "It's because I say so, that's why."

At the opposite extreme is the *permissive pattern* in which children encounter few don'ts and even fewer do's. The parents try not to assert their authority, impose few restrictions and controls, tend not to have set time schedules (for, say, bedtime or watching TV), and rarely use punishment. They also make few demands on the children—such as putting toys away, doing schoolwork, or helping with chores.

Autocratic parents brandish parental power; permissive parents abdicate it. But there is a third approach that is in some ways in between. It is called the *authoritative-reciprocal pattern* because the parents exercise their power but also accept the reciprocal obligation to respond to the child's point of view and his reasonable demands. Unlike the permissive parents, they govern; but unlike the autocratic ones, they try to govern with the consent of the governed.

Parents whose pattern is authoritative-reciprocal set rules of conduct for their children and enforce them when they have to. They are fairly demanding, assign duties, expect their children to behave maturely and "act their age," and spend a good deal of time in teaching their children how to perform appropriately. But they also encourage the child's independence and allow a good deal of verbal give and take.

DIFFERENT KINDS OF CHILDREN

Are there any differences between children that are raised in these three different styles? One investigator observed preschoolers in various settings. She found that children raised autocratically were more withdrawn, lacked independence, and were more angry and defiant (especially the boys). Interestingly enough, children at the opposite end of the spectrum had similar characteristics. Thus children whose parents were permissive were not particularly independent, and (if boys) they were more prone to anger. In addition, they seemed very imma-

"They never pushed me. If I wanted to retrieve, shake hands, or roll over, it was entirely up to me." (Drawing by Frascino; © 1971, The New Yorker Magazine, Inc.)

ture and lacked social responsibility. In contrast, the children raised in the authoritative-reciprocal mode were more independent, competent, and socially responsible. Here, as so often, the happy medium seems the best approach.

There is evidence that the parental pattern experienced when the child was three or four is related to the way the child behaves in later years. When observed at the age of eight or nine, children whose parents had been judged to be either autocratic or permissive five years earlier seemed to be relatively low in intellectual self-reliance and originality. Once again, the children raised in the authoritative-reciprocal style fared best. They were more self-reliant when faced by intellectual challenges, strove for achievement, and were socially more self-confident and at ease (Baumrind, 1977). More recent studies have shown that the benefits of the authoritative-reciprocal style extend into the high-school years, where this parental pattern is associated with better grades as well as better social adjustment (Dornbusch et al., 1987; Steinberg, Elman, and Mounts, 1989).

THE CHILD'S EFFECT ON THE PARENTS

Thus far, we have discussed socialization as something that is done *to* the child. But in recent years, developmental psychologists have become increasingly insistent that socialization is a two-way street. For the child is more than a lump of psychological clay that is shaped by various social agencies. In fact, he actively participates in his own rearing. His own behavior affects that of the parent, whose behavior then in turn affects him. To the extent that this is true, the parents don't just socialize the child. They are also socialized by him (Bell, 1968; Bell and Harper, 1977).

One of the main reasons why socialization works in both directions is that infants differ from the very day they are born. For example, there are differences in **temperament** that probably have a built-in, genetic basis (see Chapter 16). One infant may be relatively placid and passive; another may be more active and assertive. These differences persist over at least the first two years of life and may last much beyond. The mother will respond quite differently to these two infants. If we later study the correlation between what the mother did and how the child behaves, we will find a correlation. But in this case, the order of cause and effect is the reverse of the one that is actually expected. A difference in the child led to a difference in the way his parents dealt with him (Thomas, Chess, and Birch, 1970; Osofsky and Danzger, 1974; Olweus, 1980). This is another way of saying that children help to make their own environments. To the extent that they are genetically different in either temperament or ability, their parents, siblings, and eventually their peers cannot help but treat them differently (Scarr and McCartney, 1983).

Such reversed cause-and-effect relations can never be ignored as possible (although probably only partial) explanations of correlations between the way a child was reared and his personality. As an example consider the effect of physical punishment. As already mentioned, there is some evidence which suggests that parents who resort to physical punishment have children who tend to be more aggressive than average (Feshbach, 1970; Parke and Slaby, 1983). If this relationship is genuine, how should we interpret it? One possibility is that the parents provide a model for their child who learns to do to others what his parents have done unto him. But there is an alternative. Some children may be more aggressive to begin with, and they are the ones who are more likely to be spanked. The relation may be even more complex. The more aggressive child will probably be punished more severely; this will lead to more aggression in the child, which will then provoke yet further parental countermeasures.

The best guess is that all these cause-and-effect relationships exist side by side. The parents' behavior affects the child, but the child's behavior also affects the parents—a continual, interactive pattern in which the characteristics of all parties in the family act as both cause and effect.

THE DEVELOPMENT OF MORALITY

Initially, the child's social world is largely confined to the family. His first lessons in social behavior are taught in the limited family context: Pick up your toys, don't push your baby brother, and so on—circumscribed commands and prohibitions that apply to a very narrow social setting. But his social sphere soon grows to include young peers: at home, in day-care centers, in preschool settings, still later in the schools. These peers become increasingly important, and their approval is then sought as eagerly (if not more eagerly) than that of his parents. Eventually the child's social universe expands still further as he acquires rules of social thought and action that are vastly broader than the simple commands and prohibitions of his toddler years. For these rules pertain not just to the people he meets face to face but to countless others he has never met and probably will never meet. Among the most important of these rules are those of moral conduct.

Internalization *A four-year-old reproaches her doll: "Bad girl! Didn't I tell you to keep out of the dirt?" In imitating how her mother scolds her, the child is taking the first steps toward internalizing the mother's prohibitions. (Photograph by Suzanne Szasz)*

NOT DOING WRONG

All societies have prohibitions that its members must learn to obey despite various temptations to the contrary. It's easy enough to set up external sanctions that enforce the prohibitions from the outside. Children rarely steal from the cookie jar when their parents are present. The trick is to make them resist temptation when they are not being watched. The person who does not steal or cheat because he thinks that he will be caught is not moral; he's merely prudent. One aim of socialization is to instill moral values that are *internalized,* so that the individual will shun transgressions because he feels that they are wrong and not because he is afraid of being punished.

INTERNALIZATION AND SELF-PUNISHMENT

What leads to the internalization of right and wrong? Sigmund Freud believed that internalization is produced by self-punishment in the form of guilt and anxiety.★ The child kicks his little brother, and the parents punish him. As a result, the forbidden act (or, for that matter, the mere thought of that act) becomes associated with anxiety. Thus, the child will feel a pang of anxiety the next time he starts to attack his younger brother. To stop this painful feeling, he must stop

---

★ Freud called the primary agent of these internalization processes the **superego,** an unconscious remnant of the internal conflicts the child experienced during the Oedipus conflict (see Chapter 17).

that which triggered it: the thought, let alone the execution, of the forbidden behavior. In Freud's view, these internalized inhibitions are a remnant of our childhood that remains with us for the rest of our lives and makes sure that we commit no wrong. The external authorities that once punished our transgressions have long stopped watching the cookie jar. But they no longer have to because they now inhabit our minds, where we can no longer hide from them.

INTERNALIZATION AND MINIMAL SUFFICIENCY

Given this general view of the inhibition of the forbidden, one would predict that the internalization of prohibition is most pronounced in children whose parents relied on sheer power in raising them—whether this power was exercised by the use of physical punishment, or deprivation of privileges, or threats of withdrawal of love and of abandonment. But this prediction turns out to be false. For a number of studies suggest that prohibitions are *less* internalized in children whose parents primarily relied on power in its various forms than in children whose parents took pains to explain just why a misdeed was wrong and why the child ought to behave differently. The children of power-asserting (autocratic) parents were more likely to cheat for a prize when they thought no one was looking, and they were less likely to feel guilt about their misdeeds or to confess them when confronted (Hoffman, 1970).

One proposal tries to deduce these and other phenomena of socialization from the *principle of minimal sufficiency.* This states that a child will internalize a certain way of acting if there is just enough pressure to get him to behave in this new way, but not enough so that he feels he was forced to do so. This principle seems to fit a number of experimental findings. An example is a study in which children were prohibited from playing with a particularly attractive toy. For some children, the prohibition was backed with a mild threat (e.g., "I will be a little bit annoyed with you"); for others, the threat was severe (e.g., "I will be very upset and very angry with you"). When later tested in a rather different situation in which they thought they were unobserved, the mildly threatened children resisted temptation more than the severely threatened ones. Punishment led to internalization, but only if it was *not* the most memorable part of the child's experience.

The same principle may help account for some of the effects of child rearing we discussed above. We saw that the children of authoritative-reciprocal parents are more likely to internalize their parents' standards than the children of autocratic or permissive parents. This is in accord with the minimal sufficiency hypothesis. Autocratic parents supply too much force to induce their children to behave in the appropriate way, so their children become outwardly compliant but will not change their inner attitudes. Permissive parents apply no force at all, so their children never change their behavior in the first place—they won't even comply outwardly, let alone internalize. But authoritative-reciprocal parents somehow manage to strike the proper balance. They apply a force just strong enough to get their children to change their behavior, but mild enough so that the children come to believe that they performed the moral act of their own free will (Lepper, 1983).★

Minimal sufficiency *If the older sister's scolding is of minimal sufficiency, it may lead to internalization. (Photograph by Roberta Intrater)*

★ This is reminiscent of the effects of forced compliance on attitudes. As we saw in Chapter 11, subjects who are pressured into performing some action that runs counter to their own attitudes will tend to change this attitude if the pressure (the threat or the bribe) is relatively small, but will not change the attitude if the pressure is large (Festinger and Carlsmith, 1959; Aronson and Carlsmith, 1963).

DOING GOOD

Our discussion of moral action has dealt with the inhibition of forbidden acts. But moral action pertains to do's no less than to don'ts, to doing good as well as not committing evil. In a previous chapter we considered the fact that humans are capable of positive moral actions that call for some personal sacrifice and altruism (see Chapter 10). We now ask how this capacity develops in the child.

Thus far, we are still far from an answer. A number of studies show that even very young children try to help and comfort others, and occasionally share with them (Rheingold, Hay, and West, 1976; Radke-Yarrow, Zahn-Waxler, and Chapman, 1983). The question is why.

According to a Hobbesian view of human nature, such apparently unselfish acts are much more egoistic than they appear to be on the surface. Perhaps the child only gives to others in order to reap some ultimate benefit for himself, such as avoiding censure and obtaining social approval. There is some evidence that this hypothesis is false, for in fact children who are more popular and self-confident to begin with are more likely to help others than are children who are less popular. This suggests that altruism is more likely when one's own needs for social approval are already satisfied. But if so, its main motivation is probably not the desire to gain yet further social approval (Hoffman, 1975a).

EMPATHY

Such findings argue against the Hobbesian position that humans are by nature self-centered. A further argument comes from studies of *empathy* in very young infants. Empathy is a direct emotional response to another person's emotions; we see a patient writhe in pain in a hospital bed, and we ourselves experience vicarious distress (Aronfreed, 1968; see also Chapter 12). Some precursors to such empathic reactions are found even in the first two days of life. On hearing a newborn's cry, one-day-old infants cry too and their hearts beat faster (Simner, 1971; Sagi and Hoffman, 1976).

What accounts for such empathic reactions at this tender age? According to one hypothesis, the reason is classical conditioning. In this view, the response of crying becomes conditioned to the sound of crying. Initially, crying was evoked by some pain or discomfort. But soon the sound of the infant's own crying became a conditioned stimulus for further crying. Since another baby's cry resembles the infant's own, it will elicit her own cry as a conditioned response (in addition to various other distress reactions, such as increased heart rate). An alternative hypothesis is that some empathic reactions are innately given, a position that is by no means implausible given the facts of built-in alarm and distress reactions in many animals (see Chapter 10). As yet it is too early to choose between these two views. But whichever turns out to be correct, it is clear that some forerunner of what may later become a feeling for others is found at the very start of life.

FROM EMPATHIC DISTRESS TO UNSELFISH ACTION

The mere fact that one feels empathy doesn't mean that one will do anything about it. For to help one's fellows, one has to do more than just feel for them. One also has to act on this feeling. And one has to know how.

Consider a two-year-old girl who sees an adult in pain—say, an uncle who has cut his finger with a knife. In all likelihood, she will feel empathy and

Feeling distress at the distress of another
The young boy cries as the veterinarian gives an injection to his puppy. (Photograph by Janet Kelly/Reading Eagle-Times, © Reading Eagle Company)

become distressed herself. But what will her *empathic distress* make her do? A number of anecdotes suggest that she will give her uncle whatever *she* finds most comforting herself—for example, her favorite doll. While appreciating her kindly sentiments, the uncle would probably have preferred a Band-Aid or a stiff drink. But the child is as yet too young to take his perspective and doesn't realize that her uncle's needs are not the same as her own (Hoffman, 1977a, 1979, 1984).★

As we develop, we become increasingly able to tell what other people are likely to feel in a given situation and how to help if help is needed. But even that is not enough to ensure that we will act unselfishly. For helping is only one means of getting rid of the empathic distress that is caused by the sight of another person's pain. There is an easier but more callous method: One can simply look away. This often occurs in the big city, with its many homeless and victims of violence, where empathy may seem a luxury one can no longer afford. It may also occur in war or other situations where people "harden their hearts" to become immune to the sufferings of others (see Chapter 12).

Such arguments indicate that while empathy is a likely precursor of altruism, it does not guarantee it. In fact, there may be some circumstances in which empathic distress will interfere with appropriate helpful action. An interesting finding concerns a group of nurses who worked in a ward for severely ill persons. Those nurses who seemed to experience the greatest degree of empathy for their patients were the least effective. The reason was simple: They couldn't bear their patients' pain, and so they tried to have as little contact with them as possible (Stotland et al., 1978).

MORAL REASONING

Thus far, our focus has been on the development of moral behavior. What about the development of moral thought? What happens to the child's conception of right and wrong as he grows up?

KOHLBERG'S STAGES OF MORAL REASONING

An influential account of moral development was devised by Lawrence Kohlberg. His basic method is to confront subjects with a number of stories that pose a moral dilemma. An example is a story about a man whose wife will die unless treated with a very expensive drug, a drug that costs $2,000. The husband scraped together all the money he could, but it was not enough. He promised to pay the balance later, but the pharmacist still refused to give him the drug. In desperation, the husband broke into the pharmacy and stole the drug. The subjects were asked whether the husband's act was right or wrong and why (Kohlberg, 1969).

Kohlberg analyzed the subjects' answers and concluded that moral reasoning proceeds through a series of successive stages. Roughly speaking, there is a progression from a primitive morality guided by personal fear of punishment or desire for gain ("If you let your wife die, you'll get in trouble"), through stages in which right or wrong are defined by convention, by what people will say

---

★ Some authors make a distinction between *empathic distress* in which the primary focus is on the unpleasant feelings the victim's plight arouses in *us* and *sympathetic distress* in which there is a desire to help the other person—not merely to relieve one's own empathic distress but to relieve *his* distress. According to this view, empathic distress is a more primitive forerunner of sympathetic distress, which does not occur until the child is about two (Hoffman, 1984).

TABLE 14.1 KOHLBERG'S STAGES OF MORAL REASONING

Stage of moral reasoning	Moral behavior is that which:
Preconventional morality	
Level 1	Avoids punishment
Level 2	Gains reward
Conventional morality	
Level 3	Gains approval and avoids disapproval of others
Level 4	Is defined by rigid codes of "law and order"
Postconventional morality	
Level 5	Is defined by a "social contract" generally agreed upon for the public good
Level 6	Is based on abstract ethical principles that determine one's own moral code

SOURCE: Adapted from Kohlberg, 1969.

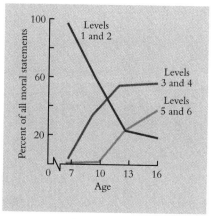

14.10 Level of moral reasoning as a function of age *With increasing age, the level of moral reasoning changes. In this figure, the percent of all moral judgments made by children at various ages falls into one of three general categories defined by Kohlberg. At seven, virtually all moral judgments are in terms of avoiding punishment or gaining reward (Kohlberg's levels 1 and 2). At ten, about half the judgments are based on criteria of social approval and disapproval or of a rigid code of laws (Kohlberg's levels 3 and 4). From thirteen on, some of the children refer to more abstract rules—a generally agreed-upon social contract or a set of abstract ethical principles (Kohlberg's levels 5 and 6). (After Kohlberg, 1963)*

("Your family will think you're an inhuman husband if you don't"), to the highest stage in which there are internalized moral principles that have become one's own ("If you didn't steal the drug, you wouldn't be blamed and you would have lived up to the outside rule of the law, but you wouldn't have lived up to your own standards of conscience"). As one might expect, there is a rough correlation between Kohlberg's levels and age. But even in adulthood only a small proportion of the subjects give answers that correspond to Kohlberg's highest level. In a recent study that made use of a revised set of Kohlberg's criteria, no subject below the age of twenty was judged to have reached Stage 5, and Stage 6 was not found at all (Colby et al., 1983; Colby and Kohlberg, 1986). Considering that Kohlberg considers this final stage to be the level that characterized such moral giants as Mahatma Gandhi and Dr. Martin Luther King, the failure of his subjects (and no doubt, most of us) to attain it is probably not too surprising (Figure 14.10; Table 14.1).

MORAL REASONING IN MEN AND WOMEN

Are there sex differences in moral orientation? An influential discussion by Carol Gilligan suggests that there may be. In her view, men tend to see morality as a matter of justice, ultimately based on abstract, rational principles by which all individuals can be treated fairly. As one eleven-year-old boy put it in describing the moral dilemmas posed by Kohlberg: "It's sort of like a math problem with humans." Women in contrast see morality in more concrete, social terms. To them, the focus is on compassion, on human relationships, on special responsibilities to those with whom one is intimately connected. Given these different emphases, one might expect women to score lower than men when moral reasoning is assessed by Kohlberg's yardstick. For as Gilligan sees it, Kohlberg's system has a built-in sex bias in which the moral outlook usually adopted by men is judged to be more advanced than that which is more characteristic of women. Kohlberg calls the highest steps on his moral staircase "postconventional morality," which is defined by just those abstract, rational principles that tend to fit in with the way in which men see the moral order. The moral outlook of women, on the other hand, with their emphasis on helping others, would be judged to be on one of Kohlberg's lower steps. Under the circumstances, it would not be surprising to find that women obtain lower scores on Kohlberg's tests than men (Gilligan, 1982).

Moral reasoning in men and women
The belief that men and women focus on different aspects of morality has ancient roots. A classical example is Sophocles's tragedy Antigone, *which revolves around the irreconcilable conflict between Antigone, who insists on burying a slain brother, and her uncle Creon, the king, who issues a decree forbidding anyone from doing so on pain of death. To Antigone, the ultimate moral obligation is to the family; to Creon, it is to the state and its laws. (From a 1982 production at the New York Shakespeare Festival, with F. Murray Abraham and Lisa Banes; photograph by Martha Swope)*

Psychologists interested in moral reasoning were quick to ask whether men really achieve "higher" levels of moral reasoning as defined by Kohlberg. It turns out that they don't. According to several authors, a systematic check of the work performed on the topic reveals no reliable sex differences in moral reasoning on Kohlberg's test; of 108 studies, only 8 showed a superiority of males over females, while 4 or 5 went in the opposite direction (Brabeck, 1983; Walker, 1984; but see Baumrind, 1986, Walker, 1989). But if so, what remains of Gilligan's critique?

Gilligan states that she herself never said that women can't reason at Kohlberg's "highest" level; the point is that they usually choose not to do so. As she sees it, the female perspective emphasizes human relationships, attachments, and personal responsibilities rather than the abstract conceptions of rights and justice emphasized by the male perspective (Gilligan, 1986). That such a difference in emphases exists is suggested by various empirical findings, including the fact that girls seem to place a greater value on going out of one's way to help other people and show more emotional empathy than do boys (Hoffman, 1977b). Just why women emphasize the perspective of care rather than of abstract justice is still unsettled. The best guess is that it is a result of different patterns of socialization that stress different values for boys and girls (Hoffman, 1984).

Is either perspective preferable to the other? Virtually everyone agrees that the answer is no and that an appropriate conception of morality must include both justice and compassion. As Kohlberg points out, both of these orientations are built into the New Testament's Golden Rule. That rule is formulated in two ways. One insists on justice: "Do unto others as you would have them do unto you." The other urges care and compassion: "Love thy neighbor as thyself" (Kohlberg and Candee, 1984).

MORAL REASONING AND CULTURAL FACTORS

Gilligan's description of the difference between the moral perspectives of men and women is paralleled by the differences found among cultural groups. A number of studies have shown that when members of technologically less advanced societies are asked to reason about moral dilemmas, they generally come up with comparatively low scores on Kohlberg's scale; they justify acts on the basis of concrete issues such as what neighbors will say or concern over one's wife, rather than more abstract conceptions of justice and morality (Kohlberg, 1969; Tietjen and Walker, 1985). How should we interpret such results? Does it mean that the inhabitants, say, of a small Turkish village are less moral than the residents of Paris or New York? A more plausible interpretation is that the Turkish villager spends his life in a small community in continual face-to-face encounters with all its members. Under the circumstances, the most likely outcome is a more concrete morality that gives the greatest weight to care, responsibility, and loyalty is just what we might expect (Simpson, 1974; Kaminsky, 1984).

MORAL REASONING AND MORAL CONDUCT

Are stages of moral reasoning related to ethical conduct? To some extent they may be. Thus a number of studies found that delinquents were at a lower stage of moral reasoning than nondelinquents of the same age and IQ. Other studies suggest that individuals at higher, principled levels of moral reasoning are less likely to cheat in an ambiguous situation in which they are unobserved and are more likely to maintain their position against the pressure of other people's views. But taken as a whole, the results suggest that the relation between moral reasoning and moral conduct is far from perfect (Blasi, 1980; Rest, 1983; Gibbs et al., 1986). To some extent, this result is reminiscent of the relatively low correlations between social attitudes and behavior we encountered in Chapter 11. Kohlberg's stages (just like attitudes) don't specifically pertain to conduct. They indicate whether an individual describes certain moral principles, but they don't tell us much about the individual's actual behavior, which may or may not be ruled by the moral principles he described (for discussion, see Rest, 1984; Blasi, 1984; Kohlberg, Levine, and Hewer, 1984).

There is also a further problem. For Kohlberg's stages don't just indicate what an individual's moral principles are. They also concern that person's ability to describe these principles and reason on the basis of them. Kohlberg has indeed shown that this ability increases with age and mental development. But this is not particularly surprising. After all, the same holds for the ability to describe and reason about various other rules of mental life—for example, those that pertain to space, to number, and to language. Seen in this light, what is really surprising is that Kohlberg's stages correlate with behavior as well as they do. One reason why they don't correlate any better may be that they have less to do with the development of morality than with the development of something we might call "metamorality"—in analogy with metacognitive processes: the ability to reflect on moral rules, regardless of whether one lives by them (see Chapters 8 and 13).

Social learning of gender roles
(Photograph by Suzanne Arms/Jeroboam)

THE DEVELOPMENT OF SEX AND GENDER

Thus far, our emphasis has been on social development considered as growth and expansion. But social development is more than that. Like physical and cognitive development, it involves growth, but this growth is not just a matter of increasing size. It is also accompanied by increasing differentiation. For as the child gets older, she becomes increasingly aware of the fact that people differ from each other and from herself. In so doing, she also gains a clearer conception of her own self and of her own personality—what she is really like, in her own eyes and in those of others.

Seen in this light, social development goes hand in hand with the development of a sense of personal identity. One of the most important elements of this is sexual identity—of being male or female and all that goes with it.

Biologically, sexual identity seems simple enough. It may refer to genetic sex: having XX or XY chromosome pairs. It may also refer to morphological (that is, structural) sex: having clitoris, vagina, and ovaries or penis, scrotum, and testes. But what does sexual identity mean psychologically? It refers to three issues. One is *gender identity*—our inner sense that we are male or female. A second is *gender role*—a whole host of external behavior patterns that a given culture deems appropriate for each sex. A third is *sexual orientation*—the inclination toward a sexual partner, which in most of us—though of course not all of us—is directed toward the opposite sex. Gender identity, gender role, and sexual orientation are among the most important determinants of a person's social existence.* How do they come about?

---

* It has become customary to distinguish between sex and gender. *Sex* generally refers to aspects of male-female differences that pertain to reproductive functions (for example, having ovaries versus testes, vagina versus penis) or genetically related factors (for example, differences in height or

GENDER ROLES

Gender roles pervade all facets of social life. The induction into one or the other of these roles begins with the very first question that is asked when a human being enters the world: "Is it a boy or a girl?" As soon as the answer is supplied—which now, due to fetal ultrasound, may be months before birth—the process of gender typing begins, and the infant is ushered onto one of two quite different social trajectories. Some of the patterns of gender typing have probably changed in the wake of modern feminism, but many differences in child rearing persist.

The stereotypes in our own culture are obvious. The infant is dressed in either pink or blue; the child plays with either dolls or trucks; at least until recently the adult woman's place was in the home, while the man's was in the marketplace—or the buffalo hunting grounds, or whatever. Society not only has different expectations about what the two sexes should *do;* it also has different conceptions of what they should *be.* In our own culture, men are expected to be more aggressive and tough, more restrained emotionally, and more interested in things than in people. In contrast, women are expected to be submissive, more emotionally expressive, and more interested in people than in things.

There is no doubt that these gender-role stereotypes have a considerable effect on how we perceive people, even newborns and very young infants. In one study, mothers of young infants were asked to participate as subjects in an experiment on "how children play." The mothers were introduced to a six-month-old baby, little "Joey" or "Janie," and they were asked to play with him or her for a few minutes. In fact, the six-month-old was a baby actor who was dressed up as a boy or girl regardless of its actual sex. The results showed that the subjects' behavior depended on whether they thought they were playing with "Joey" or "Janie." To "Joey" they offered toys such as a hammer or a rattle, while "Janie" was invariably given a doll. In addition, the subjects physically touched and handled "Joey" and "Janie" differently. In dealing with "Joey," they often bounced "him" about, thus stimulating the whole body. In contrast, their response to "Janie" was gentler and less vigorous (Smith and Lloyd, 1978).

Children soon behave as adults expect them to. Starting at about age one and a half, they begin to show gender-typed differences. By three years of age, they prefer different toys and play mainly with peers of their own sex (Huston, 1983). As they grow older, they become increasingly aware of male and female stereotypes. In one study, both male and female children had to decide whether certain characteristics were more likely in a man or a woman. Over 90 percent of a group of U.S. eleven-year-olds thought that the adjectives *weak, emotional, appreciative, gentle, soft-hearted, affected, talkative, fickle,* and *mild* probably described a woman and that the adjectives *strong, aggressive, disorderly, cruel, coarse, adventurous, independent, ambitious,* and *dominant* probably described a man. Boys and girls endorsed just about the same gender-role stereotypes (Best et al., 1977).

Many of these gender-role stereotypes are reinforced by parents and peers. When young children play with toys that are deemed to be inappropriate—as when a boy plays with a dollhouse—their parents are likely to express disapproval. This is especially so for fathers, who sternly object to any such behaviors

Gender-role stereotypes *Once parents and others recognize an infant's sex, they will treat him or her differently. Notice the difference in the cards sent to parents congratulating them on the birth of a son or daughter. (© Hallmark Cards, Inc.)*

muscular strength). It is also used to designate erotic feelings, inclinations, or practices (for example, heterosexuality and homosexuality). *Gender,* on the other hand, refers to social or psychological aspects of being seen as a man or woman or regarding oneself to be so. Thus it is one thing to be male and another to be a man; one thing to be female, another—a woman (Stoller, 1968). A special note about the term *sex difference:* This term is used here strictly to designate male-female differences, with no presuppositions about whether they have biological or cultural origins.

in their sons. By and large, girls are allowed more latitude in such matters. A girl can be a tomboy and get away with it; a boy who is a sissy is laughed at or taunted (Langlois and Downs, 1980).

CONSTITUTIONAL FACTORS AND SEX DIFFERENCES

What accounts for the difference in current gender roles? We will consider both constitutional and social factors in an attempt to understand how biology and society conspire to make boys into men and girls into women.

It's self-evident that gender roles are influenced by anatomical and physiological differences that pertain to reproduction, and there are of course differences in average size, strength, and physical endurance. But what about *psychological* differences? There is no doubt that such differences do exist and that some of them fit cultural stereotypes. The question is whether any of these differences—in aggression, independence, emotional expressiveness, social sensitivity, and so on—are biologically given, whether they accompany the sexual anatomy the way menstruation goes along with a female XX chromosome pair.

Before proceeding, two cautions: The first is that any psychological difference between the sexes is one of *averages.* The average three-year-old girl seems to be more dependent than her male counterpart; she is more likely to ask for help, to cling, and to seek affection (Emmerich, 1966). But this doesn't mean that this generalization applies to *every* boy and girl, because there are certainly many three-year-old girls who are less dependent than many three-year-old boys. After all, the same applies even to many physical differences like height and weight. Thus, while it's clear that men are on the average taller than women, it's equally clear that a considerable number of women are taller than many men.

A second caution is about interpretation. Suppose we obtain a sex difference. What accounts for it? It may indeed reflect a biological predisposition, but it may also reflect the society in which the children are raised. In our society and many others, boys are encouraged to be independent, to be "little men," and any differences in a trait like dependency may simply reflect this cultural fact. Here, as in so many other areas, nature and nurture are difficult to disentangle.

AGGRESSION

If there is one sex difference that is constitutional in origin, at least in part, it is aggression. Males are on average more active and assertive than females. This difference is apparent from the very start; male infants are more irritable and physically active than female infants, and mothers often report that their boys were more active than their girls in utero. At two or three, boys are much more likely to engage in rough-and-tumble play and mock fighting than are girls (a difference also seen in apes and monkeys; see Figure 14.11). By four or five, they are more ready to exchange insults and to greet aggression with retaliation.

The difference continues into adulthood. While acts of physical violence are relatively rare among both sexes, they are very much more common among men than women; thus among adolescents, arrests for violent crimes occur five times more often among males than females (Johnson, 1979). A similar pattern of results holds in different social classes and in such widely different cultural settings as Ethiopia, India, Kenya, Mexico, Okinawa, and Switzerland (Whiting and Whiting, 1975; Maccoby and Jacklin, 1974, 1980; Parke and Slaby, 1983).

It is probably not surprising that this sex difference is more pronounced for physical aggression than for other forms of aggression. When aggression is mea-

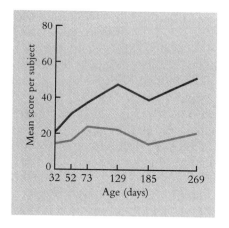

14.11   The development of rough-and-tumble play in male and female rhesus monkeys   *Roughhouse play in two male and two female rhesus monkeys during the first year of life. The scores are based on both frequency and vigor of this activity, in which monkeys wrestle, roll, or sham bite—all presumably in play, since no one ever gets hurt. Roughhouse play is considerably more pronounced in males (dark red) than in females (blue), a difference that increases during the first year of life. (After Harlow, 1962)*

14.12   Sex differences in spatial ability
Results on a spatial-mathematical test, which included questions such as "How many times between three and four o'clock do the hands of a clock make a straight line?" The curve plots the percentage of subjects who receive a particular score (with men in dark red and women in blue). As the curve shows, the men perform better than the women, though the two curves overlap considerably. (Data from Very, 1967, with test scores adjusted by a method called "normalization")

sured by rating the degree of verbal hostility or by asking how intense a shock a subject is willing to administer to another person, the difference is not as striking (Hyde, 1981). But even so, it is still quite marked.

That this sex difference in aggression—especially physical aggression—is found so early in life, is observed in so many different cultures, and is also seen in our primate relatives suggests a constitutional origin—all the more so given that aggressiveness is enhanced by the administration of male sex hormones (see Chapter 10). But a constitutional origin of a sex difference does not mean that social and cultural factors play no part—on the contrary. As we will describe below (see pp. 560–64), the various agents of socialization—parents, teachers, peers, and the cultural media—all combine to magnify whatever sex differences were there to begin with.

PATTERNS OF INTELLECTUAL APTITUDES

There is another psychological difference that is often said to be based on biological givens—a different pattern of intellectual abilities. On the average, men do better on tests of spatial and mathematical ability (Figure 14.12; Maccoby and Jacklin, 1974, 1980; Halpern, 1992). Until fairly recently, it was generally believed that the reverse held for verbal abilities. According to some recent studies, the superiority of women over men on verbal tasks may be much smaller than had previously been assumed, though this is a matter of some dispute (Hyde and Linn, 1988; Halpern, 1992).

What accounts for the sex difference in cognitive aptitudes, especially in spatial-mathematical abilities? In part, it may simply reflect a difference in the way boys and girls are brought up. But various lines of evidence suggest that social factors are only part of the story. An example is a study of SAT scores in 40,000 male and female adolescents. The investigators found the usual sex difference on spatial and mathematical tasks even when they limited their comparison to boys and girls who had taken the same high-school math courses and had expressed the same degree of interest in mathematics (Benbow and Stanley, 1983; Benbow, 1988).

A number of authors feel that such sex differences in mathematical aptitude are ultimately produced by a difference in certain spatial abilities. An example is the ability to visualize objects in space, which is often assessed by asking subjects to rotate a three-dimensional object in their imagination to decide whether it is a rotated version of another figure or whether it is its mirror image. Since a number of branches of mathematics rely on such abilities—for example, geometry, topology, trigonometry, and much of calculus—it does not seem too far-fetched to assume that the sex difference in this ability underlies those in quantitative aptitude and achievement (Burnett, Lane, and Dratt, 1979; Hunt, 1985a; Halpern, 1992).

A number of investigators have searched for a constitutional basis for the male-female difference in spatial abilities. One of several suggestions is that the key to the puzzle is in different maturation rates. There is some evidence that children who mature later tend to do better on spatial tests than children who mature earlier. An intriguing hypothesis is that this effect is related to the different functions of the two cerebral hemispheres. As we've previously seen, the right hemisphere is specialized for spatial tasks, the left for language (see Chapter 2). By making the assumption that the right hemisphere matures more slowly than the left and that neurological maturation comes to an effective end at the time of puberty, we can account for most of the evidence. The usual male-female difference in cognitive orientation would then follow from the fact that girls generally reach puberty before boys. If so, their right (spatial) hemisphere is stopped at an earlier point of neurological organization (Waber, 1977, 1979).

Social factors and sex differences *Social effects augment constitutional differences. (Photograph © Yvonne Hemsey, The Gamma Liaison Network)*

SOCIAL FACTORS AND SEX DIFFERENCES

While some psychological sex differences may have biological roots, even more important are the ways in which boys and girls are socialized. We will begin our discussion by taking a second look at the two characteristics for which there is some evidence of a biologically based sex difference: aggression and spatial aptitudes. We'll see that even here there is some reasonable evidence that social effects augment and interact with whatever constitutional differences may have been there to start with.

ARE CONSTITUTIONAL DIFFERENCES REALLY CONSTITUTIONAL?

A ready example of the interaction of culture with constitution lies in aggression. Boys may very well be more disposed toward aggression than girls, but it appears almost certain that cultural pressures magnify any preexisting sex differences. Boys are encouraged to be tough and are given toy guns, while girls are expected to be well-behaved and receive dolls and doll houses. Parents will generally allow (and even foster) a degree of aggressiveness in a boy that they would never countenance in a girl. Thus fathers often encourage their sons to fight back when another boy attacks them (Sears, Maccoby, and Levin, 1957).

This process continues in adolescence, where aggressive behavior in boys is tolerated or indulgently smiled at, while the same behavior in girls is discouraged in favor of a more dependent, approval-seeking pattern. The scales are tipped still further by the way in which the two sexes are usually portrayed by the media, with strong, silent heroes and charming, help-mate heroines. While males and females may start life with different biological dispositions toward aggression, by the time they are adults society has exaggerated this initial difference manifold (Parke and Slaby, 1983).

Similar considerations may apply to the sex difference in spatial aptitude. In our society, girls are expected to do better in English than in math. This belief is shared by teachers, parents, and the pupils themselves, who all conspire to make it come true, so that even the girl who does have the appropriate genetic potential may do worse on spatial and mathematical tests than her ability warrants. In addition, many male and female students share a widespread feeling that math-related courses and careers are a male province and that the women who succeed in them are somehow unfeminine. A recent review quotes a female mathematics professor's description of this stereotype:

> Many people on hearing the words "female mathematician" conjure up an image of a six-foot, gray-haired, tweed-suited, oxford-clad woman. This image, of course, doesn't attract the young woman who is continually bombarded with messages, both direct and indirect, to be beautiful, "feminine" and catch a man. (Quoted in Halpern, 1992, p. 216).

The ultimate upshot is similar to the gender difference in aggression. While the male-female difference in intellectual aptitudes may originally be based on built-in constitutional factors, it is certain to be greatly magnified by social expectations and stereotypes.

SEX REASSIGNMENT IN CHILDHOOD

The most dramatic examples of social influences on gender identity and gender roles come from studies of children who at birth were declared to be of one sex but who were later reassigned to the other. This can occur if the newborn has external genitalia—and often, internal reproductive organs—that are anatomically ambiguous, that is, they are not clearly male or female. Such ambiguities can result from a number of factors, ranging from drugs taken during pregnancy to specific hormonal or genetic disorders. Individuals with ambiguous genitalia are said to have *pseudohermaphroditism.★*

In such cases, parents and physicians sometimes decide to reverse the initial sex assignment. Plastic surgery is performed to make the external genitalia unambiguous, the individual begins a course of hormone therapy to complete the processes of masculinization or feminization, the sex is officially reassigned both in medical records and legal documents, and the child is reared accordingly. Because of the difficulty of constructing functioning male organs, the surgical rule for most cases is "if in doubt, make it female." The end result in these cases is a person who looks exactly like a female and can enjoy female sexual functions (the remnant of the penis becomes the clitoris, and the scrotum is fashioned to make a vagina). Since the newly constructed female lacks ovaries, she obviously cannot have children and is later told that as an adult she can become a mother by adopting a baby.

The results suggest that if the reassignment occurs early enough—according to some investigators, up to eighteen months, according to others, up to three or four years—the child adjusts to a remarkable degree. It becomes a *he* or a *she,* in part because this is how other people now regard it (Money and Ehrhardt, 1972).

The effects of reassignment   The reports of parents leave no doubt that the child is seen very differently before and after the reassignment. One case involved a child who was a genetic male with a male's XY chromosome pair and testes. But the external genitals were otherwise more similar to a female's than to a male's. At birth the child was pronounced a boy, but the decision was reversed seventeen months later, at which time there was corrective surgery. According to the parents, there was an immediate change in the way the child was now treated. Even her three-year-old brother reacted differently and showed a "marked tendency to treat her much more gently. Whereas before he was just as likely to stick his foot out to trip her as she went by, he now wants to hold her hand to make sure she doesn't fall" (Money and Ehrhardt, 1972, p. 124).

Constitutional factors in early reassignment   The findings in cases of sex reassignment suggest that social factors can override the individual's genetic makeup to a surprising extent. But they also show that constitutional factors play a role. Evidence comes from a series of studies of girls who were exposed to an abnormally high level of male hormones (androgens) in the womb, because of some malfunction during their mother's pregnancy. At birth, many of these girls were pseudohermaphrodites, with ambiguous external genitals. After appropriate plastic surgery they were raised as females. But follow-up studies showed that the excess androgen during pregnancy had some long-term psychological effects. When compared to a control group, the androgenized girls were much more likely to be "tomboys" during childhood. They chose trucks over dolls, loved to participate in energetic team sports, preferred functional slacks to feminine dresses, and had little interest in jewelry or perfume. As adolescents, they looked forward to a future in which marriage and maternity were subordinated to a career (Money and Ehrhardt, 1972; Money, 1980; Ehrhardt, 1984).

★ True *hermaphroditism* occurs when an individual has functioning reproductive tissue from both sexes, such as a testicle on one side and an ovary on the other (Simpson, 1976). In contrast, *pseudohermaphroditism* refers to individuals who have two gonads of the same kind, but have genitalia and other sex characteristics that show a mixture of male and female features.

It is generally believed that these psychological effects were produced by the prenatal masculinization of some system in the brain (probably the hypothalamus). This hypothesis fits in with the results of prenatal hormone administration in animals. For example, prenatally androgenized female monkeys act somewhat like human "tomboy" girls. Unlike normal monkey females, they engage in rough-and-tumble play with mutual chasing and mock fighting. Since monkeys have no culture that tells them about the appropriate female role, these effects are presumably based on constitutional changes that occurred during the prenatal period (Goy, 1968).

A critical period for gender identity? Until fairly recently, most practitioners felt that sex reassignment is virtually impossible after at most four or five years of age. This in turn led to the belief that there is a critical period for the establishment of gender identity (e.g., Money and Ehrhardt, 1972). But this view has been called into question by the discovery of a number of male children with a rare genetic disorder in three rural villages in the Dominican Republic. In the fetal stage, they are relatively insensitive to the effects of androgens. As a result, their external genitals at birth look much like a female's, and so they often are thought to be girls and raised as such. But puberty with its sudden upsurge in male hormone levels brings a dramatic change. The so-called girls develop male genitals, their voices deepen, and their torsos become muscular. If sex reassignment after age four or five is really as difficult or traumatic as it has been said to be, there ought to be a psychological catastrophe. But in fact, the great majority of these adolescents come to adopt their new male identity with relatively little difficulty. They change their name and take up male occupations. While they are initially anxious about sexual relationships, they ultimately seem to be fairly successful. Thus fifteen out of sixteen subjects eventually married or lived in common-law relationships (Imperato-McGinley et al., 1974, Imperato-McGinley et al., 1979).

It's hard to know how this surprising finding should be interpreted. The successful change in gender identity may be a result of the massive increase in androgen at puberty. It may also reflect the role of social factors, for these changes are by now accepted by the community and are common enough so that the villagers have coined a name for individuals with this condition: *machihembra* (first woman, then man). For machihembra, girlhood isn't a given—it's a phase. In any case, the phenomenon is an argument against the view that gender identity is essentially unchangeable after the age of five.

THEORIES OF GENDER TYPING

Social factors are evidently of great importance in fashioning our sense of being men or women, and they shape our behavior accordingly. But exactly how do these social factors exert their effects? Each of the three main theories of socialization—psychoanalysis, social learning theory, and the cognitive developmental approach—has attempted an answer (see Figure 14.13).

PSYCHOANALYTIC THEORY

According to Freud's psychoanalytic theory, the basic mechanism for determining gender identity is *identification.* The child models himself or herself on the same-sex parent in an effort to become like him or her. In Freud's view, identification is the end product of a mother-father-child triangle that he called the Oedipal conflict, which culminates at about age five or six. This identification

Male and female models (*Top: photograph by Suzanne Szasz. Bottom: photograph by Burk Uzzle/Woodfin Camp*)

14.13   Three theories of sex typing
*The figure summarizes the three major
theories of sex typing (for females).*

also has implications for sexual orientation, as we discuss below. (We will discuss
the Oedipal conflict when we discuss psychoanalytic theory; see Chapter 17).

SOCIAL LEARNING THEORY

A very different position is held by social learning theorists, who argue that children behave in gender-appropriate ways for the simplest of possible reasons:
They are rewarded if they do so and are punished if they don't. For the most
part, they learn what each sex is supposed to do by *imitation.*

But whom shall they imitate? They quickly discover that they must choose a
model of their own sex (usually a parent or caretaker). For example, a girl imitates her mother and is rewarded for rocking the baby (at that point a doll may
have to do), for prettying herself up, and for being Mommy's little helper. The
boy who imitates these maternal acts will be ridiculed and called a sissy. He will
do better by imitating his father, who rewards him for doing boylike things
(Mischel, 1970).

Why do parents push their sons and daughters into different social molds? A
social learning theorist would probably reply that the parents' behavior (as well
as that of peers, teachers, and so on) is also shaped by various reinforcers, all of
which act to maintain a particular gender-typed social structure. In effect, the
socialization of children is simply an apprenticeship for the roles they will adopt
as adults.

COGNITIVE DEVELOPMENTAL THEORY

Yet another proposal was offered by Lawrence Kohlberg, who regarded gender
typing in the context of cognitive development. Kohlberg's emphasis was on the

A four-year-old and her doll *Is she trying to live up to her gender identity or simply acting like a parent? (Photograph by Erika Stone)*

child's emerging awareness of his or her gender identity—the sense of being male or female. While social learning theory emphasizes what boys and girls must learn to *do* to fit the role of man or woman, Kohlberg focuses on what boys and girls must *understand* to recognize that they belong to the category man or woman (Kohlberg, 1966).

According to Kohlberg, the concept of gender is quite vague until the child is five or six years old. The four-year-old has only a shadowy notion of what the categories "male" and "female" mean. He has no real comprehension of how these categories pertain to genital anatomy. When presented with dolls that have either male or female genitals and varying hair length and asked to tell which are the boys and which the girls, preschoolers generally decide on the basis of hair length (McConaghy, 1979; but see Bem, 1989). This point is made rather dramatically in a story about a four-year-old boy who had been successfully taught the true meaning of gender and came to nursery school one day wearing a barrette:

> Several times that day, another little boy told Jeremy that he, Jeremy, must be a girl because "only girls wear barrettes." After trying to explain to this child that "wearing barrettes doesn't matter" and that "being a boy means having a penis and testicles," Jeremy finally pulled down his pants as a way of making his point more convincingly. The other child was not impressed. He simply said, "Everybody has a penis; only girls wear barrettes." (Bem, 1984, p. 216)

Needless to say, adults might find it rather difficult to adopt Jeremy's stringent test in deciding whether the person they're addressing is male or female. But the example highlights the confusion that many children have about the ultimate meaning of the "male" and "female" categories. A related phenomenon is the fact that four-year-olds don't really understand that gender is one of the permanent and (for all intents and purposes) unchangeable attributes of the self. Children develop a sense of gender identity by about age three. But it takes them another two years or so to achieve the concept of ***gender constancy***—the recognition that being male or female is irrevocable. When shown a picture of a girl, four-year-olds say that she could be a boy if she wanted to or if she wore a boy's haircut or wore a boy's clothes. But in Kohlberg's view, the problem is not with gender as such. For many four-year-olds also say that a cat could be a dog if it wanted to or if its whiskers were cut off. This suggests that the lack of gender constancy is just another reflection of the preschooler's failure to comprehend the underlying constancies of the universe. After all, children at this stage of cognitive development don't consistently conserve liquid quantity, mass, or number (see Chapter 13).

According to Kohlberg, the child's identification with the parent of the same sex *follows* the acquisition of gender identity. Once they recognize that they are boys or girls, they will try to live up to their sense of gender identity, to act in a manner that befits their own self-concept. They will now look for appropriate models—and the most readily available ones are usually their mothers and fathers—that can show them how to get better and better at being a male or a female.

SEXUAL ORIENTATION

The majority of men and women are ***heterosexual;*** they exclusively seek a partner of the opposite sex. But for a significant minority, the sexual orientation is otherwise. Some of them experience erotic and romantic feelings exclusively toward members of their own sex; such people are ***homosexual.***

Others experience such feelings for both their own and the opposite sex; such people are **bisexual**.★

Regardless of this variation in sexual orientation, however, virtually all gay and bisexual men think of themselves as men and are so regarded by others; the analogous point holds for lesbians (Marmor, 1975). This clearly illustrates the fact that sexual orientation, gender identity, and gender role are in principle independent.

THE PREVALENCE OF HOMOSEXUALITY

Perhaps the most comprehensive study of sexual patterns among Americans was an anonymous survey conducted in the 1940s by a research team led by biologist Alfred Kinsey. Kinsey and his associates found that 4 percent of American men are exclusively homosexual during their lifetime (Kinsey, Pomeroy, and Martin, 1948). The comparable prevalence of exclusive homosexuality among women seems to be lower—about 2 percent (Kinsey et al., 1953). But when Kinsey tallied those men and women whose orientation was predominantly homosexual but who had some heterosexual experience, the percentages increased to about 13 percent for men and 7 percent for women. Some feel that this estimate is too high, arguing that Kinsey's survey sample was not adequately representative (Reisman and Eichel, 1990). One study, using quite stringent criteria that focused entirely on actual behavior, reported only a 2 percent rate of exclusive male homosexual orientation (Hamer et al., 1993a,b), but recent surveys of both men and women in other Western cultures accord basically with Kinsey's estimates of exclusive homosexuality (e.g., ACSF Investigators, 1992; Johnson et al., 1992). In general, it's probably not surprising that studies that focus on activity (engaging in sexual behavior with members of one's own sex) and on perceived identity (regarding oneself as gay or lesbian) tend to report lower percentages than studies that ask about feeling and desire.

It's evident that a substantial number of men and women are erotically and romantically oriented toward a partner of their own sex despite the fact that our society sharply stigmatizes such behavior. This cultural taboo against homosexual behavior is by no means universal, however. According to one cross-cultural survey, two-thirds of the societies studied regarded homosexuality as normal and acceptable, at least for some people or for some age groups (Ford and Beach, 1951). In certain historical periods the practice was glorified and extolled, as in classical Greece where Pericles, the great Athenian statesman, was regarded as rather odd because he was *not* attracted to beautiful boys.

In this context it's important to realize that much of the sexual behavior of gays and lesbians revolves around feelings of romance and love just as does that of heterosexual people. There is a widely held belief that the homosexual orientation only leads to brief and furtive liaisons, especially among gay men. While this may be true for some subgroups, it does not seem to describe a majority of the gay and lesbian population. On the contrary, many gays and lesbians form lasting bonds and become couples, despite the fact that our culture does not offer any recognized route for such relationships (Mattison and McWhirter, 1987; Green and Clunis, 1988).

WHAT CAUSES HOMOSEXUALITY: ENVIRONMENTAL FACTORS?

Experience in early life Some of the attempts at an explanation of what causes homosexuality focus on the role of childhood experience. An example is

Homosexual behavior in antiquity
Among the ancient Greeks homosexual relations between men were widely practiced and accepted, as the mural from the Tomb of the Diver (c. 480 B.C.–470 B.C.), found in what was a Greek settlement in southern Italy, suggests. (Courtesy of National Archaeological Museum, Paestum, Italy)

★ Since relatively little systematic study has been directed toward bisexuality, our primary focus here will be homosexuality. (For some recent discussions, however, see Paul, 1984, 1985).

A lesbian couple (© 1991 Joan E. Biren)

Freud's theory of male homosexuality. According to Freud, homosexuality is a response to fears aroused during the Oedipal conflict. The little boy is too terrified to compete with his father for his mother's affections, and his terror generalizes to other women. He therefore tries to propitiate the father by identifying with the mother instead (after all, Father loves *her*).

There is very little evidence to support Freud's theory. In one study, about 1,000 gays and lesbians provided various items of information about their life histories. There was some difference in how gay people and heterosexuals viewed their parents. Compared to heterosexual controls, gay people had a less satisfactory relationship with their parents, especially with those of their own sex. But on closer analysis, it turned out that these familial relationships did not have much of an effect on the development of sexual orientation. If gay men don't get along too well with their fathers (although in fact many of them do), this is probably because the fathers can't accept various aspects of their sons' sexual orientation. If so, the unsatisfactory father-son relationship is a result of the son's sexual orientation, not its cause. Something of the same sort applies to the mother-daughter relationship in lesbians. Such findings give little support to the psychoanalytic framework with its emphasis on the crucial role of the early family constellation (Bell, Weinberg, and Hammersmith, 1981).

Experience in later childhood or adolescence Further evidence undermines the widely held stereotype that homosexuality is produced when a boy is "seduced" by an older man or a girl by an older woman. In the same interview study, the main predictor of eventual homosexuality was the way people *felt* about sexuality in childhood and early adolescence rather than what they *did*. Homosexual feelings and erotic fantasies usually preceded any actual homosexual encounters people might have had (Bell, Weinberg, and Hammersmith, 1981). Many individuals report that "I've been that way all my life" (Saghir and Robins, 1973), and just as future heterosexuals imagine starstruck romances with members of the opposite sex, so do those who will become homosexual imagine same-sex love and romance. Same-sex desires and the corresponding fantasies usually emerge before biological puberty, sometimes as early as age three or four (Green 1979; Hamer et al., 1993; Zuger, 1984).

But perhaps the most decisive evidence against the idea that early sexual experience determines sexual orientation comes from other cultures. In a number of cultures there are socially prescribed periods of homosexual behavior, usually between boys and older men, which begin in childhood and last through adolescence. Despite this intensive homosexual experience, which occurs amid the boys' puberty and sexual awakening, at adulthood most of the young men show the expected heterosexual orientation and pursue marriage and fatherhood (Herdt, 1990; Stoller and Herdt, 1985).

WHAT CAUSES HOMOSEXUALITY: BIOLOGICAL FACTORS?

Childhood experience does not seem to provide the answer to what causes homosexuality. As an alternative, a number of investigators have looked to biology.

Genetics and inheritance patterns One approach has considered genetic dispositions. One line of evidence comes from twin studies: A man's chance of having a homosexual orientation is fully 52 percent if his identical twin has one, but decreases to 22 percent if his gay twin brother is fraternal (Bailey and Pillard,

1991). Likewise, a woman's chance of having a homosexual orientation is 48 percent if her identical twin sister has one, but only 16 percent if her lesbian twin sister is fraternal (Bailey et al., 1993).

A potential breakthrough in understanding how sexual orientation—or at least male homosexual orientation—may be inherited comes from a team of researchers led by geneticist Dean Hamer (Hamer et al., 1993). Hamer's team obtained results which suggest that the homosexual orientation in males might largely be attributed to a gene or genes in a specific area of the X-chromosome. These results are preliminary, but even if they hold up, the question remains of just what the X-linked genes do to produce the homosexual orientation. For example, they might code for an individual's sex-hormone makeup or for specific differences in brain structures. Each of these topics has received the attention of investigators.

Hormones in adulthood   Initially, a number of investigators focused upon sex hormones on the simple assumption that male heterosexuality is correlated with male hormone levels in the bloodstream. But their results were very inconsistent. Some authors found that androgen levels tend to be lower in gay men than in heterosexuals, while others obtained no such difference (e.g., Kolodny et al., 1971; Brodie et al., 1974). In any case, male hormone levels are a very implausible candidate as the cause of male homosexuality. For, as already mentioned, the administration of androgen to gay men enhances their sexual vigor but does not change its direction—their renewed interest is still toward homosexual partners (see Chapter 10; Kinsey, Pomeroy, and Martin, 1948). Male homosexuality is evidently not caused by an insufficiency of male hormones in adulthood. It seems reasonable to assume that an analogous statement applies to lesbians. (For another discussion of the relation between homosexual orientation and neuroendocrine effects, see Gladue, Green, and Hellman, 1984.)

Hormones in the prenatal environment   A recent hypothesis proposed by Ellis and Ames suggests that hormones are indeed critical to sexual orientation but that their influence is exerted prior to birth, sometime between the second and fifth month of pregnancy (Ellis and Ames, 1987). They argue that certain neural circuits in or around the hypothalamus become sexually differentiated by the hormones circulating in the fetal bloodstream at that time. If the normal hormonal condition is disrupted, then a male fetus will be incompletely masculinized, while a female fetus will be defeminized. According to a current version of this hypothesis, these prenatal effects are primarily found in males. If so, male homosexuality should be much more frequent in both humans and animals, as it indeed seems to be.

According to Ellis and Ames, prenatal hormonal disruptions can occur for a number of reasons, including unusual stress during pregnancy and genetically produced deviations. It may well be that such a prenatal hormonal deviation is the mechanism through which the genetic disposition operates.

Differences in brain structure   Among the most dramatic recent developments in understanding sexual orientation is the finding of differences in brain structure between individuals with heterosexual and homosexual orientations. Most investigators have concentrated upon the hypothalamus and compared heterosexual to homosexual men. One study by Simon Le Vay examined an area in the anterior hypothalamus that affects sexual behavior in animals and which was previously found to be twice as large in the brains of men than in those of women (Le Vay, 1991; Allen et al., 1989). When Le Vay looked at the brains of gay men, he found that this area of the hypothalamus was about the size of the same area in heterosexual women—only about half as large as this area in the brains of the heterosexual men.★

At present, the reasons for the brain differences are unknown; they might be genetic, hormonal, or both. Nor is it known whether the structures that differ in individuals with heterosexual versus homosexual orientations are indeed themselves the crucial areas that originally determined sexual orientation; they may have developed secondarily as a function of other differences. The jury is still out—but hard at work.

Evolution and homosexuality   The preceding discussion suggests that both homosexual and heterosexual orientations are at least partially based on biological predisposition. On the face of it, this seems to pose a puzzle. For one might suppose that individuals with a homosexual orientation reproduce less than those with a heterosexual one. From the standpoint of natural selection, then, wouldn't a homosexual orientation be expected to disappear?

This point is sometimes raised as a way to claim that a homosexual orientation must be biologically disadvantageous, in the sense of reducing the number of genes its bearer will leave to posterity. This argument presupposes that people with a homosexual orientation have far fewer children than heterosexuals. But this may not be true. It is very likely that through much of human history people who would now be regarded as gay or lesbian mated with people of the opposite sex and did have children. And it is likely that much the same is true today, for many people whose basic orientation is homosexual marry even so, in part because of the great pressure exerted by the social stigma attached to homosexuality. In addition, there are many people whose orientation is bisexual and who are thus just as likely to have children as are heterosexuals. If it's true that bisexuality is genetically related to homosexuality (which seems plausible, though there is no evidence as yet), there is yet another argument against the reproductive disadvantage of homosexuality.

Some sociobiologists have proposed that a homosexual orientation may enhance biological fitness in a more subtle way. We've previously seen that reproductive success can be assessed in terms of *inclusive fitness,* which considers not just one's own offspring but also that of one's kin (see Chapter 10). For example, individuals who don't have children themselves might be more free to tend to their sisters and brothers, and nieces and nephews, and thus ensure that they thrive. The result might well be a greater (though indirect) proliferation of one's genes than would be possible through one's own children.

This caretaking role is institutionalized in the role of the *berdache* found in Native American and Eskimo villages (Williams, 1986). The berdache is a man who often dresses like a woman, has sexual relations with both single and married men in the village, and is often regarded as a shaman. He also acts as a matchmaker and marital therapist, generously distributes resources to those in need, even acting as a "spare parent" if a mother or father should die. Having a berdache in the family is considered quite beneficial to the other family members. The berdache may, as the theory suggests, also benefit his own reproductive success indirectly through the relatives whose welfare he aids (Weinrich, 1987).

★ One might ask why these studies have focused only on gay men and say nothing about lesbians. The answer is both grim and straightforward. To perform these studies requires comparisons between the brains of persons whose sexual orientation can be verified. But the only time sexual orientation is normally a part of the medical record is in diagnosed cases of HIV infection. Thus in all of these studies, the brains of the homosexual males were obtained from men who died of AIDS. A number of considerations indicate that these brain differences cannot be attributed to any overall degenerative changes resulting from the disease, since they were limited to the hypothalamic area and not found in other cerebral regions (Le Vay, 1991).

TWO SIDES OF THE COIN

So what leads to homosexuality? A biological, genetically based predisposition is very likely a major factor that determines the direction of the child's emerging sexual desire. But cultural conditions undoubtedly contribute a heavy share in shaping how children see themselves as they grow up. So as yet there is no clear answer to this question. It may well be that the question simply represents the other side of the question, "What leads to heterosexuality?" This second question is rarely asked because most people take the heterosexual preference for granted. Yet if we did know how to explain the origin of heterosexuality, we would be much closer to an understanding of how homosexuality comes about as well.

Stating the two questions in this parallel form may help us see another point. People sometimes ask whether gay men and lesbians can somehow be transformed into heterosexual men and women. The answer is that such a transformation is extremely difficult if not impossible. Nor do most gay men and lesbians wish for such a change. Like heterosexuality, homosexuality is much more than a sexual preference that can be done or undone more or less at will. It represents a fundamental part of an individual's makeup, a makeup that essentially defines him or her.

Whatever the causes of a homosexual or bisexual orientation, one thing is clear: Such an orientation is not a psychological disorder or defect. It is only abnormal in the sense of being the orientation of a minority, say, of some 10 percent or so of the population—but so is left-handedness. Gays and lesbians are neither better nor worse than heterosexuals. While their number includes great artists (e.g., Leonardo da Vinci), writers (e.g., Gertrude Stein), and warriors (e.g., Alexander the Great), the great majority of them are rather ordinary people whose names will not be recorded in history books. The same no doubt holds for left-handers—and for heterosexuals.

DEVELOPMENT AFTER CHILDHOOD

Thus far, our primary focus in describing human development has been on infancy and childhood. This emphasis reflects the orientation of the major figures in the history of the field. Thus Piaget tried to describe the growth of the mind until the achievement of formal operations at about age eleven. Freud was even more narrowly focused on childhood; to him, the most important events of social development took place before the age of five or six. Both Freud and Piaget, in common with most developmental psychologists, understood the term *development* in much the sense in which it is generally used by biology: the processes by which the newly formed organism changes until it reaches maturity.

In recent years, a number of authors have argued that this interpretation of the term *development* is too narrow. In their view, there is no reason to assume that human personality stops developing after childhood, for humans continue to change as they pass through the life cycle. The problems faced by an adolescent boy are not the same as those of a young man about to get married or become a father, let alone those of a middle-aged man at the peak of his career, or of a seventy-year-old at the close of his. This being so, it seems reasonable to chart the course of psychological development after puberty is reached in the hope that one can find some psychological milestones in adult development

Erik Erikson *A pioneer in the study of development after childhood. (© 1990 Olive Pierce/Black Star)*

TABLE 14.2   ERIKSON'S EIGHT AGES OF MAN

Approximate age	Developmental task of that stage	Psychosocial crisis of that stage
0–1 ½ years	Attachment to mother, which lays foundation for later trust in others	Trust versus mistrust
1 ½–3 years	Gaining some basic control of self and environment (e.g., toilet training, exploration)	Autonomy versus shame and doubt
3–6 years	Becoming purposeful and directive	Initiative versus guilt
6 years–puberty	Developing social, physical, and school skills	Competence versus inferiority
Adolescence	Making transition from childhood to adulthood; developing a sense of identity	Identity versus role confusion
Early adulthood	Establishing intimate bonds of love and friendship	Intimacy versus isolation
Middle age	Fulfilling life goals that involve family, career, and society; developing concerns that embrace future generations	Productivity versus stagnation
Later years	Looking back over one's life and accepting its meaning	Integrity versus despair

SOURCE: Based on Erikson, 1963.

14.14   The growth spurt at adolescence
The figure shows the percentage of total growth after birth attained between the ages 0 and 20 years for overall height (dark red) and size of genital and reproductive organs (blue) averaged for males and females. (After Tanner, 1970)

analogous to those that students of child development have tried to describe for earlier ages (Baltes, Reese, and Lipsitt, 1980).

What are the stages of development after childhood? Most later investigators have been strongly affected by proposals of the psychoanalyst Erik Erikson. According to Erikson, all human beings pass through a series of major crises as they go through the life cycle. At each stage, there is a critical confrontation between the self the individual has achieved thus far and the various demands posed by his or her social and personal setting. In all, Erikson sets out "eight ages of man," of which the first few occur in early childhood and roughly correspond to Freud's oral, anal, and phallic stages (see Chapter 17, pp. 676–80). These are followed by adolescence, early adulthood, middle age, and the final years (Erikson, 1963; see Table 14.2).

Erikson's developmental scheme has influenced many investigators of adult development. We will continue to refer to his organization as we briefly discuss some issues in the study of adolescence and adulthood.

ADOLESCENCE

The term *adolescence* is derived from the Latin for "growing up." It is a period of transition in which the individual changes from a child to an adult. There are biological changes: a physical growth spurt, a change in bodily proportions, and the attainment of sexual maturity (see Figure 14.14).

Biological maturing ultimately leads to social and economic changes: from dependence on one's family to ever-increasing independence. And of course there are the numerous psychological changes that accompany the process of growing up. These include the progressive maturing of sexual attitudes and behavior that will ultimately allow the adolescent to start his or her own family, and the acquisition of various skills that will eventually enable him or her to become a fully functioning member of adult society. In effect, adolescence is simply a protracted version of what in birds is a rather abrupt procedure—the point at which fledglings are forced to fly out of the nest and to make their own way.

THE NATURE OF THE TRANSITION

Compared to other animals, humans attain sexual maturity rather late in their development. This is just another facet of an important difference between ourselves and our animal cousins—a lengthened period of immaturity and dependence that provides time for each generation to learn from the one before. When is this period over?

Biology has set a lower limit at roughly age fifteen for girls and seventeen for boys when physical growth is more or less complete. But the point that marks the beginning of adulthood is decreed by social conditions as well as biology. As an example, a study of colonial New England families shows that the age at which sons become autonomous from their parents changed over the course of four generations. The sons of the first settlers stayed on their parents' farm until their late twenties before they married and became economically independent. As farmland became scarcer and other opportunities opened in the surrounding villages and towns, the sons left home, learned a trade, married, and became autonomous at a younger age (Greven, 1970). But with the onset of mass education in the mid-nineteenth century, this pattern was reversed again. Instead of leaving to become an apprentice or take a job, more and more youths continued to live with their families and remained in school through their late teens. This allowed them to acquire the skills required for membership in a complex, technological society, but it postponed their social and economic independence and their full entry into the adult world (Elder, 1980).

Culture evidently has an important say in the when and how of the transition period. It also sets up special occasions that mark the end of that period or highlight certain points along the way. A number of human societies have **initiation rites** that signify induction into adulthood (Figure 14.15). In some preliterate cultures, these are violent, prolonged, and painful, especially in certain puberty rites for boys that involve ceremonial beatings and circumcision. According to some anthropologists, such initiation rites are especially severe in cultures that

A   **B**

14.15 Initiation rites   *These rites signify induction into adulthood, as in (A) a bar mitzvah, or (B) a South African ceremony in which young men of about 19 are initiated into full manhood by having to live in isolation for 2 months after a ritual circumcision. During this period, they are smeared with white clay to indicate that they are in a state of transition and in contact with ancestral spirits. (A: photograph by Blair Seitz, 1986/Photo Researchers. B: photograph by A. Bernhaut/PhotoResearchers)*

571

try to emphasize the dramatic distinction between the roles of children and adults, as well as between those of men and women. In our own society, the transition to full adulthood is much more gradual, with milestones that refer not just to biological changes but also to various educational and vocational attainments. It is therefore not too surprising that we have not one initiation rite but many (none of which would ever be regarded as especially severe): confirmations and bar (or bas) mitzvahs, "sweet sixteen" parties, high-school and college graduations, and so on. Each of them represents just one more step on a protracted road to adulthood (Burton and Whiting, 1961; Muuss, 1970).

Cultural factors also determine the time at which other benchmarks of development are reached. An example is the age at which virginity is lost, which has steadily decreased in our own society during the past few decades, reflecting a change in sexual mores for both men and women. This change is undoubtedly caused by many factors, not the least of which is the existence of increasingly effective methods of birth control that allow the separation of the emotional and recreational functions of sexuality from its reproductive ones.

IS ADOLESCENCE ALWAYS TURBULENT?

There is a traditional view of adolescence which holds that it is inevitably a period of great emotional stress. This notion goes back to the romantic movement of the early nineteenth century, when major writers such as Goethe wrote influential works that featured youths in desperate conflict with a cynical, adult world that drove them to despair, suicide, or violent rebellion. This position was later endorsed by a number of psychological theorists, including Sigmund Freud and many of his followers. To Freud, adolescence was necessarily a period of conflict, since this is the time when the sexual urges repressed during the closing phase of the Oedipal conflict can no longer be denied and clash violently with the unconscious prohibitions previously set up. Further conflicts center on struggles with the older generation, especially the same-sex parent, that were repressed in childhood but now come to the fore (see Chapter 17, pp. 678–80).

This traditional view of adolescence has been seriously challenged by several modern writers who argue that the turbulence of the period is by no means inevitable. Whether there is marked emotional disturbance depends on the way the culture handles the transition. Some evidence for this view comes from studies of preliterate cultures in which the shift from childhood to adulthood is very gradual. Among the Arapesh of New Guinea, the young increasingly participate in adult activities as they get older. The child begins by tilling her parents' garden and eventually tills her own. Given the relatively simple social and economic structure of Arapesh life, the change is not very drastic. Correspondingly, there seems to be no psychological crisis among the Arapesh during adolescence (Mead, 1939).

However enviable, the gentle adolescent transition of the Arapesh is difficult to achieve in our modern industrial society. It's hard to see how a five-year-old can help his father at his job if that job happens to be computer programming. Accordingly, one might expect a fair level of disturbance during adolescence in our own society. And indeed, such emotional disturbance is a theme often sounded by the mass media and much twentieth-century American literature (for example, J. D. Salinger's *Catcher in the Rye*). But in fact, a number of studies suggest that such turbulence is by no means universal among modern American adolescents. Several investigators find that for many adolescents "development . . . is slow, gradual, and unremarkable" (Josselson, 1980, p. 189). What probably matters is the particular social and psychological setting, which surely differs from individual to individual in a complex society such as ours.

Puberty by Edward Munch, 1895 (Copyright © The Munch Museum/The Munch-Ellingsen Group/ARS, 1994)

A   B   C

14.16 Adolescent fads *New adolescent fads spring up to maintain the differentiation between the adolescents' own world and that of the adults around them. They then disappear rather quickly to be replaced by yet newer fads. The photos show some such fads prominent at various times. (A) seventies— streaking, (B) eighties—punk fashions, (C) nineties—black rap singers' hairstyles. (Photographs by T. Lowell/Black Star, © Spencer Grant/The Picture Cube, © Jeff Greenberg/The Picture Cube)*

TRYING TO FIND A PERSONAL IDENTITY

It appears that adolescence is not necessarily a time of troubles. But even so, it does pose a number of serious problems as the adolescent has to prepare to become an autonomous individual in his or her own right. A number of writers have tried to understand some characteristic adolescent behavior patterns in light of this ultimate goal.

Establishing a separate world Unlike fledglings, adolescents in our society remain in the nest for quite a while after they can fly (or perhaps more precisely, get their driver's licenses). This probably makes it all the more essential for them to establish some elements of a separation between themselves and the world of their parents. As one means to this end, many adolescents adopt all kinds of external trappings of what's "now" and what's "in," such as distinctive tastes in dance steps, clothing, and idiom (Figure 14.16). These often change with bewildering rapidity as yesterday's adolescent fads diffuse into the broader social world and become today's adult fashions (as witness men's hairstyles). When this happens, new adolescent fads spring up to maintain the differentiation (Douvan and Adelson, 1958).

The identity crisis of adolescence According to Erikson, the separation from the adult's sphere is only one manifestation of what adolescents are really trying to achieve. Their major goal throughout this period is to discover who and what they really are as they go through what he calls an ***identity crisis.*** In our complex culture, there are many social roles, and adolescence is a time to try them on to see which one fits best—which vocation, which ideology, which group membership. The adolescent's primary question is, "Who am I?" and to answer it, he strikes a succession of postures, in part for the benefit of others, who then serve as a mirror in which he can see himself. Each role, each human relationship, each worldview is first temporarily adopted on an all-or-none basis with no room for compromise. Each is at first a costume. When the adolescent finds that some costume fits, it becomes the clothes of his adult identity (Erikson, 1963).

ADULTHOOD

Erikson describes a number of further stages of personality development. In young adulthood, the healthy individual has to achieve the capacity for closeness and intimacy through love or else suffer a sense of isolation that will permit only shallow human relationships. In early middle age, he has to develop

(Top: Photograph by Roberta Intrater. Bottom: Photograph © Benn Mitchell/Image Bank)

a sense of personal creativity that extends beyond his own self. This includes a concern for others, for his work, for the community of which he is a part. And toward the end of life, there is a final crisis during which each person has to come to terms with his own life and accept it for what it was, with a sense of integrity rather than of despair. Erikson eloquently sums up this final reckoning: "It is the acceptance of one's own and only life cycle as something that had to be and that, by necessity, permitted of no substitutes. . . . healthy children will not fear life if their elders have integrity enough not to fear death" (Erikson, 1963, pp. 268–69).

RECENT ATTEMPTS TO FIND COMMON STAGES

Erikson's developmental scheme is a literary and moving account of the human odyssey through life, but in what sense is it a true description? Are the crises he listed *the* crises through which all of us must pass, and are their characteristics what he described them to be? A number of modern investigators have studied adults at various stages of their lives to find out what, if any, patterns are common to a given time of life. By and large, most of them have described a number of developmental periods that resemble some of Erikson's "ages of man" (Gould, 1978; Levinson, 1978). Others have tried to find similarities between youthful patterns and adult fulfillment when the same person is interviewed some thirty years later (Vaillant, 1977; see Chapter 16).

A stage of adult development that has received considerable attention from both Erikson and later authors is the "midlife transition" (which sometimes amounts to a midlife crisis), in which the individual reappraises what she has done with her life thus far and may reevaluate her marriage and her career. It is a period when the individual begins to see physical changes that show that the summer of life is over and its autumn has begun, a recognition that may occur earlier in women than in men (in part, because of the psychological impact of menopause). There is a shift in the way one thinks about time, from "How long have I lived?" to "How much time do I have left?" Some investigators point out that the middle-aged person is in the middle in more than one sense as she observes her children grow up and her own parents age and die:

> It is as if there are two mirrors before me, each held at a partial angle. I see part of myself in my mother who is growing old, and part of her in me. In the other mirror I see part of myself in my daughter. . . . (Neugarten and Datan, quoted in Colarusso and Nemiroff, 1981, p. 124)

HOW UNIVERSAL ARE THE STAGES OF ADULT DEVELOPMENT?

There is enough consistency in the results obtained by various investigators of adult development to suggest that the stages and transitions they describe apply fairly widely to people in our time and place. But are they universal? When we considered various stage theories of child development, we asked whether these stages occur in all cultures. The same question can be asked about adult development. Is there a midlife transition among the Arapesh? Does an Eskimo villager of fifty go through an agonizing reappraisal of what he's done with his life to date? If the answer is no, then we have to ask ourselves what the various stages described by Erikson and other students of the adult life span really are.

Thus far there is little concrete evidence one way or the other, so we can only guess. Certain adult milestones are clearly biological. In all cultures, humans reach puberty, mate, have children, begin to age, go through female menopause or male climacteric, age still further, and finally die. But the kind of crises that confront persons at different points of the life cycle surely depend on the society in which they live.

An example of the effect of social conditions on adult crises is the transition into old age. Over a century ago in the United States, different generations often lived close together as part of an extended family. There was much less segregation by age than there is now; children, parents, and grandparents frequently lived under the same roof or close to each other in the same neighborhood. In times of economic hardship, older people contributed to the family's resources even when they were too old to work—by caring for the children of working mothers, helping with the housekeeping, and so on. Older people—especially women—had yet another function: They were often sought out for advice on matters of child rearing and homekeeping. But today, the elderly have no such recognized family role. They usually live apart, are effectively segregated from the rest of society, are excluded from the workforce, and have lost their role as esteemed advisers. Given these changes, it follows that the transition into old age today is quite different from what it was 150 years ago. People still age as they did then—although the proportion of people who live into their seventies and eighties has increased radically—but they view aging differently (Hareven, 1978).

Facts of this sort suggest that various aspects of the stages proposed by students of adult development may be quite specific to our society and can therefore not be said to be universal. But if so, can we say anything about the life cycle that goes beyond the narrow specifics of our own time and social condition? Perhaps the best suggestion comes from a lecture by Erikson in which he tried to define adulthood:

> . . . In youth you find out what you *care to do* and who you *care to be*. . . . In young adulthood you learn whom you *care to be with*. . . . In adulthood, however, you learn what and whom you can *take care of*. . . . (Erikson, 1974, p. 124)

(Photograph by Eve Arnold, Magnum)

The ages of man Jacob Blessing the Sons of Joseph *by Rembrandt, 1656 (Copyright by Staatliche Museem Kassel. Photograph by M. Busing)*

Seen in this light, the later phases of the life cycle can perhaps be regarded as the culmination of the progressive expansion of the social world that characterizes the entire course of social development from early infancy on. In a way, it is a final expansion in which our concern turns from ourselves to others and from our own present to their future (and in some cases, the future of all humanity).

This may or may not be a good description of what genuine adulthood *is*. But it seems like an admirable prescription for what it *ought* to be.

SUMMARY

1. The infant's *social development* begins with the first human bond he forms—his *attachment* to his mother (or other caregiver). Studies of infant humans and monkeys indicate that this attachment is not caused by the fact that the mother feeds them, but rather because she feels so "comforting." A separation from the mother generally leads to *separation anxiety*.

2. Developmental psychologists have tried to assess the quality of the child's attachment to the mother by observing the behavior of infants and young children in the "Strange Situation." There is some evidence that the quality of attachment at about fifteen months of age predicts behavior two years later, but there is some controversy as to whether this reflects a long-term effect of the early mother-child relationship or is based on other factors, such as persisting patterns in the mother-child relationship or some continuity of childhood temperament.

3. Some theorists have proposed that the attachment to the mother can only be formed during a sensitive period in early life. In part, this position derives from work on *imprinting* in birds. According to this view, if such an early attachment is not formed,

SUMMARY

later social development may be seriously impaired, as indicated by studies of motherless monkeys and children reared in deprived orphanages. But later work on monkey isolates and adopted children suggests that this impairment is not necessarily irrevocable and that there are good reasons to reassess the belief in the all-importance of early experience.

4.   The process of *socialization* continues with child rearing by the parents. Some important differences in the way children are reared depend on the dominant values of the culture of which the parents are a part. Modern attempts to explain the mechanisms that underlie socialization include *social learning theory*, which emphasizes *modeling*, and *cognitive developmental theory*, which emphasizes the role of understanding as opposed to imitation.

5.   Freud notwithstanding, the evidence indicates that different modes of weaning or toilet training have little or no long-term effects. What seems to matter instead is the general home atmosphere, as shown by the effects of *autocratic, permissive,* and *authoritative-reciprocal* patterns of child rearing. On the other hand, how the parents treat the child is partially determined by the child's own characteristics, as suggested by studies on infant *temperament.*

6.   One aspect of moral conduct concerns the *internalization* of prohibitions. According to some theorists, punishment is more likely to lead to such internalization if the threatened punishment fits the *principle of minimal sufficiency.* Another aspect of moral conduct involves altruistic acts. Studies of *empathy* and *empathic distress* suggest that some precursors of altruism may be present in early infancy.

7.   The study of *moral reasoning* has been strongly affected by Kohlberg's analysis of progressive stages in moral reasoning. According to a later critique by Carol Gilligan, there are some important sex differences in moral orientation, with men emphasizing justice and women stressing human relationships and compassion. Related differences have been found between different cultural groups.

8.   Socialization plays a role in determining various senses of being male or female, including *gender identity, gender role,* and *sexual orientation.*

9.   Certain psychological differences between the sexes may be based on biological differences. One is physical *aggression,* which tends to be more pronounced in men. Another is a tendency for men to perform better on spatial tests of mental ability than women do. Such biologically based differences—if any—are undoubtedly magnified by socially imposed gender roles. The importance of such social factors is dramatically illustrated by the effects of *sex reassignment* in childhood.

10.   Each of the three main theories of socialization—psychoanalysis, social learning theory, and cognitive developmental theory—tries to explain how social factors shape our sense of being male or female. Psychoanalysis asserts that the basic mechanism is *identification.* Social learning theory proposes that it is *imitation* of the parent of the same sex. Cognitive developmental theorists believe that identification comes after the child acquires gender identity, which presupposes an understanding of *gender constancy.*

11.   The causes of *sexual orientation* are not yet clear. There is little evidence to support the view that *homosexuality* is produced either by a particular pattern of relations with parents in early childhood or by childhood sexual experiences. Current evidence points to *differences in brain structure* and a *genetic link.* But whatever its causes, this sexual orientation (no less than heterosexuality) is a fairly stable condition that can be changed only with great difficulty, if at all.

12.   Development continues after childhood is past. Some theorists, notably Erik Erikson, have tried to map later stages of development. One such stage is *adolescence,* which marks the transition into adulthood.

PART FIVE

INDIVIDUAL DIFFERENCES

CHAPTER 15

INTELLIGENCE: ITS NATURE AND MEASUREMENT

MENTAL TESTS 582

THE STUDY OF VARIATION ▪ EVALUATING MENTAL TESTS ▪ USING TESTS FOR SELECTION

INTELLIGENCE TESTING 589

MEASURING INTELLIGENCE ▪ AN AREA OF APPLICATION: MENTAL RETARDATION ▪ INTELLIGENCE AND AGE

WHAT IS INTELLIGENCE? THE PSYCHOMETRIC APPROACH 599

THE STRUCTURE OF MENTAL ABILITIES

WHAT IS INTELLIGENCE? THE INFORMATION-PROCESSING APPROACH 602

SIMPLE COGNITIVE CORRELATES ▪ COMPLEX COGNITIVE COMPONENTS ▪ STRATEGIES AND INTELLECTUAL FUNCTIONING

WHAT IS INTELLIGENCE? BEYOND IQ 607

PRACTICAL INTELLIGENCE ▪ THE NOTION OF MULTIPLE INTELLIGENCES ▪ THE CULTURAL CONTEXT OF INTELLIGENCE

NATURE, NURTURE, AND IQ 611

SOME POLITICAL ISSUES ▪ GENETIC FACTORS ▪ ENVIRONMENTAL FACTORS ▪ HERITABILTY ▪ GROUP DIFFERENCES IN IQ

TAKING STOCK 623

SUMMARY 624

People are different. They vary in bodily characteristics such as height, weight, strength, and hair color. They also vary along many psychological dimensions. They may be proud or humble, adventurous or timid, gregarious or withdrawn, intelligent or dull—the list of psychological distinctions is very large. Thus far such individual differences have not been our main concern. Our emphasis has been on attempts to find general psychological laws—whether in physiological function, perception, memory, learning, or social behavior—that apply to all people. To be sure, we have occasionally dealt with individual differences, as in the discussions of handedness, color blindness, and variations in child rearing. But our focus was not on these differences as such; rather, it was on what they could tell us about people in general—on how color blindness could help to explain the underlying mechanisms of color vision or how variations in child rearing might help us understand some aspects of socialization. In effect, our concern was with the nature of humankind, not with particular men and women.

We now change our emphasis and consider individual differences as a topic in its own right. We will first deal with the measurement of psychological attributes, specifically intelligence and personality traits. We will then turn to the discussion of psychopathology and attempts to treat it, a field in which the fact that people are in some ways different— sometimes all too different—is starkly clear.

I n twentieth-century industrialized society, especially in the United States, the description of individual differences is a flourishing enterprise that has produced a multitude of psychological tests to assess various personal characteristics, especially those that pertain to intellectual aptitude. As we will see, the interest in individual differences grew in part from an effort to apply evolutionary ideas to humanity itself. But even more important was the social climate of the late nineteenth century, which provided a fertile soil for such concerns. The study of individual differences makes little sense in a society in which each person's adult role is fully determined by the social circumstances of his or her birth. In a caste society there is no need for vocational counselors or personnel managers. In such a society farmers beget farmers, soldiers beget soldiers, and princes beget princes; there is no point in administering mental tests to assist in educational selection or job placement. The interest in human differences arises only if such differences matter, if there is a social system that will accommodate them.

In a complex, industrialized society like our own, with its many different socioeconomic niches and some mobility across them, there is a real use for the systematic assessment of human characteristics. Such a society will try to find a means, however imperfect, for selecting the proper person to occupy the proper niche.

Mental tests were meant to supply this means. They were devised as instruments to help in educational and occupational selection or for use in various forms of personal guidance and diagnosis. As such, they are often regarded as one of the major contributions of psychology to the world of practical affairs. However, for this very reason, the discussion of test results and applications necessarily touches upon social and political issues that go beyond the usual confines of scientific discourse. Under the circumstances, it is hardly surprising that some of the questions raised by testing, especially intelligence testing, are often debated in an emotionally charged atmosphere. Should a student be denied admission to a college because of his or her Scholastic Aptitude Test score? Are such tests fair to disadvantaged ethnic or racial groups? Are scores on such tests determined by heredity, by environment, by both? This chapter will not be able to provide definite answers to all of these questions. Some involve judgments about social and political matters; others hinge on unresolved issues of fact. Our primary purpose is to provide the background against which such questions have to be evaluated.

MENTAL TESTS

Mental tests come in different varieties. Some are tests of *achievement;* they measure what an individual can do now, his present knowledge and competence in a given area—how well he understands computer language or how well he can draw. Other tests are tests of *aptitude;* they predict what an individual will be able to do later, given the proper training and the right motivation. An example is a test of mechanical aptitude, which tries to determine the likelihood that an individual will do well as an engineer after an appropriate training period. *Intelligence tests* are sometimes considered tests of a very general cognitive aptitude, including the ability to benefit from schooling. In certain cases, a useful instrument is a *neuropsychological test* to assess learning disabilities and the effects of brain injury. Still another kind of test is a *test of personality,* which tries to assess an individual's characteristic behavior dispositions—whether she is generally outgoing or withdrawn, confident or insecure, placid or moody, and so on.

We will consider the nature of mental tests in general, regardless of what in particular they try to measure. But to understand the reasoning that underlies the construction and use of mental tests, we must first take a detour and look at the general problem of variability and of its measurement.

THE STUDY OF VARIATION

The study of how individuals differ from each other grew up in close association with the development of statistical methods. Until the nineteenth century, the term **statistics** meant little more than the systematic collection of various state records (*state*-istics) such as birth and death rates or the physical measurements of army recruits. In poring over such figures, the Belgian scientist Adolphe Quetelet (1796–1874) saw that many of them fell into a pattern. From this, he determined the **frequency distribution** of various sets of observations, that is, the frequency with which individual cases are distributed over different intervals along some measure. For example, he plotted the frequency distribution of the chest expansion of Scottish soldiers, noting the number of cases that fell into various intervals, from 33 to 33.9 inches, 34 to 34.9 inches, and so on (see Table 15.1).

**TABLE 15.1
QUETELET'S DISTRIBU-
TIONS OF CHEST MEA-
SURES OF SCOTTISH
SOLDIERS**

Measures of the chest in inches	Number of men per 10,000
33	4
34	31
35	141
36	322
37	732
38	1,305
39	1,867
40	1,882
41	1,628
42	1,148
43	645
44	160
45	87
46	38
47	7
48	2

Quetelet noticed two facts about his results. One was that his scores tended to cluster around a central value. One of the most common measures of this **central tendency** is the **mean,** or simple average, which is obtained by summing all of the values and dividing by the total number of cases. But the clustering tendency is by no means perfect, for there is **variability** around the average. All Scottish soldiers are not alike, whether in their chest sizes or anything else. An important measure of variability in a distribution is the **variance (V).** This is computed by taking the difference between each score and the mean, squaring this difference, and then taking the average of these squared differences. For many purposes, a more useful measure of variability is the **standard deviation (SD),** which is simply the square root of the variance.★

Quetelet's main contribution was the realization that, when put on a graph, the frequency distributions of various human physical attributes have a characteristic bell-shaped form. This symmetrical curve approximates the **normal curve,** which had already been studied by mathematicians in connection with games of chance. The normal curve describes the probability of obtaining certain combinations of chance events. Suppose, for example, that someone has the patience to throw six coins for over a hundred trials. How often will the coins fall to yield six heads, or five, four, three, two, one, or none? The expected distribution is shown in Figure 15.1, which also indicates what happened when a dedicated statistician actually performed the experiment. As more and more coins are thrown on any one trial, the expected distribution will approach the normal curve (Figure 15.2).

According to Quetelet, the variability found in many human characteristics can be explained in similar terms. He believed that nature aims at an ideal value—whether of height, weight, or chest size—but that it generally misses the mark, sometimes falling short and sometimes overshooting. For example, one's height depends upon a host of factors, some of which lead to an increase, others to a decrease. But each of these factors is independent of the others, and the operation of each is determined by chance. Thus nature is in effect throwing a multitude of coins to determine any one person's height. Each time the coin comes up "heads," it adds, say, a millimeter, and each time it comes up "tails," it subtracts one. The result is a frequency distribution of heights that approximates a normal curve.

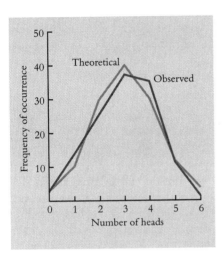

15.1   Theoretical and observed distribution of number of heads in 128 throws of six coins   *(After Anastasi, 1958)*

★ For a fuller description of these and other statistical matters that will be referred to in this chapter, see the Appendix, "Statistics: The Collection, Organization, and Interpretation of Data."

15.2   The normal curve   *(A) The probability of the number of heads that will occur in a given number of coin tosses. (B) When the number of coins tossed approaches infinity, the resulting distribution is the normal curve. The fact that this curve describes the distribution of many physical and mental attributes suggests that these attributes are affected by a multitude of independent factors, some pulling one way and some another.*

15.3 Evolution of the honeycreeper
These related species of Hawaiian honeycreepers display dramatic differences in beak size and shape. Like the finches that provided an important impetus to Darwin's theory of natural selection, these honeycreepers are thought to have evolved from a common ancestor. (Courtesy of H. Douglas Pratt)

Francis Galton *A pioneer in the study of individual differences. (Courtesy of National Library of Medicine)*

VARIABILITY AND DARWIN

After Darwin published the *Origin of Species,* variability within a species was suddenly considered in a new perspective. Darwin showed that variability provides the raw material on which natural selection can work. Suppose that the average finch on a paricular island has a fairly long and narrow beak. There is some variability; a few finches have beaks that are shorter and wider. These few will be able to crack certain hard seeds that the other finches cannot open. If these hard seeds suddenly become the primary foodstuffs in the habitat (perhaps because of a change in its climate), the short-beaked finches may find themselves at a reproductive advantage. They will outlive and thus outbreed their long-beaked comrades and eventually a new species may be born (or more precisely, hatched). Seen in this light, variability is far from being an error of nature that missed the ideal mark as Quetelet had thought. On the contrary, it is the very stuff of which evolution is made. It gives natural selection something to select *from* (Figure 15.3).

CORRELATION

Could this line of reasoning be applied to variations in human characteristics? It might, if these characteristics could be shown to be hereditary, at least in part. This assumption seemed reasonable enough for the physical attributes, such as chest size that Quetelet tabulated, but is it appropriate for mental characteristics such as intellectual ability? A half-cousin of Darwin's, Francis Galton (1822–1911), spent much of his life trying to prove that it is. Most of the subsequent work in the area rests on the statistical methods he and his followers developed to test his assertions.

An important part of Galton's program called for the assessment of similarity among relatives. It was obvious from the start that children tend to be like their parents to some extent. The problem was to find some measure of this relationship.

As an example take a person's weight. How is this related to his height? The first step is to construct a **scatter diagram** in which one axis represents weight and the other height. Each person is represented by one point corresponding to his position along the weight and height axes (see Figure 15.4A). Inspection of the scatter diagram reveals that the two variables are related: as height goes up, so does weight. But this covariation, or **correlation,** is far from perfect. We can draw a **line of best fit** through the points in the scatter diagram, which allows us to make the best prediction of a person's weight given his height. But this prediction is relatively crude, for there is considerable variability around the line of best fit.

Galton and his stiudents developed a mathematical expression that summarizes both the direction and the strength of the relationship between the two measures. This is the **correlation coefficient,** which varies between +1.00 and –1.00 and is symbolized by the letter **r.** The plus or minus sign of the correlation coefficient indicates the direction of the relationship. In the case of height and weight this direction is positive: As height increases so does weight (Figure 15.4A). With other measures, the direction is negative: As the score on one measure increases, the score on the other declines(Figure 15.4B).

The strength of the correlation is expressed by its absolute value (that is, its value regardless of sign). A correlation of $r = .00$ indicates no relation whatsoever. An example might be the relation between a student's height and his scholastic aptitude score. If we plot the scatter diagram, the points will form no

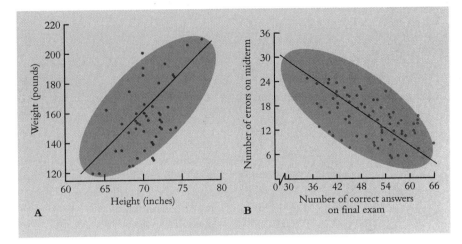

15.4   Correlation   *(A) A scatter diagram of the heights and weights of fifty male undergraduates. Note that the points fall within an ellipse, which indicates variation around the line of best fit. The correlation for these data was +.70. (Technically, there are two lines of best fit. One predicts weight from height; the other predicts height from weight. The line shown on the diagram is an average of these two.) (B) A scatter diagram of the test performances of seventy students in an introductory psychology course. The diagram plots number of errors in a midterm against number of correct answers on the final. The correlation was −.53. If errors (or correct answers) had been plotted on both exams, the correlation would, of course, have been positive.*

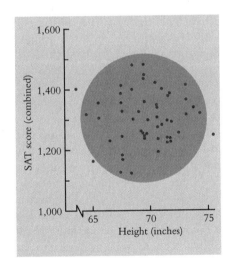

15.5   A correlation of zero   *A scatter diagram of Scholastic Aptitude Test scores and the heights of fifty undergraduate males. Not surprisingly, there was no relation, as shown by the fact that the points fall within a circle. The correlation was +.05, which for all essential purposes is equivalent to zero.*

pattern. There is thus no way of predicting a student's scholastic aptitude from his height, so there is no single line of best fit (Figure 15.5).

As the absolute value of *r* increases, the dots on the scatter diagram form an ellipse around the line of best fit. As the correlation goes up, the ellipse gets thinner and thinner. Note that as the ellipse gets thinner, there is less departure from the line of best fit. Thus, the thinner the ellipse, the less error there is as we try to predict the value of one variable (say, weight) when given the value of the other (say, height). When the absolute value of *r* reaches 1.00 (+1.00 or –1.00), the ellipse becomes a straight line. There is no more variation at all around the line of best fit; the correlation is perfect, and prediction is error-free. However, such perfect correlations are virtually never encountered in actual practice; even in the physical sciences there is bound to be some error of measurement.

While correlations are a useful index of the degree to which two variables are related, they have a limitation. The fact that two variables are correlated says nothing about the underlying causal relationship between them. Sometimes, there is none at all. Examples are correlations that are produced by some third factor. The number of umbrellas one sees on a given day is surely correlated with the number of people who wear raincoats. A Martian observing the human scene might conclude that umbrella-carrying causes raincoat-wearing or vice versa; our own earthly wisdom tells us that both are caused by rain. (For a discussion of correlation versus causation in the context of the effects of child rearing, see Chapter 14, pp. 549–50.)

EVALUATING MENTAL TESTS

An important application of the correlation techniques developed by Galton and his students was to mental testing for which they provided the underlying statistical methodology.

A   B

15.6   A test of art aptitude   *The person tested is presented with (A). Using the lines in this card as a start, he has to make a completed drawing. (B) A completed sample. The test score is based on ratings by an experienced art teacher. These scores correlated quite well (+.66) with grades in a special art course for high-school seniors. (Cronbach, 1970b. Test item from the Horn Art Aptitude Inventory, 1953; courtesy of Stoelting Co., Chicago)*

A   B

15.7   A test of mechanical comprehension   *One of the items asks, "Which man carries more weight?" (Sample item from the Bennett Test of Mechanical Comprehension; courtesy of The Psychological Corporation)*

A mental test is meant to be an objective yardstick to assess some psychological trait or capacity on which people differ (for example, artistic and mechanical aptitude; see Figures 15.6 and 15.7). But how can one tell that a given test actually accomplishes this objective?

RELIABILITY

One important criterion of the adequacy of a test is its ***reliability,*** the consistency with which it measures what it measures. Consider a bathroom scale. If the scale is in good condition, it will give virtually identical readings when the same object is repeatedly weighed. But if the scale is gradually losing its elasticity, repeated weighings will give different values. If it does this, we throw away the scale. It has proved to be unreliable.

The same logic underlies test reliability. One way of assessing this is by administering the same test twice to the same group of subjects, with, say, a few weeks in between. The correlation between test and retest scores will then be an index of the test's reliability.

One trouble with the ***test-retest method*** is that the performance on the retest may be affected by what the subject learned the first time around. For example, some people may look up the answers to questions they missed or avoid slip-ups they made the first time. To avoid these problems testers sometimes develop ***alternative forms*** of a test; reliability is then assessed by using one form on one occasion and another on a second.

Most standard psychological tests now in use have ***reliability coefficients*** (that is, test-retest correlations or correlations between alternative forms) in the .90s or in the high .80s. Tests with lower reliability are of little practical use in making decisions about enduring characteristics of individuals.

VALIDITY

High reliability alone does not guarantee that a test is a good measuring rod. Even more critical is a test's ***validity,*** which is most simply defined as the extent to which the test measures what it is supposed to measure. Again consider the spring scale. If the spring is made of good steel, the scale may be highly reliable. But suppose someone decides to use this scale to measure length. This bizarre step will produce an instrument of high reliability but virtually no validity. It measures some attribute very precisely and consistently but that attribute is not length. The weight scale is an accurate tool that happens to be irrelevant to the job at hand. As a test of length, the scale is invalid.

In the case of the spring scale, we can readily define the physical attribute that it is meant to measure and this lets us assess validity. But how can we define the psychological attribute that a mental test tries to assess?

Predictive validity   One approach is to consider the test's ***predictive validity,*** its ability to predict future performance. If a test claims to measure scholastic aptitude, a score on that test should predict later school or college performance. The same holds for tests of vocational aptitude, which ought to predict how people later succeed on the job. One index of a test's validity is the success with which it makes such predictions. This is usually measured by the correlation between the test score and some appropriate *criterion.* For scholastic aptitude, a common criterion is the grade-point average the student later attains. For vocational aptitude, it is some measure of later job proficiency. For example, aptitude tests for salespeople might be validated against their sales records.

Validity coefficients (that is, the correlations between test scores and criteria) for scholastic aptitude are generally in the neighborhood of .50 or .60, which means that the prediction is far from perfect. This is hardly surprising. For one thing, the tests probably don't provide a perfect index of one's "capacity" (ignoring for the time being just what this capacity might be). But even if they did, we would not expect validity coefficients of 1.00, for we all know that school grades depend on many factors in addition to ability (for example, motivation).

Construct validity   Predictive validity is not the only way of assessing whether a test measures what it claims to measure. Another approach is to establish that the test has **construct validity** (Cronbach and Meehl, 1955). This is the extent to which the performance on the test fits into a theoretical scheme—or construct—about the attribute the test tries to measure. For example, suppose someone tries to develop a test to assess behavioral tendencies toward depression (see Chapter 18). The validity of such a test would not be established by correlating it with any one factor, such as feelings of helplessness. Instead, the investigator would try to relate the test to a whole network of hypotheses about depression. To the extent that the results do indeed fit into this larger pattern, they confer construct validity on the test. Thus present-day chemical tests of pregnancy have both construct and predictive validity. They have construct validity because modern medical science knows enough about the hormonal changes during pregnancy to understand why the chemical reacts as it does. They also have predictive validity, for they correlate almost perfectly with the highly visible manifestations of pregnancy that appear a short time later.

STANDARDIZATION

To evaluate a test, we need another item of information in addition to its reliability and validity. We have to know something about the group on which the test was **standardized.** Suppose we learn that Rita's verbal aptitude score is 130. This number by itself provides very little information. It can, however, be interpreted by comparing it with the scores obtained by other people. These other scores provide the **norms** against which an individual's test scores are evaluated. To obtain these norms, the test is first administered to a large sample of the population on which the test is to be used. This initial group is the **standardization sample.** A crucial requirement in using tests is the comparability between the subjects who are tested and the standardization sample that yields the norms. If these two are drawn from different populations (an extreme example would be children versus adults), the test scores may not be interpretable.

UTILITY

There is one final measure of the worth of a mental test, even when the test has already been judged to be adequately valid, reliable, and standardized. This concerns the question of the test's *utility:* Is the test worth the time, energy, and cost required to admininster it? Suppose we have two tests of shyness, A and B. Both are well-standardized, but while test A has validity and reliability coefficients over .90, test B has coefficients of only .80. Test A appears to be better than test B, but there is a catch: Test A takes three days and costs $1,000 to administer, while test B is a quick ten-minute questionnaire that only costs $30. The benefits of discovering just exactly how shy you are may not be worth the additional $970; you may be perfectly happy with a ballpark result that is obtained faster and costs very much less.

USING TESTS FOR SELECTION

Suppose we have a test of good reliability, reasonable validity, and satisfactory utility. How is it used? One important application in our society is as a selection device. A well-known example is an aptitude test for pilot training developed by the Army Air Force during World War II. A large number of separate subtests were constructed for this purpose, including tests of motor coordination, reaction time, perceptual skills, and general intellectual ability. These subtests were administered to over 185,000 men who went through pilot training. The initial question was how each of these subtests correlated with the criterion—success or failure in training. The scores of each subtest were then combined to produce a composite score that gave the best estimate of the criterion. The use of this composite pilot aptitude test score led to an appreciable improvement in trainee selection. Without the test, the failure rate was 24 percent. By using the test to identify promising candidates, the failure rate was cut to 10 percent. This was accomplished by setting a ***cutoff score*** on the test below which no applicant was accepted (Flanagan, 1947).

Given a reasonable validity coefficient, the use of tests evidently helps to reduce the number of selection errors. The overall number of such errors declines as the validity coefficient of the test increases. But some errors will always be present, for validity coefficients are never at 1.00; in fact, most vocational aptitude testers count themselves lucky if they manage to obtain validity correlations of .40 or .50.

The important point is that selection errors are of two kinds. On the one hand, there are "inappropriate accepts," people who are accepted but who will fail. On the other hand, there are "inappropriate rejects," people who are rejected but who would have performed adequately. What determines which of the two kinds of errors will predominate? The answer depends upon the choice of the cutoff score. Suppose we decide to use a very stringent cutoff point. The result will be a marked reduction in the number of false accepts, but there is a price—an increased frequency of false rejects. We can reduce the number of false rejects by picking a lower cutoff score, but again there is a trade-off—a concomitant increase in the number of false accepts (Figure 15.8).

What cutoff score is the appropriate one? The answer hinges on the costs and benefits the selector assigns to each of the four possible outcomes: inappropriate accepts, inappropriate rejects, appropriate accepts, and appropriate rejects. These costs and benefits yield a ***payoff matrix*** similar to some we have already encountered (see Chapters 5 and 12).

15.8 Selection errors and cutoff scores
Applicants to pilot training are selected on the basis of an aptitude test. The line of best fit indicates the prediction of trainee performance from aptitude test score; the ellipse shows the variation around this line. The choice of a cutoff aptitude score, below which no applicant is accepted, determines the nature of selection errors. (A) A high cutoff score will increase the proportion of false rejects relative to false accepts. (B) A low cutoff score has the reverse effect.

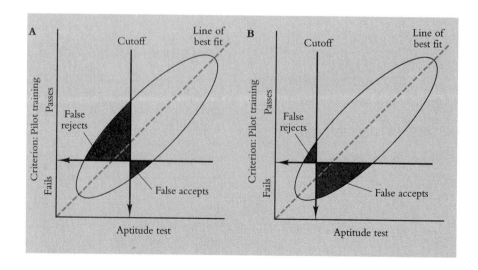

Just what these costs and benefits are depends upon a number of social, economic, and institutional values. Let us consider only the selection errors. Which is the more harmful? It obviously depends. In selecting combat pilots, there is a premium on avoiding inappropriate accepts. Pilot training is extremely costly. A trainee who doesn't make the grade represents a serious loss: in instruction time, in tying up expensive equipment, and—in case of really extreme failure—in life and limb. From the point of view of the air force, an inappropriate reject is much less serious. A rejected applicant who would in fact have succeeded as a pilot is still perfectly useful as a member of the ground crew. Under the circumstances, a high cutoff score makes good sense. In other selection situations, however, the payoff matrix may be very different. Suppose that there is a serious shortage in a particular occupation, say, engineering. If the number of applicants to engineering schools is relatively low, the schools would be well advised to set a lower cutoff point on an engineering aptitude test. Given the increased need for engineers and the reduced pool of applicants, there are good reasons to minimize inappropriate rejects. Graduating a few additional engineers may now be worth the price of a larger number of student dropouts.*

INTELLIGENCE TESTING

What is *intelligence?* In a crude sense, of course, we all have some notion of what the term refers to. The dictionary is full of adjectives that distinguish levels of intellectual functioning such as bright and dull, quick-witted and slow. Intelligence tests try to get at some attribute (or attributes) that roughly corresponds to such distinctions. One might think that the design of these tests began with a precise conception of what it was they were meant to test. But this was not the case. There was no consensus as to a definition of intelligence, and those definitions that were offered were usually so broad and all-inclusive as to be of little use. Intelligence was said to be a capacity, but what is it a capacity for? Is it a capacity for learning, for transfer, for abstract thinking, for judgment, comprehension, reason, or perhaps all of these? There was no agreement. Edward Thorndike suggested that intelligence might be defined "as the quality of mind . . . in respect to which Aristotle, Plato, Thucydides, and the like differed most from Athenian idiots of their day" (Thorndike, 1924). While this seemed sensible enough, it hardly went beyond the intuitive notions people had long before psychologists appeared on the scene.

MEASURING INTELLIGENCE

Given the difficulty in defining intelligence, devising tests for this hard-to-define attribute was an undertaking of a rather different sort from constructing a specialized aptitude test for prospective pilots. The pilot aptitude test

---

* There is a formal similarity between the selection problem just discussed and the decision subjects have to make in a detection experiment. In a detection study, a subject can make two kinds of errors: "false alarms," reporting a stimulus when in fact there is none, and "misses," failing to report a stimulus when in fact there is one. False alarms are analogous to inappropriate accepts, while misses are analogous to inappropriate rejects. In both the selection problem and the detection experiment, the choice between yea and nay is partially determined by a cutoff value, which in turn depends on a payoff matrix (see Chapter 5, p. 161).

has a rather clear-cut validity criterion. But what is the best validity criterion for intelligence tests? Since the nature of intelligence is unclear, we can't be sure of what the appropriate validity criterion might be.

But our theoretical ignorance notwithstanding, we do have intelligence tests and many of them. They were developed to fulfill certain practical needs. We may not understand exactly what it is that they assess, but the test consumers—schools, armies, industries—want them even so. The fact is that for many practical purposes these tests work quite well.

TESTING INTELLIGENCE IN CHILDREN

The pioneering step in intelligence testing was taken by a French psychologist, Alfred Binet (1857–1911). As so often in the field of individual differences, the impetus came from the world of practical affairs. By the turn of the century, compulsory elementary education was the rule among the industrialized nations. Large numbers of schoolchildren had to be dealt with, and some of them seemed untalented or even mentally retarded. If they were indeed retarded, it appeared best to send them to special schools. But mere backwardness was not deemed sufficient to justify this action; perhaps a child's prior education had been poor, or perhaps the child suffered from some illness. In 1904, the French minister of public instruction appointed a special committee, including Binet, and asked it to look into this matter. The committee concluded that there was a need for an objective diagnostic instrument to assess each child's intellectual state and to determine which pupils needed special programs. Much of what we now know about the measurement of intelligence comes from Binet's efforts to satisfy this need.

Intelligence as a general cognitive capacity Binet and his collaborator, Théophile Simon, started with the premise that intelligence is a rather general attribute that manifests itself in many spheres of cognitive functioning. This view led them to construct a test that included many tasks that varied in both content and difficulty—copying a drawing, repeating a string of digits, recognizing coins and making change, explaining absurdities. The child's performance on all these subtests yielded a composite score. Later studies showed that this composite measure correlated with the child's school grades and with the teacher's evaluations of the child's intelligence. The test evidently had some predictive validity.

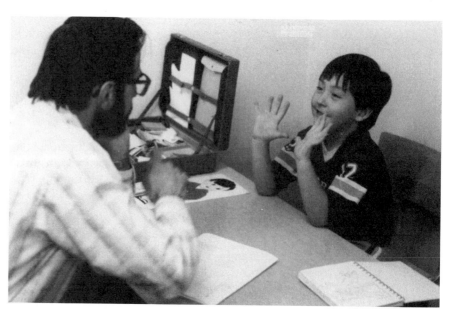

A boy taking the Stanford–Binet (Form L–M) (Photograph by Mimi Forsyth/ Monkmeyer)

Alfred Binet (Courtesy of National Library of Medicine)

The intelligence quotient, IQ Binet made another assumption about intelligence. He believed that it develops with age until maturity is reached. This fits in with our intuitive notions. We know that an average six-year-old is no intellectual match for an average nine-year-old. It's not just that she knows less; she's not as smart. This conception provided the basis for the test's scoring system. Binet and Simon first gave their test to a standardization sample composed of children of varying ages whose test performance provided the norms. Binet and Simon noted which items were passed by the average six-year-old, which by the average nine-year-old, and so on. (Items that were passed by younger but not by older children were excluded.)

This classification of the test items generated a ladder of tasks in which each rung corresponded to subtests that were passed by the average child of a given age. Testing a child's intelligence was thus tantamount to a determination of how high the child could ascend this ladder before the tasks finally became too difficult. The rung she attained indicated her **mental age** (usually abbreviated MA). If she successfully coped with all items passed by the average eight-year-old and failed all those passed by the average nine-year-old, her MA was said to be eight years.*

The MA assesses an absolute level of cognitive capacity. To determine whether a child is "bright" or "dull" one has to compare her MA with her chronological age (CA). To the extent that her MA exceeds her CA, we regard the child as "bright" or advanced; the opposite is true if the MA is below the CA. But a particular lag or advance clearly has different import depending upon the child's age. To cope with this difficulty, a German psychologist, William Stern (1871–1938), proposed the use of a ratio measure, the **intelligence quotient** or **IQ.** This is computed by dividing the MA by the CA. The resulting quotient is multiplied by 100 to get rid of decimal points. Thus,

$$IQ = MA/CA \times 100$$

By definition, an IQ of 100 indicates average intelligence; it means that the child's MA is equivalent to his CA and thus to the average score attained by his age-mates. By the same token, an IQ greater than 100 indicates that the child is above average, an IQ of less than 100 that he is below average.

Stern's quotient measure has various drawbacks. The major problem is that the top rung of Binet's mental age ladder was sixteen (in some later revisions of the test the ceiling was higher). In some ways this makes good sense, for intelligence does not grow forever, any more than height does. But since CAs keep on rising beyond the MA ceiling, the IQ (defined as a quotient) cannot help but decline. Consider the IQ of an adult. If her CA is 48 and her MA is 16, the use of the standard computation results in an IQ of 33 ($16/48 \times 100 = 33$), a score that indicates severe mental retardation—an obvious absurdity.

Eventually a new approach was adopted. In the last analysis, an intelligence score indicates how an individual stands in relation to an appropriate comparison sample—his own age-mates. The intelligence quotient expresses this comparison as a ratio, but there are more direct measures of getting at the same thing. One example is an individual's **percentile rank;** that is, the proportion of persons in his comparison group whose score is below his. A more commonly used measure that provides the same information is the **deviation IQ.** We will not go into the details of how this measure is arrived at; suffice it to say that an IQ of 100 indicates a score equal to the average of the comparison sample (and

---

* Appropriate scoring adjustments were made when the performance pattern did not work out quite as neatly; for example, if a child passed all items at the seven-year-old level, and 75 percent of those at the eight-year-old level, then her MA would be seven years and nine months.

thus a percentile rank of 50); that for most standard tests, IQs of 85 and 115 indicate percentile ranks of about 16 and 84, and IQs of 70 and 130 percentile ranks of 2 and 98.

TESTING INTELLIGENCE IN ADULTS

The Binet scales were originally meant for children, but demands soon arose for the assessment of adults' intelligence. This eventually led to the development of a test standardized on an adult population—the Wechsler Adult Intelligence Scale (Wechsler, 1958). This scale was divided into a verbal and a performance subtest. The verbal test includes items that assess general information, vocabulary, comprehension, and arithmetic. The performance test includes tasks that require the subject to assemble the cut-up parts of a familiar object so as to form the appropriate whole, to complete an incomplete drawing, or to rearrange a series of pictures so that they are in the proper sequence and tell a story (Figure 15.9).

COMPREHENSION
1. Why should we obey traffic laws and speed limits?
2. Why are antitrust laws necessary?
3. Why should we lock the doors and take the keys to our car when leaving the car parked?
4. What does this saying mean: "Kill two birds with one stone."

INFORMATION
1. Who wrote *Huckleberry Finn?*
2. Where is Finland?
3. At what temperature does paper burn?
4. What is entomology?

ARITHMETIC
1. How many 15¢ stamps can you buy for a dollar?
2. How many hours will it take a cyclist to travel 60 miles if he is going 12 miles an hour?

A. Verbal tests
3. A man bought a used stereo system for 3/4 of what it cost new. He paid $225 for it. How much did it cost new?
4. Six men can finish a job in ten days. How many men will be needed to finish the job in two and a half days?

B. Picture completion

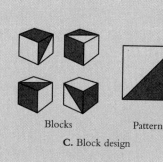

Blocks   Pattern

C. Block design

D. Object assembly

15.9   Test items similar to some in the Wechsler Adult Intelligence Scale.   *(A) Verbal tests. These include tests of information, comprehension, and arithmetic. (B) Picture completion. The task is to note the missing part. (C) Block design. The materials consist of four blocks, which are all dark green on some sides, all light green on other sides, and half dark green and half light green on the rest of the sides. The subject is shown a pattern and has to arrange the four blocks to produce this design. (D) Object assembly. The task is to arrange the cut-up pieces to form a familiar object. (Courtesy of The Psychological Corporation)*

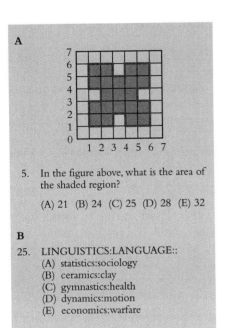

A

5. In the figure above, what is the area of the shaded region?

   (A) 21 (B) 24 (C) 25 (D) 28 (E) 32

B

25. LINGUISTICS:LANGUAGE::
    (A) statistics:sociology
    (B) ceramics:clay
    (C) gymnastics:health
    (D) dynamics:motion
    (E) economics:warfare

15.10   Two items from the Scholastic Aptitude Test (SAT) *(Courtesy of the College Entrance Examination Board and the Educational Testing Service)*

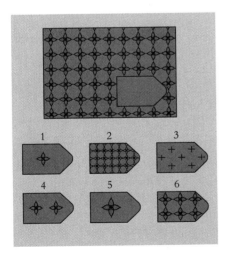

15.11   An example item from the Raven Progressive Matrices Test *The task is to select the alternative that fits into the empty slot above. (Courtesy of H. K. Lewis)*

GROUP TESTS

Both the Binet and the Wechsler scales are administered individually. This has the advantage of permitting a more careful evaluation of the person who is tested. But there is the obvious drawback that individual testing is a lengthy and expensive business. If the object is to assess a large number of people—army recruits, potential employees in large industial organizations, myriads of children in a city's schools, college applicants—the cost of administering tests individually becomes prohibitive.

Such economic facts of life led to the development of group tests of various cognitive and scholastic aptitudes, usually of the paper-and-pencil multiple-choice format. Some examples are the Scholastic Aptitude Test (SAT) taken by most college applicants, and the Graduate Record Examination (GRE), a more difficult version of the SAT designed for applicants to graduate schools (Figure 15.10). A test that emphasizes abstract, nonverbal intellectual ability is the Progressive Matrices Test (Figure 15.11).

SOME NEW DEVELOPMENTS IN INTELLIGENCE TESTING

A new test for children   In recent years, a new test for children has come to prominence, the *Kaufman Assessment Battery for Children (K-ABC)*. Like virtually all intelligence tests, this is an outgrowth of those devised by Binet and Wechsler. But it has two novel aspects. To begin with, its construction is based on some modern formulations that try to understand intelligence within the conceptual framework of information processing (see Chapters 7, 8, and 13). Some of its subtests assess the child's capacity for sequential cognitive processing, for example, his ability to recall a number of digits in the same sequence as he heard them or to copy the exact sequence in which the examiner tapped the table with his hand. Others assess his ability to process simultaneously presented information; for example, his ability to select the picture that best completes a visual analogy or to recall the location of items arranged randomly on a page. Another novelty is that the test gives particular attention to the assessment of handicapped children and is appropriate for cultural and linguistic minorities. Toward that end, it includes a nonverbal scale with questions that are presented in pantomime and have to be answered with various motor gestures. This scale is particularly useful for testing children who cannot speak English (or can't speak it well) or who are hearing-impaired, and its scores seem to be less affected by sociocultural conditions than those of the Stanford-Binet or of Wechsler's scales for children (Anastasia, 1984, 1985; Coffman, 1985; Kaufman, Kamphaus, and Kaufman, 1985; Page, 1985).

A neuropsychological test   An extension of intelligence testing in the neurological clinic tries to discover the particular cognitive deficits of a patient by asking why she gave an incorrect answer to a question. For example, most intelligence tests contain arithmetic questions that the examiner reads to the test taker. Indeed, the Wechsler Adult Intelligence Scale-Revised (WAIS-R) contains an entire arithmetic subtest in the verbal portion of the test. Thus, the test taker might be asked a question like the following:

   If it takes two bricklayers six days to build a wall, how many days would it take three bricklayers?

Here, an incorrect response may signify many things other than a weakness at arithmetic, because a correct answer requires that the examinee hear and under-

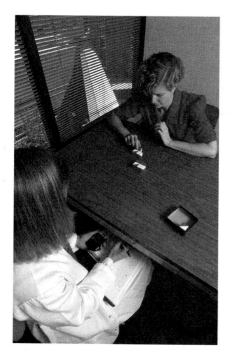

Block design test *While being timed by the test administrator, subject arranges her blocks to match the pattern of the blocks on the table. (Photograph © Will and Deni McIntyre, 1987)*

stand the question correctly (speech comprehension), keep the problem and the numbers in mind long enough to solve it (short-term memory), know how to set up the problem (mathematical reasoning), and do it quickly enough to give the answer in the allotted time (speed of problem solving), much less give the right answer on the final arithmetic.

Determining just where an individual's weakness is becomes very useful when one is trying to pinpoint cognitive impairments that may stem from learning disabilities, from normal aging, or from brain injuries or diseases (Heilman and Valenstein, 1979; Lezak, 1983; Orsini, Van Gorp, and Boone, 1988). This specialized kind of inquiry, called ***neuropsychological assessment,*** led to the development of an extension of the WAIS-R in which each standard subtest is followed by a succession of tasks that lets the neuropsychologist discover the point at which the examinee's performance falters (Kaplan et al., 1991).

For example in the arithmetic subtest all of the arithmetic questions are asked and the answers recorded and scored just in the usual way. But subsequently, the examinee is asked to return to the missed questions and attempt to answer them again. This time the questions will first be presented in written form and with no forced time limit to bypass any problems of speech comprehension or speed of responding. If the examinee can't answer the question in this form, she is asked to work out the solution on paper to lighten the memory load. If she still can't solve the problem, further steps are taken to determine whether the difficulty is in mathematical reasoning, in ignorance of the mulitplication table, and so on.

Similar methods have been used to construct tests designed specifically to assess verbal learning, abstraction, visuospatial perception, and motor functioning (Delis et al., 1988; Delis et al., 1990).

AN AREA OF APPLICATION: MENTAL RETARDATION

How valid are intelligence tests? One way of answering this question is by looking at their effectiveness in predicting school success, which as we've seen is fairly good, with correlations of around +.50. But another criterion grows out of Binet's original purpose, which was to design an instrument for the diagnosis of mental retardation. How well did he and his followers succeed? On the whole, the tests seem to perform this function rather well, at least as a first step toward diagnosis. The usual demarcation for retardation is an IQ of about 70 or below. Thus defined, about 2.5 percent of the population of the United States would be regarded as retarded (Grossman, 1983). But the test performance is by no means the only criterion of retardation. Equally important are social and cultural competence, the ability to learn and cope with the demands of society, to take care of oneself, to earn a living. This competence obviously depends in part upon the nature of the society in which a person lives. A complex technological culture like ours puts a higher premium on various intellectual skills than does an agrarian society. Someone classified as mildly retarded in twentieth-century America probably would have managed perfectly well in, say, feudal Europe.

CLASSIFYING RETARDATION

A widely used classification system distinguishes several degrees of retardation: mild (IQ of approximately 50–55 to 70), moderate (35–40 to 50–55), severe (20–25 to 35–40), and profound (20–25 and below). The more severe the retar-

TABLE 15.2 CHARACTERISTICS OF THE MENTALLY RETARDED*			
Degree of retardation	*IQ range*	*Level of functioning at school age (6–20 years)*	*Level of functioning in adulthood (21 years and over)*
Mild	50–55 to approx. 70	Can learn academic skills up to approximately sixth-grade level by late teens; can be guided toward social conformity.	Can usually achieve social and vocational skills adequate to maintain self-support, but may need guidance and assistance when under unusual social or economic stress.
Moderate	35–40 to 50–55	Can profit from training in social and occupational skills; unlikely to progress beyond second-grade level in academic subjects; may learn to travel alone in familiar places.	May achieve self-maintenance in unskilled or semiskilled work under sheltered conditions; needs supervision and guidance when under mild social or economic stress.
Severe	20–25 to 35–40	Can talk or learn to communicate; can be trained in elemental health habits; profits from systematic habit training.	May contribute partially to self-maintenance under complete supervision; can develop self-protection skills at a minimum useful level in controlled environment.
Profound	below 20–25	Some motor development present; may respond to minimal or limited training in self-help.	Some motor and speech development; may achieve very limited self-care; needs nursing care.

*Descriptive terms and score intervals are from a classificatory system recommended by the American Association for Mental Deficiency.
SOURCE: Grossman, 1983, p. 13.

dation, the less frequently it occurs: In 100 retarded persons, one would expect the degree of retardation to be mild in 90, moderate in 6, severe in 3, and profound in 1 of the cases (Robinson and Robinson, 1970).

Table 15.2 presents a description of the general level of intellectual functioning in each of these categories at various ages. Among other things, the table shows that mentally retarded persons do not have to be excluded from useful participation in society. This is especially true for those whose degree of retardation is mild, and they account for almost 90 percent of all the cases. If provided with appropriate education and training, such people can ultimately achieve an acceptable level of adjustment in adult life (Tyler, 1965).

Binet would have been pleased to learn that his tests (and their many descendants) help to diagnose mental retardation and thus aid in selecting appropriate treatment and training programs. But he would have been the first to insist that such test scores cannot be rigidly applied or used without a full knowledge of other facts about the person being tested. In addition to the test score, the diagnostician has to consider a whole set of factors, including the individual's emotional adjustment and his capacity to adjust to the everyday world in which he lives. As one author notes, "Individuals with IQs of 60 have been known to make satisfactory adjustments to the demands of daily living, while some with IQs close to 100 may require special care and guidance" (Anastasia, 1988, p. 285).

The danger of a slavish dependence on test scores is especially pronounced when diagnosing a child who belongs to a disadvantaged ethnic or racial minority or to a group with a different linguistic background. In such cases, there is a serious danger of misclassification because until recently most intelligence tests used norms that were based entirely on white, English-speaking standardization groups. To address this problem, some clinicians recommend the use of an assessment program that includes information about the child's social adjustment and sociocultural background and evaluates his test performance against norms taken from the child's own subgroup, so that the child is compared with other children who share his own background (Mercer, 1973). Some recent tests, such as the Kaufman Assessment Battery for Children, (see p. 593), are especially useful in this context, since they include nonverbal scales that are deliberately designed to minimize sociocultural biases and also have special subcultural norms for ethnic-group and parental education.

THE CAUSES OF RETARDATION

Retardation is not a condition that has one single cause. Instead, it can reflect any number of underlying factors, some of which are as yet unknown. Some forms of retardation are produced by genetic disorders or by aberrations in the chromosome structure (see pp. 613–14). Others are produced by brain damage suffered in the womb, during delivery, or after birth. Still others may reflect the composite effects of hundreds of genes. And yet others may be the result of impoverished enviromental conditions, especially during early life (Edgerton, 1979). One of the most important of these is severe malnutrition during the first two years or so of infancy (an all too common condition among infants of the very poor and of those in underdeveloped countries), which produces a profound and lasting depression of intellectual functioning (Birch et al., 1971; Stoch et al., 1982).

A number of investigators have tried to order this hodgepodge of known and unknown causal factors by arguing that cases of mental retardation can be classified into two main types—those that are produced by one factor and those that are produced by many. According to this hypothesis, **unifactor** forms correspond to the more severe varieties of retardation; these are thought to result from major pathology, such as a gene defect, chromosomal aberration, or brain damage. In contrast, mild retardation is believed to be a **multifactor** phenomenon. According to this view, mild retardation simply represents the lower portion of the distribution of intelligence. Seen in this light, intelligence in normal as well as mildly retarded persons is produced by the joint action of numerous separate factors, some genetic and others environmental. Adherents of this view believe that the lower end of the distribution consists of those unlucky cases for whom the majority of causal factors fell in the wrong direction (Zigler, 1967).

INTELLIGENCE AND AGE

What is the relation between intelligence-test performance and age? To be sure, age was the basis on which Binet standardized his original test, but he only used the age range of three to sixteen years. Numerous later investigators have extended this range by inquiring about the development of intelligence throughout the entire life span.

INTELLIGENCE IN THE INFANT

Initially, most developmental psychologists were very doubtful about the possibility of foretelling school-age intelligence from the behavior of infants below one year of age. To be sure, there were some well-established tests to assess mental development in early infancy, such as the Bayley Scales of Infant Development (see Table 15.3). To assess representative behaviors during the first year, the Bayley Scales rely heavily on various sensory-motor tasks performed by infants, such as following a moving stimulus with the eyes, reaching for an object, manipulating cubes, and so on. These tests were a fair enough measure of developmental rate in early life, but except in cases of severe retardation they proved to be of little use in predicting what happens in later years. The correlations between IQ in later childhood and performance in infancy were extremely low until the infant was at least eighteen months old (Bayley, 1970; McCall, 1979; Goodman, 1990).

Until recently, many developmental psychologists believed that the failure to predict later intellectual ability from infant performance followed from the nature of early infancy. In their view, intellectual development is essentially discontinuous; intelligence manifested in infancy is quite different from intelligence when the child starts school. But of late, this position has been challenged by, among others, Joseph Fagan, who insists that infants do differ in intellectual capacities that are genuine precursors of later intelligence. In his view, these capacities are not tapped by the Bayley Scales, which emphasize motor and sensory skills. The trick is to find a test that calls on genuine cognitive processes, such as attention and picking up information. According to Fagan, one such test is recognition of novelty. The infant is shown a stimulus until he habituates (that is, stops looking at it). He is then presented with two stimuli: the one he just looked at and another that is new. Will he prefer the novel stimulus? If he does,

TABLE 15.3 SOME CHARACTERISTIC ITEMS TO TEST MENTAL DEVELOPMENT IN INFANTS AND YOUNG CHILDREN

Item	Average age at which item is passed monthly
Turns eyes to light	2
Turns to sound	4
Lifts cup	6
Recognizes voices	8
Puts cube in cup	10
Imitates words	12
Makes tower of two cubes	14
Makes tower of three cubes	16
Puts cover on box	18
Turns doorknob	20
Names three objects	22
Names five pictures	24
Selects "big" object when asked	26
Understands three prepositions	28
Buttons one button	31
Names seven pictures	33

SOURCE: From Bayley, 1970.

he has recognized that it is different from the one he has just seen. To the extent that he can do this, he has presumably attended to various perceptual characteristics of the original stimulus, noted them, retained them, and eventually compared them to those of the new stimulus. Fagan argues that the ability to perform these various cognitive operations is related to later intelligence. As evidence he cites correlations between preference for novel stimuli at three to six months and traditional intelligence measures in later childhood (between two to seven years) that range from +.33 to +.66—very much higher than those obtained with the Bayley Scales (Fagan, 1984, 1985; for some critiques, see Kagan, 1989; McCall, 1989).

INTELLIGENCE IN LATER LIFE

Many investigators have tried to plot the growth of intelligence from middle childhood to old age. To do so, they administered the same test to people in different age groups matched by sex and socioeconomic level. Figure 15.12 presents a composite curve based on several such studies. The figure should hearten the young and bring gloom to all who are past age twenty. There is a sharp increase in mental ability between ages ten and twenty, and an accelerating decline thereafter.

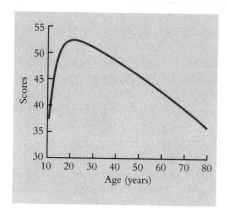

15.12 Mental test scores as related to age *The scores are based on comparisons of different age groups. They are expressed in units that allow comparisons of different tests and are based on averaged results of three different studies. (After Jones and Kaplan, 1945)*

Does intelligence really decline after twenty? Later investigators (perhaps prompted by the fact that they were over thirty) concluded that the situation could not be as bleak as that. They argued that the steep decline in intelligence across the adult years could be the by-product of an irrelevant factor: On the average, the older age groups in these studies had a lower level of education. Such a difference might have been present even though the groups were matched by years of schooling, for curricula have probably improved over time. One way of getting around this difficulty is by shifting from the **cross-sectional** method that compares people in different age groups to the **longitudinal** method in which the same people are tested at different ages. The results of such longitudinal studies suggest that age (or at least middle age) is not as deleterious to mental functioning as it seemed (Schaie and Strother, 1968; Schaie, 1979). There is a continued rise on tests for verbal meaning, for reasoning, and for educational aptitude until about age fifty. After this, there is a moderate decline.

Fluid and crystallized intelligence It appears that the precipitous decline of intelligence with age shown in Figure 15.12 was an artifact; this was avoided by the longitudinal comparisons. But does this mean that there is no decline in intelligence until age sixty or even later? Further work has shown that it depends on just what abilities are being tested. Many facets of verbal abilities do show little decline until age seventy. The results of tests of vocabulary are even more encouraging to those of later years; there is no drop in vocabulary even at age eighty-five (Blum, Jarvik, and Clark, 1970). In contrast, nonverbal abilities tapped by such tests as the Progressive Matrices decline earlier, usually around age forty (Green, 1969). The most pronounced drops are found for tests that depend on quick recall, especially when there is no memory organization available to help retrieval. An example from everyday life is memory for names, whose gradual worsening is bemoaned by many persons as they get older. An example from the laboratory is the word fluency test, in which the subject has two minutes to write down as many words as he can think of that start with a particular letter. Such mental calisthenics are best left to the young; declines in word fluency are very steep and are seen as early as thirty (Schaie and Strother, 1968).

Some authors believe that the different age curves obtained for different subtests of intelligence reflect an important distinction between two underlying intellectual abilities (Cattell, 1963). One is **_fluid intelligence,_** which is the ability to deal with essentially new problems. The other is **_crystallized intelligence,_** which is the repertoire of information, cognitive skills, and strategies acquired by the application of fluid intelligence to various fields. Examples of tasks that emphasize fluid intelligence are scrambled sentences and number series. Consider the set of words shown below:

Tree pick an climbed man our apple the to

When a person is asked to rearrange these words to make a meaningful sentence, she has to reason it out. Here fluency, speed, and flexibilty will help out greatly. The same holds for number series, such as the one below in which the task is to find the number that is next in the series:

3 8 12 15 17

In contrast, tasks that primarily rely on crystallized intelligence are exemplified by tests of vocabulary (e.g., what does "amanuensis" mean?) or of calculation (e.g., $6 \times 7 - 4 \times 5 = ?$). Such tasks depend less on processing speed and more on stored knowledge.

According to the theory, fluid intelligence declines with age, beginning in middle adulthood or earlier. But crystallized intelligence does not drop off. On the contrary, it continues to grow until old age as long as the person is in an intellectually stimulating environment. From the point of view of actual functioning in middle age and beyond, the drop in the one ability may be more than compensated for by the increase in the other. The older person has "appropriated the collective intelligence of the culture for his own use" (Horn and Cattell, 1967). By so doing, he has not only amassed a large store of knowledge, but he has also developed better ways of organizing this knowledge, of approaching problems, and of filing new information away for later use.

These cognitive achievements are similar to those we discussed in Chapter 8 in which we considered the distinction between masters and apprentices. The masters have chunked and organized the material at a different level than the apprentices. On balance, then, the slight loss in fluid intelligence can be tolerated if made up for by an increase in crystallized intelligence.

WHAT IS INTELLIGENCE? THE PSYCHOMETRIC APPROACH

We have seen that intelligence tests were developed even though there was no consensus on a definition of intelligence and thus no clear-cut validity criterion for any test that claims to measure it. But even so, many psychologists would agree that such instruments as the Stanford-Binet and the Wechsler tests do distinguish people in ways that correspond with our intuitive conceptions of the term *intelligence*. There is no doubt that either scale would easily differentiate between Aristotle and the Athenian village idiot. Can we get any further than this?

According to one group of investigators, further inquiries into the nature of intelligence can build on the fact that intelligence tests do make some distinctions between people and that these distinctions do fit our initial sense of what intelligence is about. These investigators believe that we can refine our knowledge of the nature of intelligence by a careful further study of these distinctions.

This line of reasoning underlies the *psychometric approach* to the study of intelligence. It amounts to a bootstrap operation in which one scrutinizes the results provided by the measuring instrument in order to find out what the instrument really measures.

THE STRUCTURE OF MENTAL ABILITIES

To understand the psychometric approach, consider how it addresses a central question about intelligence: Is intelligence a unitary ability? In principle one could imagine several kinds of mental ability that are quite unrelated. Perhaps different cognitive tasks draw on distinctly different cognitive gifts. It may also be that the truth is in between, that human intellectual abilities are composed of both general and more particular capacities. How can we decide among these alternatives?

The psychometric approach tries to answer these questions by starting with people's scores on various tests. These scores presumably reflect some underlying abilities—perhaps one, perhaps several. But these underlying capacities are not observable directly; they can only be inferred from the scores. Students of psychometrics have tried to perform this inference by looking at the intercorrelations among different tests.

To get an intuitive idea of this general approach, consider a man who looks at a lake and sees what appear to be serpentlike parts:

A

He can entertain various hypotheses. One is that all visible parts belong to one huge sea monster (a hypothesis that is analogous to the assumption that there is a unitary intellectual ability):

B

He might also assume that there are several such beasts (analogous to separate mental abilities):

C

Or finally, he might believe that there are as many sea animals as there are visible parts (analogous to the hypothesis that every test measures a totally different ability):

D

How can he choose among these alternatives, given that he has no way of peering below the waters? His best bet is to wait and watch how the serpentine parts change over time and space. If he does this, he can find out which parts go together. If all parts move jointly (B), the most reasonable interpretation is that they all belong to one huge sea monster. (For the purposes of our example, we will assume that sea serpents are severely arthritic and are unable to move their body portions separately.) If the first part goes with the second, while the third goes with the fourth (C), there are presumably two smaller creatures. If all parts move separately (D), the best bet is that there are as many sea serpents as there are visible parts. In effect, our sea-serpent watcher has studied a correlation pattern; this pattern allows him to infer the invisible structure (or structures) under the surface.

SPEARMAN AND THE CONCEPT OF GENERAL INTELLIGENCE

The psychometric equivalent of the joint movements of sea-serpent portions is the correlation pattern among different tests of mental abilities. As an example, consider the correlations among four subtests of the Wechsler Adult Scale: information *(I)*, comprehension *(C)*, arithmetic *(A)*, and vocabulary *(V)*. These intercorrelations are all quite high. The correlation between I and C is +.70, that between I and A is +.66, and so on. These results can be presented in the form of a **correlation matrix,** in which the intercorrelations can be read off directly (Table 15.4).

An inspection of this correlation matrix suggests that there may be a common factor that runs through all four of these subtests. In essence, those people with a greater fund of information turn out to be exactly those people who are likely to get higher scores in comprehension. They are also probably better at arithmetic, and they generally have a larger vocabulary as well. Conversely, those people who do poorly on any one of these tests, are also likely to do poorly on the others. This makes it plausible to assume that these subtests share something in common, that they all measure the same underlying attribute. This was exactly the conclusion reached by the English psychologist Charles Spearman (1863–1945), who developed the first version of **factor analysis,** a statistical technique by which one can "extract" this common factor that all of the various tests share. In Spearman's view, this factor was best described as **general intelligence,** or **g,** a mental attribute that is called upon in any intellectual task a person

TABLE 15.4 CORRELATION MATRIX OF FOUR SUBTESTS ON THE WECHSLER ADULT SCALE

	I	*C*	*A*	*V*
I (Information)	—	.70	.66	.81
C (Comprehension)		—	.49	.73
A (Arithmetic)			—	.59
V (Vocabulary)				—

NOTE: The matrix shows the correlation of each subtest with each of the other three. Note that the left-to-right diagonal (which is here indicated by the dashes) can't have any entries because it is made up of the cells that describe the correlation of each subtest with itself. The cells below the dashes are left blank because they would be redundant.

SOURCE: From Wechsler, 1958.

has to perform. According to Spearman, if one has a lot of *g,* this will help in any intellectual endeavor. If *g,* however, is in short supply, intellectual performance will suffer across the board.

Spearman pointed out that this *g*-factor alone cannot explain the correlation pattern usually found among mental tests (such as the one shown in Table 15.4). If test performance were determined by *g* and only *g,* then the correlations between any two subtests should be perfect (that is, with $r = +1.00$) except for errors of measurement. But in fact the intercorrelations fall far short of this. To explain why this is so, Spearman proposed that any test taps not only *g* but also some other ability, **s,** that is completely specific to the particular test used. Thus performance on an arithmetic subtest depends in part on *g* and in part on numerical skills (*s*) that are specific to that subtest. Since people vary along both general intelligence and these different specific factors, the intercorrelations among different tests cannot be perfect (Spearman, 1927; for further discussion, see Baron, 1985).

GROUP-FACTOR THEORIES

Spearman's theory of intelligence is sometimes described as "monarchic." As he saw it, there is one factor, *g,* that reigns supreme over all intellectual functions. But this view was soon challenged by other investigators. They argued that the intercorrelations among test scores are better explained by a *set* of underlying mental abilities rather than by one overarching *g*-factor. Spearman called this *group-factor theory* an "oligarchic" conception of intelligence, since it views intelligence as the composite of separate abilities without a sovereign capacity that enters into each. L. L. Thurstone (1887–1955), who originated most of the concepts and techniques that underlie this approach, regarded these group factors as the "primary mental abilities." Some of the more important of these are spatial, numerical, verbal, and reasoning abilities.

WHAT IS INTELLIGENCE? THE INFORMATION-PROCESSING APPROACH

The instruments devised by Binet and his successors are clearly of considerable practical importance. These tests are used in diagnosis, guidance, and selection, and so they often have an important impact on individual lives. But has this helped us to understand the processes that underlie more or less intelligent behavior? Does it explain why individuals fail (or succeed) on a particular problem? The psychometric approach provides tools whereby we can compare how people perform relative to each other; their relative standing gives us a measure of the attribute we call intelligence. But it provides little insight into the mechanisms that lead to problem solution or to failure. It tells us that some people are better and others worse at the various mental tasks posed by intelligence tests, but it doesn't tell us why.

A number of psychologists believe that the answer will come from an analysis of the relevant cognitive operations that intelligence tests call for. The basic idea is to link differences in overall test performance to more "fine grained" differences in the way individuals process information as they perceive, attend, learn, remember, and think. This general approach to the analysis of individual differences in mental abilities is reminiscent of similar attempts to study various aspects of cognition and cognitive development (see Chapters 7, 8, and 13).

SIMPLE COGNITIVE CORRELATES

Some investigators have proposed that the large-scale differences in intellectual capacity assessed by intelligence tests derive from differences in the ability to perform some remarkably low-level cognitive operations. Aptitudes in carrying out such simple operations is far from what we typically think of as intelligence. But these low-level operations are utilized again and again in intelligent performance, and so they may well be the building blocks of this performance.

Some investigators have concentrated on relatively simple cognitive operations and have tried to correlate differences in the way these are carried out with differences in intelligence-test performance. The guiding idea behind these studies is that individual differences in intellectual ability (at least in its fluid form) reflect differences in the way the nervous system functions.

Reaction time An idea that goes back to Galton is that differences in mental ability are related to speed of mental processing. To test this notion, a number of investigators have tried to correlate reaction time with intelligence-test performance. In some studies, the measure was **simple reaction time** in which the subject's job is merely to respond as quickly as she can when a stimulus appears. Others measure **choice reaction time** in which the subject's task is again to respond as quickly as possible, but now choosing between one of several responses, depending upon which stimulus is presented. In one such set-up the subject is asked to place her finger in the center of a board that contains eight small light bulbs, each with a button underneath it (see Figure 15.13). On a given trial, any one of the bulbs may light up, and the subject's task is to press the button that's underneath it as quickly as she can, thus choosing between eight possible responses (which button must be pressed?). In this task, short reaction times are correlated with higher intelligence test scores. There is some suggestion that correlations between intelligence-test scores and speed are higher for choice than for simple reaction-time tests and in fact that these correlations go up as the number of choice alternatives increases (Jensen, 1987; but see Detterman, 1987).

According to some investigators, these reaction-time measures are a way of getting at rock-bottom differences in neurological functioning, differences that may be the underpinning of Spearman's *g*. But is this really so? Reaction time is affected by many variables, including the ability to understand the experimenter's instructions, to adopt appropriate strategies for the task (say, keep your eyes on the semicircle of lights). If so, reaction time may just be another reflection of general intelligence, rather than a more direct way of measuring its underlying physiological cause (Detterman, 1987; Brody, 1992). In any case, we should note that the correlations are not very large—around −.35 or thereabouts. (The correlations are negative because higher reaction times go with lower intelligence-test scores). Reaction time may or may not tap some basic mental process that underlies mental ability, but even if it does, it can only account for a small portion of the variability in the population.

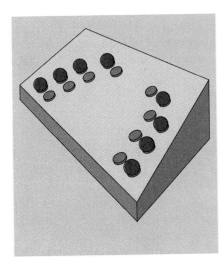

15.13 *Choice reaction time as a measure of speed of mental processing* *An apparatus for measuring choice reaction time. The subject has to place her finger in the center of a board that contains eight small light bulbs. As soon as she sees one of the bulbs light up, she has to press the button underneath it. (Jensen, 1980)*

Verbal ability and lexical access time   Other investigators have looked for one of the subcomponents of intelligence (that is, one of the group factors rather than of Spearman's *g*) in the correlation between verbal intelligence-test scores and the time it takes to look up well-known items of vocabulary in long-term memory. When we hear the word *zebra* and recognize it, we presumably have located that word in our "mental dictionary." That is, we have made contact with some memory file that includes all sorts of information about striped, horselike animals that go by that name. Many cognitive psychologists believe that this process of accessing well-established memories is a fundamental step in various mental tasks that involve language and that differences in the speed with which people perform this look-up operation may be one of the factors that underlie differences in intelligence-test performance (Hunt, Lunneborg, and Lewis, 1975; Hunt, 1976, 1985). Each individual look-up takes only a few milliseconds. But those milliseconds soon add up in tasks that involve thousands of such operations, for example, in reading or arithmetic. Thus, being quicker at this look-up process may add up to a considerable benefit, being slower to a considerable cost.

To test this general hypothesis, a number of investigators have used the **lexical identification task,** which is designed to provide a direct measure of the speed with which words are accessed in long-term memory. A subject is presented with strings of letters, such as *bread* and *blead,* and is asked to decide whether the string is a word as quickly and accurately as he can. His speed of lexical access is measured by the time it takes him to make this decision.★ The results of several studies show that memory look-up times assessed in this manner are shorter in people who do well on conventional tests of verbal intelligence than in those who do less well. The difference is especially marked when the comparison is between normal subjects and groups at the lower extremes of the population, such as brain-damaged persons (Hunt, 1978). But to a lesser extent, such differences also have been obtained within normal populations, for example, between college students with high and low scores on tests of verbal intelligence or on tests of reading comprehension (Hunt, Lunneborg, and Lewis, 1975; Jackson and McClelland, 1975, 1979).

COMPLEX COGNITIVE COMPONENTS

Simple cognitive operations such as choice reaction time and memory look-up may be correlated with intelligence-test performance, but a number of investigators doubt that studying these operations will go very far in helping us understand what intelligence really is. Intelligence may depend on the smooth operation of these simple, rock-bottom cognitive processes, but it is not equivalent to them. Consider the performance of a ballet dancer. She can't dance if she can't walk and run and jump, but dancing is more than walking, running, and jumping. It involves the intricate organization of higher-level actions such as pirouettes, combinations of ballet steps, and so on. While these cannot be performed without the lower-level operations, this doesn't mean that the two levels are identical. Much the same may be true for intelligence. To reason about a problem in arithmetic, one has to recognize the numbers (e.g., 1

★ Strictly speaking, it is the time he takes to make this yes-no decision minus the time it takes him to react to the letter strings when no decision is asked for.

means "one"), and one may have to retrieve the multiplication table from memory (e.g., $2 \times 3 = 6$). But recognizing numbers and retrieving the multiplication table are not the same as reasoning arithmetically.

Such considerations have led to attempts to study some of the higher-level rather than the lower-level cognitive processes that underlie intelligence. In attempts to discover what some of these higher-level processes are, several investigators turned to standard intelligence tests themselves. Their object was to find the *cognitive components* such tasks call for, most of which would presumably be higher-level processes (Sternberg, 1977).

One such undertaking was Robert Sternberg's analysis of *analogical reasoning.* Analogy problems are a staple of many intelligence tests, and they are often regarded as a particularly good measure of Spearman's *g*-factor. For example:

Hand is to *foot* as *finger* is to *(arm, leg, thumb, toe).*

Or to give a more difficult item:

Washington is to *one* as *Lincoln* is to *(five, ten, twenty).*

Sternberg's interpretation of how such problems are solved has the step-by-step quality of a computer program (in this it resembles other information-processing approaches to thinking and problem solving; see Chapter 8). He believes that the problem is solved in separate stages (which he calls components). The first step is the identification of some potentially relevant attributes of each term (e.g., both Washington and Lincoln were presidents; Washington was the first and Lincoln the sixteenth president). After this, the subject tries to infer some possible relations between the first and second terms of the analogy (e.g., Washington was the first president, and his portrait is on the one-dollar bill), and then she tries to map possible relations between the first and third terms (both Washington and Lincoln were presidents and both appear as portraits on U.S. currency). The last step is to decide which of the alternatives offered is the appropriate term to complete the analogy. To accomplish this, the subject takes the various relations she inferred for the *Washington/one* pair and tries to apply them to create an appropriate match for Lincoln. One such relation is *president/the first.* This doesn't fit, for Lincoln was the sixteenth president, not the fifth, tenth, or twentieth. But there is another relation that is appropriate—*portrait of Washington/one-dollar bill.* This works, for Lincoln's portrait is on the five-dollar bill, and "five" is one of the options. At this point, everything matches up, the subject makes her choice, and the analogy is solved (Sternberg, 1977; see Figure 15.14).

Will an analysis of the components of complex cognitive tasks help us to understand what intelligence really is? To answer this question, we have to know whether the components isolated by Sternberg and other investigators have some reasonable level of generality. One issue is whether they correlate reasonably well with traditional measures of intelligence. Some promising results come from a study in which subjects were presented with various tests of reasoning (Sternberg and Gardner, 1983). Some were analogies, others were classification tasks (e.g., which pair of words does *Italy* go with, *Germany/France* or *Vietnam/Korea).* There was a remarkable correspondence between decision times on these and similar tasks and the subjects' scores on several standard psychometric tests of abstract reasoning. The average correlation was -.65, a very encouraging result for the theory of complex cognitive components. (As before, the correlation was negative because shorter decision times correspond to higher reasoning scores.)

15.14 *Washington is to one as Lincoln is to five.*

STRATEGIES AND INTELLECTUAL FUNCTIONING

Concepts derived from information processing have provided still another approach to the study of individual differences in intellectual functioning. This approach asks whether subjects use various flexible *cognitive strategies* for solving problems, for learning, and for remembering. We discussed such cognitive strategies previously in the context of cognitive development (see Chapter 13). As we saw, a normal adult can master memory tasks that are generally beyond the reach of a normal six-year-old. One reason is that the adult uses a well-developed repertoire for solving problems, for learning, and for remembering. Suppose she is asked to memorize unrelated materials, such as the words

> *tulip   plumber   tiger   sweater   lily   tailor   daisy
> raincoat   monkey   butcher   zebra   jacket.*

She will surely do her best to rehearse this list of items and try to impose some kind of order upon it. For example, she might try rhythmic grouping, say, by repeating the items in threes, as in "*tulip, plumber, tiger . . . sweater, lily, tailor, . . . daisy, raincoat, monkey . . .*" and so on. Or she might try to file the words in a mental catalogue according to their semantic categories, first the flowers, then the occupations, then the animals, as in "*tulip, lily, daisy . . . plumber, tailor, butcher . . .*" and so on. Any of these organizational devices will help her do much better in later tests of recall. The six-year-old does not have such organizational tricks in her repertoire as yet and thus is much less successful at such intellectual tasks (Flavell and Wellman, 1977).

STRATEGIES AND MENTAL RETARDATION

The utilization of such cognitive strategies may account for some of the intellectual differences between adults as well. Much of the evidence comes from studies of how strategies are used for remembering (see Chapter 7). The absence of such strategies, for example, is one reason why retarded subjects do so poorly on memory tasks: They attack memory tasks with little or no resort to organization. Mentally retarded persons are less likely to rehearse, to group items in a list, or to show recall clustering by semantic categories (Brown, 1974; Campione and Brown, 1977; Campione, Brown, and Ferrara, 1982).

TRYING TO TEACH THE MISSING STRATEGIES

Is there any way of teaching retarded persons some of the strategies for problem solving and remembering that they so grossly lack? This question has important applications: If the answer is yes, then some aspects of retardation may be remediable. The results of some investigations have given a glimmer of hope. They showed that mildly retarded subjects can be trained to rehearse, for example, by being required to repeat the items cumulatively and aloud (Brown et al., 1973). This induced rehearsal leads to recall performance virtually identical to that of average adults.

These results would be extremely encouraging except for one discordant note. According to many investigators, the newly acquired strategies are often abandoned shortly after they are taught. Furthermore, the use of these strategies tends not to be generalized to tasks other than the one in which they were acquired (Campione and Brown, 1977). An example is training in the use of semantic categories, which shows little transfer to new lists with different verbal materials (Bilsky, Evans, and Gilbert, 1972).

Does this mean that trying to teach retarded persons cognitive strategies is fruitless? A number of investigators have shown that the answer is no. The newly taught strategies will transfer if the retarded person is also explicitly taught that they can be used in other situations. Suppose he is trained to use a particular mode of rehearsal, for example, grouping the items in a list by threes and repeating them out loud. He will then have to be carefully reminded to use this technique on each trial. He'll also have to be trained to use the same technique with different lists and somewhat different methods of presentation. If this is done carefully enough, the strategy will be learned and will show a reasonable degree of a transfer (Campione, Brown, and Ferrera, 1982). Similar techniques have been employed to help schoolchildren who are not retarded but who are poor at learning from texts (Brown, Campione, and Day, 1981).

Why is it that retarded persons and young children are so narrow in their use of the strategies that they won't generalize them without slow and explicit instruction? If retarded individuals learn to remember a set of names by rehearsing them aloud, why don't they apply the same principle to a shopping list? According to several writers, what is lacking is a "master plan" for dealing with memory tasks in general, a strategy for using strategies (Flavell, 1970). Normal adults adopt this higher-order strategy as a matter of course whenever they try to learn. They know that remembering telephone numbers, or traffic directions, or the months that have thirty days, are at bottom similar memory tasks. They also know that trying to learn them means using some aids to learning—rehearsal, rhythmic and semantic grouping, or whatever. Both young children and retarded persons lack this general insight. They don't recognize what all memory tasks have in common and what they all require for mastery. Young children will get it in time; retarded persons may never attain it.

WHAT IS INTELLIGENCE?
BEYOND IQ

The tests devised by Binet and his successors surely tap some aspects of what is ordinarily meant by intelligence. But no less surely some other aspects of its meaning are left out, and many of these aspects concern people's competence in dealing with the real world in which they live. People with high IQs are likely to get good grades in school, but some of them may lack "common sense," or "street smarts," or "know how," as exemplified in the stock figure of the impractical, absent-minded professor. A related ability is social competence: the ability to persuade others and to judge their moods and desires. Shrewd salespeople have this ability and so do successful politicians, even if they don't have the most spectacular IQ.

A demonstration of the separation of academic and nonacademic intelligence comes from a study of experienced racetrack handicappers who were asked to predict the favorites and their probable pay-offs in forthcoming races. This is a tricky mental task that involves complex reasoning in which such facts as track records, jockeys, track conditions, sires and dams of the horses, and so on have to be juggled and put together. On the face of it, one might suppose that the ability to perform such mental calculations is just what intelligence tests do measure. But the results proved otherwise, for the handicappers' success turned out to be completely unrelated to their IQs (Ceci and Liker, 1986).

PRACTICAL INTELLIGENCE

Some attempts have been made to develop tests for nonacademic, practical intelligence. Robert Sternberg and Richard Wagner asked business executives to rate the relative importance of various skills in heading up a company department (e.g., delegating authority, promoting communication). They found that success at the skills the executives rated most highly correlated rather well with various criteria of business success, such as percentage salary increase, and that their responses correlated only weakly with IQ if at all (Wagner, 1987; Wagner and Sternberg, 1987; Sternberg and Wagner, 1993). Sternberg and Wagner believe that this demonstrates a kind of practical intelligence that differs from the abilities measured by a standard intelligence test. In their view, this practical intelligence is based on what they call *tacit knowledge*—knowledge that is never explicitly taught but picked up along the way and that some people acquire to a greater degree than others. But it's important to realize that this practical intelligence is specific to a particular domain. The business executive acquires tacit knowledge that is relevant to running a company, but not to navigating a ship or handicapping horses.

This is probably the same phenomenon we encountered when discussing chunking in masters and beginners (see Chapter 8). Chess grandmasters can readily beat "mere" experts because they've acquired larger and better chess chunks—tacit knowledge in this very specific and specialized domain.

THE NOTION OF MULTIPLE INTELLIGENCES

A different attempt to expand the notion of intelligence to embrace abilities outside of the traditional academic domain is Howard Gardner's concept of *multiple intelligences* (Gardner, 1983). Like those who argue in favor of group-factor theories (see pp. 601–602), Gardner believes that there are several essential, independent mental capacities. He lists six such abilities (which he calls "intelligences"): linguistic, logical-mathematical, spatial, musical, bodily-kinesthetic, and personal intelligence. The first three are familiar enough, for they are assessed by most standard intelligence scales (and emerged as primary factors in Thurstone's group-factor analyses—see p. 602), and everyone knows pretty much what's meant by musical ability. By bodily-kinesthetic intelligence, Gardner refers to the ability to learn and create complex motor patterns, as in dancers and skilled athletes. By personal intelligence, he refers to the ability to understand others and oneself.

One line of evidence for Gardner's claim that these "intelligences" are largely independent of each other comes from studies of different brain lesions, which may affect some abilities (e.g., language) while leaving others unimpaired (e.g., mathematical ability). Thus certain lesions will make a person unable to recognize drawings (spatial intelligence), while others will make him unable to perform a sequence of movements (bodily-kinesthetic intelligence), and still others will produce major changes in personality (personal intelligence).

Further arguments for Gardner's theory of multiple intelligences comes from the study of *retarded savants* (formerly called *idiot savants*). These are mentally retarded persons who have some remarkable talent that seems out of keeping with their low level of general intelligence. Some display unusual artistic talent (see Figure 15.15). Others are calendar calculators; they are promptly able to come up with the right answer if asked questions like, "What was the date of the

15.15 Drawing ability in a retarded savant *A drawing by Nadia, a severely retarded child with remarkable drawing ability. This horse was drawn when she was four years old. (From Selfe, 1977)*

15.16   Unusual numerical achievements in an autistic savant   A scene from the 1988 film Rainman, which featured an autistic person with extraordinary numerical gifts that enabled him to note the exact number of matches remaining in a matchbox after the box was dropped and some were spilled on the floor, to keep track of all the cards in a casino blackjack game, etc. (From Rainman, with Dustin Hoffman and Tom Cruise; courtesy of Photofest)

third Monday in 1682?" (see Figure 15.16). Still others have unusual mechanical talents, such as the ability to build a functional full-sized merry-go-round or scale models of ships. And yet others have unusual musical skills as in the case of a woman who could play "Happy Birthday" in the style of different composers (Hill, 1978).

Some of the evidence Gardner cites in support of his general contention of independent intelligences can be questioned. For example, the incidence of retarded savants is quite low: perhaps one or two in every thousand institutionalized retarded persons (Hill, 1978). Why are such cases so rare if the various "intelligences" are really as independent as Gardner claims? Nor is it clear that the abilities of many savants are quite as extraordinary as they seem at first. Thus many calendar calculators do not possess special numerical or mathematical skills. They may do wonders with dates, but they are unable to add or subtract single digit numbers. And the savant who could play "Happy Birthday" in the style of Mozart, Verdi, or Schubert may not have been quite as musically creative as she appeared. According to one author, she may have played some appropriate bass lines she knew from memory and adjusted them to fit the harmony (Viscott, 1979). In short, while the accomplishments of these savants are unusual enough (given that they are mentally retarded), they don't come close to the musical, or artistic, or mathematical achievements of even lesser composers, artists, and mathematicians, who are generally quite intelligent in the ordinary sense of the term. That Beethoven and Michelangelo represent the absolute top of musical and artistic ability is self-evident, but a glance at the let-

Bodily-kinesthetic intelligence   The incredible precision of a ballet dancer's movements is captured in this time-lapse photograph. According to Howard Gardner, the ability to learn such complex motor patterns is one of several "multiple intelligences" that are largely independent of each other. (Photograph © Globus Studios/The Stock Market)

There are some aptitudes for which no tests have been developed thus far. (Cartoon by S. Gross, © 1983; The New Yorker Magazine, Inc.)

"Son, your mother is a remarkable woman."

ters and diaries of these giants indicates that their verbal and logical intelligence was also far from negligible, which tends to undermine the claim that these various capacities are truly independent.

Whatever the ulitmate verdict on Gardner's theory, there is no doubt that he has performed a very valuable service by drawing attention to a whole set of abilities that are all too often ignored by our society, which values (and perhaps overvalues) the kind of intelligence that helps people succeed in our educational system. Still, while it is quite clear that these various abilities should be highly esteemed, it's not clear that the same term—intelligence—should be applied to all of them.

THE CULTURAL CONTEXT OF INTELLIGENCE

Sternberg's work on practical intelligence and Gardner's on multiple intelligences point up certain limitations of standard intelligence tests. These limitations become more glaring when trying to assess intelligence in members of other cultures. To begin with, many standard intelligence tests emphasize quick and decisive responses. But not all cultures share our Western preoccupation with speed (or our taste for fast food). To give just two examples, Indians and Native Americans place a higher value on being deliberate; in effect they'd rather be right than quick. In addition, they prefer to qualify, or to say "I don't know" or "I'm not sure," unless they're absolutely certain of their answer. But such deliberations and hedging won't help their test scores; on standard intelligence tests you get more points if you guess (Sinha, 1983; Triandis, 1989).

Further factors have to do with formal Western schooling, which teaches the students the kinds of questions teachers (and tests) tend to ask. We saw previously that unschooled Kpelle subjects in Liberia group objects, not according to an abstract semantic category (e.g., tools vs. foods) but rather on the basis of the concrete situation in which the objects would be used together (e.g., a knife with an orange; see Chapter 13, pp. 528–29). A similar concreteness is seen in the response of an unschooled Russian peasant who was asked: "From Shakhimardan to Vuadil it takes three hours on foot, while to Fergana it is six hours. How much time does it take to go on foot from Vuadil to Fergana?" The reply was: "No, it's six hours from Vuadil to Shakhimardan. You're wrong. . . . It's far and you wouldn't get there in three hours." (Luria, 1976, quoted in

Sternberg, 1990, p. 229). If this had been a question on a standard intelligence test, the poor peasant would have scored poorly. But why? He had not gone to school, so he didn't know that questions of this sort are trying to get at arithmetical reasoning and nothing else, that it doesn't matter what the actual distances between the towns really are. It turned out that he was quite able to perform the relevant calculation, but couldn't accept the form in which the question was presented.

All of this makes it clear that we have to be very careful in applying the IQ measure. It is a useful instrument for predicting school success in Western cultures and probably reflects some important aspect of human cognitive functioning. But it does not reflect all such aspects. IQ can indicate an ability (or, if group factor theory is right, a set of abilities) that intelligence tests measure, and it does a pretty good job of predicting success in a Western school system. It can also indicate the speed and efficiency of various cognitive operations that are relevant to the tasks set in school. But ultimately IQ indicates mental competencies that can only be judged in their appropriate environmental and cultural context. (For further discussion, see Sternberg, 1985, 1990).

NATURE, NURTURE, AND IQ

As we've seen, while intelligence tests do a pretty good job in predicting school success in Western cultures, there is no general agreement on just what it is that they really measure. But this state of affairs has not deterred psychologists—nor indeed, the general public—from making intelligence-test performance one of the major foci of the nature-nurture controversy, debated with a stormy passion rarely found in any other area of the discipline (see Block and Dworkin, 1976; Eysenck vs. Kamin, 1981; Fancher, 1987).

SOME POLITICAL ISSUES

The vehemence of the debate over intelligence-test performance is understandable considering that mental testing is a field in which the concerns of the scientist impinge drastically upon those of the practical world. In our society, those who are well off tend to do better on intelligence tests than those who are disadvantaged. The same holds for their children. What accounts for this difference? There is some tendency for social groups to be biased in favor of different answers to this question. This bias was especially marked some eighty years ago when the prevailing social climate was much more conservative. Then—and to a lesser extent even now—advantaged groups were more likely to believe that intelligence is largely inherited. This assertion was certainly comforting to those who benefited from the status quo, since it suggested that they got what they "deserved."

In contrast, advocates for the disadvantaged took a different view. To begin with, they often disparaged the tests themselves, arguing that the tests are not fair to their own subculture. In addition, they argued that intellectual aptitudes are much more determined by nurture than nature. In their view, differences in intelligence, especially those between different ethnic and racial groups, are determined predominantly by environmental factors such as early home background and schooling. Seen in this light, the children of the poor obtain lower

"Immigration Restriction. Prop Wanted"

Anti-immigration sentiment in the United States *A cartoon that appeared in the January 23, 1903, issue of the* Philadelphia Inquirer *calling for more restrictive immigration laws. (Courtesy of the New York Public Library)*

test scores, not because they inherit deficient genes, but rather because they inherit poverty.

These contrasting views led to different prescriptions for social policy. An example of the impact of a hereditarian bias is the rationale behind the United States' immigration policy between the two World Wars. The Immigration Act of 1924 set definite quotas to minimize the influx of what were thought to be biologically "weaker stocks," specifically those from southern and eastern Europe. To "prove" the genetic intellectual inferiority of these immigrants, a congressional committee pointed to the scores of these groups on the army intelligence test, which were indeed substantially below those attained by Americans of northern European ancestry.

In actual fact, these differences were primarily related to the length of time that the immigrants had been in the United States prior to the test; their average test scores rose with every year and became indistinguishable from native-born Americans after twenty years of residence in the United States. This result undermines the hypothesis of a hereditary difference in intelligence between, say, northern and eastern Europeans. But the congressional proponents of differential immigration quotas did not analyze the results so closely. They had their own reasons for restricting immigration, such as fears of competition from cheap labor. The theory that the excluded groups were innately inferior provided a convenient justification for their policies (Kamin, 1974).

A more contemporary example of the relation between psychological theory and social policy is the argument over the value of compensatory educational programs for preschool children from disadvantaged backgrounds. Such programs have been said to be failures because they often don't lead to improvement in later scholastic performance. Assuming this is true (and this is debatable), the question is why. A highly controversial paper by Arthur Jensen suggested that the difference in intellectual performance between the advantaged and disadvantaged groups is partially caused by a genetic difference between the groups. Given this hereditarian position, Jensen argued that environmental alterations can at best mitigate the group difference; they cannot abolish it (Jensen, 1969).

Jensen's thesis has been vehemently debated on many counts, some of which we will discuss below. For now, we will only note that the failure of any given program (assuming it was really a failure) does not prove the hereditarians' claim. Perhaps the preschool experience that was provided was not of the right sort; perhaps it was inadequate to counteract the overwhelming effects of ghetto life (Hunt, 1961). In any case, there is by now a growing consensus that Jensen and others have underestimated the effectiveness of preschool education on school performance in later years (Zigler and Berman, 1983). Such preschool experiences may or may not raise the children's intelligence-test scores.[*] But regardless of their effect on IQ scores, these programs do have positive effects. Thus low-income children who have participated in such programs seem to perform more acceptably in later grades (from fourth to twelfth grades) than children who had no such experience; they are less likely to be held back in grade, less likely to drop out of school, and so on (Lazar and Darlington, 1982).

---

[*] Some preschool experiences apparently do seem to raise intelligence-test scores, both here and in underdeveloped regions elsewhere in the world, especially if they are accompanied by health measures, nutritional supplements, and efforts to help the mother, through job training, remedial education, and the like (e.g., McKay et al., 1978; Garber and Heber, 1982). Other programs were less successful, especially when evaluated some years after the preschool experience (see Coleman et al., 1966; Bronfenbrenner, 1975).

GENETIC FACTORS

Thus far, our emphasis has been on the social and political aspects of the nature-nurture issue in intelligence, the considerations that bias people to take one or another side of the issue. But what exactly are the facts? What is the evidence about the contributions of heredity and environment in producing differences within groups (for instance, among American whites) and between groups (for instance, between American whites and blacks)?

GENETIC TRANSMISSION

Before turning to the relationship between intelligence-test performance and genetic endowment, let us review a few points about the transmission of genetic characteristics, some of which were discussed in a previous chapter (see Chapter 13, pp. 499–500).

Phenotype and genotype   A key distinction in any discussion of hereditary transmission is that between **phenotype** and **genotype.** The phenotype corresponds to the overt appearance of the organism—its actual structure and behavior. But this phenotype is by no means equivalent to the organism's genotype, which describes the set of the relevant genes. One way in which a genotype may be kept from overt expression is by the interaction between genotype and environment. This interaction is especially important during the early stages in the organism's development, since a particular genetic command can only be executed if certain physical characteristics (oxygen concentration, hormone levels, temperature) both inside and outside of the developing body are within a certain range.

As an example, consider the dark markings on the paws, tail, and eartips of a Siamese cat. These markings are not present at birth, but they appear gradually as the kitten matures. The genealogical records kept by cat breeders leave no doubt that these markings in the mature animal are almost entirely determined by heredity. But this does not mean that they emerge independently of the environment. The dark markings will only appear if the kitten's extremities are kept at their normal temperature, which happens to be lower than that of the rest of the animal's body. If the extremities are deliberately warmed during early kittenhood by such devices as leggings and tail and earmuffs, they will not turn darker—in apparent defiance of the creature's genotype (Ilyin and Ilyin, 1930) Similar findings have been obtained with some other animals (see Figure 15.17).

This example underlines the fact that genes do not operate in a vacuum. They are instructions to a developing organism, instructions that will be followed only within a given range of environmental conditions. It therefore makes no sense to talk of heredity alone or environment alone, for there is no trait that does not depend upon both. There can be no organism without a genotype, and this genotype cannot ever express itself independently of the environment.

The inheritance of psychological characteristics   It is obvious that many physical characteristics (e.g., height, eye color) are determined by heredity, but the same is

15.17   The effect of temperature on coat color   *Normally only the feet, tail, ears, and nose of the Himalayan rabbit are black (A). But when an ice pack is applied to a region of the back (B), the new fur grown at an artificially low temperature also comes in black (C). (After Winchester, 1977)*

true for many psychological characteristics as well. An important example is a severe form of mental retardation, **phenylketonuria** or **PKU,** that is determined by a single gene. In the United States, about one baby in every fifteen thousand is born with this defect. PKU is caused by a deficiency in an enzyme that allows the body to transform **phenylalanine,** an amino acid (a building block of proteins), into another amino acid. When this enzyme is missing, phenylalanine is instead converted into a toxic agent that accumulates in the infant's bloodstream and damages his developing nervous system. Analyses of the incidence of PKU among the siblings of afflicted children and among others in their family trees indicate that this disorder is produced by a single recessive gene.

Although PKU is of genetic origin, it can be treated by appropriate environmental intervention. The trick is a special diet that contains very little phenylalanine. If this diet is introduced at an early enough age, retardation can be minimized, or avoided altogether.

This result demonstrates the fallacy of the popular belief that what is inherited is necessarily unchangeable. Genes lay down certain biochemical instructions that determine the development of a particular organ system. If we understand the genetic command clearly enough, we may eventually find ways to circumvent it. In the case of PKU, we are already on the way to doing so (McClearn and DeFries, 1973).

Polygenic inheritance　　Hereditary traits produced by the action of one gene pair are usually all-or-none, such as being brown-eyed or being afflicted with PKU. But how can we explain the inheritance of attributes that vary continuously, such as height and intelligence? The answer is **polygenic inheritance** in which the trait is controlled not by one but by many gene pairs. Take height. Some gene pairs pull toward increased stature, others toward lesser stature; the individual's ultimate genetic potential for height (for now, ignoring environmental effects) is then determined by the combined action of all the height-controlling gene pairs. To the extent that intelligence (or any other psychological attribute that varies continuously) is partially determined by hereditary factors the same logic applies to it.

GENETICS AND IQ

How can we find out whether differences in human intelligence (at least as measured by intelligence tests) have a genetic basis? To do so, we have to infer the underlying genotypes from the observable phenotypic performance. One strategy is to examine the similarities between relatives, an approach that dates back to Francis Galton. Galton found that personal distinction (which he called "eminence" and measured by reputation) runs in families; eminent individuals were more likely to have eminent relatives than the average person (Galton, 1869). Similar results have been repeatedly obtained with intelligence-test scores. For example, the correlation between the IQs of children and parents, or between the IQs of siblings, runs in the neighborhood of +.45 (Bouchard and McGue, 1981). From Galton's perspective, such findings document the inheritance of mental ability. But the environmentalist has a ready reply. Consider eminence. The relatives of an eminent person obviously share his or her social, educational, and financial advantages. As a result, there is a similarity of environmental background, as well as an overlapping set of genes. The same argument applies to the interpretation of the correlations between the IQs of close relatives.

A similar problem arises in another connection. IQs tend to be fairly stable; the ten-year-old with an IQ of 130 will probably get a roughly similar score at age fifteen. Supporters of the genetic theory of intelligence have often argued

15.18 Identical twins *Identical twins tend to be very much alike in both physical and mental characteristics. The photo shows two such twins, Faye and Kaye Young, who both played professional basketball for the New York Stars. As Faye put it: "We've always participated the same amount of time and done the same things and have progressed the same." (Photograph © Kathryn McLaughlin Abbe and Frances McLaughlin Gill, 1980. From Twins on Twins [New York: Clarkson N. Potter, Inc. 1980], pp. 134–35)*

that this constancy of the IQ shows that intelligence tests measure an inborn capacity, "native intelligence," which is an essentially unalterable characteristic of an individual and is genetically based. This argument has been used as a justification of such educational practices as early assignment to one or another school track. But IQ constancy is no proof that intelligence is fixed or inborn. To the extent that this constancy occurs, it only demonstrates that a child tends to maintain her relative standing among her age-mates over time. This may be because of a genetically given attribute that remains unchanged with age. But it may also be because the child's environmental advantages (or disadvantages) stay pretty much the same as time goes on. If a child is born in a slum, the odds are pretty good that she will still be there at twelve; the same holds if she is born in a palace. Once again, the evidence is inconclusive.

During the last fifty years, however, psychologists have developed a variety of research designs to disentangle hereditary and environmental factors. We will consider two main attempts to accomplish this end: the study of twins and the study of adopted children.

Twin studies **Identical twins** originate from a single fertilized egg that splits into two exact replicas that then develop into two genetically identical individuals (see Figure 15.18). In contrast, *fraternal twins* arise from two different fertilized eggs, when each of two eggs in the female reproductive tract is fertilized by a different sperm cell. Under the circumstances, the genetic similarity between fraternal twins is no greater than that between ordinary siblings. Since this is so, a comparison between identical twins and fraternal twins of the same sex is of considerable interest, if one is willing to assume that the twins' environments are no more similar if they are identical than if they are fraternal. Given this premise, it follows that if identical twins turn out to be more similar on some trait than fraternals, one can conclude that this trait is in part genetically determined.

The overall results show that the correlation between the IQs of identical twins is substantially larger than that between the IQs of fraternal twins. Based

TABLE 15.5 CORRELATIONS BETWEEN THE IQS OF FAMILY MEMBERS	
Identical twins reared together	+.86
Fraternal twins reared together	+.60
Siblings reared together	+.47
Child and biological parent by whom child is reared	+.42
Child and biological mother separated from the child by adoption	+.31
Child and unrelated adoptive mother	+.17

SOURCE: Data on twins, siblings, and children reared with biological parents from Bouchard and McGue, 1981; data on adopted children from Horn, Loehlin, and Willerman, 1979.

on roughly 10,000 twin pairs in all, the average correlations are +.86 for identicals and +.60 for fraternals (Bouchard and McGue, 1981). Some further findings on familial similarity in IQ scores are presented in Table 15.5.

On the face of it, this pattern of results seems like clear-cut evidence for a genetic component in the determination of IQ. But a number of criticisms have been leveled at these and related studies. One argument bears on the assumption that the similarity in the environments of identical and fraternal twins is essentially equal. But is it really? Since identical twins look alike, there may be a tendency to treat them the same way. Ultimately, parents and teachers may develop the same expectations for them. In contrast, fraternal twins are no more or less similar in appearance than ordinary siblings and may thus evoke a more differentiated reaction from others. If this is so, the comparison of the IQ correlations between identical and fraternal twins is not as neat a test of the nature–nurture issue as it seemed at first (Anastasi, 1971; Kamin, 1974).

In a study designed to meet this criticism, over three hundred twins were classified as identical or fraternal according to two criteria. One was by a comparison of twelve blood-type characteristics. This is a reliable and objective method for assessing genotype similarity. To be judged identical, both members of a twin pair must correspond on all of the twelve indices. Another criterion involved the subjects' own belief in whether they are identical or fraternal. This belief is presumably based on how similar the twins think they are and how similarly they feel that they are treated. In a sizable number of twins this subjective judgment did not correspond to the biological facts as revealed by the blood tests. Which of the two ways of classifying a twin is a better predictor of the similarity in intelligence-test scores? The results suggest that the primary determinant is the true genotype. When the classification was by blood tests, there was the usual effect; identical twins scored more similarly than did fraternals. But when the classification was based on the twins' own judgments, this effect was markedly reduced. This result suggests that the greater intellectual similarity of identical as compared to fraternal twins is not an artifact of different environments. The best guess is that the effect occurs because intelligence-test performance is in part genetically determined (Scarr and Carter-Saltzman, 1979).

Even more persuasive are the results obtained when considering identical twins that were reared apart. A research center in Minnesota has studied over fifty such twins who were separated in early life, reared apart during their formative years, and reunited as adults. The twins were subjected to over fifty hours of intense medical and psychological assessment, including several tests of mental ability. The results showed a correlation of about +.75, which is not substantially less than the correlations between identical twins reared together (Bouchard, Lykken, McGue, Segal, and Tellegen, 1990).

Adopted children Another line of evidence comes from studies of adopted children. One study was based on three hundred children who were adopted immediately after birth (Horn, 1983; Horn, Loehlin, and Willerman, 1979, 1982). When these children were later tested, the correlation between their IQs and those of their biological mothers (whom they had never seen) was greater than the corresponding correlation between their IQs and those of their adoptive mothers (+.28 versus +.15). Other investigators have shown that this pattern persists into adolescence. When the adopted child is tested at age fourteen, the correlation between his IQ and that of his biological mother's education is greater than that between the child's IQ and the educational level of the adoptive mother (+.31 versus +.04; Skodak and Skeels, 1949).

ENVIRONMENTAL FACTORS

There is evidently a genetic component that helps determine differences in intelligence-test performance. But heredity alone does not account for all of the variance. Environmental factors also play a role.

Some of the evidence comes from an inspection of the same kind of data that demonstrate the importance of heredity: the similarities between members of the same family. The IQs of adopted children correlate +.17 with those of their (genetically unrelated) adoptive mothers. To be sure, this correlation is fairly low and smaller than that between these same children and their biological mothers (+.31), but even so, it demonstrates that the similarity in environments exerts some effect. Another argument for the role of environment comes from the fact that the correlation between the IQ scores of fraternal twins seems to be a bit higher than the correlation of scores between ordinary siblings (+.60 versus +.47). While the similarity in the hereditary makeup of fraternal twins is no greater than that of ordinary siblings, that of their environments obviously is; if there were any changes in the family circumstances (changed economic circumstances, death of a parent, divorce), they hit both twins at the same age.

IMPOVERISHED ENVIRONMENTS

Further evidence for environmental factors comes from studies of the effects of impoverished environments. Examples of what impoverished environments can

Environmental deprivation *A migratory family from Texas in 1940 living in a trailer in an open field without water or sanitiation. The evidence suggests that the longer a child lives under such conditions the more depressed her IQ will be. (Photograph by Dorothea Lange; courtesy of the National Archives)*

do come from children who worked on canal boats in England during the 1920s and hardly attended school at all, or who lived in remote regions of the Kentucky mountains. An environmentalist would argue that these are poor conditions for the development of the intellectual skills tapped by intelligence tests. If so, exposure to such an environment should have a cumulatively adverse effect; the longer the child remains in the environment, the more depressed his IQ should be. This is precisely what was found. There was a sizable negative correlation between IQ and age. The older the child, the longer he had been in the impoverished environment, and thus the lower his IQ (Gordon, 1923; Asher, 1935).

ENRICHED ENVIRONMENTS

Impoverishing the environment is evidently harmful. Enriching it has the opposite effect. An example is a community in East Tennessee that was quite isolated from the U.S. mainstream in 1930 but became less and less so during the following decade, with the introduction of schools, roads, and radios. Between 1930 and 1940, the average IQ of individuals in this community rose by 10 points, from 82 to 92 (Wheeler, 1942).

Further evidence comes from adoption studies. We saw previously that they show the importance of genetic factors. But they also document the contribution of environment. One group of investigators studied the mean IQs of adopted children, most of whom were placed in foster homes before they were three months old. At age four, their mean IQ was 112, at age thirteen it was 117. The authors argue that these values are considerably higher than the mean IQ that would have been predicted for this group of children, given the fact that the occupational and educational levels of the biological parents were known to be below average. Since the adopting parents were above average on these indices as well as on IQ, it seems only natural to assume that the home background they provided led to an increase in the IQs of their adopted children (Skodak and Skeels, 1945, 1947, 1949). Similar results have been obtained in several other studies, both in France and in the United States (Schiff et al., 1982; Scarr and Weinberg, 1983).

HERITABILITY

When we consider the evidence as a whole, we must conclude that both genetic and environmental factors play a role in determining IQ. What is at issue is the relative weight exerted by each of these factors.

Just what is meant by the relative importance of heredity and environment in determining the variation of a trait? To answer this question, we must refer to a technical expression developed by geneticists, the **heritability ratio (H).** This is the proportion of the variance of the phenotypic expression of a trait in a given population that is attributable to genetic variation (Figure 15.19).★

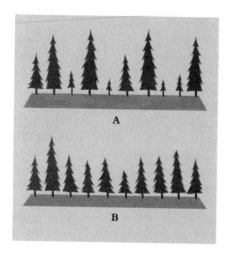

15.19 Heritability *Consider the group of evergreen trees shown in (A). They vary in height, and the degree to which they vary from each other is measured by the variance. What produces this variance? Some is presumably caused by genetic factors. To determine how much, we equalize environmental conditions—the soil, water, light, and so on (here indicated by different colors of the ground). We now take a group of seedlings randomly chosen from (A), plant them in this equalized environment, and patiently wait until they reach maturity (B). We note that the size variation in (B) is less than that in (A). This reduction in the variance reflects the fact that environmental conditions are equal for (B), so that one important source of variation has been removed. The remaining variance in (B) is entirely produced by genetic factors. We can now determine the heritability of height for (A). It is the variance in (B) (that is, the variation attributable to genetic factors) divided by the variance in (A) (that is, the total variation in the population).*

★ The idea is that the total variance of the trait (V_T)—be it height, weight, or IQ—can be considered as the sum of several constituents: the variance produced by genetic differences (V_G), the variance produced by different environments (V_E), and some others. The heritability ration, *H,* is then given by

$$H = V_G/V_T$$

The actual value of *H* for IQ (in industrialized populations like ours) is still a matter of debate, though most experts would probably agree that it falls within the range of .4 to .7.

To get a feeling for what *H* means, suppose that all children born in the United States (within a given racial-ethnic group) are raised in completely identical environments. When this environmentally equalized group is later tested, there will still be variations in IQ. These will be entirely attributable to genetic variation, for in this scenario environment would no longer be a factor. Under these conditions, *H* would necessarily equal +1.00. Conversely, let's play at science fiction and assume that there's a group of 100 children who are genetically identical. (They would presumably be clones, since the idea of identical centuplets is too unpleasant to contemplate.) When this group is later tested, any variation in their IQs must be of environmental origin since in these children heredity is equalized. As a result, *H* must necessarily be equal to 0.

There are some widely held misconceptions about the nature of heritability. Perhaps the worst is the notion that the heritability ratio applies to individuals. In popular discussions, it is sometimes said that 80 percent—or 70 percent or 40 percent, depending on the value of *H* the author accepts—of a person's intelligence is determined by heredity, the rest by environment. This is sheer nonsense. Heritability is a concept that applies only to trait variations within a particular population at a particular point in time; it does not apply to individuals. For any given person, both heredity and environment are equally important in determining whatever he or she is. As an example, consider height, for which heritability is about .90. This means that if genotype variation were eliminated (in other words, if all subjects were derived from the same fertilized egg) the remaining variance would be only 10 percent of what it is in the normal population. But it does not mean that a man whose height is six feet can thank heredity for sixty-five of his inches and credit environment with the remaining seven.

GROUP DIFFERENCES IN IQ

Thus far, we have focused on IQ differences within groups and have considered the nature-nurture debate as it pertained to these. But the real fury of the controversy rages over another issue—the differences in average IQ that are found between groups, such as different socioeconomic classes or racial-ethnic groups.

Numerous studies have shown that the average score of American blacks is about 10 to 15 IQ points below the average of the white population (Loehlin, Lindzey, and Spuhler, 1975). The fact that there is such a difference is not in dispute. What is at issue is what this difference means and how it comes about.

Before proceeding, we should emphasize that the differences are between averages. There is considerable overlap between the two distributions. From 15 to 25 percent of blacks score higher than 50 percent of whites (Shuey, 1966). The numerical variations *within* either group are clearly much greater than those *between* groups.

ARE THE TESTS CULTURE-FAIR?

Some psychologists have tried to deal with the between-group difference by explaining it away. They have suggested that it is primarily an artifact of a cultural bias built into the tests themselves (Sarason, 1973). According to this view, the intelligence tests now in use were designed to assess the cognitive skills of the white middle class. When these tests are administered to another group with different customs, values, and even dialects—such as inner-city African-American children—there cannot help but be a cultural bias that makes the yardstick no longer applicable. This point is obvious when the test item calls for verbal information, as in vocabulary or analogy tests. If different subgroups have different degrees of exposure to the relevant information, any difference in test scores becomes uninterpretable. Further problems stem from different motivations in the test-taking situation and to different attitudes toward the tester. Yet another complication is posed by different degrees of language comprehension. According to some linguists, many American blacks speak a dialect of English—so-called black English—the syntax, phonology, and lexicon of which differ in some important ways from "standard" English (e.g., Labov, 1970; see Chapter 9). Since intelligence tests are usually administered in standard English, the African-American children who take them are under a linguistic handicap.

Such considerations suggest that some component of the black-white test score difference is attributable to cultural bias, either in the tests themselves, in their administration, or both. The question is whether this accounts for all of the difference. There are reasons to believe that it does not. The evidence comes from studies in which one or another possible source of cultural bias has been eliminated or at least minimized. An example is an attempt to test African-Americans in black English. To this end, the Stanford-Binet was translated into black English and was then administered orally to black children by black examiners (Quay, 1971). The performance of these children was virtually identical to that of a group tested with the regular version. The dialect difference is evidently not the crucial variable.

BETWEEN-GROUP DIFFERENCES: HEREDITY OR ENVIRONMENT?

The **between-group** difference in average IQ is evidently not just an artifact. But what accounts for it? In the thirty years before 1965, the consensus among social scientists in the United States was that the effect resulted from the massively inferior environmental conditions that were (and in many ways still are) the lot of most African-Americans—systematic discrimination, poorer living conditions, lower life expectancies, inadequate diets and housing, and inferior schooling. But the issue was reopened in the sixties and early seventies by, among others, Arthur Jensen, who felt that the hypothesis of a genetic contribution to the between-group difference had been dismissed prematurely (Jensen, 1969, 1973, 1985).

As currently conceived, human racial groups (some authors prefer the term racial-ethnic groups) are populations whose members are more likely to interbreed than they are to mate with outsiders. This restriction on the gene flow between different subgroups may be imposed by geographical barriers, such as oceans or mountains, or by social taboos, such as prohibitions on intermarriage. The restrictions are not complete, but if they last long enough, they may result in a population that differs from other groups in the statistical frequency of various genes. This is undeniable for genes that determine such characteristics as skin color, pattern of hair growth, or various blood groups. But does the same hold for behavioral traits like intelligence-test performance? More specifically, is the difference in average black and white IQs partially attributable to different frequencies of IQ-determining genes in the two populations?

Within-group heritability   One of Jensen's arguments was based on the finding that IQ has a substantial **within-group** heritability. Jensen suggested that, given this fact, it was plausible to suppose that the between-group difference (that is, the difference between the black and white averages) could be interpreted in similar terms. A number of critics disagreed. They countered by saying that the

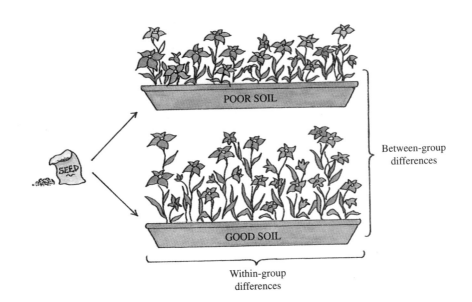

15.20 Between-group and within-group differences *Between-group differences may be caused by very different factors than within-group differences. Here, the between-group difference reflects an environmental factor (soil) while the within-group difference reflects genetic variation (seed).*

fact that within-group heritability is high does not imply that between-group differences are genetically determined (Layzer, 1972).

One writer gave an example of two samples of seed, randomly drawn from a bag that contains several genetically different varieties. One sample is placed in barren soil and the other in soil that is extremely fertile. When the plants are fully grown they will differ in height. There will be *within-group* differences as measured by the variance within each of the two samples. There will also be a *between-group* difference as indicated by a difference in the average height of the plants in the two samples. The within-group difference can be attributed to genetic variation; the samples were drawn from a genetically mixed bag so that there is high within-group heritability. But the between-group variation must be primarily of environmental origin since the two sets of seeds were planted in soils of different fertility (Lewontin, 1976; see Figure 15.20).

The moral is simple: Differences within and between groups may be produced by very different causal factors. This holds for plants and the heights they attain at maturity. And it may also apply to human racial-ethnic groups and IQ.

Matching for environment If the black-white difference in IQs is really a result of environmental factors, that difference should disappear if one compares black and white groups who are equated in these regards. It is reasonable to suppose that the relevant factors include socioeconomic variables like education, parents' education, income, occupational level, and so on. A number of studies have tried to match black and white children on indices of this kind and then compared the IQ averages of the two matched groups. The general result was that the black-white difference was markedly reduced (Loehlin, Lindzey, and Spuhler, 1975).

On the face of it, such results seem like vindications of the environmentalists' view: Equate the soil and the two sets of seeds will grow up much alike. But hereditarians will emphasize another finding. While equalizing socioeconomic variables diminishes the black-white difference, it does not abolish it. In their view, this residual difference makes the genetic hypothesis all the more plausible. But environmentalists reply that the environments of the black and white children were not truly matched, despite the social scientists' very best efforts. For matching parental education, income, and occupational level is not enough. The very fact that one child is black and the other white means that they grow

621

up in different environments, since our society is riddled with racial discrimination that will hit the one child but not the other.

A somewhat better approximation to an equalized environment is found in a study of the illegitimate offspring of U.S. servicemen stationed in Germany after World War II. The investigators compared two groups of such children whose white, German mothers were roughly similar in socioeconomic background. One group of children was fathered by black soldiers and the other by white ones. When the children were tested with a German version of the Wechsler scale, the main finding was that both groups had about the same average IQ (Eyferth, 1961). This result seems to contradict the genetic interpretation of the black-white difference, for the children received half of their genes from a black father. To maintain the genetic hypothesis, one would have to postulate a special kind of mating selection—whatever the reasons, the choice of mates might have been such that black fathers and white fathers had about the same average IQ. This possibility cannot be completely ruled out, but it does not seem very plausible (Flynn, 1980).

The effect of environmental change Some investigators have taken another tack. Instead of trying to match environments, they have asked what happens when the environment is changed. A widely cited example is Scarr and Weinberg's study of ninety-nine black children who were adopted at an early age by white middle-class parents, most of whom were college educated (Scarr and Weinberg, 1976). The mean IQ of these children was 110. This value exceeds the national average for black children by about 25 IQ points. (For further discussion, see Scarr and Carter-Saltzman, 1982; Scarr and Weinberg, 1983.)

Some tentative conclusions about between-group differences in IQ Perhaps the fairest thing to say in summarizing this debate is that there is not a single study whose results or interpretations cannot be challenged, nor is there a single argument (whether genetic or environmental) for which there is no counterargument. Under the circumstances, no conclusion can be anything but tentative. Even so, the weight of the evidence seems to tilt toward the environmentalist side, especially when one's intuitions about the effects of three hundred years of slavery and racist oppression are thrown into the balance.

But suppose that the genetic interpretation is correct after all. Suppose that some significant fraction of the black-white IQ difference is in fact determined by the genes. What then? What effects should this have on our thinking about social issues and socioeconomic policy? In this author's view, relatively little. There are several reasons for this.

First, the genetic interpretation does not imply that environmental intervention—in home or school—will have no effect. There is no one who denies that environmental factors are responsible for some proportion of the between-group variance. There are thus no grounds for abandoning appropriate educational efforts for improving cognitive skills (and presumably raising IQs). The trouble is that thus far we have only the skimpiest ideas about the kinds of environmental changes that would to the trick.

Second, what about the portion of the variance that, according to the hereditarians, is determined by the genotype? Is that unchangeable? Some participants on both sides of the controversy seem to feel that, almost by definition, environmentally determined traits are alterable while genetically determined ones are fixed. But this is far from true. Some environmentally produced effects are almost impossible to change, including some that are acquired through certain forms of learning. Examples are the long-lasting effects of imprinting (see Chapter 14) and the difficulty most adults have in shedding the phonological system of their mother tongue when trying to speak another language without an accent (see Chapter 9). Nor is it true that genetically determined traits are necessarily unchangeable. The widely cited counterexample is PKU, an inherited form of mental retardation which, as we have seen, can be treated by an appropriate diet. Conceivably, other approaches may be found to alter the effects of some of the genes that underlie the distribution of IQs.

Third, there are reasons to believe that the black-white IQ difference, regardless of what causes it, is not a major factor in producing the economic inequality between whites and blacks. To be sure, IQ is correlated with adult income, but according to at least some writers, this correlation accounts for only 12 percent of the total variance in individual incomes in the United States (Jencks et al., 1972). Given this relatively low value, the emphasis on IQ in discussions of social inequality may well be misplaced.

We should make a final point (which has been stressed by Jensen no less than by his environmentalist critics). In a democratic society the emphasis is on individuals and their own abilities and attributes. A given individual's subgroup may have a greater or smaller average gene frequency for this or the other trait, but this has no bearing on how this particular person should be judged. When people are assessed according to the average characteristics of the group to which they belong, rather than according to the characteristics that they themselves possess, one of the most essential premises of a democratic society is violated.

TAKING STOCK

What has been the upshot of the work on human individual differences in cognitive aptitudes that Francis Galton began over a hundred years ago? One consequence was the developement of a whole host of sophisticated techniques for the creation and evaluation of mental tests. Modern intelligence tests document the variabililty of certain intellectual skills, and they have found wide (though not always salutary) applications for selection and clinical guidance. People differ in their test performance, and these differences correlate substantially with success in our Western school system.

We have tests, and there is no denying their practical significance. But many questions remain about the nature of the differences they reveal. Investigators who take a psychometric perspective ask whether intelligence-test performance is best ascribed to one underlying ability or to several (Spearman's g versus group factors). Those influenced by the information-processing approach try to discover the cognitive operations that underlie this ability (or these abilities), such as speed of processing, cognitive components, or strategies. Yet other questions are raised by the fact that the term *intelligence* can also refer to mental abilities that only make sense within a given environmental and cultural context.

A rather different question goes back to the nature-nurture controversy we've encountered so often before: Are the differences revealed by intelligence tests produced by heredity or environment? As usual, the answer is both, for humans are shaped both by their genes, their environment, and the interaction between them. But while there is clear-cut evidence that genetic factors are of considerable importance in determining variation *within* groups (as shown by the comparison of identical and fraternal twins and adopted children), there is but little evidence for a genetic account of the difference *between* groups.

So far, our discussion has been concerned with differences between individuals that have to do with abilities, especially cognitive abilities. But people don't just differ in what they can do, but also in what they want to do, how they do it, and how they feel about it. Those and many other differences between people—whether they are usually sociable or solitary, pleasant or surly, anxious or self-confident—belong to the topic of human personality and are the subject matter of the field of personality, the topic to which we turn next.

SUMMARY

1. Many physical and psychological characteristics vary from one individual to another. This pattern of variation is often displayed by *frequency distributions*. The scores in a frequency distribution tend to cluster around a *central tendency*, often measured by the *mean*. The *variability* around this central tendency is indicated by the *variance*, or its square root, the *standard deviation*. The graphed frequency distributions of many physical and psychological characteristics have a shape approximating that of the *normal curve*, which describes the probability of obtaining certain combinations of chance events.

2. The extent to which two characteristics vary together is measured by the *correlation coefficient*, or *r*. Perfect correlation is indicated by an *r* of +1.00 or −1.00, no correlation by an *r* of .00.

3. An important application of the correlation technique was the development of mental testing. A mental test is meant to be an objective yardstick to assess some psychological trait or capacity on which people differ. One criterion of such a test's adequacy is its *reliability*, the consistency with which it measures what it measures, as given by *test-retest correlations* and similar indices. An even more important criterion is a test's *validity*, the extent to which it measures what it is supposed to measure. *Predictive validity* is assessed by determining the correlation between the test and an appropriate criterion. *Construct validity* is the extent to which performance on a test fits into some relevant theoretical scheme. A test's *utility* is its usefulness when weighed against the time, energy, and expense required to administer it.

4. Tests with good reliability, reasonable predictive validity, and acceptable utility may be useful as a selection device. But since validity coefficients are less than 1.00, there are inevitable selection errors, some of which are *inappropriate* accepts, while others are *inappropriate rejects*. The relative proportion of these two errors depends on the choice of a *cutoff score* below which no applicant is selected. The choice of this cutoff value depends on the selector's *payoff matrix*.

5. Alfred Binet, the originator of intelligence tests, was primarily interested in assessing children. His tests measured *mental age*, or *MA*. The relative standing of a child relative to her age-mates was determined by comparing her MA with her chronological age, or *CA*. A useful measure of this relative position is the *intelligence quotient*, or *IQ*, which equals MA / CA × 100. Modern testers prefer another measure, the *deviation IQ*. This is based on a comparison between an individual's score and that of her age-mates and can be used with both children and adults.

6. Different intelligence-test scales have been developed for various uses. Some are meant to test children, others to test adults; some can be administered individually, others in groups. Specialized tests have also been developed as instruments for *neuropsychological assessment*.

7. Intelligence tests can be used to diagnose several levels of *mental retardation*, varying from mild to profound.

8. Investigators have also studied the relation between intelligence-test performance and age. The evidence suggests a distinction between *fluid intelligence*, which declines with age, and *crystallized intelligence*, which tends to drop off more slowly if at all.

9. Investigators using the *psychometric approach* try to discover something about the underlying nature of intelligence by studying the pattern of results provided by intelli-

gence tests themselves. One issue is the structure of mental abilities. To determine whether intelligence is one unitary ability or is composed of several unrelated abilities investigators have looked at the correlations between different subtests. *Factor analysis* of these correlations led to a number of competing theories of mental structure, including Spearman's theory of *general intelligence,* or *g,* and *group-factor theory.*

10. The *information-processing approach* tries to understand individual differences in intellectual performance as differences in the cognitive processes that underlie remembering, problem solving, and thinking, as studied by cognitive psychology. One line of inquiry tries to relate Spearman's general intelligence factor *g* to differences in *choice reaction time.* Another approach focuses on a subfactor, in particular on verbal intelligence, and tries to relate it to simple cognitive operations, such as *memory look-up times.* Still another approach tries to understand the more complex *cognitive components* of the tasks posed by standard intelligence tests, as exemplified in studies of *analogical reasoning.* Yet another line of inquiry tries to relate intellectual differences to success or failure in the acquisition and use of various *cognitive strategies.*

11. Some investigators have concerned themselves with some aspects of the term *intelligence* that go beyond IQ, such as practical and social intelligence, and with the cultural spheres in which intelligence is used and assessed. Another related approach has led to the notion of *multiple intelligences,* buttressed by evidence from studies of brain lesions and of *retarded savants.*

12. Intelligence-test performance has become one of the major foci of the nature-nurture controversy, fueled in great part by various social and political forces. The factual questions concern the relative contributions of heredity and environment in producing differences within and between groups in contemporary America.

13. Intelligence-test performance seems to be determined by both environmental and genetic factors, though the issue is not regarded as fully settled by all psychologists. Evidence for the role of genetic factors comes from the fact that the correlation between IQs of *identical twins* are higher than those for *fraternal twins* and that this correlation is remarkably high even when identical twins are reared apart. Further evidence for a hereditary contribution comes from adopted children whose IQs correlate more highly with those of their biological than their adoptive parents. Evidence for environmental effects is provided by increases and decreases in the mean IQ of populations whose cultural or educational level has risen or fallen. A similar point is made by adoption studies that show IQ increases in adopted children after being placed in enriching foster homes.

14. The relative weight of genetic and environmental factors in determining the variation of a given characteristic is given by the *heritability ratio,* or *H.* The value of *H* depends in part upon the given population, for *H* only describes the degree to which the variability within this population can be attributed to genetic variance.

15. In recent years, much interest (and polemic) has focused on IQ differences between different racial-ethnic groups. The mean IQ of American blacks is about 10 to 15 points lower than that of American whites. Some authors have argued that this is in part a consequence of a genetic difference between the two groups. Environmentalists reply that the difference is markedly reduced by various environmental changes such as interracial adoption. A similar point is made by the fact that the mean IQs of illegitimate children of white German mothers fathered by U.S. soldiers after World War II are just about the same whether the fathers were black or white.

PERSONALITY I: ASSESSMENT, TRAIT THEORY, AND THE BEHAVIORAL-COGNITIVE APPROACH

METHODS OF ASSESSMENT   629

STRUCTURED PERSONALITY TESTS ■ UNSTRUCTURED PERSONALITY TESTS

THE TRAIT APPROACH   639

THE SEARCH FOR THE RIGHT TAXONOMY ■ THE TRAIT-SITUATION CONTROVERSY ■ TRAITS AND BIOLOGY

THE BEHAVIORAL-COGNITIVE APPROACH   658

RADICAL BEHAVIORISM ■ SOCIAL LEARNING THEORY

SUMMARY   666

I n the preceding chapter, our focus was on differences in cognitive ability. But people also differ in their nonintellectual attributes. They differ in their predominant desires, in their characteristic feelings, in their typical modes of expressing these needs and feelings, and in the way these affect their outlook on the world they live in. All of these distinctions fall under the general heading of personality differences.

The fact that personality differences exist is hardly a recent discovery; it was probably known since prehistoric times. Cro-Magnons surely knew that all Cro-Magnons were not the same; they probably liked some, disliked others, and spent some of their time gossiping about the Cro-Magnons in the cave next door. But it's unlikely that they did so self-consciously, unlikely that they had any explicit ideas about the ways in which one person is different from another. Such explicit formulations came later. In the main, they were the work of various writers who concerned themselves with the representation of character.

An example is a series of sketches entitled "The Characters" that was written in the fourth century B.C. by the Greek philosopher Theophrastus (ca. 370–287 B.C.). "The Characters" featured such diverse types as the Coward, the Flatterer, the Boor, and so on. At least some of his types are as recognizable today as they were in ancient Greece:

> The Garrulous man is one who will sit down close beside somebody he does not know, and begin with a eulogy of his own life, and then relate a dream he had the night before, and after that tell dish by dish what he had for supper. As he warms to his work he will remark that we are by no means the men we were, and the price of wheat has gone down, and there's a ship of strangers in town. . . . Next he will surmise that the crops would be all the better for some more rain, and tell him what he's going to grow on his farm next year, adding that it's difficult to make both ends meet . . . and "I vomited yesterday" and "What day is it today?" . . . And if you let him go on, he will never stop. . . . (Edmonds, *The Characters of Theophrastus*, 1929, pp. 48–49)

Even more influential than such literary efforts were those of the playwrights. The very origin of the word *personality* suggests a possible relationship between the dramatic rendering of character and the psychologists' attempts to describe and understand it. The word comes from *persona*, the mask that Greek and Roman actors wore to indicate the characters that they played.

In their comic drama, the Greeks and the Romans tended to think of people as types, a tradition that has continued in various forms to the present day. Their comedy created a large cast of stock characters: the handsome hero, the pretty young maiden, the restless wife, her jealous husband, the angry old man, the sly servant, the panderer, the kind-hearted prostitute, the boastful soldier, the pedant, and so on. Many of these types were resurrected in later times and other countries. An example is the comic theater of Renaissance Italy, the *commedia dell' arte,* which boasted a large stable of such stock characters, each invariably played by the same actor and always with a mask that indicated who he was. While modern movie and television actors usually don't wear masks (Batman is

Masks used by actors in Roman comic drama *(Capitolone Museums, Rome; courtesy of Scala/Art Resource)*

A

B

Characters in sixteenth and seventeenth century Italy's Commedia dell' arte *(A) Pantalone, the rich, stingy, old merchant, who is invariably deceived by his servants, his children, and his young wife. (B) Pulcinella, a sly and boisterous comic. (Courtesy of Casa Goldoni, Venezia; photographs by Paul Smit, Imago)*

one exception), they often represent stock characters even so. The hero and villain of the Western and the busybody and conniving schemer of the television soap opera are only a few of such instantly recognizable types.

Over the ages, there have been many discussions of the appropriate conception of dramatic and literary character. One concerned the use of type characters in drama and literature. Some critics argued that such characterizations are necessarily flat and two-dimensional and could not possibly do justice to an individual; in reality, even the most passionate lover is not just passionate, for he surely has other attributes as well. They therefore felt that drama and literature should avoid all such stock characters and instead only present fully rounded, complex characters, such as Hamlet, who are essentially like no one else. Such rounded characters are as difficult to describe perfectly as a person in real life, and are therefore capable of surprising us (Forster, 1927). But other critics disagreed and felt that, while simplified types could not possibly do full justice to any individual, they accomplished another and equally important aim: They showed what all people of a certain kind have in common rather than that which distinguishes them as individuals (Johnson, 1765).

Another argument concerns the relative importance of internal versus external forces in determining what a character does. Some critics insisted that all dramatic action ultimately springs from within and grows out of the character's own essential nature, while others disagreed and pointed to the role of the external situation, as in the case of realistic modern dramas, such as *Death of a Salesman,* whose heroes do what they do because their social or economic situation forces them to. Yet another issue concerns the character's self-knowledge. Do her actions spring from goals of which she is aware, or is she reacting to unconscious forces that she herself does not recognize? (Bentley, 1983).

These arguments about drama and literature are mirrored in current debates between psychologists who embrace different theories of personality. As we will see, the drama of types is a distant cousin of modern *trait theory,* which holds that personality is best understood by the description and analysis of underlying personality traits. The insistence that a character's actions are prompted by external circumstances is related to some formulations of the *behavioral-cognitive approach,* which defines personality differences by the way in which different people act and think about their actions, and insists that these acts and thoughts are largely produced by the situation that the individuals face now or have faced on previous occasions. And the belief that people may act because of unconscious impulses is of course a dominant view of *psychodynamic theory,* which argues that the crucial aspects of personality stem from deeply buried, unconscious conflicts and desires (see Chapter 17). The insistence that characters be rounded and to some extent unpredictable would be congenial to a *humanistic approach* to personality, which maintains that what is most important about people is how they achieve their own selfhood and actualize their human potentialities (see Chapter 17). Finally, that the concept of character and selfhood may differ from one culture to another is a tenet of the *sociocultural approach* to personality (see Chapter 17).

Before turning to these theories of personality, however, we must first consider some of the methods by which differences in personality have been assessed.

METHODS OF ASSESSMENT

There is an implicit assumption that underlies Theophrastus's sketches or, for that matter, any drama that uses character types, and that assumption is shared by most authors who concern themselves with personality: The personality patterns they ascribe to their characters are assumed to be essentially consistent from one time to the next, and from one situation to another. The hero is generally heroic, the villain villainous, and the garrulous talkative regardless of who is listening (or rather, trying not to listen). The traits by which modern students of personality describe people are more subtle than those that define the stock characters of the classical or Renaissance stage, but for many investigators the key postulate of this trait theory still exists. They assume that certain traits characterize a person's behavior in a variety of situations. This is just another way of saying that a knowledge of an individual's personality traits will permit us to predict what he is likely to do, even in situations in which we have never observed him (Allport, 1937).

Personality tests were devised in an attempt to supply the information that would make such prediction possible. In a way, they are analogous to an actor's audition; the director asks him to try out for a part by reading a page or two from a scene. Such an audition is a test that tries to determine (by no means perfectly) whether the actor can play a certain part. In contrast, a personality test is a test that tries to determine (again, far from perfectly) whether a person *is* that part.

Character types in the Nō drama of Japan In the traditional Nō drama of Japan, character is indicated by a mask. The mask shown in the figure is that of a mystical old man with godlike powers. Before donning the mask, the actor who performs this part must go through various rituals of purification, because after he puts it on, the actor "becomes" the god. (Photograph by George Dineen/Photo Researchers)

STRUCTURED PERSONALITY TESTS

As in the case of intelligence measurement, the impetus for the development of personality tests came from the world of practical affairs. The first personality test was meant to identify emotionally disturbed U.S. Army recruits during World War I. This test was an "adjustment inventory" consisting of a list of questions that dealt with various symptoms or problem areas (for instance, "Do you daydream frequently?" and "Do you wet your bed?"). If the subject reported many such symptoms, he was singled out for further psychiatric examination (Cronbach, 1970a).

The parallel between tests of intelligence and those of personality ends when we turn to the question of how these tests are validated. Binet and his successors had various criteria of validity: teachers' evaluations, academic performance, and, perhaps most important, chronological age. It turns out that validity criteria are much harder to come by in the field of personality measurement.

THE MMPI: CRITERION GROUPS FROM THE CLINIC

To provide an objective validity criterion, some later investigators turned to the diagnostic categories developed in clinical practice. Their object was to construct a test that could assess a person's similarity to this or the other psychiatric criterion group—paranoid patients, depressives, schizophrenics, and so on. The best-known test of this sort is the **Minnesota Multiphasic Personality Inventory,** or **MMPI,** which first appeared in 1940 (see Table 16.1; Hathaway and

TABLE 16.1 SOME MMPI SCALES WITH REPRESENTATIVE EXAMPLE ITEMS *

Scale	Criterion group	Example items
Depression	Patients with intense unhappiness and feelings of hopelessness	"I often feel that life is not worth the trouble."
Paranoia	Patients with unusual degree of suspiciousness, together with feelings of persecution and delusions of grandeur	"Several people are following me everywhere."
Schizophrenia	Patients with a diagnosis of schizophrenia, characterized by bizarre or highly unusual thoughts or behavior, by withdrawal, and in many cases by delusions and hallucinations	"I seem to hear things that other people cannot hear."
Psychopathic deviance	Patients with marked difficulties in social adjustment, with histories of delinquency and other asocial behaviors	"I often was in trouble in school, although I do not understand for what reasons."

* In the example items here shown, the response appropriate to the scale is "True." For many other items, the reverse is true. Thus, answering "False" to the item "I liked school" would contribute to the person's score on the psychopathic deviance scale.

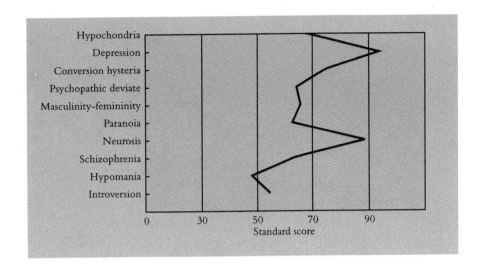

16.1 MMPI profile *The profile is of an adult male seeking help in a community health center. The scales are those described in Table 16.1. The scores are based on the performance of the standardization group. Scores above 70 will occur in about 2.5 percent of the cases; scores above 80 in about .1 percent. The profile strongly suggests considerable depression and neurotic anxiety. (After Lanyon and Goldstein, 1971)*

McKinley, 1940). The original MMPI together with its new revision the MMPI-2, are widely used in both clinical practice and research (Butcher et al., 1989; Lanyon and Goldstein, 1982; Greene, 1991) and constitute the psychological tests most frequently administered in professional settings (Lubin et al., 1985).

Constructing the MMPI The authors of the MMPI began by compiling a large set of test items taken from previously published inventories, from psychiatric examination forms, and from their own clinical hunches. The intent from the outset was to make the test "multiphasic," that is, diagnostic of a number of different kinds of psychopathology. These items were then administered to several patient groups who had already been diagnosed, as well as to a group of nonpatient subjects. The next step was to eliminate all items that did not discriminate between the patients and the non-patient controls and to retain those items that did. The end result was the MMPI—an inventory of 566 items the responses to which are collated and tallied to form ten major scales. The score on each of these scales indicates how the subject's answers compare with those of the relevant criterion group (Table 16.1).

After nearly half a century, the original MMPI was supplanted by the MMPI-2 in which the wording of many of the original MMPI questions was updated and a few questions deleted. But it contains the same scales and is scored the same way. The biggest change in the new version is its standardization group. Whereas the nonpatients used to standardize the original MMPI were almost all white, middle-aged Minnesotans, the standardization group for the MMPI-2 consisted of 2,600 individuals from diverse areas of the United States selected to be representative of the population in such factors as age, marital status, and ethnicity (Greene, 1991).

Using the MMPI Interpreting an MMPI record is a complicated business. Clinicians don't merely look at the absolute scores obtained on any one scale. Instead, they consider the various scale values in relation to each other. This is most easily done by inspecting **score profiles,** which present the scores on every scale in graphic form (Figure 16.1). In interpreting a patient's score on the depression scale, for example, a clinician compares the patient's answers against the items that differentiated a group of patients diagnosed to be in a depressive state from normal persons.

Validity scales One trouble with self-administered personality inventories is that subjects can easily misrepresent themselves. To cope with this and related problems, the originators of the MMPI added a set of further items that make up several *validity scales.* One is a simple lying scale. It contains items like "I gossip a little at times" and "Once in a while I laugh at a dirty joke." The assumption is that a person who denies a large number of such statements is either a saint (and few of those take personality tests) or is lying. Another validity scale consists of a number of bizarre statements like "There are persons who are trying to steal my thoughts and ideas" and "My soul sometimes leaves my body." To be sure, some of these statements will be endorsed by severely disturbed psychiatric patients, but even they will only agree with a small proportion of them. As a result, we can be reasonably sure that a person who checks an unusually large number of such items is either careless, has misunderstood the instructions, or is trying to fake psychiatric illness. If the score on these and similar validity scales is too high, the test record is discarded as invalid.

THE CPI: CRITERION GROUPS FROM NORMAL LIFE

While the MMPI can be employed to test normal subjects, it has some limitations when used in this way. The main problem is that the criterion groups that defined the scales were composed of psychiatric patients. This prompted the development of several new inventories constructed according to the same logic that led to the MMPI but with normal rather than with pathological criterion groups. One of the best known of these is the *California Psychological Inventory,* or *CPI.* The CPI is especially aimed at high-school and college students. It tests for various personality traits such as dominance, sociability, responsibility, a sense of wellbeing, and so on.

As an example of how scales for these and other traits were derived, consider dominance. High-school and college students were asked to name the most and the least dominant people within their social circles. The people who comprised these two extremes were then used as the criterion groups that defined the dominance-submission dimension. Other traits were defined in a similar manner, and several validity scales were added to assess the subjects' test-taking attitudes (Gough, 1975).

THE VALIDITY OF PERSONALITY INVENTORIES

The originators of the MMPI, the CPI, and other personality inventories based on criterion groups, took considerable pains to provide their instruments with a solid, empirical foundation. To evaluate the success of their efforts, we must look at the validity of these tests.

Predictive validity　The usual way to assess validity is to determine the degree to which a test can predict some real-world events. There is evidence that personality tests do indeed have some *predictive validity.* For instance, among college women during the fifties and sixties, the sociability scale of the CPI correlated with how often the subject went out on dates and whether she joined a sorority. Other scales correlate with how subjects are rated by their peers (Hase and Goldberg, 1967).

The trouble is that while personality inventories can predict behavior, their efficiency in doing so is not terribly high. The correlations between test scores and validity criteria are generally in the neighborhood of +.30. This doesn't compare very well with the validation coefficients of intelligence tests (usually assessed by correlating IQ and academic performance), which are about +.50. The contrast is even sharper if we compare the usefulness of these personality tests with the predictive efficiency of common-sense measures such as relevant past behavior in related situations. The result is simple: The best predictor of future performance (for example, of psychiatric breakdown or delinquency) is past performance. A dramatic and widely cited example is provided by a study which showed that the thickness of a mental patient's file folder correlates +.61 with the probability of his rehospitalization following his release (Lasky et al., 1959).

Construct validation The relatively low predictive validity coefficients of personality inventories may not be grounds for as much chagrin as one might assume at first. For what most personality tests try to get at is some hypothesized psychological entities, such as traits, that are presumed to underlie overt behavior. In effect, the trait—whether sociability, or psychopathic deviance, or whatever—is a theoretical concept devised by the psychologist in an effort to make sense, not just of one set of observations, but of many. To validate such a construct one has to devise and test hypotheses about the relation between the underlying trait and various behavioral effects. This is **construct validation,** an approach we discussed previously, in the context of intelligence testing (see Chapter 15).

Construct validation is often built upon a set of diverse relationships between the test scores and rather different behavioral manifestations. An example is provided by the psychopathic deviance scale (Pd) of the MMPI, a scale originally based upon those items that differentiated a group of delinquents from other groups (see Table 16.1). Not too surprisingly, normal (that is, nondelinquent) high-school students who are regarded as "least responsible" by their classmates have much higher Pd scores than students rated as "most responsible." A related fact is that high Pd scores are characteristic of school dropouts. Another set of findings shows that high Pd scorers tend to be relatively aggressive and are unlikely to be considered good natured. Rather further afield is the fact that high Pd scores are also characteristic of professional actors. Still more remote is the finding that hunters who have carelessly shot someone in a hunting accident have higher Pd scores than other hunters. On the face of it, many of these findings seem unrelated, but they do fit together if understood as different manifestations of the same underlying personality trait—psychopathic deviance. In its extreme form, this trait is characterized by shallow social and emotional ties, a disregard of social mores and conventions, a failure to consider potential dangers and to worry about the consequences of one's own actions—in short, an attitude that says, "I just don't give a damn" (Cronbach and Meehl, 1955).

The various correlations just described are all fairly small. None of these effects—being rated irresponsible, having hunting accidents, and so on—correlate strongly enough with the Pd scale to provide a decent single criterion for predictive validity. But when they are considered together, they fit into a network of relationships that does seem to give some validity to the underlying construct. Seen in this light, the fact that the individual correlations are not very strong is not surprising. "If they were, we would find the same person dropping out of school, being ill-natured, becoming a Broadway actor and shooting a fellow hunter. . . . Personality structure, even if perfectly measured, represents only a disposition rather than a determining force" (Cronbach, 1970a, p. 555). How that disposition manifests itself depends upon the particular circumstances the person is in.

Barnum effects Finding out whether a personality test predicts some relevant performance or whether it fits some theoretical construct are reasonable criteria for assessing its validity. But there is one criterion that is of little use, and that is the person's own acceptance of the test interpretation. For when that description is sufficiently broad so as to fit just about any one, many of us will be all too

"You are trustworthy, loyal, helpful, friendly, courteous, kind, obedient, cheerful, thrifty, brave, clean, reverent."

The Barnum effect *(Drawing by Chas. Addams; © 1936, 1964, The New Yorker Magazine, Inc.)*

TABLE 16.2 PERSONALITY SKETCH LIKELY TO PRODUCE A BARNUM EFFECT

1. You have a great need for other people to like and admire you.
2. You have a tendency to be critical of yourself.
3. You have a great deal of unused capacity, which you have not turned to your advantage.
4. While you have some personality weaknesses, you are generally able to compensate for them.
5. Your sexual adjustment has presented problems for you.
6. Disciplined and self-controlled outside, you tend to be worried and insecure inside.
7. You have found it unwise to be too frank in revealing yourself to others.
8. At times you are extroverted, affable, sociable, while at other times you are introverted, wary, reserved.

SOURCE: Adapted from Forer, 1949.

readily disposed to accept it. This phenomenon is called the **Barnum effect** after P. T. Barnum of circus fame, who coined the slogan "There's a sucker born every minute."

An early demonstration of the Barnum effect was performed by Bertram Forer who asked the students in one of his classes to take a personality test (Forer, 1949). This test made them list the hobbies, personal characteristics, secret hopes, and ambitions of the person they would like to be. Forer promised that within a week he would give them a brief description of their personality based on the results of the test. True to his word, he gave each subject what appeared to be a personalized interpretation: a typed personality sketch with the student's own name written on the top. The subjects were assured that their privacy would be strictly respected, since no one except they and Dr. Forer would ever know the contents of the sketch.

After reading the sketches, the students were asked to rate the effectiveness of the test in describing their personality, using a scale from 0 (poor) to 5 (perfect). They evidently thought that the test had done a good job, for their average rating was 4.3. There was only one thing wrong: Unbeknown to the subjects, Forer had given each of them the identical personality sketch.

So how could they possibly have considered the sketch a good description of their own unique personalities? We can understand what happened when we consider the kind of statements that Forer compiled to make up the sketch (see Table 16.2).

As the table shows, the statements that comprised the personality sketch were sufficiently vague to apply to just about all of the subjects. For most of them must surely have felt a desire to be liked by others, or been occasionally insecure, or worried, or concerned about their sexual adjustment, and so on. Under the circumstances, it's not really surprising that the subjects felt that the test had indeed done a good job.★ Numerous later studies confirmed Forer's general findings (e.g., Snyder, Shenkel, and Lowery, 1977; Dickson and Kelly, 1985). The moral is clear. The mere fact that people believe that a test interpretation fits them is no guarantee of the test's validity.

★ Interestingly enough, most of the statements in the sketch were taken from a newsstand astrology book. After all, astrologers (and palmists and tea-leaf readers) undoubtedly depended upon the Barnum effect for thousands of years before Barnum was born.

UNSTRUCTURED PERSONALITY TESTS

The 1940s and 1950s saw the increasing popularity of a new approach to personality assessment—the use of *projective techniques.* These techniques present the subject with a relatively unstructured task, such as making up a story to fit a picture or describing what he sees in an inkblot. In part, this approach was a protest against the highly structured paper-and-pencil tests of personality discussed above. As we saw, the MMPI and similar tests contain various safeguards to assure that the subject will not lie to the test administrator. But critics pointed out that these tests give no guarantee that the subjects will not lie to themselves. In line with psychoanalytic thinking (of which more later—see pp. 669–95), they were convinced that the deeper layers of any individual's personality contain repressed wishes, unconscious conflicts, and various hidden defense maneuvers that are not accessible by ordinary means. But how can one penetrate below the surface to find out what the subject does not know himself?

In their view, the trick is to circumvent the subject's own defenses against threatening impulses and ideas. They believed that when structuring unstructured materials the subject cannot help but unveil some deeper facets of his personality makeup. The test materials are thus considered a kind of screen upon which the subject "projects" his inner feelings, wishes, conflicts, and ideas.

The number and variety of projective techniques invented during the past sixty years is remarkable. Some require the subject to give word associations or to complete unfinished sentences, others to draw a person or to copy designs; yet others ask subjects to state three wishes. We will consider only the two that are used most widely—the *Rorschach inkblot technique* and the *Thematic Apperception Test.*

THE RORSCHACH INKBLOTS

Hermann Rorschach, a Swiss psychologist, used the perception of unstructured forms as a diagnostic tool. He used ten symmetrical inkblots, some colored and some black and white, and presented them to various groups of psychiatric patients. When the patients were asked what they saw in the inkblots, their responses seemed to differ depending upon the diagnostic group to which they

Young girl taking a Rorschach test
(Photograph by Mimi Forsyth, Monkmeyer)

belonged. Rorschach regarded these findings as tentative, but he nevertheless used them to devise a system for scoring and interpretation (Zubin, Eron, and Shumer, 1965).

Administration and scoring While there are several different systems for administering, scoring, and interpreting the Rorschach, all share certain overall features (Klopfer et al., 1954; Exner, 1974, 1978). The subject is presented with each of ten cards, one at a time, and is asked what she sees, what the blots might be (see Figure 16.2 for an example of a card similar to those used in the test). After all ten of the cards have been presented, the examiner queries the subject about each response to find out which part of the blot was used and which of its attributes determined its nature.

The scoring is according to various categories, such as the portion of the blot that is used in the response (e.g., the whole blot, a large detail, a small detail), the attributes of the stimulus that are the basis of the response (e.g., form, shading, color), and the content of the response (e.g., human figures, parts of human figures, animals or parts of animals, inanimate objects, blood).

Interpretation Rorschach experts insist that the interpretation of a Rorschach record cannot be performed in a simple cookbook fashion, for it demands the interrelation of all of its various features in all their complexity. In their view, interpretation is a subtle art that requires much talent and even more experience. Nevertheless, we can at least sketch a few of the major hypotheses about certain Rorschach signs. For example, using the entire inkblot is said to indicate integrative, conceptual thinking, whereas the use of a high proportion of small details suggests compulsive rigidity. A relatively frequent use of the white space (which then serves as figure rather than as ground) is supposed to be a sign of rebelliousness and negativism, and responses that are dominated by color suggest emotionality and impulsivity.

Assessing the validity of Rorschach interpretation is a difficult task. We will consider this issue together with similar ones raised by the other major projective technique in current use, the **Thematic Apperception Test,** or **TAT,** developed by Henry Murray and his associates (Morgan and Murray, 1935).

16.2   An inkblot of the type used in the Rorschach test *Because familiarity with the cards makes it difficult to evaluate a person's first reaction, most psychologists prefer not to print the actual inkblots used in the test. Five of the actual cards are in black and white; five others are colored.*

THE THEMATIC APPERCEPTION TEST (TAT)

To Rorschach, the content of the subject's responses was a secondary concern. What mattered to him was not so much whether a subject interpreted the inkblot as a giant moth, or a human face, or a splotch of blood. What really counted was the features of the card that were utilized—the whole card or just a part, the form or the color, and so on. In contrast, the originators of the TAT took content as their primary focus, for their emphasis was on the person's major motives and preoccupations, defenses, conflicts, and ways of interpreting the world.

Administration The TAT test materials are a number of pictures of various scenes (Figure 16.3). The subject is asked to tell a story about each picture, to describe what is happening, what led up to the scene, and what the outcome will be.

Interpretation In clinical practice, TAT interpretation is usually a rather freewheeling affair. Each story suggests a hypothesis that is then checked and elaborated (or discarded) by looking at later stories. The desired end product is a picture of the person's major motives and conflicts, pieced together by interpreting the TAT stories in the light of all available information, of which the case history is probably the most important.

Some illustrations of this impressionistic and global approach to TAT interpretation are provided by the stories elicited by one of the cards, which shows a boy looking at a violin that lies on a table in front of him. A forty-five-year-old business man, who was an important executive in his firm and believed to have an even brighter future, gave this story:

> This is a child prodigy dreaming over his violin, thinking more of the music than anything else. But of wonderment that so much music can be in the instrument and in the fingers of his own hand. . . . I would say that possibly he is in reverie about what he can be or what he can do with his music in the times that lie ahead. He is dreaming of concert halls, tours, and . . . the beauty he will be able to express and even now can express with his own talents.

A clerk in the same firm was about the same age, but had been in the same position for many years and was regarded as unlikely to advance further. He produced this story:

> . . . This is the son of a very well-known, a very good musician. . . . The father has probably died. The only thing the son has left is this violin which is undoubtedly a very good one. . . . To the son, the violin is the father and the son sits there daydreaming of the time that he will understand the music and interpret it on the violin that his father had played.

According to the interpreter, the difference in the two stories reflects the difference between the achievements and aspirations of the two men. Both presumably identify with the boy in the picture but in different ways. The successful executive concentrates upon the work to be accomplished (the music), visualizes eventual success (the concert halls), and sees himself as part of it (the fingers of his own hand). In contrast, the clerk focuses on the difference between the boy and his dead successful father whom he may not be able to emulate (very well-known, very good musician) so that he only daydreams of future success and understanding (Henry, 1973).

Interpretations of this sort are very beguiling. But are the facets of personality suggested by the test interpretation really there? Are these interpretations equally astute when the tester does not have the benefit of hindsight, when she does not know the salient facts of the subject's life history?

VALIDITY OF PROJECTIVE TECHNIQUES

By now, there must be nearly ten thousand published articles that are explicitly devoted to the Rorschach and the TAT. Considering all this effort, the upshot has been disappointing. According to some experts, these techniques have some limited validity; according to others, they have little or none (Holt, 1978; Kleinmuntz, 1982; Rorer, 1990).

Validity and the Rorschach   Individual Rorschach indices—especially those that don't refer to content—show little or no relation to external validity criteria. In one study of psychiatric patients, over thirty different measures from the Rorschach records (for instance, the number of responses using the whole inkblot) were studied to see whether there was any relation to later diagnosis. There was none. Similar results apply to nonpsychiatric populations. For example, a preponderance of responses that involve human movement is said to indicate creativity, but a group of eminent artists were no different from ordinary persons in this regard (Zubin, Eron, and Shumer, 1965).

Studies of this kind have sometimes been criticized as too "atomistic," for they focus on single aspects of a subject's Rorschach record. Wouldn't it be better to use the test as a whole and to allow the judge to read the entire record

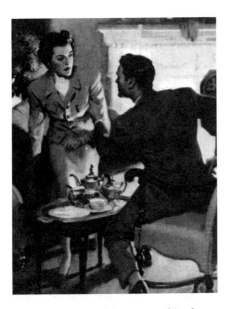

16.3   A picture of the type used in the TAT

verbatim (or even to administer the test) and then predict the criterion on the basis of this overall, global knowledge? One study that meets these conditions used twelve eminent Rorschach experts who tried to assess the personalities of various patients on the basis of their complete Rorschach records. These Rorschach-based assessments were then compared to the pooled judgment of a number of psychiatrists who had read each patient's case history, obtained in six or so interviews of several hours each. The mean correlation between the Rorschach experts' predictions and the psychiatrists' judgments was +.21. Apparently then, global assessment on the basis of the verbatim record does have some modest validity (Little and Shneidman, 1959).

Some efforts by John Exner suggest that the clinical usefulness of the Rorschach may be increased by using a more rigorous system of administration, scoring, and interpretation (Exner, 1974, 1978; Exner and Clark, 1978). The system he developed to accomplish this has led to a considerable improvement in the test's reliability, as shown by a large increase in its test-retest stability. Whether it will also increase the test's diagnostic power (that is, its validity) is as yet unclear.

Validity and the TAT The TAT has fared no better than the Rorschach in validity studies that assess its ability to predict psychiatric diagnosis. In one case study, the TAT was administered to over a hundred male veterans, some in mental hospitals and others in college. The TAT results showed no difference between normals and patients, let alone between different psychiatric groups (Eron, 1950).

While the TAT may have little value as a diagnostic tool for psychiatric classification, the test does seem to have some validity for more limited purposes. A number of studies have shown that the TAT may be a fair indicator of the presence of certain motives, though probably not of all. One group of investigators worked with subjects who had not eaten for various periods of time. When presented with TAT-like pictures, some of which suggested food or eating, hungry subjects came up with more stories whose plots concerned hunger or food-seeking than a control group of sated subjects (Atkinson and McClelland, 1948). Related findings have been obtained with various other motives, including aggression, sexual arousal, the need for achievement, and so on. The success of these efforts represents a kind of construct validation of the TAT as an assessment device for at least some motives.

Projective techniques and utility Given the verdict of these various validation studies, many projective experts have become convinced that their devices are not really tests at all, but instead are really adjuncts to a clinical interview (Zubin, Eron, and Shumer, 1965). Rorschach and TAT scores make little sense to a practitioner who has not administered the tests personally or at least read the verbatim records. They are also hard to interpret without a knowledge of the subject's background and life history. But proponents of these techniques argue that when they are used as part of the total clinical evaluation, they help to provide a richer understanding of the person. We have seen that when the Rorschach or TAT are used in this manner, they do indeed have some modest predictive validity for diagnosis. But according to some critics, predictive validity is not enough; the real issue is whether these tests have **incremental validity** (Meehl, 1959). The question is how much additional (that is, *incremental*) information these techniques provide over and above that which is contained in case histories and similar data that have to be gathered anyway. To give and score a Rorschach or a TAT is time-consuming; so if the effort is to be worthwhile, these tests ought to provide a reasonable increment in information. But the available evidence suggests they don't. Several studies have shown that when

A

B

Stock characters in the Hollywood Western (A) The hero (played by William S. Hart) and a woman in distress in Wild Bill Hickok, *and* (B) the hero (played by Roy Rogers) and the villain (played by George Hayes) in Young Buffalo Bill. (Courtesy of Movie Stills Archives)

clinical psychologists were asked to make inferences about a subject's personal characteristics, they were just as accurate with only the case history to go on as they were when provided with additional data in the form of the Rorschach or TAT records (Kostlan, 1954; Winch and More, 1956).

THE TRAIT APPROACH

Personality tests have a very practical purpose: They are meant as an aid in diagnosis and counseling. But psychologists who study the topic of personality have aims that go beyond such applications, no matter how socially useful those might be. They want to understand the kinds of differences that personality tests uncover, to find a useful framework within which to describe such differences, and to discover how they come about. In their efforts to answer these questions, they appeal to several so-called personality theories.

Most of the theories of personality that have been developed thus far aren't really theories in the conventional sense. They are not specific enough to make the clear-cut predictions that would help us choose between them. What they are instead are different orientations from which the subject of personality is approached. We will begin with the *trait approach,* which tries to describe individuals by a set of characterizing attributes.

Trait theory is first of all an attempt to be descriptive. It tries to find some way to characterize people by reference to some underlying basic traits. But just which traits are basic? The comic theaters of classical and Renaissance days—and modern trait theory—imply not merely that a particular person has a characteristic personality, but that this personality can be categorized along with those of others who are in some ways equivalent. But what are the categories along which people should be grouped together? The early playwrights (and many film makers) picked a few attributes that were easy to characterize and caricature—the tight-lipped silence of the Western hero who speaks only with his guns, the virtuous chastity of the eternal heroine, the cowardice of the braggart soldier (who in Shakespeare's hands transcends his type and becomes Falstaff). But are these the personality traits that are really primary for the description of human personality?

The trait theorists' search for an answer is a bit like an attempt to find a few general principles that underlie the multitude of masks on, say, an Italian Renaissance stage. At first glance, these masks are very different, as different as the many people we encounter in real life. Is there a way to classify these masks according to a few basic dimensions? Put another way, can we classify human personality by reference to a few fundamental traits?

Transcending type in the modern Western Some modern film makers deliberately play on the stock conceptions of earlier days, as in the recent Western Unforgiven, *in which Gene Hackman plays a sadistic sheriff and Clint Eastwood a sympathetic gunman. (Photograph © Warner Bros., Inc.; courtesy of Photofest)*

THE SEARCH FOR THE RIGHT TAXONOMY

In a way, much the same question is faced during the early stages of any science. At this point, a major task is the development of a useful *taxonomy,* or classification system. Consider the early biologists. They recognized that various creatures differ in a multitude of ways—in their size and color, in the absence or the presence of a skeleton, in the number and kind of appendages, and so on. The biologists had to decide which of these distinctions provided the most useful classification categories. The psychologist who studies personality differences faces exactly the same issues. The dictionary lists 18,000 trait names (Allport and Odbert, 1936). But without some kind of taxonomy, how can we decide which of these are basic traits, important for classifying all people?

CLASSIFICATION THROUGH LANGUAGE

One step towards a taxonomy of personality traits grew out of an examination of the language used to describe personality attributes (Allport and Odbert, 1936). Advocates of this procedure argue that the adjectives we use to describe people (e.g., shy, friendly, stingy, generous, arrogant, humble, and so on) embody the accumulated observations of many previous generations. A systematic sifting of such trait adjectives might therefore give clues about individual differences whose description has been important enough to withstand the test of time (Goldberg, 1982).

This line of reasoning led to the development of a widely used personality inventory by Raymond Cattell (1957). Cattell's starting point was a set of 4,500 terms taken from the 18,000 trait words in an unabridged dictionary. This list was drastically reduced by throwing out difficult or uncommon words and eliminating synonyms. Finally, 171 trait names were left. A group of judges was then asked to rate subjects by using these terms. Their ratings were then subjected to a *factor analysis* using methods similar to those employed in the study of intelligence-test performance—that is, by finding out which items correlated highly with one another while correlating little or not all with others. The resulting item clusters were then inspected to see what they had in common, yielding what Cattell thought were some sixteen primary dimensions of personality. Each of these dimensions was defined by a pair of adjectives that describe the opposite poles of the dimension, such as outgoing versus reserved, suspicious versus trusting, tense versus relaxed, happy-go-lucky versus sober, and so on (Cattell, 1966).

Later work by other investigators managed to reduce the number of primary dimensions to a smaller set. A widely quoted study by Warren Norman featured five major dimensions of personality, often dubbed the "Big Five": extroversion (sometimes called extraversion), emotional stability, agreeableness, conscientiousness, and cultural sensitivity. The Big-Five model is hierarchical in the sense that several lower-level traits (for example tidy/careless, persevering/fickle) can be regarded as manifestations of one of the Big-Five factors (here, conscientiousness; see Table 16.3).

NEUROTICISM AND EXTROVERSION/ INTROVERSION

Many later studies have come up with other five-factor descriptions of personality that are quite similar to Norman's (see Brody, 1988; Goldberg, 1990, 1993;

The seven dwarfs as character types
Doc, Sleepy, Grumpy, Dopey, Sneezy, Happy, and Bashful. (From Walt Disney's Snow White; *courtesy of the Kobal Collection)*

TABLE 16.3 THE NORMAN FIVE-FACTOR TAXONOMY OF PERSONALITY TRAITS

Factor names	Scale dimensions
Extroversion	Talkative/Silent
	Frank, open/Secretive
	Adventurous/Cautious
	Sociable/Reclusive
Agreeableness	Good-natured/Irritable
	Not jealous/Jealous
	Mild, gentle/Headstrong
	Cooperative/Negativistic
Conscientiousness	Fussy, tidy/Careless
	Responsible/Undependable
	Scrupulous/Unscrupulous
	Persevering/Quitting, fickle
Emotional stability	Poised/Nervous, tense
	Calm/Anxious
	Composed/Excitable
	Not hypochondriacal/Hypochondriacal
Culture	Artistically sensitive/Artistically insensitive
	Intellectual/Unreflective, narrow
	Polished, refined/Crude, boorish
	Imaginative/Simple, direct

SOURCE: Adapted from Norman, 1963.

John, 1990). But others have suggested that the underlying dimensions of personality may be even fewer. The most influential alternative is that proposed by Hans Eysenck, who tried to encompass the whole spectrum of personality differences in a space defined by just two dimensions: neuroticism/emotional stability and extroversion/introversion (which correspond to two of Norman's dimensions).

Neuroticism is equivalent to emotional instability and maladjustment. It is assessed by affirmative answers to questions like "Do you ever feel 'just miserable' for no good reason at all?" and "Do you often feel disgruntled?" *Extroversion/introversion* are terms that refer to the main direction of a person's energies, toward the outer world of material objects and other people or toward the inner world of one's own thoughts and feelings. The extrovert is sociable, impulsive, and enjoys new experiences, while the introvert tends to be more solitary, cautious, and slow to change. Extroversion is indicated by affirmative answers to questions such as "Do you like to have many social engagements?" and "Would you rate yourself as a happy-go-lucky individual?"

As Eysenck sees it, neuroticism/emotional stability and extroversion/introversion are independent dimensions. To be sure, introverts and many neurotics have something in common: They are both unsociable and withdrawn. But, in Eysenck's view, their lack of sociability has different roots. Healthy introverts are not afraid of social activities: They simply do not like them. In contrast, neurotically shy people keep to themselves because of fear: They want to be with others but are afraid of joining them.

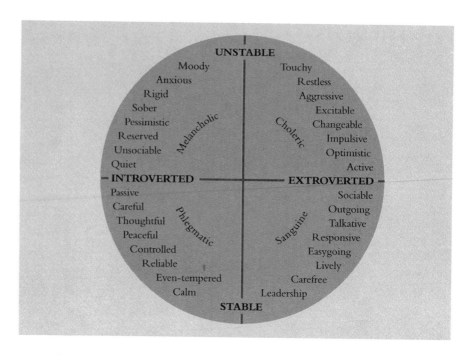

16.4 Eysenck's two-dimensional classification of personality *Two dimensions of personality—neuroticism/emotional stability and extroversion/introversion—define a space into which various trait terms may be fitted. Eysenck points out that the four quadrants of this space seem to fit Hippocrates's temperaments: introverted and stable—phlegmatic; introverted and unstable—melancholic; extroverted and stable—sanguine; and extroverted and unstable—choleric. (After Eysenck and Rachman, 1965)*

Eysenck's two-dimensional classification defines a conceptual space into which many trait terms can be fitted (see Figure 16.4). To the extent that it or similar systems succeed, they are analogous to the classification schemes that have proved so successful in the field of sensory psychology, such as, the color solid, which accommodates all possible colors on the basis of just three dimensions—brightness, hue, and saturation (see Chapter 5, pp. 185–86).

Eysenck points to an interesting relation between his own two-dimensional space and the venerable four-fold classification of temperaments proposed by the ancient Greek physician Hippocrates (ca. 400 B.C.). Hippocrates believed that there are four human temperaments that correspond to four different personality types: *sanguine* (cheerful and active), *melancholic* (gloomy), *choleric* (angry and violent), and *phlegmatic* (calm and passive). He believed that these temperaments reflected an excess of one of four bodily humors; thus sanguine people were thought to have relatively more blood, melancholy people to have an excess of black bile, phlegmatic people to have an excess of phlegm, and choleric people an excess of yellow bile (see Figure 16.5). Today the humor theory is a mere historical curiosity, but Hippocrates's four-fold classification is in some ways still with us. For the four quadrants of Eysenck's two-dimensional space seem to fit Hippocrates's four temperamental types. The category *introverted and stable* corresponds to *phlegmatic, introverted and unstable* to *melancholic, extroverted and stable* to *sanguine,* and *extroverted and unstable* to *choleric* (Eysenck and Rachman, 1965).

BIG FIVE OR BIG THREE?

A later version of Eysenck's system adds a third dimension independent of the other two, called **psychoticism**—a characteristic related to aggressive, antisocial, cold, impulsive, and self-centered attributes.★ This new dimension evidently

★ Eysenck uses the term *psychoticism* because he believes that some of the psychiatric disorders that used to be categorized under the broad psychiatric rubric *psychosis* represent the absolute extreme on this axis. The same holds for the term *neurosis,* a term now obsolete in psychiatric diagnosis but still widely current in popular usage, designating an individual plagued by disabling, anxiety-related inner conflicts.

encompasses two more of the Big-Five dimensions: agreeableness/disagreeableness and conscientiousness/irresponsibility. Eysenck believes that the fifth, which Big-Five theorists describe as cultural sensitivity and openness to experience, is related to cognitive and educational traits, including intelligence (Eysenck and Eysenck, 1975, 1983; for discussion, see Claridge, 1983).

IS FACTOR ANALYSIS THE PROPER ROAD TO A TAXONOMY?

A number of psychologists have taken issue with factor analytical approaches such as Eysenck's and those that led to the Big Five. They point out that there is no guarantee that the factors extracted by such methods are the "real" dimensions of personality, since the results of the analysis depend on what is fed into it. The factors describe the coherence among a certain set of items; if some items are added and others subtracted, the pattern of coherence (and thus the factors) may well be different.

While this critique of the factor analytic approach has some merit, there is no denying the fact that at least some of the major dimensions discovered in this manner seem to come up again and again even if different tests are used. This is especially true for the two main pillars of Eysenck's classification system, extroversion and emotional instability. In fact, there is some evidence that these two dimensions may apply not just to our own culture but to others, since much the same factor pattern was obtained in such diverse societies as Bangladesh, Brazil, Hong Kong, and Japan. (Eysenck and Eysenck, 1983; for a further discussion of personality differences and similarities in different cultures, see Chapter 17, pp. 702–703).

THE TRAIT-SITUATION CONTROVERSY

Different trait theorists may argue about the kind and number of trait dimensions with which to describe personality. Yet on one thing they all agree: There are personality traits that are stable and enduring properties of the individual. This basic credo has come under serious attack. One reason was the predictive validity of personality tests. For while tests such as the MMPI and the CPI predict behavior, they don't predict it all that accurately. Critics of the trait approach suggest that the tests don't do as well as one might wish because that which they are trying to measure—a set of stable personality traits—isn't really there. To put it another way, they contend that there is no real consistency in the way people behave at different times and in different situations.

THE ATTACK ON TRAIT THEORY

The challenge to the trait concept was launched over twenty-five years ago by Walter Mischel, whose survey of the research literature led him to conclude that

*16.5 **An early taxonomy of personality**   A medieval illustration of one of the earliest attempts to classify human personality, Hippocrates's four temperaments: sanguine (cheerful and active), melancholic (gloomy), choleric (angry and violent), and phlegmatic (calm and passive). According to Hippocrates, these temperaments reflected an excess of one of four bodily humors; thus sanguine persons were thought to have relatively more blood. Today the humor theory is a mere historical curiosity, but some aspects of Hippocrates's classification are still with us. (Courtesy of the Bettmann Archive)*

Traits versus situations Do the fighters punch each other because they want to win the prize money (situation) or because they are angry men (trait)? The blows probably hurt just as much either way. (Stag at Sharkey's. Oil on canvas, 1909, 92 × 122.6 cm. George Bellows, American, 1882–1925. © The Cleveland Museum of Art, 1994, Hinman B. Hurlbut Collection, 1133.22)

people behave much less consistently than a trait theory would predict (Mischel, 1968). A classic study concerns honesty in children (Hartshorne and May, 1928). Grade-school children were placed in a variety of settings in which they had the opportunity to lie, cheat, or steal: in athletic events, in the classroom, at home, alone, or with peers. The important finding was that the child who was dishonest in one situation (cheating on a test) was not necessarily dishonest in another setting (cheating in an athletic contest). There was some consistency, but it was rather unimpressive; a later reanalysis of the results came up with an average intercorrelation of +.30 between honest behavior in one setting and honesty in another (Burton, 1963). The more similar the two settings, the greater were the correlations. Thus honesty in one classroom situation was more consistent with honesty in another classroom situation than with honesty assessed at home.

Mischel argued that a similar lack of cross-situational consistency is found for many other behavior patterns, such as aggression, dependency, rigidity, and reactions to authority. The intercorrelations among different measures of what seems to be the same trait are often low and sometimes nonexistent. In Mischel's view, the fact that personality tests have relatively low validities is just another demonstration of the same phenomenon. A personality test taps behavior in one situation, while the validity criterion of that test assesses behavior in another context. Since cross-situational consistency tends to be low, so are validity coefficients.

SITUATIONISM

The failure to find behavioral consistency has been taken as an argument against the importance of personality characteristics in determining what a person will do. But if these are not relevant, what is? One answer is offered by *situationism,* the notion that human behavior is largely determined by the characteristics of the situation itself rather than by the characteristics of the person. That this is so for some situations is indubitable. Given a red light, most drivers stop; given a green light, most go—regardless of whether they are friendly or unfriendly, stingy or generous, dominant or submissive, and so on. Situations of this sort produce predictable reactions in virtually all of us. According to situationism, the same principle applies to much or nearly all of human behavior. Consider the enormous effect of social roles, which often define what an actor must do with little regard to who the actor is (see Chapter 11). To predict how someone will act in a courtroom, there is little point in asking whether she is sociable or extravagant with money, or whether she gets along with her mother. What we really want to know is the role that she will play—judge, prosecutor, defense attorney, or defendant. Seen in this light, what we do depends not on who we are, but on the situation in which we find ourselves.

This is not to say that situationists deny the existence of individual differences. They certainly agree that various demographic and socioeconomic factors—such as age and sex, marital status, ethnic background, occupation, and income—are powerful determinants of human behavior. Nor do they dispute the important effect of differences in ability, especially cognitive ability. As they see it, all of these factors determine the kinds of situations a person is likely to encounter (or to have encountered) and thus to learn from. But in their view, it is these situations, rather than personality traits, that determine what people actually do.

CONSISTENCY AS AN ILLUSION

If situationism is correct, the underlying consistency of the personalities of our friends and acquaintances (and perhaps our own) is more or less illusory. But if so, how can one explain the fact that most people have been subject to this particular illusion since the days of Greek drama and no doubt much before?

According to critics of trait theory, one explanation is that people's personalities seem to be stable because we repeatedly see them in the same social setting. But the critics make an even more important point. In their view, personality traits are mental constructions devised by the observer who watches another person's actions and tries to make sense out of them. They believe that people are often faced with an overload of information, which they then try to reduce and simplify (e.g., Shweder, 1975; Nisbett and Ross, 1980; Ross and Nisbett, 1991). As a result, they are prone to various kinds of errors of inference that produce the belief that there are consistent personality traits.* Critics of trait theory argue that such errors show that personality descriptions are more in the eyes of the beholders than in the people they behold (Cantor and Mischel, 1977, 1979).

IN DEFENSE OF TRAITS

The emphasis on situations provided a useful corrective to those who sought to explain everything people do as a manifestation of their own inner nature. But if pushed to the extreme, this position becomes just as questionable as the one it tried to correct. For in this form situationism can be interpreted as asserting that personality does not exist at all. Whether any psychologist has actually gone to this extreme is doubtful; certainly Mischel never did (Mischel, 1973, 1979). But the very possibility that someone might climb all the way out on this particular theoretical limb was enough to produce a spirited counterreaction against Mischel's attack on the trait concept.

Consistency over time The reaction to the situationist position took several forms. Many authors felt that even if there is little personal consistency across *situations*, there is considerable consistency over *time* (Block, 1971, 1977). Proof comes from a number of longitudinal studies that show a fair degree of behav-

Consistency as an illusion *At a class reunion people may think that their old classmates haven't changed at all. They really have changed, but they act as they once did because they have returned to the old situation. Here we see Kathleen Turner in the 1986 film* Peggy Sue Got Married, *as she once again puts on the crown and holds the flowers as "homecoming queen" at her twenty-fifth class reunion. (Courtesy of the Kobal Collection)*

* We previously considered some of these errors in our discussion of attribution processes and person perception, for example, the fundamental attribution error, illusory correlations, and oversimplified schemas and stereotypes (see Chapter 11).

ioral consistency over sizable stretches of the life span. Thus in one study, dependability in males as judged in high school correlated quite well with ratings of the same attribute made by different judges some ten or more years later (*r* = +.55; Block, 1971). In another study, male adults between seventeen and eighty-five years of age were given the same personality inventory at six- and twelve-year intervals. The correlations between their scores on the first and second administration of the inventory (on traits such as dominance, sociability, and emotional stability) ranged from +.59 to +.87 (Costa, McCrae, and Arenberg, 1980).

Consistency across situations   Others have argued that there is behavioral consistency across situations, despite Mischel's critique. According to Seymour Epstein, cross-situational consistency is much higher than Mischel had supposed. In Epstein's view, studies that seem to show low cross-situational consistency usually employ only a small sample of behaviors. As a result, the assessment of the relevant trait is necessarily unreliable. And the correlation between two (unreliable) measures of this trait cannot help but be low or nonexistent. To determine whether people behave consistently from one situation to another, the behavior in each situation (e.g., cheating in class and cheating on the athletic field) must be measured not just once, but on a number of different occasions.

To buttress his position, Epstein observed subjects' moods and behavior on about thirty days. He found that correlations from one day to any other day were very low. He then compared correlations based on the average score on any two days, then on any three days, and so on. As the number of observations increased, the correlations rose from about +.30 to +.80 (Epstein, 1979, 1980).

Epstein interprets these findings as evidence for cross-situational consistency. But Mischel and his collaborators reply that they are essentially demonstrations of consistency in time and not across situations, though this is still a matter of considerable debate (Mischel and Peake, 1983; Epstein, 1983).

The definition of consistency   Another issue concerns the definition of cross-situational consistency. Whether such consistency is found may well depend on what behaviors the experimenter defined as different or equivalent for the purposes of assessing a given trait. A number of authors argue that behavioral inconsistency is often more apparent than real, for two reactions that are at first glance quite dissimilar may turn out to be a manifestation of the same underlying trait when examined more closely (e.g., Moskowitz, 1982; Buss and Craik, 1983; Rorer and Widiger, 1983).

Consistency across situations?   *In some situations, most people behave the same way. In others, people behave differently. A major task of personality psychology is to discover whether they behave consistently across situations. (Left: Photograph by Bob Krist/Black Star. Right: Photograph by Jan Halaska/ Photo Researchers)*

Aggression in boys and men The same trait is often (though not always) expressed differently at different ages. (Left: Photograph by Wayne Miller/Magnum. Right: Photograph by Paul Kennedy/Leo de Wys)

Some examples come from the study of development. Consider aggression. In males, aggression is fairly consistent between childhood and adolescence, but it takes different overt forms at different ages. Young boys pummel each other with their fists; young men rarely do more than shout in anger (Kagan and Moss, 1962). Another example concerns the distinction between the attributes happy/outgoing and somber/reserved. When different judges were asked to assess this trait in people first studied at age six and then again at age fifteen, their ratings were quite similar, yielding correlations of about +.60. This consistency disappeared, however, when the judges were asked to rate overt behavior only. But as the author saw it, this result made sense. The five-year-old who is reserved and somber shows this by a low level of physical vitality. At ten, the same underlying attribute manifests itself as cautiousness and emotional vulnerability. Still later, during adolescence, this basic pattern goes together with a sense of inferiority (Bronson, 1966).

Here, as in so many other aspects of behavior, a superficial difference disguises a deeper sameness. At a surface level, the two sentences *John eats the apple* and *The apple is eaten by John* are obviously different. But at a deeper level, they are in many ways alike and mean much the same thing (Chapter 9).

THE INTERACTION BETWEEN PERSON AND SITUATION

A number of psychologists feel that the debate between situationists and trait theorists has focused on the wrong distinction. As originally formulated, the question was whether an individual's actions are better predicted by the situation or by personal characteristics. But there is a third alternative: The critical factor may be the *interaction* between person and situation (e.g., Magnusson and Endler, 1977).

Person-by-situation interaction The term *interaction* is used here in a technical sense. To understand what it means in this context, consider a hypothetical experiment in which we study the reactions of several pairs of individuals to two different situations. The response to be measured will be anxiety as indicated by the galvanic skin response (GSR); the two situations are waiting to take a test and being threatened with electric shock. Let's call the subjects Jane and Carol, Mary and Claire, and let us assume that the GSR scale runs from 0 (no anxiety) to 12 (maximal anxiety). Two extreme outcomes are displayed in Tables 16.4 and 16.5 on the next page.

TABLE 16.4 AN EFFECT OF SITUATION			
	Situation		Average for each person
Person	Test	Shock	
Jane	3	9	6
Carol	3	9	6
Average for situation	3	9	

TABLE 16.5 AN EFFECT OF INDIVIDUAL DIFFERENCES			
	Situation		Average for each person
Person	Test	Shock	
Mary	3	3	3
Claire	9	9	9
Average for situation	6	6	

The results shown in Tables 16.4 and 16.5 are diametrically opposed. Table 16.4 depicts a powerful situational effect. For these two subjects, Jane and Carol, shock is evidently much more frightening than the test. But there is no effect of individual differences, since Jane and Carol behave identically. In Table 16.5 we see the reverse. Here individual differences have a profound effect; Claire is evidently much more fearful than is Mary. But in this second example, situational differences are insignificant as the two situations provoke essentially the equivalent amount of fear.

These two illustrations fit the extreme positions that ascribe all behavior either to the situation or to personality. Needless to say, there are much more plausible intermediate outcomes in which both factors play a role. But our concern is with another alternative, which has quite different theoretical implications. Consider the pattern of results shown by yet another pair of subjects—Donna and Anne—as indicated in Table 16.6.

What is important about the results of Table 16.6 is that they neither exhibit situational effects as such nor the effects of individual differences as such. When we look at average GSRs, Anne and Donna prove equally fearful. The same holds for the difference between the situations; on the average, the test and the threatened shock produce equal GSRs. But there is a new twist that is obscured by the averages. The two situations produce radically different effects in the two persons. Anne is evidently much more afraid of the shock than of the test, while the opposite holds for Donna. In statistical language, a relationship of this kind, in which the effect of one variable (fear-evoking situation) depends upon another variable (individual differences) is called an interaction.

The test-shock experiment here described is a highly simplified version of a large number of studies that have actually been carried out. An example is a

TABLE 16.6 AN INTERACTION EFFECT			
	Situation		Average for each person
Person	Test	Shock	
Anne	3	9	6
Donna	9	3	6
Average for situation	6	6	

Person-by-situation interaction *Like some other fantasy heroes, Superman is utterly fearless when faced by physical danger, but is shy and timid—at least as his alter ego, Clark Kent—when around women. (Top: Courtesy of Photofest. Bottom: Courtesy of Photofest)*

study in which subjects were asked to describe their usual reaction to various threats (Endler and Hunt, 1969). Some of these perils involved loss of self-esteem (failing an examination), others physical danger (being on a high ledge on a mountain top), still others a threat whose nature was still unclear (getting a police summons). The results showed that both individual differences and situations affected behavior to some extent. Some people seemed more generally fearful than others, and some situations ("being approached by cars racing abreast") evoked more fear than others ("sitting in a restaurant").

What is more interesting, though, is that the bulk of these effects were produced by the person-by-situation interaction. Put in other words, people tend to be frightened (or angered or reassured) by different things. This finding undercuts the usefulness of general traits such as "anxiety." To predict behavior better, such traits should be qualified; for example, "anxiousness in an interpersonal setting," "anxiousness when facing physical danger," "anxiousness in the face of the unknown." By this utilization of the person-by-situation interaction, the notion of stable personality differences can be maintained. But there is a price, for the process of qualification may be endless. Consider "anxiousness when facing physical dangers." Should this be further qualified so that we separately consider "anxiousness when facing inanimate nature," "anxiousness when facing threatening strangers," and "anxiousness in the presence of animals," with the last of these subdivided into "anxiousness with cats," "anxiousness with dogs," "anxiousness with horses"? The end result of such subdivisions can only be an enormous subdivision of ever more finely drawn traits (Cronbach, 1975; Nisbett, 1977).

Reciprocal interaction We've seen that different situations may affect different people differently. But the interaction between person and situation may go deeper than this. For in many cases, the relation between situation and person is reciprocal. People often play a major role in choosing the situations they confront—the places they live in, the work they do, the friends they associate with. And those choices are partially determined by their personality traits: The extrovert will generally find a lively party, while the introvert will seek a quiet corner where she can curl up with a book. The situation may (and often does) determine a person's behavior, but the person's traits often determine what situation that person finds herself in (Snyder, 1981; Endler, 1982).

Reciprocal effects of this sort pervade the domain of human interaction. They are a commonplace in the psychiatric clinic where many unhappy individuals don't recognize that the situations that trouble them so greatly are partially of their own creation. Further examples come from developmental psychology, where many investigators point to the fact that children of different temperaments elicit different reactions from their parents (e.g., Scarr and McCartney, 1983; see Chapter 14 for a fuller discussion).

CONSISTENCY AS A TRAIT

By now there is general agreement that, when properly defined, traits do exist. We've seen that a major criterion for determining whether such traits are present is cross-situational consistency in behavior. But recently psychologists have come to realize that consistency itself—the degree to which people do much the same thing in different situations—also varies from person to person. To the extent that this is true, cross-situational consistency may be regarded as a trait in its own right.

Some people are more consistent than others In most of us, what we do is affected by both our personal characteristics and by the demands of the situation. But

TABLE 16.7 SOME REPRESENTATIVE ITEMS FROM THE SELF-MONITORING SCALE

1. I can look anyone in the eye and tell a lie with a straight face (if for a right end). (True)★

2. In different situations and with different people, I often act like very different persons. (True)

3. I have trouble changing my behavior to suit different people and different situations. (False)

4. I can only argue for ideas which I already believe. (False)

★ In the items shown, the key after each question is in the direction of self-monitoring. Thus high self-monitors would presumably answer "True" to questions 1 and 2, and "False" to questions 3 and 4.

SOURCE: Snyder, 1987.

the extent to which one or the other of these predominates varies from person to person. It goes without saying that there are some social situations that affect most people equally and allow little play for personal variations. At a funeral, everyone is quiet and restrained (Price and Bouffard, 1974; Monson, Hesley, and Chernick, 1982). What about situations that are more ambiguous? Here some people will tend to behave much more consistently than others.

Self-monitoring Some people adjust their behavior to fit the social situation more than do others. One of the factors that determines the extent to which they do this, is the degree to which they try to control the impression they make on others, so that they can be "the right person in the right place at the right time." The tendency to do this is assessed by the ***self-monitoring scale,*** developed by Mark Snyder. (For some representative items, see Table 16.7). High self-monitors care a great deal about the appearance of the self they project in a social situation. By constantly adjusting to the situation, they are necessarily inconsistent; they'll act like cultured highbrows when with art lovers and boisterous sports fans when with a group of college athletes. In effect, they always seem to ask themselves: "How can I be the person this situation calls for?" In contrast, low self-monitors are much less interested in how they appear to others. They want to be themselves whatever the social climate in which they find themselves. As a result, their behavior is much more consistent from situation to situation (Snyder, 1987).★

On the face of it, the high self-monitor seems to cut a rather less admirable figure than his low self-monitoring counterpart. But as Snyder points out, whether such value judgments apply depends on the way in which the self-monitoring pattern fits into the rest of the individual's life. The high self-monitor is probably rather pleasant to be with, and his diplomatic skill and adaptability may well be an asset in dealing with the many roles created by a

★ One might guess that high self-monitoring is just another aspect of extroversion, since the social skills of high self-monitors would seem to be closely related to the extroverted style of life. There is indeed a correlation between the self-monitoring scale and tests of extroversion, but it is very slight. It appears that the two traits are at bottom quite different. High self-monitors can readily be the life of the party, but they will only be so when it seems appropriate. They know when the situation calls for greater decorum, say, at an upper-class tea party or in an art gallery, and then they will be properly reserved. The extrovert is much more likely to be gregarious and outgoing even in such situations (Snyder, 1987).

complex society such as ours. The virtues of the low self-monitor are even more apparent; there's much to be said for the man of integrity who is the same today as he'll be tomorrow and to himself is ever true.

But at the extremes, neither approach is particularly appealing. An extremely high self-monitor may very well be a shallow, unprincipled poseur. And an extremely low self-monitor may manage to turn the virtues of his pattern into vices as consistent adherence to principle becomes blind and stubborn rigidity. To march to the music of a different drummer is not necessarily admirable. It depends on what the music is (Snyder, 1987).

PERSON CONSTANCY

In looking back it's worth noting that the trait-situation controversy has its counterpart in a similar debate we encountered when discussing social psychology (see Chapters 11 and 12). The critics of trait theory have argued that traits alone do not predict what people will do. Similar claims have been made in the social realm, where the tendency to attribute an individual's actions to his dispositional qualities and underestimate the role of the situation (the fundamental attribution error) has been noted. The difficulty in predicting behavior from attitudes and the belief that unusual acts (such as blind obedience in the Milgram experiment) reflect unusual personality characteristics also indicate that emphasizing traits can be mistaken. The person-situation debate comes up again and again, and the social psychologists—and their like-minded colleagues in the field of personality—have highlighted one pole of this polarity by emphasizing the crucial and often underrated role of the situation.

In the light of all this, what can we say about the other end of the polarity—the assumption that there is an underlying unity in how any one individual acts and thinks and feels, a basic consistency that we call "personality" and that plays a role in determining behavior? The evidence indicates that this assumption—which goes back to the ancient dramatists and before—still stands.

We all have an intuitive belief in something like "person constancy," a phenomenon analogous to "object constancy" in perception (see Chapter 6). A chair is perceived as a stable object whose size remains the same whether we are near to it or far away and whose shape remains unchanged regardless of our visual orientation. These constancies are not illusions; they reflect a genuine sta-

The extremes of the self-monitoring scale (A) Woody Allen as the high self-monitor, Zelig, the man who can fit in with anybody, anywhere, anytime. (B) Woody Allen as the hero of most of his other movies who remains Woody Allen, the ultimate low self-monitor, who stays true to himself regardless of the situation. (Pictured with Calvin Coolidge and Herbert Hoover in Zelig, 1983, courtesy of the Kobal Collection; with Diane Keaton in Annie Hall, 1977, courtesy of the Kobal Collection)

A

B

bility in the external world. The stability of persons is in some ways analogous. For we somehow manage to peer through a welter of ever-changing situations to perceive an individual's behavioral consistency. The constancy of personality is not as sturdy as that of chairs, but it has some reality even so.

To be sure, we sometimes err and may see more uniformity and coherence than is actually there so that we exaggerate person constancy in others and in ourselves (Shweder, 1975; Nisbett and Wilson, 1977; Nisbett, 1980; Kihlstrom and Cantor, 1984). But the fact that there are errors in our perception of persons, doesn't mean that their personality is entirely in our own eyes. After all, there are visual illusions, but their existence does not disprove the fact that by and large we see the world as it really is. What holds for the world of vision probably holds for person perception as well, and this is probably why trait theory has continued to have so much appeal (Kenrick and Funder, 1988). Person constancy is a fact. Jane remains Jane whether she is at home or at the office, whether it is today or yesterday or the day after tomorrow. And at some level she is different from Carol and Margaret and six billion other humans alive today, for her personality—just like theirs—is unique.

TRAITS AND BIOLOGY

To the extent that person constancy exists, we are probably justified in holding on to some version of the trait approach. People vary in their characteristic modes of behavior, and their variations can be described and assessed, however imperfectly, by the trait vocabulary. But how do such variations arise?

Thus far, we've talked about traits as if they were merely descriptive labels for broad groups of behavior patterns. But some trait theorists go further. In their view, traits are general predispositions to behave in one way or another that are ultimately rooted in the individual's biological makeup.

PERSONALITY AND TEMPERAMENT

A number of modern investigators believe that personality traits grow out of the individual's **temperament,** a characteristic reaction pattern of the individual that is present from a rather early age. Like Hippocrates who coined the term some 2,500 years ago, they believe that such temperamental patterns are largely genetic and constitutional in origin (though they obviously don't share his archaic ideas of their underlying humoral basis). Such characteristic behavior patterns may begin in the first few months of life. An example comes from a study of 141 children, observed for about a decade following birth:

> Donald exhibited an extremely high activity level almost from birth. At three months . . . he wriggled and moved about a great deal while asleep in his crib. At six months he "swam like a fish" while being bathed. At twelve months he still squirmed constantly while he was being dressed or washed. . . . At two years he was "constantly in motion, jumping and climbing." At three, he would "climb like a monkey and run like an unleashed puppy." . . . By the time he was seven, Donald was encountering difficulty in school because he was unable to sit still long enough to learn anything. . . . (Thomas, Chess, and Birch, 1970, p. 104)

More recent investigators have tried to describe temperament within the framework of traditional trait classifications. An example is a temperament scale developed by Buss and Plomin that includes two major dimensions called sociability and emotionality (Buss and Plomin, 1984). According to Buss and

Person constancy and caricature *Most artists have always believed that there is a constancy of behavioral as well as of bodily features, as illustrated in this 1743 print by William Hogarth. (Detail from "Characters and Caricaturas," subscription ticket for* Marriage à la Mode; *reproduced by courtesy of the Trustees of the British Museum)*

Plomin, these two traits are the core components of the main axes of Eysenck's system—extroversion and neuroticism/emotional stability. They feel that in young children, extroversion is best represented by sociability (which presumably affects the attachment bond between mother and child, reactions to strangers, and the like), while neuroticism (emotional instability) is mainly represented by a greater tendency to be fearful (anxiety and guilt are reactions that come in later years). In line with these views, both sociability and emotionality show a fair degree of stability over the first twenty years of life, as demonstrated by correlations of +.48 between fearfulness assessed at age five and again assessed in adulthood, and of +.53 between sociability at age six and at age fifteen (Bronson, 1966, 1967).

PERSONALITY AND THE GENES

Consistencies of this sort suggest the operation of genetic factors. Such hereditary effects are no news to animal breeders. Different strains of dogs show marked differences in temperament produced by centuries of breeding: Basset hounds are calm, terriers are excitable and aggressive, while spaniels become easily attached to people and are very peaceable (Scott and Fuller, 1965; see Figure 16.6). We wouldn't expect to find such enormous differences in human temperaments, since there are fortunately no people breeders working to create pure-bred human strains. But some fairly sizable genetic effects on human personality exist even so.

The evidence comes from the same methods that have been used to study hereditary effects in the determination of intelligence—the study of twins. In just about all cases, identical twins turn out to be more alike than fraternal twins on various personality attributes (e.g., Buss and Plomin, 1984; Zuckerman, 1987). In one study, a personality questionnaire was administered to over 12,000 pairs of twins in Sweden. The results showed average correlations of +.50 between identical twins on scores both of extroversion and of neuroticism. The corresponding correlations for fraternal twins were +.21 and +.23 (Floderus-Myrhed, Pedersen, and Rasmuson, 1980). Given these findings, there is little doubt that hereditary factors make a sizable contribution to differences in personality makeup.

A number of investigators thought that such results might help to provide a definite underpinning for the taxonomy of personality traits. The idea is simple: Those traits that are especially heritable are presumably more basic and should therefore serve as the primary categories for classification. But the facts seemed

16.6 Temperamental differences in different breeds of dogs (A) Basset hounds are calm (Photograph by Wilfong Photographic/Leo de Wys), (B) terriers are excitable, and (C) spaniels are very sociable and affectionate. (Photographs by H. Reinhard/Bruce Coleman)

A

B

C

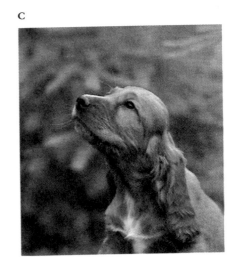

to prove otherwise. In one study, 1,700 twins of high-school age took a standard personality test, the California Psychological Inventory. As expected, the scores of identical twins were more alike than those of the fraternal twins. The trouble was that this difference was just about the same on each of the test's eighteen scales. This suggests that each of these eighteen traits—for example, dominance, sociability, self-acceptance, self-control—are about equally heritable (Loehlin and Nichols, 1976). Much the same is true for responses to questionnaires assessing altruism ("I have donated blood"), empathy ("I like to watch people open presents"), and aggressiveness ("Some people think I have a violent temper"). Identical twins proved to be more alike than fraternal twins and to just about the same extent on each of the scales (Rushton et al., 1986).

Such findings argue that virtually all personality traits are equally heritable. The only exceptions are characteristics that are generally regarded as attitudes rather than as traits, such as adherence to fundamentalist religious beliefs (Pogue-Geile and Rose, 1985). But a more recent analysis of the results by John Loehlin may cause a reassessment (Loehlin, 1982). Loehlin suggests that the equal heritability of all these traits reflects the influence of Eysenck's two "supertraits," extroversion and neuroticism, both of which are substantially heritable. In fact, heritability is quite high for specific traits that are closely related to these supertraits (for example, sociability). For traits that are not tied to extroversion or neuroticism, such as stereotyped masculinity ("I like adventure stories better than romantic stories") and persistence (e.g., "I always tried to make the best school grades I could"), the heritability is much lower (Loehlin, 1982).

Given Loehlin's reanalysis, we may have reason to return to the idea of a few basic personality dimensions that have genuine primary status. The most likely candidates seem to be extroversion and neuroticism. It's too early to judge whether this conception will hold up, but it is worth noting that a number of different approaches to the study of traits—factor analysis of personality inventories, developmental studies of temperament, and research on the hereditary basis of personality traits—all appear to converge toward the same conclusion.

THE INTERACTION BETWEEN GENES AND ENVIRONMENT

We've seen that some traits have a genetic basis. But genes alone cannot account for the variability in personality. Consider extroversion. The correlation between the extroversion scores of identical twins is roughly +.50. If heredity alone accounted for all of the differences in extroversion and if there were no error of measurement, that correlation should be +1.00. The fact that it is not indicates that environmental differences also operate to produce differences in personality. But what are the environmental differences that have this effect?

Between-family differences One environmental factor concerns **between-family differences,** such as the socioeconomic status of the parents, or the parents' religion, or their attitudes about child rearing: The Smiths live in the city and are very strict; the Browns live in the suburbs and are very permissive; and so on. A recent analysis by Plomin and Daniels suggests that, surprisingly enough, differences of this sort are relatively unimportant in determining such personality traits as extroversion, emotionality, conscientiousness, and the like. Some evidence comes from studies of adoption. If between-family differences in environment played a significant role in determining personality traits, we would expect a reasonable correlation between the trait scores of adopted children and their adoptive siblings. But the facts say otherwise. In four recent studies, the average correlation between adopted children and their adoptive siblings was +.04, that

"Separated at birth, the Mallifert twins meet accidentally." (Drawing by Chas. Addams; © 1981, The New Yorker Magazine, Inc.)

between those children and their adoptive parents was +.05 (Plomin and Daniels, 1987).

Further proof comes from a study conducted at the University of Minnesota, comparing the personality traits of pairs of twins tested as adults. Some of the twins had been reared together; others had been reared apart and had been separated for an average of over thirty years. The results for the twins that were reared together were just as expected. As usual, the median correlation between the scores of identical twins was substantially larger than that between the scores of fraternal twins, with correlations of +.51 and +.23 respectively. But surprisingly enough, the results were virtually identical for twins that were reared apart and had been separated for many years. Here the median correlations were +.50 and +.21, for identical and fraternal twins respectively. Similar results were found in a study that looked at the twins' vocational interests (Moloney, Bouchard, and Segal, 1991). On the face of it, one might have expected the correlations between the personality traits and vocational interests of the identical twins to be considerably lower, since they were raised apart—in different family environments. The fact that the results were virtually identical is a strong further argument against the importance of between-family environmental factors (Bouchard, 1984; Bouchard, Lykken, McGue, Segal, and Tellegen, 1990; Tellegen et al., 1988).

Within-family differences   Between-family environmental differences are evidently less important than one might have thought. But if so, what environmental factors do matter? According to Plomin and Daniels, the key is in **within-family differences** in the environment encountered by different children in the same family. These include various accidents and injuries that befall one child in a family but not another; for example, one sister may contract pneumonia while the other does not. Other differences concern birth order and spacing. Still others concern the fact that parents treat different children differently. Finally, there are differences in friends, teachers, and peer groups; one brother may be a member of a local boy-scout troop while the other is not, and so on. All of these are differences within the family environment; their sum total accounts for some of the differences that are found between children in the same family.

How do within-family differences come about? There are no doubt many reasons, including chance encounters, accidents, changing family fortunes that

Within-family differences   *The fact that children within the same family are often very different from each other is an ancient theme of myth and literature. Among the many examples are the biblical stories of Cain and Abel and of Jacob and Esau, and of the three daughters of Shakespeare's* King Lear, *pictured here in this painting by Edwin Abbey. (Courtesy of Metropolitan Museum of Art; gift of George A. Hearn, 1913 [13.140])*

affect younger and older children differently, and so on. But an important further factor is the reciprocal interaction between a child's genetic makeup and the environment, an interaction we've considered in another context (see p. 649). If two siblings differ genetically, they will necessarily create different environments for themselves. A very sociable, active infant is likely to evoke more social stimulation than one who is passive and somber, and this in turn is likely to reinforce her initial pattern and make her even more sociable. The same holds for emotionality. The very moody child, prone to frequent bursts of temper, may well provoke a host of adverse reactions from her frustrated parents, who will respond with a mixture of guilt, anger, and confusion; here, too, the parents' reaction is likely to reinforce the behavior that evoked their reaction in the first place (Chess, 1987). In these examples, the child's own behavioral tendencies—many of which are determined genetically—produce changes in her environment. Still further changes are produced at a somewhat later age when children actively seek out an environment that suits them—in the activities they engage in (sports, scholarship, or whatever) and the people they associate with (friends, teachers, and so on). All of these factors will combine to produce a correlation between an individual's genetic predisposition and the environment she comes to inhabit (Scarr and McCartney, 1983).

When between-family environmental differences do matter   It appears that—once genetic factors are set aside—the differences between families are of less importance than the differences within families. But this statement requires a number of important qualifications.

To begin with, between-family differences in environment do matter for intelligence. One line of evidence comes from studies of adopted children whose intelligence-test scores correlate about +.20 with those of their adopted parents (Bouchard and McGue, 1981). Further proof comes from studies in which young children have been moved from a culturally deprived to a middle-class environment with a resultant increase of 10 to 15 points in IQ (Scarr and Weinberg, 1976; Schiff et al., 1982).

Another qualification concerns the range of possible environments that are considered. All of the evidence we've considered thus far was based on samples that were limited to families whose socioeconomic level was working class or above. Within this range, between-family differences don't seem to affect personality traits very much. But this range constitutes a rather limited sample of environments. It tends not to include the environments provided by parents who are unemployed or that of parents who abuse their children or neglect them grossly. And of course it doesn't include families that belong to another culture entirely—such as a family of Masai cattle herders in East Africa or a group of villagers in New Guinea. If the range had been broadened to include

Some people seek sensations *(Top: Photograph © Helga Lade/Peter Arnold, Inc.; Bottom: Photograph © Philippe Blondel, Agence Vandystadt/Photo Researchers, Inc.)*

Others prefer a more quiet existence *(Photograph by Alan Carey/The Image Works)*

all of these, between-family environmental differences would almost surely have turned out to have major effects (Scarr, 1987).

PERSONALITY AND PHYSIOLOGICAL AROUSAL

To say that personality traits are in part inherited is to say that they have some physical basis. But just what is this physical basis? Here the search for an answer has just begun.

Extroversion-introversion   An interesting approach comes from attempts to link certain personality traits to aspects of neurophysiological arousal. The pioneer in this area is Hans Eysenck, who has tried to relate the extroversion-introversion dimension to many phenomena outside of the personality domain.

As Eysenck sees it, introversion corresponds to a higher level of central nervous system arousal than does extroversion; in effect, introverts are thought to be more awake than extroverts. As a result, they are less distractible and better able to attend to the task at hand (Harkins and Green, 1975). A related finding is that introverts are more reactive to external stimuli than extroverts are; according to Eysenck, this is one of the reasons why they shy away from the world while extroverts embrace it enthusiastically. Thus introverts have lower pain tolerance (Bartol and Costello, 1976) and when studying prefer a lower noise level and fewer opportunities for socializing (Campbell and Hawley, 1982). On the other hand, extroverts prefer to be stimulated; they seek diversion from job routine, enjoy going on trips without planned routes, and are more active sexually, both in terms of frequency and of number of different partners (Wilson, 1978). They need external stimulation more than do the naturally aroused introverts.

In a recent study, these findings were linked directly to cerebral functioning. The investigators measured the electrical reaction to auditory clicks in several areas of the brain stem that are thought to help activate the cortex.★ In line with Eysenck's theory, introverts showed a faster response—indicating greater arousal—than extroverts (Bullock and Gilliland, 1993).

Sensation-seeking   A related topic concerns **sensation seeking.** This is the tendency to seek varied and novel experiences, to look for thrills and adventure, and to be highly susceptible to boredom, as shown by affirmative answers to items such as: "I would like to try parachute jumping," "I sometimes like to do 'crazy' things just to see the effect on others," and "I wish I didn't have to waste so much of a day sleeping" (Zuckerman, 1979). While sensation seeking is related to extroversion, it is not identical with it. It focuses on the liveliness and intolerance of boredom that characterize extroversion, but it is more narrow, for it seems to have little to do with the sociability, which is another aspect of that trait.

Marvin Zuckerman, who developed the scales that contained these items, has provided convincing evidence of their validity. People who score at the high end of these scales are more likely to participate in risky sports such as scuba diving, get more restless in a monotonous, confined situation, are less likely to be afraid of snakes, and drive at faster speeds than people at the lower end (Zuckerman, 1983). A final bit of validation comes from a study on "streaking," a popular fad of the 1970s, whose practitioners took off their clothes and then ran, walked, or bicycled naked through some public area. When students were asked whether they had ever considered streaking (or had in fact streaked), their

---

★ The technical term for this reaction is *evoked potential*—an aggregate electrical response of a region of the brain evoked by a stimulus.

answer showed a substantial correlation with the sensation-seeking scales (Bacon, 1974, quoted in Zuckerman, 1979).

According to Zuckerman, the biological basis of sensation seeking is similar to that which Eysenck suggests for extroversion. In Zuckerman's view, sensation seekers are people who are underaroused in certain systems of the brain, specifically those whose neurotransmitter is norepinephrine (usually abbreviated NE). One of his lines of evidence comes from a study in which the level of NE in the spinal fluid was correlated with various measures on personality scales. The results showed a negative correlation: the greater the sensation-seeking tendency, the lower the NE level (Zuckerman et al., 1983). This fits in with the general hypothesis. Persons whose NE level is low are presumably underactive in their NE systems. In effect, they are underaroused; as a result they seek thrills and take risks to jog their depleted and sluggish NE systems into greater activity.

The need for caution   Findings of this sort, combined with the genetic evidence encourage those who seek a biological basis for personality differences. But thus far this optimism should be tempered with a dose of caution. There are correlations between some personality traits and certain physiological indices of cerebral arousal (though this is still a matter of debate, see Gale, 1984; Gale and Edwards, 1986). But even if these correlations hold up, their eventual interpretation may turn out to be rather different and considerably more complex than those currently offered (Zuckerman, 1990). So while it is apparent that some facets of our personality have a biological basis, it is as yet unclear just what that biological basis is.

Repertory roles   *Lawrence Olivier is often regarded as the prototype of the repertory actor who could play any part. He once said that "in finding a character . . . I do it from the outside in," an approach quite different from that of the Actor's Studio. (A) As Hamlet (from the 1948 film he directed), (B) as Archie Rice, a cheap music hall entertainer (from the 1960 film,* The Entertainer*), (C) as the Mahdi, the fanatical leader of a 19th-century Sudanese sect (from the 1966 film* Khartoum*). (Courtesy of Photofest)*

THE BEHAVIORAL-COGNITIVE APPROACH

Trait theory tries to explain the differences in what people do by reference to something that is within them by appealing to stable and perhaps built-in internal predispositions (that is, traits). The trait approach argues that people do what they do because of who they are: The jovial backslapper is the life of the party

A

B

C

Is personality coherent? *Some early versions of the behavioral-cognitive approach argued that the consistency of personality is an illusion. (Pablo Picasso's* Girl before a Mirror. *Boisegeloup, March 1932. Oil on canvas, 64 × 51¼". The Museum of Modern Art, New York. Mrs. Simon Guggenheim Fund. Photograph © 1994 The Museum of Modern Art, New York.)*

because he is an extreme extrovert. But there is an alternative view that takes issue with this position. This is the behavioral approach (which, as we'll see, is a view with several shadings).

In contrast to trait theory, the ***behavioral approach*** asserts that human actions are determined from without: They are reactions to the external forces that impinge upon the person. In recent times, this has often been called the ***behavioral-cognitive approach,*** since many recent adherents of the behavioral position assign increasing importance to cognitive factors such as expectations and beliefs.

In part, this position grows out of the situationist critique of trait theory we considered previously, for its adherents hold that people do what they do because of the situation in which they find themselves or in which they have found themselves on previous occasions. The life of the party acts his part precisely because he is at a party, a situation in which he will be reinforced for being outgoing and boisterous, as he has no doubt been reinforced on many previous occasions. This general view is traditionally associated with ***behaviorism,*** a very influential theoretical outlook that dominated American psychology for the first half of this century, emphasizing the role of environment and of learning, and insisting that people, no less than animals, must be studied objectively—from the outside (see Chapter 4).

If the trait approach can be likened to dramatic productions with character types who wear one mask that defines them throughout, the behavioral view corresponds to the dramatic approach of a repertory company in which every member takes many parts. Today an actor plays one role, tomorrow he learns to play another, depending upon the play. Nor is the way he plays them determined by anything from inside. Actors of the behavioral school don't worry about inner motivations or subtle subtexts. If required to enact an emotion, they pay a great deal of attention to its visible bodily manifestations; they tremble or sway or clench their fists or breathe more rapidly, depending upon the particular emotion they want to enact. For in their view, all that matters is their outer behavior, because that's all the audience ever hears or sees. Here again, they are much like behavior theorists, who believe that the only way to understand people is by studying them objectively—from the outside.

RADICAL BEHAVIORISM

Behaviorism comes in a number of different forms, some more extreme than others. The most influential modern exponent of ***radical behaviorism*** was B. F. Skinner (1904–1990). To him, the subject matter of psychology was overt behavior and nothing else, with little if any reference to inferred, internal processes such as wishes, traits, or expectations. In Skinner's view, humans—no less than rats and pigeons—behave according to the way they are prompted by the external environment. This environment may be today's—people wear overcoats in the winter and polo shirts in the summer. But more often the relevant environment is yesterday's, when a particular situation led to learning.

In some cases, the relevant learning is by ***classical conditioning.*** Some hitherto neutral stimulus is paired with some motivationally significant event and a response is then elicited; a dog salivates when it sees the food dish or a child cries when she sees the nurse who gave her a painful injection. In others, the learning is by ***operant (or instrumental) conditioning.*** A reinforcement is made contingent on some response, which will then be emitted in the future; a rat presses a lever for a food reward, or a four-year-old reverts to baby talk to get his

Radical behaviorism *(Drawing by W. Miller; © 1963, The New Yorker Magazine, Inc.)*

parent's attention. In either case, what matters is the external environment that provides the conditions for learning. (For a review, see Chapter 4, p. 118.)

Skinner's behaviorism represents a powerful and influential view of human— and, of course, of animal—nature. But can it account for the characteristic differences that we call differences in personality? Many behaviorists believe that it can. In their view, to say that people are different is just to say that they behave differently. Suppose Jane is generally sociable, while Anne is withdrawn, even when the external circumstances are the same. As Skinner sees it, there is little gained by attributing this difference to a difference in the trait of sociability. He would instead assume that there is a difference in the reinforcement histories of these two people. In the past, Jane was probably reinforced for amiable chatting, while Anne was offered little or no encouragement. Seen in this light, the so-called trait of sociability is just another case of operant learning (e.g., Skinner, 1969, 1971).

This line of argument brings up an immediate question. If reinforcement produces the difference between Jane and Anne, why do such differences often persist even when the reinforcements are changed? For persist they do. Jane will continue to smile and chatter even after her dinner party companions have become bored and stopped listening, while Anne will sit back in a corner despite everyone's best efforts to lure her out. Eventually, no doubt, both women will respond to the changed circumstances, but why does it generally take so long? Felix and Oscar of *The Odd Couple* will stay respectively fussy and sloppy no matter what, and Theophrastus's garrulous man will keep on talking and talking even though every citizen of Athens has repeatedly yawned in his face. How can Skinner (or any other behavior theorist) account for this persistence of characteristic behaviors?

If the relevant behavior were developed by operant conditioning, then, according to Skinner, its persistence would be based on the phenomenon of ***partial*** (sometimes called ***intermittent***) ***reinforcement.*** As we saw in Chapter 4, resistance to extinction is markedly increased by partial reinforcement. Rats who are rewarded every time they run down an alley will stop running after a few trials if no more reward is obtained. But the situation is quite different when they are rewarded on only some proportion of the trials. Now they'll keep on running even when there is no reward, as if they've learned that if at first you don't succeed, it generally pays to try and try again.

According to Skinner and other behaviorists, what holds for rats, holds for people too. Many behavior patterns persist because they've been rewarded only sometimes. Gamblers keep on pulling slot machine levers because the machine pays off every once in a while, and children continue to throw temper tantrums because their parents did not ignore them—and thus extinguish them—all the time. Some people consistently whine and wheedle favors; others bully; still others sulk. Wheedling worked for the one, bullying for the other, and sulking for the third; not always, but sometimes, and that is precisely why each is still persisting in the characteristic behavior pattern. Similarly for Jane and Anne, who continue to smile or sit quietly because of previous intermittent reinforcement for these behavior patterns.

Behavior theorists offer a different explanation for the persistence of classically conditioned reactions that are based on fear. The reason is that avoidance learning is generally difficult to extinguish. Consider a little girl who became intensely afraid of dogs after she was accidentally knocked down by a playful Saint Bernard. Her fear was based on classical conditioning, with the dog as the conditioned stimulus and the pain as the unconditioned stimulus. Her fear generalized, so she avoided all dogs. As a result, she was never exposed to situations in which the presence of a dog was not followed by unpleasant consequences, so the fear was never extinguished. The fear was self-perpetuating: It kept her from "testing reality" so she could never discover that it was—now—essentially groundless (see Chapter 4, p. 125, and Chapter 19, p. 777).

SOCIAL LEARNING THEORY

While impressed with radical behaviorism's successes in achieving precise experimental control in some areas of behavior (especially in the animal laboratory), many authors have had misgivings about its ability to describe, let alone to explain, the more complex aspects of human personality. To be sure, people differ in their behavior—some brag, others sulk, still others tease—but can we define these subtle, interpersonal responses as readily as we can define the response of lever pressing in a rat?

Nor is it clear that outer behavior is all that matters. Personality differences involve not only what people do but also what they think and believe and expect. The fact that Joe believes that women can't be trusted and that Carol expects to fail no matter how hard she tries are important aspects of their personalities. Such facts clearly go beyond the outwardly observable aspects of behavior, and as such they are difficult to describe in the language of radical behaviorism.

Such considerations gradually led to a liberalized behavioral approach to personality, which now accepts terms like *expectation* and *belief* as a matter of course. Those who subscribe to this modified approach are often called **social learning theorists** and include such figures as Albert Bandura and Walter Mischel.

At first glance, one might well think that social learning theorists would downplay the role of personality differences in predicting human behavior. For it was they (most prominently, Walter Mischel) who attacked trait theory by arguing that differences between situations are more important than differences between persons in determining what people do. But by now, virtually everyone—whether trait or social learning theorist—has abandoned the extremes of the trait-situation controversy and agrees that both persons and situations matter, as well as the interaction between the two. Thus social learning theorists do accept the notion of personality differences after all. But how do they express that notion?

In essence, they contend that many of the personal qualities that characterize individuals are essentially cognitive: different ways of seeing the world, thinking about it, and interacting with it acquired in the course of an individual's history. Mischel lists some of the cognitive qualities on which people may differ. One concerns the individual's **competencies**—the kinds of things a person can do and understand. Another concerns her **encoding strategies**—the way she tends to interpret situations. A third refers to her **expectancies**—her beliefs about what follows what: what acts will produce what outcomes, what events will lead to what consequences, and so on. A fourth difference concerns her **subjective values**—which outcomes she values. A final difference involves what Mischel calls **self-regulatory systems**—the way in which a person regulates her own behavior by various self-imposed goals and plans (Mischel, 1973, 1984).

CONTROL

We will consider only a few of the cognitive categories along which personalities may differ. Here we'll talk about a certain kind of expectancy: people's beliefs about the control they can exert on the world around them. But before discussing what different individuals believe about control, a few words are in order about the fact that just about all of us generally seem to desire control.

People differ in what they're consistent about The two members of the Odd Couple *are utterly consistent about being respectively fussy and neat on the one hand (Felix), and messy and sloppy on the other (Oscar). And these traits are likely to persist long after the reinforcements for such behavior are changed. (Tony Randall and Jack Klugman in the TV version of the* Odd Couple; *courtesy Photofest; © Paramount Pictures 1989)*

In a previous discussion, we saw that animals and babies behave as if they want to have a sense of control over their lives. Babies smile if an overhead mobile turns around because they made it turn; if it turns around regardless of what they do, they stop smiling. Dogs can cope with electric shocks if they can escape them; other dogs who get the same number of shocks no matter what they do will suffer from learned helplessness (see Chapter 4). What holds for animals and babies also holds for human adults. They too prefer control.

A widely cited illustration of this common desire for control is a series of studies of elderly people in a nursing home. Patients on one floor of a nursing home were given small houseplants to take care of, and they were also asked to choose the time at which they wanted to participate in some of the nursing home activities (for example, visiting friends, watching television, planning social events). Patients on another floor were also given plants but with the understanding that they would be tended by the staff. They also participated in the same activities as the first group of patients, but at times chosen by the staff rather than by them. The results were clear-cut. According to both nurses and the patients' own report, the patients that were allowed to exert control were more active and felt better than the patients who lacked this control; this difference was still apparent a year later (Langer and Rodin, 1976; Rodin and Langer, 1977).

ATTRIBUTIONAL STYLE

The actual control an individual exercises over vital events in his life is important. But no less important is the extent to which he *believes* that these events are under his control. These beliefs are intimately related to his **attributional style,** a characteristic pattern in designating the causes of whatever good or bad fortunes may befall him. This style can be measured by a specially constructed **Attributional Style Questionnaire (ASQ)** in which a subject is asked to imagine himself in a number of situations (for example, failing a test) and to indicate what would have caused those events if they had happened to him (Peterson et al., 1982).

Much of the interest in attributional style comes from its use in predicting whether a person is likely to suffer from depression, a psychological disorder that can range from a mild case of "feeling blue" to an intense, chronic, and ultimately hospitalizable condition characterized by utter dejection, apathy, hopelessness, and such physical symptoms as loss of appetite and sleeplessness (for details, see Chapter 18). Being prone to depression is correlated with a tendency to attribute unfortunate events to internal, global, and stable causes—that is, to causes that refer to something within the person, that will generalize to other situations, and that will continue over time (for example, being unattractive or unintelligent) (Peterson and Seligman, 1984).★

According to proponents of this approach, the internal-global-stable attributional style for unfortunate events creates a predisposition that makes the person vulnerable to depression. This vulnerability will then be transformed into the actual disorder by a stressful event. (For a further discussion of this approach to mental disorders, see Chapter 18.) To test this hypothesis, the investigators administered the ASQ to students enrolled in a large college class and also assessed the students' mood both before a mid-term exam and at several points thereafter (Metalsky et al., 1982; Metalsky, Halberstadt, and Abramson, 1987). The question was how a poor grade would affect the students' mood. The

Loss of control Patients in a Florida nursing home. (Photograph by Michael Heron, 1983/Woodfin Camp)

★ This attributional account of depression is a reformulation of an earlier model of depression based on helplessness (e.g., Seligman, 1975).

results were in line with the vulnerability-stress conception. A lasting depressive mood was primarily found in students who had the appropriate internal-global-stable attributional style (the vulnerability) and also received a poor grade (the stress).

SELF-CONTROL

Expectancies about control represent one category of personality differences that social learning theorists have considered. Another concerns differences in patterns of self-regulation, especially *self-control.* Control refers to an individual's ability to do what he wants to do. Self-control refers to his ability to refrain from doing some of the things he wants to do (or doing some things he would rather not do) in order to get what he really wants at some time in the future.★

An important example of self-control is *delay of gratification.* Much of our ordinary life requires us to postpone immediate rewards for the sake of some more important reward in the future. Some of the postponements involve delays of years or even decades, as in the case of a student who plans a career as a neurosurgeon or a fledgling politician who wants to become president. Others are reckoned in shorter intervals, such as waiting for a paycheck at the end of the week or waiting one's turn in a cafeteria line. Many authors have pointed out that it's hard to imagine any culture that does not require some such system of self-imposed delays, whether they involve food or sex and reproduction. Farmers have to sow before they reap, and most cultures have elaborate rule systems that prescribe the when and where of sexuality and procreation (e.g., Freud, 1930; Mischel, 1986).

What is often called "will power" is presumably just this ability to forgo some immediate gratification in order to pursue some ultimate goal. According to popular wisdom, some people have this ability to a greater degree than others. But do they really? That is, is this ability consistent over time and across different situations?

Delay of gratification *(Photograph by George Gleitman)*

Delay of gratification in young children Walter Mischel and his associates studied this ability in young children and showed that it is related to a number of personality attributes in later life (Mischel, 1974, 1984). Their subjects were children between four and five years of age who were shown two treats, one of which they had previously said they preferred to the other (for example, two marshmallows or two pretzels versus one). To obtain the more desirable treat, they had to wait for an interval of about fifteen minutes. If they didn't want to wait or grew tired of waiting during the delay interval, they were given the less desirable treat immediately but then had to forgo the more desirable one. The results showed that the length of time the children were able to wait depended on just what happened during that period. If the marshmallows were hidden from view, the subjects waited ten times longer than if they were visibly exposed (Mischel, Ebbesen, and Zeiss, 1972).

Further study showed that the mere physical presence or absence of the rewards was not the primary factor. What really mattered was what the children did and thought during the interval. If they looked at the marshmallow, or—worse—thought about eating it, they usually succumbed and stopped waiting. But they could delay if they found (or were shown) some way of distracting their attention from the desired treat—for example, by thinking of some "fun

---

★ Some manifestations of self-control involve forgoing a particular gratification altogether for the sake of some other reward or to avoid some aversive state of affairs. An example is giving up smoking.

things," such as Mommy pushing them on a swing. They could also delay if they thought about the desired objects in some way other than consuming them— for example, by focusing on the pretzels' shape and color rather than on their crunchy taste. By mentally transforming the goals in this fashion, the children managed to have their cake (or pretzel) and ultimately eat it too. By the time they were seven or eight, some of the children seemed to understand their own cognitive strategies for achieving self-control. One child explained why one mustn't look at the marshmallows: "If she's looking at them all the time, it will make her hungry . . . and she'd want to [stop waiting] . . ." (Mischel and Baker, 1975; Mischel and Moore, 1980; Mischel and Mischel, 1983; Mischel, 1984).

As Mischel points out, such results suggest that "will power" is not really the grimly heroic quality it is often said to be. At least in children, the trick is not in buckling up and bearing what's difficult and aversive, but in transforming what's unpleasant into what is pleasant while yet sticking to the task at hand (Mischel, 1986).

Childhood delay and adolescent competence These various findings show that whether a child delays gratification depends on how he construes the situation. But it apparently also depends on some qualities in the child himself. The best evidence comes from follow-up studies that have demonstrated some remarkable correlations between the children's ability to delay at four years of age and some of their characteristics ten years later as rated by their parents. The results showed that the ability to tolerate lengthy delay of gratification in early childhood augurs well for later development. It correlates significantly with academic and social competence and with general coping ability in adolescence. Thus subjects who delayed longer in early childhood were judged to be more verbally fluent, attentive, self-reliant, able to plan, and capable of thinking ahead, and less likely to go to pieces under stress than were subjects whose delay times were shorter (Mischel, Shoda, and Peake, 1988; see Figure 16.7).

Why should a four-year-old's willingness to wait fifteen minutes to get two pretzels rather than one be an indicator of such important personal characteristics as academic and social competence a full decade later? So far, we can only guess. One possibility is that some of the same cognitive characteristics that underlie this deceptively simple waiting task in childhood are similar to those demanded by successful performance in the more serious undertakings of adolescence and adulthood. To succeed in school, the student must be able to subordinate short-term goals to long-term purposes. Much the same is true of her social relations. The person who is at the whim of every momentary impulse will probably be unable to keep friendships, sustain commitments, or participate in any kind of team play, for reaching any long-term goal inevitably means some renunciation of lesser goals that beckon in the interval, whether in childhood or later life. One possibility is that there is some built-in disposition that underlies the child's behavior and also the adult's. But it may also be that the common personal quality is produced by learning. Some children may acquire certain general cognitive skills (say, at keeping their attention on distant goals without getting too frustrated in the bargain) that they can continue to apply to more complex goal-directed efforts as they get older.

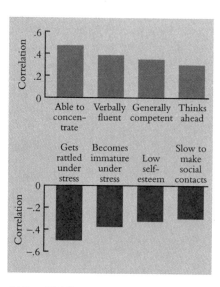

16.7 Childhood delay and adolescent competence *The figure indicates the relation between the ability to delay gratification at age four or five and personality traits at about age sixteen by showing correlations between various personality traits of adolescents as rated by their parents and the length of time they delayed gratification as preschoolers. Bars in blue show positive correlations; bars in dark red show negative correlations. (Data from Mischel, 1984)*

SOCIAL LEARNING THEORY AND BEHAVIORISM

Looking back over our discussion, it's clear that social learning theorists have taken a considerable interest in relatively stable and generalized personal characteristics, as revealed by studies of attributional style and delay of gratification. But if so, how do they differ from trait theorists? They have also moved further and further away from radical behaviorism, having become increasingly interested in all kinds of cognitive processes, such as expectations, beliefs, and plans, none of which are directly observable from the outside. In what sense do they still regard themselves as behaviorists?

There are two answers. One has to do with the situation. By now, everyone agrees that both traits and situations matter, but even so, social learning theorists, true to their behaviorist lineage, are more likely to stress the role of situational factors (or of a person-situation interaction) than trait theorists are. Thus Mischel found that delay of gratification is an index of a surprisingly stable personal attribute, but he was quick to point out that this index is strongly affected by the way the situation was set up (Was the reward visible?) and how it was construed (Did the child think about eating the reward?).

The second answer is even more important. For unlike trait theorists, who are generally inclined to believe that the major personality traits have a built-in, genetic basis, social learning theorists are more likely to assume that most such attributes are a result of learning. In this regard, social learning theory still shares the environmentalist bias that is a hallmark of American behaviorism. For both radical behaviorists and their social learning theory descendants hold to an empiricist worldview, which in its extreme form asserts that virtually anyone can become anything by proper (or in some cases, improper) training. This view was well-expressed in a widely quoted pronouncement by the founder of American behaviorism, John B. Watson:

> Give me a dozen healthy infants, well-formed, and my own specified world to bring them up in and I'll guarantee to take any one at random and train him to become any type of specialist I might select—doctor, lawyer, artist, merchant-chief, and, yes even beggarman thief, regardless of his talents, penchants, tendencies, abilities, vocations, and race of his ancestors. (Watson, 1925)

This is just another way of climbing out to the most extreme pole of the nature-nurture controversy as it pertains to individual differences. Put in terms of our theatrical metaphor, it's a way of saying that any actor can take any part at all, put on any mask whatever, as long as he's properly coached.

Needless to say, such an extreme position is no longer held by anyone. As in most other areas of psychology, there is virtually no one who believes that behavior is determined by nature alone or by nurture alone. In this sense, the nature-nurture controversy is resolved. Similarly for the trait-situation controversy. What's left are different biases. For different psychologists will still make different bets about which factors—traits or situations, a built-in, genetic disposition or the individual's learning history—will be most illuminating in understanding this or another facet of a person. Trait theorists generally make one bet, and social learning theorists make the other. But biases only play a role when we don't yet know the actual facts. For when these are in—and they are coming in ever more quickly—there will be no more room for betting.

In this chapter, we've considered the trait approach, which tries to describe differences in personality in terms of a few underlying attributes that may well be based on built-in predispositions, and the behavioral-cognitive approach, which focuses on the individual's outwardly observable acts and emphasizes the role of the situation and of learning. Both approaches have made important contributions to our understanding, but they are not the only approaches to the subject matter. In the next chapter, we will consider three further perspectives from which personality can be viewed: the psychodynamic, the humanistic, and the social-cultural. As we will see, each perspective on the field has its own validity. For like a statue, the subject matter of personality can be viewed from several different angles, all of which contribute to our overall appreciation.

SUMMARY

1.   People differ in their predominant desires, in their characteristic feelings, and in their typical modes of expressing these desires and feelings. All of these distinctions fall under the general heading of personality differences. The five main attempts to understand these differences are the *trait approach*, the *behavioral-cognitive approach*, the *psychodynamic approach*, the *humanistic approach*, and the *sociocultural approach* to personality.

2.   One approach to personality assessment is by objective personality tests, such as the *Minnesota Multiphasic Personality Inventory*, or *MMPI*. The MMPI assesses traits by means of a number of different scales, each of which measures the extent to which a person's answers approximate those of a particular psychiatric criterion group. In actual practice, MMPI records are interpreted by inspecting the person's score profile, including his response to various validity scales. The same is true of its new revision, the MMPI-2. A number of other personality inventories, such as the *California Psychological Inventory* or *CPI,* were constructed in an analogous manner but using normal rather than pathological criterion groups.

3.   The validity of personality inventories has been evaluated by using indices of *predictive validity*. The results show that while these tests predict, they don't predict very well, for their validity coefficients are relatively low. When the evaluation is based on construct validity, the results look more promising. *Barnum effects* show that the one criterion that is of little use is the person's own acceptance of the test interpretation.

4.   A very different way of assessing personality is by means of *projective techniques.* Two prominent examples are the *Rorschach inkblot test* and the *Thematic Apperception Test,* or *TAT.* While these tests are often used in clinical practice, they have been criticized because of their relatively low predictive validity and even lower utility, as shown by their low *incremental validity* coefficients.

5.   Personality *traits* are attributes that define distinctions in the predominating desires and feelings, and the typical modes of expressing these that are characteristic of different persons. The underlying assumption of trait theory is that such traits are fundamentally consistent over time and situations.

6.   One of the first tasks of the trait approach is to find an appropriate taxonomy for personality attributes. Many investigators have tried to develop such a taxonomy by the method of *factor analysis.* This method has led to the identification of five major dimensions, often called the *Big Five:* extroversion, emotional stability, agreeableness, conscientiousness, and cultural sensitivity. An alternative scheme proposed by Eysenck features two main dimensions—*neuroticism/emotional stability* and *extroversion/introversion*.

7.   The concept of stable personality traits has been seriously challenged by critics who argue that people behave much less consistently than a trait theory would lead one to predict. One alternative is *situationism,* which claims that human behavior is largely determined by the situation in which the individual finds herself. Proponents of this view believe that the underlying consistency of human personalities is more or less illusory and that personality traits are mental figments devised by an observer who watches other people's actions and tries to make sense out of them.

8.   While most observers have concluded that there is strong support for behavioral consistency over time, there is still disagreement over the degree to which there is *behavioral consistency across situations.* Some authors argue that the failure to find cross-situational consistency is caused by assessments that are based on too few observations. Others argue that many inconsistencies in behavior are apparent rather than real.

9.   Many commentators argue that behavioral consistencies will show up best if one looks at the *interaction* between person and situation. Such interactions can be reciprocal because people have a hand in creating the situations that they face.

10. Consistency of behavior can be regarded as a trait in its own right. Some people tend to be more consistent than others. To the extent that people monitor their behavior to fit the social situation, they will behave inconsistently; the tendency to do so is assessed by the *self-monitoring scale*.

11. While some trait theorists view traits as merely descriptive categories, others see them as predispositions to behave in certain ways that are ultimately rooted in the individual's biological makeup. Some evidence for this view grows out of studies of *temperament,* a characteristic reaction pattern of an individual that is present from early childhood on.

12. There is evidence that some personality traits have a genetic basis. Twin studies, for example, show that the correlations on traits such as dominance, sociability, self-acceptance, and self-control are considerably higher in identical than in fraternal twins. Some theorists believe that these effects are based on the high heritability of Eysenck's two super traits, neuroticism/emotional stability and extroversion/introversion.

13. Environmental differences also contribute to the variability on traits such as extroversion and neuroticism. But contrary to expectations, what matters are not *between-family differences* (at least for samples that are limited to this culture), but *within-family differences.* Evidence comes from the fact that the correlation between the personality traits of adopted children and their adoptive siblings is essentially zero and that the correlations between the traits of identical twins reared together are virtually identical to those of identical twins reared apart.

14. Some investigators have tried to link certain personality traits to aspects of neurophysiological arousal. According to Hans Eysenck, introversion corresponds to a higher level of central nervous system arousal than does extroversion. As a result, introverts prefer lower levels of physical and social stimulation, while extroverts prefer to enhance their level of stimulation. Much the same may hold for the trait of *sensation seeking,* which is thought to relate to underarousal of certain regions of the brain.

15. In contrast to trait theory, adherents of the *behavioral-cognitive approach* assert that people do what they do because of the situation that they are in or have been in on previous occasions. The most thoroughgoing version of this approach is the *radical behaviorism* of B. F. Skinner, which focuses on overt behavior and asserts that differences in the ways people act are produced by differences in what they have learned through either classical or operant conditioning. The fact that characteristic behavior patterns persist even when the reinforcements that produced them are no longer there may reflect the effect of partial reinforcement on resistance to extinction.

16. *Social learning theory* is a more liberalized behavioral approach to personality. Unlike radical behaviorists, social learning theorists, such as Albert Bandura and Walter Mischel, are interested in what people think no less than in what they do, which is why their orientation is sometimes called the *behavioral-cognitive approach.* But like radical behaviorists, they emphasize the role of situational factors in determining behavior. Unlike trait theorists, who tend to believe that major personality traits have a built-in basis, social learning theorists also share the radical behaviorists' belief that most such attributes are the result of learning.

17. Social learning theorists are interested in various cognitive characteristics along which personalities may differ. One of these concerns the beliefs people have about the control they can exert on the world around them. One difference concerns their characteristic *attributional style*—the causes to which they tend to attribute events that happen to them. Some of the interest in attributional style comes from its use in predicting depression. Being prone to depression is correlated with a tendency to attribute unfortunate events to internal, global, and stable causes.

18. While control refers to a person's ability to do what he wants to do, *self-control* refers to his ability to refrain from doing what he wants to do in order to get something he wants even more. There is evidence that four-year-olds who are able to tolerate *delay of gratification* for the sake of a more desirable reward show more social and academic competence in adolescence.

CHAPTER **17**

PERSONALITY II: PSYCHODYNAMIC, HUMANISTIC, AND SOCIOCULTURAL APPROACHES

THE PSYCHODYNAMIC APPROACH: FREUD AND PSYCHOANALYSIS 669

THE ORIGINS OF PSYCHOANALYTIC THOUGHT ▪ UNCONSCIOUS
CONFLICT ▪ THE ORIGINS OF UNCONSCIOUS CONFLICT ▪ WINDOWS INTO
THE UNCONSCIOUS ▪ A CRITICAL LOOK AT FREUDIAN THEORY

THE PSYCHODYNAMIC APPROACH: PERSONALITY DIFFERENCES 691

PATTERNS OF NEUROTIC CONFLICT ▪ COPING PATTERNS AND MENTAL
HEALTH

THE HUMANISTIC APPROACH 695

THE MAJOR FEATURES OF THE HUMANISTIC MOVEMENT ▪ EVALUATING
THE HUMANISTIC APPROACH

THE SOCIOCULTURAL PERSPECTIVE 702

HUMAN DIVERSITY ▪ HUMAN SAMENESS ▪ COLLECTIVISM AND
INDIVIDUALISM ▪ CULTURAL DIFFERENCES IN THE CONCEPT OF THE SELF

TAKING STOCK 710

SUMMARY 711

The preceding chapter described many of the ways in which people differ in their characteristic modes of thought, desires, and behavior—that is, in their distinctive patterns of personality. Trait theorists try to understand these differences by reference to underlying trait dimensions, while adherents of the behavioral-cognitive approach stress the importance of the situation and of learning. We will now consider several alternatives to these approaches that take another tack entirely: the *psychodynamic,* the *humanistic,* and the *sociocultural.*

THE PSYCHODYNAMIC APPROACH: FREUD AND PSYCHOANALYSIS

Adherents of the **psychodynamic approach** do not deny that some people are more sociable than others, that some are more impulsive, or emotionally labile, or whatever. But they feel that explaining such tendencies as the expression of a personality trait or as the result of simple learned patterns is rather superficial. In their view, what people do and say—and even what they consciously think—is only the tip of the iceberg. As they see it, human acts and thoughts are just the outer expression of a whole set of motives and desires that are often derived from early childhood experiences, that lie buried beneath the surface, that are generally pitted against each other, and that are for the most part unknown to the person himself. They believe that to understand a person is to understand these hidden psychological forces (often called *psychodynamic* forces) that make him an individual divided against himself.

We saw previously that the trait approach bears a certain similarity to dramatic forms that employ stock characters, such as the comedies of the classical age. In such plays, everything was exactly what it appeared to be. Once the character entered, the audience knew pretty much what to expect. If the actor wore the mask of the cowardly soldier, he would brag and run away; if he wore the mask of the miserly old man, he would jealously guard his money. In contrast, the psychodynamic perspective is related to a more modern approach to drama in which nothing is quite what it seems. In playing a character, actors who follow this approach pay attention to the *subtext,* the unspoken thoughts that go through the character's head while he speaks his lines. And many actors are interested in a still deeper subtext, which consists of thoughts and wishes of which the character is unaware. According to the psychodynamic approach, this deepest level of subtext is the essence of all human personality.

Acting with the subtext *Certain modern approaches to acting such as those developed by New York's Actor's Studio emphasize the importance of subtexts. The photo shows a scene from the film,* The Godfather, Part II, *featuring Lee Strasberg, the late head of the Actor's Studio, and Al Pacino, one of its illustrious graduates. In the scene, a gangster overlord plans a deadly double-cross of another, while telling him: "You're a wise and considerate young man." (From* The Godfather, Part II, *1974; courtesy of the Kobal Collection)*

The dramatic presentation of inner conflicts *In some cases, actors play a character who is not fully aware of her own subtext, so she, like one of Freud's patients, is really lying to herself. An example is Blanche, in this scene from Tennessee Williams's play* A Streetcar Named Desire. *She is both sexually attracted to and repelled by her brutal brother-in-law Stanley. (From the stage version of* A Streetcar Named Desire, *1947, with Marlon Brando and Jessica Tandy; photograph courtesy of the Museum of the City of New York)*

THE ORIGINS OF PSYCHOANALYTIC THOUGHT

We will begin our discussion with the views of Sigmund Freud (1856–1939), the founder of *psychoanalysis,* for all current versions of the psychodynamic approach are ultimately derived from his. Initially, our primary emphasis will be on exposition, postponing critical analysis until later.

In some ways, Freud can be regarded as a modern Hobbesian. Hobbes had insisted that at bottom humans are savage brutes whose natural impulses would inevitably lead to murder, rape, and pillage if left unchecked (see Chapter 10). To curb this beast within, they entered into a social contract in some distant past and subordinated themselves to a larger social unit, the state. Like Hobbes, Freud regarded the basic human instincts as a "seething cauldron" of pleasure seeking that blindly strives for gratification regardless of the consequences. This savage, selfish human nature has to be tamed by civilization.

Unlike Hobbes, however, Freud did not believe that the subjugation of the brute in humankind was a onetime event in political history. Rather, he argued that it occurs in every lifetime, for the social contract is renewed in the childhood of every generation. Another difference concerns the nature of the taming process. According to Hobbes, people's baser instincts are curbed by external social sanctions; they want to rob their neighbors but don't do so because they are afraid of the king's men. According to Freud, the restraints of society are incorporated internally during the first few years of childhood. The first curbs on behavior are based on a simple (and quite Hobbesian) fear of direct social consequences—of a scolding or spanking. But eventually the child inhibits her misdeeds because she feels that they are bad, and not just because she fears that she will be caught and punished. At this point, the taming force of society has become internalized. The king's men are now within us, internalized embodiments of society's dictates whose weapons—the pangs of conscience—are no less powerful for being mental.

According to Freud, the taming process is never fully complete. The forbidden impulses cannot be ruled out of existence. They can be denied for a while, but eventually they will reassert themselves, often through new and devious channels, leading to yet further repressive measures that will probably fail in their turn as well. As a result, there is constant conflict between the demands of

The Dream of Reason Produces Monsters
An engraving by Francisco Goya (1799), which suggests that the same mind that is capable of reason also produces unknown terrors. (Courtesy of the National Library of Medicine)

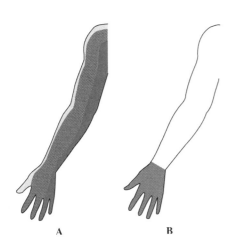

17.1 Glove anesthesia *(A) Areas of the skin of arms that send sensory information to the brain by way of different nerves. (B) A typical region of anesthesia in a patient with hysteria. If there were a nerve injury (in the spinal cord), the anesthesia would extend the length of the arm, following the nerve distribution shown in (A).*

instinct and of society, but this war goes on underground, within the individual and usually without his own knowledge. As a result, the individual is divided against himself, and his unconscious conflicts express themselves in thoughts and deeds that appear irrational but that make sense if understood in terms of the underground drama.

HYSTERIA AND HYPNOSIS

When Freud began his medical practice, many of his patients suffered from a disorder then called **hysteria.** The symptoms of hysteria presented an apparently helter-skelter catalogue of physical and mental complaints—total or partial blindness or deafness, paralysis or anesthesia of various parts of the body, uncontrollable trembling or convulsive attacks, distortions, and gaps in memory. Except for these symptoms, the patients were in no sense "insane"; they were generally lucid and did not have to be institutionalized. Was there any underlying pattern that could make sense of this confusing array of complaints?

The first clue came with the suspicion that hysterical symptoms are **psychogenic,** the results of some unknown psychological cause rather than the product of organic damage to the nervous system. This hypothesis grew out of the work of Jean Charcot (1825–1893), a French neurologist, who noticed that many of the bodily symptoms of hysteria make no anatomical sense. For example, some patients suffered from anesthesia of the hand but lost no feeling above the wrist. This **glove anesthesia** (so called, because of the shape of the affected region) could not possibly be caused by any nerve injury, since an injury to any of the relevant nerve trunks would also affect a portion of the arm above the wrist (Figure 17.1). This ruled out a simple organic interpretation and suggested that glove anesthesia has some psychological basis. While such findings showed that the hysterical symptoms are somehow psychological, they did not mean that the symptoms are therefore unreal. The patients weren't faking; their symptoms were real enough to them and often caused considerable suffering.

In collaboration with another physician, Josef Breuer (1842–1925), Freud came to believe that hysterical symptoms are a disguised means of keeping certain emotionally charged memories under mental lock and key. When such memories are finally recovered, there is **catharsis,** an explosive release of previously dammed up emotions (Freud and Breuer, 1895). Originally, Freud and Breuer tried to uncover these memories while the patients were in a hypnotic trance, but Freud eventually abandoned this method, in part because not all patients were readily hypnotized. He decided that crucial memories could be recovered even in the normal, waking state through the method of **free association.** The patients are told to say anything that enters their mind, no matter how trivial and unrelated it may seem, or how embarrassing, disagreeable, or indiscreet. Since Freud presumed that all ideas are related by an associative network, he concluded that the emotionally charged "forgotten" memories would be evoked sooner or later. But a difficulty arose, for it seemed that the patients did not really comply with Freud's request: There was a **resistance** of which the patient was often unaware.

> The patient attempts to escape . . . by every possible means. First he says nothing comes into his head, then that so much comes into his head that he can't grasp any of it. Then we observe that . . . he is giving in to his critical objections, first to this, then to that; he betrays it by the long pauses which occur in his talk. At last he admits that he really cannot say something, he is ashamed to. . . . Or else, he has thought of some thing but it concerns someone else and not himself. . . . Or else, what he has just thought of is really too unimportant, too stupid, and too absurd. . . . So it goes on, with untold variations, to which one continually replies that telling everything really means telling everything. (Freud, 1917, p. 289)

671

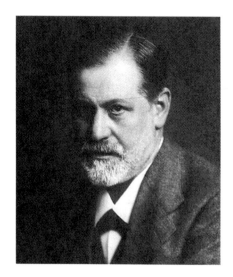

Sigmund Freud *(Courtesy of the National Library of Medicine)*

Freud believed that the intensity of resistance was often an important clue to what was really important: When a patient seemed to struggle especially hard to change a topic, to break off a train of thought, she was probably close to the recovery of an emotionally charged memory. Eventually it would come, often to the patient's great surprise. But if this was so, and if the recovery of these memories helped the patient to get better (as both Freud and his patients believed), why then did the patients resist the retrieval of these memories and thus obstruct their own cure? Freud concluded that the resistance was the overt manifestation of some powerful force that opposed the recovery of the critical memories into consciousness. Certain experiences in the patient's life—certain acts, impulses, thoughts, or memories—that were especially painful or anxiety provoking had been pushed out of consciousness, in Freud's terms *repressed,* and the same repressive forces that led to their original expulsion were mobilized to oppose their reentry into consciousness during the psychiatric session.

Freud believed that the repressed material is not really eradicated but remains in the **unconscious.**★ This is a metaphorical expression which only means that the repressed ideas still exert a powerful effect. Again and again, they push up from below, like a jack-in-the-box, fueled by the biological urges that gave rise to them in the first place or triggered by associations in the here and now. As these repressed ideas well up again, they also bring back anxiety and are therefore pushed down once more. The result is a never-ending unconscious conflict.

The task Freud set for himself was the analysis (as he called it, the **psychoanalysis**) of these conflicts, the discovery of their origins, of their effects in the present, of their removal or alleviation. But he soon came to believe that the same mechanisms that produce the symptoms of psychopathology also operate in normal persons, that his discoveries were not just a contribution to psychiatry, but laid the foundation for a general theory of human personality.

UNCONSCIOUS CONFLICT

Our sketch of Freud's theory of the nature and development of human personality will concentrate on those aspects that represent the highlights of a complex (though scientifically marred) theoretical formulation that was continually revised and modified during the course of his long career. In this description, we will separate two aspects of Freudian theory: We will begin with his conception of the mechanisms of unconscious conflict; we will then deal with Freud's theory of the origins of these conflicts in the individual's life history and of their relation to the development of sexual identity and morality.

THE ANTAGONISTS OF INNER CONFLICT

Freud's theories concern hypothesized forces whose antagonism produces unconscious conflict and the effects produced when these forces clash. But who fights whom in unconscious conflict?

★ The term *unconscious* as Freud used it is not equivalent to *nonconscious.* Freud employed it to apply to ideas or memories that in his view are actively kept out of consciousness because they are threatening or because they provoke anxiety. In contrast, the term *nonconscious* is applied to the many mental processes that go on outside of consciousness, for example, tying one's shoelaces. We are simply not aware of these mental processes in just the sense in which we are usually unaware of our heartbeat (see Chapter 8, pp. 316–18 and this chapter, pp. 689–90).

When conflict is external, the antagonists are easily identified: David and Goliath, St. George and the Dragon, and so on. But what, according to Freud, are the warring forces when the conflict is inside of the individual? In essence, they are different behavioral tendencies, such as a patient's sexually tinged desire to be at a dance and her conflicting reactions of guilt at leaving a dying father. One of the tasks Freud set himself was to classify the tendencies that participate in such conflicts, to see which of them are usually arrayed together and fight on the same side. Freud eventually devised a threefold classification of conflicting tendencies within the individual, which he regarded as three more or less distinct subsystems of the human personality: the *id,* the *ego,* and the *superego.* In some of his writings, Freud treated these three systems as if they were three separate persons inhabiting the mind. But this is only a metaphor that must not be taken literally; id, ego, and superego are just the names he gave to three sets of very different reaction patterns. They are not persons in their own right (Freud, 1923).

The id　The **id** is the most primitive portion of the personality, from which the other two are derived. It contains all of the basic biological urges: to eat, drink, eliminate, be comfortably warm, and, most of all, to gain sexual pleasure.★ The id's sole law is the **pleasure principle**—satisfaction now and not later, regardless of circumstances and whatever the cost.

　The id's blind strivings for pleasure know no distinction between self and world, between fantasy and reality, between wishing and having. Its insistent urges spill out into reflex motor action, like emptying the bladder when it is full. If that doesn't work, the clamoring for pleasure leads to primitive thoughts of gratification, fantasies of wish fulfillment that cannot be distinguished from reality.

The ego　At birth, the infant is all id. But the id's shrill clamors are soon met by the harsh facts of external reality. Some gratifications come only after a delay. The breast or the bottle are not always present; the infant has to cry to get them.

　The confrontations between hot desire and cold reality lead to a whole set of new reactions that are meant to reconcile the two. Sometimes the reconciliation is by appropriate action (saying "please"), sometimes by suppression of a forbidden impulse (not touching one's genitals). These various reactions become organized into a new subsystem of the personality—the **ego.** The ego is derived from the id and is essentially still in its service. But unlike the id, the ego obeys the **reality principle.** It tries to satisfy the id (that is, to gain pleasure), but it does so pragmatically, in accordance with the real world and its real demands. As time proceeds, the opposition between need and reality leads to the emergence of more and more skills, all directed to the same end, as well as a whole system of thoughts and memories that grows up concurrently. Eventually, this entire system becomes capable of looking at itself and now deserves the name Freud gave it, *ego* or "self." Until this point, there was no "I" but only a mass of undifferentiated strivings (named after the Latin impersonal pronoun *id,* literally "it").

The superego　The id is not the ego's only master. As the child grows older, a new reaction pattern develops from within the ego that acts as a kind of judge that decides whether the ego has been "good" or "bad." This new mental agency is the **superego,** which represents the internalized rules and admonitions of the parents and, through them, of society. Initially, the ego only has to worry

Inner conflicts as envisaged by Plato　*The Greek philosopher Plato anticipated Freud's tripartite division of the mind by over two thousand years. In one of his dialogues, he likened the soul to a chariot with two horses that often pull in opposed directions. The chariot's driver is Reason, the two horses are Spirit (our nobler emotions) and Appetite. This Renaissance medallion depicts Plato's image of the internal conflict.*

　★ These urges are sometimes called "instincts," but that is a misnomer caused by an unfortunate translation of Freud's original term.

Ego and superego in popular culture *(A) If Freud were asked to describe Walt Disney's creations in psychoanalytic terms, he would probably describe* Fantasia's *sorcerer's apprentice (a.k.a. Mickey Mouse) as the ego and the sorcerer as the superego. (From* Fantasia, *1940; photograph © The Walt Disney Company) (B) In his film* Pinocchio, *the character of Jimminy Cricket serves as a "kinder, gentler" superego. (From* Pinocchio, *1940; photograph courtesy of Photofest)*

about external reality. It may inhibit some id-inspired action but only to avert some future trouble: You don't steal cookies because you might be caught. But a little later, the forbidden act is suppressed even when there can never be any real punishment. This change occurs because the child starts to act and think as if he himself were the parent who administers praise and reproof. A three-year-old is sometimes seen to slap his own hand as he is about to play with mud or commit some other heinous deed; he sometimes mutters some self-righteous pronouncement like "Dirty. Bad." This is the beginning of the superego, the ego's second master, which praises and punishes just as the parents did. If the ego lives up to the superego's dictates, the reward is pride. But if one of the superego's rules is broken, the superego metes out punishment just as the parents scolded or spanked or withdrew their love. There is then self-reproach and a feeling of guilt.

The formation of the superego puts the ego in a difficult position, for its two masters often issue conflicting commands. The promptings of the id are all too often in forbidden directions; if the ego gives in, the superego will punish it. What's worse is that both masters are essentially infantile. We have seen that the id's demands are blind and unreasoning, but the superego's strictures are also rooted in childish irrationality. The superego was formed when the child's cognitive abilities were still quite primitive. At that time, it could only internalize what it understood then—blind do's and don'ts. As a result, the superego is essentially irrational; Freud regarded it as largely unconscious. It issues absolute imperatives that are not accessible to reason. If the ego obeys, it must throttle various urges of the id, even if those are merely expressed in a thought or a memory. To accomplish this feat, the ego must resort to repression.

In summary, Freud's threefold division of the personality is just a way of saying that our thoughts and actions are determined by the interplay of three major factors: our biological drives, the various ways we have learned to satisfy these drives and master the external world, and the commands and prohibitions of society. Freud's contribution is his insistence that the conflicts among these three forces are inside the individual, that they are derived from childhood experiences, and that they are waged without the individual's conscious awareness.

REPRESSION AND ANXIETY

We now turn to Freud's formulation (here drastically simplified) of the rules by which these inner wars are waged. In rough outline, the conflict begins when id-derived urges and various associated memories are pushed underground, are repressed. But the forbidden urges refuse to stay down. They find substitute outlets whose further consequence is a host of additional defenses that are erected to reinforce the original repression, hold off the id-derived flood, and allow the ego to maintain its self-regard (Freud, 1917, 1926; Freud, 1946).

What underlies repression? Freud came to believe that the crucial factor is intense ***anxiety,*** an emotional state akin to fear (see Chapter 3). According to Freud, various forbidden acts become associated with anxiety as the child is scolded or disciplined for performing them. The parents may resort to physical punishment, or they may merely register their disapproval with a frown or reprimand; in either case, the child is threatened with the loss of their love and becomes anxious. The next time he is about to, say, finger his penis or pinch his baby brother, he will feel a twinge of anxiety, an internal signal that his parents may leave him and that he will be abandoned and alone.

Since anxiety is intensely unpleasant, the child will do everything he can in order to remove it or to ward it off. If the cause is an external stimulus, the child's reaction is clear. He runs away and thus removes himself from the fear-inducing object. But how can he cope with a danger that comes from within?

As before, he will flee from whatever evokes fear or anxiety. But now the flight is from something inside himself. To get rid of anxiety, the child must suppress that which triggers it—the forbidden act.

Freud's concept of repression applies to the thought no less than the deed. We can understand that a four-year-old boy who is punished for kicking his baby brother will refrain from such warlike acts in the future. But why does the boy stop thinking about them, and why does he fail to remember the crucial incident, as Freud maintains? One answer is that thinking about an act is rather similar to performing it. This is especially so given the young child's limited cognitive abilities. He has not as yet fully mastered the distinction between thought and action. Nor does he know that his father can't really "read his mind," that his thoughts are private and thus immune from parental prosecution. The inhibition therefore applies not just to overt action, but to related thoughts, memories, and wishes.

SUPPLEMENTARY MECHANISMS OF DEFENSE

Repression can be regarded as the primary, initial *mechanism of defense* that protects the individual against anxiety. But repression is often incomplete. Often enough the thoughts and urges that were pushed underground refuse to stay buried and surge up again. But as they do, so does the anxiety with which they are associated. As a result, various further mechanisms of defense are brought into play to reinforce the original dam against the forbidden impulses.

One such supplementary defense mechanism is *displacement.* When a geyser is dammed up, its waters usually penetrate other cracks and fissures and eventually gush up elsewhere. According to Freud, the same holds for repressed urges, which tend to find new and often disguised outlets. An example is *displaced aggression,* which develops when fear of retaliation blocks the normal direction of discharge. The child who is reprimanded by her parent turns on her playmate or vents her anger on the innocent household cat. According to many social psychologists, the same mechanism underlies the persecution of minority groups. They become convenient scapegoats for aggressive impulses fueled by social and economic unrest.

In displacement, the forbidden impulse is rechanneled into a safer course. Certain other mechanisms of defense are attempts to supplement the original repression by blocking off the impulse altogether. An example is *reaction formation* in which the repressed wish is warded off by its diametrical opposite. The young girl who jealously hated her sister and was punished for hostile acts may turn her feelings into the very opposite; she now showers her sister with an exaggerated love and tenderness, a desperate bulwark against aggressive wishes that she cannot accept. But the repressed hostility can still be detected underneath the loving exterior; her love is overly solicitous and stifling, and the sister probably feels smothered by it.

In reaction formation, there is an attempt (albeit not terribly successful) to keep the forbidden wishes at bay. Some other mechanisms represent a different line of defense; the repressed thoughts break through but they are reinterpreted and are not recognized for what they are. One example of this is *rationalization* in which the person interprets some of his own feelings or actions in more acceptable terms. The cruel father beats his child mercilessly but is sure that he does so "for the child's own good." Countless atrocities have been committed under the same guise of altruism: Heretics have been tortured to save their immortal souls, and cities have been razed to protect the world against barbarism. Rationalization is also employed at a more everyday level, as a defense not only against repressed wishes but against any thought that would make the individual feel unworthy and anxious. An example is the sour-grapes phenome-

Rationalization The expression "sour grapes" comes from a fable by Aesop, which tells of a fox who desperately desired some grapes that hung overhead. When the fox discovered that the grapes were so high that he could not reach them, he said that he never really wanted them, for they were much too sour. (From Baby's Own Aesop *by Walter Crane, engraved and colored by Edmund Evans; reproduced from the print collection of the New York Library, Astor, Lenox, and Tilden Foundations)*

6 7 5

non. The jilted lover tells his friends that he never really cared for his lost love; eventually he comes to believe this himself.

Another example of a defense mechanism in which cognitive reorganization plays a major role is **projection.** Here the forbidden urges well up and are recognized as such. But the person does not realize that these wishes are his own; instead, he attributes them to others. "I desire you" becomes "You desire me," and "I hate you" becomes "You hate me"—desperate defenses against repressed sexual or hostile wishes that can no longer be banished from consciousness (Freud, 1911).

In yet another defense mechanism, **isolation,** the dangerous memories are allowed back into consciousness; what's held back is their relation to the patient's motives and emotions. The memories themselves are retained, but they are isolated (so to speak, compartmentalized) from the feelings that go along with them. This mechanism is sometimes seen in people who have suffered severe distress, such as concentration camp survivors or rape victims. Some of these people are able to relate their experiences in precise detail but are unable to recall the emotions that accompanied them.

THE ORIGINS OF UNCONSCIOUS CONFLICT

Freud believed that the unconscious conflicts he uncovered always derived from certain critical events in the individual's early life. His observations of his patients convinced him that these crucial events are remarkably similar from person to person. He concluded that all human beings go through a largely similar sequence of significant emotional events in their early lives, that some of the most important of these involve sexual urges, and that it is this childhood past that shapes their present (Freud, 1905).

STAGES OF PSYCHOSEXUAL DEVELOPMENT

Freud's theory of **psychosexual development** emphasizes different stages, each of which is built upon the achievements of those before. (In this regard it resembles

Hidden meanings *This painting,* Hide and Seek, *by the Russian emigré artist Pavel Tchelitchew shows the different aspects of childhood development as hiding in the branches of a gnarled tree. (*Hide and Seek, *1941–42, oil on canvas, 6′6½″ × 7′¾″, collection of the Museum of Modern Art; reproduced by permission)*

Jean Piaget's theory of cognitive growth, which we took up in Chapter 13). In Freud's view, the child starts life as a bundle of pleasure-seeking tendencies. Pleasure is obtained by the stimulation of certain zones of the body that are particularly sensitive to touch: the mouth, the anus, and the genitals. Freud called these regions *erogenous zones,* for he believed that the various pleasures associated with each of them have a common element that is sexual.* As the child develops, the relative importance of the zones shifts. Initially, most of the pleasure seeking is through the mouth (the *oral stage*). With the advent of toilet concerns, the emphasis shifts to the anus (the *anal stage*). Still later, there is an increased interest in the pleasure that can be obtained from stimulating the genitals (the *phallic stage*). The culmination of *psychosexual development* is attained in adult sexuality when pleasure involves not just one's own gratification but also the social and bodily satisfaction brought to another person (the *genital stage*).

How does the child move from one stage to the next? In part, it is a matter of physical maturation. For example, bowel control is simply impossible at birth, for the infant lacks the necessary neuromuscular readiness. But there is another element. As the child's bodily maturation proceeds, there is an inevitable change in what the parents allow, prohibit, or demand. Initially, the child nurses, then he is weaned. Initially, he is diapered, then he is toilet trained. Each change automatically produces some frustration and conflict as former ways of gaining pleasure are denied.

ORAL AND ANAL CHARACTERS

According to Freud, many patterns of adult personality can be understood as remnants of reactions at one or another stage of childhood psychosexual development. As Freud saw it, each step in this development will necessarily produce some frustration (say, as in weaning), and these frustrations may have lasting consequences. One reaction to such frustrations is *fixation,* which refers to a lingering attachment to an earlier stage of pleasure seeking even after a new stage has been attained. When fixation occurs, some remnants of the earlier pattern may hang on for a while, such as thumb-sucking in weaned infants. Another mode of response to frustration during development is *reaction formation,* through which the forbidden impulse that was pushed out of consciousness is replaced by its very opposite. Thus during toilet training, the child's forbidden urge—to relax the sphincter whenever he feels like it—leads to anxiety. One means of dealing with the conflict for the child is to do the exact opposite of what he really wants to. This reaction formation may manifest itself as constipation.

Eventually Freud became convinced that what is really important in these stages is not just the particular anatomical region, whether mouth or anus, through which the child gains pleasure at the time. More crucial are certain ways of relating to other people that are characteristic of a given stage and leave residues in adult behavior. According to one view, the degree to which the early social patterns persist is one important determinant in the shaping of adult personalities (Freud, 1940).

An example is what Freud called the *oral character,* which is said to go back to oral fixation. During the oral stage, the infant feels warm, well-fed, and protected, leading an idyllic existence in which all is given and nothing is asked for in return. According to Freud and his student Karl Abraham, certain adults are oral characters, whose relations to others recapitulate the passive dependency they enjoyed while suckling at the mother's breast (Abraham, 1927).

---

* One of his arguments for regarding oral and anal stimulation in infancy as ultimately sexual was the fact that such stimulation sometimes precedes (or replaces) sexual intercourse in adulthood.

Freud and Abraham believed that there is also an **anal character,** whose personality derives from severe conflicts during toilet training. These conflicts may lead to various forms of reaction formation in which the child inhibits rather than relaxes his bowels (Freud, 1908; Abraham, 1927). This pattern then broadens and becomes manifest in more symbolic terms. The child becomes compulsively clean and orderly ("I must not soil myself"). Another effect is obstinacy. The child asserts himself by holding back on his potty ("You can't make me if I don't want to"), a stubbornness that may soon become a more generalized "no." Another characteristic is stinginess. According to Freud, this is a general form of withholding, a refusal to part with what is one's own (that is, one's feces). This refusal also generalizes, and the child becomes obsessed with property rights and jealously hoards his possessions. Freud believed that excessive conflicts during the anal stage may lead to an adult personality that displays the three symptomatic attributes of the anal character—compulsive orderliness, stubbornness, and stinginess.

THE OEDIPUS COMPLEX

We now turn to that aspect of the theory of psychosexual development that Freud himself regarded as the most important—the family triangle of love, jealousy, and fear that is at the root of internalized morality and out of which grows the child's identification with the parent of the same sex. This is the **Oedipus complex,** named after the mythical king of Thebes who unknowingly committed two awful crimes—killing his father and marrying his mother. According to Freud, an analogous family drama is reenacted in the childhood of all men and women. Since he came to believe that the sequence of steps is somewhat different in the two sexes, we will take them up separately. We will start with his theory of how genital sexuality emerges in males (Freud, 1905).

At about three or four years of age the **phallic stage** begins. The young boy becomes increasingly interested in his penis, which becomes a source of both pride and pleasure. He masturbates and this brings satisfaction, but it is not enough. His erotic urges seek an external object. The inevitable choice is his mother (or some mother substitute). But there is an obstacle—the boy's father. The little boy wants to have his mother all to himself, as a comforter as well as an erotic partner, but this sexual utopia is out of the question. His father is a

Oedipus Rex *From a 1955 production directed by Tyrone Guthrie with Douglas Campbell in the title role, at Stratford, Ontario. (Courtesy Billy Rose Theatre Collection, The New York Public Library at Lincoln Center, Astor, Lenox, and Tilden Collections)*

"Why can't you be more like Oedipus?"
(Drawing by Chas. Addams; © 1972, The
New Yorker Magazine, Inc.)

rival, and he is bigger. The little boy wants his father to go away and not come back—in short, to die.

At this point, a new element enters into the family drama. The little boy begins to fear the father he is jealous of. According to Freud, this is because the boy is sure that the father knows of his son's hostility and that the father will surely answer hate with hate. With childish logic the little boy suspects that his punishment will fit his crime: The same organ by which he sinned will be the one that is made to suffer. The result is *castration anxiety.* As a result, the boy tries to push the hostile feelings underground, but they refuse to stay buried. They return, and the only defense that is left is projection: "I hate father" becomes "Father hates me." This naturally increases the boy's fear, which increases his hate, which is again pushed down, comes back up, and leads to yet further projection. This process spirals upward, until the father is finally seen as an overwhelming ogre who threatens to castrate his son.

As the vicious cycle continues, the little boy's anxiety eventually becomes unbearable. At this point, he throws in the towel, renounces his mother as an erotic object, and renounces genital pleasure, at least for a while. Instead, he *identifies* with his father. He concludes that by becoming like him, he will eventually enjoy an erotic partnership of the kind his father enjoys now, if not with his mother, then at least with someone much like her.

Freud believed that once the tumult of the Oedipal conflict dies down, there is a period of comparative sexual quiet which lasts from about five to twelve years of age. This is the *latency period* during which boys play only with boys, devote themselves to athletics, and want to have nothing to do with the opposite sex. All of this changes at puberty. The hormone levels rise, the sex organs mature rapidly, and the repressed sexual impulses can no longer be denied. But as these urges come out of their closet, parts of the Oedipal family skeleton come out as well, dragging along many of the fears and conflicts that had been comfortably hidden away for all these years.

According to Freud, this is one of the reasons why adolescence is so often a period of deep emotional turbulence. The boy is now physically mature, and he is strongly attracted to the opposite sex, but this very attraction frightens him, and he doesn't know why. Sexual contact with women arouses the unconscious wishes and fears that pertain to mother and father. In healthy individuals, the Oedipus complex has been resolved well enough so that these fears can be overcome. The boy can eventually accept himself as a man and achieve *genital sexuality* in which he loves a woman as herself rather than as some shadowy substitute for his mother and in which his love involves giving as well as taking.

THE ELECTRA COMPLEX

We have traced Freud's account of the male psychosexual odyssey to adult sexuality. What about the female? In Freud's view, she goes through essentially identical oral and anal phases as does the male. And in many ways, the development of her phallic interests (Freud used the same term for both sexes) is symmetrical to the male's. As he focuses his erotic interests on the mother, so she focuses hers upon the father. As he resents and eventually comes to fear the father, so she the mother. In short, there is a female version of the Oedipus complex (sometimes called the *Electra complex* after the Greek tragic heroine who goaded her brother into slaying their mother). But there is a theoretical difficulty. How does the little girl get to desire her father in the first place? Her first attachment was to the mother. But if so, what accounts for the little girl's switch of love objects?

To answer this question, Freud elaborated a far-fetched scheme that is widely regarded as one of the weakest aspects of his whole theory. He proposed that the

6 7 9

shift of attachment begins as the little girl discovers that she does not have a penis. According to Freud, she regards this lack as a catastrophe, regards herself as unworthy, and develops **penis envy.** One consequence is that she withdraws her love from the mother, whom she regards as equally unworthy. The little girl wants a penis, but how can she get one? She turns to her father who does have the desirable organ and who she believes can help her obtain a penis substitute—a child. (Why *child* equals *penis* requires even more far-fetched arguments.) From here on, the rest of the process unfolds more or less analogously to its counterpart in the boy: love of father, jealousy of mother, increasing fear of mother, eventual repression of the entire complex, and identification with the mother (Freud, 1925, 1933).

This theory of female psychosexual development has been widely attacked on both scientific and political grounds. For example, why does the girl want a penis? (And if she does, why does she blame her mother for the lack of it?) That she envies her little brother's social role in a culture in which men have more power and status is not surprising. But there is no evidence that she really envies that particular male organ as such rather than the role and status that maleness confers in many cultures.

The primal couple *Male and femal ancestor figures of the Dogon tribe in Mali, western Africa. From the psychoanalytic perspective, they can be regarded as a symbolic representation of the primal couple, the father and mother, whether in western culture or in other societies. (Photograph © Wettstein and Kauf, Museum Rietberg, Zürich)*

WINDOWS INTO THE UNCONSCIOUS

Freud arrived at his theory of unconscious conflict by studying the behavior of disturbed individuals, usually hysterics. But he soon concluded that the same clash of unconscious forces that results in neurotic symptoms is also found in the life of normal persons. Their inner conflicts are under control, with less resulting anxiety and no crippling effects, but the conflicts are present nonetheless. We will consider two areas to which Freud appealed for evidence: lapses of memory and slips of the tongue in everyday life, and the content of dreams.

ERRORS OF SPEECH AND MEMORY

Freud drew attention to what he called the "psychopathology of everyday life" in which we momentarily forget a name that might call up embarrassing memories or in which we suffer a slip of the tongue that unwittingly reveals an underlying motive (Freud, 1901). Suppressed intentions sometimes emerge to make us become "absent minded" about things we don't really want to do. Freud cites the example of a friend who wrote a letter that he forgot to send off for several days. He finally mailed it, but it was returned by the post office, for there was no address. He addressed it and sent it off again only to have it returned once more because there was no stamp.

This is not to say (though psychoanalytic writers often seem to say it) that all such slips of the tongue, mislayings of objects, and lapses of memory are motivated in Freud's sense. The host who cannot call up a guest's name when he has to introduce him to another guest is unlikely to have some hidden reason for keeping that name out of his consciousness. The name is probably blocked because of simple, and quite unmotivated, memory interference (see Chapter 7).

DREAMS

One of Freud's most influential works was his theory of dreams (Freud, 1900). He argued that dreams have a meaning that can be deciphered if one looks deeply enough. In his view, dreams concern the dreamer's past and present, and they arise from unknown regions within. He saw dreams as somewhat analogous to hysterical symptoms. On the surface, they both appear meaningless and bizarre, but they become comprehensible when understood as veiled expressions of an unconscious clash between competing motives.

Freud began with the assumption that at bottom every dream is an attempt at **wish fulfillment.** While awake, a wish is usually not acted upon right away, for there are considerations of both reality (the ego) and morality (the superego) that must be taken into account: "Is it possible?" and "Is it allowed?" But during sleep these restraining forces are drastically weakened and the wish then leads to immediate thoughts and images of gratification. In some cases the wish fulfillment is simple and direct. Starving explorers dream of sumptuous meals; men stranded in the desert dream of cool mountain streams. According to a Hungarian proverb quoted by Freud, "Pigs dream of acorns, and geese dream of maize."

Simple wish-fulfillment dreams are comparatively rare. What about the others, the strange and illogical nightly narratives that are far more usual? Freud argued that the same principle of attempted wish fulfillment could explain these as well. But here a new process comes into play. The underlying wish touches upon some forbidden matters that are associated with anxiety. As a result, various mechanisms of defense are invoked. The wish cannot be expressed directly; it is censored and is only allowed to surface in symbolic disguise. The dreamer never experiences the underlying **latent dream** that represents his own hidden wishes and concerns. What he does experience is the carefully laundered version that emerges after the defense mechanisms have done their work—the **manifest dream.** The end product is reminiscent of hysterical symptoms and various pathologies of everyday life. It represents a compromise between forbidden urges and the repressive forces that hold them down. The underlying impulse is censored, but it surreptitiously emerges in a veiled disguise.

In some dreams, the underlying wish finds expression in various displaced forms. There is **symbolism** in which one thing stands for another. Some symbols are widely shared because certain physical, functional, or linguistic similarities are recognized by most people (for example, screwdriver for penis and box for vagina). But there is no simple cipher that can be generally applied. After all,

An artist's dream   *A painting that depicts a dream in which an artist is at a friend's house when the door suddenly opens and a man to whom he was once apprenticed enters, joined by a nude woman who was one of his most beautiful models. Freud would probably have noted the Oedipal theme, considering that the dream featured a former mentor and his nude model. (The frontispiece of* Les rêves et les moyens de les diriger, *by Marquis d'Hervey de Saint Denis, 1867)*

Dreams and symbolism The 1927 German silent film The Secrets of a Soul by Georg Pabst tried to depict a case history in psychoanalytic terms. Its subject was a middle-aged man suffering from impotence. The film portrays several of the patient's dreams. In this one, he tries to plant a tree, a symbol for impregnating his wife. (Courtesy of the Museum of Modern Art/Film Stills Archive)

many physical objects are either long and pointed or round and hollow; a pat equation with male and female genitals will be of little use. Instead, most symbolic relationships depend upon the dreamer's own life experience and can only be interpreted by noting her free associations to the dream.

PSYCHOANALYTIC THEORY OF MYTHS

Freud and his students contended that as dreams are a window into the individual's unconscious, so myths, legends, and fairy tales allow us a glimpse into those hidden concerns that are shared by whole cultural groups, if not all of humanity. Indeed, psychoanalysts found an ample supply of Oedipal themes. There are numerous ogres, dragons, and monsters whom the hero must slay if he wants to reach the fair maid. The part of the villain is often taken by a cruel stepparent, a fairly transparent symbol of Oedipal hostilities.

As an example of a psychoanalytic interpretation of a fairy tale, consider Snow White and the seven dwarfs (Brown, 1940). Snow White is a child princess who is persecuted by her stepmother, the wicked queen. The queen is envious of Snow White's beauty and tries to have her killed. The child escapes and lives with seven dwarfs who work in an underground mine. The queen finally discovers Snow White and persuades her to eat part of a poisoned apple. Snow White falls as if dead. The dwarfs place her in a beautiful coffin in which she lies motionless for seven years. At this point, a handsome prince appears, opens the casket with his sword, awakens Snow White from her long sleep, and the two live happily ever after.

According to psychoanalytic authors, this fairy tale is a veiled allegory of the Oedipal sequence. The wicked queen is the mother on whom the child projects her own hate and sexual jealousy. The Oedipal conflict is temporarily resolved as the child's erotic urges go underground and remain dormant for the seven years of the latency period, symbolized both by Snow White's long sleep and by the seven dwarfs. At the end of this period, her sexuality is reawakened in adult form by the young prince. (The meaning of the sword is left as an exercise for the reader.)

Is this interpretation valid? It is hard to know by what ground rules validity

THE PSYCHODYNAMIC APPROACH: FREUD AND PSYCHOANALYSIS

can be judged. There are undoubtedly many alternative (and perhaps more plausible) interpretations of this and many other legends that psychoanalysts have tried to squeeze into their scheme. Death and resurrection are old themes in mythology that probably refer to many important natural cycles, such as the daily succession of darkness and light and the yearly alternation of winter's desolation and spring's green rebirth. Myths may also embody dim folk memories of long-past wars, dynastic conflicts, previously held religions, and various catastrophes. The psychoanalytic view may throw some light on an aspect of our cultural heritage, but it is just one light among many others. (For a critique, see Darnton, 1984.)

PSYCHOANALYSIS AND LITERATURE

Freud's approach to the interpretation of works of art and literature was very similar to the way in which he tried to understand the hidden meaning of dreams and myths. The artistic production reflects the artist's own inner conflicts and has impact upon others because it strikes the same unconscious chords in them. Perhaps the most famous example of psychoanalytic literary interpretations is Freud's analysis of Shakespeare's *Hamlet,* later elaborated by his student Ernest Jones (Jones, 1954). The central puzzle of the play is Hamlet's indecisiveness. He waits until the end of the fifth act before he finally avenges his father's death, a delay that causes his own death, as well as the death of virtually everyone else in the play, innocent as well as guilty. To Freud and Jones, the clue to Hamlet's inaction is the Oedipus complex. Hamlet is paralyzed because he must kill a man who did precisely what he himself unconsciously wanted to do, kill his father and marry his mother. According to Freud and Jones, the play grips the audience because it stirs the same latent conflicts in them.

Shakespearean scholars are by no means agreed on the virtues of this interpretation, though some find it interesting. But the issue goes further than that. Suppose we accept the interpretation that Freud and Jones offer. Is this the key to *Hamlet,* which is then shorn of all its mysteries, like a completed crossword puzzle that is discarded once it is solved? The truth is that there is no one key, there is no one meaning of *Hamlet,* for a work of art is necessarily ambiguous. As with myths and legends, this or the other interpretation may help to illuminate them, but it does not explain them away. *Hamlet* may be about Oedipal

A psychoanalytic interpretation of Little Red Riding Hood Little Red Riding Hood is the story of a pretty young girl who is sent on an errand through the forest. Her mother tells her to walk decently, without ever leaving the path. On her trip, she meets a wolf who persuades her to run off the path and pick some beautiful flowers in the forest. According to psychoanalysts, the wolf stands for male sexuality, and Little Red Riding Hood is torn between resisting temptation (staying on the right path) and giving in to it (picking the flowers). (Courtesy of the Granger Collection)

Hamlet confronting his mother in her bedroom *A scene from Lawrence Olivier's 1948 film* Hamlet. *Olivier's conception of the role of Hamlet was seriously affected by Ernest Jones's psychoanalytic interpretation of the play. His casting of a young attractive actress, Eileen Herlie, for the part of Hamlet's mother helped to underscore the Oedipal theme. (Courtesy of Universal Pictures)*

conflicts, but many hack novels have the same theme. What makes the one a great literary treasure while the others are forgotten almost immediately?

These points argue against the overenthusiastic application of psychoanalytic interpretation to literary works. But for good or ill (probably for both), Freud's impact on literature and literary criticism has been enormous. Most literary critics today have at least a passing acquaintance with Freud's basic works, and many major authors have been consciously affected by him. By now, his insights have become part of our culture and Freudian lore (often vulgarized) has become a staple of our popular literature, our stage, and our screen.

A CRITICAL LOOK AT FREUDIAN THEORY

Thus far, we have presented Freud's views with a minimum of critical comment. (Our discussions of Freud's theory of female psychosexual development and the psychoanalytic approach to myths and literature were exceptions.) We now shift our perspective to consider some of his assertions in the light of present-day thought and evidence.

METHODOLOGICAL AND CONCEPTUAL ISSUES

By what criteria can one determine whether Freud's assertions are in fact correct? Freud's own criterion was the evidence from the couch. He considered the patient's free associations, his resistances, his slips of the tongue, his dreams and then tried to weave them into a coherent pattern that somehow made sense of all the parts. But can one really draw conclusions from this kind of clinical evidence alone? Clinical practitioners cannot be totally objective no matter how hard they try. As they listen to a patient, they are more likely to hear and remember those themes that fit in with their own views than those that do not? (This point is especially pertinent to Freud who never took notes during psychoanalytic sessions.) Would a clinician with different biases have remembered the same themes?

Yet another problem is conceptual. Scientific theories lead to certain predictions; if these fail, the theory is refuted. But are Freud's assertions theories in this sense? What specific predictions do they lead to? Consider the hypothetical case of a boy raised by a harsh, rejecting mother and a weak, alcoholic father. What will the boy be like as an adult? Will he seek dominating women who will degrade him as his mother did? Will he try to find a warm, comforting wife upon whom he can become dependent and thus make up for the mothering he never had as a child? There is no way of predicting on psychoanalytic grounds. Each outcome makes perfectly good sense—after it has occurred.

Another problem with many psychoanalytic arguments is that the analyst's theory often determines whether a patient's statement should or should not be accepted at face value. Suppose a woman insists that she hates her mother. The analyst will probably believe her. But if she swears that she loves her mother, the analyst may conclude that she, like Shakespeare's lady, "doth protest too much." He may then interpret her protestations of love as meaning the exact opposite, as reflecting a reaction formation against her "real" feelings of hate. The trouble with this kind of two-way reasoning is that it becomes difficult to find any sort of disproof. (For a discussion of this and related issues, see Grünbaum, 1984.)

Such considerations suggest that if we want to test Freud's assertions, we must look for further evidence and must be more rigorous in the way in which we interpret it. We will begin by considering some criticisms from theorists who agreed with Freud's thesis that there is unconscious conflict, but who were skeptical of his particular assertions of what these conflicts are.

BIOLOGY OR CULTURE?

A number of psychoanalytically oriented theorists took strong exception to Freud's insistence that the pattern of unconscious conflicts is biologically based and will therefore be found in essentially the same form in all men and all women.

The emphasis on social factors Since Freud believed that the key to emotional development is in biology, he assumed that its progression followed a universal course. In his view, all humans pass through oral, anal, and phallic stages and suf-

A picture of Freud's consultation room
In classical psychoanalysis, the patient reclines on the couch while the analyst sits behind him, out of sight. Freud adopted this method to avoid influencing the patient's flow of associations by his own facial expressions. He also had a personal motive: "I cannot bear to be gazed at for eight hours a day." (Freud, 1913; photograph by Edmund Engelman)

fer the conflicts appropriate to each stage. This conception has been challenged by various clinical practitioners, many of whom used Freud's own psychoanalytic methods. These critics felt that Freud had overemphasized biological factors at the expense of social ones. This point was first raised by one of Freud's own students, Alfred Adler (1870–1937). It was later taken up by several likeminded authors who are often grouped together under the loose label **neo-Freudians,** including Erich Fromm (1900–1980), Karen Horney (1885–1952), and H. S. Sullivan (1892–1949).

According to the neo-Freudians, human development cannot be properly understood by focusing on the particular anatomical regions—mouth, anus, genitals—through which the child tries to gratify her instinctual desires. In their view, the important question is how humans relate, or try to relate, to others—whether by dominating, or submitting, or becoming dependent, or whatever. Their description of our inner conflicts is therefore in social terms. For example, if they see a mother who toilet trains her child very severely, they are likely to interpret her behavior as part of an overall pattern whereby she tries to push the child to early achievement; the specific frustrations of the anal stage as such are of lesser concern to them. Similarly for the sexual sphere. According to Freud, the neurotic conflict centers on the repression of erotic impulses. According to the neo-Freudian critics, the real difficulty is in the area of interpersonal relationships. Neurosis often leads to sexual symptoms, not because sex is a powerful biological motive that is pushed underground, but rather because it is one of the most sensitive barometers of interpersonal attitudes. The man who can only relate to other people by competing with them may well be unable to find sexual pleasure in his marriage bed, but the sexual malfunction is an effect of his neurotic social pattern rather than its cause.

The same emphasis on social factors highlights the neo-Freudian explanation for how these conflicts arise in the first place. In contrast to Freud, the neo-Freudians deny that these conflicts are biologically ordained; they contend, rather, that these conflicts depend upon the specific cultural conditions in which the child is reared. According to the neo-Freudians, the conflicts that Freud observed may have characterized his patients, but this does not mean that these same patterns will be found in people who live at other times and in other places.

The rejection of cultural absolutism   One set of relevant findings came from another discipline, **cultural anthropology,** which concerns itself with the practices and beliefs of different peoples throughout the world. There are evidently considerable variations in these patterns, with accompanying variations in the kind of person who is typical in each setting. Personality characteristics that are typical in our culture are by no means universal, a result that was beautifully attuned to the antibiological bias of the neo-Freudians (a point to which we will return later, see pp. 702–703).

CRITIQUE OF FREUD'S THEORIES OF DEVELOPMENT

Some related criticisms concern Freud's theories of psychosexual development. It's rather ironic that Freud, whose views of childhood development had such a powerful influence on Western thought, never himself studied children. His theories of early development were mostly based on his adult patients' recollections, dreams, and free associations. But by now of course, the study of childhood development is a flourishing enterprise (See Chapters 13 and 14). What light has it shed on the role of early childhood events in producing adult personality?

*Freud at age sixteen with his mother,
Amalie Nathanson Freud* Freud was his
mother's first-born and her favorite, a fact that
may have affected his theory of the human
family drama. As he put it, "A man who has
been the indisputable favorite of his mother
keeps for life the feeling of a conqueror, that
confidence of success that often induces real
success." (E. Jones, 1954, p. 5; photograph
courtesy of Mary Evans/Freud copyrights)

Oral and anal characters The verdict on the oral character is simple. There is little or no evidence that differences in the way the infant was fed have much of an effect on later personality (assuming adequate nutrition). Later adjustment and development appear to be much the same whether the infant was fed by breast or by bottle, was weaned early or weaned late. (For an overview, see Zigler and Child, 1972.)

Some who study childhood development contend that the concept of the anal character may have more validity. They cite evidence that the critical anal traits—neatness, obstinacy, and parsimony—do in fact correlate to a significant extent (Fisher and Greenberg, 1977). In one study, a number of undergraduates were asked to rate their own and their friends' characteristics. Their ratings showed that the three critical traits do indeed form a coherent cluster. Those students who judged themselves (or were judged by others) to be obstinate were also those who tended to be orderly and a bit stingy. More important, the students with these anal characteristics tended to have mothers with similar attributes, as shown by questionnaires administered to the mothers. These results may seem to vindicate Freud's theory, since it appears that anal children have anal mothers. But a further finding runs counter to the theory. The mothers were asked at what age they toilet-trained their children. There was no correlation whatever between this factor and the personality traits that define the anal character (Beloff, 1957).

This result fits in with other studies on the effects of toilet training. Some parents begin toilet training when their infant is as young as five months; others wait until the child is two years old. There are some slight indications that starting later makes the whole process simpler and may minimize certain childhood disorders of elimination such as bedwetting (Brazelton, 1962). But there is little evidence that shows any long-term effects growing out of toilet-training practices, either in our own or other cultures (Orlansky, 1949). For example, there seems to be no relation between the severity of toilet training in different cultures and the degree of hoarding or economic competition (Cohen, 1953). There is thus little evidence for Freud's claim that the toilet is a prep school for becoming a banker or a captain of industry.

But if so, what can we make of the fact that the three so-called anal traits form a cluster and seem to be transmitted from parent to child? Our best guess is that they are transmitted as part of a general pattern of middle-class values and attitudes, communicated by the general social atmosphere in which the child is raised, and instilled as one facet of what the parents want the child to become. Seen in this light, obstinacy, orderliness, and parsimony may well be a result of the parents pushing their child toward independence and achievement. They are not by-products of getting the child out of diapers.

The universal Oedipus complex Freud's theories of the Oedipus complex in childhood have not fared much better. Our major source of information in this area comes from studies of other cultures. On the whole, the evidence was welcome grist to the neo-Freudian mill: The Oedipus conflict is not universal but depends upon cultural variations in the family constellation.

This point was first raised some seventy years ago by the English anthropologist Bronislaw Malinowski on the basis of his observations of the Trobriand Islanders of the western Pacific (Malinowski, 1927). The family pattern of the Trobriand Islanders is quite different from our own. Among the Trobrianders, the biological father is not the head of the household. He spends time with his children and plays with them, but he exerts no authority. This role is reserved for the mother's brother, who acts as disciplinarian. The Trobriand Islanders thus separate the roles that in Freud's Vienna were played by one and the same person.

6 8 7

The Nightmare This painting by Henry Fuseli (painted in 1783 and said to have decorated Freud's office) highlights what seems to be one of the difficulties of Freud's dream theory. If all dreams are wish fulfillments, what accounts for nightmares? According to Freud, they are often dreams in which the latent dream is not sufficiently disguised. The forbidden wish is partially recognized, anxiety breaks through, and the sleeper suffers a nightmare. (Courtesy of The Detroit Institute of Arts)

According to Freud, this different family pattern should make no difference. There should still be an Oedipus complex in which the father is the hated villain, for, after all, it is he who is the little boy's sexual rival. But this did not turn out to be the case. Malinowski saw no signs of friction between sons and fathers, though he did observe a fair amount of hostility directed at the maternal uncle. The same held for dreams and folk tales. The Trobriand Islanders believe that there are prophetic dreams of death; these generally involve the death of the maternal uncle. Similarly there are no myths about evil fathers or stepfathers; again, the villain is typically the mother's brother. If we accept Freud's notion that dreams (and myths) involve unconscious wishes and preoccupations, we are forced to conclude that the Trobriand boy hates his uncle, not his father. In sum, the child has fears and fantasies about the authoritarian figure in his life, the man who bosses him around. This is the father in Freud's Austria, but the uncle on the Trobriand Islands. His fears are not about his mother's lover as such, for the Trobriand boy does not hate the father who plays this role.

FREUD'S THEORIES OF DREAMS, REPRESSION, AND DEFENSE

Thus far, we have looked at critiques that came from within the psychodynamic fold. They disagreed with Freud's theories about what internal conflicts were about and where they came from. But they accepted his notion of unconscious conflict and its effect on mental processes—acts, wishes, thoughts, perceptions—that are kept out of consciousness by an elaborate system of internal censorship. We'll now consider two lines of research that bear on this conception. One concerns Freud's theory of dreams, the other his theory of repression and defense.

Freud's theory of dreams Stated in the most general terms, Freud's theory asserts that dreams tend to reflect the current emotional preoccupations of the dreamer, including those of which he is unaware, often portrayed in a condensed and symbolic form. This is probably quite true. Thus, patients who await major surgery reveal their fears in what they dream about during the two or three nights before the operation. Their fears are rarely expressed directly; few, if any, of their dreams are about scalpels or operating rooms. The reference is indirect, in condensed and symbolized form, as in dreams about falling from tall ladders or standing on a high, swaying bridge, or about a decrepit machine that needs repair (Breger, Hunter, and Lane, 1971).

Such evidence indicates that dreams often express whatever motives are currently most important. But Freud's theory went much further than this, for it insisted that the manifest dream represents a wish fulfillment and is a censored and disguised version of the latent dream that lies underneath. This conception of dreams has been much criticized. To begin with, there is considerable doubt that all (or even many) dreams are attempts at wish fulfillments, whether disguised or open. In one study, subjects were made extremely thirsty before they went to sleep. Since thirst is hardly a forbidden urge, there is no reason to suppose an internal censorship. However, none of the subjects reported dreams of drinking. Since they were so thirsty, why didn't they gratify themselves in their dreams (Dement and Wolpert, 1958)?

Another problem is the fact that the same urge is sometimes freely expressed in dreams, but heavily disguised on other occasions. Tonight, the sleeper dreams of unabashed sexual intercourse; tomorrow night, she dreams of riding a team of wild horses. For sake of argument, let us agree that riding is a symbol for intercourse. Why should the censor disguise tomorrow what is so freely allowed tonight?

One investigator, C. S. Hall, has come up with a plausible suggestion (Hall, 1953). According to Hall, the dream symbol does not *disguise* an underlying idea; on the contrary, it *expresses* it. In Hall's view, the dream is a rather concrete mental shorthand that embodies a feeling or emotion. Riding a horse, plowing a field, planting a seed—all of these may be concrete renditions of the idea of sexual intercourse. But they are not meant to hide this idea. Their function is much the same as the cartoonist's picture of Uncle Sam or John Bull. These are representations of the United States and of England, but they are certainly not meant as disguises for them. During sleep, more specifically during REM sleep (see Chapter 3), we are incapable of the extreme complexity and abstractness of waking mental life. We are thus reduced to a more concrete and archaic form of thinking. The wishes and fears of our waking life are still present at night, and we dream about them. But the way in which these are now expressed tends to be more primitive, a concrete pictorialization that combines fragments of various waking concerns and serves as a kind of symbolic cartoon.

Such findings do not dispute Freud's belief that dreams involve complex cognitive processes many of which are hidden from view. But they argue against the central tenet of his theory: that they are disguised representations of forbidden urges that are held underground in their threatening, unmasked form.

Laboratory studies of anxiety and recall The concept of repression is the cornerstone of psychoanalytic thought. What evidence bears on this hypothesis? There have been many efforts to produce repression and related effects in the laboratory (see Eriksen and Pierce, 1968). But this task is far from easy. According to psychoanalytic theory, motivated forgetting is a defense against anxiety. One would therefore expect that materials that are associated with anxiety would be recalled less readily than neutral items. But how can the experimenter be sure that the critical material is really anxiety-provoking for the subject?

To cope with this problem, several investigators selected material to fit each subject's own pattern of anxieties. One way of doing this is by an initial word-association test. The subject is given a list of words; she has to reply to each with the first word that comes to mind. If her reaction to any one stimulus word is unusually slow or if it is accompanied by increased heart rate or a marked galvanic skin response, that word is presumably emotion-arousing for her. Using this method, one experimenter selected a set of neutral and emotional words for each subject (Jacobs, 1955). When these were later used as the responses in a paired-associate task, the subject had more trouble in producing the emotional than the neutral items. One way of explaining the result is to assume that as the emotionally loaded word was about to be retrieved from memory, it triggered anxiety, which blocked further efforts at retrieval. (For a review and methodological critique, see Holmes, 1990).

Seen in this light, repression may turn out to be a special case of retrieval failure. We have previously seen that recall is enormously dependent upon the presence of an appropriate retrieval cue. We forget the street names of the city we grew up in, but most of them come back when we revisit the city after many years. The same may hold for memories that Freud said are repressed. Perhaps they are not really held back by some imperious censor; perhaps they are rather misfiled under a hard-to-reach rubric and cannot be retrieved for this reason. One might want to add some further assumptions about the role of anxiety in maintaining this state of affairs. Perhaps anxiety blocks refiling; perhaps it impedes the use of appropriate retrieval cues (Erdelyi and Goldberg, 1979).

The retrieval-blocking interpretation of repression is part of a more general approach taken by some contemporary psychologists who have tried to fit the concept of the unconscious into the framework of modern cognitive psychology. They agree with the psychoanalysts' assertion that much of mental life is affected by processes of which we are not conscious, pointing to such phenomena as blind sight, implicit retrieval, and automatization as illustrations (see Chapter 8, pp. 296, 317–18). They do not, however, share Freud's belief that these unconscious processes are necessarily defenses against anxiety or have the sexual and aggressive quality that Freud attributed to them. To quote one author, our modern view of nonconscious mental life suggests that, while quite extensive, it is often "kinder, gentler, and more rational than the seething unconscious of Freud" (Kihlstrom, 1990).

FREUD'S CONTRIBUTIONS IN RETROSPECT

We have seen that many of Freud's beliefs have not been confirmed. There are good grounds to doubt Freud's essentially Hobbesian view of human nature. There is little evidence for his general theory of psychosexual development, even less for his male-centered conception of feminine psychology, and there is a good reason to believe that he overemphasized biological givens at the expense of cultural factors. We have also seen that Freud can be criticized not just for what he asserted but for the way in which he tried to prove his claims. By now, there is general agreement that the psychoanalytic couch is not a source of objective fact and that many of Freud's theoretical proposals are rather vague and metaphorical, so that it is not clear how one can decide whether they are right or wrong. All in all, this is a formidable set of criticisms. But even so, many psychologists would maintain that, wrong as he probably was in any number of particulars, Sigmund Freud must nevertheless be regarded as one of the giants of psychology, one of the few our field has known thus far.

There are at least two reasons. The first concerns one major conception of Freud's that still stands, however much it may have to be modified and reinterpreted—the notion that there is some kind of internal conflict of which we are often unaware. Freud was not the first to recognize that we are often torn in opposite directions and that we frequently deceive ourselves about what we want (Ellenberger, 1970). But he was the first for whom this insight was the cornerstone of an entire point of view. Whether his own therapeutic procedure, psychoanalysis, is an appropriate tool to make the unknown known and thus to restore a measure of free choice to the emotionally crippled victims of inner

*Freud looking at a bust of himself sculpted
for his seventy-fifth birthday   by O. Nem-
on (Courtesy of Wide World Photos)*

conflict is still debatable (see Chapter 19). But whether his therapy works or
not, Freud's contribution remains. He saw that we do not know ourselves, that
we are not masters of our own souls. By pointing out how ignorant we are, he
set a task for later investigators who may ultimately succeed, so that we may
then be able to follow Socrates's deceptively simple prescription for a good life,
"Know thyself."

The other major reason why Freud has a lasting place among the greats of
intellectual history is the sheer scope of his theoretical conception. His was a
view of human nature that was virtually all-embracing. It tried to encompass
both rational thought and emotional urges. It conceived of neurotic ailments as
a consequence of the same psychological forces that operate in everyday life. It
saw humans as biological organisms as well as social beings, as creatures whose
present is rooted in their past and who are simultaneously children and adults.
The range of psychological phenomena that Freud tried to comprehend within
his theory is staggering—neurotic symptoms, personality patterns, social groupings, family relations, humor, slips of the tongue, dreams, artistic productions,
aspects of religious thought. Freud's theory has many faults, but this long list
highlights some of its virtues. It dealt with matters of genuine human significance; it concerned both human beings and their works; it was an account that
was about humanity as a whole.

We now know that many of Freud's views have not been confirmed, but
there is no doubt that these views have influenced virtually all thinkers in these
areas who have come after him. For Freud was one of those rare intellectual figures who cast his shadow over a whole century. And right or wrong, he provided a guide for posterity by showing us the kinds of questions we must answer
before we can claim to have a full theory of human personality.

THE PSYCHODYNAMIC APPROACH: PERSONALITY DIFFERENCES

While the primary focus of psychodynamic theory (and of Freud's theory in
particular) is about human personality in general, it does offer many proposals
about the way in which people (especially "normal" people) differ from each

other and also how those differences come about. Freud's theory of oral and anal personalities is one example. More recent attempts at theorizing by various neo-Freudians classify and analyze personality differences in terms of the person's dominant patterns of defense. The neo-Freudians, like Freud himself, believe that anxiety is an inevitable part of human existence and that some defenses against anxiety will therefore be found in everyone. What makes people different is the pattern of defenses they have erected.

PATTERNS OF NEUROTIC CONFLICT

A major figure in the analysis of these patterns of defenses was Karen Horney (1885–1952), who argued that many people in our society suffer from **basic anxiety**—an "all-pervading feeling of being alone and helpless in a hostile world" (Horney, 1937, p. 89). Horney believed that this anxious feeling should not be traced to childhood struggles with infantile sexual conflicts. She felt that instead its roots are in our culture, which often makes incompatible demands on the individual.

According to Karen Horney, the neurotics' basic anxiety leads them to the frantic pursuit of various goals, sought less for themselves than as a way to deaden this anxiety. Some neurotics try to assuage their anxiety by seeking love, others by seeking prestige or possessions, still others by withdrawing from any genuine emotional involvements, and yet others by deadening the anxiety with alcohol or drugs (Horney, 1937, 1945, 1950). Such efforts often fail, but they generally persist and harden into enduring patterns of personality. The question is why. Horney's answer is that the neurotic conflict creates a self-perpetuating vicious circle.

An example of such a vicious circle is the neurotic search for love. If a man needs a woman's love to deaden his sense of basic anxiety, his demands for affection will be unconditional and excessive. But if so, they can't possibly be fulfilled. The slightest failure to accede to his wishes will be interpreted as a rebuff and rejection. This will increase his feelings of anxiety, which will make him even more desperate for affectionate reassurance, which will further increase the chances of rebuff, and so on. Add the fact that such rebuffs—whether real or imagined—lead to hostility, which he can't possibly acknowledge lest he lose her altogether. Add the further fact that since his basic anxiety makes him devalue himself, he may well begin to devalue her. How could she be as wonderful as he thought at first, if she loves him? As Groucho Marx once said, "I wouldn't want to belong to any club that would accept me as a member." All of these further factors combine to enhance the love-seeking neurotic's sense of anxiety, which then refuels his desperate need for love and affection.

While vicious circles of this kind are a characteristic of deeply disturbed and unhappy persons, minor versions of such circular mechanisms are found in everyday life. A student has to write an important paper. The paper worries her, so she puts it off. This makes her feel guilty, which makes her more anxious, which makes her put it off yet further, and so on (Hall et al., 1985). But as Horney points out, there are occasional "lucky circles." Some fortunate encounters in work or love may reverse the circle by increasing self-confidence, which leads to appropriate further efforts and further successes. But all too often, the neurotic's own conflicts make her unable to recognize whatever luck may come her way. Put another way, neurotic conflicts tend to perpetuate themselves, which is one reason why at least some people try to break the pattern by seeking some form of psychotherapeutic help.

Self-destructive behavior (From B. Kliban, Luminous animals. Copyright 1983, B. Kliban, Penguin Books)

COPING PATTERNS AND MENTAL HEALTH

The patterns we have just described characterize people with emotional conflicts that in some cases are quite serious. But can they help us understand normal people? Contemporary psychodynamically oriented theorists would say that they can. For in their view, unconscious conflict and defense mechanisms are found in normals as well as in people with profound emotional disorders; what distinguishes the two is the extent to which those conflicts are appropriately resolved.

Several investigators have studied characteristic patterns of defense using normal people. Much of this work was influenced by an emerging new movement in psychoanalysis, called *ego psychology,* whose initial impetus probably came from Freud's daughter Anna Freud (1895–1982). Its leaders include Heinz Hartmann (1894–1970), as well as Erik Erikson (1902–1994), whose work we encountered in a previous chapter (see Chapter 14). Adherents of this position share the neo-Freudian concern with cultural factors and interpersonal factors. But they add a further element by stressing the healthy aspects of the self as it tries to cope with the world—to deal with reality as it is rather than to distort it or hide from it. (Freud, 1946; Hartmann, 1964).★

Anna Freud *(Photograph courtesy of the Bettmann Archive)*

LONGITUDINAL STUDIES OF COPING PATTERNS

To find out how coping patterns are employed over the course of the life span, a number of investigators have performed **longitudinal studies,** that is, studies in which the same person is examined at different ages. Longitudinal studies that cover a span of twenty to thirty years represent an arduous undertaking; subjects drop out of the study for any number of reasons, and the investigators who begin the study are rarely the ones who finally complete it. In longitudinal studies of personality, the raw material is usually in the form of interview records conducted at different times. These records are later rated for various characteristics, such as certain personality traits or the use of this or another mechanism of defense.

An example of such a longitudinal study is George Vaillant's analysis of the case reports of ninety-four male college graduates studied at different points in their life span. They were extensively interviewed at age nineteen, and then again at thirty-one, and yet again at forty-seven. Vaillant studied the predominant patterns of defense—that is, ways of coping—each man used at these three ages. He classified these coping patterns according to their level of psychological maturity. At the bottom of the hierarchy were mechanisms that are often found in early childhood and during serious psychiatric breakdown—such as denial or gross distortions of external reality. Further up the ladder were patterns often seen in adolescence and in disturbed adults—such as projection, hypochondria, and irrational, emotional outbursts—"acting out." Still higher were the mechanisms studied by Freud and seen in many adults—repression, isolation, reaction formation, and the like. At the top of the hierarchy were coping patterns that Vaillant saw in "healthy" adolescents and adults—such as humor, suppression (a conscious effort to push anxiety-evoking thoughts out of mind, at least for the time being, as opposed to repression, which is an unconscious process), and altruism (in which one tries to give to others what one might wish to receive oneself).

★ A more recent and influential version of this ego-oriented position is *self-psychology,* developed by Heinz Kohut (1913–1981) (Kohut, 1978).

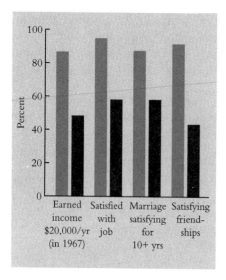

17.2 Maturity of defense mechanisms and life adjustment *Adult success at work and love, as shown by men with predominantly mature (blue) and immature (dark red) adaptive styles. (After Vaillant, 1971)*

Vaillant's findings are simple enough. It's not particularly surprising (though it is certainly reassuring) that as his subjects grew older, their coping mechanisms generally became more mature. There was growth and change, but there was also some continuity; men whose coping patterns were better integrated at nineteen, were somewhat more likely to have mature patterns in their forties, which then predicted various objective indices—satisfaction in marriage, rewarding friendships, more gratifying jobs, and better physical health (see Figure 17.2). As so often, it is by no means clear just what in those men's lives was cause and what was effect, but regardless of whether the mature coping defenses produced success in marriage and career or vice versa, it is worth knowing that the two tend to be correlated (Vaillant, 1974, 1976, 1977).

Similar results were obtained in a study by Jack Block that may be one of the most systematic longitudinal studies of personality ever undertaken. Block studied case records of some 250 men and women in junior high school, in senior high school, and in their thirties (Block, 1971). In many ways, the results were similar to those of Vaillant. Like Vaillant, Block found a general increase in overall personal adjustment. But he also found considerable evidence of continuity in characteristics such as grooming, enjoyment of social activities, self-assurance, and desire for achievement. In addition, he found a relation between the subjects' adjustment as adults and the family background from which they came. By and large, the well-adjusted adults were those who had a (psychologically) benign family atmosphere. Their mothers and fathers were active, self-assured, and warm, and took their parenting tasks seriously; they provided firm guidelines but were affectionate in doing so. In contrast, the subjects judged to be more poorly adjusted as adults came from less favorable family backgrounds. The parents were often at odds with each other, and they were either overinvolved with their child, or rejecting, dictatorial, or indifferent. As Block points out, these early histories differ widely; all they have in common is that they are unfavorable. This is quite different from those of the more well-adjusted subjects, which tend to be much more alike. There are more ways to make a machine (or a human body, or a human personality) function badly than to make it work properly. As the Russian novelist Leo Tolstoy put it in *Anna Karenina,* "Happy families are all alike; every unhappy family is unhappy in its own way" (Tolstoy, 1875, p. 1).

Block interprets these correlations in cause-and-effect terms. As he sees it, the parents provided a familial atmosphere that ultimately helped shape their child for good or ill by inducing healthy or unhealthy coping patterns. But as we saw above, this interpretation does not necessarily follow. One possibility is that the correlation was produced by a genetic similarity between child and parents. Another possibility is that the cause-and-effect relation is the reverse of the one proposed by Block; the child's own personality (in part, perhaps, based on genetic factors) may have influenced the way the parents treated her. No doubt there are other interpretations as well. Our present concern is merely to stress the enormous complexity of the issue. As yet, we have no easy solutions to the question of how any of us came to be the people we now are. (For further discussion, see Chapters 14 and 16, pp. 547–50, 652–58).

COPING AND THE UNCONSCIOUS

On the face of it, the preceding discussion of adaptive patterns may appear rather distant from the orientation of psychodynamic theorists, especially as represented by Freud. After all, Freud emphasized unconscious processes that operated in a murky underground of which we are unaware. In contrast, the coping responses of normal people seem much more ordinary, and they are at least sometimes in plain view. Is there any relation between these two?

Ego-oriented psychoanalysts—and most modern psychologists—would answer yes. For whatever their many differences, the defense mechanisms of the neurotic and the shoulder-shrugging reaction of the mature adult who refuses to worry about things he can't help anyway have one thing in common—they are both ways of trying to cope with and adapt to the strains and stresses of existence.

The fact that some of these adaptive reactions are fully conscious while others are not doesn't necessarily mean that there is a sharp break between them. For a number of psychologists have pointed out that what Freud called "unconscious mechanisms" may be regarded as ways of not attending, in line with the "kinder, gentler, and more rational" unconscious we discussed previously (see p. 690; Bowers, 1984; Erdelyi, 1985; Kihlstrom, 1987). The person who is in favor of a particular political candidate is much more likely to attend to arguments on his behalf than to arguments that favor his opponent. The first he will tend to remember; the second he is likely to forget. Similarly, the woman who has just suffered a painful divorce may prefer not to think about her ex-husband. When some topic comes up that starts to remind her about him, she will deliberately try to think about something else and may forget what it was that started the new train of thought. This method of turning away from one's own pain may not be as exotic as the complicated repressive maneuvers that Freud attributed to his patients, but it belongs to the same family.

Most of us physically avoid some situations we would rather not face; by the same token, some of us mentally avoid (that is, don't attend to) sights or thoughts or memories we find unpleasant or frightening. Seen in this light, the so-called unconscious mechanisms lose some of their mystery. They are just one more way of dealing with the world.

THE HUMANISTIC APPROACH

Improvisation *Some actors are famed for their ability to improvise on the spur of the moment. An example is Robin Williams, who improvised many of his lines in the film* Good Morning Vietnam, *1987. (Courtesy of the Kobal Collection)*

Some forty years ago, a new perspective on human motivation and personality—the **humanistic approach**—gained some prominence. According to its adherents, neither trait theorists, behaviorists, nor psychodynamic theorists have much to say about healthy, striving human beings. In their view, psychoanalysts look at people as if they are all emotional cripples, behaviorists regard them as if they are blind, unthinking robots, and trait theorists see them as material to file in sterile pigeon holes. Humanistic psychologists believe that all of these views have lost sight of what is truly human about human beings. Healthy humans want to feel free to choose and determine their own lives rather than to exist as mere pawns pushed around by stimuli from without and unconscious impulses from within. They seek more than food and sex and safety, strive for more than mere adjustment—they want to grow, to develop their potential, to become *self-actualized.*

Returning to our theatrical analogy, the humanistic approach can be likened to certain modern movements in theater that emphasize spontaneity and improvisation. Actors who belong to this school insist that what is most important is genuine, authentic feeling. At least in principle (though rarely in actual practice), such actors might depart from the playwright's words and the director's stagings to provide the audience and themselves with a sense of freedom and spontaneity. To the extent that this occurs, there is no mask left at all; the actor and the part have become one.

THE MAJOR FEATURES OF THE HUMANISTIC MOVEMENT

According to Abraham Maslow (1908–1970), the humanistic movement represents a kind of "third force" in American psychology—the other two being behaviorism and psychoanalysis. For expositional purposes, we will begin by presenting some of the major features of this movement before discussing them more critically.

A POSITIVE VIEW OF HUMAN MOTIVATION

A major contrast between humanistic psychologists and the behaviorists and psychoanalysts that they oppose is in their contrasting conception of human motivation. According to Maslow, behaviorists and psychoanalysts see human beings as engaged in a never-ending struggle to remove some internal tension or make up for some deficit. The result is an essentially pessimistic and negative conception of human nature. Seen in this light, people always want to get away from something (pain, hunger, sexual tension) rather than to gain something positive. This perspective necessarily leads to an emphasis on the physiological needs—hunger, thirst, escape from pain, sex. Maslow called these *deficiency needs*; in all such cases, we experience a lack and want to fill it. According to Maslow, an analogous deficiency sometimes underlies social needs such as the desire for prestige or security; an example is the woman who hungers for the admiration of all men around her and feels empty without it. But as Maslow pointed out, release from pain and tension does not account for everything we strive for. We sometimes seek things for their own sake, as a positive goal in themselves. There is the joy of solving a puzzle, the exhilaration of galloping on a horse, the ecstasy of fulfilled love, the quiet rapture in the contemplation of great art and music or a beautiful sunrise. All of these are experiences that human beings seek, and it is these positive, enriching experiences—rather than the filled stomach or the sexual release at orgasm—that make us most distinctively human. A hungry rat and a sexually aroused monkey seek food and orgasmic release pretty much as we do, but the joy of Beethoven's Ninth Symphony is ours alone. Maslow insisted that to understand what is truly human, psychologists must consider motives that go beyond the deficiency needs (Maslow, 1968).

Thus, Maslow proposed a *hierarchy of needs* in which the lower-order physiological needs are at the bottom, safety needs are further up, the need for attachment and love is still higher, and the desire for esteem is yet higher. At the very top of the hierarchy is the striving for self-actualization—the desire to realize oneself to the fullest (of which more later) (see Figure 17.3).

Maslow believed that people will only strive for higher-order needs (say, self-esteem or artistic achievement) when lower-order needs (such as hunger) are satisfied. By and large this is plausible enough; the urge to write poetry generally takes a back seat if one hasn't eaten for days. But as Maslow pointed out, there are exceptions. Some artists starve rather than give up their poetry or their painting, and some martyrs proclaim their faith regardless of pain or suffering. But to the extent that Maslow's assumption holds, the motive at the very top of his hierarchy—that is, the drive toward self-actualization—will become a primary concern only when all other needs beneath are satisfied.

THE SELF IN HUMANISTIC PSYCHOLOGY

Before trying to describe what Maslow and other humanistic psychologists mean by self-actualization, we should say a word about the self that is (or is not)

Spontaneity in the theater *Several modern movements emphasize spontaneity and creativity in the theater. An influential example is the theatrical school founded by the Polish director Jerzy Grotowski, who requires his actors to perform in a kind of trance, to give themselves totally in a confrontation with the play and the audience. The figure is taken from one of his productions,* The Constant Prince, *by Pedro Calderón de la Barca. (Reproduced by permission of Jerzy Grotowski)*

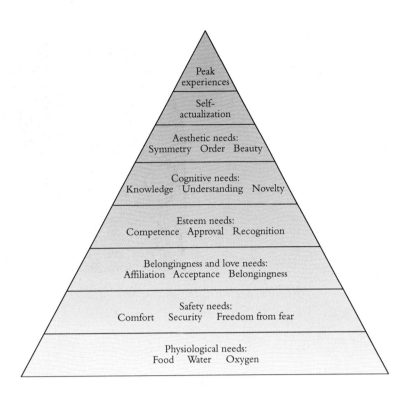

17.3   Maslow's hierarchy of needs
*People will strive for higher-order needs
(esteem or artistic achievement) generally after
lower-order needs (hunger, safety) have been
satisfied. (After Maslow, 1954)*

being actualized. We've previously encountered some issues related to the self;
social psychologists study it under the headings of self-perception theory and
self-presentation (Chapter 11, pp. 437–38), and Freud and Piaget treat it as a
developmental matter, since they believe that the "ego" emerges from an earlier
diffuse state in which there is no self at all (Chapter 13, pp. 505–506, and
Chapter 17, p. 673). To humanistic psychologists, the self is even more important, for one of their primary concerns is with subjective experience—with
what the individual thinks and feels right here and now. According to Carl
Rogers (1902–1987), a major figure in the humanistic movement, a crucial
facet of this subjective experience is the *self* or *self-concept.* This self-concept is
developed in early childhood and eventually comes to include one's sense of
oneself—the "I"—as an agent who takes (or doesn't take) actions and makes (or
doesn't make) decisions. It also includes one's sense of oneself as a kind of
object—the "me"—that is seen and thought about, and liked or disliked
(Rogers, 1959, 1961).

In the course of his work in clinical counseling, Rogers came to feel that
an important condition for adult mental health is a solid sense of personal
self-worth. Rogers believed that to achieve this the child requires **unconditional
positive regard**—the sense of being accepted and loved without condition or
reservation. But such a prescription for child rearing is difficult to follow.
For the parents can (and no doubt must) disapprove of some of the things the
child does; they are unlikely to applaud when little Janie spills ketchup all over
the new living room rug. They could still show Janie their unconditional positive regard by making it clear that while they certainly don't love her *behavior*
they do and will always love *her.* But this is much easier said than done. Most
parents probably do set some conditions on their love, no matter how subtly,
indicating that they will love her if she'll do well at school, or if she acts like a
nice girl, or whatever. Rogers believed that the likely upshot is that the child
will suppress some aspect of herself in order to feel loved and accepted. And
this in turn may lead to a sense of confusion and disquiet, and a doubt of one's
real self-worth.

Self-actualization shown through self-portraits To actualize one's self may take a whole lifetime. Some great artists have given us a graphic record of the process at different points in their lives, as in these self-portraits by Rembrandt. One was created at the age of thirty-four, when he was very successful and saw himself as a Renaissance gentleman artist and virtuoso. The other was painted at about age sixty, when he tried to reaffirm his identity through his art and portrayed himself as a painter holding the tools of his craft (Wright, 1982). (Left: Self-Portrait at the Age of thirty-four; courtesy of the National Gallery. Right: Portrait of the Artist; courtesy of English Heritage, The Iveagh Bequest)

SELF-ACTUALIZATION

Given a reasonable sense of self-worth and the satisfaction of the lower-level needs, the stage is set for the motive at the very top of Maslow's hierarchy of needs, the desire for *self-actualization.* Maslow and other humanistic psychologists describe this as the desire to realize one's potential, to fulfill oneself, to become what one can become (Maslow, 1968, 1970). But exactly what does this mean?

Maslow gave some examples by presenting case histories of a number of people that he and his collaborators regarded as "self-actualized." Some of them were individuals that he had personally interviewed; others were historical figures (for example, Thomas Jefferson and Ludwig van Beethoven) or more recent luminaries (such as Eleanor Roosevelt and Albert Einstein), whose lives were studied by means of historical or other documents. Unlike most other investigators in the field, Maslow was not interested in these subjects' specific attributes or behavior patterns; all he looked for were some overall patterns that he felt were shared by them all. As Maslow saw it, these self-actualizers had many admirable characteristics. Among other things, they were realistically oriented, accepted themselves and others, were spontaneous, cared more about the problems they were working on than about themselves, had intimate relationships with a few people rather than superficial relationships with many, and had democratic values—all in all, an admirable list of human qualities (Maslow, 1968, 1970).

According to Maslow, another characteristic of self-actualized persons is that they are more likely than other people to have what he called *peak experiences.* Peak experiences are profound and deeply felt moments in a person's life in which there is a "feeling of great ecstasy and awe . . . with the conviction that something extremely important and valuable had happened . . ." (Maslow, 1970, p. 164). Such moments might come while with a lover, or while watching the sea or a sunset, or while listening to music or watching a play—but regardless of when and where they occur, they seem to have some important and lasting effects on the individual who thereafter is likely to see himself and others in a more spontaneous and healthier way.

GROWTH

What happens to people whose self-regard is so low that the possibility of self-actualization doesn't arise? Rogers believed that new experiences in later life could provide some of the spontaneous warmth and positive regard that was lacking earlier. To that end, his therapy offered the client warmth and showed him that his feelings are accepted and that he is worthy of love (Rogers, 1980; for more details, see Chapter 19, pp. 782–83).

Rogers's approach to therapy illustrates that he—and indeed most humanistic psychologists—regard the development of human personality as a kind of growth process. They believe that, if given the appropriate conditions, people will grow so as to realize their inherent potential. They further believe that in general this potential is for good rather than for evil. In this regard, their position is the very opposite of that held by such pessimists as Hobbes and Freud, who insisted that humans cannot help but be brutes unless their baser instincts are tamed by civilization. In contrast, Rogers and Maslow felt that humans will only turn sour and ugly if they are somehow twisted and frustrated by the social conditions in which they live.

According to Rogers, people will attain a healthy sense of self if they are provided with the proper emotional climate. To grow into a healthy rose, the rose seedling needs water, sun, and soil. In the same vein, Rogers believed that to grow into emotionally healthy adulthood, the child needs warmth and acceptance, what he called **empathic understanding** (where someone seems to understand what you feel and so to speak to "feel it with you"), and to be with another person who is *genuine* (without a facade—open and trustworthy).

EVALUATING THE HUMANISTIC APPROACH

In trying to evaluate the humanistic approach to personality, we must begin by asking about its empirical and conceptual foundations.

EMPIRICAL AND CONCEPTUAL DIFFICULTIES

Consider Rogers's account of the origins of the feeling of self-worth. Is it really true that unconditional positive regard and empathic understanding are essential for the development of self-worth? We've previously noted the enormous difficulties in drawing any conclusions about the effects of child rearing on later personality development (see Chapter 14). Under the circumstances, Rogers's description of the parent-child relationships that lead to feelings of adequate or inadequate self-worth seems rather oversimplified. Nor is it clear that his form of therapy has all the beneficial effects that he claimed for it, though there is some evidence in his favor, especially for milder cases (Rogers, 1951; Rogers and Dymond, 1954).

Similar qualifications apply to a number of other assertions made by the proponents of the humanistic approach. How do we know that self-actualizers are in fact as Maslow described them to be—for example, realistically oriented, accepting of themselves and others, spontaneous, problem-centered, democratic, and so on; or that peak experiences have lasting and often beneficial effects on later life; or that self-actualizers have more such peak experiences than other people? As yet, there is no real evidence that would allow us to draw such conclusions.

An even more serious criticism is the fact that many of the core conceptions of the humanistic approach are exceedingly unclear. Just what is meant by *self-actualization,* or by "letting yourself go and being yourself," or by *unconditional positive regard,* or by a peak experience? Since these terms are only vaguely defined, it is difficult to know how to evaluate any assertions about them.

"I'm quite fulfilled. I always wanted to be a chicken." (Drawing by Joseph Farris; © 1989, The New Yorker Magazine, Inc.)

Consider Maslow's study of self-actualizers. Maslow chose a number of persons as exemplars, including a number of prominent and historical figures. But by what criteria did he select them? Among the historical figures he chose were Thomas Jefferson, Abraham Lincoln (in his later years), Eleanor Roosevelt, and Albert Einstein. Most of us would agree that these were admirable and creative people, and we can understand what is meant when someone says that they fulfilled their potential and "actualized themselves." But why can't the same term be applied to many other individuals, some of whom are far from admirable and may be veritable monsters? What about Napoleon, or Al Capone, or even Adolf Hitler? It's very likely that these persons felt that they had become what they were meant to become (at least until St. Helena, or Alcatraz, or the final days in the Berlin bunker.) But if so, why shouldn't we regard *them* as self-actualized? Given their belief that human growth has an inherent tendency toward good rather than evil, Maslow and Rogers would presumably rule out—by definition—moral monsters such as Capone or Hitler. But this line of reasoning can certainly be questioned. The development of personality may be a growth process, but this alone is not enough grounds for optimism. Given soil, sun, and water, a rose seedling will indeed become a rose. But if the seedling is a certain weed, it may self-actualize and become a full-grown stand of poison ivy.

HUMANISTIC PSYCHOLOGY AS A PROTEST MOVEMENT

It appears that many of the major tenets of the humanistic approach to personality rest on rather shaky foundations. But if so, why should we take it seriously? One answer is that the humanistic approach is best considered as a protest movement. It reacts against both behaviorism and psychoanalysis because it regards them as representatives of sterile mechanisms that treat people as marionettes pushed and pulled by forces from without and within. It reacts against trait psychology because it regards this approach as devoted to an endless cataloguing that reduces humans to mere ciphers. And it reacts against the general focus of much contemporary psychology, which it regards as narrow and pessimistic, ori-

The theater of protest The humanistic approach to personality is reminiscent of protest movements in the literary and political spheres. Examples are various modern dramatic productions that attack contemporary attitudes, as in Peter Weiss's play Marat/Sade *in which contemporary society is likened to an insane asylum. (From the 1966 film* Marat/Sade, *directed by Peter Brook; courtesy of the Kobal Collection)*

THE HUMANISTIC
APPROACH

Romanticism in the arts *The Romantic artists of the early nineteenth century stressed the full expression of the emotions. An example is this painting by Caspar David Friedrich. (*Frau in der Morgensonne; *courtesy of Museum Folkwang, Essen)*

ented toward human sickness and deficiency rather than toward health and upward striving.

In some ways, the humanistic approach to personality is reminiscent of some prior movements in the political and literary spheres. Some two hundred years ago, the Romantic poets in England and Germany elevated feeling over reason, celebrated individualism and natural man, and deplored the effects of eighteenth-century science and technology. Some, such as William Blake and Samuel Coleridge, sought peak experiences in mystical visions or in opium dreams. Others railed against the cold, mechanical science that had left the universe dry and bare. An example is John Keats's lament that "Newton has destroyed all the poetry of the rainbow by reducing it to the prismatic colors" (in Abrams, 1953, p. 303). And many of them agreed with the social philosopher Jean Jacques Rousseau (1712–1778), whose writings helped to shape the French and American Revolutions, that "man is by nature good, and . . . only our institutions have made him bad!" (in Durant and Durant, 1967, p. 19).

The similarity between these sentiments and many of the themes of the humanistic psychologists is clear enough. The Romantics protested against what they regarded as a cold, mechanical approach to nature and politics; the humanistic psychologists lodge similar complaints against contemporary approaches to psychology. This is not to say that the humanistic psychologists were directly influenced by Rousseau or the eighteenth-century Romantics, for they almost surely were not. The point is that by now Romanticism is a part of our cultural heritage that has provided a general vocabulary for many later protest movements. One example is the student revolution of the 1960s. Another is the humanistic movement in American psychology.

To be sure, the Romantic poets did much more than protest; they also made lasting contributions to literature. And Rousseau influenced the political landscape of Europe for a century after his death. Is there a corresponding positive contribution of humanistic psychology? Some critics feel that apart from Rogers's work on the practice and evaluation of psychotherapy, the humanists' concepts are as yet too vague and their assertions as yet too unproven to count as serious positive scientific accomplishments (e.g., Smith, 1950). Others argue that the humanists often serve as moral advocates rather than dispassionate scientists. They tell us what personality *should* be rather than what it is.

But there is one accomplishment of which we can be sure. The humanistic psychologists remind us of many phenomena that other approaches to the study of personality have largely ignored. People do strive for more than food and sex or prestige; they read poetry, listen to music, fall in love, have occasional peak experiences, try to actualize themselves. Whether the humanistic psychologists have really helped us to understand these elusive phenomena better than we did before is debatable. But there is no doubt that what they have done is to insist that these phenomena are there, that they constitute a vital aspect of what makes us human, and that they must not be ignored.

THE SOCIOCULTURAL PERSPECTIVE

Whatever their many differences, all of the approaches to personality we've discussed thus far have one thing in common: a focus on the individual. But surely all individuals exist in a social and cultural context that is critical in shaping and defining who they are. Yet by and large personality theorists have ignored that context and focused their efforts almost entirely on the individual, whether by categorizing him (trait theory), by studying how different situations shape him (social learning theory), by trying to uncover his hidden motives (psychodynamic theory), or by celebrating his uniqueness (humanistic psychology). None of these approaches concerns itself particularly with the culture of which the person necessarily is a part. Some modern critics feel that this is a serious lack. They point out that virtually all of the data on which modern personality theory is based come from the study of middle class western Europeans or North Americans. Can we really be sure that what holds true for these people can be generalized to people in different times, different places, and different cultures?

As we might expect, the answer is both yes and no. For it turns out that in some regards people throughout the world are very different from each other, while in other respects they are much the same.

Margaret Mead in Samoa, 1925 (Courtesy of the Institute for Intercultural Studies)

HUMAN DIVERSITY

Much of the evidence that bears on these matters comes from *cultural anthropology,* a discipline that studies ways of living that characterize different societies throughout the world. An early pioneer in this enterprise was Franz Boas (1858–1942), who convinced many anthropologists to study the preliterate cultures of the world before they disappeared altogether. Among his students were Ruth Benedict (1887–1948) and Margaret Mead (1901–1978), two of the most influential figures in this area; their work documents the enormous variety of human character and personality, shaped as they are by drastically different cultural traditions.

DIFFERENT PERSONALITY PATTERNS

Ruth Benedict's *Patterns of Culture* (1934) describes the characteristic personality patterns found in three very different preliterate societies. Among the Kwakiutl

Indians of the Canadian Northwest, the dominant theme was rivalry and boastful self-glorification. Among the Pueblo Indians of the American Southwest, the primary theme was self-control, cooperation, and very little aggression within the community. And among the Dobu Islanders, there was a great deal of mutual enmity and distrust, and a near-universal conviction that everyone practices sorcery against everyone else.

Other findings pointed to a variety of gender roles in different cultures. Thus Margaret Mead compared the personality traits of men and women in three preliterate New Guinea tribes that lived within a hundred-mile radius of one another. Among the Arapesh, both men and women were mild, cooperative, and, so to speak, "maternal" in their attitudes toward each other and especially toward children. Among the neighboring Mundugomor, both sexes were ferociously aggressive and quarrelsome. In yet another tribe, the Tchambuli, the usual sex roles were reversed: The women were the hale and hearty breadwinners who fished and went to market unadorned. While the women managed the worldly affairs, the men gossiped and pranced about, adjusted elaborate hairdos, carved and painted, and practiced intricate dance steps (Mead, 1935, 1937). Here was further evidence that the ways of modern Western society are not necessarily universal characteristics of human nature.

Of course neither Benedict nor Mead suggested that every member of a given culture exhibits the pattern they described. Not every Kwakiutl was vehemently boastful; not every Arapesh was gentle and cooperative. What they tried to describe is a typical and common personality pattern that characterizes a given cultural group.

DIFFERENT EMOTIONS

Other authors suggest that cultures differ in the typical emotions experienced by their members. As evidence they cite the fact that some societies have words that describe emotions for which we have no special terms. Thus people who live on the western Pacific island of Ifaluk often feel an emotion they call *fago,* which involves a complex mixture of compassion, love, and sadness experienced in relationships in which one person is dependent on the other (Lutz, 1986, 1988). And in Japanese culture there is an emotion called *amae,* which is a desire to be dependent and taken care of (Doi, 1973; Morsbach and Tyler, 1986).

HUMAN SAMENESS

The anthropological evidence suggests that the typical personality patterns and characteristic emotions of the Kwakiutl, Arapesh, Ifaluk, and ourselves are in many ways very different. But a number of authors point out that there are also many respects in which the dominant personalities and emotions of these various societies must be alike, for whatever their cultural differences, they all share a common humanity.

The broad pattern of evidence thus suggests that the differences between the members of various cultures are not as unbridgeable as one might have supposed. Ironically enough, these differences may actually be a tool for discovering some universal principles of human nature. That at least is the underlying rationale of the **cross-cultural method.**

UNIVERSAL PATTERNS OF PERSONALITY

Let's begin with personality patterns. Several anthropologists have criticized Benedict's and Mead's accounts as oversimplifications. For example, they take issue with some of Mead's work by pointing out that there are probably some universal sex roles after all; for example, warfare is generally conducted by the men, even among the Tchambuli. They argue that this may very well be due to biological factors, for aggression is in part under hormonal control; as androgen levels rise, both human and animal males become more aggressive (see Chapter 10). To these critics, some aspects of aggression are part of our biological nature regardless of the culture we belong to. What culture does is to determine how this aggression is to be channeled and against whom, whether it is to be valued, and how much of it will be allowed. (For recent discussions of Mead's work, see Freeman, 1983, 1986; Brady, 1983; Patience and Smith, 1986.)

Some other considerations concern personality traits. Let's assume that we could administer personality tests to some of the people studied by Mead and Benedict. Even granting that some of their descriptions may be overdrawn, one would still guess that the average Kwakiutl male would score much more highly on such traits as dominance and irritability than his Arapesh counterpart. To that extent, the typical personality patterns of the cultures surely differ. But one thing may still be the same: the *dimensions* along which these personalities vary. Some relevant evidence comes from translated personality tests administered in such diverse societies as those in Bangladesh, Brazil, Hong Kong, and Japan. When the results were factor analyzed, the pattern that emerged was much the same as that found in the United States and in Britain. This was especially true for Eysenck's two main dimensions of extroversion and neuroticism. This is not to say that people in these different cultures do not differ on these personality traits, for they certainly do. For example, extroversion scores are very much higher in the United States than in Japan. What is the same is the way the responses to the items hang together; as a result, the same dimensions of personality emerge. To use an analogy, people come in different shapes and sizes, but their diversity can nevertheless be described by just a handful of tailor's measurements. To be sure, people in Sweden tend to be taller than people in Japan, but the same measuring tape can be used for them all. (Eysenck and Eysenck, 1983; for some qualifications see Bond, 1979; Yang and Bond, 1990).

In some ways, these results should not be surprising. Traits such as extroversion and emotional stability may well be based on built-in characteristics related to temperament, which we know is in part genetically based (see Chapter 16, pp. 652–54). If so, these trait dimensions correspond to a broad framework that should in principle fit all humankind. What varies is just where within this framework a particular person falls. And this in part depends on the culture of which an individual is a member.

UNIVERSAL PATTERNS OF EMOTIONS

Similar considerations apply to the emotions. Certain emotions may be experienced more readily in one culture than they are in others. But does this mean that the emotions felt by members of various cultures are fundamentally different? When Rudyard Kipling expressed the views of Victorian British colonialists, he spoke in just such terms, insisting that "East is East and West is West and never the twain shall meet." But the best guess is that this is not really true. To begin with, there is good evidence that patterns of physiological reaction are quite similar across cultures: Feeling physically warm is generally found with the experience of joy; feeling hot, together with a quickened heart beat and tense muscles, accompanies anger; while feeling cold and clammy goes with fear. Similarly for facial expressions, which as we've seen before may well have a universal, built-in basis, despite the fact that they can be voluntarily masked or enhanced by culturally determined rules (see Chapters 10 and 11, pp. 402–404 and 443–44). In addition, there is evidence that certain events lead to pretty much the same emotions the world over; examples are bereavement and the anticipation of physical danger (Mesquita and Frijda, 1992).

Such considerations suggest that the emotions experienced by members of different cultures are not themselves quite as different as first supposed. What *is* different, however, is the set of circumstances that sets them off. In some Eastern cultures, modesty is highly valued, and being thought immodest is grounds for shame. In others, such as that of the Kwakiutl, boasting is socially approved of, and shame is felt only if one is unable to to fulfill one's boast. The Utku Eskimos report that they experience fear when confronting dangerous animals, evil spirits, and thin ice. While few of us are afraid of evil spirits, we can certainly understand why an Eskimo would fear thin ice or a polar bear.

In short, which experiences elicit which emotions partially depends on the culture one is a member of and the circumstances one finds oneself in. But the emotions as such may well be shared by all. If this is so, how can we explain that the members of some societies name emotions that our own culture has no single word for, as witness the Ifaluk *fago* and Japanese *amae*? Rudyard Kipling to the contrary, Westerners can likely sympathize with the feelings of people who experience *fago* or *amae* and may sometimes experience such feelings themselves, even if they can't name them. That the Ifaluk and the Japanese have words for these experiences and we don't merely suggests that this particular emotional complex is a common and important facet of their—but not of our own—emotional lives. This, however, does not change the emotion, what it means, or how it feels.

THE CROSS-CULTURAL METHOD: STUDIES OF THE EFFECTS OF CHILDHOOD

We've repeatedly run across the notion that what happens in early childhood determines later personality. This view is most prominently associated with Freud, but it is found in the writings of many other authors as well and permeates much of modern American thinking. Those who embrace the cross-cultural method examine this view by studying the relation between a culture's beliefs and practices—family structures, child-rearing patterns, rituals and religious thought—and the typical personality characteristics of its members. In effect, they take advantage of cultural differences to ask how—and whether—certain cultural variations, especially in the area of child rearing, shape personality.

We saw an interesting application of the cross-cultural method in Chapter 14, where we discussed the effect of socioeconomic factors on child rearing. One study demonstrated a relationship between the economy on which a society is based and its methods of child rearing: Cultures that make their living through agriculture tend to stress compliance, conformity, and responsibility in raising their children, whereas hunting and fishing societies tend to stress self-reliance and initiative (see p. 545; Barry, Child, and Bacon, 1959). Other studies demonstrated that some differences in child rearing in our own society may be associated with social class. The evidence suggests that parents encourage their children to behave at home as they themselves do at work. Since members of the working class tend to be more closely supervised than are members of the middle class, working-class parents tend to emphasize control from outside and are more likely to use physical punishment, an extreme version of physical control. Because the work of the middle class tends to be self-directed, they are inclined to encourage self-control in their children as well (see p. 545; Kohn, 1969; Hess, 1970).

COLLECTIVISM AND INDIVIDUALISM

The relations between child-rearing patterns and socioeconomic factors just described seems clear enough. But does either of the two cause the other? Most likely there is no direct cause-and-effect link. Instead, they are both strands in a complex web of patterns of thought and action handed down from one generation to the next. It is this web that constitutes the culture, and according to many anthropologists, its strands cannot be studied in isolation. As they see it, a culture is a kind of social Gestalt, whose parts only make sense by reference to the whole, much as a note takes its character from the melody in which it appears. If so, the best way to compare cultures would be along some dimension that considers the culture as a whole.

Many authors believe that current cultures and ethnic subgroups can be distinguished according to their position on the dimension of *collectivism-individualism* (Triandis, 1989). Collectivist societies include many of the societies of Latin America, and most of the cultures of Asia and Africa. Individualist societies include the dominant cultures of the United States, western Europe, Canada, and Australia.

In collectivist societies, the emphasis is on the needs, demands, and values of the family and immediate community. It is these primary groups that determine what is expected and what is frowned upon and that provide the major motives and rewards. In individualist societies, the emphasis is on a person's own private goals and aspirations. In such societies, one's important life choices—of occupation, friends, and spouse—are much less affected by the wishes of family and neighbors, for the ultimate goal is to be true to oneself. Thus students from individualist California are more likely to agree with statements that emphasize self-reliance, such as "Only those who depend on themselves get ahead in life," than are students from collectivist Hong Kong or Costa Rica. In contrast, students from Hong Kong and Costa Rica will be more likely to agree with statements that affirm a concern for one's family and close friends, such as "I would help within my means if a relative told me he (she) is in financial difficulty" and "I like to live close to my friends" (Triandis et al., 1988).

Once again, it is important to realize that terms that describe a culture don't necessarily apply to all of its members. They designate what is typical or average. There are surely some students from Hong Kong who would marry against their parents' wishes and some from California who would not. But the *average* student from Hong Kong will be more likely to behave along collectivist lines than the *average* student from California.

IN-GROUPS AND OUT-GROUPS

Collectivists and individualists (that is, members of collectivist and individualist societies) tend to differ in some further ways. Consider group pressure. On the face of it one might expect collectivists to be more subject to group pressure than individualists. But it turns out that this depends on the nature of the group. Collectivists are more affected than individualists by pressure from members of their *in-group,* a group to which they are tied by traditional bonds—their family (including second cousins and great-aunts and so on),★ classmates, close

---

★ Of course, individualists and collectivists both have families to which they have strong ties. In a collective society the family is greatly extended. Typical individualists, on the other hand, take family to mean the *nuclear* family: two parents and their children. Individualists often feel affection for their own parents, but they don't feel obliged to live with them or close to them after they've started their own families.

friends, and fellow workers. But in contrast, they are less affected than individualists by members of the **out-group,** a group that is best defined by exclusion, being constituted by those who do *not* belong to the in-group.

A related phenomenon is the permanence of an individual's social bonds. Collectivists belong to relatively few in-groups, but their bonds to those are strong and long-lasting. It's no accident that in Japan (a collectivist society) workers tend to remain in whatever organization they started out with, wearing their company's colors and singing company songs, such as "A bright heart overflowing with life links together Matsushita Electric" (Weisz, Rothbaum, and Blackburn, 1984). In contrast, members of individualist cultures belong to a whole set of overlapping in-groups, but their relation to these groups is more fragile and less enduring. In part, this is a consequence of their different values. To the individualist, what matters most is the freedom to pursue her own goals and preferences. As these change, so do her social relationships. As a result, individualists generally make friends more easily than collectivists do, but their friendships tend to be impermanent and to lack intimacy. Freedom is very precious, but for some individualists its price is loneliness.

All of this has to be qualified somewhat. It's true that members of collectivist societies are more likely to subordinate their own aspirations to the demands of their in-group than members of individualist cultures like our own. But that doesn't mean that Westerners are unable to submerge their individuality for the sake of some common good. They can and do—sometimes. This is especially true in major emergencies, such as floods, earthquakes, and similar disasters, which often bring out rare qualities of heroism and group spirit. And millions of Americans have shown in one generation after another that they, the citizens of what may well be the most individualist society on earth, are capable of the most extreme acts of self-sacrifice and collectivism in times of war. Americans are less concerned about what their neighbors think and don't sing songs in praise of General Motors, but they too are capable of collective acts and feelings.

INDIVIDUALISM AND SELF-EXPRESSION

Historians point to a number of sources for our modern concept of individualism, especially in America. Some point to special environmental factors, such as the presence of the frontier in eighteenth and nineteenth century America

Individualism versus collectivism in art
(A) After the middle ages, artists expressed their own individuality in their works, as in this self-portrait by Albrecht Dürer painted in 1499. (From Alte Pinakothek, Munich. Courtesy of Giraudon/Art Resource, New York); (B) In contrast, medieval painters, print makers, and architects saw themselves primarily as craftsmen who often dedicated themselves to some collective effort and were content to remain anonymous. Their lack of interest in individuality is illustrated in this French woodcut circa 1250, depicting the building of the biblical Tower of Babel, in which all workers look virtually alike. (From The Pierpont Morgan Library, New York; courtesy of The Pierpont Morgan Library/Art Resource, New York.) (C) Great medieval cathedrals, like Notre Dame in Paris (shown here), are the result of just such collective efforts. (Photograph courtesy of Robert McLean)

A

B

C

Japanese collectivism versus U. S. individualism (A) Tokyo school children. (Photograph © Yves Gellie/Odyssey Matrix, 1990) (B) Kindergartners from P.S. 75, New York City. (Photograph courtesy of Marian Johnson, 1994)

(Tocqueville, 1835). Others trace it to the Protestant Reformation, which insisted that each individual bears a direct relation to God (Weber, 1904–1905). Still others go further back and see its origin in the Italian Renaissance. In that period artists began the practice of signing their own works as if to say "Look here! It's mine!" Until then, painters were craftsmen whose job was simply to paint a pious picture of the Madonna or a good likeness of their patron. But since the Renaissance, the artist's task has changed, for his job now is to make his work different from that of others, to be creative and original, to express himself (Burckhardt, 1860).

John Sabini has argued that our Western individualism has much in common with the value we place on artistic creativity. We celebrate personal uniqueness, appreciate sincerity, approve of spontaneity, and applaud individual accomplishment. The unique self is regarded as a thing of value in itself, for we value self-expression, regardless of what it is that is expressed (Sabini, 1995). In this regard, we are quite different from collectivists. Americans try to excel and are asked to "be the best you can be." In contrast, collectivists like the Japanese try to become "so identified with their in-group that [their] individuality is not noticed." Where American children are urged to stand out, Japanese children are taught to "stand in" (Weisz, Rothbaum, and Blackburn, 1984; Barlund, 1975).

CULTURAL DIFFERENCES IN THE CONCEPT OF THE SELF

Some authors believe that differences among cultures indicate that our Western conception of the self and human personality has only limited applications to cultures other than our own. In their view, many other cultures don't see the individual as we do—as ultimately separate and independent from the social framework in which she lives. They neither see nor value this socially abstracted personal independence, but define the self through its interdependence with others (e.g., Markus and Kitayama, 1991). Richard Shweder and his collaborators have tried to demonstrate this difference by comparing the responses of Western and non-Western subjects when asked to describe a close acquaintance. Americans were likely to use abstract trait terms, such as, "She is friendly." In contrast, subjects in India were inclined to describe what a person does in a particular social context, as in "She brings cakes to my family on festival days," or "He has trouble giving to his family" (Shweder and Bourne, 1986).

Whether Shweder's findings really prove that different cultures have a different conception of the self is debatable; the real difference may be in how the subjects talk about people rather than in how they think about them (e.g., Sabini, 1995). A more persuasive argument comes from some detailed accounts of life on the Indonesian island of Bali, provided by the anthropologist Clifford Geertz. As Geertz describes it, Bali's culture (at least until about 1950 or so) is at one extreme end of the collectivism-individualism dimension and may well possess a different conception of selfhood (Geertz, 1983).

Consider people's names. In Bali, individuals have personal names (our equivalent of Henry or Lila), but they are rarely used. Instead, they have an elaborate system of other labels. One is a birth-order name (first-child, second-child, and so on) that parents and siblings use to address children and adolescents. Another is a complex naming system that refers to one's descendants, based on the name of one's first child (e.g., "Father of Henry"). When one's first grandchild is born, one's own name changes (e.g., "Grandfather of Ellen"). And if one lives until the first great-grandchild is born, one's name changes again (e.g., "Great-grandfather of Philip"). In addition, there is a complex system of status titles (e.g., high caste, middle caste, and so on) and social role indicators (e.g., elder of such and such a village). There is quite a difference between this and the American "Hello, I'm Joe."

This complex system of names and titles is part and parcel of a pattern of social life ruled by an elaborate system of ritual and etiquette that enters into every sphere of human existence, whether familial, economic, political, or religious. Individuality is suppressed; all that matters is the proper outward form. To quote Geertz:

> . . . Anything idiosyncratic, anything characteristic of the individual merely because he is who he is physically, psychologically, or biographically is muted in favor of his assigned place in the continuing pageant that is Balinese life. . . . Physically men come and go, mere incidents in a happenstance history, of no genuine importance even to themselves. But the masks they wear, the stage they occupy, the parts they play . . . remain, and they comprise not the facade but the substance of things, not least the self . . ." (Geertz, 1983, p. 62).

This description of Balinese life is one of the best expositions of what some authors mean when they argue that modern psychology's notions of personality and the self are a Western invention that may not apply to cultures (or at least, to all cultures) other than our own.

How does any of this bear on the various approaches to personality we discussed in this and the preceding chapter? It certainly reminds us that some aspects of these personality theories are bound up with our own individualist Western notions of what a person is. But that is to be expected. All of these theoretical approaches try to understand what makes people different: Trait theory concentrates on differences in largely built-in characteristics, social learning theory focuses on differences in what people have learned, and psychodynamic theory looks at differences in unconscious motivations. The humanistic approach is even more Western in its emphasis, for its focus is on human uniqueness, which it both studies and exalts. It is clear that all of these approaches could only arise in a culture in which people are differentiated over and above their differences

Westernization of nonwestern cultures
Solar-powered television in Nigeria. (Photograph © John Chiasson, Liaison International)

in age, gender, race, and religion. In Bali such differences are suppressed; in many other non-Western, collectivized societies they are muted. Under the circumstances, we may have to be cautious about supposing that what makes sense in the West makes sense everywhere.

In closing, let us suppose that the sociocultural critique is valid in all regards (and this is by no means undisputed, e.g., Sabini, 1995). If this were so, then our various personality theories would only make sense for people in Western societies. While this would obviously limit their range of application, we shouldn't forget that this range is still very large indeed—encompassing perhaps a billion people. And for better or worse—probably for both—that number may well get larger as much of the world becomes progressively westernized, watching U.S. television, listening to Western rock music, and wearing Western jeans.

Even so, the sociocultural critique has provided a valuable corrective. It reminds us that we are not the only society in an ever-shrinking world and that others have different perspectives, a reminder that is all the more valuable as the United States becomes increasingly aware of its own multicultural nature.

TAKING STOCK

In this and the previous chapter, we considered a number of approaches to personality. One is the trait approach, which tries to describe personality by reference to a few basic characteristics, many of which have a built-in basis. Another is the behavioral approach, which focuses on the individual's outwardly observable acts and argues that these acts are produced by the situation that the individual faces now or has faced on previous occasions. Yet another is the psychodynamic approach, which centers on submerged feelings, unconscious conflicts, and desires. Still another is the humanistic approach, which asks how people achieve selfhood and realize their potential. And we concluded with a discussion of the sociocultural perspective, which suggests that certain conceptions of human individuality and the self may be a product of our Western culture that may not apply to cultures other than our own.

Today there are relatively few theorists who would espouse any of these approaches in their most extreme form. By now most adherents of the behavioral approach have shifted to a more cognitive conception of the subject matter, most psychodynamic theorists see unconscious defenses and conscious coping mechanisms as parts of a continuum, virtually everyone grants that what people do depends on both traits and situations, and many theorists recognize that there are both cultural differences and universals.

But even so, some important differences in approach clearly remain. This is probably fortunate. For these different theoretical orientations reflect different perspectives on the same subject matter, and each of these orientations has some validity. Some aspects of personality are clearly built in (trait theory); others are learned (social learning theory); some reflect buried conflicts (psychodynamic theory); others reveal the need for self-actualization (humanistic approach); and yet others may be limited to a particular cultural worldview (the sociocultural perspective). We cannot envisage what a complete theory of personality will look like in the year 2095, but it will surely have to describe all of these aspects of human functioning, for they are all there.

In this regard, the different perspectives on personality are again similar to different approaches to the presentation of character in literature or on the stage. Is the human drama best described by the use of a number of stock types, perhaps designated by a few well-chosen masks, or by well-rounded characters that are like themselves alone and no others? There is no simple yes or no, for people are both similar to and different from each other. Is character best described by the Classicists, who stress human reason, or by the Romantics, who emphasize feeling? Again there is no answer, for both emotion and rationality are part of our very nature. Should actors portray the inner life and concentrate on what lies behind the mask, or should they focus on the outward mask, since that is what the audience sees? Here too there is no answer, for we all have both an inner and an outer life.

We are similar to others, but we are also different. We are pulled by outer and inner forces, but we are also free to make our own choices. We are rational, but we are also impelled by feeling. We are both the masks we wear and something else beneath. We are members of a particular culture, but we are also members of the human race. Each of the approaches to personality—and to dramatic character—focuses on one or another of these aspects of our nature. Each of these aspects exists. And to that extent each of the approaches is valid.

SUMMARY

1.   The *psychodynamic approach* to personality is derived from Sigmund Freud's *psychoanalytic theory*. Freud asserted that all people experience *unconscious conflicts* originating in childhood. His theories grew out of studies of a *psychogenic* mental disorder then called *hysteria*. Freud proposed that hysterical symptoms are a means of keeping *repressed* thoughts or wishes unconscious. He believed that the symptoms would be eliminated once the repressed materials were recovered and devised a procedure, *psychoanalysis,* directed toward this end.

2.   Freud distinguished three subsystems of the human personality. One is the *id,* a blind striving toward biological satisfaction that follows the *pleasure principle.* The second is the *ego,* a system of reactions that tries to reconcile id-derived needs with the actualities of the world, in accordance with the *reality principle.* A third is the *superego,* which represents the internalized rules of the parents and punishes deviations by feelings of guilt.

3.   According to Freud, internal conflict is initially prompted by *anxiety,* which becomes associated with forbidden thoughts and wishes, usually in childhood. To ward off this anxiety, the child resorts to repression and pushes the forbidden materials out of consciousness. Repression is the initial, primary *mechanism of defense* against anxiety. But the repressed materials generally surface again, together with their associated anxiety. To push these thoughts and wishes down again, further, supplementary defense mechanisms come into play, including *displacement, reaction formation, rationalization, projection,* and *isolation.*

4.   Freud believed that most adult unconscious conflicts are ultimately sexual in nature and refer to events during childhood *psychosexual development.* According to Freud, the child passes through three main stages that are characterized by the erogenous zones through which gratification is obtained: *oral, anal,* and *phallic.* In Freud's view, differences in adult personality can be understood as residues of early *fixations* and *reaction formations* that occurred during psychosexual development. An example is the *oral character,* whose nature he believed goes back to a powerful oral fixation. Another example is the *anal character,* whose attributes include compulsive neatness, obstinacy, and stinginess.

5.   During the phallic stage, the male child develops the *Oedipus complex.* He directs his sexual urges toward his mother, hates his father as a rival, and comes to dread him as he suffers increasing *castration anxiety.* He finally renounces his sexual urges, *identifies* with his father, and represses all relevant memories. At adolescence, repressed sexual urges

surface, are redirected toward adult partners, and the person generally achieves *genital sexuality*. In female children, the *Electra complex* develops, with love toward the father and rivalry toward the mother.

6. Freud tried to apply his theory of unconscious conflict to many areas of everyday life, including slips of the tongue, memory lapses, and dreams. He believed that all dreams are at bottom *wish fulfillments*. Since many of these wishes prompt anxiety, their full expression is censored. As a result, the underlying *latent dream* is transformed into the *manifest dream* in which the forbidden urges emerge in a disguised, sometimes symbolic form. A similar approach led to the psychoanalytic interpretation of myths and literature that in Freud's view provide a glimpse into the hidden concerns that are shared by whole groups of people.

7. Some early critiques of Freudian theory came from within the psychoanalytic movement. Among the most influential of these were the *neo-Freudians,* who disputed many of Freud's theories about the nature and origins of unconscious conflict. In particular, they denied the notion of a universal Oedipus complex independent of culture.

8. Attempts to find evidence for repression and unconscious conflict have not met with unqualified success. While dreams are often relevant to personal preoccupations and may feature symbolism, there is little evidence that they are disguised representations of hidden urges. Laboratory studies of repression suggest that when motivated forgetting occurs, it may be a special case of retrieval failure. There are clearly nonconscious mental activities, but they are not necessarily a defense against anxiety, nor do they have the sexual and aggressive quality that Freud attributed to them, prompting some critics to hypothesize a "kinder, gentler unconscious."

9. Later psychodynamic theorists take a neo-Freudian orientation. In contrast to Freud, they generally focus on interpersonal rather than biological forces in the individual and are generally more interested in the individual's present situation than his childhood past. An example is Karen Horney, who studied self-perpetuating vicious circles in adult neurotic conflicts. Some modern psychodynamic theorists have studied characteristic patterns of defense and coping in normal persons, which show considerable consistency over an individual's lifetime.

10. Another major orientation to personality is the *humanistic approach,* which maintains that what is most important about people is how they achieve their own selfhood and actualize their human potential. The humanistic approach emphasizes what it considers positive human motives, such as *self-actualization,* and positive personal events, such as *peak experiences,* rather than what it calls *deficiency needs.* According to Abraham Maslow, people only strive for higher-order needs when lower-order needs are satisfied.

11. A major concern of humanistic psychologists is the self. According to Carl Rogers and other humanistic psychologists, its development is essentially based on growth. In their view, given the appropriate conditions, people will grow so as to realize their potential, which is for good rather than evil. Rogers believed that children will only achieve a solid sense of personal self-worth if they have experienced a sense of *unconditional positive regard.* Some defects in a person's self can be healed later in life by providing the individual with important growth experiences she lacked before.

12. A number of authors have argued that much of modern personality theory is based on the study of middle-class western Europeans and North Americans and may not be applicable to cultures other than our own. The *sociocultural approach* is an attempt to provide a corrective. Testimony to the remarkable diversity of human beings has come from the work of *cultural anthropologists,* most prominently Ruth Benedict and Margaret Mead. Considerable diversity has been shown in characteristic personality patterns, in gender roles, and in the kinds of emotions that different cultures emphasize. But, as *cross-cultural methods* demonstrate, there is also evidence for some sameness across cultures, sameness that includes similar psychological dimensions and a universal pattern of underlying emotions.

13. A number of investigators have tried to use the *cross-cultural* method as a tool to discover the effects of child rearing on adult personality. Some have looked at socioeconomic factors and contrasted child-rearing styles in hunting and agricultural societies, and in different socioeconomic classes in our own culture.

SUMMARY

14. According to many psychologists and anthropologists, an important psychological dimension along which different cultures can be classified is *collectivism-individualism*. In collectivist societies the emphasis is on the needs, demands, and values of the family and the community. In individualist societies, including our own, the focus is on the person's private aims and aspirations, and special value is placed on self-expression. While collectivists are more affected by social pressure than individualists, this only holds if the social force is applied by the *in-group*. For individualists the in-group/out-group distinction is not so sharply drawn. Some authors interpret these and other differences as demonstrations that different cultures have different conceptions of the self.

CHAPTER 18

PSYCHOPATHOLOGY

DIFFERENT CONCEPTIONS OF MADNESS 715

PSYCHOPATHOLOGY AS DEMONIC POSSESSION ■ PSYCHOPATHOLOGY AS A DISEASE

THE UNDERLYING PATHOLOGY MODEL 722

SUBCATEGORIES OF THE PATHOLOGY MODEL ■ CLASSIFYING MENTAL DISORDERS ■ EXPLAINING DISORDER: DIATHESIS, STRESS, AND PATHOLOGY

SCHIZOPHRENIA 726

SIGNS AND SYMPTOMS ■ THE SEARCH FOR THE UNDERLYING PATHOLOGY ■ULTIMATE CAUSES OF SCHIZOPHRENIA ■ THE PATHOLOGY MODEL AND SCHIZOPHRENIA

MOOD DISORDERS 736

BIPOLAR AND UNIPOLAR SYNDROMES ■ ORGANIC FACTORS ■ PSYCHOGENIC FACTORS ■ MOOD DISORDERS AND THE DIATHESIS–STRESS CONCEPTION

ANXIETY DISORDERS 744

PHOBIAS ■ OBSESSIVE-COMPULSIVE DISORDER ■ GENERALIZED ANXIETY DISORDER ■ PANIC DISORDER ■ POST-TRAUMATIC STRESS DISORDER

DISSOCIATIVE DISORDERS 750

FACTORS UNDERLYING DISSOCIATIVE DISORDERS ■ DISSOCIATIVE DISORDERS AND THE DIATHESIS-STRESS CONCEPTION

SOMATOFORM AND PSYCHOPHYSIOLOGICAL DISORDERS 752

SOMATOFORM DISORDERS ■ PSYCHOPHYSIOLOGICAL DISORDERS

A CATEGORIZING REVIEW 756

SOCIAL DEVIANCE 757

THE SOCIOPATH ■ SOCIOPATHY AND THE DISORDER CONCEPT

THE SCOPE OF PSYCHOPATHOLOGY 759

SUMMARY 760

I n the two preceding chapters, we considered normal variations in human personality. We now turn to conditions that depart from normal functioning and are considered *malfunctions*. The study of disorders in psychological functioning is the province of **psychopathology** or, as it sometimes is called, **abnormal psychology**. There is considerable debate about how psychopathology is to be defined. Some consider it simply a problem of statistical deviance, when normal kinds of behavior reach such an extreme that we label them pathological. Others take the term *psychopathology* more literally and regard its manifestations as something akin to illness. But if these manifestations are illnesses, then what kinds of illnesses are they? Are they simply the psychological aspects of some hidden bodily disorder, such as a defect in brain function or a biochemical imbalance? Or should they be considered distinctly *mental* illnesses, whose origins are psychological, such as learned defenses against anxiety?

As we shall see, there is no one answer to these questions. The biggest reason is that the conditions that comprise psychopathology are a very mixed lot. For some, the term *illness* seems quite appropriate; for others, this is not so clear. In any case, there is little doubt that many of the conditions that come to the attention of the psychopathologist—the psychiatrist, clinical psychologist, social worker, or other mental-health specialist—often cause considerable anguish and disability.

Our conceptions of psychopathology go back to antiquity, and so we will begin by discussing some of their historical roots.

DIFFERENT CONCEPTIONS OF MADNESS

Mental disorders existed long before the mental-health profession appeared on the scene. Early mythological and religious writings are proof enough. The Greek hero, Ajax, slew a flock of sheep that he mistook for his enemies; King Saul of Judea alternated between bouts of murderous frenzy and suicidal depressions; and the Babylonian King Nebuchadnezzar walked on all fours in the belief that he was a wolf. Such phenomena were evidently not isolated instances. According to the Bible, young David feigned madness while seeking refuge from his enemies at the court of a Philistine king. This king had obviously encountered psychopathology before and upbraided his servants, "Do I lack madmen, that you have brought this fellow to play the madman in my presence?"★

★ The terms *madness* and *insanity* are sometimes used colloquially to refer to severe cases of psychopathology. *Madness* is simply archaic and doesn't refer to any particular mental illness. The term *insanity*, however, is current—but it isn't a psychological term. It is a legal term, used to refer to a

An early example of mental disorder
King Nebuchadnezzar as depicted by
William Blake (1795). (Courtesy of the Tate
Gallery, London)

18.1 Trephining *A trephined prehistoric
skull found in Peru. The patient apparently
survived the operation for a while, for there is
some evidence of bone healing. (Courtesy of
The American Museum of Natural History)*

PSYCHOPATHOLOGY AS DEMONIC POSSESSION

What leads to mental disorder? One of the earliest theories held that the afflicted person was possessed by evil spirits. It followed that the cure for the malady was to drive the devils out, and one of the earliest approaches was to provide a physical escape hatch for them. According to some anthropologists, this may explain why Stone Age people sometimes cut large holes into their fellows' skulls; many such ***trephined*** skulls have been found, often with signs that the patient managed to survive the operation. In some preliterate tribes, this operation is still performed for much the same reasons (Stewart, 1957; Figure 18.1).

Later treatment regimens attempted to calm the unruly demons or devils by music or chase them away with prayers or exorcisms. If the patient was lucky, the exorcism procedures were fairly mild; more often the techniques were less benign. One idea was to make things as uncomfortable for the evil spirit as possible so as to induce it to escape. Accordingly, the patient was chained, immersed in boiling water or ice baths, starved, or flogged. It is hardly surprising that such procedures usually drove the patient into worse and worse derangement.

PSYCHOPATHOLOGY AS A DISEASE

The demonological theory of mental illness is a thing of the past. Even in its heyday, there was an alternative view which held that such conditions

judgment by a court that one cannot be held responsible for one's actions. Of course, opinions of mental-health specialists may contribute to the court's decision, and the defense of not guilty by reason of insanity (NGRI) is occasionally used when a criminal defendant was so disabled by mental illness at the time of a crime that the focus in any sentencing is on treatment rather than incarceration (Simon and Aaronson, 1988).

resulted from natural causes and were a kind of disease. This theory of mental disorder goes back to antiquity and was held by many even during the Middle Ages, when the demonological theory was at its height (Allderidge, 1979; Neugebauer, 1979). But this belief did not necessarily lead to more humane treatment of the afflicted. It might have done so if a ready cure had been available, but until recently, there was little hope of that. As a result, the "madmen" were treated with little sympathy, for they seemed to have no common bond with the rest of humanity, and there was little likelihood that they ever would have. They were seen as a nuisance at best and a menace at worst. In either case, the interests of society seemed best served by "putting them away."

To this end, a number of special hospitals were established throughout Europe. But until the beginning of the nineteenth century (and in some cases, even later), most of these were hospitals in name only. Their real function was to serve as a place of confinement in which all kinds of social undesirables were segregated from the rest of humankind—criminals, beggars, the elderly, epileptics, incurables of all sorts, and the mentally disturbed (Rosen, 1966). After they had been in the "hospital" for a few years, it became hard to distinguish among them. Their treatment was barbaric. One author describes conditions in the major mental hospital for Parisian women at the end of the eighteenth century: "Madwomen seized by fits of violence are chained like dogs at their cell doors, and separated from keepers and visitors alike by a long corridor protected by an iron grille; through this grille is passed their food and the straw on which they sleep; by means of rakes, part of the filth that surrounds them is cleaned out" (Foucault, 1965, p. 72).

To most of their contemporaries, this treatment seemed only natural; after all, "madmen" were like dangerous animals and had to be caged. But since such animals are interesting to watch, some of the hospitals took on another function—they became zoos. At London's Bethlehem hospital (which became known as "Bedlam," for that's how it sounded when pronounced with a Cockney accent), the patients were exhibited to anyone curious enough to pay the required penny per visit. In 1814, there were 96,000 such visits (Figure 18.2).

A number of reformers gradually succeeded in eliminating the worst of these practices. Historians have given much of the credit to the French physician,

18.2 The mentally disturbed on exhibit
An eighteenth-century depiction of a tour of Bedlam. (The Madhouse, 1735/1763, William Hogarth; courtesy of the Bettmann Archive)

Philippe Pinel (1745–1826), who was put in charge of the Parisian hospital system in 1793 when the revolution was at its height. Pinel wanted to remove the inmates' chains and fetters (albeit treating inmates from upper-class families preferentially), but the government gave its permission only grudgingly (Figure 18.3). A high functionary argued with Pinel, "Citizen, are you mad yourself that you want to unchain these animals?" (Zilboorg and Henry, 1941, p. 322). The functionary's concern about the prospect of the inmates running free is echoed even today; many people attach a severe stigma to mental illness and believe that mental hospitals are a good idea, just so long as neither the hospitals nor the patients come into *their* neighborhoods.

MENTAL DISORDER AS AN ORGANIC ILLNESS

Pinel and other reformers sounded one main theme: Madness is a disease. Following from this assertion, inmates became patients who needed treatment rather than imprisonment. And developing such treatments first required discovering the causes of the disease (or rather, diseases, since it was already known that there were several varieties of mental disorder). Today, almost two hundred years after Pinel, we are still searching for the causes of most of them.

At first, the notion of mental disorder as an illness implied a bodily cause, most likely some disease of the brain. Proponents of this *somatogenic* hypothesis (from the Greek *soma,* meaning "body") could point to such relevant discoveries as the effects of cerebral strokes in impairing speech (see Chapter 2). But the somatogenic position gained its greatest impetus at the end of the nineteenth century in the discovery of the organic cause of a once widely prevalent, severe, and debilitating disorder, *general paresis.* It is characterized by a general decline in physical and psychological functions, culminating in a grossly disturbed gait and marked personality aberrations that may include childish delusions ("I am the Prince of Wales") or profound hypochondriacal depressions ("My heart has stopped beating"). Without treatment, the cognitive deterioration progresses, paralysis ensues, and death occurs within a few years (Dale, 1975).

By the end of the nineteenth century, the conviction had grown that general paresis has its roots in a syphilis infection that was contracted many years prior to

18.3   Pinel ordering the removal of the inmates' fetters *(Copyright Stock Montage, Inc.)*

DIFFERENT CONCEPTIONS OF MADNESS

Insanity as seen by an artist   *This painting undoubtedly shows aspects of what Francisco Goya saw when he visited an insane asylum in Spain, but it may also have been affected by the then current views of the classification of mental disorder. Most early descriptions included the raving maniac (here the nude men wrestling in the center), the hopeless melancholic (the despairing figures on the left), and those with grotesque delusions (the men with crowns demanding allegiance from their subjects).* (The Insane Asylum, *c. 1810, Francisco Goya, Accademia S. Fernando, Madrid; courtesy of Art Resource)*

the appearance of overt symptoms. In some untreated syphilitics (according to recent estimates, perhaps 5 percent), the outward signs of the infection may disappear, but the spirochete that caused it remains, invading and damaging the nervous system. Experimental proof came in 1897 when the Viennese physician Richard von Krafft-Ebbing inoculated several paretic patients with matter taken from syphilitic sores. None of them developed any of the early symptoms of syphilis, a clear sign that they had contracted the disease previously.★ Once the cause of the disease was known, the discovery of its cure and prevention was just a matter of time. The preferred modern treatment is penicillin. Its effectiveness is unquestioned. While general paresis at one time accounted for more than 10 percent of all admissions to mental hospitals; as of 1970, it accounted for less than 1 percent (Dale, 1975).

The discovery of the cause of general paresis was a triumph for the somatogenic view and aided many of its proponents in their claim that all mental disorders would ultimately be shown to have an organic basis, most likely in the brain. They could point to senility (a group of disorders now known as the *dementias*) in which there is atrophy of cortical cells. And they could point to a cognitive syndrome specific to chronic alcoholism, which results from the effects on the brain of a vitamin deficit produced by the alcoholism. The question became not whether there was value to the somatogenic view, but whether it could account for *all* mental disorders.

MENTAL DISORDER AS A PSYCHOLOGICAL ILLNESS

The achievements of the somatogenic approach were impressive, but by the end of the nineteenth century it became clear that it could not explain the full spectrum of mental disorders. One of the main stumbling blocks was a condition then known as *hysteria*, which we already encountered in our discussion of psychoanalysis (see Chapter 17).

★ Modern medical and scientific practitioners are considerably more sensitive than our forebears to the ethical issues raised by this and similar studies. Today such a procedure would require the patients' informed consent.

The story of hysteria (now called **conversion disorder,** see p. 671) is part of the background that led to Freud's theories. For now, we will only reiterate the key discoveries. Patients with hysteria had odd complaints that seemed organic but did not conform consistently to the clinical picture of organic disorders. For example, hysterics would appear with limbs that were routinely "paralyzed" but that moved perfectly well during hypnosis. This suggested that hysteria was a **psychogenic** disorder, that is, a disorder whose origin is psychological rather than organic. A number of cases studied by French hypnotists of the nineteenth century appeared to originate in traumatic incidents. For example, one patient trapped underneath a derailed railroad car developed hysterical paralysis of his legs. His legs were actually in perfect physical condition, but his *belief* that they had been crushed ultimately produced his symptoms. Freud's theories were cast in a similar psychogenic mold, but they were much more elaborate, centering on repressed sexual fantasies in early childhood that threatened to break into consciousness and could only be restrained by drastic defensive maneuvers of which the somatic symptom was one (see Chapter 17).

We will turn to the modern conception of hysteria later. For now, the important point is that by 1900, most theorists had become convinced that the disorder was psychogenic. In other words, there were illnesses that did not conform to a strictly somatogenic account—they seemed to have mental causes as well as mental manifestations.

EVALUATING THE SOMATOGENIC-PSYCHOGENIC DISTINCTION

The distinction between somatogenic and psychogenic disorders is sometimes criticized as artificial. The argument goes that since all behavior and mental activity are ultimately a function of the nervous system, then the distinction simply boils down to those conditions whose organic bases are known versus those that await discovery. So should we discard the distinction?

The answer is no. Undoubtedly, all our psychological processes have a neurophysiological basis. But this doesn't imply that the proper scientific explanation of all psychological phenomena is necessarily a neurophysiological one. For example, consider two people who can speak and see but who are unable to read. One of the two has a certain combination of brain lesions that disconnect the regions that control vision from those that handle language (see Chapter 2, pp. 44–45). The other person can't read because she was never taught. One could of course maintain that both conditions are organically caused. In one case, the organic basis is obvious—brain lesions. In the other, it is that certain brain pathways are missing because the person never learned to read. But it is perfectly obvious that, while the organic account is useful in the former case, it adds nothing to the latter. This is not just because our knowledge of the neurological basis of learning is limited. Even with perfect knowledge, explaining illiteracy by describing millions of synaptic connections that were never formed is altogether unwieldy. It is far simpler to say that the person can't read because she never learned.

The same arguments apply to the distinction between somatogenic and psychogenic disorders. Calling a disorder "somatogenic" reflects the claim that we can most directly explain the malfunction organically, as with the syphilitic infection in general paresis. Likewise, terming a disorder "psychogenic" asserts that it is explained most directly at the psychological level, as with a learned mode of coping with anxiety in conversion disorders. This does not deny the ultimate neurological basis of any and all psychological events; it just states that this is, for many purposes, of marginal relevance.

THE MODERN CONCEPTION OF MENTAL DISORDER

Whatever their views on the somatogenic or psychogenic distinction, most mental-health specialists agree on one thing—these conditions are *disorders*. They are called *mental* disorders because their primary symptoms are psychological, and they all represent a departure from normal psychological functioning (Wakefield, 1992). The commonly accepted definition was provided by the American Psychiatric Association in its now standard manual for categorizing such conditions, the ***Diagnostic and Statistical Manual for Mental Disorders*** (known in its most recent edition as the ***DSM-IV***). As the DSM-IV defines it:

> ". . . Each of the mental disorders is conceptualized as a clinically significant behavioral or psychological syndrome or pattern that occurs in a person and that is associated with present distress (a painful symptom) or disability (impairment in one or more important areas of functioning) or with a significantly increased risk of suffering death, pain, disability, or an important loss of freedom." (American Psychiatric Association, 1994).

Some special questions arise from the fact that the terms *psychopathology* and *abnormal psychology* are often used interchangeably. Does this mean that psychopathology necessarily involves behavior that deviates from some statistical norm? Mental-health practioners would answer no. They would concede that in actual practice mental disorder often involves aberrations from what people usually do in a given situation; the disordered person may hear voices, suffer from severe mood swings, or behave in ways that are clearly bizarre. It was surely for reasons of this sort that the term *abnormal* became a near-synonym for *psychopathological*. But most modern practitioners would argue that deviation from a statistical norm is not what defines psychopathology. Consider the Black Death, which wiped out half of the population in the fourteenth century. At that time, having the plague may well have been statistically normal. But this did not change the plague's status as a disease. The same applies to behavior. Certain patterns of behavior may qualify as a mental disorder no matter how common they are.

Psychopathology is not defined by statistical abnormality According to the psychopathology model, deviation from some statistical norm does not define psychopathology. The Black Death killed half to three-quarters of the population of many European countries during the fourteenth century, but that did not make it any less pathological. (Triumph of Death *by Pieter Bruegel the elder, Prado, Madrid; photograph courtesy of Scala/Art Resource*)

THE UNDERLYING PATHOLOGY MODEL

How can the various mental disorders be understood? Many mental-health professionals believe that one might try to understand them according to the same broad set of rules by means of which we try to understand most physical disorders, whether tuberculosis, diabetes, or whatever.

Just what are these rules? We will class them together under a very general category that we'll here call the **underlying pathology model.** (Different practitioners subscribe to different subcategories of this model of which more below.) According to this pathology model, various overt signs and symptoms are produced by an underlying cause—the pathology. The main object of the would-be healer is to discover (and ultimately to remove) the underlying pathology. After this is done, the symptoms will presumably disappear. As here used, the term *underlying pathology model* makes no particular assumption about the kind of pathology that underlies a particular mental disorder. It might be somatogenic or psychogenic or perhaps a little of both.

SUBCATEGORIES OF THE PATHOLOGY MODEL

There are a number of different approaches to psychopathology, which can be regarded as subcategories of the pathology model. We will briefly present a few of these. As we will see, some of these models are probably more appropriate to some forms of mental disorder than to others.

THE MEDICAL MODEL

Some authors endorse the **medical model,** a particular version of the pathology model, which assumes, for one thing, that the underlying pathology is organic. Its practitioners therefore employ various forms of somatic therapy such as drugs. In addition, it takes for granted that would-be healers should be members of the medical profession (Siegler and Osmond, 1974).

THE PSYCHOANALYTIC MODEL

Adherents of the **psychoanalytic model** follow the general conception of psychopathology developed by Sigmund Freud and other psychoanalysts. In their view, the manifestations of mental disorders are produced by psychological causes. The underlying pathology is a constellation of unconscious conflicts and various defenses against anxiety, often rooted in early childhood experience. Treatment is by some form of psychotherapy based on psychoanalytic principles, which allows the patient to gain insight into his own inner conflicts and thus removes the root of the pathology.

THE LEARNING MODEL

The *learning model* tends to view mental disorders as the result of some form of maladaptive learning. According to some practitioners (usually called *behavior therapists*), these faulty learning patterns are best described and treated by the laws of classical and instrumental conditioning.

A popular current variant on the learning model is the *cognitive-behavioral model,* which regards certain disorders as caused by faulty thinking habits, such as pessimistic or catastrophic thinking. Practitioners of this model, often called *cognitive therapists,* deal with disorders by changing the way in which the patient thinks about himself, his situation, and his future.

CLASSIFYING MENTAL DISORDERS

Mental disorders differ. They differ in their manifestations, their severity, their duration, and their outlook for recovery. Into how many pieces do we need to slice the mental disorders pie? To answer this question, practitioners have tried to set up classificatory schemes for mental disorders analogous to the diagnostic systems in other branches of medicine. Here, as elsewhere in science, the purpose of a taxonomy is to bring some order into what at first seems a host of diverse phenomena. If the taxonomy is valid, then conditions that have been grouped together will turn out to have the same cause, and better yet, the same treatment.

The great German psychiatrist Emil Kraepelin (1855–1925) began the practice of diagnosing mental disorders just like physical disorders. In psychopathology, as in physical medicine, the diagnostic process begins with a *clinical interview* in which the practitioner asks the patient to describe her problems and concerns, and observes the patient throughout. The first consideration is the patient's set of complaints or *symptoms.* Patients who say, "I hear voices," "I feel nervous all the time," and "I feel hopeless" are providing symptoms. The practitioner then looks for any *signs* that might accompany these symptoms. If the same patients, respectively, turn toward a stapler as though it were speaking, shake visibly, and look teary-eyed, these would be signs that parallel the patients' symptoms. Sometimes symptoms do not correspond to signs, and such discrepancies are also important. In some cases of conversion disorder, for example, a patient might state, "My head hurts so bad it's like a buzzsaw running through my brain" but the patient seems to be quite calm and unconcerned while saying it.

In physical medicine, a single symptom like "I always feel tired," or a single sign like a low red blood cell count, is rarely sufficient to reach a conclusion about what ails the patient. This is because feeling tired is a symptom of many disorders, and the low red blood cell count is a sign of many others. However, the combination may narrow the choices considerably (to disorders like anemia, among others). The same holds for psychopathology, and so the mental-health practitioner looks for a pattern of signs and symptoms that tend to go together. These patterns are called *syndromes.* An example of such a syndrome in psychopathology is a pattern of signs like disorganized speech, altered gait, and subdued facial expressions, together with symptoms like agitation, persecutory beliefs, and hallucinations. This syndrome is characteristic of schizophrenia.

The practitioner also attempts to obtain other information during the interview with the patient and, if possible or necessary, from family and friends. When did the problems start (the illness *onset*)? Has the patient's everyday func-

Emil Kraepelin (1855–1925) The major figure in psychiatric classification, Kraepelin distinguished between two groups of severe mental disorders, schizophrenia and manic-depressive psychosis (now called bipolar disorder). (Courtesy of Historical Pictures Service)

723

tioning stayed the same, improved, worsened, or been irregular with good spells and bad spells (the *course* of the illness)? Has anything extraordinary happened recently in the person's life? Has the person been abusing drugs or alcohol? Does the patient have any coexisting medical conditions that might exacerbate or mimic a mental disorder? The clinician will also observe the patient's grooming, mannerisms, speaking style and content, and overall mood and may ask the patient to engage in brief tasks that assess attention, memory, perception, judgment, and insight. Occasionally, psychological or neuropsychological testing (see Chapters 2 and 15) is used to obtain supplementary information about the patient's personality traits or intellectual and cognitive functioning.

The patient's signs and symptoms, taken together with their onset and course, will begin to point to a disorder or disorders. Finally, the practitioner renders an opinion as to the specific disorder(s), and this opinion is called the patient's ***diagnosis.*** The diagnosis is not set in stone, but serves as the practitioner's best judgment about the patient's current state. A proper diagnosis can imply the outlook for the patient, can suggest the most effective treatments, and can sometimes point to the cause (the disorder's *etiology*).

How many disorders are there? Until about twenty-five years ago, the majority of mental-health specialists believed that most mental disorders could be subsumed under three broad supercategories. First were ***organic brain syndromes,*** such as the dementias or brain damage from chronic alcoholism. Second was ***neurosis,*** which referred to any disorder that was thought to be characterized by underlying anxiety-related conflicts. Examples of neuroses were the disorders now called phobias, panic disorder, obsessive-compulsive disorder, and the dissociative disorders. Neurotic patients might be severely distressed or handicapped by their symptoms, but they had not lost contact with reality. In contrast, ***psychosis*** referred to conditions such as schizophrenia and bipolar disorder (formerly called manic-depressive illness), which in their severe forms could render the patients' thoughts, moods, and deeds grossly disturbed and no longer in touch with reality (American Psychiatric Association, 1968).

Today, the term *neurosis* is no longer widely used in psychiatric classification. A major reason was the change to diagnoses based on specific, observable criteria, such as those cited above, rather than on theoretical inferences about underlying processes. The term *psychosis* is still used, but only descriptively; it refers not to an underlying set of disorders the causes of which are inferred, but to any disorder so severe that the victim loses contact with reality. The same holds for a number of other terms that are no longer used in official diagnosis, such as *sociopathy, hysteria,* and *senility.*

This new emphasis on observable criteria was embodied in the DSM-IV. Both it and its immediate predecessors (DSM-III, 1980, and DSM-IIIR, 1987) departed from earlier diagnostic manuals in a number of ways. The most important was a greater stress on the description of disorders rather than on theories about their origin. As a result, a number of disorders that were once grouped together because of a belief—usually based on psychoanalytic theory—that they were at bottom alike are now classified under different diagnostic categories. An example is provided by various conditions that were once regarded as subcategories of neurosis, such as phobias or obsessive-compulsive disorders (see pp. 745–47). A major consequence of these changes is the substantially increased diagnostic reliability of the new manual (Matarazzo, 1983; American Psychiatric Association, 1994).

The list of disorders in DSM-IV is extensive, comprising nearly 400 disorders in 17 supercategories and covering an enormous range that includes mental retardation, the dementias, schizophrenia, mood disorders such as bipolar disorder and depression, phobias, conversion disorders, sleep disorders, and substance abuse, to mention only some of the most prominent.

EXPLAINING DISORDER: DIATHESIS, STRESS, AND PATHOLOGY

To explain how the underlying pathology approach may be applied to mental disorders, we'll first turn to the analysis of a disease that is already well understood. Our example will be an organic illness—diabetes (see Figure 18.4).

Again, our first step is to examine the overt signs and symptoms. In diabetes, the symptoms include declining strength, a marked increase in the frequency of urination, enormous thirst, and, in many cases, a voracious appetite. A frequent sign is a high sugar level in the urine. The next step is to look for the pathology underlying this syndrome. Diabetes was discovered to be a disorder of carbohydrate metabolism, produced by an insufficient secretion of insulin (see Chapter 3). These pathological conditions represent the immediate or *proximate* cause of the syndrome. But a full understanding of diabetes requires a further step, an inquiry into the more remote causes that led to the present pathology.

When the causal chain is traced backward, two general factors emerge. One is a predisposition (technically called a *diathesis*) toward the illness. The other is a set of environmental conditions that *stress* the system and precipitate the defective insulin mechanism. Obesity is one such stressor. In diabetes, the diathesis is based in part on genetic factors that create a marked susceptibility to the disease, which is then triggered or worsened by a stressor. The treatment follows from the analysis of the cause-and-effect relations. Since the diabetic's pancreas does not secrete enough insulin, this substance can be supplied from the outside (orally or by injection). Further regulation of the faulty metabolic controls is then imposed by an appropriate diet (Dolger and Seeman, 1985).

This discussion illustrates the *diathesis-stress* model, a conception that extends to mental as well as physical disorders. Many kinds of psychopathology are thought to result from the presence of a diathesis that leaves one vulnerable to a particular disorder or set of disorders and some kind of stressor that turns potentiality into actuality. The nature of the diathesis depends on the particular

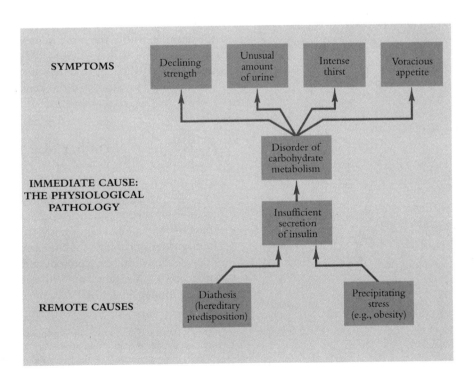

18.4 The pathology model as applied to diabetes

disorder. For some disorders, as we'll see, a diathesis may be genetic, as in schizophrenia (see pp. 732–33). For others, it may be environmental, as in phobia, which is sometimes thought to go back to an anxiety-producing incident in the patient's past (see pp. 745–46).

Figure 18.4 provides a schematic summary of our discussion of diabetes, a physical ailment with few direct psychological manifestations. The figure gives us an idea of how a disease is analyzed when it is reasonably well understood. This is the framework we will use when we ask whether a particular mental disorder is an illness and if so, in what sense. How such disorders are treated will be taken up in the next chapter. We now turn to some of the most important mental disorders.

SCHIZOPHRENIA

One of the most serious disorders in all of psychopathology is **schizophrenia** (from the Greek *schizo,* "split" and *phrene,* "mind"). The term was coined by the Swiss psychiatrist, Eugen Bleuler (1857–1939), to designate what he regarded as the main attribute of this disorder—an abnormal disintegration of mental functions (Bleuler, 1911).★

Schizophrenia is quite prevalent, being found worldwide in about 1 percent of humanity (Torrey, 1987). According to one estimate, between 1 and 2 percent of Americans will need treatment for this disorder at some period during their lifetimes. At any one time, about 400,000 people are hospitalized with this condition, accounting for about half of all of the beds in the country's mental hospitals (Babigian, 1975). The diagnosis is usually made not at the first subtle signs of the disorder but much later, when the condition has become so severe that evaluation and diagnosis in a clinic or hospital is required (Andreasen and Black, 1991; Babigian, 1975; Goldstein and Tsuang, 1990).

Many investigators believe that schizophrenia is a disease, in the straightforward, somatogenic sense of the term. To evaluate this position, we will discuss the disorder within the same framework we used when we considered a frankly organic disease, diabetes. We will discuss the pattern of signs and symptoms, the underlying pathology, the less *proximate* (that is, immediate) causes such as genetic predisposition, and the precipitating factors.

Eugen Bleuler *(Courtesy of National Library of Medicine)*

SIGNS AND SYMPTOMS

The fragmentation of mental life characteristic of schizophrenia can be seen in disruptions in cognition, of motivation and emotion, and of social relationships. Few patients who are diagnosed as schizophrenics exhibit all of these manifestations. Until fairly recently, this led to considerable disagreement in diagnosis, since different clinicians used different yardsticks to determine how many features had to be present and to what degree before someone was said to suffer from schizophrenia. With the new taxonomy introduced with DSM-III and continued in DSM-IV came more specific criteria for diagnosis, such as

---

★ This etymological derivation is responsible for a widespread confusion between schizophrenia and multiple personality ("split personality"), now called *dissociative identity disorder.* While both are varieties of psychopathology, the two conditions are wholly distinct.

Paintings by schizophrenics *Paintings by schizophrenics often have an odd, eerie quality. In many cases, the usual artistic conventions are disregarded, and the picture includes written comments, digits, and other idiosyncratic material. (A)* Saint-Adolf-Grand-Grand-God-Father *(1915), a painting by Adolf W., who was institutionalized in early adulthood and elaborated a fantastic autobiography that featured himself as Saint Adolf II, a young god who travels through space and has many adventures. (B)* Guardian Angels *by Else B., an institutionalized schizophrenic. In all her works, the legs of angels are painted as though they had fused at the top, to make sure that "nothing happens there."* (Prinzhorn, 1972; courtesy of Galerie Rothe Heidelberg)

gross distortion in the perception of reality, symptoms present for at least six months, and so on.

DISORDERS OF COGNITION

A key sign of schizophrenia is a pervasive thought disturbance. The schizophrenic doesn't "think straight"; she can't maintain one unified guiding thought, but rather skips from one idea to the next. An example is a fragment of a letter written by one of Bleuler's patients:

> I am writing on paper. The pen I am using is from a factory called "Perry & Co." This factory is in England. I assume this. Behind the name of Perry Co., the city of London is inscribed; but not the city. The city of London is in England. I know this from my school-days. Then, I always liked geography. My last teacher in that subject was Professor August A. He was a man with black eyes. I also like black eyes. There are also blue and gray eyes and other sorts too. I have heard it said that snakes have green eyes. All people have eyes. There are some, too, who are blind. These blind people are led about by a boy. (Bleuler, 1911, p. 17)

This example shows that the schizophrenic may have difficulty in suppressing irrelevant ideas that come from within. Similar problems arise with irrelevant stimuli that assail her from without. We have seen that in ordinary perception one focuses on some aspects of the world while deemphasizing others. We somehow filter out the irrelevant stimuli so that we can follow a conversation without being continually distracted by other people's voices or radiator clankings or whatever (see Chapter 6). But schizophrenics seem to be less efficient in attending selectively. They hear (and see and feel) too much, perhaps because they can't exclude what is extraneous (McGhie and Chapman, 1961).

LOSS OF PERSONAL CONTACT

A common feature of schizophrenia is a withdrawal from contact with other people. In some patients this withdrawal begins quite early; they have had few friends and little or no adolescent sexual experience. What brings on this withdrawal is still unknown. One possibility is that it is a defense against the overstimulation to which they are exposed because of their inability to filter out the irrelevant. Another possibility is that it grows out of pathological family relations during childhood and adolescence.

Whatever led up to it, the schizophrenic's withdrawal from social contacts has drastic consequences. The individual starts to inhabit an inner world that becomes more and more private. The withdrawal from others provides fewer and fewer opportunities for *social reality testing* in which one's ideas are validated against those of others. As a result, the schizophrenic's thoughts become ever more idiosyncratic, until the patient may have trouble communicating with others even if he wants to; they may very well rebuff him because they can't understand him and think he's "weird." The result is further withdrawal, which leads to further idiosyncrasy, still further withdrawal, and so on. The final consequence of this vicious cycle is a condition in which the patient can no longer distinguish between his own thoughts and fantasies and the external reality experienced by all those around him. He has lost touch with the world.

ELABORATING THE PRIVATE WORLD

In our previous discussion of personality (Chapters 16 and 17), we discussed just how much we seek consistency in others and in the world. This is no less true

Schizophrenia *The delusional world of some schizophrenics may resemble the bizarre images created by some surrealist artists. (Frederico Castellión,* The Dark Figure, *1938; courtesy of the Whitney Museum of American Art, New York; photograph by Geoffrey Clements, NY)*

for the schizophrenic, who tries to make sense of a world that is increasingly sealed off from the outside. This can result in what Bleuler called *restitutional symptoms,* which include developing elaborate, organized systems of eccentric beliefs *(delusions)* and hearing voices of people who are not there *(hallucinations).*

Delusions Once having initiated the break with the social world, many schizophrenics develop *ideas of reference.* They begin to believe that external events are specially related to them personally. The patient observes some strangers talking and concludes that they are talking about her; she sees people walk by and decides that they are following her; she hears a radio commercial and is sure that it contains a secret message aimed at her. Eventually, she may weave these false ideas, or delusions, into an entire *delusional system* in which she may believe, for example, that agents of the government are talking about her, following her everywhere, and have taken over the media to spread secrets about her. Such delusions are especially common in a subcategory called *paranoid schizophrenia.*

A common symptom of paranoid schizophrenia is a delusion of persecution. The patient is sure that "they"—the Communists or the FBI or the members of the American Medical Association or whoever—are actively spying on and plotting against her. This delusion gradually expands as the patient gathers further evidence that convinces her that her family, her ward psychiatrist, and the woman in the bed near the door are all part of the conspiracy.

Hallucinations Delusions are beliefs that result from the misinterpretation of real events. In contrast, *hallucinations* are perceptions that occur in the absence of actual sensory stimulation. This phenomenon is fairly common in schizophrenia. Usually they are *auditory hallucinations* in which the patient "hears" voices—of God, the devil, relatives, or neighbors. If the patient can make out what they say, she will report that they are talking about her, shouting obscenities at her, threatening her, or making accusations about her.

Some authors believe that such hallucinations reflect an inability to distinguish between one's own memories and perceptions, between experiences that originate from within and those that originate from without. The patients may be talking to themselves, but they will then interpret their own inner speech as originating from outside. They "heard themselves talk" and thought they heard voices (McGuigan, 1966; Green and Preston, 1981).

DISORDERS OF MOTIVATION AND EMOTION

Thus far we have emphasized the schizophrenic's thoughts. When we look at his motives and feelings, we find similar evidence of disruption and fragmentation. In the early phase of the disorder, there is often a marked emotional oversensitivity in which the slightest rejection may trigger an extreme response. As time goes on, this sensitivity declines. In many patients it dips below normal until there is virtual indifference to their own fate or that of others. This apathy is especially pronounced in long-term schizophrenics, who stare vacantly, their faces expressionless, and answer questions in a flat and toneless voice.

In some cases, emotional reaction is preserved but the emotion is strikingly inappropriate to the situation. A patient may break into giddy laughter at the news of a brother's death "because she was so pleased at receiving letters with black borders"; another becomes enraged when someone says hello (Bleuler, 1911).

DISORDERS OF BEHAVIOR

Given the disruptions in the schizophrenics' thoughts, motives, and feelings, it is hardly surprising that there is often disruption in normal movements and actions. Some patients—in a subtype of schizophrenia called *catatonic schizophrenia*—exhibit very unusual motor reactions. They can become stuporous, remaining virtually motionless for long periods of time. They may be standing or sitting or "frozen" in some unusual posture and will often maintain this position for hours on end (Figure 18.5). With no notice, they can become frenzied, running haphazardly, shouting nonsensically, and acting violently.

In another subtype, *disorganized schizophrenia* (formerly, *hebephrenia*), thought, emotion and behavior become virtually chaotic. The predominant symptoms are incoherence of speech and marked inappropriateness of behavior and emotion. In many ways, the disorganized schizophrenic is the closest match to the popular stereotype of madness. His speech is often bizarre and babbling, and while he is talking he giggles, makes silly smiles or odd grimaces, assumes odd postures, and may have sudden fits of laughing and crying. Such patients often deteriorate profoundly, lose all concern over personal appearance, and ignore the most elementary rules of social conduct; for example, they may urinate and defecate in public.

18.5   Patient with a diagnosis of catatonic schizophrenia who spent virtually all waking hours in this crouched position.   (Photograph by Bill Bridges/Globe Photos)

THE SEARCH FOR THE UNDERLYING PATHOLOGY

We have described the various manifestations that define schizophrenia. As in diabetes or any other organic disease, the next step is to look for the underlying *psychological malfunction* from which these signs and symptoms spring. Once found, then—if there is reason to suspect that the disorder is somatogenic—one searches for the organic pathology of which this psychological malfunction is an expression.

WHAT IS THE PSYCHOLOGICAL MALFUNCTION?

A widely held view is that the schizophrenic's major psychological malfunction is cognitive. The details of the proposed explanations vary, but most of them agree that the patient's major deficit is an inability to keep things in their proper context. Normal people perceive other persons, objects, and events without losing track of the context and without being distracted by extraneous stimuli; they execute plans without interference by irrelevant responses. Not so the schizophrenic, who has considerable difficulty in holding onto one line of thought or action and is forever being lured off the main path (Chapman and Chapman, 1973; Patterson et al., 1986). It may be that some of the other major symptoms of schizophrenia such as delusions and hallucinations are yet further consequences of this basic thought disturbance. Bleuler believed that these symptoms are the elaborations of the private world of a person who has lost contact with other people and can no longer distinguish between his private fantasies and external reality.

WHAT IS THE ORGANIC PATHOLOGY?

By now, most investigators believe that the core psychological malfunctions in schizophrenia are themselves expressions of an organic pathology. The search for the immediate, or proximate, causes centers on two possible kinds of malfunctions. One is physiological, emphasizing a disorder in certain neurotransmitter systems in the brain. The other is anatomical and focuses on some possible abnormalities in the brain structure of those who suffer from schizophrenia (Meltzer, 1987).

Malfunctioning neurotransmitters Some investigators believe that the immediate organic pathology involves some malfunction in one or more neurotransmitter systems in the brain. A likely neurotransmitter candidate is **dopamine,** one of a set of transmitters known as the **catecholamines** (see Chapter 2). According to the **dopamine hypothesis,** the proximate organic cause of schizophrenia is abnormally increased dopamine activity in the brain. The increased activity may result from any of several mechanisms, including an overabundance of dopamine, an oversensitivity of dopamine receptors, or the facilitation of dopamine transmission by other transmitters such as other catecholamines like norepinephrine (Van Kammen and Kelley, 1991) or serotonin (Kahn et al., 1993).

One strong line of evidence for the dopamine hypothesis comes from the effects of a number of medications known as **antipsychotics.** Among the most commonly used today are Thorazine and Haldol. These drugs are known to block dopamine at the synapse (Figure 18.6). This dopamine blockade is more pronounced in some kinds of antipsychotics than in others. As predicted by the dopamine hypothesis, the stronger the blockade, the more therapeutic the drug (Snyder, 1976).

If a decrease in dopamine activity makes schizophrenics better, an increase should presumably make them worse. This is indeed the case. One group of investigators injected small doses of a drug that increases dopamine activity into the veins of schizophrenics who were in a comparatively mild state. Within a minute, the patients' symptoms became florid. One patient began shredding a pad of paper, announcing that he had been sending and receiving messages from ancient Egypt. Others became catatonic (Davis, 1974). Related effects are seen in normal subjects who take overdoses of amphetamines. These are stimulants whose effect includes the enhancement of dopamine activity. When taken often enough and in large enough doses, they produce a temporary **amphetamine psychosis** that is in many ways quite similar to paranoid schizophrenia (Angrist et al., 1974). As the dopamine hypothesis would predict, those medications that block dopamine activity at the synapse also reduce the psychotic symptoms that follow chronic amphetamine abuse.

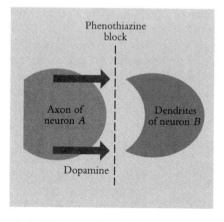

18.6 *The dopamine-blockade hypothesis of phenothiazine action*

Why should an oversensitivity to dopamine produce the psychotic reactions characteristic of schizophrenia? One possibility is that a hyperactive dopamine system is equivalent to chronic overstimulation. When dopamine-releasing neurons in the limbic system of an animal's brain are destroyed, the animal ignores sensory stimuli (Ungerstedt and Ljungberg, 1974). Perhaps the opposite is true when dopamine tracts are hyperactive. This may cause an inability to ignore anything, whether sensory messages from the outside or irrelevant thoughts from the inside, leading to that jangling, screaming cognitive overload that some schizophrenics describe in retrospective accounts of their condition.

Structural defects   The highly resolved images now permitted by magnetic resonance imaging scans (MRI; see Chapter 2, pp. 42–43) confirm that a certain proportion of schizophrenics suffer from some structural abnormalities in their brains. One such abnormality is an enlargement of the ventricles, the fluid-filled cavities within the brain. The ventricles enlarge when the brain does not fill the cranial space, which suggests a large-scale deficiency or even a progressive loss of brain tissue (Andreasen et al., 1986; Meltzer, 1987). Although abnormalities have been reported in numerous areas, the most persuasive findings involve the frontal and temporal lobes. Studies of these areas during autopsy show various abnormalities at the cellular level, for example, cell derangement and missing or abnormally sized neurons. These neuronal defects obviously affect brain function, and indeed, PET scans of brain metabolism and cerebral blood-flow studies suggest abnormally low levels of functioning in just these areas (Bloom, 1993).

Crow's two-syndrome hypothesis   Both the dopamine and the anatomical-defect hypotheses face a problem: Each fits some cases of schizophrenia, but not all. For example, many schizophrenic patients respond to dopamine-blocking medications, but a number do not. In contrast, a significant number of schizophrenics show signs of cerebral atrophy, but many do not. One proposal by British psychiatrist Timothy Crow tries to handle these facts by proposing a **two-syndrome hypothesis** of schizophrenia (Crow, 1982, 1985). This hypothesis begins by making a distinction between positive and negative symptoms. **Positive symptoms** are those that involve what the patients do (and see and think) that normals don't; they include hallucinations, delusions, and bizarre behaviors. In contrast, **negative symptoms** are those that involve a lack of normal functioning, such as apathy, poverty of speech, emotional blunting, and the inability to experience pleasure or be sociable.

According to the two-syndrome hypothesis, schizophrenia is really a composite of two underlying pathologies, which Crow named Type I and Type II. Crow proposed that Type I schizophrenia is caused by a malfunction of neurotransmitters (especially dopamine) and produces the positive symptoms of delusions, hallucinations, and thought disorders (see pp. 727–29). Type II, he suggested, is produced by cerebral damage and atrophy and leads to the negative symptoms of flat affect, social withdrawal, and apathy (see pp. 727, 729). Support for this view comes from the fact that, by and large, patients with mostly positive symptoms tend to respond well to standard antipsychotic medications and show no cerebral damage. The reverse holds for patients with negative symptoms who are generally not improved by treatment with standard antipsychotics and are more likely to show signs of cerebral damage (Crow, 1980, 1985).

Despite some intriguing evidence, these various hypotheses about the underlying organic pathology of schizophrenia are just what their name indicates—hypotheses. All face a number of difficulties of which we'll only mention a few. A problem with the dopamine hypothesis is that the antipsychotics block dopamine receptors quickly, within a matter of hours, but the therapeutic effect on schizophrenic symptoms takes weeks (Davis, 1978). One problem with the

PET scans of schizophrenics   *PET scans comparing the normal and the schizophrenic brain reveal certain abnormalities of brain structure and increased metabolic activity in different areas of the schizophrenic's brain. (NIH/Science Source/Photo Researchers)*

two-syndrome hypothesis is the fact that more recent work has shown that the relationship between negative symptoms and structural brain damage is not as clear cut as the hypothesis would predict. Another problem concerns the relationship between the two diseases. Are they two distinct diseases, or is Type II schizophrenia just a more extreme form of the condition, perhaps the endpoint of a progressive disorder that begins with the positive symptoms characteristic of the Type I syndrome (Andreasen, 1985; Andreason et al., 1989; Cannon, Mednick, and Parnas, 1990; Zorilla and Cannon, 1995)? As yet, we don't know. But whatever the final verdict, it is very likely that our eventual understanding of schizophrenia will include some reference both to biochemical malfunctions and anatomical defects.

ULTIMATE CAUSES OF SCHIZOPHRENIA

We have considered several analyses of the basic pathology in schizophrenia, including hypotheses about the underlying psychological malfunction and some guesses about organic deficits or defects. These hypotheses about pathological processes are about the proximal causes of the disorder. But what explains these psychological, physiological, or anatomical deficits? This is the question of more ***ultimate*** causes, causes that are less immediate, further back in time. As we have seen in our discussion of diabetes, we must consider both the proximal causes (a metabolic malfunction brought on by insulin insufficiency) and more ultimate ones (genetic factors, environmental effects) if we are to understand a disorder fully and make a possible diathesis-stress interpretation. We will follow the same approach in our discussion of schizophrenia.

HEREDITARY PREDISPOSITION

Does schizophrenia have a hereditary basis? This question has been studied by the same means used to assess the role of heredity in other human traits such as intelligence. The basic approach is to consider family resemblance. In schizophrenia, as in intelligence, this resemblance is considerable. For example, the likelihood that a person who has a schizophrenic sibling is schizophrenic himself or will eventually become so is about 8 percent; this compares to 1 to 2 percent lifetime risk of schizophrenia in the general population (Andreason and Black, 1991; Rosenthal, 1970).

But again, as with intelligence, studies of family resemblances aren't decisive on the nature-nurture issue, for they can be interpreted either way. More conclusive evidence requires techniques that disentangle the contributions of heredity and environment using the familiar strategies of studying twins and adopted children. It turns out that if one of a set of twins is schizophrenic, then the other twin is much more likely to be schizophrenic as well. The probability of this event, technically called ***concordance,*** is 55 percent if the twins are identical, compared to 9 percent if they are fraternal (Gottesman and Shields, 1972, 1982; Gottesman, McGuffin, and Farmer, 1987; Tsuang, Gilbertson, and Faraone, 1991; see Figure 18.7). Further evidence comes from adoption studies. Children born to schizophrenic mothers and placed in foster homes within a week or so after birth are much more likely to become schizophrenic. In fact, the odds are about 8 percent that the child of a schizophrenic mother who is adopted by nonschizophrenic parents will become schizophrenic, the same percentage as for children who remain with the schizophrenic biological parent (Kety, 1983; Kendler and Gruenberg, 1984; Tsuang et al., 1991).

MRI scans of the brains of twins *Magnetic resonance imaging (MRI) scans of the brains of two twenty-eight-year-old identical twins. One (right) is hospitalized for schizophrenia; the other (left) is well. The schizophrenic twin has enlarged cerebral ventricles; the other does not. The fact that just one twin has schizophrenia shows that heredity is not the only factor in producing this disorder. (Courtesy of Drs. E. Fuller Torey and Daniel R. Weinberger, NIMH Neuroscience Center, Washington, D.C.)*

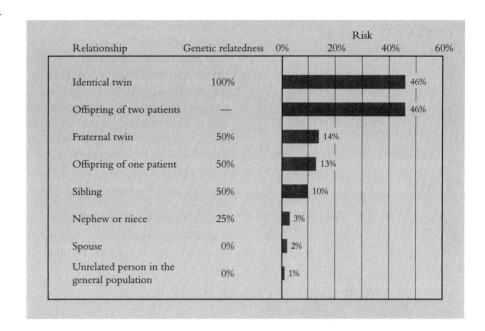

Relationship	Genetic relatedness	Risk
Identical twin	100%	46%
Offspring of two patients	—	46%
Fraternal twin	50%	14%
Offspring of one patient	50%	13%
Sibling	50%	10%
Nephew or niece	25%	3%
Spouse	0%	2%
Unrelated person in the general population	0%	1%

18.7   Genetic factors in schizophrenia
Risk estimates for schizophrenia as a function of relationship to a schizophrenic patient. (From Nicol and Gottesman, 1983)

Some contemporary investigators believe that these genetic findings coupled with some further evidence suggest that schizophrenia is a ***neurodevelopmental disorder*** (Waddington et al., 1991). According to this theory, pathological genes produce abnormalities in the brain during fetal development. These abnormalities, in turn, lead to behavioral and cognitive eccentricities from the outset that may eventuate in schizophrenia. One line of evidence comes from the fact that many cases of schizophrenia show preludes in childhood. Children at special hereditary risk for schizophrenia tend to have low activity levels, motor immaturity, and poor cuddliness; by adolescence, they have a host of subtle cognitive and perceptual deficits (Marcus et al., 1993). Those children who will later develop the negative symptoms of schizophrenia tend to manifest behavior problems such as isolation, passivity, and social unresponsiveness; those who will later develop the positive symptoms show irritability, distractibility, and aggression (Cannon, Mednick, and Parnas, 1990; Parnas and Jorgensen, 1989).

ENVIRONMENTAL INFLUENCES

The preceding discussion indicates that schizophrenia has a genetic basis. But there is no doubt that other factors also play a role. One line of evidence comes from identical twins. Their concordance for schizophrenia is considerable, but is much less than 100 percent. Since identical twins have the same genotype, there must be some nongenetic factors that also have a say in the determination of who becomes schizophrenic and who does not.

What are these nongenetic factors? As yet, there is no consensus. We will consider a few lines of evidence that relate to various potentially stress-producing situations. Some involve the person's social class and economic condition; others concern his family. According to many modern investigators, these and other stress-producing environmental factors may bring out the latent pathology in a person with a genetic predisposition toward schizophrenia and will eventually precipitate the actual disorder, much as obesity or continued emotional stress precipitates diabetes. The stronger the diathesis, the less stress is presumably required to convert the predisposition into the actual disorder (Meehl, 1962; Gottesman and Shields, 1982).

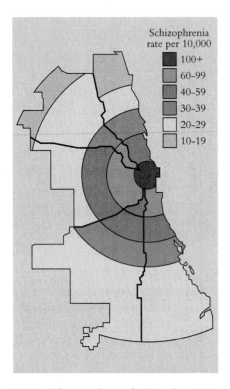

Schizophrenia rate per 10,000

100+
60–99
40–59
30–39
20–29
10–19

18.8   The prevalence of schizophrenia in different regions of a city   *A map of Chicago (1922–1934) represented by a series of concentric zones. The center zone is the business and amusement area, which is without residents except for some transients and vagabonds. Surrounding this center is a slum region inhabited largely by unskilled laborers. Further out are more stable regions: a zone largely populated by skilled workers, followed by zones of middle- and upper-middle-class apartment dwellers, and, furthest out, the upper-middle-class commuters. The map shows clearly that the incidence of schizophrenia increases the closer one gets to the city's center. (After Faris and Dunham, 1939)*

Social class   Sociologically minded investigators have emphasized social class in the etiology of schizophrenia, and they have found a sizable relationship there. The proportion of schizophrenics is much higher at the bottom of the socioeconomic hierarchy than it is at the top. According to one study, the ratio is 9 to 1 (Hollingshead and Redlich, 1958). The prevalence of schizophrenia is highest in the poorest and most dilapidated areas of cities and diminishes progressively as one moves outward toward the higher status regions (Figure 18.8). This general relation between social class and schizophrenia has been found in city after city, from New York, Omaha, New Haven, and Milwaukee in the United States to Oslo, Helsinki, London, and Taiwan abroad (Kohn, 1968).

One interpretation of this result is that poverty, inferior status, and low occupational rank lead to increased environmental stress, which sooner or later converts a genetic susceptibility toward schizophrenia into the actual disorder. According to this view, given the predisposition, one becomes a schizophrenic because one is at the lowest rung of the social ladder. But there is a logical alternative, that of *downward drift,* with schizophrenics falling to the bottom of the ladder because they cannot hold down a job or sustain a personal relationship. If so, then the lower socioeconomic status of schizophrenics is both an effect and a cause; the issue is by no means settled (Kohn, 1968).

Family environment   Some psychoanalytically oriented investigators concentrated upon the personality of the schizophrenic's parents. They painted a gloomy picture. As they described them, schizophrenics' mothers were rejecting, cold, dominating, and prudish, while their fathers were detached, humorless, weak, and passive (Arieti, 1959). Later studies concentrated on relationships within the family and found a high degree of instability and conflict. However, critics argued that this family portrait was inaccurate. The descriptions of the parents were often sketched by the same psychiatrists who treated the children and who were probably biased in favor of their patients' accounts. When these and other procedural flaws are eliminated, the schizophrenic's family didn't appear to be quite as pathological as it did at first. But signs of pathology remain even so. Objective studies in which the families of schizophrenic patients were observed in discussions of various topics (such as "When should teenagers begin dating?") showed more within-family conflict than normal controls (Fontana, 1966).

Schizophrenics evidently have less benign family backgrounds than do normal children. But this does not prove that the family environment caused the patient's disorder. It may also be an effect, and for two reasons. First, having a schizophrenic in the family can be tragic for the family. Parents often blame themselves and each other for their disturbed child and become frustrated in their attempts to "reach" their child (Torrey, 1983). In one study, the investigators observed mothers who had both a schizophrenic and a healthy daughter (Mishler and Waxler, 1968). When observed with the schizophrenic daughter, the mothers seemed unresponsive and aloof. But when observed with the healthy daughter, the mothers behaved more normally. This suggests that their unresponsiveness was not a general characteristic of their personality (and thus perhaps a cause of their child's disorder) but was instead a reaction to the schizophrenic daughter (and thus an effect of the child's disorder upon the mother's behavior). The second reason that schizophrenic children come from more disturbed families is that at least one of the parents possesses the same pathological genes that eventuated in schizophrenia in their child, whether or not the parent is schizophrenic. In fact, there is some evidence that even the nonschizophrenic parents and siblings of schizophrenics manifest biological markers for the propensity (Holtzman et al., 1988; Tsuang et al., 1991).

If poor familial relations do not cause the patient's illness, they have much to do with how well he copes with the disorder. The evidence comes from studies of schizophrenic patients who were functioning well enough to be discharged from the hospital and who went back to live with their parents or spouses. These family members were interviewed at the time of the patient's breakdown to assess the extent to which they were critical, hostile, or emotionally overinvolved and manifested these negative feelings to the patient. The greater these *expressed emotions,* the more likely the patient would eventually relapse with sufficient severity to warrant readmission to the mental hospital (Hooley, 1985). On reflection, this is hardly surprising. Parents or spouses who tell an interviewer "He is stupid. . . . The farther I am away from him the better" or, on hearing that the patient was in a mental hospital, "I thought I'd have to go there myself from the shock" will probably talk identically to the patient when he returns from the hospital. This is unlikely to ease his adjustment to his illness, and it makes the hospital look inviting by comparison. It is somewhat encouraging that family members can learn to reduce their expressed emotion through an educational program in which they learn about schizophrenia and have an opportunity to talk about their own problems. Patients whose families participated in such a program were much less likely to be readmitted than patients whose families had not (Leff et al., 1982).

Prenatal environment   In recent years, considerable attention has been focused on environmental stresses in the uterus and during delivery. An important line of evidence comes from obstetric reports on the effects of various complications during pregnancy and birth. Such complications evidently increase the likelihood that a genetic predisposition will eventually be expressed as schizophrenia (Cannon, 1991; Zorilla and Cannon, 1995). Some further studies implicate a viral infection of the mother. It appears that patients with schizophrenia are more likely to have been born shortly after an influenza epidemic, suggesting that the mother's infection (probably in the second trimester) may be a contributing stress (Sham et al., 1992). It may well be that these and other prenatal factors are the most important environmental factors that precipitate the diathesis into the full-blown disease.

THE PATHOLOGY MODEL AND SCHIZOPHRENIA

We have considered schizophrenia under the same headings that are used to analyze physical illnesses—the pattern of signs and symptoms, the underlying pathology, the role of ultimate causes such as genetic predisposition, and precipitating factors. What can we conclude? To guide our evaluation, we will refer to a schematic diagram of the main factors in the schizophrenic disorder that is analogous to the one we used to analyze diabetes (Figure 18.9).

The schizophrenic syndrome can be considered the manifestation of a psychological deficit, perhaps a defect in the ability to retain the context of one's current thoughts and actions. The best guess is that this psychological malfunction reflects an organic pathology whose exact nature is still unknown. Most investigators believe that this organic pathology has two sources: One is a biochemical defect, most likely involving some neurotransmitter system. The other is anomalous or deficient brain tissue, perhaps through progressive atrophy. The pathology that represents the proximal cause of the disorder is in turn produced by more ultimate causes. One is a hereditary diathesis. Another may be a set of

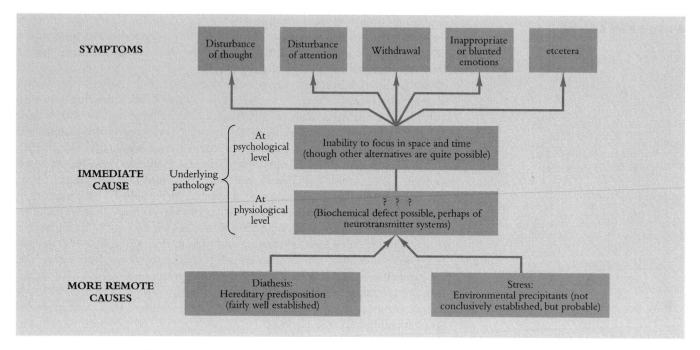

| | | Disturbance of thought | Disturbance of attention | Withdrawal | Inappropriate or blunted emotions | etcetera |

SYMPTOMS

IMMEDIATE CAUSE — Underlying pathology

At psychological level: Inability to focus in space and time (though other alternatives are quite possible)

At physiological level: ? ? ? (Biochemical defect possible, perhaps of neurotransmitter systems)

MORE REMOTE CAUSES

Diathesis: Hereditary predisposition (fairly well established)

Stress: Environmental precipitants (not conclusively established, but probable)

18.9   The pathology model as applied to schizophrenia   *The diagram shows that the causal analysis by which nonbehavioral disorders such as diabetes are described (see pp. 725–26) can be applied to mental disorders such as schizophrenia. The basic logic applies regardless of whether the disorder ultimately turns out to be in part somatogenic or not.*

environmental stresses, including socioeconomic and familial pressures, as well as problems during pregnancy and delivery, that trigger the pathological process in persons with the initial diathesis.

What is the outlook for schizophrenic patients? To date, the prospects are not very encouraging. One study tracked down 200 people who were suffering from schizophrenia in the 1930s and 1940s some 30 years later. Of these patients, 20 percent were doing well, while 45 percent were incapacitated. Sixty-seven percent had never married, and 58 percent had never worked (Andreasen and Black, 1991; Cutting, 1986).

Clearly schizophrenia is devastating in its overall impact, but we hasten to note that about one in five schizophrenics do well and continue to do well. We can hope that the odds will improve as researchers converge on the etiology of the disease and perfect new treatments. Indeed, some new treatments give grounds for optimism, as we will discuss in the next chapter.

MOOD DISORDERS

While schizophrenia can be regarded as essentially a disorder of thought, in another group of disorders the dominant disturbance is one of mood. These are the **mood disorders** (sometimes called the **affective disorders**), which are characterized by two emotional extremes—the vehement energy of mania, the despair and lethargy of depression, or both.

BIPOLAR AND UNIPOLAR SYNDROMES

An initial distinction is that between **bipolar disorder** (essentially equivalent to what was formerly called **manic-depressive psychosis**) and **major depres-**

sion. In bipolar disorder, the patient swings from one energetic and emotional extreme to the other, sometimes with intermittent periods of normality, and experiences both manic and depressive episodes that may be as short as a few hours or as long as several months or more. Bipolar disorder occurs in about 0.5 to 1 percent of the population and is diagnosed more often in women by a ratio of 3 to 2 (Andreasen and Black, 1991). Much more frequent are cases of *major depression* (sometimes called *unipolar disorder,* since the mood extreme is of one kind only). According to several estimates, about 10 percent of all men and 20 percent of all women in America will suffer from a major depressive episode (defined as one that lasts for at least two weeks) at some time during their lives (Hirschfeld and Cross, 1981; Weissman and Boyd, 1985).

MANIA

In their milder form, manic states are often hard to distinguish from buoyant spirits. The person seems to have shifted into high gear: She is more lively and infectiously merry, is extremely talkative and always on the go, is charming, utterly self-confident, and indefatigable. It is hard to see that something is wrong unless one notices that she jumps from one plan to another, seems unable to sit still for a moment, and quickly shifts from unbounded elation to brittle irritation if she meets even the smallest frustration. These pathological signs become greatly intensified as the manic episode becomes more severe (*acute* or *psychotic mania*). Now the motor is racing and all brakes are off. The person may begin to stay up all night, engage in an endless stream of talk that runs from one topic to another and knows no inhibitions of social or personal (or for that matter, sexual) propriety. Patients in the manic state are incessantly busy. They may burst into shouts of song, smash furniture out of sheer overabundance of energy, do exercises, sleep only rarely, engage in reckless sexual escapades, go on drinking or drug-abuse bouts, spend all their money on gambling, conceive grandiose plans for rebuilding the hospital or redirecting the nation's foreign policy or making millions in the stock market—a ceaseless torrent of activity that continues unabated over many days and sleepless nights and which will eventually sap the patients' health (and that of those around them) if they are not sedated.

An example of a manic episode is described in an autobiography by Clifford Beers, a man who endured a severe bipolar disorder for three years, obtained treatment, and proceeded to become a crusader for the reform of mental hospitals. Beers started to write letters about everything that was happening to him. He soon ran out of stationery, so he obtained large rolls of wrapping paper that he cut into one-foot strips and glued together to make long rolls. He started writing letters that were twenty to thirty feet long and continued to write at the rate of twelve feet per hour. He eventually tried to take over the hospital, was put in a small cell, and soon tried his hand at invention. He decided to overcome the force of gravity. He tore a carpet into strips and used the makeshift ropes to suspend his bed (with himself in it) off the floor. "So epoch-making did this discovery appear to me that I noted the exact position of the bed so that a wondering posterity might ever afterward view and revere the exact spot on the earth's surface whence one of man's greatest thoughts had winged its way to immortality" (quoted in White and Watt, 1973).

DEPRESSION

In many ways, major depression is the polar opposite of mania. The patient's mood may be utterly dejected, his outlook hopeless; he has lost interest in other people and believes he is utterly sinful or worthless. In describing the depths of his own depression, the novelist William Styron wrote:

PET scan of a rapid-cycling bipolar patient *The top and bottom row are scans obtained on days in which the patient was depressed; the middle row on a day in which he was mildly manic. Reds and yellows indicate a high rate of metabolic activity; blues and greens indicate low rates. (Courtesy Dr. John Mazziotta)*

All sense of hope vanished, along with the idea of a futurity; my brain, in thrall to its outlaw hormones, had become less an organ of thought than an instrument registering, minute by minute, varying degrees of its own suffering. The mornings themselves were becoming bad now as I wandered about lethargic . . . but afternoons were still the worst, when I'd feel the horror, like some poisonous fogbank, roll in upon my mind, forcing me into bed. There I would lie for as long as six hours, stuporous and virtually paralyzed, gazing at the ceiling and waiting for that moment of evening when, mysteriously, the crucifixion would ease up just enough to allow me to force down some food and then, like an automaton, seek an hour or two of sleep again. (Styron, 1990, pp. 58–59)

In many cases, both thought and action slow down to a crawl:

The patient . . . speaks only in response to questions and even then answers in a word, not a sentence. . . . He speaks in such a low tone that one finds oneself moving close to him and speaking more loudly as if he were the one who could not hear. He says that everything is hopeless, that he is a disgrace to his family; he recalls that when he was a boy he took a paper from the newsstand and did not pay for it. (Cohen, 1975, p. 1019)

About 20 percent of major depressions are accompanied by delusions or hallucinations. Some are variations on the theme of worthlessness: "I must weep myself to death. I cannot live. I cannot die. I have failed so. It would be better if I had not been born. . . . I am the most inferior person in the world. . . . I am subhuman" (Beck, 1967, p. 38). Others concern guilt about some unspeakable, unpardonable sin, and patients report hearing the devil tell them that they will surely burn in hell for eternity (Andreasen and Black, 1991). The extreme of major depression is a *depressive stupor* in which the person may become entirely unresponsive, rock back and forth, urinate or defecate on himself, and mutter incoherently.

Specific cognitive deficits often accompany severe major depression, including disrupted attention and short-term memory. Moreover, depressed patients often exhibit various physical manifestations that are called *vegetative symptoms.* These can include a loss of appetite and weight loss, weakness, fatigue, poor bowel functioning, sleep disorders (most often early-morning awakenings), and loss of interest in sex. It is as if both bodily and psychic batteries have run down completely.

Vegetative symptoms seem to predominate in the depressions that occur in non-Western cultures, while mood symptoms like feelings of worthlessness and sinfulness are largely confined to Western depressions. The reasons for this difference are unknown, but several hypotheses have been proposed. These include the implicit blame that individualist Western cultures affix on people who are not faring well and the various ways that the cultures handle death and mourning (Kleinman and Good, 1985).

DEPRESSION AND SUICIDE

Depression, like schizophrenia, can be lethal. Given the depressive's bottomless despair it is not surprising that suicide is a very real risk. Some attempt the act, and more than a few succeed.

Women are three times as likely to attempt suicide as men, but when men make the attempt, they are much more likely to succeed; in fact, four times as many men as women kill themselves. One reason for the difference is in the choice of methods. The methods that women tend to use don't have the absolute finality of those generally used by men. While women are more likely to cut their wrists or swallow a bottle of sleeping pills, men tend to use methods

Hamlet on depression *Probably no patient in real life has described his preoccupation with death, suicide, and dissolution as eloquently as that greatest depressive in all of English literature, Prince Hamlet:*
"O that this too too sullied flesh would melt,
Thaw, and resolve itself into a dew,
Or that the Everlasting had not fixed
His canon 'gainst self-slaughter. O God,
  O God,
How weary, stale, flat, and unprofitable
Seem to me all the uses of this world!
Fie on 't, ah fie, fie! 'Tis an unweeded
  garden
That grows to seed. . . ."
(Hamlet, Act I, scene ii, photograph from the 1948 film version of the play starring Sir Laurence Olivier).

that are irreversible, such as shooting themselves or jumping off a roof top (Fremouw, Perczel, and Ellis, 1990).

Contrary to what one might expect, the risk of suicide is relatively low while the patient is still in the depths of his depression. At that point his gloom is deepest, but so is his inertia. The risk increases as the patient begins to recover. Suicide rates are greatest during weekend leaves from the hospital and shortly after discharge (Beck, 1967). At this point the patient's mood may still be bleak, but he has regained some of his energy and ability to act. He has recovered just enough to do the one thing that will prevent all further recovery.

SEASONAL AFFECTIVE DISORDER

Many people who live in cold climates have experienced the phenomenon of "cabin fever," a lethargy that ensues as the days grow short with precious few hours of sunlight. Clinical investigators observed that this phenomenon often reached serious proportions. The typical picture is one of depressions that start in late fall when the days become shorter and remit—or even switch to mania—when the days lengthen in March or April. Such *seasonal affective disorders* are evidently linked to the amount of sunlight the patients receive (see Figure 18.10). When they travel south in the winter, their depression lifts within a few days; when they travel north in the fall or winter, their depression gets worse. And needless to say, seasonal affective disorder is nonexistent in equatorial countries where there are no seasons and all days are equally long. Given these findings, it was only natural to attempt a treatment using bright artificial lights to replace the sun on one's "dark days." According to several studies, this treatment relieves even severe seasonal depressions within a few days or weeks, but the patient will relapse just as fast if the light therapy is discontinued. It's probably not surprising that one of the first regions in which this therapy was employed was Alaska (Rosen et al., 1990; Rosenthal et al., 1984; Hellekson, Kline, and Rosenthal, 1986; Lewy et al., 1987).

What might account for this striking effect of light on mood in people with seasonal affective disorder? As yet, we don't know. But one possibility is that the effect is somehow connected with the sleeping-waking cycle and with the secretion by the pineal gland of a chemical called *melatonin* (both of which are

18.10   Seasonal affective disorder and day length   *(A) Percentage of patients with seasonal affective disorder who report being depressed in any given month. (B) Mean minutes of daylight per month. (From Rosenthal et al., 1984)*

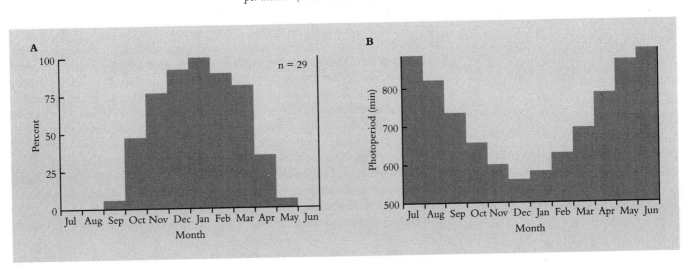

modulated by light). Indeed, there is some evidence that all depression may involve a disturbance in sleep rhythms, including the overly quick onset of REM sleep (Kupfer, Foster, and Reich, 1976; Wehr and Goodwin, 1981).

ORGANIC FACTORS

What produces the mood extremes of bipolar disorder and depression? According to one view, some of these conditions—especially the bipolar variety—are produced by some internal, organic pathology.

GENETIC COMPONENTS

The belief that such an organic pathology exists is based on several pieces of evidence. First, as in schizophrenia, certain drugs have rather specific therapeutic effects. And again, as in schizophrenia, there is good reason to suppose that at least some of the mood disorders have an important hereditary component. This is undoubtedly true for the bipolar condition. Concordances for identical twins with this affliction have been found to be some four times higher than those for fraternal twins (Andreasen and Black, 1991; Siever, Davis, and Gorman, 1991). Another line of evidence comes from detailed "genetic linkage" studies of extended families with numerous cases of bipolar disorder. In these families, the pattern of occurrence of bipolar disorder was linked to a particular enzyme deficiency as well as a type of color blindness. Both of these anomalies are due to defective genes on the X-chromosome, and the hunch is that the gene(s) causing bipolar disorder may be close by (Hodgkinson, Mullan, and Gurling, 1990).

While there is evidence that genetic factors play a role in unipolar cases as well, their contribution is probably not as powerful as it is in the bipolar condition. Further genetic evidence indicates that despite their surface similarity, the two conditions are at bottom quite different. Both tend to "breed true": People with one disorder (that is bipolar or unipolar) tend to have relatives with that condition but not the other. This suggests that there are separate inheritance pathways for each and makes it likely that they are largely separate disorders (Gershon et al., 1985; Torgersen, 1986; Wender et al., 1986).

BIOCHEMICAL HYPOTHESES

The genetic evidence is a strong argument for the view that there is some biological factor that underlies mood disorders, especially the bipolar ones. This view is further bolstered by the fact that in people suffering from bipolar disorder the switch from one mood to another is often quite divorced from external circumstances. The most plausible interpretation is that there is some internal, biological switch. But thus far, we know rather little about the biochemistry of bipolar disorder. Some investigators speculate that the disorder is due to instabilities of neuronal membranes (Hirschfeld and Goodwin, 1988; Meltzer, 1986). Such instabilities may also explain the actions of those medications that are successful in controlling the bipolar's mood swings.

Another hypothesis proposes a biochemical defect that involves the supply of some important neurotransmitters at certain critical sites of the brain. When there is a shortage, there is depression. Some investigators believe that this transmitter is **norepinephrine;** others believe that it is **serotonin;** still others suspect that both of these substances are involved (Schildkraut, 1965; Schildkraut, Green, and Mooney, 1985).

One line of evidence for the role of these neurotransmitters came from an analysis of the metabolic breakdown of these substances in the spinal fluid or the

Depression and despair *Edward Adamson, a professional artist, founded a studio in a British mental hospital for the use of the institutionalized patients. Many of their works forcefully express these patients' depression and despair, as in the case of this painting entitled* Cri de Coeur *or* Cry from the heart. *(Cri de Coeur, by Martha Smith; reproduced from Adamson, 1984)*

urine. If the level of these by-products is low, there should be a correspondingly low supply of the neurotransmitters from which they are derived. Just as predicted, the relevant metabolic by-products were in fact lower in at least some depressed patients than in controls. In addition, the norepinephrine levels in bipolar patients were below average when the patients were depressed and increased when the patients became manic (Muscettola et al., 1984; Schildkraut, Green, and Mooney, 1985). Further confirmation comes from the effect of various *antidepressant medications* all of which increase the amounts of norepinephrine and serotonin available for synaptic transmission.

In recent years, some further findings have complicated the picture. One problem is the time course of the medication effects. While the antidepressants lead to an almost immediate increase in the amount of available norepinephrine or serotonin, this increase is short-lived; within a few days, the transmitter levels subside to what they had been before the drug was first administered. But the drugs don't begin to relieve the depression until a week or two after the drug therapy was started. This means that the antidepressants may not exert their effect by increasing the supply of neurotransmitters. So how do they accomplish their mission? Some recent studies indicate that instead of increasing the supply of the neurotransmitters, the antidepressants make the relevant neurons more sensitive to them (Schildkraut, Green, and Mooney, 1985).

PSYCHOGENIC FACTORS

The organic pathology—whatever it may turn out to be—might account for the extremes of some patients' moods, the fact that they are speeded up or slowed down in virtually all respects. But can it explain the depressive's hopeless despair and self-loathing? How does an inadequate supply of norepinephrine or serotonin lead to the belief that one is the "most inferior person in the world"?

MOOD OR COGNITION?

What comes first, mood or cognition? The question is again one of cause and effect. Theorists who regard the disorder as primarily somatogenic believe that what the patient thinks follows from her mood. If a transmitter insufficiency (or some other biochemical state) makes her feel sluggish and gloomy, she looks for reasons to explain her own mood. Eventually she finds them: The world is no good and neither is she. The end result is that her cognitions match her feelings. (For an analogous approach to the nature of emotional feelings in normal people, see Chapter 11).

Does this approach really do justice to the phenomenon? Theorists who believe in a psychogenic explanation think not. They grant that mood disorders such as bipolar disorder are probably mostly constitutional, but they insist that psychological factors play a vital role in at least some cases of major depression. In their view, the patient's view that she and the world are no good comes first and her depression comes second, as an effect of these cognitions rather than as their cause.

BECK'S COGNITIVE THEORY OF DEPRESSION

This cognitive view underlies a very influential approach to the understanding and treatment of depression developed by Aaron Beck (Beck, 1967, 1976). Beck believes that the patient's condition can be traced to a trio of intensely negative

Depression *(Photograph by Rhoda Sydney, Leo de Wys)*

and irrational beliefs about himself, about his future, and about the world around him: that he is worthless, that his future is bleak, and that whatever happens around him is sure to turn out to be for the worst. According to Beck, these beliefs form the core of a negative cognitive schema in terms of which the patient interprets whatever happens to him. Facing minor setbacks, the depressive makes mountains out of molehills (insisting that he has ruined his car when he's only scratched a fender); facing major accomplishments he makes molehills out of mountains (insisting that he's inept even though he's just won an important professional prize). These negative schemas are ultimately derived from a succession of unfortunate experiences in earlier life; a harshly critical attitude in the home or in school, the loss of a parent, rejection by peers, and so on. But whatever their origins, such negative schemas become self-fulfilling; expecting defeat, the depressive eventually will be defeated. To counteract this system of essentially irrational beliefs, Beck has developed a psychological treatment called **cognitive therapy** by means of which the patients are made to confront and overcome the essential irrationality of their beliefs (we will discuss this in a later section—see Chapter 19; Beck, 1967; Beck et al., 1979).

LEARNED HELPLESSNESS AND DEPRESSIVE ATTRIBUTIONS

Whereas Beck's cognitive theory grew out of clinical observations of depressed patients, a related cognitive account, proposed by Martin Seligman, had its source in studies of animal learning. The initial findings that led to Seligman's approach concerned **learned helplessness,** first observed in the animal laboratory (Seligman, 1975; see Chapter 4).

Learned helplessness and depression   When normal dogs are placed in a shuttle box in which they have to jump from one compartment to another in order to escape an electric shock, they learn to do so with little difficulty. This contrasts with a second group of dogs who are first exposed to a series of painful shocks about which they can do absolutely nothing. When this second group is later placed in the shuttlebox, their performance is drastically different from that of normal dogs. They do not look for some means of escape. Nor do they ever find the correct response—jumping over the hurdle. Instead, they simply give up; they lie down, whimper, and passively accept their fate. They learn to become helpless (Seligman, Maier, and Solomon, 1971).

Seligman argued that learned helplessness in animals is in many ways similar to at least some forms of depression. Like the helpless dogs, depressed patients have given up. They just sit there passively, unable to take any initiative that might help them cope. Some further similarities concern the effects of antidepressant drugs. As we've seen, these drugs alleviate the symptoms of many depressed patients. It turns out that they have a similar effect on animals rendered helpless; the helplessness disappears, and the animals behave much like normals (Porsolt, LePichon, and Jalfre, 1977).

Seligman supposed that the essential similarity between the helpless dogs and the depressed people is the expectation that one's own acts are of no avail. In dogs, the cause is a series of inescapable shocks that the animals can do nothing about. In humans, the precipitating factor may be some personal catastrophe—rejection, bankruptcy, physical disease, the death of a loved one. In some people, this may lead to a generalized sense of impotence, a belief that there is nothing one can do to shape one's own destiny, that one is a passive victim with no control over events—that one is helpless.

Attributional style and depression   The helplessness interpretation of depression runs into a number of problems. To begin with, it can't explain why being help-

Sorrow   *(Vincent Van Gogh, 1882; courtesy of the Vincent Van Gogh Foundation/ National Museum Vincent Van Gogh, Amsterdam)*

less doesn't necessarily lead to depression. People who are about to undergo an operation are helpless in the sense of being utterly dependent on their surgeons, but if they believe they will recover they will generally not become depressed. A further problem is the depressive's self-hatred. If he thinks that he is helpless, then why does he blame himself? (Abramson and Sackheim, 1977). Considerations of this sort led to a revised version of the helplessness theory, which proposed that what really matters is the individual's ***attributional style,*** the way in which he habitually tries to explain events—especially bad events—that happen to him (see also Chapter 16, pp. 662–63). Does he attribute unfortunate events to internal, global, and stable causes—that is, to causes that refer to something within himself, that will generalize to other situations, and that will continue over time (for example, being unattractive or unintelligent)? If so, he has an attributional style that will predispose him to depression (Abramson, Seligman, and Teasdale, 1978). There is good evidence that this despondent explanatory style is indeed characteristic of depressed persons (as shown by results with the Attributional Style Questionnaire described in Chapter 16, p. 662; Peterson and Seligman, 1984).

A number of critics have argued that this and other cognitive theories of depression (including Beck's) confuse the symptoms with the cause (Coyne and Gotlib, 1983; Lewinsohn et al., 1985). After all, hopelessness, helplessness, and unmitigated self-blame are among the symptoms of the condition we call "depression." To say they are the cause is a bit like saying that sneezing and nose-blowing cause colds. In contrast, cognitive theorists believe that the attributional style (or the negative cognitive schema) is a predisposing condition; given this style, the depression will then be precipitated by some environmental stress. If so, the cognitive patterns should precede the depressive episode.

Evidence for this interpretation comes from studies which show that people who are not currently depressed but who exhibit the despondent explanatory style are more likely to become depressed when faced with failure or stress. Thus college students who manifested this style at the start of the semester were more likely to become depressed on learning that they received a poor grade on an examination; prison inmates who displayed it at the start of their term were more likely to become depressed after some months of imprisonment; pregnant mothers who showed it in their second trimester were more likely to become depressed three months after childbirth (Peterson and Seligman, 1984). The issue is by no means settled, for there are a number of contradictory findings. But taken as a whole, there is reason to believe that the cognitive account fits some individuals and that certain habitual ways of interpreting the world are among the factors that predispose an individual toward depression. (For some contrary evidence, see Lewinsohn et al., 1981).

A recent extension of this general approach stresses hopelessness. Its main point is that in some cases of depression, hopelessness is a major cause rather than a symptom. If the patient believes that he has absolutely nothing to look forward to and that the future is utterly bleak, he will probably start a downward spiral that will eventually have bodily manifestations and end in full-fledged depression. The precise differences between this and related psychogenic views (such as Beck's and other offshoots of the learned helplessness approach) are still being spelled out (Alloy, Hartlage, and Abramson, 1988; Abramson, Metalsky, and Alloy, 1989).

SEX DIFFERENCES IN THE INCIDENCE OF DEPRESSION

One very evident fact about depression deserves special mention. Major depression is diagnosed about twice as often in women as in men, even after accounting for differences in income and socioeconomic level. What accounts for this

Depression in women *Major depressions are diagnosed about twice as frequently in women as in men. (Photograph by Mark Antman/The Image Works)*

difference? We cannot know for certain, but there are several possibilities. Some are biological. Women may suffer more from depression because of hormonal factors, such as drops in estrogen and progesterone levels during the premenstrual period, the postpartum period, and menopause. Men's hormonal makeup, in contrast, may lead them to "act out" distress rather than to manifest it in depression.

Some other factors are behavioral. According to a recent study, when men are depressed, they try to distract themselves: "I avoid thinking of reasons why I'm depressed," or "I do something physical." In contrast, women who are depressed seem to dwell on their despondency: "I try to determine why I'm depressed," "I talk to other people about my feelings," and "I cry to relieve the tension." The result of these different ways of dealing with one's own feelings is that the initial depression is more likely to escalate and last longer in women than in men (Nolen-Hoeksema, 1987). These differences in the ways in which men and women try to cope with difficult life situations are probably based on cultural factors. The culture expects men to be self-reliant and active, while women are supposed to be more passive and dependent. To the extent that women follow this cultural expectation, they may gradually come to believe that they can't control their own fate and shouldn't even try—the very condition that renders them liable to learned helplessness and depression.

MOOD DISORDERS AND THE DIATHESIS-STRESS CONCEPTION

Major depressions are often preceded by some stressful event, whether it involves marital or professional difficulties, serious physical illness, or a death in the family (Leff, Roatsch, and Bunney, 1970; Paykel, 1982). But it's clear that environmental stress cannot be the whole story. After all, there are many people who suffer major setbacks and serious losses but who don't fall into a depressive collapse. There is evidently a diathesis—some people are more prone to mood disorders than others—that may be based on biological factors, such as an insufficiency of available norepinephrine or serotonin. But the predisposition may well be psychological in nature—such as a negative view of oneself or the world or a depressive attributional style. In either case, the diathesis makes the individual more vulnerable to later stress.

Seen in this light, psychological and biological factors are intermingled, so that the distinction between somatogenic and psychogenic origins becomes somewhat blurred. Negative cognitions and learned helplessness can produce a depletion of norepinephrine and serotonin, but the causal chain can also run the other way around. Either way, there will be a predisposition for later depression, which will be manifested in both behavior and biochemistry.

ANXIETY DISORDERS

In major depressions, the primary symptom is a profoundly dejected mood: The patient believes that her condition is awful and that there is no hope that it will ever get better. In another group of conditions, the ***anxiety disorders,*** the primary symptoms are anxiety or defenses against anxiety: The patient is chronically apprehensive, fears the worst, and must guard vigilantly against it. While such symptoms often cause serious distress and impair the person's functioning, they generally do not become so extreme as to render the person psychotic.★

PHOBIAS

A relatively common anxiety disorder is a *phobia,* which is characterized by an intense and irrational fear of some object or situation. During the nineteenth century, some of these irrational fears were catalogued and assigned exotic-sounding Greek or Latin names. Some phobias are of particular objects or events; these are the ***specific phobias.*** Examples are fear of high places (acrophobia), enclosed places (claustrophobia), crowds (ocholophobia), germs (mysophobia), cats (ailurophobia), and even the number 13 (triskaidekophobia)—the list is potentially endless. The crucial point in the definition is that the fear must be irrational—there really is no danger at all or the danger is exaggerated out of all proportion. An African villager who lives in the jungle and is worried about leopards has an understandable fear; a San Francisco apartment dweller with a similar fear has a phobia. In most cases, this irrationality is quite apparent to the sufferer, who knows that the fear is groundless but continues to be afraid all the same.

In phobia, the irrational fear exerts an enormous effect on every aspect of the sufferer's life, for he is always preoccupied with his phobia. On the face of it, it is not entirely clear why this should be so. Why can't the phobic simply avoid the situations that frighten him? If he is afraid of leopards and snakes, he should stay away from the zoo; if he is terrified of heights, he should refrain from visits to the top of the World Trade Center. Some phobias may be minor enough to be handled this easily, but most cannot. In some cases this is because the phobia tends to expand: The fear of leopards becomes a fear of the part of the city where the zoo is located, of all cats and catlike things, or of all spotted objects, and so on. Still others do not allow avoidance, such as the fear of flying in an executive who has to travel.

THE CONDITIONING ACCOUNT OF SPECIFIC PHOBIAS

What is the mechanism that underlies the specific phobias? One notion goes back to John Locke, who believed that such fears were produced by the chance association of ideas, as when a child is told stories about goblins that come by night and is forever after terrified of the dark (Locke, 1690). Several modern authors express much the same idea in the language of conditioning theory. In their view, phobias result from classical conditioning; the conditioned stimulus is the feared object (e.g., cats) and the response is the autonomic upheaval (increased heart rate, cold sweat, and so on) characteristic of fear (Wolpe, 1958).

A number of phobias may indeed develop in just this fashion. Examples include fear of dogs after dog bites, fear of heights after falling off a ladder, and fear of cars or driving after a serious automobile accident (Marks, 1969).

A

B

Phobias *(A) The fear of dirt (Painting by Vassos); and (B) the fear of heights (Painting by Leon Spilliaert).*

★ In psychiatric classification systems prior to DSM-III, anxiety disorders were listed under the general rubric *neurosis* because it was believed that these conditions, along with a number of others such as conversion disorders and dissociative states, could all be understood as the manifestation of unconscious defenses against anxiety. Because DSM-III and its successors dropped the emphasis on origins, the anxiety disorders are now grouped purely descriptively, based upon their shared signs and symptoms.

Conditioning theorists can readily explain why phobias acquired in this manner expand and spread to new stimuli. The fear response is initially conditioned to a particular stimulus. If this stimulus subsequently occurs in a new context, the fear will be evoked and thus conditioned to a whole set of new stimuli. An example is a woman who developed a fear of anesthetic masks after experiencing a terrifying sensation of suffocation while being anesthetized. This same sense of suffocation reoccurred later when she was in a stuffy, crowded elevator. This is turn led to a dread of elevators, whether empty or crowded. The phobia generalized to any and all situations in which she could not leave at will, even when playing cards (Wolpe, 1958, p. 98).

SPECIFIC PHOBIAS AND PREPAREDNESS

There is an odd fact about specific phobias that is hard to reconcile with a simple conditioning account. By and large, phobic patients are afraid of a rather limited class of stimuli, such as snakes, spiders, and heights. On the other hand, phobias of hammers, knives, stoves, and electrical outlets are extremely rare. If phobias were produced by the mere association of a traumatic event with whatever stimuli happened to be around at the time, then there should be many more fear-arousing objects and of wholly different kinds. After all, there's little doubt that in urban America more children have been shocked by an open outlet or burned by a stove than have been bitten by a snake or a spider. But if so, why the disproportionate number of snake and spider phobias? A suggestion comes from the study of acquired taste aversions, which indicates that the organism is "prepared" to learn some associations more readily than others. Rats are very quick to associate tastes with illness, but are unlikely to associate illness with tones or lights (see Chapter 4). According to the **preparedness theory of phobias,** a similar account applies to phobias. Snakes, spiders, and a number of other stimuli were exceedingly dangerous to our primate ancestors; since this is so, natural selection must have favored animals who had a built-in predisposition (that is, a preparedness) to come to fear such stimuli very quickly (Seligman, 1971).

Some evidence for this theory comes from fear-conditioning experiments on normal (that is, nonphobic) subjects in which pictures of various objects were paired with electric shock. Pictures of snakes and spiders were considerably more effective as conditioned stimuli than were pictures of flowers and mushrooms (Öhman, Eriksson, and Olofsson, 1975; Öhman, Dimberg, and Öst, 1985). These studies have come in for some criticism (e.g., McNally, 1987). One problem is that there is no way of knowing what prior fears and associations the subjects may have had before they entered the laboratory. These may have developed through contacts with other people's fears and various cultural traditions such as folklore, legends, and the like. To control for such factors, some investigators have turned to laboratory-reared monkeys who had never seen a snake before. In line with preparedness theory, they found that the animals were much more easily frightened by toy snakes than by flowers. We—and our simian cousins with whom we share a common heritage—evidently come to fear some stimuli much more readily than others (Cook and Mineka, 1989).

Prepared fears of snakes in monkeys
The sight of the snake in the foreground leads to a characteristic fear grimace in the monkey, accompanied by a quick retreat to the rear of its cage while leaving its food untouched. (Courtesy of Susan Mineka)

SOCIAL PHOBIA

Unlike the specific phobias, other phobias may be more wide-ranging to begin with. An example is **social phobia** in which the problem is fear of embarrassment or humiliation in front of others. People with social phobia will desperately try to avoid situations in which they must expose themselves to public scrutiny. They will avoid public speaking or performing because they might falter, will not eat in restaurants for fear they will choke on their food, and won't go to parties or professional meetings because they may stutter and stammer when trying to make small talk. When forced into situations of this sort, they may try to "fortify" themselves with alcohol or drugs. Thus substance abuse or dependence is a constant risk.

OBSESSIVE-COMPULSIVE DISORDER

In phobias, anxiety is aroused by external objects or situations. In contrast, anxiety in *obsessive-compulsive disorder* is produced by internal events—persistent thoughts or wishes that intrude into consciousness and cannot be stopped. An example of such an *obsession* is a mother who has recurrent thoughts of strangling her children. Several studies have found that the most common obsessive themes are of dirt and contamination, aggression and violence, religion, sex, bodily functions like elimination, and the need for balance and symmetry.

A number of *compulsions* may be understood psychodynamically, as attempts to *counteract* the anxiety-producing impulse that underlies an obsession: in Freud's terms, a way of *undoing* what should not have been done. This may explain some cases of compulsions like ritualistic cleaning, handwashing, and counting. The mother with uncontrollable thoughts of committing infanticide might feel compelled to count her children over and over again, as if to check that they are all there, that she hasn't herself done away with any. The patient is quite aware that her behavior is irrational but she can't help herself even so. Lady Macbeth knew that "what's done cannot be undone," but she nevertheless continued to wash the invisible blood off her hands.

Minor and momentary obsessional thoughts or compulsions are commonplace. After all, most people have on occasion checked the stove repeatedly. But in obsessive-compulsive disorder, such thoughts and acts are the patient's major preoccupation and are crippling. The disorder is fairly common, afflicting as many as 2 to 3 percent of the population sometime in their lives. It is also quite serious: Most cases worsen over time and are accompanied by bouts of major depression (Barlow, 1988).

There is some suggestion that there is a biological predisposition to develop obsessive-compulsive disorder. To begin with, there seems to be some genetic basis as shown by the fact that the concordance is higher for identical than for fraternal twins (Black and Noyes, 1990). The neurological mechanism apparently involves the neurotransmitter serotonin: Medications that increase serotonin activity reduce obsessive-compulsive manifestations, but just why they do this is unclear (Insel, 1990; Winslow and Insel, 1990; Zohar et al., 1988).

GENERALIZED ANXIETY DISORDER

In the anxiety disorders we have discussed thus far, anxiety is relatively focused, for it occurs in response to a fairly specific condition. In phobia, anxiety is aroused by the feared object; in obsessive-compulsive disorder, it is aroused by a thought or the belief that one hasn't performed some important act. In contrast, there are several conditions in which anxiety is not related to anything in particular, but isn't any less upsetting for all that.

In *generalized anxiety disorder,* anxiety is all-pervasive, or free-floating. The patient is constantly tense and worried, feels inadequate, is oversensitive, can't concentrate or make decisions, and suffers from insomnia. This state of affairs is generally accompanied by any number of physiological concomitants—rapid heart rate, irregular breathing, excessive sweating, and chronic diarrhea.

Generalized anxiety disorder is probably the most common of the anxiety

Compulsive hand washing in literature
A scene from the Old Vic's 1956 production of Macbeth *with Coral Browne. It shows Lady Macbeth walking in her sleep and scrubbing imaginary blood off her hands, as she relives the night in which she and her husband murdered the king. (Courtesy of the Performing Arts Research Center, The New York Public Library)*

The Scream   *(Edward Munch, 1893; courtesy Nasjonalgalleriet, Oslo)*

disorders, occurring in as many as 6 percent of the population in any one year (Weissman, 1985). However, little information is available on any genetic predisposition, and there is uncertainty about its cause. Some theorists believe it is psychogenic. A psychoanalytic interpretation holds that the disorder occurs when there are no defenses against anxiety or when those defenses are weak and collapse, so that unacceptable impulses are able to break into consciousness and to precipitate anxiety reactions. Conditioning theorists contend that generalized anxiety disorder is much like a phobia. The difference is that anxiety is conditioned to a very broad range of stimuli so that avoidance is virtually impossible (Wolpe, 1958). The trouble is that these stimuli are not easily specified, and thus the conditioning interpretation of this disorder is hard to evaluate.

Some investigators offer evidence in favor of a somatogenic interpretation. They believe that the condition is linked to certain abnormalities in the secretion of the neurotransmitter GABA (for gamma aminobutyric acid). Support comes from findings that the medications that lower anxiety work by locking onto specific receptor sites in the brain where GABA is plentiful (Costa, 1985).

PANIC DISORDER

Panic disorder is like generalized anxiety disorder in being characterized by anxiety that is not directed at anything in particular. The difference is in the frequency and intensity of the anxiety. Patients with panic disorder don't suffer from the nagging, chronic tensions and worries that beset people with generalized anxiety disorder. But when anxiety strikes them, it strikes with a vengeance.

The patient suffers sudden attacks that come out of the blue and bring terrifying bodily symptoms that she doesn't understand: labored breathing, choking, dizziness, tingling in the hands and feet, sweating, trembling, heart palpitations, and chest pain. These bodily sensations are accompanied by feelings of intense apprehension, terror, and a sense of impending doom. The patient often has an intense experience of unreality and fears that she is losing control, is going insane, or is about to die. Panic disorder is diagnosed if such attacks occur once a week or more often; based on that criterion, it is found in about 2 to 3 percent of women and 1 percent of men (Robins et al., 1984).

Panic disorders can be frightening enough, but in addition, sufferers often develop a profound fear of *having* panic attacks, especially in places such as shopping malls where they might be embarrassing or in circumstances that might prove dangerous such as driving. As a result, people with the condition can rarely venture outside their designated "safe" places—their houses or even just their bedrooms. A common result is **agoraphobia,** a fear of being alone and outside of the home, especially in a public place.★

What accounts for panic disorder? Some authors hold to a cognitive theory of the condition. They believe that it is produced by a vicious cycle that begins with a misinterpretation of certain bodily reactions to fear. In fear reactions, the sympathetic nervous system produces a number of circulatory and respiratory responses such as quicker heartbeats and faster and shallower breathing. This is normal enough, but the person with the panic disorder over reacts to her own internal sensations. She believes that the shortness of breath and quickened heart beat are a sign of an impending heart attack. This makes her more fearful, which intensifies the bodily reactions, which makes her even more fearful, and so on, spiraling upward toward the full-blown attack. This pattern becomes even worse after the patient has her first panic attack, for now every normal anxiety reaction becomes a potential signal of a further panic (Clark, 1986).

POST-TRAUMATIC STRESS DISORDER

Human beings sometimes undergo especially stressful traumatic events. One consequence can be a **post-traumatic stress disorder.** This has long been known as a disorder found in soldiers after intense combat and reached wide public attention because of its prevalence among Viet Nam war veterans (Figley, 1978). But the disorder can occur at any age and can be produced by a wide range of extreme stressors including fires, automobile accidents, rape, concentration camp incarceration, or handling bodies after airplane crashes (Wolf and Mosnaim, 1990).

Regardless of what the trauma was, the signs and symptoms of post-traumatic stress disorders are similar. Immediately after the trauma, there is usually a period of numbness during which the sufferer feels wholly estranged, socially unresponsive, and oddly unaffected by the event, a reaction technically known as **dissociation.** This initial period is often followed by recurrent nightmares and waking flashbacks of the traumatic event. These are often so intense and intrusive that the sufferer may momentarily believe that he is back *in* the situation. Below is a description of the flashbacks of soldiers who served as body handlers:

> . . . A dental X-ray technician reported seeing skulls when he saw the teeth of smiling people. A young lieutenant could not enter a local fast food establishment because the smell of burning food elicited a vomiting response. Some intrusions did not require an external stimulus. Soldiers reported seeing bodies when they closed their eyes. Their dream content consisted of nightmarish horror shows where zombie-like bodies were coming to kill the dreamer. One soldier reported seeing himself in a dream where he searched through human body parts and found his own ID tag. (Garrigan, 1987, p. 8)

★ The term is derived from the Greek word *agora* meaning "marketplace."

749

The Dead Mother, 1899–1900, *by Edward Munch (Courtesy of Eigentum der Kunsthalle, Bremen)*

Other consequences may include sleep disturbances and some changes in sympathetic nervous system and endocrine functioning. Still another may be "survival guilt" if friends or relatives were harmed or killed by the same traumatic event (Friedman, 1990). If the trauma is severe enough, the manifestations of post-traumatic disorder may remain for years and even decades, even with the best available treatments.

DISSOCIATIVE DISORDERS

Post-traumatic stress disorder shows that people can distance themselves psychologically, or *dissociate,* from ongoing events. This phenomenon is the defining feature of a number of syndromes now called **dissociative disorders.**★ An example is **dissociative amnesia** in which the individual is unable to remember some period of her life, or sometimes all events prior to the onset of the amnesia, including her own identity. Such episodes usually last less than one week (Andreasen and Black, 1991). In other cases, the dissociation produces **dissociative fugue** in which the person wanders away from home, and then, days or even months thereafter, suddenly realizes that he is in a strange place, doesn't know how he got there, and has total amnesia for the entire period.

Still more drastic are cases of **dissociative identity disorder** (formerly known as "multiple personality disorder"). Here the dissociation is so massive that it results in two or more distinct personalities. The "auxiliary" personalities, which can number from just a few to several dozen, seem to be built upon a

★ Some authors suggest that the dissociative disorders are really severe cases of post-traumatic stress disorder, or alternatively, that the dissociations seen in post-traumatic stress disorder should be reclassified under the rubric of the dissociative disorders.

nucleus of memories that already had some prior separate status. An example is a shy and inhibited person who has had fantasies of being carefree and outgoing from childhood on. These memories eventually take on the characteristics of a separate self. Once formed, the new self may appear quite suddenly, as in the famous case of Eve White, loosely depicted in the movie *The Three Faces of Eve:*

> After a tense moment of silence, her hands dropped. There was a quick, reckless smile and, in a bright voice that sparkled, she said, "Hi there, Doc." . . . There was in the newcomer a childishly daredevil air, an erotically mischievous glance, a face marvelously free from the habitual signs of care, seriousness, and underlying distress, so long familiar in her predecessor. This new and apparently carefree girl spoke casually of Eve White and her problems, always using she or her in every reference, always respecting the strict bounds of a separate identity. When asked her own name she immediately replied, "Oh, I'm Eve Black." (Thigpen and Cleckley, 1957, as described in Coleman, 1972, p. 246).

Some twenty years later, Eve White wrote an autobiography in which she described herself more fully. It turned out that at one time in her life she had as many as twenty-two subpersonalities rather than just three (Sizemore and Huber, 1988). The various personalities seen in such cases are not confined to differences in mood and attitudes. Sometimes the individual segregates different skills to different personalities, such that one plays the piano, while another cooks, and yet a third speaks French. The personalities can know of each other, have amnesia for each other, or exhibit any combinations of acquaintances.

Until twenty years ago, dissociative identity disorder was considered very rare, with fewer than 200 cases reported before 1975. Now cases number in the thousands of whom the large majority are females (Kluft, 1987). The rash of reported cases followed *Sybil,* a popular book about one case of dissociative identity disorder, subsequently made into a television movie (Schreiber, 1973). Some critics argued that the flood of dissociative identity disorder diagnoses reflected a fad among therapists who inadvertently led their patients—many of whom had read the book themselves—to develop the signs and symptoms of dissociative identity disorder. This may well have been true in some cases, but dissociative identity disorder is now considered an entirely valid diagnosis for many patients.

A movie recreation of a case of dissociative personality disorder Joanne Woodward in The Three Faces of Eve *portraying Eve White (above) and Eve Black (below). (Courtesy the Museum of Modern Art/Film Stills Archive)*

FACTORS UNDERLYING DISSOCIATIVE DISORDERS

The mechanism that underlies the dissociative disorders is still obscure. Some authors suggest that phenomena like the development of auxiliary personalities may represent an unusual form of self-dramatization, without the awareness that any role playing is going on (Ziegler, Imboden, and Rodgers, 1963; Sarbin and Allen, 1968). Others try to understand dissociation in the context of human information processing and stress its similarity to phenomena like implicit memory and procedural knowledge (Kihlstrom, 1992; see Chapter 7).

There is less debate about the psychological function played by dissociation. Most authors hold to one or another variant of Freud's view. He believed that dissociation is a defense against something the individual is unable to face. The post-traumatic stress reaction is a case in point. Rape victims sometimes report that they are outside of their own bodies watching themselves being raped. Similarly for people who watch their houses burn; they sometimes experience a strange calm and report the feeling that "it's like it's not really happening to me."

DISSOCIATIVE DISORDERS AND THE DIATHESIS-STRESS CONCEPTION

There is some evidence that dissociative disorders may fit a diathesis-stress conception. People seem to differ in their propensity to dissociate and in the intensity of the circumstances that make them do so. The evidence comes from work on hypnosis, which some investigators regard as a form of guided dissociation (Hilgard, 1986). If this is so, one might suspect that people with dissociative disorders should be more hypnotizable than others, and this indeed turns out to be the case (Ganaway, 1989). This seems to be especially so for patients with dissociative identity disorder. According to one investigator, such patients were unusually adept at self-hypnosis during childhood and created a new personality (often many more than just one) during their hypnotic trance as a form of escape from threatening traumatic events (Bliss, 1980).

The readiness toward dissociation—which may be constitutional or based on learned defense patterns—represents the predisposition or diathesis toward the disorder. To activate it into the full-fledged disorder, there has to be some unusual stress. This does indeed seem to be the case. Thus, most cases of dissociative amnesia occur after the same kinds of cataclysmic events that may lead to post-traumatic stress disorder. The same holds for dissociative fugues, which can also develop suddenly after personal misfortunes or financial pressures (Andreasen and Black, 1991).

There is reason to believe that the most serious and disabling of the dissociative conditions, dissociative identity disorder, results from the most harrowing stresses in early life. In a large percentage of the case histories, there are terrifying stories of repeated brutal physical and sexual abuse in childhood, often including incest (Putnam et al., 1986). These findings have led the majority of practioners to believe that child abuse, and especially sexual abuse, is a likely antecedent of dissociative identity disorder. But some others urge caution in accepting this interpretation, for virtually all of the reports of early childhood abuse are based on the patients' uncorroborated memories of early childhood (Frankel, 1993). As yet, the evidence is not all in.

SOMATOFORM AND PSYCHOPHYSIOLOGICAL DISORDERS

In a number of psychological disorders the predominant symptoms are bodily complaints. We will take up examples drawn from two categories of such disorders: the *somatoform* and the *psychophysiological*.

SOMATOFORM DISORDERS

It appears that while some people experience anxiety directly and others dissociate from it, still others turn it into bodily complaints. At least this is the most common interpretation of the **somatoform disorders** (those disorders that take bodily form). There are several kinds of such disorders, but in each the patient exhibits or describes concerns about his bodily functions in the absence of any known physical illness. Probably the best known of the somatoform disorders is **hypochondriasis** in which the sufferer believes he has a specific disease and goes to doctor after doctor to be evaluated for it. Somewhat similar is the person with **somatization disorder.** She brings to the doctor a host of miscellaneous aches and pains in various bodily systems that do not add up to any known syndrome in physical medicine. And then there is **somatoform pain disorder** in which the sufferer describes chronic pain for which no physical basis can be found.

The most dramatic of the somatoform disorders is **conversion disorder.** Conversion disorder (formerly known as *conversion hysteria* or *hysterical neurosis*) represented the first and most dramatic argument for the psychogenic approach to psychopathology and was the foundation on which psychoanalytic theory was built. According to Freud, people with these disorders resolve some intolerable conflict by developing an hysterical ailment, such as being unable to see or hear or move an arm, even though there is nothing organically wrong (see Chapter 17, pp. 671–72).★ The soldier who is terrified of going into battle but cannot face the idea of being a coward may become hysterically paralyzed. This allows him to give in to his impulse of refusing to march. But it also lets him do so without guilt or shame—he is not marching because he cannot march.

We will not describe the signs and symptoms of conversion disorder in any detail since we discussed it in Chapter 17. We will, however, note some very interesting oddities in the incidence of the disorder. A century ago, such cases were fairly common, but today they account for a much smaller fraction of mental disorders. How can we explain this changing fashion in psychopathological conditions? Some believe that this is due to a less restrictive family atmosphere and more permissive child rearing, especially in the sexual sphere, with a resulting decline in symptoms produced by repressed sexual and aggressive thoughts and memories (Chodoff, 1954). Others suggest that the reason is education: Because of a general increase in medical sophistication among lay persons, there are fewer people who believe that one can suddenly be struck blind or become paralyzed without some other accompanying bodily signs (say, of a stroke). In this era, hysterical blindness or paralysis would be rather transparent psychological defenses and thus much less acceptable to both the patient and those around him. Some evidence for either view is the fact that such disorders are more frequent in just those geographical areas in which one would expect a less permissive family atmosphere as well as less medical acumen: in rural regions rather than urban centers of America and among the less industrialized nations of the globe (Watson and Buranen, 1979). One historian has suggested that disorders such as chronic fatigue and somatoform pain disorder have become the conversion hysterias of the late twentieth century (Shorter, 1992).

A final problem is inherent in the diagnosis of conversion disorder itself, because it must necessarily be a diagnosis by exclusion. Before conversion can be diagnosed, all conceivable physical conditions must be ruled out. And how can a physician be absolutely certain that the patient's ailment is not organic after all? How can she ensure that the syndrome doesn't result from an underlying, quite subtle organic disorder (say, a neurological defect)? To be sure, someone may inadvertently give himself away by presenting a symptom that makes no anatomical sense, such as the glove anesthesia we described previously. But today, patients rarely exhibit such nonsensical symptoms. Diagnoses of conversion disorder might also be expected to decline not only because of increasing lay sophistication about medicine, but also due to medical advances that allow better detection of the physical disorders that might have otherwise been interpreted as cases of conversion disorders. Support for this notion comes from fol-

---

★ The term *conversion* was coined by Freud, who believed that the repressed energies that fueled the patient's unconscious conflict were converted into a somatic symptom much as a steam engine converts thermal energy into mechanical energy. Until recently, this condition was called *conversion hysteria*. The authors of DSM-III dropped the term *hysteria* because of its erroneous implication that conversion disorders were found only in women. ("Hysteria" is derived from the Greek *hystera,* for womb.)

low-up studies of patients whose symptoms were diagnosed as conversions. A fair proportion of these patients were later found to have had organic disorders after all, many of which involved neurological damage (Slater and Glithero, 1965; Watson and Buranen, 1979). And in today's medical malpractice climate, a physician diagnoses "conversion disorder" at her own risk.

PSYCHOPHYSIOLOGICAL DISORDERS

Thus far, our concern has been with psychopathological disorders whose primary symptoms are psychological. But certain other conditions can lead to genuine organic damage. For example, ulcer, high blood pressure, and asthma may be produced by organic causes, as in the case of an asthmatic allergic reaction. Yet they may also be produced (or aggravated) by emotional factors. If so, they are called *psychophysiological conditions* (or, to use an older term, *psychosomatic disorders*).

But whether their origin is organic or mental or a bit of both, their results are equally damaging. In this regard, the symptoms of a psychophysiological condition are quite different from the somatic complaints of a patient with a conversion disorder. That patient's paralysis of the legs may disappear after his underlying conflict is resolved; after all, his locomotor machinery is still intact. But the patient with a psychophysiological ulcer (or asthma or high blood pressure) has a disorder that plays for keeps. His ulcer will bleed and hurt just as much as an ulcer caused by gastric disease; if it perforates his stomach wall, he will suffer the same case of peritonitis; and if he dies, his death will be no less final.

CORONARY HEART DISEASE

Perhaps the best-documented example of a disorder brought on or aggravated by psychological factors is *coronary heart disease,* a progressively increasing blockage of the arteries that supply blood to the heart muscles. This may result in severe chest pains (angina), indicating that the muscles in a certain region of the heart don't get enough oxygen to maintain their current work load. It may also result in the death of some portion of the heart muscle tissue (a "heart attack") that received no oxygen at all. There are a number of biological factors that increase the risk of coronary heart disease, such as cholesterol level, obesity, smoking, and gender (men are more prone to the disease than women). But in addition, psychopathologists have identified certain characteristic behavior patterns that provide a major additional risk factor.

The Type A personality　One example is the *Type A behavior pattern.* People with this pattern are highly competitive and hard-driving, always in a hurry, and are irritable, impatient, and hostile. In the words of Friedman and Rosenman, the two cardiologists who first described this pattern, such individuals are "aggressively involved in a chronic, incessant struggle to achieve more and more in less and less time, and if required to do so, against the opposing efforts of other things or other persons" (Friedman and Rosenman, 1974, p. 67). In contrast, those with the *Type B behavior pattern* are less hurried and competitive, and more easygoing and friendly than their Type A counterparts. The Type A person runs up escalators whereas the Type B lets the escalator do the work. In traffic jams, the Type A fumes and curses, while the Type B in the next lane sits back and listens to a radio broadcast of a baseball game. Needless to say, many people are not extreme A or B types, but fall somewhere in between.

Several large-scale studies have shown that people with a Type A pattern are more likely to contract coronary heart disease than Type B individuals. In one

"I don't care if they are moving better over there. This is the fast lane. This is where I live." (Drawing by Handelsman; © 1983, The New Yorker Magazine, Inc.)

such study, over 3,000 men with no sign of coronary heart disease were evaluated to determine their behavior type. The single best predictor of whether these men developed coronary heart disease during the subsequent eight years was their original assessment: Type A's were twice as likely to become victims than Type B's. Could this be because Type A's smoked more, or had higher blood pressure, or had higher cholesterol levels? The answer is no, for the relation between behavior pattern and heart disease held up even when these other risk factors were statistically held constant (Rosenman et al., 1975). Further work showed that the same relation held for women. Compared to men, women—whether Type A or Type B—are much less likely to suffer coronary heart disease, for reasons that are still a matter of debate. But compared to Type B women, Type A women are more at risk; they are two to three times more likely to suffer a heart attack and this regardless of whether they are working women or not (Haynes, Feinleib, and Kannel, 1980).

Impatience or hostility?   It appears that some aspects of the Type A behavior pattern predict coronary heart disease. But just what is the crucial part of the pattern? Is it the Type A's impatience, his relentless need for achievement, or his irritability? Some recent investigations suggest that these different components of the behavior pattern are not as tightly linked—to each other or to the disease—as they were initially thought to be (Mathews, 1982; Shekelle et al., 1983). Many investigators feel that the major pathological ingredient is hostility, manifested as a combination of continual anger, cynicism, and distrust of other people, that is found in some—but by no means all—Type A's (Dembroski et al., 1989). Those who say yes to questions like "Most people are honest chiefly through fear of being caught" or "When someone does me wrong I feel I should pay him back if I can, just for the principle of the thing" are more likely to fall victim to cardiac disease than those who do not. Other facets of the Type A pattern, such as the sense of hurry and competitiveness seem to be of lesser importance (Williams, 1987; Krantz et al., 1988; Barefoot et al., 1989).

An as yet unanswered question concerns the mechanism. How does the Type A individual's impatience, his inability to relax, or, most of all, his continual hostility produce the progressive narrowing of his coronary arteries that eventually gets severe enough to lead to angina or a heart attack? One hypothesis is that the sympathetic branch of the Type A person's autonomic nervous system is in a continual state of arousal, which leads to an enhanced secretion of epinephrine (adrenaline), norepinephrine, and various steroid hormones produced by the adrenal gland. On a long-term basis, secretion of these substances has a number of adverse side effects. For example, they stimulate the formation of cholesterol deposits on the walls of the coronary arteries, which lead to the progressive narrowing of these blood vessels. If this process continues day in and day out, it is likely to culminate in coronary heart disease (Friedman and Rosenman, 1974). This is especially true for people whose general outlook is hostile and mistrustful; hostility provokes hostility and creates an environment in which every social encounter is a fight-or-flight emergency (Hardy and Smith, 1988).

THE DIATHESIS-STRESS CONCEPT AND PSYCHOPHYSIOLOGICAL DISORDERS

Emotional stress can lead to hypertension or coronary heart disease, but it can also lead to various other psychophysiological disorders such as stomach ulcers. Is there any way to predict which disorder will be produced in any one person by stress? What determines whether "she will eat her heart out" or whether "she'll tie her stomach into knots?" The answer is diathesis and stress.

There is reason to believe that the susceptibility to a given psychophysiological disorder depends on a preexisting somatic diathesis that may be of genetic origin. Given enough emotional stress, the body will cave in at its most vulnerable point. Some evidence for this view comes from studies which show that elevated blood pressure tends to run in families, in mice as well as men. In humans, a blood-pressure correlation between children and parents is seen as early as infancy. The best guess is that there is a genetic factor that is partially responsible for the initial blood-pressure elevation. This may bias the individual to respond to stress with his arterial muscles rather than with his lungs or stomach. If the stress is prolonged enough, the individual will develop chronic high blood pressure rather than suffer from asthma or an ulcer (Henry and Cassel, 1969).

A somewhat similar account applies to psychogenic peptic ulcers. This is a lesion in the lining of the stomach or duodenum whose immediate physiological cause is an oversecretion of gastric acid; in effect, the stomach or duodenum digests itself. A number of studies have shown that in some individuals, emotional stress leads to gastric oversecretion and possibly to ulcer formation (Wolf, 1971). Similar results have been reported for various animals (Sawrey, Conger, and Turrell, 1956).

Once again the question is why certain individuals respond to tension in this way. And again the answer is that one of the factors is an initial diathesis. One group of investigators measured gastric secretion levels in army recruits just prior to the stressful months of basic training. After several months some of these men developed ulcers. Everyone who did had very high gastric secretion levels before he entered basic training (Weiner et al., 1957).

A CATEGORIZING REVIEW

We have looked at a number of different mental disorders. The pathology model provides a convenient framework to review the way in which these disorders are generally considered today. This review is summarized in Table 18.1, which classifies disorders by the nature of their main symptoms and of their presumed underlying pathology (which in many cases is still controversial). Either the main symptoms or the pathology or both can be organic. But they can also be mental, that is, defined by behavioral rather than by organic attributes.

TABLE 18.1 A CLASSIFICATION OF SOME MENTAL DISORDERS

		Symptoms	
		Primarily organic	Primarily mental
Presumed underlying disorder	Primarily organic	Diabetes Measles Rickets	General paresis Schizophrenia★ Bipolar disorders★
	Primarily mental	Psycho-physiological disorders	Phobias Dissociative disorders

★Whether the underlying pathology of these disorders is primarily organic or psychogenic is still a matter of debate. In some cases, such as panic disorders, organic and behavioral causes are so intertwined that it's impossible to say which is primary.

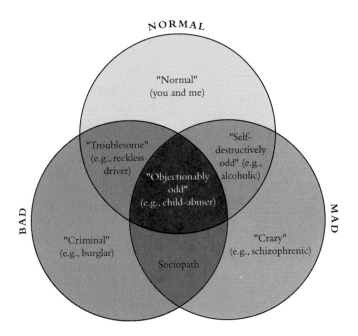

18.11 BAD, MAD, and NORMAL, and their areas of overlap *(After Stone, 1975)*

NORMAL

"Normal" (you and me)

"Troublesome" (e.g., reckless driver)

"Self-destructively odd" (e.g., alcoholic)

"Objectionably odd" (e.g., child-abuser)

BAD

MAD

"Criminal" (e.g., burglar)

"Crazy" (e.g., schizophrenic)

Sociopath

SOCIAL DEVIANCE

The conditions we've considered thus far are clearly mental disorders. There is much about them that we still don't understand, but they seem to fit reasonably well within the general underlying pathology framework nevertheless. There are a number of other diagnostic categories, however, that don't fit so readily. The psychiatric classification system includes several conditions that are certainly deviant and usually undesirable, such as antisocial personality and alcohol and drug dependence. But it is by no means clear that these are really mental disorders. Nor is it clear that the underlying pathology model is the most appropriate framework for them.

Society calls some forms of deviance criminal while calling others disorders, and it has set up institutions to deal with each—the judicial system for the first and the mental-health system for the second. In actual fact, the two classifications overlap and both shade off into normality. Figure 18.11 provides a graphic description of how the terms "normal," "bad," and "ill" are usually applied. Some kinds of persons can be classified unambiguously: you and I (definitely "normal," or at least, so we hope), a professional criminal ("bad"), and a severe case of schizophrenia ("ill"). But there are also areas of overlap. Some people occupy a gray area between normality and criminality. An example might be a person who is a habitual reckless driver. Others lie between mental disorder and normality. An example would be someone with a serious drinking problem. Still others are in the zone between criminality and mental disorder. They are somehow both "ill" and "bad" at the same time. Our present concern is with one such group of individuals, the **sociopaths,** or as they are described in DSM-IV, persons with **antisocial personality disorder.**★

★ An earlier designation was *psychopath.* Some versions of this term are still in current use. One example is the MMPI scale, which attempts to measure psychopathic deviance.

THE SOCIOPATH

The clinical picture The sociopath is an individual who gets into continual trouble with others and with society. He is grossly selfish, callous, impulsive, and irresponsible. His—or, somewhat less frequently, her—difficulties generally start with truancy from school, runaway episodes, and a wild adolescence marked by belligerence and precocious sexual experience and promiscuity (Robins, 1966). There may also be blatant infractions like fire-setting and cruelty to animals. Later on there are various minor scrapes that often escalate into increasingly serious legal and social offenses. But the distinguishing characteristics of sociopaths run deeper, because they lack any genuine feeling of love or loyalty for any person or any group. They also exhibit relatively little guilt or anxiety. As a result, the sociopath is a creature of the present whose primary object is to gratify the impulses he feels now, with little concern about the future and even less remorse about the past.

Sociopaths are not truly socialized. They are not pack animals; they are genuine loners. But they are often quite adept at the machinations and strategies of personal interaction, manifesting a superficial charm and sometimes a greater than average intelligence. In this regard, sociopaths are quite different from ordinary criminals and delinquents. Those also violate society's laws and norms, but unlike sociopaths, they generally have a society of their own, such as a juvenile gang or a crime syndicate, whose code they try to honor and to which they have some sense of loyalty. The sociopath, on the other hand, abides by no code of conduct and readily yields to the fleeting impulse of the moment (McCord and McCord, 1964). An illustration is the case of a forty-four-year-old man:

> [Roger] was reared in a well-to-do family, the only child of a doting mother. In the past ten years, Roger squandered a substantial inheritance and was beginning to "fall on hard times." Handsome, well-educated and suave in manner, he had always been skillful in charming and exploiting others, especially women. Faced with economic adversity, Roger allied himself with a group of stock promoters involved in selling essentially worthless shares of "sure-bet" Canadian mining stock. This led to other "shady deals"; and in time Roger became a full-fledged "love swindler" who intrigued, lived off, and "borrowed" thousands of dollars from a succession of wealthy and "lonely" mistresses. (Millon, 1969, p. 434)

Some possible causes of sociopathy What accounts for antisocial personality disorder? Many investigators have noted the sociopath's lack of concern for the consequences of his actions. Sociopaths are comparatively fearless. This is especially true when the danger is far off. One investigator told sociopaths and normals that they would receive a shock at the end of a ten-minute period. The subjects' apprehensiveness was assessed by their galvanic skin response (GSR). As the time grew closer, the control subjects grew increasingly nervous. In contrast, the sociopaths showed little anticipatory fear (Lippert and Senter, 1966). If future pain had just as little import when the sociopath was young, his inadequate socialization becomes partially comprehensible. Whoever tried to teach him the don'ts of childhood had no effective deterrents (Figure 18.12).

The strange fearlessness of sociopaths has been observed by several writers who have noted their "extraordinary poise," their "smooth sense of physical being," and their "relative serenity" under conditions that would produce agitation in most of us (Cleckley, 1976). How does this difference between sociopaths and normals come about? Several investigators believe that there is a difference in some underlying physiological functions. One line of evidence concerns the EEG (electrical recordings from the brain; see Chapter 3). It appears that a fairly high proportion of sociopaths have abnormal EEGs that

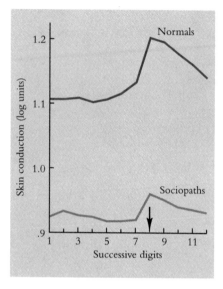

18.12 Anticipation of electric shock in normals and sociopaths *Normals and sociopaths were repeatedly presented with a series of twelve consecutive digits from 1 to 12. Whenever the digit 8 appeared, the subjects suffered an electric shock. To determine whether there were any differences in anticipatory anxiety prior to the advent of shock, the galvanic skin response (GSR) was measured. The results are shown in units of log conductance (a measure of GSR activity) for each of the 12 digits in the series. The sociopaths showed a much lower base-response level. In addition, they showed less anticipatory reaction to the digits just prior to the critical digit. (After Hare, 1965)*

resemble those of children. One possible interpretation is that this cortical immaturity of sociopaths is the physiological counterpart of their essential childishness—their desire for instant gratification and their belligerent tantrums when thwarted.

Another hypothesis is that the sociopath is cortically underaroused, as if he were not fully awake under normal conditions. Proponents of this hypothesis argue that because of this underarousal, sociopaths actively seek stimulation—they are easily bored and court thrills and danger to rouse themselves to some optimal level of stimulation, much as the rest of us might pinch our arms to keep ourselves from dozing off (Quay, 1965; Hare, 1978).★

Such physiological differences suggest that there may be a constitutional predisposition toward sociopathy. This predisposition may well be genetic, as shown by the fact that identical twins have higher concordance rates on sociopathy than fraternal twins. Early environment also plays a role. There is considerable evidence that sociopaths are more likely to have a sociopathic or alcoholic father than are normals. An additional factor is discipline; inconsistent discipline in childhood or no discipline at all correlates with sociopathy in adulthood (Robins, 1966).

SOCIOPATHY AND THE DISORDER CONCEPT

By now, we are starting to get some understanding of how sociopathy might come about. But does that justify our calling it a mental disorder? There is some doubt whether it really does. Certainly the sociopath often comes to grief, but so do ordinary criminals and for the same reason: They get caught. Why should we call the one ill and the other bad? Why should one be the province of the mental-health system while the other is the business of the courts? The question is especially pertinent given the fact that most mental-health practitioners are pessimistic about the possibility of therapy for sociopaths. An additional difficulty lies in differential diagnosis, for in actual practice it can be difficult to distinguish sociopaths from ordinary criminals. Under the circumstances, it is not obvious what is gained by classifying sociopathy as a mental disorder.

THE SCOPE OF PSYCHOPATHOLOGY

Sociopathy is only one of the questionable categories in the psychiatric catalogue. Similar questions can be raised about drug addiction or alcoholism or a number of other deviant patterns. Are these really mental disorders in the sense in which schizophrenia and obsessive-compulsive disorder are? When the term is applied so widely that it includes virtually all forms of human behavior that cause personal unhappiness, it has become so vague that it is in danger of losing its meaning.

★ This suggests a relation to sensation seeking, which shows a similar pattern (see Chapter 16, pp. 657–58).

The imperialism of modern psychopathology that makes it try to subsume ever more conditions is not solely the fault of an ambitious mental-health establishment, however. Instead, it is in part the product of a society that insists on quick and simple solutions. We think that by designating a given human or social problem a mental disorder we have somehow taken a stride toward its solution. But we've really done nothing of the sort. For calling a problem—alcoholism, sexual exhibitionism, drug addiction, or even premenstrual syndrome—a mental disorder does not necessarily make it so. Nor does it mean that we therefore know what to do about it.

SUMMARY

1. The field of *psychopathology,* which is sometimes called *abnormal psychology,* deals with a wide assortment of disorders that generally cause considerable anguish and seriously impair the person's functioning.

2. In certain periods of history, mental disorder was seen as a form of demonic possession. In others, as in our own, it was regarded as a form of illness. Some of these disorders are *somatogenic,* being the result of a bodily malfunction. An example is *general paresis,* which was discovered to result from a syphilitic infection contracted years before. Other mental disorders are thought to be *psychogenic,* resulting from psychological rather than organic causes, a view that seemed to apply to many cases then called *hysteria* (now called *conversion disorder*).

3. A very general conception of psychopathology is provided by the *underlying pathology model,* which makes psychopathology analogous to physical disorders. A given disorder has various signs and symptoms that form a pattern or *syndrome;* these, plus the course of the illness, are the bases for diagnosis and classification. The classification system now in use is set out in *DSM-IV,* the current diagnostic manual of psychiatry.

4. According to the underlying pathology model, the signs and symptoms of a disorder are thought to result from some underlying and relatively immediate (or *proximate*) cause, the pathology. Many disorders seem well described by the *diathesis-stress* conception, which proposes the interaction of various predispositions (diatheses) with various precipitants (stressors). As formulated here, the underlying pathology model is largely descriptive and makes no assertion about the nature of the signs and symptoms, their psychogenic or somatogenic causes, or the appropriate modes of treatment. Three subcategories of the underlying pathology model are the *medical model,* the *psychoanalytic model,* and the *learning model.*

5. Probably the most serious condition in psychopathology is *schizophrenia.* Its main symptoms are disorders of cognition, social withdrawal, disruption of emotional responding, and in many cases, the construction of a private world accompanied by *delusions* and *hallucinations.* Subcategories of schizophrenia used in current classification include the *paranoid, catatonic,* and *disorganized* subtypes.

6. One question about the pathology of schizophrenia is how best to characterize the schizophrenic's underlying *psychological malfunction.* Many authors believe that it is fundamentally a disorder of thought, based on an inability to retain the context of one's thoughts and actions.

7. The search for the biological basis of schizophrenia has focused on two possible kinds of pathology. One involves a malfunctioning of neurotransmitters, specifically an oversensitivity to *dopamine.* Evidence comes from the therapeutic effect of *antipsychotic medications,* which are known to block dopamine at neuron synapses. Another organic pathology involves an atrophy of brain tissue found in some schizophrenics. According to the *two-syndrome hypothesis,* schizophrenia is really a composite of two underlying pathologies. According to this hypothesis, one type (Type I schizophrenia) is caused by a

neurotransmitter malfunction and produces *positive symptoms,* such as delusions and hallucinations. The second type (called Type II schizophrenia) is caused by cerebral atrophy and leads to *negative symptoms,* such as withdrawal and apathy. Support for this view comes from the fact that patients with mostly positive symptoms respond well to standard antipsychotics and show little cerebral damage, while patients with mostly negative symptoms are not improved by standard antipsychotics and are more likely to show brain damage.

8. More ultimate causes of schizophrenia include a genetic factor. The evidence is provided by *concordance* studies of identical and fraternal twins and by studies of children of schizophrenic mothers adopted shortly after birth. But this genetic factor is only a predisposition; its conversion into the actual schizophrenic disorder depends on some precipitating environmental stress. Some investigators believe that the critical environmental factors include socioeconomic class and pathological interactions within the family. The most influential current model of schizophrenia considers it a *neurodevelopmental disorder* in which a genetic predisposition produces abnormal fetal brain development that leaves the individual vulnerable to later stress.

9. In another group of conditions, the *mood disorders,* the dominant disturbance is one of mood, as in the frenzied energy of *mania* or the despair and lethargy of *depression.* One form of mood disorder is *bipolar disorder,* with recurrent swings from one emotional extreme to the other. Another is *major depression,* in which the mood extreme is generally depression. Still another is *seasonal affective disorder,* which seems to be related to the amount of light patients are exposed to, with depressions that start in the fall and end in the spring.

10. According to one view, mood disorders, especially bipolar disorder, are produced by an organic pathology, a belief bolstered by evidence that such conditions have a genetic component. Bipolar disorder may arise from instabilities of neuronal membranes. For major depression, one hypothesis proposes a defect in the supply of certain neurotransmitters, in particular, *norepinephrine* and *serotonin.* Other investigators stress the role of psychogenic factors, such as cognitive outlook. An influential example of such a psychogenic view is the *learned helplessness theory* of depression. Some of its more recent extensions stress the role of *attributional style* and of *hopelessness.*

11. Another group of conditions are the *anxiety disorders.* One such disorder is *specific phobia,* in which there is an intense and irrational fear of some object or situation. According to the *preparedness theory,* such phobias are based on built-in predispositions to fear certain stimuli that were dangerous to our primate ancestors. Other phobias are more pervasive, such as *social phobia,* a general fear of humiliation and avoidance of relevant situations. In *obsessive-compulsive disorder,* the anxiety is produced by internal wishes or events, such as obsessions that cannot be stopped. In *generalized anxiety disorder* it is all pervasive and free floating. In *panic disorder,* which is often accompanied by *agoraphobia,* there are sudden, vehement attacks that strike out of the blue. In *post-traumatic stress disorder,* there is a reaction to especially stressful events such as fires, war, and rape, which usually starts with an initial period of *dissociation,* followed by severe aftereffects, including recurrent nightmares, waking flashbacks, and "survival guilt."

12. Another way of handling anxiety is through *dissociation.* Chief among the dissociative disorders is *dissociative identity disorder,* which has been somewhat controversially linked to early childhood sexual abuse.

13. Another group are the *somatoform disorders,* characterized by the presence of bodily signs and symptoms that have no apparent organic basis. The somatoform disorders include the classic but now-rare disorder that inspired psychoanalysis, *conversion disorder.*

14. In *psychophysiological conditions,* psychogenic causes have genuine organic consequences. An example is *coronary heart disease,* which is more likely in people with elements of the *Type A behavior pattern.*

15. The problem of defining psychopathology is acute for conditions such as *antisocial personality disorder* (or *sociopathy*) in which deviance overlaps mental disorder and criminality. The causes of sociopathy are still unknown; hypotheses include cortical immaturity, a chronic state of underarousal that leads to attempts to seek continued stimulation, and a genetic predisposition.

CHAPTER **19**

TREATMENT OF PSYCHOPATHOLOGY

BIOLOGICAL THERAPIES   763

PHARMACOTHERAPIES ■ EVALUATING A MEDICATION ■ PSYCHOSURGERY
■CONVULSIVE TREATMENTS

PSYCHOTHERAPY   772

CLASSICAL PSYCHOANALYSIS ■ PSYCHODYNAMIC THERAPY ■ BEHAVIOR
THERAPY ■ COGNITIVE-BEHAVIORAL THERAPIES ■ HUMANISTIC
THERAPIES ■ SOME COMMON THEMES ■ EXTENSIONS OF
PSYCHOTHERAPY

EVALUATING THERAPEUTIC
OUTCOME   789

DOES PSYCHOTHERAPY WORK? ■ COMPARING DIFFERENT THERAPIES

A CENTURY OF THERAPY   795

SUMMARY   796

What can be done to help those who suffer from mental disorders? There is no scarcity of therapeutic methods, each with its own adherents. Some rely on biological interventions such as medications. Others approach the condition at the psychological level through various kinds of psychotherapy. Until recently, the proven benefits of these interventions were relatively modest. Of late, the outlook is more optimistic. There are no miracle cures, but at least some disorders seem to respond reasonably well to certain biological and/or psychological treatments.

BIOLOGICAL THERAPIES

One approach to treatment is to make direct changes in various bodily systems. Such *biological therapies* characterize medicine's classical attack on any disease. Thus, once mental disorder was conceived as an illness, it was only natural to try to heal it with the traditional tools of the physician's trade. Until fairly recently, such attempts were largely unsuccessful, with the would-be cures often far worse than the disease. We already mentioned a very early example: *trephining,* the removal of pieces of skull bone, a prehistoric practice that persisted into the Middle Ages. Other early procedures involved a relentless succession of bloodlettings and purgatives, all intended somehow to restore harmony among the bodily humors. Later developments were hardly milder. For example, Benjamin Rush (1745–1813), one of the signers of the Declaration of Independence and the acknowledged father of American psychiatry, submersed patients in hot or cold water until they were just short of drowning, or twirled them on special devices at speeds that rendered them unconscious (see Figure 19.1 on the next page). Such methods were said to reestablish balance between bodily and mental functions. They almost certainly had no such salutary effects, although they were probably welcomed by hospital attendants, since such methods undoubtedly terrified the inmates and thus helped to "keep order" (Mora, 1975).

PHARMACOTHERAPIES

The bleak outlook for biological therapies did not brighten until the turn of the century. The first step was the conquest of the global, progressively disabling syndrome of general paresis, accomplished by attacking the syphilitic infection that caused it (see Chapter 18). But the major advances have come only during the last forty years or so with the discovery and development of a number of medications that seem to control, or at least moderate, the manifestations of schizophrenia and the affective and anxiety disorders.

A

B

C

19.1 Early methods for treating mental disorder *(A) A crib for violent patients. (Courtesy of Historical Pictures Service) (B) A centrifugal-force bed. (Courtesy of National Library of Medicine) (C) A swinging device. (Courtesy of Culver Pictures)*

These medications have had an enormous impact upon mental-health care. They have allowed many patients to be treated without hospitalization, and for many disorders, they are now routinely prescribed not only by psychiatrists, but by primary-care physicians, such as general and family practitioners (Olfson and Klerman, 1993).

DRUG TREATMENT OF SCHIZOPHRENIA: ANTIPSYCHOTICS

In the last chapter, we saw that one of the major arguments for a biochemical theory of schizophrenia was the effectiveness of certain drugs called **antipsychotics.** The most common of these drugs include Thorazine and Haldol. (Here, and in further text discussions, we only give the drug's trade name. Its technical name, the biochemical family it belongs to, and some related drugs that have similar effects are shown in Table 19.1.) These medications tend to reduce many of the major manifestations of schizophrenia, such as thought disorder and hallucinations. They are believed to act mainly by blocking synaptic receptors in pathways of the brain that are sensitive to dopamine. It is this blockade and the resultant decrease in dopamine activity that are generally thought to produce the therapeutic effects.

It is sometimes said that drugs like Thorazine and Haldol are not really antipsychotic agents at all but are only fancy sedatives—"chemical straitjackets"—that quiet patients down. This argument does not square with the facts. While Thorazine and similar drugs alleviate schizophrenic symptoms, such powerful sedatives as phenobarbital have no such effect. They put the patient to sleep, but when he wakes up, his delusions and hallucinations will be just as they were before. Other evidence suggests that the antipsychotics act specifically on schizophrenic signs and symptoms, but have only minor effects on those of other disorders. For example, they help to clear up the patient's disordered thought but have little effect on depression or anxiety. It is thus hardly surprising that antipsychotics are rarely used to calm down normals or patients with anxiety disorders (Davis, 1985a; Hollister and Csernansky, 1990).

The social reality of treating schizophrenics Because they allowed many schizophrenic patients to be managed outside of mental hospitals, the classic antipsychotics lent impetus to a movement called **deinstitutionalization,** which was intended to obtain better and less expensive care for patients in their own communities—at local community mental-health centers rather than at large, centralized hospitals. In part, this movement worked. Whereas in the 1950s

TABLE 19.1 SOME COMMONLY USED PSYCHOTROPIC MEDICATIONS			
Primary Function	*Drug Class*	*Chemical Name*	*Trade (Commercial) Name*
Antidepressants	MAO inhibitors	Phenelzine Tranylcypromine	Nardil Parnate
	Tricyclics	Clomipramine Imipramine	Anafranil Tofranil
	Selective serotonin reuptake inhibitors	Fluoxetine Sertaline	Prozac Zoloft
Antipsychotics	Butyrophenones	Haloperidol	Haldol
	Phenothiazines	Chlorpromazine	Thorazine
	Atypical antipsychotics	Clozapine Resperidone	Clozaril Resperdol
Antimanic medications		Lithium carbonate	Eskalith
Anxiety-reducing medications (anxiolytics)	Benzodiazepines	Chlordiazepoxide Diazepam	Librium Valium

mental hospitals housed about 600,000 patients, by the 1980s this number had dropped to 125,000. The new drugs made it possible to discharge schizophrenic patients more quickly than ever before. According to one estimate, prior to the introduction of these drugs, two out of three schizophrenic patients spent most of their lives in the state asylum. In the 1980s, their average stay was about two months (Lamb, 1984; Davis, 1985a; see Figure 19.2).

But it soon became apparent that the situation was not as hopeful as it first appeared. For while the antipsychotic medications help to alleviate the symptoms of the disorder, they still leave much to be desired as a treatment. They only hold the manifestations of schizophrenia in check so long as they are taken; they neither cure the disease nor alter its progress. They tend to work more on positive symptoms like delusions and hallucinations and do little for negative symptoms like apathy, emotional blunting, and poor sociability. In addition, they have potent side effects that can include sedation, constipation, dry mouth, blurred vision, difficulty in urination, cardiac irregularities, tremors and muscle spasms, restlessness, a shuffling gait, and a curiously inexpressive, masklike face. Some patients who take them over the long term will eventually develop permanent motor disorders (Hollister and Csernansky, 1990).

One result of all these side effects is that many schizophrenic patients refuse to take their medicines reliably, and the flare-up of their signs and symptoms can eventuate in repeated hospitalizations, producing a "revolving-door patient." Even when patients do take their antipsychotics regularly, 30 to 50 percent of patients have recurrent outbreaks of the illness and need further hospitalization or a change of dosage or type of medication (Andreasen and Black, 1991). As a consequence, although fewer schizophrenics remain in mental hospitals and do not stay in the hospital as long (Lamb, 1984; Davis, 1985a; see Figure 19.2), the number of times they are readmitted for short stays has increased by

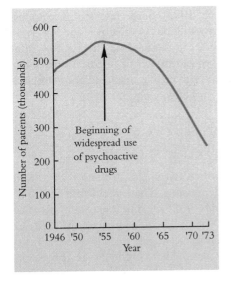

19.2 Number of residents in state and local government mental hospitals, 1946–1973 in the United States *(Based on data from U.S. Public Health Service)*

Some adverse effects of deinstitutionalization *Some of the homeless in American cities may be persons discharged from mental hospitals who are unable to make an adjustment to the world outside. (Courtesy of AP/Wide World Photos)*

80 percent since the 1960s (Rosenstein, Milazzo-Sayre, and Manderscheid, 1989).

What do schizophrenic patients do when they are discharged from the hospital? Some stay at home with their aging parents. Others live in less than ideal board-and-care homes, while still others become drifters and join the swelling ranks of the homeless. According to a recent report, some 40 percent of New York City's homeless people suffer persistent mental disorder or have a history of mental illness (Golden, 1990). Such findings make it clear that while the antipsychotic drugs help to alleviate the symptoms of schizophrenia, they do not provide a cure. Given the current inadequacy—and in many cases, the complete lack—of appropriate community services, this represents, at least for now, a failure to achieve the intentions of deinstitutionalization (Jones, 1983; Lamb, 1984; Westermeyer, 1987).

Advances in antipsychotic medications   Classic antipsychotics such as Thorazine and Haldol not only have a host of side effects; they also have another drawback: They are ineffective in up to 20 percent of patients, who tend to be the Type II schizophrenics we discussed previously (See Chapter 18, pp. 731–32).

Some new antipsychotics may circumvent some of these problems. The most commonly used of these new medications is Clozaril, which seems to reduce positive symptoms and also restores many of the deficits seen in the negative symptoms (Kane et al., 1988; Meltzer et al., 1990; Kane and Marder, 1993). In part, these new antipsychotics achieve their effect much like their classic predecessors: by blocking dopamine neurotransmission. According to some authors, their enhanced benefits—especially on negative symptoms—may be produced by their effect on other neurotransmitters, particularly norepinephrine or serotonin. It may also be produced by a more selective effect on some particular group of dopamine neurons rather than on all (Tandon and Kane, 1993).

Unfortunately, while Clozaril has its benefits, it also has some drawbacks. The main impediment to its widespread use is that, as a new drug, it is quite expensive (Reid, Pham, and Rago, 1993). Second, between 1 and 2 percent of patients taking Clozaril develop a potentially fatal blood disorder, necessitating regular and careful blood testing (Alvir et al., 1993). Some research now underway may lead to similar medications that will be as effective but less risky (Meltzer, 1993). One contender is the new drug Resperdol. There is thus considerable hope that this new generation of antipsychotic medications, when delivered to all who can benefit from them, will enable many sufferers of schizophrenia to function more independently and effectively.

DRUG TREATMENT OF DEPRESSION: ANTIDEPRESSANTS

Shortly after the introduction of antipsychotics, two major groups of drugs were found that seemed to act specifically on depression. These antidepressants were of two major classes, the **monoamine oxidase (MAO) inhibitors** such as Nardil and the **tricyclic antidepressants** such as Tofranil (see Table 19.1, p. 765). Of these, the tricyclics became the most widely used, mostly because the chemistry of MAO inhibitors requires that patients conform to difficult dietary restrictions.

Most investigators believe that both the MAO inhibitors and tricyclic antidepressants work by increasing the amount of norepinephrine and serotonin available for synaptic transmission. (The mechanisms whereby they accomplish this mission are different; for details, see Figure 19.3). These medications are very effective in counteracting depression in up to 65 percent of the patients who take them (Hollister and Csernansky, 1990). Not all of them work for all

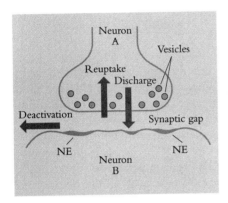

19.3   A schematic presentation of two ways in which a drug may increase the available supply of a neurotransmitter   *A neurotransmitter, norephinephrine (NE), is discharged by Neuron A into the synaptic gap and diffuses across the gap to stimulate Neuron B. The more NE accumulates at the membrane of Neuron B, the more that neuron will fire. The amount of NE at the synapse is diminished in several ways. One is* reuptake, *a process in which NE is pumped back into Neuron A. Another is* deactivation, *a process whereby certain enzymes (such as monoamine oxidase or MAO) break down the neurotransmitter and render it ineffective. Tricyclics and MAO inhibitors are antidepressants that increase the amount of available NE (and serotonin) at the synaptic junction but that accomplish this in different ways. Tricyclics do so by interfering with neurotransmitter uptake; MAO inhibitors do so by preventing MAO from breaking the transmitters down. Second-generation antidepressants like Prozac work similarly, except that they act selectively upon serotonin neurons.*

patients, however. Some patients may have somewhat different biochemical deficits and thus may do better with an MAO inhibitor than a tricyclic antidepressant, or vice versa. Furthermore, even within each class of antidepressant, some patients may respond better to one medication than another. There is some evidence that by using blood tests and the like a patient can be matched to the proper antidepressant drug (Maugh, 1981; Davis, 1985b), but the selection of medication is in most cases a matter of clinical judgment.

The use of medication for treating depression changed dramatically in 1988 with the introduction of the first "designer drug" for depression, Prozac (Kramer, 1993). Prozac was engineered in the laboratory to act minimally upon norepinephrine and maximally upon serotonin, and it became the most prominent of the new class of antidepressants known as ***selective serotonin reuptake inhibitors*** (see Table 19.1). They reduce the manifestations of depression as fast and as completely as the MAO inhibitors or the tricyclics, but they have far fewer side effects and are thus safer to prescribe—so safe that most are now prescribed (and perhaps overprescribed) not by psychiatrists but by personal physicians (Olfson and Klerman, 1993). But while these antidepressants have been regarded by many as panaceas, like all medications they, too, have their side effects. The most substantial side effect from Prozac can be a loss of sexual desire, which can occur in up to 30 percent of patients, but which can be countered in some patients with additional medication (Hollander and McCarley, 1992; Jacobsen, 1992).

Regardless of the type of antidepressant, medications are usually taken for the duration of the depressive episode and then are withdrawn cautiously. For some patients with chronic depression, antidepressant medications may be a lifelong affair. Just as the antipsychotics are not true sedatives, so the antidepressants are not stimulants. Evidence comes from the fact that these drugs do not produce euphoria in normals; they evidently have little effect on mood if there is no depression to begin with (Cole and Davis, 1975). Even so, the label "antidepressant" may give them far too little credit, because they are often quite useful in alleviating the distress of many other conditions, including panic disorder, migraine headache, school phobia, eating disorders like bulimia, and chronic pain (Hollister and Csernansky, 1990; Olfson and Klerman, 1993; Sheean, 1985). It turns out that certain antidepressants such as the tricyclic Anafranil and several selective serotonin reuptake inhibitors are also effective in many cases of obsessive-compulsive disorder (Ananth, 1985; Rapaport 1989; Dominguez, 1992).

DRUG TREATMENT OF BIPOLAR DISORDER: LITHIUM

Another pharmacological development is the use of lithium salts such as ***lithium carbonate*** in the treatment of bipolar disorder (see Table 19.1, p. 765). Most manic episodes subside within five or ten days after patients start lithium therapy. There is some further evidence that the drug can also forestall the depressive episodes in bipolar disorder. Just what accounts for these effects is largely unknown. According to one hypothesis, lithium carbonate may reregulate neurotransmission by stabilizing the influence of calcium on neuronal membranes (Meltzer, 1986; Wood and Goodwin, 1987).

DRUG TREATMENT OF ANXIETY: ANXIOLYTICS

When patients suffer from disabling anxiety, they are often treated with medications that are popularly called tranquilizers and technically known as ***anxiolytics*** (see Table 19.1, p. 765). The most common kinds of anxiolytics work by increasing neurotransmission at synapses containing the neurotransmitter GABA. Some of these medications, such as Valium and Xanax, are prescribed so often that their names have almost become household words. They are useful as short-term treatments for generalized anxiety disorder, post-traumatic stress disorder, alcohol withdrawal, insomnia, muscle spasms and tension headaches, and various other stress-related disorders. They are rarely used for long-term treatment because, unlike the medications we have reviewed thus far, they are highly addictive and interact dangerously with alcohol. Some newer anxiolytics such as Buspar are not addicting and have become popular substitutes for the older group of anxiolytics for patients who are prone to drug abuse or will have to take the medications over a long period of time.

EVALUATING A MEDICATION

How can we assess the effectiveness of a medication? We will discuss this issue in detail, because some of the issues raised by drug evaluation methods extend beyond tests of drug therapy. In large part, they apply to the evaluation of any therapeutic procedure whatever, including psychotherapy.

Suppose we want to find out whether a given drug, say Thorazine, has palliative effects on the manifestations of schizophrenia. The most obvious approach is to administer the drug to a group of schizophrenic patients for some period and then make a before-and-after assessment. In fact, many of the clinical studies are of just this kind. But a little reflection shows that relying only on this procedure would be mistaken.

CONTROLLING FOR SPONTANEOUS IMPROVEMENT

One problem with a simple before-and-after assessment is that it ignores the possibility that the patient's condition would have cleared up without treatment, whether permanently or just for a while. Such spontaneous improvements occur in many disorders (though not often in schizophrenia). To control for this factor, one has to compare two groups of patients drawn from the same population. One group would receive the drug for, say, six weeks; a control group would not. Both groups would be assessed at the start and the end of the study (and perhaps at intervals in between). Initially, they ought to be equivalent. The question is whether they will be different when the six weeks are up.

CONTROLLING FOR PLACEBO EFFECTS

Suppose that after six weeks the patients who were given Thorazine seem to be less bothered by hallucinations and delusions than the untreated controls. That the treated group fared better than the untreated one minimizes the odds that the change was due to spontaneous improvement. Indeed, one might guess at this point that the benefits of treatment were caused by the drug directly. Unfortunately, we still cannot make this claim, because we have not controlled for the possibility that the result was due to the *placebo effect.*

In medicine, the term *placebo* refers to some inert (that is, medically neutral) substance that is administered to a patient who believes it to have certain therapeutic powers, although it actually has none. Numerous studies have shown that, given this belief, many patients will make some kind of improvement after taking disguised sugar pills or receiving injections of harmless salt solutions. Such placebo effects probably account for many of the cures of ancient physicians whose medications included such items as crocodile dung, swine teeth, and moss scraped from the skull of a man who died a violent death (Shapiro, 1971).

Given the power of the placebo effect, how can we be sure that the improvement in the drug-treated group of our example is caused by the properties of the drug itself? Perhaps a sugar pill—or a bit of crocodile dung—would have done as well. To exclude this possibility, we must administer a placebo to the control patients. They will thus no longer be "untreated." On the contrary, they will receive the same attention, will be told the same thing, and will be given the same number of pills at the same time as the patients in the true drug group. There will be only one difference between the two groups: The control patients will swallow pills that, unbeknownst to them, contain only inert materials. As a result of this stratagem, we achieve simultaneous control for two factors—spontaneous improvement and placebo effects. Now that these two factors are controlled, a difference in the way the two groups appear after treatment can finally be attributed to the effect of the drug itself. Figure 19.4 shows the results of such a study, comparing the effects of Thorazine and a placebo after one, three, and six weeks of treatment. As the figure shows, Thorazine was clearly superior. But as the figure also shows, some slight improvement is found in the placebo group as well, thus highlighting the need for such a control in the evaluation of drug effectiveness.

What explains placebo effects? Some of them may be the result of **endorphins,** chemicals produced by the brain itself that act like opiates and reduce pain (see Chapter 3). Evidence for this view comes from a study in which pain was reduced by a placebo medication that the patients believed was a pain reliever. But this relief stopped as soon as the patients received a dose of a drug that is known to counteract the effects of any opiate (Levine, Gordon, and Fields, 1979).

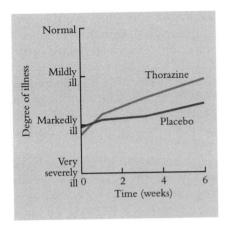

19.4 Controlling for placebo effects
Severity of illness over a six-week period during which patients were treated with either Thorazine or a placebo.

CONTROLLING FOR EXPECTATIONS

By definition, a placebo control implies that all of the patients in the group think that they are being treated with the real medicine. But to guarantee this desired state of ignorance, the physicians—and the psychologists and social workers and nurses and attendants—must also be kept in the dark about who is getting a placebo and who the real medication, for the true information may affect their ratings of the patients' progress. If they believe in the medicine's effectiveness, they may exaggerate signs of improvement in members of the medicated group.

The staff members' knowledge may also have a more indirect effect. They may unwittingly communicate it to the patients, perhaps by observing the medicated ones more closely or by being less concerned if a placebo-treated patient fails to take her morning pill. By such signals, the patients may find out whether the physicians expect them to get better or not. If so, there is no genuine placebo control. To guard against such confounding effects of expectation, modern medication evaluators use the **double-blind technique** in which neither the staff members nor the patients know who is assigned to which group. The only ones who know are the investigators who run the study.

There are still problems with using placebos in double-blind studies of medication effectiveness. First, in many cases it is unethical to give a placebo and thereby withhold an accepted treatment. Second, it is often easy to discern who is taking actual medication from those patients receiving placebos, because many medications have characteristic side effects that are hard for either the patient or the investigator to ignore. Finally, researchers seldom want to know if a new medication is better than nothing; they want to know whether it's better than the standard treatment. For all of these reasons, the most common research practice is to assess a new medication's incremental effectiveness against the best current treatment. In this kind of study, no one is deprived of an actual treatment, placebo effects are controlled with the current-treatment group, and differences in side effects are less obvious between the groups. Finally, in this kind of study even if patients respond no differently to the new medications than they do to the accepted medications, the results may have an impact, because one medication may be cheaper or safer than the other.

LIMITATIONS OF PHARMACOTHERAPY

In our discussion of common kinds of psychotropic medications, we have taken pains to indicate their effectiveness. But we have also noted their two chief limitations, that they do not help everyone and that many of them have unpleasant side effects. These side effects can be regarded simply as a cost exacted by the drugs. But how great are the drugs' benefits? Critics of pharmacotherapy contend that currently the beneficial results of drug therapy are still quite limited. This is especially so for patients taking the classic antipsychotics and antimanic medications, who must remain on a maintenance dose to minimize their disability but who often quit taking their medicine because they find the side effects so unpleasant.

This criticism is less compelling in the case of antidepressants and anxiolytics, which sometimes do for patients with mood and anxiety disorders what insulin does for patients with diabetes: They don't cure the disease, but they sometimes do a fine job of controlling it.

Despite their limitations, the modern drug therapies are a major step forward. They have restored some patients to normal functioning and have allowed those who would otherwise have spent much of their lives in hospital wards to manage, however imperfectly, in a family or community setting. No less important is the fact that these drugs—especially the antipsychotics—have completely changed the atmosphere of mental hospitals, especially the large state-run facilities. Until a few decades ago, straitjackets were common, as were feces-smeared and shriek-filled wards; today, such scenes are comparatively rare because the medications can so effectively control the more florid manifestations of mental disorder. As a result, the modern mental hospital can function more as a therapeutic center than a warehouse. It can provide important social and psychological services, including vocational counseling and psychotherapy, all of which would have been unthinkable in the "snake-pit" settings of former times.

PSYCHOSURGERY

Until the advent of the major psychotropic drugs, psychiatrists relied on several other biological therapies, all of which involved drastic assaults on the nervous system. Some of these consisted of *psychosurgery*, or surgery on the brain. In prefrontal lobotomy, for example, the neurological connections between the thalamus and the frontal lobes are severed, in whole or in part. This operation was meant to liberate the patient's thoughts from the pathological influence of his emotions, on the dubious neurological assumption that thought and emotion were localized in the frontal lobes and the thalamus, respectively. Evaluations of these early surgical procedures revealed ambiguous and even deleterious results on cognitive functions and led to extreme caution in their application (Maher, 1966; Robbin, 1958; Valenstein, 1986).

Psychosurgery has reemerged, but the psychosurgery of today has been refined considerably, both in the surgical procedures used and the patients judged suitable for them (Rappaport, 1992). The surgeries themselves now precisely locate and create lesions in very specific brain areas instead of disconnecting or destroying whole lobes or regions. In the vast majority of cases, psychosurgery is reserved for those patients who are severely disabled and show no improvement after all other medical or psychotherapeutic alternatives have been exhausted. In patients with intractable depression, severe obsessive-compulsive disorder, and chronic pain psychosurgery is often beneficial, and the risks are usually tolerable compared to the severe level of the patients' ongoing disability (Davies and Weeks, 1993; Hay et al., 1993).

CONVULSIVE TREATMENTS

Another form of biological therapy involves the deliberate production of convulsive seizures. Today, the most widely used form of the convulsive method is *electroconvulsive therapy (ECT),* sometimes colloquially called "shock treatment." For about half a second a current of moderate intensity is passed between two electrodes attached to each side of the patient's forehead. The result is a 30- to 60-second convulsive seizure similar to that seen in epilepsy (Figure 19.5). When this treatment first came into use, patients were conscious and sometimes suffered serious bruises or bone fractures while thrashing about during their convulsions. Modern ECT actually looks very mild. Patients are given a short-acting anesthetic to render them temporarily unconscious, and muscle relaxants to reduce the manifestations of the seizure to a few slight muscle twitches. The usual course of ECT treatments is six to ten sessions over a period of a week or two. After each treatment, the patient may experience a brief period of nausea and confusion but is usually fine within a few hours (Andreasen and Black, 1991).

ECT was originally meant as a treatment of schizophrenia, but evaluation studies soon showed that it is most effective in depression. Here, its efficacy is considerable. It works for as many as 70 to 80 percent of patients who have not

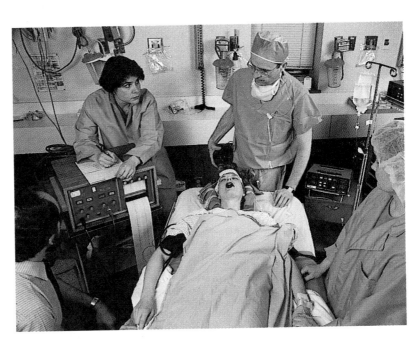

19.5   Patient about to undergo electro-convulsive shock treatment   (Photograph by James D. Wilson/Woodfin Camp)

responded to any antidepressant medication (Janicak et al., 1985; Andreasen and Black, 1991) or who cannot take such medications because of overdose potential or other medical problems. In addition, ECT seems to act more quickly than antidepressant medications usually do (Weiner, 1984b, 1985).

Despite these advantages, the use of ECT is highly controversial. The main reason is the potential for memory impairment that in some cases lasts for months or even longer (Squire, 1977; Breggin, 1979; for discussion, see Weiner, 1984a, 1984b). Under the circumstances, ECT is generally used only after drug therapy has failed or when there seems to be a serious chance of suicide. In the latter case, the fast-acting quality of ECT treatment may be an overriding advantage (Andreasen and Black, 1991). Because of the speed with which ECT brings relief, several ways of minimizing psychological or physical damage have been attempted. One is to apply the current in very brief pulses to just one cerebral hemisphere (typically, the nondominant one), which apparently lessens memory impairment and other side effects but does not diminish the therapeutic effect (Inglis, 1969; Welch et al., 1982; Squire and Zouzounis, 1986).

What accounts for the therapeutic effects of ECT? As yet, we have little more than speculation. According to one hypothesis, ECT leads to heightened activation of certain neural pathways, which increases the availability of norepinephrine and serotonin in the brain (Weiner, 1984b, 1985).

PSYCHOTHERAPY

Biological manipulations represent one approach to the treatment of psychopathology. But as we have already seen, there is another approach to the treatment of such disorders that forgoes all direct ministrations to the patient's body and instead relies on psychological means alone. Such attempts to treat mental disturbance by psychological rather than biological methods are here grouped together under the general label *psychotherapy.*

There are many different approaches to psychotherapy. A major difference among them is in their conceptions of psychopathology. Some approaches are based upon psychoanalysis and emphasize unconscious conflicts. Others rely on behavioral findings from animal and human experimentation. Still others take a cognitive approach and argue that many mental disorders arise from faulty thinking. A final, humanistic outlook espouses the importance of the concept of free will and views "disorder" as a failure to build a life that is expanding, fulfilling, and meaningful.

Given how much these perspectives differ in their basic view of psychopathology, it is hardly surprising that they differ greatly in how they say it should be treated. Here we will discuss five forms of psychotherapy that are conducted with individual patients: (1) classical psychoanalysis, (2) modern offshoots of psychoanalysis, (3) behavior therapy, (4) cognitive therapy, and (5) humanistic therapy.

CLASSICAL PSYCHOANALYSIS

Classical psychoanalysis is the method Sigmund Freud developed at the turn of this century. According to some writers, this technique is the ancestor of virtually all forms of modern psychotherapy, whether they acknowl-

An early attempt at psychotherapy   *The biblical King Saul was subject to severe bouts of rage and depression but was apparently calmed by listening to young David playing the harp. (Rembrandt's* David Playing the Harp Before Saul; *photograph © Foundation Johan Maurits van Nassau. Courtesy of Mauritshuis, The Hague)*

edge this heritage or not (London, 1964). Freud's basic assumption was that his patients' ills (in his terms, their neuroses) stemmed from unconscious defenses against unacceptable urges that date back to early childhood. By adulthood, many of these defenses are useless relics, a mental blanket the neurotic has drawn over his head that prevents him from seeing both the outer world and his own inner world as they really are. These defenses become manifest as psychological symptoms, bodily malfunctions, or tendencies to repeat outdated and by now utterly unadaptive patterns of behavior (see Chapter 17).

Freud believed that to overcome his neurosis, the patient must drop his mental blanket, must achieve access to his buried thoughts and wishes, and gain insight into why he buried them. By so doing, he will master the internal conflicts that crippled him for so long. Once these are resolved, his symptoms will presumably wither away by themselves. In effect, Freud's prescription for the neuroses is the victory of reason over passion: "Where id was, there shall ego be."

THE RECOVERY OF UNCONSCIOUS MEMORIES

The origin of psychoanalytic technique dates back to Freud's attempts to treat hysteria by helping the patient recover some emotionally charged memories (see Chapter 17). Initially, Freud and his then collaborator, Josef Breuer, probed for these memories while their patients were hypnotized. Later on it became clear that such memories could be dug up even in the normal waking state by the method of *free association.* The patient was asked to say whatever came into his mind, and sooner or later the relevant memory was likely to emerge. Various forms of *resistance,* usually unconscious, by which the patient tried to derail a given train of thought—by changing the topic, forgetting what he was about to say, and so on—often gave important clues that the patient was about to remember something he had previously tried to forget. In addition to free association, Freud later asked his patients to tell him their dreams, and he began to interpret nearly any action—whether a slip of the tongue, or the wiggling of a foot on the couch, or a particular choice of words, or whether the patient was late or early for the sessions—as clues to the identity of their neurotic conflicts.

In popularized movie or TV versions, this dredging up of forgotten memories is often presented as the essence of psychoanalysis. The distraught heroine finally remembers a childhood scene in which she was spanked for a little sister's misdeed, suddenly a weight lifts from her shoulders, she rises from the couch reborn, is ready to face life and love serenely, and will live happily—or at least unneurotically—ever after. But as Freud described it, what actually happens is much less dramatic. The discovery of the patient's unconscious conflicts comes bit by bit, as a memory surfaces here, a dream or a slip of the tongue suggests a meaning there, and as the analyst offers an occasional interpretation of the resistances that crop up in a given session. To help the patient see how all of these strands of her mental life are woven together is one of the analyst's main tasks.

EMOTIONAL INSIGHT

Psychoanalysts want their patients to attain *insight* into the motives of which they were formerly unaware, but they don't want that insight to be merely intellectual. The patient must regain access, not just to various repressed thoughts and memories, but also and more importantly, to the *feelings* that go along with them. Freud was emphatic that recollections without emotions have little therapeutic effect. Genuine self-discovery is only achieved when the patient rids himself of the repressive forces that had kept the insights from him, and this typically requires a good deal of emotional involvement. Without this involvement, the psychoanalytic process is an intellectual exercise rather than a therapy (Freud, 1913).

Freud believed that the major means for providing the necessary emotional component is the **transference** relationship in which the patient responds to the analyst in increasingly personal terms. He reacts to him as he had reacted to the major figures in his own life, and he will therefore love or hate the analyst as he loved or hated his mother, father, siblings, and, more recently, his lovers and friends. All of these feelings are transferred to the analyst, as a kind of repetition of the unresolved problems of the patient's childhood. Patients show transference reactions when they idealize and idolize their analysts, or fall in love with them, or are terrified or distrustful of them, or want to be their "best patients," or fear that they are not being "good" patients.

Freud argued that this transference relation can be a powerful therapeutic tool. It lets the analyst hold up a mirror to the patient to show him how he really feels and acts toward the important people in his life. As an example, take a person who expresses violent anger at the psychiatrist, and then is immediately seized by a feeling of total terror. What is going on? A psychoanalytic interpretation is that the patient had equated the analyst with his own tyrannical father. Having transgressed against him, he could not help but expect some awful retribution. But needless to say, the analyst will not retaliate. Instead, he may say something mildly reassuring, such as "That was hard to get out, wasn't it?" After that he will probably interpret the patient's outburst and subsequent fear and will point out the discrepancy between the actual present and the long-dead past.

Through many such experiences, the patient's anxieties are gradually extinguished. The analyst's role in all of this is to serve as a temporary stand-in for the significant characters in the patient's early family drama. But he won't let himself be drawn into the play. He will let the patient say the same old lines and go through the same old motions, but he won't respond to them as the patient's father (or mother, or brother, or whoever) did. The analyst's job is to let the patient see what he is really doing, what is really happening on his private stage. The effect is a gradual process of emotional reeducation.

A psychoanalytic session *(Photograph by Will and Demi McIntyre/Science Source/Photo Researchers)*

PSYCHODYNAMIC THERAPY

Many present-day psychotherapists still use techniques that bear Freud's imprint. Although a few still practice psychoanalysis just as Freud did, most practitioners have modified Freud's theories and procedures in various ways. Most of them—known variously as psychoanalytic, ego-analytic, or dynamic psychotherapists—subscribe to neo-Freudian views or to related approaches such as ego psychology (see Chapter 17). Like Freud, they believe that the ultimate key to what they call "neurosis" is unconscious conflict. But unlike Freud's classical form of psychoanalysis, these therapies emphasize the resolution of current problems by focusing on interpersonal and cultural factors. If early development is discussed in therapy, it centers on the patterns of interaction in one's family and the difficulties in establishing autonomy from one's parents as setting the stage for one's current problems (Eagle and Wolitsky, 1992; Liff, 1992).

These variations on Freud's theoretical themes are accompanied by corresponding alterations in therapeutic technique. In classical analysis, sessions are scheduled five times a week and may continue for five or more years. Apart from the fact that this restricts the therapy to the affluent few, some critics contend that a five-times-a-week five-years-or-more analysis can easily become a patient's last ditch defense against getting well: She escapes her real problems in the present by hiding in a never-ending stream of free associations about her past. In effect, she becomes "couchridden."

To counter this trend, many psychoanalytically oriented therapists have adopted a schedule of fewer sessions per week. They believe that this helps to keep the sessions from becoming routine and intellectualized (Alexander and French, 1946). Others have tried to condense the whole process into a few months, sometimes by defining therapeutic goals in advance or setting definite time limits (e.g., Malan 1963; Strupp and Binder, 1984). One casualty of these modifications is that venerable instrument of Freudian orthodoxy, the psychoanalytic couch. Many practitioners have dispensed with it in favor of the simpler face-to-face interview. One reason is that a prone position encourages a feeling of dependency on the all-powerful analyst from whom the patient may have difficulty being weaned (Gill, 1976; Liff, 1992).

Yet other modifications concern the relation between what goes on in the therapist's office and what happens in the patient's "real" life. For Freud, the crucial theater of operations was the analysis itself. He believed that to make sure that the patient's unconscious conflicts emerge fully there, the patient's life outside has to remain stable. He therefore insisted that his patients make no major life decisions such as getting married or divorced or changing careers while they were in analysis. In contrast, many psychoanalytic psychotherapists regard the sessions as a microcosm of the patient's entire life, and they recommend that the patient apply the lessons from therapy to the rest of her life (Alexander and French, 1946).

BEHAVIOR THERAPY

Not all psychotherapists derive their techniques from psychoanalysis. In fact, two major therapeutic approaches are reactions against psychoanalysis but for reasons that are diametrically opposed. The first is *behavior therapy,* which maintains that the theoretical notions underlying psychoanalysis are vague and untestable, while its therapeutic effectiveness is a matter of doubt. The other group consists of various humanistic therapies, which regard psychoanalysis as too mechanistic in its approach. Freud, who had a fine sense of irony, would have been wryly amused to find himself in the middle of this two-front war in which one side accuses him of being too scientific and the other of not being scientific enough.

Behavior therapists hold that the various conditions Freud called "neurosis" are caused by maladaptive learning whose remedy must be a form of reeducation. Taken by itself, this view is hardly original. What makes it different is that the behavior therapists take the emphasis on learning and relearning much more seriously than anyone had before them. They see themselves as applied scientists whose techniques for reeducating troubled people are adapted from principles of classical and instrumental conditioning discovered in the laboratories of Pavlov, Thorndike, and Skinner (see Chapter 4).

Like the learning theorists from whom they trace their descent, behavior therapists are basically tough-minded and pragmatic. They emphasize overt, observable behavior rather than hypothetical underlying causes such as unconscious thoughts and wishes, which they regard as hard to define and impossible to observe. Their concern is with what a person does, especially if it causes him distress. If so, the behavior therapists want to modify such behaviors—to get the person with agoraphobia over his fear of open places, to help the person with obsessive-compulsive disorder overcome the hand-washing rituals that are rubbing away his skin. To accomplish these ends, behavior therapists resort to various techniques for learning and unlearning—deliberate exposure to anxiety-producing stimuli, conditioning of incompatible reactions, or whatever. But their treatment does not include any attempt to have the patient gain insight into the origin of these symptoms. As these therapists see it, such insights, however valid, have no therapeutic value. What is wrong, and must be fixed, is the patient's behavior in the here and now.

EXPOSURE TECHNIQUES

One set of behavior therapy techniques is based on concepts drawn from classical conditioning. The major target of these techniques is unrealistic fear found

Desensitization *(Courtesy of Henry Gleitman and Mary Bullock)*

in cases of specific phobias such as disabling fears of heights, enclosed spaces, or cockroaches. Behavior therapists regard such fears as classically conditioned responses that are evoked by various eliciting stimuli such as looking down a flight of stairs, being in an elevator, or finding roaches in one's cupboard (see Chapters 4 and 18). Exactly how the original conditioning took place—whether in a single episode or through a series of cumulative experiences—is immaterial. What matters is how this connection between stimulus and fear can be broken, regardless of how it was forged originally.

The most obvious way of removing the classically conditioned connection is through *extinction.* Imagine a rat that has been shocked on seeing a flashing light. To extinguish the fear, all we have to do is to present the conditioned stimulus (the light) without the unconditioned stimulus (the shock). But this is easier said than done, for the animal has learned to avoid the fear-arousing stimulus and runs away as soon as the light starts flashing. As a result, it can't "test reality" and discover that the formerly dangerous stimulus no longer signals shock. Therefore, its fear won't be extinguished. What holds for the rat, also holds for the person with a phobia. He is afraid of heights, or of enclosed spaces, or of roaches. His fear makes him avoid these stimuli, which is why he can't ever find out that his terrors are unjustified. And if he tries to face the phobic stimuli, he is often so traumatized that he becomes reconditioned.

One way of getting the rat (or the person suffering from a phobia) to test reality is to make the rat expose itself to the flashing light (or the snakes, or open spaces). If the rat is forced to remain in the compartment in which it was formerly shocked and is repeatedly presented with the flashing light that is now no longer followed by shock, then its fear of the light will eventually disappear (Baum, 1970). Just this principle underlies what behavior therapists call "exposure techniques." The most widely used exposure technique is *systematic desensitization,* developed by the psychiatrist Joseph Wolpe. Its basic idea is to connect the stimuli that now evoke fear to a new response that is incompatible with fear and that will therefore displace it (Wolpe, 1958). The competing response is usually muscular relaxation, a pervasive untensing of the body's musculature that is presumably incompatible with the autonomic and skeletal reactions that accompany fear. This requires that the patient learn to relax his musculature on cue through meditation-like tensing and untensing exercises performed in the clinic and often assisted by using audiotapes at home. Once the patient can relax thoroughly on cue, the goal is to condition the relaxation to the fear-evoking stimuli, whether the stimuli is snakes, open spaces, or high roof tops (see Figure 19.6).

To establish the desired link between relaxation and the fear-evoking situation, the patient is asked to imagine this situation as vividly as possible while in deep relaxation. Such imagined encounters have enough reality for most patients to evoke a reasonable amount of anxiety (Wolpe and Lazarus, 1966). To make sure that this anxiety is not excessive, Wolpe adopted a policy of deliberate gradualism, in which the therapist sneaks up on the fear response, step by step. He first asks the patient to construct an *anxiety hierarchy* in which feared situations are arranged from least to most anxiety provoking. The patient starts out by imagining the first scene in the hierarchy (for example, being on the first floor of the Empire State Building). He imagines this scene while in a state of deep relaxation. He will stay with this scene—imagining and relaxing—until he no longer feels any qualms. After this, the next scene is imagined and thoroughly counterconditioned, and so on, until the patient finally can imagine the most frightening scene of all (leaning over the railing of the observation deck above the 102d floor) and still be able to relax.

According to Wolpe and his followers, this procedure of taking the sting out

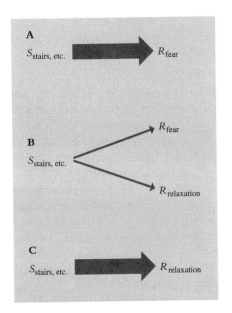

19.6 Systematic desensitization *(A) The state of affairs in phobia. Various stimuli such as flights of stairs arouse the response of fear. (B) These stimuli are conditioned to the response of relaxation. As this connection becomes stronger, the connection between the stimulus and the fear response is weakened. (C) The state of affairs when counterconditioning is complete. The relaxation response has completely displaced the old fear response.*

A

B

Behavior therapy in the real world *(A) A person with acrophobia who visits a rooftop in the presence of the therapist. (Photograph © Steve Mellon, 1994) (B) A person with agoraphobia with panic disorder who forces herself to go on a bus ride. (Photograph © Jacques Chenet, all rights reserved; courtesy of Woodfin Camp & Assoc.)*

of imagined horrors carries over almost completely into the real world. But other investigators argue that the transfer into real life is less than Wolpe claims and often lags behind the desensitization of the images. A plausible guess is that the shift from image to reality is automatic but requires some active participation on the part of the patient (Davidson, 1968). Toward this end, many patients are given homework assignments that force them to confront progressively more fear-evoking situations in the real world. While the desensitization method is most directly applicable to specific phobias, many behavior therapists believe that it is useful whenever anxiety is a major factor in the disorder and when the stimuli that trigger this disorder are known. Examples are sexual arousal disorders in men and women (Brady, 1985).

AVERSION THERAPY

Another behavior therapy technique, *aversion therapy,* tries to attach negative feelings to stimulus situations that are initially appealing so that the patient will no longer want to approach them. The object of this endeavor is to eliminate behavior patterns that both patient and therapist regard as undesirable. Examples are overeating, excessive drinking, or engaging in certain sexual deviations such as exhibitionism.

The basic procedure of aversion therapy is very simple. One pairs the stimulus that one wants to render unpleasant with some obnoxious unconditioned stimulus. An example is aversion therapy for excessive drinking. The patient takes a sip of alcohol while under the effect of a nausea-producing drug. He tastes the liquor while he desperately wants to vomit.

Whether aversion therapy works is debatable. No one doubts that it works in the therapist's office; the question is whether it is effective outside, when the shocking device is no longer attached or the nausea-producing drugs are no longer administered (Rachman and Teasdale, 1969; Emmelkamp, 1986). There is some suggestion that the nausea-producing procedure has lasting effects in some cases of alcoholism. According to one review, two-thirds of alcoholics treated in this manner remained abstinent for a year, one-third for three years (Wiens and Menustik, 1983). In effect, the patients acquired a learned taste aversion so that the actual taste and smell of alcohol became repellent (see Chapter 4).

OPERANT TECHNIQUES

Most of the behavior therapies we've discussed so far are based on classical conditioning. As such, they try to alter the significance of various stimulus events, as in making a patient realize that snakes are not really threatening. Another set of behavioral therapies is derived from the principles of instrumental conditioning and emphasizes the relation between acts and consequences (see Chapter 4). Its theme is the same as that which underlies the entire operant approach—the control of behavior through reinforcement.

An example of this approach is the use of *token economies* in certain hospital psychiatric wards. These tokens function much as money does in our economy; they can be exchanged for desirable items such as snacks or watching TV. But again, like money, they must be earned by the patient, perhaps by making his own bed, or being neatly dressed, or performing various ward chores. The overall effect seems to be positive. While the patients are certainly not cured, they become less apathetic and the general ward atmosphere is much improved (Ayllon and Azrin, 1968). The problem is that the effects of token economies do not generalize well out of the hospital or even off the ward. Thus they are probably best seen not as therapy but as ward-management techniques.

COGNITIVE-BEHAVIORAL THERAPIES

Exposure and aversion therapies focus on behaviors that are more or less overt and try to modify them by techniques based on the principles of simple learning. In exposure techniques like desensitization, the emphasis is on some external stimulus (such as heights) that is connected with anxiety, a connection the therapy tries to sever. In aversion therapy, the emphasis is on some overt response (such as excessive drinking), a response the therapy tries to eliminate. But what treatment is appropriate when the patient's problems cannot be so readily described by referring to fear-evoking stimuli or to overt, undesirable responses? Many patients' difficulties stem from anxiety that is triggered by their own thoughts and feelings. An example is the person with an obsessive-compulsive disorder whose own obsessional thoughts lead to intense anxiety that can only be relieved by ever more frantic compulsive rituals. Here the critical features of the disorder derive from covert rather than overt sources—thoughts and feelings that go on "in the patient's head." How does a behavior-oriented approach to therapy handle cases such as these?

A number of therapists deal with such problems by a frontal attack on the way the patient thinks. They try to replace the patient's irrational beliefs and attitudes that caused his emotional stress by a more appropriate mode of thinking that is in better accord with reality. This general form of therapy goes under various labels. A relatively recent version is cognitive therapy, originally developed as a treatment for depression by the psychiatrist Aaron Beck (Beck, 1967).

On the face of it, the goal of all cognitive approaches seems similar to the psychoanalytic quest for emotional insight. But cognitive therapists see themselves as more closely allied to behavior therapy. While they make little use of conditioning principles and concentrate on what the patients think rather than on what they do overtly, their techniques share many of the characteristics of behavior therapy. Cognitive therapists are extremely directive. They are primarily concerned with the patient in the present rather than with his history, and they focus on the beliefs that affect what the patient does and feels.

THE MAJOR TECHNIQUES OF COGNITIVE THERAPY

The basic technique of cognitive therapists is to confront patients with the contradictions inherent in their maladaptive beliefs. To accomplish this end, the therapist is active and even dominant throughout the proceedings, and—like many modern behavior therapists—gives the patient "homework assignments." One such task might be to discover irrational thoughts that come in the form of certain illogical phrases and sentences the patients say to themselves, such as "it's all my fault," and "if no one loves me, I'm no good," and so on. Such automatic and ultimately self-defeating thoughts may explain why patients sometimes feel unaccountably upset. For example, an event like seeing an old acquaintance across the street might lead to a wave of anxiety, with the patient in the dark about why he is anxious. But the therapist can put light on the situation—seeing the old friend triggered an automatic and irrational thought that led to the anxiety:

> The anxiety seemed incomprehensible until [the patient] "played back" his thoughts: "If I greet Bob, he many not remember me. He may snub me, it has been so long, he may not know who I am. . . ." (Ellis, 1962, quoted in Beck, 1985, p. 1436)

The job of the therapist is to help the patient identify the automatic thought and to recognize its irrationality. After all, Bob may very well remember him. And if he doesn't, it may be because Bob's memory is faulty. But suppose the patient is right, and Bob never liked him in the first place and might well have snubbed him. Is that the end of the world? Is it really necessary to be liked by everybody? Once these irrational beliefs are ferreted out, the patient has to tell himself repeatedly that they are false. If he can stop himself from such self-defeating automatisms, he will feel better, which will allow him to function at a higher level, which will make him feel better still, leading to a beneficent cycle of emotional improvement.

How does the cognitive therapist help the patient recognize the essential irrationality of the beliefs that underlie the automatic sentences that trigger his anxiety or depression? In effect, the therapist takes the role of a sympathetic Socrates who asks one question after another to show the patient that these thoughts about himself and others are irrational and self-defeating. An example is a dialogue between a therapist (T) and a student patient (P), who was in despair because she was convinced that she would not be accepted by a particular college:

> T: Why do you think you won't be able to get into the university of your choice?
> P: Because my grades are really not so hot.
> T: Well, what was your grade average?
> P: Well, pretty good until the last semester in high school.
> T: What was your grade average in general?
> P: As and Bs.
> T: Well, how many of each?
> P: Well, I guess, almost all of my grades were As, but I got terrible grades last semester.
> T: What were your grades then?
> P: I got two As and two Bs.
> T: Since your grade average would seem to me to come out to almost all As, why do you think you won't be able to get into the university?
> P: Because of competition being so tough.
> T: Have you found out what the average grades are for admissions to the college?
> P: Well, somebody told me that a B+ average would suffice.
> T: Isn't your average better than that?
> P: I guess so.
>
> (Beck et al., 1979, p. 153)

The way this treatment deals with irrational thought indicates its close affinity with behavior therapy. A fear-evoking thought is regarded as a form of behavior: The response is saying the illogical sentence to oneself.

COGNITIVE THERAPY AND PANIC DISORDER

While cognitive therapy was originally developed as a treatment for depression (Beck et al., 1979), it was eventually extended to serve as a therapy for phobias and certain other anxiety disorders (Beck, 1976, 1985). Some recent evidence suggests that it may be effective in cases of panic disorder. As we saw in the preceding chapter, panic disorder is the repeated and disabling occurrence of episodes that include palpitations, nausea, hyperventilation, feelings of apprehension, and thoughts of impending death or other catastrophe (see Chapter 18, pp. 748–49). The panic attack triggers a violent fear that feeds upon itself and produces a runaway reaction for the duration of the attack.

The most common treatment for panic disorder, and one that is quite effective, has been the administration of antidepressant medications such as Prozac. However, Beck and his coworkers have developed a cognitive treatment program that helps patients appraise their frightening bodily sensations more realistically. The therapist begins by explaining that the symptoms are not really pathological. (Needless to say, this is only appropriate if the patient has been medically cleared of any underlying physical pathology.) For example, she may explain that the sensation of dizziness may occur whenever there is a sudden drop in blood pressure (e.g., on standing up suddenly), that shortness of breath may result from some harmless, momentary biochemical change in the blood (e.g., by hyperventilation), and so on.

After this education, the therapist tries to induce the frightening physical sensation in her office to show the patient that it is really safe. If the patient is frightened when his heartbeat accelerates, she may have him repeatedly jump up and down; if he is frightened on feeling "lightheaded," she may have him hyperventilate, and so on. In one clinical study, sixteen such patients were seen for an average of fifteen sessions. At the time they started, they suffered an average of about five panic attacks per week. This number dropped to about one after six weeks and to none at all after sixteen weeks of treatment. The treatment evidently had a lasting effect, for no panic attacks were reported after a full year's follow-up (Clark, 1988; Beck, 1988).

The jury is still out on the relative worth of pharmacotherapy versus cognitive therapy for panic disorder. One important factor is cost; medication is inexpensive compared to cognitive therapy. But another factor is risk; many people cannot take antidepressant medications because of various physical conditions, and so cognitive therapy is a worthy alternative.

THERAPY AS SOCIAL EDUCATION

Most of the therapeutic techniques we have discussed thus far have goals that are essentially negative—to eliminate irrational fears, suppress unwanted behaviors, and root out illogical beliefs. These goals are certainly admirable, but do they go far enough? There is no doubt that, say, agoraphobia or compulsive drinking are millstones around a person's neck. But what happens after they are removed? Is the therapist's task to help the patient find new and more appropriate behavior patterns to take the place of the unhealthy ones he has finally managed to shuck off?

Many therapists—including most behavior therapists, cognitive therapists, and many psychodynamic therapists—believe that the answer is yes. They emphasize that the patient's anxieties had kept him from learning all kinds of interpersonal skills that are by no means easy to acquire: how to conduct an initial approach to the opposite sex, how to assert oneself without being overly aggressive, and so on. These skills have to be learned and practiced in the real world, but the patient can get a modest start in the therapist's office. In fact,

Therapy as social education (© 1950, 1952 United Feature Syndicate Inc.)

learning interpersonal skills, dealing with isolation, and solving disputes are at the heart of interpersonal therapy, which, as we will see below, is effective in treating depression (Klerman et al., 1984).

A number of techniques have been developed to help the therapist conduct this tutorial course in interpersonal relations. One technique employs **graded task assignments** in which the patient is asked to take progressively larger steps in real-life social interactions that give him trouble. We have already discussed an application of this step-by-step approach in the treatment of phobias. Another example is training in assertiveness, which would progress from tasks like maintaining eye contact with other people, to asking directions from a stranger, to complaining to a waiter about an overdone steak (Lazarus, 1971). Another technique is **modeling** in which the therapist shows the patient some effective ways of handling a particular situation. Yet another is **role playing** in which the patient and therapist act out some scenes, such as a marital confrontation, that are likely to take place at some future time.

An illustration of the use of role playing is provided by a patient who was unable to express genuine affection for his wife:

> [The therapist] says, "Tom, do you really care for me?"
> Tom says, "I would say to her that I do, but she'd complain."
> Therapist: "Don't tell me what you would do. I'm Jane. Talk to me. Tom, do you really care for me?"
> Tom (turning away, looking slightly disgusted): "Yes."
> Therapist (still as Jane): "You don't say it like you mean it."
> Tom: "Yeah, that's what she says and I usually . . ."
> Therapist (interrupting): "You're again telling me about what you'd say. I'm Jane. Tom, you don't say it like you mean it."
> Tom: "It's very hard for me to answer her when she says that."
> Therapist: "How do you feel when she says it?"
> Tom: "Angry, pushed."
> Therapist: "OK, I'm Jane. Tell me how you feel."
> Tom: "Jane, when you do that it really turns me off. Maybe if you didn't ask me so often I'd be able to say it spontaneously without feeling like a puppet . . . (then, in a tone that indicates he is now talking to the therapist as therapist) Gee, I wonder what would happen if I really said that to her."
>
> (Wachtel, 1977, pp. 234–35)

HUMANISTIC THERAPIES

A number of practitioners charge that behavior therapy (and to a lesser extent, psychoanalysis) describes human beings too mechanistically and treats them too manipulatively. These **humanistic therapists** try to deal with the individual at a more global level, not as a bundle of conditioned reflexes to be extinguished, nor as a collection of warring, unconscious impulses to be reconciled, but rather as a whole person, who must be understood as one person among many and in the context of his entire life.

CLIENT-CENTERED THERAPY

One example of a humanistically oriented approach is **client-centered therapy** (Rogers, 1951, 1970), which was developed during the early 1940s by psychologist Carl Rogers (1902–1987). One of its main premises is that the process of personality development is akin to growth. In this view, Rogers followed theorists like Abraham Maslow (1908–1970) and other adherents of a humanistic approach to personality in believing that all people have a native impulse toward the full realization of their human potential (Maslow, 1968; see Chapter 17). In this sense, he held that human nature is inherently good. But, alas, such self-actualization is fairly rare, for personality growth is often stunted. There are many people who dislike themselves, are out of touch with their own feelings, and are unable to reach out to others as genuine fellow beings. Rogers' remedy was to provide the appropriate psychological soil in which personal growth could resume; this soil was the therapeutic relationship.

Rogers believed that therapy should be essentially democratic. The Rogerian therapist does not act as an omniscient authority who sagely interprets what the patient says or dreams (as does a psychoanalyst) or who tells him what to do for his own good (as does a behavior therapist). Instead, he tries to help the patient—whom he calls a client—help himself.

Rogers initially tried to achieve this client-centered quality by a variety of **nondirective techniques** (Rogers, 1942). He would never advise or interpret directly, but would only try to clarify what the client really felt, by echoing or restating what the client himself seemed to say or feel. Rogers subsequently decided that there was no way of being truly nondirective, that one couldn't help but convey some evaluation with even the blandest nod. But more important, Rogers came to believe that the therapist's main contribution does not lie in any particular approach or technique; it is rather to supply the one crucial condition of successful therapy, himself or herself, as a genuinely involved, participating fellow person. The Rogerian therapist's main job is to let the client know that she understands how the world looks through his eyes; that she can empathize with his wishes and feelings; and, most important of all, that she accepts and values him. In Rogers' view, this awareness that another person unconditionally accepts and esteems him ultimately helps the client to accept and esteem himself (Rogers, 1961). Perhaps this is just a modern restatement of the old idea that love can redeem us all.★

Existential therapy *(Hand with Reflecting Sphere, 1935, by M.C. Escher: © M.C. Escher Heirs, courtesy of Cordon Art, Baarn, Holland)*

EXISTENTIAL THERAPY

Rogers's approach to therapy was distinctively American in its belief in an almost limitless human capacity for growth and self-improvement. Another humanistic approach to therapy originates in Europe and takes a more somber view. This is existential therapy, a movement that echoes some of the major themes sounded by a group of philosophers called "existentialists." Existential therapists are primarily concerned with what they regard as the major emotional sickness of our times, an inability to endow life with meaning. In their view, this condition is a by-product of the rootless, restless anonymity of twentieth-century Western life; it was especially prevalent in modern Europe in the wake of the despair that followed two bloody world wars and the Nazi terror. It is marked by a sense that one is alienated, lost, and dehumanized; that one is nothing but a cog in a huge, impersonal machine; that one's existence is meaningless. According to existential therapists, this feeling that everything is pointless is a common facet of many modern emotional disorders. It is this, rather than the specific symptoms of the disorders—the phobias, the obsessions, and the like—that they want to rectify (Ofman, 1985).

In essence, existential therapists try to help people achieve a personal outlook that gives meaning to their lives. How do they do this? It turns out that most

---

★ Rogers's humanistic approach has often been attacked by behavior therapists who regard him as "antiscientific." Under the circumstances, it is somewhat ironic that Rogers was one of the pioneers of psychotherapy evaluation, the first major figure in the field of psychotherapy who looked for evidence that his techniques were actually having some effect.

Alienation in the modern world *(Gov-
ernment Bureau by George Tooker, 1956,
Courtesy of the Metropolitan Museum of Art,
New York)*

existential therapists have no distinctive technique. Some use the couch and ask
the patient to free associate, while others sit face to face and have lengthy philosophical discussions. What is distinctive about them is their underlying attitude.
They try to make their patients aware of the importance of free choice. They
insist that people are persons and not objects, that human acts spring from within rather than being imposed from without, that there are always choices—even
in jail, even in a concentration camp—and that what one *is* is ultimately the
result of what one chooses to *do*. The therapist's job is to help the patient realize
that the responsibility for finding and for making her life's choices is hers and
hers alone. If and when the patient accepts this responsibility, she will no longer
be plagued by the vacuum of her own existence but will begin to feel "authentic."

Like practitioners of most other schools, existential therapists stress the role of
the therapeutic relationship in affecting the changes they want to bring about.
In their view, the key element of this relationship is what they call the encounter
in which two individuals meet as genuine persons of whose independent human
existence neither has any doubt. According to existential therapists, the experience derived from this encounter will ultimately transfer to the way in which
the patient sees herself and others (May, 1958).

In the past, the task that existential therapists set themselves was generally
held to be the province of clergymen. It was priests and ministers and rabbis
who tried to help people find some meaning in their existence. They did so
within a religious framework that defined the spiritual dimension of human life.
As religious values eroded, secular social institutions stepped in and tried to take
the clergy's place. One of these is modern humanistic psychotherapy, especially
the existentialist school. It is no accident that an influential book by a prominent
existential therapist bears the title *The Doctor and the Soul* (Frankl, 1966).

SOME COMMON THEMES

The various forms of psychotherapy differ in some important regards in
what they try to do. Psychoanalytically oriented therapists emphasize
understanding; they aim to help the patient realize the pattern of his thoughts

and actions so that he can confront his unconscious conflicts and overcome them. Behavior therapists emphasize doing. They try to help their patients eliminate undesirable responses and build desirable ones. Cognitive-behavioral therapists are most concerned with thinking. They want to enable their patients to overcome patterns of irrational and self-defeating thoughts. Humanistic therapists stress feeling. Their hope is to help their clients accept themselves, express what they want and feel in the here-and-now, and set about doing things that give their lives transcendent meaning.

These differences among the various therapeutic schools are real enough. But of late there have been trends toward a rapprochement between the different schools of therapy. Some psychoanalytically oriented practitioners have come to use techniques that were formerly the exclusive preserve of behavior therapists, such as modeling and "homework" assignments (Wachtel, 1977, 1982). And from the opposite side, many behavior therapists have come to realize that the client-therapist relation is an important part of treatment, that something like Freud's "transference" comes into play even in mechanistic conditioning therapies such as desensitization (Lazarus, 1971, 1981). The endpoint of this integration is seen in a survey of influential psychotherapists who strongly advocated what they call *technical eclecticism*—basically, doing whatever works—as the trend in therapy (Norcross and Freedheim, 1992). This eclectic orientation dovetails with recent changes in the practice of psychotherapy that were prompted by economic considerations, as we will see below (see. pp. 793–95).

But quite apart from such trends toward an eclectic approach to psychotherapy, there are some common underlying themes that run through the beliefs and practices of all the various therapies:

Emotional defusing   All psychotherapies aim at some kind of emotional reeducation. They try to help the patient rid himself of various intense and unrealistic emotional reactions, such as the fear in specific phobia. To this end, these reactions are evoked during the therapeutic session. Since this happens in the presence of an accepting, nonjudgmental therapist, the reactions are weakened.

Interpersonal learning   All major schools stress the importance of interpersonal learning and believe that the therapeutic relationship is an important tool for bringing this about. This relationship shows the patient how she generally reacts to others, and it provides a test for trying new and better ways of reacting.

Self-knowledge   Most psychotherapists try to help their patients achieve greater self-knowledge, though different therapeutic schools differ in what kind of self-knowledge they try to bring about. For psychoanalysts, the crucial emotional insights the patient must acquire refer to his own past; for Rogerians, they concern one's feelings in the present; for behavior therapists, the relevant self-understanding is the correct identification of the stimuli to which fear has been conditioned.

Therapy as a step-by-step process   There is general agreement that psychotherapy is a gradual affair and that this is so regardless of whether the therapy emphasizes insight, emotion, or overt action. There are few sudden flashes of insight or emotional understanding that change a patient overnight. Instead, each new skill or newfound insight must be laboriously applied in one life situation after another before the patient can call it her own.

Therapy as socially accepted healing   By and large, psychotherapists operate within a social context that gives them the status of officially designated healers for many mental disorders. As a result, the stage is set for a number of nonspecific gains of psychotherapy. One is an intimate, confiding relationship with another person. This alone may be a boon to some people who have no close bonds to anyone and for whom psychotherapy may amount to "the purchase of friendship" (Schofield, 1964). Another nonspecific gain is the hope that one will get better. This may lead to self-perpetuating improvements, because as the patient thinks better of himself, he may have small successes in the outside world, which may lead him to greater hope, with even better odds of continued success.

EXTENSIONS OF PSYCHOTHERAPY

In Freud's time, psychotherapy was still considered a somewhat arcane art, practiced by a few initiates (mostly physicians) and limited to a selected group of well-educated adult patients. Since then, psychotherapy has been broadened and extended to cover increasingly more terrain. One set of extensions widened the patient population to include children, retarded persons, various kinds of sociopaths, and psychotics. Another extension was a shift from the original one-therapist/one-patient formula to various modes of group therapy that feature all conceivable permutations: one therapist and several patients, several therapists and several patients, several patients and no therapist, and so on.

One early reason for treating patients in groups was that there simply weren't enough trained therapists for all the people who wanted their services; seeing clients in groups was one way of making the supply fit the demand. But group therapy was appealing for deeper reasons as well. For instance, therapy groups seemed to fill a void, at least temporarily, left by the weakening of family and religious ties of modern urbanized society.

EXPANSION OF THERAPEUTIC METHOD

Shared-problem groups   One approach is to organize a group of people all of whom have the same problem. They may all be alcoholics, or drug addicts, or ex-convicts. The members meet, share relevant advice and information, help newcomers along, exhort and support each other in their resolve to overcome their handicaps. The classic example is ***Alcoholics Anonymous (AA),*** which provides the alcoholic with a sense that he is not alone and helps him weather crises without suffering a relapse. In such we-are-all-in-the-same-boat groups, the primary aim is to manage the problem that all members share. No specific attention is paid to emotional problems that are unique to any one individual.

Therapy groups   The rules of the game are very different in groups explicitly organized for the purpose of ***group therapy.*** Here, a group of selected patients, usually around ten, are treated together under the guidance of a trained therapist. This form of therapy may have some advantages that individual treatment lacks. According to its proponents, in group therapy the therapist does not really treat the members of the group; instead, he helps them to treat each other. The specific techniques of the therapist may vary from psychoanalytically oriented insight therapy to various forms of behavior therapy to Rogerian client-centered approaches. But whatever techniques the therapist favors, the treatment of each group member really begins as she realizes that she is not all that different from the others. She learns that there are other people who are painfully shy, who have hostile fantasies about their parents, or whatever. Further benefits come from a sense of group belongingness, of support, and of encouragement. But most important of all is the fact that the group provides a ready-made laboratory in interpersonal relations. The patient can discover just

A

B

Play therapy, an extension of psychotherapy adapted for children   *(A) In play therapy, the therapist tries to help the child understand and express his feelings about his parents and other family members through play with various toys. (B) Puppets are sometimes used to act out problems, as in this example of a therapy session with victims of child abuse. (Top: photograph by Michael Heron, 1979/Monkmeyer Press. Bottom: photograph by Bart Bartholomew, 1984/ Black Star)*

"When Jud accuses Zack, here, of hostility toward his daughter, like he seems to every session, why, it's plain to me he's only rationalizing his own lack of gumption in standing up to a stepson who's usurping the loyalty of his second wife. The way he lit into him just now shows he's got this here guilt identification with Zack's present family constellation. Calling Zack egotistical ain't nothing but a disguise mechanism for concealing his secret envy of Zack's grit and all-around starch, and shows mighty poor ego boundaries of his own, it appears to me." (Drawing by Whitney Darrow, Jr.,; © 1976, The New Yorker Magazine, Inc.)

what she does that rubs others the wrong way, how she can relate to certain kinds of people more effectively, and so on (Sadock, 1975).

Marital and family therapy In the therapy groups we've considered thus far, the members are almost always strangers before the session begin. This is in marked contrast to what happens in **marital and family therapy.** Here the people seeking help know each other very well (sometimes all too well) before they enter therapy.

In recent years, family therapy has become a major therapeutic movement (Satir, 1967; Minuchin, 1974; Kerr and Bowen, 1988). It is probably no coincidence that this growth has occurred during a time of turmoil in American families, evidenced by spiraling divorce rates and reports of child and spousal abuse, and by the increasing numbers of single-parent households.

Family and marital therapists regard the family as an emotional unit that can influence the onset and continuing manifestation of many mental disorders and social problems. Seen from this perspective, the key to marital and family distress is not necessarily in the pathology of any individual spouse or family member. Rather, it lies in the relationships within the family system: between the husband and wife or the various members of the family. In a dislocated shoulder, both the upper arm and shoulder socket may be perfectly sound, but until their mutual relationship is appropriately readjusted, there will necessarily be pain and the shoulder won't be able to function. Many marital (or couple) and family therapists feel that their task is like that of the orthopedist who resets the dislocated shoulder: They try to help the couple or the family readjust their interrelations.

Many family therapists prefer to see the members of the couple or family together rather than individually. In such conjoint sessions, the therapist can act as an emotional translator who can help the spouses or family members to understand each other better. An example is this exchange between therapist (T), husband (H), and wife (W):

H: She never comes up to me and kisses me. I am always the one to make the overtures.
T: [To wife] Is this the way you see yourself behaving with your husband?
W: Yes, I would say he is the demonstrative one. I didn't know he wanted me to make the overtures.
T: Have you told your wife that you would like this from her—more open demonstration of affection?

H: Well, no, you'd think she'd know.

W: No. How would I know? You always said you don't like aggressive women.

H: I don't. I don't like dominating women.

W: Well, I thought you meant women who make the overtures. How am I to know what you want?

T: You'd have a better idea if he had been able to tell you.

(From Satir, 1967, pp. 72–73)

Some reviewers believe that this approach can be beneficial, especially when the spouses or family members are seen together rather than individually (Gurman and Kniskern, 1981; Hazelrigg, Cooper, and Borduin, 1987). But this conclusion can be questioned on various technical grounds. For example, the superiority of conjoint to individual therapy may reflect a difference in who chooses what treatment. Perhaps the Smiths who refuse to see a therapist together are more at odds with each other than the Browns who decide to see her jointly. To achieve the appropriate controls for outcome evaluation may be even more difficult in this area than in the field of individual therapy.

THE EXPANSION OF THERAPEUTIC GOALS

Group methods and other extensions made psychotherapy available to a much larger number of people. But did all of them really need it? The answer depends on what one believes the goals of therapy are.

For Freud, the matter was simple. Most of his patients were incapable of any kind of full life. They were disabled by terrorizing phobias or all-consuming compulsions and were rendered unable to work and love. Freud wanted to heal these patients so that they could once again live normally. But he never regarded his treatment as automatically producing happiness or fulfillment or the discovery of meaning in their lives. These the patients had to find for themselves, and they might very well fail to do so even when no longer saddled with their inner conflicts.

Later therapists broadened treatment goals. As we mentioned in the previous chapter, there has been a considerable tendency to group more and more behavior patterns under the rubric of mental disorder and thus make them fodder for psychotherapy. We have reached the point that people who overspend are labeled victims of "shopping addiction" and are urged to join a self-help program; women who have several unpleasant relationships are diagnosed as suffering from an excessive need to love and are referred to groups for "women who love too much," and so on.

The expansion of therapeutic goals is not only confined to getting over problems. Consider humanistic therapists such as Rogers. To be sure, Rogerian therapists try to remove or alleviate their clients' distress. But their ambitions go further. They aim at more than a cure (the goal of psychoanalysts, at least in their early days) and at more than the modification of unwanted behavior patterns (the goal of behavior therapists). Their ultimate object is to help their clients to "grow" and to "realize their human potential." But if so, then therapy can be appropriate for just about anyone, regardless of whether he suffers some form of psychopathology or not (Orne, 1975). After all, who among us can claim to have achieved his full potential?

CULTURAL COMPETENCE IN PSYCHOTHERAPY

Because the originators of the common theories and techniques we have discussed were all Europeans and North Americans, many observers have suggested that psychotherapy may ill-serve patients whose backgrounds are from other cultures. The increasing awareness of multiculturalism has led many authors to

"We're not living happily ever after." (Drawing by Chas. Addams; © 1959, 1987, The New Yorker Magazine, Inc.)

stress the importance of *cultural competence* in psychotherapy. They argue that the therapist must understand the patient's culture well enough to modify the goals of therapy to conform to the values that the patient brings to therapy.

For example, Asian-American patients put more emphasis on formality in all their affairs. Their social roles tend to be structured largely by age and sex, with a father's authority rarely challenged within the family (Sue and Kirk, 1973). The therapist whose own values place a premium on individual autonomy over family loyalties might inadvertently run afoul of the patient's cultural traditions and endanger the therapy. Another example comes from Native Americans who tend to value happiness and sharing over competition and private ownership (Bryde, 1972). Here a therapy that stresses assertiveness over conciliation and diplomacy may well backfire. Part of cultural competence in psychotherapy requires that the therapist question the patient sensitively about her cultural values and religious beliefs and the extent to which she is assimilated to the dominant culture (Atkinson, Morten, and Sue, 1983; Sue, 1980).

EVALUATING THERAPEUTIC OUTCOME

We have just surveyed what different kinds of therapists do. We now ask whether what they do does any good. This question often arouses indignant protests from therapists and patients alike. For many of them feel utterly certain that they help or have been helped. They therefore see no point in questioning what to them is obvious. But their testimonials alone are not convincing. For one thing, both patients and therapists have a serious stake in believing that psychotherapy works. If it doesn't, the patient has wasted his money and the therapist has wasted her time. Under the circumstances, neither may be the most objective judge in assessing whether there was a significant change.

But even granting that change occurred, what caused this change? At this point, our previous explanation of how medications are evaluated should raise some obvious questions. Was the change produced by the psychotherapy itself, or would it have occurred anyway? Assuming that people naturally have ups and downs in their lives, patients often seek out therapy when they are at their worst, so it is natural that they would more likely return to an "up" phase while in therapy. And, assuming that the psychotherapy did play a direct role, was the improvement caused by the therapeutic techniques themselves, or indirectly by placebo-like factors such as hope, expectations of cure, and the decision to "turn over a new leaf"?

DOES PSYCHOTHERAPY WORK?

The early impetus for discussions of psychotherapeutic outcomes came from a sharp attack launched by the British psychologist Hans Eysenck (Eysenck, 1961) on the efficacy of psychoanalysis and similar "insight" therapies. Eysenck surveyed some two dozen articles that reported the number of "neurotic" patients (mostly, patients with depression or anxiety disorders, in today's nomenclature) who improved or failed to improve after psychotherapy. Overall, about 60 percent improved, a result that might be considered fairly encouraging. But Eysenck argued that there was really nothing to cheer about.

According to Eysenck's analysis, the spontaneous recovery rate in neurotics who received no treatment was, if anything, even higher—about 70 percent. If so, psychotherapy apparently has no curative effects.

In retrospect, it appears that Eysenck's appraisal was unduly harsh. In particular, he evidently overestimated the rate of spontaneous improvement. According to one review, the median rate of patients who get better without therapy is, depending upon the diagnostic composition of the group of patients, around 30 percent compared to an average improvement rate of 60 percent for neurotic patients who received psychotherapy, a difference that constitutes what the author called "some modest evidence that psychotherapy 'works'" (Bergin, 1971, p. 229; see also Luborsky, Singer, and Luborsky, 1975).

META-ANALYSES OF THERAPY OUTCOME

Several recent analyses of the effectiveness of psychotherapy provide an even more optimistic picture. For the most part, they are based on a statistical technique called *meta-analysis* by means of which the results of many different studies can be combined. In the most comprehensive analysis of this kind, 475 different studies, comprising 25,000 patients in all, were reviewed (Smith, Glass, and Miller, 1980). In each of these studies, patients who received some kind of psychotherapy were compared with a reasonably comparable group of patients who did not. The studies differed in many respects. One factor that varied was the kind of psychotherapy, whether psychodynamic, humanistic, behavioral, or cognitive. Another factor that varied was the criterion of improvement. In some cases, the criterion was the level of a symptom: the amount of avoidance that snake phobics eventually showed toward snakes, the number of washing episodes shown by compulsive washers, and so on. In others, it was based on an improvement in functioning, such as a rise in a disturbed student's grade-point average. In still others, such as studies on depressed patients, it was concerned with an improvement in mood, as rated by scales filled out by the patient herself or by knowledgeable outsiders such as her spouse and children. Given all these differences between the studies, combining the results seemed problematic, but meta-analysis provided a method.

Consider two hypothetical studies, A and B. Let's say that Study A shows that after treatment the average snake phobic can move closer to a snake than the average patient who received no treatment. Let's assume that Study B found that depressed students who received psychotherapy show a greater increase in grade-point average (GPA) than do equivalent students in an untreated control group. On the face of it, there's no way to average the results of the two studies, for they are measured in completely different units. In the first case, the average effect of therapy—that is, the difference between the group that received treatment and the one that did not—is measured in feet (how near to the snake the patient will go); in the second, it is counted in GPA points. But here's the trick provided by meta-analysis. It is to determine the percentage of persons in the untreated group whose improvement score is below the average improvement score of the treated group. Let's suppose we find that in Study A, 85 percent of the patients are able to move closer to the snake than the average untreated patient. Let's further suppose that in Study B, 75 percent of the students who received psychotherapy get a GPA that's higher than the average GPA of the untreated students. Now we can average the scores. To be sure, feet and GPA points are like apples and oranges and cannot be compared. But the percentage relationships—in our case, 85 and 75—are comparable. Since this is so, they can be averaged across different studies.

The conclusion drawn by averaging across the 475 studies reviewed was that the "average person who receives therapy is better off at the end of it than 80 percent of the persons who do not" (Smith, Glass, and Miller, 1980, p. 87). Later analyses used somewhat more stringent criteria in eliminating studies that were methodologically suspect, and these yielded similar results (e.g., Andrews and Harvey, 1981; Shapiro and Shapiro, 1982). Further studies showed that these improvements are still found when patients are studied months or years after treatment (Nicholson and Berman, 1983).

DETERIORATION EFFECTS

Overall, it appears that patients who receive psychotherapy are better off than patients who do not. But this statement applies to averages. When we look at individuals, we find that while psychotherapy has an effect, this effect is not always for the better. A certain proportion of patients seem to get worse. Some evidence that this is so came from an inspection of the variability of post-treatment test scores (for example, self-ratings). After psychotherapy, the scores on such tests are more divergent than the scores of an untreated control group. This suggests that while some patients are improving, some others—fortunately, a smaller number, between 5 and 10 percent of patients—become worse than they were to start with (Bergin, 1967; Smith et al., 1980).

One possible cause of this ***deterioration effect*** is that psychotherapy sometimes disrupts what is stable in the patient's life and provides no substitute (Bergin, 1967; Hadley and Strupp, 1976). Sometimes the original problems worsen, or the patient begins to show new ones. For example, the therapy may lead a patient to regard her present relationship as unsatisfactory, but as she takes steps to end it she becomes severely depressed at the prospect of being alone. Many cases of deterioration in psychotherapy seem to be due to a bad therapist-patient relationship at the outset or to outright incompetence or even pathology in the therapist (Hadley and Strupp, 1976; Smith, Glass, and Miller, 1980). But investigators are hesitant to affix all blame on therapists, because some patients are quite difficult to work with for any therapist. Events in the patient's life—such as the death of a spouse or the loss of a job—can occur during therapy while not resulting from it. These kinds of events can lead to a worsening of the patient's condition while she is in therapy and lead to the appearance that the therapy caused the deterioration (Mays and Franks, 1985).

COMPARING DIFFERENT THERAPIES

The preceding discussion indicates that patients who receive psychotherapy will, on average, be better off than patients who do not. To the extent that this is so, psychotherapy works. But as we've seen, there are any number of different psychotherapies: psychodynamic, humanistic, behavioral, cognitive, and so on. Do any of them get better results than the others?

THE DODO BIRD VERDICT

Which form of psychotherapy works better than others? This question has been asked by several investigators. Their answer is unlikely to provide comfort for the adherents of any one school of psychotherapy. Most studies of psychotherapeutic outcomes suggest that the differences in the effectiveness of the various psychotherapies are slight or nonexistent. This view is sometimes called the ***dodo bird verdict*** after the dodo bird in *Alice in Wonderland* who organized a race between various Wonderland creatures and concluded that "Everyone has won and all must have prizes" (see Figure 19.7; Luborsky, Singer, and Luborsky,

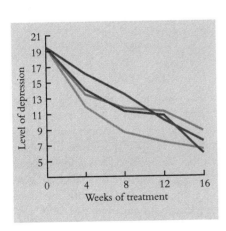

19.7 The dodo bird verdict *The figure shows the results of a study of 279 depressed patients receiving either cognitive therapy, interpersonal therapy (Klerman et al., 1984), antidepressant medication (Tofranil), or a placebo. The results after four months show that, while all treated patients were better off than the placebo controls, the particular treatment they received made little difference. (Gibbons et al., 1993)*

"Everyone has won and all must have prizes." (*From Lewis Carroll,* Alice in Wonderland, *1865/1963)*

1975). While a few reviewers feel that the behavioral and cognitive therapies have a slight advantage (e.g., Shapiro and Shapiro, 1982), many others judge that the outcome similarities far outweigh the differences (e.g., Smith, Glass, and Miller, 1980; Sloane et al., 1975; Elkin et al., 1989).

PLACEBO EFFECTS

One way to explain equivalence in therapeutic outcome is to propose that psychotherapy simply generated a placebo effect. According to this view, the patients got better because they expected to get better, in a manner quite analogous to what happens when patients ingest little blue sugar pills in the belief that they are swallowing a potent medicine (see pp. 769–70). We wouldn't expect blue sugar pills to be more helpful than red or green sugar pills; analogously, we shouldn't expect psychodynamic therapies to be more (or less) effective than, say, humanistic therapies. Whether we're dealing with sugar pills or with psychotherapies, in this view all that matters is the patients' belief in the therapy and hope for help through it.

An ingenious demonstration of a placebo effect in psychotherapy was provided in a classic study by Gordon Paul in which students who suffered from severe anxiety during public speaking were given five sessions of a bogus treatment. During each session, they took what they thought was a potent tranquilizer (it actually was a capsule of sodium bicarbonate) and performed a boring discrimination task. They were told that this task was ordinarily very stressful but would not be so for them because of the "tranquilizer." If repeated often enough, this experience would then inoculate them against anxiety-provoking situations in real life. Needless to say, all of this was a ruse, but the subjects accepted it and believed that the treatment would help them. When later tested for speech anxiety, these subjects improved considerably more than an untreated control group, providing a powerful demonstration of a psychotherapeutic placebo effect (Paul, 1966).

The mere expectation of getting better seems to help, at least in the short term and in laboratory studies of this type. But is that all there is to psychotherapy? Placebo effects wear thin over the long term: Hope fades and problems often return. Indeed, the bulk of the evidence argues that psychotherapy is more than a placebo. Several meta-analytic studies have compared the effect of placebo treatments (such as Paul's) to the effect of genuine psychotherapies. By and large, genuine psychotherapy led to more improvement than placebo treatments (Smith, Glass, and Miller, 1980; Andrews and Harvey, 1981; for a contrary view and discussion, see Prioleau, Murdock, and Brody, 1983).

Placebo effects are evidently smaller than the benefits produced by genuine psychotherapy. So we are still left with the problem of explaining the dodo bird effect.

COMMON FACTORS

One explanation centers on the shared themes that underlie many of the beliefs and practices of the various schools, such as attempts at *emotional defusing,* efforts to provide *interpersonal learning,* and an *empathic relationship* with another human being conducted within an accepted social framework (see pp. 785–86). To the extent that these features are indeed therapeutic and are common to the various schools, we would expect that they (together with some shared psychological placebo effects) will exert similar beneficial effects.

SPECIFIC FACTORS

There may also be some effects that are not so readily picked up by the outcome studies (for the most part, meta-analytic) that we've discussed thus far. These suggested that all psychotherapies are equally effective, regardless of the banner under which they are practiced. But the real issue may not be which therapy is most effective, but rather which treatment is most effective for which patient under which set of circumstances (Paul, 1967). Meta-analysis may not be the

Placebos in medieval medicine *Medieval apothecaries prescribed many "medicinal" substances that were of no proven benefit to their patients. They must have had a placebo effect, though, because the patients (that survived) kept coming back. (Courtesy of Österreichische Nationalbibliotek, Vienna)*

best way to answer this question, for it tends to lump different disorders together. Some critics feel that this is like combining apples and oranges and coming up with only moderate evidence for fruit.

According to some practitioners some treatments do have a specific effect, being more effective for some patients and some conditions than for others. They believe that psychotherapy works best and goes beyond the effect of the common factors, if specific therapies are matched to the disorder and the patient (Beutler and Clarkin, 1990; Norcross, 1991; Norcross and Freedheim, 1992). This position is sometimes called *prescriptionism,* for it argues that specific therapies be *prescribed* for patients suffering from particular mental disorders just as specific medications are prescribed for particular physical illnesses.

A number of such "prescriptions" are in current use today. They will undoubtedly be superseded by more effective ones developed in years hence, but the majority of practitioners regard them as the best to date. For example, it is widely believed that phobias and related anxiety conditions are best treated by any of the behavior therapies that try to eliminate fear, such as systematic desensitization (Emmelkamp, 1986). Similar techniques have proved useful in dealing with panic, although recent evidence suggests that cognitive therapy (especially in conjunction with antidepressant medication) is even more effective (Clark, 1988). Schizophrenia responds to the classic antipsychotics, with medication by Clozaril or Resperdol preferable if possible and medically permissible. Depression seems to be effectively treated by antidepressant medications, cognitive therapy, or interpersonal therapy, and electroconvulsive treatment tends to work if these do not. Eskalith is highly favored for bipolar disorder, with psychotherapy of no direct use. These are just a few examples of what amounts to an emerging cookbook of therapeutic prescriptions for mental disorders.

ACCOUNTABILITY FOR PSYCHOTHERAPY

While attacks such as Eysenck's provoked the initial studies of therapeutic effectiveness, a more recent impetus has been the demand for economic accountability. Beginning in the 1970s, private insurance companies that had for years reimbursed patients for both inpatient care and outpatient psychotherapy began to question the costs and benefits of each. As health maintenance organizations (HMOs) began to provide group health care, they too began to require that psychotherapists account for themselves by showing that the time they spent with patients was worth the cost. Finally, tax-funded government programs like Medicare debated whether even to finance psychotherapy (Garfield, 1992).

Did patients do any better with one kind of care than another, or with twelve years of therapy rather than twelve weeks? These questions struck at the pocketbook of both patient and practitioner, and they forced drastic changes in the practice of psychotherapy. Instead of justifying psychotherapy based on theories about psychopathology or commentaries about meaning and existence, practitioners suddenly had to show that what they practiced improved patients using the most concrete of dependent variables: How fast could the patient be discharged? How rapidly could she return to work? How long was the patient able to function without further use of professional services? If the costs of therapy were to be reimbursed, the therapy had to be the most cost-effective. And if a patient was making no progress in therapy, the solution was not to conduct more therapy but to discontinue it entirely.

The ramifications also became legal. Could a therapist be guilty of malpractice for not offering a patient the best treatment or at least a proven treatment? Indeed, this was the outcome of a widely cited court case that pitted biological against psychoanalytic approaches to the treatment of depression. The case concerned a patient who was severely depressed and was admitted to a psychoanalytically oriented private hospital where he received no antidepressant medication, only intensive psychoanalytically based psychotherapy. During his hospital stay his condition worsened: He lost forty pounds, and his overall physical condition deteriorated. Even so, the therapy was continued, and the patient's deterioration was interpreted as reflecting the difficulties of working through the patient's defenses. After seven months, the patient's family became alarmed, removed him from this hospital, and placed him in another in which he was immediately treated with antidepressant medication. He recovered within three months and began initiating the lawsuit against the first hospital (*Osheroff v. Chestnut Lodge;* see Klerman, 1990).

The lawsuit was settled out of court, but the result stirred the medical community to form a set of standards of effective treatment. One of the first concerned the acceptable care for depression. It provides that depressives are best treated by a combination of antidepressant medication and psychotherapy. If psychotherapy is attempted alone, it should be only for mild to moderate depressions and only if improvement is seen quickly; otherwise antidepressant medication must be instituted (American Psychiatric Association, 1993). These standards will probably come to govern all mental-health practitioners, and similar standards of care are expected for other disorders.

Given these legal and economic factors, most psychotherapists today rarely engage patients in long-term insight or humanistic-existential therapy. Instead, they try to provide therapies that have a reasonable chance of working and working quickly. Most psychotherapy today reflects this pragmatic concern with expense and expediency; it consists of brief problem-solving sessions, various psychoeducational interventions such as stress-management classes, and time-limited behavioral therapy (Vandenbos, Cummings, and DeLeon, 1992).

A CENTURY OF THERAPY

Where does all of this leave us? It has been more than a hundred years since Krafft-Ebbing's discovery that general paresis is caused by syphilis and since Freud and Breuer's classic studies of hysteria. What can we say today about the treatment of mental disorder?

All in all, there has been considerable progress.

Let's begin with psychotherapy. There is little doubt that psychotherapy produces some nonspecific benefits. It helps people by providing someone in whom they can confide, who lends advice about troubling matters, who listens to them, and who instills hope that they will get better. The critic may reply that such gains merely reflect placebo effects and similar matters. According to this view, the benefits are not produced by any specific psychotherapeutic technique but might just as easily have been provided by a wise uncle, the understanding family doctor, or the local clergy.

Even if this were true—and it is certainly not the whole story—it may not be relevant. For wise uncles are in short supply today. The extended family in which uncles, nieces, and grandparents lived nearby is largely a thing of the past. The same is true of the family doctor, who has vanished from the scene, together with his bedside manner. Nor do many people today have a member of the clergy as a confidant. All of this suggests that psychotherapy has come to fill a social vacuum. Some of its effect may well be placebo-like, but a placebo may be better than nothing. And for the present, the psychotherapeutic professions seem to be the officially designated dispensers of such placebos.

But this is by no means all. For over and above placebo effects there seem to be some genuine, specific psychotherapeutic benefits that produce improvement, though rarely a complete cure. The specific ingredients that bring these effects about have not been identified with certainty but they probably include emotional defusing, interpersonal learning, and some insight—all acquired within the therapeutic situation and somehow transferred to the patient's life beyond.

How about biological therapies? Here the progress has been dramatic. Antipsychotic drugs control some of the worst manifestations of schizophrenia, the antidepressants and antimanic drugs (and where appropriate, electroconvulsive therapy) do the same for the mood swings of depression and mania, as do the anxiolytics for excessive anxiety. These advances are far from what one might wish. The drugs don't begin to effect a cure, and all have side effects. But we're much further along than we were a century ago.

How far is far? As so often, it depends on where we look. If we look back and compare our current practices with those at the time of the American Revolution when Benjamin Rush dunked his patients into ice cold water or whirled them around until they were unconscious, we've come a long way. But if we look ahead to some diagnostic manual of the future in which schizophrenia, mood and anxiety disorders, and all the rest of the current DSM-IV entries have neatly catalogued therapies that are sure to work, we must recognize that we have a much longer way to go. But considering our progress over the last hundred years, there is much to celebrate.

SUMMARY

1. *Biological therapies* constitute one major form of treatment of mental disorder. Of these, the most widely used are *psychotropic medications.* The classic *antipsychotics* like Thorazine and Haldol are helpful in holding in check the major positive symptoms of schizophrenia, and new antipsychotics like Clozaril and Resperdol show promise in treating negative symptoms as well. These new antipsychotics can often produce beneficial results in schizophrenics who have not responded to classic antipsychotics.

2. *Lithium carbonate* is useful in cases of bipolar disorder, especially in forestalling or reducing the intensity of manic episodes.

3. Classic *antidepressants* such as *MAO inhibitors* and *tricyclics* counteract depression, and one particular tricyclic, Anafranil, is effective in many cases of obsessive-compulsive disorder. These classic antidepressants all have many undesirable side effects. *Selective serotonin reuptake inhibitors* like Prozac were designed to maximize their effects on serotonin neurotransmission. They have fewer side effects and are equally effective for depression and obsessive-compulsive disorder.

4. The effectiveness of pharmacological medication—as indeed of all therapies—requires careful evaluation that controls for spontaneous improvement and *placebo effects,* and that also guards against both the physicians' and the patients' expectations by use of *double-blind techniques.* Such studies have demonstrated genuine effects of certain psychotropic medications, some of which are quite specific to a particular mental disorder. These medications reduce the signs and symptoms of a disorder but do not cure it. Without maintenance doses, patients discharged from care may relapse.

5. Other biological therapies include *psychosurgery,* a procedure that was once performed rather promiscuously and to the detriment of the recipients but is now conducted much more selectively and precisely. *Electroconvulsive therapy (ECT)* is markedly effective in cases of severe and potentially suicidal depression and for cases of bipolar disorder that resist antimanic medications.

6. Another approach to the treatment of mental disorder, *psychotherapy,* relies on psychological means alone. Much of it is derived from *classical psychoanalysis* but has been expanded and diversified in both its guiding principles and techniques.

7. Psychoanalysts try to help their patients to recover repressed memories and wishes so that they can overcome crippling internal conflicts. Their tools include *free association* and the interpretation of the patient's *resistance* to it. The goal is emotional rather than mere intellectual *insight,* an achievement made possible by an analysis of the *transference* relationship between analyst and patient.

8. In *psychodynamic therapy,* therapists follow Freud's basic principles but generally place greater emphasis on current interpersonal and social problems rather than on psychosexual matters in the patient's childhood. They also tend to take a more active role in helping the patient extend the therapeutic experience to the world outside.

9. A different approach is taken by *behavior therapists* whose concern is with unwanted, overt behaviors rather than with hypothetical underlying causes. Many of the behavior therapists' techniques are derived from the principles of classical and instrumental conditioning. Therapies based on classical conditioning include *systematic desensitization,* which tries to countercondition the patient's fear by a policy of gradual exposure. Another is *aversion therapy* in which undesirable behaviors, thoughts, and desires are coupled with unpleasant stimuli. Therapies based on operant conditioning principles include the use of *token economies* in which patients are systematically reinforced for desirable behaviors.

10. Some recent offshoots of behavior therapy share its concrete and directive orientation but not its emphasis on conditioning. One example is *cognitive therapy,* which tries to change the way the patient thinks about his situation. Others include various attempts to advance the patient's social education, using techniques such as *graded task assignments, modeling,* and *role playing.*

11. Another group of practitioners, the *humanistic therapists,* charge that both behavior therapy and psychoanalysis are too mechanistic and manipulative and that they fail to deal with their patients as whole persons. An example of a humanistic approach is Rogers' *client-centered therapy,* which is largely *nondirective* and is based on the idea that therapy is a personal growth process. A related approach is *existential therapy,* whose goal is to help patients recognize the importance of personal responsibility and free choice, and to assist them in imbuing their lives with meaning.

12. The last few decades have seen an enormous extension of psychotherapy. One extension is of method. An example is *group therapy* in which patients are treated in groups rather than individually. Another example is *marital and family therapy,* whose practitioners believe that family distress is not in the pathology of any one individual but in the relationships within the family system and who therefore try to rectify these faulty relationships. Another extension concerns therapeutic goals. While the original purpose of psychotherapy was to cure pathology, some practitioners gradually broadened this goal to include personal growth and the discovery of meaning in life. Therapists are now encouraged to develop *cultural competence,* so that they can adapt their therapies to the specific cultural values and customs that patients bring with them.

13. In recent years, investigators have begun to assess the effectiveness of psychotherapies through a statistical technique called *meta-analysis* by means of which the results of many different studies can be combined. The results of such analyses indicate that the various psychotherapies are more effective than placebo treatments, which in turn are better than no treatment at all. Comparing the effect of different psychotherapies is enormously difficult, but the main finding is that therapies tend to be fairly effective and that they are effective to about the same extent (the *dodo bird verdict*).

14. The dodo-bird verdict, however, comes from studies that combine many types of patients and disorders. Work is underway to determine the extent to which therapy can be matched to the patient and the disorder. Practitioners who adopt the *prescriptionist* position believe that in addition to placebo effects and various common factors such as *emotional defusing, interpersonal learning,* and an *empathic relationship* with another person, particular therapies have some specific effects on particular conditions.

15. Economic factors and legal issues have forced psychotherapists to reexamine their own efforts and provide only those services that have demonstrated effectiveness. This is leading to the development of generally accepted professional standards of care for specific mental disorders.

EPILOGUE

We have come to the end of our journey. We have traveled through the sprawling fields of psychology, a loosely federated intellectual empire that stretches from the domains of the biological sciences on one border to those of the social sciences on the other. We have gone from one end of psychology to another. What have we learned?

In looking back over our journey, there is little doubt that we have encountered many more questions than answers. To be sure, very much more is known today about mind and behavior than was known in the days of, say, Thorndike and Köhler, let alone those of Descartes, Locke, and Kant. For by now, psychology has assuredly become a science, and in fact, a science of quite respectable accomplishments. But this does not change the fact that what we know today is just a small clearing in a vast jungle of ignorance. As we come to know more, the clearing expands, but so does the circumference that borders on the uncharted wildness.

What can we say? We can point at what we know and congratulate ourselves. Or we can consider what we do not know and bemoan our ignorance. Perhaps a wiser course is one recommended by Sigmund Freud on thinking about some aspects of human intellectual history (Freud, 1917).

Freud suggested a parallel between the psychological growth of each human child and the intellectual progress of humanity as a whole. As he saw it, the infant is initially possessed by an all-prevading sense of his own power and importance. He cries and his parents come to change or feed or rock him and so he feels that he is the cause of whatever happens around him, the sole center of a world that revolves around him alone. But this happy delusion of his own omnipotence cannot last forever. Eventually the growing infant discovers that he is not the hub of the universe. This recognition may come as a cruel blow, but he will ultimately be the better for it. For the child cannot become strong and capable without some awareness that he is not so as yet, without first accepting the fact that he can't have his way just by wishing. His first achievements will be slight—as he lifts his own cup or a bit later says his first word—but they are real enough and will lay the foundation for his later mastery of his environment.

Freud thought that a similar theme underlies the growth of humankind's awareness of the world in which we live. On two crucial occasions in our history, we had to give up some cherished beliefs in our own power and importance. With Copernicus, we had to cede our place in the center of the physical universe: the sun doesn't circle us, but we the sun. With Darwin, we had to perform a similar abdication in the biological sphere: We are not specially created but are descended from other animals. Each of these intellectual revolutions ran into vehement opposition; in large part because each represented a gigantic blow to humanity's self-love and pride. They made us face our own ignorance and insignificance. But however painful it may have been initially, each recognition of our weakness ultimately helped us gain more strength, each confession of ignorance eventually led to deeper understanding. The Copernican revolution forced us to admit our minute place in the celestial scheme of things, but this admission was the first step in a journey of ever-increasing physical horizons, a journey which in our own time brought human beings to the moon. The Darwinian revolution made us aware that we are just one biological species among millions, the product of the same evolutionary process that brought forth sea urchins and penguins as well as us. But this awareness opened the way for continually expanding explorations of the biological universe, explorations that have already given us much greater control of our own bodily condition and of the fragile environment in which humans and other species exist.

In this century we have had to suffer yet another blow to our self-pride. We learned that we are not sure of what goes on in our own minds. Modern psychology, for all its accomplishments, has made it utterly clear that thus far we know even less about our own mental processes and behavior than we know about the physical and biological world around us. Here, too, we have to confess that we are weak and ignorant. We can only hope that this confession will have some of the effects of our previous ones, that here again strength will grow out of weakness and knowledge out of folly and ignorance. If so, we may finally understand why we think and do what we think and do, so that we may ultimately master our inner selves as we have learned to master the world around us.

There are few goals in science that are worthier than this.

APPENDIX

STATISTICS: THE COLLECTION, ORGANIZATION, AND INTERPRETATION OF DATA

DESCRIBING THE DATA   A2

CATEGORICAL AND ORDINAL SCALES ■ INTERVAL SCALES ■ RATIO SCALES

COLLECTING THE DATA   A4

THE EXPERIMENT ■ THE OBSERVATIONAL STUDY ■ THE CASE STUDY

SELECTING THE SUBJECTS   A5

SAMPLE AND POPULATION ■ RANDOM AND STRATIFIED SAMPLES ■ SAMPLING RESPONSES

ORGANIZING THE DATA: DESCRIPTIVE STATISTICS   A7

THE FREQUENCY DISTRIBUTION ■ MEASURES OF CENTRAL TENDENCY ■ MEASURES OF VARIABILITY ■ CONVERTING SCORES TO COMPARE THEM ■ THE NORMAL DISTRIBUTION

DESCRIBING THE RELATION BETWEEN TWO VARIABLES: CORRELATION   A14

POSITIVE AND NEGATIVE CORRELATION ■ THE CORRELATION COEFFICIENT ■ INTERPRETING AND MISINTERPRETING CORRELATIONS

INTERPRETING DATA: INFERENTIAL STATISTICS   A18

ACCOUNTING FOR VARIABILITY ■ HYPOTHESIS TESTING ■ SOME IMPLICATIONS OF STATISTICAL INFERENCE

SUMMARY   A27

large body of psychological knowledge has been summarized in this book, and a good part of the discussion was devoted to the ways in which this knowledge was obtained. But there are certain methodological issues that were dealt with only in passing. These concern **statistical methods,** the ways in which investigators gather, organize, and interpret collections of numerical data.

Suppose some investigators want to find out whether three-year-old boys are more aggressive than three-year-old girls. To answer this question is a very big job. To start with, the investigators will have to come up with some appropriate measure of aggression. They will then have to select the subjects. The investigators presumably want to say something about three-year-olds in general, not just the particular three-year-olds in their study. To make sure that this can be done, they have to select their subjects appropriately. Even more important, their groups of boys and girls must be as comparable as possible, so that one can be reasonably sure that any differences between the two groups is attributable to the difference in sex rather than to other factors (such as intellectual development, social class, and so on).

The investigators are now ready to collect their data. But having collected them, they will have to find some way of organizing these data in a meaningful way. Suppose the study used two groups of, say, 50 boys and 50 girls, each observed on 10 separate occasions. This means that the investigators will end up with at least 1,000 separate numerical entries (say, number of aggressive acts for each child on each occasion), 500 for the boys and 500 for the girls. Something has to be done to reduce this mass of numbers into some manageable, summarized form. This is usually accomplished by some process of averaging scores.

The next step involves statistical interpretation. Suppose the investigators find that the average aggression score is greater for the boys than for the girls (it probably will be). Can they be sure that the difference between the groups is large enough not to be dismissed as a fluke, a chance event? For it is just about certain that the data contain **variability.** The children in each group will not perform equally; furthermore, the same child may very well behave differently on one occasion than another. As a result, the scores in the two groups will almost surely overlap; that is, some girls will get a higher aggression score than some boys. Could it be that the difference *between* the groups (that is, the difference between the two averages) is an accidental chance product of the variability that is seen to hold *within* the two groups? One of the key functions of statistical methods is to deal with questions of this sort, to help us draw useful general conclusions about organisms despite the unavoidable variability in their behavior.

The preceding example indicates the main tasks to which statistical methods have been applied. In this appendix, we will sketch the logic that underlies these methods as psychologists use them.

DESCRIBING THE DATA

The data with which statistics deals are numerical, so a preliminary step in statistical analysis is the reduction of the actual results of a study to numbers. Much of the power of statistics results from the fact that numbers (unlike responses to a questionnaire, videotapes of social interactions, or lists of words recalled by a subject in a memory experiment) can be manipulated with the rules of arithmetic. As a result, scientists prefer to use response measures that are in numerical form. Consider our hypothetical study of aggression and sex. The investigators who watched the subjects might rate their aggression in various situations (from, say, "extremely aggressive" to "extremely docile") or they might count the number of aggressive acts (say, hitting or insulting another child), and so on. This operation of assigning numbers to observed events (usually, a subject's responses) is called *scaling.*

There are several types of scales that will concern us. They differ by the arithmetical operations that can be performed upon them.

CATEGORICAL AND ORDINAL SCALES

Sometimes the scores assigned to individuals are merely *categorical* (also called *nominal.*) For example, when respondents to a poll are asked to name the television channel they watch most frequently, they might respond "4," "2," or "13." These numbers serve only to group the responses into categories. They can obviously not be subjected to any arithmetic operations.

Ordinal numbers convey more information, in that their relative magnitude is meaningful—not arbitrary, as in the case of categorical scales. If individuals are asked to list the ten people they most admire, the number 1 can be assigned to the most admired person, 2 to the runner-up, and so on. The smaller the number assigned, the more the person is admired. Notice that no such statement can be made of television channels: Channel 4 is not more anything than channel 2, just different from it.

Scores which are ordinally scaled cannot, however, be added or subtracted. The first two persons on the most-admired list differ in admirability by 1; so do the last two. Yet the individual who has done the ranking may admire the first person far more than the other nine, all of whom might be very similar in admirability; in other words, given an ordinal scale, differences of 1 are not necessarily equal psychologically. Imagine a child who, given this task, lists his mother first, followed by the starting lineup of the Chicago Cubs baseball team. In this example, the difference of 8 between person 2 and person 10 probably represents a smaller difference in judged admirability than the difference of 1 obtained between persons 1 and 2 (at least so the mother hopes).

INTERVAL SCALES

Scales in which equal differences between scores, or intervals, *can* be treated as equal units are called *interval scales.* Reaction time is a common psychological variable that is usually treated as an interval scale. In some memory experiments, a subject must respond as quickly as possible to each of several words, some of which he has seen earlier in the experiment; the task is to indicate whether each word has appeared before by pressing one of two buttons. An unknown, but possibly constant, part of the reaction time is simply the time required to press the response button; the rest is the time required for the decision-making process:

$$\text{reaction time} = \text{decision time} + \text{button-press time} \qquad (1)$$

Suppose a subject requires an average of 2 seconds to respond to nouns, 3 seconds to verbs, and 4 seconds to adjectives. The difference in decision time between verbs and nouns ($3 - 2 = 1$ second) is the same as the difference in decision time between adjectives and verbs ($4 - 3 = 1$ second). We can make this statement—which in turn suggests various hypotheses about the factors that underlie such differences—precisely because reaction time can be regarded as an interval scale.

RATIO SCALES

Scores based on an interval scale allow subtraction and addition. But they do not necessarily allow multiplication and division. Consider the centigrade scale of temperature. There is no doubt that the difference between 10 and 20 degrees centigrade is equal to that between 30 and 40 degrees centigrade. But can one say that 20 degrees centigrade is *twice* as high a temperature as 10 degrees centigrade? The answer is no, for the centigrade scale of temperature is only an interval scale. It is not a *ratio scale,* which allows statements such as 10 feet is 1/5 as long as 50 feet, or 15 pounds is 3 times as heavy as 5 pounds. To make such statements one needs a true zero point. Such a ratio scale with a zero point does exist for temperature—the Kelvin absolute temperature scale, whose zero point is about −273 degrees centigrade.

Some psychological variables can be described by a ratio scale. This is true of various forms of sensory intensity—brightness, loudness, and so on. For example, it makes sense to say that the rock music emanating from your neighbor's apartment is four times as loud as your roommate singing in the shower. But there are many psychological variables that cannot be so readily described in ratio terms. Let's go back to reaction time. This cannot be considered a ratio scale for the decision process. In our previous example we saw that the reaction time for adjectives was 4 seconds, while that for nouns was 2 seconds. But we cannot say that the 4-second response represents twice as much *decision* time as the 2-second response, because of the unknown time required to press the response button. Since this time is unknown, we have no zero point.

The fact that very few variables are ratio scaled does not, of course, prevent people from describing ordinal- or interval-scaled variables in ratio terms. A claim by an advertiser that drug A is "twice as effective" as drug B may mean that A works twice as fast, or for twice the time, or is successful on twice as many people, or requires only half the dose. A potential consumer needs to know the advertiser's meaning of "effective" to evaluate the claim. Similarly, a 4-second reaction time in the word-recognition experiment is certainly twice as long as a 2-second reaction time; there is no harm in saying so, as long as it is understood that we are not talking about the decision time but rather about the total reaction time.

COLLECTING THE DATA

The kinds of scales we have just discussed concern the ways in which psychological variables are described in numerical terms. The point of most psychological investigations is to see how such variables are related to various factors that may produce them. Psychologists—and most other scientists—employ three major methodological tools to achieve this end: the experiment, the observational study, and the case study.

THE EXPERIMENT

An *experiment* is a study in which the experimenter deliberately manipulates one or more variables to determine the effect of this manipulation on another variable. As an example, consider an experiment conducted to determine whether visual imagery aids memory. Participants in the experiment listen to a list of words, which they are instructed to memorize; later they are asked to recall as many words as possible. Two groups of subjects are chosen. One is the *experimental group;* this is the group to which the experimenter's manipulation is applied. It consists of subjects who are instructed to form visual images that connect each word to the preceding word. Other subjects form the *control group,* a group to which the experimenter's manipulation is not applied. These control subjects are not given imagery instructions. Many experiments have more than one experimental group (in this example, different groups might be told to do their visual imagining in different ways) or more than one control group (here, a second control group might be instructed to rehearse by repeating each word over and over).

Like many other experiments, this one can be thought of as a situation in which the experimenter varies something (here the instructions given to the subjects) and observes the effect of this variation on certain responses of the subjects (the number of words they correctly recall). The variable that is manipulated by the experimenter (imagery instructions) is called the *independent variable.* The subject's response (number of words recalled) is called the *dependent variable,* since the investigator wants to know whether it is dependent upon his manipulation of the independent variable. Speaking loosely, independent variables are sometimes regarded as causes, dependent variables as effects.

The results of our experiment are graphically presented in Figure A.1. The values of the independent variable are indicated on the horizontal, or *x*-axis, and the values of the dependent variable on the vertical, or *y*-axis. The figure displays the average number of items recalled for subjects who used visual imagery in memorizing and for those who did not. We will have more to say about this experiment presently.

A.1 The results of an experiment on memorizing *Subjects in the imagery group, who formed visual images of the words they were to memorize, recalled an average of 11 words. Subjects in the control group, who received no special instructions, recalled an average of 8 words.*

THE OBSERVATIONAL STUDY

Much psychological research departs from the experimental method in that investigators do not produce the effects directly, but only observe them. They do not so much design the experiment as discover it. Such an investigation is called an *observational study.* Consider the question "What is the effect of prenatal malnutrition on IQ?" This question can only be answered by locating children whose mothers were malnourished during pregnancy and measuring their IQs; to provide pregnant women with inadequate diets deliberately is obviously worse than unethical. But even though the investigators do not manipulate the mother's diet (or indeed, anything else), some of the methodological terms used before can still be applied. We can consider the mother's diet as the independent variable, and the child's IQ as the dependent variable. A group analogous to the experimental group would consist of children whose mothers were malnourished during pregnancy. An analogue to the control group is a group of children whose mothers' diet was adequate.

Observational studies like this one are sometimes called "experiments of nature." Because nature does not always provide exactly those control groups that the investigator might wish for, observational studies can be difficult to interpret. For example, children whose mothers were malnourished during pregnancy are often born into environments that might also be expected to have negative effects on IQ. Women whose diet is inadequate during pregnancy are likely to be poor; they are therefore less likely to provide some of the physical advantages (like good food and health care) and educational advantages (like books and nursery schools) that may well be helpful in developing intelligence.

THE CASE STUDY

In many areas of psychology, conclusions are based on only one person who is studied intensively. Such an investigation is called a *case study.* Individuals who display unusual psychological or physiological characteristics, such as rare forms of color blindness, exceptionally good or poor memory, or brain injuries, can sometimes provide information about normal vision, memory, or brain function that would be difficult or impossible to obtain from normal individuals. Take the patient known as H.M., who suffered severe amnesia after brain surgery (see Chapter 7). Before the operation his memory was normal; afterward he could remember virtually nothing about events that occurred after the operation. This patient has been extensively studied because of his unusual memory disorder. Since his amnesia is apparently the result of the destruction of a particular structure in the brain, the hippocampus, a comparison of H.M.'s performance with that of normal individuals allows us to make inferences about the role of the hippocampus in normal memory.

Some of the most famous case studies in psychology are those described by Sigmund Freud, whose extensive psychoanalytic interviews of his patients led him to develop his theories of dreams, defense mechanisms, and other psychological processes (see Chapter 17).

SELECTING THE SUBJECTS

How does one select the subjects for a psychological study? To answer the question, we have to consider the difference between a population and a sample.

SAMPLE AND POPULATION

Psychologists—again like other scientists—usually want to make statements about a larger group of persons (or animals) than the particular subjects they happen to use in their study. They want their conclusions to apply to a particular *population:* all members of a given group—say, all three-year-old boys, all schizophrenic patients, all U.S. voters, and in some cases, all humans. But they normally can't study all members of the given population. As a result, they have to select a *sample,* that is, a subset of the population they are interested in. Their hope is that the results found in the sample can be generalized to the population from which the sample is drawn.

It is important to realize that generalizations from a given sample to a particular population can only be made if the sample is representative (that is, typical) of the population to which one wants to generalize. Suppose one does a study on memory by using college students. Can one generalize the results to adults in general? Strictly speaking one cannot, for college students are on the average younger than the population at large and are more accustomed to memorizing things. Under the circumstances, the safest course may be to restrict one's generalizations to the population of college students.

Most experimenters would probably argue that college students don't differ too greatly from the general population (at least in memory skills) so that results obtained with them do apply in general, at least approximately. But there are many cases in which inadequate sampling leads to gross blunders. The classic example is a 1936 poll which predicted that Franklin D. Roosevelt would lose the presidential election. In fact, he won by a landslide. This massive error was produced by a *biased sample*—all persons polled were selected from telephone directories. But in 1936 having a telephone was much more likely among persons of higher than of lower socioeconomic status. As a result, the sample was not representative of the voting population as a whole. Since socioeconomic level affected voting preference, the poll predicted falsely.

RANDOM AND STRATIFIED SAMPLES

To ensure that one can generalize from sample to population, investigators use a *random sample.* This is a sample in which every member of the population has an equal chance of being picked—as in a jury drawn by lot from all the voters of a given district (if none are disqualified or excuse themselves). The random sampling procedure applies with special force to the assignment of subjects in an experiment. Here every effort has to be made to assign subjects randomly to the various experimental or control groups.

For some purposes, even a random sample may not be good enough. While every member of the population has an equal chance of being selected, the sample may still turn out to be atypical by chance alone. This danger of chance error becomes less and less the greater the size of the sample. But if one is forced to use a small sample (and one often is because of lack of time or money), other sampling procedures may be necessary. Suppose we want to take a poll to determine the attitudes of American voters toward legalized abortion. We can expect people's attitudes to differ depending (at least) on their age, sex, and religion. If the sample is fairly small, it is important that each subgroup of the population be (randomly) sampled in proportion to its size. This procedure is called *stratified sampling* and is common in studying psychological traits or attitudes that vary greatly among different subgroups of the population.

SAMPLING RESPONSES

The distinction between sample and population does not only apply to subjects. It also applies to the subjects' responses. Consider the investigators who studied aggressive behavior in 50 three-year-old boys. Each of these boys was observed on 10 occasions. Those 10 occasions can be regarded as a sample of all such occasions, just as the 50 boys can be regarded as a sample of all three-year-old boys (or at least of all middle-class U.S. boys). The investigators will surely want to generalize from this sample of occasions to the population of all such occasions. To make sure that such a generalization is warranted, one has to see to it that the occasions are not atypical—that the child isn't especially tired, or sick, and so on.

ORGANIZING THE DATA: DESCRIPTIVE STATISTICS

We have considered the ways in which psychologists describe the data provided by their subjects by assigning numbers to them (scaling) and the ways in which they collect these data in the first place (experiments, observational studies, case studies). Our next task is to see how these data are organized.

THE FREQUENCY DISTRIBUTION

Suppose we have designed and performed an experiment such as the imagery study described previously. The data will not automatically arrange themselves in the form shown in Figure A.1. Instead, investigators will first be faced with a list of numbers, the scores (number of words recalled correctly) for each subject in a given group. For example, if there were 10 subjects in the control group, their scores (in words correct) might have been

8, 11, 6, 7, 5, 9, 5, 9, 9, 11.

A first step in organizing the data is to list all the possible scores and the frequency with which they occurred, as shown in Table A.1. Such an arrangement is called a ***frequency distribution.***

The frequency distribution can be expressed graphically. A common means for doing this is a ***histogram,*** which depicts the frequency distribution by a series of contiguous rectangles (Figure A.2). The values of the dependent variable (here, the number of words recalled) are shown by the location of each rectangle on the horizontal or *x*-axis. The frequency of each score is shown on the verti-

TABLE A.1 FREQUENCY DISTRIBUTION

Score	Frequency
11	2
10	0
9	3
8	1
7	1
6	1
5	2

A.2 Histogram *In a histogram, a frequency distribution is graphically represented by a series of rectangles. The location of each rectangle on the* x-*axis indicates a score value, while its height shows how often that score value occurred.*

cal or y-axis, that is, by the height of each rectangle. This is simple enough for our example, but in practice graphic presentation often requires a further step. The number of possible values the dependent variable can assume is often very large. As a result, exactly equal values rarely occur, as when reaction times are measured to the nearest millisecond (thousandth of a second). To get around this, the scores are generally grouped by intervals for purposes of graphic display. The histogram might then plot the frequency of all reaction times between, say, 200 and 225 milliseconds, between 226 and 250 milliseconds, and so on.

MEASURES OF CENTRAL TENDENCY

A frequency distribution is a more concise description of the result of the experiment than the raw list of scores from which it was derived, but for many purposes we may want a description that is even more concise. We often wish to summarize an entire distribution by a single, central score; such a score is called a *measure of central tendency.* Three measures of central tendency are commonly used to express this central point of a distribution: the mode, the median, and the mean.

The *mode* is simply the score that occurs most frequently. In our example, the mode is 9. More subjects (to be exact, 3) recalled 9 words than recalled any other number of words.

The *median* is the point that divides the distribution into two equal halves, when the scores are arranged in increasing order. To find the median in our example, we first list the scores:

$$5, 5, 6, 7, 8, 9, 9, 9, 11, 11$$
$$\uparrow$$

Since there are ten scores, the median lies between the fifth and sixth scores, that is, between 8 and 9, as indicated by the arrow. Any score between 8 and 9 would divide the distribution into two equal halves, but it is conventional to choose the number in the center of the interval between them, that is, 8.5. When there is an odd number of scores this problem does not arise.

The third measure of central tendency, the *mean (M),* is the familiar arithmetic average. If N stands for the number of scores, then

$$M = \frac{\text{sum of scores}}{N}$$
$$= \frac{5+5+6+7+8+9+9+9+11+11}{10} = \frac{80}{10} = 8.0$$

Of these three measures, the mode is the least helpful, because the modes of two samples from the same population can differ greatly even if the samples have very similar distributions. If one of the 3 subjects who recalled 9 words recalled only 5 instead, the mode would have been 5 rather than 9. But the mode does have its uses. For example, in certain elections, the candidate with the most votes—the modal candidate—wins

The median and the mean differ most in the degree to which they are affected by extreme scores. If the highest score in our sample were changed from 11 to 111, the median would be unaffected, whereas the mean would jump from 8.0 to 18.0. Most people would find the median (which remains 8.5) a more compelling "average" than the mean in such a situation, since most of the scores in the distribution are close to the median, but are not close to the mean (18.0).

Distributions with extreme values at one end are said to be *skewed.* A classic example is income, since there are only a few high incomes but many low ones. Suppose we sample ten individuals from a neighborhood and find their yearly incomes (in thousands of dollars) to be:

$$5, 5, 5, 5, 10, 10, 10, 20, 20, 1,000$$

The median income for this sample is 10 ($10,000), since both the fifth and sixth scores are 10, and this value reflects the income of the typical individual. The mean income for this sample, however, is $(5 + 5 + 5 + 5 + 10 + 10 + 10 + 20 + 20 + 1,000)/10 = 109$, or $109,000. A politician who wants to demonstrate that his neighborhood has prospered might—quite honestly—use these data to claim that the average (mean) income is $109,000. If, on the other hand, he wished to plead for financial aid, he might say—with equal honesty—that the average (median) income is only $10,000. There is no single "correct" way to find an "average" in this situation, but it is obviously important to know which average (that is, which measure of central tendency) is being used.

When deviations in either direction from the mean are equally frequent, the distribution is said to be *symmetric.* In such distributions, the mean and the median are equal. Many psychological variables have symmetric distributions, but for variables with skewed distributions, like income, measures of central tendency must be chosen with care.

MEASURES OF VARIABILITY

In reducing an entire frequency distribution to an average score, we have discarded a lot of very useful information. Suppose we (or the National Weather Service) measure the temperature every day for a year in various cities and construct a frequency distribution for each city. The mean of this distribution tells us something about the city's climate. That it does not tell us everything is shown by the fact that the mean temperature in both San Francisco and Albuquerque is 56 degrees Fahrenheit. But the climates of the two cities nonetheless differ considerably, as indicated in Table A.2.

The weather displays much more variability in the course of a year in Albuquerque than in San Francisco. A simple measure of variability is the *range,* the highest score minus the lowest. The range of temperatures in San Francisco is 15, while in Albuquerque it is 42.

A shortcoming of the range as a measure of variability is that it reflects the values of only two scores in the entire sample. As an example, consider the following distributions of ages in two college classes:

Distribution *A:* 19, 19, 19, 19, 19, 20, 25
Distribution *B:* 17, 17, 17, 20, 23, 23, 23

TABLE A.2 TEMPERATURE DATA FOR TWO CITIES (DEGREES FAHRENHEIT)				
City	Lowest month	Mean	Highest month	Range
Albuquerque, New Mexico	35	56	77	42
San Francisco, California	48	56	63	15

TABLE A.3 CALCULATING VARIANCE

Score	Score − mean	(Score − mean)^2
8	$8 - 8 = 0$	$0^2 = 0$
11	$11 - 8 = 3$	$3^2 = 9$
6	$6 - 8 = -2$	$(-2)^2 = 4$
7	$7 - 8 = -1$	$(-1)^2 = 1$
5	$5 - 8 = -3$	$(-3)^2 = 9$
9	$9 - 8 = 1$	$1^2 = 1$
5	$5 - 8 = -3$	$(-3)^2 = 9$
9	$9 - 8 = 1$	$1^2 = 1$
9	$9 - 8 = 1$	$1^2 = 1$
11	$11 - 8 = 3$	$3^2 = 9$

Each distribution has a mean of 20. Intuitively, distribution A has less variability, since all scores but one are very close to the mean. Yet the range of scores is the same (6) in both distributions. The problem arises because the range is determined by only two of the seven scores in each distribution.

A better measure of variability would incorporate every score in the distribution rather than just two scores. One might think that the variability could be measured by the average difference between the various scores and the mean, that is, by:

$$\frac{\text{sum of (score} - M)}{N}$$

This hypothetical measure is unworkable, however, because some of the scores are greater than the mean and some are smaller, so that the numerator is a sum of both positive and negative terms. (In fact, it turns out that the sum of the positive terms equals the sum of the negative terms, so that the expression shown above always equals zero.) The solution to this problem is simply to square all the terms in the numerator, thus making them all positive.★ The resulting measure of variability is called the **variance (V):**

$$V = \frac{\text{sum of (score} - M)^2}{N} \tag{2}$$

The calculation of the variance for the control group in the memorization experiment is shown in Table A.3. As the table shows, the variance is obtained by subtracting the mean (M, which equals 8) from each score, squaring each result, adding all the squared terms, and dividing the resulting sum by the total number of scores (N, which equals 10), yielding a value of 4.4.

Because deviations from the mean are squared, the variance is expressed in units different from the scores themselves. If our dependent variable were a distance, measured in centimeters, the variance would be expressed in square centimeters. As we will see in the next section, it is convenient to have a measure of

---

★ An alternative solution would be to sum the absolute value of (score − M), that is, consider only the magnitude of this difference for each score, not the sign. The resulting statistic, called the *average deviation,* is little used, however, primarily because absolute values are not too easily dealt with in certain mathematical terms that underlie statistical theory. As a result, statisticians prefer to transform negative into positive numbers by squaring them.

variability that can be added to or subtracted from the mean; such a measure ought to be expressed in the same units as the original scores. To accomplish this end, we employ another measure of variability, the **standard deviation,** or **SD.** The standard deviation is derived from the variance (V); it is obtained by taking the square root of the variance. Thus

$$SD = \sqrt{V}$$

In our example, SD is about 2.1, the square root of the variance which is 4.4.

CONVERTING SCORES TO COMPARE THEM

Suppose a person takes two tests. One measures her memory span—how many digits she can remember after one presentation. The other test measures her running ability—how fast she can run 100 yards. It turns out that she can remember 8 digits and runs 100 yards in 17 seconds. Is there any way to decide whether she can remember digits better (or worse or equally well) than she can run 100 yards? On the face of it, the question seems absurd; it seems to be like comparing apples and oranges. But in fact, there is a way, for we can ask where each of these two scores is located on the two frequency distributions of other persons (presumably women of the same age) who are given the same two tasks.

PERCENTILE RANKS

One way of doing this is by transforming each of the two scores into a **percentile rank.** The percentile rank of a score indicates the percentage of all scores that lie below that given score. Let's assume that 8 digits is the 78th percentile, which means that 78 percent of the relevant comparison group remembers fewer digits. Let's further assume that a score of 17 seconds in the 100-yard dash is the 53d percentile of the same comparison group. We can now answer the question with which we started. Our subject can remember digits better than she can run 100 yards. By converting into percentile ranks we have rendered incompatible scores compatible, allowing us to compare the two.

STANDARD SCORES

For many statistical purposes there is an even better method of comparing scores or of interpreting the meaning of individual scores. This is to express them by reference to the mean and standard deviation of the frequency distribution of which they are part by converting them into **standard scores** (often called **z-scores**).

Suppose you take a test that measures aptitude for accounting and are told your score is 36. In itself, this number cannot help you decide whether to pursue or avoid a career in accounting. To interpret your score you need to know both the average score and how variable the scores are. If the mean is 30, you know you are above average, but how far above average is 6 points? This might be an extreme score or one attained by many, depending on the variability of the distribution.

Let us suppose that the standard deviation of the distribution is 3. Your score of 36 is therefore 2 standard deviations (6 points) above the mean (30). A score that is expressed this way, as so many standard deviations from the mean, is called a standard score, or z-score. The formula for calculating a z-score is:

$$z = \frac{(\text{score} - M)}{SD} \qquad (3)$$

Your aptitude of 36 has a z-score of $(36 - 30)/3 = 2$; that is, your score is 2 standard deviations above the mean.

The use of z-scores allows one to compare scores from different distributions. Still unsure whether to become an accountant, you take a screen test to help you decide whether to be an actor. Here your score is 60. This is a larger number than the 36 you scored on the earlier test, but it may not reveal much acting aptitude. Suppose the mean score on the screen test is 80, the standard deviation 20; then your z-score is $(60 - 80)/20 = -1$. In acting aptitude, you are 1 standard deviation below the mean (that is, $z = -1$); in accounting aptitude, 2 standard deviations above (that is, $z = +2$). The use of z-scores makes your relative abilities clear.

Notice that scores below the mean have negative z-scores, as in the last example. A z-score of 0 corresponds to a score that equals the mean.

Percentile rank and a z-score give similar information, but one cannot be converted into the other unless we know more about the distribution than just its mean and standard deviation. In many cases this information is available, as we shall now see.

A.3 Normal distribution *Values taken from any normally distributed variable (such as those presented in Table A.4) can be converted to z-scores by the formula z = (score − mean)/(standard deviation). The figure shows graphically the proportions that fall between various values of z.*

THE NORMAL DISTRIBUTION

Frequency histograms can have a wide variety of shapes, but many variables of psychological interest have a ***normal distribution*** (often called a ***normal curve***), which is a symmetric distribution of the shape shown in Figure A.3. The graph is smooth, unlike the histogram in Figure A.2, because it approximates the distribution of scores from a very large sample. The normal curve is bell-shaped, with most of its scores near the mean; the farther a score is from the mean, the less likely it is to occur. Among the many variables whose distributions are approximately normal are IQ, scholastic aptitude test scores (SAT), and women's heights (see Table A.4).★

These three variables, IQ, SAT score, and height, obviously cannot literally have the "same" distribution, since their means and standard deviations are different (Table A.4 gives plausible values for them). In what sense, then, can they

TABLE A.4 NORMALLY DISTRIBUTED VARIABLES

			z-scores				
Variable	Mean	Standard deviation	−2	−1	0	1	2
IQ	100	15	70	85	100	115	130
SAT	500	100	300	400	500	600	700
Height (women)	160cm	5cm	150	155	160	165	170

★ Men's heights are also normally distributed, but the distribution of the heights of all adults is not. Such a distribution would have two peaks, one for the modal height of each sex, and would thus be shaped quite differently from the normal curve. Distributions with two modes are called ***bimodal.***

all be said to be normal? The answer is that the distribution of z-scores for all these variables is the same. For example, an IQ of 115 is 15 points, or 1 standard deviation, above the IQ mean of 100; a height of 165 centimeters is 5 centimeters, or 1 standard deviation, above the height mean of 160 centimeters. Both scores, therefore, have z-scores of 1. Furthermore, the percentage of heights between 160 and 165 centimeters is the same as the percentage of IQ scores between 100 and 115, that is, it is 34 percent. This is the percentage of scores that lie between the mean and one standard deviation above the mean for any normally distributed variable.

THE PERCENTILE RANK OF A Z-SCORE

When a variable is known to have a normal distribution, a z-score can be converted directly into a percentile rank. A z-score of 1 has a percentile rank of 84, that is, 34 percent of scores lie between the mean and $z = 1$, and (because the distribution is symmetric) 50 percent of the scores lie below the mean. A z-score of -1 corresponds, in a normal distribution, to a percentile rank of 16: only 16 percent of the scores are lower. These relationships are illustrated in Figure A.3 and Table A.4.

HOW THE NORMAL CURVE ARISES

Why should variables such as height or IQ scores—and many others—form distributions that have this particular shape? Mathematicians have shown that whenever a given variable is the sum of many smaller variables, its distribution will be close to that of the normal curve. An example is height. Height can be thought of as the sum of the contributions of the many genes (and some environmental factors) that influence this trait; it therefore satisfies the general condition.

The basic idea is that the many different factors that influence a given measure (such as the genes for height) operate independently. A given gene will pull height up or push it down; the direction in which it exerts its effort is a matter of chance. If the chances are equal either way, then a good analogy to this situation is a person who tosses a coin repeatedly and counts the number of times the coin comes up heads. In this analogy, a head corresponds to a gene that tends to increase height, a tail to a gene that tends to diminish it. The more often the genetic coin falls heads, the taller the person will be.

What will the distribution of the variable "number of heads" be? Clearly, it depends on the number of tosses. If the coin is tossed only once, then there will be either 0 heads or 1 head, and these are equally likely. The resulting distribution is shown in the top panel of Figure A.4.

If the number of tosses (which we will call N) is 2, then 0, 1, or 2 heads can arise. However, not all these outcomes are equally likely: 0 heads come up only if the sequence tail-tail (TT) occurs; 2 heads only if head-head (HH) occurs; but 1 head results from either HT or TH. The distribution of heads for $N = 2$ is shown in the second panel of Figure A.4. The area above 1 head has been subdivided into two equal parts, one for each possible sequence containing a single head.★

As N increases, the distribution of the number of heads looks more and more like the normal distribution, as the subsequent panels of Figure A.4 show. When N becomes as large as the number of factors that determine height, the distribu-

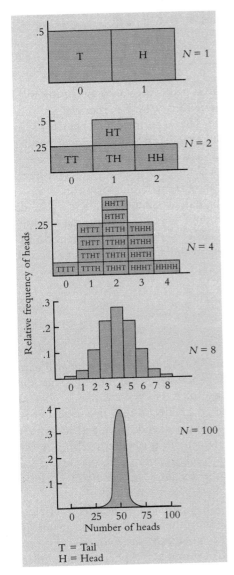

A.4   Histograms showing expected number of heads in tossing a fair coin N times *In successive panels, N = 1, 2, 4, and 8. The bottom panel illustrates the case when N = 100 and shows a smoothed curve.*

★ The distribution of the number of heads is called the **binomial distribution,** because of its relation to the binomial theorem: the number of head-tail sequences that can lead to k heads is the $(k + 1)$st coefficient of $(a + b)^N$.

tion of the number of heads is virtually identical to the normal distribution. Similar arguments justify the assumption of normality for many psychological variables.

DESCRIBING THE RELATION BETWEEN TWO VARIABLES: CORRELATION

The basic problem facing psychological investigators is to account for observed differences in some variable they are interested in. Why, for example, do some people display better memory than others? The experimental approach to the problem, described earlier, is to ask whether changes in an independent variable produce systematic changes in the dependent variable. In the memory experiment, we asked whether subjects using visual imagery as an aid to memorizing would recall more words on the average than those who did not. In an observational study, however, our approach must be different, for in such a study we do not manipulate the variables. What is often done here is to observe the relationship between two—sometimes more—variables as they occur naturally, in the hope that differences in one variable can be attributed to differences in a second.

POSITIVE AND NEGATIVE CORRELATION

Imagine that a taxicab company wants to identify drivers who will earn relatively large amounts of money (for themselves and, of course, for the company). The company's officers make the plausible guess that one relevant factor is the driver's knowledge of the local geography, so they devise an appropriate test of street names, routes from place to place, and so on, and administer the test to each driver. The question is whether this test score is related to the driver's job performance as measured by his weekly earnings. To decide one has to find out whether the test score and the earnings are *correlated*—that is, whether they tend to vary together.

In the taxicab example, the two variables will probably be *positively correlated*—as one variable (test score) increases, the other (earnings) will generally increase too. But other variables may be *negatively correlated*—when one increases, the other will tend to decrease. An example is a phenomenon called Zipf's law, which states that words that occur frequently in a language tend to be relatively short. The two variables—word length and word frequency—are negatively correlated, since one variable tends to increase as the other decreases.

Correlational data are often displayed in a *scatter plot* (or scatter diagram) in which values of one variable are shown on the horizontal axis and variables of the other on the vertical axis. Figure A.5A is a scatter plot of word frequency versus word length for the words in this sentence.★ Each word is represented by a single point. An example is provided by the word *plot*, which is 4 letters long

★ There is no point for the "word" A.5A in this sentence. The frequencies of the other words are taken from H. Kucera and W. N. Francis, *Computational Analysis of Present-Day American English* (Providence, R. I.: Brown University Press, 1967).

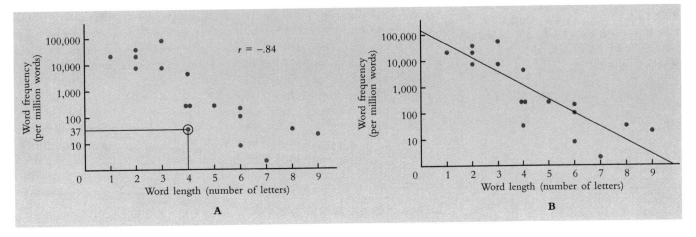

A.5 *Scatter plot of a negative correlation between word length and word frequency*

and occurs with a frequency of 37 times per million words of English text (and is represented by the circled dot). The points on the graph display a tendency to decrease on one variable as they increase on the other, although the relation is by no means perfect. It is helpful to draw a straight line through the various points in a scatter plot that comes as close as possible to all of them (Figure A.5B). The line is called a **line of best fit**, and it indicates the general trend of the data. Here, the line slopes downward because the correlation between the variables is negative.

The three panels of Figure A.6 are scatter plots showing the relation between other pairs of variables. In Figure A.6A hypothetical data from the taxicab example show that there is a positive correlation between test score and earnings (since the line of best fit slopes upward), but that test score is not a perfect predictor of on-the-job performance (since the points are fairly widely scattered around the line). Points above the line represent individuals who earn more than their test score would lead one to predict, points below the line individuals who earn less.

The examples in Figures A.5 and A.6A each illustrate moderate correlations; panels B and C of Figure A.6 are extreme cases. Figure A.6B shows data from a hypothetical experiment conducted in a fourth-grade class to illustrate the relation between metric and English units of length. The heights of five children are measured twice, once in inches and once in centimeters; each point on the scatter plot gives the two height measurements for one child. All the points in the

A.6 **Scatter plots of various correlations**
(A) The scatter plot and line of best fit show a positive correlation between a taxi-driving test and earnings. (B) A perfect positive correlation. The line of best fit passes through all the points. (C) A correlation of zero. The line of best fit is horizontal.

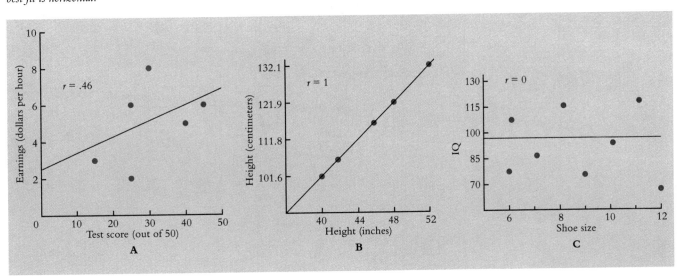

figure fall on the line of best fit, because height in centimeters always equals 2.54 times height in inches. The two variables, height in centimeters and height in inches, are perfectly correlated—one can be perfectly predicted from the other. Once you know your height in inches, there is no information to be gained by measuring yourself with a meterstick.

Figure A.6C presents a relation between IQ and shoe size. These variables are unrelated to each other; people with large shoes have neither a higher nor a lower IQ than people with small ones. The line of best fit is therefore horizontal, because the best guess of an individual's IQ is the same no matter what his or her shoe size—it is the mean IQ of the population.

THE CORRELATION COEFFICIENT

Correlations are often described by a **correlation coefficient,** denoted **r,** a number that can vary from +1.00 to −1.00 and that expresses the strength and the direction of the correlation. For positive correlations, r is positive; for negative correlations, it is negative; for variables that are completely uncorrelated, $r = 0$. The largest positive value r can have is +1.00, which represents a perfect correlation (as in Figure A.6B); the largest possible negative value is −1.00,

---

TABLE A.5 CALCULATION OF THE CORRELATION COEFFICIENT

1. Data (from Figure A.6A).

Test score (X)	Earnings (Y)
45	6
25	2
15	3
40	5
25	6
30	8

2. Find the mean and standard deviation for X and Y.

$$\text{For } X, \text{ mean} = 30, \text{ standard deviation} = 10$$
$$\text{For } Y, \text{ mean} = 5, \text{ standard deviation} = 2$$

3. Convert each X and each Y to a z-score, using $z = \dfrac{(\text{score} - M)}{SD}$

X	Y	z-score for X (z_x)	z-score for Y (z_x)	$z_x z_y$
45	6	1.5	0.5	0.75
25	2	−0.5	−1.5	0.75
15	3	−1.5	−1.0	1.50
40	5	1.0	0.0	0.00
25	6	−0.5	0.5	−0.25
30	8	0.0	1.5	0.00
				2.75

4. Find the product $z_x z_y$ for each pair of scores.

5. $r = \dfrac{\text{sum } (z_x z_y)}{N} = \dfrac{2.75}{6} = .46$

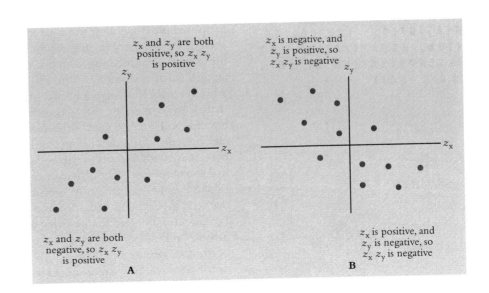

A.7 *Correlation coefficients* *(A) Two positively correlated variables. Most of the points lie in the upper-right and lower-left quadrants, where $z_x z_y$ is positive, so r is positive. (B) Two negatively correlated variables. Most of the points lie in the upper left and lower right quadrants, where $z_x z_y$ is negative, so r is negative.*

which is also a perfect correlation. The closer the points in a scatter plot come to falling on the line of best fit, the nearer *r* will be to +1.00 or −1.00 and the more confident we can be in predicting scores on one variable from scores on the other. The values of *r* for the scatter plots in Figures A.5 and A.6A are given on the figures.

The method for calculating *r* between two variables, *X* and *Y,* is shown in Table A.5 (on the previous page). The formula is:

$$r = \frac{\text{sum } (z_x z_y)}{N} \tag{4}$$

The variable z_x is the *z*-score corresponding to *X*; z_y is the *z*-score corresponding to *Y*. To find *r,* each *X* and *Y* score must first be converted to a *z*-score by subtracting the mean and then dividing by the standard deviation. Then the product of z_x and z_y is found for each pair of scores. The average of these products (the sum of the products divided by *N,* the number of pairs of scores) is the correlation coefficient *r.*

Figure A.7 illustrates why this procedure yields positive values of *r* for positively related variables and negative values of *r* for negatively related variables. For positively correlated variables, most points are either above or below the mean on both variables. If they are above the mean, both z_x and z_y will be positive; if they are below, both z_x and z_y will be negative. (This follows from the definition of a *z*-score.) In either case the product $z_x z_y$ will be positive, so *r* will be positive. For negatively correlated variables, most points that are above the mean on one variable are below the mean on the other—either z_x is positive and z_y is negative or vice versa. The product $z_x z_y$ is therefore negative, and so is *r.*

INTERPRETING AND MISINTERPRETING CORRELATIONS

It is tempting, but false, to assume that if two variables are correlated, one is the cause of the other. There is a positive correlation between years of education and annual income in the population of North American adults;

many people, including some educators, argue from these data that students should stay in school as long as possible in order to increase their eventual earning power. The difficulty with this reasoning is not the existence of counterexamples (such as Andrew Carnegie, the American industrialist and millionaire who never finished high school), which merely show that the correlation is less than 1.00. It is rather that it is difficult to infer causality from this correlation because both variables are correlated with yet a third variable. Years of schooling and income as an adult are not only correlated with each other, they are also correlated with a third variable—the parents income. Given this fact, can we make any assertions about what causes adult income? Perhaps income is determined by one's education (it probably is, in part). But perhaps the relationship between income and education is a spurious byproduct of the parents' income. Perhaps this third factor partially determines both one's education and one's income, and there is no real causal connection between the two.

Another demonstration of the fact that correlation is not equivalent to causation occurs while waiting for a bus or a subway whose schedule is unknown. There is a negative correlation between the number of minutes a rider will have to wait for the next subway and the number of people waiting when the rider enters the station: The more people who are waiting, the sooner the subway will arrive. This negative correlation is fairly substantial, but even so, one would hardly try to cut down one's waiting time by arriving at the station with fifty friends. Here, the third, causal variable (time since the last train or bus left) is fairly obvious.★ But even when it is harder to imagine just what the third variable might be, it is still possible that such a third variable exists and is responsible for the correlation. As a result, correlations can never provide solid evidence of a causal link.

INTERPRETING DATA: INFERENTIAL STATISTICS

We have seen that a psychologist collecting data encounters variability. In memory experiments, for example, different individuals recall different numbers of items, and the same person is likely to perform differently when tested twice. An investigator wishes to draw general conclusions from data in spite of this variability, or to discover the factors that are responsible for it.

ACCOUNTING FOR VARIABILITY

As an example of how variability may be explained, consider a person shooting a pistol at a target. Although he always aims at the bull's eye, the shots scatter around it (Figure A.8A). Assuming that the mean is the bull's eye, the variance of these shots is the average squared deviation of the shots from the center; suppose this variance is 100.

Now we set about explaining the variance. If the shooting was done outdoors, the wind may have increased the spread; moving the shooter to an indoor shooting range produces the tighter grouping shown in Figure A.8B. The new

★ I thank Barry Schwartz for this example.

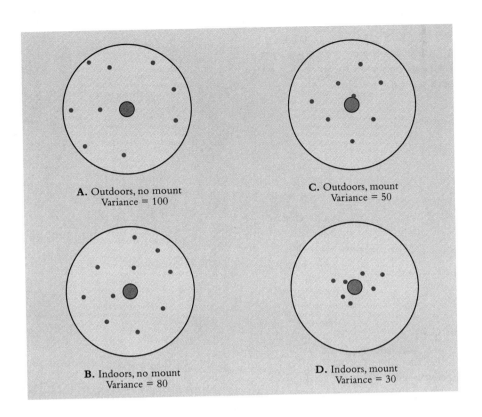

A.8   Results of target shooting under several conditions   *In each case, the bull's eye is the mean, and the variance is the average squared deviation of the shots from the bull's eye.*

variance is 80, a reduction of 20 percent—this means that the wind accounts for 20 percent of the original variance. Some of the variance may result from the unsteady hand of the shooter, so we now mount the gun. This yields a variance of 50 (Figure A.8C), a reduction of 50 percent, so 50 percent of the variance can be attributed to the shaky hand of the shooter. To find out how much of the variance can be accounted for by both the wind and the shaking, we mount the gun *and* move it indoors; now we may find a variance of only 30 (Figure A.8D). This means we have explained 70 percent of the variance, leaving 30 percent unaccounted for.★ Not all changes in the situation will reduce the variance. For example, if we find that providing the shooter with earmuffs leaves the variance unchanged, we know that none of the original variance was due to the noise of the pistol.

VARIANCE AND EXPERIMENTS

Figure A.9 (on the next page) shows how this approach can be applied to the experiment on visual imagery described earlier (see page A4). Figure A.9A shows the distribution of scores for all twenty subjects in the experiment lumped together; the total variance of this overall distribution is 6.25. But as we saw, ten of these subjects had been instructed to use visual imagery in memorizing, whereas another ten control subjects were given no special instructions. How much of the overall variance can be accounted for by the difference in these instructions? In Figure A.9B, the distributions are no longer lumped together. They are instead presented as two separate histograms; the subjects who received imagery instructions are shown in blue, while those who did not are indicated in rust. As the figure shows, there is less variability with either the imagery group or the control group than in the overall distribution that lumped both kinds of subjects together. While the variance in the overall distribution is

★ I am grateful to Paul Rozin for suggesting this example.

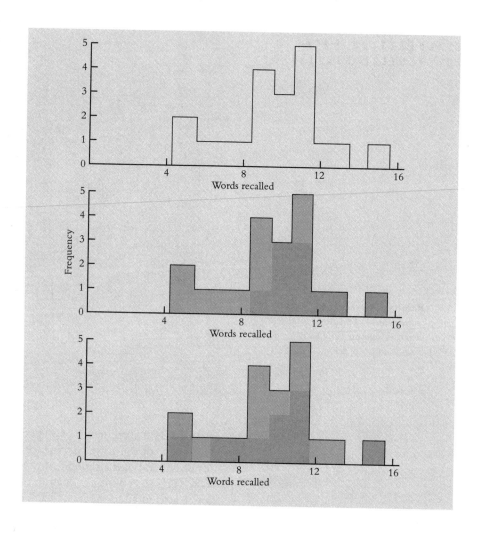

A.9 Accounting for variance in an experiment on memorizing *(A) The distribution of number of words recalled is shown for all twenty subjects lumped together; the variance of this distribution is 6.25. (B) The distributions of the experimental and control groups are displayed separately. The number of words recalled by the group that received imagery instructions is shown in blue; the number recalled by the control group that received no special instructions is shown in rust. Within each of these groups, the variance is about 4.00. (C) The distribution of words recalled is plotted separately for men and women regardless of how they were instructed. Blue indicates the number of words recalled by women, rust the number recalled by men. The variance is 6.25.*

6.25, the variance within the two subgroups averages to only 4.0. We conclude that the difference between the instructions the subjects were given accounted for 36 percent of the variance and that 64 percent (4 ÷ 6.25) still remains unexplained.

Figure A.9C shows a situation in which an independent variable (in this case, sex) accounts for little or none of the variance. In this figure, the subjects' scores are again presented as two separate histograms—one for the scores of the men (regardless of whether they were instructed to use imagery or not) and the other for the scores of the women (again, regardless of the instructions they received). The men's scores are shown in rust, the women's, in blue. Now the variance of the two subgroups (that is, men vs. women) averages to 6.25, a value identical to that found for the overall distribution. We conclude that the subject's sex accounts for none of the overall variance in memorizing performance.

VARIANCE AND CORRELATION

The technique of explaining the variance in one variable by attributing it to the effect of another variable can also be applied to correlational studies. Here, the values of one variable are explained (that is, accounted for) when the values of the other variable are known. Recall the taxicab example. In it a correlation of .46 was found between taxi drivers' earnings and their scores on a screening test. Since the correlation is neither perfect nor zero, some but not all of the variance in job performance can be explained by the aptitude test scores. The greater the magnitude of the correlation coefficient, r, the more variance is accounted for. The rule is that the proportion of variance that is explained equals r^2. If $r = .46$, one variable accounts for $(.46)^2 = .21$ of the variance of the other. (Just why this proportion is r^2 is beyond the scope of this discussion.) To put this another way, suppose all the cab drivers were identical on the one variable, their performance on the geographical text. This means that the variance on that variable would be zero. As a result, the variability on the second variable, earnings, would be reduced. The formula tells us by how much. The original variance on earnings can be determined from the data in Figure A.6A. It is 4. Its correlation with the geography test is .46. Since the effect of this variable, the geography test, is completely controlled, the variability on earnings will be $4 - (.46)^2 \times 4 = 3.16$. The drop in the variance from 4 to 3.16 is a reduction of 21 percent. The aptitude test does help us to predict taxicab earnings, for it accounts for 21 percent of the variance. But a good deal of the variance, 79 percent, is still unexplained.

HYPOTHESIS TESTING

Much behavioral research attempts to answer two-alternative questions. Does the amount of food a person eats depend on the effort required to eat it? Can people learn while they are sleeping? Is drug X more effective than aspirin? Each of these questions suggests an experiment, and the procedures described in the previous section could be used to discover how much of the variance in the dependent variable could be accounted for by the independent variable. But how can the results of such experiments lead to simple yes-or-no answers to the questions that inspired them?

TESTING HYPOTHESES ABOUT SINGLE SCORES

We will begin by testing a hypothesis about single scores. Consider the problem in interpreting a lie-detector test. In such a test, a person is asked a series of questions and various measures of physiological arousal are taken as he answers. An answer that is accompanied by an unusually high degree of arousal is taken as possible evidence that the person is lying. The question is how high is "unusually high?"

To answer this question we will first rephrase it. Can we reject the hypothesis that the given score came from the distribution of responses the same individual gave to neutral questions? (An example is "Is your name Fred?") Suppose the average arousal score to such control questions is 50, that the standard deviation of these neutral responses is 10, and that the arousal scores are normally distributed. We now look at the arousal score to the critical item. Let us say that this is 60. How likely is it that this score is from a sample drawn by chance from the population of responses to neutral questions? To find out, we convert it to a z-score by computing its distance from the mean and dividing it by the standard deviation. The resulting z-score is $(60 - 50)/10$ or 1. Since the distribution is normal, Figure A.3 tells us that 16 percent of this person's arousal scores would be as high or higher than this. Under the circumstances we don't feel justified in rejecting the hypothesis that the score in question comes from the distribution of neutral responses. Put another way, we don't feel justified in accusing the person of lying. Our feelings might be different if the score were 70 or above. For now the z-score is $(70 - 50)/10$ or 2 standard deviations above the mean of the neutral distribution. The chances that a score this high or higher is from a sample drawn from the population of neutral responses is only 2 in 100. We might now feel more comfortable in rejecting the hypothesis that this score is simply a chance event. We are more likely to assume that it is drawn from another distribution—in short, that the person is lying.

In this example we had to decide between two hypotheses. We looked at a given score (or a set of scores) obtained under a particular experimental condition (in this case, a loaded question). One hypothesis is that the experimental condition has no effect, that the score is merely a reflection of the ordinary variability around the mean of a control condition (in this case, neutral questions). This is the **null hypothesis,** the hypothesis that there really is no effect. The **alternative hypothesis** is that the null hypothesis is false, that the score is far enough away from the control mean so that we can assume that the same experimental condition has some effect. To decide between these two hypotheses, the data are expressed as a z-score, which in the context of hypothesis testing is called a **critical ratio.** Behavioral scientists generally accept a critical ratio of 2 as the cutoff point. If this ratio is 2 or greater, they generally reject the null hypothesis and assume there is an effect of the experimental condition. (Such critical ratios of 2 or more are said to be **statistically significant,** which is just another way of saying that the null hypothesis can be rejected.) Critical ratios of less than 2 are considered too small to allow the rejection of the null hypothesis.

This general procedure is not foolproof. It is certainly possible for a subject in the lie-detection example to have an arousal score of 70 (a critical ratio of 2) or higher even though he is telling the truth. According to Figure A.3, this will happen about 2 percent of the time, and the person administering the test will erroneously "detect" a lie. Raising the cutoff value to the critical ratio of 3 or 4 would make such errors less common, but would not eliminate them entirely; furthermore, such a high critical value might mean failure to discover any lies the subject does utter. One of the important consequences of the variability in psychological data can be seen here: The investigator who has to decide between two interpretations of the data (the null hypothesis and the alternative hypothesis) cannot be correct all the time.

TESTING HYPOTHESES ABOUT MEANS

In the preceding discussion, our concern was with hypotheses about single scores. We now turn to the more commonly encountered problems in which the hypotheses involve means.

In many experiments, the investigator compares two or more groups—subjects tested with or without a drug, with or without imagery instructions, and so on. Suppose we get a difference between the two groups. How do we decide whether the difference is genuine rather than a mere chance fluctuation?

Let us return to the experiment in which memory for words was tested with and without instructions to imagine the items visually. To simplify the exposition, we will here consider a modified version of the experiment in which the same subjects serve in both the imagery and the nonimagery conditions. Each subject memorizes a list of 20 words without instructions, then memorizes a second list of 20 words under instructions to visualize. What we want to know is whether the subjects show any improvement with imagery instructions. There is no separate control group in this experiment, but, because a subject's score in the imagery condition can be compared with her score in the uninstructed condition, each subject provides her own control.

Table A.6 gives data for the ten subjects in the experiment. For each subject, the table lists the number of words recalled without imagery instructions, the number recalled with such instructions, and the improvement (the difference between the two scores). The mean improvement overall is 3 words, from a mean of 8 words recalled without imagery to a mean of 11 words with imagery. But note that this does not hold for all subjects. For example, for Fred and

TABLE A.6 NUMBER OF ITEMS RECALLED WITH AND WITHOUT IMAGERY INSTRUCTION, FOR 10 SUBJECTS

Subject	Score with imagery	Score without imagery	Improvement
Alphonse	11	5	6
Betsy	15	9	6
Cheryl	11	5	6
Davis	9	9	0
Earl	13	6	7
Fred	10	11	−1
Germaine	11	8	3
Hortense	10	11	−1
Imogene	8	7	1
Jerry	12	9	3
Mean	11	8	3

Variance of improvement scores $= \dfrac{\text{sum of (score} - 3)^2}{10} = 8.8$

Standard deviation of improvement scores $= \sqrt{8.8} = 2.97$

Hortense, the "improvement" is negative—they both do better without imagery instructions. The question is whether we can conclude that there is an imagery facilitation effect overall. Put in other words, is the difference between the two conditions statistically significant?

To show how this question is answered, we will follow much the same logic as that used in the analysis of the lie-detection problem. We have a mean—the average difference score of ten subjects. What we must realize is that this mean—3—is really a sample based on the one experiment with the ten subjects we have just run. Suppose we had run the experiment again, with another set of ten subjects—not just once, but many times. Each such repetition of the experiment would yield its own mean. And each of these means would constitute another sample. But what is the population to which these samples refer? It is the set of all of these means—the average differences between imagery and non-imagery instructions obtained in each of the many repetitions of the experiment we might possibly perform. And the mean of these means—a kind of grand mean—is the mean of the population. Any conclusions we want to draw from our experiment are really assertions about this population mean. If we say that the difference we found is statistically significant, we are asserting that the population mean is a difference score that is greater than zero (and in the same direction as in the sample). Put another way, we are asserting that the difference we found is not just a fluke but is real and would be obtained again and again if we repeated the experiment, thus rejecting the null hypothesis.

The null hypothesis amounts to the claim that the mean we actually obtained could have been drawn by chance from a distribution of sample means (that is, the many means of the possible repetitions of our experiment) around a population mean of zero. To test this claim, we have to compute a critical ratio that can tell us how far from zero our own mean actually is. Like all critical ratios, this is a z-score that expresses the distance of a score from a mean in units of the standard deviation (the SD). Thus, $z = (\text{score} - M)/SD$. In our present case, the score is our obtained mean (that is, 3); the mean is the hypothetical population mean of zero (assumed by the null hypothesis). But what is the denominator? It is the standard deviation of the distribution of sample means, the means of the many experiments we might have done.

The standard deviation of such a distribution of sample means is called the **standard error** of the mean **(SE).** Its value is determined by two factors: the standard deviation of the sample and the size of that sample. Specifically,

$$SE = \frac{SD}{\sqrt{N-1}} \tag{5}$$

It is clear that the variability of a mean (and this is what the standard error measures) goes down with increasing sample size. (Why this factor turns out to be $\sqrt{N-1}$ is beyond the scope of this discussion.) A clue as to why comes from the consideration of the effects of an atypical score. Purely by chance, a sample may include an extreme case. But the larger the size of that sample, the less the effect of an extreme case on the average. If a sample of three people includes a midget, the average height will be unusually far from the population mean. But in a sample of 3,000, one midget will not affect the average very markedly.

We can now conclude our analysis of the results of the memorization experiment. The critical ratio to be evaluated is:

$$\text{Critical Ratio} = \frac{\text{obtained sample mean} - \text{population mean}}{SE}$$

Since the population mean is assumed to be zero (by the null hypothesis), this expression becomes:

$$\text{Critical Ratio} = \frac{\text{obtained sample mean}}{SE} \tag{6}$$

This critical ratio expresses the mean difference between the two experimental conditions in units of the variability of the sample mean, that is, the standard error.★ To compute the standard error, we first find the standard deviation of the improvement scores; this turns out to be 2.97, as shown in Table A.6. Then equation (5) tells us

$$SE = \frac{SD}{\sqrt{N-1}} = \frac{2.97}{\sqrt{10-1}} = .99$$

The critical ratio is now the obtained mean difference divided by the standard error, or $3/.99 = 3.03$. This is clearly larger than 2.0, so we conclude that the observed difference in memory between the imagery and control conditions is much too great to be attributed to chance factors. Thus, using visual imagery evidently does improve recall.

CONFIDENCE INTERVALS

In statistical hypothesis testing we ask whether a certain sample mean could be drawn by chance from a distribution of sample means around some assumed

---

★ There are several simplifications in this account. One is that the critical ratio described here does not have an exactly normal distribution. When the sample size is large, this effect is unimportant, but for small samples (like the one in the example) they can be material. To deal with these and related problems, statisticians often utilize measures that refer to distributions other than the normal one. An example is the *t*-test, a kind of critical ratio based on what is called the *t*-distribution.

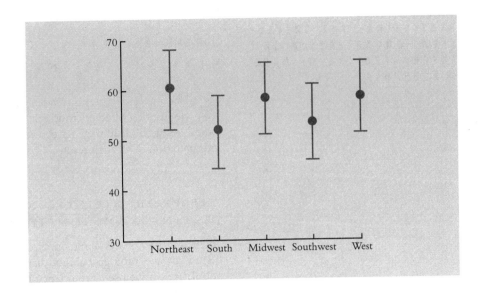

A.10   A candidate's poll results and her confidence intervals   *The results of a mythical poll conducted for a no-less-mythical presidential candidate Smith by randomly sampling 200 people in each of five regions of the United States. The figure shows the pro-Smith proportions in each region, together with the confidence intervals around them, and indicates that she is ahead in all five samples. But there are two regions where she cannot be confident that she is ahead in the population—the South and the Southwest, where the confidence intervals of the pro-Smith proportion dip below 50 percent.*

population mean. (When testing the null hypothesis, this assumed population mean is zero.) But there is another way of phrasing this question. Can we be reasonably confident that the mean of the population falls within a certain specified interval? If we know the standard error of the mean, the answer is yes. We have already seen that about 2 percent of the scores in a normal distribution are more than two standard deviations above and about 2 percent are lower than two standard deviations below the mean of that distribution. Since this is so, we can conclude that the chances are roughly 4 in 100 that the population mean is within an interval whose largest value is two standard errors above the sample mean and whose lowest value is two standard errors below. Because we can be fairly (96 percent) confident that the actual population mean will fall within this specified range, it is often called the ***confidence interval.***

As an example, consider the prediction of political elections. During election campaigns, polling organizations report the current standing of various candidates by statements such as the following: "In a poll of 1,000 registered voters, 57 percent favored candidate Smith; the margin of error was 3 percent." This margin of error is the confidence interval around the proportion (that is, ± 3 percent).

To determine this confidence interval, the pollsters compute the standard error of the proportion they found. (In this case, .57.) This standard error is analogous to the standard error of a mean we discussed in the previous section. Given an N of 1,000, this standard error happens to be .015.★ Since 2 × .015 is .03 or 3 percent, the appropriate confidence interval for our example is the interval from 54 to 60 percent. Under the circumstances, candidate Smith can be fairly confident that she has the support of at least 50 percent of the electorate since 50 percent is well *below* the poll's confidence interval (see Figure A.10).

★ The standard error of a proportion (e.g., the proportion of polled voters who express pro-X sentiments) is analogous to the standard error of the mean, and measures the precision with which our sample proportion estimates the population proportion. The formula for the standard error of a proportion p is:

$$SE_p = \sqrt{\frac{p \times (1 - p)}{N}}$$

In our example, $p = .57$ and $N = 1,000$, so $SE_p = .015$.

SOME IMPLICATIONS OF STATISTICAL INFERENCE

The methods of testing hypotheses and estimating confidence intervals that we just described are routinely employed in evaluating the results of psychological research. But they have several characteristics that necessarily affect the interpretation of all such results.

THE PROBABILISTIC NATURE OF HYPOTHESIS TESTING AND CONFIDENCE INTERVALS

Since there is always some unexplained variance in any psychological study, there is always some probability that the conclusions are wrong as applied to the population. If we use a confidence interval of ± 2 *SE*, the chances that the population mean (or proportion, or whatever) falls outside of that interval are less than 4 or 5 in 100. Do we want to be more confident than this? If so, we might use a confidence interval of ± 3 *SE*, where the equivalent chance is only 1 in 1,000. The same holds for critical ratios. We can say that a critical ratio of 2 means that a difference is statistically significant, but that only means that the chances are less than 2 in 100 that the difference as large or larger than this arose by chance. If we want to be more certain than this, we must insist that the critical ratio be larger—perhaps 3 (a chance factor of 1 in 2,000) or 4 (5 in 100,000), and so on. As long as there is some unexplained variance, there is some chance of error.

The probabilistic nature of statistical reasoning has another consequence. Even if we can come to a correct conclusion about the mean of a population (or a proportion, as in polls), we cannot generalize to individuals. Thus, a study which shows that men have higher scores than women on spatial relations tests is not inconsistent with the existence of brilliant female artists or architects. Sample means for the two groups can differ significantly, even though there is considerable overlap in the two distributions of scores.

THE CONSERVATIVE NATURE OF HYPOTHESIS TESTING

Another characteristic of statistical hypothesis testing is that it is essentially conservative. This is because of the great stress placed on the null hypothesis in reaching a decision: One has to be quite sure that the null hypothesis is false before one entertains the alternative hypothesis. There are other imaginable strategies for reaching statistical decisions, but the conservative one has a perfectly rational basis. Let's suppose that some independent variable *does* produce a difference between two groups that is quite genuine and not the result of chance, but that the critical ratio is too low to reject the null hypothesis. If so, we will have falsely concluded that no difference exists in the population. As a result, we will have failed to discover a small effect. But what of it? If the effect is interesting enough, someone else may well attempt a similar experiment and manage to find the difference we didn't uncover. On the other hand, suppose we "discover" that some independent variable has an effect when it actually does not (that is, the null hypothesis is true). By falsely rejecting the null hypothesis, we will have added an inaccurate "fact" to the store of scientific knowledge and run the risk of leading other investigators up a blind alley.

THE ROLE OF SAMPLE SIZE

A last point concerns the role of sample size in affecting the interpretations of results. The larger the sample, the smaller the standard error and the smaller the confidence interval around the mean or the proportion. This can have major effects on hypothesis testing.

Suppose that, in the population, a certain independent variable produces a very small difference. As an example, suppose that the population difference between men and women on a certain test of spatial relations is 1 percent. We would probably be unable to reject the null hypothesis (that there is no sex difference on the test) with samples of moderate size. But if the sample size were sufficiently increased, we could reject the null hypothesis. For such a sizable increase in N would lead to a decrease in the standard errors of the sample means, which in turn would lead to an increase in the critical ratio. Someone who read a report of this experiment would now learn that, by using thousands of subjects, we discovered a "significant" difference of 1 percent. A fair reaction to this bit of intelligence would be that the null hypothesis can indeed be rejected, but that the *psychological* significance of this finding is rather slight. The moral is simple. Statistical significance is required before a result can be considered reliable, but this statistical significance does not guarantee that the effect discovered is of psychological significance or of any practical importance.

SUMMARY

1. Statistical methods concern the ways in which investigators describe, gather, organize, and interpret collections of numerical data. A crucial concern of statistical endeavors is to deal with the variability that is encountered in all research.

2. An early step in the process is *scaling*, a procedure for assigning numbers to psychological responses. Scales can be *categorical*, *ordinal*, *interval*, or *ratio scales*. These differ in the degree to which they can be subjected to arithmetical operations.

3. There are three main methods for conducting psychological research: by means of an *experiment*, an *observational study*, or a *case study*. In an experiment, the investigator manipulates the *independent variable* to see how it affects the subject's response, the *dependent variable*. In an observational study, the investigator does not manipulate any variables directly but rather observes them as they occur naturally. A case study is an investigation in which one person is studied in depth.

4. An important distinction in psychological research is that between *sample* and *population*. The population is the entire group about which the investigator wants to draw conclusions. The sample is the subset (usually small) of that population that is actually tested. Generalizations from sample to population are only possible if the one is representative of the other. This requires the use of *random samples*. In some cases a special version of the random sample, the *stratified sample*, may be employed.

5. A first step in organizing the data is to arrange them in a *frequency distribution*, often displayed in graphic form, as in a *histogram*. Frequency distributions are characterized by a *central tendency* and by *variability* around this central tendency. The common measure of central tendency is the *mean*, though sometimes another measure, the *median*, may be preferable, as in cases when the distribution is *skewed*. Important measures of variability are the *variance* and the *standard deviation*.

6. One way of comparing two scores drawn from different distributions is to convert both into *percentile ranks*. Another is to transform them into *z-scores*, which express the

distance of a score from its mean in standard deviation units. The percentile rank of a z-score can be computed if the shape of that score's distribution is known. An important example is the *normal distribution,* graphically displayed by the *normal curve,* which describes the distribution of many psychological variables and is basic to much of statistical reasoning.

7. In observational studies, the relation between variables is often expressed in the form of a *correlation,* which may be positive or negative. It is measured by the *correlation coefficient,* a number that can vary from +1.00 to −1.00. While correlations reflect the extent to which two variables vary together, they do not necessarily indicate that one of them causes the other.

8. A major task of any investigator is to explain the variability of some dependent variable, usually measured by the variance. One means for doing so is to see whether that variance is reduced when a certain independent variable is controlled. If so, this independent variable is said to account for some of the variability of the dependent variable.

9. One of the main functions of statistical methods is to help test hypotheses about a population given information about the sample. An important example is the difference between mean scores obtained under two different conditions. Here the investigator has to decide between the *null hypothesis,* which asserts that the difference was obtained by chance, and the *alternative hypothesis,* which asserts that the difference is genuine and exists in the population. The decision is made by dividing the obtained mean difference by the *standard error,* a measure of the variability of that mean difference. If the resulting ratio, called the *critical ratio,* is large enough, the null hypothesis is rejected, the alternative hypothesis is accepted, and the difference is said to be *statistically significant.* A related way of making statistical decisions is by using a *confidence interval,* or margin of error. This is based on the variability of the scores from a sample and determines the interval within which the population mean or proportion probably falls.

GLOSSARY

abnormal psychology *See* psychopathology.

absolute threshold The lowest intensity of some stimulus that produces a response.

accessory structures In sensory processing, the parts of sensory systems that gather external stimulus energies and fashion the proximal stimulus, which the receptors then transduce.

accommodation (1) The process by which the lens is thickened or flattened to focus on an object. (2) In Piaget's theory of development, one of the twin processes that underlies cognitive development. *See* assimilation and accommodation.

accommodative distortion Retrospective alterations of memory to fit a schema. *See also* schema.

acetylcholine A neurotransmitter found in many parts of the nervous system. Among many other functions, it serves as an excitatory transmitter at the synaptic junctions between muscle fibers and motor neurons.

achromatic colors Colors that do not have the property of hue, such as black, white, and the neutral grays.

across-fiber theory The theory that a certain sensory quality is signaled by the pattern of neural activity across a number of different nerve fibers.

action potential A brief change in the electrical potential of an axon, which is the physical basis of the nervous impulse.

activation-synthesis hypothesis A modern account which holds that dreams are a reflection of the brain's aroused state during REM sleep, when the cerebral cortex is active but shut off from sensory input. This helps explain the content and often disjointed form of dreams.

active memory *See* working memory.

active sleep (or REM sleep) A stage of sleep during which the EEG is similar to that of the waking brain; in this stage there are rapid eye movements (REMs) and dreams occur.

actor-observer difference The difference in attributions made by actors who describe their own actions and observers who describe another person's. The former emphasizes external, situational causes; the latter, internal, dispositional factors. *See also* attribution theory, fundamental attribution error, self-serving bias.

acuity The ability to distinguish between separate points projected on the retina. Acuity is greatest in the fovea, where the receptors are closely bunched together.

acute mania *See* psychotic mania.

adaptation The process by which the sensitivity to a particular stimulus declines when it is continually presented.

adaptive value In biological terms, the extent to which an attribute increases the likelihood of viable offspring. Also, the unit of inheritance.

addiction The result of repeated drug use. The consequences are increased tolerance and withdrawal symptoms, which cause addiction to be self-perpetuating.

additive color mixture Mixing colors by stimulating the eye with two sets of wavelengths simultaneously (e.g., by focusing filtered light from two projectors on the same spot). *See also* subtractive color mixture.

adequate stimulus An electrical pulse above the threshold, or critical point, that induces an action potential in a neuron.

adrenaline *See* epinephrine.

adrenal medulla The inner core of the adrenal gland, which regulates the release of epinephrine (adrenaline) and norepinephrine into the bloodstream.

affective disorders *See* mood disorders.

afferent nerves Sensory nerves that carry messages to the brain.

agnosia A serious disturbance in the organization of sensory information produced by lesions in certain cortical association areas. An example is visual agnosia in which the patient can see but often does not recognize what it is that he sees.

agonists Drugs that enhance the activity of a neurotransmitter, often by increasing the amount of transmitter substance available (e.g., by blocking reuptake or by increasing the availability of precursors).

agoraphobia The fear of being alone and outside of the home, especially in a public place; often observed in those with panic disorder.

alarm call Special, genetically programmed cry that impels members of a given species to seek cover. A biological puzzle, since it suggests a form of altruism in which the individual appears to endanger his own survival. *See also* altruism.

algorithm In computer problem solving, a procedure in which all of the operations are specified step-by-step. *See also* heuristics.

all-or-none law A law that describes the fact that once a stimulus exceeds threshold, further increases do not increase the amplitude of the action potential.

alpha blocking The disruption of the alpha rhythm by visual stimulation or by active thought with the eyes closed.

alpha waves Fairly regular EEG waves, between eight to twelve per second, characteristic of a relaxed, waking state, usually with eyes closed.

alternative hypothesis In statistics, the hypothesis that the null hypothesis is false, that an obtained difference is so far from zero that one has to assume that the mean difference in the population is greater than zero and that the experimental condition has some effect. *See also* null hypothesis.

altruism (1) Acting so as to elevate the interests and welfare of others above one's own. (2) As used by sociobiologists, any behavior pattern that benefits individuals who are not one's own offspring (e.g., an alarm call). According to the kin-selection hypothesis, such altruism has biological survival value because the altruist's beneficiaries tend to be close relatives who carry a high proportion of his or her own genes. According to the reciprocal altruism hypothesis, altruism is based on the expectation that today's giver will be tomorrow's taker. *See also* alarm call.

Alzheimer's disease A degenerative brain disorder characterized by increasing memory loss followed by increasing disorientation and culminating in total physical and mental helplessness and death. One of the major sites of the destruction is a pathway of acetylcholine-releasing cells leading from the base of the forebrain to the cortex and hippocampus. *See also* acetylcholine.

ambiguity (in sentence meaning) The case in which a sentence (i.e., one surface structure) has two meanings (i.e., two underlying structures). (For example, "These missionaries are ready to eat" overheard in a conversation between two cannibals.)

American Sign Language (ASL) The manual-visual language system of deaf persons in America.

amphetamines Drugs that increase the availability of norepinephrine, causing increased arousal and excitement. Large doses may lead to frenetic hyperactivity and delusions.

amplitude The height of a wave crest.

anal character According to Freud, a personality type that derives from serious conflicts during the anal stage and is distinguished by three symptomatic traits: compulsive orderliness, stubbornness, and stinginess. *See also* anal stage.

analgesic A pain reliever.

analogical representation A representation that shares some of the physical characteristics of an object; for example, a picture of a mouse is an analogical representation because it looks like the small rodent it represents.

anal stage In psychoanalytic theory, the stage of psychosexual development during which the focus of pleasure is on activities related to elimination.

androgen Any male sex hormone.

angiotensin A substance produced by the kidneys when there is a decrease in the amount of liquid passing through them, activating receptors in the brain that monitor the volume of blood and other fluids in the body.

anomia A difficulty in finding words that is often experienced by people with brain injuries.

anorexia nervosa An eating disorder that primarily afflicts young women and that is characterized by an exaggerated concern with being overweight and by compulsive dieting, sometimes to the point of self-starvation and death. *See also* bulimia and obesity.

A-not-B effect The tendency of infants around nine months of age to search for a hidden object by reaching for place *A*, where it was previously hidden, rather than a new place *B*, where it was hidden most recently while the child was watching.

antagonists Drugs that impede the activity of a neurotransmitter, often by decreasing the amount available (e.g., by speeding reuptake and decreasing availability of precursors).

anterograde amnesia A memory deficit suffered after some brain damage. It is an inability to learn and remember any information imparted after the injury, with little effect on memory for information acquired previously. *See also* retrograde amnesia.

antidepressant drugs Drugs that alleviate depressive symptoms, presumably because they increase the availability of certain neurotransmitters (especially norepinephrine and serotonin) at synaptic junctions. The three major classes are monoamine oxidase (MAO) inhibitors, tricyclics, selective serotonin reuptake inhibitors.

antidiuretic hormone (ADH) A hormone secreted by one of the parts of the pituitary gland. This hormone instructs the kidneys to reabsorb more of the water that passes through them. *See also* pituitary gland.

antipsychotic drugs Drugs, e.g., Thorazine and Haldol, that alleviate the psychotic patient's symptoms, such as thought disorders and hallucinations. Also known as major tranquilizers.

antisocial personality disorder Also called psychopathy or sociopathy. The term describes persons who get into continual trouble with society, are indifferent to others, are impulsive, and have little concern for the future or remorse about the past.

anxiety An emotional state akin to fear. According to Freud, many mental illnesses center around anxiety and on attempts to ward it off by various unconscious mechanisms.

anxiety disorders *See* generalized anxiety disorder, obsessive-compulsive disorders, phobia, specific phobia.

anxiety hierarchy *See* systematic desensitization.

anxiolytics More commonly known as tranquilizers, these drugs are given to patients suffering from disabling anxiety. Most types work by increasing the activity of the neurotransmitter GABA and are highly addictive.

aphagia Refusal to eat (and in an extreme version, to drink) brought about by a lesion of the lateral hypothalamus.

aphasia A disorder of language produced by lesions in certain association areas of the cortex. A lesion in Broca's area leads to expressive aphasia, one in Wernicke's area to receptive aphasia.

apparent movement The perception of movement produced by stimuli that are stationary but flash on and off at appropriate time intervals.

appetitive stimulus In instrumental conditioning, a stimulus that the animal will do everything to attain and nothing to prevent.

apraxia A serious disturbance in the organization of voluntary action produced by lesions in certain cortical association areas, often in the frontal lobes.

artificial intelligence A field that draws on concepts from both cognitive psychology and computer science to develop artificial systems that display some aspects of human-like intelligence. Examples are computer programs that recognize patterns or solve certain kinds of problems.

assimilation and accommodation In Piaget's theory, the twin processes by means of which cognitive development proceeds. Assimilation is the process whereby the environment is interpreted in terms of the schemas the child has at the time. Accommodation is the way the child changes her schemas as she continues to interact with the environment.

association A linkage between two psychological processes as a result of past experience in which the two have occurred together. A broad term that subsumes conditioning and association of ideas among others.

association areas Regions of the cortex that are not projection areas. They tend to be involved in the integration of sensory information or of motor commands.

attachment The tendency of the young of many species to stay in close proximity to an adult, usually their mother. *See also* imprinting.

attention A collective label for all the processes by which we perceive selectively.

attitude A fairly stable, evaluative disposition that makes a person think, feel, or behave positively or negatively about some person, group, or social issue.

attribution theory A theory about the process by which we try to explain a person's behavior, attributing it to situational factors or to inferred dispositional qualities or both.

attributional style The characteristic manner in which a person explains good or bad fortunes that befall him. A particular attributional style in which bad fortunes are generally attributed to internal, global, and stable causes may create a predisposition that makes a person vulnerable to depression. *See also* depression.

attribution-of-arousal theory An approach that combines the James-Lange emphasis on bodily feedback with a cognitive approach to emotion. Various stimuli can trigger a general state of arousal, which is then interpreted in light of the subject's present situation and shaped into a specific emotional experience.

authoritarian personality A cluster of personal attributes (e.g., submission to persons above and harshness to those below) and social attitudes (e.g., prejudice against minority groups), which is sometimes held to constitute a distinct personality.

authoritative-reciprocal pattern A pattern of child rearing in which parents exercise considerable power but also respond to the child's point of view and reasonable demands. Parents following this pattern set rules of conduct and are fairly demanding, but also encourage the child's independence and self-expression.

autocratic pattern A pattern of child rearing in which the parents control the child strictly, setting stern and usually unexplained rules whose infraction leads to severe, often physical, punishment.

automatization A process whereby components of a skilled activity become subsumed under a higher-order organization and are run off automatically.

autonomic nervous system (ANS) A part of the nervous system that controls the internal organs, usually not under voluntary control.

availability heuristic A rule of thumb often used to make probability estimates, which depends on the frequency with which certain events readily come to mind. This can lead to errors, since very vivid events will be remembered out of proportion to their actual frequency of occurrence.

aversion therapy A form of behavior therapy in which the undesirable response leads to an aversive stimulus (e.g., the patient shocks himself every time he reaches for a cigarette).

aversive stimulus In instrumental conditioning, a stimulus such as an electric shock, which the animal does everything to avoid and nothing to attain.

avoidance learning Instrumental learning in which the response averts an aversive stimulus before it occurs. This poses a problem: What is the reinforcement for this kind of learning? *See also* punishment training, escape learning.

axon Part of a neuron that transmits impulses to other neurons or effectors.

backward pairing A classical conditioning procedure in which the conditioned stimulus (CS) follows the unconditioned stimulus (US). *See also* forward pairing, simultaneous pairing.

Barnum effect Describes the fact that a description of one's personality will often be uncritically accepted as valid if it is stated in sufficiently general terms.

basal ganglia In the extrapyramidal motor system, a set of subcortical structures in the cerebrum that send messages to the spinal cord through the midbrain to modulate various motor functions.

base rate *See* representativeness heuristic.

basilar membrane *See* cochlea.

behavioral-cognitive approach to personality An approach that defines personality differences by the way in which different people act and think about their actions. It tends to emphasize situational determinants and prior learning in trying to explain how such differences come about. *See also* humanistic approach, psychodynamic approach, sociocultural approach, situationism, trait theory.

behaviorism A theoretical outlook that emphasizes the role of environment and of learning, and insists that people must be studied objectively and from the outside.

behavior therapy A general approach to psychological treatment which (1) holds that the disorders to which it addresses itself are produced by maladaptive learning and must be remedied by reeducation, (2) proposes techniques for this reeducation based on principles of learning and conditioning, (3) focuses on the maladaptive behaviors as such rather than on hypothetical unconscious processes of which they may be expressions.

belongingness in learning The fact that the ease with which associations are formed depends upon the items to be associated. This holds for classical conditioning in which some CS-US combinations are more effective than others (e.g., learned taste aversions) and for instrumental conditioning in which some response-reinforcer combinations work more easily than others (e.g., specific defense reactions in avoidance conditioning of species).

between-family differences A term often used in the discussion of the role of environment. It describes environmental differences that apply to entire families, such as differences in socioeconomic status, religion, or child-rearing attitudes. For personality attributes, these seem to be less important than within-family differences. *See also* within-family differences.

between-group heritability The extent to which variation between groups (as in the difference between the mean IQs of U.S. whites and blacks) is attributable to genetic factors. *See also* heritability, within-group heritability.

bidirectional activation models Models of pattern recognition in which elements are activated as well as inhibited from both lower levels (bottom-up processing) and higher levels (top-down processing).

binocular disparity An important cue for depth perception. Each eye obtains a different view of an object, the disparity becoming less pronounced the farther the object is from the observer.

bipolar cells The intermediate neural cells in the eye that are stimulated by the receptors and excite the ganglion cells.

bipolar disorder An affective disorder in which the patient swings from one emotional extreme to another, experiencing both manic and depressive episodes. Formerly called manic-depressive psychosis.

blindsight The ability of a person with a lesion in the visual cortex to reach toward or guess at the orientation of objects projected on the part of the visual field that corresponds to this lesion, even though they report that they can see absolutely nothing in that part of their visual field.

blind spot The region of the eye that contains no visual receptors and therefore cannot produce visual sensations.

blocking effect An effect produced when two conditioned stimuli, *A* and *B*, are both presented together with the unconditioned stimulus (US). If stimulus *A* has previously been associated with the unconditioned stimulus while *B* has not, the formation of an association between stimulus *B* and the US will be impaired (that is, blocked).

bottom-up processes *See* top-down processes.

brightness A perceived dimension of visual stimuli—the extent to which they appear light or dark.

brightness contrast The perceiver's tendency to exaggerate the physical difference in the light intensities of two adjacent regions. As a result, a gray patch looks brighter on a black background, darker on a white background.

brightness ratio The ratio between the light reflected by a region and the light reflected by the area that surrounds it. According to one theory, perceived brightness is determined by this ratio.

Broca's area *See* aphasia.

bulimia An eating disorder characterized by repeated binge-and-purge bouts. In contrast to anorexics, bulimics tend to be of roughly normal weight. *See also* anorexia nervosa, obesity.

bystander effect The phenomenon that underlies many examples of failing to help strangers in distress: The larger the group a person is in (or thinks he is in), the less likely he is to come to a stranger's assistance. One reason is diffusion of responsibility (no one thinks it is *his* responsibility to act).

case study An observational study in which one person is studied intensively.

catatonic schizophrenia A subcategory of schizophrenia. Its main symptoms are peculiar motor patterns, such as periods in which the patient is immobile and maintains strange positions for hours on end.

catecholamines A family of neurotransmitters that have an activating function, including epinephrine, norepinephrine, and dopamine.

categorical scale A scale that divides responses into categories that are not numerically related. *See also* interval scale, nominal scale, ordinal scale, ratio scale.

catharsis An explosive release of hitherto dammed-up emotions that is sometimes believed to have therapeutic effects.

CAT scan (Computerized Axial Tomography) A technique for examining brain structure in living humans by constructing a composite X-ray picture based on views from all different angles.

censorship in dreams *See* Freud's theory of dreams.

central nervous system (CNS) The brain and spinal cord.

central pattern generators (CPGs) Circuits in the nervous system that orchestrate lower level reflexes and other neural activities into larger, organized acts. CPGs instigate certain crucial basic actions, such as, chewing, breathing, locomotion, etc.

central route to persuasion *See* elaboration-likelihood model of persuasion.

central tendency The tendency of scores in a frequency distribution to cluster around a central value. *See also* median, mean, and variability.

central trait A trait that is associated with many other attributes of the person who is being judged. Warm and cold are central because they are important in determining overall impressions.

cerebellum Two small hemispheres that form part of the hindbrain and control muscular coordination and equilibrium.

cerebral cortex The outermost layer of the gray matter of the cerebral hemispheres.

cerebral hemispheres Two hemispherical structures that comprise the major part of the forebrain in mammals and serve as the main coordinating center of the nervous system.

childhood amnesia The failure to remember the events of our very early childhood. This is sometimes ascribed to massive change in retrieval cues, sometimes to different ways of encoding memories in early childhood.

chlorpromazine *See* phenothiazines.

choice reaction time A measure of the speed of mental processing in which the subject has to choose between one of several responses depending upon which stimulus is presented.

chromosomes Structures in the nucleus of each cell which contain the genes, the units of hereditary transmission. A human cell has 46 chromosomes, arranged in 23 pairs. One of these pairs consists of the sex chromosomes. In males, one member of the pair is an X-chromosome, the other a Y-chromosome. In females, both members are X-chromosomes. *See also* gene, X-chromosome.

chunking A process of reorganizing (or recoding) materials in memory which permits a number of items to be packed into a larger unit.

circadian rhythm A rhythm that spans about a twenty-four-hour day, such as that of the sleep-waking cycle. Circadian rhythms in humans originate from a clock circuit in the hypothalamus that is set by information from the optic nerve about whether it is day or night.

classical conditioning A form of learning in which a hitherto neutral stimulus, the conditioned stimulus (CS) is paired with an unconditioned stimulus (US) regardless of what the animal does. In effect, what has to be learned is the relation between these two stimuli. *See also* instrumental conditioning.

classical psychoanalysis The method developed by Sigmund Freud which assumes that a patient's ills stem from unconscious defenses against unacceptable urges that date back to early childhood.

client-centered therapy A humanistic psychotherapy developed by Carl Rogers. *See also* humanistic therapies.

closure A factor in visual grouping. The perceptual tendency to fill in gaps in a figure so that it looks closed.

cochlea A coiled structure in the inner ear which contains the basilar membrane whose deformation by sound-produced pressure stimulates the auditory receptors.

cocktail-party effect The effect one experiences in settings such as noisy parties, where one tunes in to the voice of the person one is talking to and filters out the other voices as background noise. This phenomenon is the model for studying selective attention based on listening to speech.

coding The translation of stimulus information into various dimensions of sensation (e.g., intensity and quality) that are actually experienced.

cognitive development Intellectual growth from infancy to adulthood.

cognitive dissonance An inconsistency among some experiences, beliefs, attitudes, or feelings. According to dissonance theory, this sets up an unpleasant state that people try to reduce by reinterpreting some part of their experiences to make them consistent with the others.

cognitive interpretation theory of emotions A theory proposed by Schachter and Singer which asserts that emotions are an interpretation of our own autonomic arousal in the light of the situation to which we attribute it. *See also* attribution theory.

cognitive map *See* cognitive theory.

cognitive neuropsychology A field evidence of damage to certain areas of the brain and corresponding behaviors are used to make inferences about underlying psychological functions.

cognitive theory A conception of human and animal learning which holds that both humans and animals acquire items of knowledge (cognitions) such as what is where (cognitive map) or what leads to what (expectancy). This contrasts with theories of instrumental learning such as Thorndike's or

Skinner's which assert that learning consists of the strengthening or weakening of particular response tendencies.

cognitive therapy An approach to therapy that tries to change some of the patient's habitual modes of thinking about himself, his situation, and his future. It is related to behavior therapy because it regards such thought patterns as a form of behavior.

collectivism-individualism A dimension used to characterize the differences in the dominant personality patterns of different cultures. Collectivist societies emphasize the needs, demands, and values of the family and immediate community, whereas individualist societies emphasize an individual's private goals and aspirations.

common sense As used in the discussion of artificial intelligence, the term refers to an understanding of what is relevant to a problem and what is not.

complementary colors Two colors that, when additively mixed with each other in the right proportions, produce the sensation of gray.

compulsions *See* obsessive-compulsive disorders.

concept A class or category that subsumes a number of individual instances. An important way of relating concepts is through propositions, which make some assertion that relates a subject (e.g., *chickens*) and a predicate (e.g., *lay eggs*).

concordance The probability that a person who stands in a particular familial relationship to a patient (e.g., an identical twin) has the same disorder as the patient.

concrete operational period In Piaget's theory, the period from ages six or seven to about eleven. At this time, the child has acquired mental operations that allow her to abstract some essential attributes of reality, such as number and substance; but these operations are as yet applicable only to concrete events and cannot be considered entirely in the abstract.

conditioned emotional response (CER) A technique in which a conditioned stimulus evokes fear, which in turn suppresses whatever other activities that the animal is currently engaged in. For example, a rat will no longer press a lever for a food reward after several trials involving a light or tone that precedes an electrical shock.

conditioned reflex *See* conditioned response.

conditioned reinforcer An initially neutral stimulus that acquires reinforcing properties through pairing with another stimulus that is already reinforcing.

conditioned response (CR) A response elicited by some initially neutral stimulus, the conditioned stimulus (CS), as a result of pairings between that CS and an unconditioned stimulus (US). This CR is typically not identical with the unconditioned response though it often is similar to it. *See also* conditioned stimulus, unconditioned response, unconditioned stimulus.

conditioned stimulus (CS) In classical conditioning, the stimulus which comes to elicit a new response by virtue of pairings with the unconditioned stimulus. *See also* conditioned response, unconditioned response, unconditioned stimulus.

cones Visual receptors that respond to greater light intensities and give rise to chromatic (color) sensations.

confidence interval An interval around a sample mean or proportion within which the population mean or proportion is likely to fall. In common practice, the largest value of the interval is 2 standard errors above the mean or proportion, and the smallest value is 2 standard errors below it.

confirmation bias The tendency to seek evidence to confirm one's hypothesis rather than to look for evidence to see whether the hypothesis is false.

conformity The act of going along with what other people think or do.

Evidence suggests that there are two main reasons people conform: the desire to be right and the desire to be liked.

conjunction of features In a visual search procedure, a target that is composed of several different features (i.e., a red X as opposed to the feature red or the feature diagonal). Search times required to find these kinds of targets are longer and increase with the number of distractors that are displayed.

conservation of number In Piaget's theory, the understanding that the number of objects in a group remains constant despite their spatial arrangement (e.g., a child at age six realizes that there is the same number of objects in a row of six closely spaced bottles as in a row of six bottles spaced far apart).

conservation of quantity In Piaget's theory, the understanding that the quantity of a substance remains unchanged despite a visible change in appearance (thus in liquid conservation, the realization that the amount of liquid remains the same when poured from a tall, thin beaker into a short, wide jar).

construct validity The extent to which performance on a test fits into a theoretical scheme about the attribute the test tries to measure.

content morphemes Morphemes that carry the main burden of meaning (e.g., *strange*). This is in contrast to function morphemes that add details to the meaning but also serve various grammatical purposes (e.g., the suffixes *s* and *er*, the connecting words *and, or, if,* and so on).

context effects *See* top-down processes.

contiguity The togetherness in time of two events, which is sometimes regarded as the condition that leads to association.

contingency A relation between two events in which one is dependent upon another. If the contingency is greater than zero, then the probability of event *A* will be greater when event *B* is present than when it is absent.

control group A group to which the experimenter's manipulation is not applied.

convergence The movement of the eyes as they swivel toward each other to focus upon an object.

conversion disorders Formerly called conversion hysteria. A condition in which there are physical symptoms that seem to have no physical basis. They instead appear to be linked to psychological factors and are often believed to serve as a means of reducing anxiety. *See also* hysteria.

conversion hysteria *See* conversion disorders.

corpus callosum A bundle of fibers that connects the two cerebral hemispheres.

correct negative See payoff matrix.

correlation The tendency of two variables to vary together. If one goes up as the other goes up, the correlation is positive; if one goes up as the other goes down, the correlation is negative.

correlation coefficient A number, referred to as *r*, that expresses both the size and the direction of a correlation, varying from +1.00 (perfect positive correlation) through 0.00 (absence of any correlation) to −1.00 (perfect negative correlation).

counterconditioning A procedure for weakening a classically conditioned CR by connecting the stimuli that presently evoke it to a new response that is incompatible with the CR.

criterion groups Groups whose test performance sets the validity criterion for certain tests (e.g., the Minnesota Multiphasic Personality Inventory, MMPI, which uses several psychiatric criterion groups to define most of its subscales).

critical period A period in the development of an organism when it is particularly sensitive to certain environmental influences. Outside of this period, the same environmental influences have little effect (e.g., the period during which a duckling can be imprinted). After embryonic development, this phenomenon is rarely all-or-none. As a result, most developmental psychologists prefer the term *sensitive period*.

critical ratio A *z*-score used for testing the null hypothesis. It is obtained by dividing an obtained mean difference by the standard error *(SE)* so that critical ratio = obtained mean difference/*SE*. If this ratio is large enough, the null hypothesis is rejected and the difference is said to be statistically significant. *See also* standard error of the mean.

cross-cultural approach The view that people differ in some regards as a result of the cultural group of which they are a member. *See also* behavioral-cognitive approach, humanistic approach.

cross-cultural method The study of the relation between a culture's beliefs and practices and the typical personality characteristics of its members. *See also* sociocultural approach.

crystallized intelligence The repertoire of information, cognitive skills, and strategies acquired by the application of fluid intelligence to various fields. This is said to increase with age, in some cases into old age. *See also* fluid intelligence.

cultural anthropology A branch of anthropology that compares the similarities and differences among human cultures.

culture fairness of a test The extent to which test performance does not depend upon information or skills provided by one culture but not another.

curare A drug that completely paralyzes the skeletal musculature but does not affect visceral reactions.

cutoff score A score on a test used for selection below which no individual is accepted.

decay A possible factor in forgetting, producing some loss of the stored information through erosion by some as yet unknown physiological process

decibels The logarithmic units used to describe sound intensity (or amplitude).

decision making The process of forming probability estimates of events and utilizing them to choose between different courses of action.

declarative knowledge Knowing "that" (e.g., knowing someone's name) as contrasted with procedural knowledge, which is knowing "how" (e.g., knowing how to ride a bicycle).

deductive reasoning Reasoning in which one tries to determine whether some statement follows logically from certain premises, as in the analysis of syllogisms. This is in contrast with inductive reasoning in which one observes a number of particular instances and tries to determine a general rule that covers them all.

defense mechanism In psychoanalytic theory, a collective term for a number of reactions that try to ward off or lessen anxiety by various unconscious means. *See also* displacement, projection, rationalization, reaction formation, repression.

definition (of a word) A set of necessary and sufficient features shared by all members of a category which are the criteria for membership in that category.

deindividuation A weakened sense of personal identity in which self-awareness is merged in the collective goals of a group.

deinstitutionalization A movement intended to obtain better and less expensive care for schizophrenic patients in their own communities rather than at large, centralized hospitals.

delay of gratification The postponement of immediate satisfaction in

order to achieve a more important reward later on, a process that plays an important role in some behavioral-cognitive approaches to personality.

delusion Systematized false beliefs, often of grandeur or persecution.

demand characteristics (of an experiment) The cues that tell a subject what the experimenter expects of him or her.

dendrites A typically highly branched part of a neuron that receives impulses from receptors or other neurons and conducts them toward the cell body and axon.

dependent variable *See* experiment.

depolarization A drop of the membrane potential of a neuron from its resting potential. The basis of neural excitation.

depression A state of deep and pervasive dejection and hopelessness, accompanied by apathy and a feeling of personal worthlessness.

depth-of-processing approach An approach to memory that stresses the nature of encoding at the time of acquisition. It argues that deeper levels of processing (for example, attending to a word's meaning) lead to better retention and retrieval than shallower levels of processing (for example, attending to the word's sound). Thus maintenance rehearsal leads to much poorer retrieval than elaborative rehearsal. *See also* encoding, elaborative rehearsal, maintenance rehearsal.

descriptive rules *See* prescriptive rules.

deviation IQ A measure of intelligence-test performance based on an individual's standing relative to his own age-mates (e.g., an IQ of 100 is average and IQs of 70 and 130 correspond to percentile ranks of 2 and 98 respectively). *See also* Intelligence Quotient.

diathesis *See* diathesis-stress conception.

diathesis-stress conception The belief that many organic and mental disorders arise from an interaction between a diathesis (a predisposition toward an illness) and some form of precipitating environmental stress.

dichotic listening A procedure by which each ear receives a different message while the listener is asked to attend to only one.

difference threshold The amount by which a given stimulus must be increased or decreased so that the subject can perceive a just-noticeable difference (j.n.d.).

differentiation A progressive change from the general to the particular and from the simpler to the more complex which characterizes embryological development. According to some theorists, the same pattern holds for the development of behavior after birth.

diffusion of responsibility *See* bystander effect.

diminishing returns principle Applied to the perceived value of money, the principle states that the increase in the subjective value produced by every additional dollar decreases the more dollars the person has already. The same principle applies to the subjective value of other gains and losses. It also applies to the psychological magnitude of sensory qualities, as in the case of Weber's law.

directed thinking Thinking that is aimed at the solution of a problem.

direct perception In Gibson's theory, our ability to perceive information about sizes directly, without any intermediate cognitive steps.

discrimination A process of learning to respond to certain stimuli that are reinforced and not to others that are unreinforced.

discriminative stimuli In instrumental conditioning, the external stimuli that signal a particular relationship between the instrumental response and the reinforcer. For example, a green light is a positive discriminative stimulus when it signals to a pigeon that it will get food if it hops on a treadle; the reverse is true of a red light, or the negative discriminative stimulus, which indicates that this action will not lead to a food reward.

disinhibition An increase of some reaction tendency by the removal of some inhibiting influence upon it (e.g., the increased strength of a frog's spinal reflexes after decapitation).

disorganized type of schizophrenia A subtype of schizophrenia formerly called hebephrenia in which the predominant symptoms are extreme incoherence of thought and marked inappropriateness of behavior and affect.

displaced aggression *See* displacement.

displacement In psychoanalytic theory, a redirection of an impulse from a channel that is blocked into another, more available outlet (e.g., displaced aggression, as in a child who hits a sibling when punished by her parents).

display A term used by ethologists to describe genetically preprogrammed responses that serve as stimuli for the reaction of others of the same species, and thus serve as the basis of a communication system (e.g., mating rituals).

display rules A culture's rules about what facial signals may or may not be given and in what contexts.

dispositional quality Any underlying attribute that characterizes a given individual and makes her more disposed than others to engage in a particular behavior (e.g., the presence or absence of some ability or some personality trait).

dissociation (1) A term used for symptoms when a patient is impaired in one function but relatively unaffected in another. (2) In post-traumatic stress disorder, the period of numbness immediately after the trauma in which the sufferer feels estranged, socially unresponsive, and oddly unaffected by the traumatizing event.

dissociative disorders Disorders in which a whole set of mental events is stored out of ordinary consciousness. These include dissociative amnesia, fugue states and, very rarely, cases of dissociative identity disorder.

dissociative identity disorder Formerly multiple personality disorder. A dissociative disorder that results in a person developing two or more distinct personalities.

dissonance theory *See* cognitive dissonance.

distal stimulus An object or event outside (e.g., a tree) as contrasted to the proximal stimulus (e.g., the retinal image of the tree), which is the pattern of physical energies that originates from the distal stimulus and impinges on a sense organ.

distance cues The visual clues that allow us to perceive depth and the distance of objects.

distress calls The innate signals through which a human or animal infant indicates its need of aid.

doctrine of specific nerve energies The assertion that qualitative differences in sensory experience are not attributable to the differences in the stimuli that correspond to different sense modalities (e.g., light versus sound) but rather to the fact that these stimuli excite different nervous structures.

dominance hierarchies A social order developed by animals that live in groups by which certain individuals gain status and exert power over others.

dominant gene *See* gene.

door-in-the-face technique A method for achieving compliance in which a certain request is preceded by a much larger one. The refusal of the first request, and the apparent concession on the part of the requester, makes people more likely to agree to the second demand, feeling that they should now make a concession of their own.

dopamine (DA) A neurotransmitter involved in various brain structures, including those that control motor action.

dopamine hypothesis of schizophrenia Asserts that schizophrenics are oversensitive to the neurotransmitter dopamine and are therefore in a state of overarousal. Evidence for this view comes from the fact that the phenothiazines, which alleviate schizophrenic symptoms, block dopamine transmission. *See also* phenothiazines.

double-blind technique A technique for evaluating drug effects independent of the effects produced by the expectations of patients (placebo effects) and of physicians. This is done by assigning patients to a drug group or a placebo group with both patients and staff members in ignorance of who is assigned to which group. *See also* placebo effect.

drive-reduction theory A theory that claims that all built-in rewards are at bottom reductions of some noxious bodily state. The theory has difficulty in explaining motives in which one seeks stimulation, such as sex and curiosity.

drug tolerance The compensatory reaction developed after repeated use of a drug. Addicts must use increasingly larger doses to obtain the same effect that was produced previously.

DSM-III The diagnostic manual of the American Psychiatric Assocaition adopted in 1980. A major distinction between it and its predecessor is that it categorizes mental disorders by their descriptive characteristics rather than by theories about their underlying cause. Thus a number of disorders that were formerly grouped together under the general heading "neurosis" (e.g., phobias, conversion disorders) are now classified under separate headings. *See also* conversion disorders, neurosis, phobia.

DSM-III-R The diagnostic manual of the American Psychiatric Association adopted in 1987, a relatively minor revision of its predecessor, DSM-III.

DSM-IV The current diagnostic manual of the American Psychiatric Association (adopted in 1994), a substantial revision of its predecessor, DSM-III-R.

duplex theory of vision The theory that rods and cones handle different aspects of vision. The rods are the receptors for night vision; they operate at low light intensities and lead to achromatic (colorless) sensations. The cones are used in day vision; they respond at higher illumination levels and are responsible for sensations of color.

eardrum The taut membrane that transmits vibrations caused by sound waves across the middle ear to the inner ear.

effectors Organs of action; in humans, muscles and glands.

efferent nerves Nerves that carry messages to the effectors.

ego In Freud's theory, a set of reactions that try to reconcile the id's blind pleasure strivings with the demands of reality. These lead to the emergence of various skills and capacities that eventually become a system that can look at itself—an "I." *See also* id and superego.

egocentrism In Piaget's theory, a characteristic of preoperational children, an inability to see another person's point of view.

ego psychology An approach to psychology that, in addition to the neo-Freudian concern with cultural and interpersonal factors, stresses the healthy aspects of the self as it tries to cope with reality.

eidetic memory A relatively rare kind of memory characterized by relatively long-lasting and detailed images of scenes that can be scanned as if they were physically present.

elaboration-likelihood model of persuasion A theory that asserts that the factors that make for persuasion depend on the extent to which the arguments of the persuasive message are thought about (elaborated). If they are seriously thought about, the central route to persuasion will be used, and attitude change will depend on the nature of the arguments. If they are not seriously considered, the peripheral route to persuasion will be used, and attitude change will depend on more peripheral factors.

elaborative rehearsal Rehearsal in which material is actively reorganized and elaborated while in working memory. In contrast to maintenance rehearsal, this confers considerable benefit. *See also* maintenance rehearsal.

Electra complex *See* Oedipus complex.

electroconvulsive shock treatment (ECT) A somatic treatment, mostly used for cases of severe depression, in which a brief electric current is passed through the brain to produce a convulsive seizure.

electroencephalogram (EEG) A record of the summed activity of cortical cells picked up by wires placed on the skull.

embryo The earliest stage in a developing animal. In humans, up to about eight weeks after conception.

emergency reaction Intense sympathetic arousal that mobilizes an organism for a crisis.

empathic concern A feeling of sympathy and concern for the sufferings of another coupled with the desire to relieve this suffering. *See also* vicarious distress.

empathy A direct emotional response to another person's emotions.

empiricism A school of thought that holds that all knowledge comes by way of empirical experience, that is, through the senses.

encoding The form in which some information is stored.

encoding specificity principle The hypothesis that retrieval is most likely if the context at the time of recall approximates that during the original encoding.

endocrine system The system of ductless glands whose secretions are released directly into the bloodstream and affect organs elsewhere in the body (e.g., adrenal gland).

endorphin A drug produced within the brain itself whose effects and chemical composition are similar to such pain-relieving opiates as morphine.

epinephrine (adrenaline) A neurotransmitter released into the bloodstream by the adrenal medulla whose effects are similar to those of sympathetic activation (e.g., racing heart).

episodic memory Memory for particular events in one's own life (e.g., I missed the train this morning). *See also* generic memory.

erogenous zones In psychoanalytic theory, the mouth, anus, and genitals. These regions are particularly sensitive to touch. According to Freud, the various pleasures associated with each of them have a common element, which is sexual.

escape learning Instrumental learning in which reinforcement consists of the reduction or cessation of an aversive stimulus (e.g., electric shock). *See also* punishment training, avoidance learning.

estrogen A female sex hormone that dominates the first half of the female cycle through ovulation; in animals, estrus performs this function.

estrus In mammalian animals, the period in the cycle when the female is sexually receptive (in heat).

ethology A branch of biology that studies the behavior of animals under natural conditions.

excitation transfer effects The transfer of autonomic arousal from one situation to another, as when strenuous exercise leads to an increased arousal when presented with aggression-arousing or erotic stimuli.

existential therapy A humanistic therapy that emphasizes people's free will and tries to help them achieve a personal outlook to give meaning to their lives.

experiment A study in which the investigator manipulates one (or more than one) variable (the independent variable) to determine its effect on the subject's response (the dependent variable).

expert systems Computer problem-solving programs with a very narrow scope which only deal with problems in a limited domain of knowledge (e.g., the diagnosis of infectious diseases).

explicit memory Memory retrieval in which there is awareness of remembering at the time of retrieval. *See also* implicit memory.

expressive aphasia A disorder in which the patient has difficulty with the production of speech. Expressive aphasia is caused by a cortical lesion that damages one's ability to organize the movements necessary for speech production into a unified sequence.

expressive movements Movements of the face and body in animals and humans that seem to express emotion. They are usually regarded as built-in social displays.

externality hypothesis The hypothesis that some and perhaps all obese people are relatively unresponsive to their own internal hunger state but are much more susceptible to signals from without.

extinction In classical conditioning, the weakening of the tendency of CS to elicit CR by unreinforced presentations of CS. In instrumental conditioning, a decline in the tendency to perform the instrumental response brought about by unreinforced occurrences of that response.

extrapyramidal system One of the two cerebral motor control systems; it is older in evolutionary terms, and it controls relatively gross movements of the head, limbs, and trunk.

extroversion/introversion In Eysenck's system, a trait dimension that refers to the main direction of a person's energies; toward the outer world of objects and other people (extroversion) or toward the inner world of one's own thoughts and feelings (introversion).

facial feedback hypothesis The hypothesis that sensory feedback from the facial muscles will lead to subjective feelings of emotion that correspond to the particular facial pattern. *See* fundamental emotions.

factor analysis A statistical method for studying the interrelations among various tests, the object of which is to discover what the tests have in common and whether these commonalities can be ascribed to one or several factors that run through all or some of these tests.

false alarm *See* payoff matrix.

familiarity effect The fact that increased exposure to a stimulus tends to make that stimulus more likable.

family resemblance structure Overlap of features among members of a category of meaning such that no members of the category have all of the features but all members have some of them.

family therapy A general term for a number of therapies that treat the family (or a couple), operating on the assumption that the key to family or marital distress is not necessarily in the pathology of any individual spouse or family member but is rather in the interrelationships within the family or marriage system.

feature detectors Neurons in the retina or brain that respond to specific features of the stimulus, such as movement, orientation, and so on.

Fechner's law The assertion that the strength of a sensation is proportional to the logarithm of physical stimulus intensity.

feedback system A system in which some action produces a consequence that affects (feeds back on) the action. In negative feedback, the consequence stops or reverses the action (e.g., thermostat-controlled furnace). In positive feedback, the consequence strengthens the action (e.g., rocket that homes in on airplanes).

fetus A later stage in embryonic development. In humans, from about eight weeks until birth.

figure-ground organization The segregation of the visual field into a part (the figure) that stands out against the rest (the ground).

final common path The single neural output upon which two groups of nerve fibers converge.

fixation (1) In problem solving, the result of rigid mental sets that makes it difficult for people to approach a problem in new and different ways. (2) In Freud's theory of personality, the lingering attachment to an earlier stage of pleasure seeking, even after a new stage has been attained.

fixed-action patterns Term used by ethologists to describe stereotyped, species-specific behaviors triggered by genetically pre-programmed releasing stimuli.

fixed-interval schedule *See* interval schedule.

fixed-ratio schedule *See* ratio schedule.

flashbulb memories Vivid, detailed, and apparently accurate memories said to be produced by unexpected and emotionally important events.

flooding A form of behavior therapy based on concepts derived from classical conditioning in which the patient exposes himself to whatever he is afraid of, thus extinguishing his fear. *See also* implosion therapy.

flow chart (1) In computer science, a diagram that shows the step-by-step operation of a computer program. (2) In human cognition, similar diagrams that show the hypothesized flow of information as it is thought to be processed by the human mind.

fluid intelligence The ability, which is said to decline with age, to deal with essentially new problems. *See also* crystallized intelligence.

forced compliance effect An individual forced to act or speak publicly in a manner contrary to his own beliefs may change his own views in the direction of the public action. But this will happen only if his reward for the false public pronouncement is relatively small. If the reward is large, there is no dissonance and hence no attitude change. *See also* cognitive dissonance.

forebrain In mammals, the bulk of the brain. Its foremost region includes the cerebral hemispheres; its rear includes the thalamus and hypothalamus.

forgetting curve A curve showing the inverse relationship between memory and the retention interval.

forward pairing A classical conditioning procedure in which the conditioned stimulus (CS) precedes the unconditioned stimulus (US). This contrasts with simultaneous pairing, in which CS and US are presented simultaneously, and backward pairing, in which CS follows US. *See also* classical conditioning, conditioned stimulus, unconditioned stimulus.

framing A heuristic that affects the subjective desirability of an event by changing the standard of reference for judging the desirability of that event.

fraternal twins Twins that arise from two different eggs that are (simultaneously) fertilized by different sperm cells. Their genetic similarity is no greater than that between ordinary siblings. *See also* identical twins.

free association Method used in psychoanalytic therapy in which the patient is to say anything that comes to her mind, no matter how apparently trivial, unrelated, or embarrassing.

free recall A test of memory that asks for as many items in a list as a subject can recall regardless of order.

frequency distribution An arrangement in which scores are tabulated by the frequency in which they occur.

Freud's theory of dreams A theory that holds that at bottom all dreams are attempts to fulfill a wish. The wish fulfillment is in the latent dream, which represents the sleeper's hidden desires. This latent dream is censored and reinterpreted to avoid anxiety. It reemerges in more acceptable form as the manifest dream, the dream the sleeper remembers upon awakening.

frontal lobe A lobe in each cerebral hemisphere which includes the motor projection area.

function morphemes *See* content morphemes.

functional fixedness A set to think of objects in terms of their normal function.

fundamental attribution error The tendency to attribute behaviors to dispositional qualities while underrating the role of the situation. *See also* actor-observer difference, attribution theory, self-serving bias.

fundamental emotions According to some theorists, a small set of elemental, built-in emotions revealed by distinctive patterns of facial expression. *See also* facial feedback hypothesis.

galvanic skin response (GSR) A drop in the electrical resistance of the skin, widely used as an index of autonomic reaction.

ganglion (*plural* ganglia) Neural control centers that integrate messages from different receptor cells and coordinate the activity of different muscle fibers.

ganglion cells In the retina, one of the intermediate links between the receptor cells and the brain. The axons of the ganglion cells converge into a bundle of fibers that leave the eyeball as the optic nerve. *See also* bipolar cells.

gender constancy The recognition that being male or female is to all intents and purposes irrevocable.

gender identity The inner sense of being male or female. *See also* gender role, sexual orientation.

gender role The set of external behavior patterns a given culture deems appropriate for each sex. *See also* gender identity, sexual orientation.

gene The unit of hereditary transmission, located at a particular place in a given chromosome. Both members of each chromosome pair have corresponding locations at which there are genes that carry instructions about the same characteristic (e.g., eye color). If one member of a gene pair is dominant and the other is recessive, the dominant gene will exert its effect regardless of what the recessive gene calls for. The characteristic called for by the recessive gene will only be expressed if the other member of the gene pair is also recessive. *See also* chromosomes.

general intelligence (g) According to Spearman, a mental attribute that is called upon in any intellectual task a person has to perform.

generalization decrement In classical conditioning, the weakening of a response to a new stimulus compared to the response elicited by the original CS. The greater the difference between the new stimulus and the original CS, the larger the generalization decrement. In instrumental conditioning, a similar effect occurs when a new discriminating stimulus is presented instead of the original stimulus.

generalization gradient The curve that shows the relationship between the tendency to respond to a new stimulus and its similarity to the original conditioned stimulus (CS).

generalized anxiety disorder A mental disorder (formerly called anxiety neurosis) whose primary characteristic is an all-pervasive, "free-floating" anxiety. A member of the diagnostic category "anxiety disorders," which also includes phobias and obsessive-compulsive disorders. *See also* phobia, obsessive-compulsive disorders.

general paresis A psychosis characterized by progressive decline in cognitive and motor function culminating in death, reflecting a deteriorating brain condition produced by syphilitic infection.

generic memory Memory for items of knowledge as such (e.g., The capital of France is Paris), independent of the occasion on which they are learned. *See also* episodic memory.

genital stage In psychoanalytic theory, the stage of psychosexual development reached in adult sexuality in which sexual pleasure involves not only one's own gratification but also the social and bodily satisfaction brought to another person.

genotype The genetic blueprint of an organism which may or may not be overtly expressed by its phenotype. *See also* phenotype.

Gestalt An organized whole such as a visual form or a melody.

Gestalt psychology A theoretical approach that emphasizes the role of organized wholes (Gestalten) in perception and other psychological processes.

glove anesthesia A condition sometimes seen in conversion disorders, in which there is an anesthesia of the entire hand with no loss of feeling above the wrist. This symptom makes no organic sense given the anatomical arrangement of the nerve trunks and indicates that the condition has a psychological basis.

glucose A form of sugar which is the major source of energy for most bodily tissues. If plentiful, much of it is converted into glycogen and stored away.

glucose receptors Receptors in the brain (probably the hypothalamus) that detect changes in the way glucose is used as a metabolic fuel.

glycogen A stored form of metabolic energy derived from glucose. To be used, it must first be converted back into glucose.

good continuation A factor in visual grouping. Contours tend to be seen in such a way that their direction is altered as little as possible.

gradient of reinforcement The curve that describes the declining effectiveness of reinforcement, with increasing delay between the response and the reinforcer.

group-factor theory of intelligence A factor-analytic approach to intelligence test performance which argues that intelligence is the composite of separate abilities (group factors such as verbal ability, spatial ability, etc.) without a sovereign capacity that enters into each. *See also* factor analysis, general intelligence.

group therapy Psychotherapy of several persons at one time.

habituation A decline in the tendency to respond to stimuli that have become familiar. While short-term habituation dissipates in a matter of minutes, long-term habituation may persist for days or weeks.

habituation procedure A widely used method for studying infant perception. After some exposure to a visual stimulus, an infant becomes habituated and stops looking at it. The extent to which a new stimulus leads to renewed interest and resumption of looking is taken as a measure of the extent to which the infant regards this new stimulus as different from the old one to which she became habituated.

hair cells The auditory receptors in the cochlea, lodged between the basilar membrane and other membranes above.

hallucination Perceived experiences that occur in the absence of actual sensory stimulation.

hebephrenia *See* disorganized type of schizophrenia.

heritability As measured by *H,* the heritability ratio, this refers to the relative importance of heredity and environment in determining the variation of a particular trait. More specifically, *H* is the proportion of the variance of the trait in a given population that is attributable to genetic factors.

heritability ratio (H) *See* heritability.

hermaphrodite A person whose reproductive organs are anatomically ambiguous so that they are not exclusively male or female.

hertz (HZ) A measure of frequency in number of cycles per second.

heterosexuality A sexual orientation leading to a choice of sexual partners of the opposite sex.

heuristics In computer problem solving, a procedure that has often worked in the past and is likely, but not certain, to work again. *See also* algorithm.

hierarchical organization Organization in which narrower categories are subsumed under broader ones, which are subsumed under still broader ones, and so on. Often expressed in the form of a tree diagram.

hierarchy of needs According to Maslow and other adherents of the humanistic approach, human needs are arranged in a hierarchy with physiological needs such as hunger at the bottom, safety needs further up, the need for attachment and love still higher, and the desire for esteem yet higher. At the very top of the hierarchy is the striving for self-actualization. By and large, people will only strive for the higher-order needs when the lower ones are fulfilled. *See* self-actualization.

higher-order conditioning In classical conditioning, a procedure by which a new stimulus comes to elicit the conditioned response (CR) by virtue of being paired with an effective conditioned stimulus (CS) (e.g., first pairings of tone and food, then pairings of bell and tone, until finally the bell elicits salivation by itself).

hindbrain The most primitive portion of the brain, which includes the medulla and the cerebellum.

hippocampus A structure in the temporal lobe that constitutes an important part of the limbic system. One of its functions seems to involve memory.

histogram A graphic rendering of a frequency distribution which depicts the distribution by a series of contiguous rectangles. *See also* frequency distribution.

hit *See* payoff matrix.

homeostasis The body's tendency to maintain the conditions of its internal environment by various forms of self-regulation.

homogamy The tendency of like to marry like.

homosexuality A sexual orientation leading to a choice of partners of the same sex.

hue A perceived dimension of visual stimuli whose meaning is close to the term *color* (e.g., red, blue).

humanistic approach to personality Asserts that what is most important about people is how they achieve their selfhood and actualize their potentialities. *See also* behavioral-cognitive approach, cross-cultural approach, psychodynamic approach, situationism, sociocultural approach, trait theory.

humanistic therapies Methods of treatment that emphasize personal growth and self-fulfillment. They try to be relatively nondirective, since their emphasis is on helping the clients achieve the capacity for making their own choices. *See also* nondirective techniques.

hyperphagia Voracious, chronic overeating brought about by a lesion of the ventromedial region of the hypothalamus.

hypnosis A temporary, trancelike state that can be induced in normal persons. During hypnosis, various hypnotic or posthypnotic suggestions sometimes produce effects that resemble some of the symptoms of conversion disorders. *See also* conversion disorders.

hypothalamus A small structure at the base of the brain which plays a vital role in the control of the autonomic nervous system, of the endocrine system, and of the major biological drives.

hysteria An older term for a group of presumably psychogenic disorders that included conversion disorders and dissociative disorders. Since DSM-III, it is no longer used as a diagnostic category, in part because of an erroneous implication that the condition is more prevalent in women (Greek *hystera*—womb). *See also* conversion disorders, dissociative disorders, glove anesthesia.

id In Freud's theory, a term for the most primitive reactions of human personality, consisting of blind strivings for immediate biological satisfaction regardless of cost. *See also* ego and superego.

ideas of reference A characteristic of some mental disorders, notably schizophrenia, in which the patient begins to think that external events are specially related to him personally (e.g., "People walk by and follow me").

identical twins Twins that originate from a single fertilized egg that then splits into two exact replicas that develop into two genetically identical individuals. *See also* fraternal twins.

identification In psychoanalytic theory, a mechanism whereby a child models himself or herself (typically) on the same-sex parent in an effort to become like him or her.

idiot savant *See* savant.

ill-defined problems *See* well-defined problems.

imipramine A tricyclic antidepressant drug.

implicit memory Memory retrieval in which there is no awareness of remembering at the time of retrieval. *See also* explicit memory.

implicit theories of personality Beliefs about the way in which different patterns of behavior of people hang together and why they do so.

implosion therapy A form of behavior therapy related to flooding in which the patient exposes herself to whatever she is afraid of, in its most extreme form, but does so in imagination rather than in real life (e.g., a person afraid of dogs has to imagine herself surrounded by a dozen snarling Dobermans). *See* flooding.

impossible figure A figure that appears acceptable when looked at locally but poses unresolvable visual contradictions when seen as a whole.

impression management According to Goffman, the characteristic of much social interaction in which people maintain a certain image that goes along with social or professional roles.

imprinting A learned attachment that is formed at a particular period in life (the critical, or sensitive, period) and is difficult to reverse (e.g., the duckling's acquired tendency to follow whatever moving stimulus it encounters twelve to twenty-four hours after hatching).

incidental learning Learning without trying to learn (e.g., as in a study in which subjects judge a speaker's vocal quality when she recites a list of words and are later asked to produce as many of the words as they can recall). *See also* intentional learning.

incremental validity The extent to which a test adds to the predictive validity already provided by other measures (e.g., the extent to which a projective technique adds to what is already known through an ordinary interview).

independent variable *See* experiment.

induced movement Perceived movement of an objectively stationary stimulus that is enclosed by a moving framework.

inductive reasoning Reasoning in which one observes a number of particular instances and tries to determine a general rule that covers them all.

information processing A general term for the presumed operations whereby the crude raw materials provided by the senses are refashioned into items of knowledge. Among these operations are perceptual organization, comparison with items stored in memory, and so on.

insightful learning Learning by understanding the relations between components of the problem; often contrasted with "blind trial and error"

and documented by wide and appropriate transfer if tested in a new situation.

instrumental conditioning Also called operant conditioning. A form of learning in which a reinforcer (e.g., food) is given only if the animal performs the instrumental response (e.g., pressing a lever). In effect, what has to be learned is the relationship between the response and the reinforcer. *See* classical conditioning.

insulin A hormone with a crucial role in utilization of nutrients. One of its functions is to help promote the conversion of glucose into glycogen.

Intelligence Quotient (IQ) A ratio measure to indicate whether a child's mental age (MA) is ahead or behind her chronological age (CA); specifically IQ = $100 \times$ MA/CA. *See also* deviation IQ, mental age.

intentional learning Learning when informed that there will be a later test of learning. *See also* incidental learning.

interference theory of forgetting The assertion that items are forgotten because they are somehow interfered with by other items learned before or after.

intermittent reinforcement *See* partial reinforcement.

internalization The process whereby moral codes are adopted by the child so that they control his behavior even where there are no external rewards or punishments.

interneurons Neurons that receive impulses and transmit them to other neurons.

interposition A monocular depth cue in which objects that are farther away are blocked from view by any other opaque object obstructing their optical path to the eye.

interval scale A scale in which equal differences between scores can be treated as equal so that the scores can be added or subtracted. *See also* categorical scale, nominal scale, ordinal scale, ratio scale.

interval schedule A reinforcement schedule in which reinforcement is delivered for a first response made after a given interval of time has elapsed. In a fixed-interval schedule, the interval is always the same. In a variable-interval schedule, the interval varies around a specified average.

introversion *See* extroversion/introversion.

invariant Some aspect of the proximal stimulus pattern that remains unchanged despite various transformations of the stimulus.

ions Atoms or molecules that have gained or lost electrons, thus acquiring a positive or negative charge.

iris The smooth circular muscle in the eye that surrounds the pupil and contracts or dilates under reflex control in order to govern the amount of light entering.

isolation A mechanism of defense in which anxiety arousing memories are retained but without the emotion that accompanied them.

James-Lange theory of emotions A theory that asserts that the subjective experience of emotion is the awareness of one's own bodily reactions in the presence of certain arousing stimuli.

just-noticeable difference (j.n.d.) *See* difference threshold.

kinesthesis A general term for sensory information generated by receptors in the muscles, tendons, and joints which informs us of our skeletal movement.

kin-selection hypothesis *See* altruism.

Korsakoff's syndrome A brain disorder characterized by serious memory disturbances. The most common cause is extreme and chronic alcohol use.

latency General term for the interval before some reaction occurs.

latency period In psychoanalytic theory, a stage in psychosexual development in which sexuality lies essentially dormant, roughly from ages five to twelve.

latent dream *See* Freud's theory of dreams.

latent learning Learning that occurs without being manifested by performance.

lateral hypothalamus A region of the hypothalamus which is said to be a "hunger center" and to be in an antagonistic relation to a supposed "satiety center," the ventromedial region of the hypothalamus.

lateral inhibition The tendency of adjacent neural elements of the visual system to inhibit each other; it underlies brightness contrast and the accentuation of contours. *See also* brightness contrast.

lateralization An asymmetry of function of the two cerebral hemispheres. In most right-handers, the left hemisphere is specialized for language functions, while the right hemisphere is better at various visual and spatial tasks.

law of effect A theory that asserts that the tendency of a stimulus to evoke a response is strengthened if the response is followed by reward and is weakened if the response is not followed by reward. Applied to instrumental learning, this theory states that as trials proceed, incorrect bonds will weaken while the correct bond will be strengthened.

learned helplessness A condition created by exposure to inescapable aversive events. This retards or prevents learning in subsequent situations in which escape or avoidance is possible.

learned helplessness theory of depression The theory that depression is analogous to learned helplessness effects produced in the laboratory by exposing subjects to uncontrollable aversive events.

learning curve A curve in which some index of learning (e.g., the number of drops of saliva in Pavlov's classical conditioning experiment) is plotted against trials or sessions.

learning model As defined in the text, a subcategory of the pathology model that (1) views mental disorders as the result of some form of faulty learning, and (2) believes that these should be treated by behavior therapists according to the laws of classical and instrumental conditioning, or by cognitive therapists who try to affect faulty modes of thinking. *See also* behavior therapy, cognitive therapy, medical model, pathology model, psychoanalytic model.

learning set The increased ability to solve various problems, especially in discrimination learning, as a result of previous experience with problems of a similar kind.

lens The portion of the eye that bends light rays and thus projects an image on the retina.

lesions The damage incurred by an area of the brain.

lexical access The process of recognizing and understanding a word, which is presumably achieved by making contact with (accessing) the word in the mental lexicon.

lightness constancy The tendency to perceive the lightness of an object as more or less the same despite the fact that the light reflected from these objects changes with the illumination that falls upon them.

limbic system A set of brain structures including a relatively primitive portion of the cerebral cortex and parts of the thalamus and hypothalamus; it is believed to be involved in the control of emotional behavior and motivation.

line of best fit A line drawn through the points in a scatter diagram; it yields the best prediction of one variable when given the value of the other variable.

lithium carbonate A drug used in the treatment of mania and bipolar disorders.

lobotomy *See* prefrontal lobotomy.

lock-and-key model The theory that neurotransmitter molecules will only affect the postsynaptic membrane if their shape fits into that of certain synaptic receptor molecules.

longitudinal study A developmental study in which the same person is tested at various ages.

long-term habituation *See* habituation.

long-term memory Those parts of the memory system that are currently dormant and inactive, but have enormous storage capacity. *See also* stage theory of memory, working memory.

looming A rapid magnification of a form in the visual field that generally signals impending impact.

luminance ratio The ratio between the light reflected off a figure and that reflected off the background against which the figure is seen. Whatever the illumination, the ratio remains the same.

Mach bands The accentuated edges between two adjacent regions that differ in hue. This sharpening is maximal at the borders where the distance between the two regions is smallest and the contrast most striking.

Magic Number According to Miller, the number (seven plus or minus two) that represents the holding capacity of the working (or short-term) memory system.

Magnetic Resonance Imaging (MRI) A neurodiagnostic technique that relies on nuclear magnetic resonance. An MRI scan passes a high frequency alternating magnetic field through the brain and detects the different resonant frequencies of nuclei. A computer then puts this information together to form a picture of the brain that shows damaged areas.

maintenance rehearsal Rehearsal in which material remains in working memory for a while. In contrast to elaborative rehearsal, this confers little benefit. *See also* elaborative rehearsal.

major depression A unipolar disorder in which a patient suffers depressive mood extremes.

major tranquilizers *See* antipsychotic drugs.

mania Hyperactive state with marked impairment of judgment, usually accompanied by intense euphoria.

manic-depressive psychosis *See* bipolar disorder.

manifest dream *See* Freud's theory of dreams.

marital therapy *See* family therapy.

matching hypothesis The hypothesis that persons of a given level of physical attractiveness will seek out partners of a roughly similar level.

matching to sample A procedure in which an organism has to choose one of two alternative stimuli which is the same as a third sample stimulus.

maturation A programmed growth process based on changes in underlying neural structures that are relatively unaffected by environmental conditions (e.g., flying in sparrows and walking in humans).

maximum-likelihood principle The assertion that we interpret the proximal stimulus pattern as that external stimulus object that most probably produced it.

mean (M) *See* measure of central tendency.

measure of central tendency The summary of an entire distribution of experimental results in a single, central score. There are three commonly used measures: (1) the mode, or the score that occurs most frequently; (2) the median, or the point that divides the distribution into two equal halves; and (3) the mean, or the arithmetic average.

medial forebrain bundle (MFB) A bundle of fibers that runs through the base of the forebrain and parts of the hypothalamus. Electric stimulation of this bundle is usually rewarding.

median *See* measure of central tendency.

medical model As defined in the text, a subcategory of the pathology model that (1) holds that the underlying pathology is organic, and that (2) the treatment should be conducted by physicians. *See also* learning model, pathology model, psychoanalytic model.

medulla The rearmost portion of the brain, just adjacent to the spinal cord. It includes centers that help to control respiration and muscle tone.

memory search An internal process preceding memory retrieval that usually occurs very quickly and without our awareness.

memory span The number of items a person can recall after just one presentation.

memory trace The change in the nervous system left by an experience that is the physical basis of its retention in memory. What this change is, is still unknown.

mental age (MA) A score devised by Binet to represent a child's test performance. It indicates the chronological age at which 50 percent of the children in that age group will perform. If the child's MA is greater than his chronological age (CA), he is ahead of his age mentally; if his MA is lower than his CA, he lags behind.

mental images Analogical memories that reserve some of the characteristic attributes of our senses.

mental representations Internal symbols that stand for something but are not equivalent to it, such as internalized actions, images, or words.

mental retardation Usually defined as an IQ of 70 or below.

mental set The predisposition to perceive (or remember or think of) one thing rather than another.

meta-analysis A statistical technique by means of which the results of many different techniques can be combined. This has been useful in studies on the outcome of psychotherapy.

metacognition A general term for knowledge about knowledge, as in knowing that we do or don't remember something.

midbrain Part of the brain that includes some lower centers for sensory-motor integration (e.g., eye movements).

middle ear An antechamber to the inner ear which amplifies sound-produced vibrations of the eardrum and imparts them to the cochlea. *See also* cochlea.

minimal-sufficiency principle A principle of socialization that states that a child will internalize a certain way of acting if there is just enough pressure to get her to behave in this new way, but not enough so that she feels she was forced to do so.

Minnesota Multiphasic Personality Inventory (MMPI) *See* criterion groups.

miss *See* payoff matrix.

mnemonics Deliberate devices for helping memory. Many of them utilize imagery.

mode *See* measure of central tendency.

monoamine oxidase (MAO) inhibitors *See* antidepressant drugs.

monocular depth cues Various features of the visual stimulus which indicate depth, even when viewed with one eye (e.g., linear perspective and motion parallax).

monogamy A mating pattern in which a reproductive partnership is based on a special, more or less permanent tie between one male and one female.

mood disorders A group of disorders (formerly called affective disorders) whose primary characteristic is a disturbance of mood and which is characterized by two emotional extremes—the energy of mania, the despair or lethargy of depression, or both. *See also* bipolar disorder, depression, mania, unipolar disorder.

morpheme The smallest significant unit of meaning in a language (e.g., the word *boys* has two morphemes, *boy* and *s*).

motherese A whimsical term for the speech pattern that mothers and other adults generally employ when talking to infants.

motion parallax A depth cue provided by the fact that, as an observer moves, the images cast by nearby objects move more rapidly on the retina than the images cast by objects farther away.

motor neurons Neurons whose cell bodies are in the spinal cord or brain and whose axons terminate in individual muscle cells.

motor projection areas *See* projection areas.

multiple intelligences In Gardner's theory, the six essential, independent mental capacities, some of which are outside of the traditional academic notions of intelligence (i.e., linguistic, logical-mathematical, spatial, musical, bodily-kinesthetic, and personal intelligence).

multiple personality disorder *See* dissociative identity disorder.

myelin sheath A tube mainly composed of several elongated segments of fatty tissue that insulates an axon from other axons.

nalaxone A drug that inhibits the effect of morphine and similar opiates, and blocks the pain alleviation ascribed to endorphins.

nativism The view that some important aspects of perception and of other cognitive processes are innate.

natural selection The explanatory principle that underlies Darwin's theory of evolution. Some organisms produce offspring that are able to survive and reproduce while other organisms of the same species do not. Thus organisms with these hereditary attributes will eventually outnumber organisms who lack these attributes.

negative correlation The tendency of one variable to increase when a corresponding second variable decreases.

negative feedback *See* feedback system.

negative symptoms of schizophrenia Symptoms that involve a lack of normal functioning, such as apathy, poverty of speech, and emotional blunting. *See* positive symptoms of schizophrenia.

neo-Freudians A group of theorists who accept the psychoanalytic conception of unconscious conflict but who differ with Freud in (1) describing these conflicts in social terms rather than in terms of particular bodily pleasures or frustrations, and (2) maintaining that many of these conflicts arise from the specific cultural conditions under which the child was reared rather than being biologically ordained.

neophobia A term used in the study of food selection, where it refers to an animal's tendency to refuse new foods.

nerve impulse *See* action potential.

network model Theories of cognitive organization, especially of semantic memory, that assert that items of information are represented by a system of nodes linked through associative connections. *See also* node.

neurodevelopmental disorder A disorder in which pathological genes produce abnormalities in the brain during fetal development; these abnormalities in turn lead to behavioral and cognitive eccentricities.

neuron A nerve cell.

neuropsychological assessment A specialized kind of test used to pinpoint cognitive impairments that may stem from learning disabilities, aging, or brain injuries or diseases.

neurosis In psychoanalytic theory, a broad term for mental disorders whose primary symptoms are anxiety or what seem to be defenses against anxiety. Since the adoption of DSM-III, the term has been dropped as the broad diagnostic label it once was. Various disorders that were once diagnosed as subcategories of neurosis (e.g., phobia, conversion disorders, dissociative disorders) are now classified as separate disorders.

neuroticism A trait dimension that refers to emotional instability and maladjustment.

neurotransmitters Chemicals liberated at the terminal end of an axon which travel across the synapse and have an excitatory or inhibitory effect on an adjacent neuron (e.g., norepinephrine).

node A point in a network on which a number of connections converge.

nodes of Ranvier Gaps in the myelin sheath surrounding an axon that allow for a considerable increase in the transmission speed of neural impulses.

nominal scale A scale in which responses are ordered only into different categories. *See also* categorical scale, interval scale, ordinal scale, and ratio scale.

nondirective techniques A set of techniques for psychological treatment developed by Carl Rogers. As far as possible, the counselor refrains from offering advice or interpretation but only tries to clarify the patient's own feelings by echoing him or restating what he says.

nonsense syllable Two consonants with a vowel between that do not form a word. Used to study associations between relatively meaningless items.

noradrenaline *See* norepinephrine.

norepinephrine (NE) The neurotransmitter by means of which the sympathetic fibers exert their effect on internal organs. It is also the neurotransmitter of various arousing systems in the brain.

normal curve A symmetrical, bell-shaped curve that describes the probability of obtaining various combinations of chance events. It describes the frequency distributions of many physical and psychological attributes of humans and animals.

normal distribution A frequency distribution whose graphic representation has a symmetric, bell-shaped form—the normal curve. Its characteristics are often referred to when investigators test statistical hypotheses and make inferences about the population from a given sample.

norms In intelligence testing, the scores taken from a large sample of the population against which an individual's test scores are evaluated.

null hypothesis The hypothesis that an obtained difference is merely a chance fluctuation from a population in which the true mean difference is zero. *See also* alternative hypothesis.

obesity A condition of marked overweight in animals and humans; it is produced by a large variety of factors including metabolic factors (oversecretion of insulin) and behavioral conditions (overeating, perhaps a nonresponsiveness to one's own internal state).

object permanence The conviction that an object remains perceptually constant over time and exists even when it is out of sight. According to Piaget, this does not develop until infants are eight months old or more.

observational learning A mechanism of socialization in which a child observes another person who serves as a model and then proceeds to imitate what that model does.

observational study A study in which the investigator does not manipulate any of the variables but simply observes their relationship as they occur naturally.

obsessions *See* obsessive-compulsive disorders.

obsessive-compulsive disorder A disorder whose symptoms are obsessions (persistent and irrational thoughts or wishes) and compulsions (uncontrollable, repetitive acts), which seem to be defenses against anxiety. A member of a diagnostic category called anxiety disorders, which also includes generalized anxiety disorder and phobias. *See also* generalized anxiety disorder, phobia and specific phobia.

occipital lobe A lobe in each cerebral hemisphere which includes the visual projection area.

occlusion The partial concealment of one object by another object in front of it.

Oedipus complex In psychoanalytic theory, a general term for a whole cluster of impulses and conflicts that occur during the phallic phase, at around age five. In boys, a fantasied form of intense sexual love is directed at the mother, which is soon followed by hate and fear of the father. As the fear mounts, the sexual feelings are pushed underground and the boy identifies with the father. An equivalent process in girls is called the Electra complex.

olfaction The sense of smell.

olfactory epithelium The small area at the top of the nasal cavity that contains receptors that react to chemicals suspended in air.

operant In Skinner's system, an instrumental response. *See also* instrumental conditioning.

operant conditioning *See* instrumental conditioning.

opponent-process theory of color vision A theory of color vision that asserts that there are three pairs of color antagonists: red-green, blue-yellow, and white-black. Excitation of one member of a pair automatically inhibits the other member.

opponent-process theory of motivation A theory that asserts that the nervous system has the general tendency to counteract any deviation from the neutral point of the pain-pleasure dimension. If the original stimulus is maintained, there is an attenuation of the emotional state one is in; if it is withdrawn, the opponent process reveals itself, and the emotional state swings sharply in the opposite direction.

optic nerve A bundle of fibers, made up of the axons of ganglion cells, that leave the eyeball.

oral character According to Freud, a personality type based on a fixation at the oral stage of development whose symptomatic attribute is passive dependency. *See also* oral stage.

oral stage In psychoanalytic theory, the earliest stage of psychosexual development during which the primary source of bodily pleasure is stimulation of the mouth and lips, as in sucking at the breast.

ordinal scale A scale in which responses are rank-ordered by relative magnitude but in which the intervals between successive ranks are not necessarily equal. *See also* categorical scale, interval scale, nominal scale, and ratio scale.

osmoreceptors Receptors that help to control water intake by responding to the concentrations of body fluids. *See also* volume receptors.

ossicles The three small bones in the ear that transmit vibrations from the eardrum to the oval window.

out-group homogeneity effect A phenomenon related to stereotyping in which a member of a group (the in-group) tends to view members of another group (the out-group) as more alike than members of his or her own.

oval window The membrane separating the middle ear from the inner ear.

paired-associate method A procedure in which subjects learn to provide particular response terms to various stimulus items.

panic disorder A disorder characterized by sudden anxiety attacks in which there are bodily symptoms such as choking, dizziness, trembling, and chest pains, accompanied by feelings of intense apprehension, terror, and a sense of impending doom.

parallel distributed processing (PDP) Models of cognitive processing in which the relevant symbolic representations do not correspond to any one unit of the network but to the state of the network as a whole.

parallel search The simultaneous comparison of a target stimulus to several items in memory. *See also* serial search.

paranoid schizophrenia A subcategory of schizophrenia. Its dominant symptom is a set of delusions that are often elaborately systematized, usually of grandeur or persecution.

paraphrase The relation between two sentences whose meanings (underlying structures) are the same but whose surface structures differ (e.g., *The boy hit the ball/The ball was hit by the boy*).

parasympathetic system A division of the autonomic nervous system that serves vegetative functions and conserves bodily energies (e.g., slowing heart rate). Its action is antagonistic to that of the sympathetic system.

parietal lobe A lobe in each cerebral hemisphere that includes the somatosensory projection area.

Parkinson's disease A degenerative neurological disorder characterized by various difficulties of movement. Produced by degeneration of dopamine-releasing neurons in a pathway of the brain crucial for motor control.

partial reinforcement A condition in which a response is reinforced only some of the time.

partial-reinforcement effect The fact that a response is much harder to extinguish if it was acquired during partial rather than continuous reinforcement.

pathology model A term adopted in the text to describe a general conception of mental disorders which holds that (1) one can generally distinguish between symptoms and underlying causes, and (2) these causes may be regarded as a form of pathology. *See also* learning model, medical model, psychoanalytic model.

pattern recognition The process by which the perceptual system matches the form of a figure against a figure stored in memory.

payoff matrix (1) In a detection experiment, a table that shows the costs and benefits of each of the four possible outcomes: a hit, reporting the stimulus when it is present; a correct negative, reporting it as absent when it is in fact absent; a miss, failing to report it when it is present; and a false alarm, reporting it as present when it is not. (2) In the context of the use of tests for selection an analogous table that shows the costs and benefits of correct and incorrect acceptances and rejections respectively.

peak experience Profound and deeply felt moments in a person's life, sometimes said to be more common in self-actualized persons than in others. *See* self-actualization.

perceived locus of control A person's belief about the source of outcomes that befall him. That perceived source (locus) may be internal, the result of something he did, or external, the result of forces outside of his own control.

percentile rank The percentage of all the scores in a distribution that lie below a given score.

perceptual adaptation The gradual adjustment to various distortions of the perceptual world, as in wearing prisms that tilt the entire visual world in one direction.

perceptual constancies Certain constant attributes of a distal object, such as its shape and size, that we are able to perceive despite vagaries of the proximal stimulus.

perceptual hypothesis The perceiver's assumption about what the stimulus is, which is tested as the perceptual system analyzes the stimulus for appropriate features.

perceptual parsing The process of grouping various visual elements of a scene appropriately, deciding which elements go together and which do not.

period of formal operations In Piaget's theory, the period from about age eleven on, when genuinely abstract mental operations can be undertaken (e.g., the ability to entertain hypothetical possibilities).

peripheral route to persuasion *See* elaboration-likelihood model of persuasion.

periphery In vision, the area towards the outside of the retina that has a high concentration of rods, is highly sensitive to dim light, and is responsible for colorless sensations.

permissive pattern A parental style in which parents try not to assert their authority and impose few restrictions or demands on their children.

personal space The physical region all around us whose intrusion we guard against; this aspect of human behavior has been likened to territoriality in animals.

personality inventories Paper-and-pencil tests of personality that ask questions about feelings or customary behavior. *See also* projective techniques.

person-by-situation interaction The fact that the effect of a situational variable may depend on the person. Thus some people may on average be equally fearful, but while one is afraid of meeting people but unafraid of large animals, another may be afraid of large animals but be unafraid of meeting people. *See also* reciprocal interaction, situationism.

persuasive communications Messages that openly try to convince us to act a certain way or to hold a particular belief.

PET scan (Positron Emission Tomography) A technique for examining brain structure and function by recording the degree of metabolic activity of different regions of the brain.

phallic stage In psychoanalytic theory, the stage of psychosexual development during which the child begins to regard his or her genitals as a major source of gratification.

phenothiazines A group of drugs, including Thorazine, that seem to be effective in alleviating the major symptoms of schizophrenia.

phenotype The overt appearance and behavior of an organism, regardless of its genetic blueprint. *See also* genotype.

phenylalanine An amino acid that cannot be transformed due to an enzyme deficiency in those with phenylketonuria (PKU). It is instead converted into a toxic agent that accumulates in an infant's bloodstream and damages the developing nervous system. *See also* phenylketonuria.

phenylketonuria (PKU) A severe form of mental retardation detemined by a single gene. This disorder can be treated by means of a special diet (if detected early enough), despite the fact that the disorder is genetic. *See also* phenylalanine.

pheromones Special chemicals secreted by many animals which trigger particular reactions in members of the same species.

phi phenomenon *See* apparent movement.

phobia One of the anxiety disorders which is characterized by an intense and, at least on the surface, irrational fear. *See also* generalized anxiety disorder, obsessive-compulsive disorder, specific phobia.

phoneme The smallest significant unit of sound in a language. In English, it corresponds roughly to a letter of the alphabet (e.g., *apt, tap,* and *pat* are all made up of the same phonemes).

phonology The rules in a language that govern the sequence in which phonemes can be arranged.

phrase A sequence of words within a sentence that function as a unit (e.g., *The ball/rolled/down the hill*).

phrase structure The organization of sentences into phrases. Surface structure is the phrase organization of sentences as they are spoken or written. Underlying structure is the phrase organization that describes the meaning of parts of the sentence, such as doer, action, and done-to.

phrase structure description The tree diagram that shows the hierarchical structure of a sentence. The descending branches of the tree correspond to smaller and smaller units of sentence structure.

pictorial cues The monocular depth cues that the eye exploits as an optical consequence of the projection of a three-dimensional world upon a flat surface (such as, interposition, linear perspective, and relative size).

pitch The psychological dimension of sound corresponding to frequency; as frequency increases, the pitch appears to rise.

pituitary gland An endocrine gland heavily influenced by the hypothalamus. A master gland because many of its secretions trigger hormone secretions in other glands.

placebo In medical practice, a term for a chemically inert substance that the patient believes will help him.

placebo effect A beneficial effect of a treatment administered to a patient who believes it has therapeutic powers even though it has none.

place theory A theory of pitch proposed by Hermann von Helmholtz which states that different parts of the basilar membrane in the cochlea are responsive to different sound frequencies; the nervous system interprets the excitation from different basilar places as different pitches.

pleasure center According to some theorists, a special region of the brain that is triggered whenever any motive is satisfied.

pleasure principle In Freud's theory, the id's sole law, that of obtaining immediate satisfaction regardless of circumstances and whatever the cost.

pluralistic ignorance A situation in which individuals in a group don't know that there are others in the group who share their feelings.

polyandry A mating system in which one female monopolizes the reproductive efforts of several males.

polygenic inheritance Inheritance of an attribute whose expression is controlled not by one but by many gene pairs.

polygyny A mating system in which one male monopolizes the reproductive efforts of several females.

population The entire group of subjects (or test trials) about which the investigator wants to draw conclusions. *See also* sample.

positive feedback *See* feedback system.

positive reinforcement A reinforcement procedure in which a response is followed by the reduction or cessation of an aversive stimulus.

positive symptoms of schizophrenia Symptoms that center on what these patients do (or think or perceive) that normals don't, for example, hallucinations, delusions, and bizarre behaviors. *See* negative symptoms of schizophrenia.

postsynaptic membrane The membrane of the receiving cell across the synaptic gap that contains specialized receptor molecules.

postsynaptic neuron The cell receiving a neural message.

post-traumatic stress disorder A disorder sometimes experienced after an especially stressful traumatic event. Symptoms include dissociation, recurrent nightmares, flashbacks, and sleep disturbances.

potentiation In motivation, the tendency to make some behaviors, perceptions, and feelings more probable than others.

precursor A substance required for the chemical manufacture of a neurotransmitter.

predicate *See* concept.

predictive validity A measure of a test's validity based on the correlation between the test score and some criterion of behavior the test predicted (e.g., a correlation between a scholastic aptitude test and college grades).

prefrontal lobotomy A somatic treatment for severe mental disorders which surgically cuts the connections between the thalamus and the frontal lobes.

preoperational period In Piaget's theory, the period from about ages two to six during which children come to represent actions and objects internally but cannot systematically manipulate these representations or relate them to each other; the child is therefore unable to conserve quantity across perceptual transformations and also is unable to take points of view other than her own.

preparedness A built-in predisposition of an animal to form certain associations rather than others.

preparedness theory of phobias The theory that phobias grow out of a built-in predisposition (preparedness) to learn to fear certain stimuli (e.g., snakes and spiders) that may have posed serious dangers to our primate ancestors.

prescriptive rules Rules prescribed by "authorities" about how people *ought* to speak and write that often fail to conform to the facts about natural talking and understanding. This is in contrast to the structural principles of a language which describe (rather than prescribe) the principles according to which native speakers of a language actually arrange their words into sentences. Sentences formed according to these principles are called well-formed or grammatical.

presynaptic neuron The cell that sends a neural message across the synaptic gap.

primacy effect (1) In free recall, the recall superiority of the items in the first part of a list compared to those in the middle. (2) In forming an impression of another person, the phenomenon whereby attributes first noted carry a greater weight than attributes noted later on. *See* recency effect.

primary memory *See* short-term memory, working memory.

prisoner's dilemma A particular arrangement of payoffs in a two-person situation in which each individual has to choose between two alternatives without knowing the other's choice. The payoff structure is so arranged that the optimal strategy for each person depends upon whether he can trust the other or not. If trust is possible, the payoffs for each will be considerably higher than if there is no trust.

proactive inhibition Disturbance of recall of some material by other material learned previously. *See* retroactive inhibition.

procedural knowledge *See* declarative knowledge.

progesterone A female sex hormone that dominates the latter phase of the female cycle during which the uterus walls thicken to receive the embryo.

projection In psychoanalytic theory, a mechanism of defense in which various forbidden thoughts and impulses are attributed to another person rather than the self, thus warding off some anxiety (e.g., "I hate you" becomes "You hate me").

projection areas Regions of the cortex that serve as receiving stations for sensory information or as dispatching stations for motor commands.

projective techniques Devices for assessing personality by presenting relatively unstructured stimuli that elicit subjective responses of various kinds (e.g., the TAT and the Rorschach inkblot test). Their advocates believe that such tasks allow the person to "project" her own personality into her reactions. *See also* personality inventories.

proposition *See* concept.

prosopagnosia The inability to recognize faces produced by a brain lesion.

prototype The typical example of a category of meaning (e.g., robin is a prototypical bird).

proximal stimulus *See* distal stimulus.

proximity (1) In perception, the closeness of two figures. The closer together they are, the more they will tend to be grouped together perceptually; (2) the nearness of people, which is one of the most important determinants of attraction and liking.

pseudohermaphroditism The condition of individuals with ambiguous genitalia.

psychoanalysis (1) A theory of human personality formulated by Freud whose key assertions include unconscious conflict and psychosexual development. (2) A method of therapy that draws heavily on this theory of personality. Its main aim is to have the patient gain insight into his own, presently unconscious, thoughts and feelings. Therapeutic tools employed toward this end include free association, interpretation, and the appropriate use of the transference relationship between patient and analyst. *See also* free association, transference.

psychoanalytic model As defined in the text, a subcategory of the pathology model which holds that (1) the underlying pathology is a constellation of unconscious conflicts and defenses against anxiety, usually rooted in early childhood, and (2) treatment should be by some form of psychotherapy based on psychoanalytic principles.

psychodynamic approach of personality An approach to personality originally derived from psychoanalytic theory that asserts that personality differences are based on unconscious (dynamic) conflicts within the individual. *See also* behavioral-cognitive approach, humanistic approach, situationism, sociocultural approach, trait theory.

psychogenic disorders Disorders whose origins are psychological rather than organic (e.g., phobias). *See also* somatogenic mental disorders.

psychometric approach to intelligence An attempt to understand the nature of intelligence by studying the pattern of results obtained on intelligence tests.

psychopath *See* antisocial personality.

psychopathology The study of psychological disorders.

psychophysics An approach to sensory experience that relates the characteristics of physical stimuli to attributes of the sensory experience they produce.

psychophysiological disorders In these disorders (formerly called psychosomatic), the primary symptoms involve genuine organic damage whose ultimate cause is psychological (e.g., coronary heart disease).

psychophysiology An approach to sensory experience that concerns the neural consequences of a given stimulus input.

psychosexual development In psychoanalytic theory, the description of the progressive stages in the way the child gains his main source of pleasure as he grows into adulthood, defined by the zone of the body through which this pleasure is derived (oral, anal, genital) and by the object toward which this pleasurable feeling is directed (mother, father, adult sexual partner). *See also* anal stage, genital stage, oral stage, phallic stage.

psychosis A broad category that describes some of the more severe mental disorders in which the patient's thoughts and deeds no longer meet the demands of reality.

psychosocial crises In Erik Erikson's theory, a series of crises through which all persons must pass as they go through their life cycle (e.g., the identity crisis during which adolescents or young adults try to establish the separation between themselves and their parents).

psychotherapy As used here, a collective term for all forms of treatment that use psychological rather than somatic means.

punishment training An instrumental training procedure in which a response is suppressed by having its occurrence followed by an aversive event. *See also* avoidance learning, escape learning.

pyramidal system One of two motor systems that originates in the motor cortex in the brain and sends its tracts directly to the motor neurons that activate the muscles. The pyramidal system is younger in evolutionary terms and supervises the more delicate movements of the body.

quiet sleep Stages 2 to 4 of sleep during which there are no rapid eye movements and during which the EEG shows progressively less cortical arousal. Also known as non-REM sleep.

radical behaviorism An approach usually associated with B. F. Skinner that asserts that the subject matter of psychology is overt behavior, without reference to inferred, internal processes such as wishes, traits, or expectations.

random sample *See* sample.

range A measure of variability given by the highest score minus the lowest.

rationalization In psychoanalytic theory, a mechanism of defense by means of which unacceptable thoughts or impulses are reinterpreted in more acceptable and thus less anxiety-arousing terms (e.g., the jilted lover who convinces himself he never loved her anyway).

ratio scale An interval scale in which there is a true zero point, thus allowing ratio statements (e.g., this sound is twice as loud as the other). *See also* categorical scale, interval scale, nominal scale, ordinal scale.

ratio schedule A reinforcement schedule in which reinforcement is delivered for the first response made after a certain number of responses. In a fixed-ratio schedule, the number of responses required for a reward is always the same. In a variable-ratio schedule, the number of responses required varies irregularly around a specified average.

reaction formation In psychoanalytic theory, a mechanism of defense in which a forbidden impulse is turned into its opposite (e.g., hate toward a sibling becomes exaggerated love).

reaction time The interval between the presentation of a signal and the observer's response to that signal.

reality principle In Freud's theory, the set of rules that govern the ego and that dictate the way in which it tries to satisfy the id by gaining pleasure in accordance with the real world and its demands.

recall A task in which some item must be produced from memory. *See* recognition.

receiver-operating-characteristic curve (ROC curve) A graphical representation of the relationship between stimulus sensitivity and response bias.

recency effect In free recall, the recall superiority of the items at the end of the list compared to those in the middle. *See* primacy effect (in recall).

receptive aphasia A language disorder usually associated with lesions in Wernicke's area in which patients talk rapidly and grammatically but convey little information and do not understand meanings.

receptive field The retinal area in which visual stimulation affects a particular cell's firing rate.

receptor cells A special type of neuron that can respond to various external energies and translate physical stimuli into electrical changes to which other neurons can respond.

receptor molecules The specialized molecules in the postsynaptic membrane that open or close certain ion gates when activated by the correct neurotransmitter.

recessive gene *See* gene.

reciprocal altruism *See* altruism.

reciprocal inhibition The arrangement by which excitation of some neural system is accompanied by inhibition of that system's antagonist (as in antagonistic muscles).

reciprocal interaction The fact that different people seek out different situations.

reciprocity principle A basic rule of many social interactions that decrees that one must repay whatever one has been given.

recoding Changing the form in which some information is stored.

recognition A task in which a stimulus has to be identified as having been previously encountered in some context or not. *See also* recall.

reference The relations between words or sentences and objects or events in the world (e.g., "ball" refers to ball).

reflection The process by which objects give off light from an illuminating source.

reflex A simple, stereotyped reaction in response to some stimulus (e.g., limb flexion in withdrawal from pain).

rehearsal *See* elaborative rehearsal, maintenance rehearsal.

reinforced trial In classical conditioning, a trial on which the CS is accompanied by the US. In instrumental conditioning, a trial in which the instrumental response is followed by reward, cessation of punishment, or other reinforcement.

reinforcement In classical conditioning, the procedure by which the US is made contingent on the CS. In instrumental conditioning, the procedure by which the instrumental response is made contingent upon some sought-after outcome.

relative size A monocular depth cue in which far-off objects produce a smaller retinal image than nearby objects of the same size.

releasing stimulus Term used by ethologists to describe a stimulus which is genetically programmed to elicit a fixed-action pattern (e.g., a long, thin, red-tipped beak which elicits a herring gull chick's begging response). *See also* fixed-action patterns.

reliability coefficient Coefficient used in determining the consistency of mental tests that are derived from test-retest correlations or from correlations between alternative forms of a test.

REM sleep *See* active sleep.

repetition priming An increase in the likelihood that an item word is identified, recognized, or recalled by recent exposure to that item which may occur without explicit awareness.

representational thought In Piaget's theory, thought that is internalized and includes mental representations of prior experiences with objects and events.

representations Cognitions that correspond to (represent) certain events, or relations between events, in the world.

representativeness heuristic A rule of thumb in estimating the probability that an object (or event) belongs to a certain category based on the extent to which it resembles the prototype of that category regardless of the base rate at which it occurs. *See also* prototype.

repression In psychoanalytic theory, a mechanism of defense by means of which thoughts, impulses, or memories that give rise to anxiety are pushed out of consciousness.

resistance In psychoanalysis, a collective term for the patient's failures to associate freely and say whatever enters his head.

response bias A preference for one or another response in a psychophysical experiment, independent of the stimulus situation.

response rate The number of responses per unit time; this measures response strength in operant conditioning.

response suppression The inhibition of a conditioned response by conditioned fear.

resting potential The difference in charge across the membrane in a cell's normal state.

restrained-eating hypothesis The hypothesis that the oversensitivity of obese persons to external cues is caused by the disinhibition of conscious restraints on eating. *See also* externality hypothesis, setpoint hypothesis.

restructuring A reorganization of a problem, often rather sudden, which seems to be a characteristic of creative thought.

retention The survival of the memory trace over some interval of time.

retention intervals In memory experiments, the time between original learning and the time of the test.

retina The structure that contains the visual receptors and several layers of neurons further up along the pathway to the brain.

retinal image The image of an object that is projected on the retina. Its size increases with the size of that object and decreases with its distance from the eye.

retrieval The process of searching for some item in memory and of finding it. If retrieval fails, this may or may not mean that the relevant memory trace is not present; the trace simply may be inaccessible.

retrieval cue A stimulus that helps to retrieve a memory trace.

retroactive inhibition Disturbance of recall of some material by other material learned subsequently. *See also* proactive inhibition.

retrograde amnesia A memory deficit suffered after head injury or concussion in which the patient loses memory of some period prior to the injury. *See also* anterograde amnesia.

reuptake A mechanism by which a neurotransmitter is drawn back into the presynaptic terminal that released it.

rhodopsin The visual pigment used in the rods.

ROC curve *See* receiver-operating-characteristic curve.

rods Visual receptors that respond to lower light intensities and give rise to achromatic (colorless) sensations.

Rorschach inkblot test A projective technique that requires the subject to look at inkblots and say what she sees in them.

safety signal A stimulus that has been contingent on the absence of an electric shock (or another negative reinforcer) in a situation in which such shocks are sometimes delivered. *See also* contingency.

sample A subset of a population selected by the investigator for study. A random sample is one so constructed that each member of the population has an equal chance to be picked. A stratified sample is one so constructed that every relevant subgroup of the population is randomly sampled in proportion to its size. *See also* population.

saturation A perceived dimension of visual stimuli that describes the "purity" of a color—the extent to which it is rich in hue (e.g., green rather than olive).

savant A mentally retarded person who has some remarkable talent that seems out of keeping with his or her low level of general intelligence. Previously called *idiot savant,* a term now abandoned as derogatory.

scaling A procedure for assigning numbers to a subject's responses. *See also* categorical scale, interval scale, nominal scale, ordinal scale, ratio scale.

scatter diagram A graphical representation showing the relationship between two variables.

scatter plot A diagram of correlation data in which each axis represents a single variable.

schedule of reinforcement A rule that determines the occasions when a response is reinforced. *See also* ratio schedule, interval schedules.

schema (1) In theories of memory and thinking, a term that refers to a general cognitive structure in terms of which information can be organized. (2) In Piaget's theory of development, a mental pattern.

schizophrenia A group of severe mental disorders characterized by at least some of the following: marked disturbance of thought, withdrawal, inappropriate or flat emotions, delusions, and hallucinations. *See also* catatonic schizophrenia, disorganized type of schizophrenia, paranoid schizophrenia.

score profile *See* test profile.

script A subcase of a schema, which describes a characteristic scenario of behaviors in a particular setting, such as a restaurant script. *See also* schema.

seasonal affective disorder A mood disorder with a seasonal pattern, with depressions that start in the late fall when the days become shorter and end in the spring when the days lengthen.

secondary memory *See* long-term memory.

second-order conditioning *See* higher-order conditioning.

self-actualization A major concern of Maslow and other adherents of the humanistic approach, it is the realization of one's potentialities so that one becomes what one can become. *See also* hierarchy of needs, peak experience.

self-monitoring Monitoring one's own behavior so that it fits the situation.

self-perception theory A theory that asserts that we do not know our own attitudes and feelings directly but must infer them by observing our own behavior and then performing much the same attribution processes that we employ when trying to understand the behavior of others.

self-serving bias The tendency to deny responsibility for failures but take credit for successes. *See also* attribution theory, fundamental attribution error, actor-observer difference.

semantic feature The smallest significant unit of meaning within a word (e.g., male, human, and adult are semantic features of the word "man").

semantic memory The component of generic memory that concerns the meaning of words and concepts.

semantics The organization of meaning in language.

semicircular canals Three canals within the inner ear that contain a viscous liquid that moves when the head rotates, providing information about the nature and extent of the movement.

sensation According to the empiricists, the primitive experiences that the senses give us (e.g., green, bitter).

sensation seeking The tendency to seek novel experiences, look for thrills and adventure, and be highly susceptible to boredom.

sensitive period *See* critical period.

sensory adaptation The decline in sensitivity found in most sensory systems after continuous exposure to the same stimulus.

sensory code The rule (code) by which the nervous system represents sensory characteristics of the stimulus. An example is firing frequency, which is the general code for increased stimulus intensity.

sensory coding The process by which the nervous system translates various aspects of the stimulus into dimensions of our sensory experience.

sensory interaction The fact that a sensory system's response to any given stimulus rarely depends on that stimulus alone and is affected by other impinging stimuli.

sensory modalities A technical term for the sensory domains: taste, touch, kinesthesis, vision, and hearing.

sensory-motor intelligence In Piaget's theory, intelligence during the first two years of life which consists mainly of sensations and motor impulses with, at first, little in the way of internalized representations.

sensory process According to signal detection theorists, the underlying neural activity in the sensory system upon which all psychological judgments are based. *See also* signal-detection theory.

sensory projection areas *See* projection areas.

Sentence Analyzing Machinery (SAM) A set of procedures by which listeners comprehend sentences.

serial reproduction An experiment in which a drawing is presented to one subject, who reproduces it from memory for a second subject, whose reproduction is shown to a third, and so on. Each subject's memory distortions become part of the stimulus for the next subject down the line, amplifying the reconstructive alteration.

serial search The successive comparison of a target stimulus to different items in memory. *See also* parallel search.

serotonin (5HT)   A neurotransmitter involved in many of the mechanisms of sleep and emotional arousal.

servomechanisms   Industrial devices, such as home furnaces, that operate on negative feedback systems and can maintain themselves in a particular state.

set   *See* mental set.

setpoint   A general term for the level at which negative feedback tries to maintain the system. An example is the setting of a thermostat. *See also* setpoint hypothesis.

setpoint hypothesis   The hypothesis that different persons have different setpoints for weight. *See also* setpoint.

sexual dimorphism   A condition that describes a species in which there is a marked difference in the size and/or form of the two sexes as in the case of deer (antlers) or peacocks (long tail feathers).

sexual orientation   The direction of a person's choice of a sexual partner, which may be heterosexual or homosexual. *See also* gender identity, gender role.

shape constancy   The tendency to perceive the shape of objects as more or less the same despite the fact that the retinal image of these objects changes its shape as we change the angle of orientation from which we view them.

shaping   An instrumental learning procedure through which an animal (or human) is trained to perform a rather difficult response by reinforcing successive approximations to that response.

short-term habituation   *See* habituation.

short-term memory   *See* stage theory of memory.

signal-detection theory   A theory that asserts that observers who are asked to detect the presence or absence of a stimulus try to decide whether an internal sensory experience should be attributed to background noise or to a signal added to background noise. *See also* sensory process.

similarity   In perception, a principle by which we tend to group like figures, especially by color and orientation.

simple reaction time   A measurement of the speed with which a subject can respond to a stimulus.

simulation heuristic   A mental shortcut used in making decisions and evaluating outcomes that refers to imaginary replays of events or situations.

simultaneous color contrast   The effect produced by the fact that any region in the visual field tends to induce its complementary color in adjoining areas; for example, a gray patch will tend to look bluish if surrounded by yellow and yellowish if surrounded by blue.

simultaneous pairing   A classical conditioning procedure in which the conditioned stimulus (CS) and the unconditioned stimulus (US) are presented simultaneously. *See also* backward pairing, forward pairing.

sine waves   Curves that correspond to the plot of the trigonometric sine function.

situational factors   *See* attribution theory.

situationism   The view that human behavior is largely determined by the characteristics of the situation rather than those of the person. *See also* behavioral-cognitive approach, humanistic approach, psychodynamic approach, sociocultural approach, trait theory.

size constancy   The tendency to perceive the size of objects as more or less the same despite the fact that the retinal image of these objects changes in size whenever we change the distance from which we view them.

skeletal musculature   The muscles that control the skeleton, such as those of the arms and legs.

skewed   A term used to describe asymmetrical distributions of experimental results with extreme values at one end.

smooth muscles   The muscles of the internal organs that are controlled by the autonomic nervous system.

social cognition   The way in which we interpret and try to comprehend social events.

social comparison   A process of reducing uncertainty about one's own beliefs and attitudes by comparing them to those of others.

social development   A child's growth in his or her relations with other people.

social dilemma   A problem similar in structure to the prisoner's dilemma but expanded to include any number of individuals, each of whom has to decide whether to cooperate or defect. *See also* prisoner's dilemma.

social exchange theory   A theory that asserts that each partner in a social relationship gives something to the other and expects to get something in return.

social facilitation   The tendency to perform better in the presence of others than when alone. This facilitating effect works primarily for simple and/or well-practiced tasks.

social impact theory   A theory that asserts that the influence others exert on an individual increases with their number, their immediacy, and their strength (e.g., status).

social influence   A general term for interactions in which the influence of other people affects one individual.

socialization   The process whereby the child acquires the patterns of behavior characteristic of his or her society.

social learning theory   A theoretical approach to socialization and personality that is midway between behavior theories, such as Skinner's, and cognitive approaches. It stresses learning by observing others who serve as models for the child's behavior. The effect of the model may be to allow learning by imitation and also may be to show the child whether a response he already knows should or should not be performed.

social loafing   An example of the diffusion of social impact in which individuals working as a group on a common task generate less effort than they would if they had worked alone.

social phobia   A fear of embarrassment or humiliation in front of others that causes people to avoid situations in which they must expose themselves to public scrutiny. *See also* phobia, specific phobia.

sociobiology   A recent theoretical movement in biology that tries to trace social behavior to genetically based predispositions; an approach that has led to some controversy when extended to humans.

sociocultural approach   The view that people differ in at least some regards as a result of the cultural group in which they were raised and of which they are a member. *See also* behavioral-cognitive approach, humanistic approach, psychodynamic approach, trait theory, situationism.

sociopath   *See* antisocial personality.

somatic nervous system   A division of the peripheral nervous system primarily concerned with the control of the skeletal musculature and the transmission of information from the sense organs.

somatic therapies   A collective term for any treatment of mental disorders by means of some organic manipulation. This includes drug administration, any form of surgery, convulsive treatments, etc.

somatoform disorders   The generic term for disorders that take bodily form in the absence of any known physical illness.

somatogenic mental disorders Mental disorders that are produced by an organic cause. This is the case for some disorders (e.g., general paresis) but almost surely not for all (e.g., phobias). *See also* psychogenic disorders.

somatosensory area A cortical area located in the parietal lobe just behind the motor area in the frontal lobe. This region is the projection area for bodily sensations, including touch, pain, and temperature.

sound waves Successive pressure variations in the air which vary in amplitude and wavelength.

source memory The knowledge of the event from which a certain memory derived.

Spearman's theory of general intelligence (g) Spearman's account, based on factor analytic studies, ascribes intelligence-test performance to one underlying factor, general intelligence *(g)*, which is tapped by all subtests, and a large number of specific skills (*s*'s) which depend on abilities specific to each subtest. *See also* factor analysis, group-factor theory.

specificity theory An approach to sensory experience which asserts that different sensory qualities are signaled by different neurons. These neurons are somehow labeled with their quality, so that whenever they fire, the nervous system interprets their activation as that particular sensory quality.

specific phobia A fear of certain objects or events, such as a fear of heights or enclosed places.

spectral sensitivity curve A graphical representation of the eye's sensitivity to each of the separate wavelengths that constitute a light stimulus.

split brain A condition in which the corpus callosum and some other fibers are cut so that the two cerebral hemispheres are isolated.

spontaneous recovery An increase in the tendency to perform an extinguished response after a time interval in which neither conditioned stimulus (CS) nor unconditioned stimulus (US) are presented.

spreading activation model A memory model that assumes that elements in a semantic memory network are activated the smaller the distance between them.

stabilized image technique A procedure by which the retina receives a stationary image even though the eye is moving.

stage theory of memory A theoretical approach that asserts that there are several memory stores. One is short-term memory, which holds information for fairly short intervals and has a small capacity; another is long-term memory, which holds information for very long periods and has a vast capacity. According to the theory, information will only enter into long-term memory if it has been in short-term memory for a while.

standard deviation (SD) A measure of the variability of a frequency distribution which is the square root of the variance. If *V* is the variance and *SD* the standard deviation, then $SD = \sqrt{V}$. *See also* variance.

standard error of the mean A measure of the variability of the mean whose value depends both on the standard deviation *(SD)* of the distribution and the number of cases in the sample *(N)*. If *SE* is the standard error, then $SE = SD/\sqrt{N-1}$.

standardization group The group against which an individual's test score is evaluated.

standard score (z-score) A score that is expressed as a deviation from the mean in standard deviation units, which allows a comparison of scores drawn from different distributions. If *M* is the mean and *SD* the standard deviation, then $z = (score - M)/SD$.

stereotypes Simplified schemas by which people try to categorize complex groups. Group stereotypes are often negative, especially when applied to minority groups. *See also* out-group homogeniety effect.

stimulus Anything in the environment that the organism can detect and respond to.

stimulus generalization In classical conditioning, the tendency to respond to stimuli other than the original conditioned stimulus (CS). The greater the similarity between the CS and the new stimulus, the greater this tendency will be. An analogous phenomenon in instrumental conditioning is a response to stimuli other than the original discriminative stimulus.

storage capacity The amount of information that can be kept in memory. The capacity of long-term memory is much larger than that of short-term memory.

stratified sampling An experimental procedure in which each subgroup of the population is sampled in proportion to its size.

stroboscopic movement *See* apparent movement.

Stroop effect A marked decrease in the speed of naming the colors in which various color names (such as green, red, etc.) are printed when the colors and the names are different. An important example of automatization.

structural principles (of language) *See* prescriptive rules.

subjective contours Perceived contours that do not exist physically. We tend to complete figures that have gaps in them by continuing a contour along its original path.

subroutines In a hierarchical organization, the lower level operations that are controlled by higher level operations.

subtractive color mixture Mixing colors by subtracting one set of wavelengths from another set (as in mixing colors on a palette or superimposing two colored filters). *See also* additive color mixture.

successive approximations *See* shaping.

superego In Freud's theory, a set of reaction patterns within the ego that represent the internalized rules of society and that control the ego by punishing with guilt. *See also* ego, id.

surface structure *See* phrase structure.

symbolic representation A type of mental representation that does not correspond to the physical characteristics of that which it represents. Thus, the word *mouse* does not resemble the small rodent it represents.

symmetrical distribution A distribution of experimental evidence in which deviations in either direction from the mean are equally frequent.

sympathetic system A division of the autonomic nervous system that mobilizes the body's energies for emergencies (e.g., increasing heart rate). Its action is antagonistic to that of the parasympathetic system.

symptoms The outward manifestations of an underlying pathology.

synapse The juncture between the axon of one neuron and the dendrite or cell body of another.

syndrome A pattern of symptoms that tend to go together.

syntax The system by which words are arranged into meaningful phrases and sentences.

systematic desensitization A behavior therapy that tries to remove anxiety connected to various stimuli by a gradual process of counterconditioning to a response incompatible with fear, usually muscular relaxation. The stimuli are usually evoked as mental images according to an anxiety hierarchy whereby the less frightening stimuli are counterconditioned before the more frightening ones.

taste buds The receptor organs for taste.

taxonomy A classification system.

temperament In modern usage, a characteristic level of reactivity and energy, often thought to be based on constitutional factors.

temporal lobe A lobe in each cerebral hemisphere which includes the auditory projection area.

temporal summation The process whereby two or more stimuli that are individually below threshold will elicit a reflex if presented together at different spatial points on the body.

territory A term used by ethologists to describe a region a particular animal stakes out as its own. The territory holder is usually a male, but in some species the territory is held by a mating pair or by a group.

testosterone The principal male sex hormone (androgen) in mammals.

test profile A graphic indication of an individual's performance on several components of a test. This is often useful for guidance or clinical evaluation because it indicates which abilities or traits are relatively high or low in that person.

test-retest method A way of increasing test reliability by administering the same test to the same group of subjects after a certain time lag. *See also* reliability coefficients.

texture gradient A distance cue based on changes in surface texture which depend on the distance of the observer.

thalamus A part of the lower portion of the forebrain which serves as a major relay and integration center for sensory information.

Thematic Apperception Test (TAT) A projective technique in which persons are shown a set of pictures and asked to write a story about each.

theory of mind A set of interrelated concepts we use as we try to make sense of our own mental processes and those of others, including the variability of human beliefs and desires.

Thorazine *See* antipsychotic drugs.

threat displays In animals, signs of aggression that are less costly ways of intimidating the enemy than actual combat.

threshold The value a stimulus must reach to produce a response.

tip-of-the-tongue phenomenon The condition in which one keeps on feeling on the verge of retrieving a word or name but continues to be unsuccessful.

token economy An arrangement for operant behavior modification in hospital settings. Certain responses (e.g., talking to others) are reinforced with tokens which can be exchanged for desirable items.

tolerance *See* opponent-process theory of motivation.

top-down processes Processes in form recognition, which begin with higher units and then work down to smaller units (e.g., from phrases to words to letters). This is in contrast with bottom-up processes, which start with smaller component parts and then gradually build up to the higher units on top (e.g., from letters to words to phrases). One demonstration of top-down processing is provided by context effects in which knowledge or expectations affect what one sees.

trace consolidation hypothesis The hypothesis that newly acquired memory traces undergo a gradual change that makes them more and more resistant to any disturbance.

trait *See* trait theory.

trait theory The view that people differ in regard to a number of underlying attributes (traits) that partially determine behavior and that are presumed to be essentially consistent from time to time and situation to situation. It tends toward the view that many such traits are based on genetic predispositions. *See also* behavioral-cognitive approach, humanistic approach, psychodynamic approach, situationism, sociocultural approach.

transduction The process by which a receptor translates some physical stimulus (e.g., light or pressure) to give rise to an action potential in another neuron.

transference In psychoanalysis, the patient's tendency to transfer emotional reactions that were originally directed toward one's own parents (or other crucial figures in one's early life) and redirect them toward the analyst.

transposition The phenomenon whereby visual and auditory patterns (i.e., figures and melodies) remain the same even though the parts of which they are composed are changed.

tree diagram A branched diagram that represents a hierarchical structure.

tricyclics *See* antidepressant drugs.

two-syndrome hypothesis of schizophrenia The hypothesis that schizophrenia is a composite of two different syndromes, Type I and Type II. According to the hypothesis, Type I is produced by a malfunction of transmitters, especially dopamine, and produces primarily positive symptoms, while Type II is caused by cerebral damage and atrophy and leads to negative symptoms.

Type A personality A personality type characterized by extreme impatience, competitiveness, and vehement aggressiveness when thwarted. *See also* Type B personality.

Type B personality In contrast to the Type A personality, Type B is characterized by a more easygoing, less hurried, less competitive, and friendlier behavior pattern. *See also* Type A personality.

unconditioned reflex *See* unconditioned response.

unconditioned response (UR) In classical conditioning, the response that is elicited by the unconditioned stimulus without prior training. *See* conditioned response, conditioned stimulus, unconditioned stimulus.

unconditioned stimulus (US) In classical conditioning, the stimulus that elicits the unconditioned response and the presentation of which acts as reinforcement. *See* conditioned response, conditioned stimulus, unconditioned response.

unconscious inference A process postulated by Helmholtz to explain certain perceptual phenomena such as size constancy. An object is perceived to be in the distance and is therefore unconsciously perceived or inferred to be larger than it appears to be retinally. *See also* size constancy.

underlying pathology model An approach to psychopathology which asserts that various overt signs and symptoms are produced by an underlying cause that may be mental or organic or both. The therapist's objective is to discover and remove the underlying pathology, which will then cause the symptoms to disappear.

underlying structure *See* phrase structure.

unilateral neglect syndrome The result of certain lesions on the right side of the parietal lobe, which disables a patient from perceiving features in the left visual field and causes the patient to ignore the left side of his or her body.

unipolar disorder Mood disorder (usually depression) in which there is no back-and-forth swing between the two emotional extremes.

unreinforced trial In classical conditioning, a trial in which the unconditioned stimulus (US) is omitted.

validity The extent to which a test measures what it is supposed to measure. *See also* construct validity, incremental validity, predictive validity.

validity coefficient   The correlation between test scores, such as those for scholastic aptitude, and some appropriate criterion, such as the grade-point average, which provides information about a test's ability to predict future performance.

variability   The tendency of scores in a frequency distribution to scatter away from the central value. *See also* central tendency, standard deviation, variance.

variable-interval schedule   *See* interval schedule.

variable-ratio schedule   *See* ratio schedule.

variance (V)   A measure of the variability of a frequency distribution. It is computed by finding the difference between each score and the mean, squaring the result, adding all the squared deviations obtained in this manner, and dividing it by the number of cases. If V is the variance, M the mean, and N the number of scores, then $V = $ sum of $(score - M)^2/N$.

vasoconstriction   The constriction of the capillaries brought on by activation of the sympathetic division of the autonomic nervous system in response to excessive cold.

vasodilatation   The dilating of the skin's capillaries (brought on by activation of the parasympathetic division of the autonomic nervous system in response to excessive heat) that sends warm blood to the body's surface and results in heat loss by radiation.

ventral tegmental area (VTA)   A region in the midbrain thought to be involved in dopamine releasing pathways.

ventromedial region of the hypothalamus   *See* lateral hypothalamus.

vesicles   The tiny sacs in the presynaptic neuron that contain neurotransmitters.

vestibular senses   A set of receptors that provide information about the orientation and movements of the head, located in the semicircular canals and the vestibular sacs of the inner ear.

vicarious distress   The distress produced by witnessing the suffering of another. This is a less reliable motive for helping that person than empathic concern. *See also* empathic concern.

vicarious reinforcement   According to social learning theorists, a form of reinforcement said to occur when someone watches a model being rewarded or punished.

visible spectrum   The range of wavelengths to which our visual system can respond, extending from about 400 (the wavelength of the color violet) to 750 nanometers (the wavelength of the color reddish orange).

visual cliff   A device for assessing depth perception in young organisms; it consists of a glass surface that extends over an apparently deep side (the cliff) and an apparently shallow side.

visual search task   A test in which subjects have to indicate whether a certain target is present or absent in a briefly presented display.

visual segregation   *See* perceptual parsing.

volume receptors   Receptors that help to control water intake by responding to the total volume of fluids in the body. *See also* osmoreceptors.

wavelength   The distance between the crests of two successive waves that is a major determinant of perceived color.

Weber fraction   In Weber's law, the fraction given by the change in stimulus intensity divided by the standard intensity required to produce a just-noticeable increase.

Weber's law   The observation that the size of the difference threshold is proportional to the intensity of the standard stimulus.

well-defined problems   Problems in which there is a clear-cut way for deciding whether a proposed solution is correct. This is in contrast to ill-defined problems in which it is not clear what a correct solution might be.

Wernicke's area   *See* aphasia.

wish fulfillment in dreams   *See* Freud's theory of dreams.

withdrawal effects   *See* opponent-process theory of motivation.

withdrawal symptoms   A consequence of drug addiction that occurs when the drug is withheld; these effects are the opposite of those produced by the drug itself.

within-family differences   A term often used in the discussion of the role of environment. It describes differences in the environment of different members of the same family (e.g., different schools). For personality attributes, these seem to be more important than between-family differences. *See also* between-family differences.

within-group heritability   The extent to which variation within groups (e.g., among U.S. whites) is attributable to genetic factors. *See also* between-group heritability, heritability.

working memory   Also called active memory. A part of the memory system that is currently activated, but has relatively little cognitive capacity..

X-chromosome   One of the two sex chromosomes that contains the genetic commands which determine whether a given animal will be male or female. In mammalian females, both members of the pair of chromosomes are X-chromosomes; in mammalian males, there is one X-chromosome and one Y-chromosome.

Y-chromosome   *See* X-chromosome.

Young-Helmholtz theory   An explanation of the psychological properties of color that states that each of the three receptor types (short-wave, medium-wave, and long-wave) gives rise to the experience of one basic color (blue, green, or red).

z-score   *See* standard score.

zygote   The fertilized ovum resulting from the union of a sperm and an egg cell in sexual reproduction.

REFERENCES

ABRAHAM, K. 1927. The influence of oral eroticism on character formation. In Abraham, K., *Selected papers,* pp. 393–406. London: Hogarth Press.

ABRAMS, M. H. 1953. *The mirror and the lamp: Romantic theory and the critical tradition.* New York: Oxford University Press.

ABRAMSON, L. Y.; METALSKY, G. I.; AND ALLOY, L. B. 1989. Hopelessness depression: A theory-based subtype of depression. *Psychological Review* 96:358–72.

ABRAMSON, L. Y., AND SACKHEIM, H. A. 1977. A paradox in depression: Uncontrollability and self-blame. *Psychological Bulletin* 84: 835–51.

ABRAMSON, L. Y.; SELIGMAN, M. E. P.; AND TEASDALE, J. D. 1978. Learned helplessness in humans: Critique and reformulation. *Journal of Abnormal Psychology* 87:49–74.

ACSF INVESTIGATORS. 1992. AIDS and sexual behaviour in France. *Nature* 360: 407–409.

ADAMSON, E. 1984. *Art as healing.* London: Coventure Ltd.

ADOLPH, E. F. 1947. Urges to eat and drink in rats. *American Journal of Physiology* 151:110–25.

AINSWORTH, M. D. S., AND BELL, S. M. 1970. Attachment, exploration, and separation: Illustrated by the behavior of one-year-olds in a strange situation. *Child Development* 41:49–67.

AINSWORTH, M. D. S.; BLEHAR, M. C.; WATERS, E.; AND WALL, S. 1978. *Patterns of attachment.* Hillsdale, N. J.: Erlbaum.

ALBA, J. W., AND HASHER, W. 1983. Is memory schematic? *Psychological Bulletin* 93:203–31.

ALEXANDER, B. K., AND HADAWAY, B. F. 1982. Opiate addiction: The case for an adaptive orientation. *Psychological Bulletin* 92:367–81.

ALEXANDER, F., AND FRENCH, T. 1946. *Psychoanalytic theory.* New York: Ronald Press.

ALLARD, F.; GRAHAM, S.; AND PAARSALU, M. E. 1980. Perception in sport: Basketball. *Journal of Sport Psychology* 2:14–21.

ALLDERIDGE. P. 1979. Hospitals, mad houses, and asylums: Cycles in the care of the insane. *British Journal of Psychiatry* 134:321–24.

ALLEN, L. S.; HINES, M.; SHYRNE, J. E.; AND GORSKI, R. A. 1989. Two sexually dimorphic cell groups in the human brain. *Journal of Neuroscience* 9: 497–506.

ALLEN, M. 1976. Twin studies of affective illness. *Archives of General Psychiatry* 33:1476–78.

ALLEN, V. L. 1975. Social support for non-conformity. In L. Berkowitz (Ed.), *Advances in experimental social psychology,* vol. 8. New York: Academic Press.

ALLEN, V. L., AND LEVINE, J. M. 1971. Social support and conformity: The role of independent assessment. *Journal of Experimental Social Psychology* 7:48–58.

ALLOY, L. B.; HARTLAGE, S.; AND ABRAMSON, L. Y. 1988. Testing the cognitive-diathesis stress theories of depression: Issues of research design, conceptualization, and assessment. In Alloy, L. B. (Ed.), *Cognitive processes in depression.* New York: Guilford.

ALLPORT, F. 1920. The influence of the group upon association and thought. *Journal of Experimental Psychology* 3:159–82.

ALLPORT, G. W. 1937. *Personality: A psychological interpretation.* New York: Henry Holt.

ALLPORT, G. W., AND ODBERT, H. S. 1936. Trait-names: A psychological study. *Psychological Monographs* 47(Whole No. 211).

ALTMAN, I. 1973. Reciprocity of interpersonal exchange. *Journal for Theory of Social Behavior* 3: 249–61.

ALVIR, J. M.; LIEBERMAN, J. A.; SAFFERMAN, A. Z.; SCHWIMMER, J. L.; AND SCHAAF, J. A. 1993. Clozapine-induced agranulocytosis—incidence and risk factors in the United States. *New England Journal of Medicine* 32:162–67.

AMERICAN PSYCHIATRIC ASSOCIATION. 1968. *Diagnostic and statistical manual for mental disorders,* 2nd ed. Washington, D.C.: American Psychiatric Association.

AMERICAN PSYCHIATRIC ASSOCIATION. 1980. *Diagnostic and statistical manual for mental disorders,* 3rd ed. Washington, D.C.: American Psychiatric Association.

AMERICAN PSYCHIATRIC ASSOCIATION. 1987. *Diagnostic and statistical manual for mental disorders,* 3rd. ed., Revised (DSM-III-R). Washington, D.C.: American Psychiatric Association.

AMERICAN PSYCHIATRIC ASSOCIATION. 1993. Practice guidelines for major depressive disorder in adults. *American Journal of Psychiatry* 150 (Supplement):1–26.

AMERICAN PSYCHIATRIC ASSOCIATION. 1994. *Diagnostic and statistical manual for mental disorders,* 4th ed. Washington, D.C.: American Psychiatric Association.

AMOORE, J. E.; JOHNSON, J. W., Jr.; AND RUBIN, M. 1964. The sterochemical theory of odor. *Scientific American* 210:42–49.

ANAND, B. K., AND PILLAI, R. V. 1967. Activity of single neurons in the hypothalamic feeding centers: Effects of gastric distension. *Journal of Physiology* 192:63–77.

ANANTH, J. 1985. Pharmaco-therapy of obsessive-compulsive disorder, pp. 167–205. In Mavissakalian, M.; Turner, S. M.; and Michelson, L. (Eds.), *Obsessive-compulsive disorder: Psychological and pharmacological treatment.* New York: Plenum.

ANASTASI, A. 1958. *Differential psychology,* 3rd ed. New York: Macmillan.

ANASTASI, A. 1971. More on heritability: Addendum to the Hebb and Jensen interchange. *American Psychologist* 26:1036–37.

ANASTASI, A. 1984. The K-ABC in historical perspective. *Journal of Special Education* 18:357–66.

ANASTASI, A. 1985. Review of Kaufman's Assessment Battery for Children. *Ninth Mental Measurements Yearbook,* vol. 1, pp. 769–71.

ANASTASI, A. 1988. *Psychological testing,* 6th ed. New York: Macmillan.

ANDERSON, J. R. 1990. *Cognitive psychology and its implications,* 3rd ed. San Francisco: Freeman.

ANDERSON, N. H. 1965. Averaging versus adding as a stimulus-combination rule in impression formation. *Journal of Experimental Psychology* 70:394–400.

ANDERSON, R. C., AND PICHERT, J. 1978. Recall of previously unrecallable information following a shift in perspective. *Journal of Verbal Learning and Verbal Behavior* 17:1–12.

ANDREASEN, N. C. 1985. Positive vs. negative schizophrenia: A critical evaluation. *Schizophrenia Bulletin* 1985:380–89.

ANDREASEN, N. C., AND BLACK, D. W. 1991. *Introductory Textbook of Psychiatry.* Washington, D.C.: American Psychiatric Press, Inc.

ANDREASEN, N. C.; FLAUM, M.; SWAYZE, V. W. II; TYRRELL, G.; AND ARNDT, S. 1989. Positive and negative symptoms in schizophrenia. *Archives of General Psychiatry* 47:615–21,

ANDREASEN, N. C.; NASRALLAH, H. A.; DUNN, V.; OLSEN, S. C.; GROVE, W. M.; EHRHARDT, J. C.; COFFMAN, J. A.; AND CROSSETT, I. H. W. 1986. Structural abnormalities in the frontal system in schizophrenia: A magnetic resonance imaging study. *Archives of General Psychiatry* 43:136–44.

ANDRES, R. 1980. Influence of obesity on longevity in the aged. In Borek, C.; Fenoglio, C. M.; and King, D. W. (Eds.), *Aging, cancer, and cell membranes,* pp. 230–46. New York: Thieme-Stratton.

ANDREWS, G., AND HARVEY, R. 1981. Does psychotherapy benefit neurotic patients? A reanalysis of the Smith, Glass, and Miller data. *Archives of General Psychiatry* 38:1203–1208.

ANGLIN, J. M. 1975. The child's first terms of reference. In Ehrlich, S., and Tulving, E. (Eds.), *Bulletin de Psychologie,* special issue on semantic memory.

ANGRIST, B.; SATHANANTHAN, G.; WILK, S.; AND GERSHON, S. 1974. Amphetamine psychosis: Behavioral and biochemical aspects. *Journal of Psychiatric Research* 11:13–24.

ANSTIS, S. M. 1975. What does visual perception tell us about visual coding? In Gazzaniga, M. S., and Blakemore, C. (Eds.), *Handbook of psychobiology.* New York: Academic Press.

APPEL, L. F.; COOPER, R. G.; MCCARRELL, N.; SIMS-KNIGHT, J.; YUSSEN, S. R.; AND FLAVELL, J. H. 1972. The development of the distinction between perceiving and memorizing. *Child Development* 43:1365–81.

ARANOFF, M. 1976. *Word-formation in generative grammar* (Linguistic Inquiry Monograph 1). Cambridge, Mass.: MIT Press.

ARBIB, M. A. 1972. *The metaphorical brain.* New York: Wiley.

ARDREY, R. 1966. *The territorial imperative.* New York: Dell.

ARENDT, H. 1965. *Eichmann in Jerusalem: A report on the banality of evil.* New York: Viking Press.

ARIETI, S. 1959. Schizophrenia: The manifest symptomatology, the psychodynamic and formal mechanisms. In Arieti, S. (Ed.), *American handbook of psychiatry,* vol. 1, pp. 455–84. New York: Basic Books.

ARISTOTLE. CA. 330 B.C. On sleep and waking; On dreams; On prophesy in sleep. In *The works of Aristotle,* vol. 3. London: Oxford University Press, 1931.

ARMSTRONG, S. L.; GLEITMAN, L. R.; AND GLEITMAN, H. 1983. What some concepts might not be. *Cognition* 13:263–308.

ARNOLD, M. B. 1970. Perennial problems in the field of emotion. In Arnold, M. B. (Ed.), *Feelings and emotion: The Loyola symposium.* New York: Academic Press.

ARONFREED, J. 1968. *Conduct and conscience.* New York: Academic Press.

ARONFREED, J. 1969. The problem of imitation. In Lipsett, L. P., and Reese, H. W. (Eds.), *Advances in child development and behavior,* vol. 4. New York: Academic Press.

ARONSON, E. 1969. The theory of cognitive dissonance: A current perspective. In Berkowitz, L. (Ed.), *Advances in experimental social psychology,* vol. 4, pp. 1–34. New York: Academic Press.

ARONSON, E., AND CARLSMITH, J. M. 1963. The effect of the severity of threat on the devaluation of forbidden behavior. *Journal of Abnormal and Social Psychology* 66:584–88.

ARONSON, E., AND MILLS, J. 1959. The effect of severity of initiation on liking for a group. *Journal of Abnormal and Social Psychology* 59:177–81.

ARONSON, E.; TURNER, J. A.; AND CARLSMITH, J. M. 1963. Communicator credibility and communication discrepancy as determinants of opinion change. *Journal of Abnormal and Social Psychology* 67:31–36.

ASCH, S. E. 1946. Forming impressions of personality. *Journal of Abnormal and Social Psychology* 41:258–90.

ASCH, S. E. 1952. *Social psychology.* New York: Prentice-Hall.

ASCH, S. E. 1955. Opinions and social pressure. *Scientific American* 193:31–35.

ASCH, S. E. 1956. Studies of independence and conformity: A minority of one against a unanimous majority. *Psychological Monographs* 70 (9, Whole No. 416).

ASCH, S. E., AND GLEITMAN, H. 1953. Yielding to social pressure as a function of public or private commitment. Unpublished manuscript.

ASHER, E. J. 1935. The inadequacy of current intelligence tests for testing Kentucky Mountain children. *Journal of Genetic Psychology* 46:480–86.

ASLIN, R. N. 1987. Visual and auditory development in infancy. In Osofksy, J. D. (Ed.), *Handbook of infant development,* 2nd ed., pp. 5–97. New York: Wiley.

ASTON-JONES, G. 1985. Behavioral functions of locus coeruleus derived from cellular attributes. *Physiological Psychology* 13:118–26.

ATKINSON, D.; MORTEN, G.; AND SUE, D. W. 1983. *Counseling American minorities.* Dubuque, Iowa: W. C. Brown.

ATKINSON, J. W., AND MCCLELLAND, D. C. 1948. The projective expression of needs. II. The effect of different intensities of the hunger drive on thematic apperception. *Journal of Experimental Psychology* 38:643–58.

ATKINSON, R. C., AND SHIFFRIN, R. M. 1968. Human memory: A proposed system and its control. In Spence, K. W., and Spence, J. T. (Eds.), *The psychology of learning and motivation,* vol. 2, pp. 89–105. New York: Academic Press.

ATTNEAVE, F. 1971. Multistability in perception. *Scientific American* 225:62–71.

AUSTIN, J. 1962. *How to do things with words.* Oxford: Clarendon Press.

AUSTIN, J. 1970. Other minds. In Austin, J. L. *Philosophical papers,* 2nd ed. Oxford: Oxford University Press.

AVERILL, J. R. 1978. Anger. In Howe, H., and Dienstbier (Eds.), *Nebraska Symposium on Motivation.* Lincoln, Neb.: University of Nebraska Press.

AX, A. F. 1953. The physiological differentiation of fear and anger in humans. *Psychosomatic Medicine* 15:433–42.

AYLLON, T., AND AZRIN, N. H. 1968. *The token economy: A motivational system for therapy and rehabilitation.* New York: Appleton-Century-Crofts.

BABIGIAN, H. M. 1975. Schizophrenia: Epidemiology. In Freedman, A. M.; Kaplan, H. I.; and Sadock, B. J. (Eds.), *Comprehensive textbook of psychiatry—II,* vol. 1, pp. 860–66. Baltimore: Williams & Wilkins.

BADDELEY, A. D. 1976. *The psychology of human memory.* New York: Basic Books.

BADDELEY, A. D. 1978. The trouble with levels: A reexamination of Craik and Lockhart's framework for memory research. *Psychological Review* 85:139–52.

BADDELEY, A. D. 1986. *Working memory.* Oxford: Clarendon Press.

BADDELEY, A. D. 1990. *Human memory: Theory and practice.* Needham Heights, Mass.: Allyn and Bacon.

BAHRICK, H. P. 1984. Semantic memory content in permastore:50 years of memory for Spanish learned in school. *Journal of Experimental Psychology: General* 113:1–29.

BAILEY, J. M., AND PILLARD, R. C. 1991. A genetic study of male sexual orientation. *Archives of General Psychiatry* 48: 1089–96.

BAILEY, J. M.; PILLARD, R. C.; NEALE, M. C.; AND AGYEI, Y. 1993. Heritable factors influence sexual orientation in women. *Archives of General Psychiatry* 50: 217–23.

BAILLARGEON, R. 1987. Object permanence in $3\frac{1}{2}$- and $4\frac{1}{2}$-month-old infants. *Developmental Psychology* 23:655–664.

BAILLARGEON, R., AND GRABER, M. 1987. Where is the rabbit? 5½-month-old infants' representation of the height of hidden objects. *Cognitive Development* 2:375–92.

BAILLARGEON, R.; SPELKE, E. S.; AND WASSERMAN, S. 1985. Object permanence in five-month-old infants. *Cognition* 20: 191–208.

BAKER, C., AND MCCARTHY, J. (EDS.). 1981. *The logical problem of language acquisition*. Cambridge, Mass.: MIT Press.

BALDWIN, D. A. 1991. Infants' contribution to the achievement of joint reference. *Child Development* 62:875–90.

BALL, W., AND TRONICK, E. 1971. Infant responses to impending collision: optical and real. *Science* 171:818–20.

BALOGH, R. D., AND PORTER, R. H. 1986. Olfactory preferences resulting from mere exposure in human neonates. *Infant Behavior and Development* 9:395–401.

BALTES, P. B.; REESE, H. W.; AND LIPSITT, L. P. 1980. Life-span developmental psychology. In Rosenzweig, M. R., and Porter, L. W. (Eds.), *Annual Review of Psychology* 31:65–110.

BALTES, P. B., AND SCHAIE, K. W. 1976. On the plasticity of intelligence in adulthood and old age. *American Psychologist* 31:720–25.

BANCROFT, J. 1986. The roles of hormones in female sexuality. In Dennerstein and Fraser (Eds.), *Hormones and behavior* pp. 551–60. Amsterdam: International Society of Psychosomatic Obstetrics and Gynecology, Elsevier.

BANDURA, A., AND WALTERS, R. H. 1963. *Social learning and personality development*. New York: Holt, Rinehart & Winston.

BARBER, T. X. 1969. *Hypnosis: A scientific approach*. New York: Van Nostrand Reinhold.

BARD AND RIOCH, 1937. Quoted in Gallistel, R. C., 1980. *The organization of action*. Hillsdale, N.J.: Erlbaum.

BAREFOOT, J. C.; DODGE, K. A.; PETERSON, B. L.; DAHLSTROM, W. G.; AND WILLIAMS, R. B. 1989. The Cook-Medley Hostility Scale: Item content and ability to predict survival. *Psychosomatic Medicine* 51:46–57.

BARGLOW, P.; VAUGHN, B. E.; AND MOLITOR, N. 1987. Effects of maternal absence due to employment on the quality of infant-mother attachment in a low-risk sample. *Child Development* 58(4): 945–54

BARLOW, D. H. 1988. *Anxiety and its disorders*. New York: Guilford Press.

BARLOW, H. B., AND HILL, R. M. 1963. Evidence for a physiological explanation of the waterfall illusion and figural after-effects. *Nature* 200:1345–47.

BARLUND, D. C. 1975. *Public and private self in Japan and the United States*. Tokyo: Simul Press.

BARNETT, S. A. 1963. *The rat: A study in behavior*. Chicago: Aldine.

BARNOUW, V. 1963. *Culture and personality*. Homewood, Ill.: Dorsey Press.

BARON, J. 1985. What kinds of intelligence components are fundamental? In Chipman, S. F.; Segal, J. W.; and Glaser, R. (Eds.), *Thinking and learning skills. Vol. 2: Research and open questions*. Hillsdale, N.J.: Erlbaum.

BARRY, H., III; CHILD, I. L.; AND BACON, M. K. 1959. Relation of child training to subsistence economy. *American Anthropologist* 61:51–63.

BARTLETT, F. C. 1932. *Remembering: A study in experimental and social psychology*. Cambridge, England: Cambridge University Press.

BARTOL, C. R., AND COSTELLO, N. 1976. Extraversion as a function of temporal duration of electric shock: An exploratory study. *Perceptual and Motor Skills* 42:1174.

BARTOSHUK, L. 1988. Taste. In Atkinson, R. C.; Herrnstein, R. J.; Lindzey, G.; and Luce, R. D. (Eds.), *Stevens' handbook of experimental psychology: Vol. 1. Perception and motivation*, rev. ed., pp. 461–502. New York: Wiley.

BASS, B. M. 1981. *Stogdill's handbook of leadership: Theory, research, and managerial applications*, rev. ed. New York: Free Press.

BASS, B. M. 1990. *Bass and Stogdill's handbook of leadership: Theory, research, and managerial applications*, 3rd ed. New York: Free Press.

BASS, E., AND DAVIS, L. 1988. *The courage to heal*. New York: Harper and Row.

BATES, E. 1976. *Language and context: The acquisition of pragmatics*. New York: Academic Press.

BATES, E., AND MACWHINNEY, B. 1982. Functionalist approaches to grammar. In Wanner, E., and Gleitman, L. (Eds.), *Language acquisition: State of the art*. New York: Cambridge University Press.

BATESON, P. P. G. 1984. The neural basis of imprinting. In Marler, P., and Terrace, H. S. (Eds.), *The biological basis of learning*, pp. 325–39. Dahlem-Konferenzen. Berlin: Springer.

BAUM, W. M. 1970. Extinction of avoidance response following response prevention. *Psychological Bulletin* 74:276–84.

BAUMRIND, D. 1967. Child care practices anteceding three patterns of preschool behavior. *Genetic Psychology Monographs* 75: 43–88.

BAUMRIND, D. 1971. Current patterns of parental authority. *Genetic Psychology Monographs* 1.

BAUMRIND, D. 1977. *Socialization determinants of personal agency*. Paper presented at the biennial meetings of the Society for Research in Child Development, New Orleans. (Cited in Maccoby, E. E. 1980. *Social development*. New York: Harcourt Brace Jovanovich.)

BAUMRIND, D. 1986. Sex differences in moral reasoning: Response to Walker's (1984) conclusion that there are none. *Child Development* 57:511–21.

BAYER, E. 1929. Beitrge zur *Zweikomponententheorie des Hungers. Zeitschrift der Psychologie* 112:1–54.

BAYLEY, N. 1970. Development of mental abilities. In Mussen, P. H. (Ed.), *Carmichael's manual of child psychology*, 3rd ed., pp. 1163–1209. New York: Wiley.

BECK, A. T. 1967. *Depression: Causes and treatment*. Philadelphia: University of Pennsylvania Press.

BECK, A. T. 1976. *Cognitive therapy and the emotional disorders*. New York: International Universities Press.

BECK, A. T. 1985. Cognitive therapy. In Kaplan, H. I., and Sadock, J. (Eds.), *Comprehensive textbook of psychiatry*, 4th ed. Baltimore: Williams & Wilkins.

BECK, A. T. 1988. Cognitive approaches to panic disorders: Theory and therapy. In Rachman, S., and Maser, J. D. (Eds.), *Panic: psychological perspectives*. Hillsdale, N.J.: Erlbaum.

BECK, A. T.; RUSH, A. J.; SHAW, B. F.; AND EMERY, G. 1979. *Cognitive therapy of depression*. New York: Guilford Press.

BECK, J. 1966. Effect of orientation and of shape similarity on perceptual grouping. *Perception and Psychophysics* 1:300–302.

BECK, J. 1982. Textural segmentation. In Beck, J. (Ed.), *Organization and representation in perception*, pp. 285–318. Hillsdale, N.J.: Erlbaum.

BÉKÉSY, G. VON. 1957. The ear. *Scientific American* 197:66–78.

BELL, A. P.; WEINBERG, M. S.; AND HAMMERSMITH, S. K. 1981. *Sexual preference: Its development in men and women*. Bloomington, Ind.: Indiana University Press.

BELL, R. Q. 1968. A reinterpretation of the direction of effects in studies of socialization. *Psychological Review* 75:81–95.

BELL, R. Q., AND HARPER, L. V. 1977. *Child effects on adults*. Hillsdale, N.J.: Erlbaum.

BELLI, R. F. 1989. Influences of misleading postevent information: Misinformation interference and acceptance. *Journal of Experimental Psychology: General* 118:72–85.

BELLUGI, U. 1971. Simplification in children's language. In Huxley, R., and Ingram, E., (Eds.), *Language acquisition: Models and methods*. New York: Academic Press.

BELLUGI, U.; POIZNER, H.; AND KLIMA, E. S. 1983. Brain organization for language: Clues from sign aphasia. *Human Neurobiology* 2:155–71.

BELOFF, H. 1957. The structure and origin of the anal character. *Genetic Psychology Monographs* 55:141–72.

BELSKY, J. 1988. The "effects" of infant day care reconsidered. Infant Day Care, *Early Childhood Research Quarterly* (Special Issue) 3: 235–72.

BELSKY, J., AND BRAUNGART, J. M. 1991. Are insecure-avoidant infants with extensive day-care experience less stressed by and more independent in the Strange Situation? *Child Development* 62: 567–57.

BEM, D. J. 1967. Self-perception: An alternative interpretation of cognitive dissonance phenomena. *Psychological Review* 74:183–200.

BEM, D. J. 1972. Self-perception theory. In Berkowitz, L. (Ed.), *Advances in experimental social psychology,* vol. 6, pp. 2–62. New York: Academic Press.

BEM, S. L. 1984. Androgyny and gender schema theory: A conceptual and empirical integration. In Sondregger, T. B. (Ed.), *Nebraska Symposium on Motivation.* Lincoln, Neb.: University of Nebraska Press.

BEM, S. L. 1989. Genital knowledge and gender constancy in preschool children. *Child Development* 60: 649–62.

BENBOW, C. P. 1988. Sex differences in mathematical reasoning ability in intellectually talented preadolescents: Their nature, effects, and possible causes. *Behavior and Brain Sciences* 11:169–232.

BENBOW, C. P., AND STANLEY, J. C. 1983. Sex differences in mathematical reasoning: More facts. *Science* 222:1029–31.

BENEDICT, R. 1934. *Patterns of culture.* New York: Houghton Mifflin.

BENTLEY, E. 1983. *The life of the drama.* New York: Atheneum.

BERGIN, A. E. 1967. An empirical analysis of therapeutic issues. In Arbuckle, D. (Ed.), *Counseling and psychotherapy: An overview,* pp. 175–208. New York: McGraw-Hill.

BERGIN, A. E. 1971. The evaluation of therapeutic outcomes. In Bergin, A. E. and Garfield, S. L. (Eds.), *Handbook of psychotherapy and behavior change: An empirical analysis.* New York: Wiley.

BERMANT, G., AND DAVIDSON, J. M. 1974. *Biological bases of sexual behavior.* New York: Harper & Row.

BERNARD, V. W.; OTTENBERG, P.; AND REDL, F. 1965. Dehumanization: A composite psychological defense in relation to modern war. In Schwebel, M. (Ed.), *Behavioral science and human survival,* pp. 64–82. Palo Alto, Calif.: Science and Behavior Books.

BERNHEIM, K. W., AND LEWINE, R. R. J. 1979. *Schizophrenia: Symptoms, causes, treatments. New York: Norton.*

BERNSTEIN, I. L. 1978. Learned taste aversions in children receiving chemotherapy. *Science* 200:1302–1303.

BERSCHEID, E. 1985. Interpersonal attraction. In Lindzey, G., and Aronson, E. (Eds.), *Handbook of social psychology,* vol. 2, pp. 413–84. New York: Academic Press.

BERSCHEID, E.; DION, K.; WALSTER, E.; AND WALSTER, G. W. 1971. Physical attractiveness and dating choice: A test of the matching hypothesis. *Journal of Experimental Social Psychology* 7: 173-89.

BERSCHEID, E., AND WALSTER, E. 1974. Physical attractiveness. In Berkowitz, L. (Ed.), *Advances in experimental social psychology,* vol. 7. New York: Academic Press.

BERSCHEID, E., AND WALSTER, E. H. 1978. *Interpersonal attraction,* 2nd ed. Reading, Mass.: Addison-Wesley.

BERTELSEN, A.; HARVALD, B.; AND HAUGE, M. 1977. A Danish twin study of manic depressive disorders. *British Journal of Psychiatry* 130:330–51.

BEST, D. L.; WILLIAMS, J. E.; CLOUD, J. M.; DAVIS, S. W.; ROBERTSON, L. S.; EDWARDS, J. R.; GILES, E.; AND FOWLES, J. 1977. Development of sex-trait stereotypes among young children in the United States, England, and Ireland. *Child Development* 48:1375–84.

BEUTLER, L. E., AND CLARKIN, J. 1990. *Systematic treatment selection: Toward targeted treatment interventions.* New York: Brunner-Maazel.

BEVER, T. G. 1970. The cognitive basis for linguistic structures. In Hayes, J. R. (Ed.), *Cognition and the development of language,* pp. 279–362. New York: Wiley.

BICKERTON, D. 1984. The language bioprogram hypothesis. *Behavioral and Brain Sciences* 7:173–221.

BIEDERMAN, I. 1987. Recognition-by-components: A theory of human image understanding. *Psychological Review:* 94:115-47.

BIGELOW, A. 1987. Early words of blind children. *Journal of Child Language* 14(1):1–22.

BILSKY, L.; EVANS, R. A.; AND GILBERT, L. 1972. Generalization of associative clustering tendencies in mentally retarded adolescents: Effects of novel stimuli. *American Journal of Mental Deficiency* 77:77–84.

BIRCH, H. G.; PIÑEIRO, C.; ALCADE, E.; TOCA, T.; AND CRAVIOTA, J. 1971. Relation of *kwashiokor* in early childhood and intelligence at school age. *Pediatric Research* 5:579–92.

BJORK, R. A. 1970. Positive forgetting: The noninterference of items intentionally forgotten. *Journal of Verbal Learning and Verbal Behavior* 9:255–68.

BJÖRKLUND, A., AND STENEVI, U. 1984. Intracerebral implants: Neuronal replacement and reconstruction of damaged circuitries. *Annual Review of Neuroscience* 7:279–308.

BJÖRKLUND, A.; STENEVI, U.; SCHMIDT, R. H.; DUNNETT, S. B.; AND GAGE, F. H. 1983. Intracerebral grafting of neuronal suspensions I. Introduction and general methods of preparation. *Acta Physiologica Scandinavica Supplement* 522:1–8.

BLACK, D. W., AND NOYES, R. 1990. Comorbidity in obsessive-compulsive disorder, pp. 305–16. In Maser, J. D., and Cloninger, C. D. (Eds.), *Comorbidity in anxiety and mood disorders.* Washington, D.C.: American Psychiatric Press.

BLAKEMORE, C. 1977. *Mechanics of the mind.* New York: Cambridge University Press.

BLANK, M. A., AND FOSS, D. J. 1978. Semantic facilitation and lexical access during sentence processing. *Memory and Cognition* 6:644–52.

BLASI, A. 1980. Bridging moral cognition and moral action: A critical review of the literature. *Psychological Bulletin* 88:1–45.

BLASI, A. 1984. Moral identity: Its role in moral functioning. In Kurtines, W. M., and Gewirtz, L. (Eds.), *Morality, moral behavior, and moral development,* pp. 128–39. New York: Wiley.

BLASS, E. M., AND EPSTEIN, A. N. 1971. A lateral preoptic osmosensitive zone for thirst in the rat. *Journal of Comparative and Physiological Psychology* 76:378–94.

BLEULER, E. 1911. *Dementia praecox, or the group of schizophrenias.* English translation by Zinkin, J., and Lewis, N. D. C. New York: International Universities Press, 1950.

BLISS, E. L. 1980. Multiple personalities: Report of fourteen cases with implications for schizophrenia and hysteria. *Archives of General Psychiatry* 37:1388–97.

BLOCK, J. 1971. *Lives through time.* Berkeley, Calif.: Bancroft Books.

BLOCK, J. 1977. Advancing the psychology of personality: Paradigmatic shift or improving the quality of research. In Magnusson, D., and Endler, N. S. (Eds.), *Personality at the crossroads,* pp. 37–64. New York: Wiley.

BLOCK, N.J., AND DWORKIN, G. 1976. *The IQ controversy: Critical readings.* New York: Pantheon.

BLOOM, F. E. 1983. The endorphins: A growing family of pharmacologically pertinent peptides. *Annual Review of Pharmacology and Toxicology* 23:151–70.

BLOOM, F. E. 1993. Advancing a neurodevelopmental origin for shizophrenia. *Archives of General Psychiatry* 50:224–27.

BLOOM, F. E.; LAZERSON, A.; AND HOFSTADTER, L. 1988. *Brain, mind, and behavior.* New York: Freeman.

BLOOM, K. 1988. Quality of adult vocalizations affects the quality of infant vocalizations. *Journal of Child Language* 15(1):469–80.

BLOOM, L. 1970. *Language development: Form and function in emerging grammars.* Cambridge, Mass.: MIT Press.

BLOOM, P. 1990. Syntactic distinctions in child language. *Journal of Child Language* 17(2):343–56.

BLOOM, P. 1994. Possible names: The role of syntax-semantics mappings in the acquisition of nominals. In Gleitman, L. R., and Landau, B. (Eds.), *Lexical acquisition, Lingua* (Special Issue) 92:297–329.

BLOOMFIELD, L. 1933. *Language.* NY: Henry Holt.

BLUM, J. E.; JARVIK, L. F.; AND CLARK, E. T. 1970. Rate of change on selective tests of intelligence: A twenty-year longitudinal study. *Journal of Gerontology* 25:171–76.

BLURTON-JONES, N., AND KONNER, M. J. 1976. !Kung knowledge of animal behavior. In Lee, B., and DeVore, I. (Eds.), *Kalahari hunter-gatherers.* Cambridge, Mass: Harvard University Press.

BODEN, M. 1977. *Artificial intelligence and natural man.* New York: Basic Books.

BODNAR, R. J.; KELLY, D. D.; BRUTUS, M.; AND GLUSMAN, M. 1980. Stress-induced analgesia: Neural and hormonal determinants. *Neuroscience and biobehavioral reviews* 4:87–100.

BOGEN, J. E. 1969. The other side of the brain II: An appositional mind. *Bulletin of the Los Angeles Neurological Societies* 34:135–62.

BOGEN, J. E.; FISHER, E. D.; AND VOGEL, P. J. 1965. Cerebral commissurotomy: A second case report. *Journal of the American Medical Association* 194:1328–29.

BOLLES, R. C. 1970. Species-specific defense reactions and avoidance learning. *Psychological Review* 77:32–48.

BOLLES, R. C., AND BEECHER, M. D., Eds. 1988. *Evolution and learning.* Hillsdale, N.J.: Erlbaum.

BOLLES, R. C., AND FANSELOW, M. S. 1982. Endorphins and behavior. *Annual Review of Psychology* 33:87–102.

BOND, M. H. 1979. Dimensions of personality used in perceiving peers: Cross-cultural comparisons of Hong Kong, Japanese, American, and Filipino university students. *International Journal of Psychology* 14:47–56.

BOND, M. H. 1988. *The cross-cultural challenge to social psychology,* pp. 96–108. Newbury Park, Calif.: Sage Publications.

BOOTH, D. A. 1980. Acquired behavior controlling energy and output. In Stunkard, A. J. (Ed.), *Obesity,* pp. 101–43. Philadelphia: Saunders.

BORDEN, R. J. 1980. Audience influence. In Paulus, P. B. (Ed.), *Psychology of group influence,* pp. 99–132. Hillsdale, N.J.: Erlbaum.

BORER, H., AND WEXLER, K. 1987. The maturation of syntax. In Roeper, T., and Williams, E. (Eds.), *Parameter setting and language acquisition.* Dordrecht, Netherlands: Reidel.

BORG, G.; DIAMANT, H.; STROM, C.; AND ZOTTERMAN, Y. 1967. The relation between neural and perceptual intensity: A comparative study of neural and psychophysical responses to taste stimuli. *Journal of Physiology* 192:13–20.

BORING, E. G. 1930. A new ambiguous figure. *American Journal of Psychology* 42:444–45.

BORING, E. G. 1942. *Sensation and perception in the history of experimental psychology.* New York: Appleton-Century-Crofts.

BORING, E. G. 1964. Size constancy in a picture. *American Journal of Psychology* 77:494–98.

BORING, E. G.; LANGFELD, H. S.; AND WELD, H. P. 1939. *Introduction to psychology.* New York: Wiley.

BORKE, H. 1975. Piaget's mountains revisited: Changes in the egocentric landscape. *Developmental Psychology* 11:240–43.

BORNSTEIN, M. H. 1985. Perceptual development. In Bornstein, M. H., and Lamb, M. E. (Eds.), *Developmental psychology: An advanced textbook,* pp. 81–132. Hillsdale, N.J.: Erlbaum.

BOTTGER, P. C. 1984. Expertise and air time as bases of actual and perceived influence in problem-solving groups. *Journal of Applied Psychology* 69: 214–22

BOTVIN, G. J., AND MURRAY, F. B. 1975. The efficacy of peer modelling and social conflict in the acquisition of conservation. *Child Development* 46:796–97.

BOUCHARD, C.; TREMBLAY, A.; DESPRÉS, J-P.; NADEAU, A.; LUPIEN, P. L.; THÉRIAULT, G.; DUSSAULT, J.; MOORJANI, S.; PINAULT, S. M.; AND FOURNIER, G. 1990. The response to long-term overfeeding in identical twins. *New England Journal of Medicine* 322:1477–82.

BOUCHARD, T. J., JR. 1984. Twins reared apart and together: What they tell us about human diversity. In Fox, S. (Ed.), *The chemical and biological bases of individuality,* pp. 147–84. New York: Plenum.

BOUCHARD, T. J., JR.; LYKKEN, D. T.; MCGUE, M.; SEGAL, N. L.; AND TELLEGEN, A. 1990. Sources of human psychological differences: The Minnesota study of twins reared apart. *Science* 250:223–50.

BOUCHARD, T. J., JR., AND MCGUE, M. 1981. Familial studies of intelligence: A review. *Science* 212:1055–59.

BOWER, G. H. 1970a. Analysis of a mnemonic device. *American Scientist* 58:496–510.

BOWER, G. H. 1970b. Organizational factors in memory. *Cognitive Psychology* 1:18–46.

BOWER, G. H.; BLACK, J. B.; AND TURNER, T. J. 1979. Scripts in memory for text. *Cognitive Psychology* 11:177–220.

BOWER, G. H., AND WINZENZ, D. 1969. Group structure, coding and memory for digit series. *Journal of Experimental Psychology* (Monograph) 80:1–17.

BOWER, T. G. R. 1966. Slant perception and shape constancy in infants. *Science* 151:832–34.

BOWERMAN, M. 1982. Reorganizational processes in language development. In Wanner, E., and Gleitman, L. R. (Eds.), *Language development: State of the art.* New York: Cambridge University Press.

BOWERS, K. S. 1984. On being unconsciously influenced and informed. In Bowers, K. S., and Meichenbaum, D. (Eds.), *The unconscious reconsidered.* New York: Wiley.

BOWLBY, J. 1969. *Attachment and loss: Vol. 1. Attachment.* New York: Basic Books.

BOWLBY, J. 1973. *Separation and loss.* New York: Basic Books.

BOWMAKER, J. K., AND DARTNALL, H. J. A. 1980. Visual pigments and rods and cones in a human retina. *Journal of Physiology* 298:501–11.

BRABECK, M. 1983. Moral judgement: Theory and research on differences between males and females. *Developmental Review* 3:274–91.

BRADLEY, G. W. 1978. Self-serving biases in the attribution process: A reexamination of the fact or fiction question. *Journal of Personality and Social Psychology* 13:420–32.

BRADY, I. 1983. Special section. Speaking in the name of the real: Freeman and Mead on Samoa. *American Anthropologist* 85:908–47.

BRADY, J. P. 1985. Behavior therapy. In Kaplan, H. I., and Sadock, J. (Eds.), *Comprehensive textbook of psychiatry,* 4th ed, pp. 1365–73. Baltimore: Williams & Wilkins.

BRAIN, L. 1965. *Speech disorders: Aphasia, apraxia, and agnosia.* London: Butterworth.

BRAINE, M. D. S. 1963. The ontogeny of English phrase structure: The first phase. *Language* 39:3–13.

BRAINE, M. D. S. 1976. Children's first word combinations. *Monographs of the Society for Research in Child Development* 41(1, Serial No. 164).

BRANSFORD, J. D., AND JOHNSON, M. K. 1972. Contextual prerequisites for understanding. *Journal of Verbal Learning and Verbal Behavior* 11:717–26.

BRAZELTON, T. B. 1962. A child-oriented approach to toilet training. *Pediatrics* 29:121–28.

BRAZELTON, T. B. 1972. Implications of infant development among the Mayan Indians of Mexico. *Human Development* 15: 90–111.

BREGER, L.; HUNTER, I.; AND LANE, R. W. 1971. The effect of stress on dreams. *Psychological Issues* 7(3, Monograph 27):1–213.

BREGGIN, P. R. 1979. *Electroshock: Its brain-disabling effects.* New York: Springer.

BRELAND, K., AND BRELAND, M. 1951. A field of applied animal psychology. *American Psychologist* 6:202–204.

BRELAND, K., AND BRELAND, M. 1961. *American Psychologist* 16:681–84.

BRESNAN, J. 1982. *The mental representation of grammatical relations.* Cambridge, Mass.: MIT Press.

BRETHERTON, I. 1988. How to do things with one word: The ontogenesis of intentional message-making in children. In Smith, M. D., and Locke, J. L., (Eds.), *The emergent lexicon: the child's development of a linguistic vocabulary,* pp. 255–57. New York: Academic Press.

BRICKMAN, J. C., AND D'AMATO, B. 1975. Exposure effects in a free-choice situation. *Journal of Personality and Social Psychology* 32:415–20.

BRIER, A., AND ASTRACHAN, B. M. 1984. Characterization of schizophrenic patients who commit suicide. *American Journal of Psychiatry* 141:206–209.

BROADBENT, D. E. 1958. *Perception and communication.* London: Pergamon Press.

BRODIE, H. K. H.; GARTRELL, N.; DOERING, C.; AND RHUE, T. 1974. Plasma testosterone levels in heterosexual and homosexual men. *American Journal of Psychiatry* 131:82–83.

BRODY, N. 1988. *Personality.* New York: Academic Press.

BRODY, N. 1992. *Intelligence,* 2nd ed. New York: Academic Press

BRONFENBRENNER, U. 1975. Is early intervention effective? In Guttentag, M., and Struening, E. L. (Eds.), *Handbook of evaluation research,* vol. 2. Beverly Hills, Calif.: Sage.

BRONSON, W. C. 1966. Central orientations. A study of behavior organization from childhood to adolescence. *Child Development* 37: 125–55.

BRONSON, W. C. 1967. Adult derivatives of emotional expressiveness and reactivity control: Developmental continuities from childhood to adulthood. *Child Development* 38:801–17.

BROWN. A. L. 1974. The role of strategic memory in retardate-memory. In Ellis, N. R. (Ed.), *International review of research in mental retardation,* vol. 7, pp. 55–108. New York: Academic Press.

BROWN, A. L.; BRANSFORD, J. D.; FERRARA, R. A.; AND CAMPIONE, J. C. 1983. Learning, remembering, and understanding. In Mussen, P. (Ed.), *Carmichael's manual of child psychology: Vol. 3. Cognitive development* (Markman, E. M., and Flavell, J. H., volume editors). New York: Wiley.

BROWN, A. L.; CAMPIONE, J. C.; BRAY, N. W.; AND WILCOX, B. L. 1973. Keeping track of changing variables: Effects of rehearsal training and rehearsal prevention in normal and retarded adolescents. *Journal of Experimental Psychology* 101:123–31.

BROWN, A. L.; CAMPIONE, J. C.; AND DAY, J. D. 1981. Learning to learn: On training students to learn from texts. *Educational Researcher* 10:14–21.

BROWN, J. F. 1940. *The psychodynamics of abnormal behavior.* New York: McGraw-Hill.

BROWN, R. 1957. Linguistic determinism and parts of speech. *Journal of Abnormal and Social Psychology* 55:1–5.

BROWN, R. 1958. *Words and things.* New York: Free Press, Macmillan.

BROWN, R. 1965. *Social psychology.* New York: Free Press, Macmillan.

BROWN, R. 1973. *A first language: The early stage.* Cambridge, Mass.: Harvard University Press.

BROWN, R., AND BELLUGI, U. 1964. Three processes in the child's acquisition of syntax. *Harvard Educational Review* 34: 133-51.

BROWN, R.; CAZDEN, C.; AND BELLUGI-KLIMA, U. 1969. The child's grammar from 1 to 11. In Hill, J. P. (Ed.), *Minnesota Symposium on Child Psychology,* vol. 2, pp. 28–73. Minneapolis: University of Minnesota Press.

BROWN, R., AND HANLON, C. 1970. Derivational complexity and order of acquisition in child speech. In Hayes, J. R. (Ed.), *Cognition and the development of language,* pp. 11–53. New York: Wiley.

BROWN, R., AND KULIK, J. 1977. Flashbulb memories. *Cognition* 5:73–99.

BROWN, R., AND MCNEILL, D. 1966. The tip of the tongue phenomenon. *Journal of Verbal Learning and Verbal Behavior* 5:325–27.

BROWNELL, K. D.; GREENWOOD, M. R. C.; STELLAR, E.; AND SHRAGER, E. E. 1986. The effects of repeated cycles of weight loss and regain in rats. *Physiology and Behavior* 38:459–64.

BRUCE, V., AND GREEN, P. 1985. *Visual perception: Physiology, psychology, and ecology.* Hillsdale, N.J.: Erlbaum.

BRUCH, H. 1973. *Eating disorders.* New York: Basic Books.

BRUCH, H. 1978. *The golden cage.* Cambridge, Mass.: Harvard University Press.

BRUNER, J. S. 1974/1975. From communication to language—a psychological perspective. *Cognition* 3:255–78.

BRUNER, J. S., AND TAGIURI, R. 1954. The perception of people. In Lindzey, G. (Ed.), *Handbook of social psychology,* vol. 2. Reading, Mass.: Addison-Wesley.

BRYAN, W. L., AND HARTER, N. 1897. Studies in the physiology and psychology of telegraphic language. *Psychological Review* 4:27–53.

BRYAN, W. L., AND HARTER, N. 1899. Studies on the telegraphic language: The acquisition of a hierarchy of habits. *Psychological Review* 6:345–75.

BRYDE, J. F. 1972. *Indian students and guidance.* Boston: Houghton Mifflin.

BUCHANAN, B. G., AND SHORTLIFFE, E. H. (Eds.). 1985. *Rule-based expert systems: The MYCIN experiments of the Stanford Heuristics Programming Project.* Reading, Mass: Addison-Wesley.

BUGELSKI, B. R., AND ALAMPAY, D. A. 1961. The role of frequency in developing perceptual sets. *Canadian Journal of Psychology* 15:205–11.

BULLOCK, W. A., AND GILLILAND, K. 1993. Eysenck's arousal theory of introversion-extraversion: A covergent measures investigation. *Journal of Personality andSocial Psychology* 64:113–23.

BULLOUGH, E. 1912. "Psychical distance" as a factor in art and an aesthetic principle. *British Journal of Psychology* 5:87–118.

BURCKHARDT, J. 1860. *The civilization of the Renaissance in Italy.* Oxford: Phaidon Press, 1945.

BURGESS, E. W., AND WALLIN, P. 1943. Homogamy in social characteristics. *American Journal of Sociology* 49:109–24.

BURNETT, S. A.; LANE, D. M.; AND DRATT, L. M. 1979. Spatial differences and sex differences in quantitative ability. *Intelligence* 3:345–54.

BURNS, J. M. 1978. *Leadership.* New York: Harper and Row.

BURTON, R. V. 1963. Generality of honesty reconsidered. *Psychological Review* 70:481–99.

BURTON, R. V., AND WHITING, J. W. M. 1961. The absent father and cross-sex identity. *Merrill-Palmer Quarterly* 7:85–95.

BURY, J. B. 1932. *The idea of progress.* New York: Macmillan.

BUSS, A. H., AND PLOMIN, R. 1984. *Temperament: Early developing personality traits.* Hillsdale, N.J.: Erlbaum.

BUSS, D. M. 1989. Sex differences in human mate preferences: Evolutionary hypotheses tested in 37 cultures. *Behavioral and Brain Sciences* 12:1–50.

BUSS, D. M. 1992. Mate preference mechanisms: Consequences for partner choice and intrasexual competition. In Barkow, J. H.; Cosmides, L.; and Tooby, J. *The adapted mind,* pp. 249–66. New York: Oxford University Press.

BUSS, D. M., AND BARNES, M. F. 1986. Preferences in human mate selection. *Journal of Personality and Social Psychology* 50:559–70.

BUSS, D. M., AND CRAIK, K. H. 1983. Dispositional analysis of everyday conduct. *Journal of Personality* 51:393–412.

BUTCHER, J. N.; DAHLSTROM, W. G.; GRAHAM, J. R.; TELLEGEN, A. M.; AND KAEMMER, B. 1989. *MMPI-2: Manual for administration and scoring.* Minneapolis, Minn.: University of Minnesota Press.

BUTTERWORTH, G., AND COCHRAN, E. 1980. Towards a mechanism of joint visual attention in human infancy. *International Journal of Behavioral Development* 3:253–72.

BUTTERWORTH, G., AND JARRETT, N. 1991. What minds have in common is space: Spatial mechanisms serving joint visual attention in infancy. Special issue: Perspectives on the child's theory of mind. *British Journal of Developmental Psychology* 9:55–72.

BYRNE, R. 1989. Chess-playing computer closing in on champions. *New York Times,* September 26, 1989, C1 and 12.

CAIN, W. S. 1988. Olfaction. In Atkinson, R. C.; Herrnstein, R. J.; Lindzey, G.; and Luce, R. D. (Eds.), *Stevens' handbook of experimental psychology: Vol. 1. Perception and motivation,* rev. ed., pp. 409–59. New York: Wiley.

CAIRNS, R. B. 1984. Research in language comprehension. In R. C. Naremore (Ed.), *Language science.* San Diego: College-Hill Press.

CAMMALLERI, J. A.; HENDRICK, H. W.; PITTMAN, W. C., JR.; BOUT, H. D.; AND PRATHER, D. C. 1973. Effects of different styles of leadership on group accuracy. *Journal of Applied Psychology* 57: 32–37.

CAMPBELL, J. B., AND HAWLEY, C. W. 1982. Study habits and Eysenck's theory of extraversion-introversion. *Journal of Research in Personality* 16:139–46.

CAMPBELL, J. D.; TESSER, A.; AND FAIREY, P. J. 1986. Conformity and attention to the stimulus: Some temporal and contextual dynamics. *Journal of Personality and Social Psychology* 51:315–24.

CAMPFIELD, L. A., AND SMITH, F. J. 1990a. Systemic factors in the control of food intake. In Stricker, E. M. (Ed.), *Handbook of behavioral neurobiology,* vol. 10: *Neurobiology of food and fluid intake,* pp. 183–206. New York: Plenum.

CAMPFIELD, L. A., AND SMITH, F. J. 1990b. Transient declines in blood glucose signal meal initiation. *International Journal of Obesity* 14:15–33.

CAMPFIELD, L. A.; SMITH, F. J.; AND ROSENBAUM, M. 1992. Human hunger. Is there a role for blood glucose dynamics? *Appetite* 18:244.

CAMPIONE, J. C., AND BROWN, A. L. 1977. Memory and metamemory development in educable retarded children. In Kail, R. V., Jr., and Hagen, J. W. (Eds.), *Perspectives on the development of memory and cognition.* Hillsdale, N.J.: Erlbaum.

CAMPIONE, J. C.; BROWN, A. L.; AND FERRARA, R. A. 1982. Mental retardation and intelligence. In Sternberg, R. J. (Ed.), *Handbook of human intelligence,* pp. 392–492. New York: Cambridge University Press.

CAMPOS, J. J.; BARRETT, K. C.; LAMB, M. E.; GOLDSMITH, H. H.; AND STERNBERG, C. 1983. Socioemotional development. In Mussen, P. E. (Ed.), *Carmichael's manual of child psychology: Vol. 2. Infancy and developmental psychobiology* (Haith, M. M., and Campos, J. J., volume editor), pp. 783-916. New York: Wiley.

CANNON, T. D. 1991. Genetic and prenatal sources of structural brain abnormalities in schizophrenia. In Mednick, S. A.; Cannon, T. D.; Barr, C. E.; and Lyon, M. (Eds.), *Fetal neural development and adult schizophrenia.* Cambridge: Cambridge University Press.

CANNON, T. D.; MEDNICK, S. A.; AND PARNAS, J. 1990. Antecedents of predominantly negative- and predominantly positive-symptom schizophrenia in a high-risk population. *Archives of General Psychiatry* 47:622–32.

CANNON, W. B. 1927. The James-Lange theory of emotions: A critical examination and an alternative theory. *American Journal of Psychology* 39:106–24.

CANNON, W. B. 1929. *Bodily changes in pain, hunger, fear and rage,* rev. ed. New York: Appleton-Century.

CANNON, W. B. 1932 and 1960 (revised and enlarged). *The wisdom of the body.* New York: Norton.

CANTOR, J. R.; ZILLMAN, D.; AND BRYANT, J. 1975. Enhancement of experienced sexual arousal in response to erotic stimuli through misattribution of unrelated residual excitation. *Journal of Personality and Social Psychology* 32:69–75.

CANTOR, N., AND MISCHEL, W. 1977. Traits as prototypes: Effects on recognition memory. *Journal of Personality and Social Psychology* 35:38–48.

CANTOR, N., AND MISCHEL, W. 1979. Prototypes in person perception. In L. Berkowitz (Ed.), *Advances in experimental social psychology,* vol. 12. New York: Academic Press.

CAREY, S. 1978. The child as word learner. In Halle, M.; Bresnan, J.; and Miller, G. A. (Eds.), *Linguistic theory and psychological reality.* Cambridge, Mass.: MIT Press.

CAREY, S. 1982. Semantic development: State of the art. In Wanner, E., and Gleitman, L. R. (Eds.), *Language acquisition: State of the art.* New York: Cambridge University Press.

CAREY, S. 1985. *Conceptual change in childhood.* Cambridge, Mass.: MIT Press.

CAREY, S. 1994. Does learning a language require the child to reconceptualize the world? In Gleitman, L. R., and Landau, B., Lexical acquisition, *Lingua* (Special Issue) 92:143–67.

CARLSON, G., AND TANENHAUS, M. 1988. Thematic roles and language comprehension. In W. Wilkins (Ed.), *Syntax and semantics: Vol. 21. Thematic relations.* San Diego: Academic Press.

CARLSON, N. R. 1986. *Physiology of behavior,* 3rd ed. Boston: Allyn and Bacon.

CARLSON, N. R. 1991. *Physiology of behavior.* Boston: Allyn and Bacon.

CARLYLE, T. 1841. *On heroes, hero-worship, and the heroic in history.* Berkeley: University of California Press, 1992.

CARON, A. J.; CARON, R. F.; AND CARLSON, V. R. 1979. Infant perception of the invariant shape of objects varying in slant. *Child Development* 50:716–21.

CARR, D.; BULLEN, B.; KRINAR, G.; ARNOLD, M.; ROSENBLATT, M.; BEITINS, I. Z.; MARTIN, J. B.; AND MCARTHUR, J. W. 1981. Physical conditioning facilitates the exercise-induced secretion of betaendorphin and beta-lipopotrin in women. *New England Journal of Medicine* 305:560–63.

CARRINGTON, P. 1972. Dreams and schizophrenia. *Archives of General Psychiatry* 26:343–50.

CARROLL, L. 1865. *Alice in Wonderland.* Abridged by Frank, J. and illustrated by Torrey, M. M. New York: Random House, 1969.

CARTWRIGHT, R. D. 1977. *Night life: Explorations in dreaming.* Englewood Cliffs, N.J.: Prentice-Hall.

CASE, R. 1978. Intellectual development from birth to adulthood: A neo-Piagetian interpretation. In Siegler, R. S. (Ed.), *Children's thinking: What develops?,* pp. 37–72. Hillsdale, N.J.: Erlbaum.

CASE, R. 1985. *Intellectual development: Birth to adulthood.* New York: Academic Press.

CASPI, A., AND HERBENER, E. 1990. Continuity and change: Assortative marriage and the consistency of personality in adulthood. *Journal of Personality and Social Psychology* 58: 250–58.

CASSIDY, K. E. W. 1993. The development of the child's theory of mind. Unpublished doctoral dissertation. Philadelphia: University of Pennsylvania.

CATEL, J. 1953. Ein Beitrag zur Frage von Hirnenentwicklung under Menschwerdung. *Klinische Weisschriften* 31:473–75.

CATTELL, R. B. 1957. *Personality and motivation structure and measurement.* New York: Harcourt, Brace and World.

CATTELL, R. B. 1963. Theory of fluid and crystallized intelligence: A critical experiment. Journal of Educational Psychology 54: 1–22.

CATTELL, R. B. 1966. *The scientific analysis of personality.* Chicago: Aldine.

CECI, S. J., AND LIKER, J. 1986. Academic and nonacademic intelligence: An experimental separation. In Sternberg, R. J., and Wagner, R. K. (Eds.), *Practical intelligence: Nature and origins of competence in everyday life,* pp. 119–42. New York: Cambridge University Press.

CERNOCH, J. M., AND PORTER, R. H. 1985. Recognition of maternal axillary odors by infants. *Child Development* 56:1593–98.

CHAIKEN, S. 1987. The heuristic model of persuasion. In Zanna, M. P.; Olson, J. M.; and Herman, C. P. (Eds.), *Social influence: The Ontario symposium,* vol. 5, pp. 3–40. Hillsdale, N.J.: Erlbaum.

CHAMBERS, D., AND REISBERG, D. 1985. Can mental images be ambiguous? *Journal of Experimental Psychology: Human Perception and Performance* 11:317–28.

CHAPMAN, L. J., AND CHAPMAN, J. P. 1973. *Disordered thought in schizophrenia.* New York: Appleton-Century-Crofts.

CHARNESS, N. 1981. Search in chess: Age and skill differences. *Journal of General Psychology: General* 110:21–38.

CHASE, W. G., AND SIMON, H. A. 1973a. Perception in chess. *Cognitive Psychology* 4:55–81.

CHASE, W. G., AND SIMON, H. A. 1973b. The mind's eye in chess. In Chase, W. G., *Visual information processing.* New York: Academic Press.

CHENEY, D. L., AND SEYFARTH, R. M. 1980. Vocal recognition in free-ranging vervet monkeys. *Animal Behavior* 28:362–67.

CHENEY, D. L., AND SEYFARTH, R. M. 1982. Recognition of individuals within and between groups of free-ranging vervet monkeys. *American Zoologist* 22:519–29.

CHENEY, D. L., AND SEYFARTH, R. M. 1990. *How monkeys see the world.* Chicago: University of Chicago Press.

CHENEY, D. L., AND SEYFARTH, R. M. 1992. The representation of social relations by monkeys. *Cognition* 37:167–96.

CHENEY, D. L., AND WRANGHAM, R. W. 1986. Predation. In Smuts, B. B.; Cheney, D. L.; Seyfarth, R. M.; Wrangham, R. W.; and Struhsaker, T. T., *Primate societies.* Chicago: University of Chicago Press.

CHERRY, E. C. 1953. Some experiments upon the recognition of speech, with one and with two ears. *Journal of the Acoustical Society of America* 25:975–79.

CHESS, S. 1987. Let us consider the roles of temperament and of fortuitous events. Peer commentary on Plomin, R., and Daniels, D. 1987. Why are children from the same family so different from one another? *Behavioral and Brain Sciences* 10:38–39.

CHEVRIER, J., AND DELORME, A. 1983. Depth perception in Pandora's box and size illusion: Evolution with age. *Perception* 12:177–85.

CHI, M. T. H. 1978. Knowledge structures and memory development. In

Siegler, R. S. (Ed.), *Children's thinking: What develops?*, pp. 73–96. Hillsdale, N.J.: Erlbaum.

CHI, M. T. H. 1985. Changing conceptions of sources of memory development. *Human Development* 28:50–56.

CHI, M. T. H.; GLAZER, R.; AND REES, E. 1982. Expertise in problem solving. In R. Sternberg (Ed.), *Advances in the psychology of human intelligence*, vol. 1. Hillsdale, N.J.: Erlbaum.

CHODOFF, P. 1954. A reexamination of some aspects of conversion hysteria. *Psychiatry* 17:75–81.

CHOMSKY, C. 1984. From hand to mouth: A study of speech and language through touch (manuscript, Harvard University).

CHOMSKY, N. 1959. Review of B. F. Skinner. *Verbal learning, Language* 35:26–58.

CHOMSKY, N. 1965. *Aspects of the theory of syntax*. Cambridge, Mass.: MIT Press.

CHOMSKY, N. 1975. *Reflections on language*. New York: Pantheon.

CHOMSKY, N. 1980. *Rules and representations*. New York: Columbia University Press.

CHOMSKY, N. 1986. *Barriers*. Cambridge Mass.: MIT Press.

CHOMSKY, N., AND HALLE, M. 1968. *The sound patterns of English*. New York: Harper & Row.

CHRISTIE, R. 1954. Authoritarianism re-examined. In Christie, R., and Jahoda, M. (Eds.), *Studies in the scope and method of "The authoritarian personality."* New York: Free Press, Macmillan.

CIALDINI, R. B. 1984. *Influence: How and why people agree to do things*. New York: Quill.

CIALDINI, R. B.; PETTY, R. E.; AND CACIOPPO, J. T. 1981. Attitude and attitude change. In Rosenzweig, M. R., and Porter, L. W. (Eds.), *Annual Review of Psychology* 32:357–404.

CIALDINI, R. R.; VINCENT, J. E.; LEWIS, S. K.; CATALAN, J.; WHEELER, D.; AND DARBY, J. 1975. Reciprocal concession procedure for inducing compliance: The door-in-the-face technique. *Journal of Personality and Social Psychology* 31:206–15.

CLARIDGE, D. 1983. The Eysenck psychoticism scale. In Butcher, J. N., and Spielberger, C. (Eds.), *Advances in personality assessment*, vol. 2, pp. 71–114. Hillsdale, N.J.: Erlbaum.

CLARK, D. M. 1986. A cognitive approach to panic. *Behavior Research and Therapy* 24:461–70.

CLARK, D. M. 1988. A cognitive model of panic attacks. In Rachman, S., and Maser, J. D. (Eds.), *Panic: Psychological perspectives*. Hillsdale, N.J.: Erlbaum.

CLARK, E. V. 1973. What's in a word?: On the child's acquisition of semantics in his first language. In Moore, T. E. (Ed.), *Cognitive development and the acquisition of language*. New York: Academic Press.

CLARK, E. V. 1982. The young word-maker: A case study of innovation in the child's lexicon. In Wanner, E., and Gleitman, L. R. (Eds.), *Language acquisition: State of the art*. New York: Cambridge University Press.

CLARK, E. V. 1987. The Principle of contrast: A constraint on acquisition. In MacWhinney, B. (Ed.), *Mechanisms of language acquisition*, Hillsdale, N. J.: Erlbaum.

CLARK, E. V. 1993. *The lexicon in acquisition*. New York: Cambridge University Press.

CLARK, H. H. 1978. Inferring what is meant. In Levelt, W., and Flores d'Arcais, G. (Eds.), *Studies in the perception of language*. Chichester: Wiley.

CLARK, H. H. 1979. Responding to indirect speech acts. *Cognitive Psychology* 11: 430–77.

CLARK, H. H., AND CLARK, E. V. 1977. *Psychology and language: An introduction to psycholinguistics*. New York: Harcourt Brace Jovanovich.

CLARKE, A. C. 1952. An examination of the operation of residual propinquity as a factor in mate selection. *American Sociological Review* 27:17–22.

CLARKE-STEWART, A. 1978. And daddy makes three: The father's impact on mother and young child. *Child Development* 49: 466–78.

CLARKE-STEWART, A. 1989. Infant day care: Malignant or maligned. *American Psychologist* 44: 266–73.

CLARKE-STEWART, A.; PERLMUTTER, M.; and FRIEDMAN, S. 1988. *Lifelong human development*. New York: Wiley.

CLECKLEY, J. 1976. *The mask of sanity*, 5th ed. St. Louis: Mosby.

CLEMENTE, C. D., AND CHASE, M. H. 1973. Neurological substrates of aggressive behavior. *Annual Review of Physiology* 35:329–56.

COBB, S. 1941. *Foundations of neuropsychiatry*. Baltimore: Williams and Wilkins.

COFFMAN, C. E. 1985. Review of Kaufman's Assessment Battery for Children. *Ninth Mental Measurements Yearbook*, vol. 1. pp. 771–73.

COHEN, D. B., AND WOLFE, G. 1973. Dream recall and repression: Evidence for an alternative hypothesis. *Journal of Consulting and Clinical Psychology* 41:349–55.

COHEN, H. 1972. Active (REM) sleep deprivation. In Chase, M. H. (Ed.), *The sleeping brain: Perspectives in the brain sciences*, vol. 1, pp. 343–47. Los Angeles: Brain Research Institute, University of California.

COHEN, N. J., AND SQUIRE, L. R. 1980. Preserved learning and retention of pattern-analyzing skill in amnesia: Dissociation of knowing how and knowing what. *Science* 210:207–10.

COHEN, R. A. 1975. Manic-depressive illness. In Freedman, A. M.; Kaplan, H. I.; and Sadock, B. J. (Eds.), *Comprehensive textbook of psychiatry—II*, vol. 1, pp. 1012–24. Baltimore: Williams & Wilkins.

COHEN, Y. A. 1953. A study of interpersonal relations in a Jamaican community. Unpublished doctoral dissertation, Yale University.

COLARUSSO, C. A., AND NEMIROFF, R. A. 1981. *Adult development: A new dimension in psychodynamic theory and practice*. New York: Plenum Press.

COLBY, A., AND KOHLBERG, L. 1986. *The measurement of moral judgment*. New York: Cambridge University Press.

COLBY, A.; KOHLBERG, L.; GIBBS, J.; AND LIEBERMAN, M. 1983. A longitudinal study of moral judgment. *Monographs of the Society for Research in Child Development* 48 (1, Serial No. 200).

COLE, J. O., AND DAVIS, J. M. 1975. Antidepressant drugs. In Freedman, A. M.; Kaplan, H. I.; and Sadock, B. J. (Eds.), *Comprehensive textbook of psychiatry*, vol. 2. pp. 1941–56. Baltimore: Williams & Wilkins.

COLE, M. 1975. An ethnographic psychology of cognition. In Brislin, R. W.; Bochner, S.; and Lonner, W. J. (Eds.), *Cross-cultural perspectives on learning*. New York: Wiley.

COLE, M., AND COLE, S. R. 1993. *The development of children*, 2nd ed. New York: Scientific American Books.

COLE, M.; GAY, J.; GLICK, J. A.; AND SHARP, D. W. 1971. *The cultural context of learning and thinking*. New York: Basic Books.

COLEMAN, J. C. 1972. *Abnormal psychology and modern life*, 4th ed. Glenview, Ill.: Scott, Foresman.

COLEMAN, J. S.; CAMPBELL, E. Q.; HOBSON, C. J.; McPARTLAND, J.; MOOD, A.; WEINFELD, F. D.; AND YORK, R. L. 1966. *Equality of educational opportunity*. Washington, D.C.: U.S. Government Printing Office.

COLLIER, G. 1985. *Emotional expression*. Hillsdale, N.J.: Erlbaum.

COLLINS, A. M., AND LOFTUS, E. F. 1975. A spreading activation theory of semantic processing. *Psychological Review* 82:407–28.

COLLINS, A. M., AND QUILLIAN, M. R. 1969. Retrieval time from semantic memory. *Journal of Verbal Learning and Verbal Behavior* 8:240–47.

COLLIS, G. 1975. The integration of gaze and vocal behavior in the mother-infant dyad. Paper presented at Third International Child Language Symposium, London.

COLWILL, R. M., AND RESCORLA, R. A. 1985. Postconditioning devaluation of a reinforcer affects instrumental responding. *Journal of Experimental Psychology: Animal Behavior Processes* 11:120–32.

COMRIE, B. 1987. Introduction. In Comrie, B. (Ed.), *The world's major languages*. New York: Oxford University Press.

CONEL, J. L. 1939. *The postnatal development of the human cortex*, vol. 1. Cambridge, Mass.: Harvard University Press.

CONEL, J. L. 1947. *The postnatal development of the human cortex*, vol. 3. Cambridge, Mass.: Harvard University Press.

CONEL, J. L. 1955. *The postnatal development of the human cortex*, vol. 5. Cambridge, Mass.: Harvard University Press.

CONRAD, C. 1972. Cognitive economy in semantic memory. *Journal of Experimental Psychology* 92:149–54.

CONWAY, M. A.; COHEN, G.; AND STANHOPE, N. 1991. On the very long-term retention of knowledge acquired through formal education: Twelve years of cognitive psychology. *Journal of Experimental Psychology (General)* 120:395–409.

COOK, M., AND BIRCH, R. 1984. Infant perception of the shapes of tilted plane forms. *Infant Behavior and Development* 7:389–402.

COOK, M., AND MINEKA, S. 1989. Observational conditioning of fear to fear-relevant versus fear-irrelevant stimuli in rhesus monkeys. *Journal of Abnormal Psychology* 98:448–59.

COOLEY, C. H. 1902. *Human nature and the social order.* New York: Scribner's.

COOPER, J., AND FAZIO, R. H. 1984. A new look at dissonance theory. In Berkowitz, L. (Ed.), *Advances in experimental social psychology,* vol. 17. New York: Academic Press.

COOPER, J.; ZANNA, M. P.; AND GOETHALS, G. R. 1974. Mistreatment of an esteemed other as a consequence affecting dissonance reduction. *Journal of Experimental Social Psychology* 10:224–33.

COOPER, L. A., AND SHEPARD, R. N. 1973. The time required to prepare for a rotated stimulus. *Memory and Cognition* 1:246–50.

COREN, S., AND GIRGUS, J. S. 1978. *Seeing is deceiving: The psychology of visual illusions.* Hillsdale, N.J.: Erlbaum.

COREN, S.; PORAC, C.; AND WARD, L. M. 1978, 1984. *Sensation and perception.* New York: Academic Press.

COREN, S., AND WARD, L. M. 1989. *Sensation and perception,* 3rd ed. San Diego, Calif.: Harcourt Brace Jovanovich.

CORKIN, S. 1965. Tactually-guided maze-learning in man: Effects of unilateral cortical excisions and bilateral hippocampal lesions. *Neuropsychologia* 3:339–51.

CORKIN, S. 1984. Lasting consequences of bilateral medial temporal lobectomy: Clinical course and experimental findings in H. M. *Semin. Neurology* 4:249–59.

CORNSWEET, T. M. 1970. *Visual perception.* New York: Academic Press.

CORY, T. L.; ORMISTON, D. W.; SIMMEL, E.; and DAINOFF, M. 1975. Predicting the frequency of dream recall. *Journal of Abnormal Psychology* 84:261–66.

COSTA, E. 1985. Benzodiazepine-GABA interactions: A model to investigate the neurobiology of anxiety. In Tuma, A. H., and Maser, J. D. (Eds.), *Anxiety and the anxiety disorders.* Hillsdale, N.J.: Erlbaum.

COSTA, P. T., JR.; MCCRAE, R. R.; AND ARENBERG, D. 1980. Enduring dispositions in adult males. *Journal of Personality and Social Psychology* 38:793–800.

COUVILLON, P., AND BITTERMAN, M. E. 1980. Some phenomena of associative conditioning in honeybees. *Journal of comparative and physiological psychology* 94:878–85.

COWEY, A., AND STOERIG, P. 1992. Reflections on blindsight. In Milner, A. D., and Rugg, M. D. (Eds.), *The neuropsychology of consciousness,* pp. 11–38. San Diego, Calif.: Academic Press.

COWLES, J. T. 1937. Food-tokens as incentives for learning by chimpanzees. *Comparative Psychology Monographs* 14 (5, Serial No. 71).

COYLE, J. T.; PRICE, D.; AND DELONG, M. R. 1983. Alzheimer's disease: A disorder of cholinergic innervation. *Science* 219:1184–90.

COYNE, J. C., AND GOTLIB, I. H. 1983. The role of cognition in depression: A critical appraisal. *Psychological Bulletin* 94:472–505.

CRAIK, F. I. M., AND LOCKHART, R. S. 1972. Levels of processing: A framework for memory research. *Journal of Verbal Learning and Verbal Behavior* 11:671–84.

CRAIK, F. I. M., AND TULVING, E. 1975. Depth of processing and the retention of words in episodic memory. *Journal of Experimental Psychology: General* 104:268–94.

CRAIK, F. I. M., AND WATKINS, M. J. 1973. The role of rehearsal in short-term memory. *Journal of Verbal Learning and Verbal Behavior* 12:599–607.

CRAIN, S., AND FODOR, J. D. 1985. How can grammars help parsers? In Dowty, D.; Kartunnen, L.; and Zwicky, A. (Eds.), *Natural language parsing: Psychological, computational, and theoretical perspectives.* Cambridge: Cambridge University Press.

CRAIN, S., AND NAKAYAMA, M. 1986. Structure dependence in children's language. *Language* 62:522–43.

CRAIN, S., AND STEEDMAN, M. 1985. On not being led up the garden path: The use of context by the psychological syntax parser. In Dowty, D.; Kartunnen, L.; and Zwicky, A. (Eds), *Natural language parsing.* Cambridge: Cambridge University Press.

CRONBACH, L. J. 1970a. *Essentials of psychology testing,* 3rd ed. New York: Harper & Row.

CRONBACH, L. J. 1970b. Test validation. In Thorndike, R. L. (Ed.), *Educational measurement.* Washington, D.C.: American Council on Education.

CRONBACH, L. J. 1975. Beyond the two disciplines of scientific psychology. *American Psychologist* 30:116–27.

CRONBACH, L. J. 1984. *Essentials of psychological testing,* 4th ed. New York: Harper & Row.

CRONBACH, L. J., AND MEEHL, P. E. 1955. Construct validity in psychological tests. *Psychological Bulletin* 52:281–302.

CROOK, C. 1987. Taste and olfaction. In Salapatek, P., and Cohen, L. (Eds.), *Handbook of infant perception: From perception to cognition,* vol. 2, pp. 237–64. Orlando, Fla.: Academic Press.

CROW, T. J. 1980. Molecular pathology of schizophrenia: More than one disease process? *British Medical Journal* 280:66–68.

CROW, T. J. 1982. Two dimensions of pathology in schizophrenia: Dopaminergic and non-dopaminergic. *Psychopharmacology Bulletin* 18:22–29.

CROW, T. J. 1985. The two-syndrome concept: Origins and current status. *Schizophrenia Bulletin* 11:471–86.

CROWDER, R. G. 1976. *Principles of learning and memory.* Hillsdale, N.J.: Erlbaum.

CROWDER, R. G. 1982. The demise of short-term memory. *Acta Psychologica* 50:291–323.

CROWDER, R. G. 1985a. Basic theoretical concepts in human learning and cognition. In Nillson, L.-G., and Archer, T. (Eds.), *Perspectives on learning and memory.* Hillsdale, N.J.: Erlbaum.

CROWDER, R. G. 1985b. On access and the forms of memory. In Weinberger, N. M.; McGaugh, J. L.; and Lynch, G. (Eds.), *Memory systems of the brain,* pp. 442–51. New York: Guilford Press.

CRUTCHFIELD, R. S. 1955. Conformity and character. *American Psychologist* 10:191–99.

CUNNINGHAM, M. R. 1986. Measuring the physical in physical attraction: Quasi-experiments on the sociobiology of female beauty. *Journal of Personality and Social Psychology* 50:925–35.

CURTISS, S. 1977. *Genie: A linguistic study of a modern-day "wild child."* New York: Academic Press.

CUTLER, A. 1994. Segmentation problems, rhythmic solutions. In Gleitman, L. R., and Landau, B. (Eds.), Lexical acquisition, (Special Issue) *Lingua* 92:81–104.

CUTTING, J. 1986. Outcome in schizophrenia: Overview. In Kerr, T. A., and Snaith, R. P. (Eds.), *Contemporary issues in schizophrenia,* pp. 436–40. Washington, DC: American Psychiatric Press.

DALE, A. J. D. 1975. Organic brain syndromes associated with infections. In Freedman, A. M.; Kaplan, H. I.; and Sadock, B. J. (Eds.), *Comprehensive textbook of psychiatry—II,* vol. 1, pp. 1121–30. Baltimore: Williams & Wilkins.

DARLEY, J. M., AND BATSON, C. D. 1973. "From Jerusalem to Jericho": A study of situational and dispositional variables in helping behavior. *Journal of Personality and Social Psychology* 27:100–108.

DARLEY, J., AND LATANÉ, B. 1968. Bystander intervention in emergencies: Diffusion of responsibility. *Journal of Personality and Social Psychology* 10:202–14.

DARNTON, R. 1984. The meaning of Mother Goose. *New York Review of Books,* February 2, 1984, 41–47.

DARWIN, C. 1872a. *The origin of species.* New York: Macmillan, 6th ed., 1962.

DARWIN, C. 1872b. *The expression of the emotions in man and animals.* London: Appleton.

DARWIN, C. 1877. A biological sketch of a young child. *Kosmos* 1:367–76 (as cited in Bornstein, M. H. 1978. Chromatic vision in infancy. In Reese, H., and Lipsitt, L. (Eds.), *Advances in child development and behavior,* vol. 12. New York: Academic Press).

DASSER, V. 1988. A social concept in Java monkeys. *Animal Behaviour* 36(1): 225–30.

DAVIDSON, A. R., AND JACCARD, J. J. 1979. Variables that moderate the attitude-behavior relation: Results of a longitudinal survey. *Journal of Personality and Social Psychology* 37:1364–76.

DAVIDSON, J. M. 1969. Hormonal control of sexual behavior in adult rats. In Rasp, G. (Ed.), *Advances in bioscience,* vol. 1, pp. 119–69. New York: Pergamon.

DAVIDSON, J. M. 1986. Androgen replacement therapy in a wider context: Clinical and basic aspects. In Dennerstein and Fraser (Eds.), *Hormones and behavior,* pp. 433–40. Amsterdam: International Society of Psychosomatic Obstetrics and Gynecology, Elsevier.

DAVIES, K. G., AND WEEKS, R. D. 1993. Temporal lobectomy for intractable epilepsy: Experience with 58 cases over 21 years. *British Journal of Neurosurgery* 7:23–33.

DAVIS, D. E. 1964. The physiological analysis of aggressive behavior. In Etkin, W. (Ed.), *Social behavior and organization among vertebrates.* Chicago: University of Chicago Press.

DAVIS, J. M. 1974. A two-factor theory of schizophrenia. *Journal of Psychiatric Research* 11:25–30.

DAVIS, J. M. 1978. Dopamine theory of schizophrenia: A two-factor theory. In Wynne, L. C.; Cromwell, R. L.; and Matthysse, S. (Eds.), *The nature of schizophrenia.* New York: Wiley.

DAVIS, J. M. 1985a. Antipsychotic drugs. In Kaplan, H. I., and Sadock, J. (Eds.), *Comprehensive textbook of psychiatry,* 4th ed., pp. 1481–1513. Baltimore: Williams & Wilkins.

DAVIS, J. M. 1985b. Antidepressant drugs. In Kaplan, H. I., and Sadock, J. (Eds.), *Comprehensive textbook of psychiatry,* 4th ed., pp. 1513–37, Baltimore: Williams & Wilkins.

DAVIS, K. 1947. Final note on a case of extreme social isolation. *American Journal of Sociology* 52:432–37.

DAVISON, G. C. 1968. Systematic desensitization as a counter-conditioning process. *Journal of Abnormal Psychology* 73:84–90.

DAWES, R. W. 1980. Social Dilemmas. *Annual Review of Psychology* 31:169–93.

DAY, R. H., AND MCKENZIE, B. E. 1981. Infant perception of the invariant size of approaching and receding objects. *Developmental Psychology* 17:670–77.

DAY, R. H.; STUART, G. W.; AND DICKINSON, R. G. 1980. Size constancy does not fail below half a degree. *Perception and Psychophysics* 28:263–65.

DECASPER, A. J., AND FIFER, W. P. 1980. Of human bonding: Newborns prefer their mothers' voices. *Science* 208:1174–76.

DEECKE, L.; SCHEID, P.; AND KORNHUBER, H. H. 1968. Distribution of readiness potential, pre-motion positivity, and motor potential of the human cerebral cortex preceding voluntary finger movements. *Experimental Brain Research* 7:158–68.

DE GROOT, A. D. 1965. *Thought and choice in chess.* The Hague: Mouton.

DELIS, D. C.; KRAMER, J.; FREELAND, J.; AND KAPLAN, E. 1988. Integrating clinical assessment with cognitive science: Construct validation of the California Verbal Learning Test. *Journal of Consulting and Clinical Psychology* 56:123–30.

DELIS, D. C.; KRAMER, J.; FRIDLUND, A. J.; AND KAPLAN, E. 1990. A cognitive science approach to neuropsychological assessment. In McReynolds, R.; Rosen, J. C.; and Chelune, G. (Eds.), *Advances in psychological measurement,* vol. 7, pp. 101–32. New York: Plenum.

DELL, G. S. 1986. A spreading activation theory of retrieval in sentence-production. *Psychological Review* 93:283–321.

DEMBROSKI, T. M.; MACDOUGALL, J. M.; COSTA, P. T.; AND GRANDITS, G. A. 1989. Components of hostility as predictors of sudden death and myocardial infarction in the Multiple Risk Factor Intervention Trial. *Psychosomatic Medicine* 51:514–22.

DEMENT, W. C. 1974. *Some must watch while some must sleep.* San Francisco: Freeman.

DEMENT, W. C., AND KLEITMAN, N. 1957. The relation of eye movements during sleep to dream activity: An objective method for the study of dreaming. *Journal of Experimental Psychology* 53:339–46.

DEMENT, W. C., AND WOLPERT, E. A. 1958. The relationship of eye-movements, body motility, and external stimuli to dream content. *Journal of Experimental Psychology* 55:543–53.

DENNETT, D. 1978. *Brainstorms: Philosophical essays on mind and psychology.* Montgomery, Vt.: Bradford Books.

DENNET, D. C. 1991. *Consciousness explained.* Boston: Little, Brown.

DENNIS, W. 1940. Does culture appreciably affect patterns of infant behavior? *Journal of Social Psychology* 12:305–17.

DE ROUGEMONT, D. 1940. *Love in the Western world.* New York: Harcourt Brace Jovanovich.

DESCARTES, R. 1662. *Trait de l'homme.* Haldane, E. S, and Ross, G. R. T (trans.). Cambridge, Eng.: Cambridge University Press.

DESIMONE, R.; ALBRIGHT, T. D.; GROSS, C. G.; AND BRUCE, C. 1984. Stimulus-selective properties of inferior temporal neurons in the macaque. *The Journal of Neuroscience* 4:2051–62.

DETTERMAN, D. K. 1987. What does reaction time tell us about intelligence? In Vernon, P. A. (Ed.), *Speed of information processing and intelligence.* Norwood, N.J.: Ablex.

DE VALOIS, R. L. 1965. Behavioral and electrophysiological studies of primate vision. In Neff, W. D. (Ed.), *Contributions of sensory physiology,* vol. 1. New York: Academic Press.

DE VALOIS, R. L., AND DE VALOIS, K. K. 1975. Neural coding of color. In Carterette, E. C., and Friedman, M. P. (Eds.), *Handbook of perception,* vol. 5, pp. 117–62. New York: Academic Press.

DE VILLIERS, J. G. 1980. The process of rule learning in child speech: A new look. In Nelson, K. (Ed.), *Child language,* vol. 2. New York: Gardner Press.

DE VILLIERS, J. G., AND DE VILLIERS, P. A. 1973. Development of the use of word order in comprehension. *Journal of Psycholinguistic Research* 2:331–41.

DEUTSCH, J. A.; PUERTO, A.; AND WANG, M. L. 1978. The stomach signals satiety. *Science* 201:165–67.

DI VESTA, F. J.; INGERSOLL, G.; AND SUNSHINE, P. 1971. A factor analysis of imagery tests. *Journal of Verbal Learning and Verbal Behavior* 10:471–79.

DIAMOND, A. 1988. The abilities and neural mechanisms underlying A-not-B performance. *Child Development* 59:523–27.

DIAMOND, A. 1989. Developmental progression in human infants and infant monkeys, and the neural bases of A-not-B and delayed response performance. Paper presented at a meeting on "The development and neural bases of higher cognitive functions," Philadelphia, Pa., May 20–24, 1989.

DIAMOND, A., AND GOLDMAN-RAKIC, P. S. 1989. Comparative development of human infants and rhesus monkeys on Piaget's A-not-B task: Evidence for dependence on dorsolateral prefrontal cortex. *Experimental Brain Research* 74:24–40.

DIAMOND, R., AND ROZIN, P. 1984. Activation of existing memories in the amnesic syndrome. *Journal of Abnormal Psychology* 93:98–105.

DICKINSON, A. 1987. Animal conditioning and learning theory. In Eysenck, H. J., and Martin, I. (Eds.), *Theoretical Foundations of Behavior Theory.* New York: Plenum.

DICKS, H. V. 1972. *Licensed mass murder: A sociopsychological study of some S. S. killers.* New York: Basic Books.

DICKSON, D. H., AND KELLY, I. W. 1985. The "Barnum effect" in personality assessment: A review of the literature. *Psychological Reports* 57:367–82.

DIENER, E. 1979. Deindividuation: The absence of self-awareness and self-regulation in group members. In Paulus, P. (Ed.), *The psychology of group influence,* pp. 209–42. Hillsdale, N.J.: Erlbaum.

DIENER, E.; FRASER, S. C.; BEAMAN, A. L.; AND KELEM, Z. R. T. 1976. Effects of deindividuation variables on stealing among Halloween trick-or-treaters. *Journal of Personality and Social Psychology* 5:143–55.

DILGER, W. C. 1962. The behavior of lovebirds. *Scientific American* 206:88–98.

DODD, B. 1979. Lip reading in infants: Attention to speech presented in- and out-of-synchrony. *Cognitive Psychology* 11:478–84.

DOI, T. 1973. *The anatomy of dependence.* Tokyo: Kodansha.

DOLGER, H., AND SEEMAN, B. 1985. *How to live with diabetes,* 5th ed. New York: Norton.

DOMINGUEZ, R. A. 1992. Serotonergic antidepressants and their efficacy in obsessive-compulsive disorder. *Journal of Clinical Psychiatry* 53:56–59.

DOMJAN, M. 1980. Ingestional aversion learning: Unique and general processes. *Advances in the Study of Behavior* 11:275–336.

DOMJAN, M. 1983. Biological constraints on instrumental and classical conditioning: Implications for general process theory. In Bower, G. H. (Ed.), *The psychology of learning and motivation,* vol. 17. New York: Academic Press.

DORNBUSCH, S. M.; RITTER, P. L.; LEIDERMAN, P. H.; AND ROBERTS, D. F. 1987. The relation of parenting style to adolescent school performance. Schools and development, *Child Development* (Special Issue) 58: 1244–57.

DOUVAN, E., AND ADELSON, J. 1958. The psychodynamics of social mobility in adolescent boys. *Journal of Abnormal and Social Psychology* 56:31–44.

DRISCOLL, R.; DAVIS, K. E.; AND LIPITZ. 1972. Parental interference and romantic love: The Romeo and Juliet effect. *Journal of Personality and Social Psychology* 24:1–10.

DUDA, R. O., AND SHORTLIFFE, E. H. 1983. Expert systems research. *Science* 220:261–68.

DUNCKER, K. 1929. Über induzierte Bewegung. *Psychologische Forschung* 12:180–259.

DUNCKER, K. 1945. On problem solving. *Psychological Monographs* (Whole No. 270):1–113.

DURANT, W., AND DURANT, A. 1967. *The story of civilization: Part X. Rousseau and Revolution.* New York: Simon and Schuster.

DUTTON, D. G., AND ARON, A. P. 1974. Some evidence for heightened sexual attraction under conditions of high anxiety. *Journal of Personality and Social Psychology* 30:510–17.

DYER, F. C., AND GOULD, J. L. 1983. Honey bee orientation: A backup system for cloudy days. *Science* 214:1041–1042.

EAGLE, M. N., and Wolitsky, D. L. 1992. Psychoanalytic theories of psychotherapy. In Freedheim, D. K. (Ed.), *History of psychotherapy.* Washington, D.C.: American Psychological Association.

EAGLY, A. H., AND CHAIKIN, S. 1984. Cognitive theories of persuasion. In Berkowitz, L. (Ed.), *Advances in experimental social psychology,* vol. 17. New York: Academic Press.

EBBINGHAUS, H. 1885. *Memory.* New York: Teacher's College, Columbia University, 1913. (Reprint edition, New York: Dover, 1964.)

ECCLES, J. C. 1973. *The understanding of the brain.* New York: McGraw-Hill.

ECCLES, J. C. 1982. The synapse: From electrical to chemical transmission. *Annual Review of Neuroscience* 5:325–39.

EDGERTON, R. B. 1979. *Mental retardation.* Cambridge, Mass.: Harvard University Press.

EDMONDS, J. M., ed. and trans. 1929. *The characters of Theophrastus.* Cambridge, Mass.: Harvard University Press.

EFRON, R. 1990. *The decline and fall of hemispheric specialization.* Hillsdale, N.J.: Erlbaum.

EGETH, H.; JONIDES, J.; AND WALL, S. 1972. Parallel processing of multi-element displays. *Cognitive Psychology* 3:674–98.

EGGER, M. D., AND FLYNN, J. P. 1963. Effect of electrical stimulation of the amygdala on hypothalamically elicited behavior in cats. *Journal of Neurophysiology* 26:705–20.

EHRHARDT, A. A. 1984. Gender differences: A biological perspective. In Dienstbier, R. A., and Sonderegger, T. B. (Eds.), *Nebraska Symposium on Motivation,* pp. 37–58. Lincoln, Neb.: University of Nebraska.

EICH, J. E. 1980. The cue-dependent nature of state-dependent retrieval. *Memory and Cognition* 8:157–73.

EIKELBOOM, R., AND STEWART, J. 1982. Conditioning of drug-induced physiological responses. *Psychological Review* 89:507–28.

EIMAS, P. D.; SIQUELAND, E. R.; JUSCZYK, P.; AND VIGORITO, J. 1971. Speech perception in infants. *Science* 171:303–306.

EKMAN, P. 1971. Universals and cultural differences in facial expression. In Cole, J. K. (Ed.), *Nebraska Symposium on Motivation,* pp. 207–84. Lincoln, Neb.: University of Nebraska Press.

EKMAN, P. 1973. Cross-cultural studies of facial expression. In Ekman, P. (Ed.), *Darwin and facial expression,* pp. 169–222. New York: Academic Press.

EKMAN, P. 1977. Biological and cultural contributions to body and facial movement. In Blacking, J. (Ed.), *The anthropology of the body,* A. S. A. Monograph 15. London: Academic Press.

EKMAN, P. 1980. *The face of man: Expression of universal emotions in a New Guinea village.* New York: Garland STPM Press.

EKMAN, P. 1984. Expression and the nature of emotion. In Elkman, P., and Scherer, K. (Eds.), *Approaches to emotion,* pp. 319–43. Hillsdale, N.J.: Erlbaum.

EKMAN, P. 1985. *Telling lies.* New York: Norton.

EKMAN, P., AND FRIESEN, W. V. 1975. *Unmasking the face.* Englewood Cliffs, N.J.: Prentice-Hall.

EKMAN, P., AND FRIESEN, W. V. 1986. A new pan-cultural facial expression of emotion. *Motivation and Emotion* 10:159–68.

EKMAN, P.; FRIESEN, W. V.; AND O'SULLIVAN, M. 1988. Smiles when lying. *Journal of Personality and Social Psychology* 54: 414–20.

EKMAN, P., AND OSTER, H. 1979. Facial expression of emotion. *Annual Review of Psychology* 30:527–54.

EKSTRAND, B. R. 1972. To sleep, perchance to dream (about why we forget) In Duncan, C. P.; Sechrest, L.; and Melton, A. W. (Eds.), *Human memory: Festschrift for Benton J. Underwood,* pp. 59–82. New York: Appleton-Century-Crofts.

EKSTRAND, B. R.; BARRETT, T. R.; WEST, J. M.; AND MAIER, W. G. 1977. The effect of sleep on human memory. In Drucker-Colin, R., and McGaugh, J. L. (Eds.), *Neurobiology of sleep and memory.* New York: Academic Press.

ELDER, G. H., JR. 1980. Adolescence in historical perspective. In Adelson, J. (Ed.), *Handbook of adolescent psychology.* New York: Wiley.

ELKIN, I.; SHEA, M. T.; WATKINS, J. T.; IMBER, S. D.; SOTSKY, S. M.; COLLINS, J. S.; GLASS, D. R.; PILKONIS, P. A.; LEBER, W. R.; DOCHERTY, J. P.; FEISTER, S. J.; AND PARLOFF, M. B. 1989. National Institute of Mental Health treatment of depression collaborative research program: General effectiveness of treatments. *Archives of General Psychiatry* 46:971–82.

ELLENBERGER, H. F. 1970. *The discovery of the unconscious.* New York: Basic Books.

ELLIS, A. 1962. *Reason and emotion in psychotherapy.* Secaucus, N.J.: Lyle Stuart.

ELLIS, L.; AND AMES, M. A. 1987. Neurohormonal functioning and sexual orientation: A theory of homosexuality-heterosexuality. *Psychological Bulletin* 101:233–58.

ELMS, A. C., AND MILGRAM, S. 1966. Personality characteristics associated with obedience and defiance toward authoritative command. *Journal of Experimental Research in Personality* 1:282–89.

EMMELKAMP, P. M. G. 1986. Behavior therapy with adults. In Garfied, S. L., and Bergin, A. E. (Eds.), *Handbook of psychotherapy and behavior change,* 3rd ed. New York: Wiley.

EMMERICH, W. 1966. Continuity and stability in early social development, II. Teacher ratings. *Child Development* 37:17–27.

ENDLER, N. S. 1982. Interactionism comes of age. In Zanna, M. P.;

Higgins, E. T.; and Herman, C. P. (Eds.), *Consistency in social behavior. The Ontario Symposium*, vol. 2, Hillsdale, N.J.: Erlbaum.

ENDLER, N. S., AND HUNT, J. M. 1969. Generalization of contributions from sources of variance in the S-R inventories of anxiousness. *Journal of Personality* 37:1–24.

EPSTEIN, A. N.; FITZSIMONS, J. T.; AND ROLLS, B. J. 1970. Drinking induced by injection of angiotensin into the brain of the rat. *Journal of Physiology* 210:457–74.

EPSTEIN, S. 1979. The stability of behavior: I. On predicting most of the people much of the time. *Journal of Personality and Social Psychology* 37:1097–1126.

EPSTEIN, S. 1980. The stability of behavior. II. Implications for psychological reasearch. *American Psychologist* 35:790–806.

EPSTEIN, S. 1983. The stability of confusion: A reply to Mischel and Peak. *Psychological Review* 90:179–84.

EPSTEIN, W. 1961. The influence of syntactical structure on learning. *American Journal of Psychology* 74:80–85.

ERDELYI, M. H. 1985. *Psychoanalysis: Freud's cognitive psychology.* New York: Freeman.

ERDELYI, M. H., AND GOLDBERG, B. 1979. Let's not sweep repression under the rug. In Kihlstrom, J. F., and Evans, F. J. (Eds.), *Functional disorders of memory,* pp. 355–402. Hillsdale, N.J.: Erlbaum.

ERICSSON, K. A.; CHASE, W. G.; AND FALOON, S. 1980. Acquisition of a memory skill. *Science* 208:1181–82.

ERIKSEN, C. W., AND HOFFMAN, J. E. 1972. Temporal and spatial characteristics of selective encoding from multielement displays. *Perception and Psychophysics* 12:201–204.

ERIKSEN, C. W., AND PIERCE, J. 1968. Defense mechanisms. In Borgatta, E. F., and Lambert, W. W. (Eds.), *Handbook of personality theory and research,* pp. 1007–40. Chicago: Rand McNally.

ERIKSON, E. H. 1963. *Childhood and society.* New York: Norton.

ERICKSON, E. H. 1974. *Dimensions of a new identity: The Jefferson lectures in the humanities.* New York: Norton.

ERON, L. D. 1950. A normative study of the thematic apperception test. *Psychological Monographs* 64 (Whole No. 315).

ERVIN, S. 1964. Imitation and structural change in children's language. In Lenneberg, E. H. (Ed.), *New directions in the study of language.* Cambridge, Mass.: MIT Press.

ESSOCK-VITALE, S. M., AND McGUIRE, M. T. 1985. Women's lives viewed from an evolutionary perspective: II. Patterns of helping. *Ethology and Sociobiology* 6:155–73.

ESTES, W. K., AND SKINNER, B. F. 1941. Some quantitative properties of anxiety. *Journal of Experimental Psychology* 29:390–400

ETKIN, W. 1964. Reproductive behaviors. In Etkin, W. (Ed.), *Social behavior and organization among vertebrates,* pp. 75–116. Chicago: University of Chicago Press.

EVANS, F. J. 1974. The placebo response in pain reduction. *Advances in Neurology,* vol. 4, pp. 289–96. New York: Raven Press.

EXNER, J. E. 1974. The Rorschach system. New York: Grune and Stratton.

EXNER, J. E. 1978. *A comprehensive system: Current research and advanced interpretation,* vol. 2. New York: Wiley Interscience.

EXNER, J. E., AND CLARK, B. 1978. The Rorschach. In Wolman, B. B. *Clinical diagnosis of mental disorders.* New York: Plenum.

EYFERTH, K. 1961. Leistungen verschiedener Gruppen von Besatzungskindern im Hamburg-Wechsler Intelligenz Test für Kinder (HAWIK). *Archiv für die gesamte Psychologie* 113:222–41.

EYSENCK, H. J. 1961. The effects of psychotherapy. In Eysenck, H. J. (Ed.), *Handbook of abnormal psychology,* pp. 697–725. New York: Basic Books.

EYSENCK, H. J., AND EYSENCK, S. B. G. 1975. *Psychoticism as a dimension of personality.* London: Hodder and Stoughton.

EYSENCK, H. J., AND EYSENCK, S. B. G. 1983. Recent advances: The cross-cultural study of personality. In Butcher, J. N., and Spielberger, C. D. (Eds.), *Advances in personality assessment,* vol. 2, pp. 41–72. Hillsdale, N.J.: Erlbaum.

EYSENCK, H. J. VERSUS KAMIN, L. 1981. *The intelligence controversy.* New York: Wiley.

EYSENCK, H. J., AND RACHMAN, S. 1965. *The causes and cures of neurosis.* San Diego, Calif.: Robert E. Knapp.

FAGAN, J. F. 1976. Infants' recognition of invariant features of faces. *Child Development* 47:627–38.

FAGAN, J. F. 1984. The intelligent infant: Theoretical implications *Intelligence* 8:1–9.

FAGAN, J. F. 1985. A new look at infant intelligence. In Detterman, D. K. (Ed.), *Current topics in human intelligence. Vol. 1: Research Methodology.* Norwood, N.J.: Ablex.

FALLON, A. E., AND ROZIN, P. 1985. Sex differences in perceptions of desirable body shape. *Journal of Abnormal Psychology* 94:102–105.

FANCHER, R. E. 1987. *The intelligence men: Makers of the IQ controversy.* New York: Norton.

FANT, L. G. 1972. *Ameslan: An introduction to American Sign Language.* Silver Springs, Md.: National Association of the Deaf.

FARAH, M. 1990. *Visual agnosia.* Cambridge, Mass.: MIT Press.

FARIS, R. E. L., AND DUNHAM, H. W. 1939. *Mental disorders in urban areas.* Chicago: University of Chicago Press.

FEARING, F. 1930. *Reflex action: A study in the history of physiological psychology.* Baltimore: Williams & Wilkins.

FEDER, H. H. 1984. Hormones and sexual behavior. *Annual Review of Psychology* 35:165–200.

FEINGOLD, A. 1988. Matching for attractiveness in romantic partners and same-sex friends: A meta-analysis and theoretical critique. *Psychological Bulletin* 104: 226–32.

FELDMAN, H.; GOLDIN-MEADOW, S.; AND GLEITMAN, L. R. 1978. Beyond Herodotus: The creation of language by linguistically deprived deaf children. In Lock, A. (Ed.), *Action, gesture, and symbol: The emergence of language.* London: Academic Press.

FELIPE, N. J., AND SOMMER, R. 1966. Invasions of personal space. *Social Problems* 14:206–14.

FERNALD, A. 1984. The perceptual and affective salience of mothers' speech to infants. In Feagans, L.; Garvey, C.; and Golinkoff, R. (Eds.), *The origins and growth of communication.* New Brunswick: Ablex.

FERNALD, A. 1992. Human maternal vocalizations to infants as biologically relevant signals: An evolutionary perspective. In Barkow, J. H.; Cosmides, L.; and Tooby J. (Eds.), *The adapted mind: Evolutionary psychology and the generation of culture.* New York: Oxford University Press.

FERNALD, A., AND KUHL, P. 1987. Acoustic determinants of infant preference for motherese speech. *Infant Behavior and Development* 10:279–93.

FERNALD, A., AND SIMON, T. 1984. Expanded intonation contours in mothers' speech to newborns. *Developmental Psychology* 20:104–13.

FERNALD, A.; TAESCHNER, T.: DUNN, J.; PAPOUSEK, M.; DE BOYSSON-BARDIES, B.; AND FUKUI, I. 1989. A cross-linguistic study of prosodic modifications in mothers' and fathers' speech to preverbal infants. *Journal of Child Language* 16(3):477–502.

FERSTER, C. B., AND SKINNER, B. F. 1957. *Schedules of reinforcement.* New York: Appleton-Century-Crofts.

FERSTER, D. 1981. A comparison of binocular depth mechanisms in areas 17 and 18 of the cat visual cortex. *Journal of Physiology* 311:623–55.

FESHBACH, S. 1970. Aggression. In Mussen, P. H. (Ed.), *Carmichael's manual of child psychology,* 3rd ed., pp. 159–260. New York: Wiley.

FESTINGER, L. 1954. A theory of social comparison processes. *Human Relations* 7:117–40.

FESTINGER, L. 1957. *A theory of cognitive dissonance.* Evanston, Ill.: Row, Peterson.

FESTINGER, L., AND CARLSMITH, J. M. 1959. Cognitive consequences of forced compliance. *Journal of Abnormal and Social Psychology* 58:203–10.

FESTINGER, L.; PEPITONE, A.; AND NEWCOMB, T. 1952. Some consequences of deindividuation in a group. *Journal of Abnormal and Social Psychology* 47:387–89.

FESTINGER, L.; RIECKEN, H.; AND SCHACHTER, S. 1956. *When prophecy fails.* Minneapolis: University of Minnesota Press.

FIEDLER, F. E. 1978. Recent developments in research on the contingency model. In Berkowitz, L. (Ed.), *Group processes.* New York: Academic Press.

FIELD, T. 1978. Interaction behaviors of primary versus secondary caretaker fathers. *Developmental Psychology* 14:183–84.

FIGLEY, C. R. 1978. Symptoms of delayed combat stress among a college sample of Vietnam veterans. *Military Medicine* 143:107–10.

FILLMORE, C. 1968. The case for case. In Bach, E., and Harms, R. (Eds.), *Universals in linguistic theory.* New York: Holt, Rinehart and Winston.

FINE, A. 1986. Transplantation in the central nervous system. *Scientific American* (August issue, pp. 52–58).

FINKE, R. A.; PINKER, S.; AND FARAH, M. J. 1989. Reinterpreting visual patterns in imagery. *Cognitive Science* 13:51–78.

FISHER, C., GLEITMAN, H., AND GLEITMAN, L. 1991. On the semantic content of subcategorization frames. *Cognitive Psychology,* in press.

FISHER, C.; HALL, G.; RAKOWITZ, S.; AND GLEITMAN, L. R. 1994. When it is better to receive than to give. In Gleitman, L. R., and Landau, B. (Eds.), Lexical acquisition, *Lingua* (Special Issue) 92:333–75.

FISHER, S., AND GREENBERG, R. P. 1977. *The scientific credibility of Freud's theory and therapy.* New York: Basic Books.

FITZGERALD, F. T. 1981. The problem of obesity. *Annual Review of Medicine* 32:221–31.

FITZSIMONS, J. T., AND MOORE-GILLOW, M. J. 1980. Drinking and antidiuresis in response to reductions in venous return in the dog: Neural and endocrine mechanisms. *Journal of Physiology* 307:403–16.

FLANAGAN, J. C. 1947. Scientific development of the use of human resources: Progress in the Army Air Forces. *Science* 105:57–60.

FLAVELL, J. H. 1970. Developmental studies of mediated memory. In Reese, H. W., and Lipsitt, L. P. (Eds.), *Advances in child development and behavior,* vol. 5. New York: Academic Press.

FLAVELL, J. H. 1977. *Cognitive development.* Englewood Cliffs, N.J.: Prentice-Hall.

FLAVELL, J. H. 1985. *Cognitive development. 2nd ed.* Englewood Cliffs, N.J.: Prentice-Hall.

FLAVELL, J. H.; BEACH, D. H.; AND CHINSKY, J. M. 1966. Spontaneous verbal rehearsal in a memory task as a function of age. *Child Development* 37:283–99.

FLAVELL, J. H.; FLAVELL, E. R.; AND GREEN, F. L. 1983. Development of the appearance-reality distinction. *Cognitive Psychology* 15:95–120.

FLAVELL, J. H.; SHIPSTEAD, S. G.; AND CROFT, K. 1978. Young children's knowledge about visual perception: Hiding objects from others. *Child Development* 49:1208–11.

FLAVELL, J. H., AND WELLMAN, H. M. 1977. Metamemory. In Kail, R. V., Jr., and Hagen, J. W. (Eds.), *Perspectives on the development of memory and cognition,* pp. 3–34. Hillsdale, N.J.: Erlbaum.

FLODERUS-MYRHED, B.; PEDERSEN, N.; AND RASMUSON, L. 1980. Assessment of heritability for personality, based on a short form of the Eysenck Personality Inventory: A study of 12,898 twin pairs. *Behavior Genetics* 10:153–62.

FLYNN, J.; VANEGAS, H.; FOOTE, W.; AND EDWARDS, S. 1970. Neural mechanisms involved in a cat's attack on a rat. In Whalen, R. F.; Thompson, M.; Verzeano, M.; and Weinberger, N. (Eds.), *The neural control of behavior.* New York: Academic Press.

FLYNN, J. R. 1980. *Race, IQ and Jensen.* London: Routledge and Kegan Paul.

FLYNN, S. 1985. Principled theories of second language acquisition. *Studies in Second Language Acquisition* 7:99–117.

FLYNN, S. 1987. *A parameter-setting model of L2 acquisition: Experimental studies in anaphora.* Dordrecht: Reidel.

FOARD, C. F. 1975. *Recall subsequent to tip-of-the-tongue experience.* Unpublished first-year graduate research paper, University of Pennsylvania, Philadelphia.

FOCH, T. T., AND McCLEARN, G. E. 1980. Genetics, body weight, and obesity. In Stunkard, A. J. (Ed.), *Obesity,* pp. 48–71. Philadelphia: Saunders.

FODOR, J. A. 1972. Some reflections on L. S. Vygotsky's *Thought and language. Cognition* 1:83–95.

FODOR, J. A. 1975. *The language of thought.* New York: Crowell.

FODOR, J. A. 1983. *The modularity of mind.* Cambridge, Mass.: MIT Press, Bradford Books.

FODOR, J. A. 1988. *Psychosemantics.* Cambridge, Mass.: MIT Press.

FODOR, J. A. 1992. A theory of the child's theory of mind. *Cognition* 44:283–96.

FONTANA, A. F. 1966. Familial etiology of schizophrenia: Is a scientific methodology possible? *Psychological Bulletin* 66:214–77.

FORD, C. S., AND BEACH, F. A. 1951. *Patterns of sexual behavior.* New York: Harper & Row.

FORER, B. R. 1949. The fallacy of personal validation: A classroom demonstration of gullibility. *Journal of Abnormal and Social Psychology* 44:118–23.

FORSTER, E. M. 1927. *Aspects of the novel.* New York: Harcourt, Brace, and World.

FOUCAULT, M. 1965. *Madness and civilization.* New York: Random House.

FOULKE, E., AND STICHT, T. G. 1969. Review of research on the intelligibility and compression of accelerated speech. *Psychological Bulletin* 72:50–62.

FOUTS, R. S. 1972. Use of guidance in teaching sign language to a chimpanzee *(Pantroglodytes). Journal of Comparative and Physiological Psychology* 80:515–22.

FOUTS, R. S.; HIRSCH, A. D.; AND FOUTS, D. H. 1982. Cultural transmission of a human language in a chimpanzee mother–infant relationship. In Fitzgerald, H. E.; Mullins, J. A.; and Gage, P. (Eds.), *Child nurturance: Vol. 3, Studies of development in nonhuman primates,* pp. 159–69. New York: Plenum.

FOWLER, A. 1989. Language acquisition in Down's Syndrome children: Syntax and morphology. In Cicchetti, D., and Beeghly, M., *Down's Syndrome: The developmental perspectives,* 2nd ed. New York: Cambridge University Press.

FRANK, M. 1973. An analysis of hamster afferent taste nerve response functions. *Journal of General Physiology* 61:588–618.

FRANKEL, F. H. 1993. Adult reconstruction of childhood events in the multiple personality disorder literature. *American Journal of Psychiatry* 150:954–58.

FRANKL, V. E. 1966. *The doctor and the soul.* New York: Knopf.

FRAZIER, L., AND FODOR, J. D. 1978. The sausage machine: a new two-stage parsing model. *Cognition* 6:291–325.

FREARSON, W. M., AND EYSENCK, H. J. 1986. Intelligence, reaction time [RT] and a new "odd-man-out" RT paradigm. *Personality and Individual Differences* 7:807–15.

FREED, W. J.; DE MEDICACELLI, L.; AND WYATT, R. J. 1985. Promoting functional plasticity in the damaged nervous system. *Science* 227:1544–52.

FREEDMAN, J. L., AND FRASER, S. C. 1966. Compliance without pressure: The foot-in-the-door technique. *Journal of Personality and Social Psychology* 4:195–202.

FREEMAN, D. 1983. *Margaret Mead and Samoa: The making and unmaking of an anthropological myth.* Canberra: Australian National University Press.

FREEMAN, D. 1986. Rejoinder to Patience and Smith. *American Anthropologist* 88:161–67.

FREGE, G. (1892/1952). On sense and reference, In Geach, P., and Black, M. (Eds.), *Philosophical writings of Gottlob Frege.* Oxford: Oxford University Press.

FREMOUW, W. J.; DE PERCZEL, M.; AND ELLIS, T. E. 1990. *Suicide risk: Assessment and response guidelines.* Elmsford, N.Y.: Pergamon.

FRENCH, J. D. 1957. The reticular formation. *Scientific American* 196:54–60.

FREUD, A. 1946. The ego and the mechanisms of defense. London: Hogarth Press.

FREUD, S. 1900. The interpretation of dreams. In Strachey, J., trans. and ed., *The complete psychological works*, vols. 4–5. New York: Norton, 1976.

FREUD, S. 1901. The psychopathology of everyday life. Translated by Tyson, A. New York: Norton, 1971.

FREUD, S. 1905. Three essays on the theory of sexuality. In Strachey, J., trans. and ed., *The complete psychological works*, vol. 7. New York: Norton, 1976.

FREUD, S. 1908. Character and anal eroticism. In Rieff, P. (Ed.), *Collected papers of Sigmund Freud: Character and culture.* New York: Collier Books, 1963.

FREUD, S. 1911. Psychoanalytic notes upon an autobiographical account of a case of paranoia (dementia paranoides). In Strachey, J., trans. and ed., *The complete psychological works*, vol. 12. New York: Norton, 1976.

FREUD, S. 1913. *Further recommendations in the technique of psychoanalysis.* In Strachey, J., trans. and ed., *The complete psychological works*, vol. 12. New York: Norton, 1976.

FREUD, S. 1917. *A general introduction to psychoanalysis.* Translated by Riviere, J. New York: Washington Square Press, 1952.

FREUD, S. 1923. *The ego and the id.* Translated by Riviere, J. New York: Norton, 1962.

FREUD, S. 1925. Some psychical consequences of the anatomical distinction between the sexes. In Strachey, J., trans. and ed., *The complete psychological works*, vol. 19. New York: Norton, 1976.

FREUD, S. 1926. *Inhibitions, symptoms, and anxiety.* Translated and revised by Strachey, J. New York: Norton, 1959.

FREUD, S. 1930. *Civilization and its discontents.* Translated by Strachey, J. New York: Norton, 1961.

FREUD, S. 1933. *New introductory lectures on psychoanalysis.* Translated and revised by Strachey, J. New York: Norton, 1965.

FREUD, S. 1940. *An outline of psychoanalysis.* Translated by Strachey, J. New York: Norton, 1970.

FREUD, S., AND BREUER, J. 1895. Studies on hysteria. In Strachey, J., trans. and ed., *The complete psychological works*, vol. 2. New York: Norton, 1976.

FRIDLUND, A. J. 1990. Evolution and facial action in reflex, social motive, and paralanguage. In Ackles, P. K.; Jennings, J. R.; and Coles, M. G. H. (Eds.), *Advances in psychophysiology*, vol. 4. Greenwich, Conn.: JAI Press.

FRIDLUND, A. J.; EKMAN, P.; AND OSTER, H. 1983. Facial expression of emotion: Review of literature, 1970–1983. In Siegman, A. (Ed.), *Nonverbal behavior and communication.* Hillsdale, N.J.: Erlbaum.

FRIEDMAN, M., AND ROSENMAN, R. H. 1974. *Type A behavior.* New York: Knopf.

FRIEDMAN, M. I. 1990a. Body fat and the metabolic control of food intake. *International Journal of Obesity* 14:53–67.

FRIEDMAN, M. I. 1990b. Making sense out of calories. In Stricker, E. M. (Ed.), *Handbook of behavioral neurobiology*, vol. 10: *Neurobiology of food and fluid intake*, pp. 513–29.

FRIEDMAN, M. I. 1991. Metabolic control of calorie intake. In Friedman, M. I.; Tordoff, M. G.; and Kare, M. R. (Eds.), *Chemical Senses*, vol. 4: *Appetite and nutrition*, pp. 19–38. New York: Marcel Dekker.

FRIEDMAN, M. I., AND STRICKER, E. M. 1976. The physiological psychology of hunger: a physiological perspective. *Psychological Review* 83:409–31.

FRIEDMAN, M. J. 1990. Interrelationships between biological mechanisms and pharmacotherapy of posttraumatic stress disorder, pp. 205-25. In Wolf, M. E., and Mosnaim, A. D. (Eds.), *Posttraumatic stress disorder: Etiology, phenomenology, and treatment.* Washington, D.C.: American Psychiatric Press.

FRISHBERG, N. 1975. Arbitrariness and iconicity: Historical change in American Sign Language. *Language* 51:696–719.

FROMKIN, V.; KRASHEN, S.; CURTISS, S.; RIGLER, D.; AND RIGLER, M. 1974. The development of language in Genie: A case of language acquisition beyond the "critical period." *Brain and Language* 1:81–107.

FUNKENSTEIN, D. H. 1956. Norepinephrine-like and epinephrine-like substances in relation to human behavior. *Journal of Mental Diseases* 124:58–68.

GAGE, F. H., AND BJÖRKLUND, A. 1986. Cholinergic septal grafts into the hippocampal formation improve spatial learning and memory in aged rats by an atropine-sensitive mechanism. *Journal of Neuroscience* 6:2837–47.

GAGNON, J. H., AND SIMON, W. 1973. *Sexual conduct.* Chicago: Aldine.

GALEF, B. G. 1988. Imitation in animals: History, definition, and interpretation of data from the psychological laboratory. In Zentall, T. R., and Galef, B. G. (Eds.), *Social Learning: Biological and psychological perspectives.* Hillsdale, N.J.: Erlbaum.

GALLAGAN, R. 1987. Intonation with single words: purposive and grammatical use. *Journal of Child Language* 14:1–22.

GALLISTEL, C. R. 1980. *The organization of action.* Hillsdale, N.J.: Erlbaum.

GALLISTEL, C. R. 1986. The role of the dopaminergic projections in MFB self-stimulation. *Behavior and Brain Research* 20:313–21.

GALLISTEL, C. R. 1990. *The organization of learning.* Cambridge, Mass.: MIT Press (Bradford).

GALLISTEL, C. R.; SHIZGAL, P.; AND YEOMANS, J. 1981. A portrait of the substrate for self-stimulation. *Psychological Review* 88:228–73.

GALTON, F. 1869. *Hereditary genius: An inquiry into its laws and consequences.* London: Macmillan.

GALTON, F. 1883. *Inquiries into human faculty and its development.* London: Macmillan.

GANAWAY, G. K. 1989. Historical versus narrative truth: Clarifying the role of exogenous trauma in the etiology of MPD and its variants. *Dissociation* 2:205–20.

GARBER, H., AND HEBER, R. 1982. Modification of predicted cognitive development in high-risk children through early intervention. In Detterman, D. K., and Sternberg, R. J. (Eds.), *How and how much can intelligence be increased?*, pp. 121–40. Norwood, N.J.: Ablex.

GARCIA, J.; ERVIN, F. R.; AND KOELLING, R. A. 1966. Learning with prolonged delay of reinforcement. *Psychonomic Science* 5:121–22.

GARCIA, J., AND KOELLING, R. A. 1966. The relation of cue to consequence in avoidance learning. *Psychonomic Science* 4:123–24.

GARDNER, H. 1975. *The shattered mind.* New York: Vintage Press.

GARDNER, H. 1983. *Frames of mind: The theory of multiple intelligences.* New York: Basic Books.

GARDNER, R. A., AND GARDNER, B. T. 1969. Teaching sign language to a chimpanzee. *Science* 165:664–72.

GARDNER, R. A., AND GARDNER, B. T. 1975. Early signs of language in child and chimpanzee. *Science* 187:752–53.

GARDNER, R. A., AND GARDNER, B. T. 1978. Comparative psychology and language acquisition. *Annals of the New York Academy of Science* 309:37–76.

GARFIELD, S. L. 1992. Major issues in psychotherapy research. In Freedheim, D. K. (Ed.), *History of Psychotherapy.* Washington, D.C.: American Psychological Association.

GARFINKEL, P. E., AND GARNER, D. M. 1982. *Anorexia Nervosa.* New York: Bruner/Mazel.

GARRIGAN, J. L. 1987. Post-traumatic stress disorder in military disaster workers. In *The human response to the Gander military air disaster: A summary report* (Division of Neuropsychiatry Report No. 88–12). Washington, D.C.: Walter Reed Army Institute of Research.

GATHERCOLE, V. C. 1987. The constrastive hypothesis for the acquisition of word meaning: A reconsideration of the theory. *Journal of Child Language* 14(3):493–532.

GAZZANIGA, M. S. 1967. The split brain in man. *Scientific American* 217:24–29.

GAZZANIGA, M. S. 1970. *The bisected brain.* New York: Appleton-Century-Crofts.

GAZZANIGA, M. S. 1983. Right hemisphere language following brain bisection: A 20-year perspective. *American Psychologist* 38:525–37.

GEERTZ, C. 1983. Local knowledge. In *Further essays in interpretative anthropology*. New York: Basic Books.

GEFFEN, G.; BRADSHAW, J. L.; AND WALLACE, G. 1971. Interhemispheric effects on reaction time to verbal and nonverbal visual stimuli. *Journal of Experimental Psychology* 87:415–22.

GELDARD, F. A. 1972. *The human senses.* New York: Wiley.

GELMAN, R. 1972. Logical capacity of very young children: Number invariance rules. *Child Development* 43:75–90.

GELMAN, R. 1978. Cognitive development. *Annual Review of Psychology* 29:297–332.

GELMAN, R. 1982. Basic numerical abilities. In Sternberg, R. J. (Ed.), *Advances in the psychology of human intelligence,* vol. 1, pp. 181–205. Hillsdale, N.J.: Erlbaum.

GELMAN, R., AND BAILLARGEON, R. 1983. A review of some Piagetian concepts. In Mussen, P. (Ed.), *Carmichael's manual of child psychology: Vol 3: Cognitive development* (Markman, E. M., and Flavell, J. H., volume editors), pp. 167–230. New York: Wiley.

GELMAN, R., AND GALLISTEL, C. R. 1978. *The child's understanding of number.* Cambridge, Mass.: Harvard University Press.

GERARD, H. B., AND MATHEWSON, G. C. 1966. The effects of severity of initiation on liking for a group: A replication. *Journal of Experimental Social Psychology* 2:278–87.

GERARD, H. B.; WILHELMY, R. A.; AND CONOLLEY, E. S. 1968. Conformity and group size. *Journal of Personality and Social Psychology* 8:79–82.

GERGEN, K. 1973. Social psychology as history. *Journal of Personality and Social Psychology* 26:309–20.

GERKEN, L.; LANDAU, B.; AND REMEZ, R. 1990. Function morphemes in young children's speech perception and production. *Developmental Psychology* 26(2):204–16.

GERSHON, E. S.; NURNBERGER, J. I., JR.; BERRETTINI, W. H.; AND GOLDIN, L. R. 1985. Affective disorders: Genetics. In Kaplan, H. I., and Sadock, J. (Eds.), *Modern synopsis of comprehensive textbook of psychiatry,* 4th ed. Baltimore: Williams & Wilkins.

GESCHWIND, N. 1970. The organization of language and the brain. *Science* 170:940–44.

GESCHWIND, N. 1972. Language and the brain. *Scientific American* 226:76–83.

GESCHWIND, N. 1975. The apraxias: Neural mechanisms of disorders of learned movement. *American Scientist* 63:188–95.

GESELL, A. L., AND THOMPSON, H. 1929. Learning and growth in identical twins: An experimental study by the method of co-twin control. *Genetic Psychology Monographs,* vol. 6.

GIBBONS, R. D.; HEDEKER, D.; ELKIN, I.; WATERNAUX, C.; KRAEMER, H. C.; GREENHOUSE, J. B.; SHEA, M. T.; IMBER, S. D.; SOTSKY, S. M.; WATKINS, J. T. 1993. Some conceptual and statistical issues in analysis of longitudinal psychiatric data. Application to the NIMH treatment of depression Collaborative Research Program dataset. *Archives of General Psychiatry* 50:739–50.

GIBBS, J., AND SMITH, G. P. 1984. The neuroendocrinology of postprandial satiety. In Martini, L., and Ganong, W. F. (Eds.), *Frontiers in neuroendocrinology,* vol. 8. New York: Raven.

GIBBS, J. C.; CLARK, P. M.; JOSEPH, J. A.; GREEN, J. L.; GOODRICK, T. S.; AND MAKOWSKI, D. G. 1986. Relations between moral judgment, moral courage, and filed independence. *Child Development* 57:1040–43.

GIBSON, J. J. 1950. *The perception of the visual world.* Boston: Houghton Mifflin.

GIBSON, J. J. 1966. *The senses considered as perceptual systems.* Boston: Houghton Mifflin.

GIBSON, J. J. 1979. *The ecological approach to visual perception.* Boston: Houghton Mifflin.

GICK, M. L., AND HOLYOAK, K. J. 1980. Analogical problem solving. *Cognitive Psychology* 12:306–55.

GICK, M. L., AND HOLYOAK, K. J. 1983. Schema induction and analogical transfer. *Cognitive Psychology* 15:1–38.

GILLIGAN, C. 1982. *In a different voice: Psychological theory and women's development.* Cambridge, Mass.: Harvard University Press.

GILLIGAN, C. 1986. Profile of Carol Gilligan. In Scarr, S.; Weinberg, R. A.; and Levine, A. 1986. *Understanding development,* pp. 488–91. New York: Harcourt Brace Jovanovich.

GINZBERG, L. 1909. *The legends of the Jews,* vol. 1. Translated by Szold, H. Philadelphia: Jewish Publication Society of America.

GLADUE, B. A.; GREEN, R.; AND HELLMAN, R. E. 1984. Neuroendocrine responses to estrogen and sexual orientation. *Science* 225:1496–98.

GLADWIN, T. 1970. *East is a Big Bird.* Cambridge, Mass.: Belknap Press.

GLANZER, M., AND CUNITZ, A. 1966. Two storage mechanisms in free recall. *Journal of Verbal Learning and Verbal Behavior* 5:531–60.

GLEITMAN, H. 1963. Place-learning. *Scientific American* 209:116–22.

GLEITMAN, H. 1971. Forgetting of long-term memories in animals. In Honig, W. K., and James, P. H. R. (Eds.), *Animal memory,* pp. 2–46. New York: Academic Press.

GLEITMAN, H. 1985. Some trends in the study of cognition. In Koch, S., and Leary, D. E. (Eds.), *A century of psychology as science,* pp. 420–36. New York: McGraw-Hill.

GLEITMAN, H. 1990. Some reflections on drama and the dramatic experience. In Rock, I. (Ed.), *The legacy of Solomon Asch: Essays in cognition and social psychology.* Hillsdale, N.J.: Erlbaum.

GLEITMAN, L. R. 1981. Maturational determinants of language growth. *Cognition* 10:103–14.

GLEITMAN, L. R. 1986. Biological dispositions to learn language. In Demopolous, W., and Marras, A. (Eds.), *Language learning and concept acquisition.* Norwood, N.J.: Ablex.

GLEITMAN, L. R. 1990. Structural sources of verb learning. *Language Acquisition* 1:1–54.

GLEITMAN, L. R.; GLEITMAN, H.; LANDAU, B.; AND WANNER, E. 1988. Where learning begins: Initial representations for language learning. In Newmeyer, F. (Ed.), *Linguistics: The Cambridge survey: Vol. III. Language: Psychological and biological aspects.* Cambridge: Cambridge University Press.

GLEITMAN, L. R.; GLEITMAN, H.; AND SHIPLEY, E. F. 1972. The emergence of the child as grammarian. *Cognition* 1(2):137–64.

GLEITMAN, L. R., AND LANDAU, B. (Eds.), Lexical Acquisition, *Lingua* (Special Issue) 92.1994.

GLEITMAN, L. R., AND WANNER, E. 1982. Language acquisition: The state of the art. In Wanner, E., and Gleitman, L. (Eds.), *Language acquisition: The state of the art.* New York: Cambridge University Press.

GLICK, J. 1975. Cognitive development in cross-cultural perspective. In Horowitz, F. G. (Ed.), *Review of child development research,* vol. 4. Chicago: University of Chicago Press.

GLUCKSBERG, S. 1962. The influence of strength of drive on functional fixedness and perceptual recognition. *Journal of Experimental Psychology* 63:36–41.

GODDEN, D. R., AND BADDELEY, A. D. 1975. Context-dependent memory in two natural environments: On land and underwater. *British Journal of Psychology* 66:325–31.

GOFFMAN, E. 1959. *The presentation of self in everyday life.* Garden City, N.Y.: Anchor Books, Doubleday.

GOLANI, I.; WOLGIN, D. L.; AND TEITELBAUM, P. 1979. A proposed natural geometry of recovery from akinesia in the lateral hypothalamic rat. *Brain Research* 164:237–67.

GOLD, R. 1978. On the meaning of nonconservation. In Lesgold, A. M.; Pellegrino, J. W.; Fokkema, S. D.; and Glaser, R. (Eds.), *Cognitive psychology and instruction.* New York: Plenum.

GOLDBERG, L. R. 1982. From ace to zombie: Some explorations in the language of personality. In Spielberger, C., and Butcher, J. N. (Eds.), *Advances in personality assessment,* vol. 1, Hillsdale, N.J.: Erlbaum.

GOLDBERG, L. R. 1990. An alternative "description of personality": The Big-Five factor structure. *Journal of Personality and Social Psychology* 59:1216–29.

GOLDBERG, L. R. 1993. The structure of phenotypic personality traits. *American Psychologist* 48:26–34.

GOLDEN, T. 1990. Ill, possibly violent, and no place to go. *New York Times,* Monday, April 2, 1990, pp. A1 and B4.

GOLDFARB, W. 1955. Emotional and intellectual consequences of psychological deprivation in infancy: A reevaluation. In Hock, P. H., and Zubin, J. (Eds.), *Psychopathology of childhood.* New York: Grune and Stratton.

GOLDIN-MEADOW, S. 1982. Fragile and resilient properties of language learning. In Wanner, E., and Gleitman, L. R. (Eds.), *Language acquisition: State of the art.* New York: Cambridge University Press.

GOLDIN-MEADOW, S.; BUTCHER, C.; MYLANDER, C.; AND DODGE, M. 1994. Nouns and verbs in a self-styled gesture system: What's in a name? *Cognitive Psychology* (in press).

GOLDIN-MEADOW, S., AND MYLANDER, C. 1983. Gestural communication in deaf children: The non-effects of parental input. *Science* 221:372–74.

GOLDSTEIN, E. B. 1984. *Sensation and perception,* 2nd ed. Belmont, Calif.: Wadsworth.

GOLDSTEIN, E. B. 1989. *Sensation and perception,* 3rd ed. Belmont, Calif.: Wadsworth.

GOLDSTEIN, J. M., AND TSUANG, M. T. 1990. Gender and schizophrenia: An introduction and synthesis of findings. *Schizophrenia Bulletin* 16:179–83.

GOMBRICH, E. H. 1961. *Art and illusion.* Princeton, N.J.: Bollingen Series, Princeton University Press.

GOODENOUGH, D. R. 1978. Dream recall: History and current status of the field. In Arkin, A. M.; Antrobus, J. S.; and Ellman, S. J. (Eds.), *The mind in sleep: Psychology and psychophysiology.* Hillsdale, N.J.: Erlbaum.

GOODMAN, J. F. 1990. Infant intelligence: Do we, can we, should we assess it? In Reynolds, C. R., and Kamphaus. R. (Eds.), *Handbook of psychological and educational assessment.* New York: Guilford.

GORDON H. 1923. Mental and scholastic tests among retarded children. *Educational Pamphlet,* no. 44. London: Board of Education.

GOREN, C. C.; SARTY, M.; AND WU, P. Y. K. 1975. Visual following and pattern discrimination of face-like stimuli by newborn infants. *Pediatrics* 56: 544–49.

GOTTESMAN, I. I.; McGUFFIN, P.; AND FARMER, A. 1987. Clinical genetics as clues to the "real" genetics of schizophrenia (a decade of modest gains while playing for time). *Schizophrenia Bulletin* 13:23–47.

GOTTESMAN, I. I., AND SHIELDS, J. 1972. *Schizophrenia and genetics: A twin study vantage point.* New York: Academic Press.

GOTTESMAN, I. I., AND SHIELDS, J. 1982. *Schizophrenia: The epigenetic puzzle.* New York: Cambridge University Press.

GOTTLIEB, G. 1961. Developmental age as a baseline for determination of the critical period for imprinting. *Journal of Comparative and Physiological Psychology* 54:422–27.

GOTTLIEB, G. 1976. The role of experience in the development of behavior and the nervous system. In Gottlieb, G. (Ed.), *Neural and behavioral specificity,* pp. 25–56. New York: Academic Press.

GOUGH, H. G. 1975. *California psychological inventory: Manual,* rev. ed. Palo Alto, Calif.: Consulting Psychologists Press (original edition, 1957).

GOULD, J., AND GOULD, C. 1988. The insect mind: Physics or metaphysics. In Griffin, R. R. (Ed.), *Animal mind—human mind.* Berlin: Springer Verlag.

GOULD, S. J. 1977. *Ontogeny and phylogeny.* Cambridge, Mass.: Harvard University Press.

GOULD, S. J. 1978, Sociobiology: The art of storytelling. *New Scientist* 80:530–33.

GOULDNER, A. W. 1960. The norm of reciprocity: A preliminary statement. *American Sociological Review* 25:161–79.

GOY, R. W. 1968. Organizing effect of androgen on the behavior of rhesus monkeys. In Michael, R. P. (Ed.), *Endocrinology and human behavior.* London: Oxford University Press.

GRAF, P., AND MANDLER, G. 1984. Activation makes words more accessible, but not necessarily more retrievable. *Journal of Verbal Learning and Verbal Behavior* 23:553–68.

GRAF, P.; MANDLER, G.; AND HADEN, P. 1982. Simulating amnesic symptoms in normal subjects. *Science* 218:1243–44.

GRAF, P.; MANDLER, G.; AND SQUIRE, L. R. 1984. The information that amnesic patients don't forget. *Journal of Experimental Psychology: Learning, Memory, and Cognition* 10:164–78.

GRAHAM, C. H., AND HSIA, Y. 1954. Luminosity curves for normal and dichromatic subjects including a case of unilateral color blindness. *Science* 120:780.

GRANT, V. W. 1976. *Falling in love.* New York: Springer.

GRAY, S. 1977. Social aspects of body image: Perception of normalcy of weight and affect of college undergraduates. *Perceptual and Motor Skills* 45:1035–40.

GREEN, D. M. 1976. *An introduction to hearing.* New York: Academic Press.

GREEN, D. M., AND SWETS, J. A. 1966. *Signal detection theory and psychophysics.* New York: Wiley.

GREEN, G. D., AND CLUNIS, D. M. 1988. Married lesbians. Lesbianism: Affirming Nontraditional Roles, *Women and Therapy* (Special Issue) 8: 41–49.

GREEN, P., AND PRESTON, M. 1981. Reinforcement of vocal correlates of auditory hallucinations by auditory feedback: A case study. *British Journal of Psychiatry* 139:204–208.

GREEN, R. 1969. Age-intelligence relationships between ages sixteen and sixty-four: A rising trend. *Developmental Psychology* 1:618–27.

GREEN, R. 1979. Childhood cross-gender behavior and subsequent sexual preference. *American Journal of Psychiatry* 136:106–108.

GREEN, S. K.; BUCHANAN, D. R.; AND HEUER, S. K. 1984. Winners, losers, and choosers: a field investigation of dating initiation. *Personality and Social Psychology Bulletin* 10:502–11.

GREENBERG, J.; PYSZCZYNSKI, T.; AND SOLOMON, S. 1982. The self-serving attributional bias: Beyond self-presentation. *Journal of Experimental Social Psychology* 18:56–67.

GREENE, R. L. 1991. *The MMPI-2/MMPI: An interpretive manual.* Needham Heights, Mass.: Allyn and Bacon.

GREENFIELD, P. M. 1966. On culture and conservation. In Bruner, R. R.; Olver, R. R.; and Greenfield, P. M. (Eds.), *Studies in cognitive growth.* New York: Wiley.

GREENFIELD, P. M. 1976. Cross-cultural research and Piagetian theory: Paradox and progress. In Riegel, K., and Meacham, J. (Eds.), *The developing individual in a changing world,* vol. 1. The Hague: Mouton.

GREENFIELD, P. M., AND SMITH, J. H. 1976. *The structure of communication in early language development.* New York: Academic Press.

GREGORY, R. L. 1963. Distortion of visual space as inappropriate constancy scaling. *Nature* 199:678–80.

GREGORY, R. L. 1966. Visual illusions. In Foss, B. (Ed.), *New horizons in psychology.* Baltimore: Penguin Books.

GREGORY, R. L. 1974. Choosing a paradigm for perception. In Carterette, E. C., and Friedman, M. P. (Eds.), *Handbook of perception: Vol. 1. Historical and philosophical roots of perception.* New York: Academic Press.

GREVEN, P. J., Jr. 1970. *Four generations: Population, land, and family in colonial Andover, Massachusetts.* Ithaca: N.Y.: Cornell University Press.

GREVERT, P., AND GOLDSTEIN, A. 1985. Placebo analgesia, naloxone, and the role of endogenous opioids. In White, L.; Turks, B.; and Schwartz, G. E. (Eds.), *Placebo,* pp. 332–51. New York: Guilford.

GRICE, H. P. 1968. Utterer's meaning, sentence-meaning and word-meaning. *Foundations of Language* 4:225–42.

GRILL, H. J., AND BERRIDGE, K. C. 1985. Taste reactivity as a measure of the neural control of palatability. *Progress in psychobiology and physiological psychology,* vol. 11, pp. 1–61. New York: Academic Press.

GRILLNER, S., AND WALLÉN, P. 1985. Central pattern generators for locomotion, with special reference to vertebrates. *Annual Review of Neuroscience* 8:233–61.

GRIMSHAW, J. 1981. Form, function, and the language acquisition device. In Baker, C., and McCarthy, J. (Eds.), *The logical problem of language acquisition.* Cambridge, Mass.: MIT Press.

GRIMSHAW, J. 1982. Form, function, and the language acquisition device. In Baker, C. L., and McCarthy, J. J. (Eds.), *The logical problem of language acquisition.* Cambridge, Mass.: MIT Press.

GRIMSHAW, J. 1990 *Argument structure.* Cambridge, Mass.: MIT Press.

GROSSMAN, H. J. (Ed.). 1983. *Manual on terminology and classification in mental retardation,* rev. ed. Washington, D. C.: American Association for Mental Deficiency.

GROVES, P. M., AND REBEC, G. V. 1988. *Introduction to biological psychology,* 3rd ed. Dubuque, Iowa: W. C. Brown.

GRÜNBAUM, A. 1984. *The foundations of psychoanalysis: A philosophical inquiry.* Berkeley, Calif.: University of California Press.

GURMAN, A. S., AND KNISKERN, D. P. 1981. Family therapy outcome research. In Gurman, A. S., and Kniskern, D. P. (Eds.), *Handbook of family therapy.* New York: Brunner/Mazel.

GUTHRIE, G. M. 1971. Unexpected correlations and the cross-cultural method. *Journal of cross-cultural psychology* 2:315–23.

GUTTMAN, N., AND KALISH, H. I. 1956. Discriminability and stimulus generalization. *Journal of Experimental Psychology* 51: 79–88.

GUYTON, A. C. 1981. *Textbook of medical physiology.* Philadelphia: Saunders.

HABER, R. N. 1969. Eidetic images. *Scientific American* 220: 36–44.

HABER, R. N. 1983. The impending demise of the icon: A critique of the concept of iconic storage in visual information processing. *The Behavioral and Brain Sciences* 6:1–54.

HADLEY, S. W., AND STRUPP, H. H. 1976. Contemporary accounts of negative effects in psychotherapy: An integrated account. *Archives of General Psychiatry* 33:1291–1302.

HAILMAN, J. P. 1967. The ontogeny of an instinct. *Behavior Supplements* 15:1–159.

HALL, C. S. 1953. A cognitive theory of dream symbols. *Journal of General Psychology* 48:169–86.

HALL, C. S. 1966. *The meaning of dreams.* New York: McGraw-Hill.

HALL, C. S.; LINDZEY, G.; LOEHLIN, J. C.; AND MANOSEVITZ, M. 1985. *Introduction to theories of personality.* New York: Wiley.

HALL, C. S., AND VAN DE CASTLE, R. 1966. *The content analysis of dreams.* New York: Appleton-Century-Crofts.

HALL, J. A., AND TAYLOR, S. E. 1976. When love is blind: Maintaining idealized images of one's spouse. *Human Relations* 29:751–61.

HALPERN, D. 1992. *Sex differences in cognitive abilities,* 2nd ed. Hillsdale, N.J.: Erlbaum.

HALVERSON, H. M. 1931. An experimental study of prehension infants by means of systematic cinema records. *Genetic Psychology Monographs* 47:47–63.

HAMBURG, D. A.; MOOS, R. H.; AND YALOM, I. D. 1968. Studies of distress in the menstrual cycle and the postpartum period. In Michael, R. P. (Ed.), *Endocrinology and human behavior,* pp. 94–116. London: Oxford University Press.

HAMER, D.; HU, S.; MAGNUSON, V.; AND HU, N. 1993a. A linkage between DNA markers on the X-chromosome and male sexual orientation. *Science* 261(5119):321–27.

HAMER, D.; HU, S.; MAGNUSON, V.; AND HU, N. 1993b. Genetics and male sexual orientation (Response) *Science* 261(5126): 1259.

HAMILTON, D. L., AND ROSE, T. L. 1980. Illusory correlation and the maintenance of stereotypic beliefs. *Journal of Personality and Social Psychology* 39:832–45.

HAMILTON, W. D. 1964. The genetical evolution of social behavior. *Journal of Theoretical Biology* 7:1–51.

HANSEN, J. T., AND SCHULDT, W. J. 1984. Marital self-disclosure and marital satisfaction. *Journal of Marriage and the Family* 46: 923–26.

HARDY, J. D., AND SMITH, T. W. 1988. Cynical hostility and vulnerability to disease: Social support, life stress, and physiological response to conflict. *Health Psychology* 7:447–59.

HARE, R. D. 1965. Temporal gradients of fear arousal in psychopaths. *Journal of Abnormal Psychology* 70:422–45.

HARE, R. D. 1978. A research scale for the assessment of psychopathy in criminal populations. *Personality and Individual Differences* 1: 111-19.

HAREVEN, T. K. 1978. The last stage: Historical adulthood and old age. In Erikson, E. H. (Ed.), *Adulthood,* pp. 201–16. New York: Norton.

HARKINS, S., AND GREEN, R. G. 1975. Discriminability and criterion differences between extraverts and introverts during vigilance. *Journal of Research in Personality* 9:335–40.

HARLOW, H. F. 1950. Learning and satiation of response in intrinsically motivated complex puzzle performance in monkeys. *Journal of Comparative and Physiological Psychology* 43:289–94.

HARLOW, H. F. 1958. The nature of love. *American Psychologist* 13:673–85.

HARLOW, H. F. 1962. The heterosexual affectional system in monkeys. *American Psychologist* 17:1–9.

HARLOW, H. F., AND HARLOW, M. K, 1972. The young monkeys. *Readings in Psychology Today,* 2nd ed. Albany, N.Y.: Delmar Publishers, CRM Books.

HARLOW, H. F., AND NOVAK, M. A. 1973. Psychopathological perspectives. *Perspectives in Biology and Medicine* 16:461–78.

HARRIS, G. W., AND MICHAEL, R. P. 1964. The activation of sexual behavior by hypothalamic implants of estrogen. *Journal of Physiology* 171:275–301.

HARRIS, P. L. 1987. The development of search. In Salapatek, P., and Cohen, L. (Eds.), *Handbook of infant perception,* pp. 155–208. New York: Academic Press.

HARTMANN, H. 1964. *Essays on ego psychology: Selected problems in psychoanalytic theory.* New York: International Universities Press.

HARTSHORNE, H., AND MAY, M. A. 1928. *Studies in the nature of character,* vol. 1. New York: Macmillan.

HARVEY, L. O., JR., AND LEIBOWITZ, H. 1967. Effects of exposure duration, cue reduction, and temporary monocularity on size matching at short distances. *Journal of the Optical Society of America* 57:249–53.

HASE, H. D., AND GOLDBERG, L. R. 1967. Comparative validities of different strategies of constructing personality inventory scales. *Psychological Bulletin* 67:231–48.

HATFIELD, E. 1988. Passionate and companionate love. In Sternberg, R. J., and Barnes, M. L. (Eds.), *The psychology of love.* New Haven, Conn.: Yale University Press.

HATHAWAY, S. R., AND MCKINLEY, J. C. 1940. A multiphasic personality schedule (Minnesota): I. Construction of the schedule. *Journal of Psychology* 10:249–54.

HAWKES, C. H. 1992. Endorphins: The basis of pleasure? *Journal of Neurology, Neurosurgery and Psychiatry* 55:247–50.

HAY, P.; SACHDEV, P.; CUMMING, S.; SMITH, J. S.; LEE, T.; KITCHENER, P.; AND MATHESON, J. 1993. Treatment of obsessive-compulsive disorder by psychosurgery. *Acta Psychiatrica Scandinavica* 87:197–207.

HAYES, C. 1952. *The ape in our house.* London: Gollacz.

HAYNES, S. G.; FEINLEIB, M.; AND KANNEL, W. B. 1980. The relationship of psychosocial factors to coronary heart disease in the Framingham study: Eight years incidence in coronary heart disease. *American Journal of Epidemiology* 3:37–85.

HAZELRIGG, M. D.; COOPER, H. M.; AND BORDUIN, C. M. 1987. Evaluating the effectiveness of family therapies: An integrative review and analysis. *Psychological Bulletin* 101:428–42.

HEALY, A. F., AND MILLER, G. A. 1970. The verb as the main determinant of sentence meaning. *Psychonomic Science* 20:372.

HEARST, E. 1972. Psychology across the chessboard. In *Readings in Psychology Today,* 2nd ed. Albany, N.Y.: Delmar Publishers, CRM Books.

HEATH, R. 1964. Pleasure response of human subjects to direct stimulation of the brain: Physiologic and psychodynamic considerations. In Heath, R. (Ed.), *The role of pleasure in behavior,* pp. 219–43. New York: Harper & Row.

HEDIGER, H. 1968. *The psychology and behavior of animals in zoos and circuses.* New York: Dover.

HEIDER, F. 1958. *The psychology of interpersonal relationships.* New York: Wiley.

HEILMAN, K. M., AND VALENSTEIN, E. 1979. *Clinical neuropsychology.* New York: Oxford University Press.

HELLEKSON, C. J.; KLINE, J. A.; AND ROSENTHAL, N. E. 1986. Phototherapy for seasonal affective disorder in Alaska. *American Journal of Psychiatry* 143:1035–37.

HELLER, H. C.; CRANSHAW, L. I.; AND HAMMEL, H. T. 1978. The thermostat of vertebrate animals. *Scientific American* 239:102–13.

HELMHOLTZ, H. 1909. *Wissenschaftliche Abhandlungen, II*, pp. 764–843.

HELMHOLTZ, H. 1910. *Treatise on physiological optics,* vols. 2 and 3. Trans. and ed. from the 3rd German ed. Southall, J. P. Rochester, N.Y.: Optical Society of America.

HENLE, M. 1962. On the relation between logic and thinking. *Psychological Review* 69:366–78.

HENRY, J. P., AND CASSEL, J. C. 1969. Psychosocial factors in essential hypertension. *American Journal of Epidemiology* 90:171.

HENRY, W. E. 1973. *The analysis of fantasy.* Huntington, N.Y.: Robert E. Krieger.

HERING, E. 1920. *Outlines of a theory of the light sense,* pp. 150–51. Edited by Hurvich, L. M., and Jameson, D. Cambridge, Mass.: Harvard University Press.

HERDT, G. 1990. Developmental discontinuities and sexual orientation across cultures. In McWhirter, D. P.; Sanders, S. A.; and Reinisch, J. M. (Eds.), *Homosexuality/heterosexuality: Concepts of sexual orientation.* New York: Oxford University Press.

HERMAN, C. P., AND MACK, D. 1975. Restrained and unrestrained eating. *Journal of Personality* 43:647–60.

HERMAN, C. P., AND POLIVY, J. 1980. Restrained eating. In Stunkard, A. J. (Ed.), *Obesity,* pp. 208–25. Philadelphia: Saunders.

HESS, E. H. 1958. "Imprinting" in animals. *Scientific American* 198:82.

HESS, E. H. 1959. Imprinting. *Science* 130:133–41.

HESS, E. H. 1973. *Imprinting: Early experience and the developmental psychobiology of attachment.* New York: Van Nostrand.

HESS, R. D. 1970. Social class and ethnic influences on socialization. In Mussen, P. H. (Ed.), *Carmichael's manual of child psychology,* 3rd ed., vol. 2, pp. 457–558. New York: Wiley.

HESTON, L. L. 1966. Psychiatric disorders in foster home reared children of schizophrenic mothers. *British Journal of Psychiatry* 112:819–25.

HETHERINGTON, P. A., AND SEIDENBERG, M. S. 1989. Is there "catastrophic interference" in connectionist networks? In *Proceedings of the eleventh annual conference of the Cognitive Science Society,* pp. 26–33. Hillsdale, N.J.: Erlbaum.

HILGARD, E. R. 1977. *Divided consciousness: Multiple controls in human thought and action.* New York: Wiley.

HILGARD, E. R. 1986. *Divided consciousness: Multiple controls in human thought and action,* rev. ed. New York: Wiley.

HILL, A. L. 1978. Savants: Mentally retarded individuals with specific skills. In N. R. Ellis (Ed.), *International Review of Research in Mental Retardation,* vol. 9. New York: Academic Press.

HILL, C. T.; RUBIN, L.; AND PEPLAU, L. A. 1976. Breakups before marriage: The end of 103 affairs. *Journal of Social Issues* 32:147–68.

HINELINE, P. N., AND RACHLIN, H. 1969. Escape and avoidance of shock by pigeons pecking a key. *Journal of the Experimental Analysis of Behavior* 12:533–38.

HINTZMAN, D. L. 1990. Human learning and memory: Connections and dissociations. *Annual Review of Psychology* 41:109–39.

HIRSCHFELD, R. M., AND CROSS, C. K. 1981. Epidemiology of affective disorders. *Archives of General Psychiatry* 39:3546

HIRSCHFELD, R. M., AND GOODWIN, F. K. 1988. Mood disorders. In Talbott, J. A.; Hales, R. E.; and Yudofsky, S. C. (Eds.), *The American Psychiatric Press textbook of psychiatry,* vol. 7. Washington, D.C.: American Psychiatric Press.

HIRSH-PASEK, K., AND GOLINKOFF, R. M. 1991. Language comprehension: A new look at some old themes. In Krasnegor, N.; Rumbaugh, D.; Schiefelbusch, R.; and Studdert-Kennedy, M. (Eds.), *Biological and behavioral determinants of language development.* Hillsdale, N.J.: Erlbaum

HIRSH-PASEK, K.; GOLINKOFF, R.; FLETCHER; DEGASPE-BEAUBIEN; AND CAULEY. 1985. In the beginning: one-word speakers comprehend word order. Paper presented at Boston Child Language Conference, October, 1985.

HIRSH-PASEK, K.; KEMLER-NELSON, D.; JUSCZYK, P.; CASSIDY, K.; DRUSS, B.; AND KENNEDY, L. 1987. Clauses are perceptual units for young infants. *Cognition* 26:269–86.

HIRTH, D. H., AND MCCULLOUGH, D. R. 1977. Evolution of alarm signals in ungulates with special reference to white-tailed deer. *American Naturalist* 111:31–42.

HOBBES, T. 1651. *Leviathan.* Baltimore: Penguin Books, 1968.

HOBSON, J. A. 1988. *The dreaming brain.* New York: Basic Books.

HOBSON, J. A., AND MCCARLEY, R. W. 1977. The brain as a dream-state generator: An activation-synthesis hypothesis of the dream porcess. *American Journal of Psychiatry* 134:1335–68.

HOCHBERG, J. E. 1970. Attention, organization and consciousness. In Mostofsky, D. I. (Ed.), *Attention: Contemporary theory and analysis,* pp. 99–124. New York: Appleton-Century-Crofts.

HOCHBERG, J. E. 1978a. *Perception,* 2nd ed. Englewood Cliffs, N.J.: Prentice-Hall.

HOCHBERG, J. E. 1978b. Art and perception. In Carterette, E. C., and Friedman, M. P. (Eds.), *Handbook of perception,* vol. 10, pp. 225–55. New York: Academic Press.

HOCHBERG, J. E. 1980. Pictorial functions and perceptual structures. In Hagen, M. A. (Ed.), *The perception of pictures,* vol. 2, pp. 47–93. New York: Academic Press.

HOCHBERG, J. 1981. On cognition in perception: Perceptual coupling and unconscious inference. *Cognition* 10:127–34.

HOCHBERG, J. 1988. Visual perception. In Atkinson, R. C.; Herrnstein, R. J.; Lindzey, G.; and Luce, R. D. (Eds.), *Stevens' handbook of experimental psychology: Vol. 1. Perception and motivation,* rev. ed., pp. 195–276. New York: Wiley.

HODGKIN, A. L., AND HUXLEY, A. F. 1939. Action potentials recorded from inside nerve fiber. *Nature* 144: 710–11.

HODGKINSON, S.; MULLAN, M. J.; AND GURLING, H. M. 1990. The role of genetic factors in the etiology of the affective disorders. *Behavior Genetics* 20:235–50.

HOEBEL, B. G., AND TEITELBAUM, P. 1962. Hypothalamic control of feeding and self-stimulation. *Science* 135:375–77.

HOEBEL, B. G., AND TEITELBAUM, P. 1976. Weight regulation in normal and hyperphagic rats. *Journal of Physiological and Comparative Psychology* 61: 189–93.

HOFFMAN, H. S. 1978. Experimental analysis of imprinting and its behavioral effects. *The Psychology of Learning and Motivation* 12:137.

HOFFMAN, H. S., AND FLESHLER, M. 1964. An apparatus for the measurement of the startle response in the rat. *American Journal of Psychology* 77:307–308.

HOFFMAN, L. W. 1974. Effects of maternal employment on the child. A review of the research. *Developmental Psychology* 10:204–28.

HOFFMAN, M. L. 1970. Moral development. In Mussen, P. H., (Ed.), *Carmichael's manual of child psychology,* 3rd. ed., vol. 2, pp. 457–558. New York: Wiley.

HOFFMAN, M. L. 1975. Altruistic behavior and the parent-child relationship. *Journal of Personality and Social Psychology* 31:937–43.

HOFFMAN, M. L. 1977a. Empathy, its development and prosocial implications. In Keasey, C. B. (Ed.), *Nebraska Symposium on Motivation* 25:169–217.

HOFFMAN, M. L. 1977b. Sex differences in empathy and related behaviors. *Psychological Bulletin* 84:712–22.

HOFFMAN, M. L. 1979. Development of moral thought, feeling, and behavior. *American Psychologist* 34:295–318.

HOFFMAN, M. L. 1984. Empathy, its limitations, and its role in a comprehensive moral theory. In Kurtines, W. M., and Gewirtz, L. (Eds.), *Morality, moral behavior, and moral development,* pp. 283–302. New York: Wiley.

HÖHN, E. O. 1969. The phalarope. *Scientific American* 220:104.

HOLDING, D. H. 1985. *The psychology of chess skill.* Hillsdale, N.J.: Erlbaum.

HOLDING, D. H., AND REYNOLDS, R. I. 1982. Recall or evaluation of chess positions as determinants of chess skill. *Memory and Cognition* 10:237–42.

HOLLAND, P. 1984. Origins of behavior in Pavlovian conditioning. *Psychology of Learning and Motivation* 18:129–174.

HOLLANDER, E., AND MCCARLEY, A. 1992. Yohimbine treatment of sexual side effects induced by serotonin reuptake blockers. *Journal of Clinical Psychiatry* 53:197–99.

HOLLANDER, E. P. 1985. Leadership and power. In Lindzey, G., and Aronson, E. (Eds.), *Handbook of social psychology,* 3rd ed., vol. 2. New York: Random House.

HOLLINGSHEAD, A. B., AND REDLICH, F. C. 1958. *Social class and mental illness: A community study.* New York: Wiley.

HOLLIS, K. I. 1982. Pavlovian conditioning of signal-centered action patterns and autonomic behavior: A biological analysis of function. In Rosenblatt, J. S.; Hinde, R. A.; Beer, C.; and Busnel, M. (Eds.), *Advances in the study of behavior,* vol. 12, pp. 1–64. New York: Academic Press.

HOLLIS, K. L. 1984. The biological function of Pavlovian conditioning: The best defense is a good offense. *Journal of Experimental Psychology: Animal Learning and Behavior* 10:413–25.

HOLLISTER, L. E., AND CSERNANSKY, J. G. 1990. *Clinical pharmacology of psychotherapeutic drugs,* 3rd. ed. New York: Churchill-Livingstone.

HOLMES, D. 1990. The evidence for repression: An examinmation of sixty years of research. In Singer, J. (Ed.), *Repression and dissociation: Implications for personality theory, psychopathology, and health,* pp. 85–102. Chicago: University of Chicago Press.

HOLT, R. R. 1978. *Methods in clinical psychology: Vol. 1. Projective assessment.* New York: Plenum.

HOLTZMAN, P. S.; KRINGLEN, E.; MALTHYSSE, S.; FLANAGAN, S. D.; LIPTON, R. B.; CRAMER, G.; LEVIN, S.; LANGE, K.; AND LEVY, D. L. 1988. A single dominant gene can account for eye tracking dysfunctions and schizophrenia in offspring of discordant twins. *Archives of General Psychiatry* 45:641–47.

HOLTZWORTH-MUNROE, A., AND JACOBSON, N. S. 1985. Causal attributions of married couples: When do they search for causes? What do they conclude when they do? *Journal of Personality and Social Psychology* 48:1398–1412.

HOLWAY, A. F., AND BORING, E. G. 1947. Determinants of apparent visual size with distance variant. *American Journal of Psychology* 54:21–37.

HOOK, S. 1955. *The hero in history.* Boston: Beacon Press.

HOOLEY, J. M. 1985. Expressed emotion: A review of the critical literature. *Clinical Psychology Review* 5:119–39.

HORN, J. L., AND CATTELL, R. B. 1967. Age differences in fluid and crystallized intelligence. *Acta Psychologica* 26:107–29.

HORN, J. L., AND DONALDSON, G. 1976. On the myth of intellectual decline in adulthood. *American Psychologist* 31:701–19.

HORN, J. M. 1983. The Texas Adoption Project: Adopted children and their biological and adoptive parents. *Child Development* 54:268–75.

HORN, J. M.; LOEHLIN, J. C.; AND WILLERMAN, L. 1979. Intellectual resemblance among adoptive and biological relatives: The Texas Adoption Project. *Behavior Genetics* 13:459–71.

HORN, J. M.; LOEHLIN, J. C.; AND WILLERMAN, L. 1982. Aspects of the inheritance of intellectual abilities. *Behavior Genetics* 12:479–516.

HORN, L. R. 1987. Pragmatic theory. In Newmeyer, F. J., (Ed.), *Linguistics: The Cambridge survey,* vol I.: *Linguistic theory: Foundations.* New York: Cambridge University Press.

HORNE, J. A. 1988. *Why we sleep: The functions of sleep in humans and other mammals.* New York: Oxford University Press.

HORNE, R. L., AND PICARD, R. S. 1979. Psychosocial risk factors for lung cancer. *Psychosomatic Medicine* 41:503–14.

HORNEY, K. 1937. *The neurotic personality of our time.* New York: Norton.

HORNEY, K. 1945. *Our inner conflicts.* New York: Norton.

HORNEY, K. 1950. *New ways in psychoanalysis.* New York: Norton.

HOVLAND, C. I., AND WEISS, W. 1952. The influence of source credibility on communication effectiveness. *Public Opinion Quarterly* 15:635–50.

HOWARD, D. V. 1983. *Cognitive psychology.* New York: Macmillan.

HOWE, M. L., AND COURAGE, M. L. 1993. On resolving the enigma of infantile amnesia. *Psychological Bulletin* 113:305–27.

HRDY, S. B. 1988. The primate origins of sexuality. In Smith, M. S.; Hamilton, W. D.; Margulis, L.; Hrdy, S. B.; Raven, P. H.; and Hefner, P. J. (Eds.), *The evolution of sex.* San Francisco: Harper & Row.

HRDY, S. B., AND WILLIAMS, G. C. 1983. Behavioral biology and the double standard. In Wasser, S. K., (Ed.), *The social behavior of female vertebrates,* pp. 3–17. New York: Academic Press.

HUBEL, D. H. 1963. The visual cortex of the brain. *Scientific American* 209:54–62.

HUBEL, D. H., AND WIESEL, T. N. 1959. Receptive fields of single neurons in the cat's visual cortex. *Journal of Physiology* 148: 574–91.

HUBEL, D. H., AND WIESEL, T. N. 1970. Stereoscopic vision in the macaque monkey. Nature 225:41–42.

HULL, C. L. 1943. *Principles of behavior.* New York: Appleton-Century-Crofts.

HUMPHREY, G. 1951. *Thinking: An introduction to its experimental psychology.* New York: Wiley.

HUMPHREYS, L. G. 1939. The effect of random alternation of reinforcement on the acquisition and extinction of conditioned eyelid reactions. *Journal of Experimental Psychology* 25:141–58.

HUNT, E. 1976. Varieties of cognitive power. In Resnick, L. B. (Ed.), *The nature of intelligence.* Hillsdale, N.J.: Erlbaum.

HUNT, E. 1978. Mechanics of verbal ability. *Psychological Review* 85:109–30.

HUNT, E. 1985a. The correlates of intelligence. In D. K. Detterman (Ed.), *Current topics in human intelligence,* vol. 1. Norwood, N.J.: Ablex.

HUNT, E. 1985b. Verbal ability. In Sternberg, R. J. (Ed.), *Human abilities: An information processing approach,* pp. 31–58. New York: Freeman.

HUNT, E.; LUNNEBORG, C.; AND LEWIS, J. 1975. What does it mean to be high verbal? *Cognitive Psychology* 7:194–227.

HUNT, J. M. 1961. *Intelligence and experience.* New York: Ronald Press.

HUNT, M. M. 1959. *The natural history of love.* New York: Knopf.

HUNT, P., AND HILLERY, J. M. 1973. Social facilitation in a coaction setting: An examination of the effects over learning trials. *Journal of Experimental Social Psychology* 9:563–71.

HURVICH, L. M. 1981. *Color vision.* Sunderland, Mass.: Sinauer Assoc.

HURVICH, L. M., AND JAMESON, D. 1957. An opponent-process theory of color vision. *Psychological Review* 64:384–404.

HURVICH, L. M., AND JAMESON, D. 1974. Opponent processes as a model of neural organization. *American Psychologist* 29:88–102.

HUSTON, A. C. 1983. Sex-typing. In Mussen, P. (Ed.), *Carmichael's manual of child psychology: Vol. 4. Socialization, personality, and social development,* pp. 387–468. (Hetherington, E. M., volume editor). New York: Wiley.

HUSTON, T. L.; RUGGIERO, M.; CONNER, R.; AND GEIS, G. 1981. Bystander intervention into crime: A study based on naturally occurring episodes. *Social Psychology Quarterly* 44:14–23.

HUTCHINSON, R. R., AND RENFREW, J. W. 1966. Stalking attack and eating behaviors elicited from the same sites in the hypothalamus. *Journal of Comparative and Physiological Psychology* 61:360–67.

HUTTENLOCHER, J.; SMILEY, P.; AND CHARNEY, R. 1983. Emergence of action categories in the child: Evidence from verb meanings. *Psychological Review* 90:72–93.

HUTTENLOCHER, P. R. 1979. Synaptic density in human frontal cortex—developmental changes and effects of aging. *Brain Research* 163:195–205.

HYAMS, N. 1986. *Language acquisition and the theory of parameters.* Dordrecht: Reidel.

HYDE, D. M. 1959. An investigation of Piaget's theories of the development of the concept of number. Unpublished doctoral dissertation. University of London. (Quoted in Flavell, J. H., *The developmental psychology of Jean Piaget,* p. 383. New York: Van Nostrand Reinhold).

HYDE, J. S. 1981. How large are cognitive gender differences? A meta-analysis using w^2 and d. *American Psychologist* 36:892–901.

HYDE, J. S., AND LYNN, M. C. 1988. Gender differences in verbal ability: A meta-analysis. *Psychological Bulletin* 104:53–69.

ILYIN, N. A., AND ILYIN, V. N. 1930. Temperature effects on the color of the Siamese cat. *Journal of Heredity* 21:309–18.

IMPERATO-MCGINLEY, J.; GUERRERO, L.; GAUTIER, T.; AND PETERSON, R. E. 1974. Steroid 5-alpha reductase deficiency in man: An inherited form of male pseudohermaphroditism. *Science* 186: 1213–15.

IMPERATO-MCGINLEY, J.; PETERSON, R. E.; GAUTIER, T.; AND STURLA, E. 1979. Androgens and the evolution of male-gender identity among male pseudohermaphrodites with 5-alpha reductase deficiency. *The New England Journal of Medicine* 300:1233–37.

INBAU, F. E., AND REID, J. E. 1953. *Truth and deception: The polygraph ("lie detector") technique.* Baltimore: Williams & Wilkins.

INGLIS, J. 1969. Electrode placement and the effect of ECT on mood and memory in depression. *Canadian Psychiatric Association Journal* 14:463–471.

INGVAR, D. H., AND LASSEN, N. A. 1979. Activity distribution in the cerebral cortex in organic dementia as revealed by measurements of regional cerebral blood flow. *Bayer Symposium VII. Brain function in old age*, 268–77.

INHELDER, B., AND PIAGET, J. 1958. *The growth of logical thinking from childhood to adolescence.* New York: Basic Books.

INSEL, T. R. 1990. New pharmacologic approaches to obsessive compulsive disorder. *Journal of Clinical Psychiatry* (Supplement) 51:47–51.

IZARD, C. E. 1971. *The face of emotion.* New York: Appleton-Century-Crofts.

IZARD, C. E. 1977. *Human emotions.* New York: Plenum.

IZARD, C. E. 1991. *The psychology of emotions.* New York: Plenum.

IZZETT, R. 1971. Authoritarianism and attitudes toward the Vietnam War as reflected in behavioral and self-report measures. *Journal of Personality and Social Psychology* 17:145–48.

JACKENDOFF, R. 1987. The status of thematic relations in linguistic theory. *Linguistic Inquiry* 18(3):369–411.

JACKENDOFF, R. 1990. *Semantic structures.* Cambridge, Mass.: MIT Press.

JACKSON, J. M., AND LATANÉ, B. 1981. All alone in front of all those people: Stage fright as a function of the number and type of coperformers and audience. *Journal of Personality and Social Psychology* 40:73–85.

JACKSON, M., AND MCCLELLAND, J. L. 1975. Sensory and cognitive determinants of reading speed. *Journal of Verbal Learning and Verbal Behavior* 14:565–74.

JACKSON, M. D., AND MCCLELLAND, J. L. 1979. Processing determinants of reading speed. *Journal of Experimental Psychology: Experimental* 108:151–58.

JACOBS, A. 1955. Formation of new associations to words selected on the basis of reaction-time-GSR combinations. *Journal of Abnormal and Social Psychology* 51:371–77.

JACOBSEN, F. M. 1992. Fluoxetine-induced sexual dysfunction and an open trial of yohimbine. *Journal of Clinical Psychiatry* 53:119–22.

JACOBY, L. L. 1983. Remembering the data: Analyzing the interactive process in reading. *Journal of Memory and Language* 30:513–41.

JACOBY, L. L., AND DALLAS, M. 1981. On the relationship between autobiographical memory and perceptual learning. *Journal of Experimental Psychology: General* 3:306–40.

JACOBY, L. L.; KELLEY, C.; BROWN, J.; AND JASECHKO, J. 1989. Becoming famous overnight: Limits on the ability to avoid unconscious influences of the past. *Journal of Personality and Social Psychology: General* 56:326–38.

JACOBY, L. L., AND WITHERSPOON, D. 1982. Remembering without awareness. *Canadian Journal of Psychology* 36:300–24.

JAHODA, G. 1979. A cross-cultural perspective on experimental social psychology. *Personality and Social Psychology Bulletin* 5: 142–48.

JAMES, W. 1890. *Principles of psychology.* New York: Henry Holt.

JAMESON, D., AND HURVICH, L. M.. 1975. From contrast to assimilation: In art and in the eye. *Leonardo* 8:125–31.

JANICAK, P. G.; DAVIS, J. M.; GIBBONS, R. D.; ERICKSEN, S.; CHANG, S.; AND GALLAGHER, P. 1985. Efficacy of ECT: A meta-analysis. *American Journal of Psychiatry* 142:297–302.

JENCKS, C.; SMITH, M.; ACLAND, H.; BANE, M. J.; COHEN, D.; GINTIS, H.; HEYNS, B.; AND MICHELSON, S. 1972. *Inequality: A reassessment of the effect of family and schooling in America.* New York: Basic Books.

JENKINS, H. M., AND MOORE, B. R. 1973. The form of the autoshaped response with food or water reinforcers. *Journal of the Experimental Analysis of Behavior* 20:163–81.

JENKINS, J. G., AND DALLENBACH, K. M. 1924. Oblivescence during sleep and waking. *American Journal of Psychology* 35:605–12.

JENNINGS, E. E. 1972. *An anatomy of leadership: Princes, heroes, and supermen.* New York: McGraw-Hill.

JENSEN, A. R. 1965. Scoring the Stroop test. *Acta Psychologica* 24:398–408.

JENSEN, A. R. 1969. How much can we boost I. Q. and scholastic achievement? *Harvard Educational Review* 39:1–123.

JENSEN, A. R. 1973. Educability and group differences. New York: Harper & Row.

JENSEN, A. R. 1985. The nature of the black-white difference on various psychometric tests: Spearman's hypothesis. *Behavioral and Brain Sciences* 8:193–263.

JENSEN, A. R. 1987. Individual differences in the Hick paradigm. In Vernon, P. A. (Ed.), *Speed of information processing and intelligence.* Norwood, N.J.: Ablex.

JOHN, O. P. 1990. The "Big Five" taxonomy: Dimensions of personality in the natural language and in questionnaires, pp. 676–1000. In Pervin, L. A. (Ed.), *Handbook of personality: Theory and research.* New York: Guilford Press.

JOHNSON, A. M.; WADSWORTH, J.; WELLINGS, K.; BRADSHAW, S.; AND FIELD, J. 1992. Sexual lifestyles and HIV risk. *Nature* 360: 410–12.

JOHNSON, B. L., AND KILMANN, P. R. 1975. The relationship between recalled parental attitudes and internal-external control. *Journal of Clinical Psychology* 31:40–42.

JOHNSON, J., AND NEWPORT, E. 1989. Critical period efforts in second-language learning: The influence of maturational state on the acquisition of English as a second language. *Cognitive Psychology* 21:60–99.

JOHNSON, M. H., AND MORTON, J. 1991. *Biology and cognitive development: The case of face recognition.* London: Blackwell.

JOHNSON, M. K., AND RAYE, C. L. 1981. Reality monitoring. *Psychological Review* 88:67–85.

JOHNSON, R. E. 1979. *Juvenile delinquency and its origins.* New York: Cambridge University Press.

JOHNSON, S. 1765. Shakespeare criticism. In Danziger, M. K. (Ed.), *Samuel Johnson on literature.* New York: Ungar, 1979.

JONES, E. 1954. *Hamlet and Oedipus.* New York: Doubleday.

JONES, E. E., AND NISBETT, R. E. 1972. The actor and the observer: Divergent perceptions of the cause of behavior. In Jones, E. E.; Karouse, D. E.; Kelley, H. H.; Nisbett, R. E.; Valins, S.; and Weiner, B. (Eds.), *Attribution: Perceiving the causes of behavior.* Morristown, N.J.: General Learning Press.

JONES, H. E., AND KAPLAN, O. J. 1945. Psychological aspects of mental disorders in later life. In Kaplan, O. J. (Ed.), *Mental disorders in later life*, pp. 69–115. Stanford, Calif.: Stanford University Press.

JONES, R. E. 1983. Street people and psychiatry: An introduction. *Hospital Community Psychiatry* 34:807–11.

JONIDES, J. 1980. Toward a model of the mind's eye's movement. *Canadian Journal of Psychology* 34:103–12.

JONIDES, J. 1983. Further toward a model of the mind's eye's movement. *Bulletin of the Psychonomic Society* 21:247–50.

JONIDES, J., AND BAUM, D. R. 1978. Cognitive maps as revealed by distance estimates. Paper presented at the 18th annual meeting of the Psychonomic Society. Washington, D.C.

JORGENSEN, B. W., AND CERVONE, J. C. 1978. Affect enhancement in the pseudo recognition task. *Personality and Social Psychology Bulletin* 4:285–88.

JOSHI, A. K. 1983. Varieties of cooperative responses in question-answer systems. In Keifer, F. (Ed.), *Questions and answers*, pp. 229–40. Amsterdam: D. Reidel Publishing Co.

JOSHI, A. K. 1991. Natural language processing. *Science* 253:1242–49.

JOSSELSON, R. 1980. Ego development in adolescence. In Adelson, J. (Ed.), *Handbook of adolescent psychology*, pp. 188–211. New York: Wiley.

JOURARD, S. M. 1964. *The transparent self*. New York: Van Nostrand.

JOUVET, M. 1967. The stages of sleep. *Scientific American* 216:62–72.

JULESZ, B. 1978. Perceptual limits of texture discrimination and their implications to figure-ground separation. In Leeuwenberg, E. and Buffart, H. (Eds.), *Formal theories of perception*, pp. 205–16. New York: Wiley.

JULIEN, R. M. 1985. *A primer of drug action*, 4th ed. New York: Freeman.

JUSCZYK, P. 1985. On characterizing the development of speech perception. In Mehler, J., and Fox, R. (Eds.), *Neonate cognition: Beyond the blooming buzzing confusion*. Hillsdale, N.J.: Erlbaum.

KAGAN, J. 1976. Emergent themes in human development. *American Scientist* 64:186–96.

KAGAN, J. 1984. *The nature of the child*. New York: Basic Books.

KAGAN, J. 1989. Commentary. *Human Development* (Special Topic: Continuity in early cognitive development—conceptual and methodological challenges) 32:172–76.

KAGAN, J., AND MOSS, H. A. 1962. *Birth to maturity: The Fels study of psychological development*. New York: Wiley.

KAHN, R. S.; DAVIDSON, M.; SIEVER, L.; GABRIEL, S.; APTER, S.; AND DAVIS, K. L. 1993. Serotonin and treatment response to clozapine in schizophrenic patients. *American Journal of Psychiatry* 150:1337–42.

KAHNEMAN, D., AND MILLER, D. T. 1986. Norm theory: Comparing reality to its alternatives. *Psychological Review* 93:136–53.

KAHNEMAN, D., AND TVERSKY, A. 1972. Subjective probability: A judgment of representativeness. *Cognitive Psychology* 3:430–54.

KAHNEMAN, D., AND TVERSKY, A. 1973. On the psychology of prediction. *Psychological Review* 80:237–51.

KAHNEMAN, D., AND TVERSKY, A. 1982. The simulation heuristic. In Kahneman, D.; Slovic, P.; and Tversky, A. (Eds.), *Judgment under uncertainty*. New York: Cambridge University Press.

KALAT, J. W. 1984. *Biological psychology*, 2nd ed. Belmont, Calif.: Wadsworth.

KAMIN, L. J. 1965. Temporal and intensity characteristics of the conditioned stimulus. In Prokasy, W. F. (Ed.), *Classical conditioning*. New York: Appleton-Century-Crofts.

KAMIN, L. J. 1968. "Attention-like" processes in classical conditioning. In Jones, M. R. (Ed.), *Miami symposium on the prediction of behavior: Aversive stimuli*. Miami: University of Miami Press.

KAMIN, L. J. 1969. Predictability, surprise, attention and conditioning. In Campbell, B. A., and Church, R. M. (Eds.), *Punishment and aversive behavior*, pp. 279–96. New York: Appleton-Century-Crofts.

KAMIN, L. J. 1974. *The science and politics of I. Q.* New York: Wiley.

KAMINSKY, H. 1984. Moral development in historical perspective. In Kurtines, W. M., and Gewirtz, J. L. (Eds.), *Morality, moral behavior, and moral development*. New York: Wiley.

KANDEL, D. 1978. Similarity in real-life adolescent friendship pairs. *Journal of Personality and Social Psychology* 36:306–12.

KANDEL, E. R. 1979. Small systems of neurons. *Scientific American* 241:66–76.

KANE, J.; HONIGFELD, G.; SINGER, J.; AND MELTZER, H. 1988. Clozapine for the treatment-resistant schizophrenic. A double-blind comparison with chlorpromazine. *Archives of General Psychiatry* 45:789–96.

KANE, J. M., AND MARDER, S. R. 1993. Psychopharmacologic treatment of schizophrenia. *Schizophrenia Bulletin* 19:287–302.

KANIZSA, G. 1976. Subjective contours. *Scientific American* 234:48–52.

KAPLAN, E.; FINE, D.; MORRIS, R.; AND DELIS, D. C. 1991. *WAIS-R as a neuropsychological instrument*. San Antonio, Tx.: The Psychological Corporation.

KATZ, B. 1952. The nerve impulse. *Scientific American* 187:55–64.

KATZ, J. J. 1972. *Semantic theory*. New York: Harper & Row.

KATZ, J. J., AND FODOR, J. A. 1963. The structure of a semantic theory. *Language* 39:170-210.

KATZ, N.; BAKER, E.; AND MACNAMARA, J. 1974. What's in a name? A study of how children learn common and proper names. *Child Development* 45:469–73.

KAUFMAN, A. S.; KAMPHAUS; R. W.; AND KAUFMAN, N. L. 1985. The Kaufman Assessment Battery for Children (K-ABC). In Newmark, C. S. (Ed.), *Major psychological assessment instruments*. Boston: Allyn and Bacon.

KAUFMAN, L., AND ROCK, I. 1962. The moon illusion. *Scientific American* 207:120–30.

KEELE, S. W. 1982. Learning and control of coordinated motor patterns: The programming perspective. In Kelso, J. A. S. (Ed.), *Human motor behavior;* pp. 143–60. Hillsdale, N.J.: Erlbaum.

KEESEY, R. E., AND POWLEY, T. L. 1986. The regulation of body weight. *Annual Review of Psychology* 37:109–34.

KEETON, W. T. 1972 and 1980. *Biological science*, 2nd and 3rd eds. New York: Norton.

KEETON, W. T., AND GOULD, J. L. 1986 and 1993. *Biological science*, 4th ed. New York: Norton.

KEIL, F. C. 1979. *Semantic and conceptual development: An ontological perspective*. Cambridge, Mass.: Harvard University Press.

KEIL, F. C., AND BATTERMAN, N. 1984. A characteristic-to-defining shift in the development of word meaning. *Journal of Verbal Learning and Verbal Behavior* 23:221–36.

KELLER, H. 1985. *Teacher: Anne Sullivan Macy*. Westport, Conn.: Greenwood Press.

KELLEY, H. H. 1967. Attribution theory in social psychology. In Levine, D. (Ed.), *Nebraska Symposium on Motivation*, pp. 192–238. Lincoln, Neb.: University of Nebraska Press.

KELLEY, H. H., AND MICHELA, J. L. 1980. Attribution theory and research. *Annual Review of Psychology* 31:457–501.

KELLEY, H., AND THIBAUT, J. W. 1978. *Interpersonal relations: A theory of interdependence*. New York: Wiley-Interscience.

KELLEY, S., AND MIRER, T. W. 1974. The simple act of voting. *American Political Science Review* 68:572–91.

KELLMAN, P. J., AND SHIPLEY, T. F. 1991. A theory of visual interpolation in object perception. *Cognitive Psychology* 23:141–221.

KELLMAN, P. J., AND SPELKE, E. S. 1983. Perception of partially occluded objects in infancy. *Cognitive Psychology* 15:483–524.

KELLMAN, P. J.; SPELKE, E. S.; AND SHORT, K. R. 1986. Infant perception of object unity from translatory motion in depth and vertical translation. *Child Development* 57:72–86.

KELLY, M. H., AND MARTIN, S. 1994. Domain-general abilities applied to domain-specific tasks: Sensitivity to probabilities in perception, cognition, and language. In Gleitman, L. R., and Landau, B. (Eds.) Lexical acquisition, *Lingua* (Special Issue) 92:108–40.

KEMLER-NELSON, D.; JUSCZYK; P.; AND CASSIDY, K. 1989. How the prosodic cues of motherese might assist language learning. *Journal of Child Language*, pp. 55–68.

KENDLER, K. S., AND GRUENBERG, A. M. 1984. An independent analysis of the Danish adoption study of schizophrenia: VI. The relationship between psychiatric disorders as defined by DSM-III in the relatives and adoptees. *Archives of General Psychiatry* 41:555–64.

KENNY, D., AND ZACCARO, S. J. 1983. An estimate of variance due to traits in leadership. *Journal of Applied Psychology* 68: 678–85.

KENRICK, D. T., AND CIALDINI, R. B. 1977. Romantic attraction: Misattribution versus reinforcement explanations. *Journal of Personality and Social Psychology* 35:381–91.

KENRICK, D. T.; CIALDINI, R. B.; AND LINDER, D. E. 1979. Misattribution under fear-producing circumstances: Four failures to replicate. *Personality and Social Psychology Bulletin* 5:329–34.

KENRICK, D. T., AND FUNDER, D. C. 1988. Profiting from controversy: Lessons from the person-situation debate. *American Psychologist* 43:23–34.

KERR, M. E., AND BOWEN, M. 1988. *Family evaluation.* New York: Norton.

KESSEL, E. L. 1955. The mating activities of balloon flies. *Systematic Zoology* 4:97–104.

KETY, S. S. 1983. Mental illness in the biological and adoptive relatives of schizophrenic adoptees: Findings relevant to genetic and environmental factors in etiology. *Journal of American Psychiatry* 140:720–27.

KIHLSTROM, J. F. 1987. The cognitive unconscious. *Science* 237:1445–52.

KIHLSTROM, J. F. 1990. The psychological unconscious. In Pervin, L. A. (Ed.), *Handbook of Personality: Theory and Research,* pp. 445–64. New York: Guilford Press.

KIHLSTROM, J. F. 1992. Dissociation and dissociations: A comment on consciousness and cognition. *Consciousness and Cognition: An International Journal* 1:47–53.

KIHLSTROM, J. F. 1993. The recovery of memory in the laboratory and the clinic. Paper presented at the 1993 conventions of the Rocky Mountain and the Western Psychological Associations. Phoenix, Arizona.

KIHLSTROM, J. F.; BARNHARDT, T. M.; AND TATARYN, D. J. 1992. The psychological unconscious: Found, lost, and regained. *American Psychologist* 47:788–91.

KIHLSTROM, J. F., AND CANTOR, N. 1984. Mental representations of the self. In Berkowitz, L. (Ed.), *Advances in experimental social psychology,* vol. 17, pp. 1–47. New York: Academic Press.

KILHAM, W., AND MANN, L. 1974. Level of destructive obedience as a function of transmitter and executant roles in the Milgram obedience paradigm. *Journal of Personality and Social Psychology* 29:696–702.

KIMBALL, J. 1973. Seven principles of surface structure parsing in natural language. *Cognition* 2:15–47.

KIMBLE, G. A. 1961. *Hilgard and Marquis' conditioning and learning.* New York: Appleton-Century-Crofts.

KIMURA, D. 1992. Sex differences in the brain. *Scientific American* 276:118–25.

KING, H. E. 1961. Psychological effects of excitation in the limbic system. In Sheer, D. E. (Ed.), *Electrical stimulation of the brain.* Austin: University of Texas Press.

KINSEY, A. C.; POMEROY, W. B.; AND MARTIN, C. E. 1948. *Sexual behavior in the human male.* Philadelphia: Saunders.

KINSEY, A.; POMEROY, W.; MARTIN, C.; AND GEBHARD, P. 1953. *Sexual behavior in the human female.* Philadelphia: Saunders.

KINTSCH, W., AND VAN DIJK, T. 1977. Toward a model of text comprehension and production. *Psychological Review* 85:63–94.

KITCHER, P. 1985. *Vaulting ambition: Sociobiology and the quest for human nature.* Cambridge, Mass: M. I. T. Press.

KITCHER, P. 1987. Précis of *Vaulting ambition: Sociobiology and the quest for human nature* (and open peer commentary). *Behavioral and Brain Sciences* 10:61–100.

KLEINMAN, A., AND GOOD, B. 1990. *Culture and depression.* Berkeley: University of California Press.

KLEINMUNTZ, B. 1982. *Personality and psychological assessment.* New York: St. Martin's Press.

KLEITMAN, N. 1960. Patterns of dreaming. *Scientific American* 203:82–88.

KLERMAN, G. L. 1990. The psychiatric patient's right to effective treatment: Implications of Osheroff v. Chestnut Lodge. *American Journal of Psychiatry* 147:409–18.

KLERMAN, G. L.; WEISSMAN, M. M.; ROUNSAVILLE, B. J.; AND CHEVRON, E. S. 1984. *Interpersonal psychotherapy of depression.* New York: Basic Books.

KLIMA, E.; AND BELLUGI, U.; WITH BATTISON, R.; BOYES-BRAEM, P.; FISCHER, S.; FRISHBERG, N.; LANE, H.; LENTZ, E. M.; NEWKIRK, D.;

NEWPORT, E.; PEDERSEN, C.; AND SIPLE, P. 1979. *The signs of language.* Cambridge, Mass.: Harvard University Press.

KLINEBERG, O. 1940. *Social psychology.* New York: Henry Holt.

KLOPFER, B.; AINSWORTH, M.; KLOPFER, W. G.; AND HOLT, R. R. 1954. *Developments in the Rorschach technique.* Yonkers, N.Y.: World Book.

KLOPFER, P. H. 1974. *An introduction to animal behavior: Ethology's first century.* Englewood Cliffs, N.J.: Prentice-Hall.

KLUFT, R. P. 1987. An update on multiple-personality disorder. *Journal of Hospital and Community Psychiatry* 38:363–73.

KOHLBERG, L. 1963. Development of children's orientations toward a moral order. *Vita Humana* 6:11–36.

KOHLBERG, L. 1966. A cognitive developmental analysis of children's sex-role concepts and attitudes. In Maccoby, E. E. (Ed.), *The development of sex differences,* pp. 82–171. Stanford, Calif.: Stanford University Press.

KOHLBERG, L. 1969. Stage and sequence: The cognitive developmental approach to socialization. In Goslin, D. A. (Ed.), *Handbook of socialization theory of research,* pp. 347–480. Chicago: Rand McNally.

KOHLBERG, L. AND CANDEE, D. 1984. The relationship of moral judgment to moral action. In Kurtines, W. M., and Gewirtz, L. (Eds.), *Morality, moral behavior, and moral development,* pp. 52–73. New York: Wiley.

KOHLBERG, L.; LEVINE, C.; AND HEWER, A. 1984. Synopses and detailed replies to critics. In Kohlberg, L. (Ed.), *The psychology of moral development: The nature and validity of moral stages,* pp. 320–86. San Francisco: Harper & Row.

KÖHLER, W. 1925. *The mentality of apes.* New York: Harcourt Brace and World.

KÖHLER, W. 1947. *Gestalt psychology.* New York: Liveright.

KOHN, M. L. 1968. Social class and schizophrenia: A critical review. In Rosenthal, D., and Kety, S. S. (Eds.), *The transmission of schizophrenia,* pp. 155–74. London: Pergamon.

KOHN, M. L. 1969. *Class and conformity: A study in values.* Chicago: University of Chicago Press.

KOHUT, H. 1978. *The psychology of the self: A case book.* New York: International Universities Press.

KOLB, B., AND MILNER, B. 1981. Performance of complex art and facial movements after focal brain lesions. *Neuropsychologia* 19:491–503.

KOLB, B. AND WHISHAW, I. Q. 1990. *Fundamentals of human neuropsychology,* 3rd ed. New York: Freeman.

KOLERS, P. A. 1972. *Aspects of motion perception.* New York: Pergamon.

KOLERS, P. A., AND POMERANTZ, J. R. 1971. Figural change in apparent motion. *Journal of Experimental Psychology* 87:99–108.

KOLODNY, R.; MASTERS, W.; HENDRYX, J.; AND TORO, G. 1971. Plasma testosterone and semen analysis in male homosexuals. *New England Journal of Medicine* 285:1170–74.

KORIAT, A., AND LIEBLICH, I. 1974. What does a person in a TOT state know that a person in a "Don't Know" state doesn't know? *Memory and Cognition* 2:647–55.

KOSSLYN, S. M. 1980. *Image and mind.* Cambridge, Mass.: Harvard University Press.

KOSSLYN, S. M. 1984. *Ghosts in the mind's machine.* New York: Norton.

KOSSLYN, S. M.; BALL, T. M.; AND REISSER, B. J. 1978. Visual images preserve metric spatial information: Evidence from studies of image scanning. *Journal of Experimental Psychology: Human Perception and Performance* 4:1–20.

KOSTLAN, A. 1954. A method for the empirical study of psychodiagnosis. *Journal of Consulting Psychology* 18:83–88.

KOTELCHUK, M. 1976. The infant's relationship to the father: Some experimental evidence. In Lamb, M. (Ed.), *The role of the father in child development.* New York: Wiley.

KOULACK, D., AND GOODENOUGH, D. R. 1976. Dream recall and dream recall failure: An arousal-retrieval model. *Psychological Bulletin* 83:975–84.

KRAMER, P. D. 1993. *Listening to prozac.* New York: Viking.

KRANTZ, D. S.; CONTRADA, R. J.; HILL, D. R.; AND FRIEDLER, E. 1988. Environmental stress and behavioral antecedents of coronary heart disease. *Journal of Consulting and Clinical Psychology* 56:333–41.

KRASHEN, S. 1981. Second language acquisition and second language learning. London: Pergamon Press.

KREBS, J. R. 1982. Territorial defence in the great tit. *Parus Major L. Ecology* 52:2–22.

KREBS, J. R., AND DAVIES, N. B. 1987. *An introduction to behavioral ecology,* 2nd ed. Boston: Blackwell Scientific Publications.

KRECH, D., AND CRUTCHFIELD, R. 1958. *Elements of psychology.* New York: Knopf.

KUBOVY, M. 1986. *The psychology of perspective and Renaissance art.* New York: Cambridge University Press.

KUFFLER, S. W. 1953. Discharge pattern and functional organization of mammalian retina. *Journal of Neurophysiology* 16:37–68.

KUHL, P.; WILLIAMS, K.; LACERDA, F.; STEVENS, K.; AND LINDBLOM, B. 1992. Linguistic experience alters phonetic perception in infants by six months of age. *Science* 255:606–608.

KUPFER, D. J.; FOSTER, F. G.; AND REICH, L. 1976. EEG sleep changes as predictors in depression. *American Journal of Psychiatry* 133:622.

KUZNICKI, J. T., AND McCUTCHEON, N. B. 1979. Cross enhancement of the sour taste of single human taste papillae. *Journal of Experimental Psychology* 198:68–89.

LA BERGE, D. 1975. Acquisition of automatic processing in perceptual and associative learning. In Rabbitt, P. M. A., and Dormic, S. (Eds.), *Attention and performance,* vol. 5. London: Academic Press.

LABOV, W. 1970. The logic of nonstandard English. In Williams, F. (Ed.), *Language and poverty: Perspectives on a theme,* pp. 153–89. Chicago: Markham.

LACK, D. 1953. Darwin's finches. *Scientific American* 188:66–72.

LAKOFF, G., AND JOHNSON, M. 1980. *Metaphors we live by.* Chicago: University of Chicago Press.

LAMB, H. R. 1984. Deinstitutionalization and the homeless mentally ill. *Hospital Community Psychiatry* 35:899–907.

LAMB, M. E. 1977. Father-infant and mother-infant interaction in the first year of life. *Child Development* 48:167–81.

LAMB, M. E.; THOMPSON, R. M.; GARDNER, W.; CHARNOV, E. L.; AND ESTES, D. 1985. *Infant-mother attachment.* Hillsdale, N.J.: Erlbaum.

LANDAU, B. 1982. Will the real grandmother please stand up? The psychological reality of dual meaning representations. *Journal of Psycholinguistic Research* 11:47–62.

LANDAU, B. 1994. Where's what and what's where: The language of objects in space. In Gleitman, L. R., and Landau, B. (Eds.), Lexical acquisition, *Lingua* (Special Issue) 92:259–96.

LANDAU, B., AND GLEITMAN, L. R. 1985. *Language and experience: Evidence from the blind child.* Cambridge, Mass.: Harvard University Press.

LANDAU, B.; SMITH, L.; AND JONES, S. 1988. The importance of shape in early lexical learning. *Cognitive Development* 3:299–321.

LANDIS, C., AND HUNT, W. A. 1932. Adrenalin and emotion. *Psychological Review* 39:467–85.

LANGER, E. J., AND RODIN, J. 1976. The effects of choice and enhanced personal responsibility for the aged: A field experiment in an institutional setting. *Journal of Personality and Social Psychology* 34:191–98.

LANGLOIS, J. H., AND DOWNS, A. C. 1980. Mothers, fathers, and peers as socialization agents of sex-typed play behaviors in young children. *Child Development* 51:1237–1347.

LANYON, R. I., AND GOLDSTEIN, L. D. 1971. *Personality assessment.* New York: Wiley.

LANYON, R. I., AND GOLDSTEIN, L. D. 1982. *Personality assessment.* 2nd ed. New York: Wiley.

LAPIERE, R. 1934. Attitudes versus actions. *Social Forces* 13:230–37.

LASH, J. P. 1980. *Helen and Teacher: The story of Helen Keller and Anne Sullivan Macy.* New York: Delacorte Press.

LASHLEY, K. S. 1930. The mechanism of vision:1. A method for rapid analysis of pattern-vision in the rat. *Journal of Genetic Psychology* 37:453–60.

LASKY, J. J.; HOVER, G. L.; SMITH, P. A.; BOSTIAN, D. W.; DUFFENDECK, S. C.; AND NORD, C. L. 1959. Post-hospital adjustment as predicted by psychiatric patients and by their staff. *Journal of Consulting Psychology* 23:213–18.

LASSEN, N. A.; INGVAR, D. H.; AND SKINHOJ, E. 1978. Brain function and blood flow. *Scientific American* 239:62–71.

LATANÉ, B. 1981. The psychology of social impact. *American Psychologist* 36:343–56.

LATANÉ, B., AND HARKINS, S. 1976. Cross-modality matches suggest anticipated stage fright as a multiplicative power function of audience size and status. *Perception and Psychophysics* 20:482–88.

LATANÉ, B., AND NIDA, S. 1981. Group size and helping. *Psychological Bulletin* 89:308–24.

LATANÉ, B.; NIDA, S. A.; AND WILSON, D. W. 1981. The effects of group size on helping behavior. In Rushton, J. P., and Sorrentino, R. M. (Eds.), *Altruism and helping behavior: Social, personality, and developmental perspectives.* Hillsdale, N.J.: Erlbaum.

LATANÉ, B., AND RODIN, J. 1969. A lady in distress: Inhibiting effects of friends and strangers on bystander intervention. *Journal of Experimental Social Psychology* 5: 189–202.

LATANÉ, B.; WILLIAMS, K.; AND HARKINS, S. 1979. Many hands make light the work: The causes and consequences of social loafing. *Journal of Personality and Social Psychology* 37:822–32.

LAU, R. R., AND RUSSELL, D. 1980. Attributions in the sports pages. *Journal of Personality and Social Psychology* 39:29–38.

LAYZER, D. 1972. Science or superstition: A physical scientist looks at the I. Q. controversy. *Cognition* 1:265–300.

LAZAR, I., AND DARLINGTON, R. 1982. Lasting effects of early education: A report from the Consortium for Longitudinal Studies. *Monographs of the Society for Research in Child Development* 47 (2–3, Serial No. 195).

LAZARUS, A. A. 1971. *Behavior therapy and beyond.* New York: McGraw-Hill.

LAZARUS, A. A. 1981. *The practice of multi-modal therapy.* New York: McGraw-Hill.

LE BON, G. 1895. *The crowd.* New York: Viking Press, 1960.

LEASK, J.; HABER, R. N.; AND HABER, R. B. 1969. Eidetic imagery in children: II. Longitudinal and experimental results. *Psychonomic Monograph Supplements* 3(Whole No. 35):25–48.

LEATON, R. N. 1976. Long-term retention of the habituation of lick suppression and startle response produced by a single auditory stimulus. *Journal of Experimental Psychology: Animal Behavior Processes* 2:248–59.

LEECH, G. N. 1983. *Principles of pragmatics.* London: Longman.

LEEPER, R. W. 1935. A study of a neglected portion of the field of learning: The development of sensory organization. *Journal of Genetic Psychology* 46:41–75.

LEFF, J.; KUIPPERS, L.; BERKOWITZ, R.; EBERLEIN-VRIES, R.; AND STURGEON, D. 1982. A controlled trial of social intervention in the families of schizophrenic persons. *British Journal of Psychiatry* 141:121–34.

LEFF, M. J.; ROATSCH, J. F.; AND BUNNEY, W. E., JR. 1970. Environmental factors preceding the onset of severe depressions. *Psychiatry* 33:298–311.

LEMPERS, J. S.; FLAVELL, E. R.; AND FLAVELL, J. H. 1977. The development in very young children of tacit knowledge concerning visual perception. *Genetic Psychology Monographs* 95:3–53.

LENNEBERG, E. H. 1967. *Biological foundations of language.* New York: Wiley.

LEPPER, M. R. 1983. Social control processes, attributions of motivation, and the internalization of social values. In Higgins, E. T.; Ruble, D. N.; and Hartup, W. W. (Eds.), *Social cognition and social behavior: Developmental perspectives.* New York: Cambridge University Press.

LESLIE, A. M. 1992. Pretense, autism, and the theory of mind module. *Current Directions in Psychological Science* 1:18–21.

LETTVIN, J. Y.; MATURAN, H. R.; McCULLOCH, W. S.; AND PITTS, W. H. 1959. What the frog's eye tells the frog's brain. *Proceedings of the Institute of Radio Engineers* 47:1940–51.

LeVAY, S. 1991. A difference in hypothalamic structure between heterosexual and homosexual men. *Science* 253: 1034–37.

LEVELT, W. 1970. A scaling approach to the study of syntactic relations. In Flores d'Arcais, G., and Levelt, W. (Eds.), *Advances in psycholinguistics*. Amsterdam: North-Holland.

LEVINE, J. D.; GORDON, N. C.; AND FIELDS, H. L. 1979. The role of endorphins in placebo analgesia. In Bonica, J. J.; Liebesking, J. C.; and Albe-Fessard, D. (Eds.), *Advances in pain research and therapy*, vol. 3. New York: Raven.

LEVINSON, D. J. 1978. *The seasons of a man's life*. New York: Knopf.

LEVY, J. 1974. Psychobiological implications of bilateral asymmetry. In Dimond, S. J., and Beaumont, J. G. (Eds.), *Hemisphere function in the human brain*, pp. 121–83. New York: Wiley.

LEVY, J. 1979. Personal communication.

LEVY, J. 1983. Language, cognition, and the right hemisphere: A response to Gazzaniga. *American Psychologist* 38:538–41.

LEVY, J. 1985. Right brain, left brain: Facts and fiction. *Psychology Today* 19:38–44.

LEWIN, R. 1988. Cloud over Parkinson's therapy. *Science* 240:390–92.

LEWINSOHN, P. M.; HOBERMAN, H.; TERI, L.; AND HAUTZINGER, M. 1985. An integrative theory of depression. In Reiss, S., and Bootzin, R. (Eds.), *Theoretical issues in behavior therapy*. Orlando, Fla.: Academic Press.

LEWONTIN, R. C. 1976. Race and intelligence. In Block, N. J., and Dworkin, G. (Eds.), *The IQ controversy*, pp. 78–92. New York: Pantheon.

LEWONTIN, R. C.; ROSE, S.; AND KAMIN, L. J. 1984. *Not in our genes: Biology, ideology, and human nature*. New York: Random House.

LEWY, A.; SACK, L.; MILLER, S.; AND HOBAN, T. M. 1987. Antidepressant and circadian-phase shifting effects of light. *Science* 235:352–54.

LEZAK, M. D. 1983. *Neuropsychological assessment*, 2nd. ed. New York: Oxford University Press.

LIBERMAN, A. M. 1970. The grammars of speech and language. *Cognitive Psychology* 1:301–23.

LICKLEY, J. D. 1919. *The nervous system*. New York: Longman.

LIEBERMAN, P. L. 1975. *On the origins of language*. New York: Macmillan.

LIEBERT, R. M.; POULOS, R. W.; AND STRAUSS, G. D. 1974. *Developmental psychology*. Englewood Cliffs, N. J.: Prentice-Hall.

LIFF, Z. A. 1992. Psychoanalysis and dynamic techniques. In D. K. Freedheim (Ed.), *History of Psychotherapy*. Washington, D.C.: American Psychological Association.

LINDSAY, P. H., AND NORMAN, D. A. 1977. *Human information processing*, 2nd ed. New York: Academic Press.

LIPPERT, W. W., AND SENTER, R. J. 1966. Electrodermal responses in the sociopath. *Psychonomic Science* 4:25–26.

LISKE, E., AND DAVIS, W. J. 1984. Sexual behavior of the Chinese praying mantis. *Animal Behavior* 32:916.

LITTLE, K. B., AND SHNEIDMAN, E. S. 1959. Congruencies among interpretations of psychological test and anamnestic data. *Psychological Monographs* 73 (Whole No. 476).

LOCKE, J. 1690. *An essay concerning human understanding*. Edited by A. D. Woozley. Cleveland: Meridian Books, 1964.

LOEHLIN, J. C. 1982. Are personality traits differentially heritable. *Behavior Genetics* 12:417–28.

LOEHLIN, J. C.; LINDZEY, G.; AND SPUHLER, J. N. 1975. *Race difference in intelligence*. San Francisco: Freeman.

LOEHLIN, J. C., AND NICHOLS, R. C. 1976. *Heredity, environment and personality: A study of 850 sets of twins*. Austin: University of Texas Press.

LOEWI, O. 1960. An autobiographical sketch. *Perspectives in Biological Medicine* 4:2–35.

LOFTUS, E. F. 1973. Activation of semantic memory. *American Journal of Psychology* 86:331–37.

LOFTUS, E. F. 1975. Leading questions and the eyewitness report. *Cognitive Psychology* 7:560–72.

LOFTUS, E. F. 1993. The reality of repressed memories. *American Psychologist* 48:518–37.

LOFTUS, E. F., AND HOFFMAN, H. G. 1989. Misinformation and memory: The creation of new memories. *Journal of Experimental Psychology: General* 118:100–104.

LOFTUS, E. F., AND LOFTUS, G. R. 1980. On the permanence of stored information in the human brain. *American Psychologist* 35:409–20.

LOFTUS, E. F., AND ZANNI, G. 1975. Eyewitness testimony: The influence of the wording of a question. *Bulletin of the Psychonomic Society* 5:86–88.

LOGAN, G. D. 1988. Toward an instance theory of automatization. *Psychological Review* 95:492–527.

LOGUE, A. W. 1979. Taste aversion and the generality of the laws of learning. *Psychological Bulletin* 86:276–96.

LOGUE, A. W. 1986. *The psychology of eating and drinking*. New York: Freeman.

LONDON, P. 1964. *The modes and morals of psychotherapy*. New York: Holt, Rinehart & Winston.

LONDON, P. 1970. The rescuers: Motivational hypotheses about Christians who saved Jews from the Nazis. In Macauley, J., and Berkowitz, L. (Eds.), *Altruism and helping behavior*. New York: Academic Press.

LORD, R. G.; DeVADER, C. L.; AND ALLIGER, G. M. 1986. A meta-analysis of the relationship between personality traits and leadership perceptions: An application of validity generalization procedures. *Journal of Applied Psychology* 7: 401–10.

LORENZ, K. Z. 1952. *King Solomon's ring*. New York: Crowell.

LORENZ, K. Z. 1966. *On aggression*. London: Methuen.

LUBIN, B.; LARSEN, R. M.; MATARAZZO, J. D.; AND SEEVER, M. 1985. Psychological test usage patterns in five professional settings. *American Psychologist* 40:857–61.

LUBORSKY, L. I.; SINGER, B.; AND LUBORSKY, L. 1975. Comparative studies of psychotherapies. *Archives of General Psychiatry* 20:84–88.

LUCE, R. D., AND RAIFFA, H. 1957. *Games and decisions*. New York: Wiley.

LUCHINS, A. S. 1942. Mechanization in problem-solving: The effect of Einstellung. *Psychological Monographs* 54 (Whole No. 248).

LUCHINS, A. S. 1957. Primacy-recency in impression formation: The effect of Einstellung. In Hovland, C. (Ed.), *The order of presentation in persuasion*. New Haven: Yale University Press.

LUGINBUHL, J. E. R.; CROWE, D. H.; AND KAHAN, J. P. 1975. Causal attributions for success and failure. *Journal of Personality and Social Psychology* 31:86–93.

LURIA, A. R. 1966. Higher cortical functions in man. New York: Basic Books.

LURIA, A. R. 1971. *International Journal of Psychology* 6: p. 259 ff. (cited in Scribner, S. & Cole, M. 1973. Cognitive consequences of formal and informal education. *Science* 182:553–59).

LURIA, A. R. 1976. *Cognitive development: Its cultural and social foundations*. Cambridge, Mass.: Harvard University Press.

LUST, B. 1987. *Studies in the acquisition of anaphora*. Dordrecht: Reidel.

LUTZ, C. 1986. The domain of emotion words on Ifaluk. In Harr, R. (Ed.), *The social construction of emotions*, pp. 267–88. Oxford, Blackwell.

LUTZ, C. 1988. *Unnatural emotions*. Chicago: University of Chicago Press.

LYKKEN, D. T. 1979. The detection of deception. *Psychological Bulletin* 86:47–53.

LYKKEN, D. T. 1981. The lie detector and the law. *Criminal Defense* 8:19–27.

MAASS, A., AND CLARK, R. D., III. 1984. Hidden impact of minorities: Fifteen years of research on minority influence research. *Psychological Bulletin* 95:428–55.

MACCOBY, E. E. 1980. *Social development.* New York: Harcourt Brace Jovanovich.

MACCOBY, E. E., AND JACKLIN, C. N. 1974. *The psychology of sex differences.* Stanford, Calif.: Stanford University Press.

MACCOBY, E. E., AND JACKLIN, C. N. 1980. Sex differences in aggression: A rejoinder and reprise. *Child Development* 51:964–80.

MACCOBY, E. E., AND MARTIN, J. A. 1983. Socialization in the context of the family: Parent-child interaction. In Mussen, P. H. (Ed.), *Carmichael's manual of child psychology: Vol. 4. Socialization, personality and social development* (Hetherington, M. E., volume editor), pp. 1–102. New York: Wiley.

MACFARLANE, A. 1975. Olfaction in the development of social preferences in the human neonate. *Parent-infant interaction.* Amsterdam: CIBA Foundation Symposium.

MACKENZIE, N. 1965. *Dreams and dreaming.* London: Aldus Books.

MACKINTOSH, N. J. 1983. *Conditioning and associative learning.* Oxford, England: Oxford University Press.

MACNEILAGE, P. 1972. Speech physiology. In Gilbert, J. (Ed.), *Speech and cortical functioning.* New York: Academic Press.

MACNICHOL, E. F., JR. 1964. Three-pigment color vision: *Scientific American* 211:48–56.

MACNICHOL, E. F., JR. 1986. A unifying presentation of photopigment spectra. *Vision Research* 29:543–46.

MAGNUS, O., AND LAMMERS, J. 1956. The amygdaloid-nuclear complex. *Folia Psychiatrica Neurologica et Neurochirurgico Neerlandica* 59:552–82.

MAGNUSSON, D., AND ENDLER, N. S. 1977. Interactional psychology: Present status and future prospects. In Magnusson, D., and Endler, N. S. (Eds.), *Personality at the crossroads,* pp. 3–31. New York: Wiley.

MAGOUN, H. W.; HARRISON, F.; BROBECK, J. R.; AND RANSON, S. W. 1938. Activation of heat loss mechanisms by local heating of the brain. *Journal of Neurophysiology* 1:101–14.

MAHER, B. A. 1966. *Principles of psychopathology.* New York: McGraw-Hill.

MAHONEY, M. J. 1976. *Scientist as subject: The psychological imperative.* Cambridge, Mass.: Ballinger.

MAHONEY, M. J., AND DEMONBREUN, B. G. 1981. Problem-solving bias in scientists. In Tweney, R. D.; Doherty, M. E.; and Mynatt, C. R. (Eds.), *On scientific thinking,* pp. 139–44. New York: Columbia University Press.

MAIER, S. F.; LAUDENSLAGER, M. L.; AND RYAN, S. M. 1985. Stressor controllability, immune function, and endogenous opiates. In Bush, F., and Overmier, J. B. (Eds.), *Affect, conditioning, and cognition.* Hillsdale, N.J.: Erlbaum.

MAIER, S. F.; SELIGMAN, M. E. P.; AND SOLOMON, R. L. 1969. Pavlovian fear conditioning and learned helplessness: Effects on escape and avoidance behavior of (a) the CS-US contingency and (b) the independence of the US and voluntary responding. In Campbell, B. A., and Church, R. M. (Eds.), *Punishment and aversive behavior,* pp. 299–342. New York: Appleton-Century-Crofts.

MALAN, H. 1963. *A study of brief psychotherapy.* Philadelphia: Lippincott.

MALINOWSKI, B. 1926. *Crime and custom in savage society.* London: Paul, Trench, and Trubner.

MALINOWSKI, B. 1927. *Sex and repression in savage society.* New York: Meridian, 1955.

MANDLER, G. 1975. *Mind and emotion.* New York: Wiley.

MANDLER, G. 1984. *Mind and body: Psychology of emotion and stress.* New York: Norton.

MANN, F.; BOWSHER, D.; MUMFORD, J.; LIPTON, S.; AND MILES, J. 1973. Treatment of intractable pain by acupuncture. *Lancet* 2:57–60.

MANTELL, D. M., AND PANZARELLA, R. 1976. Obedience and responsibility. *British Journal of Social and Clinical Psychology* 15: 239–45.

MARCUS, J.; HANS, S. L.; AUERBACH, J. G.; AND AUERBACH, A. G. 1993. Children at risk for schizophrenia: The Jerusalem Infant Development Study. II. Neurobehavioral deficits at school age. *Archives of General Psychiatry* 50:797–809.

MARKMAN, E. 1989. *Categorization and naming in children: Problems of induction.* Cambridge, Mass.: MIT Press.

MARKMAN, E. M., AND HUTCHINSON, J. E. 1984. Children's sensitivity to constraints on word meaning: Taxonomic vs. thematic relations. *Cognitive Psychology* 16:1–27.

MARKMAN, E. M., AND WACHTEL, G. A. 1988. Children's use of mutual exclusivity to constrain the meaning of words. *Cognitive Psychology* 20:121–57.

MARKS, D. F. 1983. In defense of imagery questionnaires. *Scandinavian Journal of Psychology* 24:243–46.

MARKS, I. M. 1969. *Fears and phobias.* New York: Academic Press.

MARKUS, H. R., AND KITAYAMA, S. 1991. Culture and the self: Implications for cognition, emotion, and motivation. *Psychological Review* 98:224–53.

MARLER, P. R. 1970. A comparative approach to vocal learning: Song development in white-crowned sparrows. *Journal of Comparative and Physiological Psychology Monographs* 71(No. 2, Part 2):1–25.

MARMOR, J. 1975. Homosexuality and sexual orientation disturbances. In Freedman, A. M.; Kaplan, H. I.; and Sadock, B. J. (Eds.), *Comprehensive textbook of psychiatry—II,* vol. 2, pp. 1510–19. Baltimore: Williams & Wilkins.

MARSDEN, C. D. 1985. Defects of movement in Parkinson's disease. In Delwaide, P. J., and Agnoli, A. (Eds.), *Clinical neurophysiology in Parkinsonism.* Amsterdam: Elsevier.

MARSHALL, D. A., AND MOULTON, D. G. 1981. Olfactory sensitivity to α—ionine in humans and dogs. *Chemical Senses* 6:53–61.

MARSHALL, G. D., AND ZIMBARDO, P. G. 1979. Affective consequences of inadequately explained physiological arousal. *Journal of Personality and Social Psychology* 37:970–88.

MARSLEN-WILSON, W. 1975. Sentence perception as an interactive parallel process. *Science* 189:226–28.

MARSLEN-WILSON, W. D., AND TEUBER, H. L. 1975. Memory for remote events in anterograde amnesia: Recognition of public figures from news photographs. *Neurobiologia* 13:353–64.

MASLACH, C. 1979. Negative emotional biasing of unexplained physiological arousal. *Journal of Personality and Social Psychology* 37:953–69.

MASLOW, A. H. 1954. *Motivation and personality.* New York: Harper & Row.

MASLOW, A. H. 1968. *Toward a psychology of being,* 2nd ed. Princeton, N.J.: Van Nostrand.

MASLOW, A. H. 1970. *Motivation and personality,* 2nd ed. New York: Harper.

MATARAZZO, J. D. 1983. The reliability of psychiatric and psychological diagnosis. *Clinical Psychology Review* 3:103–45.

MATHEWS, K. A. 1982. Psychological perspectives on the type A behavior pattern. *Psychological Bulletin* 91:293–323.

MATIN, L.; PICOULT, E.; STEVENS, J.; EDWARDS, M.; AND MACARTHUR, R. 1982. Ocuparalytic illusion: Visual-field dependent spatial mislocations by humans partially paralyzed with curare. *Science* 216: 198–80.

MATSUMOTO, D., AND EKMAN, P. 1989. Japanese and Caucasian Facial Expressions of Emotion. JACFEE.

MATTHYSSE, S., ET AL. 1986. The genetic transmission of schizophrenia: Application of Mendelian latent structure analysis to eye tracking dysfunctions in schizophrenia and affective disorders. *Journal of Psychiatric Research* 20: 57–65.

MATTISON, A., AND MCWHIRTER, D. 1987. Male couples: The beginning years. Intimate Relationships: Some Social Work Perspectives on Love, *Journal of Social Work and Human Sexuality* (Special Issue) 5: 67–78.

MAUGH, T. M. 1981. Biochemical markers identify mental states. *Science* 214:39–41.

MAY, R. 1958. Contributions of existential psychotherapy. In May, R.; Angel, E.; and Ellenberger, H. F. (Eds.), *Existence,* pp. 37–91. New York: Basic Books.

MAYER, D. J.; PRICE, D. D.; RAFII, A.; AND BARBER, J. 1976. Acupuncture hypalgesia: Evidence for activation of a central control system as a mechanism of action. In Bonica, J. J., and Albe-Fessard, D. (Eds.), *Advances in pain research and therapy,* vol. 1. New York: Raven Press.

MAYER, J. 1955. Regulation of energy intake and body weight: The glucostatic theory and the lipostatic hypothesis. *Annals of the New York Academy of Sciences* 63:15–43.

MAYES, A. R. 1988. *Human organic memory disorders.* New York: Cambridge University Press.

MAYEUX, R., AND KANDEL, E. R. 1991. Disorders of language: The aphasias. In Kandel, E. R.; Schwartz, J. H.; and Jessell, T. M. (Eds.), *Principles of Neural Science,* 3rd ed. New York: Elsevier.

MAYNARD-SMITH, J. 1965. The evolution of alarm calls. *American Naturalist* 100:637–50.

MAYS, D. T., AND FRANKS, C. M. 1985. *Negative outcome in psychotherapy and what to do about it.* New York: Springer.

McBURNEY, D. H.; LEVINE, J. M.; AND CAVANAUGH, P. H. 1977. Psychophysical and social ratings of human body odor. *Personality and Social Psychology Bulletin* 3:135–38.

McBURNEY, D. H., AND SHICK, T. R. 1971. Taste and water taste of twenty-six compounds for man. *Perception and Psychophysics* 10:249–52.

McCALL, R. B. 1979. The development of intellectual functioning in infancy and the prediction of later I. Q. In Osofsky, S. D. (Ed.), *The Handbook of infant development,* pp. 707–41. New York: Wiley.

McCALL, R. B. 1989. Commentary. *Human Development* (Special Topic: Continuity in early cognitive development—Conceptual and methodological challenges) 32:177–86.

McCARTHY, R. A., AND WARRINGTON, E. K. 1990. *Cognitive neuropsychology: A clinical introduction.* New York: Academic Press.

McCLEARN, G. E., AND DeFRIES, J. C. 1973. *Introduction to behavioral genetics.* San Francisco: Freeman.

McCLELLAND, J. L., AND RUMELHART, D. E. (Eds.). 1986. Parallel Distributed Processing: Explorations in the microstructure of cognition, vol. 2. *Psychological and biological models.* Cambridge, Mass.: MIT Press.

McCLELLAND, J. L.; RUMELHART, D. E.; AND HINTON, G. E. 1986. The appeal of parallel distributed processing. In Rumelhart, D. E.; McClelland, J. L.; and the PDP Research Group, *Parallel distributed processing: Vol. 1. Foundations,* pp. 3–44. Cambridge, Mass.: MIT Press.

McCLINTOCK, M. K. 1971. Menstrual synchrony and suppression. *Nature* 229:244–45.

McCLINTOCK, M. K., AND ADLER, N. T. 1978. The role of the female during copulation in wild and domestic Norway rats (*Rattus Norvegicus*). *Behaviour* 67:67–96.

McCLOSKEY, M.; WIBLE, C. G.; AND COHEN, N. J. 1988. Is there a special flashbulb-memory mechanism? *Journal of Experimental Psychology: General* 117:171–81.

McCONAGHY, M. J. 1979. Gender constancy and the genital basis of gender: Stages in the development of constancy by gender identity. *Child Development* 50:1223–26.

McCORD, W., AND McCORD, J. 1964. *The psychopath: An essay on the criminal mind.* New York: Van Nostrand.

McEWEN, B. S.; BIEGON, A.; DAVIS, P. G.; KREY, L. C.; LUINE, V. N.; McGINNIS, M.; PADEN, C. M.; PARSONS, B.; AND RAINBOW, T. C. 1982. Steroid hormones: Humoral signals which alter brain cell properties and functions. *Recent Progress in Brain Research* 38: 41–83.

McGEOCH, J. A., AND IRION, A. L. 1952. *The psychology of human learning,* 2nd ed. New York: Longmans, Green, and Co.

McGHIE, A., AND CHAPMAN, J. 1961. Disorders of attention and perception in early schizophrenia. *British Journal of Medical Psychology* 34:103–16.

McGRATH, M. J., AND COHEN, D. B. 1978. REM sleep facilitation of adaptive waking behavior: A review of the literature. *Psychological Bulletin* 85:24–57.

McGRAW, M. B. 1935. *Growth: A study of Johnny and Jimmy.* New York: Appleton-Century.

McGUIGAN, F. J. 1966. Covert oral behavior and auditory hallucinations. *Psychophysiology* 3:421–28.

McGUIRE, W. J. 1985. The nature of attitude and attitude change. In Lindzey, G., and Aronson, E. (Eds.), *Handbook of social psychology,* 3rd ed., vol. 2. New York: Random House.

McKAY, D. G. 1973. Aspects of the theory of comprehension, memory and attention. *Quarterly Journal of Experimental Psychology* 25:22–40.

McKAY, H.; SINISTERRA, L.; McKAY, A.; GOMEZ, H.; AND LLOREDA, P. 1978. Improving cognitive ability in chronically deprived children. *Science* 200:270–78.

McKENZIE, B. E.; TOOTELL, H. E.; AND DAY, R. H. 1980. Development of size constancy during the 1st year of human infancy. *Developmental Psychology* 16:163–74.

McKOON, G., AND RATCLIFF, R. 1979. Priming in episodic and semantic memory. *Journal of Verbal Learning and Verbal Behavior* 18:463–80.

McNALLY, J. 1987. Preparedness and phobia: A review. *Psychological Bulletin* 101:283–303.

MEAD, G. H. 1934. *Mind, self, and society.* Chicago: University of Chicago Press.

MEAD, M. 1935. *Sex and temperament in three primitive societies.* New York: Morrow.

MEAD, M. 1937. *Cooperation and competition among primitive peoples.* New York: McGraw-Hill.

MEAD, M. 1939. *From the South Seas: Studies of adolescence and sex in primitive societies.* New York: Morrow.

MEEHL, P. E. 1956. Profile analysis of the MMPI in differential diagnosis. In Welsh, G. S., and Dahlstrom, W. G. (Eds.), *Basic readings on the MMPI in psychology and medicine,* pp. 291–97. Minneapolis: University of Minnesota Press.

MEEHL, P. E. 1959. Some ruminations on the validation of clinical procedures. *Canadian Journal of Psychology* 13:102–28.

MEEHL, P. D. 1962. Schizotaxia, schizotypy, schizophrenia. *American Psychologist* 17:827–38.

MEHLER, J.; JUSCZYK, P.; LAMBERTZ, G.; HALSTED, N.; BERTONCINI, J.; AND AMIEL-TISON, C. 1988. A precursor to language acquisition in young infants. *Cognition* 29:143–78.

MELTZER, H. Y. 1986. Lithium mechanisms in bipolar illness and altered intracellular calcium functions. *Biological Psychiatry* 21:492–510.

MELTZER, H. Y. 1987. Biological studies in schizophrenia. *Schizophrenia Bulletin* 13:77–111.

MELTZER, H. Y. 1993. New drugs for the treatment of schizophrenia. *Psychiatric Clinics of North America* 16:365–85.

MELZACK, R. 1973. *The puzzle of pain.* New York: Basic Books.

MENDLEWICZ, J., AND RAINER, J. D. 1977. Adoption study supporting genetic transmission in manic-depressive illness. *Nature* 268: 327–29.

MENYUK, P. 1977. *Language and maturation.* Cambridge, Mass.: MIT Press.

MENZEL, E. W. 1973. Chimpanzee spatial memory organization. *Science* 182:943–45.

MENZEL, E. W. 1978. Cognitive maps in chimpanzees. In Hulse, S. H.; Fowler, H.; and Honig, W. K. (Eds.), *Cognitive processes in animal behavior,* pp. 375–422. Hillsdale, N.J.: Erlbaum.

MERCER, J. 1973. *Labelling the mentally retarded.* Berkeley, Calif.: University of California Press.

MERVIS, C. B., AND CRISAFI, M. 1978. Order acquisition of subordinate, basic, and superordinate level categories. *Child Development* 49:988–98.

MESQUITA, B., AND FRIJDA, N. H. 1992. Cultural variations in emotion: A review. *Psychological Bulletin* 112:179–204.

METALSKY, G. I.; ABRAMSON, L. Y.; SELIGMAN, M. E. P.; SEMMEL, A.; AND PETERSON, C. 1982. Attributional style and life events in the classroom: Vulnerability and invulnerability to depressive mood reactions. *Journal of Personality and Social Psychology* 43: 612–17.

METALSKY, G. I.; HALBERSTADT, L. J.; AND ABRAMSON, L. Y. 1987. Vulnerability to depressive mood reactions: Toward a more powerful test of the diathesis-stress and causal mediation components of the reformulated theory of depression. *Journal of Personality and Social Psychology* 52:386–93.

MEYER, D. E., AND SCHVANEVELDT, R. W. 1971. Facilitation in recognizing pairs of words: Evidence of a dependence between retrieval operations. *Journal of Experimental Psychology* 90:227–34.

MICHAEL, R. P., AND KEVERNE, E. B. 1968. Pheromones in the communication of sexual status in primates. *Nature* 218:746–49.

MICHAELS, J. W.; BLOMMEL, J. M.; BROCATO, R. M.; LINKOUS, R. A.; AND ROWE, J. S. 1982. Social facilitation and inhibition in a natural setting. *Replications in Social Psychology* 2:21–24.

MILGRAM, S. 1963. Behavioral study of obedience. *Journal of Abnormal and Social Psychology* 67:371–78.

MILGRAM, S. 1965. Some conditions of obedience and disobedience to authority. *Human Relations* 18:57–76.

MILGRAM, S. 1974. *Obedience to authority.* New York: Harper & Row.

MILL, J. S. 1865. *An examination of Sir William Hamilton's philosophy.* London: Longman, Green, Longman, Roberts & Green.

MILLER, A. G. 1986. *The obedience experiments: A case study of controversy in social science.* New York: Praeger.

MILLER, D. T. 1976. Ego involvement and attribution for success and failure. *Journal of Personality and Social Psychology* 34:901–906.

MILLER, G. A. 1956. The magical number seven plus or minus two: Some limits in our capacity for processing information. *Psychological Review* 63:81–97.

MILLER, G., AND GILDEA, P. 1987. How children learn words. *Scientific American* 257:94–99.

MILLER, G., AND JOHNSON-LAIRD, P. 1976. *Language and perception.* Cambridge, Mass.: Harvard University Press.

MILLER, J. G. 1984. Culture and the development of everyday social explanation. *Journal of Personality and Social Psychology* 46:961–78.

MILLER, N. E.; BAILEY, C. J.; AND STEVENSON, J. A. F. 1950. Decreased "hunger" but increased food intake resulting from hypothalamic lesions. *Science* 112:256–59.

MILLON, T. 1969. *Modern psychopathology.* Philadelphia: Saunders.

MILNER, B. 1966. Amnesia following operation on the temporal lobes. In Whitty, C. W. M., and Zangwill, O. L. (Eds.), *Amnesia,* pp. 109–33. London: Butterworth.

MILNER, B.; CORKIN, S.; AND TEUBER, H. L. 1968. Further analysis of the hippocampal syndrome: 14-year follow-up study of H. M. *Neuropsychologia* 6:215–34.

MINEKA, S. 1979. The role of fear in theories of avoidance learning, flooding, and extinction. *Psychological Bulletin* 86:985–1010.

MINUCHIN, S. 1974. *Families and family therapy.* Cambridge, Mass.: Harvard University Press.

MISCHEL, W. 1968. *Personality and assessment.* New York: Wiley.

MISCHEL, W. 1970. Sex-typing and socialization. In Mussen, P. H. (Ed.), *Carmichael's manual of child development,* vol. 1. New York: Wiley.

MISCHEL, W. 1973. Towards a cognitive social learning reconceptualization of personality. *Psychological Review* 80:252–83.

MISCHEL, W. 1974. Processes in delay of gratification. In Berkowitz, L. (Ed.), *Advances in experimental social psychology,* vol. 7. New York: Academic Press.

MISCHEL, W. 1979. On the interface of cognition and personality: Beyond the person-situation debate. *American Psychologist* 34: 740–54.

MISCHEL, W. 1984. Convergences and challenges in the search for consistency. *American Psychologist* 39:351–64.

MISCHEL, W. 1986. *Introduction to personality,* 4th ed. New York: Holt, Rinehart & Winston.

MISCHEL, W., AND BAKER, N. 1975. Cognitive appraisals and transformations in delay behavior. *Journal of Personality and Social Psychology* 31:254–61.

MISCHEL, W.; EBBESEN, E. B.; AND ZEISS, A. R. 1972. Cognitive and attentional mechanisms in delay of gratification. *Journal of Personality and Social Psychology* 21:204–18.

MISCHEL, W., AND MISCHEL, H. N. 1983. Development of children's knowledge of self-control strategies. *Child Development* 54: 603–19.

MISCHEL, W., AND MOORE, B. 1980. The role of ideation in voluntary delay for symbolically presented awards. *Cognitive Therapy and Research* 4:211–21.

MISCHEL, W., AND PEAKE, P. K. 1983. Some facets of consistency. Replies to Epstein, Funder and Bem. *Psychological Review* 90: 394–402.

MISCHEL, W.; SHODA, Y.; AND PEAKE, P. K. 1988. The nature of adolescent competencies predicted by preschool delay of gratification. *Journal of Personality and Social Psychology* 54:687–96.

MISELIS, R. R., AND EPSTEIN, A. N. 1970. Feeding induced by 2-deoxy-D-glucose injections into the lateral ventrical of the rat. *The Physiologist* 13:262.

MISHKIN, M., AND APPENZELLER, T. 1987. The anatomy of memory. *Scientific American* 256:80–89.

MISHLER, E. G., AND WAXLER, N. E. 1968. Family interaction and schizophrenia: Alternative frameworks of interpretation. In Rosenthal, D., and Kety, S. S. (Eds.), *The transmission of schizophrenia,* pp. 213–22. New York: Pergamon.

MITA, T. H.; DERMER, M.; AND KNIGHT, J. 1977. Reversed facial images and the mere exposure hypothesis. *Journal of Personality and Social Psychology* 35:597–601.

MITCHELL, D. E.; REARDON, J.; AND MUIR, D. W. 1975. Interocular transfer of the motion after-effect in normal and stereoblind observers. *Experimental Brain Research* 22:163–73.

MITROFF, I. I. 1974. *The subjective side of science.* Amsterdam: Elsevier.

MODIGLIANI, A. 1971. Embarrassment, face work and eye contact: Testing a theory of embarrassment. *Journal of Personality and Social Psychology* 17:15–24.

MOLONEY, D. P.; BOUCHARD, T. J., JR.; AND SEGAL, N. L. 1991. A genetic and environmental analysis of the vocational interests of monozygotic and dizygotic twins reared apart. *Journal of Vocational Behavior* 39:76–109.

MONEY, J. 1980. *Love and love sickness.* Baltimore: Johns Hopkins University Press.

MONEY, J., AND EHRHARDT, A. A. 1972. *Man and woman, boy and girl.* Baltimore: Johns Hopkins University Press.

MONSON, T. C.; HESLEY, J. W.; AND CHERNICK, L. 1982. Specifying when personality traits can and cannot predict behavior: An alternative to abandoning the attempt to predict single-act criteria. *Journal of Personality and Social Psychology* 43:385–99.

MOORE, J. W. 1972. Stimulus control: Studies of auditory generalization in rabbits. In Black, A. H., and Prokasy, W. F. (Eds.), *Classical conditioning II: Current research and theory,* pp. 206–30. New York: Appleton-Century-Crofts.

MORA, F.; ROLLS, E. T.; AND BURTON, M. J. 1976. Modulation during learning of the responses of neurons in the lateral hypothalamus to the sight of food. *Experimental Neurology* 53:508–19.

MORA, G. 1975. Historical and theoretical trends in psychiatry. In Freedman, A. M.; Kaplan, H. I.; and Sadock, B. J. (Eds.), *Comprehensive textbook of psychiatry,* vol. 1, pp. 1–75. Baltimore: Williams & Wilkins.

MORAY, N. 1959. Attention in dichotic listening: Affective cues and the influence of instructions. *Quarterly Journal of Experimental Psychology* 11:56–60.

MORELAND, R. L., AND ZAJONC, R. B. 1982. Exposure effects in person perception: Familiarity, similarity, and attraction. *Journal of Experimental Social Psychology* 18:395–415.

MORET, V.; FORSTER, A.; LAVERRIERE, M.-C.; LAMBERT, H. 1991. Mechanism of analgesia induced by hypnosis and acupuncture: Is there a difference? *Pain* 45:135–40.

MORGAN, C. D., AND MURRAY, H. A. 1935. A method for investigating fantasies: The thematic apperception test. *Archives of Neurological Psychiatry* 34:289–306.

MORGAN, J. 1986. *From simple input to complex grammar,* Cambridge, Mass.: MIT Press.

MORGAN, J., AND NEWPORT, E. 1981. The role of constituent structure in the induction of an artificial language. *Journal of Verbal Learning and Verbal Behavior* 20:67–85.

MORGAN, J., AND TRAVIS, L. 1989. Limits on negative information in language input. *Journal of Child Language* 16(3):531–52.

MORRIS, D. 1967. *The naked ape.* New York: McGraw-Hill.

MORSBACH, H., AND TYLER, W. J. 1986. In Harr, R. (Ed.), *The social construction of emotions,* pp. 289–307. Oxford: Blackwell.

MORTON, J. 1969. Interaction of information in word recognition. *Psychological Review* 76:165–78.

MORTON, T. U. 1978. Intimacy and reciprocity of exchange: A comparison of spouses and strangers. *Journal of Personality and Social Psychology* 36: 72–81.

MOSCOVICI, S. 1985. Social influence and conformity. In Lindzey, G., and Aronson, E. (Ed.), *Handbook of social psychology*, 3rd ed., vol 2, pp. 347–412. New York: Random House.

MOSCOVITCH, M. 1972. Choice reaction-time study assessing the verbal behavior of the minor hemisphere in normal adults. *Journal of Comparative and Physiological Psychology* 80:66–74.

MOSCOVITCH, M. 1979. Information processing and the cerebral hemispheres. In Gazzaniga, M. S., *Handbook of behavioral neurobiology*, vol. 2, pp. 379–446. New York: Plenum.

MOSCOVITCH, M., AND ROZIN, P. 1989. Disorders of the nervous system and psychopathology. In Rosenhan, D. L., and Seligman, M. E. P. *Abnormal psychology*, 2nd ed., pp. 558–602. New York: Norton.

MOSKOWITZ, D. W. 1982. Coherence and cross-situational generality in personality: A new analysis of old problems. *Journal of Personality and Social Psychology* 43:754–68.

MULFORD, R. 1986. First words of the blind child. In Smith, M., and Locke, J. (Eds.), *The emergent lexicon: The child's development of a linguistic vocabulary.* New York: Academic Press.

MURDOCK, B. 1962. The serial position effect of free recall. *Journal of Experimental Psychology* 64:482–88.

MURPHY, J. M. 1976. Psychiatric labelling in cross-cultural perspective. *Science* 191:1019–28.

MURRAY, F. B. 1978. Teaching strategies and conservation training. In Lesgold, A. M.; Pellegrino, J. W.; Fekkeman, D.; and Glaser, R. (Eds.), *Cognitive psychology and instruction*, vol. 1. New York: Plenum.

MUSCETTOLA, G.; POTTER, W. Z.; PICKAR, D.; AND GOODWIN, F. K. 1984. Urinary 3-methoxy-4-hydroxyphenylglycol and major affective disorders. *Archives of General Psychiatry* 41:337–42.

MUUSS, R. E. 1970. Puberty rites in primitive and modern societies. *Adolescence* 5:109–28.

NADEL, L., AND ZOLA-MORGAN, S. 1984. Infantile amnesia: A neurobiological perspective. In Moscovich, M. (Ed.), *Infant memory*, pp. 145–72. New York: Plenum Press.

NAIGLES, L. 1990. Children use syntax to learn verb meanings. *Journal of Child Language* 17:357–74.

NATHAN, P. W. 1978. Acupuncture analgesia. *Trends in Neurosciences* 1:210–23.

NAUTA, W. J. H., AND FEIRTAG, M. 1986. *Fundamental neuroanatomy.* New York: Freeman.

NEIMEYER, G. J. Cognitive complexity and marital satisfaction. *Journal of Social and Clinical Psychology* 2: 258–63.

NEISSER, U. 1967. *Cognitive psychology.* New York: Appleton-Century-Crofts.

NEISSER, U. 1976. *Cognition and reality.* San Francisco: Freeman.

NEISSER, U. 1982a. *Memory observed.* San Francisco: Freeman.

NEISSER, U. 1982b. *On the trail of the tape-recorder fallacy.* Paper presented at a symposium on "The influence of hypnosis and related states on memory: Forensic implications" at the meetings of the American Association for the Advancement of Science, Washington, D. C., in January 1982.

NEISSER, U. 1986. Remembering Pearl Harbor: Reply to Thompson and Cowan. *Cognition* 23:285–86.

NEISSER, U. 1989. Domains of memory. In Solomon, P. R.; Goethals, G. R.; Kelley, C. M.; and Stephens, B. R. (Eds.), *Memory: Interdisciplinary approaches*, pp. 67–83. New York: Springer Verlag.

NELSON, K. 1973. Structure and strategy in learning to talk. *Monographs of the Society for Research in Child Development* 38: (1–2, Serial No. 149).

NEMETH, C., AND CHILES, C. 1988. Modeling courage: The role of dissent in fostering independence. *European Journal of Social Psychology* 18: 275–80.

NEUGEBAUER, R. 1979. Medieval and early modern theories of mental illness. *Archives of General Psychiatry* 36:477–84.

NEWELL, A., AND SIMON, H. A. 1972. *Human problem solving.* Englewood Cliffs, N.J.: Prentice-Hall.

NEWMEYER, F. 1983. *Linguistic theory in America,* New York: Academic Press.

NEWPORT, E. L. 1984. Constraints on learning: Studies in the acquisition of American Sign Language. *Papers and Reports on Child Language Development* 23:1–22. Stanford, Calif.: Stanford University Press.

NEWPORT, E. 1990. Maturational constraints on language learning. *Cognitive Science* 14:11–28.

NEWPORT, E. L., AND ASHBROOK, E. F. 1977. The emergence of semantic relations in American Sign Language. *Papers and Reports in Child Language Development* 13.

NEWPORT, E., GLEITMAN, H., AND GLEITMAN, L. 1977. Mother, I'd rather do it myself: Some effects and non-effects of maternal speech style. In Snow, C., and Ferguson, C. (Eds.), *Talking to children: Language input and acquisition.* New York: Cambridge University Press.

NICHOLSON, R. A., AND BERMAN, J. S. 1983. Is follow-up necessary in evaluating psychotherapy? *Psychological Bulletin* 93:261–78.

NICOL, S. E., AND GOTTESMAN, I. I. 1983. Clues to the genetics and neurobiology of schizophrenia. *American Scientist* 71:398–404.

NILSSON, L. 1974. *Behold man.* Boston: Little, Brown.

NISBETT, R. E. 1968. Taste, deprivation, and weight determinants of eating behavior. *Journal of Personality and Social Psychology* 10:107–16.

NISBETT, R. E. 1972. Eating behavior and obesity in man and animals. *Advances in Psychosomatic Medicine* 7:173–93.

NISBETT, R. E. 1977. Interaction versus main effects as goals of personality research. In Magnusson, D., and Endler, L. (Eds.), *Personality at the crossroads: Current issues in interactional psychology*, pp. 235–41. Hillsdale, N.J.: Erlbaum.

NISBETT, R. E. 1980. The trait construct in lay and professional psychology. In Festinger, L. (Ed.), *Retrospections on social psychology*, pp. 109–30. New York: Oxford University Press.

NISBETT, R. E.; CAPUTO, C.; LEGANT, P.; AND MARACEK, J. 1973. Behavior as seen by the actor and as seen by the observer. *Journal of Personality and Social Psychology* 27:154-64.

NISBETT, R., AND ROSS, L. 1980. *Human inference: Strategies and shortcomings of social judgment.* Englewood Cliffs, N.J.: Prentice-Hall.

NISBETT, R. E., AND WILSON, T. D. 1977. Telling more than we can know: Verbal reports on mental processes. *Psychological Review* 84:231–59.

NOLEN-HOEKSMA, S. 1987. Sex differences in unipolar depression: Evidence and theory. *Psychological Bulletin* 101:259–82.

NORCROSS, J. C. 1991. Prescriptive matching in psychotherapy: Psychoanalysis for simple phobias? *Psychotherapy* 28:439–43.

NORCROSS, J. C., AND FREEDHEIM, D. K. 1992. Into the future: Retrospect and prospect in psychotherapy. In Freedheim, D. K. (Ed.), *History of Psychotherapy.* Washington, D.C.: American Psychological Association.

NORMAN, W. T. 1963. Toward an adequate taxonomy of personality attributes: Replicated factor structure in peer nomination personality ratings. *Journal of Abnormal and Social Psychology* 66:574–83.

NOTTEBOHM, F. 1987. Plasticity in adult avian central nervous system: Possible relations between hormones, learning, and brain repair. In Plum, F. (Ed.), *Higher functions of the nervous system: Section I, Vol. 5. Handbook of physiology.* Washington, D. C.: American Physiological Society.

NOVAK, M. A., AND HARLOW, H. F. 1975. Social recovery of monkeys isolated for the first year of life: I. Rehabilitation and therapy. *Developmental Psychology* 11:453–65.

NOWLIS, G. H., AND FRANK, M. E. 1981. Quality coding in gustatory systems of rats and hamsters. In Norris, D. M. (Ed.), *Perception of behavioral chemicals*, pp. 58–80. Amsterdam: Elsevier.

O'KEEFE, J., AND NADEL, L. 1978. *The hippocampus as a cognitive map.* Oxford: Clarendon Press.

ODIORNE, J. M. 1957. Color changes. In Brown, M. E. (Ed.), *The physiology of fishes*, vol. 2. New York: Academic Press.

OFMAN, W. V. 1985. Existential psychotherapy. In Kaplan, H. I., and Sadock, J. (Eds.), Comprehensive textbook of psychiatry, 4th ed, pp. 1438-43. Baltimore: Williams & Wilkins.

OHANIAN, H. C. 1985 and 1993. *Physics*. New York: Norton.

ÖHMAN, A.; DIMBERG, U.; AND ÖST, L. G. 1985. Biological constraints on the fear response. In Reiss, S. and Bootsin, R. (Eds.), *Theoretical issues in behavior therapy*, pp. 123–75. New York: Academic Press.

ÖHMAN, A.; ERIKSSON, A.; AND OLOFSSON, 1975. One-trial learning and superior resistance to extinction of autonomic responses conditioned to potentially phobic stimuli. *Journal of Comparative and Physiological Psychology* 88:619–27.

OLDS, J., AND MILNER, P. 1954. Positive reinforcement produced by electrical stimulation of septal areas and other regions of rat brains. *Journal of Comparative and Physiological Psychology* 47:419–27.

OLDS, M. E., AND FOBES, T. 1981. The central basis of motivation: Intracranial self-stimulation. *Annual Review of Psychology* 32:523–74.

OLFSON, M., AND KLERMAN, G. L. 1993. Trends in the prescription of psychotropic medications. The role of physician specialty. *Medical Care* 31:559–64.

OLSON, D. J. 1991. Species differences in spatial memory among Clark's nutcrackers, scrub jays, and pigeons. *Journal of Experimental Psychology: Animal Behavior Processes* 17(4):363–76.

OLTON, D. S. 1978. Characteristics of spatial memory. In Hulse, S. H., Fowler, H., and Honig, W. K. (Eds.), *Cognitive processes in animal behavior*, pp. 341–73. Hillsdale, N.J.: Erlbaum.

OLTON, D. S. 1979. Mazes, maps, and memory. *American Psychologist* 34:583–96.

OLTON, D. S., AND SAMUELSON, R. J. 1976. Remembrance of places passed: Spatial memory in rats. *Journal of Experimental Psychology: Animal Behavior Processes* 2:97–116.

OLWEUS, D. 1980. Familial and temperamental determinants of aggressive behavior in adolescent boys: A causal analysis. *Developmental Psychology* 16:644–66.

ORBELL, J. M.; VAN DE KRAGT, A. J. C.; AND DAWES, R. M. 1988. Explaining discussion-induced cooperation. *Journal of Personality and Social Psychology* 54:811–19.

ORLANSKY, H. 1949. Infant care and personality. *Psychological Bulletin* 46:1–48.

ORNE, M. T. 1951. The mechanisms of hypnotic age regression: An experimental study. *Journal of Abnormal and Social Psychology* 58:277–99.

ORNE, M. T. 1975. Psychotherapy in contemporary America: Its development and context. In Arieti, S. (Ed.), *American handbook of psychiatry*, 2nd ed., vol. 5, pp. 1–33. New York: Basic Books.

ORNE, M. T. 1979. The use and misuse of hypnosis in court. *The International Journal of Clinical and Experimental Hypnosis* 27:311–41.

ORNE, M. T., AND HAMMER, A. G. 1974. Hypnosis. in *Encyclopaedia Brittanica*, 5th ed., pp. 133–40. Chicago: Encyclopaedia Brittannica.

ORNSTEIN, R. 1977. *The psychology of consciousness* 2nd ed. New York: Harcourt Brace Jovanovich.

ORSINI, D. L.; VAN GORP, W. G.; AND BOONE, K. B. 1988. *The neuropsychology casebook*. New York: Springer-Verlag.

OSOFSKY, J. D., AND DANZGER, B. 1974. Relationships between neonatal characteristics and mother-infant characteristics. *Developmental Psychology* 10:124–30.

OSTROM, T. M. 1977. Between-theory and within-theory conflict in explaining context effects in impression formation. *Journal of Experimental Social Psychology* 13:492–503.

PACKER, C. 1977. Reciprocal altruism in olive baboons. *Nature* 265:441–43.

PAGE, E. B. 1985. Review of Kaufman's Assessment Battery for Children. *Ninth mental measurements yearbook*, vol. 1., pp. 773–77.

PAI, M. N. 1946. Sleep-walking and sleep activities. *Journal of Mental Science* 92:756–65.

PARKE, R. D. 1981. *Fathers*. Cambridge, Mass.: Harvard University Press.

PARKE, R. D., AND SLABY, R. G. 1983. The development of aggression. In Mussen, P. H. (Ed.), *Carmichael's manual of child psychology: Vol. 4. Socialization, personality and social development* (Hetherington, M. E., volume editor), pp. 547–642. New York: Wiley.

PARNAS, J., AND JORGENSEN, A. 1989. Premorbid psychopathology in schizophrenia spectrum. *British Journal of Psychiatry* 155:623–27.

PARROTT, W. G.; SABINI, J.; AND SILVER, M. 1988. The roles of self-esteem and social interaction in embarrassment. *Personality and Social Psychology Bulletin* 14:191–202.

PASCALE-LEONE, J. 1978. Compounds, confounds and models in developmental information processing: A reply to Trabasso and Foellinger. *Journal of Experimental Child Psychology* 26:18–40.

PATIENCE, A., AND SMITH, J. W. 1986. Derek Freeman and Samoa: The making and unmaking of a biobehavioral myth. *American Anthropologist* 88:157–61.

PATTERSON, T.; SPOHN, H. E.; BOGIA, D. P.; AND HAYES, K. 1986. Thought disorder in schizophrenia: Cognitive and neuroscience approaches. *Schizophrenia Bulletin* 12:460–72.

PAUL, G. L. 1966. *Insight vs. desensitization in psychotherapy: An experiment in anxiety reduction*. Stanford, Calif.: Stanford University Press.

PAUL, G. L. 1967. Insight versus desensitization in psychotherapy two years after termination. *Journal of Consulting Psychology* 31:333–48.

PAUL, J. P. 1984. The bisexual identity: An idea without social recognition. *Journal of Homosexuality* 9: 45–63.

PAUL, J. P. 1985. Bisexuality: Reassessing our paradigms of sexuality. *Bisexualities: Theory and Research, Journal of Homosexuality* (Special Issue) 11:21–34.

PAVLOV, I. 1927. *Conditioned reflexes*. Oxford, England: Oxford University Press.

PAVLOV, I. 1928. *Lectures on conditioned reflexes*, vol 1. New York: International Publishers Co., Inc.

PAYKEL, E. S. 1982. Life events and early environment. In Paykel, E. S. (Ed.), *Handbook of affective disorders*. New York: Guilford.

PENFIELD, W. 1975. *The mystery of the mind*. Princeton, N.J.: Princeton University Press.

PENFIELD, W., AND RASMUSSEN, T. 1950. *The cerebral cortex of man*. New York: Macmillan.

PENFIELD, W., AND ROBERTS, L. 1959. *Speech and brain mechanisms*. Princeton, N.J.: Princeton University Press.

PENROSE, L. S., AND PENROSE, R. 1958. Impossible objects: A special type of visual illusion. *British Journal of Psychology* 49:31–33.

PEPITONE, A. 1976. Toward a normative and comparative biocultural social psychology. *Journal of Personality and Social Psychology* 43:641–53.

PERIN, C. T. 1943. A quantitative investigation of the delay of reinforcement gradient. *Journal of Experimental Psychology* 32:37–51.

PETERSON, C., AND SELIGMAN, M. E. P. 1984. Causal explanations as a risk factor for depression: Theory and evidence. *Psychological Review* 91:341–74.

PETERSON, C.; SEMMEL, A.; VON BAEYER, C.; ABRAMSON, L. Y.; METALSKY, G. I.; AND SELIGMAN, M. E. P. 1982. The Attributional Style Questionnaire. *Cognitive Therapy and Research* 6:287–99.

PETITTO, L., AND MARENTETTE, P. F. 1991. Babbling in the manual mode: Evidence for the ontogeny of language. *Science* 251:1493–96.

PETTY, R. E., AND CACIOPPO, J. T. 1985. The elaboration likelihood model of persuasion. In Berkowitz, L. (Ed.), *Advances in experimental social psychology*, vol. 19. New York: Academic Press.

PIAGET, J. 1951. *Play, dreams and imitation in childhood*. New York: Norton.

PIAGET, J. 1952. *The origins of intelligence in children*. New York: International University Press.

PIAGET, J. 1972. *The child's conception of the world*. Totowa, N.J.: Littlefield, Adams.

PIAGET, J., AND INHELDER, B. 1956. *The child's conception of space.* London: Routledge and Kegan Paul.

PIAGET, J., AND INHELDER, B. 1967. *The child's conception of space.* New York: Norton.

PILLEMER, D. B. 1984. Flashbulb memories of the assassination attempt on President Reagan. *Cognition* 16:63–80.

PINKER, S. 1984. *Language learnability and language development.* Cambridge, Mass: Harvard University Press.

PINKER, S. 1989. *Learnability and cognition: The acquisition of argument structure.* Cambridge, Mass: MIT Press.

PINKER, S. 1994. *The language instinct.* New York: William Morrow.

PINKER, S., AND PRINCE, A. 1988. On language and connectionism: Analysis of a parallel distributed processing model of language acquisition. *Cognition* 28(1):73–194.

PLECK, J. H. 1985. *Working wives/working husbands.* Beverly Hills, Calif: Sage.

PLOMIN, R., AND DANIELS, D. 1987. Why are children from the same family so different from one another? *Behavioral and Brain Sciences* 10:1–16.

PLUTCHIK, R. 1970. Emotions, evolution, and adaptive processes. In Arnold, M. B. (Ed.), *Feelings and emotions: The Loyola symposium.* New York: Academic Press.

PLUTCHIK, R. 1980. The evolutionary context. In Plutchik, R., and Kellerman, H. (Eds.), *Emotion: Theory, research and experience,* vol. 1. New York: Academic Press.

PLUTCHIK, R. 1984. Emotions: A general psychoevolutionary approach. In Scherer, K., and Ekman, P. *Approaches to emotion.* Hillsdale, N.J.: Erlbaum.

POGGIO, G. F., AND FISCHER, B. 1978. Binocular interaction and depth sensitivity in striate and prestriate cortex of behaving rhesus monkey. *Journal of Neurophysiology* 40:1392–1405.

POGUE-GEILE, M. F., AND ROSE, R. J. 1985. Developmental genetic studies of adult personality. *Developmental Psychology* 21: 547–57.

POLEY, W. 1974. Dimensionality in the measurement of authoritarian and political attitudes. *Canadian Journal of Behavioral Science* 6:83-94.

POMERANTZ, J. R., AND KUBOVY, M. 1981. Perceptual organization: An overview. In Kubovy, M., and Pomerantz, J. R. (Eds.), *Perceptual organization,* pp. 423–56. Hillsdale, N.J.: Erlbaum.

POMERANTZ, J. R., AND KUBOVY, M. 1986. Theoretical approaches to perceptual organization. In Boff, K. R.; Kauffman, L.; and Thomas, J. P. (Eds.), *Handbook of perception and human performance: Vol. 2. Cognitive processes and performance,* pp. 1–46. New York: Wiley.

PORAC, C., AND PORAC, S. 1981. *Lateral preferences and human behavior.* New York: Springer-Verlag.

PORSOLT, R. D.; LePICHON, M.; AND JALFRE, M. 1977. Depression: A new animal model sensitive to antidepressant treatments. *Nature* 266: 730-32.

PRASADA, S., AND PINKER, S. 1993. Generalizations of regular and irregular morphology. *Language and Cognitive Processes* 8:1–56.

PREMACK, A., AND PREMACK, D. 1972. Teaching language to an ape. *Scientific American* 227: 92-99.

PREMACK, A., AND PREMACK, D. 1983. *The mind of an ape.* New York: Norton.

PREMACK, D. 1976. *Intelligence in ape and man.* Hillsdale, N.J.: Erlbaum.

PREMACK, D. 1978. On the abstractness of human concepts: Why it would be difficult to talk to a pigeon. In Hulse, S. H.; Fowler, H.; and Honig, W. K. (Eds.), *Cognitive processes in animal behavior.* Hillsdale, N.J.: Erlbaum.

PREMACK, D. 1988. 'Does the chimpanzee have a theory of mind' revisited. In Byrne, R. W., and Whiten, A. (Eds.), *Machiavellian intelligence: Social expertise and the evolution of intellect in monkeys, apes, and humans,* pp. 160–79. Oxford: Oxford University.

PREMACK, D., AND WOODRUFF, G. 1978. Does the chimpanzee have a theory of mind? *The Behavioral and Brain Sciences* 4:515–26.

PRICE, R. H., AND BOUFFARD, B. L. 1974. Behavioral appropriateness and situational constraint. *Journal of Personality and Social Psychology* 30:579–86.

PRICE-WILLIAMS, D. R. 1981. Concrete and formal operations. In

Munroe, R. H.; Munroe, R. L.; and Whiting, B. B. (Eds.), *Handbook of cross-cultural development,* pp. 403–22. New York: Garland.

PRICE-WILLIAMS, D. R. 1985. Cultural psychology. In Lindzey, G., and Aronson, E. (Eds.), *Handbook of social psychology,* vol. 2, pp. 993–1042. New York: Academic Press.

PRICE-WILLIAMS, D., GORDON, W., AND RAMIREZ, M. 1969. Skill and conservation: A study of pottery-making children. *Developmental Psychology* 1:769.

PRINCE, E. 1981. Toward a taxonomy of given-new information. In P. Cole (Ed.), *Syntax and semantics 9 Pragmatics.* New York: Academic Press.

PRINCE, G. 1978. Putting the other half of the brain to work. *Training: The Magazine of Human Resources Development* 15:57-61.

PRINZHORN, H. 1972. *Artistry of the mentally ill.* New York: Springer-Verlag.

PRIOLEAU, L.; MURDOCK, M.; AND BRODY, N. 1983. An analysis of psychotherapy versus placebo studies. *The Behavioral and Brain Sciences* 6:275–310.

PRITCHARD, R. M. 1961. Stabilized images on the retina. *Scientific American* 204:72–78.

PROVENCE, S., AND LIPTON, R. C. 1962. *Infants in institutions.* New York: International Universities Press.

PUTNAM, F. W.; GUROFF, J. J.; SILBERMAN, E. K.; BARBAN, L.; AND POST, R. M. 1986. The clinical phenomenology of multiple personality disorder: Review of 100 recent cases. *Journal of Clinical Psychiatry* 47:285–93.

PUTNAM, H. 1975. The meaning of "meaning." In Gunderson, K. (Ed.), *Language, mind, and knowledge.* Minneapolis: University of Minnesota Press.

PUTNAM, K. E. 1979. Hypnosis and distortions in eye witness memory. *International Journal of Clinical and Experimental Hypnosis* 27:437–48.

QUAY, H. C. 1965. Psychopathic personality as pathological stimulation seeking. *American Journal of Psychiatry* 122:180–83.

QUAY, L. C. 1971. Language, dialect, reinforcement, and the intelligence test performance of Negro children. *Child Development* 42:5–15.

RACHMAN, S. J., AND TEASDALE, J. 1969. Aversion therapy: An appraisal. In Franks, C. M. (Ed.), *Behavior therapy: Appraisal and status,* pp. 279–320. New York: McGraw-Hill.

RADFORD, A. 1988. *Transformational grammar: A first course* New York: Cambridge University Press.

RADKE-YARROW, M.; ZAHN-WAXLER, C.; AND CHAPMAN, M. 1983. Children's prosocial dispositions and behavior. In Mussen, P. E. (Ed.), *Carmichael's manual of child psychology: Vol. 4. Socialization, personality, and social development* (Hetherington, E. M., volume editor), pp. 469-546. New York: Wiley.

RAPOPORT, A. 1988. Experiments with *N*-person social traps. II. Tragedy of the commons. *Journal of Conflict Resolution* 32:473–99.

RAPOPORT, J. L. 1990. *The boy who couldn't stop washing.* New York: Penguin Books.

RAPPAPORT, M., AND LEVIN, B. 1988. What to do with roles. In W. Wilkins (Ed), *Syntax and semantics: Vol. 21. Thematic relations.* San Diego: Academic Press.

RAPPAPORT, Z. H. 1992. Psychosurgery in the modern era: Therapeutic and ethical aspects. *Medicine and Law* 11:449–53.

RAVEN, B. H., AND RUBIN, J. Z. 1976. *Social psychology: People in groups.* New York: Wiley.

RAYNER, K. 1978. Eye movements in reading and information processing. *Psychological Bulletin* 85:618–60.

READ, C., AND SCHREIBER, P. 1982. Why short subjects are harder to find than long ones. In Wanner, E., and Gleitman, L. R. (Eds.), *Language acquisition: The state of the art.* New York: Cambridge University Press.

REBER, A. S. 1985. *The Penguin dictionary of psychology.* New York: Viking Penguin.

REID, W. H.; PHAM, V. A.; AND RAGO, W. 1993. Clozapine use by state programs: Public mental-health systems respond to a new medication. *Hospital and Community Psychiatry* 44:739–43.

REISBERG, D.; BARON, J.; AND KEMLER, D. G. 1980. Overcoming Stroop interference: The effects of practice on distractor potency. *Journal of Experimental Psychology: Human Perception and Performance* 6:140–50.

REISBERG, D., AND CHAMBERS, D. 1992. Neither pictures nor propositions: What can we learn from a mental image? *Canadian Journal of Psychology* 45:336–52.

REISBERG, D., AND LEAK, S. 1987. Visual imagery and memory for appearance: Does Clark Gable or George C. Scott have bushier eyebrows? *Canadian Journal of Psychology* 41:521–26.

REISENZEIN, R. 1983. The Schachter theory of emotions: Two decades later. *Psychological Bulletin* 94:239–64.

REISMAN, J. A., AND EICHEL, E. W. 1990. *Kinsey, sex and fraud.* Lafayette, La.: Huntington House.

RENNER, M. J., AND ROSENZWEIG, M. R. 1987. *Enriched and impoverished environments: Effects on brain and behavior.* New York: Springer.

RESCORLA, R. A. 1966. Predictability and number of pairings in Pavlovian fear conditioning. *Psychonomic Science* 4:383–84.

RESCORLA, R. A. 1967. Pavlovian conditioning and its proper control procedures. *Psychological Review* 74:71–80.

RESCORLA, R. A. 1980. *Pavlovian second-order conditioning.* Hillsdale, N.J.: Erlbaum.

RESCORLA, R. A. 1988. Behavioral studies of Pavlovian conditioning. *Annual Review of Neuroscience* 11: 329–52.

RESCORLA, R. A., AND HOLLAND, P. C. 1982. Behavioral studies of associative learning in animals. *Annual Reviews of Psychology* 33:265–308.

RESCORLA, R. A., AND WAGNER, A. R. 1972. A theory of Pavlovian conditioning: Variations in the effectiveness of reinforcement and non-reinforcement. In Black, A. H., and Prokasy, W. F. (Eds.), *Classical conditioning II.* New York: Appleton-Century-Crofts.

REST, J. R. 1983. Morality. In Mussen, P. E. (Ed.), *Carmichael's manual of child psychology: Vol. 4. Socialization, personality, and social development* (Hetherington, E. M., volume editor). New York: Wiley.

REST, J. R. 1984. The major components of morality. In Kurtines, W. M., and Gewirtz, L. (Eds.), *Morality, moral behavior, and moral development.* New York: Wiley.

REVLIN, R., AND LEIRER, V. O. 1980. Understanding quantified categorical expressions. *Memory and Cognition* 8:447–58.

REVUSKY, S. H. 1971. The role of interference in association over a delay. In Honig, W. K., and James, H. R. (Eds.), *Animal memory.* New York: Academic Press.

REVUSKY, S. 1977. Learning as a general process with an emphasis on data from feeding experiments. In Milgram, N. W.; Krames, L.; and Alloway, T. H. (Eds.), *Food aversion learning,* pp. 1–51. New York: Plenum.

REVUSKY, S. 1985. The general process approach to animal learning. In Johnston, T. D., and Petrewicz, A. T. (Eds.), *Issues in the ecological study of learning.* Hillsdale, N.J.: Erlbaum.

REYNOLDS, G. S. 1968. *A primer of operant conditioning.* Glenview, Ill.: Scott, Foresman.

RHEINGOLD, H. L.; HAY, D. F.; AND WEST, M. J. 1976. Sharing in the second year of life. *Child Development* 47:1148–58.

RICHARDS, W. 1977. Lessons in constancy from neurophysiology. In Epstein, W. W. (Ed.), *Stability and constancy in visual perception: Mechanisms and processes,* pp. 421–36. New York: Wiley.

RICKS, S. S. 1985. Father-infant interactions: A review of empirical research. *Family Relations* 34:505–11.

RIGGS, L. A.; RATLIFF, F.; CORNSWEET, J. C.; AND CORNSWEET, T. N. 1953. The disappearance of steadily fixated visual test objects. *Journal of the Optical Society of America* 43:495–501.

RIPS, L. J.; SHOBEN, E. J.; AND SMITH, E. E. 1973. Semantic distance and the verification of semantic relations. *Journal of Verbal Learning and Verbal Behavior* 12:1–20.

RIPS, L. J.; SMITH, E. E.; AND SHOBEN, E. J. 1978. Semantic composition in sentence verification. *Journal of Verbal Learning and Verbal Behavior* 19:705–21.

RIZZI, L. 1982. Negation, *wh*-movement, and the null subject parameter. In Rizzi, L., *Issues in Italian syntax,* pp. 117–84. Dordrecht: Foris.

ROBBIN, A. A. 1958. A controlled study of the effects of leucotomy. *Journal of Neurology, Neurosurgery and Psychiatry* 21:262–69.

ROBBINS, S. J. 1990. Mechanisms underlying spontaneous recovery in autoshaping. *Journal of Experimental Psychology: Animal Behavior Processes* 16:235–49.

ROBINS, L. N.; HELZER, J. E.; WEISSMAN, M. M.; ORVASCHEL, H.; GRUENBERG, E.; BURKE, J. D.; AND REGIER, D. A. 1984. Lifetime prevalence of specific psychiatric disorders in three sites. *Archives of General Psychiatry* 41:948–58.

ROBINS, L. R. 1966. *Deviant children grown up: A sociological and psychiatric study of sociopathic personality.* Baltimore: Williams & Wilkins.

ROBINSON, H. B., AND ROBINSON, N. M. 1970. Mental retardation. In Mussen, P. H. (Ed.), *Carmichael's manual of child psychology,* vol. 2, pp. 65–66. New York: Wiley.

ROCK, I. 1975. *An introduction to perception.* New York: Macmillan.

ROCK, I. 1977. In defense of unconscious inference. In Epstein, W. W. (Ed.), *Stability and constancy in visual perception: Mechanisms and processes,* pp. 321–74. New York: Wiley.

ROCK, I. 1983. *The logic of perception.* Cambridge, Mass.: MIT Press.

ROCK, I. 1986. The description and analysis of object and event perception. In Boff, K. R.; Kauffman, L.; and Thomas, J. P. (Eds.), *Handbook of perception and human performance: Vol. 2. Cognitive processes and performance,* pp. 1–71. New York: Wiley.

ROCK, I., AND KAUFMAN, L. 1962. The moon illusion, II. *Science* 136:1023–31.

RODIN, J. 1980. The externality theory today. In Stunkard, A. J. (Ed.), *Obesity,* pp. 226–39. Philadelphia: Saunders.

RODIN, J. 1981. Current status of the internal-external hypothesis for obesity. What went wrong? *American Psychologist* 36:361–72.

RODIN, J., AND LANGER, E. J. 1977. Long-term effects of a control-relevant intervention with the institutionalized aged. *Journal of Personality and Social Psychology* 35:897–902.

RODMAN, H. R.; GROSS, C. G.; AND ALBRIGHT, T. D. 1989. Afferent basis of visual response properties in area MT of the macaque. I. Effects of striate cortex removal. *Journal of Neuroscience* 9:2033–50.

ROEDER, K. D. 1935. An experimental analysis of the sexual behavior of the praying mantis. *Biological Bulletin* 69:203–20.

ROEDER, L. 1967. *Nerve cells and insect behavior.* Cambridge, Mass.: Harvard University Press.

ROEDIGER, H. L., III. 1980. Memory metaphors in cognitive psychology. *Memory and Cognition* 8: 231–46.

ROEDIGER, H. L., III. 1990. Implicit memory: Retention without remembering. *American Psychologist* 45:1043–56.

ROEPER, T., AND WILLIAMS, E. (Eds.). 1987. *Parameter setting.* Dordrecht: Reidel.

ROGERS, C. R. 1942. *Counseling and psychotherapy: New concepts in practice.* Boston: Houghton Mifflin.

ROGERS, C. R. 1951 and 1970. *Client-centered therapy: Its current practice, implications, and theory,* 1st and 2nd eds. Boston: Houghton Mifflin.

ROGERS, C. R. 1959. A theory of therapy, personality, and interpersonal relationships as developed in the client-centered framework. In Koch, S. (Ed.), *Psychology: A study of a science,* vol. 3. New York: McGraw-Hill.

ROGERS, C. R. 1961. *On becoming a person: A therapist's view of psychotherapy.* Boston: Houghton Mifflin.

ROGERS, C. R. 1980. *A way of being.* Boston: Houghton Mifflin.

ROGERS, C. R., AND DYMOND, R. F. 1954. *Psychotherapy and personality change: Coordinated studies in the client-centered approach.* Chicago: University of Chicago Press.

ROGOFF, B.; GAUVAIN, M.; AND ELLIS, S. 1984. Development viewed in its cultural context. In Bornstein, M. H., and Lamb, M. E. (Eds.), *Developmental psychology: An advanced textbook.* Hillsdale, N.J.: Erlbaum.

ROLAND, P. E.; LARSEN, B.; LASSEN, N. A.; AND SKINHØJ, E. 1980. Supplementary motor area and other cortical areas in organization of voluntary movements in man. *Journal of Neurophysiology* 43:539–60.

ROLLS, B. J., AND ROLLS, E. T. 1982. *Thirst.* New York: Cambridge University Press.

ROLLS, E. J. 1978. Neurophysiology of feeding. *Trends in Neurosciences* 1:1–3.

ROLLS, E. T. 1975. *The brain and reward.* New York: Pergamon.

ROLLS, E. T.; BURTON, M. J.; AND MORA, F. 1976. Hypothalamic responses associated with the sight of food. *Brain Research* 111:53–66.

ROMANES, G. J. 1882. *Animal intelligence.* London: Kegan Paul.

ROPER, T. J. 1983. Learning as a biological phenomenon. In Halliday, T. R., and Slater, P. J. B. (Eds.), *Genes, development and behavior,* vol. 3, pp. 178–212: *Animal behavior.* Oxford: Blackwell.

RORER, L. G. 1990. Personality assessment: A conceptual survey. In Pervin, L. A. (Ed.), *Handbook of personality: Theory and research,* pp. 693–722. New York: Guilford Press.

RORER, L. G., AND WIDIGER, T. A. 1983. Personality structure and assessment. In Rosenzweig, M. R., and Porter, L. W. (Eds.), *Annual Review of Psychology* 34:431–63.

ROSCH, E. H. 1973a. Natural categories. *Cognitive Psychology* 4:328–50.

ROSCH, E. H. 1973b. On the internal structure of perceptual and semantic categories. In Moore, T. E. (Ed.), *Cognitive development and the acquisition of language.* New York: Academic Press.

ROSCH, E. H. 1978. Principles of categorization. In Rosch, E., and Lloyd (Eds.), *Cognition and categorization.* Hillsdale, N.J.: Erlbaum.

ROSCH, E. H., AND MERVIS, C. B. 1975. Family resemblances: Studies in the internal structure of categories. *Cognitive Psychology* 7:573–605.

ROSCH, E. H.; MERVIS, C. B.; GRAY, W. D.; JOHNSON, D. M.; AND BOYES-BRAEM, P. 1976. Basic objects in natural categories. *Cognitive Psychology* 8:382–439.

ROSEN, G. 1966. *Madness in society.* Chicago: University of Chicago Press.

ROSEN, L. N.; TARGUM, S. D.; TERMAN, M.; BRYANT, M. J.; HOFFMAN, H.; KASPER, S. F.; HAMOVIT, J. R.; DOCHERTY, J. P.; WELCH, B.; AND ROSENTHAL, N. E. 1990. Prevalence of seasonal affective disorder at four latitudes. *Psychiatry Research* 31: 131–44.

ROSENFELD, P.; GIACALONE, R. A.; AND TEDESCHI, J. T. 1984. Cognitive dissonance and impression management explanations for effort justification. *Personality and Social Psychology Bulletin* 10: 394–401.

ROSENHAN, D. L. 1973. On being sane in insane places. *Science* 179:250–58.

ROSENMAN, R. H.; BRAND, R. J.; JENKINS, C. D.; FRIEDMAN, M.; AND STRAUS, R. 1975. Coronary heart disease in the Western Collaborative Group Study: Final follow-up experience of $8\frac{1}{2}$ years. *Journal of the American Medical Association* 233:872–77.

ROSENSTEIN, M. J.; MILAZZO-SAYRE. L. J.; AND MANDERSCHEID, R. W. 1989. Care of persons with schizophrenia: A statistical profile. *Schizophrenia Bulletin* 15:45–58.

ROSENTHAL, A. M. 1964. *Thirty-eight witnesses.* New York: McGraw-Hill.

ROSENTHAL, D. 1970. *Genetic theory and abnormal behavior.* New York: McGraw-Hill.

ROSENTHAL, D. M. 1993. Higher-order thoughts and the appendage theory of consciousness. *Philosophical Psychology* 6:155–66.

ROSENTHAL, N. E.; CARPENTER, C. J.; JAMES, S. P.; PARRY, B. L.; ROGERS, S. L. B.; AND WEHER, T. A. 1986. Seasonal affective disorder in children and adolescents. *American Journal of Psychiatry* 143:356–58.

ROSENTHAL, N. E.; SACK, D. A.; GILLIN, J. C.; LEWY, A. J.; GOODWIN, F. K.; DAVENPORT, Y.; MUELLER, P. S.; NEWSOME, D. A.; AND WEHR, T. A. 1984. Seasonal affective disorder: A description of the syndrome and preliminary findings with light therapy. *Archives of General Psychiatry* 41:72–80.

ROSENTHAL, N. E.; SACK, D. A.; SKWERER, R. G.; AND JACOBSEN, F. M., 1988. Phototherapy for seasonal-affective disorder. Seasonal-Affective Disorder: Mechanisms, Treatments, and Models. *Journal of Biological Rhythms* (Special Issue) 3(2):101–20.

ROSENZWEIG, M. R., AND BENNETT. 1972. Cerebral changes in rats exposed individually to an enriched environment. *Journal of Comparative and Physiological Psychology* 80:304–13.

ROSENZWEIG, M. R., AND LEIMAN, A. L. 1989. *Physiological psychology,* 2nd ed. New York: Random House.

ROSS, J., AND LAWRENCE, K. Q. 1968. Some observations on memory artifice. *Psychonomic Science* 13:107–108.

ROSS, L. 1977. The intuitive psychologist and his shortcomings: Distortions in the attribution process. In Berkowitz, L. (Ed.), *Advances in experimental social psychology,* vol. 10. New York: Academic Press.

ROSS, L.; AMABILE, T. M.; AND STEINMETZ, J. L. 1977. Social roles, social control, and biases in social perception processes. *Journal of Experimental Social Psychology* 35:817–29.

ROSS, L., AND NISBETT, R. E. 1991. *The person and the situation.* New York: McGraw-Hill.

ROVEE-COLLIER, C. K. 1990. The "memory system" of prelinguistic infants. In Diamond, A. (Ed.), *The development and neural bases of higher cognitive functions.* New York: The New York Academy of Sciences.

ROVEE-COLLIER, C. K., AND HAYNE, H. 1987. Reactivation of infant memory: Implications for cognitive development. In Reese, H. W. (Ed.), *Advances in child development and behavior,* vol. 20. New York: Academic Press.

ROY, A. 1982. Suicide in chronic schizophrenics. *British Journal of Psychiatry* 141:170–77.

ROZIN, P. 1976a. The evolution of intelligence and access to the cognitive unconscious. In Stellar, E., and Sprague, J. M. (Eds.), *Progress in psychobiology and physiological psychology,* vol. 6. New York: Academic Press.

ROZIN, P. 1976b. The psychobiological approach to human memory. In Rosenzweig, M. R., and Bennett, E. L., *Neural mechanisms of learning and memory,* pp. 3–48. Cambridge, Mass.: MIT Press.

ROZIN, P. 1976c. The selection of foods by rats, humans and other animals. *Advances in the study of behavior,* vol. 6, pp. 21–76. New York: Academic Press.

ROZIN, P. 1982. Human food selection: The interaction of biology, culture, and individual experience. In Barker, L. M. (Ed.), *The psychology of human food selection,* pp. 225–54. Westport, Conn.: AVI Publ. Co.

ROZIN, P., AND KALAT, J. W. 1971. Specific hungers and poison avoidance as adaptive specializations of learning. *Psychological Review* 78:459–86.

ROZIN, P., AND KALAT, J. W. 1972. Learning as a situation-specific adaptation. In Seligman, M. E. P., and Hager, J. L. (Eds.), *Biological boundaries of learning,* pp. 66–96. New York: Appleton-Century-Crofts.

ROZIN, P., AND SCHULL, J. 1988. The adaptive-evolutionary point of view in experimental psychology. In Atkinson, R. C.; Herrnstein, R. J.; Lindzey, G.; and Luce, R. D. (Eds.), *Steven's handbook of experimental psychology,* 2nd ed., vol. 1: *Perception and motivation,* pp. 503–46. New York: Wiley.

RUBIN, Z; HILL, C. T.; PEPLAU, L. A.; DUNKEL-SCHETTER, C. 1980. Self-disclosure in dating couples: Sex roles and the ethic of openness. *Journal of Marriage and the Family* 42(2): 305–17.

RUMBAUGH, D. M. (Ed.). 1977. *Language learning by a chimpanzee: The Lana Project.* New York: Academic Press.

RUMELHART, D., AND MCCLELLAND, J. 1986. On learning the past tenses of English verbs. In McClelland, J.; Rumelhart, D.; and the PDP Research Group (Eds.), *Parallel distributed processing: Explorations in the microstructure of cognition,* vol. I. Cambridge, Mass: MIT Press.

RUSHTON, J. P.; FULKER, D. W.; NEALE, M. C.; NIAS, D. K. B.; EYSENCK, H. J. 1986. Altruism and aggression: The heritability of individual differences. *Journal of Personality and Social Psychology* 50:1192–98.

RUSSEK, M. 1971. Hepatic receptors and the neurophysiological mechanisms controlling feeding behavior. In Ehrenpreis, S. (Ed.), *Neurosciences research,* vol. 4. New York: Academic Press.

RUSSELL, G. V. 1961. Interrelationship within the limbic and centrem-cephalic systems. In Sheer, D. E. (Ed.), *Electrical stimulation of the brain,* pp. 167–81. Austin, Tex.: University of Texas Press.

RUSSELL, M. J. 1976. Human olfactory communication. *Nature* 260:520–22.

RUSSELL, M. J.; SWITZ, G. M.; AND THOMPSON, K. 1980. Olfactory influence on the human menstrual cycle. *Pharmacology, Biochemistry, and Behavior* 13:737–38.

SABINI, J. 1995. *Social psychology,* 2nd ed. New York: Norton.

SABINI, J., AND SILVER, M. 1982. *Moralities of everyday life.* New York: Oxford University Press.

SACHS, J. 1967. Recognition memory for syntactic and semantic aspects of connected discourse. *Perception and Psychophysics* 2:437–42.

SACKS, O. 1985. *The man who mistook his wife for a hat.* New York: Harper & Row.

SADLER, H. H.; DAVISON, L.; CARROLL, C.; AND KOUNTZ, S. L. 1971. The living, genetically unrelated, kidney donor. *Seminars in Psychiatry* 3:86–101.

SADOCK, B. J. 1975. Group psychotherapy. In Freedman, A. M.; Kaplan, H. I.; and Sadock, B. J. (Eds.), *Comprehensive textbook of psychiatry,* vol. 2, pp. 1850–76. Baltimore: Williams & Wilkins.

SAGHIR, M. T., AND ROBINS, E. 1973. *Male and female homosexuality.* Baltimore: Williams & Wilkins.

SAGI, A., AND HOFFMAN, M. L. 1976. Empathic distress in the newborn. *Developmental Psychology* 12:175–76.

SAHLINS, M. 1976. *The use and abuse of biology.* Ann Arbor, Mich.: University of Michigan Press.

SARASON, S. B. 1973. Jewishness, blackness, and the nature nurture controversy. *American Psychologist* 28:926–71.

SARBIN, T. R., AND ALLEN, V. L. 1968. Role theory. In Lindzey, G., and Aronson, E. (Eds.), *The handbook of social psychology,* 2nd ed., vol. 1, pp. 488–567. Reading, Mass.: Addison-Wesley.

SARNOFF, C. 1957. *Medical aspects of flying motivation—a fear-of-flying casebook.* Randolph Air Base, Tex.: U. S. Air Force, Air University, School of Aviation Medicine.

SATINOFF, E. 1964. Behavioral thermoregulation in response to local cooling of the rat brain. *American Journal of Physiology* 206:1389–94.

SATINOFF, E. 1978. Neural organization and evolution of thermal regulation in mammals. *Science* 201:16–22.

SATINOFF, E., AND RUTSTEIN, J. 1970. Behavioral thermoregulation in rats with anterior hypothalamic lesions. *Journal of Comparative and Physiological Psychology* 71:77–82.

SATINOFF, E., AND SHAN, S. Y. 1971. Loss of behavioral thermoregulation after anterior hypothalamic lesions in rats. *Journal of Comparative and Physiological Psychology* 77:302–12.

SATIR, V. 1967. *Conjoint family therapy,* rev. ed. Palo Alto, Calif.: Science and Behavior Books.

SAVAGE-RUMBAUGH, E.; MCDONALD, D.; SEVCIK, R.; HOPKINS, W.; AND RUPERT, E. 1986. Spontaneous symbol acquisition and communicative use by pygmie chimpanzees. *Journal of Experimental Psychology: General* 115:211–235.

SAVAGE-RUMBAUGH, E.; RUMBAUGH, D.; SMITH, S.; AND LAWSON, J. 1980. Reference: The linguistic essential. *Science* 210:922–25.

SAVAGE-RUMBAUGH, S. 1987. A new look at ape language: Comprehension of vocal speech and syntax. *Nebraska Symposium on Motivation* 35:201–55.

SAWREY, W. L.; CONGER, J. J.; AND TURRELL, E. S. 1956. An experimental investigation of the role of psychological factors in the production of gastric ulcers in the rat. *Journal of Comparative and Physiological Psychology* 49:457–61.

SAXE, L.; DOUGHERTY, D.; AND CROSS, T. 1985. The validity of polygraph testing: Scientific analysis and public controversy. *American Psychologist* 40:355–66.

SCAIFE, M., AND BRUNER, J. S. 1975. The capacity for joint visual attention in the infant. *Nature* 253(5489): 265–66.

SCARR, S. 1987. Distinctive environments depend on genotypes. Peer commentary to article by Plomin, R., and Daniels, D. Why are children from the same family so different from one another? *Behavioral and Brain Sciences* 10:38–39.

SCARR, S., AND CARTER-SALTZMAN, L. 1979. Twin method: Defense of a critical assumption. *Behavior Genetics* 9:527–42.

SCARR, S., AND CARTER-SALTZMAN, L. 1982. Genetics and intelligence. In Sternberg, R. J. (Ed.), *Handbook of human intelligence,* pp. 792–896. New York: Cambridge University Press.

SCARR, S., AND MCCARTNEY, K. 1983. How people make their own environments: A theory of genotype-environment effects. *Child Development* 54:424–35.

SCARR, S., AND WEINBERG, R. A. 1976. IQ test performance of black children adopted by white families. *American Psychologist* 31:726–39.

SCARR, S., AND WEINBERG, R. A. 1983. The Minnesota adoption studies genetic differences and malleability. *Child Development* 54:260–67.

SCHACHER, S. 1981. Determination and differentiation in the development of the nervous system. In Kandel, E. R., and Schwartz, J. H. (Eds.), *Principles of neural science.* New York: Elsevier North Holland.

SCHACHTEL, E. G. 1947. On memory and childhood amnesia. *Psychiatry* 10:1–26.

SCHACHTER, S. 1964. The interaction of cognitive and physiological determinants of emotional state. In Berkowitz, L. (Ed.), *Advances in Experimental Social Psychology,* pp. 49–80. New York: Academic Press.

SCHACHTER, S. 1971. Some extraordinary facts about obese humans and rats. *American Psychologist* 26:129–44.

SCHACHTER, S., AND RODIN, J. 1974. *Obese humans and rats.* Washington, D. C.: Erlbaum-Halstead.

SCHACHTER, S., AND SINGER, J. 1962. Cognitive, social and physiological determinants of emotional state. *Psychological Review* 69:379–99.

SCHACHTER, S., AND SINGER, J. E. 1979. Comments on the Maslach and Marshall-Zimbardo experiments. *Journal of Personality and Social Psychology* 37:989–95.

SCHACTER, D. L. 1987. Implicit memory: History and current status. *Journal of Experimental Psychology: Learning, Memory, and Cognition* 13:501–18.

SCHACTER, D. 1992. Understanding implicit memory. *American Psychologist* 47:559–69.

SCHÄFER, S. 1977. Sociosexual behavior in male and female homosexuals: A study in sex differences. *Archives of Sexual Behavior* 6:355–64.

SCHAIE, K. 1979. The primary mental abilities in adulthood: An exploration in the development of psychometric intelligence. In Baltes, P. B., and Brim, O. G., Jr. (Eds.), *Life-span development and behavior,* vol. 2. New York: Academic Press.

SCHAIE, K., AND HERZOG, C. 1983. Fourteen-year cohort-sequential analyses of adult intellectual development. *Developmental Psychology* 19:531–43.

SCHAIE, K., AND STROTHER, C. 1968. A cross-sequential study of age changes in cognitive behavior. *Psychological Bulletin* 70:671–80.

SCHANK, R. C., AND ABELSON, R. 1977. *Scripts, plans, goals, and understanding.* Hillsdale, N.J.: Erlbaum.

SCHAPIRO, S., AND VUKOVICH, K. R. 1976. Early experience effects on cortical dendrites: A proposed model for development. *Science* 167:292–94.

SCHEERER, M. 1963. Problem solving. *Scientific American* 208:118–28.

SCHEERER, M.; GOLDSTEIN, K.; AND BORING, E. G. 1941. A demonstration of insight: The horse-rider puzzle. *American Journal of Psychology* 54:437–38.

SCHEFF, S. W., AND COTMAN, C. W. 1977. Recovery of spontaneous alternation following lesions of the entorhinal cortex in adult rats: Possible correlation to axon sprouting. *Behavioral Biology* 21:286–93.

SCHEFF, T. 1966. *Being mentally ill: A sociological theory.* Chicago: Aldine.

SCHIFF, M.; DUYME, M.; DUMARET, A.; AND TOMKIEWICZ, S. 1982. How much *could* we boost scholastic achievement and IQ scores? A direct answer from a French adoption study. *Cognition* 12: 165–96.

SCHIFF, W. 1965. Perception of impending collision. *Psychological Monographs* 79:1–26.

SCHIFFMAN, H. R. 1976. Sensation and perception: An integrated approach. New York: Wiley.

SCHIFFRIN, D. 1988. Conversational analysis. In F. Newmeyer (Ed.), *Linguistics: The Cambridge survey: Vol. IV. The socio-cultural context.* Cambridge: Cambridge University Press.

SCHILDKRAUT, J. J. 1965. The catecholamine hypothesis of affective disorders: A review of supporting evidence. *American Journal of Psychiatry* 122:509–22.

SCHILDKRAUT, J. J.; GREEN, A. I.; AND MOONEY, J. J. 1985. Affective disorders: Biochemical aspects. In Kaplan, H. I.; and Sadock, J. (Eds.), *Comprehensive textbook of psychiatry,* 4th ed. Baltimore: Williams & Wilkins.

SCHLEIDT, W. M. 1961. Ueber die Aufloesung der Flucht bor Raubvoeglns bei Truthuenern. *Naturwissenschaften* 48:141–42.

SCHLENKER, B. R. 1980. *Impression management: The self-concept, social identity and interpersonal relations.* Monterey, Calif.: Brooks/Cole.

SCHLENKER, B. R.; HALLAM, J. R.; AND McCOWN, N. E. 1983. Motives and social evaluation: Actor-observer differences in the delineation of motives for a beneficial act. *Journal of Experimental Social Psychology* 19:254–73.

SCHNEIDER, D. J. 1973. Implicit personality theory: A review. *Psychological Bulletin* 79:294–309.

SCHNEIDER, D. J.; HASTORF, A. H.; AND ELLSWORTH, P. C. 1979. *Person perception,* 2nd ed. Reading, Mass.: Addison-Wesley.

SCHOFIELD, W. 1964. *Psychotherapy: The purchase of friendship.* Englewood Cliffs, N.J.: Prentice-Hall.

SCHREIBER, F. R. 1973. *Sybil.* New York: Warner Paperback.

SCHULL, J. 1979. A conditioned opponent theory of Pavlovian conditioning and habituation. In Bower, G. (Ed.), *The psychology of learning and motivation,* vol. 13. New York: Academic Press.

SCHWARTZ, B. 1989. *Psychology of learning and behavior,* 3rd ed. New York: Norton.

SCHWARTZ, B., AND GAMZU, E. 1977. Pavlovian control of operant behavior. In Honig, W. K., and Staddon, J. E. R. (Eds.), *Handbook of operant behavior.* Englewood Cliffs, N.J.: Prentice-Hall.

SCHWARTZ, B., AND REISBERG, D. 1991. *Psychology of learning and memory.* New York: Norton.

SCHWARTZ, G. E.; WEINBERGER, D. A.; AND SINGER, J. A. 1981. Cardiovascular differentiation of happiness, sadness, anger, and fear following imagery and exercise. *Psychosomatic Medicine* 43:343–64.

SCOTT, J. P., AND FULLER, J. L. 1965. *Genetics and the social behavior of the dog.* Chicago: University of Chicago Press.

SCRIBNER, S., AND COLE, M. 1973. Cognitive consequences of formal and informal education. *Science* 182:553–59.

SEARLE, J. R. 1969. *Speech acts: An essay in the philosophy of language.* New York: Cambridge University Press.

SEARS, R. R.; MACCOBY, E. E.; AND LEVIN, H. 1957. *Patterns of child rearing.* Evanston, Ill.: Row, Peterson.

SEAY, B.; ALEXANDER, B. K.; AND HARLOW, H. F. 1964. Maternal behavior of socially deprived rhesus monkeys. *Journal of Abnormal and Social Psychology* 69:345–54.

SEIDENBERG, M. S., AND PETITTO, L. 1979. Signing behavior in apes: A critical review. *Cognition* 7:177–215.

SELFE, L. 1977. *Nadia: A case of extraordinary drawing ability in an autistic child.* New York: Academic Press.

SELFRIDGE, O. G. 1955. Pattern recognition and modern computers. In *Proceedings of Western Joint Computer Conference,* Los Angeles, Calif.

SELFRIDGE, O. G. 1959. Pandemonium: A paradigm for learning. In Blake, D. V., and Uttley, A. M. (Eds.), *Proceedings of the Symposium on the Mechanisation of Thought Processes.* London: HM Stationary Office.

SELIGMAN, M. E. P. On the generality of the laws of learning. *Psychological Review* 77: 406–18.

SELIGMAN, M. E. P. 1968. Chronic fear produced by unpredictable electric shock. *Journal of Comparative and Physiological Psychology* 66:402–11.

SELIGMAN, M. E. P. 1971. Phobias and preparedness. *Behavior Therapy* 2:307–20.

SELIGMAN, M. E. P. 1975. *Helplessness: On depression, development, and death.* San Francisco: Freeman.

SELIGMAN, M. E. P., AND HAGER, J. L. (Eds.). 1972. *Biological boundaries of learning.* New York: Appleton-Century-Crofts.

SELIGMAN, M. E. P.; KLEIN, D. C.; AND MILLER, W. R. 1976. Depression. In Leitenberg, H. (Ed.), *Handbook of behavior modification and behavior therapy.* Englewood Cliffs, N.J.: Prentice-Hall.

SELIGMAN, M. E. P., AND MAIER, S. F. 1967. Failure to escape traumatic shock. *Journal of Experimental Psychology* 74:1–9.

SELIGMAN, M. E. P.; MAIER, S. F.; AND SOLOMON, R. L. 1971. Unpredictable and uncontrollable aversive events. In Brush, F. R. (Ed.), *Aversive conditioning and learning.* New York: Academic Press.

SELLS, P. 1985. *Lectures on contemporary syntactic theories.* Stanford, Calif.: Center for the Study of Language and Information.

SENDAK, M. 1963. *Where the wild things are.* New York: Harper & Row.

SENDAK, M. 1979. *Higglety pigglety pop! or There must be more to life.* New York: Harper & Row.

SEYFARTH, R.; CHENEY, D.; AND MARLER, P. 1980. Monkey responses to three different alarm calls: Evidence of predator classification and semantic communication. *Science* 21:801–803.

SHALLICE, T., 1988. *From neuropsychology to mental structure.* Cambridge: Cambridge University Press.

SHALTER, M. D. 1984. Predator-prey behavior and habituation. In Peeke, H. V. S., and Petrinovich, L. (Eds.), *Habituation, sensitization and behavior,* pp. 423–58. New York: Academic Press.

SHAM, P. V. C.; O'CALLAGHAN, E.; TAKEI, N.; MURRAY, G. K.; HARE, E. H.; AND MURRAY, R. M. 1992. Schizophrenia following pre-natal exposure to influenza epidemics between 1939 and 1960. *British Journal of Psychiatry* 160:461–66.

SHANAB, M. E., AND YAHYA, K. A. 1977. A behavioral study of obedience in children. *Journal of Personality and Social Psychology* 35:530–36.

SHAPIRO, A. K. 1971. Placebo effects in medicine, psychotherapy, and psychoanalysis. In Bergin, A. E., and Garfield, S. L. (Eds.), *Handbook of psychotherapy and behavior change,* pp. 439–73. New York: Wiley.

SHAPIRO, C. M.; BORTZ, R.; MITCHELL, D.; BARTELL, P.; AND JOOSTE, P. 1981. Slow wave sleep: A recovery period after exercise. *Science* 214:1253–54.

SHAPIRO, D. A., AND SHAPIRO, D. 1982. Meta-analysis of comparative therapy outcome studies: A replication and refinement. *Psychological Bulletin* 92:581–604.

SHEEAN, D. 1985. Monoamine oxidase inhibitors and alprazolam in the treatment of panic disorder and agoraphobia. *Psychiatric Clinics of North America* 8:49–82.

SHEFFIELD, F. D., AND ROBY, T. B. 1950. Reward value of a nonnutritive sweet taste. *Journal of Comparative and Physiological Psychology* 43:471–81.

SHEFFIELD, F. D.; WULFF, J. J.; AND BACKER, R. 1951. Reward value of copulation without sex drive reduction. *Journal of Comparative and Physiological Psychology* 44:3–8.

SHEINGOLD, K., AND TENNEY, Y. J. 1982. Memory for a salient childhood event. In Neisser, U. (Ed.), *Memory observed,* pp. 201–12. San Francisco: Freeman.

SHEKELLE, R. B.; HONEY, S. B.; NEATON, J.; BILLINGS, J.; BORLANI, N.; GERACE, T.; JACOBS, D.; LASSER, N.; AND STANDER, J. 1983. Type A behavior pattern and coronary death in MRFIT. *American Heart Association Cardiovascular Disease Newsletter* 33:34.

SHEKELLE, R. B.; RAYNOR, W. J.; OSTFELD, A. M.; GARRON, D. C.; BIELIAVSKAS, L. A.; LIV, S. C.; MALIZA, C.; AND PAUL, O. 1981. Psychological depression and the 17-year risk of cancer. *Psychosomatic Medicine* 43:117–25.

SHEPARD, R. N., AND COOPER, L. A. 1982. *Mental images and their transformations.* Cambridge, Mass.: MIT Press.

SHERMAN, P. W. 1977. Nepotism and the evolution of alarm calls. *Science* 197:1246–54.

SHERRICK, C. E., AND CHOLEWIAK, R. W. 1986. Cutaneous sensitivity. In Boff, K. R.; Kaufman, L.; and Thomas, J. P. (Eds.), *Handbook of perception and human performance,* Chapter 12. New York: Wiley.

SHERRINGTON, C. S. 1906. *The integrative action of the nervous system,* 2nd ed. New Haven, Conn.: Yale University Press, 1947.

SHERROD, D. 1989. The influence of gender on same-sex friendships. In Hendrick, C. (Ed.), *Close relationships,* vol. 10, *Review of personality and social psychology.* Newbury Park, Calif.: Sage.

SHERRY, D. F.; JACOBS, L. F.; GAULIN, S. J. C. 1992. Spatial memory and adaptive specialization of the hippocampus. *Trends in Neurosciences* 15(8): 298-303.

SHERRY, D. F.; VACCARINO, A. L.; BUCKENHAM, K.; AND HERZ, R. S. 1989. The hippocampal complex of food storing birds. *Brain, Behavior and Evolution* 34: 308-17.

SHETTLEWORTH, S. J. 1972. Constraints on learning. In Lehrman, D. S.; Hinde, R. A.; and Shaw, E. (Eds.), *Advances in the study of behavior*, vol. 4. New York: Academic Press.

SHETTLEWORTH, S. J. 1983. Memory in food-hoarding birds. *Scientific American* 248:102–10.

SHETTLEWORTH, S. J. 1984. Learning and behavioral ecology. In Krebs, J. R., and Davies, N. B. (Eds.), *Behavioral ecology* 2nd ed., pp. 170–94. Oxford: Blackwell.

SHIPLEY, E. F., AND KUHN, I. F. 1983. A constraint on comparisons: Equally detailed alternatives. *Journal of Experimental Child Psychology* 35:195–222.

SHIPLEY, E. F.; KUHN, I. F.; AND MADDEN, E. C. 1983. Mothers' use of superordinate terms. *Journal of Child Language* 10:571–88.

SHIPLEY, E. F.; SMITH, C. S.; AND GLEITMAN, L. R. 1969. A study in the acquisition of language: Free responses to commands. *Language* 45:322–42.

SHIRLEY, M. M. 1961. *The first two years: A study of twenty-five babies.* Minneapolis: University of Minnesota Press.

SHORTER, E. 1992. *From paralysis to fatigue: A history of psychosomatic illness in the modern era.* New York: Macmillan Free Press.

SHORTLIFFE, E. H.; AXLINE, S. G.; BUCHANAN, B. G.; MERIGAN, T. C.; AND COHEN, N. S. 1973. An artificial intelligence program to advise physicians regarding antimicrobial therapy. *Computers and Biomedical Research* 6:544–60.

SHUEY, A. 1966. *The testing of Negro intelligence.* New York: Social Science Press.

SHWEDER, R. A. 1975. How relevant is an individual difference theory of personality? *Journal of Personality* 43:455–85.

SHWEDER, R. A., AND BOURNE, E. J. 1986. Does the concept of the person vary cross-culturally? In Shweder, R. A. (Ed.), *Thinking through cultures*, pp. 113-55. Cambridge, Mass.: Harvard University Press, 1991.

SICOLY, F., AND ROSS, M. 1977. Facilitation of ego-biased attributions by means of self-serving observer feedback. *Journal of Personality and Social Psychology* 35:734–41.

SIEGAL, M. 1991. *Knowing children: Experiments in conversation.* Hillsdale, N.J.: Erlbaum.

SIEGEL, R. K. 1984. Changing patterns of cocaine use: Longitudinal observations, consequences, and treatment. In Grabowski, J. (Ed.), *Cocaine: Pharmacology, effects, and treatment of abuse*, pp. 92–110. NIDA Research Monograph 50.

SIEGEL, S. 1977. Morphine tolerance acquisition as an associative process. *Journal of Experimental Psychology: Animal Behavior Processes* 3:1–13.

SIEGEL, S. 1983. Classical conditioning, drug tolerance, and drug dependence. In Israel, Y.; Glaser, F. B.; Kalant, H.; Popham, R. E.; Schmidt, W.; and Smart, R. G. (Eds.), *Research advances in alcohol and drug problems*, vol. 7. New York: Plenum.

SIEGEL, S.; HINSON, R. E.; KRANK, M. D.; AND MCCULLY, J. 1982. Heroin "overdose" death: Contribution of drug-associated environmental cues. *Science* 216:436–37.

SIEGLER, M., AND OSMOND, H. 1974. *Models of madness, models of medicine.* New York: Harper & Row.

SIEGLER, R. S. 1983. Information processing approaches to child development. In Mussen, P. H., *Handbook of child psychology: Vol. 1. History, theory, and methods* (Kessen, W., volume editor). New York: Wiley.

SIEGLER, R. S. 1989. Mechanisms of cognitive development. In Rosenzweig, M. R., and Porter, L. W. (Eds.), *Annual Review of Psychology* 40:353–79.

SIEVER, L. J.; DAVIS, K. L.; AND GORMAN, L. K. 1991. Pathogenesis of mood disorders. In Davis, K.; Klar, H.; and Coyle, J. T. (Eds.), *Foundations of psychiatry*. Philadelphia: Saunders.

SILK, J. B. 1986. Social behavior in evolutionary perspective. In Smuts, B. B.; Cheney, D. L.; Seyfarth, R. M.; Wrangham, R. W.; and Struhsaker, T. T. (Eds.), *Primate societies.* Chicago: University of Chicago Press.

SIMMEL, G. 1911. *On individuality and social form.* Levine, D. N. (editor of 1971 edition). Chicago, Ill.: University of Chicago Press.

SIMNER, M. L. 1971. Newborn's response to the cry of another infant. *Developmental Psychology* 5:136–50.

SIMON, R. J., AND AARONSON, D. E. 1988. *The insanity defense: A critical assessment of law and policy in the post-Hinckley era.* New York: Praeger.

SIMPSON, E. L. 1974. Moral development research: A case of scientific cultural bias. *Human Development* 17: 81–106.

SIMS, E. A. 1986. Energy balance in human beings: The problems of plenitude. *Vitamins and hormones: Research and applications* 43:1–101.

SINHA, D. 1983. Human assessment in the Indian context. In Irvine, S. H., and Berry, J. W. (Eds.), *Human assessment and cultural factors*, pp.17–34. New York: Plenum.

SIZEMORE, C. C., AND HUBER, R. J. 1988. The twenty-two faces of Eve. *Individual Psychology: Journal of Adlerian Theory, Research and Practice* 44:53–62.

SKEELS, H. 1966. Adult status of children with contrasting early life experiences. *Monograph of the Society for Research in Child Development* 31 (No. 3).

SKINNER, B. F. 1938. *The behavior of organisms.* New York: Appleton-Century-Crofts.

SKINNER, B. F. 1969. *Contingencies of reinforcement: A theoretical analysis.* New York: Appleton-Century-Crofts.

SKINNER, B. F. 1971. *Beyond freedom and dignity.* New York: Alfred Knopf.

SKODAK, M., AND SKEELS, H. M. 1945. A follow-up study of children in adoptive homes. *Journal of Genetic Psychology* 66:21–58.

SKODAK, M., AND SKEELS, H. M. 1947. A follow-up study of the development of one-hundred adopted children in Iowa. *American Psychologist* 2:278.

SKODAK, M., AND SKEELS, H. M. 1949. A final follow-up study of children in adoptive homes. *Journal of Genetic Psychology* 75: 85–125.

SLATER, E., AND GLITHERO, E. 1965. A follow-up of patients diagnosed as suffering from hysteria. *Journal of Psychosomatic Research* 9:9–13.

SLOANE, R. B.; STAPLES, F. R.; CRISTOL, A. H.; YORKSTON, N.J.; AND WHIPPLE, K. 1975. *Psychotherapy vs. behavior therapy.* Cambridge, Mass.: Harvard University Press.

SLOBIN, D. I. 1966. Grammatical transformations and sentence comprehension in childhood and adulthood. *Journal of Verbal Learning and Verbal Behavior* 5:219–27.

SLOVIC, P.; FISCHOFF, B.; AND LICHTENSTEIN, S. 1982. Facts versus fears: Understanding perceived risk. In Kahneman, D.; Slovic, P.; and Tversky, A. (Eds.), *Judgment under uncertainty: Heuristics and biases.* New York: Cambridge University Press.

SMEDSLUND, J. 1961. The acquisition of conservation of substance and weight in children. *Scandinavia Journal of Psychology* 2:11–20.

SMELSER, N. J. 1963. *Theory of collective behavior.* New York: Free Press, Macmillan.

SMITH, C. 1985. Sleep states and learning: A review of the animal literature. *Neuroscience and Biobehavioral Reviews* 9:157–68.

SMITH, C., AND LLOYD, B. 1978. Maternal behavior and perceived sex of infant: Revisited. *Child Development* 49:1263–65.

SMITH, D. G. 1981. The association between rank and reproductive success of male rhesus monkeys. *American Journal of Primatology* 1:83–90.

SMITH, E. E., AND MEDIN, D. L. 1981. *Categories and concepts.* Cambridge, Mass.: Harvard University Press.

SMITH, M. 1983. Hypnotic memory enhancement of witnesses: Does it work? *Psychological Bulletin* 94:387–407.

SMITH, M. B. 1950. The phenomenological approach in personality theory: Some critical remarks. *Journal of Abnormal and Social Psychology* 45:516–22.

SMITH, M. L.; GLASS, G. V.; AND MILLER, R. L. 1980. *The benefits of psychotherapy.* Baltimore: Johns Hopkins Press.

SMITH, S. M. 1979. Remembering in and out of context. *Journal of Experimental Psychology: Human Learning and Memory* 5: 460–71.

SMITH, S. M., AND BLANKENSHIP, S. E. 1989. Incubation effects. *Bulletin of the Psychonomic Society* 27(4):311–14.

SMITH, S. M., AND BLANKENSHIP, S. E. 1991. Incubation and the persistence of fixation in problem solving. *American Journal of Psychology* 104(1):61–87.

SNOW, C., AND HOEFNAGEL-HOHLE, M. 1978. The critical period for language acquisition: Evidence from second language learning. *Child Development* 49:1114–28.

SNYDER, C. R.; SHENKEL, R. J.; AND LOWERY, C. R. 1977. Acceptance of personality interpretations: The "Barnum effect" and beyond. *Journal of Consulting and Clinical Psychology* 45:104–14.

SNYDER, M. 1981. On the influence of individuals on situations. In Cantor, N., and Kihlstrom, J. F. (Eds.), *Personality, cognition, and social interaction.* Hillsdale, N.J.: Erlbaum.

SNYDER, M. 1987. *Public appearances/private realities.* New York: Freeman.

SNYDER, M., AND CUNNINGHAM, M. R. 1975. To comply or not comply: Testing the self-perception explanation of the "foot-in-the-door" phenomenon. *Journal of Personality and Social Psychology* 31:64–67.

SNYDER, M., AND ICKES, W. 1985. Personality and social behavior. In Lindzey, G., and Aronson, E. (Eds.), *Handbook of Social Psychology,* 3rd ed., vol. 2. New York: Random House.

SNYDER, M. L.; STEPHAN, W. G.; and ROSENFIELD, D. 1976. Egotism and attribution. *Journal of Personality and Social Psychology* 33:435–41.

SNYDER, S. H. 1976. The dopamine hypothesis of schizophrenia. *American Journal of Psychiatry* 133:197–202.

SNYDER, S. H., AND CHILDERS, S. R. 1979. Opiate receptors and opioid peptides. *Annual Review of Neuroscience* 2:35–64.

SOLOMON, R. C. 1981. The love lost in clichés. *Psychology Today,* October 1981, pp. 83–85, 87–88.

SOLOMON, R. L. 1980. The opponent-process theory of acquired motivation: The costs of pleasure and the benefits of pain. *American Psychologist* 35:691–712.

SOLOMON, R. L., AND CORBIT, J. D. 1974. An opponent-process theory of motivation: I. Temporal dynamics of affect. *Psychological Review* 81:119–45.

SOLOMON, R. L., AND WYNNE, L. C. 1953. Traumatic avoidance learning: Acquisition in normal dogs. *Psychological Monographs* 67 (Whole No. 354).

SPEARMAN, C. 1927. *The abilities of man.* London: Macmillan.

SPEMANN, H. 1967. *Embryonic development and induction.* New York: Hafner Publishing Company.

SPENCE, J. T., AND SPENCE, K. W. 1966. The motivational components of manifest anxiety: Drive and drive stimuli. In Spielberger, C. D. (Ed.), *Anxiety and behavior.* New York: Academic Press.

SPERBER, D., AND WILSON, D. 1986. *Relevance: Communication and cognition.* Oxford: Blackwell.

SPERLING, G. 1960. The information available in brief visual presentations. *Psychological Monographs* 74 (Whole No. 11).

SPERRY, R. W. 1974. Lateral specialization in the surgically separated hemispheres. In Schmitt, F. O., and Worden, F. G. (Eds.), *The Neuroscience Third Study Program.* Cambridge, Mass.: MIT Press.

SPERRY, R. W. 1982. Some effects of disconnecting the cerebral hemispheres. *Science* 217:1223–26.

SPIES, G. 1965. Food versus intracranial self-stimulation reinforcement in food deprived rats. *Journal of Comparative and Physiological Psychology* 60:153–57.

SPILICH, G. S.; VESONDER, G. T.; CHIESI, H. L.; AND VOSS, J. F. 1979. Text processing of domain-related information for individuals with high and low domain knowledge. *Journal of Verbal Learning and Verbal Behavior* 18:275–90.

SPIRO, R. J. 1980. Accommodative reconstruction in prose recall. *Journal of Verbal Learning and Verbal Behavior* 19:84–95.

SPITZER, R. L. 1976. More on pseudoscience in science and the case for psychiatric diagnosis. *Archives of General Psychiatry* 33:459–70.

SPOONER, A., AND KELLOGG, W. N. 1947. The backward conditioning curve. *American Journal of Psychology* 60:321–34.

SPRINGER, S. P., AND DEUTSCH, G. 1981. *Left brain, right brain.* San Francisco: Freeman.

SQUIRE L. R. 1977. ECT and memory loss. *American Journal of Psychiatry* 134:997–1001.

SQUIRE, L. R. 1986. Mechanisms of memory. *Science* 232:1612–19.

SQUIRE, L. R. 1987. *Memory and brain.* New York: Oxford University.

SQUIRE, L. R., AND COHEN, N. J. 1979. Memory and amnesia: Resistance to disruption develops for years after learning. *Behavioral Biology and Neurology* 25:115–25.

SQUIRE, L. R., AND COHEN, N. J. 1982. Remote memory, retrograde amnesia, and the neuropsychology of memory. In Cermak, L. S. (Ed.), *Human memory and amnesia,* pp. 275–304. Hillsdale, N.J.: Erlbaum.

SQUIRE, L. R., AND COHEN, N. J. 1984. *Human memory and amnesia.* In McGaugh, J.; Lynch, G.; and Weinberger, N. *Neurobiology of learning and memory.* New York: Guilford.

SQUIRE, L. R., AND ZOUZOUNIS, J. A. 1986. ECT and memory: Brief pulse versus sine wave. *American Journal of Psychiatry* 143: 596–601.

STACHER, G.; BAUER, H.; AND STEINRINGER, H. 1979. Cholecystokinin decreases appetite and activation evoked by stimuli arising from preparation of a meal in man. *Physiology and Behavior* 23:325–31.

STANLEY, B. G.; MAGDALIN, W.; AND LEIBOWITZ, S. F. 1989. A critical site for neuropeptide Y-induced eating lies in the caudolateral paraventricular/perifornical region of the hypothalamus. *Society for Neuroscience Abstracts* 15:894.

STARK, L., AND ELLIS, S. 1981. Scanpaths revisited: Cognitive models direct active looking. In Fisher, D.; Monty, R.; and Senders, I. (Eds.), *Eye movements: Cognition and visual perception,* pp. 193–226. Hillsdale, N.J.: Erlbaum.

STARKEY, P.; SPELKE, E. S.; AND GELMAN, R. 1983. Detection of intermodal numerical correspondences by human infants. *Science* 222:179–81.

STARKEY, P.; SPELKE, E. S.; AND GELMAN R. 1990. Numerical abstraction by human infants. *Cognition* 36:97–127.

STEELE, C. M., AND LIU, T. J. 1983. Dissonance processes as self-affirmation. *Journal of Personality and Social Psychology* 45:5–19.

STEINBERG, L; ELMAN, J. D.; AND MOUNTS, N. S. 1989. Authoritative parenting, psychosocial maturity, and academic success among adolescents. *Child Development* 60(6): 1424–36

STEINER, J. E. 1974. The gustafacial response: Observation on normal and anencephalic newborn infants. In Bosma, F. J. (Ed.), *Fourth symposium on oral sensation and perception: Development in the fetus and infant* (DHEW Publication No. NIH 73–546). Washington, D. C.: U. S. Government Printing Office.

STEINER, J. E. 1977. Facial expressions of the neonate infant indicating the hedonics of food-related chemical stimuli. In Weiffenbach, J. M. (Ed.), *Taste and development: The genesis of sweet preference* (DHEW Publication No. NIH 77–1068), pp. 173–88. Washington, D. C.: U. S. Government Printing Office.

STELLAR, E. 1954. The physiology of motivation. *Psychological Review* 61:5–22.

STELLAR, J. R., AND STELLAR, E. 1985. *The neurobiology of motivation and reward.* New York: Springer Verlag.

STERNBERG, R. J. 1977. *Intelligence, information processing, and analogical reasoning: The componential analysis of human abilities.* Hillsdale, N.J.: Erlbaum.

STERNBERG, R. J. 1985. General intellectual ability. In Sternberg, R. *Human abilities: An information processing approach.* New York: Freeman.

STERNBERG, R. J. 1986. A triangular theory of love. *Psychological Review* 93:119–35.

STERNBERG, R. J. 1988. *The triangle of love: Intimacy, passion, commitment.* New York: Basic Books.

STERNBERG, R. J. 1990. *Metaphors of mind.* New York: Cambridge University Press.

STERNBERG, R. J., AND DAVIDSON, J. E. 1983. Insight in the gifted. *Educational Psychologist* 18:51–57.

STERNBERG, R. J., AND GARDNER, M. K. 1983. Unities in inductive reasoning. *Journal of Experimental Psychology: General* 112: 80–116.

STERNBERG, R. J., AND WAGNER, R. K. 1993. The egocentric view of intelligence and job performance is wrong. *Current Directions in Psychological Science* 2:1–5.

STEVENS, A., AND COUPE, P. 1978. Distortions in judged spatial relations. *Cognitive Psychology* 10:422–37.

STEVENS, L., AND JONES, E. E. 1976. Defensive attributions and the Kelley cube. *Journal of Personality and Social Psychology* 34: 809–20.

STEVENS, S. S. 1955. The measurement of loudness. *Journal of the Acoustical Society of America* 27:815–19.

STEWART, K. 1951. Dream theory in Malaya. *Complex* 6:21–34.

STEWART, T. D. 1957. Stone age surgery: A general review, with emphasis on the New World. *Annual Review of the Smithsonian Institution.* Washington, D. C.: Smithsonian Institution.

STOCH, M. B.; SMYTHE, P. M.; MOODIE, A. D.; AND BRADSHAW, D. 1982. Psychosocial outcome and CT findings after gross undernourishment during infancy: A 20-year developmental study. *Developmental Medicine and Child Neurology* 24:419–36.

STOKOE, W. C., JR. 1960. Sign language structure: An outline of the visual communication systems. *Studies in Linguistics Occasional Papers* 8.

STOLLER, R. J. 1968. *Sex and gender: On the development of masculinity and femininity.* New York: Science House.

STOLLER, R. J., AND HERDT, G. H. 1985. Theories of origins of male homosexuality: A cross-cultural look. *Archives of General Psychiatry* 42: 399-404.

STONE, A. 1975. *Mental health and law: A system in transition.* (DHEW Publication No. 75176). Washington, D.C.: U.S. Government Printing Office.

STORMS, M. D. 1973. Videotape and the attribution process: Reversing actors' and observers' points of view. *Journal of Personality and Social Psychology* 27:165–75.

STOWE, L. 1987. Thematic structures and sentence comprehension. In Carlson, G., and Tanenhaus, M. (Eds.), *Linguistic structure in language processing.* Dordrecht: Reidel.

STRICKER, E. M., AND ZIGMOND, M. J. 1976. Recovery of function after damage to catecholamine-containing neurons: A neurochemical model for the lateral hypothalamic syndrome. In Sprague, J. M., and Epstein, A. N. (Eds.), *Progress in psychobiology and physiological psychology,* vol. 6, pp. 121–88. New York: Academic Press.

STROOP, J. R. 1935. Studies of interference in serial verbal reactions. *Journal of Experimental Psychology* 18:643-62.

STRUPP, H. H., AND BINDER, J. L. 1984. *Psychotherapy in a new key: A guide to time-limited dynamic psychotherapy.* New York: Basic Books.

STUART, R. B., AND MITCHELL, C. 1980. Self-help groups in the control of body weight. In Stunkard, A. J. (Ed.), *Obesity,* pp. 354–55. Philadelphia: Saunders.

STUNKARD, A. J. 1975. Obesity. In Freedman, A. M.; Kaplan, H. I.; and Sadock, B. J. (Eds.), *Comprehensive textbook of psychiatry—II,* vol. 2, pp. 1648–54. Baltimore: Williams & Wilkins.

STUNKARD, A. 1980. Psychoanalysis and psychotherapy. In Stunkard, A. J. (Ed.), *Obesity,* pp. 355–68. Philadelphia: Saunders.

STYRON, W. 1990. *Darkness visible: A memoir of madness.* New York: Random House.

SUE, D. W., AND KIRK, B. A. 1973. Psychological characteristics of Chinese-American college students. *Journal of Counseling Psychology* 19:142–48.

SULS, J. M. 1972. A two-stage model for the appreciation of jokes and cartoons: An information processing analysis. In Goldstein, J. H., and McGhee, P. E. (Eds.), *The psychology of humor,* pp. 81–100. New York: Academic Press.

SULS, J. M. 1983. Cognitive processes in humor appreciation. In McGhee, P. E., and Goldstein, J. H. (Eds.), *Handbook of humor research,* vol. 1, pp. 39–58. New York: Springer.

SULS, J. M., AND MILLER, R. L. (Eds.). 1977. *Social comparison processes: Theoretical and empirical perspectives.* New York: Washington Hemisphere Publishing Co.

SUOMI, S. J. 1989. Personal communication.

SUOMI, S. J., and HARLOW, H. F. 1971. Abnormal social behavior in young monkeys. In Helmuth, J. (Ed.), *Exceptional infant: Studies in abnormalities,* vol. 2, pp. 483–529. New York: Brunner/Mazel.

SUOMI, S., AND HARLOW, H. 1972. Social rehabilitation of isolate-reared monkeys. *Developmental Psychology* 6:487–96.

SUPALLA, I., AND NEWPORT, E. L. 1978. How many seats in a chair? The derivation of nouns and verbs in American Sign Language. In Siple, P. (Ed.), *Understanding language through sign language research.* New York: Academic Press.

SUPALLA, T. 1986. The classifier system in American Sign Language. In Craig, C. (Ed.), *Noun classes and categorization: Typological studies in language,* vol. 7. Amsterdam: John Benjamins.

SUPER, C. M. 1976. Environmental effects on motor development. *Developmental Medicine and Child Neurology* 18:561–67.

SYMONS, D. 1979. *The evolution of human sexuality.* New York: Oxford University Press.

SYMONS, D. 1993. The stuff that dreams aren't made of: Why wake-state and dream-state sensory experiences differ. *Cognition* 47:181–217.

TAKAHASHI, Y. 1979. Growth hormone secretion related to the sleep waking rhythm. In Drucker-Colín, R.; Shkurovich, M.; and Sterman, M. B. (Eds.), *The functions of sleep.* New York: Academic Press.

TANDON, R., AND KANE, J. M. 1993. Neuropharmacologic basis for clozapine's unique profile (Letter). *Archives of General Psychiatry,* 50:158–59.

TANENHAUS, M. 1988. Psycholinguistics: An overview. In Newmeyer, F. (Ed.), *Linguistics: The Cambridge survey, Vol. III, Language: Psychological and biological aspects.* Cambridge: Cambridge University Press.

TANNER, J. M. 1970. Physical growth. In Mussen, P. H. (Ed.), *Carmichael's manual of child psychology,* 3rd ed., pp. 77–105. New York: Wiley.

TAYLOR, S. E., AND FISKE, S. T. 1975. Point of view and perceptions of causality. *Journal of Personality and Social Psychology* 32:439–45.

TEACH, R. L., AND SHORTLIFFE, E. H. 1985. An analysis of physicians' attitudes. In Buchanan, B. G., and Shortliffe, E. H. (Eds.), *Rule-based expert systems: The MYCIN experiments of the Stanford Heuristics Programming Project.* Reading, Mass: Addison-Wesley.

TEITELBAUM, P. 1955. Sensory control of hypothalamic hyperphagia. *Journal of Comparative and Physiological Psychology* 48: 156–63.

TEITELBAUM, P. 1961. Disturbances in feeding and drinking behavior after hypothalamic lesions. In Jones, M. R. (Ed.), *Nebraska Symposium on Motivation,* pp. 39–65. Lincoln, Neb.: University of Nebraska Press.

TEITELBAUM, P., AND EPSTEIN, A. N. 1962. The lateral hypothalamic syndrome: Recovery of feeding and drinking after lateral hypothalamic lesions. *Psychological Review* 69:74–90.

TEITELBAUM, P., AND STELLAR, E. 1954. Recovery from failure to eat produced by hypothalamic lesions. *Science* 120:894–95.

TELLEGEN, A.; LYKKEN, D. T.; BOUCHARD, T. J.; WILCOX, K. J.; SEGAL, N. L.; AND RICH, S. 1988. Personality of twins reared apart and together. *Journal of Personality and Social Psychology* 54:1031–39.

TERRACE, H. S. 1979. *Nim.* New York: Knopf.

TERRACE, H. S.; PETITTO, L. A.; SANDERS, D. L.; AND BEVER, T. G. 1979. Can an ape create a sentence? *Science* 206:891–902.

TERVOORT, B. T. 1961. Esoteric symbolism in the communication behavior of young deaf children. *American Annals of the Deaf* 106:436–80.

TESSER, A.; CAMPBELL, J.; AND SMITH, M. 1984. Friendship choice and performance: Self-evaluation maintenance in children. *Journal of Personality and Social Psychology* 46:561–74.

THEOPHRASTUS. 319 B.C. The *characters.* Translated by Edmonds, J. M. Cambridge, Mass.: Harvard University Press, 1929.

THIGPEN, C. H., AND CLECKLEY, H. M. 1957. *The three faces of Eve.* New York: McGraw-Hill.

THOMAS, A.; CHESS, S.; AND BIRCH, H. G. 1970. The origin of personality. *Scientific American* 223:102–109.

THOMPSON, C. P., AND COWAN, T. 1986. Flashbulb memories: A nicer recollection of a Neisser recollection. *Cognition* 22:199–200.

THOMPSON, R. F. 1973. *Introduction to biopsychology.* San Francisco: Albion Publishing Co.

THOREN, P.; FLORAS, J. S.; HOFFMANN, P.; AND SEALS, D. R. 1990. Endorphins and exercise: Physiological mechanisms and clinical implications. *Medicine and Science in Sports and Exercise* 22:417–28.

THORNDIKE, E. L. 1898. Animal intelligence: An experimental study of the associative processes in animals. *Psychological Monographs* 2 (Whole No. 8).

THORNDIKE, E. L. 1899. The associative processes in animals. *Biological lectures from the Marine Biological Laboratory at Woods Hole.* Boston: Atheneum.

THORNDIKE, E. L. 1911. *Animal intelligence: Experimental studies.* New York: Macmillan.

THORNDIKE, E. L. 1924. The measurement of intelligence: Present status. *Psychological Review* 31:219–52.

TIETJEN, A. M., AND WALKER, L. J. 1985. Moral reasoning and leadership among men in a Papua New Guinea society. *Developmental Psychology* 21: 982–89.

TINBERGEN, N. 1951. *The study of instinct.* Oxford, England: Clarendon.

TIZARD, B., AND HODGES, J. 1978. The effect of early institutional rearing on the development of eight-year-old children. *Journal of Child Psychology and Psychiatry* 19:98–118.

TOCQUEVILLE, A. 1835. *Democracy in America.* Mayer, J. P., and Lerner, M. (Eds.). George Lawrence (trans.) New York: Harper and Row, 1966.

TOLMAN, E. C. 1932. *Purposive behavior in animals and men.* New York: Appleton-Century-Crofts.

TOLMAN, E. C. 1948. Cognitive maps in rats and men. *Psychological Review* 55:189–208.

TOLMAN, E. C., AND GLEITMAN, H. 1949. Studies in learning and motivation: I. Equal reinforcements in both end-boxes, followed by shock in one end-box. *Journal of Experimental Psychology* 39:810–19.

TOLMAN, E. C., AND HONZIK, C. H. 1930. Introduction and removal of reward, and maze performance in rats. *University of California Publications in Psychology* 4:257–75.

TOLSTOY, L. 1868. *War and peace,* second epilogue. Henry Gifford (Ed.), Louise Maude and Aylmer Maude (trans.). New York: Oxford University Press, 1922.

TOLSTOY, L. 1875. *Anna Karenina.* Trans. C. Garnett. New York: Random House, 1939.

TOMASELLO, M., AND FERRAR, M. 1986. Joint attention and early language. *Child Development* 57:1454–63.

TOMKINS, S. S. 1962. *Affect, imagery, consciousness,* vol. 1: *The positive affects.* New York. Springer.

TOMKINS, S. S. 1963. *Affect, imagery, consciousness,* vol. 2: *The negative affects.* New York: Springer.

TORGERSEN, S. 1986. Genetic factors in moderately severe and mild affective disorders. *Archives of General Psychiatry* 43:222–26.

TORREY, E. F. 1983. *Surviving schizophrenia: A family manual.* New York: Harper and Row.

TORREY, E. F. 1987. Prevalence studies in schizophrenia. *British Journal of Psychiatry* 150: 598–608.

TORREY, E. F. 1988. *Nowhere to go: The tragic odyssey of the homeless mentally ill.* New York: Harper and Row.

TREIBER, F., AND WILCOX, S. 1984. Discrimination of number by infants. *Infant Behavior and Development* 7:93–100.

TREISMAN, A. M. 1964. Verbal cues, language, and meaning in selective attention. *American Journal of Psychology* 77:206–19.

TREISMAN, A. M. 1986a. Properties, parts, and objects. In Boff, K. R.; Kaufman, L.; and Thomas, J. P. (Eds.), *Handbook of perception and human performance,* vol. II (Chapter 35). New York: Wiley.

TREISMAN, A. M. 1986b. Features and objects in visual processing. *Scientific American* 255:114–25.

TREISMAN, A. M. 1988. Features and objects: The Fourteenth Barlett Memorial Lecture. *Quarterly Journal of Experimental Psychology* 40A:201–37.

TREISMAN, A. M., AND GELADE, G. 1980. A feature-integration theory of attention. *Cognitive Psychology* 12:97–136.

TREISMAN, A. M., AND SCHMIDT, H. 1982. Illusory conjunction in the perception of objects. *Cognitive Psychology* 14:107–41.

TREISMAN, A. M., AND SOUTHER, J. 1985. Search assymetry: A diagnostic for preattentive processing of separable features. *Journal of Experimental Psychology: General* 114:285–310.

TRIANDIS, H. C. 1989. Cross-cultural studies of individualism and collectivism. *Nebraska Symposium on Motivation* 37:41–134. Lincoln, Neb.: University of Nebraska Press.

TRIANDIS, H. C.; BONTEMBO, R.; VILLAREAL, M. J.; ASAI, M.; AND LUCA, N. 1988. Individualism and collectivism: Cross-cultural perspectives on self-group relationships. *Journal of Personality and Social Psychology* 54:323–38.

TRIVERS, R. L. 1971. The evolution of reciprocal altruism. *Quarterly Review of Biology* 46:35–57.

TRIVERS, R. L. 1972. Parental investment and sexual selection. In Campbell, B. (Ed.), *Sexual selection and the descent of man,* pp. 139–79. Chicago: Aldine.

TRUESWELL, J.; TANEHAUS, M.; AND GARNSEY, S. 1994. Semantic influences on parsing. *Journal of Experimental Psychology: Learning, Memory, and Cognition* (in press).

TSUANG, M. T.; GILBERTSON, M. W.; AND FARAONE, S. V. 1991. The genetics of schizophrenia. *Schizophrenia Research* 4:157–71.

TSUANG, M. T.; WOOLSON, R. F.; AND FLEMING, J. A. 1979. Long-term outcome of major psychoses. I. Schizophrenia and affective disorder compared with psychiatrically symptom-free surgical conditions. *Archives of General Psychiatry* 36:1295–1306.

TULVING, E. 1972. Episodic and semantic memory. In Tulving, E., and Donaldson, W. (Eds.), *Organization and memory.* New York: Academic Press.

TULVING, E., AND OSLER, S. 1968. Effectiveness of retrieval cues in memory for words. *Journal of Experimental Psychology* 77: 593–601.

TULVING, E., AND PEARLSTONE, Z. 1966. Availability versus accessability of information in memory for words. *Journal of Verbal Learning and Verbal Behavior* 5:381–91.

TULVING, E.; SCHACTER, D. L.; AND STARK, H. A. 1982. Priming effects in word-fragment completion are independent of recognition memory. *Journal of Experimental Psychology: Learning, Memory, and Cognition* 8:336–42.

TULVING, E., AND THOMSON, D. M. 1973. Encoding specificity and retrieval processes in episodic memory. *Psychological Review* 80: 352–73.

TURING, A. M. 1950. Computing machinery and intelligence. *Mind* 59:433-60.

TURNER, A. M., AND GREENOUGH, W. T. 1985. Differential rearing effects on rat visual cortex synapses. I. Synaptic and neuronal density and synapses per neuron. *Brain Research* 329:195–203.

TVERSKY, A., AND KAHNEMAN, D. 1973. Availability: A heuristic for judging frequency and probability. *Cognitive Psychology* 5: 207–32.

TVERSKY, A., AND KAHNEMAN, D. 1974. Judgment under uncertainty: Heuristics and biases. *Science* 125:1124–31.

TVERSKY, A., AND KAHNEMAN, D. 1981. The framing of decisions and the psychology of choice. *Science* 211:453–58.

TVERSKY, B., AND TUCHIN, M. 1989. A reconciliation of the evidence on eyewitness testimony: Comments on McCloskey and Zaragoza (1985). *Journal of Experimental Psychology: General* 118:86–91.

TYLER, L. E. 1965. *The psychology of human differences.* New York: Appleton-Century-Crofts.

TZENG, O., AND WANG, W. Y. S. 1984. Search for a common neurocognitive mechanism for language and movements. *American Journal of Physiology* 246:904–11.

UNDERWOOD, B. J. 1957. Interference and forgetting. *Psychological Review* 64:49–60.

UNGERSTEDT, U., AND LJUNGBERG, T. 1974. Central dopamine neurons and sensory processing. *Journal of Psychiatry Research* 11:149–50.

U. S. PUBLIC HEALTH SERVICE, DIVISION OF CHRONIC DISEASES. 1966. *Obesity and health* (Public Health Service Publication No. 1485). Washington, D.C.: U. S. Government Printing Office.

URWIN, C. 1983. Dialogue and cognitive functioning in the early language development of three blind children. In Mills, A. E. (Ed.), *Language acquisition in the blind child.* London: Croom Helm.

VAILLANT, G. E. 1971. Theoretical hierarchy of adaptive ego mechanisms. *Archives of General Psychiatry* 24: 107-18.

VAILLANT, G. E. 1974. Natural history of male psychological health. II. Some antecedents of health adult adjustment. *Archives of General Psychiatry* 31:15–22.

VAILLANT, G. E. 1976. Natural history of male psychological health. V: Relation of choice of ego mechanisms of defense to adult adjustment. *Archives of General Psychiatry* 33:535–45.

VAILLANT, G. E. 1977. *Adaptation to life.* Boston: Little, Brown & Co.

VALENSTEIN, E. S. 1986. *Great and desperate cures.* New York: Basic Books.

VALENTA, J. G., AND RIGBY, M. K. 1968. Discrimination of the odor of stressed rats. *Science* 161:599–601.

VALINS, S. 1966. Cognitive effects of false heart-rate feedback. *Journal of Personality and Social Psychology* 4:400–408.

VAN CANTFORT, E., AND RIMPAU, J. 1982. Sign language studies with children and chimpanzees. *Sign Language Studies* 34:15–72.

VANDELL, D. L.; HENDERSON, V. K.; AND WILSON, K. S. 1988. A longitudinal study of children with day care experiences of varying quality. *Child Development* 59:1286–92.

VANDENBOS, G. R.; CUMMINGS, N. A.; AND DELEON, P. H. 1992. A century of psychotherapy: Economic and environmental influences. In Freedheim, D. K. (Ed.), *History of psychotherapy.* Washington, D.C.: American Psychological Association.

VAN HOOFF, J. A. R. A. M. 1972. A comparative approach to the phylogeny of laughter and smiling. In Hinde, R. A. (Ed.), *Non-verbal communication.* New York: Cambridge University Press.

VAN KAMMEN, D. P., AND KELLEY, M. 1991. Dopamine and norepinephrine activity in schizophrenia: An integrated perspective. *Schizophrenia Research* 4:173–91.

VAN ZOEREN, J. G., AND STRICKER, E. M. 1977. Effects of preoptic, lateral hypothalamic, or dopamine-depleting lesions on behavioral thermoregulations in rats exposed to the cold. *Journal of Comparative and Physiological Psychology* 91:989.

VAULTIN, R. G., AND BERKELEY, M. A. 1977. Responses of single cells in cat visual cortex to prolonged stimulus movement: Neural correlates of visual aftereffects. *Journal of Neurophysiology* 40: 1051–65.

VERAA, R. P., AND GRAFSTEIN, B. 1981. Cellular mechanisms for recovery from nervous system injury: A conference report. *Experimental Neurology* 71:6–75.

VERY, P. S. 1967. Differential factor structure in mathematical ability. *Genetic Psychology Monographs* 75:169–208.

VISCOTT, D. S. 1979. A musical idiot savant: A psychodynamic study, and some speculations on the creative process. *Psychiatry* 33: 494–515.

VISINTAINER, M.; VOLPICELLI, J. R.; AND SELIGMAN, M. E. P. 1982. Tumor rejection in rats after inescapable or escapable shock. *Science* 216:437–39.

VOLPICELLI, J. 1989. Psychoactive substance use disorders. In Rosenhan, D. L., and Seligman, M. E. P. *Abnormal psychology,* 2nd ed. New York: Norton.

WABER, D. P. 1977. Sex differences in mental abilities, hemispheric lateralization, and rate of physical growth at adolescence. *Developmental Psychology* 13:29–38.

WABER, D. P. 1979. Cognitive abilities and sex-related variations in the maturation of cerebral cortical functions. In Wittig, M. A., and Petersen, A. C. (Eds.), *Sex-related differences in cognitive functioning,* pp. 161–89. New York: Academic Press.

WACHTEL, P. L. 1977. *Psychoanalysis and behavior therapy: Toward an integration.* New York: Basic Books.

WACHTEL, P. L. 1982. What can dynamic therapies contribute to behavior therapy? *Behavior Therapy* 13:594–609.

WADDINGTON, J. L.; TORREY, E. F.; CROW, T. J.; AND HIRSCH, S. R. 1991. Schizophrenia, neurodevelopment, and disease. *Archives of General Psychiatry* 48:271–73.

WAGNER, A. R. 1979. Habituation and memory. In Dickinson, A., and Boakes, R. A. (Eds.), *Mechanisms of learning and memory: A memorial to Jerzy Konorski,* pp. 53–82. Hillsdale, N.J.: Erlbaum.

WAGNER, D. A. 1974. The development of short-term and incidental memory: A cross-cultural study. *Child Development* 45: 389–96.

WAGNER, D. A. 1978. Memories of Morocco: The influence of age, schooling, and environment on memory. *Cognitive Psychology* 10:1–28.

WAGNER, R. K. 1987. Tacit knowledge in everyday intelligent behavior. *Journal of Personality and Social Psychology* 52:1236–47.

WAGNER, R. K., AND STERNBERG, R. J. 1987. Tacit knowledge in managerial success. *Journal of Business and Psychology* 1:301–12.

WAID, W. M., AND ORNE, M. T. 1982. The physiological detection of deception. *American Scientist* 70:402–409.

WAKEFIELD, J. C. 1992. The concept of mental disorder: On the boundary between biological facts and social values. *American Psychologist* 47(3):373–88.

WALD, G. 1950. Eye and camera. *Scientific American* 183: 32–41.

WALDFOGEL, S. 1948. The frequency and affective character of childhood memories. *Psychological Monographs,* vol. 62 (Whole No. 291).

WALKER, L. J. 1984. Sex differences in the development of moral reasoning: A critical review. *Child Development* 55:677–91.

WALKER, L. J. 1989. Sex differences in the development of moral reasoning: A reply to Baumrind. *Child Development* 57:522–26.

WALL, P. D. 1980. Mechanisms of plasticity of connection following damage of adult mammalian nervous system. In Bach-y-Rita, P. (Ed.), *Recovery of function: Theoretical considerations for brain injury rehabilitation.* Bern: Hans Huber.

WALLACH, H. 1948. Brightness constancy and the nature of achromatic colors. *Journal of Experimental Psychology* 38:310-24.

WALLÉN, K. 1989. Mate selection: Economics and affection. Peer commentary to aritcle by Buss, D. M. Sex differences in human mate preferences: Evolutionary hypotheses tested in 37 cultures. *Behavioral and Brain Sciences* 12:3738.

WALSTER, E.; ARONSON, E.; AND ABRAHAMS, D. 1966. On increasing the persuasiveness of a low prestige communicator. *Journal of Experimental Social Psychology* 2:325–42.

WALSTER, E.; ARONSON, E.; ABRAHAMS, D.; AND ROTTMAN, L. 1966. The importance of physical attractiveness in dating behavior. *Journal of Personality and Social Psychology* 4:508–16.

WALSTER, E., AND BERSCHEID, E. 1974. A little bit about love: A minor essay on a major topic. In Huston, T. L. (Ed.), *Foundations of interpersonal attraction.* New York: Academic Press.

WALSTER (HATFIELD), E., AND WALSTER, G. W. 1978. *A new look at love.* Reading, Mass.: Addison-Wesley.

WALTERS, J. R., AND SEYFARTH, R. M. 1986. Conflict and cooperation. In Smuts, B. B.; Cheney, D. L.; Seyfarth, R. M.; Wrangham, R. W.; and Struhsaker, T. T. (Eds.), *Primate societies.* Chicago: University of Chicago Press.

WANNER, E. 1988. The parser's architecture. In Kessel, F. (Ed.), *The development of language and of language researchers: Papers presented to Roger Brown.* Hillsdale, N.J.: Erlbaum.

WANNER, E., AND MARATSOS, M. 1978. An ATN approach to comprehension. In Halle, M.; Bresnan, J.; and Miller, G. A. (Eds.), *Linguistic theory and psychological reality.* Cambridge, Mass.: MIT Press.

WAPNER, W. T.; JUDD, T.; AND GARDNER, H. 1978. Visual agnosia in an artist. *Cortex* 14:343–64.

WARREN, R. M. 1970. Perceptual restorations of missing speech sounds. *Science* 167:392–93.

WARRINGTON, E. K., AND WEISKRANTZ, L. 1978. Further analysis of the prior learning effect in amnesic patients. *Neuropsychologia* 16:169–76.

WASMAN, M., AND FLYNN, J. P. 1962. Directed attack elicited from the hypothalamus. *Archives of Neurology* 6:220–27.

WASON, P. C. 1960. On the failure to eliminate hypotheses in a conceptual task. *Quarterly Journal of Experimental Psychology* 12: 129–40.

WASON, P. C. 1968. On the failure to eliminate hypotheses—A second look. In Wason, P. C., and Johnson-Laird, P. N. (Eds.), *Thinking and reasoning*. Harmondsworth, England: Penguin Books.

WASON, P. C., AND JOHNSON-LAIRD, P. N. 1972. *Psychology of reasoning*. London: B. T. Batsford, Ltd.

WATERS, E.; WIPPMAN, J.; AND SROUFE, L. A. 1979. Attachment, positive affect, and competence in the peer group: Two studies in construct validation. *Child Development* 50:821–29.

WATKINS, L. R., AND MAYER, D. J. 1982. Organization of endogenous opiate and nonopiate pain control systems. *Science* 216: 1185–92.

WATSON, C. G., AND BURANEN, C. 1979. The frequency of conversion reaction. *Journal of Abnormal Psychology* 88:209–11.

WATSON, D. 1982. The actor and the observer: How are their perceptions of causality different? *Psychological Bulletin* 92:682–700.

WATSON, J. B. 1925. *Behaviorism*. New York: Norton.

WATSON, J. S. 1967. Memory and "contingency analysis" in infant learning. *Merrill-Palmer Quarterly* 13:55–76.

WAUGH, N. C., AND NORMAN, D. A. 1965. Primary memory. *Psychological Review* 72:89–104.

WAXMAN, S. R. 1994. The development of an appreciation of specific linkages between linguistic and conceptual organization. In Gleitman, L. R., and Landau, B. (Eds.), Lexical acquisition, *Lingua* (Special Issue) 92:229–57.

WEBB, W. B. 1972. Sleep deprivation: Total, partial, and selective. In Chase, M. H. (Ed.), *The sleeping brain*, pp. 323–62. Los Angeles: Brain Information Service, Brain Research Institute.

WEBB, W. B. 1974. Sleep as an adaptive process. *Perceptual and Motor Skills* 38:1023–27.

WEBB, W. B. 1979. Theories of sleep functions and some clinical implications. In Drucker-Colin, R.; Shkurovich, M.; and Sterman, M. B. (Eds.), *The functions of sleep*, pp. 19–36. New York: Academic Press.

WEBB, W. B. 1982. Some theories about sleep and their clinical implications. *Psychiatric Annals* 11:415–22.

WEBER, M. 1904–1905. *The Protestant ethic and the spirit of capitalism*. Parsons, T. (trans.). New York: Scribner's, 1976.

WECHSLER, D. 1958. *The measurement and appraisal of adult intelligence,* 4th ed. Baltimore: Williams & Wilkins.

WEHR, T. A., AND GOODWIN, F. K. 1981. Biological rhythms and psychiatry. In Arieti, S., and Brodie, H. K. H. (Eds.), *American Handbook of Psychiatry,* vol. 7, pp. 46–74. New York: Basic Books.

WEIGEL, R. H.; VERNON, D. T. A.; AND TOGNACCI, L. N. 1974. Specificity of the attitude as a determinant of attitude-behavior congruence. *Journal of Personality and Social Psychology* 30:724–28.

WEINER, B. 1982. The emotional consequences of causal attributions. In Clark, M. S., and Fiske, S. T. (Eds.), *Affect and cognition: The 17th annual Carnegie symposium on cognition*. Hillsdale, N.J.: Erlbaum.

WEINER, H.; THALER, M.; REISER, M. F.; AND MIRSKY, I. A. 1957. Etiology of duodenal ulcer: I. Relation of specific psychological characteristics to rate of gastric secretion. *Psychosomatic Medicine* 19:1–10.

WEINER, R. D. 1984a. Does electroconvulsive therapy cause brain damage? (with peer commentary). *The Behavioral and Brain Sciences* 7:1–54.

WEINER, R. D. 1984b. Convulsive therapy:50 years later. *American Journal of Psychiatry* 141:1078–79.

WEINER, R. D. 1985. Convulsive therapies. In Kaplan, H. I., and Sadock, J. (Eds.), *Comprehensive textbook of psychiatry*, 4th ed. Baltimore: Williams & Wilkins.

WEINGARTNER, H., AND PARKER, E. S. (Eds.). 1984. *Memory consolidation: Psychobiology of cognition*. Hillsdale, N.J.: Erlbaum.

WEINRICH, J. D. 1987. *Sexual landscapes*. New York: Scribner's.

WEINSTOCK, S. 1954. Resistance to extinction of a running response following partial reinforcement under widely spaced trials. *Journal of Comparative and Physiological Psychology* 47:318–22.

WEISBERG, R. W., AND ALBA, J. W., 1981. An examination of the alleged role of "fixation" in the solution of several "insight" problems. *Journal of Experimental Psychology: General* 110:169–92.

WEISKRANTZ, L. 1986. *Blindsight: A case study and implications*. Oxford: Clarendon Press.

WEISKRANTZ, L., AND WARRINGTON, E. K. 1979. Conditioning in amnesic patients. *Neuropsychologia* 18:177–84.

WEISS, B., AND LATIES, V. G. 1961. Behavioral thermoregulation. *Science* 133:1338–44.

WEISS, J. M. 1970. Somatic effects of predictable and unpredictable shock. *Psychosomatic Medicine* 32:397–408.

WEISS, J. M. 1977. Psychological and behavioral influences on gastrointestinal lesions in animal models. In Maser, J. D., and Seligman, M. E. P. (Eds.), *Psychopathology: Experimental models*, pp. 232–69. San Francisco: Freeman.

WEISSMAN, M. 1985. The epidemiology of anxiety disorders: Rates, risks, and familial patterns. In Tuma, A. H., and Maser, J. D. (Eds.), *Anxiety and the anxiety disorders*, pp. 275–96. Hillsdale, N.J.: Erlbaum.

WEISSMAN, M., AND BOYD, J. H. 1985. Affective disorders: Epidemiology. In Kaplan, H. I., and Sadock, J. (Eds.), *Modern synopsis of comprehensive textbook of psychiatry*, 4th ed. Baltimore: Williams & Wilkins.

WEISSTEIN, N., AND WONG, E. 1986. Figure-ground organization and the spatial and temporal responses of the visual system. In Schwab, E. C., and Nusbaum, H. C. (Eds.), *Pattern recognition by humans and machines*, vol. 2. New York: Academic Press.

WEISZ, J. R.; ROTHBAUM, F. M.; AND BLACKBURN, T. C. 1984. Standing out and standing in: The psychology of control in American and Japan. *American Psychologist* 39:955–69.

WELCH, C. A.; WEINER, R. D.; WEIR, D.; CAHILL, J. F.; ROGERS, H. J.; DAVIDSON, J.; MILLER, R. D.; AND MANDEL, M. R. 1982. Efficacy of ECT in the treatment of depression: Wave form and electrode placement considerations. *Psychopharmacological Bulletin* 18:31–34.

WELKER, W. I.; JOHNSON, J. I.; AND PUBOLS, B. H. 1964. Some morphological and physiological characteristics of the somatic sensory system in raccoons. *American Zoologist* 4:75–94.

WELLMAN, H. M. 1990. *The child's theory of mind*. Cambridge, Mass.: MIT Press.

WELLMAN, H. M., AND BARTSCH, K. 1988. Young children's reasoning about beliefs. *Cognition* 30:239–77.

WELLMAN, H. M.; RITTER, K.; AND FLAVELL, J. H. 1975. Deliberate memory behavior in the delayed reactions of very young children. *Developmental Psychology* 11:780–87.

WENDER, P. H.; KETY, S. S.; ROSENTHAL, D.; SCHULSINGER, F.; AND ORTMANN, J. 1986. Psychiatric disorders in the biological relatives of adopted individuals with affective disorders. *Archives of General Psychiatry* 43:923–29.

WERKER, J. 1991. The ontogeny of speech perception. In Mattingly, I. G., and Studdert-Kennedy, M. (Eds.), *Modularity and the motor theory of speech perception: Proceedings of a conference to honor Alvin M. Liberman*, pp. 91–109. Hillsdale, N. J.: Erlbaum.

WERKER, J., AND TEES, R. 1984. Cross-language speech perception: Evidence for perceptual reorganization during the first year of life. *Infant Behavior and Development* 7:49–63.

WERTHEIMER, MAX. 1912. Experimentelle Studien über das Gesehen von Bewegung. *Zeitschrift frPsychologie* 61:161–265.

WERTHEIMER, MAX. 1923. Untersuchungen zur Lehre von der Gestalt, II. *Psychologische Forschung* 4:301–50.

WERTHEIMER, MICHAEL. 1961. Psychomotor coordination of auditory and visual space at birth. *Science* 134:1692.

WEST, S. G.; WHITNEY, G.; AND SCHNEDLER, R. 1975. Helping a motorist in distress: The effects of sex, race, and neighborhood. *Journal of Personality and Social Psychology,* 31:691–98.

WESTERMEYER, J. 1987. Public health and chronic mental illness. *American Journal of Public Health* 77:667–68.

WETZEL, M., AND STUART, D. G. 1976. Ensemble characteristics of cat locomotion and its neural control. *Progress in Neurobiology* 7:1–98.

WEXLER, K., AND CULICOVER, P. 1980. *Formal principles of language acquisition.* Cambridge, Mass.: MIT Press.

WEXLER, K., AND MANZINI, R. 1987. Parameters and learnability in binding theory. In Roeper, T., and Williams, E. (Eds.), *Parameter setting.* Dordrecht: Reidel.

WHEELER, L.; REIS, H.; AND BOND, M. H. 1989. Collectivism-individualism in everyday social life: The middle kingdom and the melting pot. *Journal of Personality and Social Psychology* 57:79–86.

WHEELER, L. R. 1942. A comparative study of the intelligence of East Tennessee mountain children. *Journal of Educational Psychology* 33:321–34.

WHITE, G. L. 1980. Physical attractiveness and courtship progress. *Journal of Personality and Social Psychology* 39:660–68.

WHITE, L. 1985. Universal grammar as a source of explanation in second language acquisition. In Wheatley, B., et al. (Eds.), *Current approaches to second language acquisition: Proceedings of the 1984 University of Wisconsin linguistics symposium,* Indiana University Linguistics Club.

WHITE, R. W., AND WATT, N. F. 1973. *The abnormal personality,* 4th ed. New York: Ronald Press.

WHITE, S. H., AND PILLEMER, D. B. 1979. Childhood amnesia and the development of a functionally accessible memory system. In Kihlstrom, J. F., and Evans, F. J. (Eds.), *Functional disorders of memory.* Hillsdale, N.J.: Erlbaum.

WHITING, J. W. M., AND CHILD, I. L. 1953. *Child training and personality.* New Haven: Yale University.

WHITING, J. W. M., AND WHITING, B. B. 1975. *Children of six cultures: A psychocultural analysis.* Cambridge, Mass.: Harvard University Press.

WHITLOW, J. W., JR., AND WAGNER, A. R. 1984. Memory and habituation. In Peeke, H. V. S., and Petrinovich, L. (Eds.), *Habituation, sensitization, and behavior,* pp. 103–53. New York: Academic Press.

WICKELGREN, W. A. 1974. *How to solve problems.* San Francisco: Freeman.

WICKER, A. W. 1969. Attitudes versus action: The relationship of verbal and overt behavioral responses to attitude objects. *Journal of Social Issues* 25:41–78.

WIENS, A. N., AND MENUSTIK, C. E. 1983. Treatment outcome and patient characteristics in an aversion therapy program for alcoholism. *American Psychologist* 38:1089–96.

WIESENTHAL, D. L.; ENDLER, N. S.; COWARD, T. R.; AND EDWARDS, J. 1976. Reversibility of relative competence as a determinant of conformity across different perceptual tasks. *Representative Research in Social Psychology* 7:319–42.

WILCOXIN, H. C.; DRAGOIN, W. B.; AND KRAL, P. A. 1971. Illness-induced aversions in rat and quail: Relative salience of visual and gustatory cues. *Science* 171: 826–28.

WILLIAMS, C. D. 1959. The elimination of tantrum behavior by extinction procedures. *Journal of Abnormal and Social Psychology* 59:269.

WILLIAMS, D. R., AND WILLIAMS, H. 1969. Auto maintenance in the pigeon: Sustained pecking despite contingent non-reinforcement. *Journal of the Experimental Analysis of Behavior* 12:511–20.

WILLIAMS, G. C. 1966. *Adaptation and natural selection.* Princeton, N.J.: Princeton University Press.

WILLIAMS, H. L.; TEPAS, D. I.; AND MORLOCK, H. C. 1962. Evoked responses to clicks and electroencephalographic stages of sleep in man. *Science* 138:685–86.

WILLIAMS, M. D., AND HOLLAN, J. D. 1982. The process of retrieval from very long-term memory. *Cognitive Science* 5:87–119.

WILLIAMS, R. B. 1987. Psychological factors in coronary artery disease: Epidemiological evidence. *Circulation* 76 (suppl I) 117–23.

WILLIAMS, W. L. 1986. *The spirit and the flesh: Sexual diversity in American Indian culture.* Boston: Beacon Press.

WILSON, D. H.; REEVES, A. G.; GAZZANIGA, M. S.; AND CULVER, C. 1977. Cerebral commissurotomy for the control of intractable seizures. *Neurology* 27:708–15.

WILSON, E. O. 1975. *Sociobiology.* Cambridge, Mass.: Harvard University Press.

WILSON, E. O. 1978. *On human nature.* Cambridge, Mass; Harvard University Press.

WILSON, G. 1978. Introversion/extraversion. In London, H., and Exner, J. (Eds.), *Dimensions of personality.* New York: Wiley.

WILSON, G. 1985. *The psychology of the performing arts.* London and Sydney: Croom Helm.

WILSON, G. T. 1980. Behavior modification and the treatment of obesity. In Stunkard, A. J. (Ed.), *Obesity,* pp. 325–44. Philadelphia: Saunders.

WILTSCHKO, R.; NORH, D.; AND WILTSCHKO, W. 1981. Pigeons with a deficient sun compass use the magnetic compass. *Science* 214:34–45.

WIMMER, H., AND PERNER, J. 1983. Beliefs about beliefs: Representation and constraining function of wrong beliefs in young children's understanding of deception. *Cognition* 13:103–28.

WINCHESTER, A. M. 1977. *Genetics,* 5th ed. Boston: Houghton Mifflin.

WINCH, R. F., AND MORE, D. M. 1956. Does TAT add information to interviews? Statistical analysis of the increment. *Journal of Clinical Psychology* 12:316–21.

WINKLER, J., AND TAYLOR, S. E. 1979. Preference, expectation, and attributional bias: Two field experiments. *Journal of Applied Social Psychology* 2:183–97.

WINSLOW, J. T., AND INSEL, T. R. 1990. Neurobiology of obsessive-compulsive disorder: A possible role for serotonin. *Journal of Clinical Psychiatry* 51(Supplement): 27–31.

WINTER, R. 1976. *The smell book: Scents, sex, and society.* Philadelphia: Lippincott.

WISE, R. A. 1987. The role of reward pathways in the development of drug dependence. *Pharmacological Therapy* 35:227–63.

WISE, R. A., AND BOZARTH, M. A. 1987. A psychomotor stimulant theory of addiction. *Psychological Review* 94:469–92.

WISE, R. A., AND ROMPRE, P. P. 1989. Brain dopamine and reward. *Annual Review of Psychology* 40:191–226.

WISHNER, J. 1960. Reanalysis of "impressions of personality." *Psychological Review* 67:96–112.

WISHNER, J. 1974. *Psychopathology: Defective concept or defective practice?* Invited address delivered at the XVIII International Congress of Applied Psychology, Montreal, Canada.

WITTGENSTEIN, L. 1953. *Philosophical investigations.* Trans. by Anscombe, G. E. M. Oxford, England: Blackwell.

WOLF, M. E., AND MOSNAIM, A. D. 1990. *Post-traumatic stress disorder: Etiology, phenomenology, and treatment.* Washington, D.C.: American Psychiatric Press.

WOLF, S. 1971. Psychosocial influences in gastrointestinal function. In Levi, L. (Ed.), *The psychosocial environment and psychosomatic disease,* vol. 1, pp. 362–68. London: Oxford University Press.

WOLLEN, K. A.; WEBER, A.; AND LOWRY, D. 1972. Bizarreness versus interaction of mental images as determinants of learning. *Cognitive Psychology* 3:518–23.

WOLPE, J. 1958. *Psychotherapy by reciprocal inhibition.* Stanford, Calif.: Stanford University Press.

WOLPE, J., AND LAZARUS, A. A. 1966. *Behavior therapy techniques: A guide to the treatment of neuroses.* Elmsford, N.Y.: Pergamon.

WOLPERT, E. A., AND TROSMAN, H. 1958. Studies in psychophysiology of dreams: I. Experimental evocation of sequential dream episodes. *Archives of Neurology and Psychiatry* 79:603–606.

WOOD, A. J., AND GOODWIN, G. M. 1987. A review of the biochemical and neuropharmacological actions of lithium. *Psychological Medicine* 17: 579–600.

WOODRUFF, G., AND PREMACK, D. 1979. Intentional communication in the chimpanzee: The development of deception. *Cognition* 7: 333–62.

WOODS, B. T., AND TEUBER, H. L. 1978. Changing patterns of childhood aphasia. *Archives of Neurology* 3:273–80.

WOODS, R. L. 1947. *The world of dreams: An anthology.* New York: Random House.

WOODWORTH, R. S. 1938. *Experimental Psychology.* New York: Henry Holt and Co.

WYERS, E. J.; PEEKE, H. V. S.; AND HERZ, M. J. 1973. Behavioral habituation in invertebrates. In Peeke, H. V. S., and Herz, M. J. (Eds.), *Habituation: Vol. 1. Behavioral studies*. New York: Academic Press.

WYNN, K. 1992. Addition and subtraction by human infants. *Nature* 358:749–50.

YAGER, D. D., AND HOY, R. R. 1986. The Cyclopean ear: A new sense for the Praying Mantis. *Science* 231:727–29.

YAGER, D. D., AND MAY, M. L. 1990. Ultrasound-triggered, flight-gated evasive maneuvers in the Praying Mantis *Parasphendale agrionina*. *Journal of Experimental Biology* 152:41–58.

YANDO, R.; SEITZ, V.; AND ZIGLER, E. 1978. *Imitation: A developmental perspective*. Hillsdale, N.J.: Erlbaum.

YANG, K., AND BOND, M. H. 1990. Exploring implicit personality theories with indigenous or imported constructs: The Chinese case. *Journal of Personality and Social Psychology* 58:1087–95.

YARBUS, A. L. 1967. *Eye movements and vision*. Trans. by Riggs, L. A. New York: Plenum Press.

YARROW, L. J. 1961. Maternal deprivation: Toward an empirical and conceptual reevaluation. *Psychological Bulletin* 58:459–90.

YERKES, R. M., AND MORGULIS, S. 1909. Method of Pavlov in animal psychology. *Psychological Bulletin* 6:264.

YONAS, A. 1981. Infants' response to optical information for collision. In Aslin, R. N.; Alberts, J. R.; and Petersen, M. R. (Eds.), *Development of perception*, pp. 313–34. New York: Academic Press.

YUSSEN, S. R., AND LEVY, V. M. 1975. Developmental changes in predicting one's own span of memory. *Journal of Experimental Child Psychology* 19: 502–508.

ZAIDEL, E. 1976. Auditory vocabulary of the right hemisphere following brain bisection or hemidecortication. *Cortex* 12:191–211.

ZAIDEL, E. 1983. A response to Gazzaniga: Language in the right hemisphere. *American Psychologist* 38:542–46.

ZAJONC, R. B. 1965. Social facilitation. *Science* 149:269–74.

ZAJONC, R. B. 1968. Attitudinal effects of mere exposure. *Journal of Personality and Social Psychology Monograph Supplement* 9:1–27.

ZAJONC, R. B. 1980. Copresence. In Paulus, P. (Ed.), *The psychology of group influence*. Hillsdale, N.J.: Erlbaum.

ZAJONC, R. B., HEINGERTNER, A.; AND HERMAN, E. M. 1969. Social enhancement and impairment of performance in the cockroach. *Journal of Personality and Social Psychology* 13:83–92.

ZARAGOZA, M. S., AND McCLOSKEY, M. 1989. Misleading postevent information and the memory impairment hypothesis: Comment on Belli and reply to Tversky and Tuchin. *Journal of Experimental Psychology: General* 118:92–99.

ZEIGLER, H. P., AND LEIBOWITZ, H. 1957. Apparent visual size as a function of distance for children and adults. *American Journal of Psychology* 70:106–109.

ZENER, K. 1937. The significance of behavior accompanying conditioned salivary secretion for theories of the conditioned response. *American Journal of Psychology* 50:384–403.

ZENTALL, T., AND HOGAN, D. 1974. Abstract concept learning in the pigeon. *Journal of Experimental Psychology* 102:393–98.

ZIEGLER, F. J.; IMBODEN, J. B.; AND RODGERS, D. A. 1963. Contemporary conversion reactions: III. Diagnostic considerations. *Journal of the American Medical Association* 186:307–11.

ZIGLER, E. 1967. Familial mental retardation: A continuing dilemma. *Science* 155:292–98.

ZIGLER, E., AND BERMAN, W. 1983. Discerning the future of early childhood intervention. *American Psychologist* 38:894–906.

ZIGLER, E., AND CHILD, I. L. 1969. Socialization. In Lindzey, G., and Aronson, E. (Eds.), *The handbook of social psychology*, vol. 3, pp. 450–589. Reading, Mass.: Addison-Wesley.

ZIGLER, E. F.; LAMB, M. E.; AND CHILD, I. L. 1982. *Socialization and personality development*, 2nd ed. New York: Oxford University Press.

ZILBOORG, G., AND HENRY, G. W. 1941. *A history of medical psychology*. New York: Norton.

ZILLMAN, D. 1983. Transfer of excitation in emotional behavior. In Cacioppo, J. T., and Petty, R. E. (Eds.), *Social psychophysiology: A sourcebook*, pp. 215–40. New York: Guilford.

ZILLMAN, D.; KATCHER, A. H.; AND MILAVSKY, B. 1972. Excitation transfer from physical exercise to subsequent aggressive behavior. *Journal of Experimental Social Psychology* 8:247–59.

ZIMBARDO, P. G. 1969. The human choice: Individuation, reason, and order versus deindividuation, impulse and chaos. In Arnold, W. J. and Levine, E. (Eds.), *Nebraska Symposium on Motivation*, pp. 237–308. Lincoln, Neb.: University of Nebraska Press.

ZOHAR, J.; INSEL, T.; ZOHAR-KADOUCH, R. C.; HILL, J. L.; AND MURPHY, D. 1988. Serotonergic responsivity in obsessive-compulsive disorder. Effects of chronic clomipramine treatment. *Archives of General Psychiatry* 45:167–72.

ZORILLA, L. T. E., AND CANNON, T. D. 1995. Structural brain abnormalities in schizophrenia: Distribution, etiology, and implications. In Mednick, S. A. (Ed.), *Neural development in schizophrenia: Theory and research*. New York: Plenum Press.

ZUBIN, J.; ERON, L. D.; AND SHUMER, F. 1965. *An experimental approach to projective techniques*. New York: Wiley.

ZUCKERMAN, M. 1979. *Sensation seeking: Beyond the optimum level of arousal*. Hillsdale, N.J.: Erlbaum.

ZUCKERMAN, M. 1983. A biological theory of sensation seeking. In Zuckerman, M. (Ed.), *Biological bases of sensation seeking, impulsivity, and anxiety*. Hillsdale, N.J.: Erlbaum.

ZUCKERMAN, M. 1987. All parents are environmentalists until they have their second child. Peer commentary on Plomin, R., and Daniels, D. Why are children from the same family so different from one another? *Behavioral and Brain Sciences* 10:38–39.

ZUCKERMAN, M. 1990. The psychophysiology of sensation seeking. *Journal of Personality* 58:313–45.

ZUCKERMAN, M. 1991. *The psychobiology of personality*. New York: Cambridge University Press.

ZUCKERMAN, M.; BALLENGER, J. C.; JIMERSON, D. C.; MURPHY, D. L.; AND POST, R. M. 1983. A correlational test in humans of the biological models of sensation seeking and anxiety. In Zuckerman, M. (Ed.), *Biological bases of sensation seeking, impulsivity, and anxiety*, pp. 229–48. Hillsdale, N.J.: Erlbaum.

ZUGER, B. 1984. Early effeminate behavior in boys. *Journal of Nervous and Mental Disease* 172:90–96.

ACKNOWLEDGMENTS AND CREDITS

FIGURES

Chapter 1: **1.1** Courtesy of Kaiser Porcelain Ltd. **1.2A,B,C** Bugelski, B. R., and Alampay, D. A., The role of frequency in developing perceptual sets, *Canadian Journal of Psychology* 15 (1961): 205-11. Adapted by permission of the Canadian Psychological Association. **1.3A** Courtesy of Richard D.Walk. **1.3B** Courtesy of William Vandivert. **1.4A** Photograph by Ed Reschke/Peter Arnold, Inc. **1.4B** Photograph by David Gillison/Peter Arnold, Inc. **1.4C** Photograph by Fred Bavendam/Peter Arnold, Inc. **1.5A** Photograph by George H. Harrison/Grant Heilman. **1.5B** Photograph by Peter Hendrie/ The Image Bank. **1.6** Collection of Robert H. Helmick; courtesy Brooke Alexander, New York. **1.7** Dement, W. C., *Some Must Watch While Some Must Sleep.* New York: W. W. Norton & Company, Inc. Copyright © 1972, 1974, 1976 by William C. Dement. **1.8** Courtesy of William C. Dement. **1.9** Courtesy of the Staatlicher Museum für Völkerkunde, Munich. **1.10** Courtesy of The Museum of Modern Art/Film Stills Archive.

Chapter 2: **2.1** Photograph by Cabisco/Visuals Unlimited. **2.2B** Photograph by Dr. John Mazziotta, UCLA School of Medicine/Science Photo Library/ Photo Researchers. **2.4B** Photograph by Manfred Kage/Peter Arnold, Inc. **2.5C** © Guigoz/Dr. A. Privat/Petit Format/Science Source/Photo Researchers. **2.9** From *Biology: The Unity and Diversity of Life*, Fifth Edition, by Cecie Starr and Ralph Taggart, © 1989 by Wadsworth, Inc. Reprinted by permission of the publisher. **2.10** Eccles, J. C., *The Understanding of the Brain.* New York: McGraw-Hill, 1973. Adapted by permission of McGraw-Hill, Inc. **2.14** Drawing by Maura Conron. **2.15** Lewis, E. R., Everhart, T. E., and Seevi, Y. Y., Studying neural organization in aplysia with the scanning electron microscope, *Science* 165 (12 September 1969): 1140-43. Copyright 1969 by the American Association for the Advancement of Science. Reprinted by permission of the publisher and the author. **2.16** Bloom, F. E., Lazerson, A., and Hofstadter, L., *Brain, Mind and Behavior.* New York: Freeman, 1988. Adapted by permission of WNET/Thirteen. **2.17** *Physiological Psychology*, 2nd ed., by Mark Rosenzweig and Arnold Leiman. Copyright © 1989 by Random House. Reprinted by permission of McGraw-Hill, Inc. **2.19** Roeder, K., *Nerve Cells and Insect Behavior.* Cambridge, Mass.: Harvard University Press, 1972, p. 198. Adapted by permission of Harvard University Press. **2.20** Bloom, F. E., Lazerson, A., and Hofstadter, L., *Brain, Mind and Behavior.* New York: Freeman, 1988. Adapted by permission of WNET/Thirteen. **2.21** Lickley, J. D., *The Nervous System.* Essex, England: Longman, 1919. Reprinted by permission of the publisher. **2.22A** Photograph by Biophoto Associates/Photo Researchers. **2.22B** Keeton, W. T., *Biological Science*, 3rd ed. New York: W. W. Norton & Company, Inc., 1980. Copyright © 1980, 1979, 1972, 1967 by W. W. Norton & Company, Inc. Used with permission. **2.25** Bloom, F. E., Lazerson, A., and Hofstadter, L., *Brain, Mind and Behavior.* New York: Freeman, 1988. Adapted by permission of WNET/Thirteen. **2.26** Adapted with permission of Macmillan Publishing Co., Inc., from *The Cerebral Cortex of Man* by Wilder Penfield and Theodore Rasmussen. Copyright © 1950 by Macmillan Publishing Co., Inc., renewed 1978 by Theodore Rasmussen. **2.27** Cobb, S., *Foundations of Neuropsychiatry.* Baltimore, Md.: William & Wilkins, 1941. © 1941, the Williams & Wilkins Co., Baltimore. Adapted by permission of the publisher. **2.28** Photograph by Simon Fraser/Science Photo Library/Photo Researchers. **2.29** NIH/SPL/Photo Researchers. **2.30** Photograph by Dr. John Mazziotta et al./Photo Researchers. **2.31** Photograph © Paul Shambroom. **2.32** From *Higher Cortical Functions in Man* by Aleksandr Romanovich Luria. Copyright © 1966, 1979 Consultants Bureau Enterprises, Inc., and Basic Books, Inc. Reprinted by permission of Basic Books, Inc., New York. **2.33** *Physiological Psychology*, 2nd ed., by Mark Rosenzweig and Arnold Leiman. Copyright © 1989 by Random House. Reprinted by permission of McGraw-Hill. **2.34** Photograph by M. Sakka, courtesy Musée de l'Homme et Musée Depuytren, Paris. **2.37** Gazzaniga, M. S., The split brain in man, *Scientific American* 217 (August 1967): 25. Copyright © 1967 by Scientific American, Inc. All rights reserved. Drawing by Maura Conron. **2.39** After figure "Space Relations" (p. 354) from *Essentials of Psychological Testing*, 3rd edition, by Lee J. Cronbach. Copyright ©1949 by Harper & Row, Inc. Copyright © 1960, 1970 by Lee J. Cronbach. Reprinted by permission of HarperCollins Publishers. **2.40** Adapted from Björklund, A., Stenevi, U., Schmidt, R. H., Dunnett, S. B., and Gage, F. H., Intracerebral grafting of neuronal suspensions I: Induction and general methods of preparation, *Acta Physiologica Scandinavica Supplement* 522 (1983): 1-7. Reproduced by permission of Acta Physiologica Scandinavica. **2.41** Adapted from Coyle, J. T., Price, D., and Delong, M. R., Alzheimer's disease: A disorder of cholinergic innervation, *Science* 219 (1983): 1184-90. Copyright 1983 by the American Association for the Advancement of Science. Reproduced by permission of the AAAS and the author. **2.42** Courtesy of Rex Features USA.

Chapter 3: **3.3** Keeton, W. T., and Gould, J. L., *Biological Science*, 4th edition. New York: W. W. Norton & Company, Inc., 1986. Copyright © 1986, 1980, 1979, 1972, 1967 by W. W. Norton & Company, Inc. **3.4** Weiss, B., and Laties, V. G., Behavioral thermoregulation, *Science* 133 (28 April 1961): 1338-44, Fig 1. Copyright 1961 by the American Association for the Advancement of Science. Reproduced by permission of the AAAS and the author. **3.7B** Courtesy Neal E. Miller, Rockefeller University. **3.8** Photograph courtesy of Jacob Steiner. **3.9A** Laura Riley/Bruce Coleman. **3.9B** Stan Osolinski/ Oxford Scientific Films. **3.9C** Helen Williams/Photo Researchers. **3.10** Adapted from Bouchard, C., Tremblay, A., Després, J.-P., Nadeau, A., Lupien, P. J., Thèriault, G., Dussault, J., Moorjani, S., Pinault, S. M., and Fournier, G., The response to long-term overfeeding in identical twins, *New England Journal of Medicine* 322 (1990): 1477-82. Reprinted by permission of the New England Journal of Medicine. **3.11** Adapted from Nisbett, R. E., Taste, deprivation and weight determinants of eating behavior, *Journal of Personality and Social Psychology* 10 (1968): 107-16. Copyright 1968 by the American Psychological Association. Updated by permission of the author. **3.12** Herman, H. C., and Mack, D., Restrained and unrestrained eating, *Journal of Personality* 43 (1975): 647-60. Adapted by permission of Duke University Press. **3.13** Andres, R., Influence of obesity on longevity in the aged, in Borek, C., Fenoglio, C. M., and King, D. W. (Eds.), *Aging, Cancer, and Cell Membranes*, pp. 230-46. New York: Thieme-Stratton, 1980. **3.14** Reprinted by permission of Hawthorne Properties (Elsevier-Dutton Publishing Co., Inc.) from *Bodily Changes in Pain, Hunger, Fear and Rage* by W. B. Cannon. Copyright © 1929 by Appleton-Century Co.; 1957 by W. B. Cannon. **3.15** © Walter Chandoha, 1994. **3.16A** Photograph by Mary Shuford. **3.16B** Inbau, F. E., and Reid, J. E., *The Polygraph ("Lie Detector") Technique*, 2nd ed. Baltimore, Md.: Williams & Wilkins, 1977. © Professor Fred E. Inbau. **3.17** Adapted from Keeton, W. T., and Gould, J. L., *Biological Science*, 4th ed. New York: W. W. Norton, 1986. Copyright © 1986, 1980, 1979, 1972, 1967 by W.W. Norton & Company, Inc. Used with permission. **3.18** Adapted from

Bloom, F. E., Lazerson, A., and Hofstadter, L., *Brain, Mind, and Behavior.* New York: Freeman, 1988. Adapted by permission of WNET/Thirteen. **3.19A** Blakemore, C., *Mechanics of the Mind*, p. 42. New York: Cambridge University Press, 1977. Reprinted by permission of the publisher. **3.19B** Photograph © Pierre Boulat/Woodfin Camp & Associates. **3.23** Courtesy of William C. Dement. **3.24** Adapted from Kleitman, N., Patterns of dreaming, *Scientific American* 203 (November 1960): 82–88. Copyright © 1960 by Scientific American, Inc. All rights reserved. **3.26** Carlson, N. R., *Psychology of Behavior*, 4th ed., p. 295. Boston: Allyn & Bacon, 1991; graph courtesy of S. T. Inoueye. **3.27** Photograph courtesy of the University of Wisconsin Primate Laboratory. **3.28** Courtesy of Dr. M. E. Olds. **3.29** Adapted from *Physiological Psychology*, 2nd ed., by Mark Rosenzweig and Arnold Leiman. Copyright © 1989 by Random House. Reprinted by permission of McGraw-Hill.

Chapter 4: **4.2** Hoffman, H. S., and Fleshler, M., An apparatus for measurement of the startle response in the rat, *American Journal of Psychology* 77 (1964): 307–308. Copyright © 1964 by the Board of Trustees of the University of Illinois. Used with permission of the University of Illinois Press. **4.6** Pavlov, I. P., *Lectures on Conditioned Reflexes*, vol. I. New York: International Publishers Co., Inc., 1928. Adapted by permission of International Publishers Co., Inc. **4.7** Moore, J. W., Stimulus control: Studies of auditory generalization in rabbits, in Black, A. H., and Prokasy, W. F. (Eds.), *Classical Conditioning II: Current Theory and Research.* © 1972. Adapted by permission of Prentice-Hall, Inc., Englewood Cliffs, N.J. **4.12A** Photograph by Mike Salisbury. **4.12B** Photograph by Susan M. Hogue. **4.13** Drawing by Maura Conron. **4.14** From *A Primer of Operant Conditioning* by G. S. Reynolds. Copyright © 1968 by Scott, Foresman & Co. Reprinted by permission. **4.15A** Photograph courtesy of Animal Behavior Enterprises, Inc. **4.15B** Photograph by Gerald Davis/Contact Press Images. **4.16** Courtesy Yerkes Regional Primate Research Center of Emory University. **4.18, 4.19, 4.20** Ferster, C. B., and Skinner, B. F., *Schedules of Reinforcement*, pp. 56, 399. Englewood Cliffs, N.J.: Prentice-Hall, Inc., 1957. Adapted by permission of the author. **4.24** Spooner, A., and Kellogg, W. N., The backward conditioning curve, *American Journal of Psychology* 60 (1947): 321–34. Copyright © 1947 by Board of Trustees of the University of Illinois. Used with permission of the publisher, The University of Illinois Press. **4.25** Rescorla, R. A., Predictability and number of pairings in Pavlovian fear conditioning, *Psychonomic Science* 4 (1966): 383–84. **4.26** Kamin, L. J., Predictability, surprise, and conditioning, in Campbell, B. A., and Church, R. M. (Eds.), *Punishment and Aversive Behavior*, 1969. Used by permission of Prentice-Hall, Inc., Englewood Cliffs, N.J. **4.28** Colwill, R. M., and Rescorla, R. A., Postconditioning devaluation of a reinforcer affects instrumental responding, *Journal of Experimental Psychology: Animal Behavior Processes* 11 (1985): 120–32. Copyright 1985 by the American Psychological Association. Updated by permission of the American Psychological Association and the authors. **4.29** Drawing by Maura Conron. **4.30** Maier, S. F., Seligman, M. E. P., and Solomon, R. L., Pavlovian fear conditioning and learned helplessness: Effects on escape and avoidance behavior of (a) the CS-US contingency and (b) the independence of the US and voluntary responding, in Campbell, B. A., and Church, R. M. (Eds.), *Punishment and Aversive Behavior*, © 1969, p. 328. Adapted by permission of Prentice-Hall, Inc., Englewood Cliffs, N.J. **4.32** Photographs by Bruce Moore. **4.33** Olton, D. S., and Samuelson, R. J., Remembrance of places passed: Spatial memory in rats, *Journal of Experimental Psychology: Animal Behavior Processes* 2 (1976): 97–116. Copyright 1976 by the American Psychological Association. Reprinted by permission. **4.37** Figure adapted from *Why Chimps Can Read* by A. J. Premack. Copyright © 1976 by Ann J. Premack. Reprinted by permission of HarperCollins Publishers. Drawing by Maura Conron. **4.38** Premack, D., and Woodruff, G., Chimpanzee problem-solving: A test for comprehension, *Science* 202 (3 November 1978): 533–34. Copyright 1978 by American Association for the Advancement of Science.

5.1 Drawing by Maura Conron. **5.2** *The School of Athens* by Raphael, 1505; Stanza della Segnatura, Vatican; courtesy Scala/Art Resource, New York. **5.6A** Krech, D., and Crutchfield, R., *Elements of Psychology.* New York: Knopf, 1958. Adapted by permission of Hilda Krech. **5.6B** Adapted from *Biological Psychology*, 2nd ed., by James W. Kalat. © 1984 by Wadsworth, Inc. **5.7** Adapted from Carlson, N. R., *Physiology of Behavior*, 3rd ed. Boston: Allyn and Bacon, 1986. Reproduced by permission of the publisher. **5.8** Frank, M., An analysis of hamster afferent taste nerve response functions. *Journal of General Physiology* 61 (1973): 588–618. Reproduced by permission of the Rockefeller University Press. **5.10** Gibson, James J., *The Senses Considered as Perceptual Systems*, p. 80, Fig. 5.4. Boston: Houghton Mifflin Company, 1966. Reprinted by permission of the publisher. **5.11** Thompson, R. F., *Introduction to Biopsychology.* San Rafael, Calif.: Albion Publishing Company, 1973. Adapted by permission of the publisher. **5.13, 5.14A, 5.15A** Lindsay,

P. H., and Norman, D. A., *Human Information Processing*, 2nd edition, pp. 126, 133, and 136. New York: Academic Press, 1977. Adapted by permission of the author and Harcourt Brace Jovanovich. **5.14B, 5.15B, 5.17** Coren, S., and Ward, L. M., *Sensation and Perception*, 3rd ed. San Diego: Harcourt Brace Jovanovich, 1989. Adapted by permission of the author and publisher. **5.16** Wald, G., Eye and camera, *Scientific American* 183 (August 1950): 33. Copyright © 1950 by Scientific American, Inc. All rights reserved. **5.18, 5.19, 5.20** Cornsweet, T. M., *Visual Perception.* New York: Academic Press, 1970. Adapted by permission of the author and Harcourt Brace Jovanovich. **5.23** Hering, E., *Outlines of a Theory of the Light Sense*, 1920 (translated by Hurvich, L. M., and Jameson, D., 1964), pp. 150–51. Cambridge, Mass.: Harvard University Press, 1964. Adapted by permission of Harvard University Press. **5.24A** *Arcturus II* (1966) by Victor Vasarely, Hirshhorn Museum and Sculpture Garden, Smithsonian Institution, gift of Joseph H. Hirshhorn, 1972. **5.25** Coren, S., Porac, C., and Ward, L. M., *Sensation and Perception*, p. 155. New York: Academic Press, 1978. Adapted by permission of the author and Harcourt Brace Jovanovich. Also **5.25** Cornsweet, T. M., *Visual Perception*, p. 276. New York: Academic Press, 1970. Adapted by permission of the author and Harcourt Brace Jovanovich. **5.26** Schiffman, H., *Sensation and Perception.* New York: John Wiley and Sons, Inc., 1976. Adapted by permission of the publisher. **5.27** Adapted from Kuffler, S. W., Discharge pattern and functional organization of mammalian retina, *Journal of Neurophysiology* 16 (1953): 37–68. **5.31** Hurvich, L. M., *Color Vision.* Sunderland, Mass.: Sinauer Associates, 1981. Reproduced by permission of Sinauer Associates. **5.33 and 5.34** Courtesy of Munsell Color, 2441 N. Calvert Street, Baltimore, Md., 21218. **5.37** Detail and full use of Georges Seurat's *The Channel of Gravelines (Petit Fort Philippe)*, 1890, oil on canvas. © 1994 Indianapolis Museum of Art, gift of Mrs. James W. Fesler in memory of Daniel W. and Elizabeth C. Marmon. **5.43** Hurvich, L. M., and Jameson, D., An opponent-process theory of color vision, *Psychological Review* 64 (1957): 384–404. Copyright 1957 by the American Psychological Association. Adapted by permission of the author. **5.44** DeValois, R. L., and DeValois, K. K., *Neural Coding of Color*, in Carterette, E. C., and Friedman, M. P., (Eds.), *Handbook of Perception*, vol. 5. New York: Academic Press, 1975. Adapted by permission of the publisher. **5.46** Hubel, D. H., The visual cortex of the brain, *Scientific American* 209 (November 1963): 54–58. Copyright © 1963 by Scientific American, Inc. All rights reserved. **5.47** Drawing by Maura Conron.

Chapter 6: **6.1** Julian Hochberg, *Perception*, 2nd ed., 1978, p 56. Adapted by permission of Prentice-Hall, Inc., Englewood Cliffs, N.J. **6.2** Photograph by Roberta Intrater. **6.5A** Photograph by Geoff Dore/© Tony Stone Worldwide. **6.5B** Photograph © G. R. Roberts. **6.6** Figures 40 and 41 from *The Perception of the Visual World* by James J. Gibson. Copyright © 1978, 1950 by Houghton Mifflin Company. Used with permission. **6.7** Coren, S., and Ward, L. M., *Sensation and Perception*, 3rd ed. San Diego: Harcourt Brace Jovanovich. Adapted by permission of the author and Harcourt Brace Jovanovich. Drawing by Maura Conron. **6.8A** Bruce, V., and Green, P., *Visual Perception: Physiology, Psychology, and Ecology.* Hillsdale, N.J.: Erlbaum, 1985. Reprinted by permission of Lawrence Erlbaum Associates, Inc. **6.8B** Adapted from Figure 56 from *The Perception of the Visual World* by James J. Gibson. Copyright © 1978, 1950 by Houghton Mifflin Company. Used with permission. **6.10** Duncker, K., Uber induzierte Bewegung, *Psychologische Forschung* 12 (1929): 180–259. Adapted by permission of Springer-Verlag, Inc., Heidelberg. **6.12** Landau, B., Where's what and what's where: The language of objects in space. In Gleitman, L. R., and Landau, B. (Eds.), Lexical acquisition. *Lingua (Special Issue)* 92 (1994): 259–96. Drawing by Maura Conron. **6.15** Photograph by Jeffery Grosscup. **6.18** Salvador Dali's *The Trojan War*, courtesy Esquire. **6.20** Beck, J., Effect of orientation and shape similarity on perceptual grouping, *Perception and Psychophysics* 1 (1966): 300–302. Reprinted by permission of the Psychonomic Society, Inc. **6.22** Köhler, W., *Gestalt Psychology.* New York: Liveright Publishing Company, 1947. Adapted by permission of the publisher. **6.23A** Photograph by Larry Downing/Woodfin Camp & Associates. **6.24B** Photograph © Michael Fogden/Oxford Scientific Films. **6.25** Kanizsa, G., Subjective Contours, *Scientific American* 234 (1976): 48–52. Copyright 1976 by Scientific American, Inc. All rights reserved. **6.27** Drawing by Maura Conron. **6.28** Boring, E. G., A new ambiguous figure, *American Journal of Psychology* 42 (1930): 444–45; and Leeper, R. W., A study of a neglected portion of the field of learning: The development of sensory organization. *Journal of Genetic Psychology* 46 (1935): 41–75. Reproduced by permission of Lucy D. Boring. **6.29** Selfridge, O. G., Pattern recognition and modern computers, in *Proceedings of Western Joint Computer Conference*, Los Angeles, Calif., 1955. **6.31** Biederman, I., Recognition-by-components: A theory of human image understanding, *Psychological Review* 94 (1987):115–47. Copyright 1987 by the American Psychological Association. Reprinted by permission of the American Psychological Association and the author. **6.32** Rubens, A. B., and Benson, D. F., Associative visual agnosia, *Archives of Neurology* 24: 305–16,

John Shaw/Bruce Coleman. **10.16B** Courtesy of Ian Wyllie, Monks Wood Experiment Station. **10.17A** Lorenz, K., Die angeborenen Formen möglicher Erfahrung. *Zeitschrift Für Tierpsychologie* 5 (1943): 276. Adapted by permission of Paul Parey Verlagsbuchhandlung, Hamburg and Berlin. **10.17B** © Walt Disney Productions. **10.18** © Paul Ekman, 1971. **10.19B** Photograph © Tommy Thompson, 1992; courtesy of Florida School for the Deaf and Blind, St. Augustine, Florida. **10.20** Ekman, P., and Friesen, W. V., Unmasking the Face. Englewood Cliffs, N.J.: Prentice-Hall, 1975. Reprinted by permission of the author. **10.21** Wayne Lankinen/Bruce Coleman. **10.22** Georg D. Lepp/Bio-Tec Images.

Chapter 11: **11.1** Asch, S. E., Studies of independence and conformity: A minority of one against a unanimous majority, *Psychological Monographs* 70 (9, Whole No. 416), 1956. Copyright 1956 by the American Psychological Association. **11.3, 11.4, 11.5** Drawings by Maura Conron.

Chapter 12: **12.1** Drawing by Maura Conron. **12.4** Leonardo da Vinci's *La Jaconde* (Mona Lisa), Louvre, Paris; photograph courtesy of Service Photographique de la Reunion des Musées Nationaux. **12.5 and 12.6** Copyright 1965 by Stanley Milgram. From the film *Obedience*, distributed by the Pennsylvania State University, PCR.

Chapter 13: **13.1** Reproduced from Keeton, W. T., and Gould, J. L., *Biological Science*, 4th ed. New York: W. W. Norton, 1986. Copyright © 1986, 1980, 1979, 1972, 1967 by W. W. Norton & Company, Inc. Used with permission. **13.2** Liebert, R. M., Poulos, R. W., and Strauss, G. D., *Developmental Psychology*, Fig. III-10, p.81. Englewood Cliffs, N.J.: Prentice-Hall, Inc., 1974. Originally adapted from H. M. Halverston, printed by The Journal Press, 1931. Photographs by Kathy Hirsh-Pasek. **13.3** Tanner, J. M., Physical growth, in *Carmichael's Manual of Child Psychology*, 3rd ed., vol. 1, Mussen, P. H., ed., Fig. 6, p. 85. New York: John Wiley & Sons, 1970. Copyright 1970 by John Wiley & Sons. **13.4** Conel, J. L., *The Postnatal Development of the Human Cortex*, vols. 1, 3, 5. Cambridge, Mass.: Harvard University Press, 1939, 1947, 1955. **13.5** Shirley, M. M., *The First Two Years: A Study of Twenty-five Babies*, vol. II. University of Minnesota Press, Minneapolis. © 1933, 1961, University of Minnesota Press. **13.6** Photograph courtesy of M. M. Grumbach. **13.8** Reproduced from Keeton,W. T., and Gould, J. L., *Biological Science*, 4th ed. New York: W. W. Norton, 1986. Copyright © 1986, 1980, 1979, 1972, 1967 by W.W. Norton & Company, Inc. Used with permission. **13.9** Photograph by Victor Englebert/Photo Researchers. **13.10** Courtesy Dr. Mark Rosenzweig. **13.11** Photographs by Doug Goodman 1986/Monkmeyer. **13.12 and 13.14** Photographs by Chris Massey. **13.13** Photograph by Ed Boswell. **13.15** Piaget, J., and Inhelder, B., *The Child's Conception of Space*. Humanities Press International Inc., Atlantic Highlands, N.J., 1967. Adapted by permission of the publisher and Routledge & Kegan Paul Ltd. Drawing by Maura Conron. **13.16** Drawing by Maura Conron. **13.17** Photographs courtesy of Phillip Kellman. **13.18** Kellman, P. J., and Spelke, E. S., Perception of partially occluded objects in infancy, *Cognitive Psychology* 15 (1983): 483-524. Copyright 1983 by the American Psychological Association. Adapted by permission of the author. **13.19** Adapted from Baillargeon, R., Object permanence in $3\frac{1}{2}$- and $4\frac{1}{2}$-month-old infants, *Developmental Psychology* 23 (1987): 655-64. Used by permission of the author. **13.20** Photographs courtesy of Adele Diamond. **13.21** Starkey, P., Spelke, E. S., and Gelman, R., Detection of intermodal numerical correspondences by human infants, *Science* 222 (1983): 179-81. Drawing by Maura Conron. **13.22** Johnson, M. H., and Morton, J., *Biology and Cognitive Development: The Case of Face Recognition*. Cambridge, Mass.: Blackwell Publishers, 1991. **13.23** Photographs courtesy of Hilary Schmidt. **13.24** Photographs courtesy of Helene Borke. Borke, H., Piaget's mountains revisited: Changes in the egocentric landscape, *Developmental Psychology* 11 (1975): 240-43. **13.25** Photographs courtesy of Kimberly Canidy. **13.26A** Photograph by Pat Lynch/Photo Researchers. **13.26B** Photograph by Ray Ellis/Photo Researchers. **13.26C** Photograph by Chris Massey. **13.27** Case, R., 1978. Intellectual development from birth to adulthood: A neo-Piagetian interpretation, in Siegler, R., (Ed.), *Children's Thinking: What Develops*. Hillsdale, N.J.: Lawrence Erlbaum Associates, Inc. Reproduced by permission of Lawrence Erlbaum Associates, Inc.

Chapter 14: **14.1** Photograph by Martin Rogers/Stock, Boston. **14.2** Photograph by Suzanne Szasz. **14.4** Ainsworth, M., Blehar, M., Waters, E., and Wall, S., 1978. *Patterns of Attachment*, p. 34. Hillsdale, N.J.: Lawrence Erlbaum Associates, Inc. Reproduced by permission of Lawrence Erlbaum

Asscoiates, Inc. Drawing by Maura Conron. **14.5** Photographs courtesy Kathy Hirsh-Pasek. **14.6, 14.7, and 14.8** Courtesy Harry Harlow, University of Wisconsin Primate Laboratory. **14.9** Photograph by Michael Heron/Woodfin Camp. **14.10** Kohlberg, L., Development of children's orientation towards a moral order in sequence in the development of moral thought, *Vita Humana* 6 (1963): 11-36. Adapted by permission of S. Karger AG, Basel. **14.14** Tanner, J. M., Physical growth, in Mussen, P. H., (Ed.), *Carmichael's Manual of Child Psychology*, 3rd ed., vol. 1, Fig. 6, p. 85. New York: John Wiley & Sons, 1970. Reprinted by permission of the publisher. **14.15A** Photograph © Blair Seitz, 1986/Photo Researchers. **14.15B** Photograph by A. Bernhaut/Photo Researchers. **14.16A** T. Lowell/Black Star. **14.16B** © Spencer Grant/The Picture Cube. **14.16C** © Jeff Greenberg/The Picture Cube.

Chapter 15: **15.1** Reprinted with permission of Macmillan Publishing Co., Inc. from *Differential Psychology*, 3rd ed., p. 57, by Ann Anastasi. Copyright © 1958 by Macmillan Publishing Co., Inc. **15.3** Courtesy H. Douglas Pratt. **15.6** Test item from Horn Art Aptitude Inventory, 1953. Courtesy Stoelting Co., Chicago. **15.7** Sample item from the Bennett Test of Mechanical Comprehension. Copyright © 1967, 1968 by The Psychological Corporation. Reproduced by permission. All rights reserved. **15.9** Adapted by permission from the *Wechsler Adult Intelligence Scale—Revised*. Copyright © 1955, 1981 by The Psychological Corporation. All rights reserved. **15.10** SAT questions selected from *10 SAT's*, College Entrance Examinations Board (1983). Reprinted by permission of Educational Testing Service, the copyright owner of the test questions. **15.11** From the Raven Standard Progressive Matrices, by permission of J. C. Raven Limited. **15.12** Jones, H. E., and Kaplan, O. J., Psychological aspects of mental disorders in later life, in Kaplan, O. J. (Ed.), *Mental Disorders in Later Life*, 72. Stanford, Calif.: Stanford University Press, 1945. Adapted by permission of Stanford University Press. **15.13** Brody, N., *Intelligence*, 2nd Ed. New York: Academic Press, 1992. **15.15** Selfe, S. *Nadia: A Case of Extraordinary Drawing Ability in an Autistic Child*. New York: Academic Press, 1977. Reproduced by permission of Academic Press and Lorna Selfe. **15.16** Courtesy Photofest. **15.17** Based on Winchester, A. M., *Genetics*, 5th ed. Boston: Houghton Mifflin, 1977. **15.18** Photographs courtesy of Dr. Franklin A. Bryan. **15.20** Drawing by Maura Conron.

Chapter 16: **16.1** Lanyon, R. I., and Goodstein, L. D., *Personality Assessment*, p. 79. New York: John Wiley & Sons, Inc., 1971. Adapted by permission of John Wiley & Sons, Inc. **16.4** Eysnck, H. J., and Rachman, S., *The causes and cures of neurosis*, p. 16. San Diego, Calif.: Robert R. Knapp, 1965. **16.5** The Bettmann Archive. **16.6A** Wilfong Photographic/Leo de Wys, Inc. **16.6B,C** Photographs by H. Reinhard/Bruce Coleman.

Chpater 17: **17.3** "Hierarchy of Needs" from *Motivation and Personality* by Abraham H. Maslow. Copyright 1954 by Harper & Row, Publishers, Inc. Copyright © 1970 by Abraham H. Maslow. Reprinted by permission of HarperCollins Publishers.

Chapter 18: **18.1** Negative #31568. Courtesy Department of Library Services, The American Museum of Natural History. **18.2** William Hogarth's *The Madhouse, 1735/1763*; courtesy The Bettmann Archive. **18.3** © Stock Montage, Inc. **18.5** Photograph by Bill Bridges/Globe Photos. **18.7** Nicol, S. E., and Gottesman, I. I., Clues to the genetics and neurobiology of schizophrenia, *American Scientist*, 71 (1983): 398-404. Reprinted by permission of *American Scientist*, journal of Sigma Xi, The Scientific Research Society. **18.8** Data from Faris, R. E. L., and Dunham, H. W., *Mental Disorders in Urban Areas*. Chicago: University of Chicago Press, 1939. Adapted by permission of the author. **18.10** Rosenthal, N. E., Sack, D. A., Gillin, J. C., Lewy, A. J., Goodwin, F. K., Davenport, Y., Mueller, P. S., Newsome, D. A., and Wehr, T. A., Seasonal affective disorder: A description of the syndrome and preliminary findings with light therapy. *Archives of General Psychiatry* 41 (1984): 72-80. Copyright 1984, American Medical Association. **18.11** Stone, A., Mental health and law: A system in transition, U.S. Department of Health, Education and Welfare, #75176, p. 7, 1975. **18.12** Hare, R. D., Temporal gradient of fear arousal in psychopaths, *Journal of Abnormal Psychology* 70 (1965): 442-45. Copyright 1965 by the American Psychological Association. Reprinted by permission of the author.

Chapter 19: **19.1A** Courtesy Historical Pictures Service. **19.1B** Courtesy National Library of Medicine. **19.1C** Culver Pictures. **19.5** Photograph by James D. Wilson/Woodfin Camp. **19.7** Gibbons R. D., Hedeker, D., Elkin, I., Waternaux, C., Kraemer, H. C., Greenhouse, J. B., Shea, M. T., Imber, S. D.,

Sotsky, S. M., Watkins, J. T., Some conceptual and statistical issues in analysis of longitudinal psychiatric data. Application to the NIMH treatment of Depression Collaborative Research Program dataset. *Archives of General Psychiatry*, 50 (1993), 739-50.

TABLES

13.1 Lenneberg, E. H., *Biological Foundations of Language*. New York: John Wiley & Sons, 1967. Reprinted by permission of John Wiley & Sons, Inc. **14.1** Adapted from Kohlberg, L., Classification of moral judgment into levels and stages of development, in Sizer, Theodore R., *Religion and Public Education*, pp. 171-73. Copyright © 1967 Houghton Mifflin Company. Used with permission. **14.2** Erikson, E. H., *Childhood and Society*. New York: W. W. Norton & Company, Inc., 1963. Adapted by permission. **15.2** Grossman, H. J. (Ed.), *Manual on Terminology and Classification in Mental Retardation*, revised edition. Washington, D.C.: American Association on Mental Deficiency, 1983. Used with permission. **15.3** Bayley, N., Mental growth during the first three years, *Genetic Psychology Monographs* 14 (1933): 1-92. Reprinted with permission of the Helen Dwight Reed Educational Foundation. Published by Heldref Publications, 4000 Albemarle St. N.W., Washington, D.C. 20016. **15.4** Wechsler, D., *The Measurement and Appraisal of Adult Intelligence*, 4th ed. Baltimore, Md.: The Williams & Wilkins Co., 1958. © 1958 David Wechsler. Used by permission of Ruth Wechsler, executor David Wechsler estate. Table adapted from the Manual for the Wechsler Adult Intelligence Scale. Copyright © 1955 by The Psychological Corporation. **16.3** Norman, W. T., Toward an adequate taxonomy of personality attributes: Replicated factor structure in peer nomination personality ratings, *Journal of Abnormal and Social Psychology* 66 (1963): 577. Copyright 1963 by the American Psychological Association. Adapted by permission of the author.

UNNUMBERED PHOTOS AND ART

(Chapter 1 Opener) Detail of Michelangelo's *Profile with Fantastic Head-Dress*, courtesy Ashmolean Museum, Oxford, England. **9** Two illustrations from *Where the Wild Things Are*, written and illustrated by Maurice Sendak. Copyright 1963 by Maurice Sendak. Reprinted by permission of HarperCollins Publishers. **10** Pablo Picasso, *The Dream*, 1932; Scala/Art Resource. **11** *Top* Stock Montage. *Bottom* The Warder Collection. *(Part Opener I)* Detail of *The Battle of the Melvian Bridge*, Stanze di Raffaello, Vatican Palace, Vatican State; courtesy Scala/Art Resource. **16** Courtesy National Library of Medicine. **24** *Top* Photograph by David M. Phillips/Visuals Unlimited. *Bottom* Courtesy National Library of Medicine. **31** *Left* Photograph by B. Malkin/Anthro-Photo. *Right* Photograph © 1992, Comstock. **41** Courtesy of The Natural History Museum, London. **47** Photofest. **52** *Left* The Science Museum/Science & Society Picture Library. *Right* Photograph by Leonard Lessin/Peter Arnold, Inc. **62** Gift of Mrs. George von Lengerke Meyer. Courtesy Museum of Fine Arts, Boston. **65** Photograph by Jane Burton, © 1987, Bruce Coleman, Inc. **69** Photofest. **72** Pieter Bruegel The Elder, *Peasant Wedding Feast*; courtesy Kunsthistorisches Museum, Vienna. **79** Photograph by Jane Carter. **80** *Left The Venus of Willendorf*; courtesy Naturhistorisches Museum, Vienna. *Center* Peter Paul Rubens, *The Three Graces*; © Museo del Prado, Madrid. *Right* Photograph © M. Carraro/Gamma Liaison. **81** Courtesy National Library of Medicine. **88** Photograph by Grant Leduc/Monkmeyer. **92** Photographs by Takahisa Hirano/Nature Production. **93** *Jacob's Ladder*, from the Lambeth Bible; courtesy the Archbishop of Canterbury and the Trustees of Lambeth Palace Library. **94** Salvador Dali, *The Grand Paranoic*, 1936, oil on panel, 62 x 62 cm.; collection Museum Boymans-van-Beuningen, Rotterdam. **98** *Left* Georg Gerster/Comstock. *Center* Guy Sauvage, Agence Vandystadt/Photo Researchers. *Right* Photofest. **106** Photograph by Bette Splendens/Oxford Scientific Films. **108** The Bettmann Archive. **114** Courtesy of the Museum of the City of New York. **115** The Granger Collection. **118** Photograph by Nina Leen/Life Magazine, © Time Warner. **120** Photograph © Hank Morgan. **125** Photograph by Erika Stone. **126** Courtesy Psychology Department, University of California, Berkeley. **136** Courtesy of Animal Behavior Enterprises, Inc. **137** Photographs by Lincoln P. Brower. **140** Courtesy of Animal Behavior Enterprises, Inc. **141** Photograph by Susan Bradnam. **142** *Top* Photograph by Stephen Dalton/NHPA. *Center* Photograph by Joe MacDonald/Bruce Coleman, Inc. *Bottom* Photograph by Stephen Dalton/Photo Researchers, Inc. **143** The Warder Collection. *(Part Opener II)* Detail from Raphael's *School of Athens*, 1505, Stanza della Segnatura, Vatican; courtesy Scala/Art Resource, New York. **154** *Top* Courtesy National Portrait Gallery, London. *Bottom* Detail from *The Bermuda Group* by John Smibert; courtesy Yale University Art Gallery; gift of Isaac Lothrop of Plymouth, Mass. **156** Culver Pictures, Inc., New York. **158** Photographs courtesy National Library of Medicine. **166** Photograph by Ed Reschke. **171** Photograph © RDR Productions, 1981; Rex Features USA. **175** *Top* Courtesy National Library of Medicine. *Bottom* Courtesy Nobel Stiftelsen. **176** Courtesy Dr. David D. Yager and Michael L. May; © The Company of Biologists Limited. **182** Courtesy National Library of Medicine. **188** Photographs by Fritz Goro/Life Magazine, © Time Warner, Inc. **202** Claude Monet, *Terrace at Sainte-Adresse*, oil on canvas, 38⅝ x 51⅛"; reproduced by permission of the Metropolitan Museum of Art, New York; purchased with special contributions and purchase funds given or bequeathed by friends of the Museum, 1967. **207** Courtesy Omikron. **228** Photograph © Jeff M. Dunn. **230** Courtesy E. J. Gibson. **244** Photograph by Kathy Hirsh-Pasek. **246** The Kobal Collection. **249** Detail of *Netherlandish Proverbs* by Pieter Brueghel, 1559; courtesy of Gemaldegalerie, Staatliche Museen Preuischer Kulturbesitz, Berlin. **250** Paul Cezanne, *The Cardplayers*; courtesy The Metropolitan Museum of Art, bequest of Stephen C. Clark, 1960. **255** Photofest. **264** Photograph by Suzanne Szasz. **265** Marc Chagall, *I and the Village*, 1911, oil on canvas, 63⅝ x 59⅝" (192.1 x 151.4 cm); collection, The Museum of Modern Art, New York, Mrs. Simon Guggenheim Fund. **266** Photographs courtesy of The Bettmann Archive. **269** Salvador Dali, *The Persistence of Memory*, 1931, oil on canvas, 9½ x 13"; Collection, The Museum of Modern Art, New York; given anonymously. **277** *Top* Mamie Eisenhower (UPI/Bettmann); Jonas Salk (Bettmann); Adlai Stevenson (Bettmann); Nikita Khrushchev (Bettmann); Mohammed Ali (The Everett Collection/ABC); Golda Meir (Bettmann); Anwar El-Sadat (William Karel/Sygma); Betty Ford (Tony Korody/Sygma); Patty Hearst (UPI/Bettmann); Robert Bork (Michael Evans/Sygma); Walter Mondale (Bill Nation/Portland State University); Bjorn Borg (AP/Wide World). *Bottom* Marslan-Wilson, W. D., and Teuber, H. L., Memory for remote events in anterograde amnesia: Recognition of public figures from news photographs, *Neuropsychologia* 13 (1975):353-64. **282** Rembrandt's *Aristotle with a Bust of Homer*, oil on canvas, 56½ x 53¾"; courtesy The Metropolitan Museum of Art, purchased with special funds and gifts of friends of the Museum, 1961. **282** Pablo Picasso, *Portrait of Ambroise Vollard*, 1909, Pushkin Museum, Moscow; courtesy Scala/Art Resource. **303** Courtesy of Lifesmith Classic Fractals. Copyright © 1993, Lifesmith Classic Fractals, Northridge, Calif. **310** From a British National Theatre production of *Galileo* by Bertolt Brecht; photograph by Zoe Dominic. **316** *Figure 14*, Alfredo Castañeda, 1982. Courtesy Mary-Anne Martin/Fine Art, New York. **318** Photograph by John Gaps III/AP Wide World. **324** Pieter Brueghel the Elder, *Trumbau zu Babel (Tower of Babel)*; courtesy Kunsthistorisches Museum, Vienna. **325** Photograph by Leonard McCombe/Life Magazine, © Time Warner, Inc. **326** William Blake, *Adam Naming the Beasts*, courtesy The Stirling Maxwell Collection, Pollok House, Glasgow Museums & Art Galleries. **327** Henri Rousseau, *The Sleeping Gypsy*, 1897, oil on canvas, 51" x 6'7"; collection, The Museum of Modern Art, New York. Gift of Mrs. Simon Guggenheim. **332** By permission. From *Webster's Ninth New Collegiate Dictionary*. © 1990 by Merriam-Webster Inc., publisher of the Merriam-Webster® dictionaries. **333** Reproduced from Lewis Carroll's *Alice in Wonderland*, original illustrations by John Tenniel; in color for this edition by Martina Selway. Secaucus, N.J.: Castle Books. **335** *Left* Photograph by Kenneth W. Fink/Bruce Coleman. *Center* Photograph by Laura Riley/Bruce Coleman. *Right* Photograph by Des & Jen Bartlett/Bruce Coleman. **336** Reproduced from Lewis Carroll's *Alice in Wonderland*, original drawings by John Tenniel; in color for this edition by Martina Selway. Secaucus, N.J.: Castle Books. **347** Lewis Carroll's *Through the Looking Glass*, illustration by John Tenniel, courtesy of General Research Division, The New York Public Library, Astor, Lenox, and Tilden Foundations. **349, 351** Photographs by Erika Stone. **358** Photograph by Roberta Intrater. **366, 367** Courtesy of The Perkins School for the Blind. **372** Photographs courtesy of Herbert Terrace. *(Part Opener III)* Detail from Auguste Renoir's *Le Moulin de la Galette*, 1876, Louvre, Paris; photograph © R.M.N. **380** *Top* Painting by John Michael Wright; courtesy The Granger Collection. *Bottom* Painting by J. Collier; courtesy of the National Portrait Gallery, London. **381** *Top* Photograph © Ed Reschke, 1988; all rights reserved. *Bottom* Brian M. Rogers/Biofotos. **382, 383** Photographs by Nina Leen. **385** Stouffer Productions/Animals Animals. **386** Photograph © Manfred Danegger. **387** Photograph © I. Eibl-Eibesfeldt. **396** Photograph by Robert W. Hernández/The National Audubon Society Collection/Photo Researchers. **398** Courtesy of The Motion Picture and Television Photo Archive. **399** Photograph © Zefa Germany/The Stock Market, 1994. **402** *Left* © 1978 Tom McHugh/Photo Researchers. *Right* ©

NAME INDEX

Abelson, R., 269
Abraham, K., 677–78
Abrahams, D., 422
Abrams, M. H., 701
Abramson, L. Y., 662, 743
Addams, Charles, 302
Adelson, J., 573
Adler, Alfred, 448
Adler, N. T., 393, 395
Adolph, E. F., 70
Adorno, Theodor, 472
Ainsworth, Mary, 537
Alba, J. W., 273, 300
Albright, T. D., 313
Alexander, B. K., 99, 543
Alexander, F., 775
Allard, F., 296
Allderidge, P., 717
Allen, V. L., 470, 751
Alloy, L. B., 743
Allport, F., 468
Allport, G. W., 629, 640
Alvir, J. M., 766
Amabile, T. M., 434
Ames, M. A., 567
Anand, B. K., 74
Ananth, J., 767
Anastasi, A., 596, 616
Anderson, J. R., 301
Anderson, N. H., 427
Anderson, R. C., 268, 271
Andreasen, N. C., 731, 732, 736, 737, 738, 740,
    750, 752, 765, 771
Andrews, G., 791, 793
Anglin, J. M., 353
Angrist, B., 730
Anstis, S. M., 209
Aranoff, M., 330
Arbib, M. A., 47
Archimedes, 300
Ardrey, R., 389
Arenberg, D., 646
Arendt, Hannah, 473
Arieti, S., 734
Aristotle, 5, 10, 165, 480
Armstrong, S. L., 335
Arnold, M. B., 440
Aron, A. P., 465
Aronfreed, J., 547, 552
Aronson, E., 422, 423, 424, 551n
Asch, Solomon, 416–17, 427, 469–70
Ashbrook, E. F., 363
Asher, E. J., 618
Aslin, R. N., 497
Aston-Jones, G., 88
Astrachan, B. M., 736

Atkinson, J. W., 638
Atkinson, R. C., 245
Augustine, Saint, 245
Austin, J., 327, 515
Averill, J. R., 446
Ax, A. F., 443
Ayllon, T., 778
Azrin, N. H., 778

Babigian, H. M., 726
Backer, R., 96
Bacon, M. K., 545, 658, 705
Baddeley, A. D., 251, 256, 263, 283
Baer, Karl Ernst von, 494
Bahrick, H. P., 265
Bailey, 566, 567
Bailey, C. J., 73
Baillargeon, Renée, 513, 514, 517, 523
Baker, C., 356n
Baker, E., 359
Baker, N., 664
Baldwin, D. A., 349
Ball, T. M., 284
Ball, W., 206
Balogh, R. D., 169
Baltes, P. B., 570, 653n
Bancroft, J., 395
Bandura, A., 546, 661
Barber, T. X., 272
Bard, 38
Barefoot, J. C., 755
Barett, T. R., 279
Barlow, D. H., 747
Barlow, H. B., 211
Barnes, M. F., 397
Barnouw, V., 8
Barnum, P. T., 634
Baron, J., 296, 602
Barry, H., III, 545, 705
Bartlett, Frederic, 267–68
Bartol, C. R., 657
Bartoshuk, L., 167
Bartsch, K., 520
Bass, E., 273, 481
Bates, E., 349, 367
Bateson, P. P. G., 537
Batson, C. D., 460
Batterman, N., 353
Bauer, H., 70
Baum, D. R., 286
Baum, W. M., 126, 777
Baumrind, D., 548, 549
Bayer, E., 72
Bayley, N., 597, 652
Beach, D. H., 526
Beach, F. A., 398

Beck, Aaron T., 738, 739, 741–42, 743, 779–81
Beck, J., 214, 215
Beethoven, Ludwig van, 174, 300, 650, 698
Békésy, Georg von, 174
Bell, A. P., 566
Bell, R. Q., 549
Bell, S. W., 537
Belli, R. F., 271
Bellugi, U., 46, 355, 357, 363
Beloff, H., 687
Belski, 540
Bem, D. J., 438, 438n, 564
Benbow, C. P., 559
Benedict, Ruth, 702–3
Bennett, 504
Bentley, E., 628
Bergin, A. E., 790, 791
Berkeley, Bishop George, 154–55, 201, 234–35,
    291
Berkeley, M. A., 211
Berman, J. S., 791
Berman, W., 612
Bermant, G., 395
Bernard, Claude, 64
Bernard, V. W., 475
Bernstein, I. L., 139
Berridge, K. C., 47
Berscheid, E., 461, 462, 463, 464
Best, D. L., 557
Beutler, L. E., 794
Bever, T. G., 344
Bickerton, D., 373
Biederman, I., 221
Bigelow, A., 365
Bilsky, L., 607
Binder, J. L., 775
Binet, Alfred, 590–93, 595, 651, 654
Birch, H. G., 549, 596, 652
Birch, R., 232
Bischoff, Theodor, 24
Bitterman, M. E., 142
Bjork, R. A., 246
Björklund, A., 55
Black, D. W., 736, 737, 738, 740, 750, 752, 765,
    771
Black, J. B., 268
Blackburn, T. C., 707, 708
Blake, W., 701
Blank, M. A., 290
Blasi, A., 556
Blass, E. M., 69
Bleuler, Eugen, 726, 727
Bliss, E. L., 752
Block, J., 645, 694
Block, N. J., 611
Bloom, K., 349

Bloom, L., 87, 356
Bloom, P., 348, 356
Bloomfield, L., 325
Blum, J. E., 598, 653
Blurton-Jones, N., 528
Boas, Franz, 702
Boden, M., 305
Bodnar, R. J., 85
Bogen, J. E., 48, 49, 51
Bolles, Robert C., 85, 139
Bond, M. H., 455, 468, 704
Boole, George, 308–9
Boone, K. B., 594
Booth, D. A., 79
Borden, R. J., 477
Borduin, C. M., 788
Borg, G., 164
Boring, E. G., 164, 231
Bornstein, M. H., 497
Bottger, 481
Botvin, G. J., 523
Bouchard, Thomas J., Jr., 77, 614, 615, 616, 655, 656
Bouffard, B. L., 650
Bourne, E. J., 708
Bowen, M., 787
Bower, T. G. R., 232, 268
Bowerman, M., 357
Bowers, K. S., 695
Bowlby, John, 534, 539
Bowmaker, J. K., 191
Boyd, J. H., 737
Bozarth, M. A., 101
Bradley, G. W., 435
Bradshaw, J. L., 50
Brady, I., 704
Brady, J. P., 449, 778
Brain, L., 48
Braine, M. D. S., 355, 359
Bransford, J. D., 257
Brazelton, T. Berry, 503, 687
Breger, L., 689
Breggin, P. R., 772
Breland, K., 121, 140
Breland, M., 121, 140
Bresnan, J., 336
Bretherton, I., 354
Breuer, Josef, 671, 773
Brickman, J. C., 461
Brier, A., 736
Broadbent, D. E., 228, 245
Broca, Paul, 45
Brodie, H. K. H., 567
Brody, E. B., 603
Brody, N., 640, 649, 793
Bronfenbrenner, U., 612n
Bronson, W. C., 647, 653
Brown, A. L., 525, 606, 607
Brown, J. F., 682
Brown, Roger, 259, 266, 355, 359, 360–61, 473, 483–84, 486
Brownell, K. D., 78
Browning, Robert, 237
Bruce, V., 221
Bruch, H., 79, 80
Bruner, J. S., 349, 428, 516
Bryan, W. L., 294
Bryant, J., 442
Buchanan, D. R., 463
Bullock, W. A., 657
Bullough, E., 449
Bunney, W. E., Jr., 744
Buranen, C., 754
Burckhardt, J., 108
Burgess, E. W., 462
Burnett, S. A., 559
Burns, 480

Burton, M. J., 72, 74
Burton, R. V., 572, 644
Bury, J. B., 493
Buss, A. H., 652, 653
Buss, D. M., 397. 646
Butterworth, G., 516

Cabanis, Pierre, 24
Cacioppo, J. T., 422–23
Cain, W. S., 169
Cairns, R. B., 343
Calvin, John, 543
Cameron, O. G., 778
Cammalleri, 481
Campbell, J. B., 657
Campbell, J. D., 462, 469
Campfield, L. A., 71
Campione, J. C., 606, 607
Campos, J. J., 535
Candee, D., 555
Cannon, T. D., 733
Cannon, Walter B., 64, 81–83, 440
Cantor, J. R., 442
Cantor, N., 428, 645, 652
Capone, A., 700
Carey, G., 780
Carey, S., 348, 353, 359
Carlsmith, J. M., 422, 423n, 424, 551n
Carlson, G., 346
Carlson, N. R., 78
Carlson, V. R., 232
Carlyle, Thomas, 480
Caron, A. J., 232
Caron, R. F., 232
Carr, D., 87
Carrington, P., 10
Carroll, Lewis, 338
Carter-Saltzman, L., 616, 622
Cartwright, R. D., 93
Case, R., 525
Caspi, 467
Cassel, J. C., 756
Cassidy, 521
Catel, J., 496
Cattell, Raymond, 599, 640, 653
Cavanaugh, P. H., 169
Ceci, S. J., 607
Cernoch, J. M., 169
Cervone, J. C., 461
Chaikin, S., 423
Chambers, D., 285
Chapman, J. P., 727, 730
Chapman, L. J., 730
Chapman, M., 552
Charness, N., 296
Charney, R., 352
Chase, M. H., 84
Chase, W. G., 256, 295 Cheney, D. L., 405n, 406, 671
Cheng, P. W., 320
Chernick, L., 650
Cherry, E. C., 227
Chess, S., 549, 652, 656
Chevrier, J., 231
Chi, M. T. H., 353, 525
Child, I. L., 449, 545, 548, 687, 705
Childers, S. R., 87
Chinsky, J. M., 526
Chodoff, Paul, 754
Cholewiak, R. W., 166
Chomsky, C., 367
Chomsky, Noam, 325, 329, 330, 356n, 373
Chovil, 444
Christie, R., 473
Chuang-tzu, 5
Churchill, Winston, 326
Cialdini, R. B., 422, 454–55, 465

Cicero, 455
Claridge, D., 643
Clark, B., 638
Clark, D. M., 749, 781, 794
Clark, E. T., 598, 653
Clark, E. V., 327, 353, 357, 359
Clark, H. H., 327
Clark, R. D., 470
Clarke, A. C., 461
Clarkin, J., 794
Clark-Stewart, A., 539, 540
Cleckley, H. M., 751, 758
Clemente, C. D., 84
Clunis, 565
Cochran, E., 516
Cohen, D. B., 7, 92
Cohen, N. J., 260, 266, 276, 277, 292
Cohen, R. A., 738
Cohen, Y. A., 687
Colarusso, C. A., 574
Colby, A., 554
Cole, J. O., 767
Cole, M., 528, 529
Coleman, J. C., 751
Coleman, J. S., 612n
Coleridge, Samuel Taylor, 448, 701
Collier, G., 389
Collins, A. M., 289–90, 444
Collis, G., 349
Colwill, Ruth M., 132, 133
Comrie, B., 323
Conel, J. L., 496
Conger, J. J., 756
Conrad, C., 289
Cook, M., 232
Cooley, C. H., 437
Cooper, H. M., 788
Cooper, J., 424, 425
Cooper, L. A., 284, 285
Corbit, J. D., 99
Coren, S., 48
Corkin, S., 275, 276
Cory, T. L., 7
Cosmides, Leda, 456
Costa, E., 748
Costa, P. T., Jr., 646
Costello, C. G., 657
Cotman, C. W., 54
Cottrell, 468
Coupe, P., 287
Couvillon, P., 141
Cowan, T., 283
Cowles, J. T., 121 Cox, J. R., 320
Coyle, J. T., 55
Coyne, J. C., 743
Craik, F. I. M., 250, 252, 256, 257
Craik, K. H., 646
Crain, S., 346, 356
Cranshaw, L. I., 65
Crisafi, M., 358
Croft, K., 520
Cromwell, Oliver, 311
Cronbach, L. J., 587, 630, 633, 649
Crook, C., 497
Cross, C. K., 83, 737
Crow, T. J., 731
Crowder, R. G., 245, 247n, 251
Crowe, D. H., 435
Crutchfield, R. S., 418·
Csernansky, J. G., 764, 765, 766
Culicover, P., 356n
Cummings, N. A., 795
Cunningham, M. R., 438, 463
Curtis, G. C., 778
Curtiss, Susan, 362
Custer, George Armstrong, 255
Cutting, J., 736

Dale, A. J. D., 718, 719
Dallas, M., 259, 260
Dallenbach, K. M., 262
D'Amato, B., 461
Daniels, D., 655
Danzger, B., 549
Darley, J. M., 457, 459, 460
Darlington, R. B., 612
Darnton, R., 683
Dartnall, H. J. A., 191
Darwin, Charles, 115, 300, 351, 380, 381, 443, 584
Datan, 574
Davidson, A. R., 421
Davidson, J. E., 299
Davidson, J. M., 394, 395
Davies, K. G., 771
Davies, N. B., 386
Davis, D. E., 384
Davis, J. M., 361, 730, 731, 767
Davis, K. E., 466
Davis, K. L., 740, 764, 765, 766
Davis, L., 273
Davis, W. J., 35n
Davison, G. C., 778
Dawes, R. W., 486
Day, R. H., 232, 607
De Beneedittis, 87
DeCasper, A. J., 497, 535
De Chirico, Giorgio, 236–37
Deecke, L., 43
DeFries, J. C., 614
De Groot, Adrian, 295
DeLeon, 795
Delis, D. C, 594
Dell, G. S., 293
Delong, M. R., 55
Delorme, A., 231
De Medicacelli, L., 55
Dement, W. C., 6, 93, 687, 689
Dennett, D. C., 316, 520
Dennis, W., 503, 542
Dermer, M., 462
De Rougemont, D., 465n
Descartes, René, 16–17, 18, 24, 56, 61–62, 64, 105, 210, 300, 323, 329
Detterman, D. K., 603
Deutsch, G., 48, 51
Deutsch, J. A., 70
deVader, 481
De Valois, R. L., 194
De Villiers, J. G., 353, 355
De Villiers, P. A., 355
Diamond, A., 514
Diamond, R., 277
Dickinson, A., 126
Dickinson, R. G., 232
Dicks, H. V., 473
Dickson, D. H., 634
Diener, F., 483
Dilger, W. C., 384
Dimberg, U., 746
Di Vesta, F. J., 283
Doi, T., 703
Dolger, H., 725
Domingues, R. A., 767
Domjan, M., 136
Donaldson, G., 653n
Dornbusch, 549
Dougherty, D., 83
Douvan, E., 573
Downs, A. C., 558
Dragoin, W. B., 138
Dratt, L. M., 559
Driscoll, R., 466
Duda, R. O., 306
Dumaret, A., 709

Duncker, Karl, 292–93
Dunning, 436
Durant, A., 701
Durant, W., 701
Dutton, D. G., 465
Dworkin, G., 611
Dyer, F. C., 175
Dymond, R., 699

Eagle, M. N., 775
Eagly, Alice H., 423
Ebbesen, E. B., 663
Ebbinghaus, Hermann, 262
Eccles, J. C., 27
Edgerton, R. B., 596
Egeth, H., 227
Egger, M. D., 84
Ehrhardt, A. A., 502, 561, 562
Eichmann, Adolf, 473
Eikelboom, R., 115
Eimas, P. D., 350
Einstein, Albert, 698, 700
Ekman, P., 402, 404, 443, 444
Ekstrand, B. R., 262
Elder, G. H., Jr., 571
Eliot, T. S., 422
Ellenberger, H. F., 451, 690
Ellis, Albert, 567, 780
Ellis, S., 226, 524
Ellis, T. E., 739
Ellsworth, P. C., 427
Elman, 549
Elms, A. C., 473
Emmelkamp, P. M. G., 778, 794
Emmerich, W., 558
Endler, N. S., 647, 649
Epstein, A. N., 68, 69, 73
Epstein, A. W., 70
Epstein, Seymour, 646
Epstein, W., 338
Erdelyi, M. H., 695
Ericsson, K. A., 256
Eriksen, C. W., 227, 689
Erikson, Erik, 570, 573–74, 693
Eriksson, A., 746
Eron, L. D., 636, 637, 638
Ervin, F. R., 138
Ervin, S., 357
Essock-Vitale, S. M., 410
Estes, W. K., 113
Etkin, W., 391
Evans, F. J., 87
Evans, R. A., 607
Exner, J. E., 636, 638
Eyferth, K., 622
Eysenck, Hans, 603, 611, 641–43, 653, 654, 657, 789–90, 794
Eysenck, S. B. G., 704

Fagan, J. F., 232, 597–98, 652
Fairey, P. J., 469
Fallon, A. E., 79
Faloon, S., 256
Fancher, R. E., 611
Fanselow, M. S., 85
Fant, L. G., 363
Fara, M. J., 285
Farah, M., 221
Fazio, R. H., 424
Fearing, F., 24
Fechner, Gustav Theodor, 158–60
Feder, H. H., 394
Feirtag, M., 20
Feldman, H., 363
Felipe, N. J., 389
Fenton, M. B., 176

Fernald, A., 349, 351
Ferrar, M., 349
Ferrara, R. A., 606, 607
Ferster, D., 210
Feshbach, S., 549
Festinger, Leon, 418, 419, 423n, 424, 483, 551n
Fiedler, 482
Field, T., 539
Fields, H. L., 769
Fifer, W. P., 497, 535
Figley, C. R., 749
Fillmore, C., 336
Fine, A., 54
Finke, R. A., 285
Fischer, B., 209, 210
Fischoff, B., 313
Fisher, C., 336, 360
Fisher, E. D., 49
Fisher, S., 687
Fitzgerald, F. T., 79
Fitzsimons, J. T., 68
Flanagan, J. C., 316, 588
Flavell, E. R., 520, 526, 527
Flavell, J. H., 507, 520, 521, 525, 526, 527, 606, 607
Fleming, J. A., 736
Fletcher, 488
Floderus-Myrhed, B., 653
Flynn, J., 84, 369, 384
Flynn, S., 622
Fobes, T., 100
Foch, T. T., 78
Fodor, J. D., 343, 346, 519, 521
Fodor, Jerry A., 292–93, 331, 332, 358
Fontana, A. F., 734
Ford, C. S., 398
Forer, B. R., 633–34
Forster, E. M., 628
Foss, D. J., 290
Foster, F. G., 740
Foucault, Michel, 717, 789
Foulke, E., 329
Fouts, D. H., 371
Fouts, R. S., 371
Fowler, A., 368
Frank, M., 167
Frankl, V. E., 784
Fraser, S. C., 439
Frazier, L., 343
Frearson, W. M., 603
Freed, W. J., 55
Freedheim, D. K., 794
Freedman, J. L., 439
Freeman, D., 449
Frege, Gottlob, 332
Fremouw, W. J., 739
French, J. D., 88n
French, T., 775
Freud, Anna, 693
Freud, Sigmund, 8, 94, 98, 453, 533, 542–43, 548, 551, 562–63, 566, 569, 572, 589, 663, 670–92, 693, 695, 697, 699, 720, 751, 773–75, 779, 780, 785, 788
Fridlund, A. J., 402, 404, 444
Friedman, M. I., 71, 74, 77, 750, 754, 755
Friesen, W. V., 444
Frijda, N. H., 705
Fromkin, V., 361
Fromm, Erich, 448, 686
Fuller, J. L., 653
Funder, D. C., 652
Funkenstein, D. H., 442

Gage, F. H., 57
Gagnon, J. H., 398
Galanter, E., 293)
Galileo, Galilei, 16, 17

Gallagan, R., 354
Gallistel, C. R., 34, 37, 100, 101, 141, 517, 518, 563
Galton, Francis, 283, 584–86, 614
Gamzu, E., 140
Ganaway, G. K., 752
Garber, H., 612n
Garcia, J., 136–38
Gardner, Beatrice T., 371
Gardner, H., 44, 608–10
Gardner, M. K., 605
Gardner, R. Allen, 371
Garfield, S. L., 794
Garner, D. M., 80
Garnsey, S., 346
Garrigan, J. L., 749
Gathercole, V. C., 359
Gaulin, 141
Gauvain, M., 524
Gazzaniga, M. S., 49, 50
Geertz, C., 708–9
Geffen, G., 50
Gelade, G., 211
Gelman, D., 55
Gelman, R., 515, 517, 518
Genovese, Kitty, 457
Gerard, H. B., 423
Gergen, K., 480
Gerken, L., 352
Gershon, E. S., 740
Geschwind, N., 43
Gesell, A. L., 504
Giacalone, R. A., 424
Gibbs, J., 70
Gibson, James J., 204, 205, 230, 232
Gick, M. L., 299
Gilbert, L., 607
Gilbert, Sir William Schwenck, 439
Gildea, P., 330
Gilligan, Carol, 554–55
Gilliland, K., 657
Gladue, B. A., 567
Gladwin, T., 528
Glass, G. V., 790, 791, 792
Glazer, R., 353
Gleitman, Henry, 126, 132, 262, 264, 302, 335, 336, 350, 417, 449, 527, 528
Gleitman, Lila R., 335, 336, 348, 350, 351, 353, 354, 356, 359, 360, 363, 365, 367, 373, 527
Glick, J., 529
Glithero, E., 754, 781
Glucksberg, S., 298
Godden, D. R., 256
Goethals, G. R., 425
Goethe, Johann Wolfgang von, 572
Goffman, Erving, 431, 788, 789
Golani, I., 54
Gold, R., 523
Goldberg, L. R., 632, 640
Golden, T., 766
Goldfarb, W., 542
Goldin-Meadow, S., 363, 364
Goldman-Rakic, P. S., 514
Goldstein, A., 87
Goldstein, E. B., 164, 175
Goldstein, L. D., 631
Gombrich, E. H., 234, 236
Good, B., 738
Goodenough, D. R., 93
Goodman, J. F., 597
Goodwin, F. K., 740, 767
Gordon, H., 618
Gordon, W., 523
Goren, 516
Gorman, L. K., 740
Gotlib, I. H., 743

Gottesman, I. I., 732, 733, 780
Gottlieb, G., 504, 536
Gough, H. G., 632, 670
Gould, C., 175
Gould, J., 175
Gould, S. J., 494, 496, 574
Gouldner, A. W., 495
Graber, M., 514
Graf, P., 259, 260, 277
Grafstein, B., 54
Graham, C. H., 194
Graham, S., 269
Grant, V. W., 465n
Gray, S., 79
Green, 565, 631
Green, A. L., 740, 741
Green, D. M., 160, 175
Green, F. L., 527
Green, P., 221, 729
Green, R., 566, 599, 653, 657
Green, S. K., 463
Greenberg, J., 437
Greenberg, R. P., 687
Greenfield, P. M., 354, 524, 528, 529
Greenough, W. T., 505
Gregory, R. L., 216
Greven, P. J., Jr., 571
Grevert, P., 87
Grice, H. P., 328
Griggs, R. A., 320
Grill, H. J., 47
Grillner, S., 34
Grimshaw, J., 360
Gross, C. G., 317
Grossman, H. J., 594
Gruenberg, A. M., 732
Guilford, J. P., 649
Gurman, A. S., 788
Guttman, N., 120

Haber, R. B., 283
Haber, R. N., 245n, 283
Hadaway, B. F., 99
Haden, P., 260
Hager, M. E. P., 136
Hailman, J. P., 383
Halberstadt, L. J., 662
Hall, C. S., 6, 8, 689
Hall, E. T., 389
Hall, J. A., 436, 692
Hallam, J. R., 437
Halle, M., 329
Halpern, D. F., 559
Halverson, H. M., 494
Hamburg, D. A., 395
Hamer, 566
Hamilton, D. L., 430
Hamilton, W. D., 408
Hammel, H. T., 65
Hammer, A. G., 272
Hammersmith, S. K., 566
Hansen, 455
Hardy, J. D., 755
Hareven, T. K., 575
Harkins, S., 477, 479, 657
Harley, 91
Harlow, Harry, 384, 534–35, 541–42, 543
Harlow, M. K., 541
Harper, L. V., 549
Harris, G. W., 394
Harris, P. L., 507
Harter, N., 294, 296
Hartlage, S., 743
Hartmann, H., 693
Hartshorne, H., 644
Harvey, L. O., Jr., 231
Harvey, R., 791, 793

Hase, H. D., 632
Hasher, W., 273
Hastorf, A. H., 427
Hatfield, 467
Hathaway, S. R., 630
Hawkins, 87
Hawley, C. W., 657
Hay, D. F., 552
Hay, Q., 771
Hayer, C., 370
Hayne, H., 525
Haynes, S. G., 755
Hazelrigg, M. D., 788
Healy, A. F., 336
Heber, R., 612n
Hediger, H., 385
Heider, F., 432, 433, 434
Heilman, K. M., 44, 45, 594
Heingerter, A., 468
Hellekson, C. J., 739
Heller, H. C., 65
Hellman, R. E., 567
Helmholtz, Hermann von, 174, 192, 205, 207, 216, 229, 232
Henderson, V. K., 541
Henle, M., 308
Henry, 637
Henry, G. W., 718
Henry, J. P., 756
Herbener, 467
Herdt, 566
Hering, Ewald, 183
Herman, C. P., 77
Herman, E. M., 468
Herz, M. J., 106
Hesley, J. W., 650
Hess, E. H., 536
Hess, R. D., 545, 705
Heston, L. L., 732
Hetherington, P. A., 292
Heurer, S. K., 463
Hewer, A., 556
Hilgard, E. R., 272, 752
Hill, A. L., 604, 650
Hill, C. T., 462
Hill, R. M., 211
Hillery, J. M., 468
Hineline, P. N., 139
Hinton, G. E., 221
Hippocrates, 642, 652
Hirsch, A. D., 371
Hirschfield, 737
Hirsch-Pasek, K., 351, 354
Hirth, D. H., 409
Hitler, Adolf, 700
Hobbes, Thomas, 379–80, 381, 412, 456, 488, 670, 699
Hobson, J. A., 95
Hochberg, Julian E., 216, 224, 230, 236, 237
Hodges, J., 543
Hodgkinson, S., 740
Hoebel, B. G., 73
Hoefnagel-Hohle, M., 368
Hoffman, M. L., 271
Hoffman, H. S., 537
Hoffman, J. E., 227
Hoffman, M. L., 551, 552, 553, 555
Hogan, D., 146
Holding, D. H., 296, 305
Hollan, J. D., 257, 258
Holland, P. C., 106n, 113, 115
Hollander, E., 481, 767
Hollingshead, A. B., 734
Hollis, K. I., 113, 115
Hollister, L. E., 764, 765, 766
Holt, R. R., 637
Holtzman, P. S., 734

Holtzworth–Munroe, A., 436
Holway, A. F., 231
Holyoak, K. J., 299, 320
Holzberg, 436
Honzik, C. H., 132
Hook, 480
Hooley, J. M., 734
Horn, J. L., 653
Horn, J. M., 617
Horne, L. R., 328
Horne, R. L., 91, 93, 135
Horney, Karen, 448, 686
Hovland, C. I., 422
Howard, D. V., 311
Hoy, R. R., 176
Hrdy, S. B., 388, 411
Hsia, Y., 194
Hubel, David, 195, 210
Huber-Smith, M. J., 778
Hull, Clark L., 96–97
Humphrey, G., 287, 291
Humphreys, L. G., 123
Hunt, E., 559, 604
Hunt, J. M., 612, 649
Hunt, M. M., 465n
Hunt, P., 468
Hunt, W. A., 440
Hunter, I., 689
Hurvich, Leo, 193, 194, 235
Huston, T. L., 460
Hutchinson, R. R., 358, 384
Huttenlocher, J., 352
Huttenlocher, P. R., 496
Hyams, N., 356
Hyde, D. M., 522
Hyde, J. S., 559

Ickes, W., 417
Ilyin, N. A., 613
Ilyin, V. N., 613
Imboden, J. B., 751
Imperato-McGinley, J., 562
Ingersoll, G., 283
Inglis, J., 772
Ingvar, D. H., 2
Inhelder, B., 510, 511
Insel, T. R., 747
Izard, C. E., 443, 444, 445
Izzett, R., 417

Jaccard, J. J., 421
Jackendoff, R., 336
Jacklin, C. N., 558, 559
Jackson, J. M., 479
Jacobs, 141
Jacobsen, F. M., 767
Jacoby, L. L., 259, 260, 261
Jahoda, G., 488
Jalfre, M., 742
James, William, 10, 258, 439–40
Jameson, Dorothea, 193, 235
Janicak, P. G., 772
Jarrett, N., 516
Jarvik, L. F., 598
Jefferson, Thomas, 698, 700
Jencks, C., 623
Jenkins, J. G., 262
Jennings, 480
Jensen, Arthur R., 296, 603, 612, 620–21
Johnson, 516
Johnson, J., 369
Johnson, J. I., 41
Johnson, M., 335
Johnson, M. K., 257
Johnson, R. E., 558
Johnson, S., 628
Johnson-Laird, P. N., 311, 335

Johnston, 444
Jones, 444, 766
Jones, Ernest, 432, 434, 435, 683
Jones, S., 358
Jonides, J., 227, 286
Jorgensen, A., 733
Jorgensen, B. W., 461
Joshi, A. K., 307, 343
Josselson, R., 572
Jourard, 455
Jouvet, M., 90
Judd, T., 44
Julesz, B., 214
Julien, R. M., 98
Jusczyk, P., 350, 352

Kagan, J., 537, 598, 647, 652
Kahan, J. P., 435
Kahneman, D., 312–13, 314, 329, 447
Kalat, J. W., 136, 138, 139
Kalish, H. I., 120
Kamin, L. J., 113, 130–31, 411, 611, 612, 616
Kaminsky, 555
Kandel, D., 34, 462
Kane, J. M., 766
Kannel, W. B., 755
Kant, Immanuel, 156–57
Kaplan, E., 594
Katcher, A. H., 442
Katz, J. J., 332
Katz, N., 359
Kaufman, L., 235
Keats, J., 701
Keele, S. W., 294
Keil, F. C., 9, 353, 358
Keller, Helen, 365–66, 370
Kelley, H. H., 432, 433, 454
Kelley, M., 730
Kelley, S., 421
Kellman, P. J., 216, 513
Kelly, I. W., 634
Kelly, M. H., 352
Kemler-Nelson, D. G., 296, 351
Kendler, K. S., 732
Kennedy, J. F., 266, 283
Kenny, 481
Kenrick, D. T., 465, 652
Kepler, Johannes, 16
Kerr, M. E., 787
Kessel, E. L., 392
Kessey, R. E., 78
Kety, S. S., 732
Keverne, E. B., 169
Kihlstrom, J. F., 273, 652, 690, 695, 703
Kilham, W., 475
Kimball, J., 343
Kimble, G. A., 112
King, H. E., 84
King, Martin Luther, 554
Kinsey, A. C., 395, 565, 567
Kitayama, S., 708
Kitcher, P., 399, 411
Kittrie, N. N., 788–89
Kleinman, A., 738
Kleinmuntz, B., 637
Kleitman, N., 6, 93
Klerman, G. L., 767, 795
Klima, E. S., 46, 362, 363
Klinberg, O., 403
Kline, J. A., 739
Klopfer, B., 636
Kluft, R. P., 751
Knight, J., 462
Kniskern, D. P., 788
Knopman, 54
Koelling, R. A., 136–38
Kohlberg, Lawrence, 547, 553–55, 563–64

Köhler, Wolfgang, 143–45, 147
Kohn, M. L., 544, 705, 734
Kohut, Heinz, 693n
Kolb, B., 43, 44, 53
Kolers, P. A., 224
Kolodny, R., 567
Konner, M. J., 528
Koriat, A., 259
Kornhuber, H. H., 43
Kosslyn, S. M., 284
Kostlan, A., 639
Kotelchuk, M., 538
Koulack, D., 93
Kraepelin, E., 723
Kral, P. A., 138
Kramer, P. D., 767
Krantz, D. S., 755
Krashen, S., 369
Kraut, 444
Krebs, J. R., 385, 386
Kubovy, M., 216, 231n
Kuhl, P., 350
Kuhn, I. F., 358
Kulik, James, 266
Kupfer, D. J., 740
Kuznicki, J. T., 167

La Berge, D., 296
Labov, W., 620
Lakoff, G., 335
Lamb, M. E., 537, 539, 548, 765, 766
Lammers, J., 84
Landau, B., 208, 335, 352, 353, 358, 365
Landis, C., 440
Lane, D. W., 559
Lane, R. W., 689
Lange, Carl, 439
Langer, E. J., 662
Langlois, J. H., 558
Lanyon, R. I., 631
LaPiere, Richard, 420–21
Lash, J. P., 366
Lashley, Karl S., 293
Lassen, N. A., 2
Latané, Bibb, 457, 459, 477–79
Laties, V. G., 67
Lau, R. R., 436
Laudenslager, M. L., 135
Lawrence, K. Q., 254
Layzer, D., 621
Lazar, I., 612
Lazarus, A. A., 777, 781, 785
Leask, J., 283
Leaton, R. N., 107
Le Bon, Gustav, 483, 484
Leech, G. N., 328
Leeper, R. W., 219
Leff, J. P., 734
Lehuin, J.Y., 195
Leibowitz, H., 231, 232
Leiman, A. L., 54, 164
Leirer, V. O., 309
Lempers, J. S., 520
Lenneberg, E. H., 349, 367, 368, 373
LePichon, M., 742
Lepper, M. R., 551
Leslie, A. M., 519
Lettvin, J. Y., 195
LeVay, 567–68
Levelt, W. J. M., 293, 338
Levin, B., 336
Levin, H., 560
Levine, C., 556
Levine, J. D., 769
Levine, J. M., 169, 470
Levinson, D. J., 574
Levy, J., 9, 50, 51, 52

Levy, V. M., 527
Lewin, R., 55
Lewis, J., 604
Lewinsohn, P. M., 743
Lewontin, R. C., 411, 621
Lewy, A., 739
Lezak, M.D., 594
Liberman, A. M., 328
Lichenstein, S., 313
Lieberman, S., 438
Lieblich, I., 259
Liff, Z.A., 775
Liker, 607
Lincoln, A., 605, 700
Linder, D. E., 465
Lindsley, D. B., 86
Lindzey, G., 619, 621
Linn, M. C., 559
Lipitz, 466
Lippert, W. W., 758
Lipsitt, L. P., 570
Lipton, R. C., 542
Liske, E., 35n
Little, K. B., 638
Liu, T. J., 424
Ljungberg, T., 731
Lloyd, B., 558
Locke, John, 154, 180, 201, 234–35, 523, 745
Lockhart, R. S., 252
Loehlin, J. C., 617, 619, 621, 654
Loewi, O., 27
Loftus, E. F., 263, 269–70, 271, 273, 290
Loftus, G. R., 273
Logue, A. W., 79, 80, 138
London, P., 460, 773
Lord, 481
Lorenz, Konrad, 382, 384, 387, 404, 536
Lowery, C. R., 634
Lowry, D., 254
Luborsky, L., 790, 791
Luborsky, L. I., 790, 791
Lubin, B., 631
Luce, R. D., 484
Luchins, A. S., 427
Lucretius, 10
Luginbuhl, J. E. R., 435
Lunneborg, C., 604
Luria, A. R., 43, 44, 45, 529, 610
Lust, B., 356n
Lutz, C., 703
Lykken, D. T., 83, 616, 655

Maass, A., 470
McBurney, D. H., 167, 169
McCall, R. B., 597, 598
McCann, D. S., 778
McCarley, R. W., 95, 767
McCarthy, J., 356n
McCarthy, R. A., 53
McCartney, K., 549, 649, 656
McClearn, G. E., 78, 614
McClelland, D. C., 638
McClelland, J. L., 221, 290, 357
McClintock, M. K., 170, 393
McCloskey, M., 266, 271, 292
Maccoby, E. E., 540, 548, 558, 559, 560
McConaghy, M. J., 564
McCord, J., 758
McCord, W., 758
McCown, N. E., 437
McCrae, R. R., 646
McCullough, D. R., 409
McCutcheon, N. B., 167
McEwen, B. S., 394
MacFarlane, A., 535
McGhie, A., 727
McGrath, M. J., 92

McGraw, M. B., 504
McGue, M., 614, 615, 616, 655, 656
McGuigan, F. J., 729
McGuire, M. T., 410
McGuire, W. J., 422
Mach, Ernst, 182, 183–84
Machiavelli, Niccolï, 488
Mack, D., 78
McKay, A., 612n
McKay, D. G., 228
McKenzie, B. E., 5, 232
McKinley, S. R., 630
McKoon, G., 290
McNally, J., 746
MacNamara, J., 359
MacNeilage, P., 329
McNeill, D., 259
MacNichol, E. F., Jr., 191
MacWhinney, B., 349, 367
McWhirter, 565
Madison, 565
Magnus, O., 84
Magnusson, D., 647
Magoun, H. W., 66
Maher, B. A., 770
Mahoney, M. J., 311
Maier, S. F., 135, 742
Malan, H., 775
Malinowski, Bronislaw, 455–56, 687
Malthus, Thomas, 380
Manderscheid, R. W., 766
Mann, F., 85
Mann, L., 475
Manosevitz, M., 692
Mantell, 475
Manzini, R., 356
Maratsos, M., 344
Marcus, 733
Marder, 766
Marsden, 32
Marentette, P. F., 349
Markman, E. M., 358, 359
Marks, I. M., 745
Markus, 708
Marler, 144
Marler, P. R., 368
Marmor, J., 565
Marshall, D. A., 169
Marshall, G. D., 443
Marslen-Wilson, W. D., 275, 346
Martin, C. E., 395, 565, 567
Martin, J. A., 548
Martin, S., 352
Marx, G., 692
Maslach, C., 443
Maslow, Abraham, 696–700, 782
Matarazzo, J. D., 724
Mathews, K. A., 755
Mathewson, G. C., 423
Matin, L., 208
Matthyse, S., 734
Maugh, T. M., 767
May, M. A., 644
May, M. L., 176
May, R., 784
Mayer, D. J., 87
Mayer, J., 70
Mayes, A. R., 275
Maynard-Smith, J., 408
Mead, G. H., 437
Mead, Margaret, 448–49, 572, 702, 703, 704
Medin, D. L., 333, 335
Mednick, S. A., 733
Meehl, P. E., 587, 633, 638
Mehler, J., 349
Meltzer, H. Y., 730, 731, 766, 767

Melzack, R., 85
Menustik, C. E., 778
Menyuk, P., 367
Menzel, E. W., 143
Mercer, J., 596
Mervis, C. B., 333, 358
Mesquita, B., 705
Metalsky, G. I., 662, 743
Meyer, D. E., 290
Meyerowitz, 436
Michael, R. P., 169, 394
Michaels, J. W., 468
Michela, J. L., 432
Michelangelo, 650
Milavsky, B., 442
Milazzo-Sayle, L. J., 766
Milgram, Stanley, 473–74
Mill, John Stuart, 418
Miller, A. G., 475
Miller, D. T., 447, 476
Miller, George A., 246, 293, 330, 335, 336
Miller, Joan, 488
Miller, N. E., 73
Miller, R. L., 418, 790, 791, 792
Miller, W. R., 135
Millon, T., 758
Mills, J., 423
Milner, Brenda, 43, 275
Milner, Peter, 99–100
Mineka, S., 126
Minuchin, S., 787
Mirer, T. W., 421
Mischel, H. N., 664
Mischel, Walter, 428, 563, 643–44, 645, 661, 663, 665
Miselis, R. R., 70
Mishler, E. G., 734
Mita, T. H., 462
Mitchell, C., 79
Mitchell, D. E., 196
Mitroff, I. I., 311
Modigliani, A., 431
Molitor, 540
Money, J., 502, 561, 562
Monson, T. C., 650
Mooney, J. J., 740, 741
Moore, B., 664
Moore-Gillow, M. J., 68
Moos, R. H., 395
Mora, F., 72, 74
Moray, N., 228
More, D. M., 639
Moreland, R. L., 461
Moret, V., 87
Morgan, C. D., 351, 636
Morgan, J., 348
Morlock, H. C., 90
Morris, Desmond, 391
Morsbach, H., 703
Morse, Samuel, 163–64
Morton, J., 221, 455, 516
Moscovici, S., 470
Moscovitch, M., 50, 53
Moskowitz, D. W., 646
Mosnain, A. D., 749
Moss, H. A., 647
Moulton, D. G., 169
Mounts, 549
Muir, D. W., 196
Mulford, R., 365
Mullan, M. J., 740
Müller, Johannes, 164, 165
Murdock, M., 793
Murphy, J. M., 790
Murray, F. B., 523
Murray, Henry, 636
Muscettola, G., 741

Muus, R. E., 572
Mylander, C., 364

Nadel, L., 143, 265
Nakayama, M., 356
Napolean Bonaparte, 480
Nathan, P. W., 86
Nauta, W. J. H., 20
Neimeyer, 467
Neisser, U., 210, 264, 266, 267, 273
Nelson, K., 352, 353
Nemeth, 470
Nemiroff, R. A., 574
Nesse, F. M., 778
Neugarten, 574
Neugebauer, R., 717
Newcomb, T., 483
Newell, Allen, 304
Newmeyer, F., 330
Newport, Elissa, 350, 363, 369
Newton, Isaac, 16, 300, 500, 701
Nichols, R. C., 654
Nicholson, R. A., 791
Nida, S. A., 459
Nisbett, R. E., 73, 77, 78, 318, 320, 432, 434, 645, 649, 652
Nohr, D., 175
Nolen-Hoeksema, S., 744
Norcross, J. C., 794
Norman, D. A., 245
Norman, Warren T., 640–41
Nottebohm, F., 20n
Novak, M. A., 542, 543
Nowlis, G. H., 167

Odbert, H. S., 640
Odiorne, J. M., 83
Ofman, W. V., 783
Öhman, A., 746
O'Keefe, J., 143
Olds, James, 99–100
Olfson, M., 764, 767
Oliver, L. M., 320
Olofsson, 746
Olson, D. J., 141
Olton, D. S., 143
Olweus, D., 549
Orbell, J. M., 486
Orlansky, H., 548
Orlansky, H.., 687
Orne, M. T., 83, 271, 788
Ornstein, R., 51
Orsini, D. L., 594
Osler, S., 256
Osmond, H., 722
Osofsky, J. D., 549
Öst, L., 746
Oster, H., 402
Ostrom, T. M., 427
O'Sullivan, 444
Ottenberg, P., 475

Paarsalu, M. E., 296
Packer, C., 409
Pai, M. N., 5
Palmer, J. C., 270
Panzarella, 475
Parke, R. D., 539, 549, 558, 560
Parker, E. S., 275
Parnas, J., 733
Parrott, W. G., 431
Pascal-Leone, J., 525
Patience, A., 449, 704
Patterson, T., 730
Paul, Gordon, 792–93
Pavlov, Ivan P., 107–10, 115, 126, 139, 147, 156n, 523, 776

Paykel, E. S., 744
Peake, P. K., 647, 664
Pearlstone, Z., 255
Pedersen, N., 653
Peeke, H. V. S., 106
Penfield, Wilder, 1, 40
Penrose, L. S., 224
Penrose, R., 224
Pepitone, A., 483, 488
Peplau, L. A., 462
Perczel, W. J., 739
Pericles, 565
Perin, C. T., 122
Perner, J., 520, 521
Peterson, B. L., 786
Peterson, C., 662, 742, 743
Petitto, L. A., 372
Petitto, L. G., 349
Petty, R. E., 422–23
Pham, V. A., 766
Piaget, Jean, 9, 505–25, 547, 677, 697
Picard, R. S., 135
Picasso, Pablo, 236
Pichert, J., 268, 271
Pierce, J., 689
Pillai, R. V., 74
Pillard, R. C., 566
Pillemer, D. B., 265, 266
Pinel, Philippe, 718
Pinker, S., 285, 292, 348, 356n, 357, 359, 360, 373
Plato, 10, 156
Pleck, J. H., 539
Plomin, R., 652, 653, 655
Plutchik, R., 444
Poggio, G. F., 210
Pogue-Geile, M. F., 654
Poincaré, Jules-Henri, 300
Poizner, H., 46
Poley, W., 473
Polivy, J., 77
Pomerantz, J. R., 216, 224, 231n
Pomeroy, W. B., 395, 565, 567
Porac, C., 48
Porsolt, R. D., 742
Porter, R. H., 169
Powley, T. L., 78
Premack, A., 145
Premack, David, 145, 146, 371, 406, 407, 519
Preston, M., 729
Pribram, K. H., 293
Price, D. D., 55
Price, R. H., 650
Price-Williams, D. R., 488, 523, 524, 528, 530
Prince, A., 292, 357
Prince, E., 327
Prince, G., 51
Prioleau, L., 793
Provence, S., 542
Pubols, B. H., 41
Puerto, A., 70
Putnam, F. W., 752
Putnam, K. E., 272, 331
Pyszczynski, T., 437

Quay, L. C., 620, 759
Quetelet, Adolphe, 582–83
Quillian, M. R., 289

Raag, 444
Rachlin, H., 139
Rachman, S. J., 778
Radford, A., 330
Radke-Yarrow, M., 552
Rago, W., 766
Raiffa, H., 484
Ramirez, M., 523

Rapaport, A., 767
Rappaport, M., 336
Rasmuson, L., 653
Rasmussen, T., 40
Ratcliff, R., 290
Raven, B. H., 488
Rayner, K., 226
Read, C., 336
Reardon, J., 196
Reber, A. S., 464
Redl, F., 475
Redlich, F. C., 734
Rees, E., 353
Reese, H. W., 570
Reich, L., 740
Reid, W. H., 766
Reis, 455
Reisburg, D., 268, 285, 290, 296
Reisenzein, R., 443
Reisman, 565
Reisser, B. J., 284
Remez, R., 352
Renfrew, J. W., 384
Renner, M. J., 504
Rescorla, Robert A., 106n, 115, 127, 129, 130, 132, 133, 353
Rest, J. R., 556
Revlin, R., 309
Revusky, S. H., 138
Reynolds, R. I., 296
Rheingold, H. L., 552
Ricks, S. S., 539
Riecken, H., 419
Rigby, M. K., 169
Riggs, L. A., 181
Rimpau, J., 372
Rioch, 38
Rips, L. J., 289
Ritter, K., 526
Rizzi, L., 356
Roatsch, J. F., 744
Robbin, A. A., 770
Robbins, S. J., 111
Roberts, L., 1
Robins, E., 566
Robins, L. N., 749
Robins, L. R., 758, 759
Robinson, H. B., 595
Robinson, N. M., 595
Roby, T. B., 96
Rock, I., 216, 223, 230, 235
Rodgers, D. A., 751
Rodin, J., 77, 78, 662
Rodman, H. R., 317
Roeder, K. D., 35
Roediger, H. L., 245
Roeper, T., 356n
Rogers, Carl, 697–700, 782–84, 788
Rogoff, B., 524
Roland, P. E., 44
Rolls, B. J., 68, 69
Rolls, E. T., 68, 69, 72, 74
Romanes, G. J., 115
Rompre, P., 100
Roosevelt, Eleanor, 698, 700
Roper, T. J., 141
Rorer, L. G., 637, 646
Rorschach, Hermann, 635–36
Rosch, E. H., 289, 333, 334, 358
Rose, R. J., 654
Rose, R. M., 411
Rose, T. L., 430
Rosen, G., 717
Rosenbaum, M., 71
Rosenfeld, P., 424
Rosenfield, D., 435
Rosenhan, David L., 791

Rosenman, R. H., 754, 755
Rosenstein, M. J., 766
Rosenthal, 316
Rosenthal, A. M., 457
Rosenthal, D., 739
Rosenthal, N. E., 739
Rosenzweig, M. R., 54, 164, 504
Ross, J., 254
Ross, L., 433, 434, 645
Ross, M., 435
Rothbaum, F. M., 707, 708
Rovee-Collior, C. K., 525
Rousseau, Jean-Jacques, 701
Rozin, E., 168
Rozin, Paul, 53, 75, 79, 136, 138, 139, 146, 262, 277
Roy, A., 736
Rubin, 455
Rubin, J. Z., 488
Rubin, L., 462
Rumbaugh, D. M., 371
Rumelhart, D., 221, 291, 357
Rush, Benjamin, 763
Rushton, J. P., 654
Russek, M., 71
Russell, D., 436
Russell, M. J., 169, 170
Rutstein, 67
Ryan, S. M., 135

Sabini, John, 431, 446, 460n, 466, 708
Sachs, J., 340
Sackheim, H., 743
Sacks, O., 44
Sadler, H. H., 460
Sadock, B. J., 787
Saghir, M. T., 566
Sagi, A., 552
Sahlins, M., 410
Salinger, J. D., 572
Samuelson, R. J., 143
Sanders, 468
Sarason, S. B., 619
Sarbin, T. R., 751
Sarnoff, C., 113
Sarty, 516
Satinoff, E., 67
Satir, V., 787, 788
Savage-Rumbaugh, E., 371, 372
Sawrey, W. L., 756
Saxe, L., 83
Scarr, Sandra, 549, 616, 618, 622, 649, 656, 657
Schacher, S., 77, 495
Schachtel, E. G., 264
Schachter, D. L., 259
Schachter, Stanley, 419, 439, 441–42, 443, 465
Schäffer, S., 398
Schaie, K., 598
Schaife, K. W., 516
Schank, R. C., 269
Schapiro, S., 505
Scheff, S. W., 54
Scheff, T., 790
Scheid, P., 43
Schiff, M., 618, 656
Schiff, W., 206
Schiffrin, D., 327
Schildkraut, J. J., 740, 741
Schleidt, W. M., 107
Schlenker, R. B., 431, 437
Schmidt, 211
Schnedler, R., 460
Schneider, D. J., 427, 427n, 428
Schofield, W., 786
Schreiber, F. R., 751
Schreiber, P., 336
Schuldt, 455

Schull, J., 114n
Schvaneveldt, R. W., 290
Schwartz, Barry, 125, 130, 140, 268, 291
Schwartz, G. E., 443
Scott, J. P., 653
Scribner, S., 529
Searle, J. R., 327
Sears, R. R., 560
Seay, B., 543
Seeman, B., 725
Segal, M., 616, 655
Seidenberg, M. S., 292, 372
Seitz, V., 547
Selfridge, O. G., 218
Seligman, Martin, 130, 134, 135, 136, 138, 662, 742, 746
Sells, P., 330
Senter, R. J., 758
Seurat, Georges, 189
Seyfarth, R. M., 372, 388, 390, 405n, 406
Shakespeare, William, 11, 91, 283, 465, 466
Shalter, M. D., 106
Shan, 67
Shanab, 475
Shapiro, A. K., 769
Shapiro, C. M., 91
Shapiro, D., 791, 792
Shapiro, D. A., 791, 792
Sheean, D., 767
Sheffield, F. D., 96
Sheingold, K., 264
Shekelle, R. B., 135
Shenkel, R. J., 634
Shepard, R. N., 284
Sherman, P. W., 409
Sherrick, C. E., 166
Sherrington, Sir Charles, 25–26, 27, 28, 183–84
Sherrod, 455
Sherry, 141
Shettleworth, S. J., 139, 141
Shick, T. R., 167
Shields, J., 732, 733
Shiffrin, R. M., 245
Shipley, E. F., 354, 358, 527
Shipley, T. F., 216
Shipstead, S. G., 520
Shizgal, Peter, 100
Shneidman, E. S., 638
Shoben, E. J., 289
Shoda, Y., 664
Short, K. R., 513
Shortliffe, E. H., 306
Shuey, A., 619
Shumer, F., 636, 637, 638
Shweder, R. A., 645, 652, 708
Sicoly, F., 435
Siegal, M., 518
Siegel, S., 98, 114
Siegler, M., 522, 722
Silk, J. B., 388
Silver, M., 431, 446
Simmel, G., 466
Simner, M. L., 552
Simon, H. A., 295, 304, 329
Simon, Théodor, 351
Simon, W., 398
Simpson, 555
Sims, E. A., 76
Singer, B., 790, 791
Singer, J. A., 443
Singer, J. E., 439, 441–42, 443
Sinha, D., 610
Skeels, H. M., 544, 617, 618
Skinhoj, E., 2
Skinner, B. F., 113, 118–19, 121, 126, 132, 139, 523, 659–60, 776
Skodak, M., 617, 618

Slaby, R. G., 549, 558, 560
Slater, E., 754, 780, 781
Sloane, R. B., 792
Slobin, D. I., 344, 346
Slovic, P., 313
Smedslund, J., 523
Smelser, N. J., 484
Smiley, P., 352
Smith, C., 92, 558
Smith, C. S., 354
Smith, D. G., 388
Smith, E. E., 289, 333, 335
Smith, G. P., 70
Smith, J. H., 354
Smith, J. W., 449, 704
Smith, L., 358
Smith, M., 462
Smith, M. B., 701
Smith, M. L., 790, 791, 792
Smith, S. M., 256
Smith, T. W., 755
Snow, C., 368
Snyder, C. R., 634
Snyder, M., 435, 438, 473, 649, 650–51
Snyder, S. H., 87, 730
Socrates, 451
Solomon, R. L., 99, 742
Solomon, S., 437
Sommer, R., 389
Souther, J., 211
Spearman, Charles, 601–2, 604
Spelke, E. S., 513, 515
Spemann, H., 501, 503
Spence, J. T., 468n
Spence, K. W., 468n
Sperber, D., 307, 327
Sperry, R. W., 48
Spies, G., 100
Spilich, G. S., 267
Spiro, M. E., 271
Spitzer, R. L., 791
Springer, S. P., 48, 51
Spuhler, J. N., 619, 621
Squire, L. R., 260, 276, 277, 772
Stacher, G., 70
Stanley, J. C., 559
Stark, H. A., 259
Stark, L., 226
Starkey, P., 515
Staudenmeyer, H., 319
Steedman, M., 346
Steele, C. M., 424
Steinberg, 549
Steiner, J. E., 74
Steinmetz, J. L., 434
Steinringer, H., 70
Stellar, E., 73, 100
Stellar, J. R., 100
Stenevi, U., 55
Stephan, W. G., 435
Sternberg, R. J., 299
Sternberg, Robert, 464, 608, 610, 611
Stevens, A., 171, 287
Stevens, L., 435
Stevenson, J. A. F., 73
Stewart, J., 115
Stewart, K., 8
Stewart, T. D., 716
Sticht, T. G., 329
Stoch, M. B., 596
Stokoe, W. C., Jr., 362
Stoller, R. J., 557n, 566
Storms, M. D., 435
Stotland, E., 553
Stowe, L., 346
Stricker, E. M., 54, 67, 71, 73, 74
Stroop, J. R., 296

Strother, C., 598
Stroufe, L. A., 538
Strupp, H. H., 775
Stuart, D. G., 38
Stuart, G. W., 232
Stuart, R. B., 79
Styron, W., 737–38
Stunkard, A. J., 76, 79
Sullivan, H. S., 448
Sullivan, Anne, 366–67
Sullivan, Sir Arthur S., 439
Sullivan, H. S., 686
Suls, J. M., 301, 418
Sunshine, P., 283
Suomi, S. J., 542, 543
Supalla, Ted, 362, 363
Super, C. M., 503
Swets, J. A., 160
Switz, G. M., 170
Symons, D., 95, 398
Szasz, Thomas S., 790

Tagiuri, R., 428
Takahashi, Y., 91
Tanenhaus, M., 343, 346
Taplin, J., 319
Taylor, S. E., 436
Teach, R. L., 306
Teasdale, J., 778
Teasdale, J. D., 743
Tedeschi, J. T., 424
Tees, R., 350
Teitelbaum, P., 54, 73
Tellegen, A., 616, 655
Tenney, Y. J., 264
Tepas, D. I., 90
Terrace, H. S., 371
Tervoort, B. T., 363
Tess, R., 350
Tesser, A., 462, 469
Teuber, H. L., 54, 275
Theophrastus, 627, 629
Thibaut, J. W., 454
Thigpen, C. H., 751
Thomas, A., 549, 652
Thompson, C. P., 283
Thompson, H., 504
Thompson, K., 170
Thomson, D. M., 256
Thoren, Peter, 87
Thorndike, Edward L., 115–18, 121, 126, 132,
        143, 144, 147, 546, 589, 776
Thurstone, L. L., 602
Tietjen, 555
Tinbergen, Niko, 107, 382–83
Tizard, B., 542
Tocqueville, A., 708
Tognacci, L. N., 421
Tolman, Edward C., 126, 127, 131–32, 143
Tolstoy, Leo, 480, 694
Tomasello, M., 349
Tomkiewicz, S., 709
Tomkins, S. S., 443
Tooby, John, 456
Tootell, H. E., 232
Torgersen, S., 740, 778
Torrey, E. F., 734
Travis, L., 348
Treisman, A. M., 211, 227, 228
Triandis, H. C., 610, 706
Trivers, R. L., 393, 408, 409
Tronick, E., 206
Trosman, H., 93
Tsuang, M. T., 732, 736
Tuchin, M., 271
Tulving, E., 255, 256, 257, 259, 288
Turing, A. M., 304

Turner, A. M., 505
Turner, J. A., 422
Turner, T. J., 268
Turrell, E. S., 756
Tversky, A., 312–13, 314, 329, 447
Tversky, B., 271
Tyler, L. E., 595
Tyler, W. J., 703
Tzeng, O., 51

Ungerstedt, U., 731
Urwin, C., 365

Vaillant, George, 574, 693–94
Valenstein, E., 594, 770
Valenta, J. G., 169
Valins, S., 442
Van Cantfort, E., 372
Van de Castle, R., 8
van de Kragt, A. J. C., 486
Vandell, D. L., 541
Vandenbos, G. P., 795
Van Gorp, W. G., 594
Van Kammen, D. P., 730
Van Zoeren, J. G., 67
Vaughn, 540
Vaultin, R. G., 211
Veraa, R. P., 54
Vernon, D. T. A., 421
Viscott, D. S., 609
Visintainer, M., 135
Vogel, P. J., 49
Volpicelli, J. R., 98, 135
Vukovich, K. R., 505

Waber, D. P., 559
Wachtel, P. L., 359, 782, 785
Waddington, J. L., 733
Wagner, A. R., 107, 130
Wagner, D. A., 529
Wagner, R. K., 608
Waid, W. M., 83
Wakefield, J. C., 721
Waldfogel, S., 264
Walker, L. J., 555
Wall, P. D., 54
Wall, S., 227
Wallace, J. G., 50
Wallas, G., 301
Wallèn, K., 34, 397
Wallin, P., 462
Walster, E. H., 422, 461, 462, 463, 464, 465, 467
Walster, G. W., 462, 463, 465
Walters, J. R., 388, 390
Walters, R. H., 546
Wang, M. L., 70
Wang, W. Y., 51
Wanner, E., 344, 351, 356
Wapner, W. T., 44
Ward, 488
Warren, R. M., 220
Warrington, E. K., 53, 276, 277
Washington, George, 605
Wasman, M., 384
Wason, P. C., 311, 319–20
Wasserman, S., 513
Waters, E., 537
Watkins, L. R., 87
Watkins, M. J., 250
Watson, C. G., 753, 754, 781
Watson, John B., 134, 665
Watson, R. I., 44, 45
Watt, N. F., 737
Waugh, N. C., 245
Waxler, N. E., 734
Waxman, S. R., 348
Webb, W. B., 91, 93

Weber, 708
Weber, A., 254
Weber, E. H., 158–59
Wechsler, David, 592, 593, 599
Weeks, R. D., 771
Weigel, R. H., 421
Weinberg, M. S., 566
Weinberg, R. A., 618, 622, 656
Weinberger, G. E., 443
Weiner, Bernard, 445
Weiner, H., 756
Weiner, R. D., 772
Weingartner, H., 275
Weinreich, 568
Weinstock, S., 123
Weisberg, R. W., 300
Weiskrantz, L., 276, 277, 317
Weiss, B., 67
Weiss, J. M., 130
Weiss, W., 422
Weissman, M., 748
Weisstein, N., 214
Weisz, J. R., 707, 708
Welch, C. A., 772
Welker, W. I., 41
Wellman, H. M., 519, 520, 521, 525, 526, 606
Wender, P. H., 740
Werker, J., 350
Wertheimer, M., 206, 214
West, M. J., 552
West, S. G., 460
Westermeyer, J., 766
Wetzel, M., 38
Wexler, K., 356, 356n
Wheeler, 455
Wheeler, D., 455
Wheeler, L. R., 618
Whishaw, I. Q., 43, 44, 53
White, G. L., 463
White, L., 356
White, R. W., 737
White, S. H., 265
Whiting, B. B., 558
Whiting, J. W. M., 558, 572
Whitlow, J. W., Jr., 107
Whitney, G., 460
Whytt, Robert, 25
Wible, C. G., 266
Wickelgren, W. A., 301
Wicker, A. W., 421
Widiger, T. A., 646
Wiens, A. N., 778
Wiesel, Torsten, 195, 210
Wiesenthal, D. L., 469
Wilcoxin, H. C., 138
Wilde, Oscar, 303
Willerman, L., 617
Williams, 568
Williams, C. D., 124
Williams, D. R., 140
Williams, E., 356n
Williams, G. C., 388, 393
Williams, H., 140
Williams, H. L., 90
Williams, K., 479
Williams, M. D., 257
Williams, R. B., 755
Wilson, D., 307, 327
Wilson, D. H., 49
Wilson, D. W., 459
Wilson, Edward, 383, 407, 409
Wilson, G., 467, 657
Wilson, G. T., 79
Wilson, K. S., 541
Wilson, T. D., 318, 652
Wiltschko, R., 175
Wiltschko, W., 175

Wimmer, H., 520, 521
Winch, R. F., 639
Winter, R., 169
Wippman, J., 537
Wise, R. A., 100, 101
Wishner, Julius, 427n, 791
Witherspoon, D., 259
Wittgenstein, L., 333
Wolf, M. E., 749
Wolf, S., 756
Wolfe, G., 7
Wolgin, D. L., 54
Wolitsky, D. L., 775
Wollen, K. A., 254
Wolpe, Joseph, 745–46, 748, 777–78
Wolpert, E. A., 93, 689
Wong, E., 214
Wood, 767
Woodruff, G., 407, 519
Woods, R. L., 10, 54
Woodworth, R. S., 160
Woolson, R. F., 736

Wrangham, R. W., 405n
Wu, 516
Wulff, J. J., 96
Wundt, Wilhelm, 10
Wyatt, R. J., 55
Wyers, E. J., 106
Wynn, K., 515

Yager, D. D., 176
Yahya, 475
Yalom, I. D., 395
Yando, R., 547
Yang, K., 704
Yarbus, A. L., 226
Yarrow, L. J., 543
Yeomans, J., 100
Yonas, A., 206
Young, Thomas, 192
Yussen, S. R., 527

Zaccaro, 481
Zahn-Waxler, C., 552

Zaidel, E., 50
Zajonc, R. B., 461, 468–69
Zanna, M. P., 425
Zanni, G., 270
Zaragoza, M. S., 271
Zeigler, H. P., 232
Zeiss, A. R., 663
Zener, K., 113
Zentall, T., 146
Ziegler, F. J., 751
Zigler, E. F., 449, 547, 548, 596, 612, 687, 751
Zigmond, M. J., 54, 73, 74
Zilboorg, G., 718
Zillman, D., 442
Zimbardo, P. G., 443, 483
Zohar, J., 747
Zola-Morgan, S., 265
Zouzounis, J. A., 772
Zubin, J., 636, 637, 638
Zuckerman, M., 97, 653, 657, 658
Zuger, B., 566

SUBJECT INDEX

abnormal psychology, *see* psychopathology
absolute threshold, 157
    detection experiments and, 160–63
abstract concepts, 292
    in animals, 145–46
    concrete or formal operations and, 510–11
    cultural differences and, 528–29
    in moral reasoning, 554–55
    reference theory of meaning and, 331–32
abstract thought, 291–93
access to intellectual processes, 146–47
accommodation (in cognitive development), 507, 524
accommodation (in vision), 178
accommodative distortions, 271
acetylcholine, 27, 29, 30–31
achievement tests, 582
achromatic colors, 186
across-fiber pattern theory, 164
action potential, 21–23, 28
activation, 88
activation-synthesis hypothesis, 94–95
active memory, 249–55
    retrieval from, 264–66
    see also short-term memory
active (REM) sleep, 6–7, 90, 91–92, 740
active sentences, 344
actor-observer bias, 434–35
act-outcome associations, 131–33, 139–40
adaptation, 167
    in vision, 180–81, 191
adaptive value, of behavior, 381
addiction, to drugs, 97–99, 100–101, 114
additive color mixture, 189
ADH (anti-diuretic hormone), 67
adolescence, 570–72
    competence in, related to childhood ability to
        delay gratification, 664
    growth in, 495
    nature of transition in, 571–72
    search for personal identity in, 573
adoption, maternal deprivation and, 543
adoption studies:
    on bipolar disorder, 740
    on intelligence, 617, 618
    on personality, 654–55
    on schizophrenia, 732
adrenaline (epinephrine), 81–82
adrenal medulla, 81–82
adulthood, 573–75
    changes in intelligence during, 652–54
    Erikson's stages of, 573–75
    intelligence tests administered in, 592–93
    mid-life transition in, 573–74
    transition from adolescence to, 617–18
    universality of stages in, 574–75
affective disorders, *see* mood disorders

afferent nerves, 18
afterimages, negative, 190
age, memory declines and, 653
aggression, 383–89
    in animals, 384–89
    crowd behavior and, 482, 529
    at different ages, 647
    dominance hierarchies and, 387–88
    hormones and, 388, 559
    physical punishment and, 549–50
    predation and defense, 384
    sex differences in, 558–59, 560
    territoriality and, 334–35
agnosia, 44
agoraphobia, 749, 776
alarm signals, 170, 405*n*, 408
alcohol, 97–98, 101
Alcoholics Anonymous, 786
alcoholism, 778
algorithms, 304–5
all-or-none law, 23
ally effect, 470–71
alpha males, 388
alpha waves, 89
alternative hypothesis, A22
altruism, 456–60
    in animals, 407–9
    bystander effect and, 457–59, 479, 529
    in children, 552, 553
    costs of helping and, 459–60
    empathy and, 553
    kin selection and, 408–9
    reciprocal, 409, 410
    selfish benefits of, 408, 460, 552
    self-sacrifice and, 407–11
    sociobiologists' view of, 409–11
Alzheimer's disease, 55
ambiguity:
    in language, 2, 330–31, 341–42
    of reversible figures, 213–14
American Sign Language (ASL), 46, 362–63, 369
amnesia, 264, 275–76, 750
    anterograde, 275
    childhood, 264–65
    retrograde, 275–76
amphetamine psychosis, 730
amphetamines, 31, 95, 101
amplitude, of sound waves, 170, 171
anal character, 677
analgesics, 86
analogical reasoning, 299, 605
analogical representations, 281–82
anal stage, 677–78
androgens, 394, 395, 501, 561, 567
anger, 444, 445–46
angiotensin, 68
animal behavior, 382–88

aggression in, 384–89
communication in, human language vs., 323, 370–73
courtship and mating in, 3–4, 396
displays in, 3–4, 383, 387, 391, 401–2, 404–5
dominance hierarchies in, 387–88
fixed-action patterns in, 382–83
grooming in, 390
inherited predispositions in, 381, 382–83
insightful, 143–47
law of effect and, 115–17
parallels between human behavior and, 388, 389
self-sacrifice and altruism in, 407–9
sociobiological approach to, 383, 397–99, 409–11
territoriality in, 388–89
animals:
    abstract concepts in, 145–46
    cognitions in, 126, 143–47
    see also specific animals
animism, 15
anomia, 53
anonymity, hostile crowds and, 529
anorexia nervosa, 79–80
A-not-B effect, 506–7
ANS, *see* autonomic nervous system
antagonists, 30–31
    in color vision, 190–91, 192–93
anterograde amnesia, 275
antidepressant drugs, 740–41, 766–67, 825
anti-diuretic hormone (ADH), 67
antipsychotic drugs, 31–32, 764–66
antisocial personalities, *see* sociopaths
anxiety:
    basic, 692
    conversions and dissociative disorders as
        responses to, 780–83
    fear vs., 130
    free-floating, 535
    person-by-situation interaction and, 647–49
    repression and, 674–75
    superego and, 550*n*
anxiety disorders, 744–50
    behavior therapy for, 825
    cognitive therapy for, 781, 825
    generalized, 747–48, 780
    obsessive-compulsive disorders, 724, 747, 779
    panic disorder, 724, 748–49, 780, 781, 825
    pathology model and, 779–80
    see also phobias
anxiety hierarchy, 777
apathetic crowds, 529–30
apes, grooming in, 390
aphagia, 73
aphasia, 45–46
    language learning and, 367
apparent movement, 206

appeasement displays, in wolves, 387
appetitive stimulus, 119
apraxia, 43
aptitude tests, 582, 593
   cutoff scores on, 588–89
   predictive validity of, 586
arousal, autonomic:
   coronary heart disease and, 755
   drug use and, 97–98
   emergency reaction and, 82–83
   emotions and, 440–41, 465
   essential hypertension and, 783–84
   optimum level of, 95–97
   personality and, 657–58
   social facilitation and, 467–69
art, 234–37
   Egyptian, 234
   Impressionist, 235–36
   modern, 236–37
   Renaissance, 234–35
artificial intelligence, 303–8, 329
   algorithms and heuristics in, 304–5
   expert systems and, 306
   limitations of, 306–8
artificial recognition systems, 218–20
asexual reproduction, 390
"as if" emotional experiences, 449
ASL (American Sign Language), 46, 362–63, 369
ASQ (Attributional Style Questionnaire), 662–63
assimilation, in cognitive development, 507, 524
association areas of brain, 41–46
   action disorders and, 43–44
   language disorders and, 45–46
   perception and action disorders and, 43–45
   studying localization in, 41–43
associations, 107
   act-outcome, 131–33, 139–40
   in conditioning, 132–33, 136, 139–40
   in sensory processes, 155–56
attachment, mother-child, 351, 368, 503, 534–44
   absence of, 539–43
   assessing of, 537–38
   biological basis of, 399–401
   Bowlby's theory of, 535–36
   contact comfort and, 534–35
   cupboard theory of, 534
   father's role and, 538–39
   importance of early experience and, 541–44
   imprinting and, 536–37
   separation or loss and, 537–38, 543–44
attention:
   disorders of, due to lesions, 44–45
   disturbance of, in schizophrenia, 726–27
   failures of conservation and, 509–10
   filter theory of, 227–28
   in perceptual selection, 225–28
attitude (in sentence meaning), 339, 340
attitude questionnaires, 420–21
attitudes (beliefs), 420–25
   authoritarian, 472–73
   behavior and, 420–21
   changes in, 422–24, 551n
   defined, 420
   stability of, 425
attraction, 461–64
   physical attractiveness and, 463–64
   proximity or familiarity and, 461–62
   similarity and, 462
attributional style, 662–63
   depression and, 742–43
Attributional Style Questionnaire (ASQ), 662–63
attribution of traits, 432–37
   actor-observer bias and, 434–35
   cognitive constructions in, 428–31
   errors in, 433–37
   impression formation and, 426
   self-perception and, 437–38
   self-serving bias and, 435–37

audition, *see* hearing
authoritarian personalities, 472–73
authoritative-reciprocal child-rearing pattern, 548–49, 551
autocratic child-rearing pattern, 548–49, 551
automatization, 296
autonomic nervous system (ANS), 36, 81
   emergency reaction of, 82–83
   parasympathetic, 66, 74, 81, 88
     see also arousal, autonomic
   sympathetic, 66, 81, 82–84, 88
   in temperature control, 64–67
availability heuristic, 313
aversion therapy, 778
aversive conditioning, 123–26
   to tastes, 137–38
aversive stimuli, 119, 122
avoidance learning, 125–26, 660
axons, 18–19, 495
   firing frequency of, 23–24
   of ganglion cells, 178
   resting vs. action potential of, 21–23
   see also neurotransmitters

baboons, dominance hierarchies of, 387
background noise, 162
backward pairing, 127
barbiturates, 97
Barnum effects, 633–34
basal ganglia, 46
base rates, representativeness heuristics and, 313
basilar membrane, 173
bats, evolution of insect ear and, 175–76
Bayley Scales of Infant Development, 651–52
Bedlam Hospital, London, 717
behavior:
   biological bases of, 15–59
   correlation between attitudes or principles and, 420–21, 555–56
   differentiation in development of, 494
   disorders of, in schizophrenia, 729
   dreams as, 6
   emotions and, 439–41, 444
   hormonal changes and, 394–95
   inheritance of, 381, 383, 613–14
   insightful, 143–47
   mechanistic theory of, 16–17
   see also animal behavior; sexual behavior; social behavior
behavioral (behavioral-cognitive) approach to personality, 628, 658–65
   control and, 661–62
   radical behaviorism and, 659–61
   self-control and, 663–64
   social learning theory and, 661–65
behaviorism, 105, 659
   radical, 659–61, 664–65
   social learning theory and, 664–65
   see also classical conditioning; instrumental conditioning
behavior therapy, 723, 775–78, 785, 825
   aversion therapy in, 778
   flooding and implosion in, 825
   systematic desensitization in, 777–78, 825
   see also cognitive-behavioral therapies
beliefs:
   cognitive consistency and, 419–20
   interpersonal nature of, 416–18
   in social learning theory, 661
   see also attitudes
belongingness effect, in classical conditioning, 136–39
between-family differences, 654–55, 656–57
binocular depth cues, 202
binomial distributions, A13n
biological constraints on learning, 136–40
bipolar cells, 178

bipolar disorder (formerly manic-depressive psychosis), 724, 736–37
   depression in, 736–37
   drug therapies for, 740–41, 766–68
   mania in, 737
   organic factors in, 740–41
   see also depression
birds:
   alarm calls of, 408
   displays by, 3, 404–5
   fixed-action patterns in, 382–83
   habituation in, 106
   imprinting in, 536–37
   mating of, 396
   parent-child attachment in, 399
   self-sacrifice and altruism in, 407–8
   songs of, critical period for, 368
   territoriality in, 388
bitter tastes, 74, 166, 167
blacks, average IQ of whites vs., 619–23
black widow spider, venom of, 31
blindness:
   color, 194
   innate emotional expressions and, 4
   language learning and, 365–67
blind obedience, 471–77
   being another person's agent and, 475
   cognitive reinterpretations and, 475–76
   Milgram's study on, 473–76
   personality structure and, 472–73
   situation and, 473–77
blind spot, 178
blocking effect, 130–31
blood pressure, essential hypertension and, 756, 783–85
bonding, 390; *see also* attachment, mother-child; love; male-female bonding
bottom-up processing:
   in perception, 219–20, 222
brain, 37–60
   abnormalities of, in schizophrenia, 730–31
   activity of, during sleep, 6–7, 89
   anatomy of, 1–2, 36–39
   blood flow in, 1–2
   development of, 496, 503, 504–5
   evolution of, 33–34
   glucoreceptors in, 70
   hierarchical functioning of, 35–36
   homosexuality and, 567–68
   language learning and, 367
   lateralization of, 48–56
   mind and, 52–53
   plasticity of function in, 54
   pleasure centers in, 99–100
   split, 48–50
   see also cerebral cortex; cerebral hemispheres; hypothalamus; midbrain
brain stem, 36
brain surgery, 1
   neural tissue transplants, 54–55
   prefrontal lobotomy, 770
brightness, 214
   color and, 186, 193
brightness contrast, 181–85
   edges exaggerated by, 182–83
   physiological account of, 183–84
Broca's area, 45, 367
bulimia, 80–81
bystander effect, 457–59, 479, 529

California Psychological Inventory (CPI), 632, 643, 654
case studies, A5
catatonic schizophrenia, 729
catecholamines, 730
CAT (Computerized Axial Tomography) scans, 41
causative verbs, 357
CCK (cholecystokinin), 70

cell bodies, 18, 28
Central Excitatory State, 26
central nervous system (CNS), 35–36; *see also*
  brain; cerebral cortex; cerebral
  hemispheres
central pattern generators (CPGs), 34
central route to persuasion, 422–23
central selective processes, 226–28
central tendency, measures of, A8–A9
cerebellum, 36
cerebral cortex, 38–46, 84
  association areas of, 44–49
  development of, 496, 522, 560
  lesions in, *see* lesions, cortical
  in nervous system hierarchy, 38–39
  projection areas of, 39–41, 164
  schizophrenia related to damage of, 730, 731
  sex differences in intellectual aptitudes and, 559
cerebral hemispheres, 36
  lateralization of, 48–56
  selective stimulation of, 50
chess playing, 295–96
child development, *see* cognitive development; de-
    velopment; language learning; psychosex-
    ual development; social development
childhood:
  homosexuality related to experiences in, 566
  obesity and feeding patterns in, 77
  socialization in, 544–50
  childhood amnesia, 264–65
child rearing:
  authoritarian personalities and, 472–73
  cultural values and, 545
  moral behavior and, 550–51
  partial-reinforcement effect in, 124
  punishment in, 548, 549–50
  socialization and, 545, 547–50
  sociopathy and, 759
  styles of, 548–49, 551
  toilet training in, 548, 677–78
  unconditional positive regard in, 697, 699
children:
  altruism in, 552, 553
  delay of gratification in, 663–64
  development of, *see* cognitive development;
    development; language learning; physical
    development; social development
  dreams of, 8–9
  egocentrism in, 510, 519–20, 561
  eidetic imagery in, 283–84
  intelligence tests for, 590–92, 593–94
  isolated, 361–62
  memory processes in, 524–26
  parents affected by, 549–50
  temperamental differences in, 537–38, 549–50,
    652–53
  wild, 360–61
  see also attachment, mother-child; infants; new-
    borns
  chimpanzees:
    access to intellectual operations in, 146–47
    insightful behavior in, 144
    language in, 370–73
    symbol manipulation in, 145–46
    threat displays in, 386–87
  cholecystokinin (CCK), 70
  choleric personality type, 642
  chromatic colors, 185–86
  chromosomes, 499–500
    sex determination and, 499–500, 501, 556
    see also genes and genetics
  chunking, 248–49, 252–53
    in cognitive development, 524, 525
    imagery in, 254
    masters vs. beginners and, 295–96
    in problem solving, 293–96
    in skill development, 294–95
  classical conditioning, 105–15, 126, 659

acquisition of conditioned response in, 110
as adaptive reaction, 117–18
in behavior therapy, 776
belongingness in, 136–37
and biological constraints on learning, 136–38
blocking in, 130–31
cognitive view of, 127–31
contiguity in, 127–28, 129, 138
contingency in, 128–29, 138
CR–UR relation in, 113
discrimination in, 112
drug effects and, 114–15
empathy in infants and, 552
in everyday life, 112
extensions of, 112
extinction in, 111, 776
of fear, 113, 660
generalization in, 111
instrumental conditioning vs., 115, 118–19
Pavlov's discovery of, 107–9
phobias and, 746
second-order conditioning in, 110
surprise in, 130–31
client-centered therapy, 782–83
closure, in perceptual grouping, 216
CNS (central nervous system), 35–36; *see also*
    brain; cerebral cortex; cerebral
    hemispheres
cocaine, 31, 95, 101
cochlea, 173
  transduction in, 173–74
cocktail-party effect, 227
coding, *see* sensory coding
cognition:
  affective disorders and, 741–43
  in animals, 126, 143–47
  disorders of, in schizophrenia, 754–55
  dreams as, 7
  emotions and, 440–42, 444–45
  hostile crowds and, 528–29
  intelligence and, 652, 654–58
  panic disorder and, 749
  panicky crowds and, 483–84
  socialization and, 547
  see also social cognition; thinking and thought
cognitive abilities, sex differences in, 559, 560
cognitive arousal theory of emotion, 440–42,
    444–45
  criticisms of, 442–43
  love and, 465
  misattribution and, 441–42
cognitive-behavioral therapies, 723, 741, 779–82,
    785, 825
  major techniques of, 779–80
  panic disorder and, 781, 825
cognitive components of intelligence, 604–5
cognitive consistency:
  attitude stability and, 425
  beliefs and, 419–20
cognitive development, 494, 504–29, 533
  accommodation and assimilation in, 507, 524
  beginnings of representational thought in,
    507–8
  causes of, 522–28
  chunking and strategies in, 524–28
  concrete operations period in, 506, 510–11,
    521, 528, 561
  from cross-cultural perspective, 522, 528–29
  dreams and, 8–9
  environment and, 502
  formal operations period in, 506, 510–11,
    528–29
  gender typing and, 563–64
  infants' native endowment and, 511–17, 522–23
  information processing in, 524–28
  maturation and, 522–23, 525
  metacognition and, 527–28
  moral reasoning and, 553–56

object permanence and, 506–8
Piaget's theory of, 505–22, 524
preoperational period in, 508–10
qualitative changes in, 505
schemas in, 507, 524
of self-concept, 437–38, 697
sensory-motor intelligence period in, 506–8
specific learning in, 523–24
stages of, 506–11, 560–64
see also language learning
cognitive dissonance, 419, 423–25, 438n
attitude change and, 423–25
cognitive learning, 126–47
classical conditioning and, 127–31
cognitive maps, 126, 143
cognitive neuropsychologists, 52
cognitive reinterpretations, blind obedience and,
    475–76
cognitive restructuring, humor and, 301–2
cognitive tests, cross-cultural differences and,
    528–29
cognitive therapy, 723, 779–82
depression and, 741, 780, 825
panic disorder and, 781, 825
cold, as skin sense, 165–66
collateral sprouts, 54
color, 214
classificatory schema for, 185–88
color blindness, 194
color circle, 187
color mixture, 188–90
additive, 189
subtractive, 188–89
color solid, 187
color vision, 185–95
antagonist phenomena in, 190–91
classifying sensations in, 185–87
complementary hues in, 190
opponent-process theory of, 191–93
physiological basis of, 191–94
receptors in, 191, 193
simultaneous contrast in, 190
common sense, 307–8
communication:
  of animals vs. human, 392–93
  displays in, 383
  facial expressions as, 444
  of motives, 401–5
  persuasive, 422–23
  pheromones in, 169–70
  see also language; language learning; sentences;
    words
companionate love, 467
compensatory-reaction hypothesis, 114–15
competencies, 661
complementary hues, 190
complex cognition in animals, 143–47
  instrumental conditioning and, 131–35
complex sentences, 338–40
complex waves, 172
component model of pattern recognition, 219
comprehension, 342–46
  function words signaling propositional bound-
    aries in, 344
  interaction of syntax and semantics in, 346
  linguistic illusions and, 344–46
  phrase order and, 343–44
compulsions, 747, 779
Computerized Axial Tomography (CAT) scans, 41
computers, *see* artificial intelligence; information
    processing
concepts:
  in abstract thought, 292
  mental maps and, 286–87
  see also abstract concepts
concordance, in twin studies, 732
concrete operations period, 506, 510–11, 521,
    528–29, 561

conditional statements, 318–20
conditioned emotional response (CER) procedure, 113
conditioned reflexes, 108–9
conditioned reinforcement, 117–18
conditioned response (CR), 115, 127
  acquisition of, 110
  defined, 109
  extinction of, 111
  law of effect and, 116–18
  relation between UR and, 113
  shaping of, 120–21
conditioned stimulus (CS), 110
  belongingness and, 136–39
  blocking of, 130–31
  contiguity and, 127–28, 129, 130
  contingency of US and, 128–29, 132–35
  defined, 109
  surprise element and, 130–31
conditioning:
  generalized anxiety disorders and, 748
  phobias and, 746
  see also classical conditioning; instrumental conditioning
cones, 178–79, 191
confidence intervals, A24–A25
confirmation bias, 310–11
conflict:
  between species, 384
  within species, 384–89
  threat displays and, 4, 386–87
  see also aggression; unconscious conflicts
conformity, 469–71
  causes of, 469–70
  majorities and minorities in, 470–71
conformity effects, 469–71
conscious experience, short-term memory and, 245–46
consciousness, 318–19
conservation, 529
  failure of, in preoperational period, 508–10
  specific learning and, 523–24
  stage concept and, 561–64
consistency, of personality traits, 643–53
  across situations, 645–46
  criterion of, 646–47
  intermittent reinforcement and, 659–61
  lack of, 643–45
  person constancy and, 651–52
  over time, 645
  as trait, 649–51
constancies, see perceptual constancies
construct validity of mental tests, 587
  of personality inventories, 633
contact comfort, in relationships, 534–35
content words, 330
context effects, 219
contiguity, in classical conditioning, 127–28, 129, 138
contingency:
  absence of, 129–30, 133–35
  in classical conditioning, 128–29, 138
  in instrumental conditioning, 132–35
  learned taste aversions and, 138–39
  response control and, 132–33
contours, subjective, 216
contrast effects:
  brightness, 181–85
  edges exaggerated by, 182–83
  physiological account of, 183–84
  simultaneous color, 190
control, 661–62
  desire for, 661–62
  self-, 663–64
control groups, A4
control systems, 62–63
conversation, principles of, 326–28
conversion disorders, 720, 780–81

convulsive treatments, 771–72
coping patterns, 693–95
  mental health and, 693–95
coronary heart disease, 754–55
corpus callosum, 48
correct negatives, in detection experiments, 161
correlation, 584–85, A14–A18
  illusory, 429–30
  interpretation and misinterpretation of, A17–A18
  positive and negative, A14–A16
  variance and, A20–A21
correlation coefficient (r), 584–85, A16–A17
correlation matrices, 601–2
counter-attitudinal advocacy, 423n
counting, by children, 521
courtship and mating rituals, 3–4, 391–92
  of dancing flies, 392
  of peacocks, 3, 4
CPGs (central pattern generators), 34
CPI (California Psychological Inventory), 632, 643, 654
creative thinking, 300–303
credibility, 422
critical periods, 369–70, 502–3
  for gender identity, 562
  for language learning, 362, 368, 503
  see also sensitive periods
critical ratios, A22, A24
cross-cultural differences:
  in child rearing, 545
  in cognitive abilities, 529
  in emotional expression, 403–4
  in mating patterns, 398
crowd behavior, 482–86
  apathy and, 529–30
  deindividuation and, 483
  hostility and, 528–30
  panic and, 4, 483–84
crystallized intelligence, 653–54
culture:
  adolescence and, 571–72
  altruism and, 410–44
  child rearing and, 545
  cognitive development and, 522, 528–29
  dreams and, 8
  emotional expressions and, 403–4
  food preferences and, 75–76
  homosexuality and, 564
  intelligence and, 610–11
  intelligence tests and, 593, 596, 612, 619–20
  labeling theory and, 790–91
  mating patterns and, 398
  personality traits and, 643–44
  personal space and, 389
  physical attractiveness and, 463–64
cupboard theory of mother-child attachment, 534
curare, 30
curiosity, 96
cuteness, 463
cutoff scores, 588–89

dancing flies, courtship rituals of, 392
data, research:
  collection of, A1, A4–A5
  description of, A2–A3
  interpretation of, A1, A17–A25
  organization of, A1, A7–A14
deafness:
  language learning and, 362–64, 365–67, 369
decay, of memory trace, 246, 262
decision making, 311–14
  availability heuristics in, 313
  framing in, 313–14
  representativeness heuristics in, 312
declarative knowledge, 276–77
deductive reasoning, 309–11, 328
  conditional statements and, 318–20

defense, against predation, 384
defense mechanisms, 635, 674–76, 677
  coping patterns and, 693–95
defense reactions, 139
deficiency needs, 696
definitional theory of meaning, 332–33, 334–35
dehumanization of victims, 476
dehydration, by osmosis, 68
deindividuation, 483
deinstitutionalization, 764–65
delay of gratification, self-control and, 663–64
delay of reinforcement, 121–22
delusions, 728, 766
demonic possession, insanity as, 716
dendrites, 18–19, 495
depressants, 97–98
depression, 737–44
  attributional style and, 662–63, 742–43
  Beck's cognitive theory of, 741–42
  cognitive therapy for, 741–42, 780, 825
  diathesis-stress conception and, 743
  drug therapies for, 766–68, 825
  electroconvulsive shock treatment for, 771–72
  learned helplessness and, 734, 742–43
  male-female ratio in, 743–44
  organic factors in, 740–41
  psychogenic factors in, 741–44
  seasonal affective disorder and, 739–40
  suicide and, 738–39
  symptoms of, 738–41
deprivation:
  language learning and, 361–62
  sensory, 504
  sleep, 91
depth cues, 202–6
  pictorial, 156, 202–4, 235
  size constancy and, 229, 231–32
depth of processing (of memories), 252–53
depth perception, 202–6
  binocular cues in, 202
  innate factors in, 205–6
  monocular cues in, 203–4
  through motion, 205
  in very young, 2–3, 206
desensitization, systematic, 777–78, 825
detection experiments, 589n
  decision process in, 162–63
  response bias in, 160–62
  signal-detection theory and, 160–63
deterioration effects, 791
development, 490–579
  as differentiation, 494
  embryonic, 494–95, 497, 501–2, 503
  as growth, 494
  maturation in, 503–5
  motor, 493–94, 497–99, 503–4
  as orderly progression, 497–99, 503–4
  personality consistency and, 646–47
  sensitive or critical periods in, 502–3
  skill acquisition and, 294–95; see also cognitive development; language learning; physical development; psychosexual development; social development
deviation:
  average, A10n
  standard (SD), 583, A11, A24
Diagnostic and Statistical Manual for Mental Disorders (DSM-IV), 721, 724
dialects, 620
diaphragm (in eyes), 178
diathesis-stress conception, 725–26
  affective disorders and, 743
  anxiety disorders and, 780
  psychophysiological disorders and, 755–56
  schizophrenia and, 733–34
  see also pathology model of mental disorder
dichotic presentation, 227
difference threshold, 158–59

differentiation, 556
  development as, 494
  sensitive periods for, 503
  of sexual structures, 501–2
direct perception, 230
discrimination, in conditioning, 112, 119
disease concept, *see* pathology model of mental
  disorder
disinhibition, 34–35, 77–78
disorganized type schizophrenia, 729
displacement (in short-term memory), 246
display rules, 444
displays, 3–4, 383, 401–2
  appeasement, 387
  evolutionary origin of, 404
  language vs., 404–5
  of sex differences, 391
  sexual, 3–4, 390–91
  threat, 4, 386–87
dispositional factors, in attribution of traits, 432–37
dissociative disorders, 750–52, 780
  underlying factors in, 751, 751*n*
dissonance theory, 419, 423–26, 438*n*
distal stimuli, 154–55
distance cues, 156
distress calls, 400
distributions, statistical, A7–A11
  binomial, A13*n*
  frequency, A7–A8
  and measures of central tendency, A8–A9
  normal, A12–A14
  skewed, A9
  symmetric, A9
  t, A24*n*
Dodo Bird verdict, in evaluation of therapy outcome, 791–92, 825
dominance hierarchies, 387–88
dominant genes, 500
dopamine, 29, 55
  rewarding effects of self-stimulation and,
  100–101
  schizophrenia and, 31, 730
Down syndrome, 367–68
dreams, 5–10, 93–95
  activation-synthesis hypothesis and, 94–95
  as behavior, 6
  as cognition, 7
  culture's effect on, 8
  and external stimulation during sleep, 6
  function of, 94–95
  human development and, 8–9
  individual differences reflected in, 10
  internal conflict expressed in, 8
  as mental experiences, 5–6
  in psychoanalytic theory, 94, 680–82
  rapid eye movements during, 6, 93
  recall of, 7, 93–94
  recent waking experiences and, 6
  social behavior and, 7–8
drive, 88
drive-reduction theory of motivation, 96
drugs, 97–98
  addiction to, 97–99, 100–101, 114
  arousal level and, 97–98
  compensatory-reaction hypothesis and, 114–15
  neurotransmitter activity and, 31
  opponent-process theory and, 99
  tolerance to, 98
drug therapies, 763–70
  evaluating effectiveness of, 768–70
  major types of, 763–70
  for mood disorders, 740–41, 766–68, 825
  for schizophrenia, 31, 730, 763–70
DSM-IV (Diagnostic and Statistical Manual for
  Mental Disorders), 721, 724
dual-center theory of hypothalamic control, 73–74
ducks, imprinting in, 536–37
duct glands, 32*n*

duodenum, satiety signals from, 70
duplex theory of vision, 179–80

eardrums, 173
ears:
  anatomy of, 173–74
  evolution and, 175–76
  see also hearing
ECT (electroconvulsive shock treatment), 771–72
edges, contrast effects and, 182–83
EEGs, *see* electroencephalograms
effectors, 18
efferent nerves, 18
eggs, fertilized (zygotes), 390, 494, 500
ego, 673, 697
egocentrism, 510, 519–20, 561
ego psychology, 693–95, 775
Egyptian art, 234
eidetic imagery, 283–84
elaborative rehearsal, 256–57, 264
Electra complex, 679–80
electrical potentials, resting and action, 21–23, 28
electroconvulsive shock treatment (ECT), 771–72
electroencephalograms (EEGs), 7, 89
  of sociopaths, 758–59
embarrassment, 431
embryos and fetuses, 406, 494–95, 496
  development of, 494–95, 497, 501–2, 503
  differentiation of, 494–95, 501–2
  growth of, 494
  homosexuality and hormonal effects in, 567
  physical environment of, 501–2
  sensitive periods for, 503
emergency reaction, 82–83, 783–84
  central controls in, 84
  description of, 82–83
  habituation and, 106–7
  negative effects of, 84–85
emotions:
  in adolescence, 572
  in behavioral approach to personality, 659
  classical conditioning and, 113
  cognitive arousal theory of, 440–41, 444–45,
  465
  complex, 445–47
  defusing of, as therapeutic goal, 785
  disorders of, in schizophrenia, 729
  dissonance reduction and, 424
  expression of, 402–4
  facial expression and, 443–44
  fundamental, 443–45, 448
  insight into, as therapeutic goal, 774, 779
  James-Lange theory of, 439–41, 443
  love, 464–67
  pity, anger, and guilt, 445–46
  prefrontal lobotomy and, 770
  regret, 446–47
  subjective experience of, 439–49
  theater and, 448–49
empathy, 552–53, 665
  in humanistic psychology, 699
empiricism:
  cognitive development and, 511, 523–24, 560
  perception and, 205, 229–30
  sensory experience and, 154–57
  thinking and, 291, 292
  see also nativism
encoding phase of remembering, 245–55
  active memory and, 249–50
  childhood amnesia and, 264–65
  depth of processing in, 252–53
  mnemonics in, 253–54
  organization in, 248–49, 252–53
  specificity in, 255–56
  stage theory and, 245–49
encoding strategies, in social learning theory, 661
endocrine system, 32
endorphins, 85–87

  exercise and, 35, 87
  pain and, 85–87
  placebos and, 87
environment:
  assimilation-accommodation interaction with,
  507, 524
  after birth, 502–3
  before birth, 501–2
  diathesis-stress conception and, 725–26
  empiricist approach to learning and, 523–24
  enriched, 618
  heredity vs., as factor in intelligence, 611–23,
  656
  impoverished, 617–18
  interaction between heredity and, 500–505,
  613, 614, 654–57
  maturation and, 503–5
  personality and, 654–57
  schizophrenia and, 733–35
  see also culture
epilepsy, 48–49
epinephrine (adrenaline), 81–82
equipotentiality principle, 136–40
escape learning, 125
escape reaction, *see* emergency reaction
essential hypertension, 756, 783–85
estrogen, 393–94
estrus, 394, 395
ethology, 382, 412; *see also* animal behavior
evolution:
  of courtship rituals, 404
  homosexuality and, 568–69
  law of effect and, 115, 117–18
  mating systems and, 381, 395–99
  natural selection in, 380–81, 584
  origin of displays and, 404
  parent-child attachment and, 399, 400
  predispositions to behavior in, 381
  self-sacrifice or altruism and, 407–8
  variability within species and, 584
excitation, 25–26
excitation transfer effects, 442
exercise, endorphins and, 35, 87
existential therapy, 783–84
experimental extinction, 111
experimental groups, A4
experiments, A4
  variance and, A19–A20
expertise, chunking and, 295–96
expert systems, 306
expressive aphasia, 45
expressive movements, 401–2; *see also* displays
extension reflexes, 24
extensor muscles, 26
externality hypothesis, obesity and, 77–78
extinction, 111
  of avoidance responses, 126, 660
  partial reinforcement and, 123–24, 660
  in psychotherapy, 777
extrapyramidal system, 46
extroversion, 640–42, 650*n*, 653
  arousal system and, 657
  heritability of, 653
eye movements:
  in perceptual selection, 225
  rapid, in REM sleep, 6, 7, 90, 91–92, 740
eyes:
  binocular depth cues and, 202
  color of, heredity and, 500
  see also retinas; vision
eyewitness testimony, 269–71
face recognition, difficulty in, 44
facial expression:
  as communication, 444
  emotions and, 443–44
factor analysis, 601
  group-factor theories and, 602
  in taxonomy of personality traits, 643–53

false accepts and rejects, in aptitude tests, 588–89
false alarms, in detection experiments, 161
familiarity, attraction and, 461–62
family:
    extended, 575
    personality and differences within, 654–55
    schizophrenia and, 734–35
    see also attachment, mother-child; child rearing;
        children; fathers; infants; mothers; new-
        borns; parents
family resemblance structure, 333–34
family therapy, 787–88
fat cells, obesity and, 77
fathers:
    homosexual sons and, 566
    infants' relation to, 538–39
fat metabolism, 73–74
fear:
    anxiety vs., 130
    conditioned, 112, 125–26, 660
    emergency reaction and, 81–83
    panic disorder and, 748–49, 781
    panicky crowds and, 482, 483–84
    pheromones as signal of, 170
    of unknown and unfamiliar, 535–36
    unrealistic, behavior therapy for, 825
    see also phobias
featural approach to word meaning, 333
feature analysis, Pandemonium model and, 217–20
feature detectors, 194–96
Fechner's law, 159–60
feedback systems, 62–63
feeding, 69–80, 101
    anorexia nervosa or bulimia and, 79–80
    dual-center theory of, 73–74
    external signals for, 71–72
    fixed-action patterns and, 382–83
    food selection in, 74–76
    hypothalamic control centers in, 72–74
    internal signals for, 70–71
    neophobia and, 75
    obesity and, 76–79
fetuses, *see* embryos and fetuses
fighting:
    ritualized, 387
    see also aggression
figure-ground segregation, 213–14
filter theory of attention, 227–28
fixation (in psychoanalytic theory), 677, 717
fixation (mental set), 297–98
fixation point, 227
fixed-action patterns, 382–83
fixed-interval (FI) schedules of reinforcement, 123
fixed-ratio (FR) schedules of reinforcement,
    122–23
flashbulb memories, 266–67
flexion reflexes, 24
flexor muscles, 26
flooding, 825
fluid intelligence, 653–54
food intake, *see* feeding
forced compliance, 423–25, 438n, 551n
forebrain, 36, 37–38
forgetting, 262–67
    change of retrieval cues and, 264–65
    decay in, 246, 262
    interference and, 263–64
    memories immune to, 265–67
    of recent memories, 246
    retention interval and, 262, 264
forgetting curves, 262
formal operations period, 506, 510–11, 528–29
form perception, 51, 208–11
    elements of form and, 208–11
    information processing approach to, 210–11
    perceptual segregation in, 212–22
forward pairing, 127
fovea, 178

framing, 313–14
    changing losses to gains by, 314
fraternal twins, 615
free association, 773
free-floating anxiety, 535
free-floating primitives, 211
free recall, 247
frequency, of sound waves, 170–72, 174–75
frequency distributions, 162–63, 582–83, A8–A11
    central tendency of, A8–A9
    graphic representation of, A7–A8
    variability of, 582–83, A9–A11
frontal lobes, 38, 40, 45, 770
fugue states, 750
functional fixedness, 298
function words, 48, 330, 343
    boundaries between propositions signaled by,
        344
    language learning and, 352, 355, 356
fundamental attribution error, 433–34

galvanic skin response (GSR), 83
gamma-amino-butyric acid (GABA), 29
ganglia, 33
ganglion cells, 178
gaping response, in young birds, 400
gender, sex vs., 556–57n
gender constancy, 564
gender identity, 556, 564
    critical period for, 562
    development of, 562–65
    sex reassignment and, 560–62
gender roles, 557–58
    constitutional factors and, 557–58
    social factors and, 560–62
    stereotypes of, 557–58
gender typing, theories of, 562–64
    cognitive developmental, 563–64
    psychoanalytic, 562–63
    social learning, 563
general intelligence (*g*-factor), 601–2
generalization, in conditioning, 111, 112, 119–20
generalization decrement, 111
generalization gradient, 111
generalized anxiety disorders, 747–48, 780
general paresis, 718
genes and genetics:
    affective disorders and, 740
    anxiety disorders and, 778, 779–80
    behavior patterns and, 381, 383, 613–14
    dominant and recessive, 500
    environment vs., as factor in intelligence,
        611–23, 656
    homosexuality and, 566–67
    interaction between environment and, 500–505,
        613, 614, 654–57
    maturation and, 503–5
    personality and, 653–54
    phenotypes and genotypes in, 500, 613
    psychophysiological disorders and, 756
    of racial-ethnic groups, 620
    schizophrenia and, 732–33
    self-sacrifice or altruism and, 407–8, 409–11
    sex determination and, 499–500, 501–2, 556
    sex differences and, 499–500, 501–2, 556
    sexual reproduction and, 390–91
    sociopathy and, 759
    transmission mechanism in, 499–500, 613–14
genital stage, 679
genotypes, 500, 613
geons, 220–21
Gestalt psychology, 214
gestural languages, 363–64
    American Sign Language (ASL), 46, 362–63,
        369
g-factor (general intelligence), 601–2
glands, 66
glucoreceptors, 70

glucose, 70, 71, 74
glycogen, 71
good continuation, in perceptual grouping,
    215–16
graded task assignments, 782
Graduate Record Examination (GRE), 593
grammar:
    language learning and, 356n
    prescriptive rules of, 325–26
    see also syntax
grasping, in human infants, 494, 496–97
grooming, in monkeys and apes, 390
ground-figure segregation, 213–14
group-factor theories of intelligence, 602
grouping factors, in perception, 214–17
    maximum likelihood principle and, 216–17
group therapy, 786–87
growth, 494–95
    after birth, 495–97
    before birth, 495
    slow rate of, in humans, 496
GSR (galvanic skin response), 83
guilt, 425, 445–46, 551

habituation, in learning, 106–7
habituation procedure, 232, 512–13
hair cells, 173
hallucinations, 766
    in schizophrenia, 728–29
hearing, 157, 170–75, 185
    gathering of proximal stimulus in, 173–74
    in infants, 497
    loudness and, 171
    pitch and, 171–72, 174
    projection area for, 41
    selective listening and, 227
    sound as stimulus for, 170–72
heart, volume receptors in, 68
heart disease, 754–55
hebephrenia, 729
helplessness, learned, *see* learned helplessness
heredity, *see* genes and genetics
heritability ratio (*H*), 618–19
hermaphrodites, 561
heroin, 97
herring gulls, releasing stimuli in, 382–83
heterosexuality, 564
heuristics, 305, 328, 423
    availability, 313
    framing, 313
    representativeness, 312
    simulation, 447
hibernation, 65
hierarchical organization:
    in nervous system, 34, 36
    in thinking, 46–47, 293–96
hierarchy:
    dominance, 387–88
    of needs, 696–97
higher-order patterns of stimulation, 230
higher-order relationships, 146
hindbrain, 36
hippocampus, 41
histograms, A8–A9
hits, in detection experiments, 161
homeostasis, 64–65
    feeding and, 69–72, 76
    temperature control and, 64–66
    water supply and, 67–68
homogamy, 462
homosexuality, 564–69
    androgen injections and, 395, 567
    brain differences and, 567–68
    causes of, 565–69
    evolution and, 568–69
    incidence of, 564
    among men vs. women, 398–401
hopelessness, depression and, 743

hormones:
  adrenaline (epinephrine), 81–82
  aggressiveness and, 388, 559
  androgens, 394, 395, 501, 561, 567
  animal sexuality and, 393–94
  behavior affected by, 394–95
  embryonic development and, 501–2
  endocrine system and, 32
  estrogen, 393–94
  gender identity and, 561–62
  homosexuality and, 395, 567
  human sexuality and, 395
hospitals, see mental hospitals
hostile crowds, 528–30
hostility, of Type A's, 755
hues, 185–86, 192
  complementary, 190
humanistic approach to personality, 629, 695–702
  empirical and conceptual difficulties of, 699–700
  evaluation of, 699–702
  growth in, 698–99, 701, 782–83
  human motivation as viewed in, 696
  as protest movement, 700–702
  self-actualization in, 695, 696–99, 783
humanistic therapies, 699, 775–76, 782–86
humor, restructuring and, 301–2
hunger, 69–80
hyperphagia, 73
hypertension, essential, 783–85
hypnosis:
  hysteria and, 671–72
  memories recalled through, 271–72
hypothalamus, 38, 68, 84, 384, 562, 567
  feeding control and, 70, 72–73
  lateral and ventromedial regions of, 73
  in limbic system, 37–38
  sexual behavior and, 393, 394
  temperature control and, 66–67
hypotheses, in inductive reasoning, 310–11
hypothesis testing, A21–A26
  confidence intervals in, A24–A25
  conservative nature of, A26
  means and, A22–A25
  probabilistic nature of, A26
  single scores and, A21–A22
hysteria, 719, 780–81
  hypnosis and, 671–72

id, 673
ideas of reference, 728
identical twins, 615
identification, gender typing and, 562–63, 564
identity crisis of adolescence, 573
illusions, linguistic, 344–46
illusions, perceptual:
  errors of thought and, 329
  of movement, 206
illusory conjunctions, 211
illusory correlation, 429–30
imagery:
  eidetic, 283–84
  electrically triggered, 1–2
  mental, thought as, 291, 292–93
  mnemonics through, 253–54
  pictures vs., 284–85
  spatial problem solving and, 285–86
image scanning, 284
imitation:
  in gender typing, 563
  modeling and, 546
  in socialization, 546–47
immune system, learned helplessness and, 135
implicit memory, 259–61, 276–77
implicit theories of personality, 428
implosion therapy, 825
impossible figures, 224
Impressionism, 235–36

impression management, 430–31, 437
impressions of others, 426–27
  as cognitive constructions, 428–31
  first, 427–28
  forming of, 426–27
  as patterns, 426–27
imprinting, 536–37
incremental validity, 638–39
incubation, in creative thinking, 301
induced movement, 207
inductive reasoning, 310–11, 328
  probability estimates and, 312–13
infants:
  care of, mating systems and, 399–401
  dependency of, 496
  depth perception in, 2–3, 205, 206
  empathy in, 552–53
  encoding of memory in, 265
  fear of unknown and unfamiliar in, 535–36
  gender-role stereotypes and, 557
  grasping movements of, 494, 496–97
  intelligence in, 651–52
  intersensory relations in, 205, 206
  language learning in, 349–51, 498–99
  motor development in, 497–98, 503–4
  native endowment of, 496–97, 511–17, 522–23
  nervous system growth in, 495–96
  number concepts in, 514–16
  object permanence notion in, 506–7, 514
  perceptual world of, 2–3, 205, 206, 232, 511–16
  rate of growth of, 496
  reared in institutions, 542–43
  response capacities of, 496–97
  response control in, 132–33, 661–62
  sensory capacities of, 169, 497
  sensory-motor intelligence in, 506–8
  size and shape constancy in, 232
  smiling by, 4, 401
  social cognition in, 515–16
  temperamental differences in, 549–50, 652–53
  vocalization by, 349
  see also attachment, mother-child; children; newborns
inferential statistics, A18–A27
  implications of, A26–A27
information processing:
  cognitive development and, 524–25
  intelligence and, 593, 654–58
  memory and, 304, 524–25, 654–55
  thinking and, 304
  see also artificial intelligence
inhibition, of neuron excitation, 26–28
initiation rites, 571–72
inner ear, 165, 173
insanity, see psychopathology
insight:
  humor and, 301–2
  in problem solving, 300–303
  as therapeutic goal, 774, 779, 789
insightful behavior, 143–47
  abstract concepts in animals and, 145–46
  accessing what one knows and, 146–47
institutions:
  humans reared in, 542–44
  see also mental hospitals
instrumental (operant) conditioning, 115–26
  act-outcome associations in, 131–33, 139–40
  aversive stimuli in, 123–26
  classical conditioning vs., 115, 118–19
  cognitive view of, 131–35
  conditioned reinforcement in, 121
  contingency in, 132–35
  delay of reinforcement in, 121–22
  generalization and discrimination in, 119–20
  law of effect and, 115–17
  partial-reinforcement effect in, 123–24, 660
  schedules of reinforcement in, 122–24

  shaping of response in, 120–21
  Skinner box in, 118
intelligence, 589–624
  accessing what one knows in, 146–47
  age and, 591–92, 651–54
  childhood deprivation and, 596
  cognitive processes and, 654–58
  definition of, 589
  environmental factors and, 617–18, 621–23, 656
  fluid vs. crystallized, 653–54
  as general cognitive capacity, 590–91
  general (g-factor), 601–2
  genetic factors and, 611–23
  group-factor theories of, 602
  in infants, 651–52
  information-processing approach to, 642, 654–58
  metacognition and, 527
  multiple intelligences and, 608–10, 649–51
  practical, 608
  psychometric approach to, 599–602
  strategies and, 606–7
  and structure of mental abilities, 600–601
  see also artificial intelligence
intelligence quotient (IQ), 591–92
  constancy of, 614–15
  environmental vs. genetic factors in, 611–23
  group differences in, 619–23
  of immigrant groups, 611–12
intelligence tests, 582, 589–96
  for adults, 592–93
  age and, 591–92, 651–54
  for children, 590–92, 593
  cognitive processes and, 590, 654–58
  cultural factors and, 593, 596, 611–12, 619–20
  group, 593
  mental abilities measured by, 600–601
  mental retardation and, 590, 594–96
  nature-nurture controversy and, 611–23
  personality tests vs., 630, 632
  political issues and, 611–12
  of verbal vs. spatial aptitude, 51
interaction, person-by-situation, 647–49
interference, in forgetting, 263–64
internalization of moral values, 550–51
interneurons, 18, 20
interpersonal learning, in therapy, 785
interposition, 203
interval scales, A2–A3
interval schedules of reinforcement, 123
intestines, satiety signals from, 70–71
introversion, 640–42
  arousal system and, 657
ions, 23
IQ, see intelligence quotient
iris, 178
isolation, language learning and, 361–62

James-Lange theory of emotions, 439–41, 443
justification of effort, 423, 424, 438n
just-noticeable difference (j.n.d.), 158–59

Kaufman Assessment Battery for Children (K-ABC), 593, 596
kidneys, 67
kinesthesis, 165
kinship, self-sacrifice and, 408–11
knowledge:
  empiricist-nativist debate on origins of, 153–57
  intellectual growth as acquisition of, 526
  procedural vs. declarative, 276–77
  spatial, 286–87
  utilized in remembering, 267–71

labeling theory, mental disorder and, 789–91
  cross-cultural comparisons and, 790–91

language, 51, 323–75
  ambiguity in, 2, 330–31, 341–42
  in chimpanzees, 370–73
  cognitive interdependence and, 416
  comprehension of, 342–46
  creativity of, 323–25
  descriptive vs. prescriptive rules of, 325
  dialects of, 620
  disorders of, due to lesions, 45–46
  displays vs., 404–5
  gestural, 363–64
  as human capacity, 323
  as interpersonal human endeavor, 326–28
  lateralization of brain and, 49–50
  linguistic hierarchy and meaning in, 331–42
  meaningfulness of, 326
  metacognition and, 527
  morphemes in, 330
  organizing words into sentences in, 335–42
  paraphrases and opposites in, 340–41
  phonemes in, 328–29, 350
  referential nature of, 326, 331–32
  sign, 362–64, 369
  structure of, 325–26, 328–31; see also communication; meaning; phrases; propositions; sentences; words
language learning, without a model, 363–64
language learning, 347–73
  as acquisition of skill, 348
  blindness and, 365–67
  with changed endowments, 367–73
  in changed environments, 360–67
  critical periods and, 362, 368–70, 503
  deafness and, 362–64, 365–67, 369
  early social deprivation and, 361–62
  environments and, 502
  among isolated children, 361–62
  later stages of, 357–60
  Motherese in, 350–51
  in nonhumans, 370–73
  one-word stage in, 352–53
  orderly progression in, 498–99
  perceptual and conceptual biases in, 358–59
  phoneme discrimination in, 350
  propositional meaning and, 353–54
  of second language, 368–69
  and social origins of speech, 349
  sound cues in, 347–48
  species-specific predisposition for, 365
  syntax in, 357
  two-word (telegraphic) stage in, 355–56
  among wild children, 360–61
  word meanings in, 352–54, 357–60, 364–65
latency period, 679
latent learning, 132
lateral inhibition, in retina, 184–85
lateralization, 48–56
  in normal subjects, 50
  in split-brain patients, 48–50
  and verbal vs. spatial modes of thought, 51
law of effect, 115–17
  aversive reinforcement and, 125
  delay of reinforcement and, 121–22
  evolutionary theory and, 115–18
leadership, 479–82
learned helplessness, 133–35
  biological consequences of, 135
  depression and, 135, 742–43
  in dogs, 133–34
learned taste aversions, 137–38
learning, 105–49
  avoidance, 125–26, 660
  biological constraints on, 136–40
  in different species, 141–42
  habituation and, 106–7
  interpersonal, in therapy, 785
  latent, 132
  to learn, in monkeys, 145–46

skill development and, 294–95
  social, 546–47; see also classical conditioning; cognitive development; cognitive learning; instrumental conditioning; language learning; social development; social learning theory
learning model of psychopathology, 723; see also behavior therapy
left-handers, 48
left hemisphere of brain, 40, 49–50
  lateralization and, 48–51
lens, 178
lesions, cortical, 649
  in association areas, 41–46
  determining location of, 41–42
lesions, hypothalamic, 73–74
lexical identification task, 604
lexicon, mental, 333
lie detection, 83
  hypothesis testing and, A21–A22
light, as stimulus, 177
liking, see attraction
limbic system, 37–38, 84
linear perspective, 156, 203
line of best fit, 584, A15
listening, selective, 227
literature, psychoanalysis and, 683–84
lithium, 767liver, receptors in, 71
lobes of brain, 37–38, 41
lobotomy, prefrontal, 770
loci, method of, 253–54
lock-and-key model of synaptic transmission, 30
locomotion, development of, 503–4
logic:
  deductive reasoning and, 309–11
  inductive reasoning and, 310–11
  of perception, 223–24
longitudinal studies:
  on intelligence, 645–46
  on personality, 645–46, 693–94
long-term memory:
  active memory and, 249–55
  capacity of, 246
  conscious experience and, 245–46
  forgetting from, 262–67
  habituation and, 107
  impairments in, 274–76
  retrieval from, 255–61, 654–55
  stage theory and, 245–49
  transfer from short-term memory into, 246–49
looming, infants' response to, 206
loudness, wave amplitude and, 171
love, 464–67
  biological basis of, 390–99
  companionate, 467
  male-female, 390–99
  neurotic search for, 692
  parent-child, 399–401, 534–35
  romantic, 464–67; see also male-female bonding; reproduction; sexual behavior
lynchings, in American South, 528–30

Mach bands, 182, 183
madness, see psychopathology
magic number, 246
Magnetic Resonance Imaging (MRI), 42–43
maintenance rehearsal, 250–51
majorities, conformity and, 470–71
male-female bonding, 390–99
  aggression and, 386–87
  dominance hierarchies and, 388
  evolution and, 381, 395–99
  physical attractiveness and, 463
  proximity and, 461–62
  similarity and, 462
  see also reproduction; sexual behavior
mammals:
  mating of, 396

parent-child attachment in, 399, 400–401
  rate of growth of, 496
  temperature regulation in, 64–67
mania, 737
  treatment of, 766–68
manic-depressive psychosis, see bipolar disorder
manual systems of language, 363–64
  American Sign Language (ASL), 46, 362–63, 369
MAO (monoamine oxidase) inhibitors, 766–67
marital therapy, 787–88
matching, for physical attractiveness, 463
matching to sample, 145–46
mating, see male-female bonding; reproduction; sexual behavior
mating patterns, human, 396–97
maturation:
  cognitive development and, 522–23, 524–25
  environment and, 503–5
  memory capacity and, 524–25
  practice and, 503–4
maximum likelihood principle, 216–17
mean, statistical (M), 583, A8–A9, A11–A12
  defined, A8
  standard error of, A24–A25
  testing hypotheses about, A22–A26
meaning, 331–35
  ambiguity in, 341–42
  children deprived access to, 364–65
  definitional theory of, 332–33, 334–35
  in one-word stage, 352–54
  paraphrases or opposites and, 340–41
  phrase structure and illusion of, 337–38
  prototype theory of, 333–34
  as reference, 331–32
  of sentences, 335–42
  underlying structure and, 339–40
  of words, 331–35, 352–54, 357–60, 364–65
medial forebrain bundle (MFB), 100
median, statistical, A8
medical model of psychopathology, 722; see also drug therapies; somatic therapies
medulla, 36
melancholic personality type, 642
memory, without awareness, 317–18
memory, 93–94, 243–79, 356
  active, 249–55, 264–66
  age-related declines in, 653
  disordered, 274–76
  encoding of, 245–55
  flashbulb, 266–67
  imagery as aid to, 253–54
  implicit, 259–61, 276–77
  implict retrieval effect, 259–61
  information-processing approach to, 304, 524–25, 654–55
  intelligence-test performance and, 654–55
  limits of, 271–73
  maturation and, 524–25
  metacognition and, 527
  repressed memory controversy and, 272–73
  rewriting of, 271
  spatial, in animals, 143
  stage theory of, 245–49
  tape recorder theory of, 272
  unconscious, recovery of, 773–74
  utilization of prior knowledge in, 267–71
  see also encoding phase of remembering; forgetting; long-term memory; remembering; short-term memory
memory distortions, 267–71
  eyewitness testimony and, 268–69
  mechanisms leading to, 270–71
  schemas and scripts in, 268–69
memory retrieval, 255–61
  from active memory, 264–66
  cues in, 255–56
  elaborative rehearsal and, 256–57

encoding specificity and, 255–56
by hypnosis, 271–72
implicit memory and, 259–61
from long-term memory, 255–61, 654–55
memory search in, 257–59
schema-based distortions and, 270–71
memory search, 257–59
memory span, 246–48, 524–25
memory traces:
  consolidation of, 275–76
  decay of, 246, 262
menstrual cycle, 394, 395
  synchrony in, 170
mental age (MA), 591
mental disorders, see psychopathology
mental growth, see cognitive development
mental hospitals, 717–18, 788–89
  deinstitutionalization policies and, 764–65
mental maps, 285–87
  conceptual, 286–87
  picturelike, 286
mental retardation:
  causes of, 596
  cognitive strategies and, 606–7
  diagnosis and classification of, 590, 594–96
  language learning and, 367–68
  phenylketonuria, 614
mental rotation, in visual memory, 284–85
mental set, 427
  incubation effects and, 301
  in problem solving, 297–98
mental tests, 582–89
  achievement, 582
  aptitude, 582, 586–87, 593
  reliability of, 586
  standardization of, 587
  statistical methodology for, 582–85
  uses of, 588–89
  validity of, 586–87
  see also intelligence tests; personality tests; test
    scores
meta-analysis, 790–91, 825
metabolism, 73–74
  obesity and, 76–77
metacognition, 527–28
microelectrodes, 20
midbrain, 36, 37
middle ear, 173
mid-life transition, 573–74
mind, brain and, 52–53
minimal sufficiency principle, 551
Minnesota Multiphasic Personality Inventory
  (MMPI), 630–32, 643, 685
minorities:
  change effected by, 470–71
  prejudice against, 473
"misbehavior" of organisms, 140
misses, in detection experiments, 161
MMPI (Minnesota Multiphasic Personality Inventory), 630–32, 643, 685
mnemonics, 253–55
  through verbal organization, 253
  through visual imagery, 253–54
mobbing, as defense behavior, 384
mode, statistical, A8
modeling, 546, 547
  in therapy, 782
  see also imitation
modern art, 236–37
monkeys:
  curiosity of, 96
  grooming in, 390
  learning to learn in, 145–46
  motherless, 541–42, 543
monoamine oxidase (MAO) inhibitors, 766–67
monocular depth cues, 203–4
monogamy, 396, 398

mood disorders (formerly called affective disorders), 736–44
  biochemical hypotheses about, 740–41
  diathesis-stress conception and, 743
  drug therapies for, 740–41, 766–68, 825
  genetic components of, 740
  mania, 736–44, 766–68
  organic factors in, 740–41
  psychogenic factors in, 741–44
  seasonal affective disorder, 739–40
  symptom pattern in, 736–44
  see also depression
mood shifts, opponent-process theory and, 99
moral development, 551–56
moral order:
  blind obedience and, 475–76
  emotions and, 445–46
moral reasoning, 553–56
  Kohlberg's stages of, 553–54
  in men and women, 554–55
  moral conduct and, 555–56
morphemes, 330
morphine, 97
Motherese, 350–51
mothers:
  of homosexuals, 566, 567
  language learning and, 350–51, 358
  see also attachment, mother-child; child rearing;
    parents
motion parallax, 205
motivation, 61–103
  as direction, 61–62
  disorders of, in schizophrenia, 729
  drive-reduction theory of, 96
  feedback systems and, 62–63
  humanists' positive view of, 696, 739
  opponent-process theory of, 99
  and optimum level of arousal or stimulation,
    96–97
  and pleasure centers in brain, 99–100
  in problem solving, 298
  in self-serving attributional bias, 435–36
motives, communication of, 401–5
motor development, 493–94
  in infants, 497–98, 503–4
  maturation and, 503–4
  orderly progression of, 497–98, 503–4
  practice in, 503–4
  specific vs. non-specific experience and, 504–5
motor homunculus, 40
motor neurons, 19
motor pathways of nervous system, 46–47
motor projection areas, 39–41
movement:
  depth perception and, 205
  induced, 207
  perception of, 206–8
  stroboscopic, 206, 223
MRI (Magnetic Resonance Imgaging), 42–43
multiple personality, 750–51, 783
muscles, 19
  kinesthesis and, 165
  neurotransmitters and, 29–30
  reciprocal inhibition and, 26
  reflexes and, 17
  smooth, 66
muscular relaxation, in systematic desensitization,
  777–78
MYCIN, 306
myelin sheath, 19
myths, 682–83

naloxone, 87
nativism:
  cognitive development and, 522–23
  perception and, 230, 231–32
  sensory processes and, 154, 156–57
  see also empiricism

natural selection, 380–81, 404
  variability within species and, 584
  see also evolution
needs (in Maslow's theory):
  deficiency, 696
  hierarchy of, 696–97
negative afterimages, 190
negative feedback systems, 63
negative rule of if-then inference, 318–20
neo-Freudians, 775
neophobia, about food, 75–76
nerve impulses, 18, 19–23
  all-or-none law and, 23
  frequency of, 23–24, 174–75
  pitch perception and, 174
  see also neurons
nervous system, 15, 16–32, 33–57
  basic functions of, 18
  central vs. peripheral, 35–36
  endocrine system vs., 32
  evolution of, 33–34
  growth of, 495–96
  hierarchical organization of, 34, 36
  main structures of, 36–41
  motor systems of, 46–47
  negative feedback systems in, 63
  see also autonomic nervous system; brain; cere-
    bral cortex; cerebral hemispheres
neurons (nerve cells), 18–32, 495–96, 505
  chemical responsiveness of, 30
  damage to, 53–54
  electrical activity of, 19–23
  firing of, see nerve impulses
  interactions among, 24–32
  presynaptic vs. postsynaptic, 27–28
  sensory quality and, 164
  sodium pump and, 22–23
  stimulus intensity and, 23
  structure of, 18–19
  synaptic gaps between, 20, 24–25, 27–31
  temporal and spatial summation effects of,
    25–26
  types of, 19–20
neurosis, 724, 779
neuroticism, 640–42, 653
  heritability of, 653
neurotransmitters, 29–32
  affective disorders and, 740–41
  endorphins, 85–86
  hormones vs., 32
  poisons or drugs and, 30–31
  schizophrenia and, 730–31
  sensation seeking and, 657–58
  in transmission process, 27–29
newborns:
  empathy in, 552
  sensory-motor schemas of, 507
  vocalization by, 349
  see also attachment, mother-child; children;
    infants
nodes of Ranvier, 19
nondirective techniques, 783
norepinephrine (NE), 29, 32
  amphetamines or cocaine use and, 31, 98
  sensation seeking and, 657–58
normal curve, 583, A12–A13
noun phrases, 336
nucleus accumbens, 100
null hypothesis, A22, A25, A27
number, conservation of, 509–10, 561–64
numerical reasoning, 518–19
obedience, see blind obedience
obesity, 76–79
  behavioral factors in, 77–78
  bodily factors in, 76–77
  treatment of, 78–79
object permanence and, 506–7, 514
  occluded objects and, 512–14

objects, perception of, 511–13
built-in basis for, 513–16
observational learning, 546
obsessive-compulsive disorders, 724, 747, 779
occipital lobes, 38, 41
occluded objects, perception of, 512–14
Oedipal conflict, 572, 678–80
gender typing and, 562–63
homosexuality and, 566
old age, transition into, 575
olfaction, *see* smell, sense of
olfactory epithelium, 168
one-word stage, in language learning, 352
propositional meaning in, 353–54
word meaning in, 352–53
operant conditioning, *see* instrumental
conditioning
operants, 118
opiates, 97, 100–101
opponent-process theory:
color vision and, 191–93
motivation and, 99
optic flow, 205
optic nerve, 178
oral character, 677
oral stage, 678
orgasm, 96
orientation, 214, 218
perceptual selection by, 225–26
oscilloscope, 20
osmoreceptors, 68–69
osmosis, 68
ossicles, 173
ova, 390, 394
oval windows (in ears), 173, 174
ovaries, 394
overweight, 78; *see also* obesity

pain:
endorphins and, 85–87
pleasure vs., 99
as skin sensation, 165–66
Pandemonium model, 217–20
panic disorder, 724, 748–49, 780
cognitive therapy for, 781, 825
panicky crowds, 4, 483–84
prisoner's dilemma and, 485–86
parallel distributed processing, 290–92
parallel search, in memory retrieval, 264–66
paranoid schizophrenia, 728
paraphrases, 340–41
parasympathetic system, 66, 74, 81, 88
parents:
children's effects on, 549–50
gender typing and, 564
homosexuals' relations with, 566
language learning and, 350–51, 358
see also attachment, mother-child; child rearing;
family; fathers; mothers
parietal lobes, 38, 41
Parkinson's disease, 31, 55*n*
partial reinforcement, 122–24
persistence of characteristic behavior patterns
and, 660
passive sentences, 337, 343, 346
past tense, language learning and, 357
pathology model of mental disorder, 722
anxiety disorders and, 779–80
classification of mental disorders in, 723–24,
756–57
diathesis-stress conception in, 725–26
learning model and, 723
medical model and, 722
psychoanalytic model and, 722
schizophrenia and, 735–36
sociological critique of, 788–95
somatogenic-psychogenic distinction and,
718–19

subcategories of, 722
pattern recognition, 217–22
bidirectional activation in, 220–21
as bottom-up vs. top-down process, 219
component model of, 219
Pandemonium model of, 217–19
payoff matrices, 161, 484–85, 588–89
peacocks, courtship and mating rituals of, 3, 4
peak experiences, 698, 699
peptic ulcers, 756, 783
percentile ranks, 592, A11, A13
perception, 201–39
of depth, 202–6
direct, 230
disorders of, due to lesions, 44–45
empiricist-nativist debate and, 229–30
of form, 51, 208–11
illusions in, 206, 329
in infants, 2–3, 206, 232, 511–16
and interpersonal nature of reality, 416–17
logic of, 223–24
metacognition in, 527
of movement, 206–8
of objects, 511–13
pattern recognition and, 217–22
in Piaget's theory, 505–7, 511–16
problem-solving approach to, 221–24
of reality, 228–33
and representation of reality in art, 234–37
selective attention in, 225–28
visual segregation in, 212–22
see also social perception
perceptual constancies, 229–33
of size and shape, 229–33
perceptual organization, laws of, 214–16
perceptual parsing, *see* visual segregation
perceptual problem solving, 222–24
hypotheses in, 222
impossible figures and, 224–25
logic in, 223–24
perceptual selection, 225–28
and filter theory of attention, 227–28
in listening, 227
in looking, 226–27
by physical orientation, 225–26
peripheral nervous system, 36; *see also* autonomic
nervous system
peripheral route to persuasion, 423
peripheral vision, 178, 226
permastore, 266
permissive child-rearing pattern, 548, 549, 551
personal constancy, 651–52
personal identity, search for, 573
personality, 627–711
antisocial, 758–59
assessment of, 582, 628–39
behavioral approaches to, 628, 658–65, 700,
739–40
genetics and, 653–54
growth of, 699, 701, 782–83
humanistic approach to, 629, 695–702, 782–83
implicit theories of, 428
multiple, 750–51, 783
obedience and, 472–73
physiological arousal and, 657–58
psychodynamic approach to, 628–29, 669–95,
700, 739–40
sociocultural perspective and, 702–10
temperament and, 652–53
Type A and B, 754–55
see also personality traits; trait theory of personality
personality tests, 582, 629–39
Barnum effects and, 633–34
CPI, 632, 643, 654
intelligence tests vs., 630, 632
MMPI, 630–32, 635, 643
Rorschach inkblots, 635–36, 637–38

structured, 630–34
TAT, 636–37, 638–39
unstructured, 635–39
validity of, 632–33, 637–39, 643
personality traits, 627–29, 639–54
biology and, 652–58
consistency of, 643–53, 660–61
similarity of, in attraction, 462
taxonomy for, 640
see also trait theory of personality
personal space, 389
person-by-situation interaction, 647–49
perspective:
actor-observer difference in, 434–35
linear, 156, 203
persuasive communications, 422–23
PET scans (Positron Emission Tomography), 42
phallic stage, 678–79
phenotypes, 613
phenylalanine, 614
phenylketonuria (PKU), 614
pheromones, 169–70
phi phenomenon, 206
phlegmatic personality type, 642
phobias, 113, 724, 745–47, 749
avoidance learning and, 125, 126
behavioral account of, 779
behavior therapy for, 825
conditioning account of, 746
preparedness theory of, 746
psychoanalytic account of, 779
phonemes, 328–29
combining of, 329
infants' discrimination of, 350
phrases, 330–31
in Motherese, 351
order of, 343–44
structure of, 336–38, 339–40
physical attractiveness, 463–64
cultural factors and, 463–64
matching for, 463
physical development, 493, 499–505, 533
differentiation in, 494
environments at different points of, 543–46
genetic transmission in, 542–43
growth in, 494–95
maturation in, 503–4
see also embryos and fetuses
pictorial depth cues, 156, 202–4, 235
pigeons, pecking response in, 139–40
pitch, 171–72
in language learning, 350, 357
place theory of, 174
pituitary gland, 32, 66, 393
pity, 445–46
PKU (phenylketonuria), 614
placebos, 87, 768–69, 792–93
endorphins and, 87
place theory of pitch, 174
play:
with father vs. mother, 538–39
gender-role stereotypes and, 557–58 sex differences in aggression and, 559
pleasure, pain vs., 99
pleasure centers in brain, 99–100
pluralistic ignorance, 457, 529
Pointillist art, 189
point of view, egocentrism and, 510, 519–20, 561
poisons, neurotransmitter activity and, 30–31
polarization, of cell membranes, 21
polyandry, 395–96
polygenic inheritance, 614
polygraph tests, 83
polygyny, 395–96
population, samples and, A5–A6, A24–A25, A27
positive feedback systems, 62–63
positive rule of if-then inference, 318, 319–20
Positron Emission Tomography (PET scans), 42

potentiation, 4
praying mantis, ear of, 175–76
precursors, 30
predation, 384–89, 535
predicates, of sentences, 292, 335
predictive validity:
    of mental tests, 586
    of personality inventories, 632–33, 643–44
predispositional approach to mental disorders, 662–63
prefrontal lobotomy, 770
preoperational period, 506, 508–10
    egocentrism in, 510
    failures of conservation in, 508–10
preparedness theory, 136–37
    of phobias, 746
preschool programs, intelligence-test scores and, 612
pressure, as skin sense, 165
primacy effect, 247, 427
primary colors, 191, 193
primary memory, see short-term memory
primates, social cognition in, 405–7
prisoner's dilemma, 484–85
    panic and, 485–86
proactive inhibition, 263
probability estimates, 312–313; see also decision making
probability of response, 110
problem solving, 293–307, 527–28
    algorithms and heuristics in, 304–5
    analogies in, 299
    automatization in, 296
    changing representation in, 300
    by computer, see artificial intelligence
    creative thinking in, 300–303
    developing skills in, 294–95
    fixation and, 297–98
    hierarchical organization and chunking in, 293–96, 303
    masters vs. beginners in, 295–96
    mental set and, 297–98
    obstacles to, 296–303
    organization in, 292
    perceptual, 222–24
    restructuring in, 300–303
    searching for solutions in, 295–96
    set and motivation in, 298
    spatial, 285–87
    working backwards in, 299
procedural knowledge, 276–77
processing
progesterone, 394–95
prohibitions, internalization of, 550–51
projection areas, cortical, 39–41, 164
projection (defense mechanism), 473, 676
projective techniques, 635–39
    Rorschach inkblots, 635–36, 637–38
    TAT, 636–37, 638–39
    validity of, 637–39
proportions, standard error of, A25
propositional thought, in chimpanzees, 371
propositions (in abstract thought), 292–93
propositions (in sentences), 335–36
    ambiguity and, 341–42
    attitude toward, 339
    function words signaling boundaries of, 344
    in one-word stage, 353–54
    order of, 343–44
    in paraphrases and opposites, 340–41
    in two-word stage, 355–56
prosopagnosia, 44
prototype theory of meaning, 333–34
proximal stimuli, 154–55, 228
proximity:
    attraction and, 461–62
    in perceptual grouping, 214, 216
psychoanalysis, 722, 772–74, 785

classical, 772–74
    emotional insight in, 774
    modern versions of, 775
    orgins of, 670
    recovery of unconscious memories in, 773–74
psychoanalytic theory, 548
    criticisms of, 684–91
    defense mechanisms in, 674–76, 677
    development of morality and, 550–51
    dream interpretation in, 94, 682–84
    gender typing and, 562–63
    homosexuality and, 566
    literature and, 683–84
    myths and, 682–83
    neo-Freudians and, 775
    personality as viewed in, see psychodynamic approach to personality
    unconscious conflict theory in, 672–73
    see also psychosexual development
psychodynamic approach to personality, 628–29, 669–95, 700, 739–40
    coping patterns in, 693–95
    Freudian account and, 669–95
    patterns of neurotic conflict and, 692
    psychosexual development and, 676–80
    remnants of childhood patterns and, 676–80
psychogenic disorders, mental illness as, 718–19
psychological studies:
    selection of subjects for, A5–A6
    types of, A5
psychometric approach to intelligence, 599–602
    age-intelligence relationship and, 651–54
    structure of mental abilities and, 600–601
psychopathic deviance scale (Pd), 633
psychopathology, 715–60
    classificatory schemes for, 723–24, 756–57
    conversions and dissociative disorders, 720, 724, 780–83
    as disease, 716–18
    and historical conceptions of madness, 715–20, 788
    labeling theory and, 789–91
    as myth, 790
    pathology model of, 722–26
    predispositional approach to, 662–63
    psychophysiological disorders, 783–87
    social deviance and, 758–59
    sociological perspective on, 788–95
    somatogenic-psychogenic distinction in, 718–19
    symptoms of, 723–24
    treatment of, 763–96
    see also anxiety disorders; depression; mood disorders; pathology model of mental disorder; schizophrenia
psychopathy, see sociopaths
psychophysics, 157–63
    sensory intensity and, 158–59
    signal detection theory in, 160–63
psychophysiological disorders, 783–87
    coronary heart disease, 754–55
    diathesis-stress conception and, 755–56
    essential hypertension, 756, 783–85
    peptic ulcers, 756, 783
psychosexual development, 677–80
    Oedipal conflict and, 562–63, 566, 572, 678–80
psychosis, 724
psychosomatic disorders, see psychophysiological disorders
psychosurgery, 770–71
psychotherapy, 772–93
    behavior therapy, 723, 775–78, 785, 825
    classical psychoanalysis, 772–74
    client-centered therapy, 782–83
    cognitive-behavioral therapies, 723, 741, 779–82, 785, 825
    common themes in, 784–86
    deterioration effects and, 791

evaluating outcome of, 789–95
    existential therapy, 783–84
    and expansion of therapeutic goals, 788
    group therapy, 786–87
    humanistic therapies, 699, 775–76, 782–84
    marital and family therapy, 787–88
    modern versions of psychoanalysis, 775
    as social education, 781–82
psychoticism, 642n
puberty, see adolescence
puberty rites, 571–72
punishment, 535–36, 548
    aggressiveness and, 549–50
    in conditioning, 117, 124
    in psychoanalytic theory, 550–51
puzzle box, 116
pyramidal system, 46

quantity, conservation of, 508–10, 521, 561–62
quiet sleep, 6, 90, 93

racial groups, IQ differences between, 619–23
radical behaviorism, 659–61, 664–65
rage, emergency reaction and, 82–83
rapid eye movement sleep, see REM sleep
rationality and errors of thought, 328–29
rationalization, 675–76
ratio scales, A3
ratio schedules of reinforcement, 122–23
rats:
    belongingness effect in conditioning of, 137–38
    self-stimulation in, 99–100
    sexual behavior in, 394–95
reaction formation, 473, 675, 677
reaction time, 50
reading:
    automatization of, 296
reality:
    interpersonal nature of, 416–18
    perception of, 228–33
    representation of, in art, 234–37
reality testing, 126
reasoning:
    analogical, 299, 605
    deductive, 309–11, 328
    inductive, 310–11, 328
    numerical, 518–19
rebound phenomena, 191
recall, 529
    of dreams, 7, 93–94
    phrase structure and, 337–38
    see also memory retrieval; remembering
receiver-operating-characteristic (ROC) curves, 162
recency effect, 247
receptive aphasia, 45–46
receptive field, of retina, 184
receptor cells, 19
receptor organs in, 178
receptors, 18, 164
    auditory, 174
    olfactory, 168
    skin, 165–66
    taste, 166
    visual, 178, 191, 193
recessive genes, 500
reciprocal altruism, 409, 410
reciprocal inhibition, 26
reciprocal interaction, 649
reciprocity, 454–56
    built-in predisposition toward, 409
reconditioning, 111
reconstruction, memory distortions and, 269–71
redundancy principle, 69
reference, in language, 326, 331–32
reflex arc, 24
reflexes, 24
    conditioned, 108–9

reflexes (continued)
  Descartes and, 16–17, 18, 61–62
  in infants, 496–97
  simple, Sherrington's study of, 25–26
  unconditioned, 108–9
reflexive temperature control, 64–66
regret, 446–47
rehabilitation, of brain-damaged patients, 56
rehearsal, in memory, 247
  in children, 526
  elaborative, 256–57, 264
  maintenance, 250–51
  mental retardation and, 606–7
reinforced trials, 110
reinforcement, 110, 119
  act-outcome relations and, 139–40
  aversive stimuli and, 123–26
  conditioned, 121
  delay of, 121–22
  intermittent (partial), 122–24, 660
  in language learning, 348
  personality theory and, 660
  schedules of, 122–24
  in shaping of response, 120
  socialization and, 546
  in token economies, 778
relative size, as depth cue, 203
relaxation, in systematic desensitization, 777–78
releasing stimuli, 382–83
reliability, of mental tests, 586
reliability coefficients, 586
remembering:
  conceptual frameworks and, 267–71
  strategies for, 248–49, 252–59, 526, 606–7
  see also encoding phase of remembering; memory retrieval
REM (rapid eye movement) sleep, 6, 7, 90, 91–92, 740
  deprivation experiments on, 91
  dreaming during, 6, 7, 93
Renaissance art, 234–35
repetition priming, 259
representational thought, beginnings of, 507–8
representations (cognitions), 126
representativeness heuristics, 312–13
repressed memories, 272–73
repression, 673, 674
  in conversions and dissociative disorders, 780–83
reproduction, 393–95, 494–95
  animal mating systems and, 396
  asexual, 390
  dominance hierarchies and, 388
  sex determination in, 499–500
  sexual, genetic advantages of, 390–91
  timing of, 393–95
  see also male-female bonding; sexual behavior
research data, see data, research
resistance, in psychoanalytic theory, 773
resources, fighting over, 388
response amplitude, 110
response bias, 160–62
response capacities, in infants, 496–97
response control, in infants, 132–33, 661–62
response latency, 110, 116
response rate, 118
responses, see conditioned response; unconditioned response
response suppression, 113
responsibility:
  blind obedience and, 475
  diffusion of, in crowds, 458–59, 488, 529
resting potential, 21
restrained-eating hypothesis, 78
restructuring, 300–303
  creative thinking and, 300–303
  humor and, 301–2
retention interval, forgetting and, 262, 264

retinas, 154, 178
  adaptation phenomena and, 191
  brightness contrast and, 184
  perceptual constancies and, 228
  retrieval cues, 255–56
  change of, 264–65
retrieval phase of remembering, see memory retrieval
retroactive inhibition, 263
retrograde amnesia, 275–76
reuptake, 30
reversible figures, 213–14
rewards:
  in conditioning, 117
  delay of, 663–64
  see also reinforcement
rhodopsin, 180
right-handers, 48
right hemisphere, 40
  lateralization and, 49–50
ritualized fighting, 387
robins, alarm calls of, 408
ROC (receiver-operating-characteristic) curves, 162
rods, 178–79
role playing, 645, 659, 782
Romanticism, 701
romantic love, 464–67
  Romeo-and-Juliet effect, 466
  theories of emotions and, 465
rooting reflex, 497

safety signals, 130
salty tastes, 166, 167
SAM, see Sentence Analyzing Machinery
"same-different" notion, 145–46
samples and sampling, A5–A7
  biased, A5
  population and, A5–A7, A25, A27
  random and stratified, A5
  responses and, A5–A6
  size factor in, A27
  standard error and, A24–A25
sanguine personality type, 642
satiety signals, 70–71
saturation, of color, 186
scaling, statistical, A2–A3
scaling in, A2–A3
scatter plots (diagrams), 584, A14, A17
schemas:
  memory distortions and, 268–69
  in Piaget's theory, 507, 524
  in social perception, 428–31
schizophrenia, 724, 726–36
  behavioral disorders in, 729
  bizarre and morbid dreams in, 10
  catatonic, 729
  cognition disorders in, 727
  delusions in, 728
  in different cultures, 790
  drug therapies for, 31, 730, 764–66
  environmental stress and, 733–35
  family life and, 734–35
  hallucinations in, 728–29
  hereditary predisposition to, 732–33
  motivational and emotional disorders in, 729
  organic pathology in, 31, 730–32
  paranoid, 728
  pathology model and, 735–36
  social class and, 734
  subcategories of, 729
  symptoms of, 724, 726–29
  withdrawal from social contacts in, 727
scholastic aptitude tests, 587
Scholastic Aptitude Test (SAT), 593
schooling, cross-cultural differences in cognitive performance and, 529
scores, see test scores

scripts, 268
seasonal affective disorder, 739–40
secondary memory, see long-term memory
second languages, learning of, 368–69
second-order conditioning, 110
selection:
  aptitude tests in, 588–89
  see also perceptual selection
selection of subjects in, A5–A6
self:
  in humanistic psychology, 697
  induced motion of, 207
self-actualization, 695, 696–98, 699–700, 783
self-concepts, 437–38
  in humanistic psychology, 697
self-control, 663–64
self-monitoring scale, 650–51
self-perception, 437–38
  attribution and, 437–38
self-picture, 424
self-presentation, 61
  impression management and, 430–31, 437–38
self-psychology, 693n
self-regulation, 61
self-regulatory systems, 661
self-restoration, 61
self-sacrifice, 407–11; see also altruism
self-serving attributional bias, 435–37
self-stimulation, rewarding effects of, 99–100
self-worth, feelings of, 697, 699
semantic features, words as bundles of, 332
semantic memory, spreading activation model of, 290
semantic priming, 290
semantics, 331
  interaction of syntax and, 346
  theories of word meaning and, 331–35
semicircular canals, 164
sensations, 155
  color, 180, 185–87
  detection experiments on, 160–63
  intensity of, 158–59, 163
  movement, 164
  qualitative differences in, 163–64
  skin, 165–66
  smell, 168
  sound, 170–72
  taste, 166
  visual, 179–80
sensation seeking, 657–58
senses, 165–99
  adaptation phenomena in, 167
  coding in, 163–64, 167, 176
  evolution and, 175–76
  hearing, 170–75
  interaction processes in, 167, 176
  origins of knowledge and, 153–57
  psychophysics and, 157–63
  relations between, in infants, 206
  skin, 165–66
  smell, 167–70
  taste, 166–67
  transduction in, 157, 173–74, 176
  vestibular, kinesthesis and, 164
  vision, 176–97
sensitive periods, 503
  imprinting and, 536–37
  see also critical periods
sensory coding, 163–64, 176
  opponent-process theory and, 191–93
  for taste quality, 167
sensory deprivation, 504
sensory interaction, 167, 176
sensory-motor intelligence period, 506–8
  beginnings of representational thought in, 507–8
  object permanence in, 506–7
  schemas in, 507

sensory process, 162
sensory projection areas, 39, 41
sensory registers, 245*n*
Sentence Analyzing Machinery (SAM), 343–46
  function words and, 344
  linguistic illusions and, 344–46
  phrase order and, 343–44
sentences, 330–31
  in abstract thought, 292–93
  ambiguous, 341–42
  boundaries between propositions in, 344
  complex, 338–40
  comprehension of, 342–46
  meaningful relations among, 340–42
  Motherese and, 350–51
  order of phrases in, 343–44
  organizing words into, 335–42
  paraphrases and opposites, 340–41
  phrase structure in, 336–38
  simple, 338
  surface vs. underlying structure of, 338–51
  in two-word stage, 355–56
separation, from mother, 537–38
serial reproduction, 268
serial search, in memory retrieval, 264–66
serotonin, 29, 740
servomechanisms, 63
setpoints:
  for temperature, 65
  for weight, 73, 78
sex, gender vs., 556–57*n*
sex determination, 499–500, 501–2, 556
sex differences, 556–57*n*
  in aggression, 388, 558–59, 560
  constitutional factors and, 557–58
  displays of, 391
  in intellectual abilities, 559, 560
  in moral reasoning, 554–55
  reassignment and, 560–62
  social factors and, 560–62
sex drive, 96
sex reassignment, 560–62
sex roles, *see* gender identity; gender roles; sexual orientation
sexual abuse, repressed memories of, 272–73
sexual behavior, 81, 88, 96, 101
  advertising of one's sex in, 390–91
  in animals, 390–91
  choice of partner in, 392–93
  courtship and mating rituals in, 3–4, 392–97
  hormones and, 393–95
  of humans vs. animals, 395
  see also homosexuality; love; male-female bonding; reproduction
sexual orientation, 556, 564–569; *see also* homosexuality
sexual structures, development of, 501–2
shadowing, in dichotic presentation, 227
shape, 215
  constancy of, 231–32
shared-problem groups, 786
short-term memory, 245–49
  as active memory, 250
  capacity of, 246, 247, 248, 251
  conscious experience and, 245–46
  forgetting from, 246
  habituation and, 107
  impairments in, 275
  as loading platform, 246–48
  maintenance rehearsal in, 250–51
  overcoming bottleneck in, 248–49
  retrieval from, 264–66
  stage theory and, 245–49
  transfer into long-term memory from, 246–48
signal detection theory, 160–63
  decision process, 162–63
  extended to other fields, 163
  payoff matrix and, 161

response bias and, 160–62
sign language:
  American Sign Language (ASL), 48, 362–63, 369
  aphasia and, 46
  informal gestural systems and, 363–64
similarity:
  attraction and, 462
  in perceptual grouping, 214, 216
simulation heuristic, 447
simultaneous color contrast, 190
simultaneous pairing, 127
sine waves, 172
situational factors:
  in attribution of traits, 432–37
  in behavioral approach to personality, 659
  in blind obedience, 473–77
  interaction between person and, 647–49, 661–62
  personality traits and, 643–53, 661–62, 665
situationism, 644–45
  person-by-situation interaction and, 647–49
size:
  constancy of, 229–33
  relative, as depth cue, 203
skeletal movement, kinesthesis and, 164
skeletal musculature, 19
skill development, 294–95
  language learning as, 348
Skinner box, 118
skin senses and sensations, 165–66, 497
  contact comfort and, 534–35
sleep, 89–94
  awakening from, 88–89
  brain activity during, 6–7, 89
  as clock-driven process, 92
  functions of, 91–92
  REM (rapid eye movement), 6, 7, 90, 91–92, 740
  seasonal affective disorder and, 739–40
  stages of, 6–7, 89–90
  waking and, 88
  see also dreams
sleep deprivation, 91
smell, sense of, 167–70, 497
  as distance sense, 169
  as internal sense, 168
  olfactory stimulus and, 168
  pheromones and, 169–70
smiling, by infants, 4, 401
smooth muscles, 66
social behavior, 4, 379–413
  aggression and, 383–89
  attitudes and, 420–21
  beliefs and social reality in, 416–18
  biological basis of, 379–413
  built-in, 382–83
  communicating motives in, 401–5
  dreams and, 7–8
  human nature and, 379–80, 412
  male-female bond and, 390–99
  parent-child bond and, 399–401
  self-sacrifice and altruism in, 407–11
social class:
  child rearing and, 545
  schizophrenia and, 733, 734
social cognition, 416–39, 457
  attitudes and, 420–25
  attribution and, 432–37
  beliefs and, 416–18
  in infancy, 515–16
  perceiving oneself and, 437–38
  perceiving others and, 426–31
  personality differences and, 661–65
  in preschoolers, 519
  in primates, 405–7
  stereotypes and, 429–30
social comparison, 418–19

social contact, schizophrenics' withdrawal from, 727
social deprivation, 542–44
  and reversibility of effects, 543–44
social development, 494, 533–79
  attachment and, 534–44
  childhood socialization and, 545–50
  environment and, 502
  Erikson's stages of, 570–74
  morality and, 550–51
  sex and gender in, 556–69
  see also language learning; socialization
social deviance, 758–59
social dilemmas, 486
social education, in psychotherapy, 781–82
social exchange, 453–54
  altruism and, 456–57, 460
  reciprocity principle and, 454–56
social facilitation, 467–69
social impact theory, 477–79
social influence, 467–69
  blind obedience and, 471–77
  conformity and, 469–71
  by mere presence, 467–69
  social impact theory and, 477–79
social interactions, 453–89
  altruism in, 456–57
  attraction and, 461–64
  love and, 464–67
  many-on-many, 482–86
  many-on-one, 467–69
  one-on-one, 453–67
  reciprocity principle and, 454–56
  social exchange theory of, 453–54
socialization, 545–50
  child-rearing patterns and, 547–49
  children's effects on parents and, 549–50
  cultural values and, 545–50
  mechanisms of, 546–47
  sex differences and, 560–62
  see also social development
social learning theory, 546–47, 661–65
  attributional style and, 662–63
  behaviorism and, 664–65
  control and, 661–62
  self-control and, 663–64
  sex typing and, 563
social loafing, 479
social perception, 426–38
  attribution process in, 432–37
  cognitive constructions in, 428–31
  impression formation in, 426
  impression management and, 430–31, 437
  inaccuracies in, 433–37
  of oneself, 437–38
  of others, 426–31
  patterning processes in, 426–27
social policy, intelligence tests and, 611–12
social psychology, generality of, 487–88
social-reality testing, 727
social roles, personality consistency and, 644–45
sociobiology, 383
  altruism and, 409–11
  ethics and, 411
  mating patterns and, 397–99
sociocultural perspective on personality, 702–10
sociological critique of pathology model, 788–95
  care provided by mental hospitals and, 788–89
  labeling theory and, 789–91
sociopaths (antisocial personalities), 758–59
  clinical description of, 758
  pathology model and, 759
  possible causes of, 758–59
sodium pump, 22–23
somatic division, of peripheral nervous system, 36
somatic therapies, 763–72
  convulsive treatments, 771–72
  psychosurgery, 770–71

somatic therapies (continued)
    see also drug therapies
somatoform disorders, 752–54
somatogenic disorder, mental illness as, 718–19
somatosensory area, cortical, 41
songbirds:
    critical period for, 368
    sound, 170–72
    as cues in language learning, 347–48
    language learning without, 362–64
    phonemes and, 328–31, 350
    see also hearing
sound waves, 171–72
    amplitude of, 171
    frequency of, 171–72, 174–75
sour tastes, 166, 167
sparrows, critical period for development of song
    in, 368
spatial memory, in animals, 143
spatial skills, sex differences in, 559, 560
spatial summation, 26
spatial thinking, 285–87
species, learning and, 141–42
species-specific behavior patterns, 382
    in courtship, 392–93
    fixed-action patterns, 382–83
specificity theory, 164, 167
specific nerve energies, doctrine of, 164, 165
spectral sensitivity curves, 179–80
speech, 293
    context effects and, 220
    motherese, 350–51
    principles of conversation and, 326–28
    unfamiliar, difficulty in understanding of, 329
    speech production:
        aphasia and, 45–46, 49–50
        errors in, 348
        social origins of, 349
speech sounds (phonemes), 328–31
sperm, 390, 393, 495
spinal cord, 36, 37
spinal reflexes, 25
split brains, 48–50
spontaneous recovery:
    of conditioned response, 111
    habituation and, 107, 111
    psychotherapy and, 790
spreading activation model of semantic memory,
    290
stability, perception of, 207–8
stabilized images, 181
stage concept in development, 560–64
    consistency and, 561
    discreteness and, 561–63
    sequences vs., 521–22
stage fright, 477
stage theory of memory, 245–49
    overcoming short-term bottleneck in, 248–49
    problems of, 248–49
    short-term memory as loading platform in,
        246–48
standard deviation (SD), 583, A11, A24
standard error (SE), A24
standardization, of mental tests, 634
standardization samples, 587
Stanford-Binet test, 593, 620
statistical methods, 582–85, A1–A28
    conservatism in, A26–A27
    correlation in, 584–85, A14–A16, A20–A21
    data collection in, A1, A4–A5
    data interpretation in, A1, A17–A25
    data organization in, A1, A7–A14
    defined, 91
    descriptive statistics and, A7–A14
    hypothesis testing and, A21–A26
    inferential statistics and, A19–A28
    meta-analyses, 790–91
    probabilistic elements and, A26

stereotypes:
    gender-role, 557–58
    social cognition and, 429–30
stimulants, 97, 98
stimuli:
    absolute threshold and, 156, 160–63
    adaptation phenomena and, 191
    aversive, 119, 124–25
    discrimination of, 112, 119
    distal vs. proximal, 154–55
    gathering and amplification of, 176
    habituation to, 106–7
    intensity of, 23, 158–59
    light, 177
    olfactory, 168
    perceptual selection and, 225–26
    releasing, 382–83
    sensory coding and, 163–64, 176
    sensory intensity and, 158–59
    sensory interaction and, 167
    sound, 170–72
    temporal or spatial summation effects and,
        25–26
    transduction and, 157, 173–74, 176
    see also conditioned stimulus; unconditioned
        stimulus
stimulus generalization, 111, 112, 119–20
stomach, satiety signals from, 70
Strange Situation, 537–38
strategies, 529
    intellectual functioning and, 606–7
    metacognition and, 527–28
    for remembering, 526, 606–7
stress:
    in adolescence, 572
    essential hypertension and, 784–85
    during pregnancy, homosexuality and, 567
    schizophrenia and, 733–35
    see also diathesis-stress conception
stroboscopic movement, 206, 223
Stroop effect, 296
subjective contours, 216
subjects, of sentences, 292, 335
    dropping of, in two-word speech, 356
submission:
    appeasement displays and, 387
    dominance hierarchies and, 387–88
subtractive color mixture, 188–89
successive approximations, 120
suicide, 738–39
superego, 673–74
    internalization of moral values and, 550n
surface phrase structure descriptions, 337
surface structure, of sentences, 339
survival of the fittest, 380–81
sweet tastes, 74, 75, 96, 166, 167
syllogisms, 309–10, 528
symbol manipulation, in chimpanzees, 145–46
sympathetic distress, 553n
sympathetic nervous system, 66, 81–82, 88
    emergency reaction of, 82–84, 783–84
    panic disorder and, 749
symptoms, of mental disorders, 723–24
synapses, 20, 24, 25, 496, 505
    Sherrington's studies of, 25–26
    transmission at, 27–31
syndromes, 723–24
syntax, 330
    chimpanzees' abilities and, 371–72
    interaction of semantics and, 346
    in later stages of language learning, 357
    motherese and, 350–51
    in two-word speech, 355
syphilis, 719
systematic desensitization, 777–78, 825

tape recorder theory of memory, 272
taste, sense of, 166–67, 497

smell related to, 168
taste aversions, learned, 137–38
taste buds, 166
TAT (Thematic Apperception Test), 636–37,
    638–39
t-distribution, A24n
telegraphic stage, in language learning, 355–56
temperament:
    bodily humors and, 642
    differences in, 537–38, 549–50, 652–53,
        779–80
    personality and, 652–53
    see also personality; personality traits
temperature:
    homeostasis and, 64–66
    memory decay and, 262
    skin senses and, 164–65
temporal lobes, 38, 41
temporal summation, 25
territoriality:
    in humans, 388–89
    in songbirds, 388
territoriality of, 388
testosterone, 388, 394
test-retest method, 586
tests, see intelligence tests; mental tests; personality
        tests
test scores:
    conversion of, for comparison, A11–A12
    and measures of central tendency, A8–A10
    normal curves and, A12–A14
    as percentile ranks, A11, A13
    range of, A9
    single, testing hypotheses about, A21–A22
    standard (z-scores), A11–A12, A13, A23–A24
texture gradients, 204
thalamus, 37–38, 770
theater:
    emotion and, 448–49
    personality types in, 628, 639
Thematic Apperception Test (TAT), 636–37,
    638–39
therapy, see behavior therapy; cognitive-behavioral
        therapies; drug therapies; psychotherapy;
        somatic therapies
therapy groups:
    as activity, 293
    computer simulation of, 329
    empiricist view of, 291, 292
    errors of, human rationality and, 328–29
    as mental imagery, 291, 292–93
    organization in, 293–99
    parallel distributed processing in, 290–92
    reasoning and, 328
    see also cognitive development; problem solving
thinking and thought, 281–321
    abstract, 291–93
thirst, 67–68
threat, reaction to, see emergency reaction
threat displays, 4, 386–87
threshold, of neuron impulse, 21–23, 25
tip-of-the-tongue phenomenon, 258–59
toilet training, 548
    adult personality differences and, 677–78
token economies, 778
top-down processing:
    in perception, 219–22, 229
touch, see skin senses and sensations
trace consolidation, 275–76
traits, see attribution of traits; personality traits
trait theory of personality, 628–29, 639–54, 700,
    739–40
    consistency as trait in, 649–51
    criticisms of, 643–45, 661
    defense of, 645–47
    interaction between person and situation and,
        647–495

neuroticism and extroversion/introversion in, 640–42, 650n, 653, 657
person constancy and, 651–52
search for right taxonomy in, 640
social learning theory vs., 661–62, 664–65
traits vs. situations and, 643–53, 661–62, 664–65
transduction, 19, 157, 176
in cochlea, 173–74
transference, 774, 785
transfer of training, 145
transplants, of neural tissue, 54–55
treatment of psychopathology, *see* behavior therapy; cognitive-behavioral therapies; drug therapies; psychotherapy; somatic therapies
tree diagrams, of phrases, 336–38, 339–40
trephining, 716, 763
tribalism, 410
trichromatic theory, 192
trustworthiness, 422
twin studies, 615
on bipolar disorder, 740
on heritability of intelligence, 615–16, 617
on panic disorder, 778
on personality, 653–54, 655
on schizophrenia, 732, 733
on sociopathy, 759
on Type A and B personalities, 755
two-word stage, in language learning, 355–56

ulcers, 754, 756, 783
unconditioned reflexes, 108–9
unconditioned response (UR), 127
defined, 108–9
relation between CR and, 113
unconditioned stimulus (US), 110
belongingness and, 136–38
contiguity and, 127–28, 129, 138
contingency and, 128–30, 132–35
defined, 109
surprise element and, 130–31
unconscious, 8
recovery of memories in, 773–74
unconscious conflicts, 672–73
psychoanalysis and, 773–74
unconscious inference, in perception, 229
underlying structure, of sentences, 338–51
ambiguity and, 341–42
comprehension and, 342–46
unilateral neglect syndrome, 44–45
unipolar disorder, *see* depression
unique colors, 186
unreinforced trials, 110

validity, 586–87, 590
construct, 587, 633
incremental, 638–39
of personality inventories, 632–34, 643
predictive, 586–87, 632–33, 643

of projective techniques, 637–39
validity coefficients, 587, 588
validity scales, in personality inventories, 631–32
values, subjective, 661
variability, 91, 583–84
accounting for, A18–A21
correlation of, 584–85
measures for, A9–A11
natural selection and, 584
variability in, 583–84, A1, A9–A11, A18–A21
variable-interval (VI) schedules of reinforcement, 123
variable-ratio (VR) schedules of reinforcement, 123
variables:
dependent, A4
independent, A4
normal distribution of, A13–A14
variance (V), 583, A10
correlation and, A20–A21
experiments and, A4, A19–A20
vasoconstriction, 64
vasodilation, 64
venom, of black widow, 31
ventral tegmental area (VTA), 100
ventromedial hypothalamic region, 73–74
verbal organization, mnemonics through, 253
verbal skills:
age and, 653
sex differences in, 559, 560
see also language learning
verb phrases, 336
verbs:
causative, 357
past tense of, 357
vesicles, 28
vestibular senses, 164, 165
vicious circles, in patterns of neurotic conflict, 692
visible spectrum, 177
vision, 158, 176–97
acuity of, 178–79
adaptation phenomena in, 180
agnosia and, 44
brightness contrast in, 181–85
color, 185–95
duplex theory of, 179–80
in infants, 497
intersensory relations and, 205
light as stimulus in, 177–78
peripheral, 178, 226
projection area for, 41
receptors in, 178
semicircular canal system and, 165
sensory deprivation and, 504
stimulus gathered by eye in, 177–78
see also blindness; perception
visual cliff, 204
infants and, 2–3
visual imagery, mnemonics through, 253–54

visual memory:
eidetic imagery and, 283–84
rating one's own imagery and, 283–84
visual pigments, 180
visual search procedure, 227
visual search task, 211
visual segregation (parsing), 212–22
of figure and ground, 213–14
laws of perceptual organization and, 214–16
maximum likelihood principle and, 216–17
vocabulary, 404, 653
chimpanzees' capacity for, 371
development of, 352, 357–60
vocational aptitude tests, 586
cutoff scores on, 588–89

waking, 88
walking, maturation and, 503–4
warmth, as skin sense, 165–66
wavelength:
of light waves, 177, 179, 188–89, 192
of sound waves, 171
Weber fraction, 158–59
Weber's law, 158, 159
Wechsler Adult Intelligence Scale, 592, 601
Wernicke's area, 45, 367
wild children, 360–61
withdrawal, of schizophrenics, 727
withdrawal symptoms, 98, 99
within-family differences, 655–57
witness testimony:
hypnosis and, 271–72
schema-based distortions of, 269–71
wolves, appeasement displays in, 387
word fluency tests, 653
words, 330
in abstract thought, 292–93
ambiguous, 342
in children's first utterances, 352–53
combining phonemes into, 329
learning of, 357–60
meaning of, 331–35, 352–54, 357–60, 364–65
organizing into meaningful sentences, 335–42
recognition of, 220–21
sentence meanings and, 335–42
working memory, 251

X-chromosomes, 499

Y-chromosomes, 499
Young-Helmholtz theory, 192

Zipf's law, A14
z-scores, A11–A12, A13, A23–A24
zygotes, 390, 494, 500